≠ Albert Pike. ⟁
Grand Commander.

MORALS AND DOGMA

OF THE

ANCIENT AND ACCEPTED SCOTTISH RITE

OF

FREEMASONRY

PREPARED FOR THE

SUPREME COUNCIL OF THE THIRTY-THIRD DEGREE

FOR THE

SOUTHERN JURISDICTION OF THE UNITED STATES

AND

PUBLISHED BY ITS AUTHORITY.

CHARLESTON
A∴ M∴ 5632

L. H. Jenkins, Inc.
Edition Book Manufacturers
Richmond, Va.
Reprinted
October, 1928.

PREFACE.

The following work has been prepared by authority of the Supreme Council of the Thirty-third Degree, for the Southern Jurisdiction of the United States, by the Grand Commander, and is now published by its direction. It contains the Lectures of the Ancient and Accepted Scottish Rite in that jurisdiction, and is specially intended to be read and studied by the Brethren of that obedience, in connection with the Rituals of the Degrees. It is hoped and expected that each will furnish himself with a copy, and make himself familiar with it; for which purpose, as the cost of the work consists entirely in the printing and binding, it will be furnished at a price as moderate as possible. No *individual* will receive pecuniary profit from it, except the agents for its sale.

It has been copyrighted, to prevent its republication elsewhere, and the copyright, like those of all the other works prepared for the Supreme Council, has been assigned to Trustees for that Body. Whatever profits may accrue from it will be devoted to purposes of charity.

The Brethren of the Rite in the United States and Canada will be afforded the opportunity to purchase it, nor is it *forbidden* that other Masons shall; but they will not be solicited to do so.

In preparing this work, the Grand Commander has been about equally Author and Compiler; since he has extracted quite half its contents from the works of the best writers and most philosophic or eloquent thinkers. Perhaps it would have been better and more acceptable if he had extracted more and written less.

Still, perhaps half of it is his own; and, in incorporating here

iii

the thoughts and words of others, he has continually changed
and added to the language, often intermingling, in the same sentences, his own words with theirs. It not being intended for the
world at large, he has felt at liberty to make, from all accessible
sources, a Compendium of the Morals and Dogma of the Rite, to
re-mould sentences, change and add to words and phrases, combine them with his own, and use them as if they *were* his own,
to be dealt with at his pleasure and so availed of as to make the
whole most valuable for the purposes intended. He claims, therefore, little of the merit of authorship, and has not cared to distinguish his own from that which he has taken from other sources,
being quite willing that every portion of the book, in turn, may
be regarded as borrowed from some old and better writer.

The teachings of these Readings are not sacramental, so far as
they go beyond the realm of Morality into those of other domains
of Thought and Truth. The Ancient and Accepted Scottish Rite
uses the word "Dogma" in its true sense, of *doctrine,* or *teaching;*
and is not *dogmatic* in the odious sense of that term. Every one
is entirely free to reject and dissent from whatsoever herein may
seem to him to be untrue or unsound. It is only required of him
that he shall weigh what is taught, and give it fair hearing and
unprejudiced judgment. Of course, the ancient theosophic and
philosophic speculations are not embodied as part of the *doctrines*
of the Rite; but because it is of interest and profit to know what
the Ancient Intellect thought upon these subjects, and because
nothing so conclusively proves the radical difference between our
human and the animal nature, as the capacity of the human
mind to entertain such speculations in regard to itself and the
Deity. But as to these opinions themselves, we may say, in the
words of the learned Canonist, Ludovicus Gomez: "*Opiniones
secundum varietatem temporum senescant et intermoriantur,
aliœque diversœ vel prioribus contrariœ renascantur et deinde
pubescant.*"

Titles of Degrees as herein given have in some instances been changed. Correct titles are as follows:

1°—Apprentice.

2°—Fellow-craft.

3°—Master.

4°—Secret Master.

5°—Perfect Master.

6°—Intimate Secretary.

7°—Provost and Judge.

8°—Intendant of the Building.

9°—Elu of the Nine.

10°—Elu of the Fifteen.

11°—Elu of the Twelve.

12°—Master Architect.

13°—Royal Arch of Solomon.

14°—Perfect Elu.

15°—Knight of the East.

16°—Prince of Jerusalem.

17°—Knight of the East and West.

18°—Knight Rose Croix.

19°—Pontiff.

20°—Master of the Symbolic Lodge.

21°—Noachite or Prussian Knight.

22°—Knight of the Royal Axe or Prince of Libanus.

23°—Chief of the Tabernacle.

24°—Prince of the Tabernacle.

25°—Knight of the Brazen Serpent.

26°—Prince of Mercy.

27°—Knight Commander of the Temple.

28°—Knight of the Sun or Prince Adept.

29°—Scottish Knight of St. Andrew.

30°—Knight Kadosh.

31°—Inspector Inquisitor.

32°—Master of the Royal Secret.

MORALS AND DOGMA.

LODGE OF PERFECTION.

MORALS AND DOGMA.

I.

APPRENTICE.

THE TWELVE-INCH RULE AND THE COMMON GAVEL.

FORCE, unregulated or ill-regulated, is not only wasted in the void, like that of gunpowder burned in the open air, and steam unconfined by science; but, striking in the dark, and its blows meeting only the air, they recoil and bruise itself. It is destruction and ruin. It is the volcano, the earthquake, the cyclone;—not growth and progress. It is Polyphemus blinded, striking at random, and falling headlong among the sharp rocks by the impetus of his own blows.

The blind Force of the people is a Force that must be economized, and also managed, as the blind Force of steam, lifting the ponderous iron arms and turning the large wheels, is made to bore and rifle the cannon and to weave the most delicate lace. It must be regulated by Intellect. Intellect is to the people and the people's Force, what the slender needle of the compass is to the ship—its soul, always counselling the huge mass of wood and iron, and always pointing to the north. To attack the citadels built up on all sides against the human race by superstitions, despotisms, and prej-

1

udices, the Force must have a brain and a law. Then its deeds of daring produce permanent results, and there is real progress. Then there are sublime conquests. Thought is a force, and philosophy should be an energy, finding its aim and its effects in the amelioration of mankind. The two great motors are Truth and Love. When all these Forces are combined, and guided by the Intellect, and regulated by the RULE of Right, and Justice, and of combined and systematic movement and effort, the great revolution prepared for by the ages will begin to march. The POWER of the Deity Himself is in equilibrium with His WISDOM. Hence the only results are HARMONY.

It is because Force is ill regulated, that revolutions prove failures. Therefore it is that so often insurrections, coming from those high mountains that domineer over the moral horizon, Justice, Wisdom, Reason, Right, built of the purest snow of the ideal after a long fall from rock to rock, after having reflected the sky in their transparency, and been swollen by a hundred affluents, in the majestic path of triumph, suddenly lose themselves in quagmires, like a California river in the sands.

The onward march of the human race requires that the heights around it should blaze with noble and enduring lessons of courage. Deeds of daring dazzle history, and form one class of the guiding lights of man. They are the stars and coruscations from that great sea of electricity, the Force inherent in the people. To strive, to brave all risks, to perish, to persevere, to be true to one's self, to grapple body to body with destiny, to surprise defeat by the little terror it inspires, now to confront unrighteous power, now to defy intoxicated triumph—these are the examples that the nations need and the light that electrifies them.

There are immense Forces in the great caverns of evil beneath society; in the hideous degradation, squalor, wretchedness and destitution, vices and crimes that reek and simmer in the darkness in that populace below the people, of great cities. There disinterestedness vanishes, every one howls, searches, gropes, and gnaws for himself. Ideas are ignored, and of progress there is no thought. This populace has two mothers, both of them stepmothers—Ignorance and Misery. Want is their only guide—for the appetite alone they crave satisfaction. Yet even these may be employed. The lowly sand we trample upon, cast into the furnace, melted, purified by fire, may become resplendent crystal.

They have the brute force of the HAMMER, but their blows help on the great cause, when struck within the lines traced by the RULE held by wisdom and discretion.

Yet it is this very Force of the people, this Titanic power of the giants, that builds the fortifications of tyrants, and is embodied in their armies. Hence the possibility of such tyrannies as those of which it has been said, that "Rome smells worse under Vitellius than under Sulla. Under Claudius and under Domitian there is a deformity of baseness corresponding to the ugliness of the tyranny. The foulness of the slaves is a direct result of the atrocious baseness of the despot. A miasma exhales from these crouching consciences that reflect the master; the public authorities are unclean, hearts are collapsed, consciences shrunken, souls puny. This is so under Caracalla, it is so under Commodus, it is so under Heliogabalus, while from the Roman senate, under Cæsar, there comes only the rank odor peculiar to the eagle's eyrie."

It is the force of the people that sustains all these despotisms, the basest as well as the best. That force acts through armies; and these oftener enslave than liberate. Despotism there applies the RULE. Force is the MACE of steel at the saddle-bow of the knight or of the bishop in armor. Passive obedience by force supports thrones and oligarchies, Spanish kings, and Venetian senates. Might, in an army wielded by tyranny, is the enormous sum total of utter weakness; and so Humanity wages war against Humanity, in despite of Humanity. So a people willingly submits to despotism, and its workmen submit to be despised, and its soldiers to be whipped; therefore it is that battles lost by a nation are often progress attained. Less glory is more liberty. When the drum is silent, reason sometimes speaks.

Tyrants use the force of the people to chain and subjugate—that is, *enyoke* the people. Then they plough with them as men do with oxen yoked. Thus the spirit of liberty and innovation is reduced by bayonets, and principles are struck dumb by cannonshot; while the monks mingle with the troopers, and the Church militant and jubilant, Catholic or Puritan, sings Te Deums for victories over rebellion.

The military power, not subordinate to the civil power, again the HAMMER or MACE of FORCE, independent of the RULE, is an armed tyranny, born full-grown, as Athenè sprung from the brain of Zeus. It spawns a dynasty, and begins with Cæsar to rot into

Vitellius and Commodus. At the present day it inclines to *begin* where formerly dynasties *ended*.

Constantly the people put forth immense strength, only to end in immense weakness. The force of the people is exhausted in indefinitely prolonging things long since dead; in governing mankind by embalming old dead tyrannies of Faith; restoring dilapidated dogmas; regilding faded, worm-eaten shrines; whitening and rouging ancient and barren superstitions; saving society by multiplying parasites; perpetuating superannuated institutions; enforcing the worship of symbols as the actual means of salvation; and tying the dead corpse of the Past, mouth to mouth, with the living Present. Therefore it is that it is one of the fatalities of Humanity to be condemned to eternal struggles with phantoms, with superstitions, bigotries, hypocrisies, prejudices, the formulas of error, and the pleas of tyranny. Despotisms, seen in the past, become respectable, as the mountain, bristling with volcanic rock, rugged and horrid, seen through the haze of distance is blue and smooth and beautiful. The sight of a single dungeon of tyranny is worth more, to dispel illusions, and create a holy hatred of despotism, and to direct FORCE aright, than the most eloquent volumes. The French should have preserved the Bastile as a perpetual lesson; Italy should not destroy the dungeons of the Inquisition. The Force of the people maintained the Power that built its gloomy cells, and placed the living in their granite sepulchres.

The FORCE of the people cannot, by its unrestrained and fitful action, maintain and continue in action and existence a free Government once created. That Force must be limited, restrained, conveyed by distribution into different channels, and by roundabout courses, to outlets, whence it is to issue as the law, action, and decision of the State; as the wise old Egyptian kings conveyed in different canals, by sub-division, the swelling waters of the Nile, and compelled them to fertilize and not devastate the land. There must be the *jus et norma,* the law and *Rule,* or *Gauge,* of constitution and law, within which the public force must act. Make a breach in either, and the great steam-hammer, with its swift and ponderous blows, crushes all the machinery to atoms, and, at last, wrenching itself away, lies inert and dead amid the ruin it has wrought.

The FORCE of the people, or the popular will, in action and

exerted, symbolized by the GAVEL, regulated and guided by and acting within the limits of LAW and ORDER, symbolized by the TWENTY-FOUR-INCH RULE, has for its fruit LIBERTY, EQUALITY, and FRATERNITY,—liberty regulated by law; equality of rights in the eye of the law; brotherhood with its duties and obligations as well as its benefits.

You will hear shortly of the *Rough* ASHLAR and the *Perfect* ASHLAR, as part of the jewels of the Lodge. The rough Ashlar is said to be "a stone, as taken from the quarry, in its rude and natural state." The perfect Ashlar is said to be "a stone made ready by the hands of the workmen, to be adjusted by the working-tools of the Fellow-Craft." We shall not repeat the explanations of these symbols given by the York Rite. You may read them in its printed monitors. They are declared to allude to the self-improvement of the individual craftsman,—a continuation of the same superficial interpretation.

The rough Ashlar is the PEOPLE, as a mass, rude and unorganized. The perfect Ashlar, or cubical stone, symbol of perfection, is the STATE, the rulers deriving their powers from the consent of the governed; the constitution and laws speaking the will of the people; the government harmonious, symmetrical, efficient, —its powers properly distributed and duly adjusted in equilibrium.

If we delineate a cube on a plane surface thus:

we have visible *three* faces, and *nine* external lines, drawn between *seven* points. The complete cube has *three* more faces, making *six; three* more lines, making *twelve;* and *one* more point, making *eight.* As the number 12 includes the sacred numbers, 3, 5, 7, and 3 times 3, or 9, and is produced by adding the sacred number 3 to 9; while its own two figures, 1, 2, the unit or monad, and duad, added together, make the same sacred number 3; it was called the perfect number; and the cube became the symbol of perfection.

Produced by FORCE, acting by RULE; hammered in accordance

with lines measured by the Gauge, out of the rough Ashlar, it is an appropriate symbol of the Force of the people, expressed as the constitution and law of the State; and of the State itself the three visible faces represent the three departments,—the Executive, which executes the laws; the Legislative, which makes the laws; the Judiciary, which interprets the laws, applies and enforces them, between man and man, between the State and the citizens. The three invisible faces, are Liberty, Equality, and Fraternity,— the threefold soul of the State—its vitality, spirit, and intellect.

*   *   *   *   *   *

Though Masonry neither usurps the place of, nor apes religion, prayer is an essential part of our ceremonies. It is the aspiration of the soul toward the Absolute and Infinite Intelligence, which is the One Supreme Deity, most feebly and misunderstandingly characterized as an "ARCHITECT." Certain faculties of man are directed toward the Unknown—thought, meditation, prayer. The unknown is an ocean, of which conscience is the compass. Thought, meditation, prayer, are the great mysterious pointings of the needle. It is a spiritual magnetism that thus connects the human soul with the Deity. These majestic irradiations of the soul pierce through the shadow toward the light.

It is but a shallow scoff to say that prayer is absurd, because it is not possible for us, by means of it, to persuade God to change His plans. He produces foreknown and foreintended effects, by the instrumentality of the forces of nature, all of which are *His* forces. Our own are part of these. Our free agency and our will are forces. We do not absurdly cease to make *efforts* to attain wealth or happiness, prolong life, and continue health, because we cannot by any effort change what is predestined. If the effort also is predestined, it is not the less *our* effort, made of *our free will.* So, likewise, we pray. Will is a force. Thought is a force. Prayer is a force. Why should it not be of the law of God, that prayer, like Faith and Love, should have its effects? Man is not to be comprehended as a starting-point, or progress as a goal, without those two great forces, Faith and Love. Prayer is sublime. Orisons that beg and clamor are pitiful. To deny the efficacy of prayer, is to deny that of Faith, Love, and Effort. Yet the effects produced, when our hand, moved by our will, launches a pebble into the ocean, never cease; and every uttered word is registered for eternity upon the invisible air.

Every Lodge is a Temple, and as a whole, and in its details symbolic. The Universe itself supplied man with the model for the first temples reared to the Divinity. The arrangement of the Temple of Solomon, the symbolic ornaments which formed its chief decorations, and the dress of the High-Priest, all had reference to the order of the Universe, as then understood. The Temple contained many emblems of the seasons—the sun, the moon, the planets, the constellations Ursa Major and Minor, the zodiac, the elements, and the other parts of the world. It is the Master of *this* Lodge, of the Universe, Hermes, of whom Khūrūm is the representative, that is one of the lights of the Lodge.

For further instruction as to the symbolism of the heavenly bodies, and of the sacred numbers, and of the temple and its details, you must wait patiently until you advance in Masonry, in the mean time exercising your intellect in studying them for yourself. To study and seek to interpret correctly the symbols of the Universe, is the work of the sage and philosopher. It is to decipher the writing of God, and penetrate into His thoughts.

This is what is asked and answered in our catechism, in regard to the Lodge.

* * * * * *

A "Lodge" is defined to be "an assemblage of Freemasons, duly congregated, having the sacred writings, square, and compass, and a charter, or warrant of constitution, authorizing them to work." The room or place in which they meet, representing some part of King Solomon's Temple, is also called the Lodge; and it is that we are now considering.

It is said to be supported by three great columns, WISDOM, FORCE or STRENGTH, and BEAUTY, represented by the Master, the Senior Warden, and the Junior Warden; and these are said to be the columns that support the Lodge, "because Wisdom, Strength, and Beauty, are the perfections of everything, and nothing can endure without them." "Because," the York Rite says, "it is necessary that there should be Wisdom to conceive, Strength to support, and Beauty to adorn, all great and important undertakings." "Know ye not," says the Apostle Paul, "that ye are the temple of God, and that the Spirit of God dwelleth in you? If any man desecrate the temple of God, him shall God destroy, for the temple of God is holy, which temple ye are."

The Wisdom and Power of the Deity are in equilibrium. The

laws of nature and the moral laws are not the mere despotic mandates of His Omnipotent will; for, then they might be changed by Him, and order become disorder, and good and right become evil and wrong; honesty and loyalty, vices; and fraud, ingratitude, and vice, virtues. Omnipotent power, infinite, and existing alone, would necessarily not be constrained to consistency. Its decrees and laws could not be immutable. The laws of God are not obligatory on us because they are the enactments of His POWER, or the expression of His WILL; but because they express His infinite WISDOM. They are not right because they are His laws, but His laws because they are right. From the equilibrium of infinite wisdom and infinite force, results perfect harmony, in physics and in the moral universe. Wisdom, Power, and Harmony constitute one Masonic triad. They have other and profounder meanings, that may at some time be unveiled to you.

As to the ordinary and commonplace explanation, it may be added, that the wisdom of the Architect is displayed in combining, as only a skillful Architect can do, and as God has done everywhere,—for example, in the tree, the human frame, the egg, the cells of the honeycomb—strength, with grace, beauty, symmetry, proportion, lightness, ornamentation. That, too, is the perfection of the orator and poet—to combine force, strength, energy, with grace of style, musical cadences, the beauty of figures, the play and irradiation of imagination and fancy; and so, in a State, the warlike and industrial force of the people, and their Titanic strength, must be combined with the beauty of the arts, the sciences, and the intellect, if the State would scale the heights of excellence, and the people be really free. Harmony in this, as in all the Divine, the material, and the human, is the result of equilibrium, of the sympathy and opposite action of contraries; a single Wisdom above them holding the beam of the scales. To reconcile the moral law, human responsibility, free-will, with the absolute power of God; and the existence of evil with His absolute wisdom, and goodness, and mercy,— these are the great enigmas of the Sphynx.

You entered the Lodge between two columns. They represent the two which stood in the porch of the Temple, on each side of the great eastern gateway. These pillars, of bronze, four fingers breadth in thickness, were, according to the most authentic account—that in the First and that in the Second Book of Kings, confirmed in Jeremiah—eighteen cubits high, with a capital five cubits high. The shaft of each was four cubits in diameter. A cubit is one foot and $\frac{707}{1000}$. That is, the shaft of each was a little over thirty feet eight inches in height, the capital of each a little over eight feet six inches in height, and the diameter of the shaft six feet ten inches. The capitals were enriched by pomegranates of bronze, covered by bronze net-work, and ornamented with wreaths of bronze; and appear to have imitated the shape of the seed-vessel of the lotus or Egyptian lily, a sacred symbol to the Hindus and Egyptians. The pillar or column on the right, or in the south, was named, as the Hebrew word is rendered in our translation of the Bible, JACHIN: and that on the left BOAZ. Our translators say that the first word means, "*He shall establish;*" and the second, "*In it is strength.*"

These columns were imitations, by Khūrūm, the Tyrian artist, of the great columns consecrated to the Winds and Fire, at the entrance to the famous Temple of Malkarth, in the city of Tyre. It is customary, in Lodges of the York Rite, to see a celestial globe on one, and a terrestrial globe on the other; but these are not warranted, if the object be to imitate the original two columns of the Temple. The symbolic meaning of these columns we shall leave for the present unexplained, only adding that Entered Apprentices keep their working-tools in the column JACHIN; and giving you the etymology and literal meaning of the two names.

The word *Jachin,* in Hebrew, is יכין. It was probably pronounced *Ya-kayan,* and meant, as a verbal noun, *He that strengthens;* and thence, *firm, stable, upright.*

The word *Boaz* is בעז, Baaz. עז means *Strong, Strength, Power, Might, Refuge, Source of Strength, a Fort.* The ב prefixed means "*with*" or "*in,*" and gives the word the force of the Latin gerund, *roborando—Strengthening.*

The former word also means *he will establish,* or *plant in an erect position*—from the verb כון *Kūn, he stood erect.* It probably meant *Active* and *Vivifying Energy* and *Force;* and *Boaz, Stability, Permanence,* in the *passive* sense.

The Dimensions of the Lodge, our Brethren of the York Rite say, "are unlimited, and its covering no less than the canopy of Heaven." "To this object," they say, "the mason's mind is con-

2

tinually directed, and thither he hopes at last to arrive by the
aid of the theological ladder which Jacob in his vision saw
ascending from earth to Heaven; the three principal rounds of
which are denominated Faith, Hope, and Charity; and which
admonish us to have Faith in God, Hope in Immortality, and
Charity to all mankind." Accordingly a ladder, sometimes with
nine rounds, is seen on the chart, resting at the bottom on the
earth, its top in the clouds, the stars shining above it; and this is
deemed to represent that mystic ladder, which Jacob saw in his
dream, set up on the earth, and the top of it reaching to Heaven,
with the angels of God ascending and descending on it. The
addition of the three principal rounds to the symbolism, is wholly
modern and incongruous.

The ancients counted seven planets, thus arranged: the Moon,
Mercury, Venus, the Sun, Mars, Jupiter, and Saturn. There
were seven heavens and seven spheres of these planets; on all
the monuments of Mithras are seven altars or pyres, consecrated
to the seven planets, as were the seven lamps of the golden
candelabrum in the Temple. That these represented the planets,
we are assured by Clemens of Alexandria, in his Stromata, and by
Philo Judæus.

To return to its source in the Infinite, the human soul, the
ancients held, had to ascend, as it had descended, through the
seven spheres. The *Ladder* by which it reascends, has, according
to Marsilius Ficinus, in his Commentary on the Ennead of Plotinus, seven degrees or steps; and in the Mysteries of Mithras,
carried to Rome under the Emperors, the ladder, with its seven
rounds, was a symbol referring to this ascent through the spheres
of the seven planets. Jacob saw the Spirits of God ascending and
descending on it; and above it the Deity Himself. The Mithraic
Mysteries were celebrated in caves, where gates were marked at
the four equinoctial and solstitial points of the zodiac; and the
seven planetary spheres were represented, which souls needs must
traverse in descending from the heaven of the fixed stars to the
elements that envelop the earth; and seven gates were marked,
one for each planet, through which they pass, in descending or
returning.

We learn this from Celsus, in Origen, who says that the symbolic image of this passage among the stars, used in the Mithraic
Mysteries, was a ladder reaching from earth to Heaven, divided

into seven steps or stages, to each of which was a gate, and at the summit an eighth one, that of the fixed stars. The symbol was the same as that of the seven stages of Borsippa, the Pyramid of vitrified brick, near Babylon, built of seven stages, and each of a different color. In the Mithraic ceremonies, the candidate went through seven stages of initiation, passing through many fearful trials—and of these the high ladder with seven rounds or steps was the symbol.

You see the Lodge, its details and ornaments, by its Lights. You have already heard what these Lights, the greater and lesser, are said to be, and how they are spoken of by our Brethren of the York Rite.

The *Holy Bible, Square, and Compasses,* are not only styled the Great Lights in Masonry, but they are also technically called the *Furniture* of the Lodge; and, as you have seen, it is held that there is no Lodge without them. This has sometimes been made a pretext for excluding Jews from our Lodges, because they cannot regard the New Testament as a holy book. The Bible is an indispensable part of the furniture of a *Christian* Lodge, only because it is the sacred book of the Christian religion. The Hebrew Pentateuch in a Hebrew Lodge, and the Koran in a Mohammedan one, belong on the Altar; and one of these, and the Square and Compass, properly understood, are the Great Lights by which a Mason must walk and work.

The obligation of the candidate is always to be taken on the sacred book or books of his religion, that he may deem it more solemn and binding; and therefore it was that you were asked of what religion you were. We have no other concern with your religious creed.

The Square is a right angle, formed by two right lines. It is adapted only to a plane surface, and belongs only to geometry, earth-measurement, that trigonometry which deals only with planes, and with the earth, which the ancients supposed to be a plane. The Compass describes circles, and deals with spherical trigonometry, the science of the spheres and heavens. The former, therefore, is an emblem of what concerns the earth and the body; the latter of what concerns the heavens and the soul. Yet the Compass is also used in plane trigonometry, as in erecting perpendiculars; and, therefore, you are reminded that, although in this Degree both points of the Compass are under the Square, and

you are now dealing only with the moral and political meaning of
the symbols, and not with their philosophical and spiritual meanings, still the divine ever mingles with the human; with the
earthly the spiritual intermixes; and there is something spiritual
in the commonest duties of life. The nations are not bodies-
politic alone, but also souls-politic; and woe to that people which,
seeking the material only, forgets that it has a soul. Then we
have a race, petrified in dogma, which presupposes the absence of
a soul and the presence only of memory and instinct, or demoralized by lucre. Such a nature can never lead civilization. Genu-
flexion before the idol or the dollar atrophies the muscle which
walks and the will which moves. Hieratic or mercantile absorption diminishes the radiance of a people, lowers its horizon by
lowering its level, and deprives it of that understanding of the
universal aim, at the same time human and divine, which makes
the missionary nations. A free people, forgetting that it has a soul
to be cared for, devotes all its energies to its material advancement.
If it makes war, it is to subserve its commercial interests. The
citizens copy after the State, and regard wealth, pomp, and luxury
as the great goods of life. Such a nation creates wealth rapidly,
and distributes it badly. Thence the two extremes, of monstrous
opulence and monstrous misery; all the enjoyment to a few, all
the privations to the rest, that is to say, to the people; Privilege,
Exception, Monopoly, Feudality, springing up from Labor itself:
a false and dangerous situation, which, making Labor a blinded
and chained Cyclops, in the mine, at the forge, in the workshop, at
the loom, in the field, over poisonous fumes, in miasmatic cells, in
unventilated factories, founds public power upon private misery,
and plants the greatness of the State in the suffering of the individual. It is a greatness ill constituted, in which all the material
elements are combined, and into which no moral element enters.
If a people, like a star, has the right of eclipse, the light ought to
return. The eclipse should not degenerate into night.

The three lesser, or the Sublime Lights, you have heard, are the
Sun, the Moon, and the Master of the Lodge; and you have heard
what our Brethren of the York Rite say in regard to them, and
why they hold them to be Lights of the Lodge. But the Sun and
Moon do in no sense light the Lodge, unless it be symbolically,
and then the lights are not they, but those things of which they
are the symbols. Of what they are the symbols the Mason in that

Rite is not told. Nor does the Moon in any sense rule the night with regularity.

The Sun is the ancient symbol of the life-giving and generative power of the Deity. To the ancients, light was the cause of life; and God was the source from which all light flowed; the *essence* of Light, the *Invisible* Fire, developed as Flame *manifested* as light and splendor. The Sun was His manifestation and visible image; and the Sabæans worshipping the Light—God, *seemed* to worship the Sun, in whom they saw the manifestation of the Deity.

The Moon was the symbol of the passive capacity of nature to produce, the female, of which the life-giving power and energy was the male. It was the symbol of Isis, Astarte, and Artemis, or Diana. The *"Master of Life"* was the Supreme Deity, above both, and manifested through both; Zeus, the Son of Saturn, become King of the Gods; Horus, son of Osiris and Isis, become the Master of Life; Dionusos or Bacchus, like Mithras, become the author of Light and Life and Truth.

* * * * * *

The Master of Light and Life, the Sun and the Moon, are symbolized in every Lodge by the Master and Wardens: and this makes it the duty of the Master to dispense light to the Brethren, by himself, and through the Wardens, who are his ministers.

"Thy sun," says ISAIAH to Jerusalem, "shall no more go down, neither shall thy moon withdraw itself; for the LORD shall be thine everlasting light, and the days of thy mourning shall be ended. Thy people also shall be all righteous; they shall inherit the land forever." Such is the type of a free people.

Our northern ancestors worshipped this tri-une Deity; ODIN, the Almighty FATHER; FREA, his wife, emblem of universal matter; and THOR, his son, the mediator. But above all these was the Supreme God, "the author of everything that existeth, the Eternal, the Ancient, the Living and Awful Being, the Searcher into concealed things, the Being that never changeth." In the Temple of Eleusis (a sanctuary lighted only by a window in the roof, and representing the Universe), the images of the Sun, Moon, and Mercury, were represented.

"The Sun and Moon," says the learned Bro.˙. DELAUNAY, "represent the two grand principles of all generations, the active and passive, the male and the female. The Sun represents the actual light. He pours upon the Moon his fecundating rays; both shed their light upon their offspring, the Blazing Star, or HORUS, and the three form the great Equilateral Triangle, in the centre of which is the omnific letter of the Kabalah, by which creation is said to have been effected."

The ORNAMENTS of a Lodge are said to be "the Mosaic Pavement, the Indented Tessel, and the Blazing Star." The Mosaic Pavement, chequered in squares or lozenges, is said to represent the ground-floor of King Solomon's Temple; and the Indented Tessel "that beautiful tesselated border which surrounded it." The Blazing Star in the centre is said to be "an emblem of Divine Providence, and commemorative of the star which appeared to guide the wise men of the East to the place of our Saviour's nativity." But "there was no stone seen" within the Temple. The walls were covered with planks of cedar, and the floor was covered with planks of fir. There is no evidence that there was such a pavement or floor in the Temple, or such a bordering. In England, anciently, the Tracing-Board was surrounded with an indented border; and it is only in America that such a border is put around the Mosaic pavement. The tesseræ, indeed, are the squares or lozenges of the pavement. In England, also, "the indented or denticulated border" is called "tesselated," because it has four "tassels," said to represent Temperance, Fortitude, Prudence, and Justice. It was termed the Indented Trassel; but this is a misuse of words. It is a *tesserated* pavement, with an indented border round it.

The pavement, alternately black and white, symbolizes, whether so intended or not, the Good and Evil Principles of the Egyptian and Persian creed. It is the warfare of Michael and Satan, of the Gods and Titans, of Balder and Lok; between light and shadow, which is darkness; Day and Night; Freedom and Despotism; Religious Liberty and the Arbitrary Dogmas of a Church that thinks for its votaries, and whose Pontiff claims to be infallible, and the decretals of its Councils to constitute a gospel.

The edges of this pavement, if in lozenges, will necessarily be indented or denticulated, toothed like a saw; and to complete and finish it a bordering is necessary. It is completed by tassels as ornaments at the corners. If these and the bordering have any symbolic meaning, it is fanciful and arbitrary.

To find in the BLAZING STAR of five points an allusion to the

Divine Providence, is also fanciful; and to make it commemorative of the Star that is said to have guided the Magi, is to give it a meaning comparatively modern. Originally it represented SIRIUS, or the Dog-star, the forerunner of the inundation of the Nile; the God ANUBIS, companion of ISIS in her search for the body of OSIRIS, her brother and husband. Then it became the image of HORUS, the son of OSIRIS, himself symbolized also by the Sun, the author of the Seasons, and the God of Time; Son of ISIS, who was the universal nature, himself the primitive matter, inexhaustible source of Life, spark of uncreated fire, universal seed of all beings. It was HERMES, also, the Master of Learning, whose name in Greek is that of the God Mercury. It became the sacred and potent sign or character of the Magi, the PENTALPHA, and is the significant emblem of Liberty and Freedom, blazing with a steady radiance amid the weltering elements of good and evil of Revolutions, and promising serene skies and fertile seasons to the nations, after the storms of change and tumult.

In the East of the Lodge, over the Master, inclosed in a triangle, is the Hebrew letter YŌD [˒ or ﬡ]. In the English and American Lodges the Letter G∴ is substituted for this, as the initial of the word GOD, with as little reason as if the letter D., initial of DIEU, were used in French Lodges instead of the proper letter. YŌD is, in the Kabalah, the symbol of Unity, of the Supreme Deity, the first letter of the Holy Name; and also a symbol of the Great Kabalistic Triads. To understand its mystic meanings, you must open the pages of the Sohar and Siphra de Zeniutha, and other kabalistic books, and ponder deeply on their meaning. It must suffice to say, that it is the Creative Energy of the Deity, is represented as a *point,* and that point in the centre of the *Circle* of immensity. It is to us in this Degree, the symbol of that unmanifested Deity, the Absolute, who has no name.

Our French Brethren place this letter YŌD in the centre of the Blazing Star. And in the old Lectures, our ancient English Brethren said, "The Blazing Star or Glory in the centre refers us to that grand luminary, the Sun, which enlightens the earth, and by its genial influence dispenses blessings to mankind." They called it also in the same lectures, an emblem of PRUDENCE. The word *Prudentia* means, in its original and fullest signification, *Foresight;* and, accordingly, the Blazing Star has been regarded as an emblem of Omniscience, or the All-seeing Eye, which to the

Egyptian Initiates was the emblem of Osiris, the Creator. With
the YŌD in the centre, it has the kabalistic meaning of the Divine
Energy, manifested as Light, creating the Universe.

The Jewels of the Lodge are said to be six in number. Three
are called *"Movable,"* and three *"Immovable."* The SQUARE, the
LEVEL, and the PLUMB were anciently and properly called the
Movable Jewels, because they pass from one Brother to another.
It is a modern innovation to call them immovable, because they
must always be present in the Lodge. The immovable jewels are
the ROUGH ASHLAR, the PERFECT ASHLAR or CUBICAL STONE, or,
in some Rituals, the DOUBLE CUBE, and the TRACING-BOARD, or
TRESTLE-BOARD.

Of these jewels our Brethren of the York Rite say: "The
Square inculcates Morality; the *Level,* Equality; and the *Plumb,*
Rectitude of Conduct." Their explanation of the immovable
Jewels may be read in their monitors.

*   *   *   *   *   *

Our Brethren of the York Rite say that "there is represented
in every well-governed Lodge, a certain point, within a circle;
the point representing an individual Brother; the Circle, the
boundary line of his conduct, beyond which he is never to suffer
his prejudices or passions to betray him."

This is not to *interpret* the symbols of Masonry. It is said by
some, with a nearer approach to interpretation, that the point
within the circle represents God in the centre of the Universe. It
is a common Egyptian sign for the Sun and Osiris, and is still
used as the astronomical sign of the great luminary. In the Kabalah the point is YŌD, the Creative Energy of God, irradiating
with light the circular space which God, the universal Light,
left vacant, wherein to create the worlds, by withdrawing His
substance of Light back on all sides from one point.

Our Brethren add that, "this circle is embordered by two
perpendicular parallel lines, representing Saint John the Baptist
and Saint John the Evangelist, and upon the top rest the Holy
Scriptures" (an open book). "In going round this circle," they
say, "we necessarily touch upon these two lines as well as upon
the Holy Scriptures; and while a Mason keeps himself circum-
scribed within their precepts, it is impossible that he should
materially err."

It would be a waste of time to comment upon this. Some writers have imagined that the parallel lines represent the Tropics of Cancer and Capricorn, which the Sun alternately touches upon at the Summer and Winter solstices. But the tropics are not perpendicular lines, and the idea is merely fanciful. If the parallel lines ever belonged to the ancient symbol, they had some more recondite and more *fruitful* meaning. They probably had the same meaning as the twin columns Jachin and Boaz. That meaning is not for the Apprentice. The adept may find it in the Kabalah. The JUSTICE and MERCY of God are in equilibrium, and the result is HARMONY, because a Single and Perfect Wisdom presides over both.

The Holy Scriptures are an entirely modern addition to the symbol, like the terrestrial and celestial globes on the columns of the portico. Thus the ancient symbol has been denaturalized by incongruous additions, like that of Isis weeping over the broken column containing the remains of Osiris at Byblos.

*   *   *   *   *   *

Masonry has its decalogue, which is a law to its Initiates. These are its Ten Commandments:

I. ⊕∴ God is the Eternal, Omnipotent, Immutable WISDOM and Supreme INTELLIGENCE and Exhaustless LOVE.

Thou shalt adore, revere, and love Him!

Thou shalt honor Him by practising the virtues!

II. O∴ Thy religion shall be, to do good because it is a pleasure to thee, and not merely because it is a duty.

That thou mayest become the friend of the wise man, thou shalt obey his precepts!

Thy soul is immortal! Thou shalt do nothing to degrade it!

III. ⊕∴ Thou shalt unceasingly war against vice!

Thou shalt not do unto others that which thou wouldst not wish them to do unto thee!

Thou shalt be submissive to thy fortunes, and keep burning the light of wisdom!

IV. O∴ Thou shalt honor thy parents!

Thou shalt pay respect and homage to the aged!

Thou shalt instruct the young!

Thou shalt protect and defend infancy and innocence!

V. ⊕∴ Thou shalt cherish thy wife and thy children!

Thou shalt love thy country, and obey its laws!

VI. O∴ Thy friend shall be to thee a second self!
   Misfortune shall not estrange thee from him!
   Thou shalt do for his memory whatever thou wouldst do
      for him, if he were living!
VII. ⊕∴ Thou shalt avoid and flee from insincere friendships!
   Thou shalt in everything refrain from excess.
   Thou shalt fear to be the cause of a stain on thy memory!
VIII. O∴ Thou shalt allow no passions to become thy master!
   Thou shalt make the passions of others profitable lessons
      to thyself!
   Thou shalt be indulgent to error!
IX. ⊕∴ Thou shalt hear much: Thou shalt speak little: Thou
      shalt act well!
   Thou shalt forget injuries!
   Thou shalt render good for evil!
   Thou shalt not misuse either thy strength or thy superiority!
X. O∴ Thou shalt study to know men; that thereby thou
      mayest learn to know thyself!
   Thou shalt ever seek after virtue!
   Thou shalt be just!
   Thou shalt avoid idleness!

But the great commandment of Masonry is this: "A new commandment give I unto you: that ye love one another! He that saith he is in the light, and hateth his brother, remaineth still in the darkness."

Such are the moral duties of a Mason. But it is also the duty of Masonry to assist in elevating the moral and intellectual level of society; in coining knowledge, bringing ideas into circulation, and causing the mind of youth to grow; and in putting, gradually, by the teachings of axioms and the promulgation of positive laws, the human race in harmony with its destinies.

To this duty and work the Initiate is apprenticed. He must not imagine that he can effect nothing, and, therefore, despairing, become inert. It is in this, as in a man's daily life. Many great deeds are done in the small struggles of life. There is, we are told, a determined though unseen bravery, which defends itself, foot to foot, in the darkness, against the fatal invasion of necessity and of baseness. There are noble and mysterious triumphs, which no eye sees, which no renown rewards, which no flourish of trumpets salutes. Life, misfortune, isolation, abandonment, poverty, are battle-fields, which have their heroes,—heroes obscure, but sometimes greater than those who become illustrious. The Mason should struggle in the same manner, and with the same bravery, against those invasions of necessity and baseness, which come to nations as well as to men. He should meet *them*, too, foot to foot, even in the darkness, and protest against the national wrongs and follies; against usurpation and the first inroads of that hydra, Tyranny. There is no more sovereign eloquence than the truth in indignation. It is more difficult for a people to keep than to gain their freedom. The Protests of Truth are always needed. Continually, the right must protest against the fact. There is, in fact, Eternity in the Right. The Mason should be the Priest and Soldier of that Right. If his country should be robbed of her liberties, he should still not despair. The protest of the Right against the Fact persists forever. The robbery of a people never becomes prescriptive. Reclamation of its rights is barred by no length of time. Warsaw can no more be Tartar than Venice can be Teutonic. A people may endure military usurpation, and subjugated States kneel to States and wear the yoke, while under the stress of necessity; but when the necessity disappears, if the people is fit to be free, the submerged country will float to the surface and reappear, and Tyranny be adjudged by History to have murdered its victims.

Whatever occurs, we should have Faith in the Justice and over-ruling Wisdom of God, and Hope for the Future, and Loving-kindness for those who are in error. God makes visible to men His will in events; an obscure text, written in a mysterious language. Men make their translations of it forthwith, hasty, incorrect, full of faults, omissions, and misreadings. We see so short a way along the arc of the great circle! Few minds comprehend the Divine tongue. The most sagacious, the most calm, the most profound, decipher the hieroglyphs slowly; and when they arrive with their text, perhaps the need has long gone by; there are already twenty translations in the public square—the most incorrect being, as of course, the most accepted and popular. From each translation, a party is born; and from each misreading, a faction. Each party believes or pretends that it has the only true text, and each faction believes or pretends that it alone possesses the light. Moreover, factions are blind men, who aim straight, errors are excellent projectiles, striking skillfully, and with all the violence that springs from false reasoning, wherever a want of logic in those who defend the right, like a defect in a cuirass, makes them vulnerable.

Therefore it is that we shall often be discomfited in combating error before the people. Antæus long resisted Hercules; and the heads of the Hydra grew as fast as they were cut off. It is absurd to say that *Error, wounded, writhes in pain, and dies amid her worshippers.* Truth conquers slowly. There is a wondrous vitality in Error. Truth, indeed, for the most part, shoots over the heads of the masses; or if an error is prostrated for a moment, it is up again in a moment, and as vigorous as ever. It will not die when the brains are out, and the most stupid and irrational errors are the longest-lived.

Nevertheless, Masonry, which is Morality and Philosophy, must not cease to do its duty. We never know at what moment success awaits our efforts—generally when most unexpected—nor with what effect our efforts are or are not to be attended. Succeed or fail, Masonry must not bow to error, or succumb under discouragement. There were at Rome a few Carthaginian soldiers, taken prisoners, who refused to bow to Flaminius, and had a little of Hannibal's magnanimity. Masons should possess an equal greatness of soul. Masonry should be an energy; finding its aim and effect in the amelioration of mankind. Socrates should enter into Adam, and produce Marcus Aurelius, in other words, bring forth from the man of enjoyments, the man of wisdom. Masonry should not be a mere watch-tower, built upon mystery, from which to gaze at ease upon the world, with no other result than to be a convenience for the curious. To hold the full cup of thought to the thirsty lips of men; to give to all the true ideas of Deity; to harmonize conscience and science, are the province of Philosophy. Morality is Faith in full bloom. Contemplation should lead to action, and the absolute be practical; the ideal be made air and food and drink to the human mind. Wisdom is a sacred communion. It is only on that condition that it ceases to be a sterile love of Science, and becomes the one and supreme method by which to unite Humanity and arouse it to concerted action. Then Philosophy becomes Religion.

And Masonry, like History and Philosophy, has eternal duties—eternal, and, at the same time, simple—to oppose Caiaphas as Bishop, Draco or Jefferies as Judge, Trimalcion as Legislator, and Tiberius as Emperor. These are the symbols of the tyranny that degrades and crushes, and the corruption that defiles and infests. In the works published for the use of the Craft we are told that the three great tenets of a Mason's profession, are Brotherly Love, Relief, and Truth. And it is true that a Brotherly affection and kindness should govern us in all our intercourse and relations with our brethren; and a generous and liberal philanthropy actuate us in regard to all men. To relieve the distressed is peculiarly the duty of Masons—a sacred duty, not to be omitted, neglected, or coldly or inefficiently complied with. It is also most true, that Truth is a Divine attribute and the foundation of every virtue. To be true, and to seek to find and learn the Truth, are the great objects of every good Mason.

As the Ancients did, Masonry styles Temperance, Fortitude, Prudence, and Justice, the four cardinal virtues. They are as necessary to nations as to individuals. The people that would be Free and Independent, must possess Sagacity, Forethought, Foresight, and careful Circumspection, all which are included in the meaning of the word Prudence. It must be temperate in asserting its rights, temperate in its councils, economical in its expenses; it must be bold, brave, courageous, patient under reverses, undismayed by disasters, hopeful amid calamities, like Rome when she sold the field at which Hannibal had his camp. No Cannæ or Pharsalia or Pavia or Agincourt or Waterloo must discourage her. Let her Senate sit in their seats until the Gauls pluck them by the beard. She must, above all things, be just, not truckling to the strong and warring on or plundering the weak; she must act on the square with all nations, and the feeblest tribes; always keeping her faith, honest in her legislation, upright in all her dealings. Whenever such a Republic exists, it will be immortal: for rashness, injustice, intemperance and luxury in prosperity, and despair and disorder in adversity, are the causes of the decay and dilapidation of nations.

II.

THE FELLOW-CRAFT.

In the Ancient Orient, all religion was more or less a mystery and there was no divorce from it of philosophy. The popular theology, taking the multitude of allegories and symbols for realities, degenerated into a worship of the celestial luminaries, of imaginary Deities with human feelings, passions, appetites, and lusts, of idols, stones, animals, reptiles. The Onion was sacred to the Egyptians, because its different layers were a symbol of the concentric heavenly spheres. Of course the popular religion could not satisfy the deeper longings and thoughts, the loftier aspirations of the Spirit, or the logic of reason. The first, therefore, was taught to the initiated in the Mysteries. There, also, it was taught by symbols. The vagueness of symbolism, capable of many interpretations, reached what the palpable and conventional creed could not. Its indefiniteness acknowledged the abstruseness of the subject: it treated that mysterious subject mystically: it endeavored to illustrate what it could not explain; to excite an appropriate *feeling*, if it could not develop an adequate *idea;* and to make the image a mere subordinate conveyance for the conception, which itself never became obvious or familiar.

Thus the knowledge now imparted by books and letters, was of old conveyed by symbols; and the priests invented or perpetuated a display of rites and exhibitions, which were not only more attractive to the eye than words, but often more suggestive and more pregnant with meaning to the mind.

Masonry, successor of the Mysteries, still follows the ancient manner of teaching. Her ceremonies are like the ancient mystic shows,—not the reading of an essay, but the opening of a problem, requiring research, and constituting philosophy the arch-expounder. Her symbols are the instruction she gives. The lectures are endeavors, often partial and one-sided, to interpret these symbols. He who would become an accomplished Mason must not be content merely to hear, or even to understand, the lectures; he

22

must, aided by them, and they having, as it were, marked out the way for him, study, interpret, and develop these symbols for himself.

*   *   *   *   *   *

Though Masonry is identical with the ancient Mysteries, it is so only in this qualified sense: that it presents but an imperfect image of their brilliancy, the ruins only of their grandeur, and a system that has experienced progressive alterations, the fruits of social events, political circumstances, and the ambitious imbecility of its improvers. After leaving Egypt, the Mysteries were modified by the habits of the different nations among whom they were introduced, and especially by the religious systems of the countries into which they were transplanted. To maintain the established government, laws, and religion, was the obligation of the Initiate everywhere; and everywhere they were the heritage of the priests, who were nowhere willing to make the common people co-proprietors with themselves of philosophical truth.

Masonry is not the Coliseum in ruins. It is rather a Roman palace of the middle ages, disfigured by modern architectural improvements, yet built on a Cyclopæan foundation laid by the Etruscans, and with many a stone of the superstructure taken from dwellings and temples of the age of Hadrian and Antoninus.

Christianity taught the doctrine of FRATERNITY; but repudiated that of political EQUALITY, by continually inculcating obedience to Cæsar, and to those lawfully in authority. Masonry was the first apostle of EQUALITY. In the Monastery there is *fraternity* and *equality*, but no *liberty*. Masonry added that also, and claimed for man the three-fold heritage, LIBERTY, EQUALITY, and FRATERNITY.

It was but a development of the original purpose of the Mysteries, which was to teach men to know and practice their duties to themselves and their fellows, the great practical end of all philosophy and all knowledge.

Truths are the springs from which duties flow; and it is but a few hundred years since a new Truth began to be distinctly seen; that MAN IS SUPREME OVER INSTITUTIONS, AND NOT THEY OVER HIM. Man has *natural* empire over *all* institutions. They are for him, according to his development; not he for them. This seems to us a very simple statement, one to which all men, everywhere, ought to assent. But once it was a great new Truth,—not revealed until governments had been in existence for at least five thousand years. Once revealed, it imposed new duties on men. Man owed it to *himself* to be free. He owed it to his *country* to seek to give *her* freedom, or maintain her in that possession. It made Tyranny and Usurpation the enemies of the Human Race. It created a general outlawry of Despots and Despotisms, temporal and spiritual. The sphere of Duty was immensely enlarged. Patriotism had, henceforth, a new and wider meaning. Free Government, Free Thought, Free Conscience, Free Speech! All these came to be inalienable rights, which those who had parted with them or been robbed of them, or whose ancestors had lost them, had the right summarily to retake. Unfortunately, as Truths always become perverted into falsehoods, and are falsehoods when misapplied, *this* Truth became the Gospel of Anarchy, soon after it was first preached.

Masonry early comprehended this Truth, and recognized its own enlarged duties. Its symbols then came to have a wider meaning; but it also assumed the mask of Stone-masonry, and borrowed its working-tools, and so was supplied with new and apt symbols. It aided in bringing about the French Revolution, disappeared with the Girondists, was born again with the restoration of order, and sustained Napoleon, because, though Emperor, he acknowledged the right of the people to select its rulers, and was at the head of a nation refusing to receive back its old kings. He pleaded, with sabre, musket, and cannon, the great cause of the People against Royalty, the right of the French people even to make a Corsican General their Emperor, if it pleased them.

Masonry felt that this Truth had the Omnipotence of God on its side; and that neither Pope nor Potentate could overcome it. It was a truth dropped into the world's wide treasury, and forming a part of the heritage which each generation receives, enlarges, and holds in trust, and of necessity bequeaths to mankind; the personal estate of man, entailed of nature to the end of time. And Masonry early recognized it as true, that to set forth and develop a truth, or any human excellence of gift or growth, is to make greater the spiritual glory of the race; that whosoever aids the march of a Truth, and makes the thought a thing, writes in the same line with MOSES, and with Him who died upon the cross; and has an intellectual sympathy with the Deity Himself.

The best gift we can bestow on man is manhood. It is that

which Masonry is ordained of God to bestow on its votaries: not sectarianism and religious dogma; not a rudimental morality, that may be found in the writings of Confucius, Zoroaster, Seneca, and the Rabbis, in the Proverbs and Ecclesiastes; not a little and cheap common-school knowledge; but manhood and science and philosophy.

Not that Philosophy or Science is in opposition to Religion. For Philosophy is but that knowledge of God and the Soul, which is derived from observation of the manifested action of God and the Soul, and from a wise analogy. It is the intellectual guide which the religious sentiment needs. The true religious philosophy of an imperfect being, is not a system of creed, but, as Socrates thought, an infinite search or approximation. Philosophy is that intellectual and moral progress, which the religious sentiment inspires and ennobles.

As to Science, it could not walk alone, while religion was stationary. It consists of those matured inferences from experience which all other experience confirms. It realizes and unites all that was truly valuable in both the old schemes of mediation,—one *heroic,* or the system of action and effort; and the *mystical* theory of spiritual, contemplative communion. "Listen to me," says Galen, "as to the voice of the Eleusinian Hierophant, and believe that the study of Nature is a mystery no less important than theirs, nor less adapted to display the wisdom and power of the Great Creator. *Their* lessons and demonstrations were obscure, but *ours* are clear and unmistakable."

We deem that to be the best knowledge we can obtain of the Soul of another man, which is furnished by his actions and his life-long conduct. Evidence to the contrary, supplied by what another man informs us that this Soul has said to his, would weigh little against the former. The first Scriptures for the human race were written by God on the Earth and Heavens. The reading of these Scriptures is Science. Familiarity with the grass and trees, the insects and the infusoria, teaches us deeper lessons of love and faith than we can glean from the writings of Fénelon and Augustine. The great Bible of God is ever open before mankind.

Knowledge is convertible into power, and axioms into rules of utility and duty. But knowledge itself is not Power. Wisdom is Power; and her Prime Minister is Justice, which is the perfected law of Truth. The purpose, therefore, of Education and Science

3

is to make a man wise. If knowledge does not make him so, it is wasted, like water poured on the sands. To know the *formulas* of Masonry, is of as little value, by itself, as to know so many words and sentences in some barbarous African or Australasian dialect. To know even the *meaning* of the symbols, is but little, unless that adds to our wisdom, and also to our charity, which is to justice like one hemisphere of the brain to the other.

Do not lose sight, then, of the true object of your studies in Masonry. It is to add to your estate of wisdom, and not merely to your knowledge. A man may spend a lifetime in studying a single specialty of knowledge,—botany, conchology, or entomology, for instance,—in committing to memory names derived from the Greek, and classifying and reclassifying; and yet be no wiser than when he began. It is the great truths as to all that most concerns a man, as to his rights, interests, and duties, that Masonry seeks to teach her Initiates.

The wiser a man becomes, the less will he be inclined to submit tamely to the imposition of fetters or a yoke, on his conscience or his person. For, by increase of wisdom he not only better *knows* his rights, but the more highly *values* them, and is more conscious of his worth and dignity. His pride then urges him to assert his independence. He becomes better *able* to assert it also; and better able to assist others or his country, when they or she stake all, even existence, upon the same assertion. But mere knowledge makes no one independent, nor fits him to be free. It often only makes him a more useful slave. Liberty is a curse to the ignorant and brutal.

Political science has for its object to ascertain in what manner and by means of what institutions political and personal freedom may be secured and perpetuated: not license, or the mere right of every man to vote, but entire and absolute freedom of thought and opinion, alike free of the despotism of monarch and mob and prelate; freedom of action within the limits of the general law enacted for all; the Courts of Justice, with impartial Judges and juries, open to all alike; weakness and poverty equally potent in those Courts as power and wealth; the avenues to office and honor open alike to all the worthy; the military powers, *in war or peace,* in strict subordination to the civil power; arbitrary arrests for acts not known to the law as crimes, impossible; Romish Inquisitions, Star-Chambers, Military Commissions, unknown; the means of instruction within reach of the children of all; the right of Free Speech; and accountability of all public officers, civil and military.

If Masonry needed to be justified for imposing political as well as moral duties on its Initiates, it would be enough to point to the sad history of the world. It would not even need that she should turn back the pages of history to the chapters written by Tacitus: that she should recite the incredible horrors of despotism under Caligula and Domitian, Caracalla and Commodus, Vitellius and Maximin. She need only point to the centuries of calamity through which the gay French nation passed; to the long oppression of the feudal ages, of the selfish Bourbon kings; to those times when the peasants were robbed and slaughtered by their own lords and princes, like sheep; when the lord claimed the first-fruits of the peasant's marriage-bed; when the captured city was given up to merciless rape and massacre; when the State-prisons groaned with innocent victims, and the Church blessed the banners of pitiless murderers, and sang Te Deums for the crowning mercy of the Eve of St. Bartholomew.

We might turn over the pages, to a later chapter,—that of the reign of the Fifteenth Louis, when young girls, hardly more than children, were kidnapped to serve his lusts; when *lettres de cachet* filled the Bastile with persons accused of no crime, with husbands who were in the way of the pleasures of lascivious wives and of villains wearing orders of nobility; when the people were ground between the upper and the nether millstone of taxes, customs, and excises; and when the Pope's Nuncio and the Cardinal de la Roche-Ayman, devoutly kneeling, one on each side of Madame du Barry, the king's abandoned prostitute, put the slippers on her naked feet, as she rose from the adulterous bed. Then, indeed, suffering and toil were the two forms of man, and the people were but beasts of burden.

The true Mason is he who labors strenuously to help his Order effect its great purposes. Not that the Order can effect them by itself; but that it, too, can help. It also is one of God's instruments. It is a Force and a Power; and shame upon it, if it did not exert itself, and, if need be, sacrifice its children in the cause of humanity, as Abraham was ready to offer up Isaac on the altar of sacrifice. It will not forget that noble allegory of Curtius leaping, all in armor, into the great yawning gulf that opened to swallow Rome. It will TRY. It shall not be *its* fault if the day *never* comes when man will no longer have to fear a conquest, an invasion, a usurpation, a rivalry of nations with the armed hand, an interruption of civilization depending on a marriage-royal, or a birth in the hereditary tyrannies; a partition of the peoples by a Congress, a dismemberment by the downfall of a dynasty, a combat of two religions, meeting head to head, like two goats of darkness on the bridge of the Infinite: when they will no longer have to fear famine, spoliation, prostitution from distress, misery from lack of work, and all the brigandages of chance in the forest of events: when nations will gravitate about the Truth, like stars about the light, each in its own orbit, without clashing or collision; and everywhere Freedom, cinctured with stars, crowned with the celestial splendors, and with wisdom and justice on either hand, will reign supreme.

In your studies as a Fellow-Craft you must be guided by REASON, LOVE and FAITH.

We do not now discuss the differences between Reason and Faith, and undertake to define the domain of each. But it is necessary to say, that even in the ordinary affairs of life we are governed far more by what we *believe* than by what we *know;* by FAITH and ANALOGY, than by REASON. The "Age of Reason" of the French Revolution taught, we know, what a folly it is to enthrone Reason by itself as supreme. Reason is at fault when it deals with the Infinite. There we must revere and believe. Notwithstanding the calamities of the virtuous, the miseries of the deserving, the prosperity of tyrants and the murder of martyrs, we *must* believe there is a wise, just, merciful, and loving God, an Intelligence and a Providence, supreme over all, and caring for the minutest things and events. A Faith is a necessity to man. Woe to him who believes nothing!

We believe that the soul of another is of a certain nature and possesses certain qualities, that he is generous and honest, or penurious and knavish, that she is virtuous and amiable, or vicious and ill-tempered, from the countenance alone, from little more than a glimpse of it, without the means of *knowing*. We venture our fortune on the signature of a man on the other side of the world, whom we never saw, upon the belief that he is honest and trustworthy. We believe that occurrences have taken place, upon the assertion of others. We believe that one will acts upon another, and in the reality of a multitude of other phenomena that Reason cannot explain.

But we ought *not* to believe what Reason authoritatively denies, that at which the sense of right revolts, that which is absurd or self-contradictory, or at issue with experience or science, or that which degrades the character of the Deity, and would make Him revengeful, malignant, cruel, or unjust.

A man's Faith is as much his own as his Reason is. His Freedom consists as much in his faith being free as in his will being uncontrolled by power. All the Priests and Augurs of Rome or Greece had not the right to require Cicero or Socrates to believe in the absurd mythology of the vulgar. All the Imaums of Mohammedanism have not the right to require a Pagan to believe that Gabriel dictated the Koran to the Prophet. All the Brahmins that ever lived, if assembled in one conclave like the Cardinals, could not gain a right to compel a single human being to believe in the Hindu Cosmogony. No man or body of men *can* be infallible, and authorized to decide what other men shall believe, as to any tenet of faith. Except to those who first receive it, every religion and the truth of all inspired writings depend on *human* testimony and internal evidences, to be judged of by Reason and the wise analogies of Faith. Each man must necessarily have the right to judge of their truth for himself; because no one man can have any higher or better right to judge than another of equal information and intelligence.

Domitian claimed to be the Lord God; and statues and images of him, in silver and gold, were found throughout the known world. He claimed to be regarded as the God of all men; and, according to Suetonius, began his letters thus: *"Our Lord and God commands that it should be done so and so;"* and formally decreed that no one should address him otherwise, either in writing or by word of mouth. Palfurius Sura, the philosopher, who was his chief delator, accusing those who refused to recognize his divinity, however much *he* may have believed in that divinity, had not the right to demand that a single Christian in Rome or the provinces should do the same.

Reason is far from being the only guide, in morals or in political science. Love or loving-kindness must keep it company, to exclude fanaticism, intolerance, and persecution, to all of which a morality too ascetic, and extreme political principles, invariably lead. We must also have faith in ourselves, and in our fellows and the people, or we shall be easily discouraged by reverses, and our ardor cooled by obstacles. We must not listen to Reason alone. Force comes more from Faith and Love: and it is by the aid of these that man scales the loftiest heights of morality, or becomes the Saviour and Redeemer of a People. Reason must hold the helm; but these supply the motive power. They are the wings of the soul. Enthusiasm is generally unreasoning; and without it, and Love and Faith, there would have been no RIENZI, or TELL, or SYDNEY, or any other of the great patriots whose names are immortal. If the Deity had been merely and only All-wise and All-mighty, He would never have created the Universe.

*   *   *   *   *   *

It is GENIUS that gets Power; and its prime lieutenants are FORCE and WISDOM. The unruliest of men bend before the leader that has the sense to see and the will to do. It is Genius that rules with God-like Power; that unveils, with its counsellors, the hidden human mysteries, cuts asunder with its word the huge knots, and builds up with its word the crumbled ruins. At its glance fall down the senseless idols, whose altars have been on all the high places and in all the sacred groves. Dishonesty and imbecility stand abashed before it. Its single Yea or Nay revokes the wrongs of ages, and is heard among the future generations. Its power is immense, because its wisdom is immense. Genius is the Sun of the political sphere. Force and Wisdom, its ministers, are the orbs that carry its light into darkness, and answer it with their solid reflecting Truth.

Development is symbolized by the use of the Mallet and Chisel; the development of the energies and intellect, of the individual and the people. Genius may place itself at the head of an unintellectual, uneducated, unenergetic nation; but in a free country, to cultivate the intellect of those who elect, is the only mode of securing intellect and genius for rulers. The world is seldom ruled by the great spirits, except after dissolution and new birth. In periods of transition and convulsion, the Long Parliaments, the Robespierres and Marats, and the semi-respectabilities of intellect, too often hold the reins of power. The Cromwells and Napoleons come later. After Marius and Sulla and Cicero the rhetorician, CÆSAR. The great intellect is often too sharp for the granite of this life. Legislators may be very ordinary men; for legislation is very ordinary work; it is but the final issue of a million minds.

The power of the purse or the sword, compared to that of the spirit, is poor and contemptible. As to *lands,* you may have agrarian laws, and equal partition. But a man's intellect is all his own, held direct from God, an inalienable fief. It is the most potent of weapons in the hands of a paladin. If the people comprehend Force in the physical sense, how much more do they reverence the intellectual! Ask Hildebrand, or Luther, or Loyola. They fall prostrate before it, as before an idol. The mastery of mind over mind is the only conquest worth having. The other injures both, and dissolves at a breath; rude as it is, the great cable falls down and snaps at last. But this dimly resembles the dominion of the Creator. It does not need a subject like that of Peter the Hermit. If the stream be but bright and strong, it will sweep like a spring-tide to the popular heart. Not in word only, but in intellectual act lies the fascination. It is the homage to the Invisible. This power, knotted with Love, is the golden chain let down into the well of Truth, or the invisible chain that binds the ranks of mankind together.

Influence of man over man is a law of nature, whether it be by a great estate in land or in intellect. It may mean slavery, a deference to the eminent human judgment. Society hangs spiritually together, like the revolving spheres above. The free country, in which intellect and genius govern, will endure. Where they serve, and other influences govern, the national life is short. All the nations that have tried to govern themselves by their smallest, by the incapables, or merely respectables, have come to nought. Constitutions and Laws, without Genius and Intellect to govern, will not prevent decay. In that case they have the dry-rot and the life dies out of them by degrees.

To give a nation the franchise of the Intellect is the only sure mode of perpetuating freedom. This will compel exertion and generous care for the people from those on the higher seats, and honorable and intelligent allegiance from those below. Then political public life will protect all men from self-abasement in sensual pursuits, from vulgar acts and low greed, by giving the noble ambition of just imperial rule. To elevate the people by teaching loving-kindness and wisdom, with power to him who teaches best: and so to develop the free State from the rough ashlar:—this is the great labor in which Masonry desires to lend a helping hand.

All of us should labor in building up the great monument of a nation, the Holy House of the Temple. The cardinal virtues must not be partitioned among men, becoming the exclusive property of some, like the common crafts. ALL are apprenticed to the partners, Duty and Honor.

Masonry is a march and a struggle toward the Light. For the individual as well as the nation, Light is Virtue, Manliness, Intelligence, Liberty. Tyranny over the soul or body, is darkness. The freest people, like the freest man, is always in danger of relapsing into servitude. Wars are almost always fatal to Republics. They create tyrants, and consolidate their power. They spring, for the most part, from evil counsels. When the small and the base are intrusted with power, legislation and administration become but two parallel series of errors and blunders, ending in war, calamity, and the necessity for a tyrant. When the nation feels its feet sliding backward, as if it walked on the ice, the time has come for a supreme effort. The magnificent tyrants of the past are but the types of those of the future. Men and nations will always sell themselves into slavery, to gratify their passions and obtain revenge. The tyrant's plea, necessity, is always available; and the tyrant once in power, the necessity of providing for his safety makes him savage. Religion is a power, and he must control that. Independent, its sanctuaries might rebel. Then it becomes unlawful for the people to worship God in their own way, and the old spiritual despotisms revive. Men must believe as Power wills, or die; and even if they may believe as they will, all they have, lands, houses, body, and soul, are stamped with the royal brand. "I am the State," said Louis the Fourteenth to his peasants; "the very shirts on your backs are mine, and I can take them if I will."

And dynasties so established endure, like that of the Cæsars of Rome, of the Cæsars of Constantinople, of the Caliphs, the Stuarts, the Spaniards, the Goths, the Valois, until the race wears out, and ends with lunatics and idiots, who *still* rule. There is no concord among men, to end the horrible bondage. The State falls inwardly, as well as by the outward blows of the incoherent elements. The furious human passions, the sleeping human indolence, the stolid human ignorance, the rivalry of human castes, are as good for the kings as the swords of the Paladins. The worshippers have all bowed so long to the old idol, that they cannot go into the streets and choose another Grand Llama. And so the effete State floats on down the puddled stream of Time, until the tempest or the tidal sea discovers that the worm has consumed its strength, and it crumbles into oblivion.

*   *   *   *   *   *

Civil and religious Freedom must go hand in hand; and Persecution matures them both. A people content with the thoughts made for them by the priests of a church will be content with Royalty by Divine Right,—the Church and the Throne mutually sustaining each other. They will smother schism and reap infidelity and indifference; and while the battle for freedom goes on around them, they will only sink the more apathetically into servitude and a deep trance, perhaps occasionally interrupted by furious fits of frenzy, followed by helpless exhaustion.

Despotism is not difficult in any land that has only known one master from its childhood; but there is no harder problem than to perfect and perpetuate free government by the people themselves; for it is not one king that is needed: all must be kings. It is easy to set up Masaniello, that in a few days he may fall lower than before. But free government grows slowly, like the individual human faculties; and like the forest-trees, from the inner heart outward. Liberty is not only the common birth-right, but it is lost as well by non-user as by mis-user. It depends far more on the universal effort than any other human property. It has no single shrine or holy well of pilgrimage for the nation; for its waters should burst out freely from the whole soil.

The free popular power is one that is only known in its strength in the hour of adversity: for all its trials, sacrifices and expectations are its own. It is trained to think for itself, and also to act for itself. When the enslaved people prostrate themselves in the dust before the hurricane, like the alarmed beasts of the field, the free people stand erect before it, in all the strength of unity, in self-reliance, in mutual reliance, with effrontery against all but the visible hand of God. It is neither cast down by calamity nor elated by success.

This vast power of endurance, of forbearance, of patience, and of performance, is only acquired by continual exercise of all the functions, like the healthful physical human vigor, like the individual moral vigor.

And the maxim is no less true than old, that eternal vigilance is the price of liberty. It is curious to observe the universal pretext by which the tyrants of all times take away the national liberties. It is stated in the statutes of Edward II., that the justices and the sheriff should no longer be elected by the people, on account of the riots and dissensions which had arisen. The same reason was given long before for the suppression of popular election of the bishops; and there is a witness to this untruth in the yet older times, when Rome lost her freedom, and her indignant citizens declared that tumultuous liberty is better than disgraceful tranquillity.

*　　　*　　　*　　　*　　　*　　　*

With the Compasses and Scale, we can trace all the figures used in the mathematics of planes, or in what are called GEOMETRY and TRIGONOMETRY, two words that are themselves deficient in meaning. GEOMETRY, which the letter G. in most Lodges is *said* to signify, means *measurement* of *land* or the earth—or Surveying; and TRIGONOMETRY, the measurement of triangles, or figures with three sides or angles. The latter is by far the most appropriate name for the science intended to be expressed by the word "Geometry." Neither is of a meaning sufficiently wide: for although the vast surveys of great spaces of the earth's surface, and of coasts, by which shipwreck and calamity to mariners are avoided, are effected by means of triangulation;—though it was by the same method that the French astronomers measured a degree of latitude and so established a scale of measures on an immutable basis; though it is by means of the immense triangle that has for its base a line drawn in imagination between the place of the earth now and its place six months hence in space, and for its apex a planet or star, that the distance of Jupiter or Sirius from the earth is ascertained; and though there is a triangle still more vast, its base extending either way from us, with and past the horizon into immensity, and its apex infinitely distant above us; to which corresponds a similar infinite triangle below—*what is above equalling what is below, immensity equalling immensity;*— yet the Science of Numbers, to which Pythagoras attached so much importance, and whose mysteries are found everywhere in the ancient religions, and most of all in the Kabalah and in the Bible, is not sufficiently expressed by either the word "*Geometry*" or the word "*Trigonometry*." For that science includes these, with Arithmetic, and also with Algebra, Logarithms, the Integral and Differential Calculus; and by means of it are worked out the great problems of Astronomy or the Laws of the Stars.

* * * * * *

Virtue is but heroic bravery, to *do* the thing thought to be true, in spite of all enemies of flesh or spirit, in despite of all temptations or menaces. Man is accountable for the *up*rightness of his doctrine, but not for the rightness of it. Devout enthusiasm is far easier than a good action. The end of thought is action; the sole purpose of Religion is an Ethic. Theory, in political science, is worthless, except for the purpose of being realized in practice.

In every *credo,* religious or political as in the soul of man, there are two regions, the Dialectic and the Ethic; and it is only when the two are harmoniously blended, that a perfect discipline is evolved. There are men who dialectically are Christians, as there are a multitude who dialectically are Masons, and yet who are ethically Infidels, as these are ethically of the Profane, in the strictest sense:—intellectual believers, but practical atheists:— men who will write you "Evidences," in perfect faith in their logic, but cannot carry out the Christian or Masonic doctrine, owing to the strength, or weakness, of the flesh. On the other hand, there are many dialectical skeptics, but ethical believers, as there are many Masons who have never undergone initiation; and as ethics are the end and purpose of religion, so are ethical believers the most worthy. He who *does* right is better than he who *thinks* right.

But you must not act upon the hypothesis that all men are hypocrites, whose conduct does not square with their sentiments. No vice is more rare, for no task is more difficult, than systematic hypocrisy. When the Demagogue becomes a Usurper it does not follow that he was all the time a hypocrite. Shallow men only so judge of others.

The truth is, that creed has, in general, very little influence on the conduct; in religion, on that of the individual; in politics, on that of party. As a general thing, the Mahometan, in the Orient, is far more honest and trustworthy than the Christian. A Gospel of Love in the mouth, is an Avatar of Persecution in the heart. Men who believe in eternal damnation and a literal sea of fire and brimstone, incur the certainty of it, according to their creed, on the slightest temptation of appetite or passion. Predestination insists on the necessity of good works. In Masonry, at the least flow of passion, one speaks ill of another behind his back: and so far from the "Brotherhood" of Blue Masonry being real, and the solemn pledges contained in the use of the word "Brother" being complied with, extraordinary pains are taken to show that Masonry is a sort of abstraction, which scorns to interfere in worldly matters. The rule may be regarded as universal, that, where there is a choice to be made, a Mason will give his vote and influence, in politics and business, to the less qualified profane in preference to the better qualified Mason. One will take an oath to oppose any unlawful usurpation of power, and then become the ready and even eager instrument of a usurper. Another will call one "Brother," and then play toward him the part of Judas Iscariot, or strike him, as Joab did Abner, under the fifth rib, with a lie whose authorship is not to be traced. Masonry does not change human nature, and cannot make honest men out of born knaves.

While you are still engaged in preparation, and in accumulating principles for future use, do not forget the words of the Apostle James: "For if any be a hearer of the word, and not a doer, he is like unto a man beholding his natural face in a glass, for he beholdeth himself, and goeth away, and straightway forgetteth what manner of man he was; but whoso looketh into the perfect law of liberty, and continueth, he being not a forgetful hearer, but a doer of the work, this man shall be blessed in his work. If any man among you seem to be religious, and bridleth not his tongue, but deceiveth his own heart, this man's religion is vain. . . . Faith, if it hath not works, is dead, being an abstraction. A man is justified by works, and not by faith only. . . . The devils believe,—and tremble. . . . As the body without the heart is dead, so is faith without works."

*　　　*　　　*　　　*　　　*　　　*

In political science, also, free governments are erected and free constitutions framed, upon some simple and intelligible theory. Upon whatever theory they are based, no sound conclusion is to be reached except by carrying the theory out without flinching, both in argument on constitutional questions and in practice. Shrink from the true theory through timidity, or wander from it through want of the logical faculty, or transgress against it through passion or on the plea of necessity or expediency, and you have denial or invasion of rights, laws that offend against first principles, usurpation of illegal powers, or abnegation and abdication of legitimate authority.

Do not forget, either, that as the showy, superficial, impudent and self-conceited will almost always be preferred, even in utmost stress of danger and calamity of the State, to the man of solid learning, large intellect, and catholic sympathies, because he is nearer the common popular and legislative level, so the highest truth is not acceptable to the mass of mankind.

When SOLON was asked if he had given his countrymen the *best* laws, he answered, "*The best they are capable of receiving.*" This is one of the profoundest utterances on record; and yet like all great truths, so simple as to be rarely comprehended. It contains the whole philosophy of History. It utters a truth which, had it been recognized, would have saved men an immensity of vain, idle disputes, and have led them into the clearer paths of knowledge in the Past. It means this,—that all truths are *Truths of Period*, and not truths for eternity; that whatever great fact has had strength and vitality enough to make itself real, whether of religion, morals, government, or of whatever else, and to find place in this world, has been a truth *for the time, and as good as men were capable of receiving.*

So, too, with great men. The intellect and capacity of a people has a single measure,—that of the great men whom Providence gives it, and whom it *receives.* There have always been men too great for their time or their people. Every people makes *such* men only its idols, as it is capable of comprehending.

To impose ideal truth or law upon an incapable and merely *real* man, must ever be a vain and empty speculation. The laws of sympathy govern in this as they do in regard to men who are put at the head. We do not know, as yet, what qualifications the sheep insist on in a leader. With men who are too high intellectually, the mass have as little sympathy as they have with the stars. When BURKE, the wisest statesman England ever had, rose to speak, the House of Commons was depopulated as upon an agreed signal. There is as little sympathy between the mass and the highest TRUTHS. The highest truth, being incomprehensible to the man of realities, as the highest man is, and largely above his level, will be a great unreality and falsehood to an unintellectual man. The profoundest doctrines of Christianity and Philosophy would be mere jargon and babble to a Potawatomie Indian. The popular explanations of the symbols of Masonry are fitting for the multitude that have swarmed into the Temples,—being fully up to the level of their capacity. Catholicism was a vital truth in its earliest ages, but it became obsolete, and Protestantism arose, flourished, and deteriorated. The doctrines of ZOROASTER were the best which the ancient Persians were fitted to receive; those of CONFUCIUS were fitted for the Chinese; those of MOHAMMED for the idolatrous Arabs of his age. Each was Truth for the time. Each was a GOSPEL, preached by a REFORMER; and if any men are so little fortunate as to remain content therewith, when others have attained a higher truth, it is their misfortune and not their fault. They are to be pitied for it, and not persecuted.

Do not expect easily to convince men of the truth, or to lead them to think aright. The subtle human intellect can weave its mists over even the clearest vision. Remember that it is eccentric enough to ask unanimity from a jury; but to ask it from any large number of men on any point of political faith is amazing. You can hardly get two men in any Congress or Convention to agree;—nay, you can rarely get one to agree with *himself*. The political church which chances to be supreme anywhere has an indefinite number of tongues. How then can we expect men to agree as to matters beyond the cognizance of the senses? How can we compass the Infinite and the Invisible with any chain of evidence? Ask the small sea-waves what they murmur among the pebbles! How many of those words that come from the invisible shore are lost, like the birds, in the long passage? How vainly do we strain the eyes across the long Infinite! We must be content, as the children are, with the pebbles that have been stranded, since it is forbidden us to explore the hidden depths.

The Fellow-Craft is especially taught by this not to become wise in his own conceit. Pride in unsound theories is worse than ignorance. Humility becomes a Mason. Take some quiet, sober moment of life, and add together the two ideas of Pride and Man; behold him, creature of a span, stalking through infinite space in all the grandeur of littleness! Perched on a speck of the Universe, every wind of Heaven strikes into his blood the coldness of death; his soul floats away from his body like the melody from the string. Day and night, like dust on the wheel, he is rolled along the heavens, through a labyrinth of worlds, and all the creations of God are flaming on every side, further than even his imagination can reach. Is this a creature to make for himself a crown of glory, to deny his own flesh, to mock at his fellow, sprung with him from that dust to which both will soon return? Does the proud man not err? Does he not suffer? Does he not die? When he reasons, is he never stopped short by difficulties? When he acts, does he never succumb to the temptations of pleasure? When he lives, is he free from pain? Do the diseases not claim him as their prey? When he dies, can he escape the common grave? Pride is not the heritage of man. Humility should dwell with frailty, and atone for ignorance, error and imperfection.

Neither should the Mason be over-anxious for office and honor, however certainly he may feel that he has the capacity to serve the State. He should neither seek nor spurn honors. It is good to enjoy the blessings of fortune; it is better to submit without a pang to their loss. The greatest deeds are not done in the glare of light, and before the eyes of the populace. He whom God has gifted with a love of retirement possesses, as it were, an additional sense; and among the vast and noble scenes of nature, we find the balm for the wounds we have received among the pitiful shifts of policy; for the attachment to solitude is the surest preservative from the ills of life.

But Resignation is the more noble in proportion as it is the less passive. Retirement is only a morbid selfishness, if it prohibit exertions for others; as it is only dignified and noble, when it is the shade whence the oracles issue that are to instruct mankind; and retirement of this nature is the sole seclusion which a good and wise man will covet or command. The very philosophy which makes such a man covet the *quiet,* will make him eschew the *inutility* of the hermitage. Very little praiseworthy would LORD BOLINGBROKE have seemed among his haymakers and ploughmen, if among haymakers and ploughmen he had looked with an indifferent eye upon a profligate minister and a venal Parliament. Very little interest would have attached to his beans and vetches, if beans and vetches had caused him to forget that if he was happier on a farm he could be more useful in a Senate, and made him forego, in the sphere of a bailiff, all care for re-entering that of a legislator.

Remember, also, that there is an education which quickens the Intellect, and leaves the heart hollower or harder than before. There are ethical lessons in the laws of the heavenly bodies, in the properties of earthly elements, in geography, chemistry, geology, and all the material sciences. Things are symbols of Truths.

Properties are symbols of Truths. Science, not teaching moral and spiritual truths, is dead and dry, of little more real value than to commit to the memory a long row of unconnected dates, or of the names of bugs or butterflies.

Christianity, it is said, begins from the burning of the false gods by the people themselves. Education begins with the burning of our intellectual and moral idols: our prejudices, notions, conceits, our worthless or ignoble purposes. Especially it is necessary to shake off the love of worldly gain. With Freedom comes the longing for worldly advancement. In that race men are ever falling, rising, running, and falling again. The lust for wealth and the abject dread of poverty delve the furrows on many a noble brow. The gambler grows old as he watches the chances. Lawful hazard drives Youth away before its time; and this Youth draws heavy bills of exchange on Age. Men live, like the engines, at high pressure, a hundred years in a hundred months; the ledger becomes the Bible, and the day-book the Book of the Morning Prayer.

Hence flow overreachings and sharp practice, heartless traffic in which the capitalist buys profit with the lives of the laborers, speculations that coin a nation's agonies into wealth, and all the other devilish enginery of Mammon. This, and greed for office, are the two columns at the entrance to the Temple of Moloch. It is doubtful whether the latter, blossoming in falsehood, trickery, and fraud, is not even more pernicious than the former. At all events they are twins, and fitly mated; and as either gains control of the unfortunate subject, his soul withers away and decays, and at last dies out. The souls of half the human race leave them long before they die. The two greeds are twin plagues of the leprosy, and make the man unclean; and whenever they break out they spread until "they cover all the skin of him that hath the plague, from his head even to his foot." Even the raw flesh of the heart becomes unclean with it.

     *   *   *   *   *   *

Alexander of Macedon has left a saying behind him which has survived his conquests: *"Nothing is nobler than work."* Work only can keep even kings respectable. And when a king is a king indeed, it is an honorable office to give tone to the manners and morals of a nation; to set the example of virtuous conduct, and restore in spirit the old schools of chivalry, in which the young manhood may be nurtured to real greatness. Work and wages *will* go together in men's minds, in the most royal institutions. We must ever come to the idea of real work. The rest that follows labor should be sweeter than the rest which follows rest.

Let no Fellow-Craft imagine that the work of the lowly and uninfluential is not worth the doing. There is no legal limit to the possible influences of a good deed or a wise word or a generous effort. Nothing is really small. Whoever is open to the deep penetration of nature knows this. Although, indeed, no absolute satisfaction may be vouchsafed to philosophy, any more in circumscribing the cause than in limiting the effect, the man of thought and contemplation falls into unfathomable ecstacies in view of all the decompositions of forces resulting in unity. All works for all. Destruction is not annihilation, but regeneration.

Algebra applies to the clouds; the radiance of the star benefits the rose; no thinker would dare to say that the perfume of the hawthorn is useless to the constellations. Who, then, can calculate the path of the molecule? How do we know that the creations of worlds are not determined by the fall of grains of sand? Who, then, understands the reciprocal flow and ebb of the infinitely great and the infinitely small; the echoing of causes in the abysses of beginning, and the avalanches of creation? A flesh-worm is of account; the small is great; the great is small; all is in equilibrium in necessity. There are marvellous relations between beings and things; in this inexhaustible Whole, from sun to grub, there is no scorn: all need each other. Light does not carry terrestrial perfumes into the azure depths, without knowing what it does with them; night distributes the stellar essence to the sleeping plants. Every bird which flies has the thread of the Infinite in its claw. Germination includes the hatching of a meteor, and the tap of a swallow's bill, breaking the egg; and it leads forward the birth of an earth-worm and the advent of a Socrates. Where the telescope ends the microscope begins. Which of them the grander view? A bit of mould is a Pleiad of flowers—a nebula is an ant-hill of stars.

There is the same and a still more wonderful interpenetration between the things of the intellect and the things of matter. Elements and principles are mingled, combined, espoused, multiplied one by another, to such a degree as to bring the material world and the moral world into the same light. Phenomena are perpetually folded back upon themselves. In the vast cosmical changes the universal life comes and goes in unknown quantities, enveloping all in the invisible mystery of the emanations, losing no dream from no single sleep, sowing an animalcule here, crumbling a star there, oscillating and winding in curves; making a force of Light, and an element of Thought; disseminated and indivisible, dissolving all save that point without length, breadth, or thickness, The MYSELF; reducing everything to the Soul-atom; making everything blossom into God; entangling all activities, from the highest to the lowest, in the obscurity of a dizzying mechanism; hanging the flight of an insect upon the movement of the earth; subordinating, perhaps, if only by the identity of the law, the eccentric evolutions of the comet in the firmament, to the whirlings of the infusoria in the drop of water. A mechanism made of mind, the first motor of which is the gnat, and its last wheel the zodiac.

A peasant-boy, guiding Blücher by the right one of two roads, the other being impassable for artillery, enables him to reach Waterloo in time to save Wellington from a defeat that would have been a rout; and so enables the kings to imprison Napoleon on a barren rock in mid-ocean. An unfaithful smith, by the slovenly shoeing of a horse, causes his lameness, and, he stumbling, the career of his world-conquering rider ends, and the destinies of empires are changed. A generous officer permits an imprisoned monarch to end his game of chess before leading him to the block; and meanwhile the usurper dies, and the prisoner reascends the throne. An unskillful workman repairs the compass, or malice or stupidity disarranges it, the ship mistakes her course, the waves swallow a Cæsar, and a new chapter is written in the history of a world. What we call accident is but the adamantine chain of indissoluble connection between all created things. The locust, hatched in the Arabian sands, the small worm that destroys the cotton-boll, one making famine in the Orient, the other closing the mills and starving the workmen and their children in the Occident, with riots and massacres, are as much the ministers of God as the earthquake; and the fate of nations depends more on them than on the intellect of its kings and legislators. A civil war in America will end in shaking the world; and that war may be caused by the vote of some ignorant prize-fighter or crazed fanatic in a city or in a Congress, or of some stupid boor in an obscure country parish. The electricity of universal sympathy, of action and reaction, pervades everything, the planets and the motes in the sunbeam. FAUST, with his types, or LUTHER, with his sermons, worked greater results than Alexander or Hannibal. A single thought sometimes suffices to overturn a dynasty. A silly song did more to unseat James the Second than the acquittal of the Bishops. Voltaire, Condorcet, and Rousseau uttered words that will ring, in change and revolutions, throughout all the ages.

Remember, that though life is short, Thought and the influences of what we do or say are immortal; and that no calculus has yet pretended to ascertain the law of proportion between cause and effect. The hammer of an English blacksmith, smiting down an insolent official, led to a rebellion which came near being a revolution. The word well spoken, the deed fitly done, even by the feeblest or humblest, cannot help but have their effect. More or less, the effect is inevitable and eternal. The echoes of the greatest deeds may die away like the echoes of a cry among the cliffs, and what has been done seem to the human judgment to have been without result. The unconsidered act of the poorest of men may fire the train that leads to the subterranean mine, and an empire be rent by the explosion.

The power of a free people is often at the disposal of a single and seemingly an unimportant individual;—a terrible and truthful power; for such a people feel with one heart, and therefore can lift up their myriad arms for a single blow. And, again, there is no graduated scale for the measurement of the influences of different intellects upon the popular mind. Peter the Hermit held no office, yet what a work he wrought!

*　　　*　　　*　　　*　　　*　　　*

From the political point of view there is but a single principle,—the sovereignty of man over himself. This sovereignty of one's self over one's self is called LIBERTY. Where two or several of these sovereignties associate, the State begins. But in this association there is no abdication. Each sovereignty parts with a certain portion of itself to form the common right. That portion is the same for all. There is equal contribution by all to the joint sovereignty. This identity of concession which each makes to all, is EQUALITY. The common right is nothing more or less than the protection of all, pouring its rays on each. This protection of each by all, is FRATERNITY.

Liberty is the summit, Equality the base. Equality is not all vegetation on a level, a society of big spears of grass and stunted oaks, a neighborhood of jealousies, emasculating each other. It is, civilly, all aptitudes having equal opportunity; politically, all votes having equal weight; religiously, all consciences having equal rights.

Equality has an organ;—gratuitous and obligatory instruction. We must begin with the right to the alphabet. The primary school *obligatory* upon all; the higher school *offered* to all. Such is the law. From the same school for all springs equal society. Instruction! Light! all comes from Light, and all returns to it.

We must learn the thoughts of the common people, if we would be wise and do any good work. We must look at men, not so much for what Fortune has given to them with her blind old eyes, as for the gifts Nature has brought in her lap, and for the use that has been made of them. We profess to be equal in a Church and in the Lodge: we shall be equal in the sight of God when He judges the earth. We may well sit on the pavement together here, in communion and conference, for the few brief moments that constitute life.

A Democratic Government undoubtedly has its defects, because it is made and administered by men, and not by the Wise Gods. It cannot be concise and sharp, like the despotic. When its ire is aroused it develops its latent strength, and the sturdiest rebel trembles. But its habitual domestic rule is tolerant, patient, and indecisive. Men are brought together, first to differ, and then to agree. Affirmation, negation, discussion, solution: these are the means of attaining truth. Often the enemy will be at the gates before the babble of the disturbers is drowned in the chorus of consent. In the Legislative office deliberation will often defeat decision. Liberty can play the fool like the Tyrants.

Refined society requires greater minuteness of regulation; and the steps of all advancing States are more and more to be picked among the old rubbish and the new materials. The difficulty lies in discovering the right path through the chaos of confusion. The adjustment of mutual rights and wrongs is also more difficult in democracies. We do not see and estimate the relative importance of objects so easily and clearly from the level or the waving land as from the elevation of a lone peak, towering above the plain; for each looks through his own mist.

Abject dependence on constituents, also, is too common. It is as miserable a thing as abject dependence on a minister or the favorite of a Tyrant. It is rare to find a man who can speak out the simple truth that is in him, honestly and frankly, without fear, favor, or affection, either to Emperor or People.

Moreover, in assemblies of men, faith in each other is almost always wanting, unless a terrible pressure of calamity or danger from without produces cohesion. Hence the constructive power of such assemblies is generally deficient. The chief triumphs of modern days, in Europe, have been in pulling down and obliterating; not in building up. But Repeal is not Reform. Time must bring with him the Restorer and Rebuilder.

Speech, also, is grossly abused in Republics; and if the use of speech be glorious, its abuse is the most villainous of vices. Rhetoric, Plato says, is the art of ruling the minds of men. But in democracies it is too common to *hide* thought in words, to *overlay* it, to babble nonsense. The gleams and glitter of intellectual soap-and-water bubbles are mistaken for the rainbow-glories of genius. The worthless pyrites is continually mistaken for gold. Even intellect condescends to intellectual jugglery, balancing thoughts as a juggler balances pipes on his chin. In all Congresses we have the inexhaustible flow of babble, and Faction's clamorous knavery in discussion, until the divine power of speech, that privilege of man and great gift of God, is no better than the screech of parrots or the mimicry of monkeys. The mere talker, however fluent, is barren of deeds in the day of trial.

There are men voluble as women, and as well skilled in fencing with the tongue: prodigies of speech, misers in deeds. Too much talking, like too much thinking, destroys the power of action. In human nature, the thought is only made perfect by deed. Silence is the mother of both. The trumpeter is not the bravest of the brave. Steel and not brass wins the day. The great doer of great deeds is mostly slow and slovenly of speech. There are some men born and bred to betray. Patriotism is their trade, and their capital is speech. But no noble spirit can plead like Paul and be false to itself as Judas.

Imposture too commonly rules in republics; they seem to be ever in their minority; their guardians are self-appointed; and the unjust thrive better than the just. The Despot, like the night-lion roaring, drowns all the clamor of tongues at once, and speech, the birthright of the free man, becomes the bauble of the enslaved.

It is quite true that republics only occasionally, and as it were accidentally, select their wisest, or even the less incapable among the incapables, to govern them and legislate for them. If genius, armed with learning and knowledge, will grasp the reins, the people will reverence it; if it only modestly offers itself for office, it will be smitten on the face, even when, in the straits of distress and the agonies of calamity, it is indispensable to the salvation of the State. Put it upon the track with the showy and superficial, the conceited, the ignorant, and impudent, the trickster and charlatan, and the result shall not be a moment doubtful. The verdicts of Legislatures and the People are like the verdicts of juries,—sometimes right by accident.

Offices, it is true, are showered, like the rains of Heaven, upon the just and the unjust. The Roman Augurs that used to laugh in each other's faces at the simplicity of the vulgar, were also tickled with their own guile; but no Augur is needed to lead the people astray. They readily deceive themselves. Let a Republic begin as it may, it will not be out of its minority before imbecility will be promoted to high places; and shallow pretence, getting itself puffed into notice, will invade all the sanctuaries. The most unscrupulous partisanship will prevail, even in respect to judicial trusts; and the most unjust appointments constantly be made, although every improper promotion not merely confers one undeserved favor, but may make a hundred honest cheeks smart with injustice.

The country is stabbed in the front when those are brought into the stalled seats who should slink into the dim gallery. Every stamp of Honor, ill-clutched, is stolen from the Treasury of Merit.

Yet the entrance into the public service, and the promotion in it, affect both the rights of individuals and those of the nation. Injustice in bestowing or withholding office ought to be so intolerable in democratic communities that the least trace of it should be like the scent of Treason. It is not universally true that all citizens of equal character have an equal claim to knock at the door of every public office and demand admittance. When any man presents himself for service he has a right to aspire to the highest body at once, if he can show his fitness for such a beginning,—that he is fitter than the rest who offer themselves for the same post. The entry into it can only justly be made through the door of merit. And whenever any one aspires to and attains such high post, especially if by unfair and disreputable and indecent means, and is afterward found to be a signal failure, he should at once be beheaded. He is the worst among the public enemies.

When a man sufficiently reveals himself, all others should be proud to give him due precedence. When the power of promotion is abused in the grand passages of life whether by People, Legislature, or Executive, the unjust decision recoils on the judge at once. That is not only a gross, but a willful shortness of sight, that cannot discover the deserving. If one will look hard, long, and honestly, he will not fail to discern merit, genius, and qualification; and the eyes and voice of the Press and Public should condemn and denounce injustice wherever she rears her horrid head.

"The tools to the workmen!" no other principle will save a Republic from destruction, either by civil war or the dry-rot. They tend to decay, do all we can to prevent it, like human bodies. If they try the experiment of governing themselves by their smallest, they slide downward to the unavoidable abyss with tenfold velocity; and there never has been a Republic that has not followed that fatal course.

But however palpable and gross the inherent defects of democratic governments, and fatal as the results finally and inevitably are, we need only glance at the reigns of Tiberius, Nero, and Caligula, of Heliogabalus and Caracalla, of Domitian and Commodus, to recognize that the difference between freedom and despotism is as wide as that between Heaven and Hell. The cruelty, baseness, and insanity of tyrants are incredible. Let him who complains of the fickle humors and inconstancy of a free people, read Pliny's character of Domitian. If the great man in a Republic cannot win office without descending to low arts and whining beggary and the judicious use of sneaking lies, let him remain in retirement, and use the pen. Tacitus and Juvenal held no office. Let History and Satire punish the pretender as they crucify the despot. The revenges of the intellect are terrible and just.

Let Masonry use the pen and the printing-press in the free State against the Demagogue; in the Despotism against the Tyrant. History offers examples and encouragement. All history, for four thousand years, being filled with violated rights and the sufferings of the people, each period of history brings with it such protest as is possible to it. Under the Cæsars there was no insurrection, but there was a Juvenal. The arousing of indignation replaces the Gracchi. Under the Cæsars there is the exile of Syene; there is also the author of the Annals. As the Neros reign darkly they should be pictured so. Work with the graver only would be pale; into the grooves should be poured a concentrated prose that bites.

Despots are an aid to thinkers. Speech enchained is speech terrible. The writer doubles and triples his style, when silence is imposed by a master upon the people. There springs from this silence a certain mysterious fullness, which filters and freezes into brass in the thoughts. Compression in the history produces conciseness in the historian. The granitic solidity of some celebrated prose is only a condensation produced by the Tyrant. Tyranny constrains the writer to shortenings of diameter which are increases of strength. The Ciceronian period, hardly sufficient upon Verres, would lose its edge upon Caligula.

The Demagogue is the predecessor of the Despot. One springs from the other's loins. He who will basely fawn on those who have office to bestow, will betray like Iscariot, and prove a miserable and pitiable failure. Let the new Junius lash such men as they deserve, and History make them immortal in infamy; since their influences culminate in ruin. The Republic that employs and honors the shallow, the superficial, the base,

<blockquote>
"who crouch
Unto the offal of an office promised,".
</blockquote>

at last weeps tears of blood for its fatal error. Of such supreme folly, the sure fruit is damnation. Let the nobility of every great heart, condensed into justice and truth, strike such creatures like a thunderbolt! If you can do no more, you can at least condemn by your vote, and ostracise by denunciation.

It is true that, as the Czars are absolute, they have it in their power to select the best for the public service. It is true that the beginner of a dynasty generally does so; and that when monarchies are in their prime, pretence and shallowness do not thrive and prosper and get power, as they do in Republics. All do not gabble in the Parliament of a Kingdom, as in the Congress of a Democracy. The incapables do not go undetected there, *all* their lives.

But dynasties speedily decay and run out. At last they dwindle down into imbecility; and the dull or flippant Members of Congresses are at least the intellectual peers of the vast majority of kings. The great man, the Julius Cæsar, the Charlemagne, Cromwell, Napoleon, reigns of right. He is the wisest and the strongest. The incapables and imbeciles succeed and are usurpers; and fear makes them cruel. After Julius came Caracalla and Galba; after Charlemagne, the lunatic Charles the Sixth. So the Saracenic dynasty dwindled out; the Capets, the Stuarts, the Bourbons; the last of these producing Bomba, the ape of Domitian.

* * * * * *

Man is by nature cruel, like the tigers. The barbarian, and the tool of the tyrant, and the civilized fanatic, enjoy the sufferings of others, as the children enjoy the contortions of maimed flies. Absolute Power, once in fear for the safety of its tenure, cannot but be cruel.

As to ability, dynasties invariably cease to possess any after a few lives. They become mere shams, governed by ministers, favorites, or courtesans, like those old Etruscan kings, slumbering for long ages in their golden royal robes, dissolving forever at the first breath of day. Let him who complains of the shortcomings of democracy ask himself if he would prefer a Du Barry or a Pompadour, governing in the name of a Louis the Fifteenth, a Caligula making his horse a consul, a Domitian, "that most savage monster," who sometimes drank the blood of relatives, sometimes employing himself with slaughtering the most distinguished citizens before whose gates fear and terror kept watch; a tyrant of frightful aspect, pride on his forehead, fire in his eye, constantly seeking darkness and secrecy, and only emerging from his solitude to make solitude. After all, in a free government, the Laws and the Constitution are above the Incapables, the Courts correct their legislation, and posterity is the Grand Inquest that passes judgment on them. What is the exclusion of worth and intellect and knowledge from civil office compared with trials before Jeffries, tortures in the dark caverns of the Inquisition, Alvabutcheries in the Netherlands, the Eve of Saint Bartholomew, and the Sicilian Vespers?

* * * * * *

The Abbé Barruel in his *Memoirs for the History of Jacobinism,* declares that Masonry in France gave, as its secret, the

words Equality and Liberty, leaving it for every honest and religious Mason to explain them as would best suit his principles;
but retained the privilege of unveiling in the higher Degrees the
meaning of those words, as interpreted by the French Revolution.
And he also excepts English Masons from his anathemas, because
in England a Mason is a peaceable subject of the civil authorities,
no matter where he resides, engaging in no plots or conspiracies
against even the worst government. England, he says, disgusted
with an Equality and a Liberty, the consequences of which she
had felt in the struggles of her Lollards, Anabaptists, and Presby-
terians, had "purged her Masonry" from all explanations tending
to overturn empires; but there still remained adepts whom disor-
ganizing principles bound to the Ancient Mysteries.

Because true Masonry, unemasculated, bore the banners of Freedom and Equal Rights, and was in rebellion against temporal and
spiritual tyranny, its Lodges were proscribed in 1735, by an edict
of the States of Holland. In 1737, Louis XV. forbade them in
France. In 1738, Pope Clement XII. issued against them his
famous Bull of Excommunication, which was renewed by Bene-
dict XIV.; and in 1743 the Council of Berne also proscribed them.
The title of the Bull of Clement is, "The Condemnation of the
Society of Conventicles *de Liberi Muratori,* or of the Free-
masons, under the penalty of *ipso facto* excommunication, the absolution from which is reserved to the Pope alone, except at the
point of death." And by it all bishops, ordinaries, and inquisitors
were empowered to punish Freemasons, "as vehemently suspected of heresy," and to call in, if necessary, the help of the
secular arm; that is, to cause the civil authority to put them to
death.

    *   *   *   *   *   *

Also, false and slavish political theories end in brutalizing the
State. For example, adopt the theory that offices and employments in it are to be given as rewards for services rendered to
party, and they soon become the prey and spoil of faction, the
booty of the victory of faction;—and leprosy is in the flesh of the
State. The body of the commonwealth becomes a mass of corruption, like a living carcass rotten with syphilis. All unsound theories
in the end develop themselves in one foul and loathsome disease
or other of the body politic. The State, like the man, must use
constant effort to *stay* in the paths of virtue and manliness. The

habit of electioneering and begging for office culminates in bribery *with* office, and corruption *in* office.

A chosen man has a visible trust from God, as plainly as if the commission were engrossed by the notary. A nation cannot renounce the executorship of the Divine decrees. As little can Masonry. It must labor to do its duty knowingly and wisely. We must remember that, in free States, as well as in despotisms, Injustice, the spouse of Oppression, is the fruitful parent of Deceit, Distrust, Hatred, Conspiracy, Treason, and Unfaithfulness. Even in assailing Tyranny we must have Truth and Reason as our chief weapons. We must march into that fight like the old Puritans, or into the battle with the abuses that spring up in free government, with the flaming sword in one hand, and the Oracles of God in the other.

The citizen who cannot accomplish well the smaller purposes of public life, cannot compass the larger. The vast power of endurance, forbearance, patience, and performance, of a free people, is acquired only by continual exercise of all the functions, like the healthful physical human vigor. If the individual citizens have it not, the State must equally be without it. It is of the essence of a free government, that the people should not only be concerned in making the laws, but also in their execution. No man ought to be more ready to obey and administer the law than he who has helped to make it. The business of government is carried on for the benefit of all, and every co-partner should give counsel and cooperation.

Remember also, as another shoal on which States are wrecked, that free States always tend toward the depositing of the citizens in strata, the creation of castes, the perpetuation of the *jus divinum* to office in families. The more democratic the State, the more sure this result. For, as free States advance in power, there is a strong tendency toward centralization, not from deliberate evil intention, but from the course of events and the indolence of human nature. The executive powers swell and enlarge to inordinate dimensions; and the Executive is always aggressive with respect to the nation. Offices of all kinds are multiplied to reward partisans; the brute force of the sewerage and lower strata of the mob obtains large representation, first in the lower offices, and at last in Senates; and Bureaucracy raises its bald head, bristling with pens, girded with spectacles, and bunched with ribbon. The art of Government becomes like a Craft, and its guilds tend to become exclusive, as those of the Middle Ages.

Political science may be much improved as a subject of speculation; but it should never be divorced from the actual national necessity. The science of governing men must always be practical, rather than philosophical. There is not the same amount of positive or universal truth here as in the abstract sciences; what is true in one country may be very false in another; what is untrue to-day may become true in another generation, and the truth of to-day be reversed by the judgment of to-morrow. To distinguish the casual from the enduring, to separate the unsuitable from the suitable, and to make progress even possible, are the proper ends of policy. But without actual knowledge and experience, and communion of labor, the dreams of the political doctors may be no better than those of the doctors of divinity. The reign of such a caste, with its mysteries, its myrmidons, and its corrupting influence, may be as fatal as that of the despots. Thirty tyrants are thirty times worse than one.

Moreover, there is a strong temptation for the governing people to become as much slothful and sluggards as the weakest of absolute kings. Only give them the power to get rid, when caprice prompts them, of the great and wise men, and elect the little, and as to all the rest they will relapse into indolence and indifference. The central power, creation of the people, organized and cunning if not enlightened, is the perpetual tribunal set up by them for the redress of wrong and the rule of justice. It soon supplies itself with all the requisite machinery, and is ready and apt for all kinds of interference. The people may be a child all its life. The central power may not be able to suggest the best scientific solution of a problem; but it has the easiest means of carrying an idea into effect. If the purpose to be attained is a large one, it requires a large comprehension; it is proper for the action of the central power. If it be a small one, it may be thwarted by disagreement. The central power must step in as an arbitrator and prevent this. The people may be too averse to change, too slothful in their own business, unjust to a minority or a majority. The central power must take the reins when the people drop them.

France became centralized in its government more by the apathy and ignorance of its people than by the tyranny of its kings. When the inmost parish-life is given up to the direct guardianship of the State, and the repair of the belfry of a country church requires a written order from the central power, a people is in its dotage. Men are thus nurtured in imbecility, from the dawn of social life. When the central government feeds part of the people it prepares all to be slaves. When it directs parish and county affairs, they are slaves already. The next step is to regulate labor and its wages.

Nevertheless, whatever follies the free people may commit, even to the putting of the powers of legislation in the hands of the little competent and less honest, despair not of the final result. The terrible teacher, EXPERIENCE, writing his lessons on hearts desolated with calamity and wrung by agony, will make them wiser in time. Pretence and grimace and sordid beggary for votes will some day cease to avail. Have FAITH, and struggle on, against all evil influences and discouragements! FAITH is the Saviour and Redeemer of nations. When Christianity had grown weak, profitless, and powerless, the Arab Restorer and Iconoclast came, like a cleansing hurricane. When the battle of Damascus was about to be fought, the Christian bishop, at the early dawn, in his robes, at the head of his clergy, with the Cross once so triumphant raised in the air, came down to the gates of the city, and laid open before the army the Testament of Christ. The Christian general, THOMAS, laid his hand on the book, and said, "*Oh God! IF our faith be true, aid us, and deliver us not into the hands of its enemies!*" But KHALED, "*the Sword of God,*" who had marched from victory to victory, exclaimed to his wearied soldiers, "*Let no man sleep! There will be rest enough in the bowers of Paradise; sweet will be the repose never more to be followed by labor.*" The faith of the Arab had become stronger than that of the Christian, and he conquered.

The Sword is also, in the Bible, an emblem of SPEECH, or of the utterance of thought. Thus, in that vision or apocalypse of the sublime exile of Patmos, a protest in the name of the ideal, overwhelming the real world, a tremendous satire uttered in the name of Religion and Liberty, and with its fiery reverberations smiting the throne of the Cæsars, a sharp two-edged sword comes out of the mouth of the Semblance of the Son of Man, encircled by the seven golden candlesticks, and holding in his right hand seven stars. "The Lord," says Isaiah, "hath made my mouth like a sharp sword." "I have slain them," says Hosea, "by the words of my mouth." "The word of God," says the writer of the apostolic letter to the Hebrews, "is quick and powerful, and sharper than any two-edged sword, piercing even to the dividing asunder of soul and spirit." "The sword of the Spirit, which is the Word of God," says Paul, writing to the Christians at Ephesus. "I will fight against them with the sword of my mouth," it is said in the Apocalypse, to the angel of the church at Pergamos.

* * * * * *

The spoken discourse may roll on strongly as the great tidal wave; but, like the wave, it dies at last feebly on the sands. It is heard by few, remembered by still fewer, and fades away, like an echo in the mountains, leaving no token of power. It is nothing to the living and coming generations of men. It was the *written* human speech, that gave power and permanence to human thought. It is this that makes the whole human history but one individual life.

To write on the rock is to write on a solid parchment; but it requires a pilgrimage to see it. There is but one copy, and Time wears even that. To write on skins or papyrus was to give, as it were, but one tardy edition, and the rich only could procure it. The Chinese stereotyped not only the unchanging wisdom of old sages, but also the passing events. The process tended to suffocate thought, and to hinder progress; for there is continual wandering in the wisest minds, and Truth writes her last words, not on clean tablets, but on the scrawl that Error has made and often mended.

Printing made the movable letters prolific. Thenceforth the orator spoke almost visibly to listening nations; and the author wrote, like the Pope, his œcumenic decrees, *urbi et orbi,* and ordered them to be posted up in all the market-places; remaining, if he chose, impervious to human sight. The doom of tyrannies was thenceforth sealed. Satire and invective became potent as armies. The unseen hands of the Juniuses could launch the thunderbolts, and make the ministers tremble. One whisper from this giant fills the earth as easily as Demosthenes filled the Agora. It will soon be heard at the antipodes as easily as in the next street. It travels with the lightning under the oceans. It makes the mass one man, speaks to it in the same common language, and elicits a sure and single response. Speech passes into thought, and thence promptly into act. A nation becomes truly one, with one large heart and a single throbbing pulse. Men are invisibly pres-

ent to each other, as if already spiritual beings; and the thinker
who sits in an Alpine solitude, unknown to or forgotten by all the
world, among the silent herds and hills, may flash his words to all
the cities and over all the seas.

Select the thinkers to be Legislators; and avoid the gabblers.
Wisdom is rarely loquacious. Weight and depth of thought are
unfavorable to volubility. The shallow and superficial are generally voluble and often pass for eloquent. More words, less
thought,—is the general rule. The man who endeavors to say
something worth remembering in every sentence, becomes fastidi-
ous, and condenses like Tacitus. The vulgar love a more diffuse
stream. The ornamentation that does not cover strength is the
gewgaws of babble.

Neither is dialectic subtlety valuable to public men. The Christian faith has it, had it formerly more than now; a subtlety that
might have entangled Plato, and which has rivalled in a fruitless
fashion the mystic lore of Jewish Rabbis and Indian Sages. It is
not this which converts the heathen. It is a vain task to balance
the great thoughts of the earth, like hollow straws, on the finger-
tips of disputation. It is not this kind of warfare which makes
the Cross triumphant in the hearts of the unbelievers; but the
actual power that lives in the Faith.

So there is a political scholasticism that is merely useless. The
dexterities of subtle logic rarely stir the hearts of the people, or
convince them. The true apostle of Liberty, Fraternity and Equality makes it a matter of life and death. His combats are like
those of Bossuet,—combats to the death. The true apostolic fire
is like the lightning: it flashes conviction into the soul. The true
word is verily a two-edged sword. Matters of government and
political science can be fairly dealt with only by sound reason, and
the logic of common sense: not the common sense of the ignorant, but of the wise. The acutest thinkers rarely succeed in becoming leaders of men. A watchword or a catchword is more
potent with the people than logic, especially if this be the least
metaphysical. When a political prophet arises, to stir the dreaming, stagnant nation, and hold back its feet from the irretrievable
descent, to heave the land as with an earthquake, and shake the
silly-shallow idols from their seats, his words will come straight
from God's own mouth, and be thundered into the conscience. He
will reason, teach, warn, and rule. The real "Sword of the Spirit"

is keener than the brightest blade of Damascus. Such men rule
a land, in the strength of justice, with wisdom and with power.
Still, the men of dialectic subtlety often rule well, because in practice they forget their finely-spun theories, and use the trenchant
logic of common sense. But when the great heart and large intellect are left to the rust in private life, and small attorneys, brawlers
in politics, and those who in the cities would be only the clerks of
notaries, or practitioners in the disreputable courts, are made
national Legislators, the country is in her dotage. even if the
beard has not yet grown upon her chin.

In a free country, human speech must needs be free; and the
State *must* listen to the maunderings of folly, and the screechings
of its geese, and the brayings of its asses, as well as to the golden
oracles of its wise and great men. Even the despotic old kings
allowed their wise fools to say what they liked. The true alchem-
ist will extract the lessons of wisdom from the babblings of folly.
He will hear what a man has to say on any given subject, even if
the speaker end only in proving himself prince of fools. Even a
fool will sometimes hit the mark. There is some truth in all men
who are not compelled to suppress their souls and speak other
men's thoughts. The finger even of the idiot may point to the
great highway.

A people, as well as the sages, must learn to forget. If it neither
learns the new nor forgets the old, it is fated, even if it has been
royal for thirty generations. To unlearn is to learn; and also it is
sometimes needful to learn again the forgotten. The antics of
fools make the current follies more palpable, as fashions are
shown to be absurd by caricatures, which so lead to their extirpation. The buffoon and the zany are useful in their places.
The ingenious artificer and craftsman, like Solomon, searches the
earth for his materials, and transforms the misshapen matter into
glorious workmanship. The world is conquered by the head even
more than by the hands. Nor will any assembly talk forever.
After a time, when it has listened long enough, it quietly puts the
silly, the shallow, and the superficial to one side,—it thinks, and
sets to work.

The human thought, especially in popular assemblies, runs in
the most singularly crooked channels, harder to trace and follow
than the blind currents of the ocean. No notion is so absurd that
it may not find a place there. The master-workman must train

these notions and vagaries with his two-handed hammer. They twist out of the way of the sword-thrusts; and are invulnerable all over, even in the heel, against logic. The martel or mace, the battle-axe, the great double-edged two-handed sword must deal with follies; the rapier is no better against them than a wand, unless it be the rapier of ridicule.

The SWORD is also the symbol of *war* and of the *soldier*. Wars, like thunder-storms, are often necessary to purify the stagnant atmosphere. War is not a demon, without remorse or reward. It restores the brotherhood in letters of fire. When men are seated in their pleasant places, sunken in ease and indolence, with Pretence and Incapacity and Littleness usurping all the high places of State, war is the baptism of blood and fire, by which alone they can be renovated. It is the hurricane that brings the elemental equilibrium, the concord of Power and Wisdom. So long as these continue obstinately divorced, it will continue to chasten.

In the mutual appeal of nations to God, there is the acknowledgment of His might. It lights the beacons of Faith and Freedom, and heats the furnace through which the earnest and loyal pass to immortal glory. There is in war the doom of defeat, the quenchless sense of Duty, the stirring sense of Honor, the measureless solemn sacrifice of devotedness, and the incense of success. Even in the flame and smoke of battle, the Mason discovers his brother, and fulfills the sacred obligations of Fraternity.

Two, or the Duad, is the symbol of Antagonism; of Good and Evil, Light and Darkness. It is Cain and Abel, Eve and Lilith, Jachin and Boaz, Ormuzd and Ahriman, Osiris and Typhon.

THREE, or the Triad, is most significantly expressed by the equilateral and the right-angled triangles. There are *three* principal colors or rays in the rainbow, which by intermixture make *seven*. The three are the *blue,* the *yellow,* and the *red.* The Trinity of the Deity, in one mode or other, has been an article in all creeds. He creates, preserves, and destroys. He is the generative *power,* the productive *capacity*, and the *result*. The immaterial man, according to the Kabalah, is composed of *vitality*, or *life*, the breath of life; of *soul* or *mind*, and *spirit*. Salt, sulphur, and mercury are the great symbols of the alchemists. To them man was body, soul, and spirit.

FOUR is expressed by the square, or four-sided right-angled

figure. Out of the symbolic Garden of Eden flowed a river, dividing into *four* streams,—PISON, which flows around the land of gold, or light; GIHON, which flows around the land of Ethiopia or Darkness; HIDDEKEL, running eastward to Assyria; and the EUPHRATES. Zechariah saw *four* chariots coming out from between two mountains of bronze, in the first of which were *red* horses; in the second, *black;* in the third, *white;* and in the fourth, *grizzled*: "and these were the four winds of the heavens, that go forth from standing before the Lord of all the earth." Ezekiel saw the *four* living creatures, each with *four* faces and *four* wings, the faces of a *man* and a *lion,* an *ox* and an *eagle;* and the *four* wheels going upon their *four* sides; and Saint John beheld the *four* beasts, full of eyes before and behind, the LION, the young Ox, the MAN, and the flying EAGLE. *Four* was the signature of the Earth. Therefore, in the 148th Psalm, of those who must praise the Lord on the land, there are *four* times *four,* and *four* in particular of living creatures. Visible nature is described as the *four* quarters of the world, and the *four* corners of the earth. "There are *four,*" says the old Jewish saying, "which take the first place in this world: *man,* among the creatures; the *eagle* among birds; the *ox* among cattle; and the *lion* among wild beasts." Daniel saw *four* great beasts come up from the sea.

FIVE is the Duad added to the Triad. It is expressed by the five-pointed or blazing star, the mysterious Pentalpha of Pythagoras. It is indissolubly connected with the number *seven.* Christ fed His disciples and the multitude with *five* loaves and *two* fishes, and of the fragments there remained *twelve,* that is, *five* and *seven,* baskets full. Again He fed them with *seven* loaves and a few little fishes, and there remained *seven* baskets full. The *five* apparently small planets, Mercury, Venus, Mars, Jupiter, and Saturn, with the two greater ones, the Sun and Moon, constituted the *seven* celestial spheres.

SEVEN was the peculiarly sacred number. There were *seven* planets and spheres presided over by *seven* archangels. There were *seven* colors in the rainbow; and the Phœnician Deity was called the HEPTAKIS or God of *seven* rays; *seven* days of the week; and *seven* and *five* made the number of months, tribes, and apostles. Zechariah saw a golden candlestick, with *seven* lamps and *seven* pipes to the lamps, and an olive-tree on each side. Since he says, "the *seven* eyes of the Lord shall rejoice, and shall see the plummet in the hand of Zerubbabel." John, in the Apocalypse, writes *seven* epistles to the *seven* churches. In the *seven* epistles there are *twelve* promises. What is said of the churches in praise or blame, is completed in the number *three*. The refrain, *"who has ears to hear,"* etc., has *ten* words, divided by *three* and *seven*, and the *seven* by *three* and *four;* and the *seven* epistles are also so divided. In the seals, trumpets, and vials, also, of this symbolic vision, the *seven* are divided by *four* and *three*. He who sends his message to Ephesus, "holds the *seven* stars in his right hand, and walks amid the *seven* golden lamps."

In *six* days, or periods, God created the Universe, and paused on the *seventh* day. Of clean beasts, Noah was directed to take by *sevens* into the ark; and of fowls by *sevens;* because in *seven* days the rain was to commence. On the *seven*teenth day of the month, the rain began; on the *seven*teenth day of the *seventh* month, the ark rested on Ararat. When the dove returned, Noah waited *seven* days before he sent her forth again; and again *seven,* after she returned with the olive-leaf. Enoch was the *seventh* patriarch, Adam included, and Lamech lived 777 years.

There were *seven* lamps in the great candlestick of the Tabernacle and Temple, representing the *seven* planets. *Seven* times Moses sprinkled the anointing oil upon the altar. The days of consecration of Aaron and his sons were *seven* in number. A woman was unclean *seven* days after child-birth; one infected with leprosy was shut up *seven* days; *seven* times the leper was sprinkled with the blood of a slain bird; and *seven* days afterwards he must remain abroad out of his tent. *Seven* times, in purifying the leper, the priest was to sprinkle the consecrated oil; and *seven* times to sprinkle with the blood of the sacrificed bird the house to be purified. *Seven* times the blood of the slain bullock was sprinkled on the mercy-seat; and *seven* times on the altar. The *seventh* year was a Sabbath of rest; and at the end of *seven* times *seven* years came the great year of jubilee. *Seven* days the people ate unleavened bread, in the month of Abib. *Seven* weeks were counted from the time of first putting the sickle to the wheat. The Feast of the Tabernacles lasted *seven* days.

Israel was in the hand of Midian *seven* years before Gideon delivered them. The bullock sacrificed by him was *seven* years old. Samson told Delilah to bind him with *seven* green withes; and she wove the *seven* locks of his head, and afterwards shaved them off. Balaam told Barak to build for him *seven* altars. Jacob served *seven* years for Leah and *seven* for Rachel. Job had *seven* sons and *three* daughters, making the perfect number *ten*. He had also *seven* thousand sheep and *three* thousand camels. His friends sat down with him *seven* days and *seven* nights. His friends were ordered to sacrifice *seven* bullocks and *seven* rams; and again, at the end, he had *seven* sons and *three* daughters, and twice *seven* thousand sheep, and lived an hundred and forty, or twice *seven* times *ten* years. Pharaoh saw in his dream *seven* fat and *seven* lean kine, *seven* good ears and *seven* blasted ears of wheat; and there were *seven* years of plenty, and *seven* of famine. Jericho fell, when *seven* priests, with *seven* trumpets, made the circuit of the city on *seven* successive days; once each day for six days, and *seven* times on the seventh. "The *seven* eyes of the Lord," says Zechariah, "run to and fro through the whole earth." Solomon was *seven* years in building the Temple. *Seven* angels, in the Apocalypse, pour out *seven* plagues, from *seven* vials of wrath. The scarlet-colored beast, on which the woman sits in the wilderness, has *seven* heads and *ten* horns. So also has the beast that rises up out of the sea. *Seven* thunders uttered their voices. *Seven* angels sounded *seven* trumpets. *Seven* lamps of fire, the *seven* spirits of God, burned before the throne; and the Lamb that was slain had *seven* horns and *seven* eyes.

EIGHT is the first cube, that of *two*. NINE is the square of *three,* and represented by the triple triangle.

TEN includes all the other numbers. It is especially *seven* and *three;* and is called the number of perfection. Pythagoras represented it by the TETRACTYS, which had many mystic meanings. This symbol is sometimes composed of dots or points, sometimes of commas or yōds, and in the Kabalah, of the letters of the name of Deity. It is thus arranged:

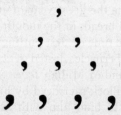

The Patriarchs from Adam to Noah, inclusive, are *ten* in number, and the same number is that of the Commandments.

TWELVE is the number of the lines of equal length that form a cube. It is the number of the months, the tribes, and the apostles; of the oxen under the Brazen Sea, of the stones on the breast-plate of the high priest.

*   *   *   *   *   *

*   *   *   *   *   *

III.

THE MASTER.

*　　　*　　　*　　　*　　　*　　　*

To understand literally the symbols and allegories of Oriental books as to ante-historical matters, is willfully to close our eyes against the Light. To translate the symbols into the trivial and commonplace, is the blundering of mediocrity.

All religious expression is symbolism; since we can *describe* only what we *see,* and the true objects of religion are THE SEEN. The earliest instruments of education were symbols; and they and all other religious forms differed and still differ according to external circumstances and imagery, and according to differences of knowledge and mental cultivation. All language is symbolic, so far as it is applied to mental and spiritual phenomena and action. All *words* have, primarily, *a material* sense, however they may afterward get, for the ignorant, a spiritual *non*-sense. "To retract," for example, is to *draw back,* and when applied to a *statement,* is symbolic, as much so as a picture of an arm drawn back, to express the same thing, would be. The very word *"spirit"* means *"breath,"* from the Latin verb *spiro, breathe.*

To present a visible symbol to the eye of another is not necessarily to inform him of the meaning which that symbol has to you. Hence the philosopher soon superadded to the symbols explanations addressed to the ear, susceptible of more precision, but less effective and impressive than the painted or sculptured forms which he endeavored to explain. Out of these explanations grew by degrees a variety of narrations, whose true object and meaning were gradually forgotten, or lost in contradictions and incongruities. And when these were abandoned, and Philosophy resorted to definitions and formulas, its language was but a more complicated symbolism, attempting in the dark to grapple with and picture ideas impossible to be expressed. For as with the visible symbol, so with the word: to utter it to you does not inform you of the *exact* meaning which it has to *me;* and thus religion and philosophy became to a great extent disputes as to the meaning

62

of words. The most abstract expression for DEITY, which language can supply, is but a *sign* or *symbol* for an object beyond our comprehension, and not more truthful and adequate than the images of OSIRIS and VISHNU, or their names, except as being less sensuous and explicit. We avoid sensuousness only by resorting to simple negation. We come at last to define spirit by saying that it is not matter. Spirit is—spirit.

A single example of the symbolism of *words* will indicate to you one branch of Masonic study. We find in the English Rite this phrase: "I will always *hail,* ever conceal, and never reveal;" and in the Catechism, these:

Q∴ "*I hail.*"

A∴ "*I conceal;*"

and ignorance, misunderstanding the word "*hail,*" has interpolated the phrase, "From whence do you *hail?*"

But the word is really "*hele,*" from the Anglo-Saxon verb ÞELAN, *helan,* to *cover, hide,* or *conceal.* And this word is rendered by the Latin verb *tegere,* to *cover* or *roof over.* "That ye fro me no thynge woll hele," says Gower. "They *hele* fro me no priuyte," says the Romaunt of the Rose. "To *heal* a house," is a common phrase in Sussex; and in the west of England, he that covers a house with slates is called a *Healer.* Wherefore, to "*heal*" means the same thing as to "*tile,*"—itself symbolic, as meaning, primarily, to *cover* a house with *tiles,*—and means to *cover, hide,* or *conceal.* Thus language too is symbolism, and words are as much misunderstood and misused as more material symbols are.

Symbolism tended continually to become more complicated; and all the powers of Heaven were reproduced on earth, until a web of fiction and allegory was woven, partly by art and partly by the ignorance of error, which the wit of man, with his limited means of explanation, will never unravel. Even the Hebrew Theism became involved in symbolism and image-worship, borrowed probably from an older creed and remote regions of Asia,—the worship of the Great Semitic Nature-God AL or ELS and its symbolical representations of JEHOVAH Himself were not even confined to poetical or illustrative language. The priests were monotheists: the people idolaters.

There are dangers inseparable from symbolism, which afford an impressive lesson in regard to the similar risks attendant on the use of language. The imagination, called in to assist the reason, usurps its place or leaves its ally helplessly entangled in its web. Names which stand for things are confounded with them; the means are mistaken for the end; the instrument of interpretation for the object; and thus symbols come to usurp an independent character as truths and persons. Though perhaps a necessary path, they were a dangerous one by which to approach the Deity; in which many, says PLUTARCH, "mistaking the sign for the thing signified, fell into a ridiculous superstition; while others, in avoiding one extreme, plunged into the no less hideous gulf of irreligion and impiety."

It is through the Mysteries, CICERO says, that we have learned the first principles of life; wherefore the term "initiation" is used with good reason; and they not only teach us to live more happily and agreeably, but they soften the pains of death by the hope of a better life hereafter.

The Mysteries were a Sacred Drama, exhibiting some legend significant of nature's changes, of the visible Universe in which the Divinity is revealed, and whose import was in many respects as open to the Pagan as to the Christian. Nature is the great Teacher of man; for it is the Revelation of God. It neither dogmatizes nor attempts to tyrannize by compelling to a particular creed or special interpretation. It presents its symbols to us, and adds nothing by way of explanation. It is the text without the commentary; and, as we well know, it is chiefly the commentary and gloss that lead to error and heresy and persecution. The earliest instructors of mankind not only adopted the lessons of Nature, but as far as possible adhered to her method of imparting them. In the Mysteries, beyond the current traditions or sacred and enigmatic recitals of the Temples, few explanations were given to the spectators, who were left, as in the school of nature, to make inferences for themselves. No other method could have suited every degree of cultivation and capacity. To employ nature's universal symbolism instead of the technicalities of language, rewards the humblest inquirer, and discloses its secrets to every one in proportion to his preparatory training and his power to comprehend them. If their philosophical meaning was above the comprehension of some, their moral and political meanings are within the reach of all.

These mystic shows and performances were not the reading of a lecture, but the opening of a problem. Requiring research, they were calculated to arouse the dormant intellect. They implied no hostility to Philosophy, because Philosophy is the great expounder of symbolism; although its ancient interpretations were often ill-founded and incorrect. The alteration from symbol to dogma is fatal to beauty of expression, and leads to intolerance and assumed infallibility.

*   *   *   *   *   *

If, in teaching the great doctrine of the divine natur᷈ of the Soul, and in striving to explain its longings after immortality, and in proving its superiority over the souls of the animals, which have no aspirations Heavenward, the ancients struggled in vain to express the *nature* of the soul, by comparing it to FIRE and LIGHT, it will be well for us to consider whether, with all our boasted knowledge, we have any better or clearer idea of its nature, and whether we have not despairingly taken refuge in having none at all. And if they erred as to its original place of abode, and under-stood literally the mode and path of its descent, these were but the accessories of the great Truth, and probably, to the Initiates, mere allegories, designed to make the idea more palpable and impressive to the mind.

They are at least no more fit to be smiled at by the self-conceit of a vain ignorance, the wealth of whose knowledge consists solely in words, than the *bosom* of Abraham, as a home for the *spirits* of the just dead; the gulf of actual fire, for the eternal torture of *spirits;* and the City of the New Jerusalem, with its walls of jasper and its edifices of pure gold like clear glass, its foundations of precious stones, and its gates each of a single pearl. "I knew a man," says PAUL, "caught up to the third Heaven; . . . . that he was caught up into Paradise, and heard ineffable words, which it is not possible for a man to utter." And nowhere is the antagon-ism and conflict between the spirit and body more frequently and forcibly insisted on than in the writings of this apostle, nowhere the Divine nature of the soul more strongly asserted. "With the mind," he says, "I serve the law of God; but with the flesh the law of sin. . . .As many as are led by the Spirit of God, are the sons of GOD. . . . The earnest expectation of the created waits for the manifestation of the sons of God. . . . The created shall be delivered from the bondage of corruption, of the flesh liable to decay, into the glorious liberty of the children of God."

*   *   *   *   *   *

Two forms of government are favorable to the prevalence of

falsehood and deceit. Under a Despotism, men are false, treacherous, and deceitful through fear, like slaves dreading the lash. Under a Democracy they are so as a means of attaining popularity and office, and because of the greed for wealth. Experience will probably prove that these odious and detestable vices will grow most rankly and spread most rapidly in a Republic. When office and wealth become the gods of a people, and the most unworthy and unfit most aspire to the former, and fraud becomes the high-way to the latter, the land will reek with falsehood and sweat lies and chicane. When the offices are open to all, merit and stern integrity and the dignity of unsullied honor will attain them only rarely and by accident. To be able to serve the country well, will cease to be a reason why the great and wise and learned should be selected to render service. Other qualifications, less honorable, will be more available. To adapt one's opinions to the popular humor; to defend, apologize for, and justify the popular follies; to advocate the expedient and the plausible; to caress, cajole, and flatter the elector; to beg like a spaniel for his vote, even if he be a negro three removes from barbarism; to profess friendship for a competitor and stab him by innuendo; to set on foot that which at third hand shall become a lie, being cousin-german to it when uttered, and yet capable of being explained away,—who is there that has not seen these low arts and base appliances put into practice, and becoming general, until success cannot be surely had by any more honorable means?—the result being a State ruled and ruined by ignorant and shallow mediocrity, pert self-conceit, the greenness of unripe intellect, vain of a school-boy's smattering of knowledge.

The faithless and the false in public and in political life, will be faithless and false in private. The jockey in politics, like the jockey on the race-course, is rotten from skin to core. Everywhere he will see first to his own interests, and whoso leans on him will be pierced with a broken reed. His ambition is ignoble, like himself; and therefore he will seek to attain office by ignoble means, as he will seek to attain any other coveted object,—land, money, or reputation.

At length, office and honor are divorced. The place that the small and shallow, the knave or the trickster, is deemed competent and fit to fill, ceases to be worthy the ambition of the great and capable; or if not, these shrink from a contest, the weapons to be used wherein are unfit for a gentleman to handle. Then the habits of unprincipled advocates in law courts are naturalized in Senates, and pettifoggers wrangle there, when the fate of the nation and the lives of millions are at stake. States are even begotten by villainy and brought forth by fraud, and rascalities are justified by legislators claiming to be honorable. Then contested elections are decided by perjured votes or party considerations; and all the practices of the worst times of corruption are revived and exaggerated in Republics.

It is strange that reverence for truth, that manliness and genuine loyalty, and scorn of littleness and unfair advantage, and genuine faith and godliness and large-heartedness should diminish, among statesmen and people, as civilization advances, and freedom becomes more general, and universal suffrage implies universal worth and fitness! In the age of Elizabeth, without universal suffrage, or Societies for the Diffusion of Useful Knowledge, or popular lecturers, or Lycæa, the statesman, the merchant, the burgher, the sailor, were all alike heroic, fearing God only, and man not at all. Let but a hundred or two years elapse, and in a Monarchy or Republic of the same race, nothing is *less* heroic than the merchant, the shrewd speculator, the office-seeker, fearing man only, and God not at all. Reverence for greatness dies out, and is succeeded by base envy of greatness. Every man is in the way of many, either in the path to popularity or wealth. There is a general feeling of satisfaction when a great statesman is displaced, or a general, who has been for his brief hour the popular idol, is unfortunate and sinks from his high estate. It becomes a misfortune, if not a crime, to be above the popular level.

We should naturally suppose that a nation in distress would take counsel with the wisest of its sons. But, on the contrary, great men seem never so scarce as when they are most needed, and small men never so bold to insist on infesting place, as when mediocrity and incapable pretence and sophomoric greenness, and showy and sprightly incompetency are most dangerous. When France was in the extremity of revolutionary agony, she was governed by an assembly of provincial pettifoggers, and Robespierre, Marat, and Couthon ruled in the place of Mirabeau, Vergniaud, and Carnot. England was governed by the Rump Parliament, after she had beheaded her king. Cromwell extinguished one body, and Napoleon the other.

Fraud, falsehood, trickery, and deceit in national affairs are the signs of decadence in States and precede convulsions or paralysis. To bully the weak and crouch to the strong, is the policy of nations governed by small mediocrity. The tricks of the canvass for office are re-enacted in Senates. The Executive becomes the dispenser of patronage, chiefly to the most unworthy; and men are bribed with offices instead of money, to the greater ruin of the Commonwealth. The Divine in human nature disappears, and interest, greed, and selfishness takes it place. That is a sad and true allegory which represents the companions of Ulysses changed by the enchantments of Circe into swine.

* * * * * *

"Ye cannot," said the Great Teacher, "serve God and Mammon." When the thirst for wealth becomes general, it will be sought for as well dishonestly as honestly; by frauds and over-reachings, by the knaveries of trade, the heartlessness of greedy speculation, by gambling in stocks and commodities that soon demoralizes a whole community. Men will speculate upon the needs of their neighbors and the distresses of their country. Bubbles that, bursting, impoverish multitudes, will be blown up by cunning knavery, with stupid credulity as its assistants and instrument. Huge bankruptcies, that startle a country like the earthquakes, and are more fatal, fraudulent assignments, engulfment of the savings of the poor, expansions and collapses of the currency, the crash of banks, the depreciation of Government securities, prey on the savings of self-denial, and trouble with their depredations the first nourishment of infancy and the last sands of life, and fill with inmates the churchyards and lunatic asylums. But the sharper and speculator thrives and fattens. If his country is fighting by a levy en masse for her very existence, he aids her by depreciating her paper, so that he may accumulate fabulous amounts with little outlay. If his neighbor is distressed, he buys his property for a song. If he administers upon an estate, it turns out insolvent, and the orphans are paupers. If his bank explodes, he is found to have taken care of himself in time. Society worships its paper-and-credit kings, as the old Hindūs and Egyptians worshipped their worthless idols, and often the most obsequiously when in actual solid wealth they are the veriest paupers. No wonder men think there ought to be another world, in which the injustices of this may be atoned for, when they see the friends of ruined families begging the wealthy sharpers to give alms to prevent the orphaned victims from starving, until they may find ways of supporting themselves.

*　　　*　　　*　　　*　　　*　　　*

States are chiefly avaricious of commerce and of territory. The latter leads to the violation of treaties, encroachments upon feeble neighbors, and rapacity toward their wards whose lands are coveted. Republics are, in this, as rapacious and unprincipled as Despots, never learning from history that inordinate expansion by rapine and fraud has its inevitable consequences in dismemberment or subjugation. When a Republic begins to plunder its neighbors, the words of doom are already written on its walls. There is a judgment already pronounced of God upon whatever is unrighteous in the conduct of national affairs. When civil war tears the vitals of a Republic, let it look back and see if it has not been guilty of injustices; and if it has, let it humble itself in the dust!

When a nation becomes possessed with a spirit of commercial greed, beyond those just and fair limits set by a due regard to a moderate and reasonable degree of general and individual prosperity, it is a nation possessed by the devil of commercial avarice, a passion as ignoble and demoralizing as avarice in the individual; and as this sordid passion is baser and more unscrupulous than ambition, so it is more hateful, and at last makes the infected nation to be regarded as the enemy of the human race. To grasp at the lion's share of commerce, has always at last proven the ruin of States, because it invariably leads to injustices that make a State detestable; to a selfishness and crooked policy that forbid other nations to be the friends of a State that cares only for itself.

Commercial avarice in India was the parent of more atrocities and greater rapacity, and cost more human lives, than the nobler ambition for extended empire of Consular Rome. The nation that grasps at the commerce of the world cannot but become selfish, calculating, dead to the noblest impulses and sympathies which ought to actuate States. It will submit to insults that wound its honor, rather than endanger its commercial interests by war; while, to subserve those interests, it will wage unjust war, on false or frivolous pretexts, its free people cheerfully allying themselves with despots to crush a commercial rival that has dared to exile its kings and elect its own ruler.

Thus the cold calculations of a sordid self-interest, in nations commercially avaricious, always at last displace the sentiments and lofty impulses of Honor and Generosity by which they rose to greatness; which made Elizabeth and Cromwell alike the protectors of Protestants beyond the four seas of England, against crowned Tyranny and mitred Persecution; and, if they had lasted, would have forbidden alliances with Czars and Autocrats and Bourbons to re-enthrone the Tyrannies of Incapacity, and arm the Inquisition anew with its instruments of torture. The soul of the avaricious nation petrifies, like the soul of the individual who makes gold his god. The Despot will occasionally act upon noble and generous impulses, and help the weak against the strong, the right against the wrong. But commercial avarice is essentially egotistic, grasping, faithless, overreaching, crafty, cold, ungenerous, selfish, and calculating, controlled by considerations of self-interest alone. Heartless and merciless, it has no sentiments of pity, sympathy, or honor, to make it pause in its remorseless career; and it crushes down all that is of impediment in its way, as its keels of commerce crush under them the murmuring and unheeded waves.

A war for a great principle ennobles a nation. A war for commercial supremacy, upon some shallow pretext, is despicable, and more than aught else demonstrates to what immeasurable depths of baseness men and nations can descend. Commercial greed values the lives of men no more than it values the lives of ants. The slave-trade is as acceptable to a people enthralled by that greed, as the trade in ivory or spices, if the profits are as large. It will by-and-by endeavor to compound with God and quiet its own conscience, by compelling those to whom it sold the slaves it bought or stole, to set them free, and slaughtering them by hecatombs if they refuse to obey the edicts of its philanthropy.

Justice in no wise consists in meting out to another that exact measure of reward or punishment which we think and decree his merit, or what we call his crime, which is more often merely his error, deserves. The justice of the father is not incompatible with forgiveness by him of the errors and offences of his child. The Infinite Justice of God does not consist in meting out exact measures of punishment for human frailties and sins. We are too apt to erect our own little and narrow notions of what is right and just into the law of justice, and to insist that God shall adopt that as His law; to measure off something with our own little tape-line, and call it God's love of justice. Continually we seek to ennoble our own ignoble love of revenge and retaliation, by misnaming it justice.

Nor does justice consist in strictly governing our conduct toward other men by the rigid rules of legal right. If there were a community anywhere, in which all stood upon the strictness of this rule, there should be written over its gates, as a warning to the unfortunates desiring admission to that inhospitable realm, the words which DANTE says are written over the great gate of Hell: "LET THOSE WHO ENTER HERE LEAVE HOPE BEHIND!" It is not just to pay the laborer in field or factory or workshop his current wages and no more, the lowest market-value of his labor, for so long only as we need that labor and he is able to work; for when sickness or old age overtakes him, that is to leave him and his family to starve; and God will curse with calamity the people in which the children of the laborer out of work eat the boiled grass of the field, and mothers strangle their children, that they may buy food for themselves with the charitable pittance given for burial expenses. The rules of what is ordinarily termed *"Justice,"* may be punctiliously observed among the fallen spirits that are the aristocracy of Hell.

* * * * * *

Justice, divorced from sympathy, is selfish indifference, not in the least more laudable than misanthropic isolation. There is sympathy even among the hair-like oscillatorias, a tribe of simple plants, armies of which may be discovered, with the aid of the microscope, in the tiniest bit of scum from a stagnant pool. For these will place themselves, as if it were by agreement, in separate companies, on the side of a vessel containing them, and seem marching upward in rows; and when a swarm grows weary of its situation, and has a mind to change its quarters, each army holds on its way without confusion or intermixture, proceeding with great regularity and order, as if under the directions of wise leaders. The ants and bees give each other mutual assistance, beyond what is required by that which human creatures are apt to regard as the strict law of justice.

Surely we need but reflect a little, to be convinced that the individual man is but a fraction of the unit of society, and that he is indissolubly connected with the rest of his race. Not only the actions, but the will and thoughts of other men make or mar his fortunes, control his destinies, are unto him life or death, dishonor or honor. The epidemics, physical and moral, contagious and infectious, public opinion, popular delusions, enthusiasms, and the other great electric phenomena and currents, moral and intellectual, prove the universal sympathy. The vote of a single and obscure man, the utterance of self-will, ignorance, conceit, or spite, deciding an election and placing Folly or Incapacity or Baseness in a Senate, involves the country in war, sweeps away our fortunes, slaughters our sons, renders the labors of a life unavailing, and pushes on, helpless, with all our intellect to resist, into the grave.

These considerations ought to teach us that justice to others and to ourselves is the same; that we cannot define our duties by mathematical lines ruled by the square, but must fill with them the great circle traced by the compasses; that the circle of humanity is the limit, and we are but the point in its centre, the drops in the great Atlantic, the atom or particle, bound by a mysterious law of attraction which we term sympathy to every other atom in the mass; that the physical and moral welfare of others cannot be indifferent to us; that we have a direct and immediate interest in the public morality and popular intelligence, in the well-being and physical comfort of the people at large. The ignorance of the people, their pauperism and destitution, and consequent degradation, their brutalization and demoralization, are all diseases; and we cannot rise high enough above the people, nor shut ourselves up from them enough, to escape the miasmatic contagion and the great magnetic currents.

Justice is peculiarly indispensable to nations. The unjust State is doomed of God to calamity and ruin. This is the teaching of the Eternal Wisdom and of history. "Righteousness exalteth a nation; but wrong is a reproach to nations." "The Throne is established by Righteousness. Let the lips of the Ruler pronounce the sentence that is Divine; and his mouth do no wrong in judgment!" The nation that adds province to province by fraud and violence, that encroaches on the weak and plunders its wards, and violates its treaties and the obligation of its contracts, and for the law of honor and fair-dealing substitutes the exigencies of greed and the base precepts of policy and craft and the ignoble tenets of expediency, is predestined to destruction; for here, as with the individual, the consequences of wrong are inevitable and eternal.

A sentence is written against all that is unjust, written by God in the nature of man and in the nature of the Universe, because it is in the nature of the Infinite God. No wrong is really successful. The gain of injustice is a loss; its pleasure, suffering. Iniquity often seems to prosper, but its success is its defeat and shame. If its consequences pass by the doer, they fall upon and crush his children. It is a philosophical, physical, and moral truth, in the form of a threat, that God visits the iniquity of the fathers upon the children, to the third and fourth generation of those who violate His laws. After a long while, the day of reckoning always comes, to nation as to individual; and always the knave deceives himself, and proves a failure.

Hypocrisy is the homage that vice and wrong pay to virtue and justice. It is Satan attempting to clothe himself in the angelic vesture of light. It is equally detestable in morals, politics, and religion; in the man and in the nation. To do injustice under the pretence of equity and fairness; to reprove vice in public and commit it in private; to pretend to charitable opinion and censoriously condemn; to profess the principles of Masonic beneficence, and close the ear to the wail of distress and the cry of suffering; to eulogize the intelligence of the people, and plot to deceive and betray them by means of their ignorance and simplicity; to prate of purity, and peculate; of honor, and basely abandon a sinking cause; of disinterestedness, and sell one's vote for place and power, are hypocrisies as common as they are infamous and disgraceful. To steal the livery of the Court of God to serve the Devil withal; to pretend to believe in a God of mercy and a Redeemer of love, and persecute those of a different faith; to devour widows' houses, and for a pretence make long prayers; to preach continence, and wallow in lust; to inculcate humility, and in pride surpass Lucifer; to pay tithe, and omit the weightier matters of the law, judgment, mercy and faith; to strain at a gnat, and swallow a camel; to make clean the outside of the cup and platter, keeping them full within of extortion and excess; to appear outwardly righteous unto men, but within be full of hypocrisy and iniquity, is indeed to be like unto whited sepulchres, which appear beautiful outward, but are within full of bones of the dead and of all uncleanness.

The Republic cloaks its ambition with the pretence of a desire and duty to "extend the area of freedom," and claims it as its "manifest destiny" to annex other Republics or the States or Provinces of others to itself, by open violence, or under obsolete, empty, and fraudulent titles. The Empire founded by a successful soldier, claims its ancient or natural boundaries, and makes necessity and its safety the plea for open robbery. The great Merchant Nation, gaining foothold in the Orient, finds a continual necessity for extending its dominion by arms, and subjugates India. The great Royalties and Despotisms, without a plea, partition among themselves a Kingdom, dismember Poland, and prepare to wrangle over the dominions of the Crescent. To maintain the balance of power is a plea for the obliteration of States. Carthage, Genoa, and Venice, commercial Cities only, must acquire territory by force or fraud, and become States. Alexander marches to the Indus; Tamerlane seeks universal empire; the Saracens conquer Spain and threaten Vienna.

The thirst for power is never satisfied. It is insatiable. Neither men nor nations ever have power enough. When Rome was the mistress of the world, the Emperors caused themselves to be worshipped as gods. The Church of Rome claimed despotism over the soul, and over the whole life from the cradle to the grave. It gave and sold absolutions for past and future sins. It claimed to be infallible in matters of faith. It decimated Europe to purge it of heretics. It decimated America to convert the Mexicans and Peruvians. It gave and took away thrones; and by excommunication and interdict closed the gates of Paradise against Nations. Spain, haughty with its dominion over the Indies, endeavored to crush out Protestantism in the Netherlands, while Philip the Second married the Queen of England, and the pair sought to win that kingdom back to its allegiance to the Papal throne. Afterward Spain attempted to conquer it with her "invincible" Armada. Napoleon set his relatives and captains on thrones, and parcelled among them half of Europe. The Czar rules over an empire more gigantic than Rome. The history of all is or will be the same,—acquisition, dismemberment, ruin. There is a judgment of God against all that is unjust.

To seek to subjugate the *will* of others and take the *soul* captive, because it is the exercise of the highest power, seems to be the highest object of human ambition. It is at the bottom of all proselyting and propagandism, from that of Mesmer to that of the Church of Rome and the French Republic. That was the apostolate alike of Joshua and of Mahomet. Masonry alone preaches Toleration, the right of man to abide by his own faith, the right of all States to govern themselves. It rebukes alike the monarch who seeks to extend his dominions by conquest, the Church that claims the right to repress heresy by fire and steel, and the confederation of States that insist on maintaining a union by force and restoring brotherhood by slaughter and subjugation.

It is natural, when we are wronged, to desire revenge; and to persuade ourselves that we desire it less for our own satisfaction than to prevent a repetition of the wrong, to which the doer would be encouraged by immunity coupled with the profit of the wrong. To submit to be cheated is to encourage the cheater to continue; and we are quite apt to regard ourselves as God's chosen instruments to inflict His vengeance, and for Him and in His stead to discourage wrong by making it fruitless and its punishment sure. Revenge has been said to be "a kind of wild justice;" but it is always taken in anger, and therefore is unworthy of a great soul, which ought not to suffer its equanimity to be disturbed by ingratitude or villainy. The injuries done us by the base are as much unworthy of our angry notice as those done us by the insects and the beasts; and when we crush the adder, or slay the wolf or hyena, we should do it without being moved to anger, and with no more feeling of revenge than we have in rooting up a noxious weed.

And if it be not in human nature not to take revenge by way of punishment, let the Mason truly consider that in doing so he is God's agent, and so let his revenge be measured by justice and tempered by mercy. The law of God is, that the consequences of wrong and cruelty and crime shall be their punishment; and the injured and the wronged and the indignant are as much His instruments to enforce that law, as the diseases and public detestation, and the verdict of history and the execration of posterity are. No one will say that the Inquisitor who has racked and burned the innocent; the Spaniard who hewed Indian infants, living, into pieces with his sword, and fed the mangled limbs to his bloodhounds; the military tyrant who has shot men without trial, the knave who has robbed or betrayed his State, the fraudulent banker or bankrupt who has beggared orphans, the public officer who has violated his oath, the judge who has sold injustice, the legislator who has enabled Incapacity to work the ruin of the State, ought not to be punished. Let them be so; and let the injured or the sympathizing be the instruments of God's just vengeance; but always out of a higher feeling than mere personal revenge.

Remember that every moral characteristic of man finds its prototype among creatures of lower intelligence; that the cruel foulness of the hyena, the savage rapacity of the wolf, the merciless
rage of the tiger, the crafty treachery of the panther, are found
among mankind, and ought to excite no other emotion, when
found in the man, than when found in the beast. Why should the
true man be angry with the geese that hiss, the peacocks that
strut, the asses that bray, and the apes that imitate and chatter,
although they wear the human form? Always, also, it remains
true, that it is more noble to forgive than to take revenge; and
that, in general, we ought too much to despise those who wrong
us, to feel the emotion of anger, or to desire revenge.

At the sphere of the *Sun*, you are in the region of LIGHT. * *
* * The Hebrew word for *gold,* ZAHAB, also means *Light*, of
which the Sun is to the Earth the great source. So, in the great
Oriental allegory of the Hebrews, the River PISON compasses the
land of *Gold* or *Light;* and the River GIHON the land of *Ethiopia*
or *Darkness*.

What light *is*, we no more know than the ancients did. According to the modern hypothesis, it is *not* composed of luminous
particles shot out from the sun with immense velocity; but that
body only impresses, on the ether which fills all space, a powerful
vibratory movement that extends, in the form of luminous waves,
beyond the most distant planets, supplying them with light and
heat. To the ancients, it was an outflowing from the Deity. To
us, as to them, it is the apt symbol of truth and knowledge. To us,
also, the upward journey of the soul through the Spheres is symbolical; but we are as little informed as they whence the soul
comes, where it has its origin, and whither it goes after death. They
endeavored to have *some* belief and faith, *some* creed, upon those
points. At the present day, men are satisfied to think nothing in
regard to all that, and only to believe that the soul is a *something*
separate from the body and out-living it, but whether existing before it, neither to inquire nor care. No one asks whether it emanates from the Deity, or is created out of nothing, or is generated
like the body, and the issue of the souls of the father and the
mother. Let us not smile, therefore, at the ideas of the ancients,
until we have a better belief; but accept their symbols as meaning
that the soul is of a Divine nature, originating in a sphere nearer
the Deity, and returning to that when freed from the enthrallment

of the body; and that it can only return there when purified of all the sordidness and sin which have, as it were, become part of its substance, by its connection with the body.

It is not strange that, thousands of years ago, men worshipped the Sun, and that to-day that worship continues among the Parsees. Originally they looked beyond the orb to the invisible God, of whom the Sun's light, seemingly identical with generation and life, was the manifestation and outflowing. Long before the Chaldæan shepherds watched it on their plains, it came up regularly, as it now does, in the morning, like a god, and again sank, like a king retiring, in the west, to return again in due time in the same array of majesty. We worship Immutability. It was that steadfast, immutable character of the Sun that the men of Baalbec worshipped. His light-giving and life-giving powers were secondary attributes. The one grand idea that compelled worship was the characteristic of God which they saw reflected in his light, and fancied they saw in its originality the changelessness of Deity. He had seen thrones crumble, earthquakes shake the world and hurl down mountains. Beyond Olympus, beyond the Pillars of Hercules, he had gone daily to his abode, and had come daily again in the morning to behold the temples they built to his worship. They personified him as BRAHMA, AMUN, OSIRIS, BEL, ADONIS, MALKARTH, MITHRAS, and APOLLO; and the nations that did so grew old and died. Moss grew on the capitals of the great columns of his temples, and he shone on the moss. Grain by grain the dust of his temples crumbled and fell, and was borne off on the wind, and still he shone on crumbling column and architrave. The roof fell crashing on the pavement, and he shone in on the Holy of Holies with unchanging rays. It was not strange that men worshipped the Sun.

There is a water-plant, on whose broad leaves the drops of water roll about without uniting, like drops of mercury. So arguments on points of faith, in politics or religion, roll over the surface of the mind. An argument that convinces one mind has no effect on another. Few intellects, or souls that are the negations of intellect, have any logical power or capacity. There is a singular obliquity in the human mind that makes the false logic more effective than the true with nine-tenths of those who are regarded as men of intellect. Even among the judges, not one in ten can argue logically. Each mind sees the truth, distorted through its own medium. Truth, to most men, is like matter in the spheroidal state. Like a drop of cold water on the surface of a red-hot metal plate, it dances, trembles, and spins, and never comes into contact with it; and the mind may be plunged into truth, as the hand moistened with sulphurous acid may into melted metal, and be not even warmed by the immersion.

*   *   *   *   *   *

The word *Khairūm* or *Khūrūm* is a compound one. Gesenius renders *Khūrūm* by the word *noble* or *free-born: Khūr* meaning *white, noble.* It also means the opening of a window, the socket of the eye. *Khri* also means *white,* or an *opening;* and *Khris,* the orb of the Sun, in *Job* viii. 13 and x. 7. *Krishna* is the Hindu Sun-God. *Khur,* the Parsi word, is the literal name of the Sun.

From *Kur* or *Khur,* the Sun, comes Khora, a name of Lower Egypt. The Sun, Bryant says in his Mythology, was called *Kur;* and Plutarch says that the Persians called the Sun *Kūros. Kurios, Lord,* in Greek, like *Adonaï, Lord,* in Phœnician and Hebrew, was applied to the Sun. Many places were sacred to the Sun, and called *Kura, Kuria, Kuropolis, Kurene, Kureschata, Kuresta,* and *Corusia* in Scythia.

The Egyptian Deity called by the Greeks *"Horus,"* was *Her-Ra.* or *Har-oeris, Hor* or *Har,* the Sun. *Hari* is a Hindu name of the Sun. *Ari-al, Ar-es, Ar, Aryaman, Areimonios,* the AR meaning *Fire* or *Flame,* are of the same kindred. *Hermes* or *Har-mes,* (*Aram, Remus, Haram, Harameias*), was Kadmos, the Divine Light or Wisdom. *Mar-kuri,* says Movers, is *Mar,* the Sun.

In the Hebrew, AOOR,   is *Light, Fire,* or the *Sun.* *Cyrus,* said Ctesias, was so named from *Kuros,* the Sun. *Kuris,* Hesychius says, was Adonis. Apollo, the Sun-god, was called *Kurraios,* from *Kurra,* a city in Phocis. The people of *Kurene,* originally Ethiopians or Cuthites, worshipped the Sun under the title of *Achoor* and *Achōr.*

We know, through a precise testimony in the ancient annals of Tsūr, that the principal festivity of *Mal-karth,* the incarnation of the Sun at the Winter Solstice, held at Tsūr, was called his *re-birth* or his *awakening,* and that it was celebrated by means of a pyre, on which the god was supposed to regain, through the aid of fire, a new life. This festival was celebrated in the month *Peritius* (*Barith*), the second day of which corresponded to the 25th of December. KHUR-UM, King of Tyre, *Movers* says, first performed this ceremony. These facts we learn from *Josephus, Servius* on the Æneid, and the *Dionysiacs* of *Nonnus;* and through a coincidence that cannot be fortuitous, the same day was at Rome the *Dies Natalis Solis Invicti,* the festal day of the invincible Sun. Under this title, HERCULES, HAR-*acles,* was worshipped at Tsūr. Thus, while the temple was being erected, the death and resurrection of a Sun-God was annually represented at Tsūr, by Solomon's ally, at the winter solstice, by the pyre of MAL-KARTH, the Tsūrian Haracles.

AROERIS or HAR-*oeris,* the elder HORUS, is from the same old root that in the Hebrew has the form *Aūr,* or, with the definite article prefixed, *Haūr,* Light, or *the* Light, splendor, flame, the Sun and his rays. The hieroglyphic of the younger HORUS was the point in a circle; of the Elder, a pair of eyes; and the festival of the thirtieth day of the month *Epiphi,* when the sun and moon were supposed to be in the same right line with the earth, was called "*The birth-day of the eyes of Horus.*"

In a papyrus published by Champollion, this god is styled "*Har-oeri,* Lord of the Solar Spirits, the beneficent eye of the Sun." Plutarch calls him "*Har-pocrates;*" but there is no trace of the latter part of the name in the hieroglyphic legends. He is the son of OSIRIS and ISIS; and is represented sitting on a throne supported by *lions;* the same word, in Egyptian, meaning *Lion* and *Sun.* So Solomon made a great throne of ivory, plated with gold, with six steps, at each arm of which was a lion, and one on each side to each step, making seven on each side.

Again, the Hebrew word חי, *Khi,* means "*living;*" and ראם *rām,* "*was, or shall be, raised or lifted up.*" The latter is the same as רום, ארום, חרם, *rōōm, arōōm, harūm,* whence *Aram,* for Syria, or *Aramæa,* High-land. *Khairūm,* therefore, would mean "*was raised up to life, or living.*"

So, in Arabic, *hrm,* an unused root, meant, "*was high,*" "*made great,*" "*exalted;*" and *Hîrm* means an *ox,* the symbol of the Sun in Taurus, at the Vernal Equinox.

KHURUM, therefore, improperly called *Hiram,* is KHUR-OM, the same as *Her-ra, Her-mes,* and *Her-acles,* the "*Heracles Tyrius Invictus,*" the personification of Light and the Son, the Mediator, Redeemer, and Saviour. From the Egyptian word *Ra* came the Coptic *Oūro,* and the Hebrew *Aūr,* Light. *Har-oeri,* is *Hor* or *Har,* the chief or *master. Hor* is also heat; and *hora,* season or hour; and hence in several African dialects, as names of the Sun, *Airo, Ayero, eer, uiro, ghurrah,* and the like. The royal name rendered *Pharaoh,* was PHRA, that is, *Pai-ra,* the Sun.

The legend of the contest between *Hor-ra* and *Set,* or *Set-nu-bi,* the same as *Bar* or *Bal,* is older than that of the strife between *Osiris* and *Typhon;* as old, at least, as the nineteenth dynasty. It is called in the Book of the Dead, "The day of the battle between Horus and Set." The later myth connects itself with Phœnicia and Syria. The body of OSIRIS went ashore at *Gebal* or *Byblos,* sixty miles above Tsūr. You will not fail to notice that in the name of each murderer of Khūrūm, that of the Evil God Bal is found.

*   *   *   *   *   *

Har-oeri was the god of TIME, as well as of Life. The Egyptian legend was that the King of Byblos cut down the tamarisk-tree containing the body of OSIRIS, and made of it a column for his palace. Isis, employed in the palace, obtained possession of the column, took the body out of it, and carried it away. Apuleius describes her as "a beautiful female, over whose divine neck her long thick hair hung in graceful ringlets;" and in the procession female attendants, with ivory combs, seemed to dress and ornament the royal hair of the goddess. The palm-tree, and the lamp in the shape of a boat, appeared in the procession. If the symbol we are speaking of is not a mere modern invention, it is to these things it alludes.

The identity of the legends is also confirmed by this hieroglyphic picture, copied from an ancient Egyptian monument, which may also enlighten you as to the Lion's grip and the Master's gavel.

אב, in the ancient Phœnician character, 𐤀 𐤁, and in the Samaritan, 𐤁 𐤀, A B, (the two letters representing the numbers 1, 2, or Unity and Duality, means *Father,* and is a primitive noun, common to all the Semitic languages.

It also means an Ancestor, Originator, Inventor, Head, Chief or Ruler, Manager, Overseer, Master, Priest, Prophet.

אבי is simply Father, when it is in construction, that is, when it precedes another word, and in English the preposition "of" is interposed, as אבי-אל, Abi-Al, the Father of Al.

Also, the final Yōd means "my"; so that אבי by itself means "My father." דויד אבי, David my father, 2 *Chron.* ii. 3.

ו, (Vav) final is the possessive pronoun "his"; and אביו, *Abiu* (which we read "Abif") means "of my father's." Its full meaning, as connected with the name of Khūrūm, no doubt is, "formerly one of my father's servants," or "slaves."

The name of the Phœnician artificer is, in Samuel and Kings, חירם and חירום—[2 *Sam.* v. 11; 1 *Kings* v. 15; 1 *Kings* vii. 40]. In Chronicles it is הורם, with the addition of אבי. [2 *Chron.* ii. 12]; and of אבין. [2 *Chron.* iv. 16].

It is merely absurd to add the word "*Abif,*" or "*Abiff,*" as part of the name of the artificer. And it is almost as absurd to add the word "*Abi,*" which was a *title* and not part of the name. Joseph says [*Gen.* xlv. 8], "God has constituted me '*Ab l'Paraah,* as Father to Paraah, *i. e.,* Vizier or Prime Minister." So Haman was called the Second Father of Artaxerxes; and when King Khūrūm used the phrase "Khūrūm Abi," he meant that the artificer he sent Schlomoh was the principal or chief workman in his line at Tsūr.

A medal copied by Montfaucon exhibits a female nursing a child, with ears of wheat in her hand, and the legend (Iao). She is seated on clouds, a star at her head, and three ears of wheat rising from an altar before her.

HORUS was the *mediator,* who was buried three days, was regenerated, and triumphed over the evil principle.

The word HERI, in Sanscrit, means *Shepherd,* as well as *Saviour.* CRISHNA is called *Heri,* as JESUS called Himself the *Good Shepherd.*

חור, *Khūr,* means an aperture of a window, a cave, or the eye. Also it means white. In Syriac, ܚܘܪ.

חר also means an opening, and noble, free-born, high-born.

82 MORALS AND DOGMA.

חרם, Khurm means consecrated, devoted; in Æthiopic ΑΖΩ! It is the name of a city, [*Josh.* xix. 38] ; and of a man, [*Ezr.* ii. 32, x. 31; *Neh.* iii. 11].

חירה, *Khirah,* means nobility, a noble race.

Buddha is declared to comprehend in his own person the essence of the Hindu Trimurti; and hence the tri-literal monosyllable *Om* or *Aum* is applied to him as being essentially the same as Brahma-Vishnu-Siva. He is the same as Hermes, Thoth, Taut, and Teutates. One of his names is Heri-maya or Hermaya, which are evidently the same name as Hermes and Khirm or Khūrm. Heri, in Sanscrit, means *Lord.*

A learned Brother places over the two symbolic pillars, from right to left, the two words 𐤀𐤁𐤂 and 𐤃𐤄𐤅 יהו and בעל, IHU and BAL: followed by the hieroglyphic equivalent, of the Sun-God, Amun-ra. Is it an accidental coincidence, that in the name of each murderer are the two names of the Good and Evil Deities of the Hebrews; for *Yu-bel* is but *Yehu-Bal* or *Yeho-Bal?* and that the three final syllables of the names, *a, o, um,* make A∴U∴M∴ the sacred word of the Hindoos, meaning the Triune-God, Life-giving, Life-preserving, Life-destroying: represented by the mystic character **Y** ?

The genuine *Acacia,* also, is the thorny tamarisk, the same tree which grew up around the body of Osiris. It was a sacred tree among the Arabs, who made of it the idol Al-Uzza, which Mohammed destroyed. It is abundant as a bush in the Desert of Thur: and of it the "crown of thorns" was composed, which was set on the forehead of Jesus of Nazareth. It is a fit type of immortality on account of its tenacity of life; for it has been known, when planted as a door-post, to take root again and shoot out budding boughs over the threshold.

*   *   *   *   *   *

Every commonwealth must have its periods of trial and transition, especially if it engages in war. It is certain at some time to be wholly governed by agitators appealing to all the baser elements of the popular nature; by moneyed corporations; by those enriched by the depreciation of government securities or paper; by small attorneys, schemers, money-jobbers, speculators and adventurers—an ignoble oligarchy, enriched by the distresses of the State, and fattened on the miseries of the people. Then all the deceitful visions of equality and the rights of man end; and the wronged and plundered State can regain a real liberty only by passing through "great varieties of untried being," purified in its transmigration by fire and blood.

In a Republic, it soon comes to pass that parties gather round the negative and positive poles of some opinion or notion, and that the intolerant spirit of a triumphant majority will allow no deviation from the standard of orthodoxy which it has set up for itself. Freedom of opinion will be professed and pretended to, but every one will exercise it at the peril of being banished from political communion with those who hold the reins and prescribe the policy to be pursued. Slavishness to party and obsequiousness to the popular whims go hand in hand. Political independence only occurs in a fossil state; and men's opinions grow out of the acts they have been constrained to do or sanction. Flattery, either of individual or people, corrupts both the receiver and the giver; and adulation is not of more service to the people than to kings. A Cæsar, securely seated in power, cares less for it than a free democracy; nor will his appetite for it grow to exorbitance, as that of a people will, until it becomes insatiate. The effect of liberty to individuals is, that they may do what they please; to a people, it is to a great extent the same. If accessible to flattery, as this is always interested, and resorted to on low and base motives, and for evil purposes, either individual or people is sure, in doing what it pleases, to do what in honor and conscience should have been left undone. One ought not even to risk congratulations, which may soon be turned into complaints; and as both individuals and peoples are prone to make a bad use of power, to flatter them, which is a sure way to mislead them, well deserves to be called a crime.

The first principle in a Republic ought to be, "that no man or set of men is entitled to exclusive or separate emoluments or privileges from the community, but in consideration of public services; which not being descendible, neither ought the offices of magistrate, legislature, nor judge, to be hereditary." It is a volume of Truth and Wisdom, a lesson for the study of nations, embodied in a single sentence, and expressed in language which every man can understand. If a deluge of despotism were to overthrow the world, and destroy all institutions under which freedom is protected, so that they should no longer be remembered among men, this sentence, preserved, would be sufficient to rekindle the fires of liberty and revive the race of free men.

But, to *preserve* liberty, another must be added: "that a free State does not confer office as a reward, especially for questionable services, unless she seeks her own ruin; but all officers are *employed* by her, in consideration solely of their will and ability to render service in the future; and therefore that the best and most competent are always to be preferred."

For, if there is to be any other rule, that of hereditary succession is perhaps as good as any. By no other rule is it possible to preserve the liberties of the State. By no other to intrust the power of making the laws to those only who have that keen instinctive sense of injustice and wrong which enables them to detect baseness and corruption in their most secret hiding-places, and that moral courage and generous manliness and gallant independence that make them fearless in dragging out the perpetrators to the light of day, and calling down upon them the scorn and indignation of the world. The flatterers of the people are never such men. On the contrary, a time always comes to a Republic, when it is not content, like Tiberius, with a single Sejanus, but must have a host; and when those most prominent in the lead of affairs are men without reputation, statesmanship, ability, or information, the mere hacks of party, owing their places to trickery and *want* of qualification, with none of the qualities of head or heart that make great and wise men, and, at the same time, filled with all the narrow conceptions and bitter intolerance of political bigotry. These die; and the world is none the wiser for what they have said and done. Their names sink in the bottomless pit of oblivion; but their acts of folly or knavery curse the body politic and at last prove its ruin.

Politicians, in a free State, are generally hollow, heartless, and selfish. Their own aggrandisement is the end of their patriotism; and they always look with secret satisfaction on the disappointment or fall of one whose loftier genius and superior talents overshadow their own self-importance, or whose integrity and incorruptible honor are in the way of their selfish ends. The influence of the small aspirants is always against the great man. *His* accession to power may be almost for a lifetime. One of themselves will be more easily displaced, and each hopes to succeed him; and so it at length comes to pass that men impudently aspire to and actually win the highest stations, who are unfit for the lowest clerkships; and incapacity and mediocrity become the surest passports to office.

The consequence is, that those who feel themselves competent and qualified to serve the people, refuse with digust to enter into the struggle for office, where the wicked and jesuitical doctrine that all is fair in politics is an excuse for every species of low villainy; and those who seek even the highest places of the State do not rely upon the power of a magnanimous spirit, on the sympathizing impulses of a great soul, to stir and move the people to generous, noble, and heroic resolves, and to wise and manly action; but, like spaniels erect on their hind legs, with fore-paws obsequiously suppliant, fawn, flatter, and actually beg for votes. Rather than descend to this, they stand contemptuously aloof, disdainfully refusing to court the people, and acting on the maxim, that "mankind has no title to demand that we shall serve them in spite of themselves."

*   *   *   *   *   *

It is lamentable to see a country split into factions, each following this or that great or brazen-fronted leader with a blind, unreasoning, unquestioning hero-worship; it is contemptible to see it divided into parties, whose sole end is the spoils of victory, and their chiefs the low, the base, the venal and the small. Such a country is in the last stages of decay, and near its end, no matter how prosperous it may seem to be. It wrangles over the volcano and the earthquake. But it is certain that no government can be conducted by the men of the people, and for the people, without a rigid adherence to those principles which our reason commends as fixed and sound. These must be the tests of parties, men, and measures. Once determined, they must be inexorable in their application, and all must either come up to the standard or declare against it. Men may betray: principles never can. Oppression is one invariable consequence of misplaced confidence in treacherous man, it is never the result of the working or application of a sound, just, well-tried principle. Compromises which bring fundamental principles into doubt, in order to unite in one party men of antagonistic creeds, are frauds, and end in ruin, the just and natural consequence of fraud. Whenever you have settled upon your theory and creed, sanction no departure from it in practice, on any ground of expediency. It is the Master's word.

Yield it up neither to flattery nor force! Let no defeat or persecution rob you of it! Believe that he who once blundered in statesmanship will blunder again; that such blunders are as fatal as crimes; and that political near-sightedness does not improve by age. There are always more impostors than seers among public men, more false prophets than true ones, more prophets of Baal than of Jehovah; and Jerusalem is always in danger from the Assyrians.

Sallust said that after a State has been corrupted by luxury and idleness, it may by its mere greatness bear up under the burden of its vices. But even while he wrote, Rome, of which he spoke, had played out her masquerade of freedom. Other causes than luxury and sloth destroy Republics. If small, their larger neighbors extinguish them by absorption. If of great extent, the cohesive force is too feeble to hold them together, and they fall to pieces by their own weight. The paltry ambition of small men disintegrates them. The want of wisdom in their councils creates exasperating issues. Usurpation of power plays its part, incapacity seconds corruption, the storm rises, and the fragments of the incoherent raft strew the sandy shores, reading to mankind another lesson for it to disregard.

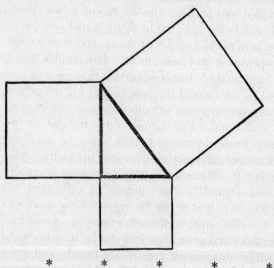

*　　　*　　　*　　　*　　　*　　　*

The Forty-seventh Proposition is older than Pythagoras. It is this: "In every right-angled triangle, the sum of the squares of the base and perpendicular is equal to the square of the hypothenuse."

The square of a number is the product of that number, multiplied by itself. Thus, 4 is the square of 2, and 9 of 3.

The first ten numbers are: 1, 2, 3, 4, 5, 6, 7, 8, 9, 10; their squares are .... 1, 4, 9, 16, 25, 36, 49, 64, 81, 100; and .... 3, 5, 7, 9, 11, 13, 15, 17, 19 are the differences between each square and that which precedes it; giving us the sacred numbers, 3, 5, 7, and 9

Of these numbers, the square of 3 and 4, added together, gives the square of 5; and those of 6 and 8, the square of 10; and if a right-angled triangle be formed, the base measuring 3 or 6 parts, and the perpendicular 4 or 8 parts, the hypothenuse will be 5 or 10 parts; and if a square is erected on each side, these squares being subdivided into squares each side of which is one part in length, there will be as many of these in the square erected on the hypothenuse as in the other two squares together.

Now the Egyptians arranged their deities in *Triads*—the FATHER or the Spirit or Active Principle or *Generative* Power; the MOTHER, or Matter, or the Passive Principle, or the *Conceptive* Power; and the SON, *Issue* or *Product,* the Universe, proceeding from the two principles. These were OSIRIS, ISIS, and HORUS. In the same way, PLATO gives us *Thought* the *Father;* Primitive *Matter* the *Mother;* and *Kosmos* the *World,* the *Son,* the Universe animated by a soul. Triads of the same kind are found in the Kabalah.

PLUTARCH says, in his book *De Iside et Osiride,* "But the better and diviner nature consists of three,—that which exists within the Intellect only, and Matter, and that which proceeds from these, which the Greeks call *Kosmos;* of which three, Plato is wont to call the Intelligible, the 'Idea, Exemplar, and Father'; Matter, 'the Mother, the Nurse, and the place and receptacle of generation'; and the issue of these two, 'the Offspring and Genesis,'" the KOSMOS, "a word signifying equally *Beauty* and *Order,* or the Universe itself." You will not fail to notice that Beauty is symbolized by the Junior Warden in the South. Plutarch continues to say that the Egyptians compared the universal nature to what they called the most beautiful and perfect triangle, as Plato does, in that nuptial diagram, as it is termed, which he has introduced into his Commonwealth. Then he adds that this triangle is right-angled, and its sides respectively as 3, 4, and 5; and he says, "We must suppose that the perpendicular is designed by them to represent the masculine nature, the base the feminine, and that the hypothenuse is to be looked upon as the offspring of both; and accordingly the first of them will aptly enough represent OSIRIS, or the prime cause; the second, ISIS, or the receptive capacity; the last, HORUS, or the common effect of the other two. For 3 is the first number which is composed of even and odd; and 4 is a square whose side is equal to the even number 2; but 5, being generated, as it were, out of the preceding numbers, 2 and 3, may be said to have an equal relation to both of them, as to its common parents."

      *   *   *   *   *   *

The *clasped hands* is another symbol which was used by PYTHAGORAS. It represented the number 10, the sacred number in which all the preceding numbers were contained; the number expressed by the mysterious TETRACTYS, a figure borrowed by him and the Hebrew priests alike from the Egyptian sacred science, and which ought to be replaced among the symbols of the Master's Degree, where it of right belongs. The Hebrews formed it thus, with the letters of the Divine name:

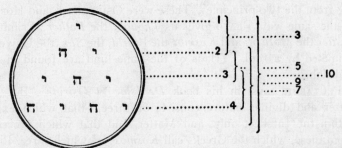

The *Tetractys* thus leads you, not only to the study of the Pythagorean philosophy as to numbers, but also to the Kabalah, and will aid you in discovering the True Word, and understanding what was meant by "The Music of the Spheres." Modern science strikingly confirms the ideas of Pythagoras in regard to the properties of numbers, and that they govern in the Universe. Long before his time, nature had extracted her cube-roots and her squares.

      *   *   *   *   *   *

All the FORCES at man's disposal or under man's control, or subject to man's influence, are his *working tools*. The friendship and sympathy that knit heart to heart are a force like the attraction of cohesion, by which the sandy particles became the solid rock. If this law of attraction or cohesion were taken away, the material worlds and suns would dissolve in an instant into thin invisible vapor. If the ties of friendship, affection, and love were annulled, mankind would become a raging multitude of wild and savage beasts of prey. The sand hardens into rock under the immense superincumbent pressure of the ocean, aided sometimes by the irresistible energy of fire; and when the pressure of calamity and danger is upon an order or a country, the members or the citizens ought to be the more closely united by the cohesion of sympathy and inter-dependence.

Morality is a force. It is the magnetic attraction of the heart toward Truth and Virtue. The needle, imbued with this mystic property, and pointing unerringly to the north, carries the mariner safely over the trackless ocean, through storm and darkness, until his glad eyes behold the beneficent beacons that welcome him to safe and hospitable harbor. Then the hearts of those who love him are gladdened, and his home made happy; and this gladness and happiness are due to the silent, unostentatious, unerring monitor that was the sailor's guide over the weltering waters. But if drifted too far northward, he finds the needle no longer true, but pointing elsewhere than to the north, what a feeling of helplessness falls upon the dismayed mariner, what utter loss of energy and courage! It is as if the great axioms of morality were to fail and be no longer true, leaving the human soul to drift helplessly, eyeless like Prometheus, at the mercy of the uncertain, faithless currents of the deep.

Honor and Duty are the pole-stars of a Mason, the Dioscuri, by never losing sight of which he may avoid disastrous shipwreck. These Palinurus watched, until, overcome by sleep, and the vessel no longer guided truly, he fell into and was swallowed up by the insatiable sea. So the Mason who loses sight of these, and is no longer governed by their beneficent and potential force, is lost, and sinking out of sight, will disappear unhonored and unwept.

The force of electricity, analogous to that of sympathy, and by means of which great thoughts or base suggestions, the utterances of noble or ignoble natures, flash instantaneously over the nerves of nations; the force of growth, fit type of immortality, lying dormant three thousand years in the wheat-grains buried with

7

their mummies by the old Egyptians; the forces of expansion and contraction, developed in the earthquake and the tornado, and giving birth to the wonderful achievements of steam, have their parallelisms in the moral world, in individuals, and nations. Growth is a necessity for nations as for men. Its cessation is the beginning of decay. In the nation as well as the plant it is mysterious, and it is irresistible. The earthquakes that rend nations asunder, overturn thrones, and engulf monarchies and republics, have been long prepared for, like the volcanic eruption. Revolutions have long roots in the past. The force exerted is in direct proportion to the previous restraint and compression. The true statesman ought to see in progress the causes that are in due time to produce them; and he who does not is but a blind leader of the blind.

The great changes in nations, like the geological changes of the earth, are slowly and continuously wrought. The waters, falling from Heaven as rain and dews, slowly disintegrate the granite mountains; abrade the plains, leaving hills and ridges of denudation as their monuments; scoop out the valleys, fill up the seas, narrow the rivers, and after the lapse of thousands on thousands of silent centuries, prepare the great alluvia for the growth of that plant, the snowy envelope of whose seeds is to employ the looms of the world, and the abundance or penury of whose crops shall determine whether the weavers and spinners of other realms shall have work to do or starve.

So Public Opinion is an immense force; and its currents are as inconstant and incomprehensible as those of the atmosphere. Nevertheless, in free governments, it is omnipotent; and the business of the statesman is to find the means to shape, control, and direct it. According as that is done, it is beneficial and conservative, or destructive and ruinous. The Public Opinion of the civilized world is International Law; and it is so great a force, though with no certain and fixed boundaries, that it can even constrain the victorious despot to be generous, and aid an oppressed people in its struggle for independence.

Habit is a great force; it is second nature, even in trees. It is as strong in nations as in men. So also are Prejudices, which are given to men and nations as the passions are,—as forces, valuable, if properly and skillfully availed of; destructive, if unskillfully handled.

Above all, the Love of Country, State Pride, the Love of Home, are forces of immense power. Encourage them all. Insist upon them in your public men. Permanency of home is necessary to patriotism. A migratory race will have little love of country. State pride is a mere theory and chimera, where men remove from State to State with indifference, like the Arabs, who camp here to-day and there to-morrow.

If you have Eloquence, it is a mighty force. See that you use it for good purposes—to teach, exhort, ennoble the people, and not to mislead and corrupt them. Corrupt and venal orators are the assassins of the public liberties and of public morals.

The Will is a force; its limits as yet unknown. It is in the power of the will that we chiefly see the spiritual and divine in man. There is a seeming identity between his will that moves other men, and the Creative Will whose action seems so incomprehensible. It is the men of *will* and *action,* not the men of pure intellect, that govern the world.

Finally, the three greatest moral forces are FAITH, which is the only true WISDOM, and the very foundation of all government; HOPE, which is STRENGTH, and insures success; and CHARITY, which is BEAUTY, and alone makes animated, united effort possible. These forces are within the reach of all men; and an association of men, actuated by them, ought to exercise an immense power in the world. If Masonry does not, it is because she has ceased to possess them.

Wisdom in the man or statesman, in king or priest, largely consists in the due appreciation of these forces; and upon the general *non*-appreciation of some of them the fate of nations often depends. What hecatombs of lives often hang upon the not weighing or not sufficiently weighing the force of an idea, such as, for example, the reverence for a flag, or the blind attachment to a form or constitution of government!

What errors in political economy and statesmanship are committed in consequence of the over-estimation or under-estimation of particular values, or the non-estimation of some among them! Everything, it is asserted, is the product of human labor; but the gold or the diamond which one accidentally finds without labor is not so. What is the value of the labor bestowed by the husbandman upon his crops, compared with the value of the sunshine and rain, without which his labor avails nothing? Commerce carried on by the labor of man, adds to the value of the products of the field, the mine, or the workshop, by their transportation to different markets; but how much of this increase is due to the rivers down which these products float, to the winds that urge the keels of commerce over the ocean!

Who can estimate the value of morality and manliness in a State, of moral worth and intellectual knowledge? These are the sunshine and rain of the State. The winds, with their changeable, fickle, fluctuating currents, are apt emblems of the fickle humors of the populace, its passions, its heroic impulses, its enthusiasms. Woe to the statesman who does not estimate these as values!

Even music and song are sometimes found to have an incalculable value. Every nation has some song of a proven value, more easily counted in lives than dollars. The Marseillaise was worth to revolutionary France, who shall say how many thousand men?

Peace also is a great element of prosperity and wealth; a value not to be calculated. Social intercourse and association of men in beneficent Orders have a value not to be estimated in coin. The illustrious examples of the Past of a nation, the memories and immortal thoughts of her great and wise thinkers, statesmen, and heroes, are the invaluable legacy of that Past to the Present and Future. And all these have not only the values of the loftier and more excellent and priceless kind, but also an actual *money*-value, since it is only when co-operating with or aided or enabled by these, that human labor creates wealth. They are of the chief elements of material wealth, as they are of national manliness, heroism, glory, prosperity, and immortal renown.

*   *   *   *   *   *

Providence has appointed the three great disciplines of *War*, the *Monarchy* and the *Priesthood,* all that the CAMP, the PALACE, and the TEMPLE may symbolize, to train the multitudes forward to intelligent and premeditated combinations for all the great purposes of society. The result will at length be free governments among men, when virtue and intelligence become qualities of the multitudes; but for ignorance such governments are impossible. Man advances only by degrees. The removal of one pressing calamity gives courage to attempt the removal of the remaining evils, rendering men more sensitive to them, or perhaps sensitive for the first time. Serfs that writhe under the whip are not disquieted about their political rights; manumitted from personal slavery, they become sensitive to political oppression. Liberated from arbitrary power, and governed by the law alone, they begin to scrutinize the law itself, and desire to be governed, not only by law, but by what they deem the best law. And when the civil or temporal despotism has been set aside, and the municipal law has been moulded on the principles of an enlightened jurisprudence, they may wake to the discovery that they are living under some priestly or ecclesiastical despotism, and become desirous of working a reformation there also.

It is quite true that the advance of humanity is slow, and that it often pauses and retrogrades. In the kingdoms of the earth we do not see despotisms retiring and yielding the ground to self-governing communities. We do not see the churches and priesthoods of Christendom relinquishing their old task of governing men by imaginary terrors. Nowhere do we see a populace that could be safely manumitted from such a government. We do not see the great religious teachers aiming to discover truth for themselves and for others; but still ruling the world, and contented and compelled to rule the world, by whatever dogma is already accredited; themselves as much bound down by this necessity to govern, as the populace by their need of government. Poverty in all its most hideous forms still exists in the great cities; and the cancer of pauperism has its roots in the hearts of kingdoms. Men there take no measure of their wants and their own power to supply them, but live and multiply like the beasts of the field,—Providence having apparently ceased to care for them. Intelligence never visits these, or it makes its appearance as some new development of villainy. War has not ceased; still there are battles and sieges. Homes are still unhappy, and tears and anger and spite make hells where there should be heavens. So much the more necessity for Masonry! So much wider the field of its labors! So much the more need for it to begin to be true to itself, to revive from its asphyxia, to repent of its apostasy to its true creed!

Undoubtedly, labor and death and the sexual passion are essential and permanent conditions of human existence, and render perfection and a millennium on earth impossible. Always,—it is the decree of Fate!—the vast majority of men must toil to live, and cannot find time to cultivate the intelligence. Man, knowing he is to die, will not sacrifice the present enjoyment for a greater one in the future. The love of woman cannot die out; and it has a terrible and uncontrollable fate, increased by the refinements of civilization. Woman is the veritable syren or goddess of the young. But society can be improved; and free government *is* possible for States; and freedom of thought and conscience is no longer *wholly* utopian. Already we see that Emperors prefer to be elected by universal suffrage; that States are conveyed to Empires by vote; and that Empires are administered with something of the spirit of a Republic, being little else than democracies with a single head, ruling through one man, one representative, instead of an assembly of representatives. And if Priesthoods still govern, they now come before the laity to prove, by stress of argument, that they *ought* to govern. They are obliged to evoke the very reason which they are bent on supplanting.

Accordingly, men become daily more free, because the freedom of the man lies in his reason. He can reflect upon his own future conduct, and summon up its consequences; he can take wide views of human life, and lay down rules for constant guidance. Thus he is relieved of the tyranny of sense and passion, and enabled at any time to live according to the whole light of the knowledge that is within him, instead of being driven, like a dry leaf on the wings of the wind, by every present impulse. Herein lies the freedom of the man as regarded in connection with the necessity imposed by the omnipotence and fore-knowledge of God. So much light, so much liberty. When emperor and church appeal to reason there is naturally universal suffrage.

Therefore no one need lose courage, nor believe that labor in the cause of Progress will be labor wasted. There is no waste in nature, either of Matter, Force, Act, or Thought. A Thought is as much the end of life as an Action; and a single Thought sometimes works greater results than a Revolution, even Revolutions themselves. Still there should not be divorce between Thought and Action. The true Thought is that in which life culminates. But all wise and true Thought produces Action. It is generative, like the light; and light and the deep shadow of the passing cloud are the gifts of the prophets of the race. Knowledge, laboriously acquired, and inducing habits of sound Thought,—the reflective character,—must necessarily be rare. The multitude of laborers cannot acquire it. Most men attain to a very low standard of it. It is incompatible with the ordinary and indispensable avocations of life. A whole world of error as well as of labor, go to make one reflective man. In the most advanced nation of Europe there are more ignorant than wise, more poor than rich, more automatic laborers, the mere creatures of habit, than reasoning and reflective men. The proportion is at least a thousand to one. Unanimity of opinion is so obtained. It only exists among the multitude who do not think, and the political or spiritual priesthood who think for that multitude, who think how to guide and govern them. When men begin to reflect, they begin to differ. The great problem is to find guides who will not seek to be tyrants. This is needed even more in respect to the heart than the head. Now, every man earns his special share of the produce of human labor, by an incessant scramble, by trickery and deceit. Useful knowledge, honorably acquired, is too often used after a fashion not honest or reasonable, so that the studies of youth are far more noble than the practices of manhood. The labor of the farmer in his fields, the generous returns of the earth, the benignant and favoring skies, tend to make him earnest, provident, and grateful; the education of the market-place makes him querulous, crafty, envious, and an intolerable niggard.

Masonry seeks to be this beneficent, unambitious, disinterested guide; and it is the very condition of all great structures that the sound of the hammer and the clink of the trowel should be always heard in some part of the building. With faith in man, hope for the future of humanity, loving-kindness for our fellows, Masonry and the Mason must always work and teach. Let each do that for which he is best fitted. The teacher also is a workman. Praiseworthy as the active navigator is, who comes and goes and makes one clime partake of the treasures of the other, and one to share the treasures of all, he who keeps the beacon-light upon the hill is also at his post.

Masonry has already helped cast down some idols from their pedestals, and grind to impalpable dust some of the links of the chains that held men's souls in bondage. That there has been progress needs no other demonstration than that you may now reason with men, and urge upon them, without danger of the rack or stake, that no doctrines can be apprehended as truths if they contradict each other, or contradict other truths given us by God. Long before the Reformation, a monk, who had found his way to heresy without the help of Martin Luther, not venturing to breathe aloud into any living ear his anti-papal and treasonable doctrines, wrote them on parchment, and sealing up the perilous record, hid it in the massive walls of his monastery. There was no friend or brother to whom he could intrust his secret or pour forth his soul. It was some consolation to imagine that in a future age some one might find the parchment, and the seed be found not to have been sown in vain. What if the truth should have to lie dormant as long before germinating as the wheat in the Egyptian mummy? Speak it, nevertheless, again and again, and let it take its chance!

The rose of Jericho grows in the sandy deserts of Arabia and on the Syrian housetops. Scarcely six inches high, it loses its leaves after the flowering season, and dries up into the form of a ball. Then it is uprooted by the winds, and carried, blown, or tossed across the desert, into the sea. There, feeling the contact of the water, it unfolds itself, expands its branches, and expels its seeds from their seed-vessels. These, when saturated with water, are carried by the tide and laid on the sea-shore. Many are lost, as many individual lives of men are useless. But many are thrown back again from the sea-shore into the desert, where, by the virtue of the sea-water that they have imbibed, the roots and leaves sprout and they grow into fruitful plants, which will, in their turns, like their ancestors, be whirled into the sea. God will not be less careful to provide for the germination of the truths you may boldly utter forth. *"Cast,"* He has said, *"thy bread upon the waters, and after many days it shall return to thee again."*

Initiation does not change: we find it again and again, and always the same, through all the ages. The last disciples of Pascalis Martinez are still the children of Orpheus; but they adore the realizer of the antique philosophy, the Incarnate Word of the Christians.

Pythagoras, the great divulger of the philosophy of numbers, visited all the sanctuaries of the world. He went into Judæa, where he procured himself to be circumcised, that he might be admitted to the secrets of the Kabalah, which the prophets Ezekiel and Daniel, not without some reservations, communicated to him. Then, not without some difficulty, he succeeded in being admitted to the Egyptian initiation, upon the recommendation of King Amasis. The power of his genius supplied the deficiencies of the imperfect communications of the Hierophants, and he himself became a Master and a Revealer.

Pythagoras defined God: a Living and Absolute Verity clothed with Light.

He said that the Word was Number manifested by Form.

He made all descend from the *Tetractys,* that is to say, from the Quaternary.

God, he said again, is the Supreme Music, the nature of which is Harmony.

Pythagoras gave the magistrates of Crotona this great religious, political and social precept:

"There is no evil that is not preferable to Anarchy."

Pythagoras said, "Even as there are three divine notions and three intelligible regions, so there is a triple word, for the Hierarchical Order always manifests itself by threes. There are the word simple, the word hieroglyphical, and the word symbolic: in other terms, there are the word that expresses, the word that conceals, and the word that signifies; the whole hieratic intelligence is in the perfect knowledge of these three degrees."

Pythagoras enveloped doctrine with symbols, but carefully eschewed personifications and images, which, he thought, sooner or later produced idolatry.

The Holy Kabalah, or tradition of the children of Seth, was carried from Chaldæa by Abraham, taught to the Egyptian priesthood by Joseph, recovered and purified by Moses, concealed under symbols in the Bible, revealed by the Saviour to Saint John, and contained, entire, under hieratic figures analogous to those of all antiquity, in the Apocalypse of that Apostle.

The Kabalists consider God as the Intelligent, Animated, Living Infinite. He is not, for them, either the aggregate of existences, or existence in the abstract, or a being philosophically definable. He is *in* all, *distinct* from all, and *greater* than all. His name even is ineffable; and yet this name only expresses the human ideal of His divinity. What God is in Himself, it is not given to man to comprehend.

God is the absolute of Faith; but the absolute of *Reason* is BEING, יהוה.   "*I am that I am,*" is a wretched translation.

Being, Existence, is by itself, and because it Is. The reason of Being, is Being itself. We may inquire, "Why does something exist?" that is, "Why does such or such a thing exist?" But we cannot, without being absurd, ask, "Why Is Being?" That would be to suppose Being before Being. If Being had a cause, that cause would necessarily Be; that is, the cause and effect would be identical.

Reason and science demonstrate to us that the modes of Existence and Being balance each other in equilibrium according to harmonious and hierarchic laws. But a hierarchy is synthetized, in ascending, and becomes ever more and more monarchial. Yet the reason cannot pause at a single chief, without being alarmed at the abysses which it seems to leave above this Supreme Monarch. Therefore it is silent, and gives place to the Faith it adores.

What is certain, even for science and the reason, is, that the idea of God is the grandest, the most holy, and the most useful of all the aspirations of man; that upon this belief morality reposes, with its eternal sanction. This belief, then, is in humanity, the most real of the phenomena of being; and if it were false, nature would affirm the absurd; nothingness would give form to life, and God would at the same time be and not be.

It is to this philosophic and incontestable reality, which is termed The Idea of God, that the Kabalists give a name. In this name all others are contained. Its cyphers contain all the numbers; and the hieroglyphics of its letters express all the laws and all the things of nature.

BEING IS BEING: the reason of Being is in Being: in the Beginning is the Word, and the Word in logic formulated Speech, the spoken Reason; the Word is in God, and is God Himself, manifested to the Intelligence. Here is what is above all the philosophies. This we must believe, under the penalty of never truly knowing anything, and relapsing into the absurd skepticism of Pyrrho. The Priesthood, custodian of Faith, wholly rests upon this basis of knowledge, and it is in its teachings we must recognize the Divine Principle of the Eternal Word.

Light is not Spirit, as the Indian Hierophants believed it to be; but only the instrument of the Spirit. It is not the body of the Protoplastes, as the Theurgists of the school of Alexandria taught, but the first physical manifestation of the Divine afflatus. God eternally creates it, and man, in the image of God, modifies and seems to multiply it.

The high magic is styled "The Sacerdotal Art," and "The Royal Art." In Egypt, Greece, and Rome, it could not but share the greatnesses and decadences of the Priesthood and of Royalty. Every philosophy hostile to the national worship and to its mysteries, was of necessity hostile to the great political powers, which lose their grandeur, if they cease, in the eyes of the multitudes, to be the images of the Divine Power. Every Crown is shattered, when it clashes against the Tiara.

Plato, writing to Dionysius the Younger, in regard to the nature of the First Principle, says: "I must write to you in enigmas, so that if my letter be intercepted by land or sea, he who shall read it may in no degree comprehend it." And then he says, "All things surround their King; they are, on account of Him, and He alone is the cause of good things, Second for the Seconds and Third for the Thirds."

There is in these few words a complete summary of the Theology of the Sephiroth. "The *King*" is AINSOPH, Being Supreme and Absolute. From this centre, *which* is *everywhere*, all things ray forth; but we especially conceive of it in three manners and in three different spheres. In the *Divine* world (AZILUTH), which is that of the First Cause, and wherein the whole Eternity of Things in the beginning existed as Unity, to be afterward, during Eternity uttered forth, clothed with form, and the attributes that constitute them matter, the First Principle is Single and First, and yet not the VERY Illimitable Deity, incomprehensible, undefinable; but Himself in so far as manifested by the Creative Thought. To compare littleness with infinity,—Arkwright, as inventor of the spinning-jenny, and not the *man* Arkwright *otherwise* and *beyond that*. All we can know of the Very God is, compared to His Wholeness, only as an infinitesimal fraction of a unit, compared with an infinity of Units.

In the World of Creation, which is that of Second Causes [the Kabalistic World BRIAH], the Autocracy of the First Principle is complete, but we conceive of it only as the Cause of the Second Causes. Here it is manifested by the Binary, and is the Creative Principle passive. Finally: in the third world, YEZIRAH, or of Formation, it is revealed in the perfect Form, the Form of Forms, the World, the Supreme Beauty and Excellence, the Created Perfection. Thus the Principle is at once the First, the Second, and the Third, since it is All in All, the Centre and Cause of all. It is not *the genius of Plato* that we here admire. We recognize only *the exact knowledge of the Initiate*.

The great Apostle Saint John did not borrow from the philosophy of Plato the opening of his Gospel. Plato, on the contrary, drank at the same springs with Saint John and Philo; and John in the opening verses of his paraphrase, states the first principles of a dogma common to many schools, but in language especially belonging to Philo, whom it is evident he had read. The philosophy of Plato, the greatest of human Revealers, could *yearn toward* the Word made man; the Gospel alone could give him to the world.

Doubt, in presence of Being and its harmonies; skepticism, in the face of the eternal mathematics and the immutable laws of Life which make the Divinity present and visible everywhere, as the Human is known and visible by its utterances of word and act,—is this not the most foolish of superstitions, and the most inexcusable as well as the most dangerous of all credulities? Thought, we know, is not a result or consequence of the organization of matter, of the chemical or other action or reaction of its particles, like effervescence and gaseous explosions. On the contrary, the fact that Thought is manifested and realized in act human or act divine, proves the existence of an Entity, or Unity, that thinks. And the Universe is the Infinite Utterance of one of an infinite number of Infinite Thoughts, which cannot but emanate from an Infinite and Thinking Source. The cause is always equal, at least, to the effect; and matter cannot think, nor could it cause itself, or exist without cause, nor could nothing *produce* either forces or things; for in void nothingness no Forces can inhere. Admit a self-existent Force, and its Intelligence, or an Intelligent cause of it is admitted, and at once GOD IS.

The Hebrew allegory of the Fall of Man, which is but a special variation of a universal legend, symbolizes one of the grandest and most universal allegories of science.

Moral Evil is Falsehood in actions; as Falsehood is Crime in words.

Injustice is the essence of Falsehood; and every false word is an injustice.

Injustice is the death of the Moral Being, as Falsehood is the poison of the Intelligence.

The perception of the Light is the dawn of the Eternal Life, in Being. The Word of God, which creates the Light, seems to be uttered by every Intelligence that can take cognizance of Forms and will look. "Let the Light BE! The Light, in fact, exists, in its condition of splendor, for those eyes alone that gaze at it; and the Soul, amorous of the spectacle of the beauties of the Universe, and applying its attention to that luminous writing of the Infinite Book, which is called "The Visible," seems to utter, as God did on the dawn of the first day, that sublime and creative word, "BE! LIGHT!"

It is not beyond the tomb, but in life itself, that we are to seek for the mysteries of death. Salvation or reprobation begins here below, and the terrestrial world too has its Heaven and its Hell. Always, even here below, virtue is rewarded; always, even here below, vice is punished; and that which makes us sometimes believe in the impunity of evil-doers is that riches, those instruments of good and of evil, seem sometimes to be given them at hazard. But woe to unjust men, when they possess the key of gold! It opens, for *them*, only the gate of the tomb and of Hell.

All the true Initiates have recognized the usefulness of toil and sorrow. "Sorrow," says a German poet, "is the dog of that unknown shepherd who guides the flock of men." To learn to suffer, to learn to die, is the discipline of Eternity, the immortal Noviciate.

The allegorical picture of Cebes, in which the Divine Comedy of Dante was sketched in Plato's time, the description whereof has been preserved for us, and which many painters of the middle age have reproduced by this description, is a monument at once philosophical and magical. It is a most complete moral synthesis, and at the same time the most audacious demonstration ever given of the Grand Arcanum, of that secret whose revelation would overturn Earth and Heaven. Let no one expect us to give them its explanation! He who passes behind the veil that hides this mystery, understands that it is in its very nature inexplicable, and that it is death to those who win it by surprise, as well as to him who reveals it.

This secret is the Royalty of the Sages, the Crown of the Initiate whom we see redescend victorious from the summit of Trials, in the fine allegory of Cebes. The Grand Arcanum makes him master of gold and the light, which are at bottom the same thing, he has solved the problem of the quadrature of the circle, he directs the perpetual movement, and he possesses the philosophical stone. Here the Adepts will understand us. There is neither interruption in the toil of nature, nor gap in her work. The Harmonies of Heaven correspond to those of Earth, and the Eternal Life accomplishes its evolutions in accordance with the same laws as the life of a dog. "God has arranged all things by weight, number, and measure," says the Bible; and this luminous doctrine was also that of Plato.

Humanity has never really had but one religion and one worship. This universal light has had its uncertain mirages, its deceitful reflections, and its shadows; but always, after the nights of Error, we see it reappear, one and pure like the Sun.

The magnificences of worship are the life of religion, and if Christ wishes poor ministers, His Sovereign Divinity does not wish paltry altars. Some Protestants have not comprehended that worship is a teaching, and that we must not create in the imagination of the multitude a mean or miserable God. Those oratories that resemble poorly-furnished offices or inns, and those worthy ministers clad like notaries or lawyer's clerks, do they not necessarily cause religion to be regarded as a mere puritanic formality, and God as a Justice of the Peace?

We scoff at the Augurs. It is so easy to scoff, and so difficult well to comprehend. Did the Deity leave the whole world without Light for two score centuries, to illuminate only a little corner of Palestine and a brutal, ignorant, and ungrateful people? Why always calumniate God and the Sanctuary? Were there never any others than rogues among the priests? Could no honest and sincere men be found among the Hierophants of Ceres or Diana, of Dionusos or Apollo, of Hermes or Mithras? Were these, then, all deceived, like the rest? Who, then, constantly deceived them, without betraying themselves, during a series of centuries?—for the cheats are not immortal! Arago said, that outside of the pure mathematics, he who utters the word "impossible," is wanting in prudence and good sense.

The true name of Satan, the Kabalists say, is that of Yahveh reversed; for Satan is not a black god, but the negation of God. The Devil is the personification of Atheism or Idolatry.

For the Initiates, this is not a *Person,* but a *Force,* created for good, but which *may* serve for evil. *It is the instrument of Liberty or Free Will.* They represent this Force, which presides over the physical generation, under the mythologic and horned form of the God PAN; thence came the he-goat of the Sabbat, brother of the Ancient Serpent, and the Light-bearer or *Phosphor,* of which the poets have made the false Lucifer of the legend.

Gold, to the eyes of the Initiates, is Light condensed. They style the sacred numbers of the Kabalah "golden numbers," and the moral teachings of Pythagoras his "golden verses." For the same reason, a mysterious book of Apuleius, in which an ass figures largely, was called "The Golden Ass."

The Pagans accused the Christians of worshipping an ass, and they did not invent this reproach, but it came from the Samaritan Jews, who, figuring the data of the Kabalah in regard to the Divinity by Egyptian symbols, also represented the Intelligence by the figure of the Magical Star adored under the name of *Remphan,* Science under the emblem of Anubis, whose name they changed to *Nibbas,* and the vulgar faith or credulity under the figure of *Thartac,* a god represented with a book, a cloak, and the head of an ass. According to the Samaritan Doctors, Christianity was the reign of *Thartac,* blind Faith and vulgar credulity erected into a universal oracle, and preferred to Intelligence and Science.

Synesius, Bishop of Ptolemaïs, a great Kabalist, but of doubtful orthodoxy, wrote:

"The people will always mock at things easy to be misunderstood; it must needs have impostures."

"A Spirit," he said, "that loves wisdom and contemplates the Truth close at hand, is forced to disguise it, to induce the multitudes to accept it. . . . Fictions are necessary to the people, and the Truth becomes deadly to those who are not strong enough to contemplate it in all its brilliance. If the sacerdotal laws allowed the reservation of judgments and the allegory of words, I would accept the proposed dignity on condition that I might be a philosopher at home, and abroad a narrator of apologues and parables. . . . . In fact, what can there be in common between the vile multitude and sublime wisdom? The truth must be kept secret, and the masses need a teaching proportioned to their imperfect reason."

Moral disorders produce physical ugliness, and in some sort realize those frightful faces which tradition assigns to the demons.

The first Druids were the true children of the Magi, and their initiation came from Egypt and Chaldæa, that is to say, from the pure sources of the primitive Kabalah. They adored the Trinity under the names of *Isis* or *Hesus,* the Supreme Harmony; of *Belen* or *Bel,* which in Assyrian means Lord, a name corresponding to that of ADONAÏ; and of *Camul* or *Camaël,* a name that in the Kabalah personifies the Divine Justice. Below this triangle of Light they supposed a divine reflection, also composed of three personified rays: first, *Teutates* or *Teuth,* the same as the *Thoth* of the Egyptians, the Word, or the Intelligence formulated; then Force and Beauty, whose names varied like their emblems. Finally, they completed the sacred Septenary by a mysterious image that represented the progress of the dogma and its future realizations. This was a young girl veiled, holding a child in her arms; and they dedicated this image to "The Virgin who will become a mother;—*Virgini parituræ.*"

Hertha or Wertha, the young Isis of Gaul, Queen of Heaven, the Virgin who was to bear a child, held the spindle of the Fates, filled with wool half white and half black; because she presides over all forms and all symbols, and weaves the garment of the Ideas.

One of the most mysterious pantacles of the Kabalah, contained in the Enchiridion of Leo III., represents an equilateral triangle reversed, inscribed in a double circle. On the triangle are written, in such manner as to form the prophetic Tau, the two Hebrew words so often found appended to the Ineffable Name, אלהם and צבאות, ALOHAYIM, or the Powers, and TSABAOTH, or the starry Armies and their guiding spirits; words also which symbolize the Equilibrium of the Forces of Nature and the Harmony of Numbers. To the three sides of the triangle belong the three great Names יהוה אדני, and אגלא, IAHAVEH, ADONAÏ, and AGLA. Above the first is written in Latin, *Formatio,* above the second *Reformatio,* and above the third, *Transformatio.* So Creation is ascribed to the FATHER, Redemption or Reformation to the SON, and Sanctification or Transformation to the HOLY SPIRIT, answering unto the mathematical laws of Action, Reaction, and Equilibrium. IAHAVEH is also, in effect, the Genesis or Formation of dogma, by the elementary signification of the four letters of the Sacred Tetragram; ADONAÏ is the realization of this dogma in the Human Form, in the Visible LORD, who is the Son of God or the perfect Man; and AGLA (formed of the initials of the four words *Ath Gebur Laulaïm Adonaï*) expresses the synthesis of the whole dogma and the totality of the Kabalistic science, clearly indicating by the hieroglyphics of which this admirable name is formed the Triple Secret of the Great Work.

Masonry, like all the Religions, all the Mysteries, Hermeticism and Alchemy, *conceals* its secrets from all except the Adepts and Sages, or the Elect, and uses false explanations and misinterpretations of its symbols to mislead those who deserve only to be misled; to conceal the Truth, which it calls Light, from them, and to draw them away from it. Truth is not for those who are unworthy or unable to receive it, or would pervert it. So God Himself incapacitates many men, by color-blindness, to distinguish colors, and leads the masses away from the highest Truth, giving them the power to attain only so much of it as it is profitable to them to know. Every age has had a religion suited to its capacity.

The Teachers, even of Christianity, are, in general, the most ignorant of the true meaning of that which they teach. There is no book of which so little is known as the Bible. To most who read it, it is as incomprehensible as the Sohar.

So Masonry jealously conceals its secrets, and intentionally leads conceited interpreters astray. There is no sight under the sun more pitiful and ludicrous at once, than the spectacle of the Prestons and the Webbs, not to mention the later incarnations of Dullness and Commonplace, undertaking to "explain" the old symbols of Masonry, and adding to and "improving" them, or inventing new ones.

To the Circle inclosing the central point, and itself traced between two parallel lines, a figure purely Kabalistic, these persons have added the superimposed Bible, and even reared on that the ladder with three or nine rounds, and then given a vapid interpretation of the whole, so profoundly absurd as actually to excite admiration.

8

IV.

SECRET MASTER.

Masonry is a succession of allegories, the mere vehicles of great lessons in morality and philosophy. You will more fully appreciate its spirit, its object, its purposes, as you advance in the different Degrees, which you will find to constitute a great, complete, and harmonious system.

If you have been disappointed in the first three Degrees, *as you have received them,* and if it has seemed to you that the performance has not come up to the promise, that the lessons of morality are not new, and the scientific instruction is but rudimentary, and the symbols are imperfectly explained, remember that the ceremonies and lessons of those Degrees have been for ages more and more accommodating themselves, by curtailment and sinking into commonplace, to the often limited memory and capacity of the Master and Instructor, and to the intellect and needs of the Pupil and Initiate; that they have come to us from an age when symbols were used, not to *reveal* but to *conceal;* when the commonest learning was confined to a select few, and the simplest principles of morality seemed newly discovered truths; and that these antique and simple Degrees now stand like the broken columns of a roofless Druidic temple, in their rude and mutilated greatness; in many parts, also, corrupted by time, and disfigured by modern additions and absurd interpretations. They are but the entrance to the great Masonic Temple, the triple columns of the portico.

You have taken the first step over its threshold, the first step toward the inner sanctuary and heart of the temple. You are in the path that leads up the slope of the mountain of Truth; and

106

it depends upon your secrecy, obedience, and fidelity, whether you will advance or remain stationary.

Imagine not that you will become indeed a Mason by learning what is commonly called the "work," or even by becoming familiar with our traditions. Masonry has a history, a literature, a philosophy. Its allegories and traditions will teach you much; but much is to be sought elsewhere. The streams of learning that now flow full and broad must be followed to their heads in the springs that well up in the remote past, and you will there find the origin and meaning of Masonry.

A few rudimentary lessons in architecture, a few universally admitted maxims of morality, a few unimportant traditions, whose real meaning is unknown or misunderstood, will no longer satisfy the earnest inquirer after Masonic truth. Let whoso is content with these, seek to climb no higher. He who desires to understand the harmonious and beautiful proportions of Freemasonry must read, study, reflect, digest, and discriminate. The true Mason is an ardent seeker after knowledge; and he knows that both books and the antique symbols of Masonry are vessels which come down to us full-freighted with the intellectual riches of the Past; and that in the lading of these argosies is much that sheds light on the history of Masonry, and proves its claim to be acknowledged the benefactor of mankind, born in the very cradle of the race.

Knowledge is the most genuine and real of human treasures; for it is Light, as Ignorance is Darkness. It is the *development* of the human soul, and its acquisition the *growth* of the soul, which at the birth of man knows nothing, and therefore, in one sense, may be said to *be* nothing. It is the seed, which has in it the *power* to grow, to acquire, and by acquiring to be developed, as the seed is developed into the shoot, the plant, the tree. "We need not pause at the common argument that by learning man excelleth man, in that wherein man excelleth beasts; that by learning man ascendeth to the heavens and their motions, where in body he cannot come, and the like. Let us rather regard the dignity and excellency of knowledge and learning in that whereunto man's nature doth most aspire, which is immortality or continuance. For to this tendeth generation, and raising of Houses and Families; to this buildings, foundations, and monuments; to this tendeth the desire of memory, fame, and celebration, and in effect the strength of all other human desires." That our influences shall survive us, and be living forces when we are in our graves; and not merely that our names shall be remembered; but rather that our works shall be read, our acts spoken of, our names recollected and mentioned when we are dead, as evidences that those influences live and rule, sway and control some portion of mankind and of the world,—this is the aspiration of the human soul. "We see then how far the monuments of genius and learning are more durable than monuments of power or of the hands. For have not the verses of Homer continued twenty-five hundred years or more, without the loss of a syllable or letter, during which time infinite palaces, temples, castles, cities, have decayed and been demolished? It is not possible to have the true pictures or statues of Cyrus, Alexander, Cæsar, no, nor of the Kings or great personages of much later years; for the originals cannot last, and the copies cannot but lose of the life and truth. But the images of men's genius and knowledge remain in books, exempted from the wrong of time, and capable of perpetual renovation. Neither are they fitly to be called images, because they generate still, and cast their seeds in the minds of others, provoking and causing infinite actions and opinions in succeeding ages; so that if the invention of the ship was thought so noble, which carrieth riches and commodities from place to place, and consociateth the most remote regions in participation of their fruits, how much more are letters to be magnified, which, as ships, pass through the vast seas of time, and make ages so distant to participate of the wisdom, illumination, and inventions, the one of the other."

To learn, to attain knowledge, to be wise, is a necessity for every truly noble soul; to teach, to communicate that knowledge, to share that wisdom with others, and not churlishly to lock up his exchequer, and place a sentinel at the door to drive away the needy, is equally an impulse of a noble nature, and the worthiest work of man.

"There was a little city," says the Preacher, the son of David, "and few men within it; and there came a great King against it and besieged it, and built great bulwarks against it. Now there was found in it a poor wise man, and he by his wisdom delivered the city; yet no man remembered that same poor man. Then, said I, wisdom is better than strength: nevertheless, the poor man's wisdom is despised, and his words are not heard." If it should chance to you, my brother, to do mankind good service, and be rewarded with indifference and forgetfulness only, still be not discouraged, but remember the further advice of the wise King. "In the morning sow the seed, and in the evening withhold not thy hand; for thou knowest not which shall prosper, this or that, or whether both shall be alike good." Sow you the seed, whoever reaps. Learn, that you may be enabled to do good; and do so because it is right, finding in the act itself ample reward and recompense.

To attain the truth, and to serve our fellows, our country, and mankind—this is the noblest destiny of man. Hereafter and all your life it is to be your object. If you desire to ascend to that destiny, advance! If you have other and less noble objects, and are contented with a lower flight, halt here! let others scale the heights, and Masonry fulfill her mission.

If you will advance, gird up your loins for the struggle! for the way is long and toilsome. Pleasure, all smiles, will beckon you on the one hand, and Indolence will invite you to sleep among the flowers, upon the other. Prepare, by secrecy, obedience, and fidelity, to resist the allurements of both!

Secrecy is indispensable in a Mason of whatever Degree. It is the first and almost the only lesson taught to the Entered Apprentice. The obligations which we have each assumed toward every Mason that lives, requiring of us the performance of the most serious and onerous duties toward those personally unknown to us until they demand our aid,—duties that must be performed, even at the risk of life, or our solemn oaths be broken and violated, and we be branded as false Masons and faithless men, teach us how profound a folly it would be to betray our secrets to those who, bound to us by no tie of common obligation, might, by obtaining them, call on us in their extremity, when the urgency of the occasion should allow us no time for inquiry, and the peremptory mandate of our obligation compel us to do a brother's duty to a base impostor.

The secrets of our brother, when communicated to us, must be sacred, if they be such as the law of our country warrants us to keep. We are required to keep none other, when the law that we are called on to obey is indeed a law, by having emanated from the only source of power, the People. Edicts which emanate from the mere arbitrary will of a despotic power, contrary to the law of God or the Great Law of Nature, destructive of the inherent rights of man, violative of the right of free thought, free speech, free conscience, it is lawful to rebel against and strive to abrogate.

For obedience to the Law does not mean submission to tyranny; nor that, by a profligate sacrifice of every noble feeling, we should offer to despotism the homage of adulation. As every new victim falls, we *may* lift our voice in still louder flattery. We *may* fall at the proud feet, we *may* beg, as a boon, the honor of kissing that bloody hand which has been lifted against the helpless. We may do more: we may bring the altar and the sacrifice, and implore the God not to ascend too soon to Heaven. This we may do, for this we have the sad remembrance that beings of a human form and soul have done. But this is all we can do. We can constrain our tongues to be false, our features to bend themselves to the semblance of that passionate adoration which we wish to express, our knees to fall prostrate; but our heart we cannot constrain. There virtue must still have a voice which is not to be drowned by hymns and acclamations; there the crimes which we laud as virtues, are crimes still, and he whom we have made a God is the most contemptible of mankind; if, indeed, we do not feel, perhaps, that we are ourselves still more contemptible.

But that law which is the fair expression of the will and judgment of the people, is the enactment of the whole and of every individual. Consistent with the law of God and the great law of nature, consistent with pure and abstract right as tempered by necessity and the general interest, as contra-distinguished from the private interest of individuals, it is obligatory upon all, because it is the work of all, the will of all, the solemn judgment of all, from which there is no appeal.

In this Degree, my brother, you are especially to learn the duty of obedience to that law. There is one true and original law, conformable to reason and to nature, diffused over all, invariable, eternal, which calls to the fulfillment of duty, and to abstinence from injustice, and calls with that irresistible voice which is felt in all its authority wherever it is heard. This law cannot be abrogated or diminished, or its sanctions affected, by any law of man. A whole senate, a whole people, cannot dissent from its paramount obligation. It requires no commentator to render it distinctly intelligible: nor is it one thing at Rome, another at Athens; one thing now, and another in the ages to come; but in all times and in all nations, it is, and has been, and will be, one and everlasting;—one as that God, its great Author and Promulgator, who is the Common Sovereign of all mankind, is Himself One. No man can disobey it without flying, as it were, from his own bosom, and repudiating his nature; and in this very act he will inflict on himself the severest of retributions, even though he escape what is regarded as punishment.

It is our duty to obey the laws of our country, and to be careful that prejudice or passion, fancy or affection, error and illusion, be not mistaken for conscience. Nothing is more usual than to pretend conscience in all the actions of man which are public and cannot be concealed. The disobedient refuse to submit to the laws, and they also in many cases pretend conscience; and so disobedience and rebellion become conscience, in which there is neither knowledge nor revelation, nor truth nor charity, nor reason nor religion. Conscience is tied to laws. Right or sure conscience is right reason reduced to practice, and conducting moral actions, while perverse conscience is seated in the fancy or affections—a heap of irregular principles and irregular defects—and is the same in conscience as deformity is in the body, or peevishness in the affections. It is not enough that the conscience be taught by nature; but it must be taught by God, conducted by reason, made operative by discourse, assisted by choice, instructed by laws and sober principles; and then it *is* right, and it *may* be sure. All the general measures of justice, are the laws of God, and therefore they constitute the general rules of government for the conscience; but necessity also hath a large voice in the arrangement of human affairs, and the disposal of human relations, and the dispositions of human laws; and these general measures, like a great river into little streams, are deduced into little rivulets and particularities, by the laws and customs, by the sentences and agreements of men, and by the absolute despotism of necessity, that will not allow perfect and abstract justice and equity to be the sole rule of civil government in an imperfect world; and that must needs be law which is for the greatest good of the greatest number.

When thou vowest a vow unto God, defer not to pay it. It is better thou shouldest not vow than thou shouldest vow and not pay. Be not rash with thy mouth, and let not thine heart be hasty to utter anything before God: for God is in Heaven, and thou art upon earth; therefore let thy words be few. Weigh well what it is you promise; but once the promise and pledge are given remember that he who is false to his obligation will be false to his family, his friends, his country, and his God.

Fides servanda est: Faith plighted is ever to be kept, was a maxim and an axiom even among pagans. The virtuous Roman said, either let not that which seems expedient be base, or if it *be* base, let it not seem expedient. What is there which that so-called expediency can bring, so valuable as that which it takes away, if it deprives you of the name of a good man and robs you of your integrity and honor? In all ages, he who violates his plighted word has been held unspeakably base. The word of a Mason, like the word of a knight in the times of chivalry, once given must be sacred; and the judgment of his brothers, upon him who violates his pledge, should be stern as the judgments of the Roman Censors against him who violated his oath. Good faith is revered among Masons as it was among the Romans, who placed its statue in the capitol, next to that of Jupiter Maximus Optimus; and we, like them, hold that calamity should always be chosen rather than baseness; and with the knights of old, that one should always die rather than be dishonored.

Be faithful, therefore, to the promises you make, to the pledges you give, and to the vows that you assume, since to break either is base and dishonorable.

Be faithful to your family, and perform all the duties of a good father, a good son, a good husband, and a good brother.

Be faithful to your friends; for true friendship is of a nature not only to survive through all the vicissitudes of life, but to continue through an endless duration; not only to stand the shock of conflicting opinions, and the roar of a revolution that shakes the world, but to last when the heavens are no more, and to spring fresh from the ruins of the universe.

Be faithful to your country, and prefer its dignity and honor to any degree of popularity and honor for yourself; consulting its interest rather than your own, and rather than the pleasure and gratification of the people, which are often at variance with their welfare.

Be faithful to Masonry, which is to be faithful to the best interests of mankind. Labor, by precept and example, to elevate the standard of Masonic character, to enlarge its sphere of influence, to popularize its teachings, and to make all men know it for the

Great Apostle of Peace, Harmony, and Good-will on earth among men; of Liberty, Equality, and Fraternity.

Masonry is useful to all men: to the learned, because it affords them the opportunity of exercising their talents upon subjects eminently worthy of their attention; to the illiterate, because it offers them important instruction; to the young, because it presents them with salutary precepts and good examples, and accustoms them to reflect on the proper mode of living; to the man of the world, whom it furnishes with noble and useful recreation; to the traveller, whom it enables to find friends and brothers in countries where else he would be isolated and solitary; to the worthy man in misfortune, to whom it gives assistance; to the afflicted, on whom it lavishes consolation; to the charitable man, whom it enables to do more good, by uniting with those who are charitable like himself; and to all who have souls capable of appreciating its importance, and of enjoying the charms of a friendship founded on the same principles of religion, morality, and philanthropy.

A Freemason, therefore, should be a man of honor and of conscience, preferring his duty to everything beside, even to his life; independent in his opinions, and of good morals; submissive to the laws, devoted to humanity, to his country, to his family; kind and indulgent to his brethren, friend of all virtuous men, and ready to assist his fellows by all means in his power.

Thus will you be faithful to yourself, to your fellows, and to God, and thus will you do honor to the name and rank of SECRET MASTER; which, like other Masonic honors, degrades if it is not deserved.

V.

PERFECT MASTER.

THE Master Khūrūm was an industrious and an honest man. What he was employed to do he did diligently, and he did it well and faithfully. *He received no wages that were not his due.* Industry and honesty are the virtues peculiarly inculcated in this Degree. They are common and homely virtues; but not for that beneath our notice. As the bees do not love or respect the drones, so Masonry neither loves nor respects the idle and those who live by their wits; and least of all those parasitic acari that live upon themselves. For those who are indolent are likely to become dissipated and vicious; and perfect honesty, which ought to be the common qualification of all, is more rare than diamonds. To do earnestly and steadily, and to do faithfully and honestly that which we have to do—perhaps this wants but little, when looked at from every point of view, of including the whole body of the moral law; and even in their commonest and homeliest application, these virtues belong to the character of a Perfect Master.

Idleness is the burial of a living man. For an idle person is so useless to any purposes of God and man, that he is like one who is dead, unconcerned in the changes and necessities of the world; and he only lives to spend his time, and eat the fruits of the earth. Like a vermin or a wolf, when his time comes, he dies and perishes, and in the meantime is nought. He neither ploughs nor carries burdens: all that he does is either unprofitable or mischievous.

It is a vast work that any man may do, if he never be idle: and it is a huge way that a man may go in virtue, if he never go out of his way by a vicious habit or a great crime: and he who per-

114

petually reads good books, if his parts be answerable, will have a
huge stock of knowledge.

St. Ambrose, and from his example, St. Augustine, divided every
day into these *tertias* of employment: eight hours they spent in
the necessities of nature and recreation: eight hours in charity,
in doing assistance to others, dispatching their business, reconciling their enmities, reproving their vices, correcting their errors,
instructing their ignorance, and in transacting the affairs of their
dioceses; and the other eight hours they spent in study and
prayer.

We think, at the age of twenty, that life is much too long for
that which we have to learn and do; and that there is an almost
fabulous distance between our age and that of our grandfather.
But when, at the age of sixty, if we are fortunate enough to reach
it, or unfortunate enough, as the case may be, and according as we
have profitably invested or wasted our time, we halt, and look back
along the way we have come, and cast up and endeavor to balance
our accounts with time and opportunity, we find that we have
made life much too short, and thrown away a huge portion of our
time. Then we, in our mind, deduct from the sum total of our
years the hours that we have needlessly passed in sleep; the work-
ing-hours each day, during which the surface of the mind's sluggish pool has not been stirred or ruffled by a single thought; the
days that we have gladly got rid of, to attain some real or fancied
object that lay beyond, in the way between us and which stood
irksomely the intervening days; the hours worse than wasted in
follies and dissipation, or misspent in useless and unprofitable
studies; and we acknowledge, with a sigh, that we could have
learned and done, in half a score of years well spent, more than
we *have* done in all our forty years of manhood.

To learn and to do!—this is the soul's work here below. The
soul grows as truly as an oak grows. As the tree takes the carbon
of the air, the dew, the rain, and the light, and the food that the
earth supplies to its roots, and by its mysterious chemistry transmutes them into sap and fibre, into wood and leaf, and flower and
fruit, and color and perfume, so the soul imbibes knowledge and
by a divine alchemy changes what it learns into its own substance,
and grows from within outwardly with an inherent force and
power like those that lie hidden in the grain of wheat.

The soul hath its senses, like the body, that may be cultivated, enlarged, refined, as itself grows in stature and proportion; and he who cannot appreciate a fine painting or statue, a noble poem, a sweet harmony, a heroic thought, or a disinterested action, or to whom the wisdom of philosophy is but foolishness and babble, and the loftiest truths of less importance than the price of stocks or cotton, or the elevation of baseness to office, merely lives on the level of commonplace, and fitly prides himself upon that inferiority of the soul's senses, which is the inferiority and imperfect development of the soul itself.

To sleep little, and to study much; to say little, and to hear and think much; to learn, that we may be able to do, and then to do, earnestly and vigorously, whatever may be required of us by duty, and by the good of our fellows, our country, and mankind,— these are the duties of every Mason who desires to imitate the Master Khūrūm.

The duty of a Mason as an honest man is plain and easy. It requires of us honesty in contracts, sincerity in affirming, simplicity in bargaining, and faithfulness in performing. Lie not at all, neither in a little thing nor in a great, neither in the substance nor in the circumstance, neither in word nor deed: that is, pretend not what is false; cover not what is true; and let the measure of your affirmation or denial be the understanding of your contractor; for he who deceives the buyer or the seller by speaking what is true, in a sense not intended or understood by the other, is a liar and a thief. A Perfect Master must avoid that which deceives, equally with that which is false.

Let your prices be according to that measure of good and evil which is established in the fame and common accounts of the wisest and most merciful men, skilled in that manufacture or commodity; and the gain such, which, without scandal, is allowed to persons in all the same circumstances.

In intercourse with others, do not do all which thou mayest lawfully do; but keep something within thy power; and, because there is a latitude of gain in buying and selling, take not thou the utmost penny that is lawful, or which thou thinkest so; for although it be lawful, yet it is not safe; and he who gains all that he can gain lawfully, this year, will possibly be tempted, next year, to gain something unlawfully.

Let no man, for his own poverty, become more oppressing and cruel in his bargain; but quietly, modestly, diligently, and patiently recommend his estate to God, and follow his interest, and leave the success to Him.

Detain not the wages of the hireling; for every degree of detention of it beyond the time, is injustice and uncharitableness, and grinds his face till tears and blood come out; but pay him exactly according to covenant, or according to his needs.

Religiously keep all promises and covenants, though made to your disadvantage, though afterward you perceive you might have done better; and let not any precedent act of yours be altered by any after-accident. Let nothing make you break your promise, unless it be unlawful or impossible; that is, either out of your nature or out of your civil power, yourself being under the power of another; or that it be intolerably inconvenient to yourself, and of no advantage to another; or that you have leave expressed or reasonably presumed.

Let no man take wages or fees for a work that he cannot do, or cannot with probability undertake; or in some sense profitably, and with ease, or with advantage manage. Let no man appropriate to his own use, what God, by a special mercy, or the Republic, hath made common; for that is against both Justice and Charity.

That any man should be the worse for us, and for our direct act, and by our intention, is against the rule of equity, of justice, and of charity. We then do not that to others, which we would have done to ourselves; for we grow richer upon the ruins of their fortune.

It is not honest to receive anything from another without returning him an equivalent therefor. The gamester who wins the money of another is dishonest. There should be no such thing as bets and gaming among Masons: for no honest man should desire that for nothing which belongs to another. The merchant who sells an inferior article for a sound price, the speculator who makes the distresses and needs of others fill his exchequer are neither fair nor honest, but base, ignoble, unfit for immortality.

It should be the earnest desire of every Perfect Master so to live and deal and act, that when it comes to him to die, he may be able to say, and his conscience to adjudge, that no man on earth is poorer, because he is richer; that what he hath he has honestly earned, and no man can go before God, and claim that by the rules of equity administered in His great chancery, this house in which we die, this land we devise to our heirs, this money that enriches those who survive to bear our name, is his and not ours, and we in that forum are only his trustees. For it is most certain that God is just, and will sternly enforce every such trust; and that to all whom we despoil, to all whom we defraud, to all from whom we take or win anything whatever, without fair consideration and equivalent, He will decree a full and adequate compensation.

Be careful, then, that thou receive no wages, here or elsewhere, that are not thy due! For if thou dost, thou wrongst some one, by taking that which in God's chancery belongs to him; and whether that which thou takest thus be wealth, or rank, or influence, or reputation or affection, thou wilt surely be held to make full satisfaction.

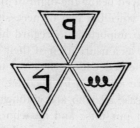

VI.

INTIMATE SECRETARY.

[Confidential Secretary.]

You are especially taught in this Degree to be zealous and faithful; to be disinterested and benevolent; and to act the peacemaker, in case of dissensions, disputes, and quarrels among the brethren.

Duty is the moral magnetism which controls and guides the true Mason's course over the tumultuous seas of life. Whether the stars of honor, reputation, and reward do or do not shine, in the light of day or in the darkness of the night of trouble and adversity, in calm or storm, that unerring magnet still shows him the true course to steer, and indicates with certainty where-away lies the port which not to reach involves shipwreck and dishonor. He follows its silent bidding, as the mariner, when land is for many days not in sight, and the ocean without path or landmark spreads out all around him, follows the bidding of the needle, never doubting that it points truly to the north. To perform that duty, whether the performance be rewarded or unrewarded, is his sole care. And it doth not matter, though of this performance there may be no witnesses, and though what he does will be forever unknown to all mankind.

A little consideration will teach us that Fame has other limits than mountains and oceans; and that he who places happiness in the frequent repetition of his name, may spend his life in propagating it, without any danger of weeping for new worlds, or necessity of passing the Atlantic sea.

If, therefore, he who imagines the world to be filled with his ac-

119

tions and praises, shall subduct from the number of his encomiasts all those who are placed below the flight of fame, and who hear in the valley of life no voice but that of necessity; all those who imagine themselves too important to regard him, and consider the mention of his name as a usurpation of their time; all who are too much or too little pleased with themselves to attend to anything external; all who are attracted by pleasure, or chained down by pain to unvaried ideas; all who are withheld from attending his triumph by different pursuits; and all who slumber in universal negligence; he will find his renown straitened by nearer bounds than the rocks of Caucasus; and perceive that no man can be venerable or formidable, but to a small part of his fellow-creatures. And therefore, that we may not languish in our endeavors after excellence, it is necessary that, as Africanus counsels his descendants, we raise our eyes to higher prospects, and contemplate our future and eternal state, without giving up our hearts to the praise of crowds, or fixing our hopes on such rewards as human power can bestow.

We are not born for ourselves alone; and our country claims her share, and our friends their share of us. As all that the earth produces is created for the use of man, so men are created for the sake of men, that they may mutually do good to one another. In this we ought to take nature for our guide, and throw into the public stock the offices of general utility, by a reciprocation of duties; sometimes by receiving, sometimes by giving, and sometimes to cement human society by arts, by industry, and by our resources.

Suffer others to be praised in thy presence, and entertain their good and glory with delight; but at no hand disparage them, or lessen the report, or make an objection; and think not the advancement of thy brother is a lessening of thy worth. Upbraid no man's weakness to him to discomfit him, neither report it to disparage him, neither delight to remember it to lessen him, or to set thyself above him; nor ever praise thyself or dispraise any man else, unless some sufficient worthy end do hallow it.

Remember that we usually disparage others upon slight grounds and little instances; and if a man be highly commended, we think him sufficiently lessened, if we can but charge one sin of folly or inferiority in his account. We should either be more severe to ourselves, or less so to others, and consider that whatsoever good any one can think or say of us, we can tell him of many unworthy and foolish and perhaps worse actions of ours, any one of which, done by another, would be enough, with *us,* to destroy his reputation.

If we think the people wise and sagacious, and just and appreciative, when they praise and make idols of *us,* let us not call them unlearned and ignorant, and ill and stupid judges, when our neighbor is cried up by public fame and popular noises.

Every man hath in his own life sins enough, in his own mind trouble enough, in his own fortunes evil enough, and in performance of his offices failings more than enough, to entertain his own inquiry; so that curiosity after the affairs of others cannot be without envy and an ill mind. The generous man will be solicitous and inquisitive into the beauty and order of a well-governed family, and after the virtues of an excellent person; but anything for which men keep locks and bars, or that blushes to see the light, or that is either shameful in manner or private in nature, this thing will not be his care and business.

It should be objection sufficient to exclude any man from the society of Masons, that he is not disinterested and generous, both in his acts, and in his opinions of men, and his constructions of their conduct. He who is selfish and grasping, or censorious and ungenerous, will not long remain within the strict limits of honesty and truth, but will shortly commit injustice. He who loves himself too much must needs love others too little; and he who habitually gives harsh judgment will not long delay to give unjust judgment.

The generous man is not careful to return no more than he receives; but prefers that the balances upon the ledgers of benefits shall be in his favor. He who hath received pay in full for all the benefits and favors that he has conferred, is like a spendthrift who has consumed his whole estate, and laments over an empty exchequer. He who requites my favors with ingratitude adds to, instead of diminishing, my wealth; and he who cannot return a favor is equally poor, whether his inability arises from poverty of spirit, sordidness of soul, or pecuniary indigence.

If he is wealthy who hath large sums invested, and the mass of whose fortune consists in obligations that bind other men to pay him money, he is still more so to whom many owe large returns of kindnesses and favors. Beyond a moderate sum each year, the wealthy man merely *invests* his means: and that which he *never* uses is still like favors unreturned and kindnesses unreciprocated, an actual and real portion of his fortune.

Generosity and a liberal spirit make men to be humane and genial, open-hearted, frank, and sincere, earnest to do good, easy and contented, and well-wishers of mankind. They protect the feeble against the strong, and the defenceless against rapacity and craft. They succor and comfort the poor, and are the guardians, under God, of his innocent and helpless wards. They value friends more than riches or fame, and gratitude more than money or power. They are noble by God's patent, and their escutcheons and quarterings are to be found in heaven's great book of heraldry. Nor can any man any more be a Mason than he can be a gentleman, unless he is generous, liberal, and disinterested. To be liberal, but only of that which is our own; to be generous, but only when we have first been just; to give, when to give deprives us of a luxury or a comfort, this is Masonry indeed.

He who is worldly, covetous, or sensual must change before he can be a good Mason. If we are governed by inclination and not by duty; if we are unkind, severe, censorious, or injurious, in the relations or intercourse of life; if we are unfaithful parents or undutiful children; if we are harsh masters or faithless servants; if we are treacherous friends or bad neighbors or bitter competitors or corrupt unprincipled politicians or overreaching dealers in business, we are wandering at a great distance from the true Masonic light.

Masons must be kind and affectionate one to another. Frequenting the same temples, kneeling at the same altars, they should feel that respect and that kindness for each other, which their common relation and common approach to one God should inspire. There needs to be much more of the spirit of the ancient fellowship among us; more tenderness for each other's faults, more forgiveness, more solicitude for each other's improvement and good fortune; somewhat of brotherly feeling, that it be not shame to use the word *"brother."*

Nothing should be allowed to interfere with that kindness and affection: neither the spirit of business, absorbing, eager, and overreaching, ungenerous and hard in its dealings, keen and bitter in its competitions, low and sordid in its purposes; nor that of ambition, selfish, mercenary, restless, circumventing, living only in the opinion of others, envious of the good fortune of others, miserably vain of its own success, unjust, unscrupulous, and slanderous.

He that does me a favor, hath bound me to make him a return of thankfulness. The obligation comes not by covenant, nor by his own express intention; but by the nature of the thing; and is a duty springing up within the spirit of the obliged person, to whom it is more natural to love his friend, and to do good for good, than to return evil for evil; because a man may forgive an injury, but he must never forget a good turn. He that refuses to do good to them whom he is bound to love, or to love that which did him good, is unnatural and monstrous in his affections, and thinks all the world born to minister to him; with a greediness worse than that of the sea, which, although it receives all rivers into itself, yet it furnishes the clouds and springs with a return of all they need . Our duty to those who are our benefactors is, to esteem and love their persons, to make them proportionable returns of service, or duty, or profit, according as we can, or as they need, or as opportunity presents itself; and according to the greatness of their kindnesses.

The generous man cannot but regret to see dissensions and disputes among his brethren. Only the base and ungenerous delight in discord. It is the poorest occupation of humanity to labor to make men think worse of each other, as the press, and too commonly the pulpit, changing places with the hustings and the tribune, do. The duty of the Mason is to endeavor to make man think better of his neighbor; to quiet, instead of aggravating difficulties; to bring together those who are severed or estranged; to keep friends from becoming foes, and to persuade foes to become friends. To do this, he must needs control his own passions, and be not rash and hasty, nor swift to take offence, nor easy to be angered.

For anger is a professed enemy to counsel. It is a direct storm, in which no man can be heard to speak or call from without; for if you counsel gently, you are disregarded; if you urge it and be vehement, you provoke it more. It is neither manly nor ingenuous. It makes marriage to be a necessary and unavoidable trouble; friendships and societies and familiarities, to be intolerable. It multiplies the evils of drunkenness, and makes the levities of wine to run into madness. It makes innocent jesting to be the beginning of tragedies. It turns friendship into hatred; it makes a man lose himself, and his reason and his argument, in disputation. It turns the desires of knowledge into an itch of wrangling. It adds insolency to power. It turns justice into cruelty, and judgment into oppression. It changes discipline into tediousness and hatred of liberal institution. It makes a prosperous man to be envied, and the unfortunate to be unpitied.

See, therefore, that first controlling your own temper, and governing your own passions, you fit yourself to keep peace and harmony among other men, and especially the brethren. Above all remember that Masonry is the realm of peace, and that *"among Masons there must be no dissension, but only that noble emulation, which can best work and best agree."* Wherever there is strife and hatred among the brethren, there is no Masonry; for Masonry is Peace, and Brotherly Love, and Concord.

Masonry is the great Peace Society of the world. Wherever it exists, it struggles to prevent international difficulties and disputes; and to bind Republics, Kingdoms, and Empires together in one great band of peace and amity. It would not so often struggle in vain, if Masons knew their power and valued their oaths.

Who can sum up the horrors and woes accumulated in a single war? Masonry is not dazzled with all its pomp and circumstance, all its glitter and glory. War comes with its bloody hand into our very dwellings. It takes from ten thousand homes those who lived there in peace and comfort, held by the tender ties of family and kindred. It drags them away, to die untended, of fever or exposure, in infectious climes; or to be hacked, torn, and mangled in the fierce fight; to fall on the gory field, to rise no more, or to be borne away, in awful agony, to noisome and horrid hospitals. The groans of the battle-field are echoed in sighs of bereavement from thousands of desolated hearths. There is a skeleton in every house, a vacant chair at every table. Returning, the soldier brings worse sorrow to his home, by the infection which he has caught, of camp-vices. The country is demoralized. The national mind is brought down, from the noble interchange of kind offices with another people, to wrath and revenge, and base pride, and the habit of measuring brute strength against brute strength, in battle. Treasures are expended, that would suffice to build ten thousand churches, hospitals, and universities, or rib and tie together a continent with rails of iron. If that treasure were sunk in the sea, it would be calamity enough; but it is put to worse use; for it is expended in cutting into the veins and arteries of human life, until the earth is deluged with a sea of blood.

Such are the lessons of this Degree. You have vowed to make them the rule, the law, and the guide of your life and conduct. If you do so, you will be entitled, because fitted, to advance in Masonry. If you do not, you have already gone too far.

VII.

PROVOST AND JUDGE.

THE lesson which this Degree inculcates is JUSTICE, in decision and judgment, and in our intercourse and dealing with other men.

In a country where trial by jury is known, every intelligent man is liable to be called on to act as a judge, either of fact alone, or of fact and law mingled; and to assume the heavy responsibilities which belong to that character.

Those who are invested with the power of judgment should judge the causes of all persons uprightly and impartially, without any personal consideration of the power of the mighty, or the bribe of the rich, or the needs of the poor. That is the cardinal rule, which no one will dispute; though many fail to observe it. But they must do more. They must divest themselves of prejudice and preconception. They must hear patiently, remember accurately, and weigh carefully the facts and the arguments offered before them. They must not leap hastily to conclusions, nor form opinions before they have heard all. They must not presume crime or fraud. They must neither be ruled by stubborn pride of opinion, nor be too facile and yielding to the views and arguments of others. In deducing the motive from the proven act, they must not assign to the act either the best or the worst motives, but those which they would think it just and fair for the world to assign to it, if they themselves had done it; nor must they endeavor to make many little circumstances, that weigh nothing separately, weigh much together, to prove their own acuteness and sagacity. These are sound rules for every juror, also, to observe.

126

In our intercourse with others, there are two kinds of injustice: the first, of those who offer an injury; the second, of those who have it in their power to *avert* an injury from those to whom it is offered, and yet do it not. So *active* injustice may be done in two ways—by force and by fraud,—of which force is lion-like, and fraud fox-like,—both utterly repugnant to social duty, but fraud the more detestable.

Every wrong done by one man to another, whether it affect his person, his property, his happiness, or his reputation, is an offense against the law of justice. The field of this Degree is therefore a wide and vast one; and Masonry seeks for the most impressive mode of enforcing the law of justice, and the most effectual means of preventing wrong and injustice.

To this end it teaches this great and momentous truth: that wrong and injustice once done cannot be undone; but are eternal in their consequences; once committed, are numbered with the irrevocable Past; that the wrong that is done *contains* its own retributive penalty as surely and as naturally as the acorn contains the oak. Its consequences are its punishment; it needs no other, and can have no heavier; they are involved in its commission, and cannot be separated from it. A wrong done to another is an injury done to our own Nature, an offence against our own souls, a disfiguring of the image of the Beautiful and Good. Punishment is not the execution of a sentence, but the occurrence of an effect. It is ordained to follow guilt, not by the decree of God as a judge, but by a law enacted by Him as the Creator and Legislator of the Universe. It is not an arbitrary and artificial annexation, but an ordinary and logical consequence; and therefore must be borne by the wrong-doer, and through him may flow on to others. It is the decision of the infinite justice of God, in the form of law.

There can be no interference with, or remittance of, or protection from, the natural effects of our wrongful acts. God will not interpose between the cause and its consequence; and in that sense there can be no forgiveness of sins. The act which has debased our soul may be repented of, may be turned from; but the injury is done. The debasement may be redeemed by after-efforts, the stain obliterated by bitterer struggles and severer sufferings; but the efforts and the endurance which might have raised the soul to the loftiest heights are now exhausted in merely regaining what it has lost. There must always be a wide difference between him who only ceases to do evil, and him who has always done well.

He will certainly be a far more scrupulous watcher over his conduct, and far more careful of his deeds, who believes that those deeds will inevitably bear their natural consequences, exempt from after intervention, than he who believes that penitence and pardon will at any time unlink the chain of sequences. Surely we shall do less wrong and injustice, if the conviction is fixed and embedded in our souls that everything done is done irrevocably, that even the Omnipotence of God cannot *uncommit* a deed, cannot make that *undone* which has *been done;* that every act of ours *must* bear its allotted fruit, according to the everlasting laws, —must remain forever ineffaceably inscribed on the tablets of Universal Nature.

If you have wronged another, you may grieve, repent, and resolutely determine against any such weakness in future. You may, so far as it is possible, make reparation. It is well. The injured party may forgive you, according to the meaning of human language; but the deed is *done;* and all the powers of Nature, were they to conspire in your behalf, could not make it *undone;* the consequences to the body, the consequences to the soul, though no man may perceive them, *are there,* are written in the annals of the Past, and must reverbrate throughout all time.

Repentance for a wrong done, bears, like every other act, its own fruit, the fruit of purifying the heart and amending the Future, but not of effacing the Past. The commission of the wrong is an irrevocable act; but it does not incapacitate the soul to do right for the future. Its consequences cannot be expunged; but its course need not be pursued. Wrong and evil perpetrated, though ineffaceable, call for no despair, but for efforts more energetic than before. Repentance is still as valid as ever; but it is valid to secure the Future, not to obliterate the Past.

Even the pulsations of the air, once set in motion by the human voice, cease not to exist with the sounds to which they gave rise. Their quickly-attenuated force soon becomes inaudible to human ears. But the waves of air thus raised perambulate the surface of earth and ocean, and in less than twenty hours, every atom of the atmosphere takes up the altered movement due to that infinitesimal portion of primitive motion which has been conveyed to it through countless channels, and which must continue to influence its path throughout its future existence. The air is one vast library, on whose pages is forever written all that man has ever said or even whispered. There, in their mutable, but unerring characters, mixed with the earliest, as well as the latest signs of mortality, stand forever recorded, vows unredeemed, promises unfulfilled; perpetuating, in the movements of each particle, all in unison, the testimony of man's changeful will. God reads that book, though we cannot.

So earth, air, and ocean are the eternal witnesses of the acts that we have done. No motion impressed by natural causes or by human agency is ever obliterated. The track of every keel which has ever disturbed the surface of the ocean remains forever registered in the future movements of all succeeding particles which may occupy its place. Every criminal is by the laws of the Almighty irrevocably chained to the testimony of his crime; for every atom of his mortal frame, through whatever changes its particles may migrate, will still retain, adhering to it through every combination, some movement derived from that very muscular effort by which the crime itself was perpetrated.

What if our faculties should be so enhanced in a future life as to enable us to perceive and trace the ineffaceable consequences of our idle words and evil deeds, and render our remorse and grief as eternal as those consequences themselves? No more fearful punishment to a superior intelligence can be conceived, than to see still in action, with the consciousness that it must continue in action forever, a cause of wrong put in motion by itself ages before.

Masonry, by its teachings, endeavors to restrain men from the commission of injustice and acts of wrong and outrage. Though it does not endeavor to usurp the place of religion, still its code of morals proceeds upon other principles than the municipal law; and it condemns and punishes offences which neither that law punishes nor public opinion condemns. In the Masonic law, to cheat and overreach in trade, at the bar, in politics, are deemed no more venial than theft; nor a deliberate lie than perjury; nor slander than robbery; nor seduction than murder.

Especially it condemns those wrongs of which the doer induces another to partake. *He* may repent; *he* may, after agonizing struggles, regain the path of virtue; *his* spirit may reachieve its purity through much anguish, after many strifes; but the weaker fellow-creature whom he led astray, whom he made a sharer in his guilt, but whom he cannot make a sharer in his repentance and amendment, whose downward course (the first step of which *he* taught) he cannot check, but is compelled to witness,—what forgiveness of sins can avail him there? *There* is his perpetual, his inevitable punishment, which no repentance can alleviate, and no mercy can remit.

Let us be just, also, in judging of other men's motives. We know but little of the real merits or demerits of any fellow-creature. We can rarely say with certainty that this man is more guilty than that, or even that this man is very good or very wicked. Often the basest men leave behind them excellent reputations. There is scarcely one of us who has not, at some time in his life, been on the edge of the commission of a crime. Every one of us can look back, and shuddering see the time when our feet stood upon the slippery crags that overhung the abyss of guilt; and when, if temptation had been a little more urgent, or a little longer continued, if penury had pressed us a little harder, or a little more wine had further disturbed our intellect, dethroned our judgment, and aroused our passions, our feet would have slipped, and we should have fallen, never to rise again.

We may be able to say—"*This* man has lied, has pilfered, has forged, has embezzled moneys intrusted to him; and *that* man has gone through life with clean hands." But we cannot say that the former has not struggled long, though unsuccessfully, against temptations under which the second would have succumbed without an effort. We can say which has the cleanest *hands* before *man;* but not which has the cleanest *soul* before *God.* We may be able to say, *this* man has committed adultery, and *that* man has been ever chaste; but we cannot tell but that the innocence of one may have been due to the coldness of his heart, to the absence of a motive, to the presence of a fear, to the slight degree of the temptation; nor but that the fall of the other may have been preceded by the most vehement self-contest, caused by the most over-mastering frenzy, and atoned for by the most hallowing repentance. Generosity as well as niggardliness may be a mere yielding to native temperament; and in the eye of Heaven, a long life of beneficence in one man may have cost less effort, and may indicate less virtue and less sacrifice of interest, than a few rare hidden acts of kindness wrung by duty out of the reluctant and unsympathizing nature of the other. There may be more real merit, more self-sacrificing effort, more of the noblest elements of moral grandeur, in a life of failure, sin, and shame, than in a career, to our eyes, of stainless integrity.

When we condemn or pity the fallen, how do we know that, tempted like him, we should not have fallen like him, as soon, and perhaps with less resistance? How can we know what *we* should do if we were out of employment, famine crouching, gaunt, and hungry, on our fireless hearth, and our children wailing for bread? *We fall not because we are not enough tempted!* He that *hath* fallen may be at heart as honest as we. How do we know that *our* daughter, sister, wife, could resist the abandonment, the desolation, the distress, the temptation, that sacrificed the virtue of their poor abandoned sister of shame? Perhaps they also have not fallen, because they have not been sorely tempted! Wisely are we directed to pray that we may not be exposed to temptation.

Human justice must be ever uncertain. How many judicial murders have been committed through ignorance of the phenomena of insanity! How many men hung for murder who were no more murderers at heart than the jury that tried and the judge that sentenced them! It may well be doubted whether the administration of human laws, in every country, is not one gigantic mass of injustice and wrong. God seeth not as man seeth; and the most abandoned criminal, black as he is before the world, may yet have continued to keep some little light burning in a corner of his soul, which would long since have gone out in that of those who walk proudly in the sunshine of immaculate fame, if they had been tried and tempted like the poor outcast.

We do not know even the *outside* life of men. We are not competent to pronounce even on their *deeds*. We do not know half the acts of wickedness or virtue, even of our most immediate fellows. We cannot say, with certainty, even of our nearest friend, that he has not committed a particular sin, and broken a particular commandment. Let each man ask his own heart! Of how many of our best and of our worst acts and qualities are our most intimate associates utterly unconscious! How many virtues does not the world give us credit for, that we do not possess; or vices condemn us for, of which we are not the slaves! It is but a small portion of our evil deeds and thoughts that ever comes to light;

and of our few redeeming goodnesses, the largest portion is known to God alone.

We shall, therefore, be just in judging of other men, only when we are charitable; and we should assume the prerogative of judging others only when the duty is forced upon us; since we are so almost certain to err, and the consequences of error are so serious. No man need covet the office of judge; for in assuming it he assumes the gravest and most oppressive responsibility. Yet you have assumed it; we all assume it; for man is ever ready to judge, and ever ready to condemn his neighbor, while upon the same state of case he acquits himself. See, therefore, that you exercise your office cautiously and charitably, lest, in passing judgment upon the criminal, you commit a greater wrong than that for which you condemn him, and the consequences of which must be eternal.

The faults and crimes and follies of other men are not unimportant to us; but form a part of our moral discipline. War and bloodshed at a distance, and frauds which do not affect our pecuniary interest, yet touch us in our feelings, and concern our moral welfare. They have much to do with all thoughtful hearts. The public eye may look unconcernedly on the miserable victim of vice, and that shattered wreck of a man may move the multitude to laughter or to scorn. But to the Mason, it is the form of sacred humanity that is before him; it is an erring fellow-being; a desolate, forlorn, forsaken soul; and his thoughts, enfolding the poor wretch, will be far deeper than those of indifference, ridicule, or contempt. All human offences, the whole system of dishonesty, evasion, circumventing, forbidden indulgence, and intriguing ambition, in which men are struggling with each other, will be looked upon by a thoughtful Mason, not merely as a scene of mean toils and strifes, but as the solemn conflicts of immortal minds, for ends vast and momentous as their own being. It is a sad and unworthy strife, and may well be viewed with indignation; but that indignation must melt into pity. For the stakes for which these gamesters play are not those which they imagine, not those which are in sight. For example, this man plays for a petty office, and gains it; but the real stake he gains is sycophancy, uncharitableness, slander, and deceit.

Good men are too proud of their goodness. They are respectable; dishonor comes not near them; their countenance has weight and influence; their robes are unstained; the poisonous breath of calumny has never been breathed upon their fair name. How easy it is for them to look down with scorn upon the poor degraded offender; to pass him by with a lofty step; to draw up the folds of their garment around them, that they may not be soiled by his touch! Yet the Great Master of Virtue did not so; but descended to familiar intercourse with publicans and sinners, with the Samaritan woman, with the outcasts and the Pariahs of the Hebrew world.

Many men think themselves better, in proportion as they can detect sin in others! When they go over the catalogue of their neighbor's unhappy derelictions of temper or conduct, they often, amidst much apparent concern, feel a secret exultation, that destroys all their own pretensions to wisdom and moderation, and even to virtue. Many even take actual pleasure in the sins of others; and this is the case with every one whose thoughts are often employed in agreeable comparisons of his own virtues with his neighbors' faults.

The power of gentleness is too little seen in the world; the subduing influences of pity, the might of love, the control of mildness over passion, the commanding majesty of that perfect character which mingles grave displeasure with grief and pity for the offender. So it is that a Mason should treat his brethren who go astray. Not with bitterness; nor yet with good-natured easiness, nor with worldly indifference, nor with the philosophic coldness, nor with a laxity of conscience, that accounts everything well, that passes under the seal of public opinion; but with charity, with pitying loving-kindness.

The human heart will not bow willingly to what is infirm and wrong in human nature. If it yields to us, it must yield to what is divine in us. The wickedness of my neighbor cannot submit to my wickedness; his sensuality, for instance, to my anger against his vices. My faults are not the instruments that are to arrest his faults. And therefore impatient reformers, and denouncing preachers, and hasty reprovers, and angry parents, and irritable relatives generally fail, in their several departments, to reclaim the erring.

A moral offence is sickness, pain, loss, dishonor, in the immortal part of man. It is guilt, and misery added to guilt. It is itself calamity; and brings upon itself, in addition, the calamity of God's disapproval, the abhorrence of all virtuous men, and the soul's own abhorrence. Deal faithfully, but patiently and tenderly, with this evil! It is no matter for petty provocation, nor for personal strife, nor for selfish irritation.

Speak kindly to your erring brother! God pities him: Christ has died for him: Providence waits for him: Heaven's mercy yearns toward him; and Heaven's spirits are ready to welcome him back with joy. Let your voice be in unison with all those powers that God is using for his recovery!

If one defrauds you, and exults at it, he is the most to be pitied of human beings. He has done himself a far deeper injury than he has done you. It is he, and not you, whom God regards with mingled displeasure and compassion; and His judgment should be your law. Among all the benedictions of the Holy Mount there is not one for this man; but for the merciful, the peace-makers, and the persecuted they are poured out freely.

We are all men of like passions, propensities, and exposures. There are elements in us all, which might have been perverted, through the successive processes of moral deterioration, to the worst of crimes. The wretch whom the execration of the thronging crowd pursues to the scaffold, is not worse than any one of that multitude might have become under similar circumstances. He is to be condemned indeed, but also deeply to be pitied.

It does not become the frail and sinful to be vindictive toward even the worst criminals. We owe much to the good Providence of God, ordaining for us a lot more favorable to virtue. We all had that within us, that might have been pushed to the same excess. Perhaps we should have fallen as he did, with less temptation. Perhaps we *have* done acts, that, in proportion to the temptation or provocation, were less excusable than his great crime. Silent pity and sorrow for the victim should mingle with our detestation of the guilt. Even the pirate who murders in cold blood on the high seas, is such a man as you or I might have been. Orphanage in childhood, or base and dissolute and abandoned parents; an un-friended youth; evil companions; ignorance and want of moral cultivation; the temptations of sinful pleasure or grinding poverty; familiarity with vice; a scorned and blighted name; seared and crushed affections; desperate fortunes; these are steps that might have led any one among us to unfurl upon the high seas the bloody flag of universal defiance; to wage war with our kind; to live the life and die the death of the reckless and remorseless **free-**

booter. Many affecting relationships of humanity plead with us to pity him. His head once rested on a mother's bosom. He was once the object of sisterly love and domestic endearment. Perhaps his hand, since often red with blood, once clasped another little loving hand at the altar. Pity him then; his blighted hopes and his crushed heart! It is proper that frail and erring creatures like us should do so; should feel the crime, but feel it as weak, tempted, and rescued creatures should. It may be that when God weighs men's crimes, He will take into consideration the temptations and the adverse circumstances that led to them, and the opportunities for moral culture of the offender; and it may be that our own offences will weigh heavier than we think, and the murderer's lighter than according to man's judgment.

On all accounts, therefore, let the true Mason never forget the solemn injunction, necessary to be observed at almost every moment of a busy life: "JUDGE NOT, LEST YE YOURSELVES BE JUDGED: FOR WHATSOEVER JUDGMENT YE MEASURE UNTO OTHERS, THE SAME SHALL IN TURN BE MEASURED UNTO YOU." Such is the lesson taught the Provost and Judge.

VIII.

INTENDANT OF THE BUILDING.

In this Degree you have been taught the important lesson, that none are entitled to advance in the Ancient and Accepted Scottish Rite, who have not by study and application made themselves familiar with Masonic learning and jurisprudence. The Degrees of this Rite are not for those who are content with the mere work and ceremonies, and do not seek to explore the mines of wisdom that lie buried beneath the surface. You still advance toward the Light, toward that star, blazing in the distance, which is an emblem of the Divine Truth, given by God to the first men, and preserved amid all the vicissitudes of ages in the traditions and teachings of Masonry. How far you will advance, depends upon yourself alone. Here, as everywhere in the world, Darkness struggles with Light, and clouds and shadows intervene between you and the Truth.

When you shall have become imbued with the morality of Masonry, with which you yet are, and for some time will be exclusively occupied,—when you shall have learned to practice all the virtues which it inculcates; when they become familiar to you as your Household Gods; then will you be prepared to receive its lofty philosophical instruction, and to scale the heights upon whose summit Light and Truth sit enthroned. Step by step men must advance toward Perfection; and each Masonic Degree is meant to be one of those steps. Each is a development of a particular duty; and in the present you are taught charity and be-

136

nevolence; to be to your brethren an example of virtue; to correct your own faults; and to endeavor to correct those of your brethren.

Here, as in all the Degrees, you meet with the emblems and the names of Deity, the true knowledge of whose character and attributes it has ever been a chief object of Masonry to perpetuate. To appreciate His infinite greatness and goodness, to rely implicitly upon His Providence, to revere and venerate Him as the Supreme Architect, Creator, and Legislator of the universe, is the first of Masonic duties.

The Battery of this Degree, and the five circuits which you made around the Lodge, allude to the five points of fellowship, and are intended to recall them vividly to your mind. To go upon a brother's errand or to his relief, even barefoot and upon flinty ground; to remember him in your supplications to the Deity; to clasp him to your heart, and protect him against malice and evil-speaking; to uphold him when about to stumble and fall; and to give him prudent, honest, and friendly counsel, are duties plainly written upon the pages of God's great code of law, and first among the ordinances of Masonry.

The first sign of the Degree is expressive of the diffidence and humility with which we inquire into the nature and attributes of the Deity; the second, of the profound awe and reverence with which we contemplate His glories; and the third, of the sorrow with which we reflect upon our insufficient observance of our duties, and our imperfect compliance with His statutes.

The distinguishing property of man is to search for and follow after truth. Therefore, when relaxed from our necessary cares and concerns, we then covet to see, to hear, and to learn somewhat; and we esteem knowledge of things, either obscure or wonderful, to be the indispensable means of living happily. Truth, Simplicity, and Candor are most agreeable to the nature of mankind. Whatever is virtuous consists either in Sagacity, and the perception of Truth; or in the preservation of Human Society, by giving to every man his due, and observing the faith of contracts; or in the greatness and firmness of an elevated and unsubdued mind; or in observing order and regularity in all our words and in all our actions; in which consist Moderation and Temperance.

Masonry has in all times religiously preserved that enlightened faith from which flow sublime Devotedness, the sentiment of Fraternity fruitful of good works, the spirit of indulgence and peace, of sweet hopes and effectual consolations; and inflexibility in the accomplishment of the most painful and arduous duties. It has always propagated it with ardor and perseverance; and therefore it labors at the present day more zealously than ever. Scarcely a Masonic discourse is pronounced, that does not demonstrate the necessity and advantages of this faith, and especially recall the two constitutive principles of religion, that *make* all religion,—love of God, and love of neighbor. Masons carry these principles into the bosoms of their families and of society. While the Sectarians of former times enfeebled the religious spirit, Masonry, forming one great People over the whole globe, and marching under the great banner of Charity and Benevolence, preserves that religious feeling, strengthens it, extends it in its purity and simplicity, as it has always existed in the depths of the human heart, as it existed even under the dominion of the most ancient forms of worship, but where gross and debasing superstitions forbade its recognition.

A Masonic Lodge should resemble a bee-hive, in which all the members work together with ardor for the common good. Masonry is not made for cold souls and narrow minds, that do not comprehend its lofty mission and sublime apostolate. Here the anathema against lukewarm souls applies. To comfort misfortune, to popularize knowledge, to teach whatever is true and pure in religion and philosophy, to accustom men to respect order and the proprieties of life, to point out the way to genuine happiness, to prepare for that fortunate period, when all the factions of the Human Family, united by the bonds of Toleration and Fraternity, shall be but one household,—these are labors that may well excite zeal and even enthusiasm.

We do not now enlarge upon or elaborate these ideas. We but utter them to you briefly, as hints, upon which you may at your leisure reflect. Hereafter, if you continue to advance, they will be unfolded, explained, and developed.

Masonry utters no impracticable and extravagant precepts, certain, because they are so, to be disregarded. It asks of its initiates nothing that it is not possible and even easy for them to perform. Its teachings are eminently practical; and its statutes can be obeyed by every just, upright, and honest man, no matter what his faith or creed. Its object is to attain the greatest practical good, without seeking to make men perfect. It does not meddle with the domain of religion, nor inquire into the mysteries of regeneration. It teaches those truths that are written by the finger of God upon the heart of man, those views of duty which have been wrought out by the meditations of the studious, confirmed by the allegiance of the good and wise, and stamped as sterling by the response they find in every uncorrupted mind. It does not dogmatize, nor vainly imagine dogmatic certainty to be attainable.

Masonry does not occupy itself with crying down this world, with its splendid beauty, its thrilling interests, its glorious works, its noble and holy affections; nor exhort us to detach our hearts from this earthly life, as empty, fleeting, and unworthy, and fix them upon Heaven, as the only sphere deserving the love of the loving or the meditation of the wise. It teaches that man has high duties to perform, and a high destiny to fulfill, on this earth; that this world is not merely the portal to another; and that this life, though not our only one, is an integral one, and the particular one with which we are here meant to be concerned; that the Present is our scene of action, and the Future for speculation and for trust; that man was sent upon the earth to live in it, to enjoy it, to study it, to love it, to embellish it, to make the most of it. It is his country, on which he should lavish his affections and his efforts. It is here his influences are to operate. It is his house, and not a tent; his home, and not *merely* a school. He is sent into this world, not to be constantly hankering after, dreaming of, preparing for another; but to do his duty and fulfill his destiny on this earth; to do all that lies in his power to improve it, to render it a scene of elevated happiness to himself, to those around him, to those who are to come after him. His life here is *part* of his immortality; and this world, also, is among the stars.

And thus, Masonry teaches us, will man best prepare for that Future which he hopes for. The Unseen cannot hold a higher place in our affections than the Seen and the Familiar. The law of our being is Love of Life, and its interests and adornments; love of the world in which our lot is cast, engrossment with the interests and affections of earth. Not a low or sensual love; not love of wealth, of fame, of ease, of power, of splendor. Not low worldliness; but the love of Earth as the garden on which the Creator has lavished such miracles of beauty; as the habitation of humanity, the arena of its conflicts, the scene of its illimitable progress, the dwelling-place of the wise, the good, the active, the loving, and the dear; the place of opportunity for the development by means of sin and suffering and sorrow, of the noblest passions, the loftiest virtues, and the tenderest sympathies.

They take very unprofitable pains, who endeavor to persuade men that they are obliged wholly to despise this world, and all that is in it, even whilst they themselves live here. God hath not taken all that pains in forming and framing and furnishing and adorning the world, that they who were made by Him to live in it should despise it. It will be enough, if they do not love it too immoderately. It is useless to attempt to extinguish all those affections and passions which are and always will be inseparable from human nature. As long as he world lasts, and honor and virtue and industry have reputation in the world, there will be ambition and emulation and appetite in the best and most accomplished men in it; and if there were not, more barbarity and vice and wickedness would cover every nation of the world, than it now suffers under.

Those only who feel a deep interest in, and affection for, this world, will work resolutely for its amelioration. Those who undervalue this life, naturally become querulous and discontented, and lose their interest in the welfare of their fellows. To serve them, and so to do our duty as Masons, we must feel that the object is worth the exertion; and be content with this world in which God has placed us, until He permits us to remove to a better one. He is here with us, and does not deem this an unworthy world.

It it a serious thing to defame and belie a whole world; to speak of it as the abode of a poor, toiling, drudging, ignorant, contemptible race. You would not so discredit your family, your friendly circle, your village, your city, your country. The world is not a wretched and a worthless one; nor is it a misfortune, but a thing to be thankful for, to be a man. If life is worthless, so also is immortality.

In society itself, in that living mechanism of human relationships that spreads itself over the world, there is a finer essence within, that as truly moves it, as any power, heavy or expansive, moves the sounding manufactory or the swift-flying car. The man-machine hurries to and fro upon the earth, stretches out its hands on every side, to toil, to barter, to unnumbered labors and enterprises; and almost always the motive, that which moves it, is something that takes hold of the comforts, affections, and hopes of social existence. True, the mechanism often works with difficulty, drags heavily, grates and screams with harsh collision. True, the essence of finer motive, becoming intermixed with baser and coarser ingredients, often clogs, obstructs, jars, and deranges the free and noble action of social life. But he is neither grateful nor wise, who looks cynically on all this, and loses the fine sense of social good in its perversions. That I can be a *friend*, that I can *have* a friend, though it were but one in the world; that fact, that wondrous good fortune, we may set against all the sufferings of our social nature. That there is such a place on earth as a *home*, that resort and sanctuary of in-walled and shielded joy, we may set against all the surrounding desolations of life. That one can be a true, social man, can speak his true thoughts, amidst all the janglings of controversy and the warring of opinions; that fact from within, outweighs all facts from without.

In the visible aspect and action of society, often repulsive and annoying, we are apt to lose the due sense of its invisible blessings. As in Nature it is not the coarse and palpable, not soils and rains, nor even fields and flowers, that are so beautiful, as the invisible spirit of wisdom and beauty that pervades it; so in society, it is the invisible, and therefore unobserved, that is most beautiful.

What nerves the arm of toil? If man minded himself alone, he would fling down the spade and axe, and rush to the desert; or roam through the world as a wilderness, and make that world a desert. His home, which he sees not, perhaps, but once or twice in a day, is the invisible bond of the world. It is the good, strong, and noble faith that men have in each other, which gives the loftiest character to business, trade, and commerce. Fraud occurs in the rush of business; but it is the exception. Honesty is the rule; and all the frauds in the world cannot tear the great bond of human confidence. If they could, commerce would furl its sails on every sea, and all the cities of the world would crumble into ruins. The bare character of a man on the other side of the world, whom you never saw, whom you never will see, you hold good for a bond of thousands. The most striking feature of the political state is not governments, nor constitutions, nor laws, nor enactments, nor the judicial power, nor the police; but the universal will of the people to be governed by the common weal. Take off that restraint, and no government on earth could stand for an hour.

Of the many teachings of Masonry, one of the most valuable is, that we should not depreciate this life. It does not hold, that when we reflect on the destiny that awaits man on earth, we ought to bedew his cradle with our tears; but, like the Hebrews, it hails the birth of a child with joy, and holds that his birthday should be a festival.

It has no sympathy with those who profess to have proved this life, and found it little worth; who have deliberately made up their minds that it is far more miserable than happy; because its employments are tedious, and their schemes often baffled, their friendships broken, or their friends dead, its pleasures palled, and its honors faded, and its paths beaten, familiar, and dull.

Masonry deems it no mark of great piety toward God to disparage, if not despise, the state that He has ordained for us. It does not absurdly set up the claims of another world, not in comparison merely, but in competition, with the claims of this. It looks upon both as parts of one system. It holds that a man may make the best of this world and of another at the same time. It does not teach its initiates to think better of other works and dispensations of God, by thinking meanly of these. It does not look upon life as so much time lost; nor regard its employments as trifles unworthy of immortal beings; nor tell its followers to fold their arms, as if in disdain of their state and species; but it looks soberly and cheerfully upon the world, as a theatre of worthy action, of exalted usefulness, and of rational and innocent enjoyment.

It holds that, with all its evils, life is a blessing. To deny that is to destroy the basis of all religion, natural and revealed. The very foundation of all religion is laid on the firm belief that God is good; and if this life is an evil and a curse, no such belief can be rationally entertained. To level our satire at humanity and human existence, as mean and contemptible; to look on this world as the habitation of a miserable race, fit only for mockery and scorn; to consider this earth as a dungeon or a prison, which has no blessing to offer but escape from it, is to extinguish the primal light of faith and hope and happiness, to destroy the basis of religion, and Truth's foundation in the goodness of God. If it indeed be so, then it matters not what else is true or not true; speculation is vain and faith is vain; and all that belongs to man's highest being is buried in the ruins of misanthropy, melancholy, and despair.

Our love of life; the tenacity with which, in sorrow and suffering, we cling to it; our attachment to our home, to the spot that gave us birth, to any place, however rude, unsightly, or barren, on which the history of our years has been written, all show how dear are the ties of kindred and society. Misery makes a greater impression upon us than happiness; because the former is not the habit of our minds. It is a strange, unusual guest, and we are more conscious of its presence. Happiness lives with us, and we forget it. It does not excite us, nor disturb the order and course of our thoughts. A great agony is an epoch in our life. We remember our afflictions, as we do the storm and earthquake, because they are out of the common course of things. They are like disastrous events, recorded because extraordinary; and with whole and unnoticed periods of prosperity between. We mark and signalize the times of calamity; but many happy days and unnoted periods of enjoyment pass, that are unrecorded either in the book of memory, or in the scanty annals of our thanksgiving. We are little disposed and less able to call up from the dim remembrances of our past years, the peaceful moments, the easy sensations, the bright thoughts, the quiet reveries, the throngs of kind affections in which life flowed on, bearing us almost unconsciously upon its bosom, because it bore us calmly and gently.

Life is not only good; but it has been glorious in the experience of millions. The glory of all human virtue clothes it. The splendors of devotedness, beneficence, and heroism are upon it; the crown of a thousand martyrdoms is upon its brow. The brightness of the soul shines through this visible and sometimes darkened life; through all its surrounding cares and labors. The humblest life may feel its connection with its Infinite Source. There is something mighty in the frail inner man; something of immortality in this momentary and transient being. The mind stretches away, on every side, into infinity. Its thoughts flash abroad, far into the boundless, the immeasurable, the infinite; far into the great, dark, teeming future; and become powers and influences in other ages. To know its wonderful Author, to bring down wisdom from the Eternal Stars, to bear upward its homage, gratitude, and love, to the Ruler of all worlds, to be immortal in our influences projected far into the slow-approaching Future, makes life most worthy and most glorious.

Life is the wonderful creation of God. It is light, sprung from void darkness; power, waked from inertness and impotence; being created from nothing; and the contrast may well enkindle wonder and delight. It is a rill from the infinite, overflowing goodness; and from the moment when it first gushes up into the light, to that when it mingles with the ocean of Eternity, that Goodness attends it and ministers to it. It is a great and glorious gift. There is gladness in its infant voices; joy in the buoyant step of its youth; deep satisfaction in its strong maturity; and peace in its quiet age. There is good for the good; virtue for the faithful; and victory for the valiant. There is, even in this humble life, an infinity for those whose desires are boundless. There are blessings upon its birth; there is hope in its death; and eternity in its prospect. Thus earth, which binds many in chains, is to the Mason both the starting-place and goal of immortality. Many it buries in the rubbish of dull cares and wearying vanities; but to the Mason it is the lofty mount of meditation, where Heaven, and Infinity and Eternity are spread before him and around him. To the lofty-minded, the pure, and the virtuous, this life is the beginning of Heaven, and a part of immortality.

God hath appointed one remedy for all the evils in the world; and that is a contented spirit. We may be reconciled to poverty and a low fortune, if we suffer contentedness and equanimity to make the proportions. No man is poor who doth not think himself so; but if, in a full fortune, with impatience he desires more, he proclaims his wants and his beggarly condition. This virtue of contentedness was the sum of all the old moral philosophy, and is of most universal use in the whole course of our lives, and the only instrument to ease the burdens of the world and the enmities of sad chances. It is the great reasonableness of complying with the Divine Providence, which governs all the world, and hath so ordered us in the administration of His great family. It is fit that God should dispense His gifts as He pleases; and if we murmur here, we may, at the next melancholy, be troubled that He did not make us to be angels or stars.

We ourselves make our fortunes good or bad; and when God lets loose a Tyrant upon us, or a sickness, or scorn, or a lessened fortune, if we fear to die, or know not how to be patient, or are proud, or covetous, then the calamity sits heavy on us. But if we know how to manage a noble principle, and fear not death so much as a dishonest action, and think impatience a worse evil than a fever, and pride to be the greatest disgrace as well as the greatest folly, and poverty far preferable to the torments of avarice, we may still bear an even mind and smile at the reverses of fortune and the ill-nature of Fate.

If thou hast lost thy land, do not also lose thy constancy; and if thou must die sooner than others, or than thou didst expect, yet do not die impatiently. For no chance is evil to him who is content, and to a man nothing is miserable unless it be unreasonable. No man can make another man to be his slave, unless that other hath first enslaved himself to life and death, to pleasure or pain, to hope or fear; command these passions, and you are freer than the Parthian Kings.

When an enemy reproaches us, let us look on him as an impartial relator of our faults; for he will tell us truer than our fondest friend will, and we may forgive his anger, whilst we make use of the plainness of his declamation. The ox, when he is weary, treads truest; and if there be nothing else in abuse, but that it makes us to walk warily, and tread sure for fear of our enemies, that is better than to be flattered into pride and carelessness.

If thou fallest from thy employment in public, take sanctuary in an honest retirement, being indifferent to thy gain abroad, or thy safety at home. When the north wind blows hard, and it rains sadly, we do not sit down in it and cry; but defend ourselves against it with a warm garment, or a good fire and a dry roof. So when the storm of a sad mischance beats upon our spirits, we may turn it into something that is good, if we resolve to make it so; and with equanimity and patience may shelter ourselves from its inclement pitiless pelting. If it develop our patience, and give occasion for heroic endurance, it hath done us good enough to recompense us sufficiently for all the temporal affliction; for so a wise man shall overrule his stars; and have a greater influence upon his own content, than all the constellations and planets of the firmament.

Compare not thy condition with the few above thee, but to secure thy content, look upon those thousands with whom thou wouldst not, for any interest, change thy fortune and condition. A soldier must not think himself unprosperous, if he be not successful as Alexander or Wellington; nor any man deem himself unfortunate that he hath not the wealth of Rothschild; but rather let the former rejoice that he is not lessened like the many generals who went down horse and man before Napoleon, and the latter that he is not the beggar who, bareheaded in the bleak winter wind holds out his tattered hat for charity. There may be many who are richer and more fortunate; but many thousands who are very miserable, compared to thee.

After the worst assaults of Fortune, there will be something left to us,—a merry countenance, a cheerful spirit, and a good conscience, the Providence of God, our hopes of Heaven, our charity for those who have injured us; perhaps a loving wife, and many friends to pity, and some to relieve us; and light and air, and all the beauties of Nature; we can read, discourse, and meditate; and having still these blessings, we should be much in love with sorrow and peevishness to lose them all, and prefer to sit down on our little handful of thorns.

Enjoy the blessings of this day, if God sends them, and the evils of it bear patiently and calmly; for this day only is ours: we are dead to yesterday, and we are not yet born to the morrow. When our fortunes are violently changed, our spirits are unchanged, if they always stood in the suburbs and expectation of sorrows and reverses. The blessings of immunity, safeguard, liberty, and integrity deserve the thanksgiving of a whole life. We are quit from a thousand calamities, every one of which, if it were upon us, would make us insensible of our present sorrow, and glad to receive it in exchange for that other greater affliction.

Measure your desires by your fortune and condition, not your fortunes by your desires: be governed by your needs, not by your fancy; by nature, not by evil customs and ambitious principles. It is no evil to be poor, but to be vicious and impatient. Is that beast better, that hath two or three mountains to graze on, than the little bee that feeds on dew or manna, and lives upon what falls every morning from the store-houses of Heaven, clouds and Providence?

There are some instances of fortune and a fair condition that cannot stand with some others; but if you desire this, you must lose that, and unless you be content with one, you lose the comfort of both. If you covet learning, you must have leisure and a retired life; if honors of State and political distinctions, you must be ever abroad in public, and get experience, and do all men's business, and keep all company, and have no leisure at all. If you will be rich, you must be frugal; if you will be popular, you must be bountiful; if a philosopher, you must despise riches. If you would be famous as Epaminondas, accept also his poverty, for it added lustre to his person, and envy to his fortune, and his virtue without it could not have been so excellent. If you would have the reputation of a martyr, you must needs accept his persecution; if of a benefactor of the world, the world's injustice; if truly great, you must expect to see the mob prefer lesser men to yourself.

God esteems it one of His glories, that He brings good out of evil; and therefore it were but reason we should trust Him to govern His own world as He pleases; and that we should patiently wait until the change cometh, or the reason is discovered.

A Mason's contentedness must by no means be a mere contented selfishness, like his who, comfortable himself, is indifferent to the discomfort of others. There will always be in this world wrongs to forgive, suffering to alleviate, sorrow asking for sympathy, necessities and destitution to relieve, and ample occasion for the exercise of active charity and beneficence. And he who sits unconcerned amidst it all, perhaps enjoying his own comforts and luxuries the more, by contrasting them with the hungry and ragged destitution and shivering misery of his fellows, is not contented, but selfish and unfeeling.

It is the saddest of all sights upon this earth, that of a man lazy and luxurious, or hard and penurious, to whom want appeals in vain, and suffering cries in an unknown tongue. The man whose hasty anger hurries him into violence and crime is not half so unworthy to live. He is the faithless steward, that embezzles what God has given him in trust for the impoverished and suffering among his brethren. The true Mason must be and must have a right to be content with himself; and he can be so only when he lives not for himself alone, but for others also, who need his assistance and have a claim upon his sympathy.

"Charity is the great channel," it has been well said, "through which God passes all His mercy upon mankind. For we receive absolution of our sins in proportion to our forgiving our brother. This is the rule of our hopes and the measure of our desire in this world; and on the day of death and judgment, the great sentence upon mankind shall be transacted according to our alms, which is the other part of charity. God himself is love; and every degree of charity that dwells in us is the participation of the Divine nature."

These principles Masonry reduces to practice. By them it expects you to be hereafter guided and governed. It especially inculcates them upon him who employs the labor of others, forbidding him to discharge them, when to want employment is to starve; or to contract for the labor of man or woman at so low a price that by over-exertion they must sell him their blood and life at the same time with the labor of their hands.

These Degrees are also intended to teach *more* than morals. The symbols and ceremonies of Masonry have more than one meaning. They rather *conceal* than *disclose* the Truth. They *hint* it only, at least; and their varied meanings are only to be discovered by reflection and study. · Truth is not only symbolized by Light, but as the ray of light is separable into rays of different colors, so is truth separable into kinds. It is the province of Masonry to teach *all* truths—not moral truth alone, but political and philosophical, and even religious truth, so far as concerns the great and essential principles of each. The sphinx was a symbol. To whom has it disclosed its inmost meaning? Who knows the symbolic meaning of the pyramids?

You will hereafter learn who are the chief foes of human liberty symbolized by the assassins of the Master Khūrūm; and in their fate you may see foreshadowed that which we earnestly hope will hereafter overtake those enemies of humanity, against whom Masonry has struggled so long.

IX.

ELECT OF THE NINE.

[Elu of the Nine.]

ORIGINALLY created to reward fidelity, obedience, and devotion, this Degree was consecrated to bravery, devotedness, and patriotism; and your obligation has made known to you the duties which you have assumed. They are summed up in the simple mandate, "Protect the oppressed against the oppressor; and devote yourself to the honor and interests of your Country."

Masonry is not "speculative," nor theoretical, but experimental; not sentimental, but practical. It requires self-renunciation and self-control. It wears a stern face toward men's vices, and interferes with many of our pursuits and our fancied pleasures. It penetrates beyond the region of vague sentiment; beyond the regions where moralizers and philosophers have woven their fine theories and elaborated their beautiful maxims, to the very depths of the heart, rebuking our littlenesses and meannesses, arraigning our prejudices and passions, and warring against the armies of our vices.

It wars against the passions that spring out of the bosom of a world of fine sentiments, a world of admirable sayings and foul practices, of good maxims and bad deeds; whose darker passions are not only restrained by custom and ceremony, but hidden even from itself by a veil of beautiful sentiments. This terrible solecism has existed in all ages. Romish sentimentalism has often covered infidelity and vice; Protestant straightness often lauds spirituality and faith, and neglects homely truth, candor, and generosity; and ultra-liberal Rationalistic refinement sometimes soars

149

to heaven in its dreams, and wallows in the mire of earth in its deeds.

There may be a world of Masonic sentiment; and yet a world of little or no Masonry. In many minds there is a vague and general sentiment of Masonic charity, generosity, and disinterestedness, but no practical, active virtue, nor habitual kindness, self-sacrifice, or liberality. Masonry plays about them like the cold though brilliant lights that flush and eddy over Northern skies. There are occasional flashes of generous and manly feeling, transitory splendors, and momentary gleams of just and noble thought, and transient coruscations, that light the Heaven of their imagination; but there is no vital warmth in the heart; and it remains as cold and sterile as the Arctic or Antarctic regions. They *do* nothing; they gain no victories over themselves; they make no progress; they are still in the Northeast corner of the Lodge, as when they first stood there as Apprentices; and they do not cultivate Masonry, with a cultivation, determined, resolute, and regular, like their cultivation of their estate, profession, or knowledge. Their Masonry takes its chance in general and inefficient sentiment, mournfully barren of results; in words and formulas and fine professions.

Most men have *sentiments,* but not *principles.* The former are temporary sensations, the latter permanent and controlling impressions of goodness and virtue. The former are general and involuntary, and do not rise to the character of virtue. Every one feels them. They flash up spontaneously in every heart. The latter are rules of action, and shape and control our conduct; and it is these that Masonry insists upon.

We approve the right; but pursue the wrong. It is the old story of human deficiency. No one abets or praises injustice, fraud, oppression, covetousness, revenge, envy, or slander; and yet how many who condemn these things, are themselves guilty of them. It is no rare thing for him whose indignation is kindled at a tale of wicked injustice, cruel oppression, base slander, or misery inflicted by unbridled indulgence; whose anger flames in behalf of the injured and ruined victims of wrong; to be in some relation unjust, or oppressive, or envious, or self-indulgent, or a careless talker of others. How wonderfully indignant the penurious man often is, at the avarice or want of public spirit of another!

A great Preacher well said, "Therefore thou art inexcusable. O

Man, whosoever thou art, that judgest; for wherein thou judgest another, thou condemnest thyself: for thou that judgest, doest the same things." It is amazing to see how men can talk of virtue and honor, whose life denies both. It is curious to see with what a marvellous facility many bad men quote Scripture. It seems to comfort their evil consciences, to use good words; and to gloze over bad deeds with holy texts, wrested to their purpose. Often, the more a man talks about Charity and Toleration, the less he has of either; the more he talks about Virtue, the smaller stock he has of it. The mouth speaks out of the abundance of the heart; but often the very reverse of what the man practises. And the vicious and sensual often express, and in a sense feel, strong disgust at vice and sensuality. Hypocrisy is not so common as is imagined.

Here, in the Lodge, virtue and vice are matters of reflection and feeling only. There is little opportunity here, for the practice of either; and Masons yield to the argument here, with facility and readiness; because nothing is to follow. It is easy, and safe, here, to *feel* upon these matters. But to-morrow, when they breathe the atmosphere of worldly gains and competitions, and the passions are again stirred at the opportunities of unlawful pleasure, all their fine emotions about virtue, all their generous abhorrence of selfishness and sensuality, melt away like a morning cloud.

For the time, their emotions and sentiments are sincere and real. Men may be really, in a certain way, interested in Masonry, while fatally deficient in virtue. It is not always hypocrisy. Men pray most fervently and sincerely, and yet are constantly guilty of acts so bad and base, so ungenerous and unrighteous, that the crimes that crowd the dockets of our courts are scarcely worse.

A man may be a good sort of man in general, and yet a very bad man in particular: good in the Lodge and bad in the world; good in public, and bad in his family; good at home, and bad on a journey or in a strange city. Many a man earnestly desires to be a good Mason. He says so, and is sincere. But if you require him to resist a certain passion, to sacrifice a certain indulgence, to control his appetite at a particular feast, or to keep his temper in a dispute, you will find that he does not wish to be a good Mason, *in that particular case;* or, wishing, is not able to resist his worse impulses.

The *duties* of life are more than life. The law imposeth it upon

every citizen, that he prefer the urgent service of his country before the safety of his life. If a man be commanded, saith a great
writer, to bring ordnance or munition to relieve any of the King's
towns that are distressed, then he cannot for any danger of tempest justify the throwing of them overboard; for there it holdeth
which was spoken by the Roman, when the same necessity of
weather was alleged to hold him from embarking: *"Necesse est ut
eam, non ut vivam:"* it needs that I go: it is not necessary I should
live.

How ungratefully he slinks away, who dies, and does nothing to
reflect a glory to Heaven! How barren a tree he is, who lives, and
spreads, and cumbers the ground, yet leaves not one seed, not one
good work to generate another after him! All cannot leave alike;
yet all may leave *something*, answering their proportions and their
kinds. Those are dead and withered grains of corn, out of which
there will not one ear spring. He will hardly find the way to
Heaven, who desires to go thither alone.

Industry is never wholly unfruitful. If it bring not joy with
the incoming profit, it will yet banish mischief from thy busied
gates. There is a kind of good angel waiting upon Diligence that
ever carries a laurel in his hand to crown her. How unworthy
was that man of the world who never did aught, but only lived
and died! That we have liberty to do anything, we should account it a gift from the favoring Heavens; that we have minds
sometimes inclining us to use that liberty well, is a great bounty
of the Deity.

Masonry is action, and not inertness. It requires its Initiates to
WORK, actively and earnestly, for the benefit of their brethren,
their country, and mankind. It is the patron of the oppressed, as
it is the comforter and consoler of the unfortunate and wretched.
It seems to it a worthier honor to be the instrument of advancement and reform, than to enjoy all that rank and office and lofty
titles can bestow. It is the advocate of the common people in
those things which concern the best interests of mankind. It
hates insolent power and impudent usurpation. It pities the poor,
the sorrowing, the disconsolate; it endeavors to raise and improve
the ignorant, the sunken, and the degraded.

Its fidelity to its mission will be accurately evidenced, by the
extent of the efforts it employs, and the means it sets on foot, to
improve the people at large and to better their condition; chiefest

of which, within its reach, is to aid in the education of the children of the poor. An intelligent people, informed of its rights, will soon come to know its power, and cannot long be oppressed; but if there be not a sound and virtuous populace, the elaborate ornaments at the top of the pyramid of society will be a wretched compensation for the want of solidity at the base. It is never safe for a nation to repose on the lap of ignorance: and if there ever was a time when public tranquillity was insured by the absence of knowledge, that season is past. Unthinking stupidity cannot sleep, without being appalled by phantoms and shaken by terrors. The improvement of the mass of the people is the grand security for popular liberty; in the neglect of which, the politeness, refinement, and knowledge accumulated in the higher orders and wealthier classes will some day perish like dry grass in the hot fire of popular fury.

It is not the mission of Masonry to engage in plots and conspiracies against the civil government. It is not the fanatical propagandist of any creed or theory; nor does it proclaim itself the enemy of kings. It is the apostle of liberty, equality, and fraternity; but it is no more the high-priest of republicanism than of constitutional monarchy. It contracts no entangling alliances with any sect of theorists, dreamers, or philosophers. It does not know those as its Initiates who assail the civil order and all lawful authority, at the same time that they propose to deprive the dying of the consolations of religion. It sits apart from all sects and creeds, in its own calm and simple dignity, the same under every government. It is still that which it was in the cradle of the human race, when no human foot had trodden the soil of Assyria and Egypt, and no colonies had crossed the Himalayas into Southern India, Media, or Etruria.

It gives no countenance to anarchy and licentiousness; and no illusion of glory, or extravagant emulation of the ancients inflames it with an unnatural thirst for ideal and Utopian liberty. It teaches that in rectitude of life and sobriety of habits is the only sure guarantee for the continuance of political freedom; and it is chiefly the soldier of the sanctity of the laws and the rights of conscience.

It recognizes it as a truth, that necessity, as well as abstract right and ideal justice, must have its part in the making of laws, the administration of affairs, and the regulation of relations in

11

society. It sees, indeed, that necessity rules in all the affairs of man. It knows that where any man, or any number or race of men, are so imbecile of intellect, so degraded, so incapable of self-control, so inferior in the scale of humanity, as to be unfit to be intrusted with the highest prerogatives of citizenship, the great law of necessity, for the peace and safety of the community and country, requires them to remain under the control of those of larger intellect and superior wisdom. It trusts and believes that God will, in his own good time, work out his own great and wise purposes; and it is willing to wait, where it does not see its own way clear to some certain good.

It hopes and longs for the day when all the races of men, even the lowest, will be elevated, and become fitted for political freedom; when, like all other evils that afflict the earth, pauperism, and bondage or abject dependence, shall cease and disappear. But it does not preach revolution to those who are fond of kings, nor rebellion that can end only in disaster and defeat, or in substituting one tyrant for another, or a multitude of despots for one.

Wherever a people is fit to be free and to govern itself, and generously strives to be so, there go all its sympathies. It detests the tyrant, the lawless oppressor, the military usurper, and him who abuses a lawful power. It frowns upon cruelty, and a wanton disregard of the rights of humanity. It abhors the selfish employer, and exerts its influence to lighten the burdens which want and dependence impose upon the workman, and to foster that humanity and kindness which man owes to even the poorest and most unfortunate brother.

It can never be employed, in any country under Heaven, to teach a toleration for cruelty, to weaken moral hatred for guilt, or to deprave and brutalize the human mind. The dread of punishment will never make a Mason an accomplice in so corrupting his countrymen, and a teacher of depravity and barbarity. If anywhere, as has heretofore happened, a tyrant should send a satirist on his tyranny to be convicted and punished as a libeller, in a court of justice, a Mason, if a juror in such a case, though in sight of the scaffold streaming with the blood of the innocent, and within hearing of the clash of the bayonets meant to overawe the court, would rescue the intrepid satirist from the tyrant's fangs, and send his officers out from the court with defeat and disgrace.

Even if all law and liberty were trampled under the feet of Jacobinical demagogues or a military banditti, and great crimes were perpetrated with a high hand against all who were deservedly the objects of public veneration; if the people, overthrowing law, roared like a sea around the courts of justice, and demanded the blood of those who, during the temporary fit of insanity and drunken delirium, had chanced to become odious to it, for true words manfully spoken, or unpopular acts bravely done, the Masonic juror, unawed alike by the single or the many-headed tyrant, would consult the dictates of duty alone, and stand with a noble firmness between the human tigers and their coveted prey.

The Mason would much rather pass his life hidden in the recesses of the deepest obscurity, feeding his mind even with the visions and imaginations of good deeds and noble actions, than to be placed on the most splendid throne of the universe, tantalized with a denial of the practice of all which can make the greatest situation any other than the greatest curse. And if he has been enabled to lend the slightest step to any great and laudable designs; if he has had any share in any measure giving quiet to private property and to private conscience, making lighter the yoke of poverty and dependence, or relieving deserving men from oppression; if he has aided in securing to his countrymen that best possession, peace; if he has joined in reconciling the different sections of his own country to each other, and the people to the government of their own creating; and in teaching the citizen to look for his protection to the laws of his country, and for his comfort to the good-will of his countrymen; if he has thus taken his part with the best of men in the best of their actions, he may well shut the book, even if he might wish to read a page or two more. It is enough for his measure. He has not lived in vain.

Masonry teaches that all power is delegated for the good, and not for the injury of the People; and that, when it is perverted from the original purpose, the compact is broken, and the right ought to be resumed; that resistance to power usurped is not merely a duty which man owes to himself and to his neighbor, but a duty which he owes to his God, in asserting and maintaining the rank which He gave him in the creation. This principle neither the rudeness of ignorance can stifle nor the enervation of refinement extinguish. It makes it base for a man to suffer when he

ought to act; and, tending to preserve to him the original desti-
nations of Providence, spurns at the arrogant assumptions of
Tyrants and vindicates the independent quality of the race of
which we are a part.

The wise and well-informed Mason will not fail to be the votary
of Liberty and Justice. He will be ready to exert himself in their
defence, wherever they exist. It cannot be a matter of indifference to him when his own liberty and that of other men, with
whose merits and capacities he is acquainted, are involved in the
event of the struggle to be made; but his attachment will be to
the cause, as the cause of man; and not merely to the country.
Wherever there is a people that understands the value of political
justice, and is prepared to assert it, that is his country; wherever
he can most contribute to the diffusion of these principles and the
real happiness of mankind, that is his country. Nor does he desire for any country any other benefit than justice.

The true Mason identifies the honor of his country with his
own. Nothing more conduces to the beauty and glory of one's
country than the preservation against all enemies of its civil and
religious liberty. The world will never willingly let die the names
of those patriots who in her different ages have received upon
their own breasts the blows aimed by insolent enemies at the
bosom of their country.

But also it conduces, and in no small measure, to the beauty and
glory of one's country, that justice should always be administered
there to all alike, and neither denied, sold, nor delayed to any one;
that the interest of the poor should be looked to, and none starve
or be houseless, or clamor in vain for work; that the child and the
feeble woman should not be overworked, or even the apprentice or
slave be stinted of food or overtasked or mercilessly scourged; and
that God's great laws of mercy, humanity, and compassion should
be everywhere enforced, not only by the statutes, but also by the
power of public opinion. And he who labors, often against reproach and obloquy, and oftener against indifference and apathy,
to bring about that fortunate condition of things when that great
code of divine law shall be everywhere and punctually obeyed, is
no less a patriot than he who bares his bosom to the hostile steel
in the ranks of his country's soldiery.

For fortitude is not only seen resplendent on the field of battle
and amid the clash of arms, but he displays its energy under

every difficulty and against every assailant. He who wars against cruelty, oppression, and hoary abuses, fights for his country's honor, which these things soil; and her honor is as important as her existence. Often, indeed, the warfare against those abuses which disgrace one's country is quite as hazardous and more discouraging than that against her enemies in the field; and merits equal, if not greater reward.

For those Greeks and Romans who are the objects of our admiration employed hardly any other virtue in the extirpation of tyrants, than that love of liberty, which made them prompt in seizing the sword, and gave them strength to use it. With facility they accomplish the undertaking, amid the general shout of praise and joy; nor did they engage in the attempt so much as an enterprise of perilous and doubtful issue, as a contest the most glorious in which virtue could be signalized; which infallibly led to present recompense; which bound their brows with wreaths of laurel, and consigned their memories to immortal fame.

But he who assails hoary abuses, regarded perhaps with a superstitious reverence, and around which old laws stand as ramparts and bastions to defend them; who denounces acts of cruelty and outrage on humanity which make every perpetrator thereof his personal enemy, and perhaps make him looked upon with suspicion by the people among whom he lives, as the assailant of an established order of things of which he assails only the abuses, and of laws of which he attacks only the violations,—he can scarcely look for present recompense, nor that his living brows will be wreathed with laurel. And if, contending against a dark array of long-received opinions, superstitions, obloquy, and fears, which most men dread more than they do an army terrible with banners, the Mason overcomes, and emerges from the contest victorious; or if he does *not* conquer, but is borne down and swept away by the mighty current of prejudice, passion, and interest; in either case, the loftiness of spirit which he displays merits for him more than a mediocrity of fame.

He has already lived too long who has survived the ruin of his country; and he who can enjoy life after such an event deserves not to have lived at all. Nor does he any more deserve to live who looks contentedly upon abuses that disgrace, and cruelties that dishonor, and scenes of misery and destitution and brutalization that disfigure his country; or sordid meanness and ignoble revenges that make her a by-word and a scoff among all generous nations; and does not endeavor to remedy or prevent either.

Not often is a country at war; nor can every one be allowed the privilege of offering his heart to the enemy's bullets. But in these patriotic labors of peace, in preventing, remedying, and reforming evils, oppressions, wrongs, cruelties, and outrages, every Mason can unite; and every one can effect something, and share the honor and glory of the result.

For the cardinal names in the history of the human mind are few and easily to be counted up; but thousands and tens of thousands spend their days in the preparations which are to speed the predestined change, in gathering and amassing the materials which are to kindle and give light and warmth, when the fire from Heaven shall have descended on them. Numberless are the sutlers and pioneers, the engineers and artisans, who attend the march of intellect. Many move forward in detachments, and level the way over which the chariot is to pass, and cut down the obstacles that would impede its progress; and these too have their reward. If they labor diligently and faithfully in their calling, not only will they enjoy that calm contentment which diligence in the lowliest task never fails to win; not only will the sweat of their brows be sweet, and the sweetener of the rest that follows; but, when the victory is at last achieved, they will come in for a share in the glory; even as the meanest soldier who fought at Marathon or at King's Mountain became a sharer in the glory of those saving days; and within his own household circle, the approbation of which approaches the nearest to that of an approving conscience, was looked upon as the representative of all his brother-heroes; and could tell such tales as made the tear glisten on the cheek of his wife, and lit up his boy's eyes with an unwonted sparkling eagerness. Or, if he fell in the fight, and his place by the fireside and at the table at home was thereafter vacant, that place was sacred; and he was often talked of there in the long winter evenings; and his family was deemed fortunate in the neighborhood, because it had had a hero in it, who had fallen in defence of his country.

Remember that life's length is not measured by its hours and days, but by that which we have done therein for our country and kind. A useless life is short, if it last a century; but that of Alexander was long as the life of the oak, though he died at thirty-five. We may do much in a few years, and we may do nothing in a lifetime. If we but eat and drink and sleep, and let everything go on around us as it pleases; or if we live but to amass wealth or gain office or wear titles, we might as well not have lived at all; nor have we any right to expect immortality.

Forget not, therefore, to what you have devoted yourself in this Degree: defend weakness against strength, the friendless against the great, the oppressed against the oppressor! Be ever vigilant and watchful of the interests and honor of your country! and may the Grand Architect of the Universe give you that strength and wisdom which shall enable you well and faithfully to perform these high duties!

X.

ILLUSTRIOUS ELECT OF THE FIFTEEN.

[Elu of the Fifteen.]

This Degree is devoted to the same objects as those of the Elu of Nine; and also to the cause of Toleration and Liberality against Fanaticism and Persecution, political and religious; and to that of Education, Instruction, and Enlightenment against Error, Barbarism, and Ignorance. To these objects you have irrevocably and forever devoted your hand, your heart, and your intellect; and whenever in your presence a Chapter of this Degree is opened, you will be most solemnly reminded of your vows here taken at the altar.

Toleration, holding that every other man has the same right to his opinion and faith that we have to ours; and liberality, holding that as no human being can with certainty say, in the clash and conflict of hostile faiths and creeds, what is truth, or that *he* is *surely* in possession of it, so every one should feel that it is quite possible that another equally honest and sincere with himself, and yet holding the contrary opinion, may himself be in possession of the truth, and that whatever one firmly and conscientiously believes, *is* truth, *to him*—these are the mortal enemies of that fanaticism which persecutes for opinion's sake, and initiates crusades against whatever it, in its imaginary holiness, deems to be contrary to the law of God or verity of dogma. And education, instruction, and enlightenment are the most certain means by which fanaticism and intolerance can be rendered powerless.

No true Mason scoffs at honest convictions and an ardent zeal in the cause of what one believes to be truth and justice. But he

160

does absolutely deny the right of any man to assume the prerogative of Deity, and condemn another's faith and opinions as deserving to be punished because heretical. Nor does he approve the course of those who endanger the peace and quiet of great nations, and the best interest of their own race by indulging in a chimerical and visionary philanthropy—a luxury which chiefly consists in drawing their robes around them to avoid contact with their fellows, and proclaiming themselves holier than they.

For he knows that such follies are often more calamitous than the ambition of kings; and that intolerance and bigotry have been infinitely greater curses to mankind than ignorance and error. Better *any* error than persecution! Better *any* opinion than the thumb-screw, the rack, and the stake! And he knows also how unspeakably absurd it is, for a creature to whom himself and everything around him are mysteries, to torture and slay others, because they cannot think as he does in regard to the profoundest of those mysteries, to understand which is utterly beyond the comprehension of either the persecutor or the persecuted.

Masonry is not a religion. He who makes of it a religious belief, falsifies and denaturalizes it. The Brahmin, the Jew, the Mahometan, the Catholic, the Protestant, each professing his peculiar religion, sanctioned by the laws, by time, and by climate, must needs retain it, and cannot have two religions; for the social and sacred laws adapted to the usages, manners, and prejudices of particular countries, are the work of men.

But Masonry teaches, and has preserved in their purity, the cardinal tenets of the old primitive faith, which underlie and are the foundation of all religions. All that ever existed have had a basis of truth; and all have overlaid that truth with errors. The primitive truths taught by the Redeemer were sooner corrupted, and intermingled and alloyed with fictions than when taught to the first of our race. Masonry is the universal morality which is suitable to the inhabitants of every clime, to the man of every creed. It has taught no doctrines, except those truths that tend directly to the well-being of man; and those who have attempted to direct it toward useless vengeance, political ends, and Jesuitism, have merely perverted it to purposes foreign to its pure spirit and real nature.

Mankind outgrows the sacrifices and the mythologies of the childhood of the world. Yet it is easy for human indolence to linger near these helps, and refuse to pass further on. So the un-adventurous Nomad in the Tartarian wild keeps his flock in the same close-cropped circle where they first learned to browse, while the progressive man roves ever forth "to fresh fields and pastures new."

The latter is the true Mason; and the best and indeed the only good Mason is he who with the power of business does the work of life; the upright mechanic, merchant, or farmer, the man with the power of thought, of justice, or of love, he whose whole life is one great act of performance of Masonic duty. The natural use of the strength of a strong man or the wisdom of a wise one, is to do the *work* of a strong man or a wise one. The natural work of Masonry is practical life; the use of all the faculties in their proper spheres, and for their natural function. Love of Truth, justice, and generosity as attributes of God, must appear in a life marked by these qualities; that is the only effectual ordinance of Masonry. A profession of one's convictions, joining the Order, assuming the obligations, assisting at the ceremonies, are of the same value in science as in Masonry; the natural form of Masonry is goodness, morality, living a true, just, affectionate, self-faithful life, from the motive of a good man. It is loyal obedience to God's law.

The good Mason does the good thing which comes in his way, and because it comes in his way; from a love of duty, and not merely because a law, enacted by man or God, commands his *will* to do it. He is true to his mind, his conscience, heart, and soul, and feels small temptation to do to others what he would not wish to receive from them. He will deny himself for the sake of his brother near at hand. His *desire* attracts in the line of his *duty*, both being in conjunction. Not in vain does the poor or the oppressed look up to him. You find such men in all Christian sects, Protestant and Catholic, in all the great religious parties of the civilized world, among Buddhists, Mahometans, and Jews. They are kind fathers, generous citizens, unimpeachable in their business, beautiful in their daily lives. You see their Masonry in their work and in their play. It appears in all the forms of their activity, individual, domestic, social, ecclesiastical, or political. True Masonry within must be morality without. It must become *eminent* morality, which is philanthropy. The true Mason loves not only his kindred and his country, but all mankind; not only the good, but also the evil, among his brethren. He has more goodness than the channels of his daily life will hold. It runs over the banks, to water and to feed a thousand thirsty plants. Not content with the duty that lies along his track, he goes out to seek it; not only *willing*, he has a salient *longing* to do good, to spread his truth, his justice, his generosity, his Masonry over all the world. His daily life is a profession of his Masonry, published in perpetual good-will to men. He *can* not be a persecutor.

Not more naturally does the beaver build or the mocking-bird sing his own wild, gushing melody, than the true Mason lives in this beautiful outward life. So from the perennial spring swells forth the stream, to quicken the meadow with new access of green, and perfect beauty bursting into bloom. Thus Masonry does the work it was meant to do. The Mason does not sigh and weep, and make grimaces. He lives right on. If his life is, as whose is not, marked with errors, and with sins, he ploughs over the barren spot with his remorse, sows with new seed, and the old desert blossoms like a rose. He is not confined to set forms of thought, of action, or of feeling. He accepts what his mind regards as true, what his conscience decides is right, what his heart deems generous and noble; and all else he puts far from him. Though the ancient and the honorable of the Earth bid him bow down to them, his stubborn knees bend only at the bidding of his manly soul. His Masonry is his freedom before God, not his bondage unto men. His mind acts after the universal law of the intellect, his conscience according to the universal moral law, his affections and his soul after the universal law of each, and so he is strong with the strength of God, in this four-fold way communicating with Him.

The old theologies, the philosophies of religion of ancient times, will not suffice us now. The duties of life are to be done; we are to do them, consciously obedient to the law of God, not atheistically, loving only our selfish gain. There are sins of trade to be corrected. Everywhere morality and philanthropy are needed. There are errors to be made way with, and their place supplied with new truths, radiant with the glories of Heaven. There are great wrongs and evils, in Church and State, in domestic, social, and public life, to be righted and outgrown. Masonry cannot in our age forsake the broad way of life. She must journey on in the open street, appear in the crowded square, and teach men by her deeds, her life more eloquent than any lips.

This Degree is chiefly devoted to TOLERATION; and it inculcates in the strongest manner that great leading idea of the Ancient Art, that a belief in the one True God, and a moral and virtuous life, constitute the only religious requisites needed to enable a man to be a Mason.

Masonry has ever the most vivid remembrance of the terrible and artificial torments that were used to put down new forms of religion or extinguish the old. It sees with the eye of memory the ruthless extermination of all the people of all sexes and ages, because it was their misfortune not to know the God of the Hebrews, or to worship Him under the wrong name, by the savage troops of Moses and Joshua. It sees the thumb-screws and the racks, the whip, the gallows, and the stake, the victims of Diocletian and Alva, the miserable Covenanters, the Non-Conformists, Servetus burned, and the unoffending Quaker hung. It sees Cranmer hold his arm, now no longer erring, in the flame until the hand drops off in the consuming heat. It sees the persecutions of Peter and Paul, the martyrdom of Stephen, the trials of Ignatius, Polycarp, Justin, and Irenæus; and then in turn the sufferings of the wretched Pagans under the Christian Emperors, as of the Papists in Ireland and under Elizabeth and the bloated Henry. The Roman Virgin naked before the hungry lions; young Margaret Graham tied to a stake at low-water mark, and there left to drown, singing hymns to God until the savage waters broke over her head; and all that in all ages have suffered by hunger and nakedness, peril and prison, the rack, the stake, and the sword,—it sees them all, and shudders at the long roll of human atrocities. And it sees also the oppression still practised in the name of religion— men shot in a Christian jail in Christian Italy for reading the Christian Bible; in almost every Christian State, laws forbidding freedom of speech on matters relating to Christianity; and the gallows reaching its arm over the pulpit.

The fires of Moloch in Syria, the harsh mutilations in the name of Astarte, Cybele, Jehovah; the barbarities of imperial Pagan Torturers; the still grosser torments which Roman-Gothic Christians in Italy and Spain heaped on their brother-men; the fiendish cruelties to which Switzerland, France, the Netherlands, England, Scotland, Ireland, America, have been witnesses, are none too powerful to warn man of the unspeakable evils which follow from mistakes and errors in the matter of religion, and especially from investing the God of Love with the cruel and vindictive passions of erring humanity, and making blood to have a sweet savor in his nostrils, and groans of agony to be delicious to his ears.

Man never had the right to usurp the unexercised prerogative of God, and condemn and punish another for his belief. Born in a Protestant land, we are of that faith. If we had opened our eyes to the light under the shadows of St. Peter's at Rome, we should have been devout Catholics; born in the Jewish quarter of Aleppo, we should have contemned Christ as an imposter; in Constantinople, we should have cried *"Allah il Allah,* God is great and Mahomet is his prophet!" Birth, place, and education give us our faith. Few believe in any religion because they have examined the evidences of its authenticity, and made up a formal judgment, upon weighing the testimony. Not one man in ten thousand knows anything about the *proofs* of his faith. We believe what we are taught; and those are most fanatical who know least of the evidences on which their creed is based. Facts and testimony are not, except in very rare instances, the ground-work of faith. It is an imperative law of God's Economy, unyielding and inflexible as Himself, that man shall accept without question the belief of those among whom he is born and reared; the faith so made a part of his nature resists all evidence to the contrary; and he will disbelieve even the evidence of his own senses, rather than yield up the religious belief which has grown up in him, flesh of his flesh and bone of his bone.

What is truth to *me* is not truth to *another.* The same arguments and evidences that convince one mind make no impression on another. This difference is in men at their birth. No man is entitled positively to assert that *he* is right, where other men, equally intelligent and equally well-informed, hold directly the opposite opinion. Each thinks it impossible for the other to be sincere, and each, as to that, is equally in error. *"What is truth?"* was a profound question, the most suggestive one ever put to man. Many beliefs of former and present times seem incomprehensible. They startle us with a new glimpse into the human soul, that mysterious thing, more mysterious the more we note its workings. Here is a man superior to myself in intellect and learning; and yet he sincerely believes what seems to me too absurd to merit confutation; and I cannot conceive, and sincerely do not believe, that he is both sane and honest. *And yet he is both.* His reason is as perfect as mine, and he is as honest as I.

The fancies of a lunatic are realities, *to him.* Our dreams are realities *while they last;* and, in the Past, no more *un*real than what we have acted in our waking hours. No man can say that he hath as sure possession of the truth as of a chattel. When men entertain opinions diametrically opposed to each other, and each is honest, who shall decide which hath the Truth; and how can either say with certainty that *he* hath it? We know not what *is* the truth. That we ourselves believe and feel absolutely certain that our own belief is true, is in reality not the slightest proof of the fact, seem it never so certain and incapable of doubt to us. No man is responsible for the rightness of his faith; but only for the *up*rightness of it.

Therefore no man hath or ever had a right to persecute another for his belief; for there cannot be two antagonistic rights; and if one can persecute another, because he himself is satisfied that the belief of that other is erroneous, the other has, for the same reason, equally as certain a right to persecute him.

The truth comes to us tinged and colored with our prejudices and our preconceptions, which are as old as ourselves, and strong with a divine force. It comes to us as the image of a rod comes to us through the water, bent and distorted. An argument sinks into and convinces the mind of one man, while from that of another it rebounds like a ball of ivory dropped on marble. It is no merit in a man to have a particular faith, excellent and sound and philosophic as it may be, when he imbibed it with his mother's milk. It is no more a merit than his prejudices and his passions.

The sincere Moslem has as much right to persecute us, as we to persecute him; and therefore Masonry wisely requires no more than a belief in One Great All-Powerful Deity, the Father and Preserver of the Universe. Therefore it is she teaches her votaries that toleration is one of the chief duties of every good Mason, a component part of that charity without which we are mere hollow images of true Masons, mere sounding brass and tinkling cymbals.

No evil hath so afflicted the world as intolerance of religious opinion. The human beings it has slain in various ways, if once and together brought to life, would make a nation of people; left to live and increase, would have doubled the population of the civilized portion of the globe; among which civilized portion it chiefly is that religious wars are waged. The treasure and the human labor thus lost would have made the earth a garden, in which, but for his evil passions, man might now be as happy as in Eden.

No man truly obeys the Masonic law who *merely* tolerates those whose religious opinions are opposed to his own. Every man's opinions are his own private property, and the rights of all men to maintain each his own are perfectly equal. Merely to *tolerate*, to *bear with* an opposing opinion, is to assume it to be heretical; and assert the *right* to persecute, if we would; and claim our *toleration* of it as a merit. The Mason's creed goes further than that. No man, it holds, has any right in any way to interfere with the religious belief of another. It holds that each man is absolutely sovereign as to his own belief, and that belief is a matter absolutely foreign to all who do not entertain the same belief; and that, if there were any right of persecution at all, it would in all cases be a mutual right; because one party has the same right as the other to sit as judge in his own case; and God is the only magistrate that can rightfully decide between them. To that great Judge, Masonry refers the matter; and opening wide its portals, it invites to enter there and live in peace and harmony, the Protestant, the Catholic, the Jew, the Moslem; every man who will lead a truly virtuous and moral life, love his brethren, minister to the sick and distressed, and believe in the ONE, *All-Powerful, All-Wise, everywhere-Present* GOD, *Architect, Creator,* and *Preserver of all things,* by whose universal law of Harmony ever rolls on this universe, the great, vast, infinite circle of successive Death and Life:—to whose INEFFABLE NAME let all true Masons pay profoundest homage! for whose thousand blessings poured upon us, let us feel the sincerest gratitude, now, henceforth, and forever!

We may well be tolerant of each other's creed; for in every faith there are excellent moral precepts. Far in the South of Asia, Zoroaster taught this doctrine: "On commencing a journey, the Faithful should turn his thoughts toward Ormuzd, and confess him, in the purity of his heart, to be King of the World; he should love him, do him homage, and serve him. He must be upright and charitable, despise the pleasures of the body, and avoid pride and haughtiness, and vice in all its forms, and especially falsehood, one of the basest sins of which man can be guilty. He must forget injuries and not avenge himself. He must honor the memory of his parents and relatives. At night, before retiring to sleep, he should rigorously examine his conscience, and repent of the faults which weakness or ill-fortune had caused him to commit." He was required to pray for strength to persevere in the Good, and to obtain forgiveness for his errors. It was his duty to confess his faults to a Magus, or to a layman renowned for his virtues, or to the Sun. Fasting and maceration were prohibited; and, on the contrary, it was his duty suitably to nourish the body and to maintain its vigor, that his soul might be strong to resist the Genius of Darkness; that he might more attentively read the Divine Word, and have more courage to perform noble deeds.

And in the North of Europe the Druids taught devotion to friends, indulgence for reciprocal wrongs, love of deserved praise, prudence, humanity, hospitality, respect for old age, disregard of the future, temperance, contempt of death, and a chivalrous deference to woman. Listen to these maxims from the Hava Maal, or Sublime Book of Odin:

"If thou hast a friend, visit him often; the path will grow over with grass, and the trees soon cover it, if thou dost not constantly walk upon it. He is a faithful friend, who, having but two loaves, gives his friend one. Be never first to break with thy friend; sorrow wrings the heart of him who has no one save himself with whom to take counsel. There is no virtuous man who has not some vice, no bad man who has not some virtue. Happy he who obtains the praise and good-will of men; for all that depends on the will of another is hazardous and uncertain. Riches flit away in the twinkling of an eye; they are the most inconstant of friends; flocks and herds perish, parents die, friends are not immortal, thou thyself diest; I know but one thing that doth not die, the judgment that is passed upon the dead. Be humane toward those whom thou meetest on the road. If the guest that cometh to thy house is a-cold, give him fire; the man who has journeyed over the mountains needs food and dry garments. Mock not at the aged; for words full of sense come often from the wrinkles of age. Be moderately wise, and not over-prudent. Let no one seek to know his destiny, if he would sleep tranquilly. There is no malady more cruel than to be discontented with our lot. The glutton eats his own death; and the wise man laughs at the fool's greediness. Nothing is more injurious to the young than excessive drinking; the more one drinks the more he loses his reason; the bird of forgetfulness sings before those who intoxicate themselves, and wiles away their souls. Man devoid of sense believes he will live always if he avoids war; but, if the lances spare him, old age will give him no quarter. Better live well than live long. When a man lights a fire in his house, death comes before it goes out."

And thus said the Indian books: "Honor thy father and mother. Never forget the benefits thou hast received. Learn while thou art young. Be submissive to the laws of thy country. Seek the company of virtuous men. Speak not of God but with respect. Live on good terms with thy fellow-citizens. Remain in thy proper place. Speak ill of no one. Mock at the bodily infirmities of none. Pursue not unrelentingly a conquered enemy. Strive to acquire a good reputation. Take counsel with wise men. The more one learns, the more he acquires the faculty of learning. Knowledge is the most permanent wealth. As well be dumb as ignorant. The true use of knowledge is to distinguish good from evil. Be not a subject of shame to thy parents. What one learns in youth endures like the engraving upon a rock. He is wise who knows himself. Let thy books be thy best friends. When thou attainest an hundred years, cease to learn. Wisdom is solidly planted, even on the shifting ocean. Deceive no one, not even thine enemy. Wisdom is a treasure that everywhere commands its value. Speak mildly, even to the poor. It is sweeter to forgive than to take vengeance. Gaming and quarrels lead to misery. There is no true merit without the practice of virtue. To honor our mother is the most fitting homage we can pay the Divinity. There is no tranquil sleep without a clear conscience. He badly understands his interest who breaks his word."

Twenty-four centuries ago these were the Chinese Ethics:

"The Philosopher [Confucius] said, 'SAN! my doctrine is simple, and easy to be understood.' THSENG-TSEU replied, 'that is certain.' The Philosopher having gone out, the disciples asked what their master had meant to say. THSENG-TSEU responded, 'The doctrine of our Master consists solely in being upright of heart, and loving our neighbor as we love ourself.'"

About a century later, the Hebrew law said, "If any man hate his neighbor . . . then shall ye do unto him, as he had thought to

12

do unto his brother . . . Better is a neighbor that is near, than a brother afar off . . . Thou shalt love thy neighbor as thyself."

In the same fifth century before Christ, SOCRATES the Grecian said, "Thou shalt love thy neighbor as thyself."

Three generations earlier, ZOROASTER had said to the Persians: "Offer up thy grateful prayers to the Lord, the most just and pure Ormuzd, the supreme and adorable God, who thus declared to his Prophet Zerdusht: 'Hold it not meet to do unto others what thou wouldst not desire done unto thyself; do that unto the people, which, when done to thyself, is not disagreeable unto thee.'"

The same doctrine had been long taught in the schools of Babylon, Alexandria, and Jerusalem. A Pagan declared to the Pharisee HILLEL that he was ready to embrace the Jewish religion, if he could make known to him in a few words a summary of the whole law of Moses. "That which thou likest not done to thyself," said Hillel, "do it not unto thy neighbor. Therein is all the law: the rest is nothing but the commentary upon it."

"Nothing is more natural," said CONFUCIUS, "nothing more simple, than the principles of that morality which I endeavor, by salutary maxims, to inculcate in you . . . It is humanity; which is to say, that universal charity among all of our species, without distinction. It is uprightness; that is, that rectitude of spirit and of heart, which makes one seek for truth in everything, and desire it, without deceiving one's self or others. It is, finally, sincerity or good faith; which is to say, that frankness, that openness of heart, tempered by self-reliance, which excludes all feints and all disguising, as much in speech as in action."

To diffuse useful information, to further intellectual refinement, sure forerunner of moral improvement, to hasten the coming of the great day, when the dawn of general knowledge shall chase away the lazy, lingering mists of ignorance and error, even from the base of the great social pyramid, is indeed a high calling, in which the most splendid talents and consummate virtue may well press onward, eager to bear a part. From the Masonic ranks ought to go forth those whose genius and not their ancestry ennoble them, to open to all ranks the temple of science, and by their own example to make the humblest men emulous to climb steps no longer inaccessible, and enter the unfolded gates burning in the sun.

The highest intellectual cultivation is perfectly compatible with the daily cares and toils of working-men. A keen relish for the most sublime truths of science belongs alike to every class of mankind. And, as philosophy was taught in the sacred groves of Athens, and under the Portico, and in the old Temples of Egypt and India, so in our Lodges ought Knowledge to be dispensed, the Sciences taught, and the Lectures become like the teachings of Socrates and Plato, of Agassiz and Cousin.

Real knowledge never permitted either turbulence or unbelief; but its progress is the forerunner of liberality and enlightened toleration. Whoso dreads these may well tremble; for he may be well assured that their day is at length come, and must put to speedy flight the evil spirits of tyranny and persecution, which haunted the long night now gone down the sky. And it is to be hoped that the time will soon arrive, when, as men will no longer suffer themselves to be led blindfolded in ignorance, so will they no more yield to the vile principle of judging and treating their fellow-creatures, not according to the intrinsic merit of their *actions*, but according to the accidental and involuntary coincidence of their *opinions*.

Whenever we come to treat with entire respect those who conscientiously differ from ourselves, the only practical effect of a difference will be, to make us enlighten the ignorance on one side or the other, from which it springs, by instructing them, if it be theirs; ourselves, if it be our own; to the end that the only kind of unanimity may be produced which is desirable among rational beings,—the agreement proceeding from full conviction after the freest discussion.

The Elu of Fifteen ought therefore to take the lead of his fellow-citizen, not in frivolous amusements, not in the degrading pursuits of the ambitious vulgar; but in the truly noble task of enlightening the mass of his countrymen, and of leaving his own name encircled, not with barbaric splendor, or attached to courtly gewgaws, but illustrated by the honors most worthy of our rational nature; coupled with the diffusion of knowledge, and gratefully pronounced by a few, at least, whom his wise beneficence has rescued from ignorance and vice.

We say to him, in the words of the great Roman: "Men in no respect so nearly approach to the Deity, as when they confer benefits on men. To serve and do good to as many as possible,—there is nothing greater in your fortune than that you should be able, and nothing finer in your nature, than that you should be desirous to do this." This is the true mark for the aim of every man and Mason who either prizes the enjoyment of pure happiness, or sets a right value upon a high and unsullied renown. And if the benefactors of mankind, when they rest from their noble labors, shall be permitted to enjoy hereafter, as an appropriate reward of their virtue, the privilege of looking down upon the blessings with which their exertions and charities, and perhaps their toils and sufferings have clothed the scene of their former existence, it will not, in a state of exalted purity and wisdom, be the founders of mighty dynasties, the conquerors of new empires, the Cæsars, Alexanders, and Tamerlanes; nor the mere Kings and Counsellors, Presidents and Senators, who have lived for their party chiefly, and for their country only incidentally, often sacrificing to their own aggrandizement or that of their faction the good of their fellow-creatures;—it will not be they who will be gratified by contemplating the monuments of their inglorious fame; but those will enjoy that delight and march in that triumph, who can trace the remote effects of their enlightened benevolence in the improved condition of their species, and exult in the reflection, that the change which they at last, perhaps after many years, survey, with eyes that age and sorrow can make dim no more,—of Knowledge become Power,—Virtue sharing that Empire,—Superstition dethroned, and Tyranny exiled, is, if even only in some small and very slight degree, yet still in *some* degree, the fruit, precious if costly, and though late repaid yet long enduring, of their own self-denial and strenuous exertion, of their own mite of charity and aid to education wisely bestowed, and of the hardships and hazards which they encountered here below.

Masonry requires of its Initiates and votaries nothing that is impracticable. It does not demand that they should undertake to climb to those lofty and sublime peaks of a theoretical and imaginary unpractical virtue, high and cold and remote as the eternal snows that wrap the shoulders of Chimborazo, and at least as inaccessible as they. It asks that alone to be done which is easy to be done. It overtasks no one's strength, and asks no one to go beyond his means and capacities. It does not expect one whose business or profession yields him little more than the wants of himself and his family require, and whose time is necessarily occupied by his daily vocations, to abandon or neglect the business by which he and his children live, and devote himself and his means to the diffusion of knowledge among men. It does not expect him to publish books for the people, or to lecture, to the ruin of his private affairs, or to found academies and colleges, build up libraries, and entitle himself to statues.

But it does require and expect every man of us to do something, within and according to his means; and there is no Mason who *cannot* do *some* thing, if not alone, then by combination and association.

If a Lodge cannot aid in founding a school or an academy it can still do something. It can educate one boy or girl, at least, the child of some poor or departed brother. And it should never be forgotten, that in the poorest unregarded child that seems abandoned to ignorance and vice *may* slumber the virtues of a Socrates, the intellect of a Bacon or a Bossuet, the genius of a Shakespeare, the capacity to benefit mankind of a Washington; and that in rescuing him from the mire in which he is plunged, and giving him the means of education and development, the Lodge that does it may be the direct and immediate means of conferring upon the world as great a boon as that given it by John Faust the boy of Mentz; may perpetuate the liberties of a country and change the destinies of nations, and write a new chapter in the history of the world.

For we never know the importance of the act we do. The daughter of Pharaoh little thought what she was doing for the human race, and the vast unimaginable consequences that depended on her charitable act, when she drew the little child of a Hebrew woman from among the rushes that grew along the bank of the Nile, and determined to rear it as if it were her own.

How often has an act of charity, costing the doer little, given to the world a great painter, a great musician, a great inventor! How often has such an act developed the ragged boy into the benefactor of his race! On what small and apparently unimportant circumstances have turned and hinged the fates of the world's great conquerors. There is no law that limits the returns that shall be reaped from a single good deed. The widow's mite may not only be as acceptable to God, but may produce as great results as the rich man's costly offering. The poorest boy, helped by benevolence, may come to lead armies, to control senates, to decide on peace and war, to dictate to cabinets; and his magnificent thoughts and noble words may be law many years hereafter to millions of men yet unborn.

But the opportunity to effect a great good does not often occur to any one. It is worse than folly for one to lie idle and inert, and expect the accident to befall him, by which his influences shall live forever. He can expect that to happen, only in consequence of one or many or all of a long series of acts. He can expect to benefit the world only as men attain other results; by continuance, by persistence, by a steady and uniform habit of laboring for the enlightenment of the world, to the extent of his means and capacity.

For it is, in all instances, by steady labor, by giving enough of application to our work, and having enough of time for the doing of it, by regular pains-taking, and the plying of constant assiduities, and not by any process of legerdemain, that we secure the strength and the staple of real excellence. It was thus that Demosthenes, clause after clause, and sentence after sentence, elaborated to the uttermost his immortal orations. It was thus that Newton pioneered his way, by the steps of an ascending geometry, to the mechanism of the Heavens, and Le Verrier added a planet to our Solar System.

It is a most erroneous opinion that those who have left the most stupendous monuments of intellect behind them, were not differently exercised from the rest of the species, but only differently gifted; that they signalized themselves only by their talent, and hardly ever by their industry; for it is in truth to the most strenuous application of those commonplace faculties which are diffused among all, that they are indebted for the glories which now encircle their remembrance and their name.

We must not imagine it to be a vulgarizing of genius, that it should be lighted up in any other way than by a direct inspiration from Heaven; nor overlook the steadfastness of purpose, the devotion to some single but great object, the unweariedness of labor that is given, not in convulsive and preternatural throes, but by little and little as the strength of the mind may bear it; the accumulation of many small efforts, instead of a few grand and gigantic, but perhaps irregular movements, on the part of energies that are marvellous; by which former alone the great results are brought out that write their enduring records on the face of the earth and in the history of nations and of man.

We must not overlook these elements, to which genius owes the best and proudest of her achievements; nor imagine that qualities so generally possessed as patience and pains-taking, and resolute industry, have no share in upholding a distinction so illustrious as that of the benefactor of his kind.

We must not forget that great results are most ordinarily produced by an aggregate of many contributions and exertions; as it is the invisible particles of vapor, each separate and distinct from the other, that, rising from the oceans and their bays and gulfs, from lakes and rivers, and wide morasses and overflowed plains, float away as clouds, and distill upon the earth in dews, and fall in showers and rain and snows upon the broad plains and rude mountains, and make the great navigable streams that are the arteries along which flows the life-blood of a country.

And so Masonry can do much, if each Mason be content to do his share, and if their united efforts are directed by wise counsels to a common purpose. "It is for God and for Omnipotency to do mighty things in a moment; but by degrees to grow to greatness is the course that He hath left for man."

If Masonry will but be true to her mission, and Masons to their promises and obligations—if, re-entering vigorously upon a career of beneficence, she and they will but pursue it earnestly and unfalteringly, remembering that our contributions to the cause of charity and education then deserve the greatest credit when it costs us something, the curtailing of a comfort or the relinquishment of a luxury, to make them—if we will but give aid to what were once Masonry's great schemes for human improvement, not fitfully and spasmodically, but regularly and incessantly, as the vapors rise and the springs run, and as the sun rises and the stars come up into the heavens, then we may be sure that great results will be attained and a great work done. And then it will most surely be seen that Masonry is not effete or impotent, nor degenerated nor drooping to a fatal decay.

XI.

SUBLIME ELECT OF THE TWELVE;

OR

PRINCE AMETH.

[Elu of the Twelve.]

THE duties of a Prince Ameth are, to be earnest, true, reliable, and sincere; to protect the people against illegal impositions and exactions; to contend for their political rights, and to see, as far as he may or can, that those bear the burdens who reap the benefits of the Government.

You are to be true unto all men.

You are to be frank and sincere in all things.

You are to be earnest in doing whatever it is your duty to do.

And no man must repent that he has relied upon your resolve, your profession, or your word.

The great distinguishing characteristic of a Mason is sympathy with his kind. He recognizes in the human race one great family, all connected with himself by those invisible links, and that mighty net-work of circumstance, forged and woven by God.

Feeling that sympathy, it is his first Masonic duty to serve his fellow-man. At his first entrance into the Order, he ceases to be isolated, and becomes one of a great brotherhood, assuming new duties toward every Mason that lives, as every Mason at the same moment assumes them toward him.

Nor are those duties on his part confined to Masons alone. He assumes many in regard to his country, and especially toward the great, suffering masses of the common people; for they too are his brethren, and God hears them, inarticulate as the moanings of their misery are. By all proper means, of persuasion and influ-

176

ence, and otherwise, if the occasion and emergency require, he is bound to defend them against oppression, and tyrannical and illegal exactions.

He labors equally to defend and to improve the people. He does not flatter them to mislead them, nor fawn upon them to rule them, nor conceal his opinions to humor them, nor tell them that they can never err, and that their voice is the voice of God. He knows that the safety of every free government, and its continuance and perpetuity depend upon the virtue and intelligence of the common people; and that, unless their liberty is of such a kind as arms can neither procure nor take away; unless it is the fruit of manly courage, of justice, temperance, and generous virtue—unless, being such, it has taken deep root in the minds and hearts of the people at large, there will not long be wanting those who will snatch from them by treachery what they have acquired by arms or institutions.

He knows that if, after being released from the toils of war, the people neglect the arts of peace; if their peace and liberty be a state of warfare; if war be their only virtue, and the summit of their praise, they will soon find peace the most adverse to their interests. It will be only a more distressing war; and that which they imagined liberty will be the worst of slavery. For, unless by the means of knowledge and morality, not frothy and loquacious, but genuine, unadulterated, and sincere, they clear the horizon of the mind from those mists of error and passion which arise from ignorance and vice, they will always have those who will bend their necks to the yoke as if they were brutes; who, notwithstanding all their triumphs, will put them up to the highest bidder, as if they were mere booty made in war; and find an exuberant source of wealth and power, in the people's ignorance, prejudice, and passions.

The people that does not subjugate the propensity of the wealthy to avarice, ambition, and sensuality, expel luxury from them and their families, keep down pauperism, diffuse knowledge among the poor, and labor to raise the abject from the mire of vice and low indulgence, and to keep the industrious from starving in sight of luxurious festivals, will find that it has cherished, in that avarice, ambition, sensuality, selfishness, and luxury of the one class, and that degradation, misery, drunkenness, ignorance, and brutalization of the other, more stubborn and intractable despots at home than it ever encountered in the field; and even its very bowels will be continually teeming with the intolerable progeny of tyrants.

These are the first enemies to be subdued; this constitutes the campaign of Peace; these are triumphs, difficult indeed, but bloodless; and far more honorable than those trophies which are purchased only by slaughter and rapine; and if not victors in this service, it is in vain to have been victorious over the despotic enemy in the field.

For if any people thinks that it is a grander; a more beneficial, or a wiser policy, to invent subtle expedients by stamps and imposts, for increasing the revenue and draining the life-blood of an impoverished people; to multiply its naval and military force; to rival in craft the ambassadors of foreign states; to plot the swallowing up of foreign territory; to make crafty treaties and alliances; to rule prostrate states and abject provinces by fear and force; than to administer unpolluted justice to the people, to relieve the condition and raise the estate of the toiling masses, redress the injured and succor the distressed and conciliate the discontented, and speedily restore to every one his own; then that people is involved in a cloud of error, and will too late perceive, when the illusion of these mighty benefits has vanished, that in neglecting these, which it thought inferior considerations, it has only been precipitating its own ruin and despair.

Unfortunately, every age presents its own special problem, most difficult and often impossible to solve; and that which this age offers, and forces upon the consideration of all thinking men, is this—how, in a populous and wealthy country, blessed with free institutions and a constitutional government, are the great masses of the manual-labor class to be enabled to have steady work at fair wages, to be kept from starvation, and their children from vice and debauchery, and to be furnished with that degree, not of mere reading and writing, but of *knowledge*, that shall fit them intelligently to do the duties and exercise the privileges of freemen; even to be intrusted with the dangerous right of suffrage?

For though we do not know why God, being infinitely merciful as well as wise, has so ordered it, it seems to be unquestionably his law, that even in civilized and Christian countries, the large mass of the population shall be fortunate, if, during their whole life, from infancy to old age, in health and sickness, they have enough of the commonest and coarsest food to keep themselves and their children from the continual gnawing of hunger—enough of the commonest and coarsest clothing to protect themselves and their little ones from indecent exposure and the bitter cold; and if they have over their heads the rudest shelter.

And He seems to have enacted this law—which no human community has yet found the means to abrogate—that when a country becomes populous, capital shall concentrate in the hands of a limited number of persons, and labor become more and more at its mercy, until mere manual labor, that of the weaver and iron-worker, and other artisans, eventually ceases to be worth more than a bare subsistence, and often, in great cities and vast extents of country, not even that, and goes or crawls about in rags, begging, and starving for want of work.

While every ox and horse can find work, and is worth being fed, it is not always so with man. To be employed, to have a chance to work at anything like fair wages, becomes the great engrossing object of a man's life. The capitalist can live without employing the laborer, and discharges him whenever that labor ceases to be profitable. At the moment when the weather is most inclement, provisions dearest, and rents highest, he turns him off to starve. If the day-laborer is taken sick, his wages stop. When old, he has no pension to retire upon. His children cannot be sent to school; for before their bones are hardened they must get to work lest they starve. The man, strong and able-bodied, works for a shilling or two a day, and the woman shivering over her little pan of coals, when the mercury drops far below zero, after her hungry children have wailed themselves to sleep, sews by the dim light of her lonely candle, for a bare pittance, selling her life to him who bargained only for the work of her needle.

Fathers and mothers slay their children, to have the burial-fees, that with the price of one child's life they may continue life in those that survive. Little girls with bare feet sweep the street-crossings, when the winter wind pinches them, and beg piteously for pennies of those who wear warm furs. Children grow up in squalid misery and brutal ignorance; want compels virgin and wife to prostitute themselves; women starve and freeze, and lean up against the walls of workhouses, like bundles of foul rags, all night long, and night after night, when the cold rain falls, and there chances to be no room for them within; and hundreds of families are crowded into a single building, rife with horrors and teeming with foul air and pestilence; where men, women and children huddle together in their filth; all ages and all colors sleeping indiscriminately together; while, in a great, free, Republican State, in the full vigor of its youth and strength, one person in every seventeen is a pauper receiving charity.

How to deal with this apparently inevitable evil and mortal disease is by far the most important of all social problems. What is to be done with pauperism and over-supply of labor? How is the life of any country to last, when brutality and drunken semi-barbarism vote, and hold offices in their gift, and by fit representatives of themselves control a government? How, if not wisdom and authority, but turbulence and low vice are to exalt to senatorships miscreants reeking with the odors and pollution of the hell, the prize-ring, the brothel, and the stock-exchange, where gambling is legalized and rascality is laudable?

Masonry will do all in its power, by direct exertion and co-operation, to improve and inform as well as to protect the people; to better their physical condition, relieve their miseries, supply their wants, and minister to their necessities. Let every Mason in this good work do all that may be in his power.

For it is true now, as it always was and always will be, that to be free is the same thing as to be pious, to be wise, to be temperate and just, to be frugal and abstinent, and to be magnanimous and brave; and to be the opposite of all these is the same as to be a slave. And it usually happens, by the appointment, and, as it were, retributive justice of the Deity, that that people which cannot govern themselves, and moderate their passions, but crouch under the slavery of their lusts and vices, are delivered up to the sway of those whom they abhor, and made to submit to an involuntary servitude.

And it is also sanctioned by the dictates of justice and by the constitution of Nature, that he who, from the imbecility or derangement of his intellect, is incapable of governing himself, should, like a minor, be committed to the government of another.

Above all things let us never forget that mankind constitutes one great brotherhood; all born to encounter suffering and sorrow, and therefore bound to sympathize with each other.

For no tower of Pride was ever yet high enough to lift its possessor above the trials and fears and frailities of humanity. No human hand ever built the wall, nor ever shall, that will keep out affliction, pain, and infirmity. Sickness and sorrow, trouble and death, are dispensations that level everything. They know none, high nor low. The chief wants of life, the great and grave necessities of the human soul, give exemption to none. They make all poor, all weak. They put supplication in the mouth of every human being, as truly as in that of the meanest beggar.

But the principle of misery is not an evil principle. We err, and the consequences teach us wisdom. All elements, all the laws of things around us, minister to this end; and through the paths of painful error and mistake, it is the design of Providence to lead us to truth and happiness. If erring only taught us to err; if mistakes confirmed us in imprudence; if the miseries caused by vicious indulgence had a natural tendency to make us more abject slaves of vice, then suffering would be wholly evil. But, on the contrary, all tends and is designed to produce amendment and improvement. Suffering is the discipline of virtue; of that which is infinitely better than happiness, and yet embraces in itself all essential happiness. It nourishes, invigorates, and perfects it. Virtue is the prize of the severely-contested race and hard-fought battle; and it is worth all the fatigue and wounds of the conflict. Man should go forth with a brave and strong heart, to battle with calamity. He is to master it, and not let it become *his* master. He is not to forsake the post of trial and of peril; but to stand firmly in his lot, until the great word of Providence shall bid him fly, or bid him sink. With resolution and courage the Mason is to do the work which it is appointed for him to do, looking through the dark cloud of human calamity, to the end that rises high and bright before him. The lot of sorrow is great and sublime. None suffer forever, nor for nought, nor without purpose. It is the ordinance of God's wisdom, and of His Infinite Love, to procure for us infinite happiness and glory.

Virtue is the truest liberty; nor is he free who stoops to passions; nor he in bondage who serves a noble master. Examples are the best and most lasting lectures; virtue the best example. He that hath done good deeds and set good precedents, in sincerity, is happy. Time shall not outlive his worth. He lives truly after death, whose good deeds are his pillars of remembrance; and no day but adds some grains to his heap of glory. Good works are seeds, that after sowing return us a continual harvest; and the memory of noble actions is more enduring than monuments of marble.

Life is a school. The world is neither prison nor penitentiary, nor a palace of ease, nor an amphitheatre for games and spectacles; but a place of instruction, and discipline. Life is given for moral and spiritual training; and the entire course of the great school of life is an education for virtue, happiness, and a future existence. The periods of Life are its terms; all human conditions, its forms; all human employments, its lessons. Families are the primary departments of this moral education; the various circles of society, its advanced stages; Kingdoms and Republics, its universities.

Riches and Poverty, Gayeties and Sorrows, Marriages and Funerals, the ties of life bound or broken, fit and fortunate, or untoward and painful, are all lessons. Events are not blindly and carelessly flung together. Providence does not school one man, and screen another from the fiery trial of its lessons. It has neither rich favorites nor poor victims. One event happeneth to all. One end and one design concern and urge all men.

The prosperous man has been at school. Perhaps he has thought that it was a great thing, and he a great personage; but he has been merely a pupil. He thought, perhaps, that he was Master, and had nothing to do, but to direct and command; but there was ever a Master above him, the Master of Life. *He* looks not at our splendid state, or our many pretensions, nor at the aids and appliances of our learning; but at our learning itself. He puts the poor and the rich upon the same form; and knows no difference between them, but their progress.

If from prosperity we have learned moderation, temperance, candor, modesty, gratitude to God, and generosity to man, then we are entitled to be honored and rewarded. If we have learned selfishness, self-indulgence, wrong-doing, and vice, to forget and overlook our less fortunate brother, and to scoff at the providence of God, then we are unworthy and dishonored, though we have been nursed in affluence, or taken our degrees from the lineage of an hundred noble descents; as truly so, in the eye of Heaven, and of all right-thinking men, as though we lay, victims of beggary and disease, in the hospital, by the hedge, or on the dung-hill. The most ordinary human equity looks not at the school, but at the scholar; and the equity of Heaven will not look beneath that mark.

The poor man also is at school. Let him take care that he

learn, rather than complain. Let him hold to his integrity, his candor, and his kindness of heart. Let him beware of envy, and of bondage, and keep his self-respect. The body's toil is nothing. Let him beware of the mind's drudgery and degradation. While he betters his condition if he can, let him be more anxious to better his soul. Let him be willing, while poor, and even if always poor, to learn poverty's great lessons, fortitude, cheerfulness, contentment, and implicit confidence in God's Providence. With these, and patience, calmness, self-command, disinterestedness, and affectionate kindness, the humble dwelling may be hallowed, and made more dear and noble than the loftiest palace. Let him, above all things, see that he lose not his independence. Let him not cast himself, a creature poorer than the poor, an indolent, helpless, despised beggar, on the kindness of others. Every man should choose to have God for his Master, rather than man; and escape not from this school, either by dishonesty or alms-taking, lest he fall into that state, worse than disgrace, where he can have no resepct for himself.

The ties of Society teach us to love one another. That is a miserable society, where the absence of affectionate kindness is sought to be supplied by punctilious decorum, graceful urbanity, and polished insincerity; where ambition, jealousy, and distrust rule, in place of simplicity, confidence, and kindness.

So, too, the social state teaches modesty and gentleness; and from neglect, and notice unworthily bestowed on others, and injustice, and the world's failure to appreciate us, we learn patience and quietness, to be superior to society's opinion, not cynical and bitter, but gentle, candid, and affectionate still.

Death is the great Teacher, stern, cold, inexorable, irresistible; whom the collected might of the world cannot stay or ward off. The breath, that parting from the lips of King or beggar, scarcely stirs the hushed air, cannot be bought, or brought back for a moment, with the wealth of Empires. What a lesson is this, teaching our frailty and feebleness, and an Infinite Power beyond us! It is a fearful lesson, that never becomes familiar. It walks through the earth in dread mystery, and lays it hands upon all. It is a universal lesson, that is read everywhere and by all men. Its message comes every year and every day. The past years are crowded with its sad and solemn mementoes; and death's finger traces its handwriting upon the walls of every human habitation.

It teaches us Duty; to act our part well; to fulfill the work assigned us. When one is dying, and after he is dead, there is but one question: *Has he lived well?* There is no evil in death but that which life makes.

There are hard lessons in the school of God's Providence; and yet the school of life is carefully adjusted, in all its arrangements and tasks, to man's powers and passions. There is no extravagance in its teachings; nor is anything done for the sake of present effect. The whole course of human life is a conflict with difficulties; and, if rightly conducted, a progress in improvement. It is never too late for man to learn. Not part only, but the whole, of life is a school. There never comes a time, even amidst the decays of age, when it is fit to lay aside the eagerness of acquisition, or the cheerfulness of endeavor. Man walks, all through the course of life, in patience and strife, and sometimes in darkness; for, from patience is to come perfection; from strife, triumph is to issue; from the cloud of darkness the lightning is to flash that shall open the way to eternity.

Let the Mason be faithful in the school of life, and to all its lessons! Let him not learn nothing, nor care not whether he learns or not. Let not the years pass over him, witnesses of only his sloth and indifference; or see him zealous to acquire everything but virtue. Nor let him labor only for himself; nor forget that the humblest man that lives is his brother, and hath a claim on his sympathies and kind offices; and that beneath the rough garments which labor wears may beat hearts as noble as throb under the stars of princes.

> God, who counts by souls, not stations,
> Loves and pities you and me;
> For to Him all vain distinctions
> Are as pebbles on the sea.

Nor are the other duties inculcated in this Degree of less importance. Truth, a Mason is early told, is a Divine attribute and the foundation of every virtue; and frankness, reliability, sincerity, straightforwardness, plain-dealing, are but different modes in which Truth develops itself. The dead, the absent, the innocent, and those that trust him, no Mason will deceive willingly. To all these he owes a nobler justice, in that they are the most certain trials of human Equity. Only the most abandoned of men, said

Cicero, will deceive him, who would have remained uninjured if he had not trusted. All the noble deeds that have beat their marches through succeeding ages have proceeded from men of truth and genuine courage. The man who is always true is both virtuous and wise; and thus possesses the greatest guards of safety: for the law has not power to strike the virtuous; nor can fortune subvert the wise.

The bases of Masonry being morality and virtue, it is by studying one and practising the other, that the conduct of a Mason becomes irreproachable. The good of Humanity being its principal object, disinterestedness is one of the first virtues that it requires of its members; for that is the source of justice and beneficence.

To pity the misfortunes of others; to be humble, but without meanness; to be proud, but without arrogance; to abjure every sentiment of hatred and revenge; to show himself magnanimous and liberal, without ostentation and without profusion; to be the enemy of vice; to pay homage to wisdom and virtue; to respect innocence; to be constant and patient in adversity, and modest in prosperity; to avoid every irregularity that stains the soul and distempers the body—it is by following these precepts that a Mason will become a good citizen, a faithful husband, a tender father, an obedient son, and a true brother; will honor friendship, and fulfill with ardor the duties which virtue and the social relations impose upon him.

It is because Masonry imposes upon us these duties that it is properly and significantly styled *work;* and he who imagines that he becomes a Mason by merely taking the first two or three Degrees, and that he may, having leisurely stepped upon that small elevation, thenceforward worthily wear the honors of Masonry, without labor or exertion, or self-denial or sacrifice, and that there is nothing to be *done* in Masonry, is strangely deceived.

Is it true that nothing remains to be done in Masonry?

Does one Brother no longer proceed by law against another Brother of his Lodge, in regard to matters that could be easily settled within the Masonic family circle?

Has the duel, that hideous heritage of barbarism, interdicted among Brethren by our fundamental laws, and denounced by the municipal code, yet disappeared from the soil we inhabit? Do Masons of high rank religiously refrain from it; or do they not, bowing to a corrupt public opinion, submit to its arbitrament, despite the scandal which it occasions to the Order, and in violation of the feeble restraint of their oath?

Do Masons no longer form uncharitable opinions of their Brethren, enter harsh judgments against them, and judge themselves by one rule and their Brethren by another?

Has Masonry any well-regulated system of charity? Has it done that which it should have done for the cause of education? Where are its schools, its academies, its colleges, its hospitals, and infirmaries?

Are political controversies now conducted with no violence and bitterness?

Do Masons refrain from defaming and denouncing their Brethren who differ with them in religious or political opinions?

What grand social problems or useful projects engage our attention at our communications? Where in our Lodges are lectures habitually delivered for the real instruction of the Brethren? Do not our sessions pass in the discussion of minor matters of business, the settlement of points of order and questions of mere administration, and the admission and advancement of Candidates, whom after their admission we take no pains to instruct?

In what Lodge are our ceremonies explained and elucidated; corrupted as they are by time, until their true features can scarcely be distinguished; and where are those great primitive truths of revelation taught, which Masonry has preserved to the world?

We have high dignities and sounding titles. Do their possessors qualify themselves to enlighten the world in respect to the aims and objects of Masonry? Descendants of those Initiates who governed empires, does your influence enter into practical life and operate efficiently in behalf of well-regulated and constitutional liberty?

Your debates should be but friendly conversations. You need concord, union, and peace. Why then do you retain among you men who excite rivalries and jealousies; why permit great and violent controversy and ambitious pretensions? How do your own words and acts agree? If your Masonry is a nullity, how can you exercise any influence on others?

Continually you praise each other, and utter elaborate and high-wrought eulogies upon the Order. Everywhere you assume that you are what you should be, and nowhere do you look upon yourselves as you are. Is it true that all our actions are so many acts of homage to virtue? Explore the recesses of your hearts; let us examine ourselves with an impartial eye, and make answer to our own questioning! Can we bear to ourselves the consoling testimony that we always rigidly perform our duties; that we even *half* perform them?

Let us away with this odious self-flattery! Let us be men, if we cannot be sages! The laws of Masonry, above others excellent, cannot wholly change men's natures. They enlighten them, they point out the true way; but they can lead them in it, only by repressing the fire of their passions, and subjugating their selfishness. Alas, these conquer, and Masonry is forgotten!

After praising each other all our lives, there are always excellent Brethren, who, over our coffins, shower unlimited eulogies. Every one of us who dies, however useless his life, has been a model of all the virtues, a very child of the celestial light. In Egypt, among our old Masters, where Masonry was more cultivated than vanity, no one could gain admittance to the sacred asylum of the tomb until he had passed under the most solemn judgment. A grave tribunal sat in judgment upon all, even the kings. They said to the dead, "Whoever thou art, give account to thy country of thy actions! What hast thou done with thy time and life? The law interrogates thee, thy country hears thee, Truth sits in judgment on thee!" Princes came there to be judged, escorted only by their virtues and their vices. A public accuser recounted, the history of the dead man's life, and threw the blaze of the torch of truth on all his actions. If it were adjudged that he had led an evil life, his memory was condemned in the presence of the nation, and his body was denied the honors of sepulture. What a lesson the old Masonry taught to the sons of the people!

Is it true that Masonry is effete; that the acacia, withered, affords no shade; that Masonry no longer marches in the advance-guard of Truth? No. Is freedom yet universal? Have ignorance and prejudice disappeared from the earth? Are there no longer enmities among men? Do cupidity and falsehood no longer exist? Do toleration and harmony prevail among religious and political sects? There are works yet left for Masonry to accomplish, greater than the twelve labors of Hercules; to advance ever

resolutely and steadily; to enlighten the minds of the people, to
reconstruct society, to reform the laws, and to improve the public
morals. The eternity in front of it is as infinite as the one behind. And Masonry cannot cease to labor in the cause of social
progress, without ceasing to be true to itself, without ceasing to be
Masonry.

T. D. J. C. G.

XII

GRAND MASTER ARCHITECT.

[Master Architect.]

THE great duties that are inculcated by the lessons taught by the working-instruments of a Grand Master Architect, demanding so much of us, and taking for granted the capacity to perform them faithfully and fully, bring us at once to reflect upon the dignity of human nature, and the vast powers and capacities of the human soul; and to that theme we invite your attention in this Degree. Let us begin to rise from earth toward the Stars.

Evermore the human soul struggles toward the light, toward God, and the Infinite. It is especially so in its afflictions. Words go but a little way into the depths of sorrow. The thoughts that writhe there in silence, that go into the stillness of Infinitude and Eternity, have no emblems. Thoughts enough come there, such as no tongue ever uttered. They do not so much want human sympathy, as higher help. There is a loneliness in deep sorrow which the Deity alone can relieve. Alone, the mind wrestles with the great problem of calamity, and seeks the solution from the Infinite Providence of Heaven, and thus is led directly to God.

There are many things in us of which we are not distinctly conscious. To waken that slumbering consciousness into life, and so to lead the soul up to the Light, is one office of every great ministration to human nature, whether its vehicle be the pen, the pencil, or the tongue. We are unconscious of the intensity and awfulness of the life within us. Health and sickness, joy and sorrow, success and disappointment, life and death, love and loss, are

189

familiar words upon our lips; and we do not know to what depths they point within us.

We seem never to know what *any* thing means or is worth until we have lost it. Many an organ, nerve, and fibre in our bodily frame performs its silent part for years, and we are quite unconscious of its value. It is not until it is injured that we discover that value, and find how essential it was to our happiness and comfort. We never know the full significance of the words, "property," "ease," and "health;" the wealth of meaning in the fond epithets, "parent," "child," "beloved," and "friend," until the thing or the person is taken away; until, in place of the bright, visible being, comes the awful and desolate shadow, where *nothing* is: where we stretch out our hands in vain, and strain our eyes upon dark and dismal vacuity. Yet, in that vacuity, we do not *lose* the object that we loved. It becomes only the more real to us. Our blessings not only brighten when they depart, but are fixed in enduring reality; and love and friendship receive their everlasting seal under the cold impress of death.

A dim consciousness of infinite mystery and grandeur lies beneath all the commonplace of life. There is an awfulness and a majesty around us, in all our little worldliness. The rude peasant from the Apennines, asleep at the foot of a pillar in a majestic Roman church, seems not to hear or see, but to dream only of the herd he feeds or the ground he tills in the mountains. But the choral symphonies fall softly upon his ear, and the gilded arches are dimly seen through his half-slumbering eyelids.

So the soul, however given up to the occupations of daily life, cannot quite lose the sense of where it is, and of what is above it and around it. The scene of its actual engagements may be small; the path of its steps, beaten and familiar; the objects it handles, easily spanned, and quite worn out with daily uses. So it may be, and amidst such things that we all live. So we live our little life; but Heaven is above us and all around and close to us; and Eternity is before us and behind us; and suns and stars are silent witnesses and watchers over us. We are enfolded by Infinity. Infinite Powers and Infinite spaces lie all around us. The dread arch of Mystery spreads over us, and no voice ever pierced it. Eternity is enthroned amid Heaven's myriad starry heights; and no utterance or word ever came from those far-off and silent spaces. Above, is that awful majesty; around us, everywhere, it stretches off into infinity; and beneath it is this little struggle of life, this poor day's conflict, this busy ant-hill of Time.

But from that ant-hill, not only the talk of the streets, the sounds of music and revelling, the stir and tread of a multitude, the shout of joy and the shriek of agony go up into the silent and all-surrounding Infinitude; but also, amidst the stir and noise of visible life, from the inmost bosom of the visible man, there goes up an imploring call, a beseeching cry, an asking, unuttered, and unutterable, for revelation, wailingly and in almost speechless agony praying the dread arch of mystery to break, and the stars that roll above the waves of mortal trouble, to speak; the enthroned majesty of those awful heights to find a voice; the mysterious and reserved heavens to come near; and all to tell us what they alone know; to give us information of the loved and lost; to make known to us what we are, and whither we are going.

Man is encompassed with a dome of incomprehensible wonders. In him and about him is that which should fill his life with majesty and sacredness. Something of sublimity and sanctity has thus flashed down from heaven into the heart of every one that lives. There is no being so base and abandoned but hath some traits of that sacredness left upon him; something, so much perhaps in discordance with his general repute, that he hides it from all around him; some sanctuary in his soul, where no one may enter; some sacred inclosure, where the memory of a child is, or the image of a venerated parent, or the remembrance of a pure love, or the echo of some word of kindness once spoken to him; an echo that will never die away.

Life is no negative, or superficial or worldly existence. Our steps are evermore haunted with thoughts, far beyond their own range, which some have regarded as the reminiscences of a pre-existent state. So it is with us all, in the beaten and worn track of this worldly pilgrimage. There is more here, than the world we live in. It is not all of life to live. An unseen and infinite presence is here; a sense of something greater than we possess; a seeking, through all the void wastes of life, for a good beyond it; a crying out of the heart for interpretation; a memory of the dead, touching continually some vibrating thread in this great tissue of mystery.

We all not only have better intimations, but are capable of better things than we know. The pressure of some great emergency would develop in us powers, beyond the worldly bias of our spirits; and Heaven so deals with us, from time to time, as to call forth those better things. There is hardly a family in the world so selfish, but that, if one in it were doomed to die—one, to be selected by the others,—it would be utterly impossible for its members, parents and children, to choose out that victim; but that each would say, "I will die; but I cannot choose." And in how many, if that dire extremity had come, would not one and another step forth, freed from the vile meshes of ordinary selfishness, and say, like the Roman father and son, "Let the blow fall on me!" There are greater and better things in us all, than the world takes account of, or than *we* take note of; if we would but find them out. And it is one part of our Masonic culture to *find* these traits of power and sublime devotion, to revive these faded impressions of generosity and self-sacrifice, the almost squandered bequests of God's love and kindness to our souls; and to induce us to yield ourselves to their guidance and control.

Upon all conditions of men presses down one impartial law. To all situations, to all fortunes, high or low, the *mind* gives their character. They are, in effect, not what they are in themselves, but what they are to the feeling of their possessors. The King may be mean, degraded, miserable; the slave of ambition, fear, voluptuousness, and every low passion. The Peasant may be the real Monarch, the moral master of his fate, a free and lofty being, more than a Prince in happiness, more than a King in honor.

Man is no bubble upon the sea of his fortunes, helpless and irresponsible upon the tide of events. Out of the same circumstances, different men bring totally different results. The same difficulty, distress, poverty, or misfortune, that breaks down one man, builds up another and makes him strong. It is the very attribute and glory of a man, that he can bend the circumstances of his condition to the intellectual and moral purposes of his nature, and it is the power and mastery of his will that chiefly distinguish him from the brute.

The faculty of moral will, developed in the child, is a new element of his nature. It is a new power brought upon the scene, and a ruling power, delegated from Heaven. Never was a human being sunk so low that he had not, by God's gift, the power to rise. Because God commands him to rise, it is certain that he *can* rise.

Every man has the power, and should use it, to make all situations, trials, and temptations instruments to promote his virtue and happiness; and is so far from being the creature of circumstances, that *he* creates and controls *them,* making them to be all that they are, of evil or of good, to him as a moral being.

Life is what we make it, and the world is what we make it. The eyes of the cheerful and of the melancholy man are fixed upon the same creation; but very different are the aspects which it bears to them. To the one, it is all beauty and gladness; the waves of ocean roll in light, and the mountains are covered with day. Life, to him, flashes, rejoicing, upon every flower and every tree that trembles in the breeze. There is more to him, everywhere, than the eye sees; a presence of profound joy on hill and valley, and bright, dancing water. The other idly or mournfully gazes at the same scene, and everything wears a dull, dim, and sickly aspect. The murmuring of the brooks is a discord to him, the great roar of the sea has an angry and threatening emphasis, the solemn music of the pines sings the requiem of his departed happiness; the cheerful light shines garishly upon his eyes and offends him. The great train of the seasons passes before him like a funeral procession; and he sighs, and turns impatiently away. The eye makes that which it looks upon; the ear makes its own melodies and discords; the world without reflects the world within.

Let the Mason never forget that life and the world are what we make them by our social character; by our adaptation, or want of adaptation to the social conditions, relationships, and pursuits of the world. To the selfish, the cold, and the insensible, to the haughty and presuming, to the proud, who demand more than they are likely to receive, to the jealous, ever afraid they shall not receive enough, to those who are unreasonably sensitive about the good or ill opinions of others, to all violators of the social laws, the rude, the violent, the dishonest, and the sensual,—to all these, the social condition, from its very nature, will present annoyances, disappointments, and pains, appropriate to their several characters. The benevolent affections will not revolve around selfishness; the cold-hearted must expect to meet coldness; the proud, haughtiness; the passionate, anger; and the violent, rudeness. Those who forget the rights of others, must not be surprised if their own are forgotten; and those who stoop to the lowest embraces of sense must not wonder, if others are not concerned to find their prostrate honor, and lift it up to the remembrance and respect of the world.

To the gentle, many will be gentle; to the kind, many will be kind. A good man will find that there is goodness in the world; an honest man will find that there is honesty in the world; and a man of principle will find principle and integrity in the minds of others.

There are no blessings which the mind may not convert into the bitterest of evils; and no trials which it may not transform into the noblest and divinest blessings. There are no temptations from which assailed virtue may not gain strength, instead of falling before them, vanquished and subdued. It is true that temptations have a great power, and virtue often falls; but the might of these temptations lies not in themselves, but in the feebleness of our own virtue, and the weakness of our own hearts. We rely too much on the strength of our ramparts and bastions, and allow the enemy to make his approaches, by trench and parallel, at his leisure. The offer of dishonest gain and guilty pleasure makes the honest man more honest, and the pure man more pure. They raise his virtue to the height of towering indignation. The fair occasion, the safe opportunity, the tempting chance become the defeat and disgrace of the tempter. The honest and upright man does not wait until temptation has made its approaches and mounted its batteries on the last parallel.

But to the impure, the dishonest, the false-hearted, the corrupt, and the sensual, occasions come every day, and in every scene, and through every avenue of thought and imagination. He is prepared to capitulate before the first approach is commenced; and sends out the white flag when the enemy's advance comes in sight of his walls. He *makes* occasions; or, if opportunities come not, evil *thoughts* come, and he throws wide open the gates of his heart and welcomes those bad visitors, and entertains them with a lavish hospitality.

The business of the world absorbs, corrupts, and degrades one mind, while in another it feeds and nurses the noblest independence, integrity, and generosity. Pleasure is a poison to some, and a healthful refreshment to others. To one, the world is a great harmony, like a noble strain of music with infinite modulations; to another, it is a huge factory, the clash and clang of whose machinery jars upon his ears and frets him to madness. Life is sub-

stantially the same thing to all who partake of its lot. Yet some
rise to virtue and glory; while others, undergoing the same discipline, and enjoying the same privileges, sink to shame and perdition.

Thorough, faithful, and honest endeavor to improve, is always
successful, and the highest happiness. To sigh sentimentally over
human misfortune, is fit only for the mind's childhood; and the
mind's misery is chiefly its own fault; appointed, under the good
Providence of God, as the punisher and corrector of its fault. In
the long run, the mind will be happy, just in proportion to its
fidelity and wisdom. When it is miserable, it has planted the
thorns in its own path; it grasps them, and cries out in loud complaint; and that complaint is but the louder *confession* that the
thorns which grew there, *it* planted.

A certain kind and degree of spirituality enter into the largest
part of even the most ordinary life. You can carry on no business, without some faith in man. You cannot even dig in the
ground, without a reliance on the unseen result. You cannot
think or reason or even step, without confiding in the inward,
spiritual principles of your nature. All the affections and bonds,
and hopes and interests of life centre in the spiritual; and you
know that if that central bond were broken, the world would rush
to chaos.

Believe that there is a God; that He is our father; that He has
a paternal interest in our welfare and improvement; that He has
given us powers, by means of which we may escape from sin and
ruin; that He has destined us to a future life of endless progress
toward perfection and a knowledge of Himself—believe this, as
every Mason should, and you can live calmly, endure patiently,
labor resolutely, deny yourselves cheerfully, hope steadfastly, and
be conquerors in the great struggle of life. Take away any one
of these principles, and what remains for us? Say that there is
no God; or no way opened for hope and reformation and triumph,
no heaven to come, no rest for the weary, no home in the bosom
of God for the afflicted and disconsolate soul; or that God is but
an ugly blind *Chance* that stabs in the dark; or a *some*what that
is, when attempted to be defined, a *no*what, emotionless, passion-
less, the Supreme *Apathy* to which all things, good and evil, are
alike indifferent; or a jealous God who revengefully visits the sins
of the fathers on the children, and when the fathers have eaten

sour grapes, sets the children's teeth on edge; an arbitrary supreme *Will*, that has made it *right* to be virtuous, and wrong to lie and steal, because It *pleased* to *make* it so rather than otherwise, retaining the power to reverse the law; or a fickle, vacillating, inconstant Deity, or a cruel, bloodthirsty, savage Hebrew or Puritanic one; and we are but the sport of chance and the victims of despair; hapless wanderers upon the face of a desolate, forsaken, or accursed and hated earth; surrounded by darkness, struggling with obstacles, toiling for barren results and empty purposes, distracted with doubts, and misled by false gleams of light; wanderers with no way, no prospect, no home; doomed and deserted mariners on a dark and stormy sea, without compass or course, to whom no stars appear; tossing helmless upon the weltering, angry waves, with no blessed haven in the distance whose guiding-star invites us to its welcome rest.

The religious faith thus taught by Masonry is indispensable to the attainment of the great ends of life; and must therefore have been designed to be a part of it. We are made for this faith; and there must be something, somewhere, for us to believe in. We cannot grow healthfully, nor live happily, without it. It is therefore *true*. If we could cut off from any soul all the principles taught by Masonry, the faith in a God, in immortality, in virtue, in essential rectitude, that soul would sink into sin, misery, darkness, and ruin. If we could cut off all sense of these truths, the man would sink at once to the grade of the animal.

No man can suffer and be patient, can struggle and conquer, can improve and be happy, otherwise than as the swine are, without conscience, without hope, without a reliance on a just, wise, and beneficent God. We must, of necessity, embrace the great truths taught by Masonry, and live by them, to live happily. *"I put my trust in God,"* is the protest of Masonry against the belief in a cruel, angry, and revengeful God, to be feared and not reverenced by His creatures.

Society, in its great relations, is as much the creation of Heaven as is the system of the Universe. If that bond of gravitation that holds all worlds and systems together, were suddenly severed, the universe would fly into wild and boundless chaos. And if we were to sever all the moral bonds that hold society together; if we could cut off from it every conviction of Truth and Integrity, of an authority above it, and of a conscience within it, it would immediately rush to disorder and frightful anarchy and ruin. The religion we teach is therefore as really a principle of things, and as certain and true, as gravitation.

Faith in moral principles, in virtue, and in God, is as necessary for the guidance of a man, as instinct is for the guidance of an animal. And therefore this faith, as a principle of man's nature, has a mission as truly authentic in God's Providence, as the principle of instinct. The pleasures of the soul, too, must depend on certain principles. They must recognize a soul, its properties and responsibilities, a conscience, and the sense of an authority above us; and these are the principles of faith. No man can suffer and be patient, can struggle and conquer, can improve and be happy, without conscience, without hope, without a reliance on a just, wise, and beneficent God. We must of necessity embrace the great truths taught by Masonry, and live by them, to live happily. Everything in the universe has fixed and certain laws and principles for its action;—the star in its orbit, the animal in its activity, the physical man in his functions. And he has likewise fixed and certain laws and principles as a spiritual being. His soul does not die for want of aliment or guidance. For the rational soul there is ample provision. From the lofty pine, rocked in the darkening tempest, the cry of the young raven is heard; and it would be most strange if there were no answer for the cry and call of the soul, tortured by want and sorrow and agony. The total rejection of all moral and religious belief would strike out a principle from human nature, as essential to it as gravitation to the stars, instinct to animal life, the circulation of the blood to the human body.

God has ordained that life shall be a social state. We are members of a civil community. The life of that community depends upon its moral condition. Public spirit, intelligence, uprightness, temperance, kindness, domestic purity, will make it a happy community, and give it prosperity and continuance. Wide-spread selfishness, dishonesty, intemperance, libertinism, corruption, and crime, will make it miserable, and bring about dissolution and speedy ruin. A whole people lives one life; one mighty heart heaves in its bosom; it is one great pulse of existence that throbs there. One stream of life flows there, with ten thousand intermingled branches and channels, through all the homes of human love. One sound as of many waters, a rapturous jubilee or a mournful sighing, comes up from the congregated dwellings of a whole nation.

The Public is no vague abstraction; nor should that which is done against that Public, against public interest, law, or virtue, press but lightly on the conscience. It is but a vast expansion of individual life; an ocean of tears, an atmosphere of sighs, or a great whole of joy and gladness. It suffers with the suffering of millions; it rejoices with the joy of millions. What a vast crime does he commit,—private man or public man, agent or contractor, legislator or magistrate, secretary or president,—who dares, with indignity and wrong, to strike the bosom of the Public Welfare, to encourage venality and corruption, and shameful sale of the elective franchise, or of office; to sow dissension, and to weaken the bonds of amity that bind a Nation together! What a huge iniquity, he who, with vices like the daggers of a parricide, dares to pierce that mighty heart, in which the ocean of existence is flowing!

What an unequalled interest lies in the virtue of every one whom we love! In his virtue, nowhere but in his virtue, is garnered up the incomparable treasure. What care we for brother or friend, compared with what we care for his honor, his fidelity, his reputation, his kindness? How venerable is the rectitude of a parent! How sacred his reputation! No blight that can fall upon a child, is like a parent's dishonor. Heathen or Christian, every parent would have his child do well; and pours out upon him all the fullness of parental love, in the one desire that he *may* do well; that he may be worthy of his cares, and his freely bestowed pains; that he may walk in the way of honor and happiness. In that way he cannot walk one step without virtue. Such is life, in its relationships. A thousand ties embrace it, like the fine nerves of a delicate organization; like the strings of an instrument capable of sweet melodies, but easily put out of tune or broken, by rudeness, anger, and selfish indulgence.

If life could, by any process, be made insensible to pain and pleasure; if the human heart were hard as adamant, then avarice, ambition, and sensuality might channel out their paths in it, and make it their beaten way; and none would wonder or protest. If we could be patient under the load of a mere worldly life; if we could bear that burden as the beasts bear it; then, *like* beasts, we might bend all our thoughts to the earth; and no call from the great Heavens above us would startle us from our plodding and earthly course.

But we art *not* insensible brutes, who can refuse the call of reason and conscience. The soul is capable of remorse. When the great dispensations of life press down upon us, we weep, and suffer and sorrow. And sorrow and agony desire other companionships than worldliness and irreligion. We are not willing to bear those burdens of the heart, fear, anxiety, disappointment, and trouble, without any object or use. We are not willing to suffer, to be sick and afflicted, to have our days and months lost to comfort and joy, and overshadowed with calamity and grief, without advantage or compensation; to barter away the dearest treasures, the very sufferings, of the heart; to sell the life-blood from failing frame and fading cheek, our tears of bitterness and groans of anguish, for nothing. Human nature, frail, feeling, sensitive, and sorrowing, cannot bear to suffer for nought.

Everywhere, human life is a great and solemn dispensation. Man, suffering, enjoying, loving, hating, hoping, and fearing, chained to the earth and yet exploring the far recesses of the universe, has the power to commune with God and His angels. Around this great action of existence the curtains of Time are drawn; but there are openings through them which give us glimpses of eternity. God looks down upon this scene of human probation. The wise and the good in all ages have interposed for it, with their teachings and their blood. Everything that exists around us, every movement in nature, every counsel of Providence, every interposition of God, centres upon one point—the fidelity of man. And even if the ghosts of the departed and remembered could come at midnight through the barred doors of our dwellings, and the shrouded dead should glide through the aisles of our churches and sit in our Masonic Temples, their teachings would be no more eloquent and impressive than the dread realities of life; than those memories of misspent years, those ghosts of departed opportunities, that, pointing to our conscience and eternity, cry continually in our ears, *"Work while the day lasts! for the night of death cometh, in which no man can work."*

There are no tokens of public mourning for the calamity of the soul. Men weep when the body dies; and when it is borne to its last rest, they follow it with sad and mournful procession. But for the dying soul there is no open lamentation; for the lost soul there are no obsequies.

And yet the mind and soul of man have a value which nothing else has. They are worth a care which nothing else is worth; and to the single, solitary individual, they ought to possess an interest which nothing else possesses. The stored treasures of the heart, the unfathomable mines that are in the soul to be wrought, the broad and boundless realms of Thought, the freighted argosy of man's hopes and best affections, are brighter than gold and dearer than treasure.

And yet the mind is in reality little known or considered. It is *all* which man permanently *is*, his inward being, his divine energy, his immortal thought, his boundless capacity, his infinite aspiration; and nevertheless, few value it for what it is worth. Few see a brother-mind in others, through the rags with which poverty has clothed it, beneath the crushing burdens of life, amidst the close pressure of worldly troubles, wants and sorrows. Few acknowledge and cheer it in that humble blot, and feel that the nobility of earth, and the commencing glory of Heaven are there.

Men do not feel the worth of their own souls. They are proud of their mental powers; but the intrinsic, inner, infinite *worth* of their own minds they do not perceive. The poor man, admitted to a palace, feels, lofty and immortal being as he is, like a mere ordinary thing amid the splendors that surround him. He sees the carriage of wealth roll by him, and forgets the intrinsic and eternal dignity of his own mind in a poor and degrading envy, and feels as an humbler creature, because others are above him, not in mind, but in mensuration. Men respect themselves, according as they are more wealthy, higher in rank or office, loftier in the world's opinion, able to command more votes, more the favorites of the people or of Power.

The difference among men is not so much in their nature and intrinsic power, as in the faculty of communication. Some have the capacity of uttering and embodying in words their thoughts. All men, more or less, *feel* those thoughts. The glory of genius and the rapture of virtue, when rightly revealed, are diffused and shared among unnumbered minds. When eloquence and poetry speak; when those glorious arts, statuary, painting, and music, take audible or visible shape; when patriotism, charity, and virtue speak with a thrilling potency, the hearts of thousands glow with a kindred joy and ecstasy. If it were not so, there would be no eloquence; for eloquence is that to which other hearts respond; it is the faculty and power of *making* other hearts respond. No one is so low or degraded, as not sometimes to be touched with the beauty of goodness. No heart is made of materials so common, or even base, as not sometimes to respond, through every chord of it, to the call of honor, patriotism, generosity, and virtue. The poor African Slave will die for the master or mistress, or in defence of the children, whom he loves. The poor, lost, scorned, abandoned, outcast woman will, without expectation of reward, nurse those who are dying on every hand, utter strangers to her, with a contagious and horrid pestilence. The pickpocket will scale burning walls to rescue child or woman, unknown to him, from the ravenous flames.

Most glorious is this capacity! A power to commune with God and His Angels; a reflection of the Uncreated Light; a mirror that can collect and concentrate upon itself all the moral splendors of the Universe. It is the soul alone that gives any value to the things of this world; and it is only by raising the soul to its just elevation above all other things, that we can look rightly upon the purposes of this earth. No sceptre nor throne, nor structure of ages, nor broad empire, can compare with the wonders and grandeurs of a single thought. That alone, of all things that have been made, comprehends the Maker of all. That alone is the key which unlocks all the treasures of the Universe; the power that reigns over Space, Time, and Eternity. That, under God, is the Sovereign Dispenser to man of all the blessings and glories that lie within the compass of possession, or the range of possibility. Virtue, Heaven, and Immortality exist not, nor ever will exist for us except as they exist and will exist, in the perception, feeling, and thought of the glorious mind.

My Brother, in the hope that you have listened to and understood the Instruction and Lecture of this Degree, and that you feel the dignity of your own nature and the vast capacities of your own soul for good or evil, I proceed briefly to communicate to you the remaining instruction of this Degree.

The Hebrew word, in the old Hebrew and Samaritan character, suspended in the East, over the five columns, is Adonaï, one of the names of God, usually translated Lord; and which the Hebrews, in reading, always substitute for the True Name, which is for them ineffable.

The five columns, in the five different orders of architecture, are emblematical to us of the five principal divisions of the Ancient and Accepted Scottish Rite:

1.—The *Tuscan,* of the three blue Degrees, or the primitive Masonry.

2.—The *Doric,* of the ineffable Degrees, from the fourth to the fourteenth, inclusive.

3.—The *Ionic,* of the fifteenth and sixteenth, or second temple Degrees.

4.—The *Corinthian,* of the seventeenth and eighteenth Degrees, or those of the new law.

5.—The *Composite,* of the philosophical and chivalric Degrees intermingled, from the nineteenth to the thirty-second, inclusive.

The North Star, always fixed and immutable for us, represents the point in the centre of the circle, or the Deity in the centre of the Universe. It is the especial symbol of duty and of faith. To it, and the seven that continually revolve around it, mystical meanings are attached, which you will learn hereafter, if you should be permitted to advance, when you are made acquainted with the philosophical doctrines of the Hebrews.

The Morning Star, rising in the East, Jupiter, called by the Hebrews Tsadōc or Tsydyk, *Just,* is an emblem to us of the ever-approaching dawn of perfection and Masonic light.

The three great lights of the Lodge are symbols to us of the Power, Wisdom, and Beneficence of the Deity. They are also symbols of the first three *Sephiroth,* or Emanations of the Deity, according to the Kabalah, *Kether,* the omnipotent divine *will; Chochmah,* the divine intellectual *power* to *generate* thought, and *Binah,* the divine intellectual *capacity* to *produce* it—the two latter, usually translated *Wisdom* and *Understanding,* being the *active* and the *passive,* the *positive* and the *negative,* which we do not yet endeavor to explain to you. They are the columns Jachin and Boaz, that stand at the entrance to the Masonic Temple.

In another aspect of this Degree, the Chief of the Architects [רב בנים, Rab Banaim,] symbolizes the constitutional executive head and chief of a free government; and the Degree teaches us that no free government can long endure, when the people cease to select for their magistrates the best and the wisest of their statesmen; when, passing these by, they permit factions or sordid interests to select for them the small, the low, the ignoble, and the obscure, and into such hands commit the country's destinies. There is, after all, a "divine right" to govern; and it is vested in the ablest, wisest, best, of every nation. "Counsel is mine, and sound wisdom: I am understanding: I am power: by me kings do reign, and princes decree justice; by me princes rule, and nobles, even all the magistrates of the earth."

For the present, my Brother, let this suffice. We welcome you among us, to this peaceful retreat of virtue, to a participation in our privileges, to a share in our joys and our sorrows.

XIII.

ROYAL ARCH OF SOLOMON.

WHETHER the legend and history of this Degree are historically true, or but an allegory, containing in itself a deeper truth and a profounder meaning, we shall not now debate. If it be but a legendary myth, you must find out for yourself what it means. It is certain that the word which the Hebrews are not now permitted to pronounce was in common use by Abraham, Lot, Isaac, Jacob, Laban, Rebecca, and even among tribes foreign to the Hebrews, before the time of Moses; and that it recurs a hundred times in the lyrical effusions of David and other Hebrew poets.

We know that for many centuries the Hebrews have been forbidden to pronounce the Sacred Name; that wherever it occurs, they have for ages read the word *Adonaï* instead; and that under it, when the masoretic points, which represent the vowels, came to be used, they placed those which belonged to the latter word. The possession of the true pronunciation was deemed to confer on him who had it extraordinary and supernatural powers; and the Word itself, worn upon the person, was regarded as an amulet, a protection against personal danger, sickness, and evil spirits. We know that all this was a vain superstition, natural to a rude people, necessarily disappearing as the intellect of man became enlightened; and wholly unworthy of a Mason.

It is noticeable that this notion of the sanctity of the Divine Name or Creative Word was common to all the ancient nations. The Sacred Word HOM was supposed by the ancient Persians (who were among the earliest emigrants from Northern India) to

204

be pregnant with a mysterious power; and they taught that by its utterance the world was created. In India it was forbidden to pronounce the word AUM or OM, the Sacred Name of the One Deity, manifested as Brahma, Vishna, and Seeva.

These superstitious notions in regard to the efficacy of the Word, and the prohibition against pronouncing it, could, being errors, have formed no part of the pure primitive religion, or of the esoteric doctrine taught by Moses, and the full knowledge of which was confined to the Initiates; unless the whole was but an ingenious invention for the concealment of some other Name or truth, the interpretation and meaning whereof was made known only to the *select few*. If so, the common notions in regard to the Word grew up in the minds of the people, like other errors and fables among all the ancient nations, out of original truths and symbols and allegories misunderstood. So it has always been that allegories, intended as vehicles of truth, to be understood by the sages, have become or bred errors, by being literally accepted.

It is true, that before the masoretic points were invented (which was after the beginning of the Christian era), the pronunciation of a word in the Hebrew language could not be known from the characters in which it was written. It was, therefore, *possible* for that of the name of the Deity to have been forgotten and lost. It is certain that its true pronunciation is not that represented by the word Jehovah; and therefore that *that* is not the true name of Deity, nor the Ineffable Word.

The ancient symbols and allegories always had more than one interpretation. They always had a *double* meaning, and sometimes *more* than two, one serving as the envelope of the other. Thus the *pronunciation* of the word was a symbol; and that pronunciation and the word itself were lost, when the knowledge of the true nature and attributes of God faded out of the minds of the Jewish people. That is *one* interpretation—*true, but not the inner and profoundest one.*

Men were figuratively said to forget the *name* of God, when they lost that *knowledge,* and worshipped the heathen deities, and burned incense to them on the high places, and passed their children through the fire to Moloch.

Thus the attempts of the ancient Israelites and of the Initiates to ascertain the True Name of the Deity, and its pronunciation, and the loss of the True Word, are an allegory, in which are rep-

resented the general ignorance of the true nature and attributes
of God, the proneness of the people of Judah and Israel to worship other deities, and the low and erroneous and dishonoring
notions of the Grand Architect of the Universe, which all shared
except a few favored persons; for even Solomon built altars and
sacrificed to Astarat, the goddess of the Tsidunim, and Malcūm,
the Aamūnite god, and built high places for Kamūs, the Moabite
deity, and Malec the god of the Beni-Aamūn. The true nature of
God was unknown to them, like His name; and they worshipped
the calves of Jeroboam, as in the desert they did that made for
them by Aarūn.

The mass of the Hebrews did not believe in the existence of one
only God until a late period in their history. Their early and
popular ideas of the Deity were singularly low and unworthy.
Even while Moses was receiving the law upon Mount Sinai, they
forced Aarūn to make them an image of the Egyptian god Apis,
and fell down and adored it. They were ever ready to return to
the worship of the gods of the Mitzraim; and soon after the death
of Joshua they became devout worshippers of the false gods of all
the surrounding nations. "Ye have borne," Amos, the prophet,
said to them, speaking of their forty years' journeying in the desert, under Moses, "the tabernacle of your Malec and Kaiūn your
idols, the star of your god, which ye made to yourselves."

Among them, as among other nations, the conceptions of God
formed by individuals varied according to their intellectual and
spiritual capacities; poor and imperfect, and investing God with
the commonest and coarest attributes of humanity, among the
ignorant and coarse; pure and lofty among the virtuous and richly
gifted. These conceptions gradually improved and became purified and ennobled, as the nation advanced in civilization—being
lowest in the historical books, amended in the prophetic writings,
and reaching their highest elevation among the poets.

Among *all* the ancient nations there was one faith and one
idea of Deity for the enlightened, intelligent, and educated, and
another for the common people. To this rule the Hebrews were no
exception. Yehovah, to the mass of the people, was like the gods
of the nations around them, except that he was the *peculiar* God,
first of the family of Abraham, of that of Isaac, and of that of
Jacob, and afterward the *National* God; and, as they believed,
more powerful than the other gods of the same nature worshipped

by their neighbors—"Who among the Baalim is like unto thee, O Yehovah?"—expressed their whole creed.

The Deity of the early Hebrews talked to Adam and Eve in the garden of delight, as he walked in it in the cool of the day; he conversed with Kayin; he sat and ate with Abraham in his tent; that patriarch required a visible token, before he would believe in his positive promise; he permitted Abraham to expostulate with him, and to induce him to change his first determination in regard to Sodom; he wrestled with Jacob; he showed Moses his person, though not his face; he dictated the minutest police regulations and the dimensions of the tabernacle and its furniture, to the Israelites; he insisted on and delighted in sacrifices and burnt-offerings; he was angry, jealous, and revengeful, as well as wavering and irresolute; he allowed Moses to reason him out of his fixed resolution utterly to destroy his people; he commanded the performance of the most shocking and hideous acts of cruelty and barbarity. He hardened the heart of Pharaoh; he repented of the evil that he had said he would do unto the people of Nineveh; and he did it not, to the disgust and anger of Jonah.

Such were the popular notions of the Deity; and either the priests had none better, or took little trouble to correct these notions; or the popular intellect was not enough enlarged to enable them to entertain any higher conceptions of the Almighty.

But such were not the ideas of the intellectual and enlightened few among the Hebrews. It is certain that *they* possessed a knowledge of the true nature and attributes of God; as the same class of men did among the other nations—Zoroaster, Menu, Confucius, Socrates, and Plato. But their doctrines on this subject were esoteric; they did not communicate them to the people at large, but only to a favored few; and as they were communicated in Egypt and India, in Persia and Phœnicia, in Greece and Samothrace, in the greater mysteries, to the Initiates.

The communication of this knowledge and other secrets, some of which are perhaps lost, constituted, under other names, what we now call *Masonry,* or *Free* or *Frank-Masonry.* That knowledge was, in one sense, *the Lost Word,* which was made known to the Grand Elect, Perfect, and Sublime Masons. It would be folly to pretend that the *forms* of Masonry were the same in those ages as they are now. The present name of the Order, and its titles, and the names of the Degrees now in use, were not then known.

Even Blue Masonry cannot trace back its *authentic* history, *with its present Degrees,* further than the year 1700, *if so far.* But, by whatever *name* it was known in this or the other country, Masonry existed as it now exists, the same in spirit and at heart, not only when Solomon builded the temple, but centuries before—before even the first colonies emigrated into Southern India, Persia, and Egypt, from the cradle of the human race.

The Supreme, Self-existent, Eternal, All-wise, All-powerful, Infinitely Good, Pitying, Beneficent, and Merciful Creator and Preserver of the Universe was the same, by whatever name he was called, to the intellectual and enlightened men of all nations. The name was nothing, if not a symbol and representative hiero-glyph of his nature and attributes. The name AL represented his remoteness *above* men, his *inaccessibility;* BAL and BALA, his *might;* ALOHIM, his various *potencies;* IHUH, *existence* and the *generation* of things. None of his names, among the Orientals, were the symbols of a divinely infinite love and tenderness, and all-embracing mercy. As MOLOCH or MALEK he was but an omnipotent *monarch,* a tremendous and irresponsible *Will;* as ADONAÏ, only an arbitrary LORD and *Master;* as AL *Shadaï, potent* and a DESTROYER.

To communicate true and correct ideas in respect of the Deity was one chief object of the mysteries. In them, Khūrūm the King, and Khūrūm the Master, obtained their knowledge of him and his attributes; and in them that knowledge was taught to Moses and Pythagoras.

Wherefore nothing forbids you to consider the whole legend of this Degree, like that of the Master's, an allegory, representing the perpetuation of the knowledge of the True God in the sanctuaries of initiation. By the subterranean vaults you may understand the places of initiation, which in the ancient ceremonies were gen-erally under ground. The Temple of Solomon presented a sym-bolic image of the Universe; and resembled, in its arrangements and furniture, all the temples of the ancient nations that practised the mysteries. The system of numbers was intimately connected with their religions and worship, and has come down to us in Ma-sonry; though the esoteric meaning with which the numbers used by us are pregnant is unknown to the vast majority of those who use them. Those numbers were especially employed that had a reference to the Deity, represented his attributes, or figured in the frame-work of the world, in time and space, and formed more or less the bases of that frame-work. These were universally regarded as sacred, being the expression of order and intelligence, the utterances of Divinity Himself.

The Holy of Holies of the Temple formed a cube; in which, drawn on a plane surface, there are 4+3+2=9 *lines* visible, and three sides or faces. It corresponded with the number *four*, by which the ancients presented *Nature,* it being the number of substances or corporeal forms, and of the elements, the cardinal points and seasons, and the *secondary* colors. The number *three* everywhere represented the Supreme Being. Hence the name of the Deity, engraven upon the *triangular* plate, and that sunken into the *cube* of agate, taught the ancient Mason, and teaches us, that the true knowledge of God, of His nature and His attributes, is written by Him upon the leaves of the great Book of Universal Nature, and may be read there by all who are endowed with the requisite amount of intellect and intelligence. This knowledge of God, so written there, and of which Masonry has in all ages been the interpreter, is *the Master Mason's Word.*

Within the Temple, all the arrangements were mystically and symbolically connected with the same system. The vault or ceiling, starred like the firmament, was supported by twelve columns, representing the twelve months of the year. The border that ran around the columns represented the zodiac, and one of the twelve celestial signs was appropriated to each column. The brazen sea was supported by twelve oxen, three looking to each cardinal point of the compass.

And so in our day every Masonic Lodge represents the Universe. Each extends, we are told, from the rising to the setting sun, from the South to the North, from the surface of the Earth to the Heavens, and from the same to the centre of the globe. In it are represented the sun, moon, and stars; three great torches in the East, West, and South, forming a triangle, give it light; and, like the Delta or Triangle suspended in the East, and inclosing the Ineffable Name, indicate, by the mathematical equality of the angles and sides, the beautiful and harmonious proportions which govern in the aggregate and details of the Universe; while those sides and angles represent, by their number, three, the Trinity of Power, Wisdom, and Harmony, which presided at the building of this marvellous work. These three great lights also represent the great mystery of the three principles, of creation, dissolution or destruction, and reproduction or regeneration, consecrated by all creeds in their numerous Trinities.

The luminous pedestal, lighted by the perpetual flame within, is a symbol of that light of *Reason,* given by God to man, by which he is enabled to read in the Book of Nature the record of the thought, the revelation of the attributes of the Deity.

The three Masters, Adoniram, Joabert, and Stolkin, are types of the True Mason, who seeks for knowledge from pure motives, and that he may be the better enabled to serve and benefit his fellow-men; while the discontented and presumptuous Masters who were buried in the ruins of the arches represent those who strive to acquire it for unholy purposes, to gain power over their fellows, to gratify their pride, their vanity, or their ambition.

The Lion that guarded the Ark and held in his mouth the key wherewith to open it, figuratively represents Solomon, the Lion of the Tribe of Judah, who preserved and communicated the key to the true knowledge of God, of His laws, and of the profound mysteries of the moral and physical Universe.

ENOCH ['חֲנוֹךְ Khanōc], we are told, walked with God three hundred years, after reaching the age of sixty-five—"walked with God, and he was no more, for God had taken him." His name signified in the Hebrew, INITIATE or INITIATOR. The legend of the columns, of granite and brass or bronze, erected by him, is probably symbolical. That of bronze, which survived the flood, is supposed to symbolize the mysteries, of which Masonry is the legitimate successor—from the earliest times the custodian and depository of the great philosophical and religious truths, unknown to the world at large, and handed down from age to age by an unbroken current of tradition, embodied in symbols, emblems, and allegories.

The legend of this Degree is thus, partially, interpreted. It is of little importance whether it is in anywise historical. For its value consists in the lessons which it inculcates, and the duties which it prescribes to those who receive it. The parables and allegories of the Scriptures are not less valuable than history. Nay, they are more so, because ancient history is little instructive, and truths are concealed in and symbolized by the legend and the myth.

There are profounder meanings concealed in the symbols of this Degree, connected with the philosophical system of the Hebrew

Kabalists, which you will learn hereafter, if you should be so fortunate as to advance. They are unfolded in the higher Degrees. The *lion* [אֲרִי, אריה, *Arai, Araiah,* which also means the *altar*] still holds in his mouth the key of the enigma of the sphynx.

But there is one application of this Degree, that you are now entitled to know; and which, remembering that Khūrūm, the Master, is the symbol of human freedom, you would probably discover for yourself.

. It is not enough for a people to *gain* its liberty. It must *secure* it. It must not intrust it to the keeping, or hold it at the pleasure, of any one man. The keystone of the Royal Arch of the great Temple of Liberty is a fundamental law, charter, or constitution; the expression of the fixed habits of thought of the people, embodied in a written instrument, or the result of the slow accretions and the consolidation of centuries; the same in war as in peace; that cannot be hastily changed, nor be violated with impunity, but is sacred, like the Ark of the Covenant of God, which none could touch and live.

A permanent constitution, rooted in the affections, expressing the will and judgment, and built upon the instincts and settled habits of thought of the people, with an independent judiciary, an elective legislature of two branches, an executive responsible to the people, and the right of trial by jury, will guarantee the liberties of a people, if it be virtuous and temperate, without luxury, and without the lust of conquest and dominion, and the follies of visionary theories of impossible perfection.

Masonry teaches its Initiates that the pursuits and occupations of this life, its activity, care, and ingenuity, the predestined developments of the nature given us by God, tend to promote His great design, in making the world; and are not at war with the great purpose of life. It teaches that everything is beautiful in its time, in its place, in its appointed office; that everything which man is put to do, if rightly and faithfully done, naturally helps to work out his salvation; that if he obeys the genuine principles of his calling, he will be a good man: and that it is only by neglect and non-performance of the task set for him by Heaven, by wandering into idle dissipation, or by violating their beneficent and lofty spirit, that he becomes a bad man. The appointed action of life is the great training of Providence; and if man yields himself to it, he will need neither churches nor ordinances, except for the *expression* of his religious homage and gratitude.

For there is a religion of toil. It is not all drudgery, a mere stretching of the limbs and straining of the sinews to tasks. It has a meaning and an intent. A living heart pours life-blood into the toiling arm; and warm affections inspire and mingle with man's labors. They are the *home* affections. Labor toils a-field, or plies its task in cities, or urges the keels of commerce over wide oceans; but home is its centre; and thither it ever goes with its earnings, with the means of support and comfort for others; offerings sacred to the thought of every true man, as a sacrifice at a golden shrine. Many faults there are amidst the toils of life; many harsh and hasty words are uttered; but still the toils go on, weary and hard and exasperating as they often are. For in that home is age or sickness, or helpless infancy, or gentle childhood, or feeble woman, that must not want. If man had no other than mere selfish impulses, the scene of labor which we behold around us would not exist.

The advocate who fairly and honestly presents his case, with a feeling of true self-respect, honor, and conscience, to help the tribunal on towards the right conclusion, with a conviction that God's justice reigns there, is acting a religious part, leading that day a religious life; or else right and justice are no part of religion. Whether, during all that day, he has once appealed, in form or in terms, to his conscience, or not; whether he has once spoken of religion and God, or not; if there has been the inward purpose, the conscious intent and desire, that sacred justice should triumph, he has that day led a good and *religious* life, and made a most essential contribution to that religion of life and of society, the cause of equity between man and man, and of truth and right action in the world.

Books, to be of religious tendency in the Masonic sense, need not be books of sermons, of pious exercises, or of prayers. Whatever inculcates pure, noble, and patriotic sentiments, or touches the heart with the beauty of virtue, and the excellence of an upright life, accords with the religion of Masonry, and is the Gospel of literature and art. That Gospel is preached from many a book and painting, from many a poem and fiction, and review and newspaper; and it is a painful error and miserable narrowness, not to recognize these wide-spread agencies of Heaven's providing; not to see and welcome these many-handed coadjutors, to the great and good cause. The oracles of God do not speak from the pulpit alone.

There is also a religion of society. In business, there is much more than sale, exchange, price, payment; for there is the sacred faith of man in man. When we repose perfect confidence in the integrity of another; when we feel that he will not swerve from the right, frank, straightforward, conscientious course, for any temptation; his integrity and conscientiousness are the image of God to us; and when we believe in *it,* it is as great and generous an act, as when we believe in the rectitude of the Deity.

In gay assemblies for amusement, the good affections of life gush and mingle. If *they* did not, these gathering-places would be as dreary and repulsive as the caves and dens of outlaws and robbers. When friends meet, and hands are warmly pressed, and the eye kindles and the countenance is suffused with gladness, there is a religion between their hearts; and each loves and worships the True and Good that is in the other. It is not policy, or self-interest, or selfishness that spreads such a charm around that meeting, but the halo of bright and beautiful affection.

The same splendor of kindly liking, and affectionate regard, shines like the soft overarching sky, over all the world; over all places where men meet, and walk or toil together; not over lovers' bowers and marriage-altars alone, not over the homes of purity and tenderness alone; but over all tilled fields, and busy workshops, and dusty highways, and paved streets. There is not a worn stone upon the sidewalks, but has been the altar of such offerings of mutual kindness; nor a wooden pillar or iron railing against which hearts beating with affection have not leaned. How many soever other elements there are in the stream of life flowing through these channels, *that* is surely here and everywhere; honest, heartfelt, disinterested, inexpressible affection.

Every Masonic Lodge is a temple of religion; and its teachings are instruction in religion. For here are inculcated disinterestedness, affection, toleration, devotedness, patriotism, truth, a generous sympathy with those who suffer and mourn, pity for the fallen, mercy for the erring, relief for those in want, Faith, Hope, and Charity. Here we meet as brethren, to learn to know and love each other. Here we greet each other gladly, are lenient to each other's faults, regardful of each other's feelings, ready to relieve each other's wants. This is the true religion revealed to the ancient patriarchs; which Masonry has taught for many centuries, and which it will continue to teach as long as time endures. If unworthy passions, or selfish, bitter, or revengeful feelings, contempt, dislike, hatred, enter here, they are intruders and not welcome, strangers uninvited, and not guests.

Certainly there are many evils and bad passions, and much hate and contempt and unkindness everywhere in the world. We cannot refuse to see the evil that is in life. But *all* is not evil. We still see God in the world. There is good amidst the evil. The hand of mercy leads wealth to the hovels of poverty and sorrow. Truth and simplicity live amid many wiles and sophistries. There are good hearts underneath gay robes, and under tattered garments also.

Love clasps the hand of love, amid all the envyings and distractions of showy competition; fidelity, pity, and sympathy hold the long night-watch by the bedside of the suffering neighbor, amidst the surrounding poverty and squalid misery. Devoted men go from city to city to nurse those smitten down by the terrible pestilence that renews at intervals its mysterious marches. Women well-born and delicately nurtured nursed the wounded soldiers in hospitals, before it became fashionable to do so; and even poor lost women, whom God alone loves and pities, tend the plague-stricken with a patient and generous heroism. Masonry and its kindred Orders teach men to love each other, feed the hungry, clothe the naked, comfort the sick, and bury the friendless dead. Everywhere God finds and blesses the kindly office, the pitying thought, and the loving heart.

There is an element of good in all men's lawful pursuits and a divine spirit breathing in all their lawful affections. The ground on which they tread is holy ground. There is a natural religion of life, answering, with however many a broken tone, to the religion of nature. There is a beauty and glory in Humanity, in man, answering, with however many a mingling shade, to the loveliness of soft landscapes, and swelling hills, and the wondrous glory of the starry heavens.

Men may be virtuous, self-improving, and religious *in* their employments. Precisely for that, those employments were made. All their social relations, friendship, love, the ties of family, were made to be holy. They may be religious, not by a kind of protest and resistance against their several vocations; but by conformity to their true spirit. Those vocations do not *exclude* religion; but *demand* it, for their own perfection. They may be religious laborers, whether in field or factory; religious physicians, lawyers, sculptors, poets, painters, and musicians. They may be religious in all the toils and in all the amusements of life. Their life may be a religion; the broad earth its altar; its incense the very breath of life; its fires ever kindled by the brightness of Heaven.

Bound up with our poor, frail life, is the mighty thought that spurns the narrow span of all visible existence. Ever the soul reaches outward, and asks for freedom. It looks forth from the narrow and grated windows of sense, upon the wide immeasurable creation; it knows that around it and beyond it lie outstretched the infinite and everlasting paths.

Everything within us and without us ought to stir our minds to admiration and wonder. We are a mystery encompassed with mysteries. The connection of mind with matter is a mystery; the wonderful telegraphic communication between the brain and every part of the body, the power and action of the will. Every familiar step is more than a story in a land of enchantment. The power of movement is as mysterious as the power of thought. Memory, and dreams that are the indistinct echoes of dead memories are alike inexplicable. Universal harmony springs from infinite complication. The momentum of every step we take in our dwelling contributes in part to the order of the Universe. We are connected by ties of thought, and even of matter and its forces, with the whole boundless Universe and all the past and coming generations of men.

The humblest object beneath our eye as completely defies our scrutiny as the economy of the most distant star. Every leaf and every blade of grass holds within itself secrets which no human penetration will ever fathom. No man can tell what is its principle of life. No man can know what his power of secretion is. Both are inscrutable mysteries. Wherever we place our hand we lay it upon the locked bosom of mystery. Step where we will, we tread upon wonders. The sea-sands, the clods of the field, the water-worn pebbles on the hills, the rude masses of rock, are traced over and over, in every direction, with a handwriting older and more significant and sublime than all the ancient ruins, and all the overthrown and buried cities that past generations have left upon the earth; for it is the handwriting of the Almighty.

A Mason's great business with life is to read the book of its teaching; to find that life is not the doing of drudgeries, but the hearing of oracles. The old mythology is but a leaf in that book; for it peopled the world with spiritual natures; and science, many-leaved, still spreads before us the same tale of wonder.

We shall be just as happy hereafter, as we are pure and upright, and no more, just as happy as our character prepares us to be, and no more. Our moral, like our mental character, is not formed in a moment; it is the habit of our minds; the result of many thoughts and feelings and efforts, bound together by many natural and strong ties. The great law of Retribution is, that all coming experience is to be affected by every present feeling; every future moment of being must answer for every present moment; one moment, sacrificed to vice, or lost to improvement, is *forever* sacrificed and lost; an hour's delay to enter the right path, is to put us back so far, in the everlasting pursuit of happiness; and every sin, even of the best men, is to be thus answered for, if not according to the full measure of its ill-desert, yet according to a rule of unbending rectitude and impartiality.

The law of retribution presses upon every man, whether he thinks of it or not. It pursues him through all the courses of life, with a step that never falters nor tires, and with an eye that never sleeps. If it were not so, God's government would not be impartial; there would be no discrimination; no moral dominion; no light shed upon the mysteries of Providence.

Whatsoever a man soweth, that, and not something else, shall he reap. That which we are doing, good or evil, grave or gay, that which we do to-day and shall do to-morrow; each thought, each feeling, each action, each event; every passing hour, every breathing moment; all are contributing to form the character, according to which we are to be judged. Every particle of influence that goes to form that aggregate,—our character,—will, in that future scrutiny, be sifted out from the mass; and, particle by particle, with ages perhaps intervening, fall a distinct contribution to the sum of our joys or woes. Thus every idle word and idle hour will give answer in the judgment.

Let us take care, therefore, what we sow. An evil temptation comes upon us; the opportunity of unrighteous gain, or of unhallowed indulgence, either in the sphere of business or pleasure, of society or solitude. We yield; and plant a seed of bitterness and sorrow. To-morrow it will threaten discovery. Agitated and alarmed, we cover the sin, and bury it deep in falsehood and hypocrisy. In the bosom where it lies concealed, in the fertile soil of kindred vices, that sin dies not, but thrives and grows; and other and still other germs of evil gather around the accursed root; until, from that single seed of corruption, there springs up in the soul all that is horrible in habitual lying, knavery, or vice. Loathingly, often, we take each downward step; but a frightful power urges us onward; and the hell of debt, disease, ignominy, or remorse gathers its shadows around our steps even on earth; and are yet but the beginnings of sorrows. The evil deed may be done in a single moment; but conscience never dies, memory never sleeps; guilt never can become innocence; and remorse can never whisper peace.

Beware, thou who art tempted to evil! Beware what thou layest up for the future! Beware what thou layest up in the archives of eternity! Wrong not thy neighbor! lest the thought of him thou injurest, and who suffers by thy act, be to thee a pang which years will not deprive of its bitterness! Break not into the house of innocence, to rifle it of its treasure; lest when many years have passed over thee, the moan of its distress may not have died away from thine ear! Build not the desolate throne of ambition in thy heart; nor be busy with devices, and circumventings, and selfish schemings; lest desolation and loneliness be on thy path, as it stretches into the long futurity! Live not a useless, an impious, or an injurious life! for bound up with that life is the immutable principle of an endless retribution, and elements of God's creating, which will never spend their force, but continue ever to unfold with the ages of eternity. Be not deceived! God has formed thy nature, thus to answer to the future. His law can never be abrogated, nor His justice eluded; and forever and ever it will be true, that *"Whatsoever a man soweth, that also he shall reap."*

XIV.

GRAND ELECT, PERFECT, AND SUBLIME MASON.

[Perfect Elu.]

It is for each individual Mason to discover the secret of Masonry, by reflection upon its symbols and a wise consideration and analysis of what is said and done in the work. Masonry does not *inculcate* her truths. She *states* them, once and briefly; or hints them, perhaps, darkly; or interposes a cloud between them and eyes that would be dazzled by them. *"Seek,* and ye shall *find,"* knowledge and the truth.

The practical object of Masonry is the physical and moral amelioration and the intellectual and spiritual improvement of individuals and society. Neither can be effected, except by the dissemination of truth. It is falsehood in doctrines and fallacy in principles, to which most of the miseries of men and the misfortunes of nations are owing. Public opinion is rarely right on any point; and there are and always will be important truths to be substituted in that opinion in the place of many errors and absurd and injurious prejudices. There are few truths that public opinion has not at some time hated and persecuted as heresies; and few errors that have not at some time seemed to it truths radiant from the immediate presence of God. There are moral maladies, also, of man and society, the treatment of which requires not only boldness, but also, and more, prudence and discretion; since they are more the fruit of false and pernicious doctrines, moral, political, and religious, than of vicious inclinations.

Much of the Masonic secret manifests itself, without speech

218

revealing it, to him who even partially comprehends all the Degrees in proportion as he receives them; and particularly to those who advance to the highest Degrees of the Ancient and Accepted Scottish Rite. That Rite raises a corner of the veil, even in the Degree of Apprentice; for it there declares that Masonry is a *worship*.

Masonry labors to improve the social order by enlightening men's minds, warming their hearts with the love of the good, inspiring them with the great principle of human fraternity, and requiring of its disciples that their language and actions shall conform to that principle, that they shall enlighten each other, control their passions, abhor vice, and pity the vicious man as one afflicted with a deplorable malady.

It is the universal, eternal, immutable religion, such as God planted it in the heart of universal humanity. No creed has ever been long-lived that was not built on this foundation. It is the base, and they are the superstructure. "Pure religion and undefiled before God and the Father is this, to visit the fatherless and widows in their affliction, and to keep himself unspotted from the world." "Is not *this* the fast that I have chosen? to loose the bands of wickedness, to undo the heavy burdens, and to let the oppressed go free, and that ye break every yoke?" The ministers of this religion are all Masons who comprehend it and are devoted to it; its sacrifices to God are good works, the sacrifices of the base and disorderly passions, the offering up of self-interest on the altar of humanity, and perpetual efforts to attain to all the moral perfection of which man is capable.

To make honor and duty the steady beacon-lights that shall guide your life-vessel over the stormy seas of time; to do that which it is right to do, not because it will insure you success, or bring with it a reward, or gain the applause of men, or be "the best policy," more prudent or more advisable; but because it *is* right, and therefore *ought* to be done; to war incessantly against error, intolerance, ignorance, and vice, and yet to pity those who err, to be tolerant even of intolerance, to teach the ignorant, and to labor to reclaim the vicious, are some of the duties of a Mason.

A good Mason is one that can look upon death, and see its face with the same countenance with which he hears its story; that can endure all the labors of his life with his soul supporting his body, that can equally despise riches when he hath them and when he hath them not; that is, not sadder if they are in his neighbor's exchequer, nor more lifted up if they shine around about his own walls; one that is not moved with good fortune coming to him, nor going from him; that can look upon another man's lands with equanimity and pleasure, as if they were his own; and yet look upon his own, and use them too, just as if they were another man's; that neither spends his goods prodigally and foolishly, nor yet keeps them avariciously and like a miser; that weighs not benefits by weight and number, but by the mind and circumstances of him who confers them; that never thinks his charity expensive, if a worthy person be the receiver; that does nothing for opinion's sake, but everything for conscience, being as careful of his thoughts as of his acting in markets and theatres, and in as much awe of himself as of a whole assembly; that is, bountiful and cheerful to his friends, and charitable and apt to forgive his enemies; that loves his country, consults its honor, and obeys its laws, and desires and endeavors nothing more than that he may do his duty and honor God. And such a Mason may reckon his life to be the life of a man, and compute his months, not by the course of the sun, but by the zodiac and circle of his virtues.

The whole world is but one republic, of which each nation is a family, and every individual a child. Masonry, not in anywise derogating from the differing duties which the diversity of states requires, tends to create a new people, which, composed of men of many nations and tongues, shall all be bound together by the bonds of science, morality, and virtue.

Essentially philanthropic, philosophical, and progressive, it has for the basis of its dogma a firm belief in the existence of God and his providence, and of the immortality of the soul; for its object, the dissemination of moral, political, philosophical, and religious truth, and the practice of all the virtues. In every age, its device has been, "Liberty, Equality, Fraternity," with constitutional government, *law, order, discipline,* and *subordination* to legitimate authority—*government* and not *anarchy.*

But it is neither a political party nor a religious sect. It embraces all parties and all sects, to form from among them all a vast fraternal association. It recognizes the dignity of human nature, and man's right to such freedom as he is fitted for; and it knows nothing that should place one man below another, except ignorance, debasement, and crime, and the necessity of subordination to lawful will and authority.

It is philanthropic; for it recognizes the great truth that all men are of the same origin, have common interests, and should co-operate together to the same end.

Therefore it teaches its members to love one another, to give to each other mutual assistance and support in all the circumstances of life, to share each other's pains and sorrows, as well as their joys and pleasures; to guard the reputations, respect the opinions, and be perfectly tolerant of the errors, of each other, in matters of faith and beliefs.

It is philosophical, because it teaches the great Truths concerning the nature and existence of one Supreme Deity, and the existence and immortality of the soul. It revives the Academy of Plato, and the wise teachings of Socrates. It reiterates the maxims of Pythagoras, Confucius, and Zoroaster, and reverentially enforces the sublime lessons of Him who died upon the Cross.

The ancients thought that universal humanity acted under the influence of two opposing Principles, the Good and the Evil: of which the Good urged men toward Truth, Independence, and Devotedness; and the Evil toward Falsehood, Servility, and Selfishness. Masonry represents the Good Principle and constantly wars against the evil one. It is the Hercules, the Osiris, the Apollo, the Mithras, and the Ormuzd, at everlasting and deadly feud with the demons of ignorance, brutality, baseness, falsehood, slavishness of soul, intolerance, superstition, tyranny, meanness, the insolence of wealth, and bigotry.

When despotism and superstition, twin-powers of evil and darkness, reigned everywhere and seemed invincible and immortal, it invented, to avoid persecution, the mysteries, that is to say, the allegory, the symbol, and the emblem, and transmitted its doctrines by the secret mode of initiation. Now, retaining its ancient symbols, and in part its ancient ceremonies, it displays in every civilized country its banner, on which in letters of living light its great principles are written; and it smiles at the puny efforts of kings and popes to crush it out by excommunication and interdiction.

Man's views in regard to God, will contain only so much positive truth as the human mind is capable of receiving; whether that truth is attained by the exercise of reason, or communicated by revelation. It must necessarily be both limited and alloyed, to bring it within the competence of finite human intelligence. Being finite, we can form no correct or adequate idea of the Infinite; being material, we can form no clear conception of the Spiritual. We do believe in and know the infinity of Space and Time, and the spirituality of the Soul; but the *idea* of that infinity and spirituality eludes us. Even Omnipotence cannot infuse infinite conceptions into finite minds; nor can God, without first entirely changing the conditions of our being, pour a complete and full knowledge of His own nature and attributes into the narrow capacity of a human soul. Human intelligence could not grasp it, nor human language express it. The visible is, necessarily, the measure of the invisible.

The consciousness of the individual reveals *itself* alone. His knowledge cannot pass beyond the limits of his own being. His conceptions of other things and other beings *are only his conceptions.* They are not those things or beings *themselves.* The living principle of a living Universe must be INFINITE; while all *our* ideas and conceptions are *finite,* and applicable only to finite beings.

The Deity is thus not an object of *knowledge,* but of *faith;* not to be approached by the *understanding,* but by the *moral sense;* not to be *conceived,* but to be *felt.* All attempts to embrace the Infinite in the conception of the Finite are, and must be only accommodations to the frailty of man. Shrouded from human comprehension in an obscurity from which a chastened imagination is awed back, and Thought retreats in conscious weakness, the Divine Nature is a theme on which man is little entitled to dogmatize. Here the philosophic Intellect becomes most painfully aware of its own insufficiency.

And yet it is here that man most dogmatizes, classifies and describes God's attributes, makes out his map of God's nature, and his inventory of God's qualities, feelings, impulses, and passions; and then hangs and burns his brother, who, as dogmatically as he, makes out a different map and inventory. The common understanding has no humility. *Its* God is an *incarnate* Divinity. Imperfection imposes its own limitations on the Illimitable, and clothes the Inconceivable Spirit of the Universe in forms that come within the grasp of the senses and the intellect, and are derived from that infinite and imperfect nature which is but God's creation.

We are all of us, though not all equally, mistaken. The cherished dogmas of each of us are not, as we fondly suppose, the pure truth of God; but simply our own special form of error, our guesses at truth, the refracted and fragmentary rays of light that have fallen upon our own minds. Our little systems have their day, and cease to be; they are but broken lights of God; and He is more than they. Perfect truth is not attainable anywhere. We style this Degree that of Perfection; and yet what it teaches is imperfect and defective. Yet we are not to relax in the pursuit of truth, nor contentedly acquiesce in error. It is our duty always to press forward in the search; for though absolute truth is unattainable, yet the amount of error in our views is capable of progressive and perpetual diminution; and thus Masonry is a continual struggle toward the light.

All errors are not equally innocuous. That which is most injurious is to entertain unworthy conceptions of the nature and attributes of God; and it is this that Masonry symbolizes by ignorance of the True Word. The true word of a Mason is, not the entire, perfect, absolute truth in regard to God; but the highest and noblest conception of Him that our minds are capable of forming; and this *word* is Ineffable, because one man cannot communicate to another his own conception of Deity; since every man's conception of God must be proportioned to his mental cultivation, and intellectual powers, and moral excellence. God is, as man conceives Him, the reflected image of man himself.

For every man's conception of God must vary with his mental cultivation and mental powers. If any one contents himself with any *lower* image than his intellect is capable of grasping, then he contents himself with that which is false *to him*, as well as false *in fact*. If lower than he can reach, he must needs *feel* it to be false. And if we, of the nineteenth century after Christ, adopt the conceptions of the nineteenth century before Him; if *our* conceptions of God are those of the ignorant, narrow-minded, and vindictive Israelite; then we think worse of God, and have a lower, meaner, and more limited view of His nature, than the faculties which He has bestowed are capable of grasping. The highest view we can form is nearest to the truth. If we acquiesce in any lower one, we acquiesce in an untruth. We feel that it is an affront and an indignity to Him, to conceive of Him as cruel, short-sighted, capricious, and unjust; as a jealous, an angry, a vindictive Being.

When we examine our conceptions of His character, if we can conceive of a loftier, nobler, higher, more beneficent, glorious, and magnificent character, then this latter is to us the true conception of Deity; *for nothing can be imagined more excellent than He.*

Religion, to obtain currency and influence with the great mass of mankind, must needs be alloyed with such an amount of error as to place it far below the standard attainable by the higher human capacities. A religion as pure as the loftiest and most cultivated human reason could discern, would not be comprehended by, or effective over, the less educated portion of mankind. What is Truth to the philosopher, would not be Truth, nor have the effect of Truth, to the peasant. The religion of the many must necessarily be more incorrect than that of the refined and reflective few, not so much in its essence as in its forms, not so much in the spiritual idea which lies latent at the bottom of it, as in the symbols and dogmas in which that idea is embodied. The truest religion would, in many points, not be comprehended by the ignorant, nor consolatory to them, nor guiding and supporting for them. The doctrines of the Bible are often not clothed in the language of strict truth, but in that which was fittest to convey to a rude and ignorant people the practical essentials of the doctrine. A perfectly pure faith, free from all extraneous admixtures, a system of noble theism and lofty morality, would find too little preparation for it in the common mind and heart, to admit of prompt reception by the masses of mankind; and Truth might not have reached us, if it had not borrowed the wings of Error.

The Mason regards God as a Moral Governor, as well as an Original Creator; as a God at hand, and not merely one afar off in the distance of infinite space, and in the remoteness of Past or Future Eternity. He conceives of Him as taking a watchful and presiding interest in the affairs of the world, and as influencing the hearts and actions of men.

To him, God is the great Source of the World of Life and Matter; and man, with his wonderful corporeal and mental frame, His direct work. He believes that God has made men with different intellectual capacities; and enabled some, by superior intellectual power, to see and originate truths which are hidden from the mass of men. He believes that when it is His will that mankind should make some great step forward, or achieve some pregnant discovery, He calls into being some intellect of more than ordinary magnitude and power, to give birth to new ideas, and grander conceptions of the Truths vital to Humanity.

We hold that God has so ordered matters in this beautiful and harmonious, but mysteriously-governed Universe, that one great mind after another will arise, from time to time, as such are needed, to reveal to men the truths that are wanted, and the amount of truth than can be borne. He so arranges, that nature and the course of events shall send men into the world, endowed with that higher mental and moral organization, in which grand truths, and sublime gleams of spiritual light will spontaneously and inevitably arise. These speak to men by inspiration.

Whatever Hiram really was, he is the type, perhaps an imaginary type, to us, of humanity in its highest phase; an exemplar of what man may and should become, in the course of ages, in his progress toward the realization of his destiny; an individual gifted with a glorious intellect, a noble soul, a fine organization, and a perfectly balanced moral being; an earnest of what humanity may be, and what we believe it will hereafter be in God's good time; *the possibility of the race made real.*

The Mason believes that God has arranged this glorious but perplexing world with a purpose, and on a plan. He holds that every man sent upon this earth, and especially every man of superior capacity, has a duty to perform, a mission to fulfill, a baptism to be baptized with; that every great and good man possesses some portion of God's truth, which he must proclaim to the world, and which must bear fruit in his own bosom. In a true and simple sense, he believes all the pure, wise, and intellectual to be inspired, and to be so for the instruction, advancement, and elevation of mankind. That kind of inspiration, like God's omnipresence, is not limited to the few writers claimed by Jews, Christians, or Moslems, but is co-extensive with the race. It is the consequence of a faithful use of our faculties. Each man is its subject, God is its source, and Truth its only test. It differs in degrees, as the intellectual endowments, the moral wealth of the soul, and the degree of cultivation of those endowments and faculties differ. It is limited to no sect, age, or nation. It is wide as the world and common as God. It was not given to a few men, in the infancy of mankind, to monopolize inspiration, and bar God out of the soul. We are not born in the dotage and decay of the world. The stars are beautiful as in their prime; the most ancient Heavens are fresh and strong. God is still everywhere in nature. Wherever a heart beats with love, wherever Faith and Reason utter their oracles, there is God, as formerly in the hearts of seers and prophets. No soil on earth is so holy as the good man's heart; nothing is so full of God. This inspiration is not given to the learned alone, not alone to the great and wise, but to every faithful child of God. Certain as the open eye drinks in the light, do the pure in heart see God; and he who lives truly, feels Him as a presence within the soul. The conscience is the very voice of Deity.

Masonry, around whose altars the Christian, the Hebrew, the Moslem, the Brahmin, the followers of Confucius and Zoroaster, can assemble as brethren and unite in prayer to the one God who is above *all* the Baalim, must needs leave it to each of its Initiates to look for the foundation of his faith and hope to the written scriptures of his own religion. For itself it finds those truths definite enough, which are written by the finger of God upon the heart of man and on the pages of the book of nature. Views of religion and duty, wrought out by the meditations of the studious, confirmed by the allegiance of the good and wise, stamped as sterling by the response they find in every uncorrupted mind, commend themselves to Masons of every creed, and may well be accepted by all.

The Mason does not pretend to dogmatic certainty, nor vainly imagine such certainty attainable. He considers that if there were no written revelation, he could safely rest the hopes that animate him and the principles that guide him, on the deductions of reason and the convictions of instinct and consciousness. He can find a sure foundation for his religious belief, in these deductions of the intellect and convictions of the heart. For reason proves to him the existence and attributes of God; and those spiritual instincts which he feels are the voice of God in his soul, infuse into his mind a sense of his relation to God, a conviction of the beneficence of his Creator and Preserver, and a hope of future existence; and his reason and conscience alike unerringly point to virtue as the highest good, and the destined aim and purpose of man's life.

He studies the wonders of the Heavens, the frame-work and revolutions of the Earth, the mysterious beauties and adaptations of animal existence, the moral and material constitution of the human creature, so fearfully and wonderfully made; and is satisfied that God IS; and that a Wise and Good Being is the author of the starry Heavens above him, and of the moral world within him; and his mind finds an adequate foundation for its hopes, its worship, its principles of action, in the far-stretching Universe, in the glorious firmament, in the deep, full soul, bursting with unutterable thoughts.

These are truths which every reflecting mind will unhesitatingly receive, as not to be surpassed, nor capable of improvement; and fitted, if obeyed, to make earth indeed a Paradise, and man only a little lower than the angels. The worthlessness of ceremonial observances, and the necessity of active virtue; the enforcement of purity of heart as the security for purity of life, and of the government of the thoughts, as the originators and forerunners of action; universal philanthropy, requiring us to love all men, and to do unto others that and that only which we should think it right, just, and generous for them to do unto us; forgiveness of injuries; the necessity of self-sacrifice in the discharge of duty; humility; genuine sincerity, and *being* that which we *seem* to be; all these sublime precepts need no miracle, no voice from the clouds, to recommend them to our allegiance, or to assure us of their divine origin. They command obedience by virtue of their inherent rectitude and beauty; and have been, and are, and will be the law in every age and every country of the world. God revealed them to man in the beginning.

To the Mason, God is our Father in Heaven, to be Whose especial children is the sufficient reward of the peacemakers, to see Whose face the highest hope of the pure in heart; Who is ever at hand to strengthen His true worshippers; to Whom our most fervent love is due, our most humble and patient submission; Whose most acceptable worship is a pure and pitying heart and a beneficent life; in Whose constant presence we live and act, to Whose merciful disposal we are resigned by that death which, we hope and believe, is but the entrance to a better life; and Whose wise decrees forbid a man to lap his soul in an elysium of mere indolent content.

As to our feelings toward Him and our conduct toward man, Masonry teaches little about which men can differ, and little from which they can dissent. He is our *Father;* and we are all *brethren.* This much lies open to the most ignorant and busy, as fully as to those who have most leisure and are most learned. This needs no Priest to teach it, and no authority to indorse it; and if every man did that only which is consistent with it, it would exile barbarity, cruelty, intolerance, uncharitableness, perfidy, treachery, revenge, selfishness, and all their kindred vices and bad passions beyond the confines of the world.

The true Mason, sincerely holding that a Supreme God created and governs this world, believes also that He governs it by laws, which, though wise, just, and beneficent, are yet steady, unwavering, inexorable. He believes that his agonies and sorrows are ordained for *his* chastening, *his* strengthening, *his* elaboration and development; because they are the necessary results of the operation of laws, the best that could be devised for the happiness and purification of the species, and to give occasion and opportunity for the practice of all the virtues, from the homeliest and most common, to the noblest and most sublime; or perhaps not even that, but the best adapted to work out the vast, awful, glorious, eternal designs of the Great Spirit of the Universe. He believes that the ordained operations of nature, which have brought misery to him, have, from the very unswerving tranquility of their career, showered blessings and sunshine upon many another path; that the unrelenting chariot of Time, which has crushed or maimed him in its allotted course, is pressing onward to the accomplishment of those serene and mighty purposes, to have contributed to which, even as a victim, is an honor and a recompense. He takes this view of Time and Nature and God, and yet bears his lot without murmur or distrust; because it is a portion of a system, the best possible, because ordained by God. He does not believe that God loses sight of *him,* while superintending the march of the great harmonies of the Universe; nor that it was not foreseen, when the Universe was created, its laws enacted, and the long succession of its operations pre-ordained, that in the great march of those events, he would suffer pain and undergo calamity. He believes that his individual good entered into God's consideration, as well as the great cardinal results to which the course of all things is tending.

Thus believing, he has attained an eminence in virtue, the highest, amid *passive* excellence, which humanity can reach. He finds his reward and his support in the reflection that he is an unreluctant and self-sacrificing co-operator with the Creator of the Universe; and in the noble consciousness of being worthy and capable of so sublime a conception, yet so sad a destiny. He is then truly entitled to be called a Grand Elect, Perfect, and Sublime Mason. He is content to fall early in the battle, if his body may but form a stepping-stone for the future conquests of humanity.

It cannot be that God, Who, we are certain, is perfectly good, can choose us to suffer pain, unless either we are ourselves to receive from it an antidote to what is evil in ourselves, or else as such pain is a necessary part in the scheme of the Universe, which as a whole is good. In either case, the Mason receives it with submission. He would not suffer unless it was ordered so. Whatever his creed, if he believes that God is, and that He cares for His creatures, he cannot doubt that; nor that it would not have been so ordered, unless it was either better for himself, or for some other persons, or for some things. To complain and lament is to murmur against God's will, and worse than unbelief.

The Mason, whose mind is cast in a nobler mould than those of the ignorant and unreflecting, and is instinct with a diviner life,—who loves truth more than rest, and the peace of Heaven rather than the peace of Eden,—to whom a loftier being brings severer cares,—who knows that man does not live by pleasure or content alone, but by the presence of the power of God,—must cast behind him the hope of any other repose or tranquillity, than that which is the last reward of long agonies of thought; he must relinquish all prospect of any Heaven save that of which trouble is the avenue and portal; he must gird up his loins, and trim his lamp, for a work that must be done, and must not be negligently done. If he does not like to live in the furnished lodgings of tradition, he must build his own house, his own system of faith and thought, for himself.

The hope of success, and not the hope of reward, should be our stimulating and sustaining power. Our object, and not ourselves, should be our inspiring thought. Selfishness is a sin, when temporary, and for time. Spun out to eternity, it does not become celestial prudence. We should toil and die, not for Heaven or Bliss, but for Duty.

In the more frequent cases, where we have to join our efforts to those of thousands of others, to contribute to the carrying forward of a great cause; merely to till the ground or sow the seed for a very distant harvest, or to prepare the way for the future advent of some great amendment; the amount which each one contributes to the achievement of ultimate success, the portion of the

price which justice should assign to each as his especial production, can never be accurately ascertained. Perhaps few of those
who have ever labored, in the patience of secrecy and silence, to
bring about some political or social change, which they felt convinced would ultimately prove of vast service to humanity, lived
to see the change effected, or the anticipated good flow from it.
Fewer still of them were able to pronounce what appreciable
weight their several efforts contributed to the achievement of the
change desired. Many will doubt, whether, in truth, these exertions have any influence whatever; and, discouraged, cease all
active effort.

Not to be thus discouraged, the Mason must labor to elevate
and purify his *motives,* as well as sedulously cherish the conviction, assuredly a true one, that in this world there is no such thing
as effort thrown away; that in all labor there is profit; that all
sincere exertion, in a righteous and unselfish cause, is *necessarily*
followed, in spite of all appearance to the contrary, by an appropriate and proportionate success; that *no* bread cast upon the
waters can be wholly lost; that *no* seed planted in the ground can
fail to quicken in due time and measure; and that, however we
may, in moments of despondency, be apt to doubt, not only
whether our cause will triumph, but whether, if it does, we shall
have contributed to its triumph,—there is One, Who has not
only seen every exertion we have made, but Who can assign
the exact degree in which each soldier has assisted to gain the
great victory over social evil. No good work is done wholly in
vain.

The Grand Elect, Perfect, and Sublime Mason will in nowise
deserve that honorable title, if he has not that strength, that will,
that self-sustaining energy; that Faith, that feeds upon no earthly
hope, nor ever thinks of victory, but, content in its own consummation, combats because it ought to combat, rejoicing fights, and
still rejoicing falls.

The Augean Stables of the World, the accumulated uncleanness
and misery of centuries, require a mighty river to cleanse them
thoroughly away; every drop we contribute aids to swell that
river and augment its force, in a degree appreciable by God,
though not by man; and he whose zeal is deep and earnest, will
not be over-anxious that his individual drops should be distinguishable amid the mighty mass of cleansing and fertilizing

waters; far less that, for the sake of distinction, it should flow in ineffective singleness away.

The true Mason will not be careful that his name should be inscribed upon the mite which he casts into the treasury of God. It suffices him to know that if he has labored, with purity of purpose, in any good cause, he *must* have contributed to its success; that the *degree* in which he has contributed is a matter of infinitely small concern; and still more, that the consciousness of having so contributed, however obscurely and unnoticed, is his sufficient, even if it be his sole, reward. Let every Grand Elect, Perfect, and Sublime Mason cherish this faith. It is a duty. It is the brilliant and never-dying light that shines within and through the symbolic pedestal of alabaster, on which reposes the perfect cube of agate, symbol of duty, inscribed with the divine name of God. He who industriously sows and reaps is a good laborer, and worthy of his hire. But he who sows that which shall be reaped by others, by those who will know not of and care not for the sower, is a laborer of a nobler order, and, worthy of a more excellent reward.

The Mason does not exhort others to an ascetic undervaluing of this life, as an insignificant and unworthy portion of existence; for that demands feelings which are unnatural, and which, therefore, if attained, must be morbid, and if merely professed, insincere; and teaches us to look rather to a future life for the compensation of social evils, than to this life for their cure; and so does injury to the cause of virtue and to that of social progress. Life is real, and is earnest, and it is full of duties to be performed. It is the beginning of our immortality. Those only who feel a deep interest and affection for this world will work resolutely for its amelioration; those whose affections are transferred to Heaven, easily acquiesce in the miseries of earth, deeming them hopeless, befitting, and ordained; and console themselves with the idea of the amends which are one day to be theirs. It is a sad truth, that those most decidedly given to spiritual contemplation, and to making religion rule in their hearts, are often most apathetic toward all improvement of this world's systems, and in many cases virtual conservatives of evil, and hostile to political and social reform, as diverting men's energies from eternity.

The Mason does not war with his own instincts, macerate the body into weakness and disorder, and disparage what he sees to be beautiful, knows to be wonderful, and feels to be unspeakably dear and fascinating. He does not put aside the nature which God has given him, to struggle after one which He has *not* bestowed. He knows that man is sent into the world, not a spiritual, but a composite being, made up of body and mind, the body having, as is fit and needful in a material world, its full, rightful, and allotted share. His life is guided by a full recognition of this fact. He does not deny it in bold words, and admit it in weaknesses and inevitable failings. He believes that his spirituality will come in the next stage of his being, when he puts on the spiritual body; that his body will be dropped at death; and that, until then, God meant it to be commanded and controlled, but not neglected, despised, or ignored by the soul, under pain of heavy consequences.

Yet the Mason is not indifferent as to the fate of the soul, after its present life, as to its continued and eternal being, and the character of the scenes in which that being will be fully developed. These are to him topics of the profoundest interest, and the most ennobling and refining contemplation. They occupy much of his leisure; and as he becomes familiar with the sorrows and calamities of this life, as his hopes are disappointed and his visions of happiness here fade away; when life has wearied him in its race of hours; when he is harassed and toil-worn, and the burden of his years weighs heavy on him, the balance of attraction gradually inclines in favor of another life; and he clings to his lofty speculations with a tenacity of interest which needs no injunction, and will listen to no prohibition. They are the consoling privilege of the aspiring, the wayworn, the weary, and the bereaved.

To him the contemplation of the Future lets in light upon the Present, and develops the higher portions of his nature. He endeavors rightly to adjust the respective claims of Heaven and earth upon his time and thought, so as to give the proper proportions thereof to performing the duties and entering into the interests of this world, and to preparation for a better; to the cultivation and purification of his own character, and to the public service of his fellow-men.

The Mason does not dogmatize, but entertaining and uttering his own convictions, he leaves every one else free to do the same; and only hopes that the time will come, even if after the lapse of ages, when all men shall form one great family of brethren, and one law alone, the law of love, shall govern God's whole Universe.

Believe as you may, my brother; if the Universe is not, to you, without a God, and if man is not like the beast that perishes, but hath an immortal soul, we welcome you among us, to wear, as we wear, with humility, and conscious of your demerits and short-comings, the title of Grand Elect, Perfect, and Sublime Mason.

It was not without a secret meaning, that *twelve* was the number of the Apostles of Christ, and *seventy-two* that of his Disciples: that John addressed his rebukes and menaces to the *Seven* churches, the number of the Archangels and the Planets. At Babylon were the Seven Stages of Bersippa, a pyramid of Seven stories, and at Ecbatana Seven concentric inclosures, each of a different color. Thebes also had Seven gates, and the same number is repeated again and again in the account of the flood. The Sephiroth, or Emanations, *ten* in number, three in one class, and seven in the other, repeat the mystic numbers of Pythagoras. Seven Amschaspands or planetary spirits were invoked with Ormuzd: Seven inferior Rishis of Hindustan were saved with the head of their family in an ark: and Seven ancient personages alone returned with the British just man, Hu, from the dale of the grievous waters. There were Seven Heliadæ, whose father Helias, or the Sun, once crossed the sea in a golden cup; Seven Titans, children of the older Titan, Kronos or Saturn; Seven Corybantes; and Seven Cabiri, sons of Sydyk; Seven primeval Celestial spirits of the Japanese, and Seven Karfesters who escaped from the deluge and began to be the parents of a new race, on the summit of Mount Albordi. Seven Cyclopes, also, built the walls of Tiryus.

Celsus, as quoted by Origen, tells us that the Persians represented by symbols the two-fold motion of the stars, fixed and planetary, and the passage of the Soul through their successive spheres. They erected in their holy caves, in which the mystic rites of the Mithriac Initiations were practised, what he denominates a high *ladder,* on the Seven steps of which were Seven gates or portals, according to the number of the Seven principal heavenly bodies. Through these the aspirants passed, until they reached the summit of the whole; and this passage was styled a transmigration through the spheres.

Jacob saw in his dream a *ladder* planted or set on the earth, and its top reaching to Heaven, and the Malaki Alohim ascending and descending on it, and above it stood IHUH, declaring Himself to be Ihuh-Alhi Abraham. The word translated *ladder,* is סלם *Salam,* from סלל, *Salal,* raised, elevated, reared up, exalted, piled up into a heap, *Aggeravit.* סללה Salalah, means a heap, rampart, or other accumulation of earth or stone, artificially made; and סלע, *Salaa* or *Salo,* is a rock or cliff or boulder, and the name of the city of Petra. There is no ancient Hebrew word to designate a pyramid.

The symbolic mountain Meru was ascended by Seven steps or stages; and all the pyramids and artificial tumuli and hillocks thrown up in flat countries were imitations of this fabulous and mystic mountain, for purposes of worship. These were the "High Places" so often mentioned in the Hebrew books, on which the idolaters sacrificed to foreign gods.

The pyramids were sometimes square, and sometimes round. The sacred Babylonian tower [מגדל, Magdol], dedicated to the great Father Bal, was an artificial hill, of pyramidal shape, and Seven stages, built of brick, and each stage of a different color, representing the Seven planetary spheres by the appropriate color of each planet. Meru itself was said to be a single mountain, terminating in three peaks, and thus a symbol of the Trimurti. The great Pagoda at Tanjore was of six stories, surmounted by a temple as the seventh, and on this three spires or towers. An ancient pagoda at Deogur was surmounted by a tower, sustaining the mystic egg and a trident. Herodotus tells us that the Temple of Bal at Babylon was a tower composed of Seven towers, resting on an eighth that served as basis, and successively diminishing in size from the bottom to the top; and Strabo tells us it was a pyramid.

Faber thinks that the Mithriac *ladder* was really a pyramid with Seven stages, each provided with a narrow door or aperture, through each of which doors the aspirant passed, to reach the summit, and then descended through similar doors on the opposite side of the pyramid; the ascent and descent of the Soul being thus represented.

Each Mithriac cave and all the most ancient temples were intended to symbolize the Universe, which itself was habitually called the Temple and habitation of Deity. Every temple was the world in miniature; and so the whole world was one grand temple. The most ancient temples were roofless; and therefore the Persians, Celts, and Scythians strongly disliked artificial covered edifices. Cicero says that Xerxes burned the Grecian temples, on the express ground that the whole world was the Magnificent Temple and Habitation of the Supreme Deity. Macrobius says that the entire Universe was judiciously deemed by many the Temple of God. Plato pronounced the real Temple of the Deity to be the world; and Heraclitus declared that the Universe, variegated with animals and plants and stars was the only genuine Temple of the Divinity.

How completely the Temple of Solomon was symbolic, is manifest, not only from the continual reproduction in it of the sacred numbers and of astrological symbols in the historical descriptions of it; but also, and yet more, from the details of the imaginary reconstructed edifice, seen by Ezekiel in his vision. The Apocalypse completes the demonstration, and shows the kabalistic meanings of the whole. The Symbola Architectonica are found on the most ancient edifices; and these mathematical figures and instruments, adopted by the Templars, and identical with those on the gnostic seals and abraxæ, connect their dogma with the Chaldaic, Syriac, and Egyptian Oriental philosophy. The secret Pythagorean doctrines of numbers were preserved by the monks of Thibet, by the Hierophants of Egypt and Eleusis, at Jerusalem, and in the circular Chapters of the Druids; and they are especially consecrated in that mysterious book, the Apocalypse of Saint John.

All temples were surrounded by pillars, recording the number of the constellations, the signs of the zodiac, or the cycles of the planets; and each one was a microcosm or symbol of the Universe, having for roof or ceiling the starred vault of Heaven.

All temples were originally open at the top, having for roof the sky. Twelve pillars described the belt of the zodiac. Whatever the number of the pillars, they were mystical everywhere. At Abury, the Druidic temple reproduced all the cycles by its columns. Around the temples of Chilminar in Persia, of Baalbec, and of Tukhti Schlomoh in Tartary, on the frontier of China, stood *forty* pillars. On each side of the temple at Pæstum were fourteen, recording the Egyptian cycle of the dark and light sides of the moon, as described by Plutarch; the whole thirty-eight that surrounded them recording the two meteoric cycles so often found in the Druidic temples.

The theatre built by Scaurus, in Greece, was surrounded by 360 columns; the Temple at Mecca, and that at Iona in Scotland, by 360 stones.

Morals and Dogma

Chapter of Rose Croix

XV.

KNIGHT OF THE EAST OR OF THE SWORD.

[Knight of the East, of the Sword, or of the Eagle.]

THIS Degree, like all others in Masonry, is symbolical. Based upon historical truth and authentic tradition, it is still an allegory. The leading lesson of this Degree is Fidelity to obligation, and Constancy and Perseverance under difficulties and discouragement.

Masonry is engaged in her crusade,—against ignorance, intolerance, fanaticism, superstition, uncharitableness, and error. She does not sail with the trade-winds, upon a smooth sea, with a steady free breeze, fair for a welcoming harbor; but meets and must overcome many opposing currents, baffling winds, and dead calms.

The chief obstacles to her success are the apathy and faithlessness of her own selfish children, and the supine indifference of the world. In the roar and crush and hurry of life and business, and the tumult and uproar of politics, the quiet voice of Masonry is unheard and unheeded. The first lesson which one learns, who engages in any great work of reform or beneficence, is, that men are essentially careless, lukewarm, and indifferent as to everything that does not concern their own personal and immediate

237

welfare. It is to single men, and not to the united efforts of many, that all the great works of man, struggling toward perfection, are owing. The enthusiast, who imagines that he can inspire with his own enthusiasm the multitude that eddies around him, or even the few who have associated themselves with him as co-workers, is grievously mistaken; and most often the conviction of his own mistake is followed by discouragement and disgust. To do all, to pay all, and to suffer all, and then, when despite all obstacles and hindrances, success is accomplished, and a great work done, to see those who opposed or looked coldly on it, claim and reap all the praise and reward, is the common and almost universal lot of the benefactor of his kind.

He who endeavors to serve, to benefit, and improve the world, is like a swimmer, who struggles against a rapid current, in a river lashed into angry waves by the winds. Often they roar over his head, often they beat him back and baffle him. Most men yield to the stress of the current, and float with it to the shore, or are swept over the rapids; and only here and there the stout, strong heart and vigorous arms struggle on toward ultimate success.

It is the motionless and stationary that most frets and impedes the current of progress; the solid rock or stupid dead tree, rested firmly on the bottom, and around which the river whirls and eddies: the Masons that doubt and hesitate and are discouraged; that disbelieve in the capability of man to improve; that are not disposed to toil and labor for the interest and well-being of general humanity; that expect others to do all, even of that which they do not oppose or ridicule; while they sit, applauding and doing nothing, or perhaps prognosticating failure.

There were many such at the rebuilding of the Temple. There were prophets of evil and misfortune—the lukewarm and the indifferent and the apathetic; those who stood by and sneered; and those who thought they did God service enough if they now and then faintly applauded. There were ravens croaking ill omen, and murmurers who preached the folly and futility of the attempt. The world is made up of such; and they were as abundant then as they are now.

But gloomy and discouraging as was the prospect, with lukewarmness within and bitter opposition without, our ancient brethren persevered. Let us leave them engaged in the good work, and whenever to us, as to them, success is uncertain, remote. and contingent, let us still remember that the only question for us to ask, as true men and Masons, is, what does duty require; and not what will be the result and our reward if we do our duty. Work on, with the Sword in one hand, and the Trowel in the other!

Masonry teaches that God is a Paternal Being, and has an interest in his creatures, such as is expressed in the title *Father;* an interest unknown to all the systems of Paganism, untaught in all the theories of philosophy; an interest not only in the glorious beings of other spheres, the Sons of Light, the dwellers in Heavenly worlds, but in us, poor, ignorant, and unworthy; that He has pity for the erring, pardon for the guilty, love for the pure, knowledge for the humble, and promises of immortal life for those who trust in and obey Him.

Without a belief in Him, life is miserable, the world is dark, the Universe disrobed of its splendors, the intellectual tie to nature broken, the charm of existence dissolved, the great hope of being lost; and the mind, like a star struck from its sphere, wanders through the infinite desert of its conceptions, without attraction, tendency, destiny, or end.

Masonry teaches, that, of all the events and actions, that take place in the universe of worlds and the eternal succession of ages, there is not one, even the minutest, which God did not forever foresee, with all the distinctness of immediate vision, combining all, so that man's free will should be His instrument, like all the other forces of nature.

It teaches that the soul of man is formed by Him for a purpose; that, built up in its proportions, and fashioned in every part, by infinite skill, an emanation from His spirit, its nature, necessity, and design are virtue. It is so formed, so moulded, so fashioned, so exactly balanced, so exquisitely proportioned in every part, that sin introduced into it is misery; that vicious thoughts fall upon it like drops of poison; and guilty desires, breathing on its delicate fibres, make plague-spots there, deadly as those of pestilence upon the body. It is made for virtue, and not for vice; for purity as its end, rest, and happiness. Not more vainly would we attempt to make the mountain sink to the level of the valley, the waves of the angry sea turn back from its shores and cease to thunder upon the beach, the stars to halt in their swift courses, than to change any one law of our own nature. And one of those laws, uttered by God's voice, and speaking through every nerve and fibre, every force and element, of the moral constitution He has given us, is that we must be upright and virtuous; that if tempted we must resist; that we must govern our unruly passions, and hold in hand our sensual appetites. And this is not the dictate of an arbitrary will, nor of some stern and impracticable law; but it is part of the great firm law of harmony that binds the Universe together: not the mere enactment of arbitrary will; but the dictate of Infinite Wisdom.

We know that God is good, and that what He does is right. This known, the works of creation, the changes of life, the destinies of eternity, are all spread before us, as the dispensations and counsels of infinite love. This known, we then know that the love of God is working to issues, like itself, beyond all thought and imagination good and glorious; and that the only reason why we do not understand it, is that it is *too* glorious for us to understand. God's love takes care for all, and nothing is neglected. It watches over all, provides for all, makes wise adaptations for all; for age, for infancy, for maturity, for childhood; in every scene of this or another world; for want, weakness, joy, sorrow, and even for sin. All is good and well and right; and shall be so forever. Through the eternal ages the light of God's beneficence shall shine hereafter, disclosing all, consummating all, rewarding all that deserve reward. Then we shall see, what now we can only believe. The cloud will be lifted up, the gate of mystery be passed, and the full light shine forever; the light of which that of the Lodge is a symbol. Then that which caused us trial shall yield us triumph; and that which made our heart ache shall fill us with gladness; and we shall then feel that there, as here, the only true happiness is to learn, to advance, and to improve; which could not happen unless we had commenced with error, ignorance, and imperfection. We must pass through the darkness, to reach the light.

XVI.

PRINCE OF JERUSALEM.

WE no longer expect to rebuild the Temple at Jerusalem. To us it has become but a symbol. To us the whole world is God's Temple, as is every upright heart. To establish all over the world the New Law and Reign of Love, Peace, Charity, and Toleration, is to build that Temple, most acceptable to God, in erecting which Masonry is now engaged. No longer needing to repair to Jerusalem to worship, nor to offer up sacrifices and shed blood to propitiate the Deity, man may make the woods and mountains his Churches and Temples, and worship God with a devout gratitude, and with works of charity and beneficence to his fellow-men. Wherever the humble and contrite heart silently offers up its adoration, under the overarching trees, in the open, level meadows, on the hill-side, in the glen, or in the city's swarming streets; there is God's House and the New Jerusalem.

The Princes of Jerusalem no longer sit as magistrates to judge between the people; nor is their number limited to five. But their duties still remain substantially the same, and their insignia and symbols retain their old significance. Justice and Equity are still their characteristics. To reconcile disputes and heal dissensions, to restore amity and peace, to soothe dislikes and soften prejudices, are their peculiar duties; and they know that the peacemakers are blessed.

Their emblems have been already explained. They are part of the language of Masonry; the same now as it was when Moses learned it from the Egyptian Hierophants.

Still we observe the spirit of the Divine law, as thus enunciated to our ancient brethren, when the Temple was rebuilt, and the book of the law again opened:

"Execute true judgment; and show mercy and compassion every man to his brother. Oppress not the widow nor the fatherless, the stranger nor the poor; and let none of you imagine evil against his brother in his heart. Speak ye every man the truth

241

to his neighbor; execute the judgment of Truth and Peace in your gates; and love no false oath; for all these I hate, saith the Lord.

"Let those who have power rule in righteousness, and Princes in judgment. And let him that is a judge be as an hiding-place from the wind, and a covert from the tempest; as rivers of water in a dry place; as the shadow of a great rock in a weary land. Then the vile person shall no more be called liberal; nor the churl bountiful; and the work of justice shall be peace; and the effect of justice, quiet and security; and wisdom and knowledge shall be the stability of the times. Walk ye righteously and speak uprightly; despise the gains of oppression, shake from your hands the contamination of bribes; stop not your ears against the cries of the oppressed, nor shut your eyes that you may not see the crimes of the great; and you shall dwell on high, and your place of defence be like munitions of rocks."

Forget not these precepts of the old Law; and especially do not forget, as you advance, that every Mason, however humble, is your brother, and the laboring man your peer! Remember always that all Masonry is work, and that the trowel is an emblem of the Degrees in this Council. Labor, when rightly understood, is both noble and ennobling, and intended to develop man's moral and spiritual nature, and not to be deemed a disgrace or a misfortune.

Everything around us is, in its bearings and influences, moral. The serene and bright morning, when we recover our conscious existence from the embraces of sleep; when, from that image of Death God calls us to a new life, and again gives us existence, and His mercies visit us in every bright ray and glad thought, and call for gratitude and content; the silence of that early dawn, the hushed silence, as it were, of expectation; the holy eventide, its cooling breeze, its lengthening shadows, its falling shades, its still and sober hour; the sultry noontide and the stern and solemn midnight; and Spring-time, and chastening Autumn; and Summer, that unbars our gates, and carries us forth amidst the ever-renewed wonders of the world; and Winter, that gathers us around the evening hearth:—all these, as they pass, touch by turns the springs of the spiritual life in us, and are conducting that life to good or evil. The idle watch-hand often points to something within us; and the shadow of the gnomon on the dial often falls upon the conscience.

A life of labor is not a state of inferiority or degradation. The Almighty has not cast man's lot beneath the quiet shades, and amid glad groves and lovely hills, with no task to perform; with nothing to do but to rise up and eat, and to lie down and rest. He has ordained that *Work* shall be done, in all the dwellings of life, in every productive field, in every busy city, and on every wave of every ocean. And this He has done, because it has pleased Him to give man a nature destined to higher ends than indolent repose and irresponsible profitless indulgence; and because, for developing the energies of such a nature, work was the necessary and proper element. We might as well ask why He could not make two and two be six, as why He could not develop these energies without the instrumentality of work. They are equally impossibilities.

This, Masonry teaches, as a great Truth; a great moral landmark, that ought to guide the course of all mankind. It teaches its toiling children that the scene of their daily life is all spiritual, that the very implements of their toil, the fabrics they weave, the merchandise they barter, are designed for spiritual ends; that so believing, their daily lot may be to them a sphere for the noblest improvement. That which we do in our intervals of relaxation, our church-going, and our book-reading, are especially designed to prepare our minds for the *action* of Life. We are to hear and read and meditate, that we may *act* well; and the *action* of Life is itself the great field for spiritual improvement. There is no task of industry or business, in field or forest, on the wharf or the ship's deck, in the office or the exchange, but has spiritual ends. There is no care or cross of our daily labor, but was especially ordained to nurture in us patience, calmness, resolution, perseverance, gentleness, disinterestedness, magnanimity. Nor is there any tool or implement of toil, but is a part of the great spiritual instrumentality.

All the relations of life, those of parent, child, brother, sister, friend, associate, lover and beloved, husband, wife, are moral, throughout every living tie and thrilling nerve that bind them together. They cannot subsist a day nor an hour without putting the mind to a trial of its truth, fidelity, forbearance, and disinterestedness.

A great city is one extended scene of moral action. There is no blow struck in it but has a purpose, ultimately good or bad, and therefore moral. There is no action performed, but has a motive; and motives are the special jurisdiction of morality. Equipages, houses, and furniture are symbols of what is moral, and they in a thousand ways minister to right or wrong feeling. Everything that belongs to us, ministering to our comfort or luxury, awakens in us emotions of pride or gratitude, of selfishness or vanity; thoughts of self-indulgence, or merciful remembrances of the needy and the destitute.

Everything acts upon and influences us. God's great law of sympathy and harmony is potent and inflexible as His law of gravitation. A sentence embodying a noble thought stirs our blood; a noise made by a child frets and exasperates us, and influences our actions.

A world of spiritual objects, influences, and relations lies around us all. We all vaguely deem it to be so; but he only lives a charmed life, like that of genius and poetic inspiration, who communes with the spiritual scene around him, hears the voice of the spirit in every sound, sees its signs in every passing form of things, and feels its impulse in all action, passion, and being. Very near to us lies the mines of wisdom; unsuspected they lie all around us. There is a secret in the simplest things, a wonder in the plainest, a charm in the dullest.

We are all naturally seekers of wonders. We travel far to see the majesty of old ruins, the venerable forms of the hoary mountains, great water-falls, and galleries of art. And yet the world-wonder is all around us; the wonder of setting suns, and evening stars, of the magic spring-time, the blossoming of the trees, the strange transformations of the moth; the wonder of the Infinite Divinity and of His boundless revelation. There is no splendor beyond that which sets its morning throne in the golden East; no dome sublime as that of Heaven; no beauty so fair as that of the verdant, blossoming earth; no place, however invested with the sanctities of old time, like that home which is hushed and folded within the embrace of the humblest wall and roof.

And all these are but the symbols of things far greater and higher. All is but the clothing of the spirit. In this vesture of time is wrapped the immortal nature: in this show of circumstance and form stands revealed the stupendous reality. Let man but be, as he is, a living soul, communing with himself and with

God, and his vision becomes eternity; his abode, infinity; his home, the bosom of all-embracing love.

The great problem of Humanity is wrought out in the humblest abodes; no more than this is done in the highest. A human heart throbs beneath the beggar's gabardine; and that and no more stirs with its beating the Prince's mantle. The beauty of Love, the charm of Friendship, the sacredness of Sorrow, the heroism of Patience, the noble Self-sacrifice, these and their like, alone, make life to be life indeed, and are its grandeur and its power. They are the priceless treasures and glory of humanity; and they are not things of condition. All places and all scenes are alike clothed with the grandeur and charm of virtues such as these.

The million occasions will come to us all, in the ordinary paths of our life, in our homes, and by our firesides, wherein we may act as nobly, as if, all our life long, we led armies, sat in senates, or visited beds of sickness and pain. Varying every hour, the million occasions will come in which we may restrain our passions, subdue our hearts to gentleness and patience, resign our own interest for another's advantage, speak words of kindness and wisdom, raise the fallen, cheer the fainting and sick in spirit, and soften and assuage the weariness and bitterness of their mortal lot. To every Mason there will be opportunity enough for these. They cannot be written on his tomb; but they will be written deep in the hearts of men, of friends, of children, of kindred all around him, in the book of the great account, and, in their eternal influences, on the great pages of the Universe.

To such a destiny, at least, my Brethren, let us all aspire! These laws of Masonry let us all strive to obey! And so may our hearts become true temples of the Living God! And may He encourage our zeal, sustain our hopes, and assure us of success!

XVII.

KNIGHT OF THE EAST AND WEST.

THIS is the first of the Philosophical Degrees of the Ancient
and Accepted Scottish Rite; and the beginning of a course of instruction which will fully unveil to you the heart and inner mysteries of Masonry. Do not despair because you have often seemed
on the point of attaining the inmost light, and have as often been
disappointed. In all time, truth has been hidden under symbols,
and often under a succession of allegories: where veil after veil
had to be penetrated before the true Light was reached, and the
essential truth stood revealed. The Human Light is but an imperfect reflection of a ray of the Infinite and Divine.

We are about to approach those ancient Religions which once
246

ruled the minds of men, and whose ruins encumber the plains of the great Past, as the broken columns of Palmyra and Tadmor lie bleaching on the sands of the desert. They rise before us, those old, strange, mysterious creeds and faiths, shrouded in the mists of antiquity, and stalk dimly and undefined along the line which divides Time from Eternity; and forms of strange, wild, startling beauty mingled in the vast throngs of figures with shapes monstrous, grotesque, and hideous.

The religion taught by Moses, which, like the laws of Egypt, enunciated the principle of exclusion, borrowed, at every period of its existence, from all the creeds with which it came in contact. While, by the studies of the learned and wise, it enriched itself with the most admirable principles of the religions of Egypt and Asia, it was changed, in the wanderings of the People, by everything that was most impure or seductive in the pagan manners and superstitions. It was one thing in the times of Moses and Aaron, another in those of David and Solomon, and still another in those of Daniel and Philo.

At the time when John the Baptist made his appearance in the desert, near the shores of the Dead Sea, all the old philosophical and religious systems were approximating toward each other. A general lassitude inclined the minds of all toward the quietude of that amalgamation of doctrines for which the expeditions of Alexander and the more peaceful occurrences that followed, with the establishment in Asia and Africa of many Grecian dynasties and a great number of Grecian colonies, had prepared the way. After the intermingling of different nations, which resulted from the wars of Alexander in three-quarters of the globe, the doctrines of Greece, of Egypt, of Persia, and of India, met and intermingled everywhere. All the barriers that had formerly kept the nations apart, were thrown down; and while the People of the West readily connected their faith with those of the East, those of the Orient hastened to learn the traditions of Rome and the legends of Athens. While the Philosophers of Greece, all (except the disciples of Epicurus) more or less Platonists, seized eargerly upon the beliefs and doctrines of the East,—the Jews and Egyptians, before then the most exclusive of all peoples, yielded to that eclecticism which prevailed among their masters, the Greeks and Romans.

Under the same influences of toleration, even those who embraced Christianity, mingled together the old and the new, Christianity and Philosophy, the Apostolic teachings and the traditions of Mythology. The man of intellect, devotee of one system, rarely displaces it with another in all its purity. The people take such a creed as is offered them. Accordingly, the distinction be-- tween the esoteric and the exoteric doctrine, immemorial in other creeds, easily gained a foothold among many of the Christians; and it was held by a vast number, even during the preaching of Paul, that the writings of the Apostles were incomplete; that they contained only the germs of another doctrine, which must receive from the hands of philosophy, not only the systematic arrange- ment which was wanting, but all the development which lay con- cealed therein. The writings of the Apostles, they said, in address- ing themselves to mankind in general, enunciated only the articles of the vulgar faith; but transmitted the mysteries of knowledge to superior minds, to the Elect,—mysteries handed down from gen- eration to generation in esoteric traditions; and to this science of the mysteries they gave the name of Γνῶσις [Gnōsis].

The Gnostics derived their leading doctrines and ideas from Plato and Philo, the Zend-avesta and the Kabalah, and the Sacred books of India and Egypt; and thus introduced into the bosom of Christianity the cosmological and theosophical speculations, which had formed the larger portion of the ancient religions of the Orient, joined to those of the Egyptian, Greek, and Jewish doctrines, which the Neo-Platonists had equally adopted in the Occident.

Emanation from the Deity of all spiritual beings, progressive degeneration of these beings from emanation to emanation, re- demption and return of all to the purity of the Creator; and, after the re-establishment of the primitive harmony of all, a for- tunate and truly divine condition of all, in the bosom of God; such were the fundamental teachings of Gnosticism. The genius of the Orient, with its contemplations, irradiations, and intuitions, dictated its doctrines. Its language corresponded to its origin. Full of imagery, it had all the magnificence, the inconsistencies, and the mobility of the figurative style.

Behold, it said, the light, which emanates from an immense centre of Light, that spreads everywhere its benevolent rays; so do the spirits of Light emanate from the Divine Light. Behold, all the springs which nourish, embellish, fertilize, and purify the Earth: they emanate from one and the same ocean; so from the bosom of the Divinity emanate so many streams, which form and fill the universe of intelligences. Behold numbers, which all emanate from one primitive number, all resemble it, all are composed of its essence, and still vary infinitely; and utterances, decomposable into so many syllables and elements, all contained in the primitive Word, and still infinitely various; so the world of Intelligences emanated from a Primary Intelligence, and they all resemble it, and yet display an infinite variety of existences.

It revived and combined the old doctrines of the Orient and the Occident; and it found in many passages of the Gospels and the Pastoral letters, a warrant for doing so. Christ himself spoke in parables and allegories, John borrowed the enigmatical language of the Platonists, and Paul often indulged in incomprehensible rhapsodies, the meaning of which could have been clear to the Initiates alone.

It is admitted that the cradle of Gnosticism is probably to be looked for in Syria, and even in Palestine. Most of its expounders wrote in that corrupted form of the Greek used by the Hellenistic Jews, and in the Septuagint and the New Testament; and there was a striking analogy between their doctrines and those of the Judæo-Egyptian Philo, of Alexandria; itself the seat of three schools, at once philosophic and religious—the Greek, the Egyptian, and the Jewish.

Pythagoras and Plato, the most mystical of the Grecian Philosophers (the latter heir to the doctrines of the former), and who had travelled, the latter in Egypt, and the former in Phœnicia, India, and Persia, also taught the esoteric doctrine and the distinction between the initiated and the profane. The dominant doctrines of Platonism were found in Gnosticism. Emanation of Intelligences from the bosom of the Deity; the going astray in error and the sufferings of spirits, so long as they are remote from God, and imprisoned in matter; vain and long-continued efforts to arrive at the knowledge of the Truth, and re-enter into their primitive union with the Supreme Being; alliance of a pure and divine soul with an irrational soul, the seat of evil desires; angels or demons who dwell in and govern the planets, having but an imperfect knowledge of the ideas that presided at the creation; regeneration of all beings by their return to the κόσμος νοητός, [kosmos noëtos], the world of Intelligences, and its Chief, the Supreme Being; sole possible mode of re-establishing that primi-

tive harmony of the creation, of which the music of the spheres
of Pythagoras was the image; these were the analogies of the two
systems; and we discover in them some of the ideas that form a
part of Masonry; in which, in the present mutilated condition of
the symbolic Degrees, they are disguised and overlaid with fiction
and absurdity, or present themselves as casual hints that are passed by wholly unnoticed.

The distinction between the esoteric and exoteric doctrines (a
distinction purely Masonic), was always and from the very earliest
times preserved among the Greeks. It remounted to the fabulous
times of Orpheus; and the mysteries of Theosophy were found in
all their traditions and myths. And after the time of Alexander,
they resorted for instruction, dogmas, and mysteries, to all the
schools, to those of Egypt and Asia, as well as those of Ancient
Thrace, Sicily, Etruria, and Attica.

The Jewish-Greek School of Alexandria is known only by two
of its Chiefs, Aristobulus and Philo, both Jews of Alexandria in
Egypt. Belonging to Asia by its origin, to Egypt by its residence,
to Greece by its language and studies, it strove to show that all
truths embedded in the philosophies of other countries were transplanted thither from Palestine. Aristobulus declared that all the
facts and details of the Jewish Scriptures were so many allegories,
concealing the most profound meanings, and that Plato had borrowed from them all his finest ideas. Philo, who lived a century
after him, following the same theory, endeavored to show that the
Hebrew writings, by their system of allegories, were the true
source of all religious and philosophical doctrines. According to
him, the literal meaning is for the vulgar alone. Whoever has
meditated on philosophy, purified himself by virtue, and raised
himself by contemplation, to God and the intellectual world, and
received their inspiration, pierces the gross envelope of the letter,
discovers a wholly different order of things, and is initiated into
mysteries, of which the elementary or literal instruction offers but
an imperfect image. A historical fact, a figure, a word, a letter, a
number, a rite, a custom, the parable or vision of a prophet, veils
the most profound truths; and he who has the key of science will
interpret all according to the light he possesses.

Again we see the symbolism of Masonry, and the search of the
Candidate for light. "Let men of narrow minds withdraw," he
says, "with closed ears. We transmit the divine mysteries to

those who have received the sacred initiation, to those who practise true piety, and who are not enslaved by the empty trappings of words or the preconceived opinions of the pagans."

To Philo, the Supreme Being was the Primitive Light, or the Archetype of Light, Source whence the rays emanate that illuminate Souls. He was also the Soul of the Universe, and as such acted in all its parts. He Himself fills and limits His whole Being. His Powers and Virtues fill and penetrate all. These Powers [Δυνάμεις, dunameis] are Spirits distinct from God, the "Ideas" of Plato personified. He is without beginning, and lives in the prototype of Time [αιων, aion].

His image is THE WORD [Λογος], a form more brilliant than fire; that not being the *pure* light. This Logos dwells in God; for the Supreme Being makes to Himself within His Intelligence the types or ideas of everything that is to become reality in this World. The Logos is the vehicle by which God acts on the Universe, and may be compared to the speech of man.

The Logos being the World of Ideas [κοσμος νοητός], by means whereof God has created visible things, He is the most ancient God, in comparison with the World, which is the youngest production. The Logos, *Chief of Intelligence,* of which He is the general representative, is named *Archangel, type* and *representative* of all spirits, even those of mortals. He is also styled the man-type and primitive man, Adam Kadmon.

God only is Wise. The wisdom of man is but the reflection and image of that of God. He is the Father, and His WISDOM the mother of creation: for He united Himself with WISDOM [Σοφια, Sophia], and communicated to it the germ of creation, and it brought forth the material world. He created the ideal world only, and caused the material world to be made real after its type, by His Logos, which is His speech, and at the same time the Idea of Ideas, the Intellectual World. The Intellectual City was but the *Thought* of the Architect, who meditated the creation, according to that plan of the Material City.

The Word is not only the Creator, but occupies the place of the Supreme Being. Through Him all the Powers and Attributes of God act. On the other side, as first representative of the Human Family, He is the Protector of men and their Shepherd.

God gives to man the Soul or Intelligence, which exists before the body, and which he unites with the body. The reasoning

Principle comes from God through the Word, and communes with God and with the Word; but there is also in man an irrational Principle, that of the inclinations and passions which produce disorder, emanating from inferior spirits who fill the air as ministers of God. The body, taken from the Earth, and the irrational Principle that animates it concurrently with the rational Principle, are hated by God, while the rational soul which He has given it, is, as it were, captive in this prison, this coffin, that encompasses it. The present condition of man is not his primitive condition, when he was the image of the Logos. He has fallen from his first estate. But he may raise himself again, by following the directions of WISDOM [Σοφια] and of the Angels which God has commissioned to aid him in freeing himself from the bonds of the body, and combating Evil, the existence whereof God has permitted, *to furnish him the means of exercising his liberty*. The souls that are purified, not by the Law but by light, rise to the Heavenly regions, to enjoy there a perfect felicity. Those that persevere in evil go from body to body, the seats of passions and evil desires. The familiar lineaments of these doctrines will be recognized by all who read the Epistles of St. Paul, who wrote after Philo, the latter living till the reign of Caligula, and being the contemporary of Christ.

And the Mason is familiar with these doctrines of Philo: that the Supreme Being is a centre of Light whose rays or emanations pervade the Universe; for that is the Light for which all Masonic journeys are a search, and of which the sun and moon in our Lodges are only emblems: that Light and Darkness, chief enemies from the beginning of Time, dispute with each other the empire of the world; which we symbolize by the candidate wandering in darkness and being brought to light: that the world was created, not by the Supreme Being, but by a secondary agent, who is but His WORD [the Λογος], and by types which are but his ideas, aided by an INTELLIGENCE, or WISDOM [Σοφια], which gives one of His Attributes; in which we see the occult meaning of the necessity of recovering "the Word"; and of our two columns of STRENGTH and WISDOM, which are also the two parallel lines that bound the circle representing the Universe: that the visible world is the image of the invisible world; that the essence of the Human Soul is the image of God, and it existed before the body; that the object of its terrestrial life is to disengage itself of its body or its sepulchre; and that it will ascend to the Heavenly regions whenever it shall be purified; in which we see the meaning, now almost forgotten in our Lodges, of the mode of preparation of the candidate for apprenticeship, and his tests and purifications in the first Degree, according to the Ancient and Accepted Scottish Rite.

Philo incorporated in his eclecticism neither Egyptian nor Oriental elements. But there were other Jewish Teachers in Alexandria who did both. The Jews of Egypt were slightly jealous of, and a little hostile to, those of Palestine, particularly after the erection of the sanctuary at Leontopolis by the High-Priest Onias; and therefore they admired and magnified those sages, who, like Jeremiah, had resided in Egypt. "The wisdom of Solomon" was written at Alexandria, and, in the time of St. Jerome, was attributed to Philo; but it contains principles at variance with his. It personifies Wisdom, and draws between its children and the Profane, the same line of demarcation that Egypt had long before taught to the Jews. That distinction existed at the beginning of the Mosaic creed. Moshah himself was an Initiate in the mysteries of Egypt, as he was compelled to be, as the adopted son of the daughter of Pharaoh, *Thouoris,* daughter of *Sesostris-Ramses;* who, as her tomb and monuments show, was, in the right of her infant husband, Regent of Lower Egypt or the Delta at the time of the Hebrew Prophet's birth, reigning at Heliopolis. She was also, as the reliefs on her tomb show, a Priestess of HATHOR and NEITH, the two great primeval goddesses. As her adopted son, living in her Palace and presence forty years, and during that time scarcely acquainted with his brethren the Jews, the law of Egypt compelled his initiation: and we find in many of his enactments the intention of preserving, between the common people and the Initiates, the line of separation which he found in Egypt. Moshah and Aharun his brother, the whole series of High-Priests, the Council of the 70 Elders, Salomoh and the entire succession of Prophets, were in possession of a higher science; and of that science Masonry is, at least, the lineal descendant. It was familiarly known as THE KNOWLEDGE OF THE WORD.

AMŪN, at first the God of Lower Egypt only, where Moshah was reared [a word that in Hebrew means Truth], was the Supreme God. He was styled *"the Celestial Lord, who sheds Light on hidden things."* He was the source of that divine life, of which the *crux ansata* is the symbol; and the source of all power. He united all the attributes that the Ancient Oriental Theosophy assigned to the Supreme Being. He was the πλήρωμα (Pleroma), or *"Fullness of things,"* for He comprehended in Himself everything; and the LIGHT; for he was the Sun-God. He was unchangeable in the midst of everything phenomenal in his worlds. He *created* nothing; but everything *emanated* from Him; and of Him all the other Gods were but manifestations.

The Ram was His living symbol; which you see reproduced in this Degree, lying on the book with seven seals on the tracing-board. He caused the creation of the world by the Primitive Thought [Εννοια, Ennoia], or *Spirit* [Πνευμα, Pneuma], that issued from him by means of his *Voice* or the WORD; and which *Thought* or *Spirit* was personified as the Goddess NEITH. She, too, was a divinity of *Light,* and mother of the Sun; and the Feast of Lamps was celebrated in her honor at Sais. The Creative *Power,* another manifestation of Deity, proceeding to the creation conceived of in her, the Divine *Intelligence,* produced with its Word the Universe, symbolized by an egg issuing from the mouth of KNEPH; from which egg came PHTHA, image of the Supreme Intelligence as realized in the world, and the type of that manifested in man; the principal agent, also, of Nature, or the creative and productive Fire. PHRE or RE, the Sun, or Celestial Light, whose symbol was ⊙, the point within a circle, was the son of PHTHA; and TIPHE, his wife, or the celestial firmament, with the seven celestial bodies, animated by spirits of genii that govern them, was represented on many of the monuments, clad in blue or yellow, her garments sprinkled with stars, and accompanied by the sun, moon, and five planets; and she was the type of Wisdom, and they of the Seven Planetary Spirits of the Gnostics, that with her presided over and governed the sublunary world.

In this Degree, unknown for a hundred years to those who have practised it, these emblems reproduced refer to these old doctrines. The lamb, the yellow hangings strewed with stars, the seven columns, candlesticks, and seals all recall them to us.

The Lion was the symbol of ATHOM-RE, the Great God of Upper Egypt; the Hawk, of RA or PHRE; the Eagle, of MENDES; the Bull, of APIS; and three of these are seen under the platform on which our altar stands.

The first HERMES was the INTELLIGENCE or WORD of God. Moved with compassion for a race living without law, and wishing

to teach them that they sprang from His bosom, and to point out
to them the way that they should go [the books which the first
Hermes, the same with Enoch, had written on the mysteries of
divine science, in the sacred characters, being unknown to those
who lived after the flood], God sent to man OSIRIS and ISIS, accompanied by THOTH, the incarnation or terrestrial repetition of
the first HERMES; who taught men the arts, science, and the ceremonies of religion; and then ascended to Heaven or the Moon.
OSIRIS was the Principle of Good. TYPHON, like AHRIMAN, was
the principle and source of all that is evil in the moral and physical order. Like the Satan of Gnosticism, he was confounded
with Matter.

From Egypt or Persia the new Platonists borrowed the idea,
and the Gnostics received it from them, that man, in his terrestrial career, is successively under the influence of the Moon, of
Mercury, of Venus, of the Sun, of Mars, of Jupiter, and of
Saturn, until he finally reaches the Elysian Fields; an idea again
symbolized in the Seven Seals.

The Jews of Syria and Judea were the direct precursors of
Gnosticism; and in their doctrines were ample oriental elements.
These Jews had had with the Orient, at two different periods, intimate relations, familiarizing them with the doctrines of Asia, and
especially of Chaldea and Persia;—their forced residence in Central Asia under the Assyrians and Persians; and their voluntary
dispersion over the whole East, when subjects of the Seleucidæ
and the Romans. Living near two-thirds of a century, and many
of them long afterward, in Mesopotamia, the cradle of their race;
speaking the same language, and their children reared with those
of the Chaldeans, Assyrians, Medes, and Persians, and receiving
from them their names (as the case of Danayal, who was called
Bæltasatsar, proves), they necessarily adopted many of the doctrines of their conquerors. Their descendants, as Azra and Na-
hamaiah show us, hardly desired to leave Persia, when they were
allowed to do so. They had a special jurisdiction, and governors
and judges taken from their own people; many of them held high
office, and their children were educated with those of the highest
nobles. Danayal was the friend and minister of the King, and
the Chief of the College of the Magi at Babylon; if we may believe the book which bears his name, and trust to the incidents
related in its highly figurative and imaginative style. Mordecai,

too, occupied a high station, no less than that of Prime Minister, and Esther or Astar, his cousin, was the Monarch's wife.

The Magi of Babylon were expounders of figurative writings, interpreters of nature, and of dreams,—astronomers and divines; and from their influences arose among the Jews, after their rescue from captivity, a number of sects, and a new exposition, the mystical interpretation, with all its wild fancies and infinite caprices. The *Aions* of the Gnostics, the *Ideas* of Plato, the *Angels* of the Jews, and the *Demons* of the Greeks, all correspond to the *Ferouers* of Zoroaster.

A great number of Jewish families remained permanently in their new country; and one of the most celebrated of their schools was at Babylon. They were soon familiarized with the doctrine of Zoroaster, which itself was more ancient than Kuros. From the system of the Zend-Avesta they borrowed, and subsequently gave large development to, everything that could be reconciled with their own faith; and these additions to the old doctrine were soon spread, by the constant intercourse of commerce, into Syria and Palestine.

In the Zend-Avesta, God is Illimitable Time. No origin can be assigned to Him: He is so entirely enveloped in His glory, His nature and attributes are so inaccessible to human Intelligence, that He can be only the object of a silent Veneration. Creation took place by emanation from Him. The first emanation was the primitive *Light,* and from that the King of Light, Ormuzd. By the "Word," *Ormuzd* created the world pure. He is its preserver and judge; a Being Holy and Heavenly; Intelligence and Knowledge; the First-born of Time without limits; and invested with all the Powers of the Supreme Being.

Still he is, strictly speaking, the *Fourth* Being. He had a *Ferouer,* a pre-existing Soul [in the language of Plato, a *type* or *ideal*]; and it is said of Him, that He existed from the beginning, in the primitive *Light.* But, that *Light* being but an element, and His *Ferouer* a type, he is, in ordinary language, *the First-born* of ZEROUANE-AKHERENE. Behold, again, "The Word" of Masonry; the *Man,* on the Tracing-Board of this Degree; the Light toward which all Masons travel.

He created after his own image, six Genii called *Amshaspands,* who surround his Throne, are his organs of communication with inferior spirits and men, transmit to Him their prayers, solicit for them His favors, and serve them as models of purity and perfection. Thus we have the *Demiourgos* of Gnosticism, and the six *Genii* that assist him. These are the Hebrew Archangels of the Planets.

The names of these *Amshaspands* are Bahman, Ardibehest, Schariver, Sapandomad, Khordad, and Amerdad.

The fourth, the Holy SAPANDOMAD, created the first man and woman.

Then ORMUZD created 28 *Izeds,* of whom MITHRAS is the chief. They watch, with *Ormuzd* and the *Amshaspands,* over the happiness, purity, and preservation of the world, which is under their government; and they are also models for mankind and interpreters of men's prayers. With *Mithras* and *Ormuzd,* they make a *pleroma* [or complete number] of 30, corresponding to the thirty Aions of the Gnostics, and to the *ogdoade, dodecade,* and *decade* of the Egyptians. *Mithras* was the Sun-God, invoked with, and soon confounded with him, becoming the object of a special worship, and eclipsing *Ormuzd* himself.

The third order of pure spirits is more numerous. They are the *Ferouers,* the THOUGHTS of Ormuzd, or the IDEAS which he conceived before proceeding to the creation of things. They too are superior to men. They protect them during their life on earth; they will purify them from evil at their resurrection. They are their tutelary genii, from the fall to the complete regeneration.

AHRIMAN, second-born of the Primitive Light, emanated from it, pure like ORMUZD; but, proud and ambitious, yielded to jealousy of the First-born. For his hatred and pride, the Eternal condemned him to dwell, for 12,000 years, in that part of space where no ray of light reaches; the black empire of darkness. In that period the struggle between *Light* and *Darkness, Good* and *Evil,* will be terminated.

AHRIMAN scorned to submit, and took the field against ORMUZD. To the good spirits created by his Brother, he opposed an innumerable army of Evil Ones. To the seven *Amshaspands* he opposed seven *Archdevs,* attached to the seven Planets; to the *Izeds* and *Ferouers* an equal number of *Devs,* which brought upon the world all moral and physical evils. Hence *Poverty, Maladies, Impurity, Envy, Chagrin, Drunkenness, Falsehood, Calumny,* and their horrible array.

The image of Ahriman was the Dragon, confounded by the

Jews with Satan and the Serpent-Tempter. After a reign of 3000 years, Ormuzd had created the Material World, in six periods, calling successively into existence the Light, Water, Earth, plants, animals, and Man. But Ahriman concurred in creating the earth and water; for darkness was already an element, and Ormuzd could not exclude its Master. So also the two concurred in producing Man. Ormuzd produced, by his Will and Word, a Being that was the type and source of universal life for everything that exists under Heaven. He placed in man a pure principle, or Life, proceeding from the Supreme Being. But Ahriman destroyed that pure principle, in the form wherewith it was clothed; and when Ormuzd had made, of its recovered and purified essence, the first man and woman, Ahriman seduced and tempted them with wine and fruits; the woman yielding first.

Often, during the three latter periods of 3000 years each, Ahriman and Darkness are, and are to be, triumphant. But the pure souls are assisted by the Good Spirits; the Triumph of Good is decreed by the Supreme Being, and the period of that triumph will infallibly arrive. When the world shall be most afflicted with the evils poured out upon it by the spirits of perdition, three Prophets will come to bring relief to mortals. SOSIOSCH, the principal of the Three, will regenerate the earth, and restore to it its primitive beauty, strength, and purity. He will judge the good and the wicked. After the universal resurrection of the good, he will conduct them to a home of everlasting happiness. Ahriman, his evil demons, and all wicked men, will also be purified in a torrent of melted metal. The law of Ormuzd will reign everywhere; all men will be happy; all, enjoying unalterable bliss, will sing with Sosiosch the praises of the Supreme Being.

These doctrines, the details of which were sparingly borrowed by the Pharisaic Jews, were much more fully adopted by the Gnostics; who taught the restoration of all things, their return to their original pure condition, the happiness of those to be saved, and their admission to the feast of Heavenly Wisdom.

The doctrines of Zoroaster came originally from Bactria, an Indian Province of Persia. Naturally, therefore, it would include Hindu or Buddhist elements, as it did. The fundamental idea of Buddhism was, matter subjugating the intelligence, and intelligence freeing itself from that slavery. Perhaps something came to Gnosticism from China. "Before the chaos which preceded the birth of Heaven and Earth," says Lao-Tseu, "a single Being existed, immense and silent, immovable and ever active—the mother of the Universe. I know not its name: but I designate it by the word *Reason*. Man has his *type* and *model* in the Earth; Earth in Heaven; Heaven in Reason; and Reason in Itself." Here again are the *Ferouers,* the *Ideas,* the *Aions*—the REASON or INTELLIGENCE [Εννοια], SILENCE [Σιγή], WORD [Λογος], and WISDOM [Σοφια] of the Gnostics.

The dominant system among the Jews after their captivity was that of the Pharoschim or Pharisees. Whether their name was derived from that of the Parsees, or followers of Zoroaster, or from some other source, it is certain that they had borrowed much of their doctrine from the Persians. Like them they claimed to have the exclusive and mysterious knowledge, unknown to the mass. Like them they taught that a constant war was waged be-- tween the Empire of Good and that of Evil. Like them they at- tributed the sin and fall of man to the demons and their chief; and like them they admitted a special protection of the righteous by inferior beings, agents of Jehovah. All their doctrines on these subjects were at bottom those of the Holy Books; but singularly developed; and the Orient was evidently the source from which those developments came.

They styled themselves *Interpreters;* a name indicating their claim to the exclusive possession of the true meaning of the Holy Writings, by virtue of the oral tradition which Moses had re- ceived on Mount Sinaï, and which successive generations of Ini- tiates had transmitted, as they claimed, unaltered, unto them. Their very costume, their belief in the influences of the stars, and in the immortality and transmigration of souls, their system of angels and their astronomy, were all foreign.

Sadduceeism arose merely from an opposition essentially Jewish, to these foreign teachings, and that mixture of doctrines, adopted by the Pharisees, and which constituted the popular creed.

We come at last to the *Essenes* and *Therapeuts,* with whom this Degree is particularly concerned. That intermingling of oriental and occidental rites, of Persian and Pythagorean opinions, which we have pointed out in the doctrines of Philo, is unmistak- able in the creeds of these two sects.

They were less distinguished by metaphysical speculations than by simple meditations and moral practices. But the latter always partook of the Zoroastrian principle, that it was necessary to free the soul from the trammels and influences of matter; which led to a system of abstinence and maceration entirely opposed to the ancient Hebrai cideas, favorable as they were to physical pleasures.

In general, the life and manners of these mystical associations, as Philo and Josephus describe them, and particularly their prayers at sunrise, seem the image of what the Zend-Avesta prescribes to the faithful adorer or Ormuzd; and some of their observances cannot otherwise be explained.

The Therapeuts resided in Egypt, in the neighborhood of Alexandria; and the Essenes in Palestine, in the vicinity of the Dead Sea. But there was nevertheless a striking coincidence in their ideas, readily explained by attributing it to a foreign influence. The Jews of Egypt, under the influence of the School of Alexandria, endeavored in general to make their doctrines harmonize with the traditions of Greece; and thence came, in the doctrines of the Therapeuts, as stated by Philo, the many analogies between the Pythagorean and Orphic ideas, on one side, and those of Judaism on the other: while the Jews of Palestine, having less communication with Greece, or contemning its teachings, rather imbibed the Oriental doctrines, which they drank in at the source and with which their relations with Persia made them familiar. This attachment was particularly shown in the Kabalah, which belonged rather to Palestine than to Egypt, though extensively known in the latter; and furnished the Gnostics with some of their most striking theories.

It is a significant fact, that while Christ spoke often of the Pharisees and Sadducees, He never once mentioned the Essenes, between whose doctrines and His there was so great a resemblance, and, in many points, so perfect an identity. Indeed, they are not named, nor even distinctly alluded to, anywhere in the New Testament.

John, the son of a Priest who ministered in the Temple at Jerusalem, and whose mother was of the family of Aharun, was in the deserts until the day of his showing unto Israel. He drank neither wine nor strong drink. Clad in hair-cloth, and with a girdle of leather, and feeding upon such food as the desert afforded, he preached, in the country about Jordan, the baptism of repentance, for the remission of sins; that is, the necessity of repentance proven by *reformation*. He taught the people charity and liberality; the publicans, justice, equity, and fair dealing; the soldiery, peace, truth, and contentment; to do violence to none, accuse none falsely, and be content with their pay. He inculcated the necessity of a virtuous life, and the folly of trusting to their descent from Abraham.

He denounced both Pharisees and Sadducees as a generation of vipers, threatened with the anger of God. He baptized those who confessed their sins. He preached in the desert; and therefore in the country where the Essenes lived, professing the same doctrines. He was imprisoned before Christ began to preach. Matthew mentions him without preface or explanation; as if, apparently, his history was too well known to need any. "In those days," he says, "came John the Baptist, preaching in the wilderness of Judea." His disciples frequently fasted; for we find them with the Pharisees coming to Jesus to inquire why *His* Disciples did not fast as often as they; and He did not denounce *them,* as His habit was to denounce the Pharisees; but answered them kindly and gently.

From his prison, John sent two of his disciples to inquire of Christ: "Art thou he that is to come, or do we look for another?" Christ referred them to his miracles as an answer; and declared to the people that John was a prophet, and more than a prophet, and that no greater man had ever been born; but that the humblest Christian was his superior. He declared him to be Elias, who was to come.

John had denounced to Herod his marriage with his brother's wife as unlawful; and for this he was imprisoned, and finally executed to gratify her. His disciples buried him; and Herod and others thought he had risen from the dead and appeared again in the person of Christ. The people all regarded John as a prophet; and Christ silenced the Priests and Elders by asking them whether he was inspired. They feared to excite the anger of the people by saying that he was not. Christ declared that he came "in the way of righteousness"; and that the lower classes believed him, though the Priests and Pharisees did not.

Thus John, who was often consulted by Herod, and to whom that monarch showed great deference, and was often governed by his advice; whose doctrine prevailed very extensively among the people and the publicans, taught *some* creed older than Christianity. That is plain: and it is equally plain, that the very large

body of the Jews that adopted his doctrines, were neither Pharisees nor Sadducees, but the humble, common people. They must,
therefore, have been Essenes. It is plain, too, that Christ applied
for baptism as a sacred rite, well known and long practiced. It
was becoming to him, he said, to fulfill all righteousness.

In the 18th chapter of the Acts of the Apostles we read thus:
"And a certain Jew, named Apollos, born at Alexandria, an eloquent man, and mighty in the Scriptures, came to Ephesus. This
man *was instructed in the way of the Lord,* and, being fervent in
spirit, *he spake and taught diligently the things of the Lord, knowing only the baptism of John;* and he began to speak boldly in
the synagogue; whom, when Aquilla and Priscilla had heard, they
took him unto them, and expounded unto him *the way of God*
more perfectly."

Translating this from the symbolic and figurative language
into the true ordinary sense of the Greek text, it reads thus: "And
a certain Jew, named Apollos, an Alexandrian by birth, an eloquent
man, and of extensive learning, came to Ephesus. He had learned
in the mysteries the true doctrine in regard to God; and, being a
zealous enthusiast, he spoke and taught diligently the truths in
regard to the Deity, having received no other baptism than that
of John." He knew nothing in regard to Christianity; for he
had resided in Alexandria, and had just then come to Ephesus;
being, probably, a disciple of Philo, and a Therapeut.

"That, in all times," says St. Augustine, "is the Christian religion, which to know and follow is the most sure and certain
health, called according to that name, but not according to the
thing itself, of which it is the name; for the thing itself, which
is now called the Christian religion, *really was known to the Ancients,* nor was wanting at any time from the beginning of the
human race, until the time when Christ came in the flesh; from
whence the true religion, which had previously existed, began to
be called Christian; and this in our days is the Christian religion,
not as having been wanting in former times, but as having, in
later times, received this name." The disciples were first called
"Christians," at Antioch, when Barnabas and Paul began to
preach there.

The Wandering or Itinerant Jews or Exorcists, who assumed
to employ the Sacred Name in exorcising evil spirits, were no
doubt Therapeutæ or Essenes.

"And it came to pass," we read in the 19th chapter of the Acts, verses 1 to 4, "that while Apollos was at Corinth, Paul, having passed through the upper parts of Asia Minor, came to Ephesus; and finding certain *disciples,* he said to them, 'Have ye received the Holy Ghost since ye became Believers?' And they said unto him, 'We have not so much as heard that there *is* any Holy Ghost.' And he said to them, 'In what, then, were you baptized?' And they said 'In John's baptism.' Then said Paul, 'John indeed baptized with the baptism of repentance, saying to the people that they should believe in Him who was to come after him, that is, in Jesus Christ. When they heard this, they were baptized in the name of the Lord Jesus."

This faith, taught by John, and so nearly Christianity, could have been nothing but the doctrine of the Essenes; and there can be no doubt that John belonged to that sect. The place where he preached, his macerations and frugal diet, the doctrines he taught, all prove it conclusively. There was no other sect to which he *could* have belonged; certainly none so numerous as his, *except* the Essenes.

We find, from the two letters written by Paul to the brethren at Corinth, that City of Luxury and Corruption, that there were contentions among them. Rival sects had already, about the 57th year of our era, reared their banners there, as followers, some of Paul, some of Apollos, and some of Cephas. Some of them denied the resurrection. Paul urged them to adhere to the doctrines taught by himself, and had sent Timothy to them to bring them afresh to their recollection.

According to Paul, Christ was to come again. He was to put an end to all other Principalities and Powers, and finally to Death, and then be Himself once more merged in God; *who should then be all in all.*

The forms and ceremonies of the Essenes were symbolical. They had, according to Philo the Jew, four Degrees; the members being divided into two Orders, the *Practici* and *Therapeutici;* the latter being the contemplative and medical Brethren; and the former the active, practical, business men. They were Jews by birth; and had a greater affection for each other than the members of any other sect. Their brotherly love was intense. They fulfilled the Christian law, "Love one another." They despised riches. No one was to be found among them, having more than another. The possessions of one were intermingled with those of the others; so that they all had but one patrimony, and were brethren. Their piety toward God was extraordinary. Before sunrise they never spake a word about profane matters; but put up certain prayers which they had received from their forefathers. At dawn of day, and before it was light, their prayers and hymns ascended to Heaven. They were eminently faithful and true, and the Ministers of Peace. They had mysterious ceremonies, and initiations into their mysteries; and the Candidate promised that he would ever practise fidelity to all men, and especially to those in authority, "because no one obtains the government without God's assistance."

Whatever they said, was firmer than an oath; but they avoided swearing, and esteemed it worse than perjury. They were simple in their diet and mode of living, bore torture with fortitude, and despised death. They cultivated the science of medicine and were very skillful. They deemed it a good omen to dress in white robes. They had their own courts, and passed righteous judgments. They kept the Sabbath more rigorously than the Jews.

Their chief towns were Engaddi, near the Dead Sea, and Hebron. Engaddi was about 30 miles southeast from Jerusalem, and Hebron about 20 miles south of that city. Josephus and Eusebius speak of them as an ancient sect; and they were no doubt the first among the Jews to embrace Christianity: with whose faith and doctrine their own tenets had so many points of resemblance, and were indeed in a great measure the same. Pliny regarded them as a very ancient people.

In their devotions they turned toward the rising sun; as the Jews generally did toward the Temple. But they were no idolaters; for they observed the law of Moses with scrupulous fidelity. They held all things in common, and despised riches, their wants being supplied by the administration of Curators or Stewards. The Tetractys, composed of round dots instead of jods, was revered among them. This being a Pythagorean symbol, evidently, shows their connection with the school of Pythagoras; but their peculiar tenets more resemble those of Confucius and Zoroaster; and probably were adopted while they were prisoners in Persia; which explains their turning toward the Sun in prayer.

Their demeanor was sober and chaste. They submitted to the superintendence of governors whom they appointed over themselves. The whole of their time was spent in labor, meditation, and prayer; and they were most sedulously attentive to every call of justice and humanity, and every moral duty. They believed in the unity of God. They supposed the souls of men to have fallen, by a disastrous fate, from the regions of purity and light, into the bodies which they occupy; during their continuance in which they considered them confined as in a prison. Therefore they did not believe in the resurrection of the body; but in that of the soul only. They believed in a future state of rewards and punishments; and they disregarded the ceremonies or external forms enjoined in the law of Moses to be observed in the worship of God; holding that the words of that lawgiver were to be understood in a mysterious and recondite sense, and not according to their literal meaning. They offered no sacrifices, except at home; and by meditation they endeavored, as far as possible, to isolate the soul from the body, and carry it back to God.

Eusebius broadly admits "that the ancient Therapeutæ were Christians; and that their ancient writings were our Gospels and Epistles."

The Essenes were of the Eclectic Sect of Philosophers, and held Plato in the highest esteem; they believed that true philosophy, the greatest and most salutary gift of God to mortals, was scattered, in various portions, through all the different Sects; and that it was, consequently, the duty of every wise man to gather it from the several quarters where it lay dispersed, and to employ it, thus reunited, in destroying the dominion of impiety and vice.

The great festivals of the Solstices were observed in a distinguished manner by the Essenes; as would naturally be supposed, from the fact that they reverenced the Sun, not as a god, but as a symbol of light and fire; the fountain of which, the Orientals supposed God to be. They lived in continence and abstinence, and had establishments similar to the monasteries of the early Christians.

The writings of the Essenes were full of mysticism, parables, enigmas, and allegories. They believed in the esoteric and exoteric meanings of the Scriptures; and, as we have already said, they had a warrant for that in the Scriptures themselves. They found it in the Old Testament, as the Gnostics found it in the New. The Christian writers, and even Christ himself, recognized it as a truth, that all Scripture had an inner and an outer meaning. Thus we find it said as follows, in one of the Gospels:

"Unto you it is given to know the mystery of the Kingdom of God; but unto men *that are without*, all these things are done in parables; that seeing, they may see and not perceive, and hearing they may hear and not understand. . . . And the disciples came and said unto him, 'Why speakest Thou the truth in parables?'— He answered and said unto them, 'Because it is given unto *you* to know the mysteries of the Kingdom of Heaven, but to *them* it is not given.' "

Paul, in the 4th chapter of his Epistle to the Galatians, speaking of the simplest facts of the Old Testament, asserts that they are *an allegory*. In the 3d chapter of the second letter to the Corinthians, he declares himself a minister of the New Testament, appointed by God; "Not of the letter, but of the spirit; for the letter killeth." Origen and St. Gregory held that the Gospels were not to be taken in their literal sense; and Athanasius admonishes us that "Should we understand sacred writ according to the letter, we should fall into the most enormous blasphemies."

Eusebius said, "Those who preside over the Holy Scriptures, philosophize over them, and expound their literal sense by allegory."

The sources of our knowledge of the Kabalistic doctrines, are the books of Jezirah and Sohar, the former drawn up in the second century, and the latter a little later; but containing materials much older than themselves. In their most characteristic elements, they go back to the time of the exile. In them, as in the teachings of Zoroaster, everything that exists emanated from a source of infinite LIGHT. Before everything, existed THE ANCIENT OF DAYS, the KING OF LIGHT; a title often given to the Creator in the *Zend-Avesta* and the code of the *Sabæans*. With the idea so expressed is connected the pantheism of India. THE KING OF LIGHT, THE ANCIENT, is ALL THAT IS. He is not only the real cause of all Existences; he is Infinite [AINSOPH]. He is HIMSELF: there is nothing in Him that We can call *Thou*.

In the Indian doctrine, not only is the Supreme Being the real cause of all, but he is the only real Existence: all the rest is illusion. In the Kabalah, as in the Persian and Gnostic doctrines, He is the Supreme Being unknown to all, the "Unknown Father." The world is his revelation, and subsists only in Him. His attributes are reproduced there, with different modifications, and in different degrees, so that the Universe is His Holy Splendor: it is but His Mantle; but it must be revered in silence. All beings have emanated from the Supreme Being: The nearer a being is to Him, the more perfect it is; the more remote in the scale, the less its purity.

A ray of Light, shot from the Deity, is the cause and principle of all that exists. It is at once Father and Mother of All, in the sublimest sense. It penetrates everything; and without it nothing can exist an instant. From this double FORCE, designated by the two parts of the word I∴ H∴ U∴ H∴ emanated the FIRST-BORN of God, the Universal FORM, in which are contained all beings; the Persian and Platonic Archetype of things, united with the Infinite by the primitive ray of Light.

This First-Born is the Creative Agent, Conservator, and animating Principle of the Universe. It is THE LIGHT OF LIGHT. It possesses the three Primitive Forces of the Divinity, LIGHT, SPIRIT, and LIFE [Φώς, Πνευμά, and Ζωη]. As it has received what it gives, Light and Life, it is equally considered as the generative and conceptive Principle, the Primitive Man, ADAM KADMON. As such, it has revealed itself in ten emanations or *Sephiroth,* which are not ten different beings, nor even beings at all; but sources of life, vessels of Omnipotence, and types of Creation. They are *Sovereignty* or *Will, Wisdom, Intelligence, Benignity, Severity, Beauty, Victory, Glory, Permanency,* and *Empire.* These are attributes of God; and this idea, that God reveals Himself by His attributes, and that the human mind cannot perceive or discern God Himself, in his works, but only his mode of manifesting Himself, is a profound Truth. We know of the Invisible only what the Visible reveals.

Wisdom was called NOUS and LOGOS [and Νοῦς Λόγος], INTELLECT or the WORD. *Intelligence,* source of the oil of anointing, responds to the Holy Ghost of the Christian Faith.

Beauty is represented by green and yellow. *Victory* is YAHOVAH-TSABAOTH, the column on the right hand, the column *Jachin: Glory* is the column *Boaz,* on the left hand. And thus our symbols appear again in the Kabalah. And again the LIGHT, the object of our labors, appears as the creative power of Deity. The circle, also, was the special symbol of the first Sephirah, Kether, or the Crown.

We do not further follow the Kabalah in its four Worlds of Spirits, *Aziluth, Briah, Yezirah,* and *Asiah,* or of *emanation, creation, formation,* and *fabrication,* one inferior to and one emerging from the other, the superior always enveloping the inferior; its doctrine that, in all that exists, there is nothing purely material; that all comes from God, and in all He proceeds by irradiation; that everything subsists by the Divine ray that penetrates creation; and all is united by the Spirit of God, which is the life of life; so that all is God; the Existences that inhabit the four worlds, inferior to each other in proportion to their distance from the Great King of Light: the contest between the good and evil Angels and Principles, to endure until the Eternal Himself comes to end it and re-establish the primitive harmony; the four distinct parts of the Soul of Man; and the migrations of impure souls, until they are sufficiently purified to share with the Spirits of Light the contemplation of the Supreme Being whose Splendor fills the Universe.

The WORD was also found in the Phœnician Creed. As in all those of Asia, a WORD of God, written in starry characters, by the planetary Divinities, and communicated by the Demi-Gods, as a profound mystery, to the higher classes of the human race, to be communicated by them to mankind, created the world. The faith of the Phœnicians was an emanation from that ancient worship of the Stars, which in the creed of Zoroaster alone, is connected with a faith in one God. Light and Fire are the most important agents in the Phœnician faith. There is a race of children of the Light. They adored the Heaven with its Lights, deeming it the Supreme God.

Everything emanates from a Single Principle, and a Primitive Love, which is the Moving Power of All and governs all. Light, by its union with Spirit, whereof it is but the vehicle or symbol, is the Life of everything, and penetrates everything. It should therefore be respected and honored everywhere; for everywhere it governs and controls.

The Chaldaic and Jerusalem Paraphrasts endeavored to render the phrase, DEBAR-YAHOVAH [דבר יהוה], the Word of God, a personalty, wherever they met with it. The phrase, "And God created man," is, in the Jerusalem Targum, "And the Word of IHUH created man."

So, in xxviii. Gen. 20. 21, where Jacob says: "If God [אלהים זהיה

IHIH ALHIM] will be with me . . . then shall IHUH be my ALHIM
והיה יהוה לי לאלהים; UHIH IHUH LI LALHIM] ; and this stone
shall be God's House [יהיה בית אלהים. . IHIH BITH ALHIM]:
Onkelos paraphrases it, "If the word of IHUH will be my help
. . . . then the word of IHUH shall be my God."

So, in iii. Gen. 8, for "The Voice of the Lord God" [יהוה אלהים,
IHUH ALHIM], we have, "The Voice of the Word of IHUH."

In ix. Wisdom, 1, "O God of my Fathers and Lord of Mercy!
who has made all things with thy word. . ἐν λόγου σου."

And in xviii. Wisdom, 15, "Thine Almighty Word [Λογος] leaped down from Heaven."

Philo speaks of the Word as being the same with God. So in
several places he calls it " δεύτερος Θεὶος Λόγος," the Second Divinity; "εἰχὼν τὸυ Θεοῦ," the Image of God: the Divine Word that
made all things: "the ὕπαρχος," substitute, of God; and the like.

Thus, when John commenced to preach, had been for ages
agitated, by the Priests and Philosophers of the East and West,
the great questions concerning the eternity or creation of matter:
immediate or intermediate creation of the Universe by the Supreme God; the origin, object, and final extinction of evil; the
relations between the intellectual and material worlds, and between God and man; and the creation, fall, redemption, and
restoration to his first estate, of man.

The Jewish doctrine, differing in this from all the other Oriental
creeds, and even from the Alohaÿistic legend with which the book
of Genesis commences, attributed the creation to the immediate
action of the Supreme Being. The Theosophists of the other
Eastern Peoples interposed more than one intermediary between
God and the world. To place between them but a single Being,
to suppose for the production of the world but a single intermediary, was, in their eyes, to lower the Supreme Majesty. The
interval between God, who is perfect Purity, and matter, which is
base and foul, was too great for them to clear it at a single step.
Even in the Occident, neither Plato nor Philo could thus impoverish the Intellectual World.

Thus, Cerinthus of Ephesus, with most of the Gnostics, Philo,
the Kabalah, the Zend-Avesta, the Puranas, and all the Orient,
deemed the distance and antipathy between the Supreme Being
and the material world too great, to attribute to the former the
creation of the latter. Below, and emanating from, or created

by, the Ancient of Days, the Central Light, the Beginning, or First Principle [Ἀρχή], one, two, or more Principles, Existences, or Intellectual Beings were imagined, to some one or more of whom [without any immediate creative act on the part of the Great Immovable, Silent Deity], the immediate creation of the material and mental universe was due.

We have already spoken of many of the speculations on this point. To some, the world was created by the Logos or Word, first manifestation of, or emanation from, the Deity. To others, the beginning of creation was by the emanation of a ray of Light, creating the principle of *Light* and *Life*. The Primitive Thought, creating the inferior Deities, a succession of Intelligences, the Iynges of Zoroaster, his *Amshaspands, Izeds,* and *Ferouers,* the *Ideas* of Plato, the *Aions* of the Gnostics, the *Angels* of the Jews, the *Nous,* the *Demiourgos,* the Divine Reason, the *Powers* or *Forces* of Philo, and the Alohayim, Forces or Superior Gods of the ancient legend with which Genesis begins,— to these and other intermediaries the creation was owing. No restraints were laid on the Fancy and the Imagination. The veriest Abstractions became Existences and Realities. The attributes of God, personified, became Powers, Spirits, Intelligences.

God was the *Light of Light, Divine Fire,* the *Abstract Intellectuality,* the *Root* or *Germ* of the Universe. *Simon Magus,* founder of the Gnostic faith, and many of the early Judaizing Christians, admitted that the manifestations of the Supreme Being, as Father, or Jehovah, Son or Christ, and Holy Spirit, were only so many different *modes* of Existence, or *Forces* [δυναμεις] of the same God. To others they were, as were the multitude of Subordinate Intelligences, real and distinct beings.

The Oriental imagination revelled in the creation of these Inferior Intelligences, Powers of Good and Evil, and Angels. We have spoken of those imagined by the Persians and the Kabalists. In the Talmud, every star, every country, every town, and almost every tongue has a Prince of Heaven as its Protector. Jehuel is the guardian of fire, and Michael of water. Seven spirits assist each; those of fire being *Seraphiel, Gabriel, Nitriel, Tammael, Tchimschiel, Hadarniel,* and *Sarniel.* These seven are represented by the square columns of this Degree, while the columns Jachin and Boaz represent the angels of fire and water. But the columns are not representatives of these alone.

To Basilides, God was without name, uncreated, at first containing and concealing in Himself the Plenitude of His Perfections;
and when these are by Him displayed and manifested, there result
as many particular Existences, all analogous to Him, and still and
always Him. To the Essenes and the Gnostics, the East and the
West both devised this faith; that the Ideas, Conceptions, or
Manifestations of the Deity were so many Creations, so many Beings, all God, nothing without Him, but more than what we now
understand by the word *ideas*. They emanated from and were
again merged in God. They had a kind of middle existence between our modern ideas, and the intelligences or ideas, elevated to
the rank of genii, of the Oriental mythology.

These personified attributes of Deity, in the theory of Basilides,
were the Πρωτόγονος or *First-born,* Νοῦς [*Nous* or *Mind*] : from
it emanates Λογος [*Logos,* or THE WORD] from it Φρόνησις :
[*Phronesis, Intellect*] : from it Σοφια [*Sophia, Wisdom*] : from it
Δύναμις [*Dunamis, Power*] : and from it Διχαιοσύνη [*Dikaiosune,
Righteousness*] : to which latter the Jews gave the name of Ειρηνη
[*Eirene, Peace,* or *Calm*], the essential characteristics of Divinity,
and harmonious effect of all His perfections. The whole number
of successive emanations was 365, expressed by the Gnostics, in
Greek letters, by the mystic word ΑΒΡΑΞΑΣ [*Abraxas*] ; designating God as manifested, or the aggregate of his manifestations;
but not the Supreme and Secret God Himself. These three hundred and sixty-five Intelligences compose altogether the Fullness
or *Plenitude* [Πληρωμα] of the Divine Emanations.

With the Ophites, a sect of the Gnostics, there were seven inferior spirits [inferior to Ialdabaoth, the Demiourgos or Actual Cre-
ator] : *Michaël, Surièl, Raphaël, Gabriel, Thauthabaoth, Erataoth,*
and *Athaniel,* the genii of the stars called the Bull, the Dog, the
Lion, the Bear, the Serpent, the Eagle, and the Ass that formerly
figured in the constellation Cancer, and symbolized respectively
by those animals; as *Ialdabaoth, Iao, Adonaï, Eloï, Oraï,* and *As-
taphaï* were the genii of Saturn, the Moon, the Sun, Jupiter,
Venus, and Mercury.

The WORD appears in all these creeds. It is the *Ormuzd* of
Zoroaster. the *Ainsoph* of the Kabalah, the *Nous* of Platonism
and Philonism, and the *Sophia* or *Demiourgos* of the Gnostics.

And all these creeds, while admitting these different manifestations of the Supreme Being, held that His identity was immutable

and permanent. That was Plato's distinction between the Being always the same [τὸ ὄν] and the perpetual flow of things incessantly changing, the Genesis.

The belief in dualism in some shape, was universal. Those who held that everything emanated from God, aspired to God, and re-entered into God, believed that, among those emanations were two adverse Principles, of Light and Darkness, Good and Evil. This prevailed in Central Asia and in Syria; while in Egypt it assumed the form of Greek speculation. In the former, a second Intellectual Principle was admitted, active in its Empire of Darkness, audacious against the Empire of Light. So the Persians and Sabeans understood it. In Egypt, this second Principle was Matter, as the word was used by the Platonic School, with its sad attributes, Vacuity, Darkness, and Death. In their theory, matter could be animated only by the low communication of a principle of divine life. It resists the influences that would spiritualize it. That resisting Power is Satan, the rebellious Matter, Matter that does not partake of God.

To many there were two Principles; the Unknown Father, or Supreme and Eternal God, living in the centre of the Light, happy in the perfect purity of His being; the other, eternal Matter, that inert, shapeless, darksome mass, which they considered as the source of all evils, the mother and dwelling-place of Satan.

To Philo and the Platonists, there was a Soul of the world, creating visible things, and active in them, as agent of the Supreme Intelligence; realizing therein the ideas communicated to Him by that Intelligence, and which sometimes excel His conceptions, but which He executes without comprehending them.

The Apocalypse or Revelations, by whomever written, belongs to the Orient and to extreme antiquity. It reproduces what is far older than itself. It paints, with the strongest colors that the Oriental genius ever employed, the closing scenes of the great struggle of Light, and Truth, and Good, against Darkness, Error, and Evil; personified in that between the New Religion on one side, and Paganism and Judaism on the other. It is a particular application of the ancient myth of Ormuzd and his Genii against Ahriman and his Devs; and it celebrates the final triumph of Truth against the combined powers of mèn and demons. The ideas and imagery are borrowed from every quarter; and allusions are found in it to the doctrines of all ages. We are continually reminded of the Zend-Avesta, the Jewish Codes, Philo, and the Gnosis. The Seven Spirits surrounding the Throne of the Eternal, at the opening of the Grand Drama, and acting so important a part throughout, everywhere the first instruments of the Divine Will and Vengeance, are the Seven Amshaspands of Parsism; as the Twenty-four Ancients, offering to the Supreme Being the first supplications and the first homage, remind us of the Mysterious Chiefs of Judaism, foreshadow the Eons of Gnosticism, and reproduce the twenty-four Good Spirits created by Ormuzd and inclosed in an egg.

The Christ of the Apocalypse, First-born of Creation and of the Resurrection, is invested with the characteristics of the Ormuzd and Sosiosch of the Zend-Avesta, the Ainsoph of the Kabalah and the Carpistes [Καρπιότης] of the Gnostics. The idea that the true Initiates and Faithful become Kings and Priests, is at once Persian, Jewish, Christian, and Gnostic. And the definition of the Supreme Being, that He is at once Alpha and Omega, the beginning and the end—He that was, and is, and is to come, *i. e.,* Time illimitable, is Zoroaster's definition of Zerouane-Akherene.

The depths of Satan which no man can measure; his triumph for a time by fraud and violence; his being chained by an angel; his reprobation and his precipitation into a sea of metal; his names of the Serpent and the Dragon; the whole conflict of the Good Spirits or celestial armies against the bad; are so many ideas and designations found alike in the Zend-Avesta, the Kabalah, and the Gnosis.

We even find in the Apocalypse that singular Persian idea, which regards some of the lower animals as so many Devs or vehicles of Devs.

The guardianship of the earth by a good angel, the renewing of the earth and heavens, and the final triumph of pure and holy men, are the same victory of Good over Evil, for which the whole Orient looked.

The gold, and white raiments of the twenty-four Elders are, as in the Persian faith, the signs of a lofty perfection and divine purity.

Thus the Human mind labored and struggled and tortured itself for ages, to explain to itself what it felt, without confessing it, to be inexplicable. A vast crowd of indistinct abstractions, hovering in the imagination, a train of words embodying no tangible meaning, an inextricable labyrinth of subtleties, was the result.

But one grand idea ever emerged and stood prominent and unchangeable over the weltering chaos of confusion. God is great, and good, and wise. Evil and pain and sorrow are temporary, and for wise and beneficent purposes. They *must* be consistent with God's goodness, purity, and infinite perfection; and there *must* be a mode of explaining them, if we could but find it out; as, in all ways we will endeavor to do. Ultimately, Good will prevail, and Evil be overthrown. God alone *can* do this, and He *will* do it, by an Emanation from Himself, assuming the Human form and redeeming the world.

Behold the object, the end, the result, of the great speculations and logomachies of antiquity; the ultimate annihilation of evil, and restoration of Man to his first estate, by a Redeemer, a Masayah, a Christos, the incarnate Word, Reason, or Power of Deity.

This Redeemer is the Word or Logos, the Ormuzd of Zoroaster, the Ainsoph of the Kabalah, the Nous of Platonism and Philonism; He that was in the Beginning with God, and was God, and by Whom everything was made. That He was looked for by all the People of the East is abundantly shown by the Gospel of John and the Letters of Paul; wherein scarcely anything seemed necessary to be said in proof that such a Redeemer was to come; but all the energies of the writers are devoted to showing that Jesus was that Christos whom all the nations were expecting; the "Word," the Masayah, the Anointed or Consecrated One.

In this Degree the great contest between good and evil, in anticipation of the appearance and advent of the Word or Redeemer is symbolized; and the mysterious esoteric teachings of the Essenes and the Cabalists. Of the practices of the former we gain but glimpses in the ancient writers; but we know that, as their doctrines were taught by John the Baptist, they greatly resembled those of greater purity and more nearly perfect, taught by Jesus; and that not only Palestine was full of John's disciples, so that the Priests and Pharisees did not dare to deny John's inspiration; but his doctrine had extended to Asia Minor, and had made converts in luxurious Ephesus, as it also had in Alexandria in Egypt; and that they readily embraced the Christian faith, of which they had before not even heard.

These old controversies have died away, and the old faiths have faded into oblivion. But Masonry still survives, vigorous and strong, as when philosophy was taught in the schools of Alexandria and under the Portico; teaching the same old truths as the Essenes taught by the shores of the Dead Sea, and as John the Baptist preached in the Desert; truths imperishable as the Deity, and undeniable as Light. Those truths were gathered by the Essenes from the doctrines of the Orient and the Occident, from the Zend-Avesta and the Vedas, from Plato and Pythagoras, from India, Persia, Phœnicia, and Syria, from Greece and Egypt, and from the Holy Books of the Jews. Hence we are called Knights of the East and West, because their doctrines came from both. And these doctrines, the wheat sifted from the chaff, the Truth separated from Error, Masonry has garnered up in her heart of hearts, and through the fires of persecution, and the storms of calamity, has brought them and delivered them unto us. That God is One, immutable, unchangeable, infinitely just and good; that Light will finally overcome Darkness,—Good conquer Evil,· and Truth be victor over Error;—these, rejecting all the wild and useless speculations of the Zend-Avesta, the Kabalah, the Gnostics, and the Schools, are the religion and Philosophy of Masonry.

Those speculations and fancies it is useful to study; that knowing in what worthless and unfruitful investigations the mind may engage, you may the more value and appreciate the plain, simple, sublime, universally-acknowledged truths, which have in all ages been the Light by which Masons have been guided on their way; the Wisdom and Strength that like imperishable columns have sustained and will continue to sustain its glorious and magnificent Temple.

XVIII.

KNIGHT ROSE CROIX.

[Prince Rose Croix.]

EACH of us makes such applications to his own faith and creed, of the symbols and ceremonies of this Degree, as seems to him proper. With these special interpretations we have here nothing to do. Like the legend of the Master Khūrūm, in which some see figured the condemnation and sufferings of Christ; others those of the unfortunate Grand Master of the Templars; others those of the first Charles, King of England; and others still the annual descent of the Sun at the winter Solstice to the regions of darkness, the basis of many an ancient legend; so the ceremonies of this Degree receive different explanations; each interpreting them for himself, and being offended at the interpretation of no other.

In no other way could Masonry possess its character of Universality; that character which has ever been peculiar to it from its origin; and which enables two Kings, worshippers of different Deities, to sit together as Masters, while the walls of the first temple arose; and the men of Gebal, bowing down to the Phœnician Gods, to work by the side of the Hebrews to whom those Gods were abomination; and to sit with them in the same Lodge as brethren.

276

You have already learned that these ceremonies have one general significance, to every one, of every faith, who believes in God, and the soul's immortality.

The primitive men met in no Temples made with human hands. "God," said Stephen, the first Martyr, "dwelleth not in Temples made with hands." In the open air, under the overarching mysterious sky, in the great World-Temple, they uttered their vows and thanksgivings, and adored the God of Light; of that Light that was to them the type of Good, as darkness was the type of Evil.

All antiquity solved the enigma of the existence of Evil, by supposing the existence of a Principle of Evil, of Demons, fallen Angels, an Ahriman, a Typhon, a Siva, a Lok, or a Satan, that, first falling themselves, and plunged in misery and darkness, tempted man to his fall, and brought sin into the world. All believed in a future life, to be attained by purification and trials; in a state or successive states of reward and punishment; and in a Mediator or Redeemer, by whom the Evil Principle was to be overcome, and the Supreme Deity reconciled to His creatures. The belief was general, that He was to be born of a Virgin, and suffer a painful death. The Indians called him Chrishna; the Chinese, Kioun-tse; the Persians, Sosiosch; the Chaldeans, Dhouvanai; the Egyptians, Har-Oeri; Plato, Love; and the Scandinavians, Balder.

Chrishna, the Hindoo Redeemer, was cradled and educated among Shepherds. A Tyrant, at the time of his birth, ordered all the male children to be slain. He performed miracles, say his legends, even raising the dead. He washed the feet of the Brahmins, and was meek and lowly of spirit. He was born of a Virgin; descended to Hell, rose again, ascended to Heaven, charged his disciples to teach his doctrines, and gave them the gift of miracles.

The first Masonic Legislator whose memory is preserved to us by history, was Buddha, who, about a thousand years before the Christian era, reformed the religion of Manous. He called to the Priesthood all men, without distinction of caste, who felt themselves inspired by God to instruct men. Those who so associated themselves formed a Society of Prophets under the name of Samaneans. They recognized the existence of a single uncreated God, in whose bosom everything grows, is developed and transformed. The worship of this God reposed upon the obedience of all the beings He created. His feasts were those of the Solstices. The doctrines of Buddha pervaded India, China, and Japan. The Priests of Brahma, professing a dark and bloody creed, brutalized by Superstition, united together against Buddhism, and with the aid of Despotism, exterminated its followers. But their blood fertilized the new doctrine, which produced a new Society under the name of Gymnosophists; and a large number, fleeing to Ireland, planted their doctrines there, and there erected the round towers, some of which still stand, solid and unshaken as at first, visible monuments of the remotest ages.

The Phœnician Cosmogony, like all others in Asia, was the Word of God, written in astral characters, by the planetary Divinities, and communicated by the Demi-gods, as a profound mystery, to the brighter intelligences of Humanity, to be propagated by them among men. Their doctrines resembled the Ancient Sabeism, and being the faith of Hiram the King and his namesake the Artist, are of interest to all Masons. With them, the First Principle was half material, half spiritual, a dark air, animated and impregnated by the spirit; and a disordered chaos, covered with thick darkness. From this came the Word, and thence creation and generation; and thence a race of men, children of light, who adored Heaven and its Stars as the Supreme Being; and whose different gods were but incarnations of the Sun, the Moon, the Stars, and the Ether. *Chrysor* was the great igneous power of Nature, and *Baal* and *Malakarth* representations of the Sun and Moon, the latter word, in Hebrew, meaning Queen.

Man had fallen, but not by the tempting of the serpent. For, with the Phœnicians, the serpent was deemed to partake of the Divine Nature, and was sacred, as he was in Egypt. He was deemed to be immortal, unless slain by violence, becoming young again in his old age, by entering into and consuming himself. Hence the Serpent in a circle, holding his tail in his mouth, was an emblem of eternity. With the head of a hawk he was of a Divine Nature, and a symbol of the sun. Hence one Sect of the Gnostics took him for their good genius, and hence the brazen serpent reared by Moses in the Desert, on which the Israelites looked and lived.

"Before the chaos, that preceded the birth of Heaven and Earth," said the Chinese Lao-Tseu, "a single Being existed, im-

mense and silent, immutable and always acting; the mother of
the Universe. I know not the name of that Being, but I designate
it by the word Reason. Man has his model in the earth, the
earth in Heaven, Heaven in Reason, and Reason in itself."

"I am," says Isis, "Nature; parent of all things, the sovereign
of the Elements, the primitive progeny of Time, the most exalted
of the Deities, the first of the Heavenly Gods and Goddesses, the
Queen of the Shades, the uniform countenance; who dispose
with my rod the numerous lights of Heaven, the salubrious breezes
of the sea, and the mournful silence of the dead; whose single
Divinity the whole world venerates in many forms, with various
rites and by many names. The Egyptians, skilled in ancient lore,
worship me with proper ceremonies, and call me by my true name,
Isis the Queen."

The Hindu Vedas thus define the Deity:

"He who surpasses speech, and through whose power speech is
expressed, know thou that He is Brahma; and not these perishable things that man adores.

"He whom Intelligence cannot comprehend, and He alone, say
the sages, through whose Power the nature of Intelligence can be
understood, know thou that He is Brahma; and not these perishable things that man adores.

"He who cannot be seen by the organ of sight, and through
whose power the organ of seeing sees, know thou that He is
Brahma; and not these perishable things that man adores.

"He who cannot be heard by the organ of hearing, and through
whose power the organ of hearing hears, know thou that He is
Brahma; and not these perishable things that man adores.

"He who cannot be perceived by the organ of smelling, and
through whose power the organ of smelling smells, know thou that
He is Brahma; and not these perishable things that man adores."

"When God resolved to create the human race," said *Arius,*
"He made a Being that He called The WORD, The Son, *Wisdom,*
to the end that this Being might give existence to men." This
WORD is the *Ormuzd* of Zoroaster, the *Ainsoph* of the Kabalah,
the Noῦς of Plato and Philo, the *Wisdom* or *Demiourgos* of the
Gnostics.

That is the True Word, the knowledge of which our ancient
brethren sought as the priceless reward of their labors on the
Holy Temple: the Word of Life, the Divine Reason, "in whom

was Life, and that Life the Light of men"; "which long shone in darkness, and the darkness comprehended it not;" the Infinite Reason that is the Soul of Nature, immortal, of which the Word of this Degree reminds us; and to believe wherein and revere it, is the peculiar duty of every Mason.

"In the beginning," says the extract from some older work, with which John commences his Gospel, "was the Word, and the Word was near to God, and the Word was God. All things were made by Him, and without Him was not anything made that was made. In Him was Life, and the life was the Light of man; and the light shineth in darkness, and the darkness did not contain it."

It is an old tradition that this passage was from an older work. And Philostorgius and Nicephorus state, that when the Emperor Julian undertook to rebuild the Temple, a stone was taken up, that covered the mouth of a deep square cave, into which one of the laborers, being let down by a rope, found in the centre of the floor a cubical pillar, on which lay a roll or book, wrapped in a fine linen cloth, in which, in capital letters, was the foregoing passage.

However this may have been, it is plain that John's Gospel is a polemic against the Gnostics; and, stating at the outset the current doctrine in regard to the creation by the Word, he then addresses himself to show and urge that this Word was Jesus Christ.

And the first sentence, fully rendered into our language, would read thus: "When the process of emanation, of creation or evolution of existences inferior to the Supreme God began, the Word came into existence and was: and this word was [τρος τον Θεον] *near to* God; *i. e.* the immediate or first emanation from God: and it was God Himself, developed or manifested in that particular mode, and in action. And by that Word everything that is was created."—And thus Tertullian says that God made the World out of nothing, by means of His Word, Wisdom, or Power.

To Philo the Jew, as to the Gnostics, the Supreme Being was the *Primitive Light,* or *Archetype of Light,—Source* whence the rays emanate that illuminate Souls. He is the *Soul* of the World, and as such acts everywhere. He himself fills and bounds his whole existence, and his forces fill and penetrate everything. His Image is the WORD [LOGOS], a form more brilliant than fire, which is not pure light. This WORD dwells in God; for it is within His Intelligence that the Supreme Being frames for Himself the

Types of Ideas of all that is to assume reality in the Universe. The WORD is the Vehicle by which God acts on the Universe; the World of Ideas by means whereof God has created visible things; the more Ancient God, as compared with the Material World; Chief and General Representative of all Intelligences; the Archangel, type and representative of all spirits, even those of Mortals; the type of Man; the primitive man himself. These ideas are borrowed from Plato. And this WORD is not only the Creator ["*by Him was everything made that was made*"], but acts *in the place* of God; and through him act all the Powers and Attributes of God. And also, as first representative of the human race, he is the protector of Men and their Shepherd, the "Ben H'Adam," or Son of Man.

The actual condition of Man is not his primitive condition, that in which he was the image of the Word. His unruly passions have caused him to fall from his original lofty estate. But he may rise again, by following the teachings of Heavenly Wisdom, and the Angels whom God commissions to aid him in escaping from the entanglements of the body; and by fighting bravely against Evil, the existence of which God has allowed solely to furnish him with the means of exercising his free will.

The Supreme Being of the Egyptians was *Amūn,* a secret and concealed God, the Unknown Father of the Gnostics, the Source of Divine Life, and of all force, the Plenitude of all, comprehending all things in Himself, the original Light. He *creates* nothing; but everything *emanates* from Him: and all other Gods are but his manifestations. From Him, by the utterance of a Word, emanated *Neith,* the Divine Mother of all things, the Primitive THOUGHT, the FORCE that puts everything in movement, the SPIRIT everywhere extended, *the Deity of Light and Mother of the Sun.*

Of this Supreme Being, *Osiris* was the image, Source of all Good in the moral and physical world, and constant foe of Typhon, the Genius of Evil, the Satan of Gnosticism, brute matter, deemed to be always at feud with the spirit that flowed from the Deity; and over whom Har-Oeri, the Redeemer, Son of Isis and Osiris, is finally to prevail.

In the Zend-Avesta of the Persians the Supreme Being is *Time without limit,* ZERUANE AKHERENE.—No origin could be assigned to Him; for He was enveloped in His own Glory, and

His Nature and Attributes were so inaccessible to human Intelligence, that He was but the object of a silent veneration. The commencement of Creation was by emanation from Him. The first
emanation was the Primitive Light, and from this Light emerged
Ormuzd, the *King of Light,* who, by the WORD, created the World
in its purity, is its Preserver and Judge, a Holy and Sacred Being, Intelligence and Knowledge, Himself Time without limit,
and wielding all the powers of the Supreme Being.

In this Persian faith, as taught many centuries before our era,
and embodied in the Zend-Avesta, there was in man a pure Principle, proceeding from the Supreme Being, produced by the Will
and Word of Ormuzd. To that was united an impure principle,
proceeding from a foreign influence, that of Ahriman, the Dragon,
or principle of Evil. Tempted by Ahriman, the first man and
woman had fallen; and for twelve thousand years there was to be
war between *Ormuzd* and the Good Spirits created by him, and
Ahriman and the Evil ones whom he had called into existence.

But pure souls are assisted by the Good Spirits, the Triumph of
the Good Principle is determined upon in the decrees of the Supreme Being, and the period of that triumph will infallibly arrive.
At the moment when the earth shall be most afflicted with the
evils brought upon it by the Spirits of perdition, three Prophets
will appear to bring assistance to mortals. Sosiosch, Chief of the
Three, will regenerate the world, and restore to it its primitive
Beauty, Strength, and Purity. He will judge the good and the
wicked. After the universal resurrection of the Good, the pure
Spirits will conduct them to an abode of eternal happiness. Ahriman, his evil Demons, and all the world, will be purified in a torrent of liquid burning metal. The Law of Ormuzd will rule
everywhere: all men will be happy: all, enjoying an unalterable
bliss, will unite with Sosiosch in singing the praises of the Supreme Being.

These doctrines, with some modifications, were adopted by the
Kabalists and afterward by the Gnostics.

Apollonius of Tyana says: "We shall render the most appropriate worship to the Deity, when to that God whom we call the
First, who is One, and separate from all, and after whom we recognize the others, we present no offerings whatever, kindle to Him
no fire, dedicate to Him no sensible thing; for he needs nothing,
even of all that natures more exalted than ours could give. The

earth produces no plant, the air nourishes no animal, there is in short nothing, which would not be impure in his sight. In addressing ourselves to Him, we must use only the higher word, that, I mean, which is not expressed by the mouth,—the silent inner word of the spirit. . . . . From the most Glorious of all Beings, we must seek for blessings, by that which is most glorious in ourselves; and that is the spirit, which needs no organ."

Strabo says: "This one Supreme Essence is that which embraces us all, the water and the land, that which we call the Heavens, the World, the Nature of things. This Highest Being should be worshipped, without any visible image, in sacred groves. In such retreats the devout should lay themselves down to sleep, and expect signs from God in dreams."

Aristotle says: "It has been handed down in a mythical form, from the earliest times to posterity, that there are Gods, and that The Divine compasses entire nature. All besides this has been added, after the mythical style, for the purpose of persuading the multitude, and for the interest of the laws and the advantage of the State. Thus men have given to the Gods human forms, and have even represented them under the figure of other beings, in the train of which fictions followed many more of the same sort. But if, from all this, we separate the original principle, and consider it alone, namely, that the first Essences are Gods, we shall find that this has been divinely said; and since it is probable that philosophy and the arts have been several times, so far as that is possible, found and lost, such doctrines may have been preserved to our times as the remains of ancient wisdom."

Porphyry says: "By images addressed to sense, the ancients represented God and his powers—by the visible they typified the invisible for those who had learned to read, in these types, as in a book, a treatise on the Gods. We need not wonder if the ignorant consider the images to be nothing more than wood or stone; for just so, they who are ignorant of writing see nothing in monuments but stone, nothing in tablets but wood, and in books but a tissue of papyrus."

Apollonius of Tyana held, that birth and death are only in appearance; that which separates itself from the *one* substance (the *one* Divine essence), and is caught up by matter, seems to be born; that, again, which releases itself from the bonds of matter, and is reunited with the one Divine Essence, seems to die. There is, at most, an alteration between becoming visible and becoming invisible. In all there is, properly speaking, but the one essence, which alone acts and suffers, by becoming all things to all; the Eternal God, whom men wrong, when they deprive Him of what properly can be attributed to Him only, and transfer it to other names and persons.

The New Platonists substituted the idea of the Absolute, for the Supreme Essence itself;—as the first, simplest principle, anterior to all existence; of which nothing determinate can be predicated; to which no consciousness, no self-contemplation can be ascribed; inasmuch as to do so, would immediately imply a quality, a distinction of subject and object. This Supreme Entity can be known only by an intellectual intuition of the Spirit, transcending itself, and emancipating itself from its own limits.

This mere logical tendency, by means of which men thought to arrive at the conception of such an absolute, the ὄν, was united with a certain mysticism, which, by a transcendent state of feeling, communicated, as it were, to this abstraction what the mind would receive as a reality. The absorption of the Spirit into that superexistence (τὸ ἐπέκεινα τῆς οὐσίας), so as to be entirely identified with it, or such a revelation of the latter to the spirit raised above itself, was regarded as the highest end which the spiritual life could reach.

The New Platonists' idea of God, was that of One Simple Original Essence, exalted above all plurality and all becoming; the only true Being; unchangeable, eternal [Εἷς ὤν ἐνὶ τῷ νῦν τὸ ἀεὶ πεπλήρωκε καὶ μόνον ἐστι τὸ κατὰ τοῦτον ὄντως ὤν.] : from whom all Existence in its several gradations has emanated— the world of Gods, as nearest akin to Himself, being first, and at the head of all. In these Gods, that perfection, which in the Supreme Essence was inclosed and unevolved, is expanded and becomes knowable. They serve to exhibit in different forms the image of that Supreme Essence, to which no soul can rise, except by the loftiest flight of contemplation; and after it has rid itself from all that pertains to sense—from all manifoldness. They are the mediators between man (amazed and stupefied by manifoldness) and the Supreme Unity.

Philo says: "He who disbelieves the miraculous, simply as the miraculous, neither knows God, nor has he ever sought after Him; for otherwise he would have understood, by looking at that truly great and awe-inspiring sight, the miracle of the Universe, that these miracles (in God's providential guidance of His people) are but child's play for the Divine Power. But the truly miraculous has become despised through familiarity. The universal, on the contrary, although in itself insignificant, yet, through our love of novelty, transports us with amazement."

In opposition to the anthropopathism of the Jewish Scriptures, the Alexandrian Jews endeavored to purify the idea of God from all admixture of the Human. By the exclusion of every human passion, it was sublimated to a something devoid of all attributes, and wholly transcendental; and the mere Being [ὄυ], the Good, in and by itself, the Absolute of Platonism, was substituted for the personal Deity [יהוה] of the Old Testament. By soaring upward, beyond all created existence, the mind, disengaging itself from the Sensible, attains to the intellectual intuition of this Absolute Being; of whom, however, it can predicate nothing but existence, and sets aside all other determinations as not answering to the exalted nature of the Supreme Essence.

Thus Philo makes a distinction between those who are in the proper sense Sons of God, having by means of contemplation raised themselves to the highest Being, or attained to a knowledge of Him, in His immediate self-manifestation, and those who know God only in his mediate revelation through his operation—such as He declares Himself in creation—in the revelation still veiled in the letter of Scripture—those, in short, who attach themselves simply to the Logos, and consider this to be the Supreme God; who are the sons of the Logos, rather than of the True Being, (ὄυ)

"God," says Pythagoras, "is neither the object of sense, nor subject to passion, but invisible, only intelligible, and supremely intelligent. In His body He is like the *light,* and in His soul He resembles truth. He is the universal *spirit* that pervades and diffuseth itself over all nature. All beings receive their *life* from Him. There is but one only God, who is not, as some are apt to imagine, seated above the world, beyond the orb of the Universe; but being Himself all in all, He sees all the beings that fill His immensity; the only Principle, the *Light* of Heaven, the Father of all. He *produces everything;* He orders and disposes everything; He is the REASON, the LIFE, and the MOTION of all being."

"I am the LIGHT of the world; he that followeth Me shall not walk in DARKNESS, but shall have the LIGHT OF LIFE." So said the Founder of the Christian Religion, as His words are reported by John the Apostle.

God, say the sacred writings of the Jews, appeared to Moses in a FLAME OF FIRE, in the midst of a bush, which was not consumed. He descended upon Mount Sinai, as the smoke of a *furnace;* He went before the children of Israel, by day, in a pillar of cloud, and, by night, in a pillar of *fire,* to give them *light.* "Call *you* on the name of *your* Gods," said Elijah the Prophet to the Priests of Baal, "and I will call upon the name of ADONAI; and the God that answereth *by fire,* let him be God."

According to the Kabalah, as according to the doctrines of Zoroaster, everything that exists has emanated from a source of infinite light. Before all things, existed *the Primitive Being,* THE ANCIENT OF DAYS, *the Ancient King of Light;* a title the more remarkable, because it is frequently given to the Creator in the Zend-Avesta, and in the Code of the Sabeans, and occurs in the Jewish Scriptures.

The world was His Revelation, God revealed; and subsisted only in Him. His attributes were there reproduced with various modifications and in different degrees; so that the Universe was His Holy Splendor, His Mantle. He was to be adored in silence; and perfection consisted in a nearer approach to Him.

Before the creation of worlds, the PRIMITIVE LIGHT filled all space, so that there was no void. When the Supreme Being, existing in this Light, resolved to display His perfections, or manifest them in worlds, He withdrew within Himself, formed around Him a void space, and shot forth His first emanation, a ray of light; the cause and principle of everything that exists, uniting both the generative and conceptive power, which penetrates everything, and without which nothing could subsist for an instant.

Man fell, seduced by the Evil Spirits most remote from the Great King of Light; those of the fourth world of spirits, Asiah, whose chief was Belial. They wage incessant war against the pure Intelligences of the other worlds, who, like the Amshaspands, Izeds, and Ferouers of the Persians are the tutelary guardians of man. In the beginning, all was unison and harmony; full of the same divine light and perfect purity. The Seven Kings of Evil fell, and the Universe was troubled. Then the Creator took from the Seven Kings the principles of Good and of Light, and divided them among the four worlds of Spirits, giving to the first three the Pure Intelligences, united in love and harmony, while to the fourth were vouchsafed only some feeble glimmerings of light.

When the strife between these and the good angels shall have continued the appointed time, and these Spirits enveloped in darkness shall long and in vain have endeavored to absorb the Divine light and life, then will the Eternal Himself come to correct them. He will deliver them from the gross envelopes of matter that hold them captive, will re-animate and strengthen the ray of light or spiritual nature which they have preserved, and re-establish throughout the Universe that primitive Harmony which was its bliss.

Marcion, the Gnostic, said, "The Soul of the True Christian, adopted as a child by the Supreme Being, to whom it has long been a stranger, receives from Him the Spirit and Divine life. It is led and confirmed, by this gift, in a pure and holy life, like that of God; and if it so completes its earthly career, in charity, chastity, and sanctity, it will one day be disengaged from its material envelope, as the ripe grain is detached from the straw, and as the young bird escapes from its shell. Like the angels, it will share in the bliss of the Good and Perfect Father, re-clothed in an aerial body or organ, and made like unto the Angels in Heaven."

You see, my brother, what is the meaning of Masonic "Light." You see why the EAST of the Lodge, where the initial letter of the Name of the Deity overhangs the Master, is the place of Light. Light, as contradistinguished from darkness, is Good, as contradistinguished from Evil: and it is that Light, the true knowledge of Deity, the Eternal Good, for which Masons in all ages have sought. Still Masonry marches steadily onward toward that Light that shines in the great distance, the Light of that day when Evil, overcome and vanquished, shall fade away and disappear forever, and Life and Light be the one law of the Universe, and its eternal Harmony.

The Degree of Rose ✠ teaches three things;—the unity, immutability and goodness of God; the immortality of the Soul; and the ultimate defeat and extinction of evil and wrong and sorrow, by a Redeemer or Messiah, yet to come, if he has not already appeared.

It replaces the three pillars of the old Temple, with three that have already been explained to you,—Faith [in God, mankind, and man's self], Hope [in the victory over evil, the advancement of

Humanity, and a hereafter], and Charity [relieving the wants. and tolerant of the errors and faults of others]. To be trustful, to be hopeful, to be indulgent; these, in an age of selfishness, of ill opinion of human nature, of harsh and bitter judgment, are the most important Masonic Virtues, and the true supports of every Masonic Temple. And they are the old pillars of the Temple under different names. For he only is wise who judges others charitably; he only is strong who is hopeful; and there is no beauty like a firm faith in God, our fellows and ourself.

The second apartment, clothed in mourning, the columns of the Temple shattered and prostrate, and the brethren bowed down in the deepest dejection, represents the world under the tyranny of the Principle of Evil; where virtue is persecuted and vice reward- ed; where the righteous starve for bread, and the wicked live sumptuously and dress in purple and fine linen; where insolent ignorance rules, and learning and genius serve; where King and Priest trample on liberty and the rights of conscience; where free- dom hides in caves and mountains, and sycophancy and servility fawn and thrive; where the cry of the widow and the orphan starving for want of food, and shivering with cold, rises ever to Heaven, from a million miserable hovels; where men, willing to labor, and starving, they and their children and the wives of their bosoms, beg plaintively for work, when the pampered capitalist stops his mills; where the law punishes her who, starving, steals a loaf, and lets the seducer go free; where the success of a party justifies murder, and violence and rapine go unpunished; and where he who with many years' cheating and grinding the faces of the poor grows rich, receives office and honor in life, and after death brave funeral and a splendid mausoleum:—this world, where, since its making, war has never ceased, nor man paused in the sad task of torturing and murdering his brother; and of which ambition, avarice, envy, hatred, lust, and the rest of Ahriman's and Typhon's army make a Pandemonium: this world, sunk in sin, reeking with baseness, clamorous with sorrow and misery. If any see in it also a type of the sorrow of the Craft for the death of Hiram, the grief of the Jews at the fall of Jerusalem, the misery of the Templars at the ruin of their order and the death of De Molay, or the world's agony and pangs of woe at the death of the Redeemer, it is the right of each to do so.

The third apartment represents the consequences of sin and

vice, and the hell made of the human heart, by its fiery passions. If any see in it also a type of the Hades of the Greeks, the Gehenna of the Hebrews, the Tartarus of the Romans, or the Hell of the Christians, or only of the agonies of remorse and the tortures of an upbraiding conscience, it is the right of each to do so.

The fourth apartment represents the Universe, freed from the insolent dominion and tyranny of the Principle of Evil, and brilliant with the true Light that flows from the Supreme Deity; when sin and wrong, and pain and sorrow, remorse and misery shall be no more forever; when the great plans of Infinite Eternal Wisdom shall be fully developed; and all God's creatures, seeing that all apparent evil and individual suffering and wrong were but the drops that went to swell the great river of infinite goodness, shall know that vast as is the power of Deity, His goodness and beneficence are infinite as His power. If any see in it a type of the peculiar mysteries of any faith or creed, or an allusion to any past occurrences, it is their right to do so. Let each apply its symbols as he pleases. To all of us they typify the universal rule of Masonry,—of its three chief virtues, Faith, Hope and Charity; of brotherly love and universal benevolence. We labor here to no other end. These symbols need no other interpretation.

The obligations of our Ancient Brethren of the Rose ✠ were to fulfill all the duties of friendship, cheerfulness, charity, peace, liberality, temperance and chastity: and scrupulously to avoid impurity, haughtiness, hatred, anger, and every other kind of vice. They took their philosophy from the old Theology of the Egyptians, as Moses and Solomon had done, and borrowed its hieroglyphics and the ciphers of the Hebrews. Their principal rules were, to exercise the profession of medicine charitably and without fee, to advance the cause of virtue, enlarge the sciences, and induce men to live as in the primitive times of the world.

When this Degree had its origin, it is not important to inquire; nor with what different rites it has been practised in different countries and at various times. It is of very high antiquity. Its ceremonies differ with the degrees of latitude and longitude, and it receives variant interpretations. If we were to examine all the different ceremonials, their emblems, and their formulas, we should see that all that belongs to the primitive and essential elements of the order, is respected in every sanctuary. All alike practise virtue, that it may produce fruit. All labor, like us, for the ex-

tirpation of vice, the purification of man, the development of the
arts and sciences, and the relief of humanity.

None admit an adept to their lofty philosophical knowledge, and
mysterious sciences, until he has been purified at the altar of the
symbolic Degrees. Of what importance are differences of opinion
as to the age and genealogy of the Degree, or variance in the practice, ceremonial and liturgy, or the shade of color of the banner
under which each tribe of Israel marched, if all revere the Holy
Arch of the symbolic Degrees, first and unalterable source of Free-
Masonry; if all revere our conservative principles, and are with us
in the great purposes of our organization?

If, anywhere, brethren of a particular religious belief have been
excluded from this Degree, it merely shows how gravely the purposes and plan of Masonry may be misunderstood. For whenever
the door of any Degree is closed against him who believes in one
God and the soul's immortality, on account of the other tenets of
his faith, that Degree is Masonry no longer. No Mason has the
right to interpret the symbols of this Degree for another, or to refuse him its mysteries, if he will not take them with the explanation and commentary superadded.

Listen, my brother, to *our* explanation of the symbols of the
Degree, and then give them such further interpretation as you
think fit.

The *Cross* has been a sacred symbol from the earliest Antiquity.
It is found upon all the enduring monuments of the world, in
Egypt, in Assyria, in Hindostan, in Persia, and on the Buddhist
towers of Ireland. Buddha was said to have died upon it. The
Druids cut an oak into its shape and held it sacred, and built their
temples in that form. Pointing to the four quarters of the world,
it was the symbol of universal nature. It was on a cruciform tree,
that Chrishna was said to have expired, pierced with arrows. It
was revered in Mexico.

But its peculiar meaning in this Degree, is that given to it by
the Ancient Egyptians. *Thoth* or *Phtha* is represented on the oldest monuments carrying in his hand the *Crux Ansata,* or *Ankh,*
[a Tau cross, with a ring or circle over it]. He is so seen on the
double tablet of Shufu and Noh Shufu, builders of the greatest of
the Pyramids, at Wady Meghara, in the peninsula of Sinai. It was
the hieroglyphic for *life,* and with a triangle prefixed meant *life-
giving.* To us therefore it is the symbol of *Life*—of that life

that emanated from the Deity, and of that Eternal Life for which we all hope; through our faith in God's infinite goodness.

The ROSE was anciently sacred to Aurora and the Sun. It is a symbol of *Dawn,* of the resurrection of Light and the renewal of life, and therefore of the dawn of the first day, and more particularly of the resurrection: and the Cross and Rose together are therefore hieroglyphically to be read, *the Dawn of Eternal Life* which all Nations have hoped for by the advent of a Redeemer.

The *Pelican* feeding her young is an emblem of the large and bountiful beneficence of Nature, of the Redeemer of fallen man, and of that humanity and charity that ought to distinguish a Knight of this Degree.

The *Eagle* was the living Symbol of the Egyptian God *Mendes* or *Menthra,* whom *Sesostris-Ramses* made one with *Amun-Re,* the God of Thebes and Upper Egypt, and the representative of the Sun, the word RE meaning *Sun* or *King.*

The *Compass* surmounted with a *crown* signifies that notwithstanding the high rank attained in Masonry by a Knight of the Rose Croix, equity and impartiality are invariably to govern his conduct.

To the word INRI, inscribed on the Crux Ansata over the Master's Seat, many meanings have been assigned. The Christian Initiate reverentially sees in it the initials of the inscription upon the cross on which Christ suffered—*Iesus Nazarenus Rex Iudæorum.* The sages of Antiquity connected it with one of the greatest secrets of Nature, that of universal regeneration. They interpreted it thus, *Igne Natura renovatur integra;* [entire nature is renovated by fire]: The Alchemical or Hermetic Masons framed for it this aphorism, *Igne nitrum roris invenitur.* And the Jesuits are charged with having applied to it this odious axiom, *Justum necare reges impios.* The four letters are the initials of the Hebrew words that represent the four elements—*Iammim,* the seas or water; *Nour,* fire; *Rouach,* the air, and *Iebeschah,* the dry earth. How we read it, I need not repeat to you.

The CROSS, **X,** was the Sign of the Creative Wisdom or Logos, the Son of God. Plato says, "He expressed him upon the Universe in the figure of the letter X. The next Power to the Supreme God was decussated or figured in the shape of a Cross on the Universe." Mithras signed his soldiers on the forehead with a

Cross. ✗ is the mark of 600, the mysterious cycle of the Incarnations.

We constantly see the Tau and the Resh united thus ₱. These two letters, in the old Samaritan, as found in Arius, stand, the first for 400, the second for 200=600. This is the Staff of Osiris, also, and his monogram, and was adopted by the Christians as a Sign. On a medal ₱ of Constantius is this inscription, *"In hoc signo victor eris* ✶ *."* An inscription in the Duomo at Milan reads, *"*✗*. et* ₱*. Christi · Nomina · Sancta · Teneï."*

The Egyptians used as a Sign of their God Canobus, a ⊤ or a ✠ indifferently. The Vaishnavas of India have also the same Sacred Tau, which they also mark with Crosses, thus ✠, and with triangles, thus, ✡. The vestments of the priests of Horus were covered with these Crosses ✳. So was the dress ╈ ╈ of the Lama of Thibet. The Sectarian marks of the Jains are ╈ ╈. The distinctive badge of the Sect of Xac Japonicus is 卍. It is the Sign of Fo, identical with the Cross of Christ.

On the ruins of Mandore, in India, among other mystic emblems, are the mystic triangle, and the interlaced triangle, ✡. This is also found on ancient coins and medals, excavated from the ruins of Oojein and other ancient cities of India.

You entered here amid gloom and into shadow, and are clad in the apparel of sorrow. Lament, with us, the sad condition of the Human race, in this vale of tears! the calamities of men and the agonies of nations! the darkness of the bewildered soul, oppressed by doubt and apprehension!

There is no human soul that is not sad at times. There is no thoughtful soul that does not at times despair. There is perhaps none, of all that think at all of anything beyond the needs and interests of the body, that is not at times startled and terrified by the awful questions which, feeling as though it were a guilty thing for doing so, it whispers to itself in its inmost depths. Some Demon seems to torture it with doubts, and to crush it with despair, asking whether, after all, it is certain that its convictions are true, and its faith well founded: whether it is indeed sure that a God of Infinite Love and Beneficence rules the Universe, or only some great remorseless Fate and iron Necessity, hid in impenetrable gloom, and to which men and their sufferings and sorrows, their hopes and joys, their ambitions and deeds, are of no more interest or importance than the motes that dance in the sunshine; or a

Being that amuses Himself with the incredible vanity and folly, the writhings and contortions of the insignificant insects that compose Humanity, and idly imagine that they resemble the Omnipotent. "What are we," the Tempter asks, "but puppets in a show-box? O Omnipotent destiny, pull our strings gently! Dance us mercifully off our miserable little stage!"

"Is it not," the Demon whispers, "merely the inordinate vanity of man that causes him now to pretend to himself that he is like unto God in intellect, sympathies and passions, as it was that which, at the beginning, made him believe that he was, in his bodily shape and organs, the very image of the Deity? Is not his God merely his own shadow, projected in gigantic outlines upon the clouds? Does he not create for himself a God out of himself, by merely adding indefinite extension to his own faculties, powers, and passions?"

"Who," the Voice that will not be always silent whispers, "has ever thoroughly satisfied himself with his own arguments in respect to his own nature? Who ever demonstrated to himself, with a conclusiveness that elevated the belief to certainty, that he was an immortal spirit, dwelling only temporarily in the house and envelope of the body, and to live on forever after that shall have decayed? Who ever has demonstrated or ever can demonstrate that the intellect of Man differs from that of the wiser animals, otherwise than in degree? Who has ever done more than to utter nonsense and incoherencies in regard to the difference between the instincts of the dog and the reason of Man? The horse, the dog, the elephant, are as conscious of their identity as we are. They think, dream, remember, argue with themselves, devise, plan, and *reason.* What is the intellect and intelligence of the man but the intellect of the animal in a higher degree or larger quantity?" In the *real* explanation of a single thought of a dog, all metaphysics will be condensed.

And with still more terrible significance, the Voice asks, in what respect the masses of men, the vast swarms of the human race, have proven themselves either wiser or better than the animals in whose eyes a higher intelligence shines than in *their* dull, unintellectual orbs; in what respect they have proven themselves worthy of or suited for an immortal life. Would that be a prize of any value to the vast majority? Do they show, here upon earth, any capacity to improve, any fitness for a state of existence in which they could not crouch to power, like hounds dreading the lash, or tyrannize over defenceless weakness; in which they could not hate, and persecute, and torture, and exterminate; in which they could not trade, and speculate, and over-reach, and entrap the unwary and cheat the confiding and gamble and thrive, and sniff with self-righteousness at the short-comings of others, and thank God that they were not like other men? What, to immense numbers of men, would be the value of a Heaven where they could not lie and libel, and ply base avocations for profitable returns?

Sadly we look around us, and read the gloomy and dreary records of the old dead and rotten ages. More than eighteen centuries have staggered away into the spectral realm of the Past, since Christ, teaching the Religion of Love, was crucified, that it might become a Religion of Hate; and His Doctrines are not yet even nominally accepted as true by a fourth of mankind. Since His death, what incalculable swarms of human beings have lived and died in total unbelief of all that we deem essential to Salvation! What multitudinous myriads of souls, since the darkness of idolatrous superstition settled down, thick and impenetrable, upon the earth, have flocked up toward the eternal Throne of God, to receive His judgment?

The Religion of Love proved to be, for seventeen long centuries, as much the Religion of Hate, and infinitely more the Religion of Persecution, than Mahometanism, its unconquerable rival. Heresies grew up before the Apostles died; and God hated the Nicolaïtans, while John, at Patmos, proclaimed His coming wrath. Sects wrangled, and each, as it gained the power, persecuted the other, until the soil of the whole Christian world was watered with the blood, and fattened on the flesh, and whitened with the bones, of martyrs, and human ingenuity was taxed to its utmost to invent new modes by which tortures and agonies could be prolonged and made more exquisite.

"By what right," whispers the Voice, "does this savage, merciless, persecuting animal, to which the sufferings and writhings of others of its wretched kind furnish the most pleasurable sensations, and the mass of which care only to eat, sleep, be clothed, and wallow in sensual pleasures, and the best of which wrangle, hate, envy, and, with few exceptions, regard their own interests alone,— with what right does it endeavor to delude itself into the conviction that it is *not* an animal, as the wolf, the hyena, and the tiger are, but a somewhat nobler, a spirit destined to be immortal, a spark of the essential Light, Fire and Reason, which are God? What other immortality than one of selfishness could this creature enjoy? Of what other is it capable? Must not immortality commence *here* and is not *life* a part of it? How shall death change the base nature of the base soul? Why have not those other animals that only faintly imitate the wanton, savage, human cruelty and thirst for blood, the same right as man has, to expect a resurrection and an Eternity of existence, or a Heaven of Love?

The world improves. Man ceases to persecute,—when the persecuted become too numerous and strong, longer to submit to it. That source of pleasure closed, men exercise the ingenuities of their cruelty on the animals and other living things below them. To deprive other creatures of the life which God gave them, and this not only that we may eat their flesh for food, but out of mere savage wantonness, is the agreeable employment and amusement of man, who prides himself on being the Lord of Creation, and a little lower than the Angels. If he can no longer use the rack, the gibbet, the pincers, and the stake, he can hate, and slander, and delight in the thought that he will, hereafter, luxuriously enjoying the sensual beatitudes of Heaven, see with pleasure the writhing agonies of those justly damned for daring to hold opinions contrary to his own, upon subjects totally beyond the comprehension both of them and him.

Where the armies of the despots cease to slay and ravage, the armies of "Freedom" take their place, and, the black and white commingled, slaughter and burn and ravish. Each age re-enacts the crimes as well as the follies of its predecessors, and still war licenses outrage and turns fruitful lands into deserts, and God is thanked in the Churches for bloody butcheries, and the remorseless devastators, even when swollen by plunder, are crowned with laurels and receive ovations.

Of the whole of mankind, not one in ten thousand has any aspirations beyond the daily needs of the gross animal life. In this age and in all others, all men except a few, in most countries, are born to be mere beasts of burden, co-laborers with the horse and the ox. Profoundly ignorant, even in "civilized" lands, they think and reason like the animals by the side of which they toil. For them, God, Soul, Spirit, Immortality, are mere words, without any real meaning. The God of nineteen-twentieths of the Christian world is only Bel, Moloch, Zeus, or at best Osiris, Mithras, or Adonaï, under another name, worshipped with the old Pagan ceremonies and ritualistic formulas. It is the Statue of Olympian Jove, worshipped as the Father, in the Christian Church that was a Pagan Temple; it is the Statue of Venus, become the Virgin Mary. For the most part, men do not in their hearts believe that God is either just or merciful. They fear and shrink from His lightnings and dread His wrath. For the most part, they only *think* they believe that there is another life, a judgment, and a punishment for sin. Yet they will none the less persecute as Infidels and Atheists those who do not believe what they themselves imagine they believe, and which yet they do *not* believe, because it is incomprehensible to them in their ignorance and want of intellect. To the vast majority of mankind, God is but the reflected image, in infinite space, of the earthly Tyrant on his Throne, only more powerful, more inscrutable, and more implacable. To curse Humanity, the Despot need only *be,* what the popular mind has, in every age, imagined God.

In the great cities, the lower strata of the populace are equally without faith and without hope. The others have, for the most part, a mere blind faith, imposed by education and circumstances, and not as productive of moral excellence or even common honesty as Mohammedanism. *"Your property will be safe here,"* said the Moslem; *"There are no Christians here."* The philosophical and scientific world becomes daily more and more unbelieving. Faith and Reason are not opposites, in equilibrium; but antagonistic and hostile to each other; the result being the darkness and despair of scepticism, avowed, or half-veiled as rationalism.

Over more than three-fourths of the habitable globe, humanity still kneels, like the camels, to take upon itself the burthens to be tamely borne for its tyrants. If a Republic occasionally rises like a Star, it hastens with all speed to set in blood. The kings need not make war upon it, to crush it out of their way. It is only necessary to let it alone, and it soon lays violent hands upon itself. And when a people long enslaved shake off its fetters, it may well be incredulously asked,

Shall the braggart shout
For some blind glimpse of Freedom, link itself,
Through madness, hated by the wise, to law,
System and Empire?

Everywhere in the world labor is, in some shape, the slave of capital; generally, a slave to be fed only so long as he can work; or, rather, only so long as his work is profitable to the owner of the human chattel. There are famines in Ireland, strikes and starvation in England, pauperism and tenement-dens in New York, misery, squalor, ignorance, destitution, the brutality of vice and the insensibility to shame, of despairing beggary, in all the human cesspools and sewers everywhere. Here, a sewing-woman famishes and freezes; there, mothers murder their children, that those spared may live upon the bread purchased with the burial allowances of the dead starveling; and at the next door young girls prostitute themselves for food.

Moreover, the Voice says, this besotted race is not satisfied with seeing its multitudes swept away by the great epidemics whose causes are unknown, and of the justice or wisdom of which the human mind cannot conceive. It must also be ever at war. There has not been a moment since men divided into Tribes, when all the world was at peace. Always men have been engaged in murdering each other somewhere. Always the armies have lived by the toil of the husbandman, and war has exhausted the resources, wasted the energies, and ended the prosperity of Nations. Now it loads unborn posterity with crushing debt, mortgages all estates, and brings upon States the shame and infamy of dishonest repudiation.

At times, the baleful fires of war light up half a Continent at once; as when all the Thrones unite to compel a people to receive again a hated and detestable dynasty, or States deny States the right to dissolve an irksome union and create for themselves a separate government. Then again the flames flicker and die away, and the fire smoulders in its ashes, to break out again, after a time, with renewed and a more concentrated fury. At times, the storm, revolving, howls over small areas only; at times its lights are seen, like the old beacon-fires on the hills, belting the whole globe. No sea, but hears the roar of cannon; no river, but runs red with blood; no plain, but shakes, trampled by the hoofs of charging squadrons; no field, but is fertilized by the blood of the dead; and everywhere man slays, the vulture gorges, and the wolf howls in the ear of the dying soldier. No city is not tortured by shot and shell; and no people fail to enact the horrid blasphemy of thanking a God of Love for victories and carnage. Te

Deums are still sung for the Eve of St. Bartholomew and the
Sicilian Vespers. Man's ingenuity is racked, and all his inventive
powers are tasked, to fabricate the infernal enginery of destruction, by which human bodies may be the more expeditiously and
effectually crushed, shattered, torn, and mangled; and yet hypo-
critical Humanity, drunk with blood and drenched with gore,
shrieks to Heaven at a single murder, perpetrated to gratify a revenge not more unchristian, or to satisfy a cupidity not more
ignoble, than those which are the promptings of the Devil in the
souls of Nations.

When we have fondly dreamed of Utopia and the Millennium,
when we have begun almost to believe that man is *not,* after all, a
tiger half tamed, and that the smell of blood will *not* wake the savage within him, we are of a sudden startled from the delusive
dream, to find the thin mask of civilization rent in twain and
thrown contemptuously away. We lie down to sleep, like the peasant on the lava-slopes of Vesuvius. The mountain has been so
long inert, that we believe its fires extinguished. Round us hang
the clustering grapes, and the green leaves of the olive tremble in
the soft night-air over us. Above us shine the peaceful, patient
stars. The crash of a new eruption wakes us, the roar of the subterranean thunders, the stabs of the volcanic lightning into the
shrouded bosom of the sky; and we see, aghast, the tortured Titan
hurling up its fires among the pale stars, its great tree of smoke
and cloud, the red torrents pouring down its sides. The roar and
the shriekings of Civil War are all around us: the land is a pandemonium: man is again a Savage. The great armies roll along their
hideous waves, and leave behind them smoking and depopulated
deserts. The pillager is in every house, plucking even the morsel
of bread from the lips of the starving child. Gray hairs are
dabbled in blood, and innocent girlhood shrieks in vain to Lust for
mercy. Laws, Courts, Constitutions, Christianity, Mercy, Pity,
disappear. God seems to have abdicated, and Moloch to reign in
His stead; while Press and Pulpit alike exult at universal murder,
and urge the extermination of the Conquered, by the sword and
the flaming torch; and to plunder and murder entitles the human
beasts of prey to the thanks of Christian Senates.

Commercial greed deadens the nerves of sympathy of Nations,
and makes them deaf to the demands of honor, the impulses of
generosity, the appeals of those who suffer under injustice. Elsewhere, the universal pursuit of wealth dethrones God and pays

divine honors to Mammon and Baalzebub. Selfishness rules supreme: to win wealth becomes the whole business of life. The villanies of legalized gaming and speculation become epidemic; treachery is but evidence of shrewdness; office becomes the prey of successful faction; the Country, like Actæon, is torn by its own hounds, and the villains it has carefully educated to their trade, most greedily plunder it, when it is *in extremis*.

By what right, the Voice demands, does a creature always engaged in the work of mutual robbery and slaughter, and who makes his own interest his God, claim to be of a nature superior to the savage beasts of which he is the prototype?

Then the shadows of a horrible doubt fall upon the soul that would fain love, trust and believe; a darkness, of which this that surrounded you was a symbol. It doubts the truth of Revelation, its own spirituality, the very existence of a beneficent God. It asks itself if it is not idle to hope for any great progress of Humanity toward perfection, and whether, when it advances in one respect, it does not retrogress in some other, by way of compensation: whether advance in civilization is not increase of selfishness: whether freedom does not necessarily lead to license and anarchy: whether the destitution and debasement of the masses does not inevitably follow increase of population and commercial and manufacturing prosperity. It asks itself whether man is not the sport of a blind, merciless Fate: whether all philosophies are not delusions, and all religions the fantastic creations of human vanity and self-conceit; and, above all, whether, when Reason is abandoned as a guide, the faith of Buddhist and Brahmin has not the same claims to sovereignty and implicit, unreasoning credence, as any other.

He asks himself whether it is not, after all, the evident and palpable injustices of this life, the success and prosperity of the Bad, the calamities, oppressions, and miseries of the Good, that are the bases of all beliefs in a future state of existence? Doubting man's capacity for indefinite progress here, he doubts the possibility of it anywhere; and if he does not doubt whether God exists, and is just and beneficent, he at least cannot silence the constantly recurring whisper, that the miseries and calamities of men, their lives and deaths, their pains and sorrows, their extermination by war and epidemics, are phenomena of no higher dignity, significance, and importance, in the eye of God, than what things of the same nature occur to other organisms of matter; and that the fish of the ancient seas, destroyed by myriads to make room for other species, the contorted shapes in which they are found as fossils testifying to their agonies; the coral insects, the animals and birds and vermin slain by man, have as much right as he to clamor at the injustice of the dispensations of God, and to demand an immortality of life in a new universe, as compensation for their pains and sufferings and untimely death in this world.

This is not a picture painted by the imagination. Many a thoughtful mind has so doubted and despaired. How many of us can say that our own faith is so well grounded and complete that we never hear those painful whisperings within the soul? Thrice blessed are they who never doubt, who ruminate in patient contentment like the kine, or doze under the opiate of a blind faith; on whose souls never rests that Awful Shadow which is the absence of the Divine Light.

To explain to themselves the existence of Evil and Suffering, the Ancient Persians imagined that there were two Principles or Deities in the Universe, the one of Good and the other of Evil, constantly in conflict with each other in struggle for the mastery, and alternately overcoming and overcome. Over both, for the SAGES, was the One Supreme; and for *them* Light was in the end to prevail over Darkness, the Good over the Evil, and even Ahriman and his Demons to part with their wicked and vicious natures and share the universal Salvation. It did not occur to them that the existence of the Evil Principle, by the consent of the Omnipotent Supreme, presented the same difficulty, and left the existence of Evil as unexplained as before. The human mind is always content, if it can remove a difficulty a step further off. It cannot believe that the world rests on nothing, but is devoutly content when taught that it is borne on the back of an immense elephant, who himself stands on the back of a tortoise. Given the tortoise, Faith is always satisfied; and it has been a great source of happiness to multitudes that they could believe in a Devil who could relieve God of the odium of being the Author of Sin.

But not to all is Faith sufficient to overcome this great difficulty. They say, with the Suppliant, "*Lord! I believe!*"—but like him they are constrained to add, "*Help Thou my unbelief!*"—Reason must, for these, co-operate and coincide with Faith, or they remain still in the darkness of doubt,—most miserable of all conditions of the human mind.

Those, only, who care for nothing beyond the interests and pursuits of this life, are uninterested in these great Problems. The animals, also, do not consider them. It is the characteristic of an immortal Soul, that it should seek to satisfy itself of its immortality, and to understand this great enigma, the Universe. If the Hottentot and the Papuan are not troubled and tortured by these doubts and speculations, they are not, for that, to be regarded as either wise or fortunate. The swine, also, are indifferent to the great riddles of the Universe, and are happy in being wholly unaware that it is the vast Revelation and Manifestation, in Time and Space, of a Single Thought of the Infinite God.

Exalt and magnify Faith as we will, and say that it begins where Reason ends, it must, after all, have a foundation, either in Reason, Analogy, the Consciousness, or human testimony. The worshipper of Brahma also has implicit Faith in what seems to us palpably false and absurd. His faith rests neither in Reason, Analogy, or the Consciousness, but on the testimony of his Spiritual teachers, and of the Holy Books. The Moslem also believes, on the positive testimony of the Prophet; and the Mormon also can say, "*I believe this, because it is impossible.*" No faith, however absurd or degrading, has ever wanted these foundations, testimony, and the books. Miracles, proven by unimpeachable testimony have been used as a foundation for Faith, in every age; and the modern miracles are better authenticated, a hundred times, than the ancient ones.

So that, after all, Faith must flow out from some source within us, when the evidence of that which we are to believe is not presented to our senses, or it will in no case be the assurance of the truth of what is believed.

The Consciousness, or inhering and innate conviction, or the instinct divinely implanted, of the verity of things, is the highest possible evidence, if not the *only real* proof, of the verity of certain things, but only of truths of a limited class.

What we call the Reason, that is, our imperfect human reason, not only may, but assuredly will, lead us *away* from the Truth in regard to things invisible and especially those of the Infinite, if we determine to believe nothing but that which *it* can demonstrate, or *not* to believe that which it can by its processes of logic prove to be contradictory, unreasonable, or absurd. Its tape-line cannot measure the arcs of Infinity. For example, to the Human reason,

an Infinite Justice and an Infinite Mercy or Love, in the same
Being, are inconsistent and impossible. One, it can demonstrate,
necessarily excludes the other. So it can *demonstrate* that as the
Creation had a beginning, it necessarily follows that an Eternity
had elapsed before the Deity began to create, during which He
was inactive.

When we gaze, of a moonless clear night, on the Heavens glittering with stars, and know that each fixed star of all the myriads
is a Sun, and each probably possessing its retinue of worlds, all
peopled with living beings, we sensibly feel our own unimportance
in the scale of Creation, and at once reflect that much of what has
in different ages been religious faith, could never have been believed, if the nature, size, and distance of those Suns, and of our
own Sun, Moon, and Planets, had been known to the Ancients as
they are to us.

To them, all the lights of the firmament were created only to
give light to the earth, as its lamps or candles hung above it. The
earth was supposed to be the only inhabited portion of the Universe. The world and the Universe were synonymous terms. Of
the immense size and distance of the heavenly bodies, men had
no conception. The Sages had, in Chaldæa, Egypt, India, China,
and in Persia, and therefore the sages always had, an esoteric
creed, taught only in the mysteries and unknown to the vulgar.
No Sage, in either country, or in Greece or Rome, believed the
popular creed. To them the Gods and the Idols of the Gods were
symbols, and symbols of great and mysterious truths.

The Vulgar imagined the attention of the Gods to be continually centred upon the earth and man. The Grecian Divinities inhabited Olympus, an insignificant mountain of the Earth. There
was the Court of Zeus, to which Neptune came from the Sea, and
Pluto and Persephoné from the glooms of Tartarus in the unfathomable depths of the Earth's bosom. God came down from
Heaven and on Sinai dictated laws for the Hebrews to His servant
Moses. The Stars were the guardians of mortals whose fates and
fortunes were to be read in their movements, conjunctions, and
oppositions. The Moon was the Bride and Sister of the Sun, at
the same distance above the Earth, and, like the Sun, made for
the service of mankind alone.

If, with the great telescope of Lord Rosse, we examine the vast
nebulæ of Hercules, Orion, and Androméda, and find them re-

solvable into Stars more numerous than the sands on the sea-shore; if we reflect that each of these Stars is a Sun, like and even many times larger than ours,—each, beyond a doubt, with its retinue of worlds swarming with life;—if we go further in imagi-nation, and endeavor to conceive of all the infinities of space, filled with similar suns and worlds, we seem at once to shrink into an incredible insignificance.

The Universe, which is the uttered Word of God, is *infinite* in extent. There is no empty space beyond creation on any side. The Universe, which is the Thought of God pronounced, never was *not,* since God never was inert; nor WAS, without thinking and creating. The forms of creation change, the suns and worlds live and die like the leaves and the insects, but the Universe itself is infinite and eternal, because God Is, Was, and Will forever Be, and never did *not* think and create.

Reason is fain to admit that a Supreme Intelligence, infinitely powerful and wise, must have created this boundless Universe; but it also tells us that we are as unimportant in it as the zoöphytes and entozoa, or as the invisible particles of animated life that float upon the air or swarm in the water-drop.

The foundations of our faith, resting upon the imagined inter-est of God in our race, an interest easily supposable when man believed himself the only intelligent created being, and therefore eminently worthy the especial care and watchful anxiety of a God who had only this earth to look after, and *its* house-keeping alone to superintend, and who was content to create, in all the infinite Universe, only one single being, possessing a soul, and not a mere animal, are rudely shaken as the Universe broadens and expands for us; and the darkness of doubt and distrust settles heavy upon the Soul.

The modes in which it is ordinarily endeavored to satisfy our doubts, only increase them. To *demonstrate* the necessity for a cause of the creation, is equally to demonstrate the necessity of a cause for that cause. The argument from plan and design only removes the difficulty a step further off. We rest the world on the elephant, and the elephant on the tortoise, and the tortoise on —nothing.

To tell us that the animals possess instinct only and that Rea-son belongs to us alone, in no way tends to satisfy us of the radi-cal difference between us and them. For if the mental phenomena exhibited by animals that think, dream, remember, argue from cause to effect, plan, devise, combine, and communicate their thoughts to each other, so as to act rationally in concert,—if their love, hate, and revenge, can be conceived of as results of the organization of matter, like color and perfume, the resort to the hypothesis of an immaterial Soul to explain phenomena of the same kind, only more perfect, manifested by the *human* being, is supremely absurd. That organized matter can think or even *feel*, at all, is the great insoluble mystery. "Instinct" is but a word without a meaning, or else it means inspiration. It is either the animal itself, or God *in* the animal, that thinks, remembers, and reasons; and instinct, according to the common acceptation of the term, would be the greatest and most wonderful of mysteries,— no less a thing than the direct, immediate, and continual promptings of the Deity,—for the animals are not machines, or automata moved by springs, and the ape is but a dumb Australian.

Must we *always* remain in this darkness of uncertainty, of doubt? Is there *no* mode of escaping from the labyrinth except by means of a blind faith, which explains nothing, and in many creeds, ancient and modern, sets Reason at defiance, and leads to the belief either in a God without a Universe, a Universe without a God, or a Universe which is itself a God?

We read in the Hebrew Chronicles that Schlomoh the wise King caused to be placed in front of the entrance to the Temple two huge columns of bronze, one of which was called YAKAYIN and the other BAHAZ; and these words are rendered in our version *Strength* and *Establishment*. The Masonry of the Blue Lodges gives no explanation of these symbolic columns; nor do the Hebrew Books advise us that they were symbolic. If not so intended as symbols, they were subsequently understood to be such.

But as we are certain that everything *within* the Temple was symbolic, and that the whole structure was intended to represent the Universe, we may reasonably conclude that the columns of the portico also had a symbolic signification. It would be tedious to repeat all the interpretations which fancy or dullness has found for them.

The key to their true meaning is not undiscoverable. The perfect and eternal distinction of the two primitive terms of the creative syllogism, in order to attain to the demonstration of their harmony by the analogy of contraries, is the second grand principle of that occult philosophy veiled under the name "*Kabalah*," and indicated by all the sacred hieroglyphs of the Ancient Sanctuaries, and of the rites, so little understood by the mass of the Initiates, of the Ancient and Modern Free-Masonry.

The Sohar declares that everything in the Universe proceeds by the mystery of "the Balance," that is, of Equilibrium. Of the Sephiroth, or Divine Emanations, Wisdom and Understanding, Severity and Benignity, or Justice and Mercy, and Victory and Glory, constitute pairs.

Wisdom, or the Intellectual Generative *Energy,* and Understanding, or the *Capacity* to be impregnated by the Active Energy and produce intellection or thought, are represented symbolically in the Kabalah as male and female. So also are Justice and Mercy. Strength is the intellectual Energy or Activity; Establishment or Stability is the intellectual Capacity to produce, a passivity. They are the POWER of *generation* and the CAPACITY of *production*. By WISDOM, it is said, God creates, and by UNDERSTANDING establishes. These are the two Columns of the Temple, contraries like the Man and Woman, like Reason and Faith, Omnipotence and Liberty, Infinite Justice and Infinite Mercy, Absolute Power or Strength to do even what is most unjust and unwise, and Absolute Wisdom that makes it impossible to do it; Right and Duty. They were the columns of the intellectual and moral world, the monumental hieroglyph of the antinomy necessary to the grand law of creation.

There must be for every Force a Resistance to support it, to every light a shadow, for every Royalty a Realm to govern, for every affirmative a negative.

For the Kabalists, Light represents the Active Principle, and Darkness or Shadow is analogous to the Passive Principle. Therefore it was that they made of the Sun and Moon emblems of the two Divine Sexes and the two creative forces; therefore, that they ascribed to woman the Temptation and the first sin, and then the first labor, the maternal labor of the redemption, because it is from the bosom of the darkness itself that we see the Light born again. The Void attracts the Full; and so it is that the abyss of poverty and misery, the Seeming Evil, the seeming empty nothingness of life, the temporary rebellion of the creatures, eternally attracts the overflowing ocean of being, of riches, of pity, and of love. Christ completed the Atonement on the Cross by descending into Hell.

Justice and Mercy are contraries. If each be infinite, their co-existence seems impossible, and being equal, one cannot even annihilate the other and reign alone. The mysteries of the Divine Nature are beyond our finite comprehension; but so indeed are the mysteries of our own finite nature; and it is certain that in all nature harmony and movement are the result of the equilibrium of opposing or contrary forces.

The analogy of contraries gives the solution of the most interesting and most difficult problem of modern philosophy,—the definite and permanent accord of Reason and Faith, of Authority and Liberty of examination, of Science and Belief, of Perfection in God and Imperfection in Man. If science or knowledge is the Sun, Belief is the Man; it is a reflection of the day in the night. Faith is the veiled Isis, the Supplement of Reason, in the shadows which precede or follow Reason. It emanates from the Reason, but can never confound it nor be confounded with it. The encroachments of Reason upon Faith, or of Faith on Reason, are eclipses of the Sun or Moon; when they occur, they make useless both the Source of Light and its reflection, at once.

Science perishes by systems that are nothing but beliefs; and Faith succumbs to reasoning. For the two Columns of the Temple to uphold the edifice, they must remain separated and be parallel to each other. As soon as it is attempted by violence to bring them together, as Samson did, they are overturned, and the whole edifice falls upon the head of the rash blind man or the revolutionist whom personal or national resentments have in advance devoted to death.

Harmony is the result of an alternating preponderance of forces. Whenever this is wanting in government, government is a failure, because it is either Despotism or Anarchy. All theoretical governments, however plausible the theory, end in one or the other. Governments that are to endure are not made in the closet of Locke or Shaftesbury, or in a Congress or a Convention. In a Republic, forces that seem contraries, that indeed are contraries, alone give movement and life. The Spheres are held in their orbits and made to revolve harmoniously and unerringly, by the concurrence, which seems to be the opposition, of two contrary forces. If the centripetal force should overcome the centrifugal, and the equilibrium of forces cease, the rush of the Spheres to the Central Sun would annihilate the system. Instead of consolidation, the whole would be shattered into fragments.

Man is a free agent, though Omnipotence is above and all around him. To be free to do good, he must be free to do evil. The Light necessitates the Shadow. A State is free like an individual in any government worthy of the name. The State is less potent than the Deity, and therefore the freedom of the individual citizen is consistent with its Sovereignty. These are opposites, but not antagonistic. So, in a union of States, the freedom of the States is consistent with the Supremacy of the Nation. When either obtains the permanent mastery over the other, and they cease to be *in equilibrio,* the encroachment continues with a velocity that is accelerated like that of a falling body, until the feebler is annihilated, and then, there being no resistance to support the stronger, it rushes into ruin.

So, when the equipoise of Reason and Faith, in the individual or the Nation, and the alternating preponderance cease, the result is, according as one or the other is permanent victor, Atheism or Superstition, disbelief or blind credulity; and the Priests either of Unfaith or of Faith become despotic.

"Whomsoever God loveth, him he chasteneth," is an expression that formulates a whole dogma. The trials of life are the blessings of life, to the individual or the Nation, if either has a Soul that is truly worthy of salvation. *"Light and darkness,"* said Zoroaster, *"are the world's eternal ways."* The Light and the Shadow are everywhere and always in proportion; the Light being the reason of being of the Shadow. It is by trials only, by the agonies of sorrow and the sharp discipline of adversities, that men and Nations attain initiation. The agonies of the garden of Gethsemane and those of the Cross on Calvary preceded the Resurrection and were the means of Redemption. It is with prosperity that God afflicts Humanity.

The Degree of Rose ✠ is devoted to and symbolizes tne final triumph of truth over falsehood, of liberty over slavery, of light over darkness, of life over death, and of good over evil. The great truth it inculcates is, that notwithstanding the existence of Evil, God is infinitely wise, just, and good: that though the affairs of the world proceed by no rule of right and wrong known to us in the narrowness of our views, yet all *is* right, for it is the work of

God; and all evils, all miseries, all misfortunes, are but as drops in
the vast current that is sweeping onward, guided by Him, to a
great and magnificent result: that, at the appointed time, He will
redeem and regenerate the world, and the Principle, the Power,
and the existence of Evil will then cease; that this will be brought
about by such means and instruments as He chooses to employ;
whether by the merits of a Redeemer that has already appeared,
or a Messiah that is yet waited for, by an incarnation of Himself,
or by an inspired prophet, it does not belong to us as Masons to
decide. Let each judge and believe for himself.

In the mean time, we labor to hasten the coming of that day.
The morals of antiquity, of the law of Moses and of Christianity,
are ours. We recognize every teacher of Morality, every Reformer, as a brother in this great work. The Eagle is to us the symbol
of Liberty, the Compasses of Equality, the Pelican of Humanity,
and our order of Fraternity. Laboring for these, with Faith,
Hope, and Charity as our armor, we will wait with patience for
the final triumph of Good and the complete manifestation of the
Word of God.

No one Mason has the right to measure for another, within the
walls of a Masonic Temple, the degree of veneration which he
shall feel for any Reformer, or the Founder of any Religion. We
teach a belief in no particular creed, as we teach unbelief in none.
Whatever higher attributes the Founder of the Christian Faith
may, in our belief, have had or not have had, none can deny that
He taught and practised a pure and elevated morality, even at the
risk and to the ultimate loss of His life. He was not only the
benefactor of a disinherited people, but a model for mankind. De-
votedly He loved the children of Israel. To them He came, and
to them alone He preached that Gospel which His disciples afterward carried among foreigners. He would fain have freed the
chosen People from their spiritual bondage of ignorance and degradation. As a lover of all mankind, laying down His life for the
emancipation of His Brethren, He should be to all, to Christian, to
Jew, and to Mahometan, an object of gratitude and veneration.

The Roman world felt the pangs of approaching dissolution.
Paganism, its Temples shattered by Socrates and Cicero, had
spoken its last word. The God of the Hebrews was unknown beyond the limits of Palestine. The old religions had failed to give
happiness and peace to the world. The babbling and wrangling

philosophers had confounded all men's ideas, until they doubted of everything and had faith in nothing: neither in God nor in his goodness and mercy, nor in the virtue of man, nor in themselves. Mankind was divided into two great classes,—the master and the slave; the powerful and the abject, the high and the low, the tyrants and the mob; and even the former we 'e satiated with the servility of the latter, sunken by lassitude and despair to the lowest depths of degradation.

When, lo, a voice, in the inconsiderable Roman Province of Judea proclaims a new Gospel—a new "God's Word," to crushed, suffering, bleeding humanity. Liberty of Thought, Equality of all men in the eye of God, universal Fraternity! a new doctrine, a new religion; the old Primitive Truth uttered once again!

Man is once more taught to look upward to his God. No longer to a God hid in impenetrable mystery, and infinitely remote from human sympathy, emerging only at intervals from the darkness to smite and crush humanity: but a God, good, kind, beneficent, and merciful: a Father, loving the creatures He has made, with a love immeasureable and exhaustless; Who feels for us, and sympathizes with us, and sends us pain and want and disaster only that they may serve to develop in us the virtues and excellences that befit us to live with Him hereafter.

Jesus of Nazareth, the "Son of man," is the expounder of the new Law of Love. He calls to Him the humble, the poor, the Pariahs of the world. The first sentence that He pronounces blesses the world, and announces the new gospel: "Blessed are they that mourn for they shall be comforted." He pours the oil of consolation and peace upon every crushed and bleeding heart. Every sufferer is His proselyte. He shares their sorrows, and sympathizes with all their afflictions.

He raises up the sinner and the Samaritan woman, and teaches them to hope for forgiveness. He pardons the woman taken in adultery. He selects his disciples not among the Pharisees or the Philosophers, but among the low and humble, even of the fishermen of Galilee. He heals the sick and feeds the poor. He lives among the destitute and the friendless. "Suffer little children," He said, "to come unto me; for of such is the kingdom of Heaven! Blessed are the humble-minded, for theirs is the kingdom of Heaven; the meek, for they shall inherit the Earth; the merciful, for they shall obtain mercy; the pure in heart, for they shall see

God; the peace-makers, for they shall be called the children of God! First be reconciled to they brother, and *then* come and offer thy gift at the altar. Give to him that asketh thee, and from him that would borrow of thee turn not away! Love your enemies; bless them that curse you; do good to them that hate you; and pray for them which despitefully use you and persecute you! All things whatsoever ye would that men should do to you, do ye also unto them; for this is the law and the Prophets! He that taketh not his cross, and followeth after Me, is not worthy of Me. A new commandment I give unto you, that ye love one another: as I have loved you, that ye also love one another: by this shall all know that ye are My disciples. Greater love hath no man than this, that a man lay down his life for his friend."

The Gospel of Love He sealed with His life. The cruelty of the Jewish Priesthood, the ignorant ferocity of the mob, and the Roman indifference to barbarian blood, nailed Him to the cross, and He expired uttering blessings upon humanity.

Dying thus, He bequeathed His teachings to man as an inestimable inheritance. Perverted and corrupted, they have served as a basis for many creeds, and been even made the warrant for intolerance and persecution. We here teach them in their purity. They are our Masonry; for to them good men of all creeds can subscribe.

That God is good and merciful, and loves and sympathizes with the creatures He has made; that His finger is visible in all the movements of the moral, intellectual, and material universe; that we are His children, the objects of His paternal care and regard; that all men are our brothers, whose wants we are to supply, their errors to pardon, their opinions to tolerate, their injuries to forgive; that man has an immortal soul, a free will, a right to freedom of thought and action; that all men are equal in God's sight; that we best serve God by humility, meekness, gentleness, kindness, and the other virtues which the lowly can practise as well as the lofty; this is "the new Law," the "Word," for which the world had waited and pined so long; and every true Knight of the Rose ✠ will revere the memory of Him who taught it, and look indulgently even on those who assign to Him a character far above his own conceptions or belief, even to the extent of deeming Him Divine.

Hear Philo, the Greek Jew. "The contemplative soul, unequally guided, sometimes toward abundance and sometimes toward barrenness, though ever advancing, is illuminated by the primitive ideas, the rays that emanate from the Divine Intelligence, whenever it ascends toward the Sublime Treasures. When, on the contrary, it descends, and is barren, it falls within the domain of those Intelligences that are termed Angels. . . for, when the soul is deprived of the light of God, which leads it to the knowledge of things, it no longer enjoys more than a feeble and secondary light, which gives it, not the understanding of things, but that of words only, as in this baser world. . . ."

". . . Let the narrow-souled withdraw, having their ears sealed up! We communicate the divine mysteries to those only who have received the sacred initiation, to those who practise true piety, and who are not enslaved by the empty pomp of words, or the doctrines of the pagans. . . ."

". . . O, ye Initiates, ye whose ears are purified, receive this in your souls, as a mystery never to be lost! Reveal it to no Profane! Keep and contain it within yourselves, as an incorruptible treasure, not like gold or silver, but more precious than everything besides; for it is the knowledge of the Great Cause, of Nature, and of that which is born of both. And if you meet an Initiate, besiege him with your prayers, that he conceal from you no new mysteries that he may know, and rest not until you have obtained them! For me, although I was initiated in the Great Mysteries by Moses, the Friend of God, yet, having seen Jeremiah, I recognized him not only as an Initiate, but as a Hierophant; and I follow his school."

We, like him, recognize all Initiates as our Brothers. We belong to no one creed or school. In all religions there is a basis of Truth; in all there is pure Morality. All that teach the cardinal tenets of Masonry we respect; all teachers and reformers of mankind we admire and revere.

Masonry also has her mission to perform. With her traditions reaching back to the earliest times, and her symbols dating further back than even the monumental history of Egypt extends, she invites all men of all religions to enlist under her banners and to war against evil, ignorance, and wrong. You are now her knight, and to her service your sword is consecrated. May you prove a worthy soldier in a worthy cause!

Morals and Dogma.

—————

Council of Kadosh.

XIX.

GRAND PONTIFF.

THE true Mason labors for the benefit of those who are to come after him, and for the advancement and improvement of his race. That is a poor ambition which contents itself within the limits of a single life. All men who deserve to live, desire to survive their funerals, and to live afterward in the good that they have done mankind, rather than in the fading characters written in men's memories. Most men desire to leave some work behind them that may outlast their own day and brief generation. That is an instinctive impulse, given by God, and often found in the rudest human heart; the surest proof of the soul's immortality, and of the fundamental difference between man and the wisest brutes. To plant the trees that, after we are dead, shall shelter our children, is as natural as to love the shade of those our fathers planted. The rudest unlettered husbandman, painfully conscious of his own inferiority, the poorest widowed mother, giving her life-blood to those who pay only for the work of her needle, will toil and stint themselves to educate their child, that he may take a higher station in the world than they;—and of such are the world's greatest benefactors.

In his influences that survive him, man becomes immortal, before the general resurrection. The Spartan mother, who, giving her son his shield, said, "WITH IT, OR UPON IT!" afterward shared the government of Lacedæmon with the legislation of Lycurgus; for she too made a law, that lived after her; and she inspired the Spartan soldiery that afterward demolished the walls of Athens, and aided Alexander to conquer the Orient. The widow who gave Marion the fiery arrows to burn her own house, that it might no longer shelter the enemies of her infant country, the house where she had lain upon her husband's bosom, and where her children had been born, legislated more effectually for her State than Locke or Shaftesbury, or than many a Legislature has done, since that State won its freedom.

It was of slight importance to the Kings of Egypt and the

312

Monarchs of Assyria and Phœnicia, that the son of a Jewish woman, a foundling, adopted by the daughter of Sesostris Ramses, slew an Egyptian that oppressed a Hebrew slave, and fled into the desert, to remain there forty years. But Moses, who might otherwise have become Regent of Lower Egypt, known to us only by a tablet on a tomb or monument, became the deliverer of the Jews, and led them forth from Egypt to the frontiers of Palestine, and made for them a law, out of which grew the Christian faith; and so has shaped the destinies of the world. He and the old Roman lawyers, with Alfred of England, the Saxon Thanes and Norman Barons, the old judges and chancellors, and the makers of the canons, lost in the mists and shadows of the Past,—these are our legislators; and we obey the laws that they enacted.

Napoleon died upon the barren rock of his exile. His bones, borne to France by the son of a King, rest in the Hôpital des Invalides, in the great city on the Seine. His Thoughts still govern France. He, and not the People, dethroned the Bourbon, and drove the last King of the House of Orleans into exile. He, in his coffin, and not the People, voted the crown to the Third Napoleon; and he, and not the Generals of France and England, led their united forces against the grim Northern Despotism.

Mahomet announced to the Arabian idolaters the new creed, *"There is but one God, and Mahomet, like Moses and Christ, is His Apostle."* For many years unaided, then with the help of his family and a few friends, then with many disciples, and last of all with an army, he taught and preached the Koran. The religion of the wild Arabian enthusiast converting the fiery Tribes of the Great Desert, spread over Asia, built up the Saracenic dynasties, conquered Persia and India, the Greek Empire, Northern Africa, and Spain, and dashed the surges of its fierce soldiery against the battlements of Northern Christendom. The law of Mahomet still governs a fourth of the human race; and Turk and Arab, Moor and Persian and Hindu, still obey the Prophet, and pray with their faces turned toward Mecca; and he, and not the living, rules and reigns in the fairest portions of the Orient.

Confucius still enacts the law for China; and the thoughts and ideas of Peter the Great govern Russia. Plato and the other great Sages of Antiquity still reign as the Kings of Philosophy, and have dominion over the human intellect. The great Statesmen of the Past still preside in the Councils of Nations. Burke still lingers in the House of Commons; and Berryer's sonorous tones will long ring in the Legislative Chambers of France. The influences of Webster and Calhoun, conflicting, rent asunder the American States, and the doctrine of each is the law and the oracle speaking from the Holy of Holies for his own State and all consociated with it: a faith preached and proclaimed by each at the cannon's mouth and consecrated by rivers of blood.

It has been well said, that when Tamerlane had builded his pyramid of fifty thousand human skulls, and wheeled away with his vast armies from the gates of Damascus, to find new conquests, and build other pyramids, a little boy was playing in the streets of Mentz, son of a poor artisan, whose apparent importance in the scale of beings was, compared with that of Tamerlane, as that of a grain of sand to the giant bulk of the earth; but Tamerlane and all his shaggy legions, that swept over the East like a hurricane, have passed away, and become shadows; while printing, the wonderful invention of John Faust, the boy of Mentz, has exerted a greater influence on man's destinies and overturned more thrones and dynasties than all the victories of all the blood-stained conquerors from Nimrod to Napoleon.

Long ages ago, the Temple built by Solomon and our Ancient Brethren sank into ruin, when the Assyrian Armies sacked Jerusalem. The Holy City is a mass of hovels cowering under the dominion of the Crescent; and the Holy Land is a desert. The Kings of Egypt and Assyria, who were contemporaries of Solomon, are forgotten, and their histories mere fables. The Ancient Orient is a shattered wreck, bleaching on the shores of Time. The Wolf and the Jackal howl among the ruins of Thebes and of Tyre, and the sculptured images of the Temples and Palaces of Babylon and Nineveh are dug from their ruins and carried into strange lands. But the quiet and peaceful Order, of which the Son of a poor Phœnician Widow was one of the Grand Masters, with the Kings of Israel and Tyre, has continued to increase in stature and influence, defying the angry waves of time and the storms of persecution. Age has not weakened its wide foundations, nor shattered its columns, nor marred the beauty of its harmonious proportions. Where rude barbarians, in the time of Solomon, peopled inhospitable howling wildernesses, in France and Britain, and in that New World, not known to Jew or Gentile, until the glories of the Orient had faded, that Order has builded new Temples, and teaches to its millions of Initiates those lessons of peace, good-will, and toleration, of reliance on God and confidence in man, which it learned when Hebrew and Giblemite worked side by side on the slopes of Lebanon, and the Servant of Jehovah and the Phœnician Worshipper of Bel sat with the humble artisan in Council at Jerusalem.

It is the Dead that govern. The Living only obey. And if the Soul sees, after death, what passes on this earth, and watches over the welfare of those it loves, then must its greatest happiness consist in seeing the current of its beneficent influences widening out from age to age, as rivulets widen into rivers, and aiding to shape the destinies of individuals, families, States, the World; and its bitterest punishment, in seeing its evil influences causing mischief and misery, and cursing and afflicting men, long after the frame it dwelt in has become dust, and when both name and memory are forgotten.

We know not who among the Dead control our destinies. The universal human race is linked and bound together by those influences and sympathies, which in the truest sense do make men's fates. Humanity is the unit, of which the man is but a fraction. What other men in the Past have done, said, thought, makes the great iron network of circumstance that environs and controls us all. We take our faith on trust. We think and believe as the Old Lords of Thought command us; and Reason is powerless before Authority.

We would make or annul a particular contract; but the Thoughts of the dead Judges of England, living when their ashes have been cold for centuries, stand between us and that which we would do, and utterly forbid it. We would settle our estate in a particular way; but the prohibition of the English Parliament, its uttered Thought when the first or second Edward reigned, comes echoing down the long avenues of time, and tells us we shall not exercise the power of disposition as we wish. We would gain a particular advantage of another; and the thought of the old Roman lawyer who died before Justinian, or that of Rome's great orator Cicero, annihilates the act, or makes the intention ineffectual. This act, Moses forbids; that, Alfred. We would sell our land; but certain marks on a perishable paper tell us that our father or remote ancestor ordered otherwise; and the arm of the dead, emerging from the grave, with peremptory gesture prohibits the alienation. About to sin or err, the thought or wish of our dead mother, told us when we were children, by words that died upon the air in the utterance, and many a long year were forgotten, flashes on our memory, and holds us back with a power that is resistless.

Thus we obey the dead; and thus shall the living, when *we* are dead, for weal or woe, obey *us*. The Thoughts of the Past are the Laws of the Present and the Future. That which we say and do, if its effects last not beyond our lives, is unimportant. That which shall live when we are dead, as part of the great body of law enacted by the dead, is the only act worth doing, the only Thought worth speaking. The desire to do something that shall benefit the world, when neither praise nor obloquy will reach us where we sleep soundly in the grave, is the noblest ambition entertained by man.

It is the ambition of a true and genuine Mason. Knowing the slow processes by which the Deity brings about great results, he does not expect to reap as well as sow, in a single lifetime. It is the inflexible fate and noblest destiny, with rare exceptions, of the great and good, to work, and let others reap the harvest of their labors. He who does good, only to be repaid in kind, or in thanks and gratitude, or in reputation and the world's praise, is like him who loans his money, that he may, after certain months, receive it back with interest. To be repaid for eminent services with slander, obloquy, or ridicule, or at best with stupid indifference or cold ingratitude, as it is common, so it is no misfortune, except to those who lack the wit to see or sense to appreciate the service, or the nobility of soul to thank and reward with eulogy, the benefactor of his kind. His influences live, and the great Future will obey; whether it recognize or disown the lawgiver.

Miltiades was fortunate that he was exiled; and Aristides that he was ostracized, because men wearied of hearing him called "The Just." Not the Redeemer was unfortunate; but those only who repaid Him for the inestimable gift He offered them, and for a life passed in toiling for their good, by nailing Him upon the cross, as though He had been a slave or malefactor. The persecutor dies and rots, and Posterity utters his name with execration: but his victim's memory he has unintentionally made glorious and immortal.

If not for slander and persecution, the Mason who would benefit his race must look for apathy and cold indifference in those whose good he seeks, in those who ought to seek the good of others. Except when the sluggish depths of the Human Mind are broken up and tossed as with a storm, when at the appointed time a great Reformer comes, and a new Faith springs up and grows with supernatural energy, the progress of Truth is slower than the growth of oaks; and he who plants need not expect to gather. The Redeemer, at His death, had twelve disciples, and one betrayed and one deserted and denied Him. It is enough for us to know that the fruit will come in its due season. When, or who shall gather it, it does not in the least concern us to know. It is our business to plant the seed. It is God's right to give the fruit to whom He pleases; and if not to us, then is our action by so much the more noble.

To sow, that others may reap; to work and plant for those who are to occupy the earth when we are dead; to project our influences far into the future, and live beyond our time; to rule as the Kings of Thought, over men who are yet unborn; to bless with the glorious gifts of Truth and Light and Liberty those who will neither know the name of the giver, nor care in what grave his unregarded ashes repose, is the true office of a Mason and the proudest destiny of a man.

All the great and beneficent operations of Nature are produced by slow and often imperceptible degrees. The work of destruction and devastation only is violent and rapid. The Volcano and the Earthquake, the Tornado and the Avalanche, leap suddenly into full life and fearful energy, and smite with an unexpected blow. Vesuvius buried Pompeii and Herculaneum in a night; and Lisbon fell prostrate before God in a breath, when the earth rocked and shuddered; the Alpine village vanishes and is erased at one bound of the avalanche; and the ancient forests fall like grass before the mower, when the tornado leaps upon them. Pestilence slays its thousands in a day; and the storm in a night strews the sand with shattered navies.

The Gourd of the Prophet Jonah grew up, and was withered, in a night. But many years ago, before the Norman Conqueror stamped his mailed foot on the neck of prostrate Saxon England, some wandering barbarian, of the continent then unknown to the world, in mere idleness, with hand or foot, covered an acorn with a little earth, and passed on regardless, on his journey to the dim

Past. He died and was forgotten; but the acorn lay there still, the mighty force within it acting in the darkness. A tender shoot stole gently up; and fed by the light and air and frequent dews, put forth its little leaves, and lived, because the elk or buffalo chanced not to place his foot upon and crush it. The years marched onward, and the shoot became a sapling, and its green leaves went and came with Spring and Autumn. And still the years came and passed away again, and William, the Norman Bastard, parcelled England out among his Barons, and still the sapling grew, and the dews fed its leaves, and the birds builded their nests among its small limbs for many generations. And still the years came and went, and the Indian hunter slept in the shade of the sapling, and Richard Lion-Heart fought at Acre and Ascalon, and John's bold Barons wrested from him the Great Charter; and lo! the sapling had become a tree; and still it grew, and thrust its great arms wider abroad, and lifted its head still higher toward the Heavens; strong-rooted, and defiant of the storms that roared and eddied through its branches; and when Columbus ploughed with his keels the unknown Western Atlantic, and Cortez and Pizarro bathed the cross in blood; and the Puritan, the Huguenot, the Cavalier, and the follower of Penn sought a refuge and a resting-place beyond the ocean, the Great Oak still stood, firm-rooted, vigorous, stately, haughtily domineering over all the forest, heedless of all the centuries that had hurried past since the wild Indian planted the little acorn in the forest;—a stout and hale old tree, with wide circumference shading many a rood of ground; and fit to furnish timbers for a ship, to carry the thunders of the Great Republic's guns around the world. And yet, if one had sat and watched it every instant, from the moment when the feeble shoot first pushed its way to the light until the eagles built among its branches, he would never have seen the tree or sapling *grow*.

Many long centuries ago, before the Chaldæan Shepherds watched the Stars, or Shufu built the Pyramids, one could have sailed in a seventy-four where now a thousand islands gem the surface of the Indian Ocean; and the deep-sea lead would nowhere have found any bottom. But below these waves were myriads upon myriads, beyond the power of Arithmetic to number, of minute existences, each a perfect living creature, made by the Almighty Creator, and fashioned by Him for the work it had to do. There they toiled beneath the waters, each doing its allotted work, and wholly ignorant of the result which God intended. They lived and died, incalculable in numbers and almost infinite in the succession of their generations, each adding his mite to the gigantic work that went on there under God's direction. Thus hath He chosen to create great Continents and Islands; and still the coral-insects live and work, as when they made the rocks that underlie the valley of the Ohio.

Thus God hath chosen to create. Where now is firm land, once chafed and thundered the great primeval ocean. For ages upon ages the minute shields of infinite myriads of infusoria, and the stony stems of encrinites sunk into its depths, and there, under the vast pressure of its waters, hardened into limestone. Raised slowly from the Profound by His hand, its quarries underlie the soil of all the continents, hundreds of feet in thickness; and we, of these remains of the countless dead, build tombs and palaces, as the Egyptians, whom we call ancient, built their pyramids.

On all the broad lakes and oceans the Great Sun looks earnestly and lovingly, and the invisible vapors rise ever up to meet him. No eye but God's beholds them as they rise. There, in the upper atmosphere, they are condensed to mist, and gather into clouds, and float and swim around in the ambient air. They sail with its currents, and hover over the ocean, and roll in huge masses round the stony shoulders of great mountains. Condensed still more by change of temperature, they drop upon the thirsty earth in gentle showers, or pour upon it in heavy rains, or storm against its bosom at the angry Equinoctial. The shower, the rain, and the storm pass away, the clouds vanish, and the bright stars again shine clearly upon the glad earth. The rain-drops sink into the ground, and gather in subterranean reservoirs, and run in subterranean channels, and bubble up in springs and fountains; and from the mountain-sides and heads of valleys the silver threads of water begin their long journey to the ocean. Uniting, they widen into brooks and rivulets, then into streams and rivers; and, at last, a Nile, a Ganges, a Danube, an Amazon, or a Mississippi rolls between its banks, mighty, majestic, and resistless, creating vast alluvial valleys to be the granaries of the world, ploughed by the thousand keels of commerce and serving as great highways, and as the impassable boundaries of rival nations; ever returning to the ocean the drops that rose from it in vapor, and descended in rain and snow and hail upon the level plains and lofty moun-

tains; and causing him to recoil for many a mile before the headlong rush of their great tide.

So it is with the aggregate of Human endeavor. As the invisible particles of vapor combine and coalesce to form the mists and
clouds that fall in rain on thirsty continents, and bless the great
green forests and wide grassy prairies, the waving meadows and
the fields by which men live; as the infinite myriads of drops that
the glad earth drinks are gathered into springs and rivulets and
rivers, to aid in levelling the mountains and elevating the plains,
and to feed the large lakes and restless oceans; so all Human
Thought, and Speech and Action, all that is done and said and
thought and suffered upon the Earth combine together, and flow
onward in one broad resistless current toward those great results
to which they are determined by the will of God.

We build slowly and destroy swiftly. Our Ancient Brethren
who built the Temples at Jerusalem, with many myriad blows
felled, hewed, and squared the cedars, and quarried the stones, and
carved the intricate ornaments, which were to be the Temples.
Stone after stone, by the combined effort and long toil of Apprentice, Fellow-Craft, and Master, the walls arose; slowly the roof
was framed and fashioned; and many years elapsed before, at
length, the Houses stood finished, all fit and ready for the Worship
of God, gorgeous in the sunny splendors of the atmosphere of
Palestine. So they were built. A single motion of the arm of a
rude, barbarous Assyrian Spearman, or drunken Roman or Gothic
Legionary of Titus, moved by a senseless impulse of the brutal
will, flung in the blazing brand; and, with no further human
agency, a few short hours sufficed to consume and melt each Temple to a smoking mass of black unsightly ruin.

Be patient, therefore, my Brother, and wait!

> *The issues are with God: To do,*
> *Of right belongs to us.*

Therefore faint not, nor be weary in well-doing! Be not discouraged at men's apathy, nor disgusted with their follies, nor
tired of their indifference! Care not for returns and results; but
see only what there is to do, and do it, leaving the results to God!
Soldier of the Cross! Sworn Knight of Justice, Truth, and Toleration! Good Knight and True! be patient and work!

The Apocalypse, that sublime Kabalistic and prophetic Sum-

mary of all the occult figures, divides its images into three Sep-
tenaries, after each of which there is silence in Heaven. There
are Seven Seals to be opened, that is to say, Seven mysteries to
know, and Seven difficulties to overcome, Seven trumpets to
sound, and Seven cups to empty.

The Apocalypse is, to those who receive the nineteenth Degree,
the Apotheosis of that Sublime Faith which aspires to God alone,
and despises all the pomps and works of Lucifer. LUCIFER, the
Light-bearer! Strange and mysterious name to give to the Spirit
of Darkness! Lucifer, the Son of the Morning! Is it *he* who
bears the *Light,* and with its splendors intolerable blinds feeble,
sensual, or selfish Souls? Doubt it not! for traditions are full of
Divine Revelations and Inspirations: and Inspiration is not of
one Age nor of one Creed. Plato and Philo, also, were inspired.

The Apocalypse, indeed, is a book as obscure as the Sohar.

It is written hieroglyphically with numbers and images; and
the Apostle often appeals to the intelligence of the Initiated.
"Let him who hath knowledge, understand! let him who understands, calculate!" he often says, after an allegory or the mention
of a number. Saint John, the favorite Apostle, and the Depositary
of all the Secrets of the Saviour, therefore did not write to be
understood by the multitude.

The Sephar Yezirah, the Sohar, and the Apocalypse are the
completest embodiments of Occultism. They contain more meanings than words; their expressions are figurative as poetry and
exact as numbers. The Apocalypse sums up, completes, and surpasses all the Science of Abraham and of Solomon. The visions
of Ezekiel, by the river Chebar, and of the new Symbolic Temple,
are equally mysterious expressions, veiled by figures of the enigmatic dogmas of the Kabalah, and their symbols are as little understood by the Commentators, as those of Free Masonry.

The Septenary is the Crown of the Numbers, because it unites
the Triangle of the Idea to the Square of the Form.

The more the great Hierophants were at pains to conceal their
absolute Science, the more they sought to add grandeur to and
multiply its symbols. The huge pyramids, with their triangular
sides of elevation and square bases, represented their Metaphysics,
founded upon the knowledge of Nature. That knowledge of Nature had for its symbolic key the gigantic form of that huge
Sphinx, which has hollowed its deep bed in the sand, while keep-

ing watch at the feet of the Pyramids. The Seven grand monuments called the Wonders of the World, were the magnificent
Commentaries on the Seven lines that composed the Pyramids,
and on the Seven mystic gates of Thebes.

The Septenary philosophy of Initiation among the Ancients
may be summed up thus:

Three Absolute Principles which are but One Principle: four
elementary forms which are but one; all forming a Single Whole,
compounded of the Idea and the Form.

The three Principles were these:

1°. BEING IS BEING.

In Philosophy, identity of the Idea and of Being or Verity; in
Religion, the first Principle, THE FATHER.

2°. BEING IS REAL.

In Philosophy, identity of Knowing and of Being or Reality;
in Religion, the LOGOS of Plato, the *Demiourgos,* the WORD.

3°. BEING IS LOGIC.

In Philosophy, identity of the Reason and Reality; in Religion,
Providence, the Divine Action that makes real the Good, that
which in Christianity we call THE HOLY SPIRIT.

The *union* of all the Seven colors is the *White,* the analogous
symbol of the GOOD: the *absence* of all is the *Black,* the analogous
symbol of the EVIL. There are three primary colors, *Red, Yellow,*
and *Blue;* and four secondary, *Orange, Green, Indigo,* and *Vio-
let;* and all these God displays to man in the rainbow; and they
have their analogies also in the moral and intellectual world. The
same number, *Seven,* continually reappears in the Apocalypse,
compounded of *three* and *four;* and these numbers relate to the
last Seven of the Sephiroth, three answering to BENIGNITY or
MERCY, SEVERITY or JUSTICE, and BEAUTY or HARMONY; and
four to *Netzach, Hōd, Yesōd,* and *Malakoth,* VICTORY, GLORY,
STABILITY, and DOMINATION. The same numbers also represent
the *first* three Sephiroth, KETHER, KHOKMAH, and BAINAH, or
Will, Wisdom, and *Understanding,* which, with DAATH or *Intellection* or *Thought,* are also four, DAATH not being regarded as a
Sephirah, not as the Deity acting, or as a potency, energy, or attribute, but as the Divine Action.

The Sephiroth are commonly figured in the Kabalah as constituting a human form, the ADAM KADMON or MACROCOSM. Thus
arranged, the universal law of Equipoise is three times exempli-

fied. From that of the Divine Intellectual, Active, Masculine
ENERGY, and the Passive CAPACITY to produce Thought, the
action of THINKING results. From that of BENIGNITY and SE-
VERITY, HARMONY flows; and from that of VICTORY or an Infinite overcoming, and GLORY, which, being Infinite, would seem to
forbid the existence of obstacles or opposition, results STABILITY
or PERMANENCE, which is the perfect DOMINION of the Infinite
WILL.

The last nine Sephiroth are included in, at the same time that
they have flowed forth from, the first of all, KETHER, or the
CROWN. Each also, in succession flowed from, and yet still remains included in, the one preceding it. The Will of God *includes*
His Wisdom, and His Wisdom *is* His Will specially developed and
acting. This Wisdom is the LOGOS that creates, mistaken and
personified by Simon Magus and the succeeding Gnostics. By
means of its utterance, the letter YŌD, it creates the worlds, first
in the Divine Intellect as an Idea, which invested with form became the fabricated World, the Universe of material reality. YŌD
and HE, two letters of the Ineffable Name of the Manifested
Deity, represent the Male and the Female, the Active and the
Passive in Equilibrium, and the VAV completes the Trinity and
the Triliteral Name יהן, the Divine Triangle, which with the
repetition of the *He* becomes the Tetragrammaton.

Thus the ten Sephiroth contain all the Sacred Numbers, *three,
five, seven,* and *nine,* and the perfect Number *Ten,* and correspond
with the Tetractys of Pythagoras.

BEING IS BEING, אהיה אשר אהיה, *Ahayah Asar Ahayah.* This
is the Principle, the "BEGINNING."

In the Beginning was, that is to say, IS, WAS, and WILL BE,
the WORD, that is to say, the REASON that *Speaks.*

Εν αρχη ην 'Ο Λογος!

The Word is the reason of belief, and in it also is the expression
of the Faith which makes Science a living thing. The Word,
Λογος, is the Source of Logic. Jesus is the Word Incarnate. The
accord of the Reason with Faith, of Knowledge with Belief, of
Authority with Liberty, has become in modern times the veritable
enigma of the Sphinx.

It is WISDOM that, in the Kabalistic Books of the Proverbs and
Ecclesiasticus, is the Creative Agent of God. Elsewhere in the
Hebrew writings it is דבר יהוה, *Debar Iahavah,* the Word of God.

It is by His uttered Word that God reveals Himself to us; not alone in the visible and invisible but intellectual creation, but also in our convictions, consciousness, and instincts. Hence it is that certain beliefs are universal. The conviction of all men that God is good led to a belief in a Devil, the fallen *Lucifer* or *Light-bearer,* Shaitan the Adversary, Ahriman and Tuphōn, as an attempt to explain the existence of Evil, and make it consistent with the Infinite Power, Wisdom, and Benevolence of God.

Nothing surpasses and nothing equals, as a Summary of all the doctrines of the Old World, those brief words engraven by HERMES on a Stone, and known under the name of *"The Tablet of Emerald:"* the Unity of Being and the Unity of the Harmonies, ascending and descending, the progressive and proportional scale of the Word; the immutable law of the Equilibrium, and the proportioned progress of the universal analogies; the relation of the Idea to the Word, giving the measure of the relation between the Creator and the Created, the necessary mathematics of the Infinite, proved by the measures of a single corner of the Finite;—all this is expressed by this single proposition of the Great Egyptian Hierophant:

"What is Superior is as that which is Inferior, and what is Below is as that which is Above, to form the Marvels of the Unity."

XX.

GRAND MASTER OF ALL SYMBOLIC LODGES.

THE true Mason is a practical Philosopher, who, under religious emblems, in all ages adopted by wisdom, builds upon plans traced by nature and reason the moral edifice of knowledge. He ought to find, in the symmetrical relation of all the parts of this rational edifice, the principle and rule of all his duties, the source of all his pleasures. He improves his moral nature, becomes a better man, and finds in the reunion of virtuous men, assembled with pure views, the means of multiplying his acts of beneficence. Masonry and Philosophy, without being one and the same thing, have the same object, and propose to themselves the same end, the worship of the Grand Architect of the Universe, acquaintance and familiarity with the wonders of nature, and the happiness of humanity attained by the constant practice of all the virtues.

As Grand Master of all Symbolic Lodges, it is your especial duty to aid in restoring Masonry to its primitive purity. You have become an instructor. Masonry long wandered in error. Instead of improving, it degenerated from its primitive simplicity, and retrograded toward a system, distorted by stupidity and ignorance, which, unable to construct a beautiful machine, made a complicated one. Less than two hundred years ago, its organization was simple, and altogether moral, its emblems, allegories, and ceremonies easy to be understood, and their purpose and object readily to be seen. It was then confined to a very small number of Degrees. Its constitutions were like those of a Society of Essenes, written in the first century of our era. There could be seen the primitive Christianity, organized into Masonry, the school of Pythagoras without incongruities or absurdities; a Masonry simple and significant, in which it was not necessary to torture the mind to discover reasonable interpretations; a Masonry at once religious and philosophical, worthy of a good citizen and an enlightened philanthropist.

Innovators and inventors overturned that primitive simplicity.

325

Ignorance engaged in the work of making Degrees, and trifles and gewgaws and pretended mysteries, absurd or hideous, usurped the place of Masonic Truth. The picture of a horrid vengeance, the poniard and the bloody head, appeared in the peaceful Temple of Masonry, without sufficient explanation of their symbolic meaning. Oaths out of all proportion with their object, shocked the candidate, and then became ridiculous, and were wholly disregarded. Acolytes were exposed to tests, and compelled to perform acts, which, if real, would have been abominable; but being mere chimeras, were preposterous, and excited contempt and laughter only. Eight hundred Degrees of one kind and another were invented: Infidelity and even Jesuitry were taught under the mask of Masonry. The rituals even of the respectable Degrees, copied and mutilated by ignorant men, became nonsensical and trivial; and the words so corrupted that it has hitherto been found impossible to recover many of them at all. Candidates were made to degrade themselves, and to submit to insults not tolerable to a man of spirit and honor.

Hence it was that, practically, the largest portion of the Degrees claimed by the Ancient and Accepted Scottish Rite, and before it by the Rite of Perfection, fell into disuse, were merely communicated, and their rituals became jejune and insignificant. These Rites resembled those old palaces and baronial castles, the different parts of which, built at different periods remote from one another, upon plans and according to tastes that greatly varied, formed a discordant and incongruous whole. Judaism and chivalry, superstition and philosophy, philanthropy and insane hatred and longing for vengeance, a pure morality and unjust and illegal revenge, were found strangely mated and standing hand in hand within the Temples of Peace and Concord; and the whole system was one grotesque commingling of incongruous things, of contrasts and contradictions, of shocking and fantastic extravagances, of parts repugnant to good taste, and fine conceptions overlaid and disfigured by absurdities engendered by ignorance, fanaticism, and a senseless mysticism.

An empty and sterile pomp, impossible indeed to be carried out, and to which no meaning whatever was attached, with far-fetched explanations that were either so many stupid platitudes or themselves needed an interpreter; lofty titles, arbitrarily assumed, and to which the inventors had not condescended to attach any explanation that should acquit them of the folly of assuming temporal rank, power, and titles of nobility, made the world laugh, and the Initiate feel ashamed.

Some of these titles we retain; but they have with us meanings entirely consistent with that Spirit of Equality which is the foundation and peremptory law of its being of all Masonry. The *Knight*, with us, is he who devotes his hand, his heart, his brain, to the Science of Masonry, and professes himself the Sworn Soldier of Truth: the *Prince* is he who aims to be *Chief* [*Princeps*], *first, leader,* among his equals, in virtue and good deeds: the *Sovereign* is he who, one of an order whose members are all Sovereigns, is Supreme only because the law and constitutions are so, which he administers, and by which he, like every other brother, is governed. The titles, *Puissant, Potent, Wise, and Venerable,* indicate that power of Virtue, Intelligence, and Wisdom, which those ought to strive to attain who are placed in high office by the suffrages of their brethren: and all our other titles and designations have an esoteric meaning, consistent with modesty and equality, and which those who receive them should fully understand. As Master of a Lodge it is your duty to instruct your Brethren that they are all so many constant lessons, teaching the lofty qualifications which are required of those who claim them, and not merely idle gewgaws worn in ridiculous imitation of the times when the Nobles and Priests were masters and the people slaves: and that, in all true Masonry, the Knight, the Pontiff, the Prince, and the Sovereign are but the first among their equals: and the cordon, the clothing, and the jewel but symbols and emblems of the virtues required of all good Masons.

The Mason kneels, no longer to present his petition for admittance or to receive the answer, no longer to a man as his superior, who is but his brother, but to his God; to whom he appeals for the rectitude of his intentions, and whose aid he asks to enable him to keep his vows. No one is degraded by bending his knee to God at the altar, or to receive the honor of Knighthood·as Bayard and Du Guesclin knelt. To kneel for other purposes, Masonry does not require. God gave to man a head to be borne erect, a port upright and majestic. We assemble in our Temples to cherish and inculcate sentiments that conform to that loftiness of bearing which the just and upright man is entitled to maintain, and we do not require those who desire to be admitted among us, ignominiously to bow the head. We respect man, because we respect ourselves that he may conceive a lofty idea of his dignity as a human being free and independent. If modesty is a virtue, humility and obsequiousness to man are base: for there is a noble pride which is the most real and solid basis of virtue. Man should humble himself before the Infinite God; but not before his erring and imperfect brother.

As Master of a Lodge, you will therefore be exceedingly careful that no Candidate, in any Degree, be required to submit to any degradation whatever; as has been too much the custom in some of the Degrees: and take it as a certain and inflexible rule, to which there is *no* exception, that real Masonry requires of no man anything to which a Knight and Gentleman cannot honorably, and without feeling outraged or humiliated submit.

The Supreme Council for the Southern Jurisdiction of the United States at length undertook the indispensable and long-delayed task of revising and reforming the work and rituals of the thirty Degrees under its jurisdiction. Retaining the essentials of the Degrees and all the means by which the members recognize one another, it has sought out and developed the leading idea of each Degree, rejected the puerilities and absurdities with which many of them were disfigured, and made of them a connected system of moral, religious, and philosophical instruction. Sectarian of no creed, it has yet thought it not improper to use the old allegories, based on occurrences detailed in the Hebrew and Christian books, and drawn from the Ancient Mysteries of Egypt, Persia, Greece, India, the Druids and the Essenes, as vehicles to communicate the Great Masonic Truths; as it has used the legends of the Crusades, and the ceremonies of the orders of Knighthood.

It no longer inculcates a criminal and wicked vengeance. It has not allowed Masonry to play the assassin: to avenge the death either of Hiram, of Charles the 1st, or of Jaques De Molay and the Templars. The Ancient and Accepted Scottish Rite of Masonry has now become, what Masonry at first was meant to be, a Teacher of Great Truths, inspired by an upright and enlightened reason, a firm and constant wisdom, and an affectionate and liberal philanthropy.

It is no longer a system, over the composition and arrangement of the different parts of which, want of reflection, chance, ignorance, and perhaps motives still more ignoble presided; a system unsuited to our habits, our manners, our ideas, or the world-wide philanthropy and universal toleration of Masonry; or to bodies small in number, whose revenues should be devoted to the relief of the unfortunate, and not to empty show; no longer a heterogeneous aggregate of Degrees, shocking by its anachronisms and contradictions, powerless to disseminate light, information, and moral and philosophical ideas.

As Master, you will teach those who are under you, and to whom you will owe your office, that the decorations of many of the Degrees are to be dispensed with, whenever the expense would interfere with the duties of charity, relief, and benevolence; and to be indulged in only by wealthy bodies that will thereby do no wrong to those entitled to their assistance. The essentials of all the Degrees may be procured at slight expense; and it is at the option of every Brother to procure or not to procure, as he pleases, the dress, decorations, and jewels of any Degree other than the 14th, 18th, 30th, and 32d.

We teach the truth of none of the legends we recite. They are to us but parables and allegories, involving and enveloping Masonic instruction; and vehicles of useful and interesting information. They represent the different phases of the human mind, its efforts and struggles to comprehend nature, God, the government of the Universe, the permitted existence of sorrow and evil. To teach us wisdom, and the folly of endeavoring to explain to ourselves that which we are not capable of understanding, we reproduce the speculations of the Philosophers, the Kabalists, the Mystagogues and the Gnostics. Every one being at liberty to apply our symbols and emblems as he thinks most consistent with truth and reason and with his own faith, we give them such an interpretation only as may be accepted by all. Our Degrees may be conferred in France or Turkey, at Pekin, Ispàhan, Rome, or Geneva, in the city of Penn or in Catholic Louisiana, upon the subject of an absolute government or the citizen of a Free State, upon Sectarian or Theist. To honor the Deity, to regard all men as our Brethren, as children, equally dear to Him, of the Supreme Creator of the Universe, and to make himself useful to society and himself by his labor, are its teachings to its Initiates in all the Degrees.

Preacher of Liberty, Fraternity, and Equality, it desires them to be attained by making men fit to receive them, and by the moral power of an intelligent and enlightened People. It lays no plots and conspiracies. It hatches no premature revolutions; it encourages no people to revolt against the constituted authorities; but recognizing the great truth that freedom follows fitness for freedom as the corollary follows the axiom, it strives to *prepare* men to govern themselves.

Where domestic slavery exists, it teaches the master humanity and the alleviation of the condition of his slave, and moderate correction and gentle discipline; as it teaches them to the master of the apprentice: and as it teaches to the employers of other men, in mines, manufactories, and workshops, consideration and humanity for those who depend upon their labor for their bread, and to whom want of employment is starvation, and overwork is fever, consumption, and death.

As Master of a Lodge, you are to inculcate these duties on your brethren. Teach the employed to be honest, punctual, and faithful as well as respectful and obedient to all proper orders: but also teach the employer that every man or woman who desires to work, has a right to have work to do; and that they, and those who from sickness or feebleness, loss of limb or of bodily vigor, old age or infancy, are not able to work, have a right to be fed, clothed, and sheltered from the inclement elements: that he commits an awful sin against Masonry and in the sight of God, if he closes his workshops or factories, or ceases to work his mines, when they do not yield him what he regards as sufficient profit, and so dismisses his workmen and workwomen to starve; or when he reduces the wages of man or woman to so low a standard that they and their families cannot be clothed and fed and comfortably housed; or by overwork must give him their blood and life in exchange for the pittance of their wages: and that his duty as a Mason and Brother peremptorily requires him to continue to employ those who else will be pinched with hunger and cold, or resort to theft and vice: and to pay them fair wages, though it may reduce or annul his profits or even eat into his capital; for God hath but loaned him his wealth, and made him His almoner and agent to invest it.

Except as mere symbols of the moral virtues and intellectual qualities, the tools and implements of Masonry belong exclusively to the first three Degrees. They also, however, serve to remind the Mason who has advanced further, that his new rank is based upon the humble labors of the symbolic Degrees, as they are improperly termed, inasmuch as all the Degrees are symbolic.

Thus the Initiates are inspired with a just idea of Masonry, to-wit, that it is essentially WORK; both teaching and practising LABOR; and that it is altogether emblematic. Three kinds of work are necessary to the preservation and protection of man and society: manual labor, specially belonging to the three blue Degrees; labor in arms, symbolized by the Knightly or chivalric Degrees; and intellectual labor, belonging particularly to the Philosophical Degrees.

We have preserved and multiplied such emblems as have a true and profound meaning. We reject many of the old and senseless explanations. We have not reduced Masonry to a cold metaphysics that exiles everything belonging to the domain of the imagination. The ignorant, and those *half*-wise in reality, but *over*-wise in their own conceit, may assail our symbols with sarcasms; but they are nevertheless ingenious veils that cover the Truth, respected by all who know the means by which the heart of man is reached and his feelings enlisted. The Great Moralists often had recourse to allegories, in order to instruct men without repelling them. But we have been careful not to allow our emblems to be too obscure, so as to require far-fetched and forced interpretations. In our days, and in the enlightened land in which we live, we do not need to wrap ourselves in veils so strange and impenetrable, as to prevent or hinder instruction instead of furthering it; or to induce the suspicion that we have concealed meanings which we communicate only to the most reliable adepts, because they are contrary to good order or the well-being of society.

The Duties of the Class of *Instructors,* that is, the Masons of the Degrees from the 4th to the 8th, inclusive, are, particularly, to perfect the younger Masons in the words, signs and tokens and other work of the Degrees they have received; to explain to them the meaning of the different emblems, and to expound the moral instruction which they convey. And upon their report of proficiency alone can their pupils be allowed to advance and receive an increase of wages.

The Directors of the Work, or those of the 9th, 10th, and 11th Degrees are to report to the Chapters upon the regularity, activity and proper direction of the work of bodies in the lower Degrees, and what is needed to be enacted for their prosperity and usefulness. In the Symbolic Lodges, they are particularly charged to stimulate the zeal of the workmen, to induce them to engage in new labors and enterprises for the good of Masonry, their country and mankind, and to give them fraternal advice when they fall short of their duty; or, in cases that require it, to invoke against them the rigor of Masonic law.

The Architects, or those of the 12th, 13th, and 14th, should be selected from none but Brothers well instructed in the preceding Degrees; zealous, and capable of discoursing upon that Masonry; illustrating it, and discussing the simple questions of moral philosophy. And one of them, at every communication, should be prepared with a lecture, communicating useful knowledge or giving good advice to the Brethren.

The Knights, of the 15th and 16th Degrees, wear the sword. They are bound to prevent and repair, as far as may be in their power, all injustice, both in the world and in Masonry; to protect the weak and to bring oppressors to justice. Their works and lectures must be in this spirit. They should inquire whether Masonry fulfills, as far as it ought and can, its principal purpose, which is to succor the unfortunate. That it may do so, they should prepare propositions to be offered in the Blue Lodges calculated to attain that end, to put an end to abuses, and to prevent or correct negligence. Those in the Lodges who have attained the rank of Knights, are most fit to be appointed Almoners, and charged to ascertain and make known who need and are entitled to the charity of the Order.

In the higher Degrees those only should be received who have sufficient reading and information to discuss the great questions of philosophy. From them the Orators of the Lodges should be selected, as well as those of the Councils and Chapters. They are charged to suggest such measures as are necessary to make Masonry entirely faithful to the spirit of its institution, both as to its charitable purposes, and the diffusion of light and knowledge; such as are needed to correct abuses that have crept in, and offences against the rules and general spirit of the Order; and such as will tend to make it, as it was meant to be, the great Teacher of Mankind.

As Master of a Lodge, Council, or Chapter, it will be your duty to impress upon the minds of your Brethren these views of the general plan and separate parts of the Ancient and Accepted Scottish Rite; of its spirit and design; its harmony and regularity; of the duties of the officers and members; and of the particular lessons intended to be taught by each Degree.

Especially you are not to allow any assembly of the body over which you may preside, to close, without recalling to the minds of the Brethren the Masonic virtues and duties which are represented upon the Tracing Board of this Degree. That is an imperative duty. Forget not that, more than three thousand years ago, ZORO-ASTER said: "*Be good, be kind, be humane, and charitable; love your fellows; console the afflicted; pardon those who have done you wrong.*" Nor that more than two thousand three hundred years ago CONFUCIUS repeated, also quoting the language of those who had lived before himself: "*Love thy neighbor as thyself: Do not to others what thou wouldst not wish should be done to thyself: Forgive injuries. Forgive your enemy, be reconciled to him, give him assistance, invoke God in his behalf!*"

Let not the morality of your Lodge be inferior to that of the Persian or the Chinese Philosopher.

Urge upon your Brethren the teaching and the unostentatious practice of the morality of the Lodge, without regard to times, places, religions, or peoples.

Urge them to love one another, to be devoted to one another, to be faithful to the country, the government, and the laws: for to serve the country is to pay a dear and sacred debt:

To respect all forms of worship, to tolerate all political and religious opinions; not to blame, and still less to condemn the religion of others: not to seek to make converts; but to be content if they have the religion of Socrates; a veneration for the Creator, the religion of good works, and grateful acknowledgment of God's blessings:

To fraternize with all men; to assist all who are unfortunate; and to cheerfully postpone their own interests to that of the Order:

To make it the constant rule of their lives, to think well, to speak well, and to act well:

To place the sage above the soldier, the noble, or the prince: and take the wise and good as their models:

To see that their professions and practice, their teachings and conduct, do always agree:

To make this also their motto: Do that which thou oughtest to do; let the result be what it will.

Such, my Brother, are some of the duties of that office which you have sought to be qualified to exercise. May you perform them well; and in so doing gain honor for yourself, and advance the great cause of Masonry, Humanity, and Progress.

XXI.

NOACHITE, OR PRUSSIAN KNIGHT.

You are especially charged in this Degree to be modest and humble, and not vain-glorious nor filled with self-conceit. Be not wiser in your own opinion than the Deity, nor find fault with His works, nor endeavor to improve upon what He has done. Be modest also in your intercourse with your fellows, and slow to entertain evil thoughts of them, and reluctant to ascribe to them evil intentions. A thousand presses, flooding the country with their evanescent leaves, are busily and incessantly engaged in maligning the motives and conduct of men and parties, and in making one man think worse of another; while, alas, scarcely one is found that ever, even accidentally, labors to make man think better of his fellow.

Slander and calumny were never so insolently licentious in any country as they are this day in ours. The most retiring disposition, the most unobtrusive demeanor, is no shield against their poisoned arrows. The most eminent public service only makes their vituperation and invective more eager and more unscrupulous, when he who has done such service presents himself as a candidate for the people's suffrages.

The evil is wide-spread and universal. No man, no woman, no household, is sacred or safe from this new Inquisition. No act is so pure or so praiseworthy, that the unscrupulous vender of lies who lives by pandering to a corrupt and morbid public appetite will not proclaim it as a crime. No motive is so innocent or so laudable, that he will not hold it up as villainy. Journalism pries into the interior of private houses, gloats over the details of domestic tragedies of sin and shame, and deliberately invents and industriously circulates the most unmitigated and baseless falsehoods, to coin money for those who pursue it as a trade, or to effect a temporary result in the wars of faction.

We need not enlarge upon these evils. They are apparent to all and lamented over by all, and it is the duty of a Mason to do all

334

in his power to lessen, if not to remove them. With the errors and even sins of other men, that do not personally affect us or ours, and need not our condemnation to be odious, we have nothing to do; and the journalist has no patent that makes him the Censor of Morals. There is no obligation resting on us to trumpet forth our disapproval of every wrongful or injudicious or improper act that every other man commits. One would be ashamed to stand on the street corners and retail them orally for pennies.

One ought, in truth, to write or speak against no other one in this world.. Each man in it has enough to do, to watch and keep guard over himself. Each of us is sick enough in this great Lazaretto: and journalism and polemical writing constantly remind us of a scene once witnessed in a little hospital; where it was horrible to hear how the patients mockingly reproached each other with their disorders and infirmities: how one, who was wasted by consumption, jeered at another who was bloated by dropsy: how one laughed at another's cancer of the face; and this one again at his neighbor's lock-jaw or squint; until at last the delirious fever-patient sprang out of his bed, and tore away the coverings from the wounded bodies of his companions, and nothing was to be seen but hideous misery and mutilation. Such is the revolting work in which journalism and political partisanship, and half the world outside of Masonry, are engaged.

Very generally, the censure bestowed upon men's acts, by those who have appointed and commissioned themselves Keepers of the Public Morals, is undeserved. Often it is not only undeserved, but praise is deserved instead of censure, and, when the latter is not undeserved, it is always extravagant, and therefore unjust.

A Mason will wonder what spirit they are endowed withal, that can basely libel at a man, even, that is fallen. If they had any nobility of soul, they would with him condole his disasters, and drop some tears in pity of his folly and wretchedness: and if they were merely human and not brutal, Nature did grievous wrong to human bodies, to curse them with souls so cruel as to strive to add to a wretchedness already intolerable. When a Mason hears of any man that hath fallen into public disgrace, he should have a mind to commiserate his mishap, and not to make him more disconsolate. To envenom a name by libels, that already is openly tainted, is to add stripes with an iron rod to one that is flayed with whipping; and to every well-tempered mind will seem most in-human and unmanly.

Even the man who does wrong and commits errors often has a quiet home, a fireside of his own, a gentle, loving wife and inno-cent children, who perhaps do not know of his past errors and lapses—past and long repented of; or if they do, they love him the better, because, being mortal, he hath erred, and being in the image of God, he hath repented. That every blow at this husband and father lacerates the pure and tender bosoms of that wife and those daughters, is a consideration that doth not stay the hand of the brutal journalist and partisan: but he strikes home at these shrinking, quivering, innocent, tender bosoms; and then goes out upon the great arteries of cities, where the current of life pulsates, and holds his head erect, and calls on his fellows to laud him and admire him, for the chivalric act he hath done, in striking his dagger through one heart into another tender and trusting one.

If you seek for high and strained carriages, you shall, for the most part, meet with them in low men. Arrogance is a weed that ever grows on a dunghill. It is from the rankness of that soil that she hath her height and spreadings. To be modest and unaffected with our superiors is duty; with our equals, courtesy; with our in-feriors, nobleness. There is no arrogance so great as the pro-claiming of other men's errors and faults, by those who under-stand nothing but the dregs of actions, and who make it their business to besmear deserving fames. Public reproof is like strik-ing a deer in the herd: it not only wounds him, to the loss of blood, but betrays him to the hound, his enemy.

The occupation of the spy hath ever been held dishonorable, and it is none the less so, now that with rare exceptions editors and partisans have become perpetual spies upon the actions of other men. Their malice makes them nimble-eyed, apt to note a fault and publish it, and, with a strained construction, to deprave even those things in which the doer's intents were honest. Like the crocodile, they slime the way of others, to make them fall; and when that has happened, they feed their insulting envy on the life-blood of the prostrate. They set the vices of other men on high, for the gaze of the world, and place their virtues under-ground, that none may note them. If they cannot wound upon proofs, they will do it upon likelihoods: and if not upon them, they manufacture lies, as God created the world, out of nothing; and so corrupt the fair tempter of men's reputations; knowing that the multitude will believe them, because affirmations are apter to win belief, than negatives to uncredit them; and that a lie travels faster than an eagle flies, while the contradiction limps after it at a snail's pace, and, halting, never overtakes it. Nay, it is contrary to the morality of journalism, to allow a lie to be contradicted in the place that spawned it. And even if that great favor is conceded, a slander once raised will scarce ever die, or fail of finding many that will allow it both a harbor and trust.

This is, beyond any other, the age of falsehood. Once, to be suspected of equivocation was enough to soil a gentleman's escutcheon; but now it has become a strange merit in a partisan or statesman, always and scrupulously to tell the truth. Lies are part of the regular ammunition of all campaigns and controversies, valued according as they are profitable and effective; and are stored up and have a market price, like saltpetre and sulphur; being even more deadly than they.

If men weighed the imperfections of humanity, they would breathe less condemnation. Ignorance gives disparagement a louder tongue than knowledge does. Wise men had rather know, than tell. Frequent dispraises are but the faults of uncharitable wit: and it is from where there is no judgment, that the heaviest judgment comes; for self-examination would make all judgments charitable. If we even do know vices in men, we can scarce show ourselves in a nobler virtue than in the charity of concealing them: if that be not a flattery persuading to continuance. And it is the basest office man can fall into, to make his tongue the defamer of the worthy man.

There is but one rule for the Mason in this matter. If there be virtues, and he is called upon to speak of him who owns them, let him tell them forth impartially. And if there be vices mixed with them, let him be content the world shall know them by some other tongue than his. For if the evil-doer deserve no pity, his wife, his parents, or his children, or other innocent persons who love him may; and the bravo's trade, practised by him who stabs the defenceless for a price paid by individual or party, is really no more respectable now than it was a hundred years ago, in Venice. Where we want experience, Charity bids us think the best, and leave what we know not to the Searcher of Hearts; for mistakes, suspicions, and envy often injure a clear fame; and there is least danger in a charitable construction.

And, finally, the Mason should be humble and modest toward the Grand Architect of the Universe, and not impugn His Wisdom, nor set up his own imperfect sense of Right against His Providence and dispensations, nor attempt too rashly to explore the Mysteries of God's Infinite Essence and inscrutable plans, and of that Great Nature which we are not made capable to understand.

Let him steer far away from all those vain philosophies, which endeavor to account for all that is, without admitting that there is a God, separate and apart from the Universe which is his work: which erect Universal Nature into a God, and worship it alone: which annihilate Spirit, and believe no testimony except that of the bodily senses: which, by logical formulas and dextrous collocation of words, make the actual, living, guiding, and protecting God fade into the dim mistiness of a mere abstraction and unreality, itself a mere logical formula.

Nor let him have any alliance with those theorists who chide the delays of Providence and busy themselves to hasten the slow march which it has imposed upon events: who neglect the practical, to struggle after impossibilities: who are wiser than Heaven; know the aims and purposes of the Deity, and can see a short and more direct means of attaining them, than it pleases Him to employ: who would have no discords in the great harmony of the Universe of things; but equal distribution of property, no subjection of one man to the will of another, no compulsory labor, and still no starvation, nor destitution, nor pauperism.

Let him not spend his life, as they do, in building a new Tower of Babel; in attempting to change that which is fixed by an inflexible law of God's enactment: but let him, yielding to the Superior Wisdom of Providence, content to believe that the march of events is rightly ordered by an Infinite Wisdom, and leads, though we cannot see it, to a great and perfect result,—let him be satisfied to follow the path pointed out by that Providence, and to labor for the good of the human race in that mode in which God has chosen to enact that that good shall be effected: and above all, let him build no Tower of Babel, under the belief that by ascending he will mount so high that God will disappear or be superseded by a great monstrous aggregate of material forces, or mere glittering, logical formula; but, evermore, standing humbly and reverently upon the earth and looking with awe and confidence toward Heaven, let him be satisfied that there is a *real* God; a *person,* and not a formula; a Father and a protector, who loves, and sympathizes, and compassionates; and that the eternal ways by which He rules the world are infinitely wise, no matter how far they may be above the feeble comprehension and limited vision of man.

XXII.

KNIGHT OF THE ROYAL AXE

OR

PRINCE OF LIBANUS.

SYMPATHY with the great laboring classes, respect for labor itself, and resolution to do some good *work* in our day and generation, these are the lessons of this Degree, and they are purely Masonic. Masonry has made a working-man and his associates the Heroes of her principal legend, and himself the companion of Kings. The idea is as simple and true as it is sublime. From first to last, Masonry is *work*. It venerates the Grand *Architect* of the Universe. It commemorates the *building* of a Temple. Its principal emblems are *the working tools* of Masons and Artisans. It preserves the name of the first *worker* in *brass* and *iron* as one of its pass-words. When the Brethren meet together, they are at *labor*. The Master is the *overseer* who sets the craft *to work* and gives them proper instruction. Masonry is the apotheosis of WORK.

It is the hands of brave, forgotten men that have made this great, populous, cultivated world a world for *us*. It is *all* work, and *forgotten* work. The *real* conquerors, creators, and eternal proprietors of every great and civilized land are all the heroic souls that ever were in it, each in his degree: all the men that ever felled a forest-tree or drained a marsh, or contrived a wise scheme, or did or said a true or valiant thing therein. Genuine work alone, done faithfully, is eternal, even as the Almighty Founder and World-builder Himself. All work is noble: a life of ease is not for any man, nor for any God. The Almighty Maker is not like one who, in old immemorial ages, having made his machine of a Universe, sits ever since, and sees it *go*. Out of that belief comes Atheism. The faith in an Invisible, Unnameable, Directing Deity, present everywhere in all that we see, and work, and suffer, is the essence of all faith whatsoever.

The life of all Gods figures itself to us as a Sublime Earnest-

340

ness,—of Infinite battle against Infinite labor Our highest religion is named the Worship of Sorrow. For the Son of Man there is no noble crown, well-worn, or even ill-worn, but is a crown of thorns. Man's highest destiny is not to be happy, to love pleasant things and find them. His only true *un*happiness should be that he cannot work, and get his destiny as a man fulfilled. The day passes swiftly over, our life passes swiftly over, and the night cometh, wherein no man can work. That night once come, our happiness and unhappiness are vanished, and become as things that never were. But our work is not abolished, and has not vanished. It remains, or the want of it remains, for endless Times and Eternities.

Whatsoever of morality and intelligence; what of pateince, perseverance, faithfulness, of method, insight, ingenuity, energy; in a word, whatsoever of STRENGTH a man has in him, will lie written in the WORK he does. To work is to try himself against Nature and her unerring, everlasting laws: and they will return true verdict as to him. The noblest Epic is a mighty Empire slowly built together, a mighty series of heroic deeds, a mighty conquest over chaos. Deeds are greater than words. They have a life, mute, but undeniable; and grow. They people the vacuity of Time, and make it green and worthy.

Labor is the truest emblem of God, the Architect and Eternal Maker; noble Labor, which is yet to be the King of this Earth, and sit on the highest Throne. Men without duties to do, are like trees planted on precipices; from the roots of which all the earth has crumbled. Nature owns no man who is not also a Martyr. She scorns the man who sits screened from all work, from want, danger, hardship, the victory over which is work; and has all his work and battling done by other men; and yet there are men who pride themselves that they and theirs have done no work time out of mind. So neither have the swine.

The chief of men is he who stands in the van of men, fronting the peril which frightens back all others, and if not vanquished would devour them. Hercules was worshipped for twelve labors. The Czar of Russia became a toiling shipwright, and worked with his axe in the docks of Saardam; and something came of that. Cromwell worked, and Napoleon; and effected somewhat.

There is a perennial nobleness and even sacredness in work. Be he never so benighted and forgetful of his high calling, there is always hope in a man who actually and earnestly works: in Idleness alone is there perpetual Despair. Man perfects himself by working. Jungles are cleared away. Fair seed-fields rise instead, and stately cities; and withal, the man himself first ceases to be a foul unwholesome jungle and desert thereby. Even in the meanest sort of labor, the whole soul of man is composed into a kind of real harmony, the moment he begins to work. Doubt, Desire, Sorrow, Remorse, Indignation, and even Despair shrink murmuring far off into their caves, whenever the man bends himself resolutely against his task. Labor is life. From the inmost heart of the worker rises his God-given Force, the Sacred Celestial Life-essence, breathed into him by Almighty God; and awakens him to all nobleness, as soon as work fitly begins. By it man learns Patience, Courage, Perseverance, Openness to light, readiness to own himself mistaken, resolution to do better and improve. Only by labor will man continually learn the virtues. There is no Religion in stagnation and inaction; but only in activity and exertion. There was the deepest truth in that saying of the old monks, "*laborare est orare*." "He prayeth best who loveth best all things both great and small;" and can man love except by working earnestly to benefit that being whom he loves?

"Work; and therein have well-being," is the oldest of Gospels; unpreached, inarticulate, but ineradicable, and enduring forever. To make Disorder, wherever found, an eternal enemy; to attack and subdue him, and make order of him, the subject not of Chaos, but of Intelligence and Divinity, and of ourselves; to attack ignorance, stupidity and brute-mindedness, wherever found, to smite it wisely and unweariedly, to rest not while we live and it lives, in the name of God, this is our duty as Masons; commanded us by the Highest God. Even He, with his unspoken voice, more awful than the thunders of Sinai, or the syllabled speech of the Hurricane, speaks to us. The Unborn Ages; the old Graves, with their long-moldering dust speak to us. The deep Death-Kingdoms, the Stars in their never-resting course, all Space and all Time, silently and continually admonish us that we too must work while it is called to-day. Labor, wide as the Earth, has its summit in Heaven. To toil, whether with the sweat of the brow, or of the brain or heart, is worship,—the noblest thing yet discovered beneath the Stars. Let the weary cease to think that labor is a curse and doom pronounced by Deity. Without it there could be no true excellence in human nature. Without it, and pain, and sorrow, where would be the human virtues? Where Patience, Perseverance, Submission, Energy, Endurance, Fortitude, Bravery, Disinterestedness, Self-Sacrifice, the noblest excellencies of the Soul?

Let him who toils complain not, nor feel humiliated! Let him look up, and see his fellow-workmen there, in God's Eternity; they *alone* surviving there. Even in the weak human memory they long survive, as Saints, as Heroes, and as Gods: they *alone* survive, and people the unmeasured solitudes of Time.

To the primeval man, whatsoever good came, descended on him (as in mere fact, it ever does) direct from God; whatsoever duty lay visible for him, this a Supreme God had prescribed. For the primeval man, in whom dwelt Thought, this Universe was all a Temple, life everywhere a Worship.

Duty is with us ever; and evermore forbids us to be idle. To work with the hands or brain, according to our requirements and our capacities, to do that which lies before us to do, is more honorable than rank and title. Ploughers, spinners and builders, inventors, and men of science, poets, advocates, and writers, all stand upon one common level, and form one grand, innumerable host, marching ever onward since the beginning of the world: each entitled to our sympathy and respect, each a man and our brother.

It was well to give the earth to man as a dark mass, whereon to labor. It was well to provide rude and unsightly materials in the ore-bed and the forest, for him to fashion into splendor and beauty. It was well, not because of that splendor and beauty; but because the act creating them is better than the things themselves; because exertion is nobler than enjoyment; because the laborer is greater and more worthy of honor than the idler. Masonry stands up for the nobility of labor. It is Heaven's great ordinance for human improvement. It has been broken down for ages; and Masonry desires to build it up again. It has been broken down, because men toil only because they must, submitting to it as, in some sort, a degrading necessity; and desiring nothing so much on earth as to escape from it. They fulfill the great law of labor in the letter, but break it in the spirit: they fulfill it with the muscles, but break it with the mind.

Masonry teaches that every idler ought to hasten to some field of labor, manual or mental, as a chosen and coveted theatre of improvement; but he is not impelled to do so, under the teachings

of an imperfect civilization. On the contrary, he sits down, folds
his hands, and blesses and glorifies himself in his idleness. It is
time that this opprobrium of toil were done away. To be ashamed
of toil; of the dingy workshop and dusty labor-field; of the hard
hand, stained with service more honorable than that of war; of
the soiled and weather-stained garments, on which Mother Nature
has stamped, midst sun and rain, midst fire and steam, her own
heraldic honors; to be ashamed of these tokens and titles, and
envious of the flaunting robes of imbecile idleness and vanity, is
treason to Nature, impiety to Heaven, a breach of Heaven's great
Ordinance. TOIL, of brain, heart, or hand, is the only true manhood and genuine nobility.

Labor is a more beneficent ministration than man's ignorance
comprehends, or his complainings will admit. Even when its .end
is hidden from him, it is not mere blind drudgery. It is all a
training, a discipline, a development of energies, a nurse of virtues,
a school of improvement. From the poor boy who gathers a few
sticks for his mother's hearth, to the strong man who fells the oak
or guides the ship or the steam-car, every human toiler, with every
weary step and every urgent task, is obeying a wisdom far above
his own wisdom, and fulfilling a design far beyond his own design.

The great law of human industry is this: that industry, working
either with the hand or the mind, the application of our powers
to some task, to the achievement of some result, lies at the foundation of all human improvement. We are not sent into the world
like animals, to crop the spontaneous herbage of the field, and
then to lie down in indolent repose: but we are sent to dig
the soil and plough the sea; to do the business of cities and the
work of manufactories. The world is the great and appointed
school of industry. In an artificial state of society, mankind is
divided into the idle and the laboring classes; but such was not
the design of Providence.

Labor is man's great function, his peculiar distinction and his
privilege. From being an animal, that eats and drinks and sleeps
only, to become a worker, and with the hand of ingenuity to pour
his own thoughts into the moulds of Nature, fashioning them into
forms of grace and fabrics of convenience, and converting them
to purposes of improvement and happiness, is the greatest possible
step in privilege.

The Earth and the Atmosphere are man's laboratory. With

spade and plough, with mining-shafts and furnaces and forges, with fire and steam; midst the noise and whirl of swift and bright machinery, and abroad in the silent fields, man was made to be ever working, ever experimenting. And while he and all his dwellings of care and toil are borne onward with the circling skies, and the splendors of Heaven are around him, and their infinite depths image and invite his thought, still in all the worlds of philosophy, in the universe of intellect, man must be a worker. He is nothing, he can be nothing, can achieve nothing, fulfill nothing, without working. Without it, he can gain neither lofty improvement nor tolerable happiness. The idle must hunt down the hours as their prey. To them Time is an enemy, clothed with armor; and they must kill him, or themselves die. It never yet did answer, and it never will answer, for any man to do nothing, to be exempt from all care and effort, to lounge, to walk, to ride, and to feast alone. No man can live in that way. God made a law against it: which no human power can annul, no human ingenuity evade.

The idea that a property is to be acquired in the course of ten or twenty years, which shall suffice for the rest of life; that by some prosperous traffic or grand speculation, all the labor of a whole life is to be accomplished in a brief portion of it; that by dexterous management, a large part of the term of human existence is to be exonerated from the cares of industry and self-denial, is founded upon a grave mistake, upon a misconception of the true nature and design of business, and of the conditions of human well-being. The desire of accumulation for the sake of securing a life of ease and gratification, of escaping from exertion and self-denial, is wholly wrong, though very common.

It is better for the Mason to live while he lives, and enjoy life as it passes: to live richer and die poorer. It is best of all for him to banish from the mind that empty dream of future indolence and indulgence; to address himself to the business of life, as the school of his earthly education; to settle it with himself now that independence, if he gains it, is not to give him exemption from employment. It is best for him to know, that, in order to be a happy man, he must always be a laborer, with the mind or the body, or with both: and that the reasonable exertion of his powers, bodily and mental, is not to be regarded as mere drudgery, but as a good discipline, a wise ordination, a training in this primary school of our being, for nobler endeavors, and spheres of higher activity hereafter.

There are reasons why a Mason may lawfully and even earnestly desire a fortune. If he can fill some fine palace, itself a work of art, with the productions of lofty genius; if he can be the friend and helper of humble worth; if he can seek it out, where failing health or adverse fortune presses it hard, and soften or stay the bitter hours that are hastening it to madness or to the grave; if he can stand between the oppressor and his prey, and bid the fetter and the dungeon give up their victim; if he can build up great institutions of learning, and academies of art; if he can open fountains of knowledge for the people, and conduct its streams in the right channels; if he can do better for the poor than to bestow alms upon them—even to think of them, and devise plans for their elevation in knowledge and virtue, instead of forever opening the old reservoirs and resources for their improvidence; if he has sufficient heart and soul to do all this, or part of it; if wealth would be to him the handmaid of exertion, facilitating effort, and giving success to endeavor; then may he lawfully, and yet warily and modestly, desire it. But if it is to do nothing for him, but to minister ease and indulgence, and to place his children in the same bad school, then there is no reason why he should desire it.

What is there glorious in the world, that is not the product of labor, either of the body or of the mind? What is history, but its record? What are the treasures of genius and art, but its work? What are cultivated fields, but its toil? The busy marts, the rising cities, the enriched empires of the world are but the great treasure-houses of labor. The pyramids of Egypt, the castles and towers and temples of Europe, the buried cities of Italy and Mexico, the canals and railroads of Christendom, are but tracks, all round the world, of the mighty footsteps of labor. Without it antiquity would not have been. Without it, there would be no memory of the past, and no hope for the future.

Even utter indolence reposes on treasures that labor at some time gained and gathered. He that does nothing, and yet does not starve, has still his significance; for he is a standing proof that *somebody* has at *some time* worked. But not to such does Masonry do honor. It honors the Worker, the Toiler; him who produces and not alone consumes; him who puts forth his hand to add to the treasury of human comforts, and not alone to take away. It honors him who goes forth amid the struggling elements to fight his battle, and who shrinks not, with cowardly effeminacy, behind pillows of ease. It honors the strong muscle, and the manly nerve, and the resolute and brave heart, the sweating brow, and the toiling brain. It honors the great and beautiful offices of humanity, manhood's toil and woman's task; paternal industry and maternal watching and weariness; wisdom teaching and patience learning; the brow of care that presides over the State, and many-handed labor that toils in workshop, field, and study, beneath its mild and beneficent sway.

God has not made a world of rich men; but rather a world of poor men; or of men, at least, who must toil for a subsistence. That is, then, the best condition for man, and the grand sphere of human improvement. If the whole world could acquire wealth, (and one man is as much entitled to it as another, when he is born); if the present generation could lay up a complete provision for the next, as some men desire to do for their children; the world would be destroyed at a single blow. All industry would cease with the necessity for it; all improvement would stop with the demand for exertion; the dissipation of fortunes, the mischiefs of which are now countervailed by the healthful tone of society, would breed universal disease, and break out into universal license; and the world would sink, rotten as Herod, into the grave of its own loathsome vices.

Almost all the noblest things that have been achieved in the world, have been achieved by poor men; poor scholars, poor professional men, poor artisans and artists, poor philosophers, poets, and men of genius. A certain staidness and sobriety, a certain moderation and restraint, a certain pressure of circumstances, are good for man. His body was not made for luxuries. It sickens, sinks, and dies under them. His mind was not made for indulgence. It grows weak, effeminate, and dwarfish, under that condition. And he who pampers his body with luxuries and his mind with indulgence, bequeaths the consequences to the minds and bodies of his descendants, without the wealth which was their cause. For wealth, without a law of entail to help it, has always lacked the energy even to *keep* its own treasures. They drop from its imbecile hand. The third generation almost inevitably goes down the rolling wheel of fortune, and there learns the energy necessary to rise again, if it rises at all; heir, as it is, to the bodily diseases, and mental weaknesses, and the soul's vices of its ancestors, and *not* heir to their wealth. And yet we are, almost all of us, anxious to put our children, or to insure that our grand-children shall be put, on this road to indulgence, luxury, vice, degradation, and ruin; this heirship of hereditary disease, soul malady, and mental leprosy.

If wealth were employed in promoting mental culture at home and works of philanthropy abroad; if it were multiplying studies of art, and building up institutions of learning around us; if it were in every way raising the intellectual character of the world, there could scarcely be too much of it. But if the utmost aim, effort, and ambition of wealth be, to procure rich furniture, and provide costly entertainments, and build luxurious houses, and minister to vanity, extravagance, and ostentation, there could scarcely be too little of it. To a certain extent it may laudably be the minister of elegancies and luxuries, and the servitor of hospi-tality and physical enjoyment: but just in proportion as its tendencies, divested of all higher aims and tastes, are running that way, they are running to peril and evil.

Nor does that peril attach to individuals and families alone. It stands, a fearful beacon, in the experience of Cities, Republics, and Empires. The lessons of past times, on this subject, are emphatic and solemn. The history of wealth has always been a history of corruption and downfall. The people never existed that could stand the trial. Boundless profusion is too little likely to spread for any people the theatre of manly energy, rigid self-denial, and lofty virtue. You do not look for the bone and sinew and strength of a country, its loftiest talents and virtues, its martyrs to patriotism or religion, its men to meet the days of peril and disaster, among the children of ease, indulgence, and luxury.

In the great march of the races of men over the earth, we have always seen opulence and luxury sinking before poverty and toil and hardy nurture. That is the law which has presided over the great processions of empire. Sidon and Tyre, whose mer-chants possessed the wealth of princes; Babylon and Palmyra, the seats of Asiatic luxury; Rome, laden with the spoils of a world, overwhelmed by her own vices more than by the hosts of her enemies; all these, and many more, are examples of the destruc-tive tendencies of immense and unnatural accumulation: and men must become more generous and benevolent, not more selfish and effeminate, as they become more rich, or the history of modern wealth will follow in the sad train of all past examples.

All men desire distinction, and feel the need of some ennobling object in life. Those persons are usually most happy and satisfied in their pursuits, who have the loftiest ends in view. Artists, mechanicians, and inventors, all who seek to find principles or develop beauty in their work, seem most to enjoy it. The farmer who labors for the beautifying and scientific cultivation of his estate, is more happy in his labors than one who tills his own land for a mere subsistence. This is one of the signal testimonies which all human employments give to the high demands of our nature. To gather wealth never gives such satisfaction as to bring the humblest piece of machinery to perfection: at least, when wealth is sought for display and ostentation, or mere luxury, and ease, and pleasure; and not for ends of philanthropy, the relief of kindred, or the payment of just debts, or as a means to attain some other great and noble object.

With the pursuits of multitudes is connected a painful conviction that they neither supply a sufficient object, nor confer any satisfactory honor. Why work, if the world is soon not to know that such a being ever existed; and when one can perpetuate his name neither on canvas nor on marble, nor in books, nor by lofty eloquence, nor statesmanship?

The answer is, that every man has a work to do in himself, greater and sublimer than any work of genius; and works upon a nobler material than wood or marble—upon his own soul and intellect, and may so attain the highest nobleness and grandeur known on earth or in Heaven; may so be the greatest of artists, and of authors, and his life, which is far more than speech, may be eloquent.

The great author or artist only portrays what every man should *be*. He *conceives,* what we should *do*. He conceives, and represents moral beauty, magnanimity, fortitude, love, devotion, forgiveness, the soul's greatness. He portrays virtues, commended to our admiration and imitation. To embody these portraitures in our lives is the practical realization of those great ideals of art. The magnanimity of Heroes, celebrated on the historic or poetic page; the constancy and faith of Truth's martyrs; the beauty of love and piety glowing on the canvas; the delineations of Truth and Right, that flash from the lips of the Eloquent, are, in their essence only that which every man may feel and practise in the daily walks of life. The work of virtue is nobler than any work of genius; for it is a nobler thing to *be* a hero than to *describe* one, to *endure* martyrdom than to *paint* it, to *do* right than to *plead* for it. Action is greater than writing. A good man is a nobler object of contemplation than a great author. There are but two things worth living for: to do what is worthy of being written; and to write what is worthy of being read; and the greater of these is *the doing*.

Every man has to do the noblest thing that any man can do or describe. There is a wide field for the courage, cheerfulness, energy, and dignity of human existence. Let therefore no Mason deem his life doomed to mediocrity or meanness, to vanity or unprofitable toil, or to any ends less than immortal. No one can truly say that the grand prizes of life are for others, and he can do nothing. No matter how magnificent and noble an act the author can describe or the artist paint, it will be still nobler for you to go and *do* that which one describes, or *be* the model which the other draws.

The loftiest action that ever was described is not more magnanimous than that which we may find occasion to do, in the daily walks of life; in temptation, in distress, in bereavement, in the solemn approach to death. In the great Providence of God, in the great ordinances of our being, there is opened to every man a sphere for the noblest action. It is not even in extraordinary situations, where all eyes are upon us, where all our energy is aroused, and all our vigilance is awake, that the highest efforts of virtue are usually demanded of us; but rather in silence and seclusion, amidst our occupations and our homes; in wearing sickness, that makes no complaint; in sorely-tried honesty, that asks no praise; in simple disinterestedness, hiding the hand that resigns its advantage to another.

Masonry seeks to ennoble common life. Its work is to go down into the obscure and unsearched records of daily conduct and feeling; and to portray, not the ordinary virtue of an extraordinary life; but the more extraordinary virtue of ordinary life. What is done and borne in the shades of privacy, in the hard and beaten path of daily care and toil, full of uncelebrated sacrifices; in the suffering, and sometimes insulted suffering, that wears to the world a cheerful brow; in the long strife of the spirit, resisting pain, penury, and neglect, carried on in the inmost depths of the heart;—what is done, and borne, and wrought, and won there, is a higher glory, and shall inherit a brighter crown.

On the volume of Masonic life one bright word is written, from

which on every side blazes an ineffable splendor. That word is
DUTY.

To aid in securing to all labor permanent employment and its
just reward: to help to hasten the coming of that time when no
one shall suffer from hunger or destitution, because, though willing and able to work, he can find no employment, or because he
has been overtaken by sickness in the midst of his labor, are part
of your duties as a Knight of the Royal Axe. And if we can succeed in making some small nook of God's creation a little more
fruitful and cheerful, a little better and more worthy of Him,—or
in making some one or two human hearts a little wiser, and more
manful and hopeful and happy, we shall have done *work,* worthy
of Masons, and acceptable to our Father in Heaven.

XXIII

CHIEF OF THE TABERNACLE.

AMONG most of the Ancient Nations there was, in addition to their public worship, a private one styled the Mysteries; to which those only were admitted who had been prepared by certain ceremonies called initiations.

The most widely disseminated of the ancient worships were those of Isis, Orpheus, Dionusos, Ceres and Mithras. Many barbarous nations received the knowledge of the Mysteries in honor of these divinities from the Egyptians, before they arrived in Greece; and even in the British Isles the Druids celebrated those of Dionusos, learned by them from the Egyptians.

The Mysteries of Eleusis, celebrated at Athens in honor of Ceres, swallowed up, as it were, all the others. All the neighboring nations neglected their own, to celebrate those of Eleusis; and in a little while all Greece and Asia Minor were filled with the Initiates. They spread into the Roman Empire, and even beyond its limits, "those holy and august Eleusinian Mysteries," said Cicero, "in which the people of the remotest lands are initiated." Zosimus says that they embraced the whole human race; and Aristides termed them the common temple of the whole world.

There were, in the Eleusinian feasts, two sorts of Mysteries, the great, and the little. The latter were a kind of preparation for the former; and everybody was admitted to them. Ordinarily there was a novitiate of three, and sometimes of four years.

Clemens of Alexandria says that what was taught in the great Mysteries concerned the Universe, and was the completion and perfection of all instruction; wherein things were seen as they were, and nature and her works were made known.

The ancients said that the Initiates would be more happy after death than other mortals; and that, while the souls of the Profane on leaving their bodies, would be plunged in the mire, and remain buried in darkness, those of the Initiates would fly to the Fortunate Isles, the abode of the Gods.

Plato said that the object of the Mysteries was to re-establish the soul in its primitive purity, and in that state of perfection which it had lost. Epictetus said, "whatever is met with therein has been instituted by our Masters, for the instruction of man and the correction of morals."

Proclus held that initiation elevated the soul, from a material, sensual, and purely human life, to a communion and celestial intercourse with the Gods; and that a variety of things, forms, and species were shown Initiates, representing the first generation of the Gods.

Purity of morals and elevation of soul were required of the Initiates. Candidates were required to be of spotless reputation and irreproachable virtue. Nero, after murdering his mother, did not dare to be present at the celebration of the Mysteries: and Antony presented himself to be initiated, as the most infallible mode of proving his innocence of the death of Avidius Cassius.

The Initiates were regarded as the only fortunate men. "It is upon us alone," says Aristophanes, "shineth the beneficent day-star. We alone receive pleasure from the influence of his rays; we, who are initiated, and who practise toward citizen and stranger every possible act of justice and piety." And it is therefore not surprising that, in time, initiation came to be considered as necessary as baptism afterward was to the Christians; and that not to have been admitted to the Mysteries was held a dishonor.

"It seems to me," says the great orator, philosopher, and moralist, Cicero, "that Athens, among many excellent inventions, divine and very useful to the human family, has produced none comparable to the Mysteries, which for a wild and ferocious life have substituted humanity and urbanity of manners. It is with good reason they use the term *initiation;* for it is through them that we in reality have learned the first principles of life; and they not only teach us to live in a manner more consoling and agreeable, but they soften the pains of death by the hope of a better life hereafter."

Where the Mysteries originated is not known. It is supposed that they came from India, by the way of Chaldæa, into Egypt, and thence were carried into Greece. Wherever they arose, they were practised among all the ancient nations; and, as was usual, the Thracians, Cretans, and Athenians each claimed the honor of invention, and each insisted that they had borrowed nothing from any other people.

In Egypt and the East, all religion, even in its most poetical forms, was more or less a mystery; and the chief reason why, in Greece, a distinct name and office were assigned to the Mysteries, was because the superficial popular theology left a want unsatisfied, which religion in a wider sense alone could supply. They were practical acknowledgments of the insufficiency of the popular religion to satisfy the deeper thoughts and aspirations of the mind. The vagueness of symbolism might perhaps reach what a more palpable and conventional creed could not. The former, by its indefiniteness, acknowledged the abstruseness of its subject; it treated a mysterious subject mystically; it endeavored to illustrate what it could not explain; to excite an appropriate feeling, if it could not develop an adequate idea; and made the image a mere subordinate conveyance for the conception, which itself never became too obvious or familiar.

The instruction now conveyed by books and letters was of old conveyed by symbols; and the priest had to invent or to perpetuate a display of rites and exhibitions,. which were not only more attractive to the eye than words, but often to the mind more suggestive and pregnant with meaning.

Afterward, the institution became rather moral and political, than religious. The civil magistrates shaped the ceremonies to political ends in Egypt; the sages who carried them from that country to Asia, Greece, and the North of Europe, were all kings or legislators. The chief magistrate presided at those of Eleusis, represented by an officer styled *King:* and the Priest played but a subordinate part.

The Powers revered in the Mysteries were all in reality Nature-Gods; none of whom could be consistently addressed as mere heroes, because their nature was confessedly super-heroic. The Mysteries, only in fact a more solemn expression of the religion of the ancient poetry, taught that doctrine of the Theocracia or Divine Oneness, which even poetry does not entirely conceal. They were not in any open hostility with the popular religion, but only a more solemn exhibition of its symbols; or rather a part of itself in a more impressive form. The essence of all Mysteries, as of all polytheism, consists in this, that the conception of an unapproachable Being, single, eternal, and unchanging, and that

of a God of Nature, whose manifold power is immediately revealed to the senses in the incessant round of movement, life, and
death, fell asunder in the treatment, and were separately symbolized. They offered a perpetual problem to excite curiosity, and
contributed to satisfy the all-pervading religious sentiment, which`
if it obtain no nourishment among the simple and intelligible, finds
compensating excitement in a reverential contemplation of the
obscure.

Nature is as free from dogmatism as from tyranny; and the
earliest instructors of mankind not only adopted her lessons, but
as far as possible adhered to her method of imparting them.
They attempted to reach the understanding through the eye; and
the greater part of all religious teaching was conveyed through
this ancient and most impressive mode of "exhibition" or demonstration. The Mysteries were a sacred drama, exhibiting some
legend significant of Nature's change, of the visible Universe in
which the divinity is revealed, and whose import was in many
respects as open to the Pagan, as to the Christian. Beyond the
current traditions or sacred recitals of the temple, few explanations were given to the spectators, who were left, as in the school
of nature, to make inferences for themselves.

The method of indirect suggestion, by allegory or symbol, is a
more efficacious instrument of instruction than plain didactic
language; since we are habitually indifferent to that which is
acquired without effort: "The initiated are few, though many
bear the thyrsus." And it would have been impossible to provide
a lesson suited to every degree of cultivation and capacity, unless
it were one framed after Nature's example, or rather a representation of Nature herself, employing her universal symbolism instead
of technicalities of language, inviting endless research, yet rewarding the humblest inquirer, and disclosing its secrets to every one in
proportion to his preparatory training and power to comprehend
them.

Even if destitute of any formal or official enunciation of those
important truths, which even in a cultivated age it was often found
inexpedient to assert except under a veil of allegory, and which
moreover lose their dignity and value in proportion as they are
learned mechanically as dogmas, the shows of the Mysteries certainly contained suggestions if not lessons, which in the opinion
not of one competent witness only, but of many, were adapted to
elevate the character of the spectators. enabling them to augur

something of the purposes of existence, as well as of the means of improving it, to live better and to die happier.

Unlike the religion of books or creeds, these mystic shows and performances were not the reading of a lecture, but the opening of a problem, implying neither exemption from research, nor hostility to philosophy: for, on the contrary, philosophy is the great Mystagogue or Arch-Expounder of symbolism: though the interpretations by the Grecian Philosophy of the old myths and symbols were in many instances as ill-founded, as in others they are correct.

No better means could be devised to rouse a dormant intellect, than those impressive exhibitions, which addressed it through the imagination: which, instead of condemning it to a prescribed routine of creed, invited it to seek, compare, and judge. The alteration from symbol to dogma is as fatal to beauty of expression, as that from faith to dogma is to truth and wholesomeness of thought.

The first philosophy often reverted to the natural mode of teaching; and Socrates, in particular, is said to have eschewed dogmas, endeavoring, like the Mysteries, rather to awaken and develop in the minds of his hearers the ideas with which they were already endowed or pregnant, than to fill them with ready-made adventitious opinions.

So Masonry still follows the ancient manner of teaching. Her symbols are the instruction she gives; and the lectures are but often partial and insufficient one-sided endeavors to interpret those symbols. He who would become an accomplished Mason, must not be content merely to hear or even to understand the lectures, but must, aided by them, and they having as it were marked out the way for him, study, interpret, and develop the symbols for himself.

The earliest speculation endeavored to express far more than it could distinctly comprehend; and the vague impressions of the mind found in the mysterious analogies of phenomena their most apt and energetic representations. The Mysteries, like the symbols of Masonry, were but an image of the eloquent analogies of Nature; both those and these revealing no new secret to such as were or are unprepared, or incapable of interpreting their significance.

Everywhere in the old Mysteries, and in all the symbolisms and ceremonial of the Hierophant was found the same mythical personage, who, like Hermes, or Zoroaster, unites Human Attributes with Divine, and is himself the God whose worship he introduced, teaching rude men the commencements of civilization through the influence of song, and connecting with the symbol of his death, emblematic of that of Nature, the most essential consolations of religion.

The Mysteries embraced the three great doctrines of Ancient Theosophy. They treated of God, Man, and Nature. Dionusos, whose Mysteries Orpheus is said to have founded, was the God of Nature, or of the moisture which is the life of Nature, who prepares in darkness the return of life and vegetation, or who is himself the Light and Change evolving their varieties. He was theologically one with Hermes, Prometheus, and Poseidon. In the Egean Islands he is Butes, Dardanus, Himeros, or Imbros. In Crete he appears as Iasius or Zeus, whose worship remaining unveiled by the usual forms of mystery, betrayed to profane curiosity the symbols, which, if irreverently contemplated, were sure to be misunderstood. In Asia he is the long-stoled Bassareus coalescing with the Sabazius of the Phrygian Corybantes: the same with the mystic Iacchus, nursling or son of Ceres, and with the dismembered Zagreus, son of Persephoné.

In symbolical forms the Mysteries exhibited THE ONE, of which THE MANIFOLD is an infinite illustration, containing a moral lesson, calculated to guide the soul through life, and to cheer it in death. The story of Dionusos was profoundly significant. He was not only creator of the world, but guardian, liberator, and Savior of the soul. God of the many-colored mantle, he was the resulting manifestation personified, the all in the many, the varied year, life passing into innumerable forms.

The spiritual regeneration of man was typified in the Mysteries by the second birth of Dionusos as offspring of the Highest; and the agents and symbols of that regeneration were the elements that affected Nature's periodical purification—the air, indicated by the mystic fan or winnow; the fire, signified by the torch; and the baptismal water, for water is not only cleanser of all things, but the genesis or source of all.

These notions, clothed in ritual, suggested the soul's reformation and training, the moral purity formally proclaimed at Eleusis. He only was invited to approach, who was "of clean hands and ingenuous speech, free from all pollution, and with a clear conscience." "Happy the man," say the initiated in Euripides and

Aristophanes, "who purifies his life, and who reverently conse-crates his soul in the thiäsos of the God. Let him take heed to his lips that he utter no profane word; let him be just and kind to the stranger, and to his neighbor; let him give way to no vicious excess, lest he make dull and heavy the organs of the spirit. Far from the mystic dance of the thiäsos be the impure, the evil speaker, the seditious citizen, the selfish hunter after gain, the traitor; all those, in short, whose practices are more akin to the riot of Titans than to the regulated life of the Orphici, or the Curetan order of the Priests of Idæan Zeus."

The votary, elevated beyond the sphere of his ordinary faculties, and unable to account for the agitation which overpow-ered him, seemed to become divine in proportion as he ceased to be human; to be a dæmon or god. Already, in imagination, the initiated were numbered among the beatified. They alone enjoy-ed the true life, the Sun's true lustre, while they hymned their God beneath the mystic groves of a mimic Elysium, and were really renovated or regenerated under the genial influence of their dances.

"They whom Proserpina guides in her mysteries," it was said, "who imbibed her instruction and spiritual nourishment, rest from their labors and know strife no more. Happy they who witness and comprehend these sacred ceremonies! They are made to know the meaning of the riddle of existence by observing its aim and termination as appointed by Zeus; they partake a benefit more valuable and enduring than the grain bestowed by Ceres; for they are exalted in the scale of intellectual existence, and obtain sweet hopes to console them at their death."

No doubt the ceremonies of initiation were originally few and simple. As the great truths of the primitive revelation faded out of the memories of the masses of the People, and wickedness became rife upon the earth, it became necessary to discriminate, to require longer probation and satisfactory tests of the candi-dates, and by spreading around what at first were rather schools of instruction than mysteries, the veil of secrecy, and the pomp of ceremony, to heighten the opinion of their value and importance.

Whatever pictures later and especially Christian writers may draw of the Mysteries, they must, not only originally, but for many ages, have continued pure; and the doctrines of natural religion and morals there taught, have been of the highest importance;

because both the most virtuous as well as the most learned and philosophic of the ancients speak of them in the loftiest terms. That they ultimately became degraded from their high estate, and corrupted, we know.

The rites of initiation became progressively more complicated. Signs and tokens were invented by which the Children of Light could with facility make themselves known to each other. Different Degrees were invented, as the number of Initiates enlarged, in order that there might be in the inner apartment of the Temple a favored few, to whom alone the more valuable secrets were entrusted, and who could wield effectually the influence and power of the Order.

Originally the Mysteries were meant to be the beginning of a new life of reason and virtue. The initiated or esoteric companions were taught the doctrine of the One Supreme God, the theory of death and eternity, the hidden mysteries of Nature, the prospect of the ultimate restoration of the soul to that state of perfection from which it had fallen, its immortality, and the states of reward and punishment after death. The uninitiated were deemed Profane, unworthy of public employment or private confidence, sometimes proscribed as Atheists, and certain of everlasting punishment beyond the grave.

All persons were initiated into the lesser Mysteries; but few attained the greater, in which the true spirit of them, and most of their secret doctrines were hidden. The veil of secrecy was impenetrable, sealed by oaths and penalties the most tremendous and appalling. It was by initiation only, that a knowledge of the Hieroglyphics could be obtained, with which the walls, columns, and ceilings of the Temples were decorated, and which, believed to have been communicated to the Priests by revelation from the celestial deities, the youth of all ranks were laudably ambitious of deciphering.

The ceremonies were performed at dead of night, generally in apartments under-ground, but sometimes in the centre of a vast pyramid, with every appliance that could alarm and excite the candidate. Innumerable ceremonies, wild and romantic, dreadful and appalling, had by degrees been added to the few expressive symbols of primitive observances, under which there were instances in which the terrified aspirant actually expired with fear.

The pyramids were probably used for the purposes of initiation, as were caverns, pagodas, and labyrinths; for the ceremonies required many apartments and cells, long passages and wells. In Egypt a principal place for the Mysteries was the island of Philæ on the Nile, where a magnificent Temple of Osiris stood, and his relics were said to be preserved.

With their natural proclivities, the Priesthood, that select and exclusive class, in Egypt, India, Phœnicia, Judea and Greece, as well as in Britain and Rome, and wherever else the Mysteries were known, made use of them to build wider and higher the fabric of their own power. The purity of no religion continues long. Rank and dignities succeed to the primitive simplicity. Unprincipled, vain, insolent, corrupt, and venal men put on God's livery to serve the Devil withal; and luxury, vice, intolerance, and pride depose frugality, virtue, gentleness, and humility, and change the altar where they should be servants, to a throne on which they reign.

But the Kings, Philosophers, and Statesmen, the wise and great and good who were admitted to the Mysteries, long postponed their ultimate self-destruction, and restrained the natural tendencies of the Priesthood. And accordingly Zosimus thought that the neglect of the Mysteries after Diocletian abdicated, was the chief cause of the decline of the Roman Empire; and in the year 364, the Proconsul of Greece would not close the Mysteries, notwithstanding a law of the Emperor Valentinian, lest the people should be driven to desperation, if prevented from performing them; upon which, as they believed, the welfare of mankind wholly depended. They were practised in Athens until the 8th century, in Greece and Rome for several centuries after Christ; and in Wales and Scotland down to the 12th century.

The inhabitants of India originally practised the Patriarchal religion. Even the later worship of Vishnu was cheerful and social; accompanied with the festive song, the sprightly dance, and the resounding cymbal, with libations of milk and honey, garlands, and perfumes from aromatic woods and gums.

There perhaps the Mysteries commenced; and in them, under allegories, were taught the primitive truths. We cannot, within the limits of this lecture, detail the ceremonies of initiation; and shall use general language, except where something from those old Mysteries still remains in Masonry.

The Initiate was invested with a cord of three threads, so twined as to make three times three, and called *zennar*. Hence comes our cable-tow. It was an emblem of their tri-une Deity, the remembrance of whom we also preserve in the three chief officers of our Lodges, presiding in the three quarters of that Universe which our Lodges represent; in our three greater and three lesser lights, our three movable and three immovable jewels, and the three pillars that support our Lodges.

The Indian Mysteries were celebrated in subterranean caverns and grottos hewn in the solid rock; and the Initiates adored the Deity, symbolized by the solar fire. The candidate, long wandering in darkness, truly wanted Light, and the worship taught him was the worship of God, the Source of Light. The vast Temple of Elephanta, perhaps the oldest in the world, hewn out of the rock, and 135 feet square, was used for initiations; as were the still vaster caverns of Salsette, with their 300 apartments.

The periods of initiation were regulated by the increase and decrease of the moon. The Mysteries were divided into four steps or Degrees. The candidate might receive the first at eight years of age, when he was invested with the zennar. Each Degree dispensed something of perfection. "Let the wretched man," says the Hitopadesa, "practise virtue, whenever he enjoys one of the three or four religious Degrees; let him be even-minded with all created things, and that disposition will be the source of virtue."

After various ceremonies, chiefly relating to the unity and trinity of the Godhead, the candidate was clothed in a linen garment without a seam, and remained under the care of a Brahmin until he was twenty years of age, constantly studying and practising the most rigid virtue. Then he underwent the severest probation for the second Degree, in which he was sanctified by the sign of the cross, which, pointing to the four quarters of the compass, was honored as a striking symbol of the Universe by many nations of antiquity, and was imitated by the Indians in the shape of their temples.

Then he was admitted to the Holy Cavern, blazing with light, where, in costly robes, sat, in the East, West, and South, the three chief Hierophants, representing the Indian tri-une Deity. The ceremonies there commenced with an anthem to the Great God of Nature; and then followed this apostrophe: "O mighty Being! greater than Brahma! we bow down before Thee as the

primal Creator! Eternal God of Gods! The World's Mansion!
Thou art the Incorruptible Being, distinct from all things transient! Thou art before all Gods, the Ancient Absolute Existence,
and the Supreme Supporter of the Universe! Thou art the
Supreme Mansion; and by Thee, O Infinite Form, the Universe
was spread abroad."

The candidate, thus taught the first great primitive truth, was
called upon to make a formal declaration, that he would be tract-
able and obedient to his superiors; that he would keep his body
pure; govern his tongue, and observe a passive obedience in receiving the doctrines and traditions of the Order; and the firmest
secrecy in maintaining inviolable its hidden and abstruse mysteries. Then he was sprinkled with water (whence our *baptism*);
certain words, now unknown, were whispered in his ear; and he
was divested of his shoes, and made to go three times around the
cavern. Hence our three circuits; hence we were neither barefoot
nor shod: and the words were the Pass-words of that Indian
Degree.

The Gymnosophist Priests came from the banks of the Euphrates into Ethiopia, and brought with them their sciences and
their doctrines. Their principal College was at Meroe, and their
Mysteries were celebrated in the Temple of Amun, renowned for
his oracle. Ethiopia was then a powerful State, which preceded
Egypt in civilization, and had a theocratic government. Above
the King was the Priest, who could put him to death in the name
of the Deity. Egypt was then composed of the Thebaid only.
Middle Egypt and the Delta were a gulf of the Mediterranean.
The Nile by degrees formed an immense marsh, which, afterward
drained by the labor of man, formed Lower Egypt; and was for
many centuries governed by the Ethiopian Sacerdotal Caste, of
Arabic origin; afterward displaced by a dynasty of warriors. The
magnificent ruins of Axoum, with its obelisks and hierogyphics,
temples, vast tombs and pyramids, around ancient Meroe, are far
older than the pyramids near Memphis.

The Priests, taught by Hermes, embodied in books the occult
and hermetic sciences, with their own discoveries and the revelations of the Sibyls. They studied particularly the most abstract
sciences, discovered the famous geometrical theorems which Pythagoras afterward learned from them, calculated eclipses, and
regulated, nineteen centuries before Cæsar, the Julian year. They

descended to practical investigations as to the necessities of life, and made known their discoveries to the people; they cultivated the fine arts, and inspired the people with that enthusiasm which produced the avenues of Thebes, the Labyrinth, the Temples of Karnac, Denderah, Edfou, and Philæ, the monolithic obelisks, and the great Lake Moeris, the fertilizer of the country.

The wisdom of the Egyptian Initiates, the high sciences and lofty morality which they taught, and their immense knowledge, excited the emulation of the most eminent men, whatever their rank and fortune; and led them, despite the complicated and terrible trials to be undergone, to seek admission into the Mysteries of Osiris and Isis.

From Egypt, the Mysteries went to Phœnicia, and were celebrated at Tyre. Osiris changed his name, and become Adoni or Dionusos, still the representative of the Sun; and afterward these Mysteries were introduced successively into Assyria, Babylon, Persia, Greece, Sicily, and Italy. In Greece and Sicily, Osiris took the name of Bacchus, and Isis that of Ceres, Cybele, Rhea and Venus.

Bar Hebraeus says: "Enoch was the first who invented books and different sorts of writing. The ancient Greeks declare that Enoch is the same as Mercury Trismegistus [Hermes], and that he taught the sons of men the art of building cities, and enacted some admirable laws. . . He discovered the knowledge of the Zodiac, and the course of the Planets; and he pointed out to the sons of men, that they should worship God, that they should fast, that they should pray, that they should give alms, votive offerings, and tenths. He reprobated abominable foods and drunkenness, and appointed festivals for sacrifices to the Sun, at each of the Zodiacal Signs."

Manetho extracted his history from certain pillars which he discovered in Egypt, whereon inscriptions had been made by Thoth, or the first Mercury [or Hermes], in the sacred letters and dialect: but which were after the flood translated from that dialect into the Greek tongue, and laid up in the private recesses of the Egyptian Temples. These pillars were found in subterranean caverns, near Thebes and beyond the Nile, not far from the sounding statue of Memnon, in a place called Syringes; which are described to be certain winding apartments underground; made, it is said, by those who were skilled in ancient rites; who, foreseeing the coming of the Deluge, and fearing lest the memory of their ceremonies should be obliterated, built and contrived vaults, dug with vast labor, in several places.

From the bosom of Egypt sprang a man of consummate wisdom, initiated in the secret knowledge of India, of Persia, and of Ethiopia, named Thoth or Phtha by his compatriots, Taaut by the Phœnicians, Hermes Trismegistus by the Greeks, and Adris by the Rabbins. Nature seemed to have chosen him for her favorite, and to have lavished on him all the qualities necessary to enable him to study her and to know her thoroughly. The Deity had, so to say, infused into him the sciences and the arts, in order that he might instruct the whole world.

He invented many things· necessary for the uses of life, and gave them suitable names; he taught men how to write down their thoughts and arrange their speech; he instituted the ceremonies to be observed in the worship of each of the Gods; he observed the course of the stars; he invented music, the different bodily exercises, arithmetic, medicine, the art of working in metals, the lyre with three strings; he regulated the three tones of the voice, the *sharp*, taken from autumn, the *grave* from winter, and the *middle* from spring, there being then but three seasons. It was he who taught the Greeks the mode of interpreting terms and things, whence they gave him the name of Ἑρμῆς [*Hermes*], which signifies *Interpreter*.

In Egypt he instituted hieroglyphics: he selected a certain number of persons whom he judged fitted to be the depositaries of his secrets, of such only as were capable of attaining the throne and the first offices in the Mysteries; he united them in a body, created them *Priests of the Living God,* instructed them in the sciences and arts, and explained to them the symbols by which they were veiled. Egypt, 1500 years before the time of Moses, revered in the Mysteries ONE SUPREME GOD, called the ONLY UN-CREATED. Under Him it paid homage to seven principal deities. It is to Hermes, who lived at that period, that we must attribute the concealment or *veiling* [*velation*] of the Indian worship, which Moses *unveiled* or *revealed,* changing nothing of the laws of Hermes, except the plurality of his mystic Gods.

The Egyptian Priests related that Hermes, dying, said: "Hitherto I have lived an exile from my true country: now I return thither. Do not weep for me: I return to that celestial country whither each goes in his turn. There is God. This life is but a death." This is precisely the creed of the old Buddhists of Samaneans, who believed that from time to time God sent Buddhas on earth, to reform men, to wean them from their vices, and lead them back into the paths of virtue.

Among the sciences taught by Hermes, there were secrets which he communicated to the Initiates only upon condition that they should bind themselves, by a terrible oath, never to divulge them, except to those who, after long trial, should be found worthy to succeed them. The Kings even prohibited the revelation of them on pain of death. This secret was styled the Sacerdotal Art, and included alchemy, astrology, magism [magic], the science of spirits, etc. He gave them the key to the Hieroglyphics of all these secret sciences, which were regarded as sacred, and kept concealed in the most secret places of the Temple.

The great secrecy observed by the initiated Priests, for many years, and the lofty sciences which they professed, caused them to be honored and respected throughout all Egypt, which was regarded by other nations as the college, the sanctuary, of the sciences and arts. The mystery which surrounded them strongly excited curiosity. Orpheus metamorphosed himself, so to say, into an Egyptian. He was initiated into Theology and Physics. And he so completely made the ideas and reasonings of his teachers his own, that his Hymns rather bespeak an Egyptian Priest than a Grecian Poet: and he was the first who carried into Greece the Egyptian fables.

Pythagoras, ever thirsty for learning, consented even to be circumcised, in order to become one of the Initiates: and the occult sciences were revealed to him in the innermost part of the sanctuary.

The Initiates in a particular science, having been instructed by fables, enigmas, allegories, and hieroglyphics, wrote mysteriously whenever in their works they touched the subject of the Mysteries, and continued to conceal science under a veil of fictions.

When the destruction by Cambyses of many cities, and the ruin of nearly all Egypt, in the year 528 before our era, dispersed most of the Priests into Greece and elsewhere, they bore with them their sciences, which they continued to teach enigmatically, that is to say, ever enveloped in the obscurities of fables and hieroglyphics; to the end that the vulgar herd, seeing, might see nothing, and hearing, might comprehend nothing. All the writers drew from this source: but these Mysteries, concealed under so many unexplained envelopes, ended in giving birth to a swarm of absurdities, which, from Greece, spread over the whole earth.

In the Grecian Mysteries, as established by Pythagoras, there were three Degrees. A preparation of five years' abstinence and silence was required. If the candidate was found to be passionate or intemperate, contentious, or ambitious of worldly honors and distinctions, he was rejected.

In his lectures, Pythagoras taught the mathematics, as a medium whereby to prove the existence of God from observation and by means of reason; grammar, rhetoric, and logic, to cultivate and improve that reason, arithmetic, because he conceived that the ultimate benefit of man consisted in the science of numbers, and geometry, music, and astronomy, because he conceived that man is indebted to them for a knowledge of what is really good and useful.

He taught the true method of obtaining a knowledge of the Divine laws of purifying the soul from its imperfections, of searching for truth, and of practising virtue; thus imitating the perfections of God. He thought his system vain, if it did not contribute to expel vice and introduce virtue into the mind. He taught that the two most excellent things were, to speak the truth, and to render benefits to one another. Particularly he inculcated Silence, Temperance, Fortitude, Prudence, and Justice. He taught the immortality of the soul, the Omnipotence of God, and the necessity of personal holiness to qualify a man for admission into the Society of the Gods.

Thus we owe the particular mode of instruction in the Degree of Fellow-Craft to Pythagoras; and that Degree is but an imperfect reproduction of his lectures. From him, too, we have many of our explanations of the symbols. He arranged his assemblies due East and West, because he held that Motion began in the East and proceeded to the West. Our Lodges are said to be due East and West, because the Master represents the rising Sun, and of course must be in the East. The pyramids, too, were built precisely by the four cardinal points. And our expression, that our Lodges extend upward to the Heavens, comes from the Persian and Druidic custom of having to their Temples no roofs but the sky.

Plato developed and spiritualized the philosophy of Pythagoras.

Even Eusebius the Christian admits, that he reached to the vestibule of Truth, and stood upon its threshold.

The Druidical ceremonies undoubtedly came from India; and the Druids were originally Buddhists. The word *Druidh,* like the word *Magi,* signifies wise or learned men; and they were at once philosophers, magistrates, and divines.

There was a surprising uniformity in the Temples, Priests, doctrines, and worship of the Persian Magi and British Druids. The Gods of Britain were the same as the Cabiri of Samothrace. Osiris and Isis appeared in their Mysteries, under the names of Hu and Ceridwen; and like those of the primitive Persians, their Temples were enclosures of huge unhewn stones, some of which still remain, and are regarded by the common people with fear and veneration. They were generally either circular or oval. Some were in the shape of a circle to which a vast serpent was attached. The circle was an Eastern symbol of the Universe, governed by an Omnipotent Deity whose centre is everywhere, and his circumference nowhere: and the egg was an universal symbol of the world. Some of the Temples were winged, and some in the shape of a cross; the winged ones referring to Kneph, the winged Serpent-Deity of Egypt; whence the name of *Navestock,* where one of them stood. Temples in the shape of a cross were also found in Ireland and Scotland. The length of one of these vast structures, in the shape of a serpent, was nearly three miles.

The grand periods for initiation into the Druidical Mysteries, were quarterly; at the equinoxes and solstices. In the remote times when they originated, these were the times corresponding with the 13th of February, 1st of May, 19th of August, and 1st of November. The time of annual celebration was May-Eve, and the ceremonial preparations commenced at midnight, on the 29th of April. When the initiations were over, on May-Eve, fires were kindled on all the cairns and cromlechs in the island, which burned all night to introduce the sports of May-day. The festival was in honor of the Sun. The initiations were performed at midnight; and there were three Degrees.

The Gothic Mysteries were carried Northward from the East, by Odin; who, being a great warrior, modelled and varied them to suit his purposes and the genius of his people. He placed over their celebration twelve Hierophants, who were alike Priests, Counsellors of State, and Judges from whose decision there was no appeal.

He held the numbers three and nine in peculiar veneration, and was probably himself the Indian Buddha. Every thrice-three months, thrice-three victims were sacrificed to the tri-une God.

The Goths had three great festivals; the most magnificent of which commenced at the winter solstice, and was celebrated in honor of Thor, the Prince of the Power of the Air. That being the longest night in the year, and the one after which the Sun comes Northward, it was commemorative of the Creation; and they termed it mother-night, as the one in which the creation of the world and light from the primitive darkness took place. This was the *Yule, Juul,* or *Yeol* feast, which afterward became Christmas. At this feast the initiations were celebrated. Thor was the Sun, the Egyptian Osiris and Kneph, the Phœnician Bel or Baal. The initiations were had in huge intricate caverns, terminating, as all the Mithriac caverns did, in a spacious vault, where the candidate *was brought to light.*

Joseph was undoubtedly initiated. After he had interpreted Pharaoh's dream, that Monarch made him his Prime Minister, let him ride in his second chariot, while they proclaimed before him, ABRECH !* and set him over the land of Egypt. In addition to this, the King gave him a new name, Tsapanat-Paänakh, and married him to Asanat, daughter of Potai Parang, a Priest of An or Hieropolis, where was the Temple of Athom-Re, the Great God of Egypt; thus completely naturalizing him. He could not have contracted this marriage, nor have exercised that high dignity, without being first initiated in the Mysteries. When his Brethren came to Egypt the second time, the Egyptians of his court could not eat with them, as that would have been abomination, though they ate with Joseph; who was therefore regarded not as a foreigner, but as one of themselves: and when he sent and brought his brethren back, and charged them with taking his cup, he said, "Know ye not that a man like me practises divination?" thus assuming the Egyptian of high rank initiated into the Mysteries, and as such conversant with the occult sciences.

So also must Moses have been initiated: for he was not only brought up in the court of the King, as the adopted son of the King's daughter, until he was forty years of age; but he was instructed in all the learning of the Egyptians, and married after-

---

* An Egyptian word, meaning, *"Bow down."*

ward the daughter of Yethrū, a Priest of An likewise. Strabo and Diodorus both assert that he was himself a Priest of Heliopolis. Before he went into the Desert, there were intimate relations between him and the Priesthood; and he had successfully commanded, Josephus informs us, an army sent by the King against the Ethiopians. Simplicius asserts that Moses received from the Egyptians, in the Mysteries, the doctrines which he taught to the Hebrews: and Clemens of Alexandria and Philo say that he was a Theologian and Prophet, and interpreter of the Sacred Laws. Manetho, cited by Josephus, says he was a Priest of Heliopolis, and that his true and original (Egyptian) name was Asersaph or Osarsiph.

And in the institution of the Hebrew Priesthood, in the powers and privileges, as well as the immunities and sanctity which he conferred upon them, he closely imitated the Egyptian institutions; making *public* the worship of that Deity whom the Egyptian Initiates worshipped in private; and strenuously endeavoring to keep the people from relapsing into their old mixture of Chaldaic and Egyptian superstition and idol-worship, as they were ever ready and inclined to do; even Aharūn, upon their first clamorous discontent, restoring the worship of Apis; as an image of which Egyptian God he made the golden calf.

The Egyptian Priests taught in their great Mysteries, that there was one God, Supreme and Unapproachable, who had *conceived* the Universe by His Intelligence, before He *created* it by His Power and Will. They were no Materialists nor Pantheists; but taught that Matter was not eternal or co-existent with the great First Cause, but created by Him.

The early Christians, taught by the founder of their Religion, but in greater perfection, those primitive truths that from the Egyptians had passed to the Jews, and been preserved among the latter by the Essenes, received also the institution of the Mysteries; adopting as their object the building of the symbolic Temple, preserving the old Scriptures of the Jews as their sacred book, and as the fundamental law, which furnished the new veil of initiation with the Hebraic words and formulas, that, corrupted and disfigured by time and ignorance, appear in many of our Degrees.

Such, my Brother, is the doctrine of the first Degree of the Mysteries, or that of Chief of the Tabernacle, to which you have now been admitted, and the moral lesson of which is, devotion to the service of God, and disinterested zeal and constant endeavor for the welfare of men. You have here received only hints of the true objects and purposes of the Mysteries. Hereafter, if you are permitted to advance, you will arrive at a more complete understanding of them and of the sublime doctrines which they teach. Be content, therefore, with that which you have seen and heard, and await patiently the advent of the greater light.

XXIV.

PRINCE OF THE TABERNACLE.

SYMBOLS were the almost universal language of ancient theology. They were the most obvious method of instruction; for, like nature herself, they addressed the understanding through the eye; and the most ancient expressions denoting communication of religious knowledge, signify ocular exhibition. The first teachers of mankind borrowed this method of instruction; and it comprised an endless store of pregnant hieroglyphics. These lessons of the olden time were the riddles of the Sphynx, tempting the curious by their quaintness, but involving the personal risk of the adventurous interpreter. "The Gods themselves," it was said, "disclose their intentions to the wise, but to fools their teaching is unintelligible;" and the King of the Delphic Oracle was said not to *declare,* nor on the other hand to *conceal;* but emphatically to *"intimate* or *signify."*

The Ancient Sages, both barbarian and Greek, involved their meaning in similar indirections and enigmas; their lessons were conveyed either in visible symbols, or in those "parables and dark sayings of old," which the Israelites considered it a sacred duty to hand down unchanged to successive generations. The explanatory tokens employed by man, whether emblematical objects or actions, symbols or mystic ceremonies, were like the mystic signs and portents either in dreams or by the wayside, supposed to be significant of the intentions of the Gods; both required the aid of anxious thought and skillful interpretation. It was only by a correct appreciation of analogous problems of nature, that the will of Heaven could be understood by the Diviner, or the lessons of Wisdom become manifest to the Sage.

The Mysteries were a series of symbols; and what was *spoken* there consisted wholly of accessory explanations of the act or image; sacred commentaries, explanatory of established symbols; with little of those independent traditions embodying physical or moral speculation, in which the elements or planets were the

371

actors, and the creation and revolutions of the world were intermingled with recollections of ancient events: and yet with so
much of that also, that nature became her own expositor through
the medium of an arbitrary symbolical instruction; and the
ancient views of the relation between the human and divine
received dramatic forms.

There has ever been an intimate alliance between the two systems, the symbolic and the philosophical, in the allegories of the
monuments of all ages, in the symbolic writings of the priests of
all nations, in the rituals of all secret and mysterious societies;
there has been a constant series, an invariable uniformity of principles, which come from an aggregate, vast, imposing, and true,
composed of parts that fit harmoniously only there.

Symbolical instruction is recommended by the constant and
uniform usage of antiquity; and it has retained its influence
throughout all ages, as a system of mysterious communication.
The Deity, in his revelations to man, adopted the use of material
images for the purpose of enforcing sublime truths; and Christ
taught by symbols and parables. The mysterious knowledge of
the Druids was embodied in signs and symbols. Taliesin, describing his initiation, says: "The secrets were imparted to me
by the old Giantess (*Ceridwen,* or *Isis*), without the use of audible language." And again he says, "I am a *silent* proficient."

Initiation was a school, in which were taught the truths of
primitive revelation, the existence and attributes of one God, the
immortality of the Soul, rewards and punishments in a future life,
the phenomena of Nature, the arts, the sciences, morality, legislation, philosophy, and philanthropy, and what we now style
psychology and metaphysics, with animal magnetism, and the
other occult sciences.

All the ideas of the Priests of Hindostan, Persia, Syria, Arabia,
Chaldæa, Phœnicia, were known to the Egyptian Priests. The
rational Indian philosophy, after penetrating Persia and Chaldæa,
gave birth to the Egyptian Mysteries. We find that the use of
Hieroglyphics was preceded in Egypt by that of the easily understood symbols and figures, from the mineral, animal, and vegetable kingdoms, used by the Indians, Persians, and Chaldæans to
express their thoughts; and this primitive philosophy was the
basis of the modern philosophy of Pythagoras and Plato.

All the philosophers and legislators that made Antiquity illustrious, were pupils of the initiation; and all the beneficent modifications in the religions of the different people instructed by them were owing to their institution and extension of the Mysteries. In the chaos of popular superstitions, those Mysteries alone kept man from lapsing into absolute brutishness. Zoroaster and Confucius drew their doctrines from the Mysteries. Clemens of Alexandria, speaking of the Great Mysteries, says: "Here ends all instruction. Nature and all things are seen and known." Had moral truths alone been taught the Initiate, the Mysteries could never have deserved nor received the magnificent eulogiums of the most enlightened men of Antiquity,—of Pindar, Plutarch, Isocrates, Diodorus, Plato, Euripides, Socrates, Aristophanes, Cicero, Epictetus, Marcus Aurelius, and others;—philosophers hostile to the Sacerdotal Spirit, or historians devoted to the investigation of Truth. No: all the sciences were taught there; and those oral or written traditions briefly communicated, which reached back to the first age of the world.

Socrates said, in the Phædo of Plato: "It well appears that those who established the Mysteries, or secret assemblies of the initiated, were no contemptible personages, but men of great genius, who in the early ages strove to teach us, under enigmas, that he who shall go to the invisible regions without being purified, will be precipitated into the abyss; while he who arrives there, purged of the stains of this world, and accomplished in virtue, will be admitted to the dwelling-place of the Deity. . . The initiated are certain to attain the company of the Gods."

Pretextatus, Proconsul of Achaia, a man endowed with all the virtues, said, in the 4th century, that to deprive the Greeks of those Sacred Mysteries which bound together the whole human race, would make life insupportable.

Initiation was considered to be a mystical death; a descent into the infernal regions, where every pollution, and the stains and imperfections of a corrupt and evil life were purged away by fire and water; and the perfect *Epopt* was then said to be *regenerated, new-born*, restored to a *renovated* existence of *life, light, and purity;* and placed under the Divine Protection.

A new language was adapted to these celebrations, and also a language of hieroglyphics, unknown to any but those who had received the highest Degree. And to them ultimately were confined the learning, the morality, and the political power of every people among which the Mysteries were practised. So effectually was the knowledge of the hieroglyphics of the highest Degree hidden from all but a favored few, that in process of time their meaning was entirely lost, and none could interpret them. If the same hieroglyphics were employed in the higher as in the lower Degrees, they had a different and more abstruse and figurative meaning. It was pretended, in later times, that the sacred hieroglyphics and language were the same that were used by the Celestial Deities. Everything that could heighten the mystery of initiation was added, until the very name of the ceremony possessed a strange charm, and yet conjured up the wildest fears. The greatest rapture came to be expressed by the word that signified to pass through the Mysteries.

The Priesthood possessed one third of Egypt. They gained much of their influence by means of the Mysteries, and spared no means to impress the people with a full sense of their importance. They represented them as the beginning of a new life of reason and virtue: the initiated, or esoteric companions were said to entertain the most agreeable anticipations respecting death and eternity, to comprehend all the hidden mysteries of Nature, to have their souls restored to the original perfection from which man had fallen; and at their death to be borne to the celestial mansions of the Gods. The doctrines of a future state of rewards and punishments formed a prominent feature in the Mysteries; and they were also believed to assure much temporal happiness and good-fortune, and afford absolute security against the most imminent dangers by land and sea. Public odium was cast on those who refused to be initiated. They were considered profane, unworthy of public employment or private confidence; and held to be doomed to eternal punishment as impious. To betray the secrets of the Mysteries, to wear on the stage the dress of an Initiate, or to hold the Mysteries up to derision, was to incur death at the hands of public vengeance.

It is certain that up to the time of Cicero, the Mysteries still retained much of their original character of sanctity and purity. And at a later day, as we know, Nero, after committing a horrible crime, did not dare, even in Greece, to aid in the celebration of the Mysteries; nor at a still later day was Constantine, the Christian Emperor, allowed to do so, after his murder of his relatives.

Everywhere, and in all their forms, the Mysteries were

funereal; and celebrated the mystical death and restoration to life of some divine or heroic personage: and the details of the legend and the mode of the death varied in the different Countries where the Mysteries were practised.

Their explanation belongs both to astronomy and mythology; and the Legend of the Master's Degree is but another form of that of the Mysteries, reaching back, in one shape or other, to the remotest antiquity.

Whether Egypt originated the legend, or borrowed it from India or Chaldæa, it is now impossible to know. But the Hebrews received the Mysteries from the Egyptians; and of course were familiar with *their legend*,—known as it was to those Egyptian Initiates, Joseph and Moses. It was the fable (or rather the *truth* clothed in allegory and figures) of OSIRIS, the Sun, Source of Light and Principle of Good, and TYPHON, the Principle of Darkness and Evil. In all the histories of the Gods and Heroes lay couched and hidden astronomical details and the history of the operations of visible Nature; and those in their turn were also symbols of higher and profounder truths. None but rude uncultivated intellects could long consider the Sun and Stars and the Powers of Nature as Divine, or as fit objects of Human Worship; and *they* will consider them so while the world lasts; and ever remain ignorant of the great Spiritual Truths of which these are the hieroglyphics and expressions.

A brief summary of the Egyptian legend will serve to show the leading idea on which the Mysteries among the Hebrews were based.

Osiris, said to have been an ancient King of Egypt, was the Sun; and Isis, his wife, the Moon: and his history recounts, in poetical and figurative style, the annual journey of the Great Luminary of Heaven through the different Signs of the Zodiac.

In the absence of Osiris, Typhon, his brother, filled with envy and malice, sought to usurp his throne; but his plans were frustrated by Isis. Then he resolved to kill Osiris. This he did, by persuading him to enter a coffin or sarcophagus, which he then flung into the Nile. After a long search, Isis found the body, and concealed it in the depths of a forest; but Typhon, finding it there, cut it into fourteen pieces, and scattered them hither and thither. After tedious search, Isis found thirteen pieces, the fishes having eaten the other (the privates), which she replaced of wood, and buried the body at Philæ; where a temple of surpassing magnificence was erected in honor of Osiris.

Isis, aided by her son Orus, Horus or Har-oeri, warred against Typhon, slew him, reigned gloriously, and at her death was reunited to her husband, in the same tomb.

Typhon was represented as born of the earth; the upper part of his body covered with feathers, in stature reaching the clouds, his arms and legs covered with scales, serpents darting from him on every side, and fire flashing from his mouth. Horus, who aided in slaying him, became the God of the Sun, answering to the Grecian Apollo; and Typhon is but the anagram of Python, the great serpent slain by Apollo.

The word Typhon, like Eve, signifies *a serpent,* and *life.** By its form the serpent symbolizes life, which circulates through all nature. When, toward the end of autumn, the Woman (Virgo), in the constellations seems (upon the Chaldæan sphere) to crush with her heel the head of the serpent, this figure foretells the coming of winter, during which life seems to retire from all beings, and no longer to circulate through nature. This is why Typhon signifies also a serpent, the symbol of winter, which, in the Catholic Temples, is represented surrounding the Terrestrial Globe, which surmounts the heavenly cross, emblem of redemption. If the word Typhon is derived from *Tupoul,* it signifies a tree which produces apples (*mala,* evils), the Jewish origin of the fall of man. Typhon means also one who supplants, and signifies the human passions, which expel from our hearts the lessons of wisdom. In the Egyptian Fable, Isis wrote the sacred word for the instruction of men, and Typhon effaced it as fast as she wrote it. In morals, his name signifies *Pride, Ignorance,* and *Falsehood.*

When Isis first found the body, where it had floated ashore near Byblos, a shrub of *erica* or tamarisk near it had, by the virtue of the body, shot up into a tree around it, and protected it; and hence our sprig of acacia. Isis was also aided in her search by Anubis, in the shape of a dog. He was Sirius or the Dog-Star, the friend and counsellor of Osiris, and the inventor of language, grammar, astronomy, surveying, arithmetic, music, and medical science; the first maker of laws; and who taught the worship of the Gods, and the building of Temples.

---

* צפעני Tsapanai, in Hebrew, means a serpent.

In the Mysteries, the nailing up of the body of Osiris in the chest or ark was termed the *aphanism,* or disappearance [of the Sun at the Winter Solstice, below the Tropic of Capricorn], and the recovery of the different parts of his body by Isis, the *Euresis,* or finding. The candidate went through a ceremony representing this, in all the Mysteries everywhere. The main facts in the fable were the same in all countries; and the prominent Deities were everywhere a male and a female.

In Egypt they were Osiris and Isis: in India, Mahadeva and Bhavani: in Phœnicia, Thammuz (or Adonis) and Astarte: in Phrygia, Atys and Cybele: in Persia, Mithras and Asis: in Samothrace and Greece, Dionusos or Sabazeus and Rhea: in Britain, Hu and Ceridwen: and in Scandinavia, Woden and Frea: and in every instance these Divinities represented the Sun and the Moon.

The mysteries of Osiris, Isis, and Horus, seem to have been the model of all other ceremonies of initiation subsequently established among the different peoples of the world. Those of Atys and Cybele, celebrated in Phrygia; those of Ceres and Proserpine, at Eleusis and many other places in Greece, were but copies of them. This we learn from Plutarch, Diodorus Siculus, Lactantius, and other writers; and in the absence of direct testimony should necessarily infer it from the similarity of the adventures of these Deities; for the ancients held that the Ceres of the Greeks was the same as the Isis of the Egyptians; and Dionusos or Bacchus as Osiris.

In the legend of Osiris and Isis, as given by Plutarch, are many details and circumstances other than those that we have briefly mentioned; and all of which we need not repeat here. Osiris married his sister Isis; and labored publicly with her to ameliorate the lot of men. He taught them agriculture, while Isis invented laws. He built temples to the Gods, and established their worship. Both were the patrons of artists and their useful inventions; and introduced the use of iron for defensive weapons and implements of agriculture, and of gold to adorn the temples of the Gods. He went forth with an army to conquer men to civilization, teaching the people whom he overcame to plant the vine and sow grain for food.

Typhon, his brother, slew him when the sun was in the sign of the Scorpion, that is to say, at the Autumnal Equinox. They had been rival claimants, says Synesius, for the throne of Egypt, as Light and Darkness contend ever for the empire of the world. Plutarch adds, that at the time when Osiris was slain, the moon was at its full; and therefore it was in the sign opposite the Scorpion, that is, the Bull, the sign of the Vernal Equinox.

Plutarch assures us that it was to represent these events and details that Isis established the Mysteries, in which they were reproduced by images, symbols, and a religious ceremonial, whereby they were imitated: and in which lessons of piety were given, and consolations under the misfortunes that afflict us here below. Those who instituted these Mysteries meant to strengthen religion and console men in their sorrows by the lofty hopes found in a religious faith, whose principles were represented to them covered by a pompous ceremonial, and under the sacred veil of allegory.

Diodorus speaks of the famous columns erected near Nysa, in Arabia, where, it was said, were two of the tombs of Osiris and Isis. On one was this inscription: "I am Isis, Queen of this country. I was instructed by Mercury. No one can destroy the laws which I have established. I am the eldest daughter of Saturn, most ancient of the Gods. I am the wife and sister of Osiris the King. I first made known to mortals the use of wheat. I am the mother of Orus the King. In my honor was the city of Bubaste built. Rejoice, O Egypt, rejoice, land that gave me birth!" . . . And on the other was this: "I am Osiris the King, who led my armies into all parts of the world, to the most thickly inhabited countries of India, the North, the Danube, and the Ocean. I am the eldest son of Saturn: I was born of the brilliant and magnificent egg, and my substance is of the same nature as that which composes light. There is no place in the Universe where I have not appeared, to bestow my benefits and make known my discoveries." The rest was illegible.

To aid her in the search for the body of Osiris, and to nurse her infant child Horus, Isis sought out and took with her Anubis, son of Osiris, and his sister Nephte. He, as we have said, was Sirius, the brightest star in the Heavens. After finding him, she went to Byblos, and seated herself near a fountain, where she had learned that the sacred chest had stopped which contained the body of Osiris. There she sat, sad and silent, shedding a torrent of tears. Thither came the women of the Court of Queen Astarte, and she spoke to them, and dressed their hair, pouring upon it deliciously perfumed ambrosia. This known to the Queen, Isis was engaged as nurse for her child, in the palace, one of the columns of which was made of the erica or tamarisk, that had grown up over the chest containing Osiris, cut down by the King, and unknown to him, still enclosing the chest: which column Isis afterward demanded, and from it extracted the chest and the body, which, the latter wrapped in thin drapery and perfumed, she carried away with her.

Blue Masonry, ignorant of its import, still retains among its emblems one of a woman weeping over a broken column, holding in her hand a branch of acacia, myrtle, or tamarisk, while Time, we are told, stands behind her combing out the ringlets of her hair. We need not repeat the vapid and trivial explanation there given, of this representation of *Isis,* weeping at Byblos, over the column torn from the palace of the King, that contained the body of Osiris, while Horus, the God of Time, pours ambrosia on her hair.

Nothing of this recital was historical; but the whole was an allegory or sacred fable, containing a meaning known only to those who were initiated into the Mysteries. All the incidents were astronomical, with a meaning still deeper lying behind *that* explanation, and so hidden by a double veil. The Mysteries, in which these incidents were represented and explained, were like those of Eleusis in their object, of which Pausanias, who was initiated, says that the Greeks, from the remotest antiquity, regarded them as the best calculated of all things to lead men to piety: and Aristotle says they were the most valuable of all religious institutions, and thus were called mysteries par excellence; and the Temple of Eleusis was regarded as, in some sort, the common sanctuary of the whole earth, where religion had brought together all that was most imposing and most august.

The object of all the Mysteries was to inspire men with piety, and to console them in the miseries of life. That consolation, so afforded, was the hope of a happier future, and of passing, after death, to a state of eternal felicity.

Cicero says that the Initiates not only received lessons which made life more agreeable, but drew from the ceremonies happy hopes for the moment of death. Socrates says that those who were so fortunate as to be admitted to the Mysteries, possessed, when dying, the most glorious hopes for eternity. Aristides says that they not only procure the Initiates consolations in the present life, and means of deliverance from the great weight of their evils, but also the precious advantage of passing after death to a happier state.

Isis was the Goddess of Sais; and the famous Feast of Lights was celebrated there in her honor. There were celebrated the Mysteries, in which were represented the death and subsequent restoration to life of the God Osiris, in a secret ceremony and scenic representation of his sufferings, called the Mysteries of Night.

The Kings of Egypt often exercised the functions of the Priesthood; and they were initiated into the sacred science as soon as they attained the throne. So at Athens, the First Magistrate, or Archon-King, superintended the Mysteries. This was an image of the union that existed between the Priesthood and Royalty, in those early times when legislators and kings sought in religion a potent political instrument.

Herodotus says, speaking of the reasons why animals were deified in Egypt: "If I were to explain these reasons, I should be led to the disclosure of those holy matters which I particularly wish to avoid, and which, but from necessity, I should not have discussed at all." So he says, "The Egyptians have at Sais the tomb of a certain personage, whom I do not think myself permitted to specify. It is behind the Temple of Minerva." [The latter, so called by the Greeks, was really Isis, whose was the often-cited enigmatical inscription, "I am what was and is and is to come. No mortal hath yet unveiled me."] So again he says: "Upon this lake are represented by night the accidents which happened to him whom I dare not name. The Egyptians call them their Mysteries. Concerning these, at the same time that I confess myself sufficiently informed, I feel myself compelled to be silent. Of the ceremonies also in honor of Ceres, I may not venture to speak, further than the obligations of religion will allow me."

It is easy to see what was the great object of initiation and the Mysteries; whose first and greatest fruit was, as all the ancients testify, to civilize savage hordes, to soften their ferocious manners, to introduce among them social intercourse, and lead them into a way of life more worthy of men. Cicero considers the establishment of the Eleusinian Mysteries to be the greatest of all the benefits conferred by Athens on other commonwealths: their effects having been, he says, to civilize men, soften their savage and ferocious manners, and teach them the true principles of morals, which *initiate* man into the only kind of life worthy of him. The same philosophic orator, in a passage where he apostrophizes Ceres and Proserpine, says that mankind owes these Goddesses the first elements of moral life, as well as the first means of sustenance of physical life; knowledge of the laws, regulation of morals, and those examples of civilization which have improved the manners of men and cities.

Bacchus in Euripides says to Pentheus, that his new institution (the Dionysiac Mysteries) deserved to be known, and that one of its great advantages was, that it proscribed all impurity: that these were the Mysteries of Wisdom, of which it would be imprudent to speak to persons not initiated: that they were established among the Barbarians, who in that showed greater wisdom than the Greeks, who had not yet received them.

This double object, political and religious,—one teaching our duty to men, and the other what we owe to the Gods; or rather, respect for the Gods calculated to maintain that which we owe the laws, is found in that well-known verse of Virgil, borrowed by him from the ceremonies of initiation: "Teach me to respect Justice and the Gods." This great lesson, which the Hierophant impressed on the Initiates, after they had witnessed a representation of the Infernal regions, the Poet places after his description of the different punishments suffered by the wicked in Tartarus, and immediately after the description of that of Sisyphus.

Pausanias, likewise, at the close of the representation of the punishments of Sisyphus and the daughters of Danaus, in the Temple at Delphi, makes this reflection; that the crime or impiety which in them had chiefly merited this punishment, was the contempt which they had shown for the Mysteries of Eleusis. From this reflection of Pausanias, who was an Initiate, it is easy to see that the Priests of Eleusis, who taught the dogma of punishment in Tartarus, included among the great crimes deserving these punishments, contempt for and disregard of the Holy Mysteries; whose object was to lead men to piety, and thereby to respect for justice and the laws, chief object of their institution, if not the only one, and to which the needs and interest of religion itself were subordinate; since the latter was but a means to lead more surely to the former; for the whole force of religious opinions being in the hands of the legislators to be wielded, they were sure of being better obeyed.

The Mysteries were not merely simple lustrations and the observation of some arbitrary formulas and ceremonies; nor a means of reminding men of the ancient condition of the race prior to civilization: but they led men to piety by instruction in morals and as to a future life; which at a very early day, if not originally, formed the chief portion of the ceremonial.

Symbols were used in the ceremonies, which referred to agriculture, as Masonry has preserved the ear of wheat in a symbol and in one of her words; but their principal reference was to astronomical phenomena. Much was no doubt said as to the condition of brutality and degradation in which man was sunk before the institution of the Mysteries; but the allusion was rather metaphysical, to the ignorance of the uninitiated, than to the wild life of the earliest men.

The great object of the Mysteries of Isis, and in general of all the Mysteries, was a great and truly politic one. It was to ameliorate our race, to perfect its manners and morals, and to restrain society by stronger bonds than those that human laws impose. They were the invention of that ancient science and wisdom which exhausted all its resources to make legislation perfect; and of that philosophy which has ever sought to secure the happiness of man, by purifying his soul from the passions which can trouble it, and as a necessary consequence introduce social disorder. And that they were the work of genius is evident from their employment of all the sciences, a profound knowledge of the human heart, and the means of subduing it.

It is a still greater mistake to imagine that they were the inventions of charlatanism, and means of deception. They may in the lapse of time have degenerated into imposture and schools of false ideas; but they were not so at the beginning; or else the wisest and best men of antiquity have uttered the most willful falsehoods. In process of time the very allegories of the Mysteries themselves, Tartarus and its punishments, Minos and the other judges of the dead, came to be misunderstood, and to be false because they were so; while at first they were true, because they were recognized as merely the arbitrary forms in which truths were enveloped.

The object of the Mysteries was to procure for man a real felicity on earth by the means of virtue; and to that end he was taught that his soul was immortal; and that error, sin, and vice must needs, by an inflexible law, produce their consequences. The rude representation of physical torture in Tartarus was but an image of the certain, unavoidable, eternal consequences that flow by the law of God's enactment from the sin committed and the vice indulged in. The poets and mystagogues labored to propagate these doctrines of the soul's immortality and the certain punishment of sin and vice, and to accredit them with the people, by teaching them the former in their poems, and the latter in the sanctuaries; and they clothed them with the charms, the one of poetry, and the other of spectacles and magic illusions.

They painted, aided by all the resources of art, the virtuous man's happy life after death, and the horrors of the frightful prisons destined to punish the vicious. In the shades of the sanctuaries, these delights and horrors were exhibited as spectacles, and the Initiates witnessed religious dramas, under the name of *initiation* and *mysteries.* Curiosity was excited by secrecy, by the difficulty experienced in obtaining admission, and by the tests to be undergone. The candidate was amused by the variety of the scenery, the pomp of the decorations, the appliances of machinery. Respect was inspired by the gravity and dignity of the actors and the majesty of the ceremonial; and fear and hope, sadness and delight, were in turns excited.

The Hierophants, men of intellect, and well understanding the disposition of the people and the art of controlling them, used every appliance to attain that object, and give importance and impressiveness to their ceremonies. As they covered those ceremonies with the veil of Secrecy, so they preferred that Night should cover them with its wings. Obscurity adds to impressiveness, and assists illusion; and they used it to produce an effect upon the astonished Initiate. The ceremonies were conducted in caverns dimly lighted: thick groves were planted around the Temples, to produce that gloom that impresses the mind with a religious awe.

The very word *mystery,* according to Demetrius Phalereus, was a metaphorical expression that denoted the secret awe which darkness and gloom inspired. The night was almost always the time fixed for their celebration; and they were ordinarily termed *nocturnal* ceremonies. Initiations into the Mysteries of Samothrace took place at night; as did those of Isis, of which Apuleius speaks.

Euripides makes Bacchus say, that *his* Mysteries were celebrated at night, because there is in night something august and imposing.

Nothing excites men's curiosity so much as Mystery, concealing things which they desire to know: and nothing so much increases curiosity as obstacles that interpose to prevent them from indulging in the gratification of their desires. Of this the Legislators and Hierophants took advantage, to attract the people to their sanctuaries, and to induce them to seek to obtain lessons from which they would perhaps have turned away with indifference, if they had been pressed upon them. In this spirit of mystery they professed to imitate the Deity, who hides Himself from our senses, and conceals from us the springs by which He moves the Universe. They admitted that they concealed the highest truths under the veil of allegory, the more to excite the curiosity of men, and to urge them to investigation. The secrecy in which they buried their Mysteries, had that end. Those to whom they were confided, bound themselves, by the most fearful oaths, never to reveal them. They were not allowed even to speak of these important secrets with any others than the initiated; and the penalty of death was pronounced against any one indiscreet enough to reveal them, or found in the Temple without being an Initiate; and any one who had betrayed those secrets, was avoided by all, as excommunicated.

Aristotle was accused of impiety, by the Hierophant Eurymedon, for having sacrificed to the manés of his wife, according to the rite used in the worship of Ceres. He was compelled to flee to Chalcis; and to purge his memory from this stain, he directed, by his will, the erection of a Statue to that Goddess. Socrates, dying, sacrificed to Esculapius, to exculpate himself from the suspicion of Atheism. A price was set on the head of Diagoras, because he had divulged the Secret of the Mysteries. Andocides was accused of the same crime, as was Alcibiades, and both were cited to answer the charge before the inquisition at Athens, where the People were the Judges. Æschylus the Tragedian was accused of having represented the Mysteries on the stage; and was acquitted only on proving that he had never been initiated.

Seneca, comparing Philosophy to initiation, says that the most sacred ceremonies could be known to the adepts alone: but that many of their precepts were known even to the Profane. Such was the case with the doctrine of a future life, and a state of rewards and punishments beyond the grave. The ancient legislators clothed this doctrine in the pomp of a mysterious ceremony, in mystic words and magical representations, to impress upon the mind the truths they taught, by the strong influence of such scenic displays upon the senses and imagination.

In the same way they taught the origin of the soul, its fall to the earth past the spheres and through the elements, and its final return to the place of its origin, when, during the continuance of its union with earthly matter, the sacred fire, which formed its essence, had contracted no stains, and its brightness had not been marred by foreign particles, which, denaturalizing it, weighed it down and delayed its return. These metaphysical ideas, with difficulty comprehended by the mass of the Initiates, were represented by figures, by symbols, and by allegorical analogies; no idea being so abstract that men do not seek to give it expression by, and translate it into, sensible images.

The attraction of Secrecy was enhanced by the difficulty of obtaining admission. Obstacles and suspense redoubled curiosity. Those who aspired to the initiation of the Sun and in the Mysteries of Mithras in Persia, underwent many trials. They commenced by easy tests and arrived by degrees at those that were most cruel, in which the life of the candidate was often endangered. Gregory Nazianzen terms them *tortures* and mystic *punishments*. No one can be initiated, says Suidas, until after he has proven, by the most terrible trials, that he possesses a virtuous soul, exempt from the sway of every passion, and at it were impassible. There were twelve principal tests; and some make the number larger.

The trials of the Eleusinian initiations were not so terrible; but they were severe; and the suspense, above all, in which the aspirant was kept for several years [the memory of which is retained in Masonry by the *ages* of those of the different Degrees], or the interval between admission to the *inferior* and initiation in the *great* Mysteries, was a species of torture to the curiosity which it was desired to excite. Thus the Egyptian Priests tried Pythagoras before admitting him to know the secrets of the sacred science. He succeeded, by his incredible patience and the courage with which he surmounted all obstacles, in obtaining admission to their society and receiving their lessons. Among the Jews. the Essenes admitted none among them, until they had passed the tests or several Degrees.

By initiation, those who before were *fellow-citizens* only, became *brothers,* connected by a closer bond than before, by means of a religious fraternity, which, bringing men nearer together, united them more strongly: and the weak and the poor could more readily appeal for assistance to the powerful and the wealthy, with whom religious association gave them a closer fellowship.

The Initiate was regarded as the favorite of the Gods. For him alone Heaven opened its treasures. Fortunate during life, he could, by virtue and the favor of Heaven, promise himself after death an eternal felicity.

The Priests of the Island of Samothrace promised favorable winds and prosperous voyages to those who were initiated. It was promised them that the CABIRI, and Castor and Pollux, the DIOSCURI, should appear to them when the storm raged, and give them calms and smooth seas: and the Scholiast of Aristophanes says that those initiated in the Mysteries there were just men, who were privileged to escape from great evils and tempests.

The Initiate in the Mysteries of Orpheus, after he was purified, was considered as released from the empire of evil, and transferred to a condition of life which gave him the happiest hopes. "I have emerged from evil," he was made to say, "and have attained good." Those initiated in the Mysteries of Eleusis believed that the Sun blazed with a pure splendor for them alone. And, as we see in the case of Pericles, they flattered themselves that Ceres and Proserpine inspired them and gave them wisdom and counsel.

Initiation dissipated errors and banished misfortune: and after having filled the heart of man with joy during life, it gave him the most blissful hopes at the moment of death. We owe it to the Goddesses of Eleusis, says Socrates, that we do not lead the wild life of the earliest men: and to them are due the flattering hopes which initiation gives us for the moment of death and for all eternity. The benefit which we reap from these august ceremonies, says Aristides, is not only present joy, a deliverance and enfranchisement from the old ills; but also the sweet hope which we have in death of passing to a more fortunate state. And Theon says that participation of the Mysteries is the finest of all things, and the source of the greatest blessings. The happiness promised there was not limited to this mortal life; but it extended beyond the grave. There a new life was to commence, during which the Initiate was to enjoy a bliss without alloy and without limit. The Corybantes promised eternal life to the Initiates of the Mysteries of Cybele and Atys.

Apuleius represents Lucius, while still in the form of an ass, as addressing his prayers to Isis, whom he speaks of as the same as Ceres, Venus, Diana, and Proserpine, and as illuminating the walls of many cities simultaneously with her feminine lustre, and substituting her quivering light for the bright rays of the Sun. She appears to him in his vision as a beautiful female, "over whose divine neck her long thick hair hung in graceful ringlets." Addressing him, she says, "The parent of Universal nature attends thy call. The mistress of the Elements, initiative germ of generations, Supreme of Deities, Queen of departed spirits, first inhabitant of Heaven, and uniform type of all the Gods and Goddesses, propitiated by thy prayers, is with thee. She governs with her nod the luminous heights of the firmament, the salubrious breezes of the ocean; the silent deplorable depths of the shades below; one Sole Divintiy under many forms, worshipped by the different nations of the Earth under many titles, and with various religious rites."

Directing him how to proceed, at her festival, to re-obtain his human shape, she says: "Throughout the entire course of the remainder of thy life, until the very last breath has vanished from thy lips, thou art devoted to my service. . . . Under my protection will thy life be happy and glorious: and when, thy days being spent, thou shalt descend to the shades below, and inhabit the Elysian fields, there also, even in the subterranean hemisphere, shalt thou pay frequent worship to me, thy propitious patron: and yet further: if through sedulous obedience, religious devotion to my ministry, and inviolable chastity, thou shalt prove thyself a worthy object of divine favor, then shalt thou feel the influence of the power that I alone possess. The number of thy days shall be prolonged beyond the ordinary decrees of fate."

In the procession of the festival, Lucius saw the image of the Goddess, on either side of which were female attendants, that, "with ivory combs in their hands, made believe, by the motion of their arms and the twisting of their fingers, to comb and ornament the Goddess' royal hair." Afterward, clad in linen robes, came the initiated. "The hair of the women was moistened by perfume, and enveloped in a transparent covering; but the men, terrestrial stars, as it were, of the great religion, were thoroughly shaven, and their bald heads shone exceedingly."

Afterward came the Priests, in robes of white linen. The first bore a lamp in the form of a boat, emitting flame from an orifice in the middle: the second, a small altar: the third, a golden palm-tree: and the fourth displayed the figure of a left hand, the palm open and expanded, "representing thereby a symbol of equity and fair-dealing, of which the left hand, as slower than the right hand, and more void of skill and craft, is therefore an appropriate emblem."

After Lucius had, by the grace of Isis, recovered his human form, the Priest said to him, "Calamity hath no hold on those whom our Goddess hath chosen for her service, and whom her majesty hath vindicated." And the people declared that he was fortunate to be "thus after a manner born again, and at once be-trothed to the service of the Holy Ministry."

When he urged the Chief Priest to initiate him, he was answer-ed that there was not "a single one among the initiated, of a mind so depraved, or so bent on his own destruction, as, without receiv-ing a special command from Isis, to dare to undertake her minis-try rashly and sacrilegiously, and thereby commit an act certain to bring upon himself a dreadful injury." "For," continued the Chief Priest, "the gates of the shades below, and the care of our life being in the hands of the Goddess,—*the ceremony of initiation into the Mysteries is,* as it were, *to suffer death,* with the precarious chance of resuscitation. Wherefore the Goddess, in the wisdom of her Divinity, hath been accustomed to select as persons to whom the secrets of her religion can with propriety be entrusted, those who, standing as it were on the utmost limit of the course of life they have completed, *may through her Providence be in a manner born again,* and commence the career of a new existence."

When he was finally to be initiated, he was conducted to the nearest baths, and after having bathed, the Priest first solicited forgiveness of the Gods, and then sprinkled him all over with the clearest and purest water, and conducted him back to the Temple; "where," says Apuleius, "after giving me some instruction, that mortal tongue is not permitted to reveal, he bade me for the suc-ceeding ten days restrain my appetite, eat no animal food, and drink no wine."

These ten days elapsed, the Priest led him into the inmost recesses of the Sanctuary. "And here, studious reader," he continues, "peradventure thou wilt be sufficiently anxious to know all that was said and done, which, were it lawful to divulge, I would tell thee; and, wert thou permitted to hear, thou shouldst know. Nevertheless, although the disclosure would affix the penalty of rash curiosity to my tongue as well as thy ears, yet will I, for fear thou shouldst be too long tormented with religious longing, and suffer the pain of protracted suspense, tell the truth notwithstanding. Listen then to what I shall relate. *I approached the abode of death; with my foot I pressed the threshold of Proserpine's Palace. I was transported through the elements, and conducted back again. At midnight I saw the bright light of the sun shining. I stood in the presence of the Gods, the Gods of Heaven and of the Shades below; ay, stood near and worshipped.* And now have I told thee such things that, hearing, thou necessarily canst not understand; and being beyond the comprehension of the Profane, I can enunciate without committing a crime."

After night had passed, and the morning had dawned, the usual ceremonies were at an end. Then he was consecrated by twelve stoles being put upon him, clothed, crowned with palm-leaves, and exhibited to the people. The remainder of that day was celebrated as his birthday and passed in festivities; and on the third day afterward, the same religious ceremonies were repeated, including a religious breakfast, *"followed by a final consummation of ceremonies."*

A year afterward, he was warned to prepare for initiation into the Mysteries of "the Great God, Supreme Parent of all the other Gods, the invincible OSIRIS." "For," says Apuleius, "although there is a strict connexion between the religions of both Deities, AND EVEN THE ESSENCE OF BOTH DIVINITIES IS IDENTICAL, the ceremonies of the respective initiations are considerably different."

Compare with this hint the following language of the prayer of Lucius, addressed to Isis; and we may judge what doctrines were taught in the Mysteries, in regard to the Deity: "O Holy and Perpetual Preserver of the Human Race! ever ready to cherish mortals by Thy munificence, and to afford Thy sweet maternal affection to the wretched under misfortune; Whose bounty is never at rest, neither by day nor by night, nor throughout the very minutest particle of duration; Thou who stretchest forth Thy health-bearing right hand over the land and over the sea for the protection of mankind, to disperse the storms of life, to unravel the inextricable entanglement of the web of fate, to mitigate the tempests of fortune, and restrain the malignant influences of the stars,—*the Gods in Heaven adore Thee, the Gods in the shades below do Thee homage, the stars obey Thee, the Divinities rejoice in Thee, the elements and the revolving seasons serve Thee!* At Thy nod the winds breathe, clouds gather, seeds grow, buds germinate; *in obedience to Thee the Earth revolves* AND THE SUN GIVES US LIGHT. IT IS THOU WHO GOVERNEST THE UNIVERSE AND TREADEST TARTARUS UNDER THY FEET."

Then he was initiated into the nocturnal Mysteries of Osiris and Serapis: and afterward into those of Ceres at Rome: but of the ceremonies in these initiations, Apuleius says nothing.

Under the Archonship of Euclid, bastards and slaves were excluded from initiation; and the same exclusion obtained against the Materialists or Epicureans who denied Providence and consequently the utility of initiation. By a natural progress, it came at length to be considered that the gates of Elysium would open only for the Initiates, whose souls had been purified and regenerated in the sanctuaries. But it was never held, on the other hand, that initiation alone sufficed. We learn from Plato, that it was also necessary for the soul to be purified from every stain: and that the purification necessary was such as gave virtue, truth, wisdom, strength, justice, and temperance.

Entrance to the Temples was forbidden to all who had committed homicide, even if it were involuntary. So it is stated by both Isocrates and Theon. Magicians and Charlatans who made trickery a trade, and impostors pretending to be possessed by evil spirits, were excluded from the sanctuaries. Every impious person and criminal was rejected; and Lampridius states that before the celebration of the Mysteries, public notice was given, that none need apply to enter but those against whom their consciences uttered no reproach, and who were certain of their own innocence.

It was required of the Initiate that his heart and hands should be free from any stain. Porphyry says that man's soul, at death, should be enfranchised from all the passions, from hate, envy, and the others; and, in a word, *be as pure as it is required to be in the Mysteries.* Of course it is not surprising that parricides and perjurers, and others who had committed crimes against God or man, could not be admitted.

In the Mysteries of Mithras, a lecture was repeated to the Initiate on the subject of Justice. And the great moral lesson of the Mysteries, to which all their mystic ceremonial tended, expressed in a single line by Virgil, was *to practise Justice and revere the Deity;*—thus recalling men to justice, by connecting it with the justice of the Gods, who require it and punish its infraction. The Initiate could aspire to the favors of the Gods, only because and while he respected the rights of society and those of humanity. "The sun," says the chorus of Initiates in Aristophanes, "burns with a pure light for us alone, who, admitted to the Mysteries, observe the laws of piety in our intercourse with strangers and our fellow-citizens." The rewards of initiation were attached to the practice of the social virtues. It was not enough to be initiated merely. It was necessary to be faithful to the *laws* of initiation, which imposed on men duties in regard to their kind. Bacchus allowed none to participate in his Mysteries, but men who conformed to the rules of piety and justice. Sensibility, above all, and compassion for the misfortunes of others, were precious virtues, which initiation strove to encourage. "Nature," says Juvenal, "has created us compassionate, since it has endowed us with tears. Sensibility is the most admirable of our senses. What man is truly worthy of the torch of the Mysteries; who such as the Priest of Ceres requires him to be, if he regards the misfortunes of others as wholly foreign to himself?"

All who had not used their endeavors to defeat a conspiracy; and those who had on the contrary fomented one; those citizens who had betrayed their country, who had surrendered an advantageous post or place, or the vessels of the State, to the enemy; all who had supplied the enemy with money; and in general, all who had come short of their duties as honest men and good citizens, were excluded from the Mysteries of Eleusis. To be admitted there, one must have lived equitably, and with sufficient good fortune not to be regarded as hated by the Gods.

Thus the Society of the Initiates was, in its principle, and according to the true purpose of its institution, a society of virtuous men, who labored to free their souls from the tyranny of the passions, and to develop the germ of all the social virtues. And this was the meaning of the idea, afterward misunderstood, that entry into Elysium was only allowed to the Initiates: because entrance to the sanctuaries was allowed to the virtuous only, and Elysium was created for virtuous souls alone.

The precise nature and details of the doctrines as to a future life, and rewards and punishments there, developed in the Mysteries, is in a measure uncertain. Little direct information in regard to it has come down to us. No doubt, in the ceremonies, there was a scenic representation of Tartarus and the judgment of the dead, resembling that which we find in Virgil: but there is as little doubt that these representations were explained to be allegorical. It is not our purpose here to repeat the descriptions given of Elysium and Tartarus. That would be aside from our object. We are only concerned with the great fact that the Mysteries taught the doctrine of the soul's immortality, and that, in some shape, suffering, pain, remorse, and agony, ever follow sin as its consequences.

Human ceremonies are indeed but imperfect symbols; and the alternate baptisms in fire and water intended to purify us into immortality, are ever in this world interrupted at the moment of their anticipated completion. Life is a mirror which reflects only to deceive, a tissue perpetually interrupted and broken, an urn forever fed, yet never full.

All initiation is but introductory to the great change of death. Baptism, anointing, embalming, obsequies by burial or fire, are preparatory symbols, like the initiation of Hercules before descending to the Shades, pointing out the mental change which ought to precede the renewal of existence. Death is the true initiation, to which sleep is the introductory or minor mystery. It is the final rite which united the Egyptian with his God, and which opens the same promise to all who are duly prepared for it.

The body was deemed a prison for the soul; but the latter was not condemned to eternal banishment and imprisonment. The Father of the Worlds permits its chains to be broken, and has provided in the course of Nature the means of its escape. It was a doctrine of immemorial antiquity, shared alike by Egyptians, Pythagoreans, the Orphici, and by that characteristic Bacchic Sage, "the Preceptor of the Soul," Silenus, that death is far better than life; that the real death belongs to those who on earth are immersed in the Lethe of its passions and fascinations, and that the true life commences only when the soul is emancipated for its return.

And in this sense, as presiding over life and death, Dionusos is in the highest sense *the* LIBERATOR: since, like Osiris, he frees the soul, and guides it in its migrations beyond the grave, preserving it from the risk of again falling under the slavery of matter or of some inferior animal form, the purgatory of Metempsychosis; and exalting and perfecting its nature through the purifying discipline of his Mysteries. "The great consummation of all philosophy," said Socrates, professedly quoting from traditional and mystic sources, "is *Death:* He who pursues philosophy aright, *is studying how to die."*

All soul is part of the Universal Soul, whose totality is Dionusos; and it is therefore he who, as Spirit of Spirits, leads back the vagrant spirit to its home, and accompanies it through the purifying processes, both real and symbolical, of its earthly transit. He is therefore emphatically the *Mystes* or Hierophant, the great Spiritual Mediator of Greek religion.

The human soul is itself δαιμόνιος a God *within* the mind, capable through its own power of rivalling the canonization of the Hero, of making itself immortal by the practice of the good, and the contemplation of the beautiful and true. The removal to the Happy Islands could only be understood mythically; everything earthly must die; Man, like Œdipus, is wounded from his birth, his real elysium can exist only beyond the grave. Dionusos died and descended to the shades. His passion was the great Secret of the Mysteries; as Death is the Grand Mystery of existence. His death, typical of Nature's Death, or of her periodical decay and restoration, was one of the many symbols of the *palingenesia* or second birth of man.

Man descended from the elemental Forces or Titans [Elohim], who fed on the body of the Pantheistic Deity creating the Universe by self-sacrifice, commemorates in sacramental observance this mysterious passion; and while partaking of the raw flesh of the victim, seems to be invigorated by a fresh draught from the fountain of universal life, to receive a new pledge of regenerated existence. Death is the inseparable antecedent of life; the seed dies in order to produce the plant, and earth itself is rent asunder and dies at the birth of Dionusos. Hence the significancy of the *phallus,* or of its inoffensive substitute, the obelisk, rising as an emblem of resurrection by the tomb of buried Deity at Lerna or at Sais.

Dionusos-Orpheus descended to the Shades to recover the lost Virgin of the Zodiac, to bring back his mother to the sky as Thyone; or what has the same meaning, to consummate his eventful marriage with Persephone, thereby securing, like the nuptials of his father with Semele or Danaë, the perpetuity of Nature. His under-earth office is the depression of the year, the wintry aspect in the alternations of bull and serpent, whose united series makes up the continuity of Time, and in which, physically speaking, the stern and dark are ever the parents of the beautiful and bright.

It was this aspect, sombre for the moment, but bright by anticipation, which was contemplated in the Mysteries: the human sufferer was consoled by witnessing the severer trials of the Gods; and the vicissitudes of life and death, expressed by apposite symbols, such as the sacrifice or submersion of the Bull, the extinction and re-illumination of the torch, excited corresponding emotions of alternate grief and joy, that play of passion which was present at the origin of Nature, and which accompanies all her changes.

The greater Eleusiniæ were celebrated in the month Boëdromion, when the seed was buried in the ground, and when the year, verging to its decline, disposes the mind to serious reflection. The first days of the ceremonial were passed in sorrow and anxious silence, in fasting and expiatory or lustral offices. On a sudden, the scene was changed: sorrow and lamentation were discarded, the glad name of Iacchus passed from mouth to mouth, the image of the God, crowned with myrtle and bearing a lighted torch, was borne in joyful procession from the Ceramicus to Eleusis, where, during the ensuing night, the initiation was completed by an imposing revelation. The first scene was in the προναος, or outer court of the sacred enclosure, where amidst utter darkness, or while the meditating God, the star illuminating the Nocturnal Mystery, alone carried an unextinguished torch, the candidates were overawed with terrific sounds and noises, while they painfully groped their way, as in the gloomy cavern of the soul's sublunar migration; a scene justly compared to the passage of the Valley of the Shadow of Death. For by the immutable law exemplified in the trials of Psyche, man must pass through the terrors of the under-world, before he can reach the height of Heaven. At length the gates of the *adytum* were thrown open, a supernatural light streamed from the illuminated statue of the Goddess, and enchanting sights and sounds, mingled with songs and dances, exalted the communicant to a rapture of supreme felicity, realizing, as far as sensuous imagery could depict, the anticipated reunion with the Gods.

In the dearth of direct evidence as to the detail of the ceremonies enacted, or of the meanings connected with them, their tendency must be inferred from the characteristics of the contemplated deities with their accessory symbols and mythi, or from direct testimony as to the value of the Mysteries generally.

The ordinary phenomena of vegetation, the death of the seed in giving birth to the plant, connecting the sublimest hopes with the plainest occurrences, was the simple yet beautiful formula assumed by the great mystery in almost all religions, from the Zend-Avesta to the Gospel. As Proserpina, the divine power is as the seed decaying and destroyed; as Artemis, she is the principle of its destruction; but Artemis Proserpina is also Corē Soteria, the Saviour, who leads the Spirits of Hercules and Hyacinthus to Heaven.

Many other emblems were employed in the Mysteries,—as the dove, the myrtle-wreath, and others, all significant of life rising out of death, and of the equivocal condition of dying yet immortal man.

The horrors and punishments of Tartarus, as described in the Phædo and the Æneid, with all the ceremonies of the judgments of Minos, Eacus, and Rhadamanthus, were represented, sometimes more and sometimes less fully, in the Mysteries; in order to impress upon the minds of the Initiates this great lesson,—that we should be ever prepared to appear before the Supreme Judge, with a heart pure and spotless; as Socrates teaches in the Gorgias. For the soul stained with crimes, he says, to descend to the Shades, is the bitterest ill. To adhere to Justice and Wisdom, Plato holds, is our duty, that we may some day take that lofty road that leads toward the heavens, and avoid most of the evils to which the soul is exposed in its subterranean journey of a thousand years. And so in the Phædo, Socrates teaches that we should seek here below to free our soul of its passions, in order to be ready to enter our appearance, whenever Destiny summons us to the Shades.

Thus the Mysteries inculcated a great moral truth, veiled with a fable of huge proportions and the appliances of an impressive spectacle, to which, exhibited in the sanctuaries, art and natural magic lent all they had that was imposing. They sought to strengthen men against the horrors of death and the fearful idea of utter annihilation. Death, says the author of the dialogue, entitled *Axiochus,* included in the works of Plato, is but a passage to a happier state; but one must have lived well, to attain that most fortunate result. So that the doctrine of the immortality of the soul was consoling to the virtuous and religious man alone; while to all others it came with menaces and despair, surrounding them with terrors and alarms that disturbed their repose during all their life.

For the material horrors of Tartarus, allegorical to the Initiate, were real to the mass of the Profane; nor in latter times, did, perhaps many Initiates read rightly the allegory. The triple-walled prison, which the condemned soul first met, round which swelled and surged the fiery waves of Phlegethon, wherein rolled roaring, huge, blazing rocks; the great gate with columns of adamant, which none save the Gods could crush; Tisiphone, their warder, with her bloody robes; the lash resounding on the mangled bodies of the miserable unfortunates, their plaintive groans, mingled in horrid harmony with the clashings of their chains; the Furies, lashing the guilty with their snakes; the awful abyss where Hydra howls with its hundred heads, greedy to devour; Tityus, prostrate, and his entrails fed upon by the cruel vulture: Sisyphus, ever rolling his rock; Ixion on his wheel; Tantalus tortured by eternal thirst and hunger, in the midst of water and with declicious fruits touching his head; the daughters of Danaus at their eternal, fruitless task; beasts biting and venomous reptiles stinging; and devouring flame eternally consuming bodies ever renewed in endless agony; all these sternly impressed upon the people the terrible consequences of sin and vice, and urged them to pursue the paths of honesty and virtue.

And if, in the ceremonies of the Mysteries, these material horrors were explained to the Initiates as mere symbols of the unimaginable torture, remorse, and agony that would rend the immaterial soul and rack the immortal spirit, they were feeble and insufficient in the same mode and measure only, as all material images and symbols fall short of that which is beyond the cognizance of our senses: and the grave Hierophant, the imagery, the paintings, the dramatic horrors, the funeral sacrifices, the august mysteries, the solemn silence of the sanctuaries, were none the less impressive, because they were known to be but symbols, that with material shows and images made the imagination to be the teacher•of the intellect.

So, too, it was represented, that except for the gravest sins there was an opportunity for expiation; and the tests of *water, air,* and *fire* were represented; by means of which, during the march of many years, the soul could be purified, and rise toward the ethereal regions; that ascent being more or less tedious and laborious, according as each soul was more or less clogged by the gross impediments of its sins and vices. Herein was shadowed forth, (how distinctly taught the Initiates we know not), the doctrine that pain and sorrow, misfortune and remorse, are the inevitable *consequences* that flow from sin and vice, as effect flows from cause; that by each sin and every act of vice the soul drops back and loses ground in its advance toward perfection: and that the ground so lost is and will be in reality never so recovered as that the sin shall be as if it never had been committed; but that throughout all the eternity of its existence, each soul shall be conscious that every act of vice or baseness it did on earth has made the distance greater between itself and ultimate perfection.

We see this truth glimmering in the doctrine, taught in the Mysteries, that though slight and ordinary offences could be expiated by penances, repentance, acts of beneficence, and prayers, grave crimes were mortal sins, beyond the reach of all such remedies. Eleusis closed her gates against Nero: and the Pagan Priests told Constantine that among all their modes of expiation there was none so potent as could wash from *his* soul the dark spots left by the murder of his wife, and his multiplied perjuries and assassinations.

The object of the ancient initiations being to ameliorate mankind and to perfect the intellectual part of man, the nature of the human soul, its origin, its destination, its relations to the body and to universal nature, all formed part of the mystic science; and to them in part the lessons given to the Initiate were directed. For it was believed that initiation tended to his perfection, and to preventing the divine part within him, overloaded with matter gross and earthy, from being plunged into gloom, and impeded in its return to the Deity. The soul, with them, was not a mere conception or abstraction; but a reality including in itself life and thought; or, rather, of whose essence it was to live and think.

It was material; but not brute, inert, inactive, lifeless, motionless, formless, lightless matter. It was held to be active, reasoning, thinking; its natural home in the highest regions of the Universe, whence it descended to illuminate, give form and movement to, vivify, animate, and carry with itself the baser matter; and whither it unceasingly tends to reascend, when and as soon as it can free itself from its connection with that matter. From that substance, divine, infinitely delicate and active, essentially luminous, the souls of men were formed, and by it alone, uniting with and organizing their bodies, men *lived*.

This was the doctrine of Pythagoras, who learned it when he received the Egyptian Mysteries: and it was the doctrine of all who, by means of the ceremonial of initiation, thought to purify the soul. Virgil makes the spirit of Anchises teach it to Æneas: and all the expiations and lustrations used in the Mysteries were but symbols of those intellectual ones by which the soul was to be purged of its vice-spots and stains, and freed of the incumbrance of its earthly prison, so that it might rise unimpeded to the source from which it came.

Hence sprung the doctrine of the transmigration of souls; which Pythagoras taught as an allegory, and those who came after him received literally. Plato, like him, drew his doctrines from the East and the Mysteries, and undertook to translate the language of the symbols used there, into that of Philosophy; and to prove by argument and philosophical deduction, what, *felt* by the consciousness, the Mysteries taught by symbols as an indisputable fact,—the immortality of the soul. Cicero did the same; and followed the Mysteries in teaching that the Gods were but mortal men, who for their great virtues and signal services had deserved that their souls should, after death, be raised to that lofty rank.

It being taught in the Mysteries, either by way of allegory, the meaning of which was not made known except to a select few, or, perhaps only at a later day, as an actual reality, that the souls of the vicious dead passed into the bodies of those animals to whose nature their vices had most affinity, it was also taught that the soul could avoid these transmigrations, often successive and numerous, by the practice of virtue, which would acquit it of them, free it from the circle of successive generations, and restore it at once to its source. Hence nothing was so ardently prayed for by the Initiates, says Proclus, as this happy fortune, which, delivering them from the empire of Evil, would restore them to their true life, and conduct them to the place of final rest. To this doctrine probably referred those figures of animals and monsters which were exhibited to the Initiate, before allowing him to see the sacred light for which he sighed.

Plato says, that souls will not reach the term of their ills, until the revolutions of the world have restored them to their primitive condition, and purified them from the stains which they have contracted by the contagion of fire, earth, and air. And he held that they could not be allowed to enter Heaven, until they had distinguished themselves by the practice of virtue in some one of three several bodies. The Manicheans allowed five: Pindar, the same number as Plato; as did the Jews.

And Cicero says, that the ancient soothsayers, and the interpreters of the will of the Gods, in their religious ceremonies and initiations, taught that we expiate here below the crimes committed in a prior life; and for that are born. It was taught in these Mysteries, that the soul passes through several states, and that the pains and sorrows of this life are an expiation of prior faults.

This doctrine of transmigration of souls obtained, as Porphyry informs us, among the Persians and Magi. It was held in the East and the West, and that from the remotest antiquity. Herodotus found it among the Egyptians, who made the term of the circle of migrations from one human body, through animals, fishes, and birds, to another human body, three thousand years. Empedocles even held that souls went into plants. Of these, the laurel was the noblest, as of animals the lion; both being consecrated to the Sun, to which, it was held in the Orient, virtuous souls were to return. The Curds, the Chinese, the Kabbalists, all held the same doctrine. So Origen held, and the Bishop Synesius, the latter of whom had been initiated, and who thus prayed to God: "O Father, grant that my soul, reunited to the light, may not be plunged again into the defilements of earth!" So the Gnostics held; and even the Disciples of Christ inquired if the man who was born blind, was not so punished for some sin that he had committed before his birth.

Virgil, in the celebrated allegory in which he develops the doctrines taught in the Mysteries, enunciated the doctrine, held by most of the ancient philosophers, of the pre-existence of souls, in the eternal fire from which they emanate; that fire which animates the stars, and circulates in every part of Nature: and the purifications of the soul, by fire, water, and air, of which he speaks, and which three modes were employed in the Mysteries of Bacchus, were symbols of the passage of the soul into different bodies.

The relations of the human soul with the rest of nature were a chief object of the science of the Mysteries. The man was there brought face to face with entire nature. The world, and the spherical envelope that surrounds it, were represented by a mystic egg, by the side of the image of the Sun-God whose Mysteries were celebrated. The famous Orphic egg was consecrated to Bacchus in his Mysteries. It was, says Plutarch, an image of the Universe, which engenders everything, and contains everything in its bosom. "Consult," says Macrobius, "the Initiates of the Mysteries of Bacchus, who honor with special veneration the sacred egg." The rounded and almost spherical form of its shell, he says, which encloses it on every side, and confines within itself the principles of life, is a symbolic image of the world; and the world is the universal principle of all things.

This symbol was borrowed from the Egyptians, who also consecrated the egg to Osiris, germ of Light, himself born, says Diodorus, from that famous egg. In Thebes, in Upper Egypt, he was represented as emitting it from his mouth, and causing to issue from it the first principle of heat and light, or the Fire-God, Vulcan, or Phtha. We find this egg even in Japan, between the horns of the famous Mithriac Bull, whose attributes Osiris, Apis, and Bacchus all borrowed.

Orpheus, author of the Grecian Mysteries, which he carried from Egypt to Greece, consecrated this symbol: and taught that matter, uncreated and informous, existed from all eternity, unorganized, as chaos; containing in itself the Principles of all Existences confused and intermingled, light with darkness, the dry with the humid, heat with cold; from which, it after long ages taking the shape of an immense egg, issued the purest matter, or first substance, and the residue was divided into the four elements, from which proceeded heaven and earth and all things else. This grand Cosmogonic idea he taught in the Mysteries; and thus the Hierophant explained the meaning of the mystic egg, seen by the Initiates in the Sanctuary.

Thus entire Nature, in her primitive organization, was presented to him whom it was wished to instruct in her secrets and initiate in her mysteries; and Clemens of Alexandria might well say that initiation was a real physiology.

So Phanes, the Light-God, in the Mysteries of the New Orphics, emerged from the egg of chaos: and the Persians had the great egg of Ormuzd. And Sanchoniathon tells us that in the Phœnician theology, the matter of chaos took the form of an egg; and he adds: "Such are the lessons which the Son of Thabion, first Hierophant of the Phœnicians, turned into allegories, in which physics and astronomy intermingled, and which he taught to the other Hierophants, whose duty it was to preside at orgies and initiations; and who, seeking to excite the astonishment and admiration of mortals, faithfully transmitted these things to their successors and the Initiates."

In the Mysteries was also taught the division of the Universal Cause into an Active and a Passive cause; of which two, Osiris and Isis,—the heavens and the earth were symbols. These two First Causes, into which it was held that the great Universal First Cause at the beginning of things divided itself, were the two great Divinities, whose worship was, according to Varro, inculcated upon the Initiates at Samothrace. "As is taught," he says, "in the initiation into the Mysteries at Samothrace, Heaven and Earth are regarded as the two first Divinities. They are the potent Gods worshipped in that Island, and whose names are consecrated in the books of our Augurs. One of them is male and the other female; and they bear the same relation to each other as the soul does to the body, humidity to dryness." The Curetes, in Crete, had builded an altar to Heaven and to Earth; whose Mysteries they celebrated at Gnossus, in a cypress grove.

These two Divinities, the Active and Passive Principles of the Universe, were commonly symbolized by the generative parts of man and woman; to which, in remote ages, no idea of indecency was attached; the *Phallus* and *Cteis,* emblems of generation and production, and which, as such, appeared in the Mysteries. The Indian Lingam was the union of both, as were the boat and mast and the point within a circle: all of which expressed the same philosophical idea as to the Union of the two great Causes of Nature, which concur, one actively and the other passively, in the generation of all beings: which were symbolized by what we now term *Gemini,* the Twins, at that remote period when the Sun was in that Sign at the Vernal Equinox, and when they were Male and Female; and of which the Phallus was perhaps taken from the generative organ of the Bull, when about twenty-five hundred years before our era he opened that equinox, and became to the Ancient World the symbol of the creative and generative Power.

The Initiates at Eleusis commenced, Proclus says, by invoking the two great causes of nature, the Heavens and the Earth, on which in succession they fixed their eyes, addressing to each a prayer. And they deemed it their duty to do so, he adds, because they saw in them the Father and Mother of all generations. The concourse of these two agents of the Universe was termed in theological language a *marriage*. Tertullian, accusing the Valentinians of having borrowed these symbols from the Mysteries of Eleusis, yet admits that in those Mysteries they were explained in a manner consistent with decency, as representing the powers of nature. He was too little of a philosopher to comprehend the sublime esoteric meaning of these emblems, which will, if you advance, in other Degrees be unfolded to you.

The Christian Fathers contented themselves with reviling and ridiculing the use of these emblems. But as they in the earlier times created no indecent ideas, and were worn alike by the most innocent youths and virtuous women, it will be far wiser for us to seek to penetrate their meaning. Not only the Egyptians, says Diodorus Siculus, but every other people that consecrate this symbol (the Phallus), deem that they thereby do honor to the Active Force of the universal generation of all living things. For the same reason, as we learn from the geographer Ptolemy, it was revered among the Assyrians and Persians. Proclus remarks that in the distribution of the Zodiac among the twelve great Divinities, by ancient astrology, six signs were assigned to the male and six to the female principle.

There is another division of nature, which has in all ages struck all men, and which was not forgotten in the Mysteries; that of Light and Darkness, Day and Night, Good and Evil; which mingle with, and clash against, and pursue or are pursued by each other throughout the Universe. The Great Symbolic Egg distinctly reminded the Initiates of this great division of the world. Plutarch, treating of the dogma of a Providence, and of that of the two principles of Light and Darkness, which he regarded as the basis of the Ancient Theology, of the Orgies and the Mysteries, as well among the Greeks as the Barbarians,—a doctrine whose origin, according to him, is lost in the night of time,—cites, in support of his opinion, the famous Mystic Egg of the disciples of Zoroaster and the Initiates in the Mysteries of Mithras.

To the Initiates in the Mysteries of Eleusis was exhibited the spectacle of these two principles, in the successive scenes of Darkness and Light which passed before their eyes. To the profoundest darkness, accompanied with illusions and horrid phantoms, succeeded the most brilliant light, whose splendor blazed round the statue of the Goddess. The candidate, says Dion Chrysostomus, passed into a mysterious temple, of astonishing magnitude and beauty, where were exhibited to him many mystic scenes; where his ears were stunned with many voices; and where Darkness and Light successively passed before him. And Themistius in like manner describes the Initiate, when about to enter into that part of the sanctuary tenanted by the Goddess, as filled with fear and religious awe, wavering, uncertain in what direction to advance through the profound darkness that envelopes him. But when the Hierophant has opened the entrance to the inmost sanctuary, and removed the robe that hides the Goddess, he exhibits her to the Initiate, resplendent with divine light. The thick shadow and gloomy atmosphere which had environed the candidate vanish; he is filled with a vivid and glowing enthusiasm, that lifts his soul out of the profound dejection in which it was plunged; and the purest light succeeds to the thickest darkness.

In a fragment of the same writer, preserved by Stobæus, we learn that the Initiate, up to the moment when his initiation is to be consummated, is alarmed by every kind of sight: that astonishment and terror take his soul captive; he trembles; cold sweat flows from his body; until the moment when the Light is shown him,—a most astounding Light,—the brilliant scene of Elysium, where he sees charming meadows overarched by a clear sky, and festivals celebrated by dances; where he hears harmonious voices, and the majestic chants of the Hierophants; and views the sacred spectacles. Then, absolutely free, and enfranchised from the dominion of all ills, he mingles with the crowd of Initiates, and, crowned with flowers, celebrates with them the holy orgies, in the brilliant realms of ether, and the dwelling-place of Ormuzd.

In the Mysteries of Isis, the candidate first passed through the dark valley of the shadow of death; then into a place representing the elements or sublunary world, where the two principles clash and contend; and was finally admitted to a luminous region, where the sun, with his most brilliant light, put to rout the shades of night. Then he himself put on the costume of the Sun-God, or the Visible Source of Ethereal Light, in whose Mysteries he was initiated; and passed from the empire of darkness to that of light. After having set his feet on the threshold of the palace of Pluto, he ascended to the Empyrean, to the bosom of the Eternal Principle of Light of the Universe, from which all souls and intelligences emanate.

Plutarch admits that this theory of two Principles was the basis of all the Mysteries, and consecrated in the religious ceremonies and Mysteries of Greece. Osiris and Typhon, Ormuzd and Ahriman, Bacchus and the Titans and Giants, all represented these principles. Phanes, the luminous God that issued from the Sacred Egg, and Night, bore the sceptres in the Mysteries of the New Bacchus. Night and Day were two of the eight Gods adored in the Mysteries of Osiris. The sojourn of Proserpine and also of Adonis, during six months of each year in the upper world, abode of light, and six months in the lower or abode of darkness, allegorically represented the same division of the Universe.

The connection of the different initiations with the Equinoxes which separate the Empire of the Nights from that of the Days, and fix the moment when one of these principles begins to prevail over the other, shows that the Mysteries referred to the continual contest between the two principles of light and darkness, each alternately victor and vanquished. The very object proposed by them shows that their basis was the theory of the two principles and their relations with the soul. "We celebrate the august Mysteries of Ceres and Proserpine," says the Emperor Julian, "at the Autumnal Equinox, to obtain of the Gods that the soul may not experience the malignant action of the Power of Darkness that is then about to have sway and rule in Nature." Sallust the Philosopher makes almost the same remark as to the relations of the soul with the periodical march of light and darkness, during an annual revolution; and assures us that the mysterious festivals of Greece related to the same. And in all the explanations given by Macrobius of the Sacred Fables in regard to the Sun, adored under the names of Osiris, Horus, Adonis, Atys, Bacchus, etc., we invariably see that they refer to the theory of the two Principles, Light and Darkness, and the triumphs gained by one over the other. In April was celebrated the first triumph obtained by the light of day over the length of the nights; and the ceremonies of mourning and rejoicing had, Macrobius says, as their object, the vicissitudes of the annual administration of the world.

This brings us naturally to the tragic portion of these religious scenes, and to the allegorical history of the different adventures of the Principle, Light, victor and vanquished by turns, in the combats waged with Darkness during each annual period. Here we reach the most mysterious part of the ancient initiations, and that most interesting to the Mason who laments the death of his Grand Master Khir-Om. Over it Herodotus throws the august veil of mystery and silence. Speaking of the Temple of Minerva, or of that Isis who was styled the Mother of the Sun-God, and whose Mysteries were termed *Isiac,* at Sais, he speaks of a Tomb in the Temple, in the rear of the Chapel and against the wall; and says, "It is the tomb of a man, whose name respect requires me to conceal. Within the Temple were great obelisks of stone [*phalli*], and a circular lake paved with stones and revetted with a parapet. It seemed to me as large as that at Delos" [where the Mysteries of Apollo were celebrated]. "In this lake the Egyptians celebrate, during the night, what they style the Mysteries, in which are represented the sufferings of the God of whom I have spoken above." This God was Osiris, put to death by Typhon, and who descended to the Shades and was restored to life; of which he had spoken before.

We are reminded, by this passage, of the Tomb of Khir-Om, his death, and his rising from the grave, symbolical of restoration of life; and also of the brazen Sea in the Temple at Jerusalem. Herodotus adds: "I impose upon myself a profound silence in regard to these Mysteries, with most of which I am acquainted. As little will I speak of the initiations of Ceres, known among the Greeks as Thesmophoria. What I shall say will not violate the respect which I owe to religion."

Athenagoras quotes this passage to show that not only the Statue but the Tomb of Osiris was exhibited in Egypt, and a tragic representation of his sufferings; and remarks that the Egyptians had mourning ceremonies in honor of their Gods, whose deaths they lamented; and to whom they afterward sacrificed as having passed to a state of immortality.

It is, however, not difficult, combining the different rays of light that emanate from the different Sanctuaries, to learn the genius and the object of these secret ceremonies. We have hints, and not details.

We know that the Egyptians worshipped the Sun, under the name of Osiris. The misfortunes and tragical death of this God were an allegory relating to the Sun. Typhon, like Ahriman, represented Darkness. The sufferings and death of Osiris in the Mysteries of the Night were a mystic image of the phenomena of Nature, and the conflict of the two great Principles which share the empire of Nature, and most influenced our souls. The Sun is neither born, dies, nor is raised to life: and the recital of these events was but an allegory, veiling a higher truth.

Horus, son of Isis, and the same as Apollo or the Sun, also died and was restored again to life and to his mother; and the priests of Isis celebrated these great events by mourning and joyous festival succeeding each other.

In the Mysteries of Phœnicia, established in honor of Thammuz or Adoni, also the Sun, the spectacle of his death and resurrection was exhibited to the Initiates. As we learn from Meursius and Plutarch, a figure was exhibited representing the corpse of a young man. Flowers were strewed upon his body, the women mourned for him; a tomb was erected to him. And these feasts, as we learn from Plutarch and Ovid, passed into Greece.

In the Mysteries of Mithras, the Sun-God, in Asia Minor, Armenia and Persia, the death of that God was lamented, and his resurrection was celebrated with the most enthusiastic expressions of joy. A corpse, we learn from Julian Firmicus, was shown the Initiates, representing Mithras dead; and afterward his resurrection was announced; and they were then invited to rejoice that the dead God was restored to life, and had by means of his sufferings secured their salvation. Three months before, his birth had been celebrated, under the emblem of an infant, born on the 25th of December, or the eighth day before the Kalends of January.

In Greece, in the Mysteries of the same God, honored under the name of Bakchos, a representation was given of his death, slain by the Titans; of his descent into hell, his subsequent resurrection, and his return toward his Principle or the pure abode whence he had descended to unite himself with matter. In the islands of Chios and Tenedos, his death was represented by the sacrifice of a man, actually immolated.

The mutilation and sufferings of the same Sun-God, honored in Phrygia under the name of Atys, caused the tragic scenes that were, as we learn from Diodorus Siculus, represented annually in the Mysteries of Cybele, mother of the Gods. An image was borne there, representing the corpse of a young man, over whose tomb tears were shed, and to whom funeral honors were paid.

At Samothrace, in the Mysteries of the Cabiri or great Gods, a representation was given of the death of one of them. This name was given to the Sun, because the Ancient Astronomers gave the name of Gods Cabiri and of Samothrace to the two Gods in the Constellation Gemini; whom others term Apollo and Hercules, two names of the Sun. Athenion says that the young Cabirus so slain was the same as the Dionusos or Bakchos of the Greeks. The Pelasgi, ancient inhabitants of Greece, and who settled Samothrace, celebrated these Mysteries, whose origin is unknown: and they worshipped Castor and Pollux as patrons of navigation.

The tomb of Apollo was at Delphi, where his body was laid, after Python, the Polar Serpent that annually heralds the coming of autumn, cold, darkness, and winter, had slain him, and over whom the God triumphs, on the 25th of March, on his return to the lamb of the Vernal Equinox.

In Crete, Jupiter Ammon, or the Sun in Aries, painted with the attributes of that equinoctial sign, the Ram or Lamb;—that Ammon who, Martianus Copella says, is the same as Osiris, Adoni, Adonis, Atys, and the other Sun-Gods,—had also a tomb, and a religious initiation; one of the principal ceremonies of which consisted in clothing the Initiate with the skin of a white lamb. And in this we see the origin of the apron of white sheep-skin, used in Masonry.

All these deaths and resurrections, these funeral emblems, these anniversaries of mourning and joy, these cenotaphs raised in different places to the Sun-God, honored under different names, had but a single object, the allegorical narration of the events which happened here below to the Light of Nature, that sacred fire from which our souls were deemed to emanate, warring with Matter and the dark Principle resident therein, ever at variance with the Principle of Good and Light poured upon itself by the Supreme Divinity. All these Mysteries, says Clemens of Alexandria, displaying to us murders and tombs alone, all these religious tragedies, had a common basis, variously ornamented: and that basis was the fictitious death and resurrection of the Sun, Soul of the World, principle of life and movement in the Sublunary World, and source of our intelligences, which are but a portion of the Eternal Light blazing in that Star, their chief centre.

It was in the Sun that Souls, it was said, were purified: and to it they repaired. It was one of the gates of the soul, through which the theologians, says Porphyry, say that it re-ascends toward the home of Light and the Good. Wherefore, in the Mysteries of Eleusis, the Dadoukos (the first officer after the Hierophant, who represented the Grand Demiourgos or Maker of the Universe), who was posted in the interior of the Temple, and there received the candidates, represented the Sun.

It was also held that the vicissitudes experienced by the Father of Light had an influence on the destiny of souls; which, of the same substance as he, shared his fortunes. This we learn from the Emperor Julian and Sallust the Philosopher. They are afflicted when he suffers: they rejoice when he triumphs over the Power of Darkness which opposes his sway and hinders the happiness of Souls, to whom nothing is so terrible as darkness. The fruit of the sufferings of the God, father of light and Souls, slain by the Chief of the Powers of Darkness, and again restored to life, was received in the Mysteries. "His death works your Salvation;" said the High Priest of Mithras. That was the great secret of this religious tragedy, and its expected fruit;—the resurrection of a God, who, repossessing Himself of His dominion over Darkness, should associate with Him in His triumph those virtuous Souls that by their purity were worthy to share His glory; and that strove not against the divine force that drew them to Him, when He had thus conquered.

To the Initiate were also displayed the spectacles of the chief agents of the Universal Cause, and of the distribution of the world, in the detail of its parts arranged in most regular order. The Universe itself supplied man with the model of the first Temple reared to the Divinity. The arrangement of the Temple of Solomon, the symbolic ornaments which formed its chief decorations, and the dress of the High Priest,—all, as Clemens of Alexandria, Josephus and Philo state, had reference to the order of the world. Clemens informs us that the Temple contained many emblems of the Seasons, the Sun, the Moon, the planets, the constellations Ursa Major and Minor, the zodiac, the elements, and the other parts of the world.

Josephus, in his description of the High Priest's Vestments, protesting against the charge of impiety brought against the Hebrews by other nations, for contemning the Heathen Divinities, declares it false, because, in the construction of the Tabernacle, in the vestments of the Sacrificers, and in the Sacred vessels, the whole World was in some sort represented. Of the three parts, he says, into which the Temple was divided, two represent Earth and Sea, open to all men, and the third, Heaven, God's dwelling-place, reserved for Him alone. The twelve loaves of Shew-bread signify the twelve months of the year. The Candlestick represented the twelve signs through which the Seven Planets run their courses; and the seven lights, those planets; the veils, of four colors, the four elements; the tunic of the High Priest, the earth; the Hyacinth, nearly blue, the Heavens; the ephod, of four colors, the whole of nature; the gold, Light; the breast-plate, in the middle, this earth in the centre of the world; the two Sardonyxes, used as clasps, the Sun and Moon; and the twelve precious stones of the breast-plate arranged by threes, like the Seasons, the twelve months, and the twelve signs of the zodiac. Even the loaves were arranged in two groups of six, like the zodiacal signs above and below the Equator. Clemens, the learned Bishop of Alexandria, and Philo, adopt all these explanations.

Hermes calls the Zodiac, the Grent Tent,—Tabernaculum. In the Royal Arch Degree of the American Rite, the Tabernacle has four veils, of different colors, to each of which belongs a banner. The colors of the four are White, Blue, Crimson, and Purple, and the banners bear the images of the Bull, the Lion, the Man, and the Eagle, the Constellations answering 2500 years before our era to the Equinoctial and Solstitial points: to which belong four stars, Aldebarán, Regulus, Fomalhaut, and Antares. At each of these veils there are three words: and to each division of the Zodiac, belonging to each of these Stars, are three Signs. The four signs, Taurus, Leo, Scorpio, and Aquarius, were termed the *fixed* signs, and are appropriately assigned to the four veils.

So the Cherubim, according to Clemens and Philo, represented the two hemispheres; their wings, the rapid course of the firmament, and of time which revolves in the Zodiac. "For the Heavens fly;" says Philo, speaking of the wings of the Cherubim: which were winged representations of the Lion, the Bull, the Eagle, and the Man; of two of which, the human-headed, winged bulls and lions, so many have been found at Nimroud; adopted as beneficent symbols, when the Sun entered Taurus at the Vernal Equinox and Leo at the Summer Solstice: and when, also, he entered Scorpio, for which, on account of its malignant influences, Aquila, the eagle was substituted, at the autumnal equinox; and Aquarius (the water-bearer) at the Winter Solstice.

So, Clemens says, the candlestick with seven branches represented the seven planets, like which the seven branches were arranged and regulated, preserving that musical proportion and system of harmony of which the sun was the centre and connection. They were arranged, says Philo, by threes, like the planets above and those below the sun; between which two groups was the branch that represented him, the mediator or moderator of the celestial harmony. He is, in fact, the fourth in the musical scale, as Philo remarks, and Martianus Capella in his hymn to the Sun.

Near the candlestick were other emblems representing the heavens, earth, and the vegetative matter out of whose bosom the vapors arise. The whole temple was an abridged image of the world. There were candlesticks with four branches, symbols of the elements and the seasons; with twelve, symbols of the signs; and even with three hundred and sixty, the number of days in the year, without the supplementary days. Imitating the famous Temple of Tyre, where were the great columns consecrated to the winds and fire, the Tyrian artist placed two columns of bronze at the entrance of the porch of the temple. The hemispherical brazen sea, supported by four groups of bulls, of three each, looking to the four cardinal points of the compass, represented the bull of the Vernal Equinox, and at Tyre were consecrated to Astarte; to whom Hiram, Josephus says, had builded a temple, and who wore on her head a helmet bearing the image of a bull. And the throne of Solomon, with bulls adorning its arms, and supported on lions, like those of Horus in Egypt and of the Sun at Tyre; likewise referred to the Vernal Equinox and Summer Solstice.

Those who in Thrace adored the sun, under the name of Saba-Zeus, the Grecian Bakchos, builded to him, says Macrobius, a temple on Mount Zelmisso, its round form representing the world and the sun. A circular aperture in the roof admitted the light, and introduced the image of the sun into the body of the sanctuary, where he seemed to blaze as in the heights of Heaven, and to dissipate the darkness within that temple which was a representative symbol of the world. There the passion, death, and resurrection of Bakchos were represented.

So the Temple of Eleusis was lighted by a window in the roof. The sanctuary so lighted, Dion compares to the Universe, from which he says it differed in size alone; and in it the great lights of nature played a great part and were mystically represented. The images of the Sun, Moon, and Mercury were represented there, (the latter the same as Anubis who accompanied Isis); and they are still the three lights of a Masonic Lodge; except that for Mercury, the Master of the Lodge has been absurdly substituted.

Eusebius names as the principal Ministers in the Mysteries of Eleusis, first, the *Hierophant,* clothed with the attributes of the Grand Architect (Demiourgos) of the Universe. After him came the *Dadoukos,* or torch-bearer, representative of the Sun: then the altar-bearer, representing the Moon: and last, the *Hieroceryx,* bearing the caduceus, and representing Mercury. It was not permissible to reveal the different emblems and the mysterious pageantry of initiation to the Profane; and therefore we do not know the attributes, emblems, and ornaments of these and other officers; of which Apuleius and Pausanias dared not speak.

We know only that everything recounted there was marvellous; everything done there tended to astonish the Initiate: and that eyes and ears were equally astounded. The Hierophant, of lofty height, and noble features, with long hair, of a great age, grave and dignified, with a voice sweet and sonorous, sat upon a throne, clad in a long trailing robe; as the Motive-God of Nature was held to be enveloped in His work and hidden under a veil which no mortal can raise. Even His name was concealed, like that of the Demiourgos, whose name was ineffable.

The Dadoukos also wore a long robe, his hair long, and a bandeau on his forehead. Callias, when holding that office, fighting on the great day of Marathon, clothed with the insignia of his office, was taken by the Barbarians to be a King. The Dadoukos led the procession of the Initiates, and was charged with the purifications.

We do not know the functions of the *Epibomos* or assistant at the altar, who represented the moon. That planet was one of the two homes of souls, and one of the two great gates by which they descended and reascended. Mercury was charged with the conducting of souls through the two great gates; and in going from the sun to the moon they passed immediately by him. He admitted or rejected them as they were more or less pure, and therefore the Hieroceryx or Sacred Herald, who represented Mercury, was charged with the duty of excluding the Profane from the Mysteries.

The same officers are found in the procession of Initiates of Isis, described by Apuleius. All clad in robes of white linen, drawn tight across the breast, and close-fitting down to the very feet, came, first, one bearing a lamp in the shape of a boat; second, one carrying an altar; and third, one carrying a golden palm-tree and the caduceus. These are the same as the three officers at Eleusis, after the Hierophant. Then one carrying an open hand, and pouring milk on the ground from a golden vessel in the shape of a woman's breast. The hand was that of justice: and the milk alluded to the Galaxy or Milky Way, along which souls descended and remounted. Two others followed, one bearing a winnowing fan, and the other a water-vase; symbols of the purification of souls by air and water; and the third purification, by earth, was represented by an image of the animal that cultivates it, the cow or ox, borne by another officer.

Then followed a chest or ark, magnificently ornamented, containing an image of the organs of generation of Osiris, or perhaps of both sexes; emblems of the original generating and producing Powers. When Typhon, said the Egyptian fable, cut up the body of Osiris into pieces, he flung his genitals into the Nile, where a fish devoured them. Atys mutilated himself, as his Priests afterward did in imitation of him; and Adonis was in that part of his body wounded by the boar: all of which represented the loss by the Sun of his vivifying and generative power, when he reached the Autumnal Equinox (the Scorpion that on old monuments bites those parts of the Vernal Bull), and descended toward the region of darkness and Winter.

Then, says Apuleius, came "one who carried in his bosom an object that rejoiced the heart of the bearer, a venerable effigy of the Supreme Deity, neither bearing resemblance to man, cattle, bird, beast, or any living creature: an exquisite invention, venerable from the novel originality of the fashioning; a wonderful,

ineffable symbol of religious mysteries, to be looked upon in profound silence. Such as it was, its figure was that of a small urn
of burnished gold, hollowed very artistically, rounded at the bottom, and covered all over the outside with the wonderful hieroglyphics of the Egyptians. The spout was not elevated, but
extended laterally, projecting like a long rivulet; while on the
opposite side was the handle, which, with similar lateral extension, bore on its summit an asp, curling its body into folds, and
stretching upward, its wrinkled, scaly, swollen throat."

The salient basilisk, or royal ensign of the Pharaohs, often
occurs on the monuments—a serpent in folds, with his head raised
erect above the folds. The basilisk was the Phœnix of the ser-
pent-tribe; and the vase or urn was probably the vessel, shaped
like a cucumber, with a projecting spout, out of which, on the
monuments of Egypt, the priests are represented pouring streams
of the *cruz ansata* or Tau Cross, and of *sceptres,* over the kings.

In the Mysteries of Mithras, a sacred cave, representing the
whole arrangement of the world, was used for the reception of the
Initiates. Zoroaster, says Eubulus, first introduced this custom
of consecrating caves. They were also consecrated, in Crete, to
Jupiter; in Arcadia, to the Moon and Pan; and in the Island
of Naxos, to Bacchus. The Persians, in the cave where the Mysteries of Mithras were celebrated, fixed the seat of that God,
Father of Generation, or Demiourgos, near the equinoctial point
of Spring, with the Northern portion of the world on his right,
and the Southern on his left.

Mithras, says Porphyry, presided over the Equinoxes, seated on
a Bull, the symbolical animal of the Demiourgos, and bearing a
sword. The equinoxes were the gates through which souls passed
to and fro, between the hemisphere of light and that or darkness.
The milky way was also represented, passing near each of these
gates: and it was, in the old theology, termed the pathway of
souls. It is, according to Pythagoras, vast troops of souls that
form that luminous belt.

The route followed by souls, according to Porphyry, or rather
their progressive march in the world, lying through the fixed stars
and planets, the Mithriac cave not only displayed the zodiacal
and other constellations, and marked gates at the four equinoctial
and solstitial points of the zodiac, whereat souls enter into and
escape from the world of generations; and through which they

pass to and fro between the realms of light and darkness; but it represented the seven planetary spheres which they needs must traverse, in descending from the heaven of the fixed stars to the elements that envelop the earth; and seven gates were marked, one for each planet, through which they pass, in descending or returning.

We learn this from Celsus, in Origen; who says that the symbolical image of this passage among the Stars, used in the Mithriac Mysteries, was a ladder, reaching from earth to Heaven, divided into seven steps or stages, to each of which was a gate, and at the summit an eighth, that of the fixed stars. The first gate, says Celsus, was that of Saturn, and of lead, by the heavy nature whereof his dull slow progress was symbolized. The second, of tin, was that of Venus, symbolizing her soft splendor and easy flexibility. The third, of brass, was that of Jupiter, emblem of his solidity and dry nature. The fourth, of iron, was that of Mercury, expressing his indefatigable activity and sagacity. The fifth, of copper, was that of Mars, expressive of his inequalities and variable nature. The sixth, of silver, was that of the Moon: and the seventh, of gold, that of the Sun. This order is not the real order of these Planets; but a mysterious one, like that of the days of the Week consecrated to them, commencing with Saturday, and *retrograding* to Sunday. It was dictated, Celsus says, by certain harmonic relations, those of the fourth.

Thus there was an intimate connection between the Sacred Science of the Mysteries, and ancient astronomy and physics; and the grand spectacle of the Sanctuaries was that of the order of the Known Universe, or the spectacle of Nature itself, surrounding the soul of the Initiate, as it surrounded it when it first descended through the planetary gates, and by the equinoctal and solstitial doors, along the Milky Way, to be for the first time immured in its prison-house of matter. But the Mysteries also represented to the candidate, by sensible symbols, the invisible forces which move this visible Universe, and the virtues, qualities, and powers attached to matter, and which maintain the marvellous order observed therein. Of this Porphyry informs us.

The world, according to the philosophers of antiquity, was not a purely material and mechanical machine. A great Soul, diffused everywhere, vivified all the members of the immense body of the Universe; and an Intelligence, equally great, directed all its movements, and maintained the eternal harmony that resulted there-from. Thus the Unity of the Universe, represented by the symbolic egg, contained in itself two units, the Soul and the Intelligence, which pervaded all its parts: and they were to the Universe, considered as an animated and intelligent being, what intelligence and the soul of life are to the individuality of man.

The doctrine of the Unity of God, in this sense, was taught by Orpheus. Of this his hymn or palinode is a proof; fragments of which are quoted by many of the Fathers, as Justin, Tatian, Clemens of Alexandria, Cyril, and Theodoret, and the whole by Eusebius, quoting from Aristobulus. The doctrine of the LOGOS (word) or the Noos (intellect), his incarnation, death, resurrection or transfiguration; of his union with matter, his division in the visible world, which he pervades, his return to the original Unity, and the whole theory relative to the origin of the soul and its destiny, were taught in the Mysteries, of which they were the great object.

The Emperor Julian explains the Mysteries of Atys and Cybele by the same metaphysical principles, respecting the demiurgical Intelligence, its descent into matter, and its return to its origin: and extends this explanation to those of Ceres. And so likewise does Sallust the Philosopher, who admits in God a secondary intelligent Force, which descends into the generative matter to organize it. These mystical ideas naturally formed a part of the sacred doctrine and of the ceremonies of initiation, the object of which, Sallust remarks, was to unite man with the World and the Deity; and the final term of perfection whereof was, according to Clemens, the contemplation of nature, of real beings, and of causes. The definition of Sallus is correct. The Mysteries were practised as a means of perfecting the soul, of making it to know its own dignity, of reminding it of its noble origin and immortality, and consequently of its relations with the Universe and the Deity.

What was meant by *real* beings, was *invisible* beings, *genii*, the *faculties* or *powers* of nature; everything not a part of the *visible* world, which was called, by way of opposition, *apparent* existence. The theory of Genii, or Powers of Nature, and its Forces, personified, made part of the Sacred Science of initiation, and of that religious spectacle of different beings exhibited in the Sanctuary. It resulted from that belief in the providence and superintendence of the Gods, which was one of the primary bases of initiation. The administration of the Universe by Subaltern Genii, to whom it is confided, and by whom good and evil are dispensed in the world, was a consequence of this dogma, taught in the Mysteries of Mithras, where was shown that famous egg, shared between Ormuzd and Ahriman, each of whom commissioned twenty-four Genii to dispense the good and evil found therein; they being under twelve Superior Gods, six on the side of Light and Good, and six on that of Darkness and Evil.

This doctrine of the Genii, depositaries of the Universal Providence, was intimately connected with the Ancient Mysteries, and adopted in the sacrifices and initiations both of Greeks and Barbarians. Plutarch says that the Gods, by means of Genii, who are intermediates between them and men, draw near to mortals in the ceremonies of initiation, at which the Gods charge them to assist, and to distribute punishment and blessing. Thus not the Deity, but His ministers, or a Principle and Power of Evil, were deemed the authors of vice and sin and suffering: and thus the Genii or angels differed in character like men, some being good and some evil; some Celestial Gods, Archangels, Angels, and some Infernal Gods, Demons and fallen Angels.

At the head of the latter was their Chief, Typhon, Ahriman, or Shaitan, the Evil Principle; who, having wrought disorder in nature, brought troubles on men by land and sea, and caused the greatest ills, is at last punished for his crimes. It was these events and incidents, says Plutarch, which Isis desired to represent in the ceremonial of the Mysteries, established by her in memory of her sorrows and wanderings, whereof she exhibited an image and representation in her Sanctuaries, where also were afforded encouragements to piety and consolation in misfortune. The dogma of a Providence, he says, administering the Universe by means of intermediary Powers, who maintain the connection of man with the Divinity, was consecrated in the Mysteries of the Egyptians, Phrygians, and Thracians, of the Magi and the Disciples of Zoroaster; as is plain by their initiations, in which mournful and funereal ceremonies mingled. It was an essential part of the lessons given the Initiates, to teach them the relations of their own souls with Universal Nature, the greatest lessons of all, meant to dignify man in his own eyes, and teach him his place in the Universe of things.

Thus the whole system of the Universe was displayed in all its parts to the eyes of the Initiate; and the symbolic cave which represented it was adorned and clothed with all the attributes of that Universe. To this world so organized, endowed with a double force, active and passive, divided between light and darkness, moved by a living and intelligent Force, governed by Genii or Angels who preside over its different parts, and whose nature and character are more lofty or low in proportion as they possess a greater or less portion of dark matter,—to this world descends the soul, emanation of the ethereal fire, and exiled from the luminous region above the world. It enters into this dark matter, wherein the hostile Principles, each seconded by his troops of Genii, are ever in conflict, there to submit to one or more organizations in the body which is its prison, until it shall at last return to its place of origin, its true native country, from which during this life it is an exile.

But one thing remained,—to represent its return, through the constellations and planetary spheres, to its original home. The celestial fire, the philosophers said, soul of the world and of fire, an universal principle, circulating above the Heavens, in a region infinitely pure and wholly luminous, itself pure, simple, and unmixed, is above the world by its specific lightness. If any part of it (say a human soul) descends, it acts against its nature in doing so, urged by an inconsiderate desire of the intelligence, a perfidious love for matter which causes it to descend, to know what passes here below, where good and evil are in conflict. The Soul, a simple substance, when unconnected with matter, a ray or particle of the Divine Fire, whose home is in Heaven, ever turns toward that home, while united with the body, and struggles to return thither.

Teaching this, the Mysteries strove to recall man to his divine origin, and point out to him the means of returning thither. The great science acquired in the Mysteries was knowledge of man's self, of the nobleness of his origin, the grandeur of his destiny, and his superiority over the animals, which can never acquire this knowledge, and whom he resembles so long as he does not reflect upon his existence and sound the depths of his own nature.

By doing and suffering, by virtue and piety and good deeds, the soul was enabled at length to free itself from the body, and ascend along the path of the Milky Way, by the gate of Capricorn and by the seven spheres, to the place whence by many gradations and successive lapses and enthralments it had descended. And thus the theory of the spheres, and of the signs and intelligences which preside there, and the whole system of astronomy, were connected with that of the soul and its destiny; and so were taught in the Mysteries, in which were developed the great principles of physics and metaphysics as to the origin of the soul, its condition here below, its destination, and its future fate.

The Greeks fix the date of the establishment of the Mysteries of Eleusis at the year 1423 B. C., during the reign of Erechtheus at Athens. According to some authors, they were instituted by Ceres herself; and according to others, by that Monarch, who brought them from Egypt, where, according to Diodorus of Sicily, he was born. Another tradition was, that Orpheus introduced them into Greece, together with the Dionisiac ceremonies, copying the latter from the Mysteries of Osiris, and the former from those of Isis.

Nor was it at Athens only, that the worship and Mysteries of Isis, metamorphosed into Ceres, were established. The Bœotians worshipped the Great or Cabiric Ceres, in the recesses of a sacred grove, into which none but Initiates could enter; and the ceremonies there observed, and the sacred traditions of their Mysteries, were connected with those of the Cabiri in Samothrace.

So in Argos, Phocis, Arcadia, Achaia, Messenia, Corinth, and many other parts of Greece, the Mysteries were practised, revealing everywhere their Egyptian origin and everywhere having the same general features; but those of Eleusis, in Attica, Pausanius informs us, had been regarded by the Greeks, from the earliest times, as being as far superior to all the others, as the Gods are to mere Heroes.

Similar to these were the Mysteries of Bona Dea, the Good Goddess, whose name, say Cicero and Plutarch, it was not permitted to any man to know, celebrated at Rome from the earliest times of that city. It was these Mysteries, practised by women alone, the secrecy of which was impiously violated by Clodius. They were held at the Kalends of May; and, according to Plutarch, much of the ceremonial greatly resembled that of the Mysteries of Bakchos.

The Mysteries of Venus and Adonis belonged principally to Syria and Phœnicia, whence they passed into Greece and Sicily. Venus or Astarte was the Great Female Deity of the Phœnicians, as Hercules, Melkarth or Adoni was their Chief God. Adoni, called by the Greeks Adonis, was the lover of Venus. Slain by a wound in the thigh inflicted by a wild boar in the chase, the flower called anemone sprang from his blood. Venus received the corpse and obtained from Jupiter the boon that her lover should thereafter pass six months of each year with her, and the other six in the Shades with Proserpine; an allegorical description of the alternate residence of the Sun in the two hemispheres. In these Mysteries his death was represented and mourned, and after this maceration and mourning were concluded, his resurrection and ascent to Heaven were announced.

Ezekiel speaks of the festivals of Adonis under the name of those of Thammuz, an Assyrian Deity, whom every year the women mourned, seated at the doors of their dwellings. These Mysteries, like the others, were celebrated in the Spring, at the Vernal Equinox, when he was restored to life; at which time, when they were instituted, the Sun (ADON, Lord, or Master) was in the Sign Taurus, the domicile of Venus. He was represented with horns, and the hymn of Orpheus in his honor styles him "the two-horned God;" as in Argos Bakchos was represented with the feet of a bull.

Plutarch says that Adonis and Bakchos were regarded as one and the same Deity; and that this opinion was founded on the great similarity in very many respects between the Mysteries of these two Gods.

The Mysteries of Bakchos were known as the Sabazian, Orphic, and Dionysiac Festivals. They went back to the remotest antiquity among the Greeks, and were attributed by some to Bakchos himself, and by others to Orpheus. The resemblance in ceremonial between the observances established in honor of Osiris in Egypt, and those in honor of Bakchos in Greece, the mythological traditions of the two Gods, and the symbols used in the festivals of each, amply prove their identity. Neither the name of Bakchos, nor the word *orgies* applied to his feasts, nor the sacred words used in his Mysteries, are Greek, but of foreign origin. Bakchos was an Oriental Deity, worshipped in the East, and his orgies celebrated there, long before the Greeks adopted them. In the earliest times he was worshipped in India, Arabia, and Bactria.

He was honored in Greece with public festivals, and in simple or complicated Mysteries, varying in ceremonial in various places, as was natural, because his worship had come thither from different countries and at different periods. The people who celebrated the complicated Mysteries were ignorant of the meaning of many words which they used, and of many emblems which they revered. In the Sabazian Feasts, for example [from Saba-Zeus, an oriental name of this Deity], the words EVOI, SABOI, were used, which are in nowise Greek; and a serpent of gold was thrown into the bosom of the Initiate, in allusion to the fable that Jupiter had, in the form of a serpent, had connection with Proserpina, and begotten Bakchos, the bull; whence the enigmatical saying, repeated to the Initiates, that a bull engendered a dragon or serpent, and the serpent in turn engendered the bull, who became Bakchos: the meaning of which was, that the bull [Taurus, which then opened the Vernal Equinox, and the Sun in which Sign, figuratively represented by the Sign itself, was Bakchos, Dionusos, Saba-Zeus, Osiris, etc.], and the Serpent, another constellation, occupied such relative positions in the Heavens, that when one rose the other set, and *vice versa*.

The serpent was a familiar symbol in the Mysteries of Bakchos. The Initiates grasped them with their hands, as Orphiucus does on the celestial globe, and the Orpheo-telestes, or purifier of candidates did the same, crying, as Demosthenes taunted Æschines with doing in public at the head of the women whom his mother was to imitate, EVOI, SABOI, HYES ATTÊ, ATTÊ, HYES!

The Initiates in these Mysteries had preserved the ritual and ceremonies that accorded with the simplicity of the earliest ages, and the manners of the first men. The rules of Pythagoras were followed there. Like the Egyptians, who held wool unclean, they buried no Initiate in woolen garments. They abstained from bloody sacrifices; and lived on fruits or vegetables or inanimate things. They imitated the life of the contemplative Sects of the Orient; thus approximating to the tranquility of the first men, who lived exempt from trouble and crimes in the bosom of a profound peace. One of the most precious advantages promised by their initiation was, to put a man in communion with the Gods, by purifying his soul of all the passions that interfere with that enjoyment, and dim the rays of divine light that are communicated to every soul capable of receiving them, and that imitate their purity. One of the degrees of initiation was the state of inspiration to which the adepts were claimed to attain. The Initiates in the Mysteries of the Lamb, at Pepuza, in Phrygia, professed to be inspired, and prophesied; and it was claimed that the soul, by means of these religious ceremonies, purified of all stain, could see the Gods in this life, and certainly, in all cases, after death.

The sacred gates of the Temple, where the ceremonies of initiation were performed, were opened but once in each year, and no stranger was ever allowed to enter it. Night threw her veil over these august Mysteries, which could be revealed to no one. There the sufferings of Bakchos were represented, who, like Osiris, died, descended to hell and rose to life again; and raw flesh was distributed to the Initiates, which each ate, in memory of the death of the Deity, torn in pieces by the Titans.

These Mysteries also were celebrated at the Vernal Equinox; and the emblem of generation, to express the active energy and generative power of the Divinity, was a principal symbol. The Initiates wore garlands and crowns of myrtle and laurel.

In these Mysteries, the aspirant was kept in terror and darkness to perform the three days and nights; and was then made Αφα νισμος, or ceremony representing the death of Bakchos, the same mythological personage with Osiris. This was effected by confining him in a close cell, that he might seriously reflect, in solitude and darkness, on the business he was engaged in: and his mind be prepared for the reception of the sublime and mysterious truths of primitive revelation and philosophy. This was a symbolic death; the deliverance from it, regeneration; after which he was called διφυης or twin-born. While confined in the cell, the pursuit of Typhon after the mangled body of Osiris, and the search of Rhea or Isis for the same, were enacted in his hearing; the initiated crying aloud the names of that Deity derived from the Sanscrit. Then it was announced that the body was found; and the aspirant was liberated amid shouts of joy and exultation.

Then he passed through a representation of Hell and Elysium. "Then," said an ancient writer, "they are entertained with hymns and dances, with the sublime doctrines of sacred knowledge, and with wonderful and holy visions. And now become perfect and initiated, they are FREE, and no longer under restraint; but, crowned and triumphant, they walk up and down the regions of the blessed, converse with pure and holy men, and celebrate the sacred Mysteries at pleasure." They were taught the nature and objects of the Mysteries, and the means of making themselves known, and received the name of *Epopts;* were fully instructed in the nature and attributes of the Divinity, and the doctrine of a future state; and made acquainted with the unity and attributes of the Grand Architect of the Universe, and the true meaning of the fables in regard to the Gods of Paganism: the great Truth being often proclaimed, that "Zeus is the primitive Source of all things; there is ONE God; ONE power, and ONE rule over all." And after full explanation of the many symbols and emblems that surrounded them, they were dismissed with the barbarous words Κογξ and Ομπαξ, corruptions of the Sanscrit words, *Kanska Aom Pakscha;* meaning, *object of our wishes, God, Silence,* or *Worship the Deity in Silence.*

Among the emblems used was the rod of Bakchos; which once, it was said, he cast on the ground, and it became a serpent; and at another time he struck the rivers Orontes and Hydaspes with it, and the waters receded and he passed over dry-shod. Water was obtained, during the ceremonies, by striking a rock with it. The Bakchæ crowned their heads with serpents, carried them in vases and baskets, and at the Ευρησις, or finding, of the body of Osiris, cast one, alive, into the aspirant's bosom.

The Mysteries of Atys in Phrygia, and those of Cybele his mistress, like their worship, much resembled those of Adonis and Bakchos, Osiris and Isis. Their Asiatic origin is universally admitted, and was with great plausibility claimed by Phrygia, which contested the palm of antiquity with Egypt. They, more than any other people, mingled allegory with their religious worship, and were great inventors of fables; and their sacred traditions as to Cybele and Atys, whom all admit to be Phrygian Gods, were very various. In all, as we learn from Julius Firmicus, they represented by allegory the phenomena of nature, and the succession of physical facts, under the veil of a marvellous history.

Their feasts occurred at the equinoxes, commencing with lamentation, mourning, groans, and pitiful cries for the death of Atys; and ending with rejoicings at his restoration to life.

We shall not recite the different versions of the legend of Atys and Cybele, given by Julius Firmicus, Diodorus, Arnobius, Lactantius, Servius, Saint Augustine, and Pausanias. It is enough to say that it is in substance this: that Cybele, a Phrygian Princess, who invented musical instruments and dances, was enamored of Atys, a youth; that either he in a fit of frenzy mutilated himself or was mutilated by her in a paroxysm of jealousy; that he died,

and afterward, like Adonis, was restored to life. It is the Phœnician fiction as to the Sun-God, expressed in other terms, under
other forms, and with other names.

Cybele was worshipped in Syria, under the name of Rhea.
Lucian says that the Lydian Atys there established her worship
and built her temple. The name of Rhea is also found in the
ancient cosmogony of the Phœnicians by Sanchoniathon. It was
Atys the Lydian, says Lucian, who, having been mutilated, first
established the Mysteries of Rhea, and taught the Phrygians, the
Lydians, and the people of Samothrace to celebrate them. Rhea,
like Cybele, was represented drawn by lions, bearing a drum, and
crowned with flowers. According to Varro, Cybele represented
the earth. She partook of the characteristics of Minerva, Venus,
the Moon, Diana, Nemesis, and the Furies; was clad in precious
stones; and her High Priest wore a robe of purple and a tiara of
gold.

The Grand Feast of the Syrian Goddess, like that of the Mother
of the Gods at Rome, was celebrated at the Vernal Equinox.
Precisely at that equinox the Mysteries of Atys were celebrated,
in which the Initiates were taught to expect the rewards of a
future life, and the flight of Atys from the jealous fury of Cybele
was described, his concealment in the mountains and in a cave,
and his self-mutilation in a fit of delirium; in which act his priests
imitated him. The feast of the passion of Atys continued three
days; the first of which was passed in mourning and tears; to
which afterward clamorous rejoicings succeeded; by which, Macrobius says, the Sun was adored under the name of Atys. The
ceremonies were all allegorical, some of which, according to the
Emperor Julian, could be explained, but more remained covered
with the veil of mystery. Thus it is that symbols outlast their
explanations, as many have done in Masonry, and ignorance and
rashness substitute new ones.

In another legend, given by Pausanias, Atys dies, wounded like
Adonis by a wild boar in the organs of generation; a mutilation
with which all the legends ended. The pine-tree under which he
was said to have died, was sacred to him; and was found upon
many monuments, with a bull and a ram near it; one the sign of
exaltation of the Sun, and the other of that of the Moon.

The worship of the Sun under the name of Mithras belonged to
Persia, whence that name came, as did the erudite symbols of that

worship. The Persians, adorers of Fire, regarded the Sun as the most brilliant abode of the fecundating energy of that element, which gives life to the earth, and circulates in every part of the Universe, of which it is, as it were, the soul. This worship passed from Persia into Armenia, Cappadocia, and Cilicia, long before it was known at Rome. The Mysteries of Mithras flourished more than any others in the imperial city. The worship of Mithras commenced to prevail there under Trajan. Hadrian prohibited these Mysteries, on account of the cruel scenes represented in their ceremonial: for human victims were immolated therein, and the events of futurity looked for in their palpitating entrails. They reappeared in greater splendor than ever under Commodus, who with his own hand sacrificed a victim to Mithras: and they were still more practised under Constantine and his successors, when the Priests of Mithras were found everywhere in the Roman Empire, and the monuments of his worship appeared even in Britain.

Caves were consecrated to Mithras, in which were collected a multitude of astronomical emblems; and cruel tests were required of the Initiates.

The Persians built no temples; but worshipped upon the summits of hills, in enclosures of unhewn stones. They abominated images, and made the Sun and Fire emblems of the Deity. The Jews borrowed this from them, and represented God as appearing to Abraham in a flame of fire, and to Moses as a fire at Horeb and on Sinai.

With the Persians, Mithras, typified in the Sun, was the invisible Deity, the Parent of the Universe, the Mediator. In Zoroaster's cave of initiation, the Sun and Planets were represented over-head, in gems and gold, as also was the Zodiac. The Sun appeared emerging from the back of Taurus. Three great pillars, Eternity, Fecundity, and Authority, supported the roof; and the whole was an emblem of the Universe.

Zoroaster, like Moses, claimed to have conversed face to face, as man with man, with the Deity; and to have received from Him a system of pure worship, to be communicated only to the virtuous, and those who would devote themselves to the study of Philosophy. His fame spread over the world, and pupils came to him from every country. Even Pythagoras was his scholar.

After his novitiate, the candidate entered the cavern of initiation, and was received on the point of a sword presented to his naked left breast, by which he was slightly wounded. Being crowned with olive, anointed with balsam of benzoin, and otherwise prepared, he was purified with fire and water, and went through seven stages of initiation. The symbol of these stages was a high ladder with seven rounds or steps. In them, he went through many fearful trials, in which darkness displayed a principal part. He saw a representation of the wicked in Hades; and finally emerged from darkness into light. Received in a place representing Elysium, in the brilliant assembly of the initiated, where the Archimagus presided, robed in blue, he assumed the obligations of secrecy, and was entrusted with the Sacred Words, of which the Ineffable Name of God was the chief.

Then all the incidents of his initiation were explained to him: he was taught that these ceremonies brought him nearer the Deity; and that he should adore the consecrated Fire, the gift of that Deity and His visible residence. He was taught the sacred characters known only to the initiated; and instructed in regard to the creation of the world, and the true philosophical meaning of the vulgar mythology; and especially of the legend of Ormuzd and Ahriman, and the symbolic meaning of the six Amshaspands created by the former: *Bahman,* the Lord of Light; *Ardibehest,* the Genius of Fire; *Shariver,* the Lord of Splendor and Metals; *Stapandomad,* the Source of Fruitfulness; *Khordad,* the Genius of Water and Time; and *Amerdad,* the protector of the Vegetable World, and the prime cause of growth. And finally he was taught the true nature of the Supreme Being, Creator of Ormuzd and Ahriman, the Absolute First Cause, styled ZERUANE AKHERENE.

In the Mithriac initiation were several Degrees. The first, Tertullian says, was that of Soldier of Mithras. The ceremony of reception consisted in presenting the candidate a crown, supported by a sword. It was placed near his head, and he repelled it, saying, "Mithras is my crown." Then he was declared the soldier of Mithras, and had the right to call the other Initiates fellow-soldiers or companions in arms. Hence the title *Companions* in the Royal Arch Degree of the American Rite.

Then he passed, Porphyry says, through the Degree of the Lion, —the constellation Leo, domicile of the Sun and symbol of Mithras, found on his monuments. These ceremonies were termed at Rome Leontic and Heliac; and *Coracia* or *Hiero-Coracia,* of the Raven, a bird consecrated to the Sun, and a sign placed in the

Heavens below the Lion, with the Hydra, and also appearing on the Mithriac monuments.

Thence he passed to a higher Degree, where the Initiates were called *Perses* and children of the Sun. Above them were the *Fathers,* whose chief or Patriarch was styled Father of Fathers, or *Pater Patratus.* The Initiates also bore the title of *Eagles* and *Hawks,* birds consecrated to the Sun in Egypt, the former sacred to the God Mendes, and the latter the emblem of the Sun and Royalty.

The little island of Samothrace was long the depositary of certain august Mysteries, and many went thither from all parts of Greece to be initiated. It was said to have been settled by the ancient Pelasgi, early Asiatic colonists in Greece. The Gods adored in the Mysteries of this island were termed CABIRI, an oriental word, from *Cabar,* great. Varro calls the Gods of Samothrace, *Potent Gods.* In Arabic, Venus is called *Cabar.* Varro says that the Great Deities whose Mysteries were practised there, were Heaven and Earth. These were but symbols of the Active and Passive Powers or Principles of universal generation. The two Twins, Castor and Pollux, or the Dioscuri, were also called the Gods of Samothrace; and the Scholiast of Apollonius, citing Mnaseas, gives the names of Ceres, Proserpine, Pluto, and Mercury, as the four Cabiric Divinities worshipped at Samothrace, as Axieros, Axiocersa, Axiocersus, and Casmillus. Mercury was, there as everywhere, the minister and messenger of the Gods; and the young servitors of the altars and the children employed in the Temples were called Mercuries or Casmilli, as they were in Tuscany, by the Etrusci and Pelasgi, who worshipped the Great Gods.

Tarquin the Etruscan was an Initiate of the Mysteries of Samothrace; and Etruria had its Cabiri as Samothrace had. For the worship of the Cabiri spread from that island into Etruria, Phrygia, and Asia Minor: and it probably came from Phœnicia into Samothrace: for the Cabiri are mentioned by Sanchoniathon; and the word *Cabar* belongs to the Hebrew, Phœnician, and Arabic languages.

The Dioscuri, tutelary Deities of Navigation, with Venus, were invoked in the Mysteries of Samothrace. The constellation Auriga, or Phaëton, was also honored there with imposing ceremonies. Upon the Argonautic expedition, Orpheus, an Initiate of these

Mysteries, a storm arising, counselled his companions to put into Samothrace. They did so, the storm ceased, and they were initiated into the Mysteries there, and sailed again with the assurance of a fortunate voyage, under the auspices of the Dioscuri, patrons of sailors and navigation.

But much more than that was promised the Initiates. The Hierophants of Samothrace made something infinitely greater to be the object of their initiations; to wit, the consecration of men to the Deity, by pledging them to virtue; and the assurance of those rewards which the justice of the Gods reserves for Initiates after death. This, above all else, made these ceremonies august, and inspired everywhere so great a respect for them, and so great a desire to be admitted to them. That originally caused the island to be styled *Sacred*. It was respected by all nations. The Romans, when masters of the world, left it its liberty and laws. It was an asylum for the unfortunate, and a sanctuary inviolable. There men were absolved of the crime of homicide, if not committed in a temple.

Children of tender age were initiated there, and invested with the sacred robe, the purple cincture, and the crown of olive, and seated upon a throne, like other Initiates. In the ceremonies was represented the death of the youngest of the Cabiri, slain by his brothers, who fled into Etruria, carrying with them the chest or ark that contained his genitals: and there the Phallus and the sacred ark were adored. Herodotus says that the Samothracian Initiates understood the object and origin of this reverence paid the Phallus, and why it was exhibited in the Mysteries. Clemens of Alexandria says that the Cabiri taught the Tuscans to revere it. It was consecrated at Heliopolis in Syria, where the Mysteries of a Divinity having many points of resemblance with Atys and Cybele were represented. The Pelasgi connected it with Mercury; and it appears on the monuments of Mithras; always and everywhere a symbol of the life-giving power of the Sun at the Vernal Equinox.

In the Indian Mysteries, as the candidate made his three circuits, he paused each time he reached the South, and said, "I copy the example of the Sun, and follow his beneficent course." Blue Masonry has retained the Circuits, but has utterly lost the explanation; which is, that in the Mysteries the candidate invariably represented the Sun, descending Southward toward the reign of the Evil Principle, Ahriman, Siba, or Typhon (darkness and winter) ; there figuratively to be slain, and after a few days to rise again from the dead, and commence to ascend to the Northward.

Then the death of Sita was bewailed; or that of Cama, slain by Iswara, and committed to the waves on a chest, like Osiris and Bacchus; during which the candidate was terrified by phantoms and horrid noises.

Then he was made to personify Vishnu, and perform his avatars, or labors. In the first two he was taught in allegories the legend of the Deluge: in the first he took three steps at right angles, representing the three huge steps taken by Vishnu in that avatar; and hence the three steps in the Master's Degree ending at right angles.

The nine avatars finished, he was taught the necessity of faith, as superior to sacrifices, acts of charity, or mortifications of the flesh. Then he was admonished against five crimes, and took a solemn obligation never to commit them. He was then introduced into a representation of Paradise; the Company of the Members of the Order, magnificently arrayed, and the Altar with a fire blazing upon it, as an emblem of the Deity.

Then a new name was given him, and he was invested in a white robe and tiara, and received the signs, tokens, and lectures. A cross was marked on his forehead, and an inverted level, or the Tau Cross, on his breast. He received the sacred cord, and divers amulets or talismans; and was then invested with the sacred Word or Sublime Name, known only to the initiated, the Triliteral A. U. M.

Then the multitude of emblems was explained to the candidate; the arcana of science hidden under them, and the different virtues of which the mythological figures were mere personifications. And he thus learned the meaning of those symbols, which, to the uninitiated, were but a maze of unintelligible figures.

The third Degree was a life of seclusion, after the Initiate's children were capable of providing for themselves; passed in the forest, in the practice of prayers and ablutions, and living only on vegetables. He was then said to be born again.

The fourth was absolute renunciation of the world, self-contemplation and self-torture; by which Perfection was thought to be attained, and the soul merged in the Deity.

In the second Degree, the Initiate was taught the Unity of the

Godhead, the happiness of the patriarchs, the destruction by the Deluge, the depravity of the heart, and the necessity of a mediator, the instability of life, the final destruction of all created things, and the restoration of the world in a more perfect form. They inculcated the Eternity of the Soul, explained the meaning of the doctrine of the Metempsychosis, and held the doctrine of a state of future rewards and punishments: and they also earnestly urged that sins could only be atoned for by repentance, reformation, and voluntary penance; and not by mere ceremonies and sacrifices.

The Mysteries among the Chinese and Japanese came from India, and were founded on the same principles and with similar rites. The word given to the new Initiate was O-MI-TO Fo, in which we recognize the original name A. U. M., coupled at a much later time with that of Fo, the Indian Buddha, to show that he was the Great Deity Himself.

The equilateral triangle was one of their symbols; and so was the mystical **Y**; both alluding to the Triune God, and the latter being the ineffable name of the Deity. A ring supported by two serpents was emblematical of the world, protected by the power and wisdom of the Creator; and that is the origin of the two parallel lines (into which time has changed the two serpents), that support the circle in our Lodges.

Among the Japanese, the term of probation for the highest Degree was twenty years.

The main features of the Druidical Mysteries resembled those of the Orient.

The ceremonies commenced with a hymn to the sun. The candidates were arranged in ranks of *threes, fives,* and *sevens,* according to their qualifications; and conducted nine times around the Sanctuary, from East to West. The candidate underwent many trials, one of which had direct reference to the legend of Osiris. He was placed in a boat, and sent out to sea alone, having to rely on his own skill and presence of mind to reach the opposite shore in safety. The death of HU was represented in his hearing, with every external mark of sorrow, while he was in utter darkness. He met with many obstacles, had to prove his courage, and expose his life against armed enemies; represented various animals, and at last, attaining the permanent light, he was instructed by the Arch-Druid in regard to the Mysteries, and in the morality of the

Order, incited to act bravely in war, taught the great truths of
the immortality of the soul and a future state, solemnly enjoined
not to neglect the worship of the Deity, nor the practice of rigid
morality; and to avoid sloth, contention, and folly.

The aspirant attained only the exoteric knowledge in the first
two Degrees. The third was attained only by a few, and they persons of rank and consequence, and after long purification, and
study of all the arts and sciences known to the Druids, in solitude,
for nine months. This was the symbolical death and burial of
these Mysteries.

The dangerous voyage upon the actual open sea, in a small boat
covered with a skin, on the evening of the 29th of April, was the
last trial, and closing scene, of initiation. If he declined this
trial, he was dismissed with contempt. If he made it and succeeded, he was termed thrice-born, was eligible to all the dignities
of the State, and received complete instruction in the philosophical and religious doctrines of the Druids.

The Greeks also styled the Εποπτης, Τριγονος, thrice-born;
and in India perfection was assigned to the Yogee who had accomplished many births.

The general features of the initiations among the Goths were
the same as in all the Mysteries. A long probation, of fasting and
mortification, circular processions, representing the march of the
celestial bodies, many fearful tests and trials, a descent into the
infernal regions, the killing of the God *Balder* by the Evil Principle, *Lok,* the placing of his body in a boat and sending it abroad
upon the waters; and, in short, the Eastern Legend, under different names, and with some variations.

The Egyptian Anubis appeared there, as the dog guarding the
gates of death. The candidate was immured in the representation of a tomb; and when released, goes in search of the body of
Balder, and finds him, at length, restored to life, and seated upon
a throne. He was obligated upon a naked sword (as is still the
custom in the *Rit Moderne*), and *sealed* his obligation by drinking mead *out of a human skull.*

Then all the ancient primitive truths were made known to him,
so far as they had survived the assaults of time: and he was informed as to the generation of the Gods, the creation of the
world, the deluge, and the resurrection, of which that of Balder
was a type.

He was marked with the sign of the cross, and a ring was given to him as a symbol of the Divine Protection; and also as an emblem of Perfection; from which comes the custom of giving a ring to the Aspirant in the 14th Degree.

The point within a Circle, and the Cube, emblem of Odin, were explained to him; and lastly, the nature of the Supreme God, "the author of everything that existeth, the Eternal, the Ancient, the Living and Awful Being, the Searcher into concealed things, the Being that never changeth;" with whom Odin the Conqueror was by the vulgar confounded: and the Triune God of the Indians was reproduced, as ODIN, the Almighty FATHER, FREA, (*Rhea* or *Phre*), his wife (emblem of universal *matter*), and *Thor* his son (the Mediator). Here we recognize *Osiris, Isis,* and *Hor* or *Horus.* Around the head of Thor, as if to show his eastern origin, twelve stars were arranged in a circle.

He was also taught the ultimate destruction of the world, and the rising of a new one, in which the brave and virtuous shall enjoy everlasting happiness and delight: as the means of securing which happy fortune, he was taught to practise the strictest morality and virtue.

The Initiate was prepared to receive the great lessons of all the Mysteries, by long trials, or by abstinence and chastity. For many days he was required to fast and be continent, and to drink liquids calculated to diminish his passions and keep him chaste.

Ablutions were also required, symbolical of the purity necessary to enable the soul to escape from its bondage in matter. Sacred baths and preparatory baptisms were used, lustrations, immersions, lustral sprinklings, and purifications of every kind. At Athens they bathed in the Ilissus, which thence became a sacred river; and before entering the Temple of Eleusis, all were required to wash their hands in a vase of lustral water placed near the entrance. Clean hands and a pure heart were required of the candidates. Apuleius bathed seven times in the sea, symbolical of the Seven Spheres through which the Soul must reascend: and the Hindus must bathe in the sacred river Ganges.

Clemens of Alexandria cites a passage of Menander, who speaks of a purification by sprinkling three times with salt and water. Sulphur, resin, and the laurel also served for purification, as did air, earth, water, and fire. The Initiates at Heliopolis, in Syria, says Lucian, sacrificed the sacred lamb, symbol of Aries, then the sign of the Vernal Equinox; ate his flesh, as the Israelites did at

the Passover; and then touched his head and feet to theirs, and
knelt upon the fleece. Then they bathed in warm water, drank of
the same, and slept upon the ground.

There was a distinction between the lesser and greater Mysteries. One must have been for some years admitted to the former,
before he could receive the latter, which were but a preparation
for them, the Vestibule of the Temple, of which those of Eleusis
were the Sanctuary. There, in the lesser Mysteries, they were
prepared to receive the holy truths taught in the greater. The
Initiates in the lesser were called simply *Mystes,* or Initiates; but
those in the greater, *Epoptes,* or Seers. An ancient poet says that
the former were an imperfect shadow of the latter, as sleep is of
Death. After admission to the former, the Initiate was taught
lessons of morality, and the rudiments of the sacred science, the
most sublime and secret part of which was reserved for the
Epopt, who saw the Truth in its nakedness, while the Mystes only
viewed it through a veil and under emblems fitter to excite than
to satisfy his curiosity.

Before communicating the first secrets and primary dogmas of
initiation, the priests required the candidate to take a fearful oath
never to divulge the secrets. Then he made his vows, prayers, and
sacrifices to the Gods. The skins of the victims consecrated to
Jupiter were spread on the ground, and he was made to set his
feet upon them. He was then taught some enigmatic formulas, as
answers to questions, by which to make himself known. He was
then enthroned, invested with a purple cincture, and crowned with
flowers, or branches of palm or olive.

We do not certainly know the time that was required to elapse
between the admission to the Lesser and Greater Mysteries of
Eleusis. Most writers fix it at five years. It was a singular mark
of favor when Demetrius was made Mystes and Epopt in one and
the same ceremony. When at length admitted to the Degree of
Perfection, the Initiate was brought face to face with entire nature,
and learned that the soul was the whole of man; that earth was
but his place of exile; that Heaven was his native country; that
for the soul to be born is really to die; and that death was for it
the return to a new life. Then he entered the sanctuary; but he
did not receive the whole instruction at once. It continued through
several years. There were, as it were, many apartments, through
which he advanced by degrees, and between which thick veils in-

tervened. There were Statues and Paintings, says Proclus, in the inmost sanctuary, showing the forms assumed by the Gods. Finally the last veil fell, the sacred covering dropped from the image of the Goddess, and she stood revealed in all her splendor, surrounded by a divine light, which, filling the whole sanctuary, dazzled the eyes and penetrated the soul of the Initiate. Thus is symbolized the final revelation of the true doctrine as to the nature of Deity and of the soul, and of the relations of each to matter.

This was preceded by frightful scenes, alternations of fear and joy, of light and darkness; by glittering lightning and the crash of thunder, and apparitions of spectres, or magical illusions, impressing at once the eyes and ears. This Claudian describes, in his poem on the rape of Proserpine, where he alludes to what passed in her Mysteries. "The temple is shaken," he cries; "fiercely gleams the lightning, by which the Deity announces his presence. Earth trembles; and a terrible noise is heard in the midst of these terrors. The Temple of the Son of Cecrops resounds with long-continued roars; Eleusis uplifts her sacred torches; the serpents of Triptolemus are heard to hiss; and fearful Hecate appears afar."

The celebration of the Greek Mysteries continued, according to the better opinion, for nine days.

On the first the Initiates met. It was the day of the full moon, of the month Boëdromion; when the moon was full at the end of the sign Aries, near the Pleiades and the place of her exaltation in Taurus.

The second day there was a procession to the sea, for purification by bathing.

The third was occupied with offerings, expiatory sacrifices, and other religious rites, such as fasting, mourning, continence, etc. A mullet was immolated, and offerings of grain and living animals made.

On the fourth they carried in procession the mystic wreath of flowers, representing that which Proserpine dropped when seized by Pluto, and the Crown of Ariadne in the Heavens. It was borne on a triumphal car drawn by oxen; and women followed bearing mystic chests or boxes, wrapped with purple cloths, containing grains of sesame, pyramidal biscuits, salt, pomegranates and the mysterious serpent, and perhaps the mystic phallus.

On the fifth was the superb procession of torches, commemorative of the search for Proserpine by Ceres; the Initiates marching by trios, and each bearing a torch; while at the head of the procession marched the Dadoukos.

The sixth was consecrated to Iakchos, the young Light-God, son of Ceres, reared in the sanctuaries and bearing the torch of the Sun-God. The chorus in Aristophanes terms him the luminous star that lights the nocturnal initiation. He was brought from the sanctuary, his head crowned with myrtle, and borne from the gate of the Ceramicus to Eleusis, along the sacred way, amid dances, sacred songs, every mark of joy, and mystic cries of *Iakchos*.

On the seventh there were gymnastic exercises and combats, the victors in which were crowned and rewarded.

On the eighth was the feast of Æsculapius.

On the ninth the famous libation was made for the souls of the departed. The Priests, according to Athenæus, filled two vases, placed one in the East and one in the West, toward the gates of day and night, and overturned them, pronouncing a formula of mysterious prayers. Thus they invoked Light and Darkness, the two great principles of nature.

During all these days no one could be arrested, nor any suit brought, on pain of death, or at least a heavy fine: and no one was allowed, by the display of unusual wealth or magnificence, to endeavor to rival this sacred pomp. Everything was for religion.

Such were the Mysteries; and such the Old Thought, as in scattered and widely separated fragments it has come down to us. The human mind still speculates upon the great mysteries of nature, and still finds its ideas anticipated by the ancients, whose profoundest thoughts are to be looked for, not in their philosophies, but in their symbols, by which they endeavored to express the great ideas that vainly struggled for utterance in words, as they viewed the great circle of phenomena,—Birth, Life, Death, or Decomposition, and New Life out of Death and Rottenness,— to them the greatest of mysteries. Remember, while you study their symbols, that they had a profounder sense of these wonders than we have. To them the transformations of the worm were a greater wonder than the stars; and hence the poor dumb scarabæus or beetle was sacred to them. Thus their faiths are condensed into symbols or expanded into allegories, which they understood, but were not always able to explain in language; for there are thoughts and ideas which no language ever spoken by man has words to express.

XXV.

KNIGHT OF THE BRAZEN SERPENT.

THIS Degree is both philosophical and moral. While it teaches the necessity of reformation as well as repentance, as a means of obtaining mercy and forgiveness, it is also devoted to an explanation of the symbols of Masonry; and especially to those which are connected with that ancient and universal legend, of which that of Khir-Om Abi is but a variation; that legend which, representing a murder or a death, and a restoration to life, by a drama in which figure Osiris, Isis and Horus, Atys and Cybele, Adonis and Venus, the Cabiri, Dionusos, and many another representative of the active and passive Powers of Nature, taught the Initiates in the Mysteries that the rule of Evil and Darkness is but temporary, and that that of Light and Good will be eternal.

Maimonides says: "In the days of Enos, the son of Seth, men fell into grievous errors, and even Enos himself partook of their infatuation. Their language was, that since God has placed on high the heavenly bodies, and used them as His ministers, it was evidently His will that they should receive from man the same

435

veneration as the servants of a great prince justly claim from the subject multitude. Impressed with this notion, they began to build temples to the Stars, to sacrifice to them, and to worship them, in the vain expectation that they should thus please the Creator of all things. At first, indeed, they did not suppose the Stars to be the only Deities, but adored in conjunction with them the Lord God Omnipotent. In process of time, however, that great and venerable Name was totally forgotten, and the whole human race retained no other religion than the idolatrous worship of the Host of Heaven."

The first learning in the world consisted chiefly in symbols. The wisdom of the Chaldæans, Phœnicians, Egyptians, Jews; of Zoroaster, Sanchoniathon, Pherecydes, Syrus, Pythagoras, Socrates, Plato, of all the ancients, that is come to our hand, is symbolic. It was the mode, says Serranus on Plato's Symposium, of the Ancient Philosophers, to represent truth by certain symbols and hidden images.

"All that can be said concerning the Gods," says Strabo, "must be by the exposition of old opinions and fables; it being the custom of the ancients to wrap up in enigma and allegory their thoughts and discourses concerning Nature; which are therefore not easily explained."

As you learned in the 24th Degree, my Brother, the ancient Philosophers regarded the soul of man as having had its origin in Heaven. That was, Macrobius says, a settled opinion among them all; and they held it to be the only true wisdom, for the soul, while united with the body, to look ever toward its source, and strive to return to the place whence it came. Among the fixed stars it dwelt, until, seduced by the desire of animating a body, it descended to be imprisoned in matter. Thenceforward it has no other resource than recollection, and is ever attracted toward its birth-place and home. The means of return are to be sought for in itself. To re-ascend to its source, it must do and suffer in the body.

Thus the Mysteries taught the great doctrine of the divine nature and longings after immortality of the soul, of the nobility of its origin, the grandeur of its destiny, its superiority over the animals who have no aspirations heavenward. If they struggled in vain to express its *nature*, by comparing it to Fire and Light,— if they erred as to its original place of abode, and the mode of its descent, and the path which, descending and ascending, it pursued among the stars and spheres, these were the accessories of the Great Truth, and mere allegories designed to make the idea more impressive, and, as it were, tangible, to the human mind.

Let us, in order to understand this old Thought, first follow the soul in its descent. The sphere or Heaven of the fixed stars was that Holy Region, and those Elysian Fields, that were the native domicile of souls, and the place to which they re-ascended, when they had recovered their primitive purity and simplicity. From that luminous region the soul set forth, when it journeyed toward the body; a destination which it did not reach until it had undergone three degradations, designated by the name of Deaths; and until it had passed through the several spheres and the elements. All souls remained in possession of Heaven and of happiness, so long as they were wise enough to avoid the contagion of the body, and to keep themselves from any contact with matter. But those who, from that lofty abode, where they were lapped in eternal light, have looked longingly toward the body, and toward that which we here below call *life,* but which is to the soul a real *death;* and who have conceived for it a secret desire,—those souls, victims of their concupiscence, are attracted by degrees toward the inferior regions of the world, by the mere weight of thought and of that terrestrial desire. The soul, perfectly incorporeal, does not at once invest itself with the gross envelope of the body, but little by little, by successive and insensible alterations, and in proportion as it removes further and further from the simple and perfect substance in which it dwelt at first. It first surrounds itself with a body composed of the substance of the stars; and afterward, as it descends through the several spheres, with ethereal matter more and more gross, thus by degrees descending to an earthly body; and its number of degradations or deaths being the same as that of the spheres which it traverses.

The Galaxy, Macrobius says, crosses the Zodiac in two opposite points, Cancer and Capricorn, the tropical points in the sun's course, ordinarily called the Gates of the Sun. These two tropics, before his time, corresponded with those constellations, but in his day with Gemini and Sagittarius, in consequence of the precession of the equinoxes; but the *signs* of the Zodiac remained unchanged; and the Milky Way crossed at the *signs* Cancer and Capricorn, though not at those *constellations.*

Through these *gates* souls were supposed to descend to earth and re-ascend to Heaven. One, Macrobius says, in his dream of Scipio, was styled the Gate of Men; and the other, the Gate of the Gods. Cancer was the former, because souls descended by it to the earth; and Capricorn the latter, because by it they re-ascended to their seats of immortality, and became Gods. From the Milky Way, according to Pythagoras, diverged the route to the dominions of Pluto. Until they left the Galaxy, they were not deemed to have commenced to descend toward the terrestrial bodies. From that they departed, and to that they returned. Until they reached the sign Cancer, they had not left it, and were still Gods. When they reached Leo, they commenced their apprenticeship for their future condition; and when they were at Aquarius, the sign opposite Leo, they were furthest removed from human life.

The soul, descending from the celestial limits, where the Zodiac and Galaxy unite, loses its spherical shape, the shape of all Divine Nature, and is lengthened into a cone, as a point is lengthened into a line; and then, an indivisible monad before, it divides itself and becomes a duad—that is, unity becomes division, disturbance, and conflict. Then it begins to experience the disorder which reigns in matter, to which it unites itself, becoming, as it were, intoxicated by draughts of grosser matter: of which inebriation the cup of Bakchos, between Cancer and Leo, is a symbol. It is for them the cup of forgetfulness. They assemble, says Plato, in the fields of oblivion, to drink there the water of the river Ameles, which causes men to forget everything. This fiction is also found in Virgil. "If souls," says Macrobius, "carried with them into the bodies they occupy all the knowledge which they had acquired of divine things, during their sojourn in the Heavens, men would not differ in opinion as to the Deity; but some of them forget more, and some less, of that which they had learned."

We smile at these notions of the ancients; but we must learn to look through these material images and allegories, to the ideas, struggling for utterance, the great speechless thoughts which they envelop: and it is well for us to consider whether we ourselves have yet found out any *better* way of representing to ourselves the soul's origin and its advent into this body, so entirely foreign to it; if, indeed, we have ever thought about it at all; or have not ceased to think, in despair.

The highest and purest portion of matter, which nourishes and constitutes divine existences, is what the poets term *nectar,* the beverage of the Gods. The lower, more disturbed and grosser portion, is what intoxicates souls. The ancients symbolized it as the River Lethe, dark stream of oblivion. How de *we* explain the soul's forgetfulness of its antecedents, or reconcile that utter absence of remembrance of its former condition, with its essential immortality? In truth, we for the most part dread and shrink from any attempt at explanation of it to ourselves.

Dragged down by the heaviness produced by this inebriating draught, the soul falls along the zodiac and the milky way to the lower spheres, and in its descent not only takes, in each sphere, a new envelope of the material composing the luminous bodies of the planets, but receives there the different faculties which it is to exercise while it inhabits the body.

In Saturn, it acquires the power of reasoning and intelligence, or what is termed the logical and contemplative faculty. From Jupiter it receives the power of action. Mars gives it valor, enterprise, and impetuosity. From the Sun it receives the senses and imagination, which produce sensation, perception, and thought. Venus inspires it with desires. Mercury gives it the faculty of expressing and enunciating what it thinks and feels. And, on entering the sphere of the Moon, it acquires the force of generation and growth. This lunary sphere, lowest and basest to divine bodies, is first and highest to terrestrial bodies. And the lunary body there assumed by the soul, while, as it were, the sediment of celestial matter, is also the first substance of animal matter.

The celestial bodies, Heaven, the Stars, and the other Divine elements, ever aspire to rise. The soul reaching the region which mortality inhabits, tends toward terrestrial bodies, and is deemed to die. Let no one, says Macrobius, be surprised that we so frequently speak of the *death* of this soul, which yet we call immortal. It is neither annulled nor destroyed by such death: but merely enfeebled for a time; and does not thereby forfeit its prerogative of immortality; for afterward, freed from the body, when it has been purified from the vice-stains contracted during that connection, it is re-established in all its privileges, and returns to the luminous abode of its immortality.

On its return, it restores to each sphere through which it ascends, the passions and earthly faculties received from them: to the Moon, the faculty of increase and diminution of the body; to Mercury, fraud, the architect of evils; to Venus, the seductive love of pleasure; to the Sun, the passion for greatness and empire; to Mars, audacity and temerity; to Jupiter, avarice; and to Saturn, falsehood and deceit: and at last, relieved of all, it enters naked and pure into the eighth sphere or highest Heaven.

All this agrees with the doctrine of Plato, that the soul cannot re-enter into Heaven, until the revolutions of the Universe shall have restored it to its primitive condition, and purified it from the effects of its contact with the four elements.

This opinion of the pre-existence of souls, as pure and celestial substances, before their union with our bodies, to put on and animate which they descend from Heaven, is one of great antiquity. A modern Rabbi, Manasseh Ben Israel, says it was always the belief of the Hebrews. It was that of most philosophers who admitted the immortality of the soul: and therefore it was taught in the Mysteries; for, as Lactantius says, they could not see how it was possible that the soul should exist *after* the body, if it had not existed *before* it, and if its nature was not independent of that of the body. The same doctrine was adopted by the most learned of the Greek Fathers, and by many of the Latins: and it would probably prevail largely at the present day, if men troubled themselves to think upon this subject at all, and to inquire whether the soul's immortality involved its prior existence.

Some philosophers held that the soul was incarcerated in the body, by way of punishment for sins committed by it in a prior state. How they reconciled this with the same soul's unconsciousness of any such prior state, or of sin committed there, does not appear. Others held that God, of his mere will, sent the soul to inhabit the body. The Kabalists united the two opinions. They held that there are four worlds, *Aziluth, Briarth, Jezirath,* and *Aziath;* the world of *emanation,* that of *creation,* that of *forms,* and the *material* world; one above and more perfect than the other, in that order, both as regards their own nature and that of the beings who inhabit them. All souls are originally in the world Aziluth, the Supreme Heaven, abode of God, and of pure and immortal spirits. Those who descend from it without fault of their own, by God's order, are gifted with a divine fire, which preserves them from the contagion of matter, and restores them to Heaven so soon as their mission is ended. Those who descend through their own fault, go from world to world, insensibly losing their love of Divine things, and their self-contemplation; until they reach the world Aziath, falling by their own weight. This is a pure Platonism, clothed with the images and words peculiar to the Kabalists. It was the doctrine of the Essenes, who, says Porphyry, "believe that souls descend from the most subtile ether, attracted to bodies by the seductions of matter." It was in substance the doctrine of Origen; and it came from the Chaldæans, who largely studied the theory of the Heavens, the spheres, and the influences of the signs and constellations.

The Gnostics made souls ascend and descend through eight Heavens, in each of which were certain Powers that opposed their return, and often drove them back to earth, when not sufficiently purified. The last of these Powers, nearest the luminous abode of souls, was a serpent or dragon.

In the ancient doctrine, certain Genii were charged with the duty of conducting souls to the bodies destined to receive them, and of withdrawing them from those bodies. According to Plutarch, these were the functions of Proserpine and Mercury. In Plato, a familiar Genius accompanies man at his birth, follows and watches him all his life, and at death conducts him to the tribunal of the Great Judge. These Genii are the media of communication between man and the Gods; and the soul is ever in their presence. This doctrine is taught in the oracles of Zoroaster: and these Genii were the Intelligences that resided in the planets.

Thus the secret science and mysterious emblems of initiation were connected with the Heavens, the Spheres, and the Constellations: and this connection must be studied by whomsoever would understand the ancient mind, and be enabled to interpret the allegories, and explore the meaning of the symbols, in which the old sages endeavored to delineate the ideas that struggled within them for utterance, and could be but insufficiently and inadequately expressed by language, whose words are images of those things alone that can be grasped by and are within the empire of the senses.

It is not possible for us thoroughly to appreciate the feelings with which the ancients regarded the Heavenly bodies, and the ideas to which their observation of the Heavens gave rise, because we cannot put ourselves in their places, look at the stars with their eyes in the world's youth, and divest ourselves of the knowledge which even the commonest of us have, that makes us regard the Stars and Planets and all the Universe of Suns and Worlds, as a mere inanimate machine and aggregate of senseless orbs, no more astonishing, except in degree, than a clock or an orrery. *We* wonder and are amazed at the Power and Wisdom (to most men it seems only a kind of Infinite *Ingenuity*) of the MAKER: they wondered at the *Work,* and endowed *it* with Life and Force and mysterious Powers and mighty Influences.

Memphis, in Egypt, was in Latitude 29° 5″ North, and in Longitude 30° 18′ East. Thebæ, in Upper Egypt, in Latitude 25° 45′ North, and Longitude 32° 43′ East. Babylon was in Latitude 32° 30′ North, and Longitude 44° 23′ East: while Saba, the ancient Sabæan capital of Ethiopia, was about in Latitude 15° North.

Through Egypt ran the great River Nile, coming from beyond Ethiopia, its source in regions wholly unknown, in the abodes of heat and fire, and its course from South to North. Its inundations had formed the alluvial lands of Upper and Lower Egypt, which they continued to raise higher and higher, and to fertilize by their deposits. At first, as in all newly-settled countries, those inundations, occurring annually and always at the same period of the year, were calamities: until, by means of levees and drains and artificial lakes for irrigation, they became blessings, and were looked for with joyful anticipation, as they had before been awaited with terror. Upon the deposit left by the Sacred River, as it withdrew into its banks, the husbandman sowed his seed; and the rich soil and the genial sun insured him an abundant harvest.

Babylon lay on the Euphrates, which ran from Southeast to Northwest, blessing, as all rivers in the Orient do, the arid country through which it flowed; but its rapid and uncertain overflows bringing terror and disaster.

To the ancients, as yet inventors of no astronomical instruments, and looking at the Heavens with the eyes of children, this earth was a level plain of unknown extent. About its boundaries there was speculation, but no knowledge. The inequalities of its surface were the irregularities of a plane. That it was a globe, or that anything lived on its under surface, or on what it rested, they had no idea. Every twenty-four hours the sun came up from beyond the Eastern rim of the world, and travelled across the sky, over the earth, always South of, but sometimes nearer and sometimes further from the point overhead; and sunk below the world's Western rim. With him went light, and after him followed darkness.

And every twenty-four hours appeared in the Heavens another body, visible chiefly at night, but sometimes even when the sun shone, which likewise, as if following the sun at a greater or less distance, travelled across the sky; sometimes as a thin crescent, and thence increasing to a full orb resplendent with silver light; and sometimes more and sometimes less to the Southward of the point overhead, within the same limits as the Sun.

Man, enveloped by the thick darkness of profoundest night, when everything around him has disappeared, and he seems alone with himself and the black shades that surround him, feels his existence a blank and nothingness, except so far as memory recalls to him the glories and splendors of light. Everything is dead to him, and he, as it were, to Nature. How crushing and overwhelming the thought, the fear, the dread, that *perhaps* that darkness may be eternal, and that day may possibly never return; if it ever occurs to his mind, while the solid gloom closes up against him like a wall! What then can restore him to like, to energy, to activity, to fellowship and communion with the great world which God has spread around him, and which perhaps in the darkness may be passing away? LIGHT restores him to himself and to nature which seemed lost to him. Naturally, therefore, the primitive men regarded light as the principle of their real existence, without which life would be but one continued weariness and despair. This necessity for light, and its actual creative energy, were felt by all men: and nothing was more alarming to them than its absence. It became their first Divinity, a single ray of which, flashing into the dark tumultuous bosom of chaos, caused man and all the Universe to emerge from it. So all the poets sung who imagined Cosmogonies; such was the first dogma of Orpheus, Moses, and the Theologians. Light was Ormuzd, adored by the Persians, and Darkness Ahriman, origin of all evils. Light was the life of the Universe, the friend of man, the substance of the Gods and of the Soul.

The sky was to them a great, solid, concave arch; a hemisphere of unknown material, at an unknown distance above the flat level earth; and along it journeyed in their courses the Sun, the Moon, the Planets, and the Stars.

The Sun was to them a great globe of fire, of unknown dimensions, at an unknown distance. The Moon was a mass of softer light; the stars and planets lucent bodies, armed with unknown and supernatural influences.

It could not fail to be soon observed, that at regular intervals the days and nights were equal; and that two of these intervals measured the same space of time as elapsed between the successive inundations, and between the returns of spring-time and harvest. Nor could it fail to be perceived that the changes of the moon occurred regularly; the same number of days always elapsing between the first appearance of her silver crescent in the West at evening and that of her full orb rising in the East at the same hour; and the same again, between that and the new appearance of the crescent in the West.

It was also soon observed that the Sun crossed the Heavens in a different line each day, the days being longest and the nights shortest when the line of his passage was furthest North, and the days shortest and nights longest when that line was furthest South: that his progress North and South was perfectly regular, marking four periods that were always the same,—those when the days and nights were equal, or the Vernal and Autumnal Equinoxes; that when the days were longest, or the Summer Solstice; and that when they were shortest, or the Winter Solstice.

With the Vernal Equinox, or about the 25th of March of our Calendar, they found that there unerringly came soft winds, the return of warmth, caused by the Sun turning back to the Northward from the middle ground of his course, the vegetation of the new year, and the impulse to amatory action on the part of the animal creation. Then the Bull and the Ram, animals most valuable to the agriculturist, and symbols themselves of vigorous generative power, recovered their vigor, the birds mated and builded their nests, the seeds germinated, the grass grew, and the trees put forth leaves. With the Summer Solstice, when the Sun reached the extreme northern limit of his course, came great heat, and burning winds, and lassitude and exhaustion; then vegetation withered, man longed for the cool breezes of Spring and Autumn, and the cool water of the wintry Nile or Euphrates, and the Lion sought for that element far from his home in the desert.

With the Autumnal Equinox came ripe harvests, and fruits of the tree and vine, and falling leaves, and cold evenings presaging wintry frosts; and the Principle and Powers of Darkness, prevailing over those of Light, drove the Sun further to the South, so that the nights grew longer than the days. And at the Winter Solstice the earth was wrinkled with frost, the trees were leafless, and the Sun, reaching the most Southern point in his career, seemed to hesitate whether to continue descending, to leave the world to darkness and despair, or to turn upon his steps and retrace his course to the Northward, bringing back seed-time and Spring, and green leaves and flowers, and all the delights of love.

Thus, naturally and necessarily, time was divided, first into days, and then into moons or months, and years; and with these divisions and the movements of the Heavenly bodies that marked them, were associated and connected all men's physical enjoyments and privations. Wholly agricultural, and in their frail habitations greatly at the mercy of the elements and the changing seasons, the primitive people of the Orient were most deeply interested in the recurrence of the periodical phenomena presented by the two great luminaries of Heaven, on whose regularity all their prosperity depended.

And the attentive observer soon noticed that the smaller lights of Heaven were, apparently, even more regular than the Sun and Moon, and foretold with unerring certainty, by their risings and settings, the periods of recurrence of the different phenomena and seasons on which the physical well-being of all men depended. They soon felt the necessity of distinguishing the individual stars, or groups of stars, and giving them names, that they might understand each other, when referring to and designating them. Necessity produced designations at once natural and artificial. Observing that, in the circle of the year, the renewal and periodical appearance of the productions of the earth were constantly associated, not only with the courses of the Sun, but also with the rising and setting of certain Stars, and with their position relatively to the Sun, the centre to which they referred the whole starry host, the mind naturally connected the celestial and terrestrial objects that were *in fact* connected: and they commenced by giving to particular Stars or groups of Stars the names of those terrestrial objects which seemed connected with them; and for those which still remained unnamed by this nomenclature, they, to complete a system, assumed arbitrary and fanciful names.

Thus the Ethiopian of Thebes or Saba styled those Stars under which the Nile commenced to overflow, Stars of Inundation, or that *poured out water* (AQUARIUS).

Those Stars among which the Sun was, when he had reached the Northern Tropic and began to *retreat* Southward, were termed, from his retrograde motion, the Crab (CANCER).

As he approached, in Autumn, the middle point between the Northern and Southern extremes of his journeying, the days and nights became equal; and the Stars among which he was then found were called Stars of the Balance (LIBRA).

Those stars among which the Sun was, when the Lion, driven from the Desert by thirst, came to slake it at the Nile, were called Stars of the Lion (LEO).

Those among which the Sun was at harvest, were called those of the Gleaning Virgin, holding a Sheaf of Wheat (VIRGO).

Those among which he was found in February, when the Ewes brought forth their young, were called Stars of the Lamb (ARIES).

Those in March, when it was time to plough, were called Stars of the Ox (TAURUS).

Those under which hot and burning winds came from the desert, venomous like poisonous reptiles, were called Stars of the Scorpion (SCORPIO).

Observing that the annual return of the rising of the Nile was always accompanied by the appearance of a beautiful Star, which at that period showed itself in the direction of the sources of that river, and seemed to warn the husbandman to be careful not to be surprised by the inundation, the Ethiopian compared this act of that Star to that of the Animal which by barking gives warning of danger, and styled it the Dog (SIRIUS).

Thus commencing, and as astronomy came to be more studied, imaginary figures were traced all over the Heavens, to which the different Stars were assigned. Chief among them were those that lay along the path which the Sun travelled as he climbed toward the North and descended to the South: lying within certain limits and extending to an equal distance on each side of the line of equal nights and days. This belt, curving like a Serpent, was termed the Zodiac, and divided into twelve Signs.

At the Vernal Equinox, 2455 years before our Era, the Sun was entering the sign and constellation Taurus, or the Bull; having passed through, since he commenced, at the Winter Solstice, to ascend Northward, the Signs Aquarius, Pisces and Aries; on entering the first of which he reached the lowest limit of his journey Southward.

From TAURUS, he passed through Gemini and Cancer, and reached LEO when he arrived at the terminus of his journey Northward. Thence, through Leo, Virgo, and Libra, he entered SCORPIO at the Autumnal Equinox, and journeyed Southward through Scorpia, Sagittarius, and Capricornus to AQUARIUS, the terminus of his journey South.

The path by which he journeyed through these signs became the *Ecliptic;* and that which passes through the two equinoxes, the *Equator.*

They knew nothing of the immutable laws of nature; and whenever the Sun commenced to tend Southward, they feared lest he might continue to do so, and by degrees disappear forever, leaving the earth to be ruled forever by darkness, storm, and cold.

Hence they rejoiced when he commenced to re-ascend after the Winter Solstice, struggling against the malign influences of Aquarius and Pisces, and amicably received by the Lamb. And when at the Vernal Equinox he entered Taurus, they still more rejoiced at the assurance that the days would again be longer than the nights, that the season of seed-time had come, and the Summer and harvest would follow.

And they lamented when, after the Autumnal Equinox, the malign influence of the venomous Scorpion, and vindictive Archer, and the filthy and ill-omened He-Goat dragged him down toward the Winter Solstice.

Arriving there, they said he had been slain, and had gone to the realm of darkness. Remaining there three days, he rose again, and again ascended Northward in the heavens, to redeem the earth from the gloom and darkness of Winter, which soon became emblematical of sin, and evil, and suffering; as the Spring, Summer, and Autumn became emblems of happiness and immortality.

Soon they personified the Sun, and worshipped him under the name of OSIRIS, and transmuted the legend of his descent among the Winter Signs, into a fable of his death, his descent into the infernal regions, and his resurrection.

The Moon became ISIS, the wife of Osiris; and Winter, as well as the desert or the ocean into which the Sun descended, became TYPHON, the Spirit or Principle of Evil, warring against and destroying Osiris.

From the journey of the Sun through the twelve signs came the legend of the twelve labors of Hercules, and the incarnations of Vishnu and Buddha. Hence came the legend of the murder of Khūrūm, representative of the Sun, by the three Fellow-crafts, symbols of the three Winter signs, Capricornus, Aquarius, and Pisces, who assailed him at the three gates of Heaven and slew him at the Winter Solstice. Hence the search for him by the nine Fellow-crafts, the other nine signs, his finding, burial, and resurrection.

The celestial Taurus, opening the new year, was the Creative Bull of the Hindús and Japanese, breaking with his horn the egg out of which the world is born. Hence the bull Apis was worshipped by the Egyptians, and reproduced as a golden calf by Aaron in the desert. Hence the cow was sacred to the Hindús. Hence, from the sacred and beneficent signs of Taurus and Leo, the human-headed winged lions and bulls in the palaces at Kouyounjik and Nimroud, like which were the Cherubim set by Solomon in his Temple: and hence the twelve brazen or bronze oxen, on which the laver of brass was supported.

The Celestial Vulture or Eagle, rising and setting with the Scorpion, was substituted in its place, in many cases, on account of the malign influences of the latter: and thus the four great periods of the year were marked by the Bull, the Lion, the Man (Aquarius) and the Eagle; which were upon the respective standards of Ephraim, Judah, Reuben, and Dan; and still appear on the shield of American Royal Arch Masonry.

Afterward the Ram or Lamb became an object of adoration, when, in his turn, he opened the equinox, to deliver the world from the wintry reign of darkness and evil.

Around the central and simple idea of the annual death and resurrection of the Sun a multitude of circumstantial details soon clustered. Some were derived from other astronomical phenomena; while many were merely poetical ornaments and inventions.

Besides the Sun and Moon, those ancients also saw a beautiful Star, shining with a soft, silvery light, always following the Sun at no great distance when he set, or preceding him when he rose. Another of a red and angry color, and still another more kingly and brilliant than all, early attracted their attention, by their free movements among the fixed hosts of Heaven: and the latter by his unusual brilliancy, and the regularity with which he rose and set. These were Venus, Mars, and Jupiter. Mercury and Saturn could scarcely have been noticed in the world's infancy, or until astronomy began to assume the proportions of a science.

In the projection of the celestial sphere by the astronomical priests, the zodiac and constellations, arranged in a circle, presented their halves in diametrical opposition; and the hemisphere of Winter was said to be adverse, opposed, contrary, to that of Summer. Over the angels of the latter ruled a king (OSIRIS or ORMUZD), enlightened, intelligent, creative, and beneficent. Over the fallen angels or evil genii of the former, the demons or Devs of the subterranean empire of darkness and sorrow, and its stars, ruled also a chief. In Egypt the Scorpion first ruled, the sign next the Balance, and long the chief of the Winter signs; and then the Polar Bear or Ass, called Typhon, that is, *deluge,* on account of the rains which inundated the earth while that constellation domineered. In Persia, at a later day, it was the serpent, which, personified as Ahriman, was the Evil Principle of the religion of Zoroaster.

The Sun does not arrive at the same moment in each year at the equinoctial point on the equator. The explanation of his anticipating that point belongs to the science of astronomy; and to that we refer you for it. The consequence is, what is termed the precession of the equinoxes, by means of which the Sun is constantly changing his place in the zodiac, at each vernal equinox; so that now, the signs retaining the names which they had 300 years before Christ, they and the constellations do not correspond; the Sun being now in the *constellation* Pisces, when he is in the *sign* Aries.

The annual amount of precession is 50 seconds and a little over [50″ 1.]. The period of a complete Revolution of the Equinoxes, 25,856 years. The precession amounts to 30° or a sign, in 2155.6 years. So that, as the sun now enters Pisces at the Vernal Equinox, he entered Aries at that period, 300 years B. C., and Taurus 2455 B. C. And the division of the Ecliptic, now *called* Taurus, lies in the Constellation Aries; while the *sign* Gemini is in the *Constellation* Taurus. Four thousand six hundred and ten years before Christ, the sun entered Gemini at the Vernal Equinox.

At the two periods, 2455 and 300 years before Christ, and now, the entrances of the sun at the Equinoxes and Solstices into the signs, were and are as follows:—

B. C. 2455.

Vern. Equinox, he entered	Taurus	. . .	from Aries.
Summer Solstice . . .	Leo	. . . .	from Cancer.
Autumnal Equinox . .	Scorpio	. . .	from Libra.
Winter Solstice . . .	Aquarius	. .	from Capricornus.

B. C. 300.

Vern. Eq.	Aries	. . .	from Pisces.
Summer Sols.	Cancer	. . .	from Gemini.
Autumn Eq.	Libra	. . .	from Virgo.
Winter Sols.	Capricornus	.	from Sagittarius.

1872.

Vern. Eq.	Pisces	. . .	from Aquarius.
Sum. Sols.	Gemini	. . .	from Taurus.
Aut. Eq.	Virgo	. . .	from Leo.
Winter Sols.	Sagittarius	. .	from Scorpio.

From confounding *signs* with *causes* came the worship of the sun and stars. "If," says Job, "I beheld the sun when it shined, or the moon progressive in brightness; and my heart hath been secretly enticed, or my mouth hath kissed my hand, this were an iniquity to be punished by the Judge; for I should have denied the God that is above."

Perhaps we are not, on the whole, much wiser than those simple men of the old time. For what do we know of *effect* and *cause,* except that one thing regularly or habitually *follows* another?

So, because the heliacal rising of Sirius *preceded* the rising of the Nile, it was deemed to *cause* it; and other stars were in like manner held to *cause* extreme heat, bitter cold, and watery storm.

A religious reverence for the zodiacal Bull [TAURUS] appears, from a very early period, to have been pretty general,—perhaps it was universal, throughout Asia; from that chain or region of Caucasus to which it gave name; and which is still known under the appellation of Mount Taurus, to the Southern extremities of the Indian Peninsula; extending itself also into Europe, and through the Eastern parts of Africa.

This evidently originated during those remote ages of the world, when the colure of the vernal equinox passed across the stars in the head of the sign Taurus [among which was Aldebarán]; a period when, as the most ancient monuments of all the oriental nations attest, the light of arts and letters first shone forth.

The Arabian word AL-DE-BARÁN, means the *foremost*, or *leading,* star: and it could only have been so named, when it *did* precede, or *lead,* all others. The year then opened with the sun in Taurus; and the multitude of ancient sculptures, both in Assyria and Egypt, wherein the bull appears with lunette or crescent horns, and the disk of the sun between them, are direct allusions to the important festival of the first new moon of the year: and there was everywhere an annual celebration of the festival of the first new moon, when the year opened with Sol and Luna in Taurus.

David sings: "Blow the trumpet in *the New Moon;* in the time appointed; on our solemn feast-day: for this is a statute unto Israel, and a law of the God of Jacob. This he ordained to Joseph, for a testimony, when he came out of the land of Egypt."

The reverence paid to Taurus continued long after, by the precession of the Equinoxes, the colure of the vernal equinox had come to pass through Aries. The Chinese still have a temple, called "The Palace of the horned Bull"; and the same symbol is worshipped in Japan and all over Hindostan. The Cimbrians carried a brazen bull with them, as the image of their God, when they overran Spain and Gaul; and the representation of the Creation, by the Deity in the shape of a bull, breaking the shell of an egg with his horns, meant Taurus, opening the year, and bursting the symbolical shell of the annually-recurring orb of the new year.

Theophilus says that the Osiris of Egypt was supposed to be dead or absent fifty days in each year. Landseer thinks that this was because the Sabæan priests were accustomed to see, in the lower latitudes of Egypt and Ethiopia, the first or chief stars of the Husbandman [BoöTES] sink achronically beneath the Western horizon; and then to begin their lamentations, or hold forth the signal for others to weep: and when his prolific virtues were supposed to be transferred to the vernal sun, bacchanalian revelry became devotion.

Before the colure of the Vernal Equinox had passed into Aries, and after it had left Aldebarán and the Hyades, the Pleiades were, for seven or eight centuries, the leading stars of the Sabæan year. And thus we see, on the monuments, the disk and crescent, sym-

bols of the sun and moon in conjunction, appear successively,—
first on the head, and then on the neck and back of the Zodiacal
Bull, and more recently on the forehead of the Ram.

The diagrammatical character or symbol, still in use to denote
Taurus, ♉, is this very crescent and disk: a symbol that has come
down to us from those remote ages when this memorable conjunction in Taurus, by marking the commencement, at once of the
Sabæan year and of the cycle of the Chaldean Saros, so pre-eminently distinguished that sign as to become its characteristic symbol. On a bronze bull from China, the crescent is attached to the
back of the Bull, by means of a cloud, and a curved groove is provided for the occasional introduction of the disk of the sun, when
solar and lunar time were coincident and conjunctive, at the commencement of the year, and of the lunar cycle. When that was
made, the year did not open with the stars in the *head* of the Bull,
but when the colure of the vernal equinox passed across the middle or later degrees of the asterism Taurus, and the Pleiades were,
in China, as in Canaan, the leading stars of the year.

The crescent and disk combined always represent the conjunctive Sun and Moon; and when placed on the head of the Zodiacal
Bull, the commencement of the cycle termed Saros by the Chaldeans, and Metonic by the Greeks; and supposed to be alluded to
in Job, by the phrase, "Mazzaroth in his season"; that is to say,
when the first new Moon and new Sun of the year were coincident, which happened once in eighteen years and a fraction.

On the sarcophagus of Alexander, the same symbol appears on
the head of a Ram, which, in the time of that monarch, was the
leading sign. So too in the sculptured temples of the Upper Nile,
the crescent and disk appear, not on the head of Taurus, but on
the forehead of the Ram or the Ram-headed God, whom the Grecian Mythologists called Jupiter Ammon, really the Sun in Aries.

If we now look for a moment at the individual stars which
composed and were near to the respective constellations, we may
find something that will connect itself with the symbols of the
Ancient Mysteries and of Masonry.

It is to be noticed that when the Sun is *in* a particular constellation, no part of that constellation will be seen, except just before
sunrise and just after sunset; and then only the edge of it: but
the constellations *opposite* to it will be visible. When the Sun is
in Taurus, for example, that is, when Taurus *sets with* the Sun,

Scorpio rises as he sets, and continues visible throughout the night. And if Taurus rises and sets with the Sun to-day, he will, six months hence, rise at sunset and set at sunrise; for the stars thus gain on the Sun two hours a month.

Going back to the time when, watched by the Chaldean shepherds, and the husbandmen of Ethiopia and Egypt,

> "The milk-white Bull with golden horns
> "Led on the new-born year,"

we see in the neck of TAURUS, the Pleiades, and in his face the Hyades, "which Grecia from their showering names," and of whom the brilliant Aldebarán is the chief; while to the southwestward is that most splendid of all the constellations, Orion, with Betelgueux in his right shoulder, Bellatrix in his left shoulder, Rigel on the left foot, and in his belt the three stars known as the Three Kings, and now as the Yard and Ell. Orion, ran the legend, persecuted the Pleiades; and to save them from his fury, Jupiter placed them in the Heavens, where he still pursues them, but in vain. They, with Arcturus and the Bands of Orion, are mentioned in the Book of Job. They are usually called the Seven Stars, and it is said there *were* seven, before the fall of Troy; though now only six are visible.

The Pleiades were so named from a Greek word signifying *to sail*. In all ages they have been observed for signs and seasons. Virgil says that the sailors gave names to "the Pleiades, Hyades, and the Northern Car: *Pleiadas, Hyadas, Claramque Lycaonis Arcton.*" And Palinurus, he says,—

> *Arcturum, pluviasque Hyadas, Geminosque Triones,*
> *Armatumque auro circumspicit Oriona,*—

studied Arcturus and the rainy Hyades and the Twin Triones, and Orion cinctured with gold.

Taurus was the prince and leader of the celestial host for more than two thousand years; and when his head set with the Sun about the last of May, the Scorpion was seen to rise in the Southeast.

The Pleiades were sometimes called *Vergiliæ,* or the Virgins of Spring; because the Sun entered this cluster of stars in the season of blossoms. Their Syrian name was *Succoth,* or *Succothbeneth,* derived from a Chaldean word signifying to *speculate* or *observe*.

The *Hyades* are five stars in the form of a V, 11° southeast of the Pleiades. The Greeks counted them as seven. When the Vernal Equinox was in Taurus, Aldebarán led up the starry host; and as he rose in the East, Aries was about 27° high.

When he was close upon the meridian, the Heavens presented their most magnificent appearance. Capella was a little further from the meridian, to the north; and Orion still further from it to the southward. Procyon, Sirius, Castor and Pollux had climbed about half-way from the horizon to the meridian. Regulus had just risen upon the ecliptic. The Virgin still lingered below the horizon. Fomalhaut was half-way to the meridian in the Southwest; and to the Northwest were the brilliant constellations, Perseus, Cepheus, Cassiopeia, and Andromeda; while the Pleiades had just passed the meridian.

ORION is visible to all the habitable world. The equinoctial line passes through the centre of it. When Aldebarán rose in the East, the Three Kings in Orion followed him; and as Taurus set, the Scorpion, by whose sting it was said Orion died, rose in the East.

Orion rises at noon about the 9th of March. His rising was accompanied with great rains and storms, and it became very terrible to mariners.

In Boötes, called by the ancient Greeks *Lycaon,* from *lukos,* a wolf, and by the Hebrews, Caleb Anubach, the Barking Dog, is the Great Star ARCTURUS, which, when Taurus opened the year, corresponded with a season remarkable for its great heat.

Next comes GEMINI, the Twins, two human figures, in the heads of which are the bright Stars CASTOR and POLLUX, the Dioscuri, and the Cabiri of Samothrace, patrons of navigation; while South of Pollux are the brilliant Stars SIRIUS and PROCYON, the greater and lesser Dog: and still further South, Canopus, in the Ship Argo.

Sirius is apparently the largest and brightest Star in the Heavens. When the Vernal Equinox was in Taurus, he rose heliacally, that is, just before the Sun, when, at the Summer Solstice, the Sun entered Leo, about the 21st of June, fifteen days previous to the swelling of the Nile. The heliacal rising of Canopus was also a precursor of the rising of the Nile. Procyon was the forerunner of Sirius, and rose before him.

There are no important Stars in CANCER. In the Zodiacs of Esne and Dendera, and in most of the astrological remains of

Egypt, the sign of this constellation was a beetle (*Scarabæus*), which thence became sacred, as an emblem of the gate through which souls descended from Heaven. In the crest of Cancer is a cluster of Stars formerly called *Præsepe*, the Manger, on each side of which is a small Star, the two of which were called *Aselli* little asses.

In *Leo* are the splendid Stars, REGULUS, directly on the ecliptic, and DENEBOLA in the Lion's tail. Southeast of Regulus is the fine Star COR HYDRÆ.

The combat of Hercules with the Nemæan lion was his first labor. It was the first sign into which the Sun passed, after falling below the Summer Solstice; from which time he struggled to re-ascend.

The Nile overflowed in this sign. It stands first in the Zodiac of Dendera, and is in all the Indian and Egyptian Zodiacs.

In the left hand of VIRGO (Isis or Ceres) is the beautiful Star SPICA Virginis, a little South of the ecliptic. VINDEMIATRIX, of less magnitude, is in the right arm; and Northwest of Spica, in Boötes (the husbandman, Osiris), is the splendid star ARCTURUS.

The division of the first Decan of the Virgin, Aben Ezra says, represents a beautiful Virgin with flowing hair, sitting in a chair, with two ears of corn in her hand, and suckling an infant. In an Arabian MS. in the Royal Library at Paris, is a picture of the Twelve Signs. That of Virgo is a young girl with an infant by her side. Virgo was Isis; and her representation, carrying a child (Horus) in her arms, exhibited in her temple, was accompanied by this inscription: "I AM ALL THAT IS, THAT WAS, AND THAT SHALL BE; and the fruit which I brought forth is the Sun."

Nine months after the Sun enters Virgo, he reaches the Twins. When Scorpio begins to rise, Orion sets: when Scorpio comes to the meridian, Leo begins to set, Typhon reigns, Osiris is slain, and Isis (the Virgin) his sister and wife, follows him to the tomb, weeping.

The Virgin and Boötes, setting heliacally at the Autumnal Equinox, delivered the world to the wintry constellations, and introduced into it the genius of Evil, represented by Ophiucus, the Serpent.

At the moment of the Winter Solstice, the Virgin rose heliacally (*with* the Sun), having the Sun (Horus) in her bosom.

In LIBRA are four Stars of the second and third magnitude, which we shall mention hereafter. They are Zuben-es-Chamali, Zuben-el-Gemabi, Zuben-hak-rabi, and Zuben-el-Gubi. Near the last of these is the brilliant and malign Star, ANTARES in Scorpio.

In SCORPIO, ANTARES, of the 1st magnitude, and remarkably red, was one of the four great Stars, FOMALHAUT, in Cetus, ALDEBARAN in Taurus, REGULUS in Leo, and ANTARES, that formerly answered to the Solstitial and Equinoctial points, and were much noticed by astronomers. This sign was sometimes represented by a Snake, and sometimes by a Crocodile, but generally by a Scorpion, which last is found on the Mithriac Monuments, and on the Zodiac of Dendera. It was considered a sign accursed, and the entrance of the Sun into it commenced the reign of Typhon.

In Sagittarius, Capricornus, and Aquarius there are no Stars of importance.

Near Pisces is the brilliant Star FOMALHAUT. No sign in the Zodiac is considered of more malignant influence than this. It was deemed indicative of *Violence* and *Death*. Both the Syrians and Egyptians abstained from eating fish, out of dread and abhorhence; and when the latter would represent anything as odious, or express hatred by Hieroglyphics, they painted a fish.

In Auriga is the bright Star CAPELLA, which to the Egyptians never set.

And, circling ever round the North Pole are Seven Stars, known as Ursa Major, or the Great Bear, which have been an object of universal observation in all ages of the world. They were venerated alike by the Priests of Bel, the Magi of Persia, the Shepherds of Chaldea, and the Phœnician navigators, as well as by the astronomers of Egypt. Two of them, MERAK and DUBHE, always point to the North Pole.

The Phœnicians and Egyptians, says Eusebius, were the first who ascribed divinity to the Sun, Moon, and Stars, and regarded them as the sole causes of the production and destruction of all beings. From them went abroad over all the world all known opinions as to the generation and descent of the Gods. Only the Hebrews looked beyond the visible world to an invisible Creator. All the rest of the world regarded as Gods those luminous bodies that blaze in the firmament, offered them sacrifices, bowed down

before them, and raised neither their souls nor their worship
above the visible heavens.

The Chaldeans, Canaanites, and Syrians, among whom Abraham
lived, did the same. The Canaanites consecrated horses and chariots to the Sun. The inhabitants of Emesa in Phœnicia adored
him under the name of Elagabalus; and the Sun, as Hercules, was
the great Deity of the Tyrians. The Syrians worshipped, with fear
and dread, the Stars of the Constellation Pisces, and consecrated
images of them in their temples. The Sun as Adonis was worshipped in Byblos and about Mount Libanus. There was a magnificent
Temple of the Sun at Palmyra, which was pillaged by the soldiers
of Aurelian, who rebuilt it and dedicated it anew. The Pleiades,
under the name of Succoth-Beneth, were worshipped by the Babylonian colonists who settled in the country of the Samaritans. Saturn, under the name of Remphan, was worshipped among the
Copts. The planet Jupiter was worshipped as Bel or Baal; Mars
as Malec, Melech, or Moloch; Venus as Ashtaroth or Astarte, and
Mercury as Nebo, among the Syrians, Assyrians, Phœnicians,
and Canaanites.

Sanchoniathon says that the earliest Phœnicians adored the Sun,
whom they deemed sole Lord of the Heavens; and honored him
under the name of BEEL-SAMIN, signifying *King of Heaven.* They
raised columns to the elements, fire, and air or wind, and worshipped them; and Sabæism, or the worship of the Stars, flourished everywhere in Babylonia. The Arabs, under a sky always clear
and serene, adored the Sun, Moon, and Stars. Abulfaragius so informs us, and that each of the twelve Arab Tribes invoked a particular Star as its Patron. The Tribe Hamyar was consecrated to
the Sun, the Tribe Cennah to the Moon; the Tribe Misa was
under the protection of the beautiful Star in Taurus, Aldebarán;
the Tribe Tai under that of Canopus; the Tribe Kais, of Sirius;
the Tribes Lachamus and Idamus, of Jupiter; the Tribe Asad, of
Mercury; and so on.

The Saracens, in the time of Heraclius, worshipped Venus,
whom they called CABAR, or The Great; and they swore by the
Sun, Moon, and Stars. Shahristan, an Arabic author, says that
the Arabs and Indians before his time had temples dedicated to
the seven Planets. Abulfaragius says that the seven great primitive nations, from whom all others descended, the Persians, Chaldæans, Greeks, Egyptians, Turks, Indians, and Chinese, all originally were Sabæists, and worshipped the Stars. They all, he
says, like the Chaldæans, prayed, turning toward the North Pole.

three times a day, at Sunrise, Noon, and Sunset, bowing themselves three times before the Sun. They invoked the Stars and the
Intelligences which inhabited them, offered them sacrifices, and
called the fixed stars and planets gods. Philo says that the Chaldæans regarded the stars as sovereign arbiters of the order of the
world, and did not look beyond the visible causes to any invisible
and intellectual being. They regarded NATURE as the great divinity, that exercised its powers through the action of its parts,
the Sun, Moon, Planets, and Fixed Stars, the successive revolutions of the seasons, and the combined action of Heaven and
Earth. The great feast of the Sabæans was when the Sun reached
the Vernal Equinox: and they had five other feasts, at the times
when the five minor planets entered the signs in which they had
their exaltation.

Diodorus Siculus informs us that the Egyptians recognized two
great Divinities, primary and eternal, the Sun and Moon, which
they thought governed the world, and from which everything receives its nourishment and growth: that on them depended all
the great work of generation, and the perfection of all effects produced in nature. We know that the two great Divinities of Egypt
were Osiris and Isis, the greatest agents of nature; according to
some, the Sun and Moon, and according to others, Heaven and
Earth, or the active and passive principles of generation.

And we learn from Porphyry that Chæremon, a learned priest
of Egypt, and many other learned men of that nation, said that the
Egyptians recognized as gods the stars composing the zodiac, and
all those that by their rising or setting marked its divisions; the
subdivisions of the signs into decans, the horoscope and the stars
that presided therein, and which were called Potent Chiefs of
Heaven: that considering the Sun as the Great God, Architect,
and Ruler of the World, they explained not only the fable of
Osiris and Isis, but generally all their sacred legends, by the stars,
by their appearance and disappearance, by their ascension, by the
phases of the moon, and the increase and diminution of her light;
by the march of the sun, the division of time and the heavens into
two parts, one assigned to darkness and the other to light; by the
Nile and, in fine, by the whole round of physical causes.

Lucian tells us that the bull Apis, sacred to the Egyptians, was
the image of the celestial Bull, or Taurus; and that Jupiter
Ammon, horned like a ram, was an image of the constellation
Aries. And Clemens of Alexandria assures us that the four prin-

cipal sacred animals, carried in their processions, were emblems of the four signs or cardinal points which fixed the seasons at the equinoxes and solstices, and divided into four parts the yearly march of the sun. They worshipped fire also, and water, and the Nile, which river they styled Father, Preserver of Egypt, sacred emanation from the Great God Osiris; and in their hymns in which they called it the god crowned with millet (which grain, represented by the *pschent,* was part of the head-dress of their kings), bringing with him abundance. The other elements were also revered by them: and the Great Gods, whose names are found inscribed on an ancient column, are the Air, Heaven, the Earth, the Sun, the Moon, Night, and Day. And, in fine, as Eusebius says, they regarded the Universe as a great Deity, composed of a great number of gods, the different parts of itself.

The same worship of the Heavenly Host extended into every part of Europe, into Asia Minor, and among the Turks, Scythians, and Tartars. The ancient Persians adored the Sun as Mithras, and also the Moon, Venus, Fire, Earth, Air, and Water; and, having no statues or altars, they sacrificed on high places to the Heavens and to the Sun. On seven ancient *pyrea* they burned incense to the Seven Planets, and considered the elements to be divinities. In the Zend-Avesta we find invocations addressed to Mithras, the stars, the elements, trees, mountains, and every part of nature. The Celestial Bull is invoked there, to which the Moon unites herself; and the four great stars, Taschter, Satevis, Haftorang, and Venant, the great Star Rapitan, and the other constellations which watch over the different portions of the earth.

The Magi, like a multitude of ancient nations, worshipped fire, above all the other elements and powers of nature. In India, the Ganges and the Indus were worshipped, and the Sun was the Great Divinity. They worshipped the Moon also, and kept up the sacred fire. In Ceylon, the Sun, Moon, and other planets were worshipped: in Sumatra, the Sun, called Iri, and the Moon, called Handa. And the Chinese built Temples to Heaven, the Earth, and genii of the air, of the water, of the mountains, and of the stars, to the sea-dragon, and to the planet Mars.

The celebrated Labyrinth was built in honor of the Sun; and its twelve palaces, like the twelve superb columns of the Temple at Hieropolis, covered with symbols relating to the twelve signs and the occult qualities of the elements, were consecrated to the twelve gods or tutelary genii of the signs of the Zodiac. The figure of the pyramid and that of the obelisk, resembling the shape of a flame, caused these monuments to be consecrated to the Sun and to Fire. And Timæus of Locria says: "The equilateral triangle enters into the composition of the pyramid, which has four equal faces and equal angles, and which in this is like fire, the most subtle and mobile of the elements." They and the obelisks were erected in honor of the Sun, termed in an inscription upon one of the latter, translated by the Egyptian Hermapion, and to be found in Ammianus Marcellinus, "Apollo the strong, Son of God, He who made the world, true Lord of the diadems, who possesses Egypt and fills it with His glory."

The two most famous divisions of the Heavens, by seven, which is that of the planets, and by twelve, which is that of the signs, are found on the religious monuments of all the people of the ancient world. The twelve Great Gods of Egypt are met with everywhere. They were adopted by the Greeks and Romans; and the latter assigned one of them to each sign of the Zodiac. Their images were seen at Athens, where an altar was erected to each; and they were painted on the porticos. The People of the North had their twelve *Azes,* or Senate of twelve great gods, of whom Odin was chief. The Japanese had the same number, and like the Egyptians divided them into classes, seven, who were the most ancient, and five, afterward added: both of which numbers are well known and consecrated in Masonry.

There is no more striking proof of the universal adoration paid the stars and constellations, than the arrangement of the Hebrew camp in the Desert, and the allegory in regard to the twelve Tribes of Israel, ascribed in the Hebrew legends to Jacob. The Hebrew camp was a quadrilateral, in sixteen divisions, of which the central four were occupied by images of the four elements. The four divisions at the four angles of the quadrilateral exhibited the four signs that the astrologers called *fixed,* and which they regard as subject to the influence of the four great Royal Stars, Regulus in Leo, Aldebaran in Taurus, Antares in Scorpio, and Fomalhaut in the mouth of Pisces, on which falls the water poured out by Aquarius; of which constellations the Scorpion was represented in the Hebrew blazonry by the Celestial Vulture or Eagle, that rises at the same time with it and is its paranatellon. The other signs were arranged on the four faces of the quadilateral, and in the parallel and interior divisions.

There is an astonishing coincidence between the characteristics assigned by Jacob to his sons, and those of the signs of the Zodiac, or the planets that have their domicile in those signs.

Reuben is compared to running water, unstable, and that cannot excel; and he answers to Aquarius, his ensign being a man. The water poured out by Aquarius flows toward the South Pole, and it is the first of the four Royal Signs, ascending from the Winter Solstice.

The Lion (Leo) is the device of *Judah;* and Jacob compares him to that animal, whose constellation in the Heavens is the domicile of the Sun; the Lion of the Tribe of Judah; by whose grip, when that of apprentice and that of fellow-craft,—of Aquarius at the Winter Solstice and of Cancer at the Vernal Equinox, —had not succeeded in raising him, Khūrūm was lifted out of the grave.

Ephraim, on whose ensign appears the Celestial Bull, Jacob compares to the ox. *Dan,* bearing as his device a Scorpion, he compares to the Cerastes or horned Serpent, synonymous in astrological language with the vulture or pouncing eagle; and which bird was often substituted on the flag of Dan, in place of the venomous scorpion, on account of the terror which that reptile inspired, as the symbol of Typhon and his malign influences; wherefore the Eagle, as its paranatellon, that is, rising and setting at the same time with it, was naturally used in its stead. Hence the four famous figures in the sacred pictures of the Jews and Christians, and in Royal Arch Masonry, of the Lion, the Ox, the Man, and the Eagle, the four creatures of the Apocalypse, copied there from Ezekiel, in whose reveries and rhapsodies they are seen revolving around blazing circles.

The Ram, domicile of Mars, chief of the Celestial Soldiery and of the twelve Signs, is the device of *Gad,* whom Jacob characterizes as a warrior, chief of his army.

Cancer, in which are the stars termed *Aselli,* or little asses, is the device of the flag of *Issachar,* whom Jacob compares to an ass.

Capricorn, of old represented with the tail of a fish, and called by astronomers the Son of Neptune, is the device of *Zebulon,* of whom Jacob says that he dwells on the shore of the sea.

Sagittarius, chasing the Celestial Wolf, is the emblem of *Benjamin,* whom Jacob compares to a hunter: and in that constellation the Romans placed the domicile of Diana the huntress. Virgo, the domicile of Mercury, is borne on the flag of *Naphtali,* whose eloquence and agility Jacob magnifies, both of which are attributes of the Courier of the Gods. And of *Simeon* and *Levi* he speaks as united, as are the two fishes that make the Constellation Pisces, which is their armorial emblem.

Plato, in his Republic, followed the divisions of the Zodiac and the planets. So also did Lycurgus at Sparta, and Cecrops in the Athenian Commonwealth. Chun, the Chinese legislator, divided China into twelve Tcheou, and specially designated twelve mountains. The Etruscans divided themselves into twelve Cantons. Romulus appointed twelve Lictors. There were twelve tribes of Ishmael and twelve disciples of the Hebrew Reformer. The New Jerusalem of the Apocalypse has twelve gates.

The Souciet, a Chinese book, speaks of a palace composed of four buildings, whose gates looked toward the four corners of the world. That on the East was dedicated to the new moons of the months of Spring; that on the West to those of Autumn; that on the South to those of Summer; and that on the North to those of Winter: and in this palace the Emperor and his grandees sacrificed a lamb, the animal that represented the Sun at the Vernal Equinox.

Among the Greeks, the march of the Choruses in their theatres represented the movements of the Heavens and the planets, and the Strophe and Anti-Strophe imitated, Aristoxenes says, the movements of the Stars. The number five was sacred among the Chinese, as that of the planets other than the Sun and Moon. Astrology consecrated the numbers twelve, seven, thirty, and three hundred and sixty; and everywhere *seven,* the number of the planets, was as sacred as *twelve,* that of the signs, the months, the oriental cycles, and the sections of the horizon. We shall speak more at large hereafter, in another Degree, as to these and other numbers, to which the ancients ascribed mysterious powers.

The Signs of the Zodiac and the Stars appeared on many of the ancient coins and medals. On the public seal of the Locrians, Ozoles was Hesperus, or the planet Venus. On the medals of Antioch on the Orontes was the ram and crescent; and the Ram was the special Deity of Syria, assigned to it in the division of the earth among the twelve signs. On the Cretan coins was the Equinoctial Bull; and he also appeared on those of the Mamertins and of Athens. Sagittarius appeared on those of the Persians. In

India the twelve signs appeared upon the ancient coins. The
Scorpion was engraved on the medals of the Kings of Comagena,
and Capricorn on those of Zeugma, Anazorba, and other cities.
On the medals of Antoninus are found nearly all the signs of the
Zodiac.

Astrology was practised among all the ancient nations. In
Egypt, the book of Astrology was borne reverentially in the religious processions; in which the few sacred animals were also
carried, as emblems of the equinoxes and solstices. The same
science flourished among the Chaldeans, and over the whole of
Asia and Africa. When Alexander invaded India, the astrologers
of the Oxydraces came to him to disclose the secrets of their
science of Heaven and the Stars. The Brahmins whom Apollonius
consulted, taught him the secrets of Astronomy, with the ceremonies and prayers whereby to appease the gods and learn the
future from the stars. In China, astrology taught the mode of
governing the State and families. In Arabia it was deemed the
mother of the sciences; and old libraries are full of Arabic books
on this pretended science. It flourished at Rome. Constantine
had his horoscope drawn by the astrologer Valens. It was a
science in the middle ages, and even to this day is neither forgotten
nor unpractised. Catherine de Medici was fond of it. Louis XIV.
consulted his horoscope, and the learned Casini commenced his
career as an astrologer.

The ancient Sabæans established feasts in honor of each planet,
on the day, for each, when it entered its place of *exaltation,* or
reached the particular degree in the particular sign of the zodiac
in which astrology had fixed the place of its exaltation; that is, the
place in the Heavens where its influence was supposed to be greatest, and where it acted on Nature with the greatest energy. The
place of exaltation of the Sun was in Aries, because, reaching that
point, he awakens all Nature, and warms into life all the germs of
vegetation; and therefore his most solemn feast among all nations,
for many years before our Era, was fixed at the time of his entrance into that sign. In Egypt, it was called the Feast of Fire and
Light. It was the Passover, when the Paschal Lamb was slain and
eaten, among the Jews, and Neurouz among the Persians. The
Romans preferred the place of *domicile* to that of exaltation; and
celebrated the feasts of the planets under the signs that were their
houses. The Chaldeans, whom, and not the Egyptians, the Sabæans followed in this, preferred the places of exaltation.

Saturn, from the length of time required for his apparent revolution, was considered the most remote, and the Moon the nearest planet. After the Moon came Mercury and Venus, then the Sun, and then Mars, Jupiter, and Saturn.

So the risings and settings of the Fixed Stars, and their conjunctions with the Sun, and their first appearance as they emerged from his rays, fixed the epochs for the feasts instituted in their honor; and the Sacred Calendars of the ancients were regulated accordingly.

In the Roman games of the circus, celebrated in honor of the Sun and of entire Nature, the Sun, Moon, Planets, Zodiac, Elements, and the most apparent parts and potent agents of Nature were personified and represented, and the courses of the Sun in the Heavens were imitated in the Hippodrome; his chariot being drawn by four horses of different colors, representing the four elements and seasons. The courses were from East to West, like the circuits round the Lodge, and seven in number, to correspond with the number of planets. The movements of the Seven Stars that revolve around the pole were also represented, as were those of Capella, which by its heliacal rising at the moment when the Sun reached the Pleiades, in Taurus, announced the commencement of the annual revolution of the Sun.

The intersection of the Zodiac by the colures at the Equinoctial and Solstitial points, fixed four periods, each of which has, by one or more nations, and in some cases by the same nation at different periods, been taken for the commencement of the year. Some adopted the Vernal Equinox, because then day began to prevail over night, and light gained a victory over darkness. Sometimes the Summer Solstice was preferred; because then day attained its maximum of duration, and the acme of its glory and perfection. In Egypt, another reason was, that then the Nile began to overflow, at the heliacal rising of Sirius. Some preferred the Autumnal Equinox, because then the harvests were gathered, and the hopes of a new crop were deposited in the bosom of the earth. And some preferred the Winter Solstice, because then, the shortest day having arrived, their length commenced to increase, and Light began the career destined to end in victory at the Vernal Equinox.

The Sun was figuratively said to *die* and be *born again* at the Winter Solstice; the games of the Circus, in honor of the invincible God-Sun, were then celebrated, and the Roman year, established or reformed by Numa, commenced. Many peoples of Italy commenced their year, Macrobius says, at that time; and represented by the four ages of man the gradual succession of periodical increase and diminution of day, and the light of the Sun; likening him to an infant born at the Winter Solstice, a young man at the Vernal Equinox, a robust man at the Summer Solstice, and an old man at the Autumnal Equinox.

This idea was borrowed from the Egyptians, who adored the Sun at the Winter Solstice, under the figure of an infant.

The image of the Sign in which each of the four seasons commenced, became the form under which was figured the Sun of that particular season. The Lion's skin was worn by Hercules; the horns of the Bull adorned the forehead of Bacchus; and the autumnal serpent wound its long folds round the Statue of Serapis, 2500 years before our era; when those Signs corresponded with the commencement of the Seasons. When other constellations replaced them at those points, by means of the precession of the Equinoxes, those attributes were changed. Then the Ram furnished the horns for the head of the Sun, under the name of Jupiter Ammon. He was no longer born exposed to the waters of Aquarius, like Bacchus, nor enclosed in an urn like the God Canopus; but in the Stables of Augeas or the Celestial Goat. He then completed his triumph, mounted on an ass, in the constellation Cancer, which then occupied the Solstitial point of Summer.

Other attributes the images of the Sun borrowed from the constellations which, by their rising and setting, fixed the points of departure of the year, and the commencements of its four principal divisions.

First the Bull and afterward the Ram (called by the Persians the Lamb), was regarded as the regenerator of Nature, through his union with the Sun. Each, in his turn, was an emblem of the Sun overcoming the winter darkness, and repairing the disorders of Nature, which every year was regenerated under these Signs, after the Scorpion and Serpent of Autumn had brought upon it barrenness, disaster, and darkness. Mithras was represented sitting on a Bull; and that animal was an image of Osiris: while the Greek Bacchus armed his front with its horns, and was pictured with its tail and feet.

The Constellations also became noteworthy to the husbandman, which by their rising or setting, at morning or evening, indicated the coming of this period of renewed fruitfulness and new life. Capella, or the kid Amalthea, whose horn is called that of abundance, and whose place is over the equinoctial point, or Taurus; and the Pleiades, that long indicated the Seasons, and gave rise to a multitude of poetic fables, were the most observed and most celebrated in antiquity.

The original Roman year commenced at the Vernal Equinox. July was formerly called *Quintilis,* the 5th month, and August *Sextilis,* the 6th, as *September* is still the 7th month, *October* the 8th, and so on. The Persians commenced their year at the same time, and celebrated their great feast of Neurouz when the Sun entered Aries and the Constellation Perseus rose,—Perseus, who first brought down to earth the heavenly fire consecrated in their temples: and all the ceremonies then practised reminded men of the renovation of Nature and the triumph of Ormuzd, the Light-God, over the powers of Darkness and Ahriman their Chief.

The Legislator of the Jews fixed the commencement of their year in the month Nisan, at the Vernal Equinox, at which season the Israelites marched out of Egypt and were relieved of their long bondage; in commemoration of which Exodus, they ate the Paschal Lamb at that Equinox. And when Bacchus and his army had long marched in burning deserts, they were led by a Lamb or Ram into beautiful meadows, and to the Springs that watered the Temple of Jupiter Ammon. For, to the Arabs and Ethiopians, whose great Divinity Bacchus was, nothing was so perfect a type of Elysium as a Country abounding in springs and rivulets.

Orion, on the same meridian with the Stars of Taurus, died of the sting of the celestial Scorpion, that rises when he sets; as dies the Bull of Mithras in Autumn: and in the Stars that correspond with the Autumnal Equinox we find those malevolent genii that ever war against the Principle of good, and that take from the Sun and the Heavens the fruit-producing power that they communicate to the earth.

With the Vernal Equinox, dear to the sailor as to the husbandman, came the Stars that, with the Sun, open navigation, and rule the stormy Seas. Then the Twins plunge into the solar fires, or disappear at setting, going down with the Sun into the bosom of the waters. And these tutelary Divinities of mariners, the Dioscuri or Chief Cabiri of Samothrace, sailed with Jason to possess themselves of the golden-fleeced ram, or Aries, whose rising in the morning announced the Sun's entry into Taurus, when the Serpent-bearer Jason rose in the evening, and, in aspect with the Dioscuri, was deemed their brother. And Orion, son of Neptune, and most potent controller of the tempest-tortured ocean, announcing sometimes calm and sometimes tempest, rose after Taurus, rejoicing in the forehead of the new year.

The Summer Solstice was not less an important point in the Sun's march than the Vernal Equinox, especially to the Egyptians, to whom it not only marked the end and term of the increasing length of the days and of the domination of light, and the *maximum* of the Sun's elevation; but also the annual recurrence of that phenomenon peculiar to Egypt, the rising of the Nile, which, ever accompanying the Sun in his course, seemed to rise and fall as the days grew longer and shorter, being lowest at the Winter Solstice, and highest at that of Summer. Thus the Sun seemed to regulate its swelling; and the time of his arrival at the solstitial point being that of the first rising of the Nile, was selected by the Egyptians as the beginning of a year which they called the Year of God, and of the Sothiac Period, or the period of Sothis, the Dog-Star, who, rising in the morning, fixed that epoch, so important to the people of Egypt. This year was also called the Heliac, that is the Solar year, and the Canicular year; and it consisted of three hundred and sixty-five days, without intercalation; so that at the end of four years, or of four times three hundred and sixty-five days, making 1460 days, it needed to add a day, to make four complete revolutions of the Sun. To correct this, some Nations made every fourth year consist, as we do now, of 366 days: but the Egyptians preferred to add nothing to the year of 365 days, which, at the end of 120 years, or of 30 times 4 years, was short 30 days or a month; that is to say, it required a month more to complete the 120 revolutions of the Sun, though so many were counted, that is, so many years. Of course the commencement of the 121st year would not correspond with the Summer Solstice, but would precede it by a month: so that, when the Sun arrived at the Solstitial point whence he at first set out, and whereto he must needs return, to make in reality 120 years, or 120 complete revolutions, the first month of the 121st year would have ended.

Thus, if the commencement of the year went back 30 days every 120 years, this commencement of the year, continuing to recede, would, at the end of 12 times 120 years, or of 1460 years, get back to the Solstitial point, or primitive point of departure of the period. The Sun would then have made but 1459 revolutions, though 1460 were counted; to make up which, a year more would need to be added. So that the Sun would not have made his 1460 revolutions until the end of 1461 years of 365 days each,—each revolution being in reality not 365 days exactly, but 365¼.

This period of 1461 years, each of 365 days, bringing back the commencement of the Solar year to the Solstitial point, at the rising of Sirius, after 1460 complete Solar revolutions, was called in Egypt the *Sothiac* period, the point of departure whereof was the Summer Solstice, first occupied by the Lion and afterward by Cancer, under which sign is Sirius, which opened the period. It was, says Porphyry, at this Solstitial New Moon, accompanied by the rising of Seth or the Dog-Star, that the beginning of the year was fixed, and that of the generation of all things, or, as it were, the natal hour of the world.

Not Sirius alone determined the period of the rising of the Nile. Aquarius, his urn, and the stream flowing from it, in opposition to the sign of the Summer Solstice then occupied by the Sun, opened in the evening the march of Night, and received the full Moon in his cup. Above him and with him rose the feet of Pegasus, struck wherewith the waters flow forth that the Muses drink. The Lion and the Dog, indicating, were supposed to *cause* the inundation, and so were worshipped. While the Sun passed through Leo, the waters doubled their depth; and the sacred fountains poured their streams through the heads of lions. Hydra, rising between Sirius and Leo, extended under three signs. Its head rose with Cancer, and its tail with the feet of the Virgin and the beginning of Libra; and the inundation continued while the Sun passed along its whole extent.

The successive contest of light and darkness for the possession of the lunar disk, each being by turns victor and vanquished, exactly resembled what passed upon the earth by the action of the Sun and his journeys from one Solstice to the other. The lunary revolution presented the same periods of light and darkness as the year, and was the object of the same religious fictions. Above the Moon, Pliny said, everything is pure, and filled with eternal light. There ends the cone of shadow which the earth projects, and which produces night; there ends the sojourn of night and darkness; to it the air extends; but there we enter the pure substance.

The Egyptians assigned to the Moon the demiurgic or creative force of Osiris, who united himself to her in the spring, when the Sun communicated to her the principles of generation which she afterward disseminated in the air and all the elements. The Persians considered the Moon to have been impregnated by the Celestial Bull, first of the signs of spring. In all ages, the Moon has been supposed to have great influence upon vegetation, and the birth and growth of animals; and the belief is as widely entertained now as ever, and that influence regarded as a mysterious and inexplicable one. Not the astrologers alone, but Naturalists like Pliny, Philosophers like Plutarch and Cicero, Theologians like the Egyptian Priests, and Metaphysicians like Proclus, believed firmly in these lunar influences.

"The Egyptians," says Diodorus Siculus, "acknowledged two great gods, the Sun and Moon, or Osiris and Isis, who govern the world and regulate its administration by the dispensation of the seasons. . . . Such is the nature of these two great Divinities, that they impress an active and fecundating force, by which the generation of beings in effected; the Sun, by heat and that spiritual principle that forms the breath of the winds; the Moon by humidity and dryness; and both by the forces of the air which they share in common. By this beneficial influence everything is born, grows, and vegetates. Wherefore this whole huge body, in which nature resides, is maintained by the combined action of the Sun and Moon, and their five qualities,—the principles spiritual, fiery, dry, humid, and airy."

So five primitive powers, elements, or elementary qualities, are united with the Sun and Moon in the Indian theology,—air, spirit, fire, water, and earth: and the same five elements are recognized by the Chinese. The Phœnicians, like the Egyptians, regarded the Sun and Moon and Stars as sole causes of generation and destruction here below.

The Moon, like the Sun, changed continually the track in which she crossed the Heavens, moving ever to and fro between the upper and lower limits of the Zodiac; and her different places, phases, and aspects there, and her relations with the Sun and the constellations, have been a fruitful source of mythological fables.

All the planets had what astrology termed their *houses*, in the

Zodiac. The House of the Sun was in Leo, and that of the Moon in Cancer. Each other planet had two signs; Mercury had Gemini and Virgo; Venus, Taurus and Libra; Mars, Aries and Scorpio; Jupiter, Pisces and Sagittarius; and Saturn, Aquarius and Capricornus. From this distribution of the signs also came many mythological emblems and fables; as also many came from the places of exaltation of the planets. Diana of Ephesus, the Moon, wore the image of a crab on her bosom, because in that sign was the Moon's domicile; and lions bore up the throne of Horus, the Egyptian Apollo, the Sun personified, for a like reason: while the Egyptians consecrated the tauriform scarabæus to the Moon, because she had her place of exaltation in Taurus; and for the same reason Mercury is said to have presented Isis with a helmet like a bull's head.

A further division of the Zodiac was of each sign into three parts of 10° each, called Decans, or, in the whole Zodiac, 36 parts, among which the seven planets were apportioned anew, each planet having an equal number of Decans, except the first, which, opening and closing the series of planets five times repeated, necessarily had one Decan more than the others. This subdivision was not invented until after Aries opened the Vernal Equinox; and accordingly Mars, having his house in Aries, opens the series of decans and closes it; the planets following each other, five times in succession, in the following order, Mars, the Sun, Venus, Mercury, the Moon, Saturn, Jupiter, Mars, etc.; so that to each sign are assigned three planets, each occupying 10 degrees. To each Decan a God or Genius was assigned, making thirty-six in all, one of whom, the Chaldeans said, came down upon earth every ten days, remained so many days, and re-ascended to Heaven. This division is found on the Indian sphere, the Persian, and that Barbaric one which Aben Ezra describes. Each genius of the Decans had a name and special characteristics. They concur and aid in the effects produced by the Sun, Moon, and other planets charged with the administration of the world: and the doctrine in regard to them, secret and august as it was held, was considered of the gravest importance; and its principles, Firmicus says, were not entrusted by the ancients, inspired as they were by the Deity, to any but the Initiates, and to them only with great reserve, and a kind of fear, and when cautiously enveloped with an obscure veil, that they might not come to be known by the profane.

With these Decans were connected the *paranatellons* or those stars *outside* of the Zodiac, that rise and set at the same moment with the several divisions of 10° of each sign. As there were anciently only forty-eight celestial figures or constellations, of which twelve were in the Zodiac, it follows that there were, outside of the Zodiac, thirty-six other asterisms, paranatellons of the several thirty-six Decans. For example, as when Capricorn set, Sirius and Procyon, or Canis Major and Canis Minor, rose, they were the Paranatellons of Capricorn, though at a great distance from it in the heavens. The rising of Cancer was known from the setting of Corona Borealis and the rising of the Great and Little Dog, its three paranatellons.

The risings and settings of the Stars are always spoken of as connected with the Sun. In that connection there are three kinds of them, cosmical, achronical, and heliacal, important to be distinguished by all who would understand this ancient learning.

When any Star rises or sets with the same degree of the same sign of the Zodiac that the Sun occupies at the time, it rises and sets simultaneously with the Sun, and this is termed rising or setting *cosmically;* but a star that so rises and sets can never be seen, on account of the light that precedes, and is left behind by the Sun. It is therefore necessary, in order to know *his* place in the Zodiac, to observe stars that rise just before or set just after him.

A Star that is in the East when night commences, and in the West when it ends, is said to rise and set *achronically*. A Star so rising or setting was in *opposition* to the Sun, rising at the end of evening twilight, and setting at the beginning of morning twilight, and this happened to each Star but once a year, because the Sun moves from West to East, with reference to the Stars, one degree a day.

When a Star rises as night ends in the morning, or sets as night commences in the evening, it is said to rise or set *heliacally*, because the Sun (*Helios*) seems to touch it with his luminous atmosphere. A Star thus re-appears after a disappearance, often, of several months, and thenceforward it rises an hour earlier each day, gradually emerging from the Sun's rays, until at the end of three months it precedes the Sun six hours, and rises at midnight. A Star sets heliacally, when no longer remaining visible above the western horizon after sunset, the day arrives when they cease to

be seen setting in the West. They so remain invisible, until the
Sun passes so far to the Eastward as not to eclipse them with his
light; and then they re-appear, but in the East, about an hour
and a half before sunrise: and this is their *heliacal* rising. In
this interval, the cosmical rising and setting take place.

Besides the relations of the constellations and their paranatellons with the houses and places of exaltation of the Planets, and
with their places in the respective Signs and Decans, the Stars
were supposed to produce different effects according as they rose
or set, and according as they did so either cosmically, achronically,
or heliacally; and also according to the different seasons of the
year in which these phenomena occurred; and these differences
were carefully marked on the old Calendars; and many things in
the ancient allegories are referable to them.

Another and most important division of the Stars was into
good and bad, beneficent and malevolent. With the Persians, the
former, of the Zodiacal Constellations, were from Aries to Virgo,
inclusive; and the latter from Libra to Pisces, inclusive. Hence
the good Angels and Genii, and the bad Angels, Devs, Evil Genii,
Devils, Fallen Angels, Titans, and Giants of the Mythology. The
other thirty-six Constellations were equally divided, eighteen on
each side, or, with those of the Zodiac, twenty-four.

Thus the symbolic Egg, that issued from the mouth of the
invisible Egyptian God KNEPH; known in the Grecian Mysteries
as the Orphic Egg; from which issued the God CHUMONG of the
Coresians, and the Egyptian OSIRIS, and PHANES, God and Principle of Light; from which, broken by the Sacred Bull of the
Japanese, the world emerged; and which the Greeks placed at the
feet of BACCHUS TAURI-CORNUS; the Magian Egg of ORMUZD,
from which came the Amshaspands and Devs; was divided into
two halves, and equally apportioned between the Good and Evil
Constellations and Angels. Those of Spring, as for example Aries
and Taurus, Auriga and Capella, were the beneficent stars; and
those of Autumn, as the Balance, Scorpio, the Serpent of Ophiucus, and the Dragon of the Hesperides, were types and subjects of
the Evil Principle, and regarded as malevolent causes of the ill
effects experienced in Autumn and Winter. Thus are explained
the mysteries of the journeyings of the human soul through the
spheres, when it descends to the earth by the Sign of the Serpent,
and returns to the Empire of light by that of the Lamb or Bull.

The creative action of Heaven was manifested, and all its demiurgic energy developed, most of all at the Vernal Equinox, to which refer all the fables that typify the victory of Light over Darkness, by the triumphs of Jupiter, Osiris, Ormuzd, and Apollo. Always the triumphant god takes the form of the Bull, the Ram, or the Lamb. Then Jupiter wrests from Typhon his thunderbolts, of which that malignant Deity had possessed himself during the Winter. Then the God of Light overwhelms his foe, pictured as a huge Serpent. Then Winter ends; the Sun, seated on the Bull and accompanied by Orion, blazes in the Heavens. All nature rejoices at the victory; and Order and Harmony are everywhere re-established, in place of the dire confusion that reigned while gloomy Typhon domineered, and Ahriman prevailed against Ormuzd.

The universal Soul of the World, motive power of Heaven and of the Spheres, it was held, exercises its creative energy chiefly through the medium of the Sun, during his revolution along the signs of the Zodiac, with which signs unite the paranatellons that modify their influence, and concur in furnishing the symbolic attributes of the Great Luminary that regulates Nature and is the depository of her greatest powers. The action of this Universal Soul of the World is displayed in the movements of the Spheres, and above all in that of the Sun, in the successions of the risings and settings of the Stars, and in their periodical returns. By these are explainable all the metamorphoses of that Soul, personified as Jupiter, as Bacchus, as Vishnu, or as Buddha, and all the various attributes ascribed to it; and also the worship of those animals that were consecrated in the ancient Temples, representatives on earth of the Celestial Signs, and supposed to receive by transmission from them the rays and emanations which in them flow from the Universal Soul.

All the old Adorers of Nature, the Theologians, Astrologers, and Poets, as well as the most distinguished Philosophers, supposed that the Stars were so many animated and intelligent beings, or eternal bodies, active causes of effect here below, animated by a living principle, and directed by an intelligence that was itself but an emanation from and a part of the life and universal intelligence of the world: and we find in the hierarchical order and distribution of their eternal and divine Intelligences, known by the names of Gods, Angels, and Genii, the same distributions and the same divisions as those by which the ancients divided the visible Universe and distributed its parts. And the famous divisions by seven and by twelve, appertaining to the planets and the signs of the zodiac, is everywhere found in the hierarchical order of the Gods, and Angels, and the other Ministers that are the depositaries of that Divine Force which moves and rules the world.

These, and the other Intelligences assigned to the other Stars, have absolute dominion over all parts of Nature; over the elements, the animal and vegetable kingdoms, over man and all his actions, over his virtues and vices, and over good and evil, which divide between them his life. The passions of his soul and the maladies of his body,—these and the entire man are dependent on the heavens and the genii that there inhabit, who preside at his birth, control his fortunes during life, and receive his soul or active and intelligent part when it is to be re-united to the pure life of the lofty Stars. And all through the great body of the world are disseminated portions of the universal Soul, impressing movement on everything that seems to move of itself, giving life to the plants and trees, directing by a regular and settled plan the organization and development of their germs, imparting constant mobility to the running waters and maintaining their eternal motion, impelling the winds and changing their direction or stilling them, calming and arousing the ocean, unchaining the storms, pouring out the fires of volcanoes, or with earthquakes shaking the roots of huge mountains and the foundations of vast continents; by means of a force that, belonging to Nature, is a mystery to man.

And these invisible Intelligences, like the stars, are marshalled in two great divisions, under the banners of the two Principles of Good and Evil, Light and Darkness; under Ormuzd and Ahriman, Osiris and Typhon. The Evil Principle was the motive power of brute matter; and it, personified as Ahriman and Typhon, had its hosts and armies of Devs and Genii, Fallen Angels and Malevolent Spirits, who waged continual wage with the Good Principle, the Principle of Empyreal Light and Splendor, Osiris, Ormuzd, Jupiter or Dionusos, with his bright hosts of Amshaspands, Izeds, Angels, and Archangels; a warfare that goes on from birth until death, in the soul of every man that lives.

We have heretofore, in the 24th Degree, recited the principal incidents in the legend of Osiris and Isis, and it remains but to point out the astronomical phenomena which it has converted into mythological facts.

The Sun, at the Vernal Equinox, was the fruit-compelling star that by his warmth provoked generation and poured upon the sublunary world all the blessings of Heaven; the beneficent god, tutelary genius of universal vegetation, that communicates to the dull earth new activity, and stirs her great heart, long chilled by Winter and his frosts, until from her bosom burst all the greenness and perfume of spring, making her rejoice in leafy forests and grassy lawns and flower-enamelled meadows, and the promise of abundant crops of grain and fruits and purple grapes in their due season.

He was then called Osiris, Husband of Isis, God of Cultivation and Benefactor of Men, pouring on them and on the earth the choicest blessings within the gift of the Divinity. Opposed to him was Typhon, his antagonist in the Egyptian mythology, as Ahriman was the foe of Ormuzd, the Good Principle, in the theology of the Persians.

The first inhabitants of Egypt and Ethiopia, as Diodorus Siculus informs us, saw in the Heavens two first eternal causes of things, or great Divinities, one the Sun, whom they called Osiris, and the other the Moon, whom they called Isis; and these they considered the causes of all the generations of earth. This idea, we learn from Eusebius, was the same as that of the Phœnicians. On these two great Divinities the administration of the world depended. All sublunary bodies received from them their nourishment and increase, during the annual revolution which they controlled, and the different seasons into which it was divided.

To Osiris and Isis, it was held, were owing civilization, the discovery of agriculture, laws, arts of all kinds, religious worship, temples, the invention of letters, astronomy, the gymnastic arts, and music; and thus they were the universal benefactors. Osiris travelled to civilize the countries which he passed through, and communicate to them his valuable discoveries. He built cities, and taught men to cultivate the earth. Wheat and wine were his first presents to men. Europe, Asia, and Africa partook of the blessings which he communicated, and the most remote regions of India remembered him, and claimed him as one of their great gods.

You have learned how Typhon, his brother, slew him. His body was cut into pieces, all of which were collected by Isis, except his organs of generation, which had been thrown into and devoured in the waters of the river that every year fertilized Egypt. The other portions were buried by Isis, and over them she erected a tomb. Thereafter she remained single, loading her subjects with blessings. She cured the sick, restored sight to the blind, made the paralytic whole, and even raised the dead. From her Horus or Apollo learned divination and the science of medicine.

Thus the Egyptians pictured the beneficent action of the two luminaries that, from the bosom of the elements, produced all animals and men, and all bodies that are born, grow, and die in the eternal circle of generation and destruction here below.

When the Celestial Bull opened the new year at the Vernal Equinox, Osiris, united with the Moon, communicated to her the seeds of fruitfulness which she poured upon the air, and therewith impregnated the generative principles which gave activity to universal vegetation. Apis, represented by a bull, was the living and sensible image of the Sun or Osiris, when in union with Isis or the Moon at the Vernal Equinox, concurring with her in provoking everything that lives to generation. This conjunction of the Sun with the Moon at the Vernal Equinox, in the constellation Taurus, required the Bull Apis to have on his shoulder a mark resembling the Crescent Moon. And the fecundating influence of these two luminaries was expressed by images that would now be deemed gross and indecent, but which then were not misunderstood.

Everything good in Nature comes from Osiris,—order, harmony, and the favorable temperature of the seasons and celestial periods. From Typhon come the stormy passions and irregular impulses that agitate the brute and material part of man; maladies of the body, and violent shocks that injure the health and derange the system; inclement weather, derangement of the seasons, and eclipses. Osiris and Typhon were the Ormuzd and Ahriman of the Persians; principles of good and evil, of light and darkness, ever at war in the administration of the Universe.

Osiris was the image of generative power. This was expressed by his symbolic statues, and by the sign into which he entered at the Vernal Equinox. He especially dispensed the humid principle of Nature, generative element of all things; and the Nile and all moisture were regarded as emanations from him, without which there could be no vegetation.

That Osiris and Isis were the Sun and Moon, is attested by

many ancient writers; by Diogenes Laertius, Plutarch, Lucian, Suidas, Macrobius, Martianus Capella, and others. His power was symbolized by an Eye over a Sceptre. The Sun was termed by the Greeks the Eye of Jupiter, and the Eye of the World; and his is the All-Seeing Eye in our Lodges. The oracle of Claros styled him King of the Stars and of the Eternal Fire, that engenders the year and the seasons, dispenses rain and winds, and brings about daybreak and night. And Osiris was invoked as the God that resides in the Sun and is enveloped by his rays, the invisible and eternal force that modifies the sublunary world by means of the Sun.

Osiris was the same God known as Bacchus, Dionusos, and Serapis. Serapis is the author of the regularity and harmony of the world. Bacchus, jointly with Ceres (identified by Herodotus with Isis) presides over the distribution of all our blessings; and from the two emanates everything beautiful and good in Nature. One furnishes the germ and principle of every good; the other receives and preserves it as a deposit; and the latter is the function of the Moon in the theology of the Persians. In each theology, Persian and Egyptian, the Moon acts directly on the earth; but she is fecundated, in one by the Celestial Bull and in the other by Osiris, with whom she is united at the Vernal Equinox, in the sign Taurus, the place of her exaltation or greatest influence on the earth. The force of Osiris, says Plutarch, is exercised through the Moon. She is the passive cause relatively to him, and the active cause relatively to the earth, to which she transmits the germs of fruitfulness received from him.

In Egypt the earliest movement in the waters of the Nile began to appear at the Vernal Equinox, when the new Moon occurred at the entrance of the Sun into the constellation Taurus; and thus the Nile was held to receive its fertilizing power from the combined action of the equinoctial Sun and the new Moon, meeting in Taurus. Osiris was often confounded with the Nile, and Isis with the earth; and Osiris was deemed to act on the earth, and to transmit to it his emanations, through both the Moon and the Nile; whence the fable that his generative organs were thrown into that river. Typhon, on the other hand, was the principle of aridity and barrenness; and by his mutilation of Osiris was meant that drought which caused the Nile to retire within his bed and shrink up in Autumn.

Elsewhere than in Egypt, Osiris was the symbol of the refreshing rains that descend to fertilize the earth; and Typhon the burning winds of Autumn; the stormy rains that rot the flowers, the plants, and leaves; the short, cold days; and everything injurious in Nature, and that produces corruption and destruction.

In short, Typhon is the principle of corruption, of darkness, of the lower world from which come earthquakes, tumultuous commotions of the air, burning heat, lightning, and fiery meteors, and plague and pestilence. Such too was the Ahriman of the Persians; and this revolt of the Evil Principle against the Principle of Good and Light, has been represented in every cosmogony, under many varying forms. Osiris, on the contrary, by the intermediation of Isis, fills the material world with happiness, purity, and order, by which the harmony of Nature is maintained. It was said that he died at the Autumnal Equinox, when Taurus or the Pleiades rose in the evening, and that he rose to life again in the Spring, when vegetation was inspired with new activity.

Of course the two signs of Taurus and Scorpio will figure most largely in the mythological history of Osiris, for they marked the two equinoxes, 2500 years before our Era; and next to them the other constellations, near the equinoxes, that fixed the limits of the duration of the fertilizing action of the Sun; and it is also to be remarked that Venus, the Goddess of Generation, has her domicile in Taurus, as the Moon has there her place of exaltation.

When the Sun was in Scorpio, Osiris lost his life, and that fruitfulness which, under the form of the Bull, he had communicated, through the Moon, to the Earth. Typhon, his hands and feet horrid with serpents, and whose habitat in the Egyptian planisphere was under Scorpio, confined him in a chest and flung him into the Nile, under the 17th degree of Scorpio. Under that sign he lost his life and virility; and he recovered them in the Spring, when he had connection with the Moon. When he entered Scorpio, his light diminished, Night reassumed her dominion, the Nile shrunk within its banks, and the earth lost her verdure and the trees their leaves. Therefore it is that on the Mithriac Monuments, the Scorpion bites the testicles of the Equinoctial Bull, on which sits Mithras, the Sun of Spring and God of Generation; and that, on the same monuments, we see two trees, one covered with young leaves, and at its foot a little bull and a torch burning; and the other loaded with fruit, and at its foot a Scorpion, and a torch reversed and extinguished.

Ormuzd or Osiris, the beneficent Principle that gives the world light, was personified by the Sun, apparent source of light. Darkness, personified by Typhon or Ahriman, was his natural enemy. The Sages of Egypt described the necessary and eternal rivalry or opposition of these principles, ever pursuing one the other, and one dethroning the other in every annual revolution, and at a particular period, one in the Spring under the Bull, and the other in Autumn under the Scorpion, by the legendary history of Osiris and Typhon, detailed to us by Diodorus and Synesius; in which history were also personified the Stars and constellations Orion, Capella, the Twins, the Wolf, Sirius, and Hercules, whose risings and settings noted the advent of one or the other equinox.

Plutarch gives us the positions in the Heavens of the Sun and Moon, at the moment when Osiris was murdered by Typhon. The Sun, he says, was in the Sign of the Scorpion, which he then entered at the Autumnal Equinox. The Moon was full, he adds; and consequently, as it rose at sunset, it occupied Taurus, which, opposite to Scorpio, rose as it and the Sun sank together, so that she was then found alone in the sign Taurus, where, six months before, she had been in union or conjunction with Osiris, the Sun, receiving from him those germs of universal fertilization which he communicated to her. It was the sign through which Osiris first ascended into his empire of light and good. It rose with the Sun on the day of the Vernal Equinox; it remained six months in the luminous hemisphere, ever preceding the Sun and above the horizon during the day; until in Autumn, the Sun arriving at Scorpio, Taurus was in complete opposition with him, rose when he set, and completed its entire course above the horizon during the night; presiding, by rising in the evening, over the commencement of the long nights. Hence in the sad ceremonies commemorating the death of Osiris, there was borne in procession a golden bull covered with black crape, image of the darkness into which the familiar sign of Osiris was entering, and which was to spread over the Northern regions, while the Sun, prolonging the nights, was to be absent, and each to remain under the dominion of Typhon, Principle of Evil and Darkness.

Setting out from the sign Taurus, Isis, as the Moon, went seeking for Osiris through all the superior signs, in each of which she

became full in the successive months from the Autumnal to the
Vernal Equinox, without finding him in either. Let us follow her
in her allegorical wanderings.

Osiris was slain by Typhon his rival, with whom conspired a
Queen of Ethiopia, by whom, says Plutarch, were designated the
winds. The paranatellons of Scorpio, the sign occupied by the
Sun when Osiris was slain, were the Serpents, reptiles which supplied the attributes of the Evil Genii and of Typhon, who himself bore the form of a serpent in the Egyptian planisphere. And
in the division of Scorpio is also found Cassiopeia, Queen of Ethiopia, whose setting brings stormy winds.

Osiris descended to the shades or infernal regions. There he
took the name of Serapis, identical with Pluto, and assumed his
nature. He was then in conjunction with Serpentarius, identical
with Æsculapius, whose form he took in his passage to the lower
signs, where he takes the names of Pluto and Ades.

Then Isis wept for the death of Osiris, and the golden bull covered with crape was carried in procession. Nature mourned the
impending loss of her Summer glories, and the advent of the empire of night, the withdrawing of the waters, made fruitful by the
Bull in Spring, the cessation of the winds that brought rains to
swell the Nile, the shortening of the days, and the despoiling of
the earth. Then Taurus, directly opposite the Sun, entered into
the cone of shadow which the earth projects, by which the Moon
is eclipsed at full, and with which, making night, the Bull rises
and descends as if covered with a veil, while he remains above
our horizon.

The body of Osiris, enclosed in a chest or coffin, was cast into
the Nile. Pan and the Satyrs, near Chemmis, first discovered his
death, announced it by their cries, and everywhere created sorrow
and alarm. Taurus, with the full Moon, then entered into the
cone of shadow, and under him was the Celestial River, most
properly called the Nile, and below, Perseus, the God of Chemmis,
and Auriga, leading a she-goat, himself identical with Pan, whose
wife Aiga the she-goat was styled.

Then Isis went in search of the body. She first met certain
children who had seen it, received from them their information,
and gave them in return the gift of divination. The second full
Moon occurred in Gemini, the Twins, who presided over the oracles
of Didymus, and one of whom was Apollo, the God of Divination

She learned that Osiris had, through mistake, had connection with her sister Nephte, which she discovered by a crown of leaves of the melilot, which he had left behind him. Of this connection a child was born, whom Isis, aided by her dogs, sought for, found, reared, and attached to herself, by the name of Anubis, her faithful guardian. The third full Moon occurs in Cancer, domicile of the Moon. The paranatellons of that sign are, the crown of Ariadne or Proserpine, made of leaves of the melilot, Procyon and Canis Major, one star of which was called the Star of Isis, while Sirius himself was honored in Egypt under the name of Anubis.

Isis repaired to Byblos, and seated herself near a fountain, where she was found by the women of the Court of a King. She was induced to visit his Court, and became the nurse of his son. The fourth full Moon was in Leo, domicile of the Sun, or of Adonis, King of Byblos. The paranatellons of this sign are the flowing water of Aquarius, and Cepheus, King of Ethiopia, called Regulus, or simply The King. Behind him rise Cassiopeia his wife, Queen of Ethiopia, Andromeda his daughter, and Perseus his son-in-law, all paranatellons in part of this sign, and in part of Virgo.

Isis suckled the child, not at her breast, but with the end of her finger, at night. She burned all the mortal parts of its body, and then, taking the shape of a swallow, she flew to the great column of the palace, made of the tamarisk-tree that grew up round the coffin containing the body of Osiris, and within which it was still enclosed. The fifth full Moon occurred in Virgo, the true image of Isis, and which Eratosthenes calls by that name. It pictured a woman suckling an infant, the son of Isis, born near the Winter Solstice. This sign has for paranatellons the mast of the Celestial Ship, and the swallow-tailed fish or swallow above it, and a portion of Perseus, son-in-law of the King of Ethiopia.

Isis, having recovered the sacred coffer, sailed from Byblos in a vessel with the eldest son of the King, toward Boutos, where Anubis was, having charge of her son Horus; and in the morning dried up a river, whence arose a strong wind. Landing, she hid the coffer in a forest. Typhon, hunting a wild boar by moonlight, discovered it, recognized the body of his rival, and cut it into fourteen pieces, the number of days between the full and new Moon, and in every one of which days the Moon loses a portion of the light that at the commencement filled her whole disk. The sixth full Moon occurred in Libra, over the divisions separating which

from Virgo are the Celestial Ship, Perseus, son of the King of
Ethiopia and Boötes, said to have nursed Horus. The river of
Orion that sets in the morning is also a paranatellon of Libra, as
are Ursa Major, the Great Bear or Wild Boar of Erymanthus, and
the Dragon of the North Pole, or the celebrated Python from
which the attributes of Typhon were borrowed. All these surround the full Moon of Libra, last of the Superior Signs, and the
one that precedes the new Moon of Spring, about to be reproduced
in Taurus, and there be once more in conjunction with the Sun.

Isis collects the scattered fragments of the body of Osiris, buries
them, and consecrates the phallus, carried in pomp at the *Pamylia*,
or feasts of the Vernal Equinox, at which time the congress of
Osiris and the Moon was celebrated. Then Osiris had returned
from the shades, to aid Horus his son and Isis his wife against
the forces of Typhon. He thus reappeared, say some, under the
form of a wolf, or, others say, under that of a horse. The Moon,
fourteen days after she is full in Libra, arrives at Taurus and
unites herself to the Sun, whose fires she thereafter for fourteen
days continues to accumulate on her disk from new Moon to full.
Then she unites with herself all the months in that superior portion of the world where light always reigns, with harmony and
order, and she borrows from him the force which is to destroy the
germs of evil that Typhon had, during the winter, planted everywhere in nature. This passage of the Sun into Taurus, whose
attributes he assumes on his return from the lower hemisphere or
the shades, is marked by the rising in the evening of the Wolf and
the Centaur, and by the heliacal setting of Orion, called the Star of
Horus, and which thenceforward is in conjunction with the Sun
of Spring, in his triumph over the darkness or Typhon.

Isis, during the absence of Osiris, and after she had hidden the
coffer in the place where Typhon found it, had rejoined that malignant enemy; indignant at which, Horus her son deprived her of
her ancient diadem, when she rejoined Osiris as he was about to
attack Typhon: but Mercury gave her in its place a helmet shaped
like the head of a bull. Then Horus, as a mighty warrior, such as
Orion was described, fought with and defeated Typhon; who, in
the shape of the Serpent or Dragon of the Pole, had assailed his
father. So, in Ovid, Apollo destroys the same Python, when Io,
fascinated by Jupiter, is metamorphosed into a cow, and placed in
the sign of the Celestial Bull, where she becomes Isis. The equi-

noctial year ends at the moment when the Sun and Moon, at the Vernal Equinox, are united with Orion, the Star of Horus, placed in the Heavens under Taurus. The new Moon becomes young again in Taurus, and shows herself as a crescent, for the first time, in the next sign, Gemini, the domicile of Mercury. Then Orion, in conjunction with the Sun, with whom he rises, precipitates the Scorpion, his rival, into the shades of night, causing him to set whenever he himself re-appears on the eastern horizon, with the Sun. Day lengthens and the germs of evil are by degrees eradicated: and Horus (from *Aur,* Light) reigns triumphant, symbolizing, by his succession to the characteristics of Osiris, the eternal renewal of the Sun's youth and creative vigor at the Vernal Equinox.

Such are the coincidences of astronomical phenomena with the legend of Osiris and Isis; sufficing to show the origin of the legend, overloaded as it became at length with all the ornamentation natural to the poetical and figurative genius of the Orient.

Not only into this legend, but into those of all the ancient nations, enter the Bull, the Lamb, the Lion, and the Scorpion or the Serpent; and traces of the worship of the Sun yet linger in all religions. Everywhere, even in our Order, survive the equinoctial and solstitial feasts. Our ceilings still glitter with the greater and lesser luminaries of the Heavens, and our lights, in their number and arrangement, have astronomical references. In all churches and chapels, as in all Pagan temples and pagodas, the altar is in the East; and the ivy over the east windows of old churches is the Hedera Helix of Bacchus. Even the cross had an astronomical origin; and our Lodges are full of the ancient symbols.

The learned author of the Sabæan Researches, Landseer, advances another theory in regard to the legend of Osiris; in which he makes the constellation Boötes play a leading part. He observes that, as none of the stars were visible at the same time with the Sun, his actual place in the Zodiac, at any given time, could only be ascertained by the Sabæan astronomers by their observations of the stars, and of their heliacal and achronical risings and settings. There were many solar festivals among the Sabæans, and part of them agricultural ones; and the concomitant signs of those festivals were the risings and settings of the stars of the Husbandman, Bear-driver, or Hunter, Boötes. His stars were,

among the Hierophants, the established nocturnal indices or signs
of the Sun's place in the ecliptic at different seasons of the year,
and the festivals were named, one, that of the *Aphanism* or disappearance; another, that of the *Zetesis,* or search, etc., of Osiris
or Adonis, that is, of *Boötes.*

The returns of certain stars, as connected with their concomitant seasons of spring (or seed-time) and harvest, seemed to the
ancients, who had not yet discovered that gradual change, resulting from the apparent movement of the stars in longitude, which
has been termed the precession of the equinoxes, to be eternal
and immutable; and those periodical returns were to the initiated,
even more than to the vulgar, celestial oracles, announcing the
approach of those important changes, upon which the prosperity,
and even the very existence of man must ever depend; and the
oldest of the Sabæan constellations seem to have been, an astronomical *Priest,* a *King,* a *Queen,* a *Husbandman,* and a *Warrior;*
and these more frequently recur on the Sabæan cylinders than any
other constellations whatever. The *King* was *Cepheus* or *Chepheus*
of Ethiopia: the *Husbandman, Osiris, Bacchus, Sabazeus, Noah*
or *Boötes.* To the latter sign, the Egyptians were nationally, tra-
ditionally and habitually grateful; for they conceived that from
Osiris all the greatest of terrestrial enjoyments were derived. The
stars of the Husbandman were the signal for those successive
agricultural labors on which the annual produce of the soil
depended; and they came in consequence to be considered and
hailed, in Egypt and Ethiopia, as the genial stars of terrestrial
productiveness; to which the oblations, prayers, and vows of the
pious Sabæan were regularly offered up.

Landseer says that the stars in Boötes, reckoning down to those
of the 5th magnitude inclusive, are *twenty-six,* which, seeming
achronically to disappear in succession, produced the fable of the
cutting of Osiris into twenty-six pieces by Typhon. There are
more stars than this in the constellation; but no more that the
ancient votaries of Osiris, even in the clear atmosphere of the
Sabæan climates, could observe without telescopes.

Plutarch says Osiris was cut into *fourteen* pieces: Diodorus,
into *twenty-six;* in regard to which, and to the whole legend,
Landseer's ideas, varying from those commonly entertained, are
as follows:

Typhon, Landseer thinks, was the *ocean,* which the ancients fabled or believed surrounded the Earth, and into which all the stars in their turn appear successively to sink; [perhaps it was DARKNESS personified, which the ancients called TYPHON. He was hunting by moonlight, says the old legend, when he met with Osiris].

The ancient Saba must have been near latitude 15° north. Axoum is nearly in 14°, and the Western Saba or Meroë is to the north of that. Forty-eight centuries ago, Aldebaran, the leading star of the year, had, at the Vernal Equinox, attained at daylight in the morning, an elevation of about 14 degrees, sufficient for him to have ceased to be *combust,* that is, to have emerged from the Sun's rays, so as to be visible. The ancients allowed *twelve* days for a star of the first magnitude to emerge from the solar rays; and there is less twilight, the further South we go.

At the same period, too, Cynosura was not the pole-star, but Alpha Draconis was; and the stars rose and set with very different degrees of obliquity from those of their present risings and settings. By having a globe constructed with circumvolving poles, capable of any adjustment with regard to the colures, Mr. Landseer ascertained that, at that remote period, in lat. 15° north, the 26 stars in Boötes, or 27, including Arcturus, did not set anchronically in succession; but several set simultaneously in couples, and six by threes simultaneously; so that, in all, there were but *fourteen* separate settings or disappearances, corresponding with the fourteen pieces into which Osiris was cut, according to Plutarch. Kappa, Iota, and Theta, in the uplifted western hand, disappeared together, and last of all. They really skirted the horizon; but were invisible in that low latitude, for the three or four days mentioned in some of the versions; while the *Zetesis* or search was proceeding, and the women of Phœnicia and Jerusalem sat weeping for the Wonder, Thammuz; after which they immediately reappeared, below and to the eastward of *a* Draconis.

And, on the very morning after the achronical departure of the last star of the Husbandman, Aldebaran rose heliacally, and became visible in the East in the morning before day.

And precisely at the moment of the heliacal rising of Arcturus, also rose Spica Virginis. One is near the middle of the Husbandman, and the other near that of the Virgin; and Arcturus may have been the part of Osiris which Isis did not recover with the other pieces of the body.

At Dedan and Saba it was thirty-six days, from the beginning of the *aphanism,* i. e., the *disappearances* of these stars, to the heliacal rising of Aldebaran. During these days, or forty at Medina, or a few more at Babylon and Byblos, the stars of the Husbandman successively sank out of sight, during the *crepusculum* or short-lived morning twilight of those Southern climes. They disappear during the glancings of the dawn, the special season of ancient sidereal observation.

Thus the forty days of mourning for Osiris were measured out by the period of the departure of his Stars. When the last had sunken out of sight, the vernal season was ushered in; and the Sun arose with the splendid Aldebaran, the Tauric leader of the Hosts of Heaven; and the whole East rejoiced and kept holiday.

With the exception of the Stars χ, ι and δ, Boötes did not begin to reappear in the Eastern quarter of the Heavens till after the lapse of about four months. Then the Stars of Taurus had declined Westward, and Virgo was rising heliacally. In that latitude, also, the Stars of Ursa Major [termed anciently the Ark of Osiris] set; and Benetnasch, the last of them, returned to the Eastern horizon, with those in the head of Leo, a little before the Summer Solstice. In about a month, followed the Stars of the Husbandman; the chief of them, Ras, Mirach, and Arcturus, being very nearly simultaneous in their heliacal rising.

Thus the Stars of Boötes rose in the East immediately after Vindemiatrix, and as if under the genial influence of its rays; he had his annual career of prosperity; he revelled orientally for a quarter of a year, and attained his meridian altitude with Virgo; and then, as the Stars of the Water-Urn rose, and Aquarius began to pour forth his annual deluge, he declined Westward, preceded by the Ark of Osiris. In the East, he was the sign of that happiness in which Nature, the great Goddess of passive production, rejoiced. Now, in the West, as he declines toward the Northwestern horizon, his generative vigor gradually abates; the Solar year grows old; and as his Stars descend beneath the Western Wave, Osiris dies, and the world mourns.

The Ancient Astronomers saw all the great Symbols of Masonry in the Stars. Sirius still glitters in our Lodges as the Blazing Star, (*l'Etoile Flamboyante*). The Sun is still symbolized by the point within a Circle; and, with the Moon and Mercury or Anubis, in the three Great Lights of the Lodge. Not only to these, but to the figures and numbers exhibited by the Stars, were ascribed peculiar and divine powers. The veneration paid to numbers had its source there. The three Kings in Orion are in a straight line, and equidistant from each other, the two extreme Stars being 3° apart, and each of the three distant from the one nearest it 1° 30'. And as the number *three* is peculiar to apprentices, so the straight line is the first principle of Geometry, having length but no breadth, and being but the extension of a point, and an emblem of Unity, and thus of Good, as the divided or broken line is of Duality or Evil. Near these Stars are the Hyades, *five* in number, appropriate to the Fellow-Craft; and close to them the Pleiades, of the master's number, *seven;* and thus these three sacred numbers, consecrated in Masonry as they were in the Pythagorean philosophy, always appear together in the Heavens, when the Bull, emblem of fertility and production, glitters among the Stars, and Aldebaran leads the Hosts of Heaven (*Tsbauth*).

Algenib in Perseus and Almaach and Algol in Andromeda form a right-angled triangle, illustrate the 47th problem, and display the Grand Master's square upon the skies. Denebola in Leo, Arcturus in Boötes, and Spica in Virgo form an equilateral triangle, universal emblem of Perfection, and the Deity with His Trinity of Infinite Attributes, Wisdom, Power, and Harmony; and that other, the generative, preserving, and destroying Powers. The Three Kings form, with Rigel in Orion, two triangles included in one: and Capella and Menkalina in Auriga, with Bellatrix and Betelgueux in Orion, form two isosceles triangles with β Tauri, that is equidistant from each pair; while the first four make a right-angled parallelogram,—the oblong square so often mentioned in our Degrees.

Julius Firmicus, in his description of the Mysteries, says, "But in those funerals and lamentations which are annually celebrated in honor of Osiris, their defenders pretend a physical reason. They call the seeds of fruit, Osiris; the Earth, Isis; the natural heat, Typhon: and because the fruits are ripened by the natural heat, and collected for the life of man, and are separated from their marriage to the earth, and are sown again when Winter approaches, this they would have to be the death of Osiris: but when the fruits, by the genial fostering of the earth, begin again to be generated by a new procreation, this is the finding of Osiris."

No doubt the decay of vegetation and the falling of the leaves, emblems of dissolution and evidences of the action of that Power that changes Life into Death, in order to bring Life again out of Death, were regarded as signs of that Death that seemed coming upon all Nature; as the springing of leaves and buds and flowers in the spring was a sign of restoration to life: but these were all secondary, and referred to the Sun as first cause. It was *his* figurative death that was mourned, and not theirs; and that with that death, as with his return to life, many of the stars were connected.

We have already alluded to the relations which the twelve signs of the Zodiac bear to the legend of the Master's Degree. Some other coincidences may have sufficient interest to warrant mention.

Khir-Om was assailed at the East, West, and South Gates of the Temple. The two equinoxes were called, we have seen, by all the Ancients, the Gates of Heaven, and the Syrians and Egyptians considered the Fish (the Constellation near Aquarius, and one of the Stars whereof is Fomalhaut) to be indicative of violence and death.

Khir-Om lay several days in the grave; and, at the Winter Solstice, for five or six days, the length of the days did not perceptibly increase. Then, the Sun commencing again to climb Northward, as Osiris was said to arise from the dead, so Khir-Om was raised, by the powerful attraction of the Lion (Leo), who waited for him at the Summer Solstice, and drew him to himself.

The names of the three assassins may have been adopted from three Stars that we have already named. We search in vain in the Hebrew or Arabic for the names *Jubelo, Jubela,* and *Jubelum.* They embody an utter absurdity, and are capable of no explanation in those languages. Nor are the names *Gibs, Gravelot, Hobhen,* and the like, in the Ancient and Accepted Rite, any more plausible, or better referable to any ancient language. But when, by the precession of the Equinoxes, the Sun was in Libra at the Autumnal Equinox, he met in that sign, where the reign of Typhon commenced, three Stars forming a triangle,—*Zuben-es Chamali* in the West, *Zuben-Hak-Rabi* in the East, and *Zuben-El-Gubi* in the South, the latter immediately below the Tropic of Capricorn, and so within the realm of Darkness. From these names, those of the murderers have perhaps been corrupted. In Zuben-Hak-Rabi we may see the original of Jubelum Akirop; and in Zuben-El-Gubi, that of Jubelo Gibs: and time and ignorance may even have transmuted the words Es Chamali into one as little like them as Gravelot.

Isis, the Moon personified, sorrowing sought for her husband. Nine or twelve Fellow-Crafts (the Rites vary as to the number), in white aprons, were sent to search for Khir-Om, in the Legend of the Master's Degree; or, in this Rite, the Nine Knights Elu. Along the path that the Moon travels are nine conspicuous Stars, by which nautical men determine their longitude at Sea;—Arietis, Aldebaran, Pollux, Regulus, Spica Virginis, Antares, Altair, Fomalhaut, and Markab. These might well be said to accompany Isis in her search.

In the York Rite, *twelve* Fellow-Crafts were sent to search for the body of Khir-Om and the murderers. Their number corresponds with that of the Pleiades and Hyades in Taurus, among which Stars the Sun was found when Light began to prevail over Darkness, and the Mysteries were held. These Stars, we have shown, received early and particular attention from the astronomers and poets. The Pleiades were the Stars of the ocean to the benighted mariner; the Virgins of Spring, heralding the season of blossoms.

As six Pleiades only are now visible, the number twelve may have been obtained by them, with Aldebaran, and five far more brilliant Stars than any other of the Hyades, in the same region of the Heavens, and which were always spoken of in connection with the Pleiades;—the Three Kings in the belt of Orion, and Bellatrix and Betelgueux on his shoulders; brightest of the flashing starry hosts.

"Canst thou," asks Job, "bind the sweet influences of the Pleiades or loose the bands of Orion?" And in the book of Amos we find these Stars connected with the victory of Light over Darkness: "Seek Him," says that Seer, "that maketh the Seven Stars (the familiar name of the Pleiades), and Orion, AND TURNETH THE SHADOW OF DEATH INTO MORNING."

An old legend in Masonry says that a dog led the Nine Elus to the cavern where Abiram was hid. Boötes was anciently called Caleb Anubach, a Barking Dog; and was personified in Anubis, who bore the head of a dog, and aided Isis in her search. Arcturus, one of his Stars, fiery red, as if fervent and zealous, is also connected by Job with the Pleiades and Orion. When Taurus opened the year, Arcturus rose after the Sun, at the time of the Winter Solstice, and seemed searching him through the darkness, until, sixty days afterward, he rose at the same hour. Orion then

also, at the Winter Solstice, rose at noon, and at night seemed to
be in search of the Sun.

So, referring again to the time when the Sun entered the Autumnal Equinox, there are nine remarkable Stars that come to the
meridian nearly at the same time, rising as Libra sets, and so
seeming to chase that Constellation. They are Capella and Menkalina in the Charioteer, Aldebaran in Taurus, Bellatrix, Betelgueux, the Three Kings, and Rigel in Orion. Aldebaran passes
the meridian first, indicating his right to his peculiar title of
Leader. Nowhere in the heavens are there, near the same meridian, so many splendid Stars. And close behind them, but further South, follows Sirius, the Dog-Star, who showed the nine
Elus the way to the murderer's cave.

Besides the division of the signs into the ascending and descending series (referring to the upward and downward progress
of the soul), the latter from Cancer to Capricorn, and the former
from Capricorn to Cancer, there was another division of them not
less important; that of the six superior and six inferior signs; the
former, 2455 years before our era, from Taurus to Scorpio, and
300 years before our era, from Aries to Libra; and the latter,
2455 years B. C. from Scorpio to Taurus, and 300 years B. C.
from Libra to Aries; of which we have already spoken, as the two
Hemispheres, or Kingdoms of Good and Evil, Light and Darkness; of Ormuzd and Ahriman among the Persians, and Osiris
and Typhon among the Egyptians.

With the Persians, the first six Genii, created by Ormuzd, presided over the first six signs, Aries, Taurus, Gemini, Cancer, Leo,
and Virgo: and the six evil Genii, or Devs, created by Ahriman,
over the six others, Libra, Scorpio, Sagittarius, Capricornus,
Aquarius, and Pisces. The soul was fortunate and happy under
the Empire of the first six; and began to be sensible of evil, when
it passed under the Balance or Libra, the seventh sign. Thus the
soul entered the realm of Evil and Darkness when it passed into
the Constellations that belong to and succeed the Autumnal Equinox; and it re-entered the realm of Good and Light, when it
arrived, returning, at those of the Vernal Equinox. It lost its
felicity by means of the Balance, and regained it by means of the
Lamb. This is a necessary consequence of the premises; and it
is confirmed by the authorities and by emblems still extant.

Sallust the Philosopher, speaking of the Feasts of Rejoicing celebrated at the Vernal Equinox, and those of Mourning, in memory of the rape of Proserpine, at the Autumnal Equinox, says that the former were celebrated, because then is effected, as it were, the return of the soul toward the Gods; that the time when the principle of Light recovered its superiority over that of Darkness, or day over night, was the most favorable one for souls that tend to re-ascend to their Principle; and that when Darkness and the Night again become victors, was most favorable to the descent of souls toward the infernal regions.

For that reason, the old astrologers, as Firmicus states, fixed the locality of the river Styx in the 8th degree of the Balance. And he thinks that by Styx was allegorically meant the earth.

The Emperor Julian gives the same explanation, but more fully developed. He states, as a reason why the august Mysteries of Ceres and Proserpine were celebrated at the Autumnal Equinox, that at that period of the year men feared lest the impious and dark power of the Evil Principle, then commencing to conquer, should do harm to their souls. They were a precaution and means of safety, thought to be necessary at the moment when the God of Light was passing into the opposite or adverse region of the world; while at the Vernal Equinox there was less to be feared, because then that God, present in one portion of the world, *recalled souls to Him,* he says, *and showed Himself to be their Saviour.* He had a little before developed that theological idea, of the attractive force which the Sun exercises over souls, drawing them to him and raising them to his luminous sphere. He attributes this effect to him at the feasts of Atys, dead and restored to life, or the feasts of Rejoicing, which at the end of three days succeeded the mourning for that death; and he inquires why those Mysteries were celebrated at the Vernal Equinox. The reason, he says, is evident. As the sun, arriving at the equinoctial point of Spring, drawing nearer to us, increases the length of the days, that period seems most appropriate for those ceremonies. For, besides that there is a great affinity between the substance of Light and the nature of the Gods, the Sun has that occult force of attraction, by which he draws matter toward himself, by means of his warmth, making plants to shoot and grow, etc.; and why can he not, by the same divine and pure action of his rays, attract and draw to him fortunate souls? Then, as light is analogous to the Divine Nature, and favorable to souls struggling to return to

their First Principle, and as that light so increases at the Vernal
Equinox, that the days prevail in duration over the nights, and as
the Sun has an attractive force, besides the visible energy of his
rays, it follows that souls are attracted toward the solar light. He
does not further pursue the explanation; because, he says, it belongs to a mysterious doctrine, beyond the reach of the vulgar
and known only to those who understand the mode of action of
Deity, like the Chaldean author whom he cites, who had treated
of the Mysteries of Light, or the God with seven rays.

Souls, the Ancients held, having emanated from the Principle
of Light, partaking of its destiny here below, cannot be indifferent to nor unaffected by these revolutions of the Great Luminary,
alternately victor and overcome during every Solar revolution.

This will be found to be confirmed by an examination of some
of the Symbols used in the Mysteries. One of the most famous
of these was THE SERPENT, the peculiar Symbol also of this Degree. The Cosmogony of the Hebrews and that of the Gnostics
designated this reptile as the author of the fate of Souls. It was
consecrated in the Mysteries of Bacchus and in those of Eleusis.
Pluto overcame the virtue of Proserpine under the form of a serpent; and, like the Egyptian God Serapis, was always pictured
seated on a serpent, or with that reptile entwined about him. It
is found on the Mithriac Monuments, and supplied with attributes
of Typhon to the Egyptians. The sacred basilisc, in coil, with
head and neck erect, was the royal ensign of the Pharaohs. Two
of them were entwined around and hung suspended from the
winged Globe on the Egyptian Monuemnts. On a tablet in one
of the Tombs at Thebes, a God with a spear pierces a serpent's
head. On a tablet from the Temple of Osiris at Philæ is a tree,
with a man on one side, and a woman on the other, and in front
of the woman an erect basilisc, with horns on its head and a disk
between the horns. The head of Medusa was encircled by winged
snakes, which, the head removed, left the Hierogram or Sacred
Cypher of the Ophites or Serpent-worshippers. And the Serpent,
in connection with the Globe or circle, is found upon the monuments of all the Ancient Nations.

Over Libra, the sign through which souls were said to descend
or fall, is found, on the Celestial Globe, the Serpent, grasped by
Serpentarius, the Serpent-bearer. The head of the reptile is under
Corona Borealis, the Northern Crown, called by Ovid, *Libera,* or

Proserpine; and the two Constellations rise, with the Balance, after the Virgin (or Isis), whose feet rest on the eastern horizon at Sunrise on the day of the equinox. As the Serpent extends over both signs, Libra and Scorpio, it has been the gate through which souls descend, during the whole time that those two signs in succession marked the Autumnal Equinox. To this alluded the Serpent, which, in the Mysteries of Bacchus Saba-Zeus, was flung into the bosom of the Initiate.

And hence came the enigmatical expression, *the Serpent engenders the Bull, and the Bull the Serpent;* alluding to the two adverse constellations, answering to the two equinoxes, one of which rose as the other set, and which were at the two points of the heavens through which souls passed, ascending and descending. By the Serpent of Autumn, souls fell; and they were regenerated again by the Bull on which Mithras sate, and whose attributes Bacchus-Zagreus and the Egyptian Osiris assumed, in their Mysteries, wherein were represented the fall and regeneration of souls, by the Bull slain and restored to life.

Afterward the regenerating Sun assumed the attributes of *Aries* or the Lamb; and in the Mysteries of Ammon, souls were regenerated by passing through that sign, after having fallen through the Serpent.

The Serpent-bearer, or Ophicus, was Æsculapius, God of Healing. In the Mysteries of Eleusis, that Constellation was placed in the eighth Heaven: and on the eighth day of those Mysteries, the feast of Æsculapius was celebrated. It was also termed Epidaurus, or the feast of the Serpent of Epidaurus. The Serpent was sacred to Æsculapius; and was connected in various ways with the mythological adventures of Ceres.

So the libations to Souls, by pouring wine on the ground, and looking toward the two gates of Heaven, those of day and night, referred to the ascent and descent of Souls.

Ceres and the Serpent, Jupiter Ammon and the Bull, all figured in the Mysteries of Bacchus. Suppose Aries, or Jupiter Ammon occupied by the Sun setting in the West;—Virgo (Ceres) will be on the Eastern horizon, and in her train the Crown, or Proserpine. Suppose Taurus setting;—then the Serpent is in the East; and reciprocally; so that Jupiter Ammon, or the Sun of Aries, causes the Crown to rise after the Virgin, in the train of which comes the Serpent. Place reciprocally the Sun at the other equinox,

with the balance in the West, in conjunction with the Serpent
under the Crown; and we shall see the Bull and the Pleiades rise
in the East. Thus are explained all the fables as to the generation of the Bull by the Serpent and of the Serpent by the Bull,
the biting of the testicles of the Bull by the Scorpion, on the
Mithriac Monuments; and that Jupiter made Ceres with child by
tossing into her bosom the testicles of a Ram.

In the Mysteries of the bull-horned Bacchus, the officers held
serpents in their hands, raised them above their heads, and cried
aloud "Eva!" the generic oriental name of the serpent, and the
particular name of the constellation in which the Persians placed
Eve and the serpent. The Arabians call it *Hevan,* Ophiucus
himself, *Hawa,* and the brilliant star in his head, *Ras-al-Hawa.*
The use of this word *Eva* or *Evoë* caused Clemens of Alexandria
to say that the priests in the Mysteries invoked *Eve,* by whom evil
was brought into the world.

The mystic winnowing-fan, encircled by erpents, was used in
the feasts of Bacchus. In the Isiac Mysteries a basilisc twined
round the handle of the mystic vase. The Ophites fed a serpent
in a mysterious ark, from which they took him when they celebrated the Mysteries, and allowed him to glide among the sacred
bread. The Romans kept serpents in the Temples of Bona Dea
and Æsculapius. In the Mysteries of Apollo, the pursuit of Latona by the serpent Python was represented. In the Egyptian
Mysteries, the dragon Typhon pursued Isis.

According to Sanchoniathon, Taaut, the interpreter of Heaven
to men, attributed something divine to the nature of the dragon
and serpents, in which the Phœnicians and Egyptians followed
him. They have more vitality, more spiritual force, than any
other creature; of a fiery nature, shown by the rapidity of their
motions, without the limbs of other animals. They assume many
shapes and attitudes, and dart with extraordinary quickness and
force. When they have reached old age, they throw off that age
and are young again, and increase in size and strength, for a certain period of years.

The Egyptian Priests fed the sacred serpents in the temple at
Thebes. Taaut himself had in his writings discussed these mysteries in regard to the serpent. Sanchoniathon said in another
work, that the serpent was immortal, and re-entered into himself;
which, according to some ancient theosophists, particularly those

of India, was an attribute of the Deity. And he also said that the serpent never died, unless by a violent death.

The Phœnicians called the serpent *Agathodemon* [the good spirit] ; and Kneph was the Serpent-God of the Egyptians.

The Egyptians, Sanchoniathon said, represented the serpent with the head of a hawk, on account of the swift flight of that bird : and the chief Hierophant, the sacred interpreter, gave very mysterious explanations of that symbol ; saying that such a serpent was a very divine creature, and that, opening his eyes, he lighted with their rays the whole of first-born space : when he closes them, it is darkness again. In reality, the hawk-headed serpent, genius of light, or good genius, was the symbol of the Sun.

In the hieroglyphic characters, a snake was the letter T or DJ. It occurs many times on the Rosetta stone. The horned serpent was the hieroglyphic for a God.

According to Eusebius, the Egyptians represented the world by a blue circle, sprinkled with flames, within which was extended a serpent with the head of a hawk. Proclus says they represented the four quarters of the world by a cross, and the soul of the world, or Kneph, by a serpent surrounding it in the form of a circle.

We read in Anaxagoras, that Orpheus said, that the water, and the vessel that produced it, were the primitive principles of things, and together gave existence to an animated being, which was a serpent, with two heads, one of a lion and the other of a bull, between which was the figure of a God whose name was Hercules or Kronos : that from Hercules came the egg of the world, which produced Heaven and earth, by dividing itself into two hemispheres : and that the God Phanes, which issued from that egg, was in the shape of a serpent.

The Egyptian Goddess *Ken,* represented standing naked on a lion, held two serpents in her hand. She is the same as the *Astarte* or *Ashtaroth* of the Assyrians. *Hera,* worshipped in the Great Temple at Babylon, held in her right hand a serpent by the head ; and near *Khea,* also worshipped there, were two large silver serpents.

In a sculpture from Kouyunjik, two serpents attached to poles are near a fire-altar, at which two eunuchs are standing. Upon it is the sacred fire, and a bearded figure leads a wild goat to the sacrifice.

The serpent of the Temple of Epidaurus was sacred to *Æsculapius,* the God of Medicine, and 462 years after the building of the city, was taken to Rome after a pestilence.

The Phœnicians represented the God *Nomu* (*Kneph* or *Amun-Kneph*) by a serpent. In Egypt, a Sun supported by two asps was the emblem of *Horhat* the good genius; and the serpent with the winged globe was placed over the doors and windows of the Temples as a tutelary God. Antipater of Sidon calls *Amun* "the renowned Serpent," and the Cerastes is often found embalmed in the Thebaid.

On ancient Tyrian coins and Indian medals, a serpent was represented, coiled round the trunk of a tree. *Python,* the Serpent Deity, was esteemed oracular; and the tripod at Delphi was a triple-headed serpent of gold.

The portals of all the Egyptian Temples are decorated with the hierogram of the Circle and the Serpent. It is also found upon the Temple of Naki-Rustan in Persia; on the triumphal arch at Pechin, in China; over the gates of the great Temple of Chaundi Teeva, in Java; upon the walls of Athens; and in the Temple of Minerva at Tegea. The Mexican hierogram was formed by the intersecting of two great Serpents, which described the circle with their bodies, and had each a human head in its mouth.

All the Buddhists crosses in Ireland had serpents carved upon them. Wreaths of snakes are on the columns of the ancient Hindu Temple at Burwah-Sangor.

Among the Egyptians, it was a symbol of Divine Wisdom, when extended at length; and, with its tail in its mouth, of Eternity.

In the ritual of Zoroaster, the Serpent was a symbol of the Universe. In China, the ring between two Serpents was the symbol of the world governed by the power and wisdom of the Creator. The Bacchanals carried serpents in their hands or round their heads.

The Serpent entwined round an Egg, was a symbol common to the Indians, the Egyptians, and the Druids. It referred to the creation of the Universe. A Serpent with an egg in his mouth was a symbol of the Universe containing within itself the germ of all things that the Sun develops.

The property possessed by the Serpent, of casting its skin, and apparently renewing its youth, made it an emblem of eternity and immortality. The Syrian women still employ it as a charm against barrenness, as did the devotees of Mithras and Saba-Zeus. The Earth-born civilizers of the early world, Fohi, Cecrops, and Erechtheus, were half-man, half-serpent. The snake was the guardian of the Athenian Acropolis. NAKHUSTAN, the brazen serpent of the wilderness, became naturalized among the Hebrews as a token of healing power. "Be ye," said Christ, "wise as serpents, and harmless as doves."

The Serpent was as often a symbol of malevolence and enmity. It appears among the emblems of Siva-Roudra, the power of desolation and death: it is the bane of Aëpytus, Idom, Archemorus, and Philoctetes: it gnaws the roots of the tree of life in the Eddas, and bites the heel of unfortunate Eurydice. In Hebrew writers it is generally a type of evil; and is particularly so in the Indian and Persian Mythologies. When the Sea is churned by Mount Mandar rotating within the coils of the Cosmical Serpent Vasouki, to produce the Amrita or water of immortality, the serpent vomits a hideous poison, which spreads through and infects the Universe, but which Vishnu renders harmless by swallowing it. Ahriman in serpent-form invades the realm of Ormuzd; and the Bull, emblem of life, is wounded by him and dies. It was therefore a religious obligation with every devout follower of Zoroaster to exterminate reptiles, and other impure animals, especially serpents. The moral and astronomical significance of the Serpent were connected. It became a maxim of the Zend-Avesta, that Ahriman, the Principle of Evil, made the Great Serpent of Winter, who assaulted the creation of Ormuzd.

A serpent-ring was a well-known symbol of time: and to express dramatically how time preys upon itself, the Egyptian priests fed vipers in a subterranean chamber, as it were in the sun's Winter abode on the fat of bulls, or the year's plenteousness. The dragon of Winter pursues Ammon, the golden ram, to Mount Casius. The Virgin of the zodiac is bitten in the heel by Serpens, who, with Scorpio, rises immediately behind her; and as honey, the emblem of purity and salvation, was thought to be an antidote to the serpent's bite, so the bees of Aristæus, the emblems of nature's abundance, are destroyed through the agency of the serpent, and regenerated within the entrails of the Vernal Bull.

The Sun-God is finally victorious. Chrishna crushes the head of the serpent Calyia; Apollo destroys Python, and Hercules that Lernæan monster whose poison festered in the foot of Philoctetes, of Mopsus, of Chiron, or of Sagittarius. The infant Hercules destroys the pernicious snakes detested of the gods, and ever, like St. George of England and Michael the Archangel, wars against hydras and dragons.

The eclipses of the sun and moon were believed by the orientals to be caused by the assaults of a dæmon in dragon-form; and they endeavored to scare away the intruder by shouts and menaces. This was the original Leviathan or Crooked Serpent of old, transfixed in the olden time by the power of Jehovah, and suspended as a glittering trophy in the sky; yet also the Power of Darkness supposed to be ever in pursuit of the Sun and Moon. When it finally overtakes them, it will entwine them in its folds, and prevent their shining. In the last Indian Avatara, as in the Eddas, a serpent vomiting flames is expected to destroy the world. The serpent presides over the close of the year, where it guards the approach to the golden fleece of Aries, and the three apples or seasons of the Hesperides; presenting a formidable obstacle to the career of the Sun-God. The Great Destroyer of snakes is occasionally married to them; Hercules with the northern dragon begets the three ancestors of Scythia; for the Sun seems at one time to rise victorious from the contest with darkness, and at another to sink into its embraces. The northern constellation Draco, whose sinuosities wind like a river through the wintry bear, was made the astronomical cincture of the Universe, as the serpent encircles the mundane egg in Egyptian hieroglyphics.

The Persian Ahriman was called "The old serpent, the liar from the beginning, the Prince of Darkness, and the rover up and down." The Dragon was a well-known symbol of the waters and of great rivers; and it was natural that by the pastoral Asiatic Tribes, the powerful nations of the alluvial plains in their neighborhood who adored the dragon or Fish, should themselves be symbolized under the form of dragons; and overcome by the superior might of the Hebrew God, as monstrous Leviathans maimed and destroyed by him. Ophioneus, in the old Greek Theology, warred against Kronos, and was overcome and cast into his proper element, the sea. There he is installed as the Sea-God Oannes or Dragon, the Leviathan of the watery half of creation, the dragon who vomited a flood of water after the persecuted woman of the Apocalypse, the monster who threatened to devour Hesione and Andromeda, and who for a time became the grave of Hercules and

Jonah; and he corresponds with the obscure name of *Rahab,* whom Jehovah is said in Job to have transfixed and overcome.

In the Spring, the year or Sun-God appears as Mithras or Europa mounted on the Bull; but in the opposite half of the Zodiac he rides the emblem of the waters, the winged horse of Nestor or Poseidon: and the Serpent, rising heliacally at the Autumnal Equinox, besetting with poisonous influence the cold constellation Sagittarius, is explained as the reptile in the path who "bites the horse's heels, so that his rider falls backward." The same serpent, the Oannes Aphrenos or Musaros of Syncellus, was the Midgard Serpent which Odin sunk beneath the sea, but which grew to such a size as to encircle the whole earth.

For these Asiatic symbols of the contest of the Sun-God with the Dragon of darkness and Winter were imported not only into the Zodiac, but into the more homely circle of European legend; and both Thor and Odin fight with dragons, as Apollo did with Python, the great scaly snake, Achilles with the Scamander, and Bellerophon with the Chimæra. In the apocryphal book of Esther, dragons herald "a day of darkness and obscurity"; and St. George of England, a problematic Cappadocian Prince, was originally only a varying form of Mithras. Jehovah is said to have "cut Rahab and wounded the dragon." The latter is not only the type of earthly desolation, the dragon of the deep waters, but also the leader of the banded conspirators of the sky, of the rebellious stars, which, according to Enoch, "came not at the right time"; and his tail drew a third part of the Host of Heaven, and cast them to the earth. Jehovah "divided the sea by his strength, and broke the heads of the Dragons in the waters." And according to the Jewish and Persian belief, the Dragon would, in the latter days, the Winter of time, enjoy a short period of licensed impunity, which would be a season of the greatest suffering to the people of the earth; but he would finally be bound or destroyed in the great battle of Messiah; or, as it seems intimated by the Rabbinical figure of being eaten by the faithful, be, like Ahriman or Vasouki, ultimately absorbed by and united with the Principle of good.

Near the image of Rhea, in the Temple of Bel at Babylon, were two large serpents of silver, says Diodorus, each weighing thirty talents; and in the same temple was an image of Juno, holding in her right hand the head of a serpent. The Greeks called Bel

Beliar; and Hesychius interprets that word to mean a dragon or great serpent. We learn from the book of Bel and the Dragon, that in Babylon was kept a great, live serpent, which the people worshipped.

The Assyrians, the Emperors of Constantinople, the Parthians, Scythians, Saxons, Chinese, and Danes all bore the serpent as a standard, and among the spoils taken by Aurelian from Zenobia were such standards, *Persici Dracones.* The Persians represented Ormuzd and Ahriman by two serpents, contending for the mundane egg. Mithras is represented with a lion's head and human body, encircled by a serpent. In the Sadder is this precept: "When you kill serpents, you will repeat the Zend-Avesta, and thence you will obtain great merit; for it is the same as if you had killed so many devils."

Serpents encircling rings and globes, and issuing from globes, are common in the Persian, Egyptian, Chinese, and Indian monuments. Vishnu is represented reposing on a coiled serpent, whose folds form a canopy over him. Mahadeva is represented with a snake around his neck, one around his hair, and armlets of serpents on both arms. Bhairava sits on the coils of a serpent, whose head rises above his own. Parvati has snakes about her neck and waist. Vishnu is the Preserving Spirit, Mahadeva is Siva, the Evil Principle, Bhairava is his son, and Parvati his consort. The King of Evil Demons was called in Hindū Mythology, *Naga,* the King of Serpents, in which name we trace the Hebrew *Nachash,* serpent.

In Cashmere were seven hundred places where carved images of serpents were worshipped; and in Thibet the great Chinese Dragon ornamented the Temples of the Grand Lama. In China, the dragon was the stamp and symbol of royalty, sculptured in all the Temples, blazoned on the furniture of the houses, and interwoven with the vestments of the chief nobility. The Emperor bears it as his armorial device; it is engraved on his sceptre and diadem, and on all the vases of the imperial palace. The Chinese believe that there is a dragon of extraordinary strength and sovereign power, in Heaven, in the air, on the waters, and on the mountains. The God Fohi is said to have had the form of a man, terminating in the tail of a snake, a combination to be more fully explained to you in a subsequent Degree.

The dragon and serpent are the 5th and 6th signs of the Chinese Zodiac; and the Hindus and Chinese believe that, at every eclipse, the sun or moon is seized by a huge serpent or dragon, the serpent *Asootee* of the Hindus, which enfolds the globe and the constellation Draco; to which also refers "the War in Heaven, when Michael and his Angels fought against the dragon."

Sanchoniathon says that Taaut was the author of the worship of serpents among the Phœnicians. He "consecrated," he says, "the species of dragons and serpents; and the Phœnicians and Egyptians followed him in this superstition." He was "the first who made an image of Cœlus"; that is, who represented the Heavenly Hosts of Stars by visible symbols; and was probably the same as the Egyptian Thoth. On the Tyrian coins of the age of Alexander, serpents are represented in many positions and attitudes, coiled around trees, erect in front of altars, and crushed by the Syrian Hercules.

The seventh letter of the Egyptian alphabet, called *Zeuta* or *Life,* was sacred to Thoth, and was expressed by a serpent standing on his tail; and that Deity, the God of healing, like Æsculapius, to whom the serpent was consecrated, leans on a knotted stick around which coils a snake. The Isiac tablet, describing the Mysteries of Isis, is charged with serpents in every part, as her emblems. The *Asp* was specially dedicated to her, and is seen on the heads of her statues, on the bonnets of her priests, and on the tiaras of the Kings of Egypt. Serapis was sometimes represented with a human head and serpentine tail: and in one engraving two minor Gods are represented with him, one by a serpent with a bull's head, and the other by a serpent with the radiated head of a lion.

On an ancient sacrificial vessel found in Denmark, having several compartments, a serpent is represented attacking a kneeling boy, pursuing him, retreating before him, appealed to beseechingly by him, and conversing with him. We are at once reminded of the Sun at the new year represented by a child sitting on a lotus, and of the relations of the Sun of Spring with the Autumnal Serpent, pursued by and pursuing him, and in conjunction with him. Other figures on this vessel belong to the Zodiac.

The base of the *tripod* of the Pythian Priestess was a triple-headed serpent of brass, whose body, folded in circles growing wider and wider toward the ground, formed a conical column, while the three heads, disposed triangularly, upheld the *tripod*

of gold. A similar column was placed on a pillar in the Hippodrome at Constantinople, by the founder of that city; one of the
heads of which is said to have been broken off by Mahomet the
Second, by a blow with his iron mace.

The British God Hu was called "The Dragon—Ruler of the
World," and his car was drawn by serpents. His ministers were
styled *adders*. A Druid in a poem of Taliessin says, "I am a Druid,
I am an *Architect,* I am a Prophet, I am a *Serpent* (Gnadi)."
The Car of the Goddess Ceridwen also was drawn by serpents.

In the elegy of Uther Pendragon, this passage occurs in a description of the religious rites of the Druids: "While the Sanctuary is earnestly invoking *The Gliding King,* before whom *the Fair
One* retreats, upon the evil that covers the huge stones; whilst
the Dragon moves round over the places which contain vessels
of drink-offering, whilst the drink-offering is in *the Golden
Horns,*" in which we readily discover the mystic and obscure allusion to the Autumnal Serpent pursuing the Sun along the circle
of the Zodiac, to the celestial cup or crater, and the Golden horns
of Virgil's milk-white Bull; and, a line or two further on, we find
the Priest imploring the victorious *Beli,* the Sun-God of the
Babylonians.

With the serpent, in the Ancient Monuments, is very often
found associated the Cross. The Serpent upon a Cross was an
Egyptian Standard. It occurs repeatedly upon the Grand Stair-
case of the Temple of Osiris at Philæ; and on the pyramid of
Ghizeh are represented two kneeling figures erecting a Cross, on
the top of which is a serpent erect. The *Crux Ansata* was a Cross
with a coiled Serpent above it; and it is perhaps the most common
of all emblems on the Egyptian Monuments, carried in the hand
of almost every figure of a Deity or a Priest. It was, as we learn
by the monuments, the form of the iron tether-pins, used for making fast to the ground the cords by which young animals were
confined: and as used by shepherds, became a symbol of Royalty
to the Shepherd Kings.

A Cross like a Teutonic or Maltese one, formed by four curved
lines within a circle, is also common on the Monuments, and represented the Tropics and the Colures.

The Caduceus, borne by Hermes or Mercury, and also by Cybele,
Minerva, Anubis, Hercules Ogmius the God of the Celts, and the
personified Constellation Virgo, was a winged wand, entwined by

two serpents. It was originally a simple Cross, symbolizing the equator and equinoctial Colure, and the four elements proceeding from a common centre. This Cross, surmounted by a circle, and that by a crescent, became an emblem of the Supreme Deity— or of the active power of generation and the passive power of production conjoined,—and was appropriated to Thoth or Mercury. It then assumed an improved form, the arms of the Cross being changed into wings, and the circle and crescent being formed by two snakes, springing from the wand, forming a circle by crossing each other, and their heads making the horns of the crescent; in which form it is seen in the hands of Anubis.

The triple Tau, in the centre of a circle and a triangle, typifies the Sacred Name; and represents the Sacred Triad, the Creating, Preserving, and Destroying Powers; as well as the three great lights of Masonry. If to the Masonic point within a Circle, and the two parallel lines, we add the single Tau Cross, we have the Ancient Egyptian Triple Tau.

A column in the form of a cross, with a circle over it, was used by the Egyptians to measure the increase of the inundations of the Nile. The Tau and Triple Tau are found in many Ancient Alphabets.

With the Tau or the Triple Tau may be connected, within two circles, the double cube, or perfection; or the perfect ashlar.

The *Crux Ansata* is found on the sculptures of Khorsabad; on the ivories from Nimroud, of the same age, carried by an Assyrian Monarch; and on cylinders of the later Assyrian period.

As the single Tau represents the one God, so, no doubt, the Triple Tau, the origin of which cannot be traced, was meant to represent the Trinity of his attributes, the three Masonic pillars, WISDOM, STRENGTH, and HARMONY.

The Prophet Ezekiel, in the 4th verse of the 9th chapter, says: "And the Lord said unto him, 'Go through the midst of the city, through the midst of Jerusalem, and mark the letter TAU upon the foreheads of those that sigh and mourn for all the abominations that be done in the midst thereof." So the Latin Vulgate, and the probably most ancient copies of the Septuagint translate the passage. This *Tau* was in the form of the cross of this Degree, and it was the emblem of *life* and *salvation*. The Samaritan *Tau* and the Ethiopic *Tavvi* are the evident prototype of the Greek τ; and we learn from Tertullian, Origen, and St. Jerome, that the Hebrew *Tau* was anciently written in the form of a Cross.

In ancient times the mark *Tau* was set on those who had been acquitted by their judges, as a symbol of innocence. The military commanders placed it on soldiers who escaped unhurt from the field of battle, as a sign of their safety under the Divine Protection.

It was a sacred symbol among the Druids. Divesting a tree of part of its branches, they left it in the shape of a Tau Cross, preserved it carefully, and consecrated it with solemn ceremonies. On the tree they cut deeply the word THAU, by which they meant God. On the right arm of the Cross, they inscribed the word HESULS, on the left BELEN or BELENUS, and on the middle of the trunk THARAMIS. This represented the sacred *Triad*.

It is certain that the Indians, Egyptians, and Arabians paid veneration to the sign of the Cross, thousands of years before the coming of Christ. Everywhere it was a sacred symbol. The Hindus and the Celtic Druids built many of their Temples in the form of a Cross, as the ruins still remaining clearly show, and particularly the ancient Druidical Temple at Classerniss in the Island of Lewis in Scotland. The Circle is of 12 Stones. On each of the sides, east, west, and south, are three. In the centre was the image of the Deity; and on the north an avenue of twice nineteen stones, and one at the entrance. The Supernal Pagoda at Benares is in the form of a Cross; and the Druidical subterranean grotto at New Grange in Ireland.

The Statue of Osiris at Rome had the same emblem. Isis and Ceres also bore it; and the caverns of initiation were constructed in that shape with a pyramid over the *Sacellum*.

Crosses were cut in the stones of the Temple of Serapis in Alexandria; and many Tau Crosses are to be seen in the sculptures of Alabastion and Esné, in Egypt. On coins, the symbol of the Egyptian God Kneph was a Cross within a Circle.

The Crux Ansata was the particular emblem of Osiris, and his sceptre ended with that figure. It was also the emblem of Hermes, and was considered a Sublime Hieroglyphic, possessing mysterious powers and virtues, as a wonder-working amulet.

The Sacred Tau occurs in the hands of the mummy-shaped figures between the forelegs of the row of Sphynxes, in the great avenue leading from Luxor to Karnac. By the Tau Cross the

Cabalists expressed the number 10, a perfect number, denoting Heaven, and the Pythagorean Tetractys, or incommunicable name of God. The Tau Cross is also found on the stones in front of the door of the Temple of Amunoth III, at Thebes, who reigned about the time when the Israelites took possession of Canaan: and the Egyptian Priests carried it in all the sacred processions.

Tertullian, who had been initiated, informs us that the Tau was inscribed on the forehead of every person who had been admitted into the Mysteries of Mithras.

As the simple Tau represented Life, so, when the Circle, symbol of Eternity, was added, it represented Eternal Life.

At the Initiation of a King, the Tau, as the emblem of life and key of the Mysteries, was impressed upon his lips.

In the Indian Mysteries, the Tau Cross, under the name of *Tiluk,* was marked upon the body of the candidate, as a sign that he was set apart for the Sacred Mysteries.

On the upright tablet of the King, discovered at Nimroud, are the names of thirteen Great Gods (among which are YAV and BEL) ; and the left-hand character of every one is a cross composed of two cuneiform characters.

The Cross appears upon an Ancient Phœnician medal found in the ruins of Citium ; on the very ancient Buddhist Obelisk near Ferns in Ross-shire ; on the Buddhist Round Towers in Ireland, and upon the splendid obelisk of the same era at Forres in Scotland.

Upon the façade of a temple at Kalabche in Nubia are three regal figures, each holding a Crux Ansata.

Like the Subterranean Mithriatic Temple at New Grange in Scotland, the Pagodas of Benares and Mathura were in the form of a Cross. Magnificent Buddhist Crosses were erected, and are still standing, at Clonmacnoise, Finglas, and Kilcullen in Ireland. Wherever the monuments of Buddhism are found, in India, Ceylon, or Ireland, we find the Cross : for Buddha or Boudh was represented to have been crucified.

All the planets known to the Ancients were distinguished by the Mystic Cross, in conjunction with the solar or lunar symbols ; Saturn by a cross over a crescent, Jupiter by a cross under a crescent, Mars by a cross resting obliquely on a circle, Venus by a cross under a circle, and Mercury by a cross surmounted by a circle and that by a crescent.

The Solstices, Cancer and Capricorn, the two Gates of Heaven, are the two pillars of Hercules, beyond which he, the Sun, never journeyed: and they still appear in our Lodges, as the two great columns, Jachin and Boaz, and also as the two parallel lines that bound the circle, with a point in the centre, emblem of the Sun, between the two tropics of Cancer and Capricorn.

The Blazing Star in our Lodges, we have already said, represents Sirius, Anubis, or Mercury, Guardian and Guide of Souls. Our Ancient English brethren also considered it an emblem of the Sun. In the old Lectures they said: "The Blazing Star or Glory in the centre refers us to that Grand Luminary the Sun, which enlightens the Earth, and by its genial influence dispenses blessings to mankind." It is also said in those lectures to be an emblem of Prudence. The word *Prudentia* means, in its original and fullest signification, *Foresight:* and accordingly the Blazing Star has been regarded as an emblem of Omniscience, or the All-Seeing Eye, which to the Ancients was the Sun.

Even the Dagger of the Elu of Nine is that used in the Mysteries of Mithras; which, with its blade black and hilt white, was an emblem of the two principles of Light and Darkness.

Isis, the same as Ceres, was, as we learn from Eratosthenes, the Constellation Virgo, represented by a woman holding an ear of wheat. The different emblems which accompany her in the description given by Apuleius, a serpent on either side, a golden vase, with a serpent twined round the handle, and the animals that marched in procession, the bear, the ape, and Pegasus, represented the Constellations that, rising with the Virgin, when on the day of the Vernal Equinox she stood in the Oriental gate of Heaven, brilliant with the rays of the full moon, seemed to march in her train.

The cup, consecrated in the Mysteries both of Isis and Eleusis, was the Constellation Crater or the Cup. The sacred vessel of the Isiac ceremony finds its counterpart in the Heavens. The Olympic robe presented to the Initiate, a magnificent mantle, covered with figures of serpents and animals, and under which were twelve other sacred robes, wherewith he was clothed in the sanctuary, alluded to the starry Heaven and the twelve signs: while the seven preparatory immersions in the sea alluded to the seven spheres, through which the soul plunged, to arrive here below and take up its abode in a body.

The Celestial Virgin, during the last three centuries that preceded the Christian era, occupied the horoscope or Oriental point, and that gate of Heaven through which the Sun and Moon ascended above the horizon at the two equinoxes. Again it occupied it at midnight, at the Winter Solstice, the precise moment when the year commenced. Thus it was essentially connected with the march of times and seasons, of the Sun, the Moon, and day and night, at the principal epochs of the year. At the equinoxes were celebrated the greater and lesser Mysteries of Ceres. When souls descended past the Balance, at the moment when the Sun occupied that point, the Virgin rose before him; she stood at the gates of day and opened them to him. Her brilliant Star, Spica Virginis, and Arcturus, in Boötes, northwest of it, heralded his coming. When he had returned to the Vernal Equinox, at the moment when souls were generated, again it was the Celestial Virgin that led the march of the signs of night; and in her stars came the beautiful full moon of that month. Night and day were in succession introduced by her, when they began to diminish in length; and souls, before arriving at the gates of Hell, were also led by her. In going through these signs, they passed the Styx in the 8th Degree of Libra. She was the famous Sibyl who initiated Eneas, and opened to him the way to the infernal regions.

This peculiar situation of the Constellation Virgo, has caused it to enter into all the sacred fables in regard to nature, under different names and the most varied forms. It often takes the name of Isis or the Moon, which, when at its full at the Vernal Equinox, was in union with it or beneath its feet. Mercury (or Anubis) having his domicile and exaltation in the sign Virgo, was, in all the sacred fables and Sanctuaries, the inseparable companion of Isis, without whose counsels she did nothing.

This relation between the emblems and mysterious recitals of the initiations, and the Heavenly bodies and order of the world, was still more clear in the Mysteries of Mithras, adored as the Sun in Asia Minor, Cappadocia, Armenia, and Persia, and whose Mysteries went to Rome in the time of Sylla. This is amply proved by the descriptions we have of the Mithriac cave, in which were figured the two movements of the Heavens, that of the fixed Stars and that of the Planets, the Constellations, the eight mystic gates of the spheres, and the symbols of the elements. So on a celebrated monument of that religion, found at Rome, were fig-

ured, the Serpent or Hydra under Leo, as in the Heavens, the
Celestial Dog, the Bull, the Scorpion, the Seven Planets, represented by seven altars, the Sun, Moon, and emblems relating to
Light, to Darkness, and to their succession during the year, where
each in turn triumphs for six months.

The Mysteries of Atys were celebrated when the Sun entered
Aries; and among the emblems was a ram at the foot of a tree
which was being cut down.

Thus, if not the whole truth, it is yet a large part of it, that the
Heathen Pantheon, in its infinite diversity of names and personifications, was but a multitudinous, though in its origin unconscious
allegory, of which physical phenomena, and principally the Heavenly Bodies, were the fundamental types. The glorious images of
Divinity which formed Jehovah's Host, were the Divine Dynasty
or real theocracy which governed the early world; and the men of
the golden age, whose looks held commerce with the skies, and
who watched the radiant rulers bringing Winter and Summer to
mortals, might be said with poetic truth to live in immediate communication with Heaven, and, like the Hebrew Patriarchs, to see
God face to face. Then the Gods introduced their own worship
among mankind: then Oannes, Oe or Aquarius rose from the Red
Sea to impart science to the Babylonians; then the bright Bull
legislated for India and Crete; and the Lights of Heaven, personified as Liber and Ceres, hung the Bœotian hills with vine-
yards, and gave the golden sheaf to Eleusis. The children of men
were, in a sense, allied or married, to those sons of God who sang
the jubilee of creation; and the encircling vault with its countless
Stars, which to the excited imagination of the solitary Chaldean
wanderer appeared as animated intelligences, might naturally be
compared to a gigantic ladder, on which, in their rising and setting, the Angel luminaries appeared to be ascending and descending between earth and Heaven. The original revelation died out
of men's memories; they worshipped the Creature instead of the
Creator; and holding all earthly things as connected by eternal
links of harmony and sympathy with the heavenly bodies, they
united in one view astronomy, astrology, and religion. Long
wandering thus in error, they at length ceased to look upon the
Stars and external nature as Gods; and by directing their attention to the microcosm or narrower world of self, they again became acquainted with the True Ruler and Guide of the Universe,

and used the old fables and superstitions as symbols and allegories, by which to convey and under which to hide the great truths which had faded out of most men's remembrance.

In the Hebrew writings, the term "Heavenly Hosts" includes not only the counsellors and emissaries of Jehovah, but also the celestial luminaries; and the stars, imagined in the East to be animated intelligences, presiding over human weal and woe, are identified with the more distinctly impersonated messengers or angels, who execute the Divine decrees, and whose predominance in Heaven is in mysterious correspondence and relation with the powers and dominions of the earth. In Job, the Morning Stars and the Sons of God are identified; they join in the same chorus of praise to the Almighty; they are both susceptible of joy; they walk in brightness, and are liable to impurity and imperfection in the sight of God. The Elohim originally included not only foreign superstitious forms, but also all that host of Heaven which was revealed in poetry to the shepherds of the desert, now as an encampment of warriors, now as careering in chariots of fire, and now as winged messengers, ascending and descending the vault of Heaven, to communicate the will of God to mankind.

"The Eternal," says the Bereshith Rabba to Genesis, "called forth Abraham and his posterity out of the dominion of the stars; by nature, the Israelite was a servant to the stars, and born under their influence, as are the heathen; but by virtue of the law given on Mount Sinai, he became liberated from this degrading servitude." The Arabs had a similar legend. The Prophet Amos explicitly asserts that the Israelites, in the desert, worshipped, not Jehovah, but Moloch, or a Star-God, equivalent to Saturn. The Gods El or Jehovah were not merely planetary or solar. Their symbolism, like that of every other Deity, was coextensive with nature, and with the mind of man. Yet the astrological character is assigned even to Jehovah. He is described as seated on the pinnacle of the Universe, leading forth the Hosts of Heaven, and telling them unerringly by name and number. His stars are His sons and His eyes, which run through the whole world, keeping watch over men's deeds. The stars and planets were properly the angels. In Pharisaic tradition, as in the phraseology of the New Testament, the Heavenly Host appears as an Angelic Army, divided into regiments and brigades, under the command of imaginary chiefs, such as Massaloth, Legion, Kartor Gistra, etc.,—each Gistra being captain of 365,000 myriads of stars. The Seven Spirits which stand before the throne, spoken of by several Jewish writers, and generally presumed to have been immediately derived from the Persian Amshaspands, were ultimately the seven planetary intelligences, the original model of the seven-branched golden candlestick exhibited to Moses on God's mountain. The stars were imagined to have fought in their courses against Sisera. The heavens were spoken of as holding a predominance over earth, as governing it by signs and ordinances, and as containing the elements of that astrological wisdom, more especially cultivated by the Babylonians and Egyptians.

Each nation was supposed by the Hebrews to have its own guardian angel, and its own provincial star. One of the chiefs of the Celestial Powers, at first Jehovah Himself in the character of the Sun, standing in the height of Heaven, overlooking and governing all things, afterward one of the angels or subordinate planetary genii of Babylonian or Persian mythology, was the patron and protector of their own nation, "the Prince that standeth for the children of thy people." The discords of earth were accompanied by a warfare in the sky; and no people underwent the visitation of the Almighty, without a corresponding chastisement being inflicted on its tutelary angel.

The fallen Angels were also fallen Stars; and the first allusion to a feud among the spiritual powers in early Hebrew Mythology, where Rahab and his confederates are defeated, like the Titans in a battle against the Gods, seems to identify the rebellious Spirits as part of the visible Heavens, where the "high ones on high" are punished or chained, as a signal proof of God's power and justice. God, it is said—

"Stirs the sea with His might—by His understanding He smote Rahab—His breath clears the face of Heaven—His hand pierced the crooked Serpent. . . . God withdraws not His anger; beneath Him bow the confederates of Rahab."

Rahab always means a sea-monster: probably some such legendary monstrous dragon, as in almost all mythologies is the adversary of Heaven and demon of eclipse, in whose belly, significantly called the belly of Hell, Hercules, like Jonah, passed three days, ultimately escaping with the loss of his hair or rays. Chesil, the rebellious giant Orion, represented in Job as riveted to the sky, was compared to Ninus or Nimrod, the mythical founder of Nineveh (City of Fish) the mighty hunter, who slew lions and panthers before the Lord. Rahab's confederates are probably the "High ones on High," the Chesilim or constellations in Isaiah, the Heavenly Host or Heavenly Powers, among whose number were found folly and disobedience.

"I beheld," says Pseudo-Enoch, "seven stars like great blazing mountains, and like Spirits, entreating me. And the angel said, This place, until the consummation of Heaven and Earth, will be the prison of the Stars and of the Host of Heaven. These are the Stars which overstepped God's command before their time arrived; and came not at their proper season; therefore was he offended with them, and bound them, until the time of the consummation of their crimes in the secret year." And again: "These Seven Stars are those which have transgressed the commandment of the Most High God, and which are here bound until the number of the days of their crimes be completed."

The Jewish and early Christian writers looked on the worship of the sun and the elements with comparative indulgence. Justin Martyr and Clemens of Alexandria admit that God had appointed the stars as legitimate objects of heathen worship, in order to preserve throughout the world some tolerable notions of natural religion. It seemed a middle point between Heathenism and Christianity; and to it certain emblems and ordinances of that faith seemed to relate. The advent of Christ was announced by a Star from the East; and His nativity was celebrated on the shortest day of the Julian Calendar, the day when, in the physical commemorations of Persia and Egypt, Mithras or Osiris was newly found. It was then that the acclamations of the Host of Heaven, the unfailing attendants of the Sun, surrounded, as at the spring-dawn of creation, the cradle of His birth-place, and that, in the words of Ignatius, "a star, with light inexpressible, shone forth in the Heavens, to destroy the power of magic and the bonds of wickedness; for God Himself had appeared, in the form of man, for the renewal of eternal life."

But however infinite the variety of objects which helped to develop the notion of Deity, and eventually assumed its place, substituting the worship of the creature for that of the creator; of parts of the body, for that of the soul, of the Universe, still the notion itself was essentially one of unity. The idea of one

God, of a creative, productive, governing unity, resided in the
earliest exertion of thought: and this monotheism of the primitive ages, makes every succeeding epoch, unless it be the present,
appear only as a stage in the progress of degeneracy and aberration.
Everywhere in the old faiths we find the idea of a supreme or presiding Deity. Amun or Osiris presides among the many gods of
Egypt; Pan, with the music of his pipe, directs the chorus of the
constellations, as Zeus leads the solemn procession of the celestial
troops in the astronomical theology of the Pythagoreans. "Amidst
an infinite diversity of opinions on all other subjects," says Maximus Tyrius, "the whole world is unanimous in the belief of one
only almighty King and Father of all."

There is always a Sovereign Power, a Zeus or Deus, Mahadeva
or Adideva, to whom belongs the maintenance of the order of
the Universe. Among the thousand gods of India, the doctrine of
Divine Unity is never lost sight of; and the ethereal Jove, worshipped by the Persian in an age long before Xenophanes or
Anaxagoras, appears as supremely comprehensive and independent of planetary or elemental subdivisions, as the "Vast One" or
"Great Soul" of the Vedas.

But the simplicity of belief of the patriarchs did not exclude
the employment of symbolical representations. The mind never
rests satisfied with a mere feeling. That feeling ever strives to
assume precision and durability as an idea, by some *outward* de-
lineation of its thought. Even the ideas that are above and beyond the senses, as all ideas of God are, require the aid of the
senses for their expression and communication. Hence come the
representative forms and symbols which constitute the external
investiture of every religion; attempts to express a religious sentiment that is essentially *one,* and that vainly struggles for adequate
external utterance, striving to tell to one man, to *paint* to him, an
idea existing in the mind of another, and essentially incapable of
utterance or description, in a language all the words of which
have a sensuous meaning. Thus, the idea being perhaps the same
in all, its expressions and utterances are infinitely various, and
branch into an infinite diversity of creeds and sects.

All religious expression is symbolism; since we can describe
only what we see; and the true objects of religion are unseen.
The earliest instruments of education were symbols; and they
and all other religious forms differed and still differ according to

external circumstances and imagery, and according to differences of knowledge and mental cultivation. To present a visible symbol to the eye of another is not to inform him of the meaning which that symbol has to *you*. Hence the philosopher soon superadded to these symbols, explanations addressed to the ear, susceptible of more precision, but less effective, obvious, and impressive than the painted or sculptured forms which he despised. Out of these explanations grew by degrees a variety of narratives, whose true object and meaning were gradually forgotten. And when these were abandoned, and philosophy resorted to definitions and formulas, its language was, but a more refined symbolism, grappling with and attempting to picture ideas impossible to be expressed. For the most abstract expression for Deity which language can supply, is but a *sign* or *symbol* for an object unknown, and no more truthful and adequate than the terms Osiris and Vishnu, except as being less sensuous and explicit. To say that He is a *Spirit,* is but to say that He is not matter. *What* spirit is, we can only define as the Ancients did, by resorting, as if in despair, to some sublimized species of matter, as Light, Fire, or Ether.

No symbol of Deity can be appropriate or durable except in a relative or moral sense. We cannot exalt words that have only a sensuous meaning, *above* sense. To call Him a *Power* or a *Force,* or an *Intelligence,* is merely to deceive ourselves into the belief that we use words that have a meaning to us, when they have none, or at least no more than the ancient visible symbols had. To call Him *Sovereign, Father, Grand Architect of the Universe, Extension, Time, Beginning, Middle, and End, whose face is turned on all sides, the Source of life and death,* is but to present other men with symbols by which we vainly endeavor to communicate to them the same vague ideas which men in all ages have impotently struggled to express. And it may be doubted whether we have succeeded either in communicating, or in forming in our own minds, any more distinct and definite and true and adequate idea of the Deity, with all our metaphysical conceits and logical subtleties, than the rude ancients did, who endeavored to symbolize and so to express His attributes, by the Fire, the Light, the Sun and Stars, the Lotus and the Scarabæus; all of them types of what, except by types, more or less sufficient, could not be expressed at all.

The primitive man recognized the Divine Presence under a

variety of appearances, without losing his faith in this unity and Supremacy. The invisible God, manifested and on one of His many sides visible, did not cease to be God to him. He recognized Him in the evening breeze of Eden, in the whirlwind of Sinai, in the Stone of Beth-El: and identified Him with the fire or thunder or the immovable rock adored in Ancient Arabia. To him the image of the Deity was reflected in all that was pre-eminent in excellence. He saw Jehovah, like Osiris and Bel, in the Sun as well as in the Stars, which were His children, His eyes, "which run through the whole world, and watch over the Sacred Soil of Palestine, from the year's commencement to its close." He was the sacred fire of Mount Sinai, of the burning bush, of the Persians, those Puritans of Paganism.

Naturally it followed that Symbolism soon became more complicated, and all the powers of Heaven were reproduced on earth, until a web of fiction and allegory was woven, which the wit of man, with his limited means of explanation, will never unravel. Hebrew Theism itself became involved in symbolism and image-worship, to which all religions ever tend. We have already seen what was the symbolism of the Tabernacle, the Temple, and the Ark. The Hebrew establishment tolerated not only the use of emblematic vessels, vestments, and cherubs, of Sacred Pillars and Seraphim, but symbolical representations of Jehovah Himself, not even confined to poetical or illustrative language.

"Among the Adityas," says Chrishna, in the Bagvat Ghita, "I am Vishnu, the radiant Sun among the Stars; among the waters, I am ocean; among the mountains, the Himalaya; and among the mountain-tops, Meru." The Psalms and Isaiah are full of similar attempts to convey to the mind ideas of God, by ascribing to Him sensual proportions. He rides on the clouds, and sits on the wings of the wind. Heaven is His pavilion, and out of His mouth issue lightnings. Men cannot worship a mere abstraction. They require some outward form in which to clothe their conceptions, and invest their sympathies. If they do not shape and carve or paint visible images, they have invisible ones, perhaps quite as inadequate and unfaithful, within their own minds.

The incongruous and monstrous in the Oriental images came from the desire to embody the Infinite, and to convey by multiplied, because individually inadequate symbols, a notion of the Divine Attributes to the understanding. Perhaps we should find that we mentally do the same thing, and make within ourselves images quite as incongruous, if judged of by our own limited conceptions, if we were to undertake to analyze and gain a clear idea of the mass of infinite attributes which we assign to the Deity; and even of His infinite Justice and infinite Mercy and Love.

We may well say, in the language of Maximus Tyrius: "If, in the desire to obtain some faint conception of the Universal Father, the Nameless Lawgiver, men had recourse to words or names, to silver or gold, to animals or plants, to mountain-tops or flowing rivers, every one inscribing the most valued and most beautiful things with the name of Deity, and with the fondness of a lover clinging with rapture to each trivial reminiscence of the Beloved, why should we seek to reduce this universal practice of symbolism, necessary, indeed, since the mind often needs the excitement of the imagination to rouse it into activity, to one monotonous standard of formal propriety? Only let the image duly perform its task, and bring the divine idea with vividness and truth before the mental eye; if this be effected, whether by the art of Phidias, the poetry of Homer, the Egyptian Hieroglyph, or the Persian element, we need not cavil at external differences, or lament the seeming fertility of unfamiliar creeds, *so long as the great essential is attained,* THAT MEN ARE MADE TO REMEMBER, TO UNDERSTAND, AND TO LOVE."

Certainly, when men regarded Light and Fire as something spiritual, and above all the corruptions and exempt from all the decay of matter; when they looked upon the Sun and Stars and Planets as composed of this finer element, and as themselves great and mysterious Intelligences, infinitely superior to man, living Existences, gifted with mighty powers and wielding vast influences, those elements and bodies conveyed to them, when used as symbols of Deity, a far more adequate idea than they can now do to us, or than we can comprehend, now that Fire and Light are familiar to us as air and water, and the Heavenly Luminaries are lifeless worlds like our own. Perhaps they gave them ideas as adequate as we obtain from the mere *words* by which we endeavor to symbolize and shadow forth the ineffable mysteries and infinite attributes of God.

There are, it is true, dangers inseparable from symbolism, which countervail its advantages, and afford an impressive lesson in regard to the similar risks attendant on the use of language. The imagination, invited to assist the reason, usurps its place, or leaves its ally helplessly entangled in its web. Names which stand for things are confounded with them; the means are mistaken for the end: the instrument of interpretation for the object; and thus symbols come to usurp an independent character as truths and persons. Though perhaps a necessary path, they were a dangerous one by which to approach the Deity; in which "many," says Plutarch, "mistaking the sign for the thing signified, fell into a ridiculous superstition; while others, in avoiding one extreme, plunged into the no less hideous gulf of irreligion and impiety."

All great Reformers have warred against this evil, deeply feeling the intellectual mischief arising out of a degraded idea of the Supreme Being: and have claimed for their own God an existence or personality distinct from the objects of ancient superstition; disowning in His name the symbols and images that had profaned His Temple. But they have not seen that the utmost which can be effected by human effort, is to substitute impressions relatively correct, for others whose falsehood has been detected, and to replace a gross symbolism by a purer one. Every man, without being aware of it, worships a conception of his own mind; for all symbolism, as well as all language, shares the subjective character of the ideas it represents. The epithets we apply to God only recall either visible or intellectual symbols to the eye or mind. The modes or forms of manifestation of the reverential feeling that constitutes the religious sentiment, are incomplete and progressive; each term and symbol predicates a partial truth, remaining always amenable to improvement or modification, and, in its turn, to be superseded by others more accurate and comprehensive.

Idolatry consists in confounding the symbol with the thing signified, the substitution of a material for a mental object of worship, after a higher spiritualism has become possible; an ill-judged preference of the inferior to the superior symbol, an inadequate and sensual conception of the Deity: and every religion and every conception of God is idolatrous, in so far as it is imperfect, and as it substitutes a feeble and temporary idea in the shrine of that Undiscoverable Being who can be known only in part, and who can therefore be honored, even by the most enlightened among His worshippers, only in proportion to their limited powers of understanding and imagining to themselves His perfections.

Like the belief in a Deity, the belief in the soul's immortality is rather a natural feeling, an adjunct of self-consciousness, than a dogma belonging to any particular age or country. It gives eternity to man's nature, and reconciles its seeming anomalies and contradictions; it makes him strong in weakness and perfectable in imperfection; and it alone gives an adequate object for his hopes and energies, and value and dignity to his pursuits. It is concurrent with the belief in an infinite, eternal Spirit, since it is chiefly through consciousness of the dignity of the mind within us, that we learn to appreciate its evidences in the Universe.

To fortify, and as far as possible to impart this hope, was the great aim of ancient wisdom, whether expressed in forms of poetry or philosophy; as it was of the Mysteries, and as it is of Masonry. Life rising out of death was the great mystery, which symbolism delighted to represent under a thousand ingenious forms. Nature was ransacked for attestations to the grand truth which seems to transcend all other gifts of imagination, or rather to be their essence and consummation. Such evidences were easily discovered. They were found in the olive and the lotus, in the evergreen myrtle of the *Mystæ* and of the grave of Polydorus, in the deadly but self-renewing serpent, the wonderful moth emerging from the coffin of the worm, the phenomena of germination, the settings and risings of the sun and stars, the darkening and growth of the moon, and in sleep, "the minor mystery of death."

The stories of the birth of Apollo from Latona, and of dead heroes, like Glaucus, resuscitated in caves, were allegories of the natural alternations of life and death in nature, changes that are but expedients to preserve her virginity and purity inviolable in the general sum of her operations, whose aggregate presents only a majestic calm, rebuking alike man's presumption and his despair. The typical death of the Nature-God, Osiris, Atys, Adonis, Hiram, was a profound but consolatory mystery: the healing charms of Orpheus were connected with his destruction; and his bones, those valued pledges of fertility and victory, were, by a beautiful contrivance, often buried within the sacred precincts of his immortal equivalent.

In their doctrines as to the immortality of the soul, the Greek Philosophers merely stated with more precision ideas long before extant independently among themselves, in the form of symbolical suggestion. Egypt and Ethiopia in these matters learned from

India, where, as everywhere else, the origin of the doctrine was as remote and untraceable as the origin of man himself. Its natural expression is found in the language of Chrishna, in the Bagvat Ghita: "I myself never was non-existent, nor thou, nor these princes of the Earth; nor shall we ever hereafter cease to be. . . The soul is not a thing of which a man may say, it hath been, or is about to be, or is to be hereafter; for it is a thing without birth; it is pre-existent, changeless, eternal, and is not to be destroyed with this mortal frame."

According to the dogma of antiquity, the thronging forms of life are a series of purifying migrations, through which the divine principle re-ascends to the unity of its source. Inebriated in the bowl of Dionusos, and dazzled in the mirror of existence, the souls, those fragments or sparks of the Universal Intelligence, forgot their native dignity, and passed into the terrestrial frames they coveted. The most usual type of the spirit's descent was suggested by the sinking of the Sun and Stars from the upper to the lower hemisphere. When it arrived within the portals of the proper empire of Dionusos, the God of this World, the scene of delusion and change, its individuality became clothed in a material form; and as individual bodies were compared to a garment, the world was the investiture of the Universal Spirit. Again, the body was compared to a vase or urn, the soul's recipient; the world being the mighty bowl which received the descending Deity. In another image, ancient as the Grottoes of the Magi and the denunciations of Ezekiel, the world was as a dimly illuminated cavern, where shadows seem realities, and where the soul becomes forgetful of its celestial origin in proportion to its proneness to material fascinations. By another, the period of the Soul's embodiment is as when exhalations are condensed, and the aerial element assumes the grosser form of water.

But if vapor falls in water, it was held, water is again the birth of vapors, which ascend and adorn the Heavens. If our mortal existence be the death of the spirit, our death may be the renewal of its life; as physical bodies are exalted from earth to water, from water to air, from air to fire, so the man may rise into the Hero, the Hero into the God. In the course of Nature, the soul, to recover its lost estate, must pass through a series of trials and migrations. The scene of those trials is the Grand Sanctuary of Initiations, the world: their primary agents are the elements; and Dionusos, as Sovereign of Nature, or the sensuous world personified, is official Arbiter of the Mysteries, and guide of the soul, which he introduces into the body and dismisses from it. He is the Sun, that liberator of the elements, and his spiritual mediation was suggested by the same imagery which made the Zodiac the supposed path of the spirits in their descent and their return, and Cancer and Capricorn the gates through which they passed.

He was not only Creator of the World, but guardian, liberator, and Saviour of the Soul. Ushered into the world amidst lightning and thunder, he became the Liberator celebrated in the Mysteries of Thebes, delivering earth from Winter's chain, conducting the nightly chorus of the Stars and the celestial revolution of the year. His symbolism was the inexhaustible imagery employed to fill up the stellar devices of the Zodiac: he was the Vernal Bull, the Lion, the Ram, the Autumnal Goat, the Serpent: in short, the varied Deity, the resulting manifestation personified, the all in the many, the varied year, life passing into innumerable forms; essentially inferior to none, yet changing with the seasons, and undergoing their periodical decay.

He mediates and intercedes for man, and reconciles the Universal Unseen Mind with the individualized spirit of which he is emphatically the Perfecter; a consummation which he effects, first through the vicissitudes of the elemental ordeal, the alternate fire of Summer and the showers of Winter, "the trials or test of an immortal Nature"; and secondarily and symbolically through the Mysteries. He holds not only the cup of generation, but also that of wisdom or initiation, whose influence is contrary to that of the former, causing the soul to abhor its material bonds, and to long for its return. The first was the Cup of Forgetfulness; while the second is the Urn of Aquarius, quaffed by the returning spirit, as by the returning Sun at the Winter Solstice, and emblematic of the exchange of wordly impressions for the recovered recollections of the glorious sights and enjoyments of its preexistence. Water nourishes and purifies; and the urn from which it flows was thought worthy to be a symbol of Deity, as of the Osiris-Canobus who with living water irrigated the soil of Egypt; and also an emblem of Hope that should cheer the dwellings of the dead.

The second birth of Dionusos, like the rising of Osiris and Atys from the dead, and the raising of Khūrūm, is a type of the spiritual regeneration of man. Psyche (the Soul), like Ariadne, had

two lovers, an earthly and an immortal one. The immortal suitor
is Dionusos, the Eros-Phanes of the Orphici, gradually exalted by
the progress of thought, out of the symbol of Sensuality into the
torch-bearer of the Nuptials of the Gods; the Divine Influence
which physically called the world into being, and which, awakening the soul from its Stygian trance, restores it from earth to
Heaven.

Thus the scientific theories of the ancients, expounded in the
Mysteries, as to the origin of the soul, its descent, its sojourn here
below, and its return, were not a mere barren contemplation of
the nature of the world, and of the intelligent beings existing there.
They were not an idle speculation as to the order of the world,
and about the soul, but a study of the means for arriving at the
great object proposed,—the perfecting of the soul; and, as a
necessary consequence, that of morals and society. This Earth, to
them, was not the Soul's home, but its place of exile. Heaven
was its home, and there was its birth-place. To it, it ought incessantly to turn its eyes. Man was not a terrestrial plant. His roots
were in Heaven. The soul had lost its wings, clogged by the
viscosity of matter. It would recover them when it extricated
itself from matter and commenced its upward flight.

Matter being, in their view, as it was in that of St. Paul, the
principle of all the passions that trouble reason, mislead the intelligence, and stain the purity of the soul, the Mysteries taught
man how to enfeeble the action of matter on the soul, and to
restore to the latter its natural dominion. And lest the stains
so contracted should continue after death, lustrations were used,
fastings, expiations, macerations, continence, and above all, initiations. Many of these practices were at first merely symbolical,—
material signs indicating the moral purity required of the Initiates; but they afterward came to be regarded as actual productive causes of that purity.

The effect of initiation was meant to be the same as that of
philosophy, to purify the soul of its passions, to weaken the
empire of the body over the divine portion of man, and to give
him here below a happiness anticipatory of the felicity to be one
day enjoyed by him, and of the future vision by him of the Divine
Beings. And therefore Proclus and the other Platonists taught
"that the Mysteries and initiations withdrew souls from this mortal and material life, to re-unite them to the gods; and dissipated

for the adepts the shades of ignorance by the splendors of the Deity." Such were the precious fruits of the last Degree of the Mystic Science,—to see Nature in her springs and sources, and to become familiar with the causes of things and with real existences.

Cicero says that the soul must exercise itself in the practice of the virtues, if it would speedily return to its place of origin. It should, while imprisoned in the body, free itself therefrom by the contemplation of superior beings, and in some sort be divorced from the body and the senses. Those who remain enslaved, subjugated by their passions and violating the sacred laws of religion and society, will re-ascend to Heaven, only after they shall have been purified through a long succession of ages.

The Initiate was required to emancipate himself from his passions, and to free himself from the hindrances of the senses and of matter, in order that he might rise to the contemplation of the Deity, or of that incorporeal and unchanging light in which live and subsist the causes of created natures. "We must," says Porphyry, "flee from everything sensual, that the soul may with ease re-unite itself with God, and live happily with Him." "This is the great work of initiation," says Hierocles,—"to recall the soul to what is truly good and beautiful, and make it familiar therewith, and they its own; to deliver it from the pains and ills it endures here below, enchained in matter as in a dark prison; to facilitate its return to the celestial splendors, and to establish it in the Fortunate Isles, by restoring it to its first estate. Thereby, when the hour of death arrives, the soul, freed of its mortal garmenting, which it leaves behind it as a legacy to earth, will rise buoyantly to its home among the Stars, there to re-take its ancient condition, and approach toward the Divine nature as far as man may do."

Plutarch compares Isis to knowledge, and Typhon to ignorance, obscuring the light of the sacred doctrine whose blaze lights the soul of the Initiate. No gift of the gods, he holds, is so precious as the knowledge of the Truth, and that of the Nature of the gods, so far as our limited capacities allow us to rise toward them. The Valentinians termed initiation LIGHT. The Initiate, says Psellus, becomes an Epopt, when admitted to see THE DIVINE LIGHTS. Clemens of Alexandria, imitating the language of an Initiate in the Mysteries of Bacchus, and inviting this Initiate, whom he terms blind like Tiresias, to come to see Christ, Who will blaze upon his eyes with greater glory than the Sun, exclaims: "Oh Mysteries most truly holy! Oh pure Light! When the torch of the Dadoukos gleams, Heaven and the Deity are displayed to my eyes! I am initiated, and become holy!" This was the true object of initiation; to be sanctified, and TO SEE, that is, to have just and faithful conceptions of the Deity, the knowledge of Whom was THE LIGHT of the Mysteries. It was promised the Initiate at Samothrace, that he should become pure and just. Clemens says that by baptism, souls are *illuminated,* and led to *the pure light* with which mingles no darkness, nor anything material. The Initiate, become an Epopt, was called A SEER. "HAIL, NEW-BORN LIGHT!" the Initiates cried in the Mysteries of Bacchus.

Such was held to be the effect of complete initiation. It lighted up the soul with rays from the Divinity, and became for it, as it were, the eye with which, according to the Pythagoreans, it contemplates the field of Truth; in its mystical abstractions, wherein it rises superior to the body, whose action on it, it annuls for the time, to re-enter into itself, so as entirely to occpy itself with the view of the Divinity, and the means of coming to resemble Him

Thus enfeebling the dominion of the senses and the passions over the soul, and as it were freeing the latter from a sordid slavery, and by the steady practice of all the virtues, active and contemplative, our ancient brethren strove to fit themselves to return to the bosom of the Deity. Let not our objects as Masons fall below theirs. We use the symbols which they used; and teach the same great cardinal doctrines that they taught, of the existence of an intellectual God, and the immortality of the soul of man. If the details of their doctrines as to the soul seem to us to verge on absurdity, let us compare them with the common notions of our own day, and be silent. If it seems to us that they regarded the symbol in some cases as the thing symbolized, and worshipped the *sign* as if it were itself Deity, let us reflect how insufficient are our own ideas of Deity, and how we worship those ideas and images formed and fashioned in our own minds, and not the Deity Himself: and if we are inclined to smile at the importance they attached to lustrations and fasts, let us pause and inquire whether the same weakness of human nature does not exist to-day, causing rites and ceremonies to be regarded as *actively* efficient for the salvation of souls.

And let us ever remember the words of an old writer, with which we conclude this lecture: "It is a pleasure to stand on the shore, and to see ships tossed upon the sea: a pleasure to stand in the window of a castle, and see a battle and the adventures thereof: but no pleasure is comparable to the standing on the vantage-ground of Truth (a hill not to be commanded, and where the air is always clear and serene), and to see the errors and wanderings, and mists and tempests, in the vale below; *so always that this prospect be with pity, and not with swelling or pride.* Certainly it is Heaven upon Earth to have a man's mind move in charity, rest in Providence, AND TURN UPON THE POLES OF TRUTH."

XXVI.

PRINCE OF MERCY, OR SCOTTISH TRINITARIAN.

WHILE you were veiled in darkness, you heard repeated by the Voice of the Great Past its most ancient doctrines. None has the right to object, if the Christian Mason sees foreshadowed in Chrishna and Sosiosch, in Mithras and Osiris, the Divine WORD that, as he believes, became Man, and died upon the cross to redeem a fallen race. Nor can *he* object if others see reproduced, in the WORD of the beloved Disciple, that was in the beginning with God, and that was God, and by Whom everything was made, only the LOGOS of Plato, and the WORD or Uttered THOUGHT or first Emanation of LIGHT, or the Perfect REASON of the Great, Silent, Supreme, Uncreated Deity, believed in and adored by all.

We do not undervalue the importance of any Truth. We utter no word that can be deemed irreverent by any one of any faith. We do not tell the Moslem that it is only important for him to believe that there is but one God, and wholly unessential whether Mahomet was His prophet. We do not tell the Hebrew that the Messiah whom he expects was born in Bethlehem nearly two thousand years ago; and that he is a heretic because he will not so believe. And as little do we tell the sincere Christian that Jesus of Nazareth was but a man like us, or His history but the unreal revival of an older legend. To do either is beyond our jurisdiction. Masonry, of no one age, belongs to all time; of no one religion, it finds its great truths in all.

To every Mason, there is a GOD; ONE, Supreme, Infinite in Goodness, Wisdom, Foresight, Justice, and Benevolence; Creator, Disposer, and Preserver of all things. How, or by what intermediates He creates and acts, and in what way He unfolds and manifests Himself, Masonry leaves to creeds and Religions to inquire.

To every Mason, the soul of man is immortal. Whether it

emanates from and will return to God, and what its continued mode of existence hereafter, each judges for himself. Masonry was not made to settle that.

To every Mason, WISDOM or INTELLIGENCE, FORCE or STRENGTH, and HARMONY, or FITNESS and BEAUTY, are the Trinity of the attributes of God. With the subtleties of Philosophy concerning them Masonry does not meddle, nor decide as to the reality of the supposed Existences which are their Personifications: nor whether the Christian Trinity be such a personification, or a Reality of the gravest import and significance.

To every Mason, the Infinite Justice and Benevolence of God give ample assurance that Evil will ultimately be dethroned, and the Good, the True, and the Beautiful reign triumphant and eternal. It teaches, as it feels and knows, that Evil, and Pain, and Sorrow exist as part of a wise and beneficent plan, all the parts of which work together under God's eye to a result which shall be perfection. Whether the existence of evil is rightly explained in this creed or in that, by Typhon the Great Serpent, by Ahriman and his Armies of Wicked Spirits, by the Giants and Titans that war against Heaven, by the two co-existent Principles of Good and Evil, by Satan's temptation and the fall of Man, by Lok and the Serpent Fenris, it is beyond the domain of Masonry to decide, nor does it need to inquire. Nor is it within its Province to determine how the ultimate triumph of Light and Truth and Good, over Darkness and Error and Evil, is to be achieved; nor whether the Redeemer, looked and longed for by all nations, hath appeared in Judea, or is yet to come.

It reverences all the great reformers. It sees in Moses, the Lawgiver of the Jews, in Confucius and Zoroaster, in Jesus of Nazareth, and in the Arabian Iconoclast, Great Teachers of Morality, and Eminent Reformers, if no more: and allows every brother of the Order to assign to each such higher and even Divine Character as his Creed and Truth require.

Thus Masonry disbelieves no truth, and teaches unbelief in no creed, except so far as such creed may lower its lofty estimate of the Deity, degrade Him to the level of the passions of humanity, deny the high destiny of man, impugn the goodness and benevolence of the Supreme God, strike at those great columns of Masonry, Faith, Hope, and Charity, or inculcate immorality, and disregard of the active duties of the Order.

Masonry is a worship; but one in which all civilized men can unite; for it does not undertake to explain or dogmatically to settle those great mysteries, that are above the feeble comprehension of our human intellect. It trusts in God, and HOPES; it BELIEVES, like a child, and is humble. It draws no sword to compel others to adopt its belief, or to be happy with its hopes. And it WAITS with patience to understand the mysteries of Nature and Nature's God hereafter.

The greatest mysteries in the Universe are those which are ever going on around us; so trite and common to us that we never note them nor reflect upon them. Wise men tell us of the *laws* that regulate the motions of the spheres, which, flashing in huge circles and spinning on their axes, are also ever darting with inconceivable rapidity through the infinities of Space; while we atoms sit here, and dream that all was made for *us*. They tell us learnedly of centripetal and centrifugal *forces*, gravity and attraction, and all the other sounding terms invented to hide a *want* of meaning. There are other forces in the Universe than those that are mechanical.

Here are two minute seeds, not much unlike in appearance, and two of larger size. Hand them to the learned Pundit, Chemistry, who tells us how combustion goes on in the lungs, and plants are fed with phosphorus and carbon, and the alkalies and silex. Let her decompose them, analyze them, torture them in all the ways she knows. The net result of each is a little sugar, a little fibrin, a little water—carbon, potassium, sodium, and the like—one cares not to know what.

We hide them in the ground: and the slight rains moisten them, and the Sun shines upon them, and little slender shoots spring up and grow;—and what a miracle is the mere growth!—the force, the power, the *capacity* by which the little feeble shoot, that a small worm can nip off with a single snap of its mandibles, extracts from the earth and air and water the different elements, so learnedly catalogued, with which it increases in stature, and rises imperceptibly toward the sky.

One grows to be a slender, fragile, feeble stalk, soft of texture, like an ordinary weed; another a strong bush, of woody fibre, armed with thorns, and sturdy enough to bid defiance to the winds: the third a tender tree, subject to be blighted by the frost, and looked down upon by all the forest; while another spreads its rugged arms abroad, and cares for neither frost nor ice, nor the snows that for months lie around its roots.

But lo! out of the brown foul earth, and colorless invisible air, and limpid rain-water, the chemistry of the seeds has extracted *colors*—four different shades of green, that paint the leaves which put forth in the spring upon our plants, our shrubs, and our trees. Later still come the flowers—the vivid colors of the rose, the beautiful brilliance of the carnation, the modest blush of the apple, and the splendid white of the orange. Whence come the *colors* of the leaves and flowers? By what process of chemistry are *they* extracted from the carbon, the phosphorus, and the lime? Is it any greater miracle to make something out of nothing?

Pluck the flowers. Inhale the delicious *perfumes;* each perfect, and all delicious. Whence have *they* come? By what combination of acids and alkalies could the chemist's laboratory produce *them?*

And now on two comes the fruit—the ruddy apple and the golden orange. Pluck them—open them! The texture and fabric how totally different! The *taste* how entirely dissimilar—the *perfume* of each distinct from its flower and from the other. Whence the taste and this new perfume? The same earth and air and water have been made to furnish a different taste to each fruit, a different perfume not only to each fruit, but to each fruit and its own flower.

Is it any more a problem whence come thought and will and perception and all the phenomena of the mind, than this, whence come the colors, the perfumes, the taste, of the fruit and flower?

And lo! in each fruit new seeds, each gifted with the same wondrous power of reproduction—each with the same wondrous *forces* wrapped up in it to be again in turn evolved. Forces that had lived three thousand years in the grain of wheat found in the wrappings of an Egyptian mummy; forces of which learning and science and wisdom know no more than they do of the nature and laws of action of God. What can *we* know of the nature, and how can *we* understand the powers and mode of operation of the human soul, when the glossy leaves, the pearl-white flower, and the golden fruit of the orange are miracles wholly beyond our comprehension?

We but hide our ignorance in a cloud of words;—and the words too often are mere combinations of sounds without any meaning.

What is the centrifugal force? A *tendency* to go in a particular direction! What external "*force*," then, produces that tendency?

What force draws the needle round to the north? What force moves the muscle that raises the arm, when the will determines it shall rise? Whence comes the *will* itself? Is it spontaneous—a first cause, or an effect? These too are miracles; inexplicable as the creation, or the existence and self-existence of God.

Who will explain to us the passion, the peevishness, the anger, the memory, and affections of the small canary-wren? the consciousness of identity and the dreams of the dog? the reasoning powers of the elephant? the wondrous instincts, passions, government, and civil policy, and modes of communication of ideas of the ant and bee?

Who has yet made us to understand, with all his learned words, how heat comes to us from the Sun, and light from the remote Stars, setting out upon its journey earth-ward from some, at the time the Chaldeans commenced to build the Tower of Babel? Or how the image of an external object comes to and fixes itself upon the retina of the eye; and when there, how that mere empty, unsubstantial image becomes transmuted into the wondrous thing that we call SIGHT? Or how the waves of the atmosphere striking upon the tympanum of the ear—those thin, invisible waves—produce the equally wondrous phenomenon of HEARING, and become the roar of the tornado, the crash of the thunder, the mighty voice of the ocean, the chirping of the cricket, the delicate sweet notes and exquisite trills and variations of the wren and mocking-bird, or the magic melody of the instrument of Paganini?

Our senses are mysteries to us, and we are mysteries to ourselves. Philosophy has taught us nothing as to the *nature* of our sensations, our perceptions, our cognizances, the origin of our thoughts and ideas, but *words*. By no effort or degree of reflection, never so long continued, can man become conscious of a personal identity in himself, separate and distinct from his body and his brain. We torture ourselves in the effort to gain an idea of ourselves, and weary with the exertion. Who has yet made us understand how, from the contact with a foreign body, the image in the eye, the wave of air impinging on the ear, particular particles entering the nostrils, and coming in contact with the palate, come sensations in the nerves, and from that, perception in the mind, of the animal or the man?

What do we know of Substance? Men even doubt yet whether it exists. Philosophers tell us that our senses make known to us only the *attributes* of substance, extension, hardness, color, and the like; but not *the thing itself* that *is* extended, solid, black or white; as we know the *attributes* of the Soul, its thoughts and its perceptions, and not the Soul itself which perceives and thinks.

What a wondrous mystery is there in heat and light, existing, we know not how, within certain limits, narrow in comparison with infinity, beyond which on every side stretch out infinite space and the blackness of unimaginable darkness, and the intensity of inconceivable cold! Think only of the mighty Power required to maintain warmth and light in the central point of such an infinity, to whose darkness that of Midnight, to whose cold that of the last Arctic Island is nothing. And yet God is everywhere.

And what a mystery are the effects of heat and cold upon the wondrous fluid that we call water! What a mystery lies hidden in every flake of snow and in every crystal of ice, and in their final transformation into the invisible vapor that rises from the ocean or the land, and floats above the summits of the mountains!

What a multitude of wonders, indeed, has chemistry unveiled to our eyes! Think only that if some single law enacted by God were at once repealed, that of attraction or affinity or cohesion, for example, the whole material world, with its solid granite and adamant, its veins of gold and silver, its trap and porphyry, its huge beds of coal, our own frames and the very ribs and bones of this apparently indestructible earth, would instantaneously dissolve, with all Suns and Stars and Worlds throughout all the Universe of God, into a thin invisible vapor of infinitely minute particles or atoms, diffused throughout infinite space; and with them light and heat would disappear; unless the Deity Himself be, as the Ancient Persians thought, the Eternal Light and the Immortal Fire.

The mysteries of the Great Universe of God! How *can* we with our limited mental vision expect to grasp and comprehend them! Infinite SPACE, stretching out from us every way, without limit: infinite TIME, without beginning or end; and WE, HERE, and NOW, in the centre of each! An infinity of suns, the nearest of which only *diminish* in size, viewed with the most powerful telescope: each with its retinue of worlds; infinite numbers of such suns, so remote from us that their light would not reach us, journeying during an infinity of time, while the light that *has* reached us, from some that we *seem* to see, has been upon its journey for fifty centuries: our world spinning upon its axis, and rushing ever in its circuit round the sun; and it, the sun, and all our system revolving round some great central point; and that, and suns, stars, and worlds evermore flashing onward with incredible rapidity through illimitable space: and then, in every drop of water that we drink, in every morsel of much of our food, in the air, in the earth, in the sea, incredible multitudes of living creatures, invisible to the naked eye, of a minuteness beyond belief, yet organized, living, feeding, *perhaps* with consciousness of identity, and memory and instinct.

Such are some of the mysteries of the great Universe of God. And yet we, whose life and that of the world on which we live form but a point in the centre of infinite Time: we, who nourish animalculæ within, and on whom vegetables grow without, would fain learn how God created this Universe, would understand His Powers, His Attributes, His Emanations, His Mode of Existence and of Action; would fain know the plan according to which all events proceed, that plan profound as God Himself; would know the laws by which He controls His Universe; would fain *see* and *talk* to Him face to face, as man talks to man: and we try not to *believe,* because we do not *understand.*

He commands us to love one another, to love our neighbor as ourself; and we dispute and wrangle, and hate and slay each other, because we cannot be of one opinion as to the Essence of His Nature, as to His Attributes; whether He became man born of a woman, and was crucified; whether the Holy Ghost is of the *same* substance with the Father, or only of a *similar* substance; whether a feeble old man is God's Vicegerent; whether some are elected from all eternity to be saved, and others to be condemned and punished; whether punishment of the wicked after death is to be eternal; whether this doctrine or the other be heresy or truth;—drenching the world with blood, depopulating realms, and turning fertile lands into deserts; until, for religious war, persecution, and bloodshed, the Earth for many a century has rolled round the Sun, a charnel-house, steaming and reeking with human gore, the blood of brother slain by brother for opinion's sake, that has soaked into and polluted all her veins, and made her a horror to her sisters of the Universe.

And if men were all Masons, and obeyed with all their heart

her mild and gentle teachings, that world would be a paradise; while intolerance and persecution make of it a hell. For this is the Masonic Creed: BELIEVE, in God's Infinite Benevolence, Wisdom, and Justice: HOPE, for the final triumph of Good over Evil, and for Perfect Harmony as the final result of all the concords and discords of the Universe: and be CHARITABLE as God is, toward the unfaith, the errors, the follies, and the faults of men: for all make one great brotherhood.

INSTRUCTION.

Sen.'. W.'. Brother Junior Warden, are you a Prince of Mercy?

Jun.'. W.'. I have seen the Delta and the Holy NAMES upon it, and am an AMETH like yourself, in the TRIPLE COVENANT, of which we bear the mark.

Qu.'. What is the first Word upon the Delta?

Ans.'. The Ineffable Name of Deity, the true mystery of which is known to the Ameth alone.

Qu.'. What do the three sides of the Delta denote to us?

Ans.'. To us, and to all Masons, the three Great Attributes or Developments of the Essence of the Deity; WISDOM, or the Reflective and Designing Power, in which, when there was naught but God, the Plan and Idea of the Universe was shaped and formed: FORCE, or the Executing and Creating Power, which instantaneously acting, realized the Type and Idea framed by Wisdom; and the Universe, and all Stars and Worlds, and Light and Life, and Men and Angels and all living creatures WERE; and HARMONY, or the Preserving Power, Order, and Beauty, maintaining the Universe in its State, and constituting the law of Harmony, Motion, Proportion, and Progression:—WISDOM, which *thought* the plan; STRENGTH, which *created:* HARMONY, which *upholds* and *preserves:*—the Masonic Trinity, three Powers and one Essence: the three columns which support the Universe, Physical, Intellectual, and Spiritual, of which every Masonic Lodge is a type and symbol:—while to the Christian Mason, they represent the Three that bear record in Heaven, the FATHER, the WORD, and the HOLY SPIRIT, which three are ONE.

Qu.'. What do the three Greek letters upon the Delta, *I.'. H.'. .'.* [*Iota, Eta,* and *Sigma*] represent?

Ans.'. Three of the Names of the Supreme Deity among the Syrians, Phœnicians. and Hebrews . . . IHUH [יהוה]; *Self-Ex-*

istence . . . AL [‚ א] : *the Nature-God, or Soul of the Universe. . .*
SHADAI [שׁדי] *Supreme Power.* Also three of the Six Chief Attributes of God, among the Kabbalists:—WISDOM [IEH], the *Intellect,* (Νοῦς) of the Egyptians, the *Word* (Λόγος) of the Platonists, and the *Wisdom* (Σοφία) of the Gnostics: . . MAGNIFI-
CENCE [AL], the Symbol of which was the Lion's Head: . . and
VICTORY and GLORY [*Tsabaoth*], which are the two columns
JACHIN and BOAZ, that stand in the Portico of the Temple of
Masonry. To the Christian Mason they are the first three letters
of the name of the Son of God, Who died upon the cross to redeem mankind.

Qu.˙. What is the first of the THREE COVENANTS, of which we
bear the mark?

Ans.˙. That which God made with Noah; when He said, "I
will not again curse the earth any more for man's sake, neither
will I smite any more everything living as I have done. While
the Earth remaineth, seed-time and harvest, and cold and heat,
and Winter and Summer, and day and night shall not cease. I
will establish My covenant with you, and with your seed after you,
and with every living creature. All mankind shall no more be
cut off by the waters of a flood, nor shall there any more be a
flood to destroy the earth. This is the token of My covenant: I
do set My bow in the cloud, and it shall be for a token of a covenant between Me and the earth: an everlasting covenant between
Me and every living creature on the earth."

Qu.˙. What is the second of the Three Covenants?

Ans.˙. That which God made with Abraham; when He said, "I
am the Absolute Uncreated God. I will make My covenant between Me and thee, and thou shalt be the Father of Many Nations,
and Kings shall come from thy loins. I will establish My covenant between Me and thee, and thy descendants after thee, to the
remotest generations, for an everlasting covenant; and I will be
thy God and their God, and will give thee the land of Canaan for
an everlasting possession."

Qu.˙. What is the third Covenant?

Ans.˙. That which God made with all men by His prophets;
when He said: "I will gather all nations and tongues, and they
shall come and see My Glory. I will create new Heavens and a
new earth; and the former shall not be remembered, nor come
into mind. The Sun shall no more shine by day, nor the Moon
by night; but the Lord shall be an everlasting light and splendor.

His Spirit and His Word shall remain with men forever. The heavens shall vanish away like vapor, and the earth shall wax old like a garment, and they that dwell therein shall die; but my salvation shall be forever, and my righteousness shall not end; and there shall be Light among the Gentiles, and salvation unto the ends of the earth. The redeemed of the Lord shall return, and everlasting joy be on their heads, and sorrow and mourning shall flee away."

Qu.∴ What is the symbol of the Triple Covenant?

Ans.∴ The Triple Triangle.

Qu.∴ Of what else is it the symbol to us?

Ans.∴ Of the Trinity of Attributes of the Deity; and of the triple essence of Man, the Principle of Life, the Intellectual Power, and the Soul or Immortal Emanation from the Deity.

Qu.∴ What is the first great Truth of the Sacred Mysteries?

Ans.∴ No man hath seen God at any time. He is One, Eternal, All-Powerful, All-Wise, Infinitely Just, Merciful, Benevolent, and Compassionate, Creator and Preserver of all things, the Source of Light and Life, coextensive with Time and Space; Who thought, and with the Thought created the Universe and all living things, and the souls of men: THAT IS:—the PERMANENT; while everything beside is a perpetual genesis.

Qu.∴ What is the second great Truth of the Sacred Mysteries?

Ans.∴ The Soul of Man is Immortal; not the result of organization, nor an aggregate of modes of action of matter, nor a succession of phenomena and perceptions; but an EXISTENCE, one and identical, a living spirit, a spark of the Great Central Light, that hath entered into and dwells in the body; to be separated therefrom at death, and return to God who gave it: that doth not disperse nor vanish at death, like breath or a smoke, nor can be annihilated; but still exists and possesses activity and intelligence, even as it existed in God, before it was enveloped in the body.

Qu.∴ What is the third great Truth in Masonry?

Ans.∴ The impulse which directs to right conduct, and deters from crime, is not only older than the ages of nations and cities, but coeval with that Divine Being Who sees and rules both Heaven and earth. Nor did Tarquin less violate that Eternal Law, though in his reign there might have been no written law at Rome against such violence; for the principle that impels us to right conduct, and warns us against guilt, springs out of the nature of things. It did not begin to be law when it was first *written*, nor was it *originated;* but it is coeval with the Divine Intelligence itself. The consequence of virtue is not to be made the end thereof; and laudable performances must have deeper roots, motives, and instigations, to give them the stamp of virtues.

Qu.∴ What is the fourth great Truth in Masonry?

Ans.∴ The moral truths are as absolute as the metaphysical truths. Even the Deity cannot make it that there should be effects without a cause, or phenomena without substance. As little could He make it to be sinful and evil to respect our pledged word, to love truth, to moderate our passions. The principles of Morality are axioms, like the principles of Geometry. The moral laws are the necessary relations that flow from the nature of things, and they are not created by, but have existed eternally in God. Their continued existence does not depend upon the exercise of His WILL. Truth and Justice are of His ESSENCE. Not because we are feeble and God omnipotent, is it our duty to obey His law. We may be forced, but are not under obligation, to obey the stronger. God is the principle of Morality, but not by His mere will, which, abstracted from all other of His attributes, would be neither just nor unjust. Good is the expression of His will, in so far as that will is itself the expression of eternal, absolute, uncreated justice, which is *in* God, which His will did not create; but which it executes and promulgates, as *our* will proclaims and promulgates and executes the idea of the good which is in us. He has given us the law of Truth and Justice; but He has not arbitrarily instituted that law. Justice is inherent in His will, because it is contained in His intelligence and wisdom, in His very nature and most intimate essence.

Qu.∴ What is the fifth great Truth in Masonry?

Ans.∴ There is an essential distinction between Good and Evil, what is just and what is unjust; and to this distinction is attached, for every intelligent and free creature, the absolute obligation of conforming to what is good and just. Man is an intelligent and free being,—free, because he is conscious that it is his duty, and because it is *made* his duty, to obey the dictates of truth and justice, and therefore he must necessarily have the power of doing so, which involves the power of *not* doing so;—capable of comprehending the distinction between good and evil, justice and injustice, and the obligation which accompanies it, and of naturally adhering to that obligation, independently of any contract or positive law; capable also of resisting the temptations which urge him toward evil and injustice, and of complying with the sacred law of eternal justice.

That man is not governed by a resistless Fate or inexorable Destiny; but is free to choose between the evil and the good: that Justice and Right, the Good and Beautiful, are of the essence of the Divinity, like His Infinitude; and therefore they are laws to man: that we are conscious of our freedom to act, as we are conscious of our identity, and the continuance and connectedness of our existence; and have the same evidence of one as of the other; and if we can put *one* in doubt, we have no certainty of *either*, and everything is unreal: that we can deny our free will and free agency, only upon the ground that they are in the nature of things impossible; which would be to deny the Omnipotence of God.

Qu∴. What is the sixth great Truth of Masonry?

Ans∴. The necessity of practising the moral truths, is *obligation.* The moral truths, necessary in the eye of reason, are obligatory on the will. The moral obligation, like the moral truth that is its foundation, is *absolute.* As the necessary truths are not more or less necessary, so the obligation is not more or less obligatory. There are degrees of importance among different obligations; but none in the obligation itself. We are not *nearly* obliged, *almost* obliged. We are *wholly* so, or not at all. If there be any place of refuge to which we can escape from the obligation, it ceases to exist. If the obligation is absolute, it is immutable and universal. For if that of to-day may not be that of to-morrow, if what is obligatory on *me* may not be obligatory on *you,* the obligation would differ from itself, and be variable and contingent. This fact is the principle of all morality. That every act contrary to right and justice, deserves to be repressed by force, and punished when committed, equally in the absence of any law or contract: that man naturally recognizes the distinction between the merit and demerit of actions, as he does that between justice and injustice, honesty and dishonesty; and feels, without being taught, and in the absence of law or contract, that it is wrong for vice to be rewarded or go unpunished, and for virtue to be punished or left unrewarded: and that, the Deity being infinitely just and good, it must follow as a necessary and inflexible law that punishment shall be the result of Sin, its inevitable and natural effect and corollary, and not a mere arbitrary vengeance.

Qu.·. What is the seventh great Truth in Masonry?

Ans.·. The immutable law of God requires, that besides respecting the absolute rights of others, and being merely just, we should do good, be charitable, and obey the dictates of the generous and noble sentiments of the soul. Charity is a law, because our conscience is not satisfied nor at ease if we have not relieved the suffering, the distressed, and the destitute. It is to *give* that which he to whom you give has no right to *take* or *demand*. To be charitable is obligatory on us. We are the Almoners of God's bounties. But the obligation is not so precise and inflexible as the obligation to be *just*. Charity knows neither rule nor limit. It goes beyond all obligation. Its beauty consists in its liberty. "He that loveth not, knoweth not God; FOR GOD IS LOVE. If we love one another, God dwelleth in us, and His love is perfected in us. God is love; and he that dwelleth in love, dwelleth in God, and God in him." To be kindly affectioned one to another with brotherly love; to relieve the necessities of the needy, and be generous, liberal, and hospitable; to return to no man evil for evil; to rejoice at the good fortune of others, and sympathize with them in their sorrows and reverses; to live peaceably with all men, and repay injuries with benefits and kindness; these are the sublime dictates of the Moral Law, taught from the infancy of the world, by Masonry.

Qu.·. What is the eighth great Truth in Masonry?

Ans.·. That the laws which control and regulate the Universe of God, are those of motion and harmony. We see only the isolated incidents of things, and with our feeble and limited capacity and vision cannot discern their connection, nor the mighty chords that make the apparent discord perfect harmony. Evil is merely apparent, and all is in reality good and perfect. For pain and sorrow, persecution and hardships, affliction and destitution, sickness and death are but the means, by which alone the noblest virtues could be developed. Without them, and without sin and error, and wrong and outrage, as there can be no effect without an adequate cause, there could be neither patience under suffering and distress; nor prudence in difficulty; nor temperance to avoid excess; nor courage to meet danger; nor truth, when to speak the truth is hazardous; nor love, when it is met with ingratitude; nor charity for the needy and destitute; nor forbearance and forgiveness of injuries; nor toleration of erroneous opinions; nor charitable judgment and construction of men's motives and actions; nor patriotism, nor heroism, nor honor, nor self-denial, nor generosity. These and most other virtues and excellencies would have no existence, and even their names be unknown; and the poor virtues that still existed, would scarce deserve the name; for life would be one flat, dead, low level, above which none of the lofty elements of human nature would emerge; and man would lie lapped in contented indolence and idleness, a mere worthless negative, instead of the brave, strong soldier against the grim legions of Evil and rude Difficulty.

Qu.∴ What is the ninth great Truth in Masonry?

Ans.∴ The great leading doctrine of this Degree;—that the JUSTICE, the WISDOM, and the MERCY of God are alike infinite, alike perfect, and yet do not in the least jar nor conflict one with the other; but form a Great Perfect Trinity of Attributes, three and yet one: that, the principle of merit and demerit being absolute, and every good action deserving to be rewarded, and every bad one to be punished, and God being as just as He is good; and yet the cases constantly recurring in this world, in which crime and cruelty, oppression, tyranny, and injustice are prosperous, happy, fortunate, and self-contented, and rule and reign, and enjoy all the blessings of God's beneficence, while the virtuous and good are unfortunate, miserable, destitute, pining away in dungeons, perishing with cold, and famishing with hunger, slaves of oppression, and instruments and victims of the miscreants that govern; so that this world, if there were no existence beyond it, would be one great theatre of wrong and injustice, proving God wholly disregardful of His own necessary law of merit and demerit;—it follows that there must be another life in which these apparent wrongs shall be repaired: That all the powers of man's soul tend to infinity; and his indomitable instinct of immortality, and the universal hope of another life, testified by all creeds, all poetry, all traditions, establish its certainty; for man is not an orphan; but hath a Father near at hand: and the day must come when Light and Truth, and the Just and Good shall be victorious, and Darkness, Error, Wrong, and Evil be annihilated, and known no more forever: That the Universe is one great Harmony, in which, according to the faith of all nations, deep-rooted in all hearts in the primitive ages, Light will ultimately prevail over Darkness, and the Good Principle over the Evil: and the myriad souls that have emanated from the Divinity, purified and ennobled by the struggle here below, will again return to perfect bliss in the bosom of God, to offend against Whose laws will then be no longer possible.

Qu.·. What, then, is the one great lesson taught to us, as Masons, in this Degree?

Ans.·. That to that state and realm of Light and Truth and Perfection, which is absolutely certain, all the good men on earth are tending; and if there is a law from whose operation none are exempt, which inevitably conveys their bodies to darkness and to dust, there is another not less certain nor less powerful, which conducts their spirits to that state of Happiness and Splendor and Perfection, the bosom of their Father and their God. The wheels of Nature are not made to roll backward. Everything presses on to Eternity. From the birth of Time an impetuous current has set in, which bears all the sons of men toward that interminable ocean. Meanwhile, Heaven is attracting to itself whatever is congenial to its nature, is enriching itself by the spoils of the Earth, and collecting within its capacious bosom whatever is pure, permanent, and divine, leaving nothing for the last fire to consume but the gross matter that creates concupiscence; while everything fit for that good fortune shall be gathered and selected from the ruins of the world, to adorn that Eternal City.

Let every Mason then obey the voice that calls him thither. Let us seek the things that are above, and be not content with a world that must shortly perish, and which we must speedily quit, while we neglect to prepare for that in which we are invited to dwell forever. While everything within us and around us reminds us of the approach of death, and concurs to teach us that this is not our rest, let us hasten our preparations for another world, and earnestly implore that help and strength from our Father, which alone can put an end to that fatal war which our desires have too long waged with our destiny. When these move in the same direction, and that which God's will renders unavoidable shall become our choice, all things will be ours; life will be divested of its vanity, and death disarmed of its terrors.

Qu.·. What are the symbols of the purification necessary to make us perfect Masons?

Ans.·. Lavation with pure water, or baptism; because to cleanse the body is emblematical of purifying the soul; and because it conduces to the bodily health, and virtue is the health of the soul, as sin and vice are its malady and sickness:—unction, or anointing with oil; because thereby we are set apart and dedicated to the service and priesthood of the Beautiful, the True, and the Good:—and robes of white, emblems of candor, purity, and truth.

Qu∴ What is to us the chief symbol of man's ultimate redemption and regeneration?

Ans∴ The fraternal supper, of bread which nourishes, and of wine which refreshes and exhilarates, symbolical of the time which is to come, when all mankind shall be one great harmonious brotherhood; and teaching us these great lessons: that as matter changes ever, but no single atom is annihilated, it is not rational to suppose that the far nobler soul does not continue to exist beyond the grave: that many thousands who have died before us might claim to be joint owners with ourselves of the particles that compose our mortal bodies; for matter ever forms new combinations; and the bodies of the ancient dead, the patriarchs before and since the flood, the kings and common people of all ages, resolved into their constituent elements, are carried upon the wind over all continents, and continually enter into and form part of the habitations of new souls, creating new bonds of sympathy and brotherhood between each man that lives and all his race. And thus, in the bread we eat, and in the wine we drink to-night *may* enter into and form part of us the identical particles of matter that once formed parts of the material bodies called Moses, Confucius, Plato, Socrates, or Jesus of Nazareth. In the truest sense, we eat and drink the bodies of the dead; and cannot say that there is a single atom of our blood or body, the ownership of which some other soul might not dispute with us. It teaches us also the infinite beneficence of God who sends us seedtime and harvest, each in its season, and makes His showers to fall and His sun to shine alike upon the evil and the good: bestowing upon us unsolicited His innumerable blessings, and asking no return. For there are no angels stationed upon the watchtowers of creation to call the world to prayer and sacrifice; but He bestows His benefits in silence, like a kind friend who comes at night, and, leaving his gifts at the door, to be found by us in the morning, goes quietly away and asks no thanks, nor ceases his kind offices for our ingratitude. And thus the bread and wine teach us that our Mortal Body is no more WE than the house in which we live, or the garments that we wear; but the Soul is I, the ONE, identical, unchangeable, immortal emanation from the Diety, to return to God and be forever happy, in His good time; as our mortal bodies, dissolving, return to the elements from which they came, their particles coming and going ever in perpetual genesis. To our Jewish Brethren, this supper is symbolical of the Passover: to the Christian Mason, of that eaten by Christ and His Disciples, when, celebrating the Passover, He broke bread and gave it to them, saying, "Take! eat! this is My body:" and giving them the cup, He said, "Drink ye all of it! for this is My blood of the New Testament, which is shed for many for the remission of sins;" thus symbolizing the perfect harmony and union between Himself and the faithful; and His death upon the cross for the salvation of man.

The history of Masonry is the history of Philosophy. Masons do not pretend to set themselves up for instructors of the human race: but, though Asia produced and preserved the Mysteries, Masonry has, in Europe and America, given regularity to their doctrines, spirit, and action, and developed the moral advantages which mankind may reap from them. More consistent, and more simple in its mode of procedure, it has put an end to the vast allegorical pantheon of ancient mythologies, and itself become a science.

None can deny that Christ taught a lofty morality. "Love one another: forgive those that despitefully use you and persecute you: be pure of heart, meek, humble, contented: lay not up riches on earth, but in Heaven: submit to the powers lawfully over you: become like these little children, or ye cannot be saved, for of such is the Kingdom of Heaven: forgive the repentant; and cast no stone at the sinner, if you too have sinned: do unto others as ye would have others do unto you:" such, and not abstruse questions of theology, were His simple and sublime teachings.

The early Christians followed in His footsteps. The first preachers of the faith had no thought of domination. Entirely animated by His saying, that he among them should be first, who should serve with the greatest devotion, they were humble, modest, and charitable, and they knew how to communicate this spirit of the inner man to the churches under their direction. These churches were at first but spontaneous meetings of all Christians inhabiting the same locality. A pure and severe morality, mingled with religious enthusiasm, was the characteristic of each, and excited the admiration even of their persecutors. Everything was in common among them; their property, their joys, and their sorrows. In the silence of night they met for instruction and to pray together. Their love-feasts, or fraternal repasts, ended these reunions, in which all differences in social position and rank were effaced in the presence of a paternal Divinity. Their sole object was to make men better, by bringing them back to a simple worship, of which universal morality was the basis; and to end those numerous and cruel sacrifices which everywhere inundated with blood the altars of the gods. Thus did Christianity reform the world, and obey the teachings of its founder. It gave to woman her proper rank and influence; it regulated domestic life; and by admitting the slaves to the love-feasts, it by degrees raised them above that oppression under which half of mankind had groaned for ages.

This, in its purity, as taught by Christ Himself, was the true primitive religion, as communicated by God to the Patriarchs. It was no new religion, but the reproduction of the oldest of all; and its true and perfect morality is the morality of Masonry, as is the morality of every creed of antiquity.

In the early days of Christianity, there was an initiation like those of the pagans. Persons were admitted on special conditions only. To arrive at a complete knowledge of the doctrine, they had to pass three degrees of instruction. The initiates were consequently divided into three classes; the first, *Auditors,* the second, *Catechumens,* and the third, *the Faithful.* The Auditors were a sort of novices, who were prepared by certain ceremonies and certain instruction to receive the dogmas of Christianity. A portion of these dogmas was made known to the Catechumens; who, after particular purifications, received baptism, or the initiation of the *theogenesis* (*divine generation*); but in the grand mysteries of that religion, the incarnation, nativity, passion, and resurrection of Christ, none were initiated but *the Faithful.* These doctrines, and the celebration of the Holy Sacraments, particularly the Eucharist, were kept with profound secrecy. These Mysteries were divided into two parts; the first styled the Mass of the Catechumens; the second, the Mass of the Faithful. The celebration of the Mysteries of Mithras was also styled *a mass;* and the ceremonies used were the same. There were found all the sacraments of the Catholic Church, even the breath of confirmation. The Priest of Mithras promised the Initiates deliverance from sin, by means of confession and baptism, and a future life of happiness or misery. He celebrated the oblation of bread, image of the resurrection. The baptism of newly-born children, extreme unction, confession of sins,—all belonged to the Mithriac rites. The candidate was purified by a species of baptism, a mark was impressed upon his forehead, he offered bread and water, pronouncing certain mysterious words.

During the persecutions in the early ages of Christianity, the Christians took refuge in the vast catacombs which stretched for miles in every direction under the city of Rome, and are supposed to have been of Etruscan origin. There, amid labyrinthine windings, deep caverns, hidden chambers, chapels, and tombs, the persecuted fugitives found refuge, and there they performed the ceremonies of the Mysteries.

The Basilideans, a sect of Christians that arose soon after the time of the Apostles, practised the Mysteries, with the old Egyptian legend. They symbolized Osiris by the Sun, Isis by the Moon, and Typhon by Scorpio; and wore crystals bearing these emblems, as amulets or talismans to protect them from danger; upon which were also a brilliant star and the serpent. They were copied from the talismans of Persia and Arabia, and given to every candidate at his initiation.

Irenæus tells us that the Simonians, one of the earliest sects of the Gnostics, had a Priesthood of the Mysteries.

Tertullian tells us that the Valentinians, the most celebrated of all the Gnostic schools, imitated, or rather perverted, the Mysteries of Eleusis. Irenæus informs us, in several curious chapters, of the Mysteries practised by the Marcosians; and Origen gives much information as to the Mysteries of the Ophites; and there is no doubt that all the Gnostic sects had Mysteries and an initiation. They all claimed to possess a secret doctrine, coming to them directly from Jesus Christ, different from that of the Gospels and Epistles, and superior to those communications, which in their eyes, were merely exoteric. This secret doctrine they did not communicate to every one; and among the extensive sect of the Basilideans hardly one in a thousand knew it, as we learn from Irenæus. We know the name of only the highest class of their Initiates. They were styled *Elect* or *Elus* ['Ἐκλεκτοί], and Strangers to the World [ξένοι ἐν κόσμῳ]. They had at least three Degrees—the *Material*, the *Intellectual*, and the *Spiritual*, and the lesser and greater Mysteries; and the number of those who attained the highest Degree was quite small.

Baptism was one of their most important ceremonies; and the Basilideans celebrated the 10th of January, as the anniversary of the day on which Christ was baptized in Jordan.

They had the ceremony of laying on of hands, by way of purification; and that of the mystic banquet, emblem of that to which they believed the Heavenly Wisdom would one day admit them, in the fullness of things [Πλήρωμα].

Their ceremonies were much more like those of the Christians than those of Greece; but they mingled with them much that was borrowed from the Orient and Egypt: and taught the primitive truths, mixed with a multitude of fantastic errors and fictions.

The discipline of the secret was the concealment (*occultatio*) of certain tenets and ceremonies. So says Clemens of Alexandria.

To avoid persecution, the early Christians were compelled to use great precaution, and to hold meetings of the Faithful [*of the Household of Faith*] in private places, under concealment by darkness. They assembled in the night, and they guarded against the intrusion of false brethren and profane persons, spies who might cause their arrest. They conversed together figuratively, and by the use of symbols, lest cowans and eavesdroppers might overhear: and there existed among them a favored class, or Order, who were initiated into certain Mysteries which they were bound by solemn promise not to disclose, or even converse about, except with such as had received them under the same sanction. They were called *Brethren, the Faithful, Stewards of the Mysteries, Superintendents, Devotees of the Secret,* and ARCHITECTS.

In the *Hierarchiæ*, attributed to St. Dionysius the Areopagite, the first Bishop of Athens, the tradition of the sacrament is said to have been divided into three Degrees, or grades, *purification, initiation,* and *accomplishment* or *perfection;* and it mentions also, as part of the ceremony, *the bringing to sight.*

The Apostolic Constitutions, attributed to Clemens, Bishop of Rome, describe the early church, and say: "These regulations must on no account be communicated to all sorts of persons, because of the Mysteries contained in them." They speak of the Deacon's duty to keep the doors, that none uninitiated should enter at the oblation. *Ostiarii,* or doorkeepers, kept guard, and gave notice of the time of prayer and church-assemblies; and also by private signal, in times of persecution, gave notice to those within, to enable them to avoid danger. The Mysteries were open to the *Fideles* or *Faithful* only; and no spectators were allowed at the communion.

Tertullian, who died about A. D. 216, says in his *Apology:* "None are admitted to the religious Mysteries without an oath of secrecy. We appeal to your Thracian and Eleusinian Mysteries; and we are especially bound to this caution, because if we prove faithless, we should not only provoke Heaven, but draw upon our heads the utmost rigor of human displeasure. And should strangers betray us? They know nothing but by report and hearsay. Far hence, ye Profane! is the prohibition from all holy Mysteries."

Clemens, Bishop of Alexandria, born about A. D. 191, says, in his *Stromata,* that he cannot explain the Mysteries, because he should thereby, according to the old proverb, put a sword into the hands of a child. He frequently compares the Discipline of the Secret with the heathen Mysteries, as to their internal and recondite wisdom.

Whenever the early Christians happened to be in company with strangers, more properly termed *the Profane,* they never spoke of their sacraments, but indicated to one another what they meant by means of symbols and secret watchwords, disguisedly, and as by direct communication of mind with mind, and by enigmas.

Origen, born A. D. 134 or 135, answering Celsus, who had objected that the Christians had a concealed doctrine said: "Inasmuch as the essential and important doctrines and principles of Christianity are openly taught, it is foolish to object that there are other things that are recondite; for this is common to Christian discipline with that of those philosophers in whose teaching some things were exoteric and some esoteric: and it is enough to say that it was so with some of the disciples of Pythagoras."

The formula which the primitive church pronounced at the moment of celebrating its Mysteries, was this: "Depart, ye Profane! Let the Catechumens, and those who have not been admitted or initiated, go forth."

Archelaus, Bishop of Cascara in Mesopotamia, who, in the year 278, conducted a controversy with the Manichæans, said: "These Mysteries the church now communicates to him who has passed through the introductory Degree. They are not explained to the Gentiles at all; nor are they taught openly in the hearing of Catechumens: but much that is spoken is in disguised terms, that the

Faithful [Πιστοί], who possess the knowledge, may be still more informed, and those who are not acquainted with it, may suffer no disadvantage."

Cyril, Bishop of Jerusalem, was born in the year 315, and died in 386. In his *Catechesis* he says: "The Lord spake in parables to His hearers in general; but to His disciples He explained in private the parables and allegories which He spoke in public. The splendor of glory is for those who are early enlightened: obscurity and darkness are the portion of the unbelievers and ignorant. Just so the church discovers its Mysteries to those who have advanced beyond the class of Catechumens: we employ obscure terms with others."

St. Basil, the Great Bishop of Cæsarea, born in the year 326, and dying in the year 376, says: "We receive the dogmas transmitted to us by writing, and those which have descended to us from the Apostles, beneath the mystery of oral tradition: for several things have been handed to us without writing, lest the vulgar, too familiar with our dogmas, should lose a due respect for them. . . . This is what the uninitiated are not permitted to contemplate; and how should it ever be proper to write and circulate among the people an account of them?"

St. Gregory Nazianzen, Bishop of Constantinople, A. D. 379, says: "You have heard as much of the Mystery as we are allowed to speak openly in the ears of all; the rest will be communicated to you in private; and that you must retain within yourself. . . . Our Mysteries are not to be made known to strangers."

St. Ambrose, Archbishop of Milan, who was born in 340, and died in 393, says in his work *De Mysteriis:* "All the Mystery should be kept concealed, guarded by faithful silence, lest it should be inconsiderately divulged to the ears of the Profane. . . . . It is not given to all to contemplate the depths of our Mysteries. . . . . that they may not be seen by those who ought not to behold them; nor received by those who cannot preserve them." And in another work: "He sins against God, who divulges to the unworthy the Mysteries confided to him. The danger is not merely in violating truth, but in telling truth, if he allow himself to give hints of them to those from whom they ought to be concealed.....Beware of casting pearls before swine!....Every Mystery ought to be kept secret; and, as it were, to be covered over by silence, lest it should rashly be divulged to the ears of the Profane. Take heed that you do not incautiously reveal the Mysteries!"

St. Augustine, Bishop of Hippo, who was born in 347, and died in 430, says in one of his discourses: "Having dismissed the Catechumens, we have retained you only to be our hearers; because, besides those things which belong to all Christians in common, we are now to discourse to you of sublime Mysteries, which none are qualified to hear, but those who, by the Master's favor, are made partakers of them.....To have taught them openly, would have been to betray them." And he refers to the Ark of the Covenant, and says that it signified a Mystery, or secret of God, shadowed over by the cherubim of glory, and honored by being veiled.

St. Chrysostom and St. Augustine speak of initiation more than fifty times. St. Ambrose writes to those who are initiated; and initiation was not merely baptism, or admission into the church, but it referred to initiation into the Mysteries. To the baptized and initiated the Mysteries of religion were unveiled; they were kept secret from the Catechumens; who were permitted to hear the Scriptures read and the ordinary discourses delivered, in which the Mysteries, reserved for the Faithful, were never treated of. When the services and prayers were ended, the Catechumens and spectators all withdrew.

Chrysostom, Bishop of Constantinople, was born in 354, and died in 417. He says: "I wish to speak openly: but I dare not, on account of those who are not initiated. I shall therefore avail myself of disguised terms, discoursing in a shadowy manner..... Where the holy Mysteries are celebrated, we drive away all uninitiated persons, and then close the doors." He mentions the acclamations of the initiated; "which," he says, "I here pass over in silence; for it is forbidden to disclose such things to the Profane." Palladius, in his life of Chrysostom, records, as a great outrage, that, a tumult having been excited against him by his enemies, they forced their way into the *penetralia,* where the uninitiated beheld what was not proper for them to see; and Chrysostom mentions the same circumstance in his epistle to Pope Innocent.

St. Cyril of Alexandria, who was made Bishop in 412, and died in 444, says in his 7th Book against Julian: "These Mysteries are so profound and so exalted, that they can be comprehended by those only who are enlightened. I shall not, therefore, attempt to speak of what is so admirable in them, lest by discovering them to

the uninitiated, I should offend against the injunction not to give
what is holy to the impure, nor cast pearls before such as cannot
estimate their worth.....I should say much more, if I were not
afraid of being heard by those who are uninitiated: because men
are apt to deride what they do not understand. And the ignorant,
not being aware of the weakness of their minds, condemn what
they ought most to venerate."

Theodoret, Bishop of Cyropolis in Syria, was born in 393, and
made Bishop in 420. In one of his three Dialogues, called the
Immutable, he introduces *Orthodoxus,* speaking thus: "Answer
me, if you please, in mystical or obscure terms: for perhaps there
are some persons present who are not initiated into the Mysteries." And in his preface to Ezekiel, tracing up the secret discipline to the commencement of the Christian era, he says: "These
Mysteries are so august, that we ought to keep them with the
greatest caution."

Minucius Felix, an eminent lawyer of Rome, who lived in 212,
and wrote a defence of Christianity, says: "Many of them [the
Christians] know each other by tokens and signs (*notis et insigni-
bus*), and they form a friendship for each other, almost before
they become acquainted."

The Latin Word, *tessera,* originally meant a square piece of
wood or stone, used in making tesselated pavements; afterward a
tablet on which anything was written, and then a cube or die.
Its most general use was to designate a piece of metal or wood,
square in shape, on which the watchword of an Army was inscribed; whence *tessera* came to mean the watchword itself. There
was also a *tessera hospitalis,* which was a piece of wood cut into
two parts, as a pledge of friendship. Each party kept one of the
parts; and they swore mutual fidelity by Jupiter. To break the
tessera was considered a dissolution of the friendship. The early
Christians used it as a Mark, the watchword of friendship. With
them it was generally in the shape of a fish, and made of bone. On
its face was inscribed the word Ἰχθῦς, a fish, the initials of which
represented the Greek words, Ἰησοῦς Χριστὸς Θεοῦ Υἱὸς Σωτήρ;
Jesus Christ, the Son of God, the Saviour.

St. Augustine (*de Fide et Symbolis*) says: "This is the faith
which in a few words is given to the *Novices* to be kept by a symbol; these few words are known to all the Faithful; that by believing they may be submissive to God; by being thus submissive, they

may live rightly; by living rightly, they may purify their hearts and with a pure heart may understand what they believe."

Maximus Taurinus says: "The tessera is a symbol and sign by which to distinguish between the Faithful and the Profane."

There are *three* Degrees in Blue Masonry; and in addition to the two words of two syllables each, embodying the binary, three, of three syllables each. There were three Grand Masters, the two Kings, and Khir-Om the Artificer. The candidate gains admission by three raps, and three raps call up the Brethren. There are three principal officers of the Lodge, three lights at the Altar, three gates of the Temple, all in the East, West, and South. The three lights represent the Sun, the Moon, and Mercury; Osiris, Isis, and Horus; the Father, the Mother, and the Child; Wisdom, Strength, and Beauty; Hakamah, Binah, and Daath; Gedulah, Geburah, and Tepareth. The candidate makes three circuits of the Lodge: there were three assassins of Khir-Om, and he was slain by three blows while seeking to escape by the three gates of the Temple. The ejaculation at his grave was repeated three times. There are three divisions of the Temple, and three, five, and seven Steps. A Master works with Chalk, Charcoal, and a vessel of Clay; there are three movable and three immovable jewels. The Triangle appears among the Symbols: the two parallel lines enclosing the circle are connected at top, as are the Columns Jachin and Boaz, symbolizing the equilibrium which explains the great Mysteries of Nature.

This continual reproduction of the number three is not accidental, nor without a profound meaning: and we shall find the same repeated in all the Ancient philosophies.

The Egyptian Gods formed Triads, the third member in each proceeding from the other two. Thus we have the Triad of Thebes, Amun, Maut, and Kharso; that of Philae, Osiris, Isis, and Horus; that of Elephantinē and the Cataracts, Neph, Satē, and Anoukē.

Osiris, Isis, and Horus were the Father, Mother, and Son; the latter being Light, the Soul of the World, the Son, the Protogonos or First-Begotten.

Sometimes this Triad was regarded as Spirit, or the *active* Principle or Generative Power; Matter, or the Passive Principle or Productive Capacity; and the Universe, which proceeds from the two Principles.

We also find in Egypt this Triad or Trinity; Ammon-Ra, the Creator: Osiris-Ra, the Giver of Fruitfulness: Horus-Ra, the

Queller of Light; symbolized by the Summer, Autumn, and Spring Sun. For the Egyptians had but three Seasons, the three gates of the Temple; and on account of the different effects of the Sun on those three Seasons, the Deity appears in these three forms.

The Phœnician Trinity was Ulomos, Chusoros, and the Egg out of which the Universe proceeded.

The Chaldean Triad consisted of Bel, [the Persian Zervana Akherana], Oromasdes, and Ahriman; the Good and Evil Principle alike outflowing from the Father, by their equilibrium and alternating preponderance to produce harmony. Each was to rule, in turn, for equal periods, until finally the Evil Principle should itself become good.

The Chaldean and Persian oracles of Zoroaster give us the Triad, Fire, Light, and Ether.

Orpheus celebrates the Triad of Phanes, Ouranos, and Kronos. Corry says the Orphic Trinity consisted of Metis, Phanes, and Ericapaeus; Will, Light or Love, and Life. Acusilaus makes it consist of Metis, Eros, and Æther: Will, Love, and Ether. Phereycides of Syros, of Fire, Water, and Air or Spirit. In the two former we readily recognize Osiris and Isis, the Sun and the Nile.

The first three of the Persian Amshaspands were BAHMAN, the Lord of LIGHT; Ardibehest, the Lord of FIRE; and Shariver, the Lord of SPLENDOR. These at once lead us back to the Kabala.

Plutarch says: "The better and diviner nature consists of three; the Intelligible (i. e. that which exists within the Intellect only as yet), and Matter; το Νοητος and Ὑλη, and that which proceeds from these, which the Greeks call Kosmos: of which Plato calls the Intelligible, the Idea, the Exemplar, the Father: Matter, the Mother, the Nurse, and the receptacle and place of generation: and the issue of these two, the Offspring and Genesis."

The Pythagorean fragments say: "Therefore, before the Heaven was made, there existed Idea and Matter, and God the Demiourgos [workman or active instrument], of the former. He made the world out of matter, perfect, only-begotten, with a soul and intellect, and constituted it a divinity."

Plato gives us Thought, the Father; Primitive Matter, the Mother; and Kosmos, the Son, the issue of the two Principles. Kosmos is the ensouled Universe.

With the later Platonists, the Triad was Potence, Intellect, and Spirit, Philo represents Sanchoniathon's as Fire, Light, and

Flame, the three Sons of Genos; but this is the Alexandrian, not the Phœnician idea.

Aurelius says the Demiourgos or Creator is triple, and the three Intellects are the three Kings: He who exists; He who possesses; He who beholds. The first is that which exists by its essence; the second exists in the first, and contains or possesses in itself the Universal of things; all that afterward becomes: the third beholds this Universal, formed and fashioned intellectually, and so having a separate existence. The Third exists in the Second, and the Second in the First.

The most ancient Trinitarian doctrine on record is that of the Brahmins. The Eternal Supreme Essence, called PARABRAHMA, BRAHM, PARATMA, produced the Universe by self-reflection, and first revealed himself as BRAHMA, the *Creating* Power, then as VISHNU, the *Preserving* Power, and lastly as SIVA, the *Destroying* and *Renovating* Power; the three Modes in which the Supreme Essence reveals himself in the material Universe; but which soon came to be regarded as three distinct Deities. These three Deities they styled the TRIMURTI, or TRIAD.

The Persians received from the Indians the doctrine of the three principles, and changed it to that of a principle of Life, which was individualized by the Sun, and a principle of Death, which was symbolized by cold and darkness; parallel of the moral world; and in which the continual and alternating struggle between light and darkness, life and death, seemed but a phase of the great struggle between the good and evil principles, embodied in the legend of ORMUZD and AHRIMAN. MITHRAS, a Median reformer, was deified after his death, and invested with the attributes of the Sun; the different astronomical phenomena being figuratively detailed as actual incidents of his life; in the same manner as the history of BUDDHA was invented among the Hindūs.

The Trinity of the Hindūs became among the Ethiopians and Abyssinians NEPH-AMON, PHTHA, and NEITH—the God CREATOR, whose emblem was a ram—MATTER, or the primitive mud, symbolized by a globe or an egg, and THOUGHT, or the LIGHT which contains the germ of everything; triple manifestation of one and the same God (ATHOM), considered in three aspects, as the *creative power, goodness,* and *wisdom.* Other Deities were speedily invented; and among them OSIRIS, represented by the Sun, ISIS, his wife, by the Moon or Earth, TYPHON, his Brother, the Principle of Evil and Darkness, who was the son of Osiris and Isis. And the Trinity of OSIRIS, ISIS, and HORUS became subsequently the Chief Gods and objects of worship of the Egyptians.

The ancient Etruscans (a race that emigrated from the Rhætian Alps into Italy, along whose route evidences of their migration have been discovered, and whose language none have yet succeeded in reading) acknowledged only one Supreme God; but they had images for His different attributes, and temples to these images. Each town had one National Temple, dedicated to the three great attributes of God, STRENGTH, RICHES, and WISDOM, or *Tina, Talna,* and *Minerva.* The National Deity was always a Triad under one roof; and it was the same in Egypt, where one Supreme God alone was acknowledged, but was worshipped as a Triad, with different names in each different home. Each city in Etruria might have as many gods and gates and temples as it pleased; but three sacred gates, and one Temple to three Divine Attributes were obligatory, wherever the laws of Tages (or Taunt or Thoth) were received. The only gate that remains in Italy, of the olden time, undestroyed, is the Porta del Circo at Volterra; and it has upon it the three heads of the three National Divinities, one upon the keystone of its magnificent arch, and one above each side-pillar.

The Buddhists hold that the God SAKYA of the Hindūs, called in Ceylon, GAUTAMA, in India beyond the Ganges, SOMONAKODOM, and in China, CHY-KIA, or FO, constituted a Trinity [TRIRATNA], of BUDDHA, DHARMA, and SANGA,—*Intelligence, Law,* and *Union* or *Harmony.*

The Chinese Sabæans represented the Supreme Deity as composed of CHANG-TI, the *Supreme Sovereign;* TIEN, the *Heavens;* and TAO, the *Universal Supreme Reason* and *Principle of Faith;* and that from Chaos, an immense silence, an immeasurable void. without perceptible forms, alone, infinite, immutable, moving in a circle in illimitable space, without change or alteration, when vivified by the Principle of Truth, issued all Beings, under the influence of TAO, Principle of Faith, who produced one, one produced two, two produced three, and three produced all that is.

The Sclavono-Vendes typified the Trinity by the three heads of the God TRIGLAV; and the Pruczi or Prussians by the Tri-une God, PERKOUN, PIKOLLOS, and POTRIMPOS, the Deities of *Light* and *Thunder,* of *Hell* and the *Earth,* its fruits and animals: and the Scandinavians by ODIN, FREA, and THOR.

In the KABALAH, or the Hebrew traditional philosophy, the Infinite Deity, beyond the reach of the Human Intellect, and without Name, Form, or Limitation, was represented as developing Himself, in order to create, and by self-limitation, in ten emanations or out-flowings, called SEPHIROTH, or *rays.* The first of these, in the world AZILUTH, that is, within the Deity, was KETHER, or the *Crown,* by which we understand the Divine Will or Potency. Next came, as a pair, HAKEMAH and BAINAH, ordinarily translated "Wisdom" and "Intelligence," the former termed the FATHER, and the latter the MOTHER. HAKEMAH is the active *Power* or *Energy* of Deity, by which He produces within Himself Intellection or Thinking: and BAINAH, the passive *Capacity,* from which, acted on by the Power, the Intellection flows. This Intellection is called DAATH: and it is the "WORD," of Plato and the Gnostics; the *unuttered* word, *within* the Deity. Here is the origin of the Trinity of the Father, the Mother or Holy Spirit, and the Son or Word.

Another Trinity was composed of the fourth Sephirah, GEDULAH or KHASED, *Benignity* or *Mercy,* also termed FATHER (*Aba*) ; the fifth, GEBURAH, *Severity* or Strict *Justice,* also termed the MOTHER (*Imma*) ; and the sixth, the SON or *Issue* of these, TIPHARETH, *Beauty* or *Harmony.* "Everything," says the SOHAR, "proceeds according to the Mystery of the Balance"—that is, by the equilibrium of Opposites: and thus from the Infinite Mercy and the Infinite Justice, in equilibrium, flows the perfect Harmony of the Universe. Infinite POWER, which is Lawless, and Infinite WISDOM, in Equilibrium, also produce BEAUTY or HARMONY, as Son, Issue, or Result—the Word, or utterance of the Thought of God. Power and Justice or Severity are the *same:* Wisdom and Mercy or Benignity are the same;—in the Infinite Divine Nature.

According to Philo of Alexandria, the Supreme Being, Primitive Light or Archetype of Light, uniting with WISDOM [Σοφια], the mother of Creation, forms in Himself the types of all things, and acts upon the Universe through the WORD [Λογος . . Logos], who dwells in God, and in whom all His powers and attributes develop themselves; a doctrine borrowed by him from Plato.

Simon Magus and his disciples taught that the Supreme Being or Centre of Light produced first of all, three couples of united

Existences, of both sexes, [Συζυγίας ... Suzugias], which were the origins of all things: REASON and INVENTIVENESS; SPEECH and THOUGHT; CALCULATION and REFLECTION: [Νοῦς and Επίνοια, Φωνή and Εννοια, Λογισμὸς and Ενθύμησις... Nöus and Epinoia, Phône and Ennoia, Logismos and Enthumēsis] ; of which Ennoia or WISDOM was the first produced, and Mother of all that exists.

Other Disciples of Simon, and with them most of the Gnostics, adopting and modifying the doctrine, taught that the Πλήρωμα .. Plerōma, or PLENITUDE of Superior Intelligences, having the Supreme Being at their head, was composed of eight Eons [Αἰώνης .. Aiōnes] of different sexes; .. PROFUNDITY and SILENCE; SPIRIT and TRUTH; the WORD and LIFE; MAN and the CHURCH: [Βυθὸς and Σιγὴ; Πνεῦμα and Αλήθεια; Λόγος and Ζωή; ῎Ανθρωπος and ᾽Εκκλησία .... Buthos and Sigē; Pneuma and Aletheia; Logos and Zōe; Anthrōpos and Ekklēsia].

Bardesanes, whose doctrines the Syrian Christians long embraced, taught that the unknown Father, happy in the Plenitude of His Life and Perfections, first produced a Companion for Himself [Σύζυγος ... Suzugos], whom He placed in the Celestial Paradise and who became, by Him, the Mother of CHRISTOS, Son of the Living God: i. e. (laying aside the allegory), that the Eternal conceived, in the silence of His decrees, the Thought of revealing Himself by a Being who should be His image or His Son: that to the Son succeeded his Sister and Spouse, the Holy Spirit, and they produced four Spirits of the elements, male and female, Maio and Jabseho, Nouro and Rucho; then Seven Mystic Couples of Spirits, and Heaven and Earth, and all that is; then seven spirits governing the planets, twelve governing the Constellations of the Zodiac, and thirty-six Starry Intelligences whom he called Deacons: while the Holy Spirit [*Sophia Achamoth*], being both the Holy Intelligence and the Soul of the physical world, went from the Plerōma into that material world and there mourned her degradation, until CHRISTOS, her former spouse, coming to her with his Divine Light and Love, guided her in the way to purification, and she again united herself with him as his primitive Companion.

Basilides, the Christian Gnostic, taught that there were seven emanations from the Supreme Being: The First-born, Thought, the Word, Reflection, Wisdom, Power, and Righteousness

Πρωτογονος,   Νους,   Λογος,   Φρονησις,   Σοφια,   Δυναμις, and Διχαιοσύνη Protogonos, Nous, Logos, Phronesis, Sophia, Dunamis, and Dikarosunē] ; from whom emanated other Intelligences in succession, to the number, in all, of three hundred and sixty-five; which were God manifested, and composed the Plenitude of the Divine Emanations, or the God Abraxas; of which the Thought [or Intellect, Novς . . Nous] united itself, by baptism in the river Jordan, with the man Jesus, servant [διάκονος . Diakonos] of the human race; but did not suffer with Him; and the disciples of Basilides taught that the Noῦς, put on the appearance only of humanity, and that Simon of Cyrene was crucified in His stead and ascended into Heaven.

Basilides held that out of the unrevealed God, who is at the head of the world of emanations, and exalted above all conception or designation [Ὁ ἀκατονόμαστος, ἄῤῥητος], were evolved seven living, self-subsistent, ever-active hyposatized powers:

First: The Intellectual Powers.

1st. Nous . . . . Noῦς . . . . . The Mind.
2d. Logos . . . . Λόγος . . . . The Reason.
3d. Phronesis .Φρόνησις . . . The Thinking Power.
4th. Sophia . .Σοφία. . . . . Wisdom.

Second: The Active or Operative Power.

5th. Dunamis .Δυναμις . . . . Might, accomplishing the purposes of Wisdom.

Third: The Moral Attributes.

6th. Dikaiosunē . Διχαιοσύνη Holiness or Moral Perfection.
7th. Eirēnē . . . Εἰρήνη. . . Inward Tranquility.

These Seven Powers (Δυνάμεις . . Dunameis), with the Primal Ground out of which they were evolved, constituted in his scheme the Πρωτη Ὀγδοὰς [Prote Ogdoas], or First Octave, the root of all Existence. From this point, the spiritual life proceeded to evolve out of itself continually many gradations of existence, each lower one being still the impression, the *antetype,* of the immediate higher one. He supposed there were 365 of these regions or gradations, expressed by the mystical word Αβραξας [Abraxas]. The αβραξας is thus interpreted, by the usual method of reckoning Greek letters numerically.... α,1 ..β,2..ρ,100..α,1 ..ξ

60..α,1 ..ς,200=365: which is the whole Emanation-World, as the development of the Supreme Being.

In the system of Basilides, Light, Life, Soul, and Good were opposed to Darkness, Death, Matter, and Evil, throughout the whole course of the Universe.

According to the Gnostic view, God was represented as the immanent, incomprehensible and original source of all perfection; the unfathomable Abyss ($\beta \upsilon \theta o s$ .. buthos), according to Valentinus, exalted above all possibility of designation; of whom, properly speaking, nothing can be predicated; the $\dot{\alpha} \varkappa \alpha \tau o \nu \acute{o} \mu \alpha \sigma \tau o \varsigma$ of Basilides, the $\ddot{\omega} \nu$ of Philo. From this incomprehensible Essence of God, an *immediate* transition to finite things is inconceivable. *Self-limitation* is the first beginning of a communication of life on the part of God—the first passing of the hidden Deity into manifestation; and from this proceeds all further self-developing manifestation of the Divine Essence. From this primal link in the chain of life there are evolved, in the first place, the manifold powers or attributes inherent in the divine Essence, which, until that first self-comprehension, were all hidden in the Abyss of His Essence. Each of these attributes presents the whole divine Essence under one particular aspect; and to each, therefore, in this respect, the title of God may appropriately be applied. These Divine Powers evolving themselves to self-subsistence, become thereupon the germs and principles of all further developments of life. The life contained in them unfolds and individualizes itself more and more, but in such a way that the successive grades of this evolution of life continually sink lower and lower; the spirits become feebler, the further they are removed from the first link in the series.

The first manifestation they termed $\pi \rho \acute{\omega} \tau \eta$ $\varkappa \alpha \tau \acute{\alpha} \lambda \eta \psi \iota \varsigma$ $\dot{\epsilon} \alpha \upsilon$-$\tau o \tilde{\upsilon}$ [*prote katalepsis heautou*] or $\pi \rho \tilde{\omega} \tau o \nu$ $\varkappa \alpha \tau \alpha \lambda \eta \pi \tau \grave{o} \nu$ $\tau o \tilde{\upsilon}$ $\theta \epsilon o \upsilon$ [*proton Kataleptou tou Theou*]; which was hypostatically represented in a $\nu o \tilde{\upsilon} \varsigma$ or $\lambda \acute{o} \gamma o \varsigma$, [*Nous* or *Logos*].

In the Alexandrian Gnosis, the Platonic notion of the $\ddot{\upsilon} \lambda \eta$ [Hule] predominates. This is the dead, the unsubstantial—the boundary that limits from without the evolution of life in its gradually advancing progression, whereby the Perfect is ever evolving itself into the less Perfect. This $\ddot{\upsilon} \lambda \eta$ again, is represented under various images;—at one time as the darkness that exists alongside of the light; at another, as the void [$\varkappa \acute{\epsilon} \nu \omega \mu \alpha$, $\varkappa \epsilon \nu \grave{o} \nu$

....Kenoma, Kenon], in opposition to the Fullness, [Πλήρωμα
....Plēroma] of the Divine Life; or as the shadow that accompanies the light; or as the chaos, or the sluggish, stagnant, dark
water. This matter, dead in itself, possesses by its own nature no
inherent tendency; as life of every sort is foreign to it, itself makes
no encroachment on the Divine. As, however, the evolutions of
the Divine Life (the essences developing themselves out of the
progressive emanation) become feebler, the further they are
removed from the first link in the series; and as their connection
with the first becomes looser at each successive step, there arises
at the last step of the evolution, an imperfect, defective product,
which, unable to retain its connection with the chain of Divine
Life, sinks from the World of Eons into the material chaos: or,
according to the same notion, somewhat differently expressed
[according to the Ophites and to Bardesanes], a drop from the
fullness of the Divine life bubbles over into the bordering void.
Hereupon the dead matter, by commixture with the living principle, which it wanted, first of all receives animation. But, at the
same time, also, the divine, the living, becomes corrupted by mingling with the chaotic mass. Existence now multiplies itself.
There arises a subordinate, defective life; there is ground for a
new world; a creation starts into being, beyond the confines of
the world of emanation. But, on the other hand, since the chaotic
principle of matter has acquired vitality, there now arises a more
distinct and more active opposition to the God-like—a barely negative, blind, ungodly nature-power, which obstinately resists all
influence of the Divine; hence, as products of the spirit of the
ὕλη, (of the πνεῦμα ὑλικον .. Pneuma Hulikon), are Satan, malignant spirits, wicked men, in none of whom is there any reasonable or moral principle, or any principle of a rational will; but blind
passions alone have the ascendency. In them there is the same conflict, as the scheme of Platonism supposes, between the soul under
the guidance of Divine reason [the νοῦς .. Nous], and the soul
blindly resisting reason—between the πρόνοια [pronoia] and the
αναγη [anagē], the Divine Principle and the natural.

The Syrian Gnosis assumed the existence of an active, turbulent
kingdom of evil, or of darkness, which, by its encroachments on
the kingdom of light, brought about a commixture of the light
with the darkness, of the God-like with the ungodlike.

Even among the Platonists, some thought that along with an

organized, inert matter, the substratum of the corporeal world, there existed from the beginning a blind, lawless motive power, an ungodlike soul, as its original motive and active principle. As the inorganic matter was organized into a corporeal world, by the plastic power of the Deity, so, by the same power, law and reason were communicated to that turbulent, irrational soul. Thus the chaos of the ὕλη was transformed into an organized world, and that blind soul into a rational principle, a mundane soul, animating the Universe. As from the latter proceeds all rational, spiritual life in humanity, so from the former proceeds all that is irrational, all that is under the blind sway of passion and appetite; and all malignant spirits are its progeny.

In one respect *all* the Gnostics agreed: they *all* held, that there was a world purely emanating out of the vital development of God, a creation evolved directly out of the Divine Essence, far exalted above any outward creation produced by God's plastic power, and conditioned by pre-existing matter. They agreed in holding that the framer of *this lower world* was not the Father of *that higher world* of emanation; but the Demiurge [Δεμιουρ- γος], a being of a kindred nature with the Universe framed and governed by him, and far inferior to that higher system and the Father of it.

But some, setting out from ideas which had long prevailed among certain Jews of Alexandria, supposed that the Supreme God created and governed the world by His ministering spirits, by the angels. At the head of these angels stood one who had the direction and control of all; therefore called the Artificer and Governor of the World. This Demiurge they compared with the plastic, animating, mundane spirit of Plato and Platonists [the δεύτερος θεὸς . . Deuteros Theos; the θεὸς γενητὸς . . . Theos Genetós], who, moreover, according to the Timæus of Plato, strives to represent the IDEA of the Divine Reason, in that which is *becoming* (as contradistinguished from that which *is*) and temporal. This angel is a representative of the Supreme God, on the lower stage of existence: he does not act independently, but merely according to the ideas inspired in him by the Supreme God; just as the plastic, mundane soul of the Platonists creates all things after the pattern of the ideas communicated by the Supreme Reason [Νοῦς. . . . Nous—the ὅ ἔστι ζῷον. . . . ho esti zōon—the παράδειγμα. paradeigma, of the Divine Reason hypostatized].

But these ideas transcend his limited essence; he cannot understand them; he is merely their unconscious organ; and therefore
is unable himself to comprehend the whole scope and meaning of
the work which he performs. As an organ under the guidance of
a higher inspiration, he reveals higher truths than he himself can
comprehend. The mass of the Jews, they held, recognized not the
angel, by whom, in all the Theophanies of the Old Testament,
God *revealed* Himself; they knew not the Demiurge in his true
relation to the hidden Supreme God, *who never reveals Himself* in
the sensible world. They confounded the type and the archetype,
the symbol and the idea. They rose no higher than the Demiurge;
they took him to be the Supreme God Himself. But the spiritual
men among them, on the contrary, clearly perceived, or at least
divined, the ideas veiled under Judaism; they rose beyond the
Demiurge, to a knowledge of the Supreme God; and are therefore
properly His worshippers [θεραπευταί . . Therapeutai].

Other Gnostics, who had not been followers of the Mosaic religion, but who had, at an earlier period, framed to themselves an
oriental Gnosis, regarded the Demiurge as a being absolutely
hostile to the Supreme God. He and his angels, notwithstanding
their finite nature, wish to establish their independence: they will
tolerate no foreign rule within their realm. Whatever of a higher
nature descends into their kingdom, they seek to hold imprisoned
there, lest it should raise itself above their narrow precincts.
Probably, in this system, the kingdom of the Demiurgic Angels
corresponded, for the most part, with that of the deceitful Star-
Spirits, who seek to rob man of his freedom, to beguile him by
various arts of deception, and who exercise a tyrannical sway
over the things of this world. Accordingly, in the system of these
Sabæans, the seven Planet-Spirits, and the twelve Star-Spirits
of the zodiac, who sprang from an irregular connection between
the cheated Fetahil and the Spirit of Darkness, play an important part in everything that is bad. The Demiurge is a limited
'and limiting being, proud, jealous, and revengeful; and this his
character betrays itself in the Old Testament, which, the Gnostics
held, came from him. They transferred to the Demiurge himself, whatever in the idea of God, as presented by the Old Testament, appeared to them defective. Against his will and rule the
ὕλη was continually rebelling, revolting without control against
the dominion which he, the fashioner, would exercise over it,

casting off the yoke imposed on it, and destroying the work he had begun. The same jealous being, limited in his power, ruling with despotic sway, they imagined they saw in nature. He strives to check the germination of the divine seeds of life which the Supreme God of Holiness and Love, who has no connection whatever with the sensible world, has scattered among men. That perfect God was at most known and worshipped in Mysteries by a few spiritual men.

The Gospel of St. John is in great measure a polemic against the Gnostics, whose different sects, to solve the great problems, the creation of a material world by an immaterial Being, the fall of man, the incarnation, the redemption and restoration of the spirits called men, admitted a long series of intelligences, intervening in a series of spiritual operations; and which they designated by the names, *The Beginning, the Word, the Only-Begotten, Life, Light,* and *Spirit* [Ghost]: in Greek, Ἀρχή, Λόγος, Μονογενής, Ζωή, Φῶς and Πνεῦμα [Archē, Logos, Monogenēs, Zōe, Phōs, and Pneuma]. St. John, at the beginning of his Gospel, avers that it was Jesus Christ who existed in the Beginning; that He was the WORD of God by which everything was made; that He was the Only-Begotten, the Life and the Light, and that He diffuses among men the Holy Spirit [or Ghost], the Divine Life and Light.

So the Plēroma [Πλήρωμα], Plenitude or Fullness, was a favorite term with the Gnostics, and Truth and Grace were the Gnostic Eons; and the Simonians, Dokētēs, and other Gnostics held that the Eon Christ Jesus was never really, but only apparently clothed with a human body: but St. John replies that the Word did really become Flesh, and dwelt among us; and that in Him were the Plēroma and Truth and Grace.

In the doctrine of Valentinus, reared a Christian at Alexandria, God was a perfect Being, an Abyss [Βυθὸς .. Buthos], which no intelligence could sound, because no eye could reach the invisible and ineffable heights on which He dwelt, and no mind could comprehend the duration of His existence; He has always been; He is the Primitive Father and Beginning [the Προπάτωρ and Προαρχή.. Propatōr and Proarchē]: He will BE always, and does not grow old. The development of His Perfections produced the intellectual world. After having passed infinite ages in repose and silence, He manifested Himself by His Thought, source of all His manifestations, and which received from Him the germ of His creations. Being of His Being, His Thought ["Εννοια..Ennoia] is also termed Χάρις [Charis], Grace or Joy, and Σιγή, or "Αρρη-τον [Sigē or Arrēton], Silence or the Ineffable. Its first manifestation was Νους [Nous], the Intelligence, first of the Eons, commencement of all things, first revelation of the Divinity, the Μονογενὴς [Monogenēs], or Only-Begotten: next, Truth ['Αλή-θεια.. Alētheia], his companion. Their manifestations were the Word [Λόγος.. Logos] and Life [Ζωὴ..Zoē]; and theirs, Man and the Church [Ανθροπος and 'Εκκλησία.. Anthrōpos and Ekklēsia]: and from these, other twelve, six of whom were Hope, Faith, Charity, Intelligence, Happiness, and Wisdom; or, in the Hebrew, *Kesten, Kina, Amphe, Ouananim, Thaedes,* and *Oubina.* The harmony of the Eons, struggling to know and be united to the Primitive God, was disturbed, and to redeem and restore them, the Intelligence [Νοῦς] produced Christ and the Holy Spirit His companion; who restored them to their first estate of happiness and harmony; and thereupon they formed the Eon Jesus, born of a Virgin, to whom the Christos united himself in baptism, and who, with his Companion Sophia-Achamoth, saved and redeemed the world.

The Marcosians taught that the Supreme Deity produced by His words the Λόγος [Logos] or Plenitude of Eons: His first utterance was a syllable of four letters, each of which became a being; His second of four, His third of ten, and His fourth of twelve: thirty in all, which constituted the Πλήρωμα [Plēroma].

The Valentinians, and others of the Gnostics, distinguished three orders of existences:—1st. The divine germs of life, exalted by their nature above matter, and akin to the Σοφία [Sophia], to the mundane soul and to the Plēroma:—the spiritual natures, φύσεις πνευματικαί [Phuseis Pneumatikai]: 2d. The natures originating in the life, divided from the former by the mixture of the ὕλη,—the psychical natures, φύσεις ψυχικαὶ [Phuseis Psuchi-kai]; with which begins a perfectly new order of existence, an image of that higher mind and system, in a subordinate grade; and finally, 3d. The Ungodlike or Hylic Nature, which resists all amelioration, and whose tendency is only to destroy—the nature of blind lust and passion.

The nature of the πνευματικὸν [pneumatikon], the spiritual, is essential relationship with God (the ὁμοούσιον τῷ θεῷ.. Homo-ousion tō Theō): hence the life of Unity, the undivided, the absolutely simple (οὐσία ἑνική. μονοειδής . . Ousia henike, monoeides).

The essence of the ψυχικοί [psuchikoi] is disruption into multiplicity, manifoldness; which, however, is subordinate to a higher unity, by which it allows itself to be guided, first unconsciously, then consciously.

The essence of the ὑλικοί [Hulikoi] (of whom Satan is the head), is the direct opposite to all unity; disruption and disunion in itself, without the least sympathy, without any point of coalescence whatever for unity; together with an effort to destroy all unity, to extend its own inherent disunion to everything, and to rend everything asunder. This principle has no power to posit anything; but only to negative: it is unable to create, to produce, to form, but only to destroy, to decompose.

By Marcus, the disciple of Valentinus, the idea of a Λογος του οντος [Logos Tou Ontos], of a WORD, manifesting the hidden Divine Essence, in the Creation, was spun out into the most subtle details—the entire creation being, in his view, a continuous *utterance* of the Ineffable. The way in which the germs of divine life [the σπέρματα πνευματικὰ . . spermata pneumatika], which lie shut up in the Eons, continually unfold and individualize themselves more and more, is represented as a spontaneous analysis of the several *names* of the Ineffable, into their several *sounds*. An *echo* of the Plēroma falls down into the ὕλη [Hulē], and becomes the forming of a new but lower creation.

One formula of the pneumatical baptism among the Gnostics ran thus: "In the NAME which is hidden from all the Divinities and Powers" [of the Demiurge], "The Name of Truth" [the Ἀλήθεια [Aletheia], self-manifestation of the Buthos], which Jesus of Nazareth has put on in the light-zones of Christ, the living Christ, through the Holy Ghost, for the redemption of the angels,—the Name by which all things attain to Perfection." The candidate then said: "I am established and redeemed; I am redeemed in my soul from this world, and from all that belongs to it, by the name of יהוה, who has redeemed the Soul of Jesus by the living Christ." The assembly then said: "Peace (or Salvation) to all on whom this name rests!"

The boy Dionusos, torn in pieces, according to the Bacchic Mysteries, by the Titans, was considered by the Manicheans as simply representing the Soul, swallowed up by the powers of darkness,—the divine life rent into fragments by matter:—that part of the luminous essence of the primitive man [the πρῶτος ἄνθρωπος [Protos Anthropos] of Mani, the πράων ἄνθρωπος [Praōn Anthrōpos] of the Valentinians, the Adam Kadmon of the Kabalah; and the Kaiomorts of the Zendavesta], swallowed up by the powers of darkness; the Mundane Soul, mixed with matter—the seed of divine life, which had fallen into matter, and had thence to undergo a process of purification and development.

The Γνῶσις [Gnosis] of Carpocrates and his son Epiphanes consisted in the knowledge of one Supreme Original being, the highest unity, from whom all existence has emanated, and to whom it strives to return. The finite spirits that rule over the several portions of the Earth, seek to counteract this universal tendency to unity; and from their influence, their laws, and arrangements, proceeds all that checks, disturbs, or limits the original communion, which is the basis of nature, as the outward manifestation of that highest Unity. These spirits, moreover, seek to retain under their dominion the souls which, emanating from the highest Unity, and still partaking of its nature, have lapsed into the corporeal world, and have there been imprisoned in bodies, in order, under their dominion, to be kept within the cycle of migration. From these finite spirits, the popular religions of different nations derive their origin. But the souls which, from a reminiscence of their former condition, soar upward to the contemplation of that higher Unity, reach to such perfect freedom and repose, as nothing afterward can disturb or limit, and rise superior to the popular deities and religions. As examples of this sort, they named Pythagoras, Plato, Aristotle, and Christ. They made no distinction between the latter and the wise and good men of every nation. They taught that any other soul which could soar to the same height of contemplation, might be regarded as equal with Him.

The Ophites commenced their system with a Supreme Being, long unknown to the Human race, and still so the greater number of men; the Βυθὸς [Buthos], or Profundity, Source of Light, and of Adam-Kadmon, the Primitive Man, made by the Demiourgos, but perfected by the Supreme God by the communication to him of the Spirit [Πνεῦμα . . Pneuma]. The first emanation was the Thought of the Supreme Deity [the Ἔννοια . . Ennoia], the conception of the Universe in the Thought of God.

This Thought, called also Silence (Σιγη . . Sigē), produced the Spirit [Πνευμα . . Pneuma], Mother of the Living, and Wisdom of God. Together with this Primitive Existence, Matter existed also (the Waters, Darkness, Abyss, and Chaos), eternal like the Spiritual Principle. Buthos and His Thought, uniting with Wisdom, made her fruitful by the Divine Light, and she produced a perfect and an imperfect being, *Christos,* and a Second and inferior wisdom, *Sophia-Achamoth,* who falling into chaos remained entangled there, became enfeebled, and lost all knowledge of the Superior Wisdom that gave her birth. Communicating movement to Chaos, she produced Ialdabaoth, the Demiourgos, Agent of Material Creation, and then ascended toward her first place in the scale of creation. Ialdabaoth produced an angel that was his image, and this a second, and so on in succession to the sixth after the Demiourgos: the seven being *reflections* one of the other, yet different and inhabiting seven distinct regions. The names of the six thus produced were IAO, SABAOTH, ADONAI, ELOI, ORAI, and ASTAPHAI. Ialdabaoth, to become independent of his mother, and to pass for the Supreme Being, made the world, and man, in his own image; and his mother caused the Spiritual principle to pass from him into man so made; and henceforward the contest between the Demiourgos and his mother, between light and darkness, good and evil, was concentrated in man; and the image of Ialdabaoth, reflected upon matter, became the Serpent-Spirit, Satan, the Evil Intelligence. Eve, created by Ialdabaoth, had by his Sons children that were angels like themselves. The Spiritual light was withdrawn from man by Sophia, and the world surrendered to the influence of evil; until the Spirit, urged by the entreaties of Wisdom, induced the Supreme Being to send Christos to redeem it. Compelled, despite himself, by his Mother, Ialdabaoth caused the man Jesus to be born of a Virgin, and the Celestial Saviour, uniting with his Sister, Wisdom, descended through the regions of the seven angels, appeared in each under the form of its chief, concealed his own, and entered with his sister into the man Jesus at the baptism in Jordan. Ialdabaoth, finding that Jesus was destroying his empire and abolishing his worship, caused the Jews to hate and crucify Him; before which happened, Christos and Wisdom had ascended to the celestial regions. They restored Jesus to life and gave Him an ethereal body, in which He remained eighteen months on earth, and receiving from Wisdom the perfect knowledge [Γνωσις . . Gnosis], communicated it to a small number of His apostles, and then arose to the intermediate region inhabited by Ialdabaoth, where, unknown to him, He sits at his right hand, taking from him the Souls of Light purified by Christos. When nothing of the Spiritual world shall remain subject to Ialdabaoth, the redemption will be accomplished, and the end of the world, the completion of the return of Light into the Plenitude, will occur.

Tatian adopted the theory of Emanation, of Eons, of the existence of a God too sublime to allow Himself to be known, but displaying Himself by Intelligences emanating from His bosom. The first of these was His spirit [Πνευμα . . Pneuma], God Himself, God thinking, God conceiving the Universe. The second was the Word [Λογος . . Logos], no longer merely the Thought or Conception, but the Creative Utterance, manifestation of the Divinity, but emanating from the Thought or Spirit; the First-Begotten, author of the visible creation. This was the Trinity, composed of the Father, Spirit, and Word.

The Elxaïtes adopted the Seven Spirits of the Gnostics; but named them Heaven, Water, Spirit, The Holy Angels of Prayer, Oil, Salt, and the Earth.

The opinion of the Doketes as to the human nature of Jesus Christ, was that most generally received among the Gnostics. They deemed the intelligences of the Superior World too pure and too much the antagonists of matter, to be willing to unite with it: and held that Christ, an Intelligence of the first rank, in appearing upon the earth, did not become confounded with matter, but took upon Himself only the *appearance* of a body, or at the most used it only as an envelope.

Noëtus termed the Son the first Utterance of the Father; the Word, not by Himself, as an Intelligence, and unconnected with the flesh, a real Son; but a Word, and a perfect Only-Begotten; light emanated from the Light; water flowing from its spring; a ray emanated from the Sun.

Paul of Samosata taught that Jesus Christ was the Son of Joseph and Mary; but that the Word, Wisdom, or Intelligence of God, the Νους [Nous] of the Gnostics, had united itself with Him, so that He might be said to be at once the Son of God, and God Himself.

Arius called the Saviour the first of creatures, non-emanated from God, but really created, by the direct will of God, before time

and the ages. According to the Church, Christ was of the same
nature as God; according to some dissenters, of the same nature
as man. Arius adopted the theory of a nature analogous to both.
When God resolved to create the Human race, He made a Being
which He called THE WORD, THE SON, WISDOM [Λόγος, Υἱὸς,
Σοφία .. Logos, Uios, Sophia], to the end that He might give
existence to men. This WORD is the Ormuzd of Zoroaster, the
Ensoph of the Kabalah, the Νοῦς [Nous] of Platonism and Philonism, and the Σοφια or Δεμιουργος [Sophia or Demiourgos]
of the Gnostics. He distinguished the Inferior Wisdom, or the
daughter, from the Superior Wisdom; the latter being *in* God,
inherent in His nature, and incapable of communication to any
creature: the second, by which the Son was made, communicated
itself to Him, and therefore He Himself was entitled to be called
the Word and the Son.

Manes, founder of the Sect of the Manicheans, who had lived
and been distinguished among the Persian Magi, profited by the
doctrines of Scythianus, a Kabalist or Judaizing Gnostic of the
times of the Apostles; and knowing those of Bardesanes and Har-
monius, derived his doctrines from Zoroasterism, Christianity, and
Gnosticism. He claimed to be the Παράκλητος [Parakletos] or
Comforter, in the Sense of a Teacher, organ of the Deity, but not
in that of the Holy Spirit or Holy Ghost: and commenced his
Epistola Fundamenti in these words: "Manes, Apostle of Jesus
Christ, elect of God the Father; Behold the Words of Salvation,
emanating from the living and eternal fountain." The dominant
idea of his doctrine was Pantheism, derived by him from its source
in the regions of India and on the confines of China: that the
cause of all that exists is in God; and at last, God is all in all.
All souls are equal—God is in all, in men, animals, and plants.
There are two Gods, one of Good and the other of Evil, each independent, eternal, chief of a distinct Empire; necessarily, and of
their very natures, hostile to one another. The Evil God, Satan, is
the Genius of matter alone. The God of Good is infinitely his
Superior, the True God; while the other is but the chief of all
that is the Enemy of God, and must in the end succumb to His
Power. The Empire of Light alone is eternal and true; and this
Empire is a great chain of Emanations, all connected with the
Supreme Being which they make manifest; all HIM, under different forms, chosen for one end, the triumph of the Good. In each

of His members lie hidden thousands of ineffable treasures. Excellent in His Glory, incomprehensible in His Greatness, the Father has joined to Himself those fortunate and glorious Eons [Αιωνες . . Aionēs], whose Power and Number it is impossible to determine. This is Spinoza's Infinity of Infinite Attributes of God. Twelve Chief Eons, at the head of all, were the Genii of the twelve Constellations of the Zodiac, and called by Manes, Olamin. Satan, also, Lord of the Empire of Darkness, had an Army of Eons or Demons, emanating from his Essence, and reflecting more or less his image, but divided and inharmonious among themselves. A war among them brought them to the confines of the Realm of Light. Delighted, they sought to conquer it. But the Chief of the Celestial Empire created a Power which he placed on the frontiers of Heaven to protect his Eons, and destroy the Empire of Evil. This was the Mother of Life, the Soul of the World, an Emanation from the Supreme Being, too pure to come in immediate contact with matter. It remained in the highest region; but produced a Son, the first Man [the *Kaiomorts*, Adam-Kadmon, Πρῶτος Ανθρωπος [Protos Anthropos,] and Hivil-Zivah; of the Zend-Avesta, the Kabalah, the Gnosis, and Sabeism] ; who commenced the contest with the Powers of Evil, but, losing part of his panoply, of his Light, his Son and many souls born of the Light, who were devoured by the darkness, God sent to his assistance the living Spirit, or the Son of the First Man [Υἱὸς 'Ανθρώπου . . . Uios Anthropou], or Jesus Christ. The Mother of Life, general Principle of Divine Life, and the first Man, Primitive Being that reveals the Divine Life, are too sublime to be connected with the Empire of Darkness. The Son of Man or Soul of the World, enters into the Darkness, becomes its captive, to end by tempering and softening its savage nature. The Divine Spirit, after having brought back the Primitive Man to the Empire of Light, raises above the world that part of the Celestial Soul that remained unaffected by being mingled with the Empire of Darkness. Placed in the region of the Sun and Moon, this pure soul, the Son of Man, the Redeemer or Christ, labors to deliver and attract to Himself that part of the Light or of the Soul of the First Man diffused through matter; which done, the world will cease to exist. To retain the rays of Light still remaining among his Eons, and ever tending to escape and return, by concentrating them, the Prince of Darkness, with their consent, made

Adam, whose soul was of the Divine Light, contributed by the Eons, and his body of matter, so that he belonged to both Empires, that of Light and that of Darkness. To prevent the light from escaping at once, the Demons forbade Adam to eat the fruit of "knowledge of good and evil," by which he would have known the Empire of Light and that of Darkness. He obeyed; an Angel of Light induced him to transgress, and gave him the means of victory; but the Demons created Eve, who seduced him into an act of Sensualism, that enfeebled him, and bound him anew in the bonds of matter. This is repeated in the case of every man that lives.

To deliver the soul, captive in darkness, the Principle of Light, or Genius of the Sun, charged to redeem the Intellectual World, of which he is the type, came to manifest Himself among men. Light appeared in the darkness, but the darkness comprehended it not; according to the words of St. John. The Light could not unite with the darkness. It but put on the *appearance* of a human body, and took the name of Christ in the Messiah, only to accommodate itself to the language of the Jews. The Light did its work, turning the Jews from the adoration of the Evil Principle, and the Pagans from the worship of Demons. But the Chief of the Empire of Darkness caused Him to be crucified by the Jews. Still He suffered in appearance only, and His death gave to all souls the symbol of their enfranchisement. The person of Jesus having disappeared, there was seen in His place a cross of Light, over which a celestial voice pronounced these words: "The cross of Light is called The Word, Christ, The Gate, Joy, The Bread, The Sun, The Resurrection, Jesus, The Father, The Spirit, Life, Truth, and Grace."

With the Priscillianists there were two principles, one the Divinity, the other, Primitive Matter and Darkness; each eternal. Satan is the son and lord of matter; and the secondary angels and demons, children of matter. Satan created and governs the visible world. But the soul of man emanated from God, and is of the same substance with God. Seduced by the evil spirits, it passes through various bodies, until, purified and reformed, it rises to God and is strengthened by His light. These powers of evil hold mankind in pledge; and to redeem this pledge, the Saviour, Christ the Redeemer, came and died upon the cross of expiation, thus discharging the written obligation. He, like all souls, was of the same substance with God, a manifestation of the Divinity, not forming a second person; unborn, like the Divinity, and nothing else than the Divinity under another form.

It is useless to trace these vagaries further; and we stop at the frontiers of the realm of the three hundred and sixty-five thousand emanations of the Mandaïtes from the Primitive Light, Fira or Ferho and Yavar; and return contentedly to the simple and sublime creed of Masonry.

Such were some of the ancient notions concerning the Deity; and taken in connection with what has been detailed in the preceding Degrees, this Lecture affords you a true picture of the ancient speculations. From the beginning until now, those who have undertaken to solve the great mystery of the creation of a material universe by an Immaterial Deity, have interposed between the two, and between God and man, divers manifestations of, or emanations from, or personified attributes or agents of, the Great Supreme God, who is coexistent with Time and coextensive with Space.

The universal belief of the Orient was, that the Supreme Being did not Himself create either the earth or man. The fragment which commences the Book of Genesis, consisting of the first chapter and the three first verses of the second, assigns the creation or rather the *formation* or *modelling* of the world from matter already existing in confusion, not to IHUH, but to the ALHIM, well known as Subordinate Deities, Forces, or Manifestations, among the Phœnicians. The second fragment imputes it to IHUH-ALHIM,* and St. John assigns the creation to the Λογος or WORD; and asserts that CHRIST was that WORD, as well as LIGHT and LIFE, other emanations from the Great Primeval Deity, to which other faiths had assigned the work of creation.

An absolute existence, wholly immaterial, in no way within the reach of our senses; a cause, but not an effect, that never was not, but existed during an infinity of eternities, before there was anything else except Time and Space, is wholly beyond the reach of our conceptions. The mind of man has wearied itself in speculations as to His nature, His essence, His attributes; and ended in being no wiser than it began. In the impossibility of conceiving of immateriality, we feel at sea and lost whenever we go beyond the domain of matter. And yet we know that there *are* Powers,

---

The Substance, or *Very Self,* of which the Alohayim are the manifestations.

Forces, Causes, that are themselves *not* matter. We give them names, but *what* they really are, and what their essence, we are wholly ignorant.

But, fortunately, it does not follow that we may not *believe,* or even *know,* that which we cannot *explain* to ourselves, or that which is beyond the reach of our comprehension. If we believed only that which our intellect can grasp, measure, comprehend, and have distinct and clear ideas of, we should believe scarce anything. The senses are not the witnesses that bear testimony to us of the loftiest truths.

Our greatest difficulty is, that language is not adequate to express our ideas; because our words refer to *things,* and are images of what is substantial and material. If we use the word *"emanation,"* our mind involuntarily recurs to something material, *flowing out* of some other thing that is material; and if we *reject* this idea of materiality, nothing is left of the emanation but an unreality. The word "thing" itself suggests to us that which is material and within the cognizance and jurisdiction of the senses. If we cut away from it the idea of materiality, it presents itself to us as *no* thing, but an intangible unreality, which the mind vainly endeavors to grasp. *Existence* and *Being* are terms that have the same color of materiality; and when we speak of a *Power* or *Force,* the mind immediately images to itself one physical and material thing acting upon another. Eliminate that idea; and the Power or Force, devoid of physical characteristics, seems as unreal as the shadow that dances on a wall, itself a mere *absence* of light; as spirit is to us merely that which is *not matter.*

Infinite space and infinite time are the two primary ideas. We formulize them thus: add body to body and sphere to sphere, until the imagination wearies; and still there will remain beyond, a void, empty, unoccupied SPACE, limitless, because it *is* void. Add event to event in continuous succession, forever and forever, and there will still remain, before and after, a TIME in which there was and will be no event, and also endless because it too *is* void.

Thus these two ideas of the boundlessness of space and the endlessness of time seem to *involve* the ideas that matter and events are limited and finite. We cannot conceive of an *infinity* of worlds or of events; but only of an *indefinite* number of each; for, as we struggle to conceive of their *infinity,* the thought ever occurs in despite of all our efforts—there must be *space* in which there are *no* worlds; there must have been *time* when there were no events.

We cannot conceive how, if this earth moves millions of millions of miles a million times repeated, it is still *in the centre of space;* nor how, if we lived millions of millions of ages and centuries, we should still be in the centre of eternity—with still as much *space* on one side as on the other; with still as much *time* before us as behind; for that seems to say that the world has not moved nor we lived at all.

Nor can we comprehend how an infinite series of worlds, added together, is no larger than an infinite series of atoms; or an infinite series of centuries no longer than an infinite series of seconds; both being alike infinite, and therefore one series containing no more nor fewer units than the other.

Nor have we the capacity to form in ourselves any idea of that which is *immaterial.* We use the word, but it conveys to us only the idea of the absence and negation of materiality; which vanishing, Space and Time alone, infinite and boundless, seem to us to be left.

We cannot form any conception of an effect without a cause. We cannot but believe, indeed we know, that, how far soever we may have to run back along the chain of effects and causes, it cannot be *infinite;* but we must come at last to *something* which is not an effect, but the first cause: and yet the fact is literally beyond our comprehension. The mind refuses to grasp the idea of *self*-existence, of existence without a beginning. As well expect the hair that grows upon our head to understand the nature and immortality of the soul.

It does not need to go so far in search of mysteries; nor have we any right to disbelieve or doubt the existence of a Great First Cause, itself no effect, because we cannot comprehend it; because the words we use do not even express it to us adequately.

We rub a needle for a little while, on a dark, inert mass of iron ore, that had lain idle in the earth for many centuries. Something is thereby communicated to the steel—we term it a *virtue,* a *power,* or a *quality*—and then we balance it upon a pivot; and, lo! drawn by some invisible, mysterious Power, one pole of the needle turns to the North, and there the same Power keeps the same pole for days and years; will keep it there, perhaps, as long as the world lasts, carry the needle where you will, and no matter what seas or mountains intervene between it and the North Pole of the world. And this Power, thus acting, and indicating to the mariner his course over the trackless ocean, when the stars shine not for many days, saves vessels from shipwreck, families from distress, and those from sudden death on whose lives the fate of nations and the peace of the world depend. But for it, Napoleon might never have reached the ports of France on his return from Egypt, nor Nelson lived to fight and win at Trafalgar. Men call this Power *Magnetism,* and then complacently think that they have explained it all; and yet they have but given a new *name* to an unknown thing, to *hide* their ignorance. What is this wonderful Power? It is a real, actual, *active* Power: that we know and see. But what its *essence* is, or how it acts, we do not know, any more than we know the essence or the mode of action of the Creative Thought and Word of God.

And again, what *is* that which we term *galvanism* and *electricity,*—which, evolved by the action of a little acid on two metals, aided by a magnet, circles the earth in a second, sending from land to land the *Thoughts* that govern the transactions of individuals and nations? The mind has formed no notion of matter, that will include *it;* and no name that we can give it, helps us to understand its essence and its being. It *is* a Power, like Thought and the Will. We know no more.

What is this power of *gravitation* that makes everything upon the earth tend to the centre? How does it reach out its invisible hands toward the erratic meteor-stones, arrest them in their swift course, and draw them down to the earth's bosom? It *is* a *power*. We know no more.

What is that *heat* which plays so wonderful a part in the world's economy?—that *caloric,* latent everywhere, within us and without us, produced by combustion, by intense pressure, and by swift motion? Is it substance, matter, spirit, or immaterial, a mere Force or State of Matter?

And what is *light?* A *substance,* say the books,—*matter,* that travels to us from the sun and stars, each ray separable into seven, by the prism, of distinct colors, and with distinct peculiar qualities and actions. And *if* a substance, what is its essence, and what power is inherent in it, by which it journeys incalculable myriads of miles, and reaches us ten thousand years or more after it leaves the stars?

All power is equally a mystery. Apply intense cold to a drop of water in the centre of a globe of iron, and the globe is shattered as the water freezes. Confine a little of the same limpid element in a cylinder which Enceladus or Typhon could not have riven asunder, and apply to it intense heat, and the vast power that couched latent in the water shivers the cylinder to atoms. A little shoot from a minute seed, a shoot so soft and tender that the least bruise would kill it, forces its way downward into the hard earth, to the depth of many feet, with an energy wholly incomprehensible. What are these mighty forces, locked up in the small seed and the drop of water?

Nay, what is LIFE itself, with all its wondrous, mighty energies,—that power which maintains the heat within us, and prevents our bodies, that decay so soon without it, from resolution into their original elements—Life, that constant miracle, the nature and essence whereof have eluded all the philosophers; and all their learned dissertations on it are a mere jargon of words?

No wonder the ancient Persians thought that Light and Life were one,—both emanations from the Supreme Deity, the archetype of light. No wonder that in their ignorance they worshipped the Sun. God breathed into man the spirit of life,—not matter, but an emanation from Himself; not a creature *made* by Him, nor a distinct existence, but a *Power,* like His own Thought: and light, to those great-souled ancients, also seemed no creature, and no gross material substance, but a pure emanation from the Deity, immortal and indestructible like Himself.

What, indeed, is REALITY? Our dreams are as real, while they last, as the occurrences of the daytime. We see, hear, feel, act, experience pleasure and suffer pain, as vividly and actually in a dream as when awake. The occurrences and transactions of a year are crowded into the limits of a second: and the dream remembered is as real as the past occurrences of life.

The philosophers tell us that we have no cognizance of *substance* itself, but only of its *attributes:* that when we see that which we call a block of marble, our perceptions give us information only of something extended, solid, colored, heavy, and the like; but not of the very *thing* itself, to which these attributes belong. And yet the attributes do not exist without the substance. They are not substances, but adjectives. There is no such *thing* or *existence* as hardness, weight or color, by itself, detached from any subject, moving first here, then there, and attaching itself to this and to the other subject. And yet, they say, the attributes are not the subject.

So Thought, Volition, and Perception are not the soul, but its *attributes;* and we have no cognizance of the soul *itself,* but only of *them,* its manifestations. Nor of God; but only of His Wisdom, Power, Magnificence, Truth, and other attributes.

And yet we know that there *is* matter, a soul within our body, a God that lives in the Universe.

Take, then, the attributes of the soul. I am conscious that I exist and am the same identical person that I was twenty years ago. I am conscious that my body is not I,—that if my arms were lopped away, this *person* that I call ME, would still remain, complete, entire, identical as before. But I cannot ascertain, by the most intense and long-continued reflection, what I am, nor where within my body I reside, nor whether I am a point, or an expanded substance. I have no power to examine and inspect. I exist, will, think, perceive. *That* I know, and nothing more. I think a noble and sublime Thought. What is that Thought? It is not Matter, nor Spirit. It is not a Thing; but a *Power* and *Force.* I make upon a paper certain conventional marks, that *represent* that Thought. There is no Power or Virtue in the *marks* I write, but only in the Thought which they tell to others. I die, but the Thought still lives. It is a Power. It acts on men, excites them to enthusiasm, inspires patriotism, governs their conduct, controls their destinies, disposes of life and death. The words I speak are but a certain succession of particular sounds, that by conventional arrangement communicate to others the Immaterial, Intangible, Eternal Thought. The fact that Thought continues to exist an instant, after it makes its appearance in the soul, proves it immortal: for there is nothing conceivable that can destroy it. The spoken words, being mere sounds, may vanish into thin air, and the written ones, mere marks, be burned, erased, destroyed: but the THOUGHT itself lives still, and must live on forever.

A Human Thought, then, is an actual EXISTENCE, and a FORCE and POWER, capable of acting upon and controlling matter as well as mind. Is not the existence of a God, who is the immaterial soul of the Universe, and whose THOUGHT, embodied or not embodied in His WORD, is an Infinite Power, of Creation and production, destruction and preservation, quite as comprehensible as the existence of a Soul, of a Thought separated from the Soul, of the Power of that Thought to mould the fate and influence the Destinies of Humanity?

And yet we know not when that Thought comes, nor what it is. It is not WE. We do not mould it, shape it, fashion it. It is neither our mechanism nor our invention. It appears spontaneously, flashing, as it were, into the soul, making that soul the involuntary instrument of its utterance to the world. It comes to us, and seems a stranger to us, seeking a home.

As little can we explain the mighty power of the human WILL. Volition, like Thought, seems spontaneous, an effect without a cause. Circumstances *provoke* it, and serve as its *occasion,* but do not *produce* it. It springs up in the soul, like Thought, as the waters gush upward in a spring. Is it the manifestation of the soul, merely making apparent what passes *within* the soul, or an emanation from it, going abroad and acting outwardly, itself a real Existence, as it is an admitted Power? We can but own our ignorance. It is certain that it acts on other souls, controls, directs them, shapes their action, legislates for men and nations: and yet it is not material nor visible; and the laws it writes merely inform one soul of what has passed within another.

God, therefore, is a mystery, only as everything that surrounds us, and as we ourselves, are mysteries. We know that there is and must be a FIRST CAUSE. His attributes, severed from Himself, are unrealities. As color and extension, weight and hardness, do not exist apart from matter as separate existences and substantives, spiritual or immaterial; so the Goodness, Wisdom, Justice, Mercy, and Benevolence of God are not independent existences, personify them as men may, but *attributes* of the Deity, the *adjectives* of One Great Substantive. But we know that He must be Good, True, Wise, Just, Benevolent, Merciful: and in all these, and all His other attributes, Perfect and Infinite; because we are conscious that these are laws imposed on us by the very nature of things, necessary, and without which the Universe would be confusion and the existence of a God incredible. They are of His *essence,* and necessary, as His existence is.

He is the Living, Thinking, Intelligent SOUL of the Universe, the PERMANENT, the STATIONARY [Εστως . . Estos], of Simon Magus, the ONE that always IS [To Ον. To ON] of Plato, as contradistinguished from the perpetual flux and reflux, or *Genesis,* of *things.*

And, as the Thought of the Soul, emanating *from* the Soul, becomes audible and visible in Words, so did THE THOUGHT OF GOD, springing up within Himself, immortal *as* Himself, when once conceived,—immortal *before,* because *in* Himself, utter Itself in THE WORD, its manifestation and mode of communication, and thus create the Material, Mental, Spiritual Universe, which, like Him, never *began* to exist.

This is the *real* idea of the Ancient Nations: GOD, the Almighty Father, and Source of All; His THOUGHT, *conceiving* the whole Universe, and *willing* its creation: His WORD, *uttering* that THOUGHT, and thus becoming the Creator or Demiourgos, in whom was Life and Light, and that Light the Life of the Universe.

Nor did that Word *cease* at the single act of Creation; and having set going the great machine, and enacted the laws of its motion and progression, of birth and life, and change and death, cease to exist, or remain thereafter in inert idleness.

FOR THE THOUGHT OF GOD LIVES AND IS IMMORTAL. Embodied in the WORD, is not only *created,* but it *preserves.* It conducts and controls the Universe, all spheres, all worlds, all actions of mankind, and of every animate and inanimate creature. It speaks in the soul of every man who lives. The Stars, the Earth, the Trees, the Winds, the universal voice of Nature, tempest, and avalanche, the Sea's roar and the grave voice of the waterfall, the hoarse thunder and the low whisper of the brook, the song of birds, the voice of love, the speech of men, all are the alphabet in which it communicates itself to men, and informs them of the will and law of God, the Soul of the Universe. And thus most truly *did* "THE WORD BECOME FLESH AND DWELL AMONG MEN."

God, the unknown FATHER [Πατὴρ Ἄγνωστος . . Pater Agnōstos], known to us only by His Attributes; the ABSOLUTE I AM:.. The THOUGHT of God [Ἔννοια . Ennoia], and the WORD [Λόγος.... Logos], Manifestation and expression of the Thought; .... Behold THE TRUE MASONIC TRINITY; the UNIVERSAL SOUL, the THOUGHT *in* the Soul, the WORD, or Thought expressed; the THREE IN ONE, of a Trinitarian Ecossais.

Here Masonry pauses, and leaves its Initiates to carry out and develop these great Truths in such manner as to each may seem

most accordant with reason, philosophy, truth, and his religious
faith. It declines to act as Arbiter between them. It looks calmly
on, while each multiplies the intermediates between the Deity and
Matter, and the personifications of God's manifestations and attributes, to whatever extent his reason, his conviction, or his fancy
dictates.

While the Indian tells us that PARABRAHMA, BRAHM, and PA-
RATMA were the first Triune God, revealing Himself as BRAHMA,
VISHNU, and SIVA, *Creator, Preserver, and Destroyer;* ....

The Egyptian, of AMUN-RE, NEITH, and PHTHA, *Creator,
Matter, Thought* or *Light;* the Persian of *his* Trinity of Three
Powers in ORMUZD, Sources of *Light, Fire,* and *Water*; the Buddhists of the God SAKYA, a Trinity composed of BUDDHA, DHARMA,
and SANGA,—*Intelligence, Law,* and *Union* or *Harmony;* the
Chinese Sabeans of *their* Trinity of *Chang-ti,* the Supreme Sovereign; *Tien,* the Heavens; and *Tao,* the Universal Supreme Reason and Principle of all things; who produced the Unit; that, two;
two, three; and three, all that is; ....

While the Sclavono-Vend typifies *his* Trinity by the three heads
of the God *Triglav;* the Ancient Prussian points to *his* Triune
God, *Perkoun, Pikollos,* and *Potrimpos,* Deities of Light and
Thunder, of Hell and of the Earth; the Ancient Scandinavian to
Odin, Frea, and *Thor;* and the old Etruscans to TINA, TALNA, and
MINERVA, *Strength, Abundance,* and *Wisdom;* ....

While Plato tells us of the *Supreme Good,* the *Reason* or *Intellect,* and the *Soul* or *Spirit;* and Philo of the *Archetype of Light,
Wisdom* [Σοφια], and the *Word* [Λογος]; the Kabalists, of
the Triads of the Sephiroth; ....

While the disciples of Simon Magus, and the many sects of the
Gnostics, confuse us with their *Eons, Emanations, Powers, Wisdom Superior* and *Inferior, Ialdabaoth, Adam-Kadmon,* even to
the three hundred and sixty-five thousand emanations of the Mal-
daïtes; ....

And while the pious Christian believes that the WORD dwelt in
the Mortal Body of Jesus of Nazareth, and suffered upon the
Cross; and that the HOLY GHOST was poured out upon the Apostles, and now inspires every truly Christian Soul: ....

While all these faiths assert their claims to the exclusive possession of the Truth, Masonry inculcates its old doctrine, and no
more: .... That God is ONE; that HIS THOUGHT uttered in His

WORD, created the Universe, and preserves it by those Eternal Laws which are the expression of that Thought: that the Soul of Man, breathed into him by God, is immortal as His Thoughts are; that he is free to do evil or to choose good, responsible for his acts and punishable for his sins: that all evil and wrong and suffering are but temporary, the discords of one great Harmony, and that in His good time they will lead by infinite modulations to the great, harmonic final chord and cadence of Truth, Love, Peace, and Happiness, that will ring forever and ever under the Arches of Heaven, among all the Stars and Worlds, and in all souls of men and Angels.

XXVII.

KNIGHT COMMANDER OF THE TEMPLE

This is the first of the really Chivalric Degrees of the Ancient and Accepted Scottish Rite. It occupies this place in the Calendar of the Degrees between the 26th and the last of the Philosophical Degrees, in order, by breaking the continuity of these, to relieve what might otherwise become wearisome; and also to remind you that, while engaged with the speculations and abstractions of philosophy and creeds, the Mason is also to continue engaged in the active duties of this great warfare of life. He is not only a Moralist and Philosopher, but a Soldier, the Successor of those Knights of the Middle Age, who, while they wore the Cross, also wielded the Sword, and were the Soldiers of Honor, Loyalty, and Duty.

Times change, and circumstances; but Virtue and Duty remain the same. The Evils to be warred against but take another shape, and are developed in a different form.

There is the same need now of truth and loyalty as in the days of Frederic Barbarossa.

The characters, religious and military, attention to the sick and wounded in the Hospital, and war against the Infidel in the field, are no longer blended; but the same duties, to be performed in another shape, continue to exist and to environ us all.

The innocent virgin is no longer at the mercy of the brutal Baron or licentious man-at-arms; but purity and innocence still need protectors.

War is no longer the apparently natural State of Society; and for most men it is an empty obligation to assume, that they will not recede before the enemy; but the same high duty and obligation still rest upon all men.

Truth, in act, profession, and opinion, is rarer now than in the days of chivalry. Falsehood has become a current coin, and circulates with a certain degree of respectability; because it has an actual value. It is indeed the great Vice of the Age—it, and its twin-sister, Dishonesty. Men, for political preferment, profess

578

whatever principles are expedient and profitable. At the bar, in the pulpit, and in the halls of legislation, men argue against their own convictions, and, with what they term *logic,* prove to the satisfaction of others that which they do not themselves believe. Insincerity and duplicity are valuable to their possessors, like estates in stocks, that yield a certain revenue: and it is no longer the *truth* of an opinion or a principle, but the net *profit* that may be realized from it, which is the measure of its value.

The Press is the great sower of falsehood. To slander a political antagonist, to misrepresent all that he says, and, if that be impossible, to invent for him what he does *not* say; to put in circulation whatever baseless calumnies against him are necessary to defeat him,—these are habits so common as to have ceased to excite notice or comment, much less surprise or disgust.

There was a time when a Knight would die rather than utter a lie, or break his Knightly word. The Knight Commander of the Temple revives the old Knightly spirit; and devotes himself to the old Knightly worship of Truth. No profession of an opinion not his own, for expediency's sake or profit, or through fear of the world's disfavor; no slander of even an enemy; no coloring or perversion of the sayings or acts of other men; no insincere speech and argument for any purpose, or under any pretext, must soil his fair escutcheon. Out of the Chapter, as well as in it, he must speak the Truth, and *all* the Truth, no more and no less; or else speak not at all.

To purity and innocence everywhere, the Knight Commander owes protection, as of old; against bold violence, or those, more guilty than murderers, who by art and treachery seek to slay the soul; and against that want and destitution that drive too many to sell their honor and innocence for food.

In no age of the world has man had better opportunity than now to display those lofty virtues and that noble heroism that so distinguished the three great military and religious Orders, in their youth, before they became corrupt and vitiated by prosperity and power.

When a fearful epidemic ravages a city, and death is inhaled with the air men breathe; when the living scarcely suffice to bury the dead,—most men flee in abject terror, to return and live, respectable and influential, when the danger has passed away. But the old Knightly spirit of devotion and disinterestedness and contempt of death still lives, and is not extinct in the human heart. Everywhere a few are found to stand firmly and unflinchingly at their posts, to front and defy the danger, not for money, or to be honored for it, or to protect their own household; but from mere humanity, and to obey the unerring dictates of duty. They nurse the sick, breathing the pestilential atmosphere of the hospital. They explore the abodes of want and misery. With the gentleness of woman, they soften the pains of the dying, and feed the lamp of life in the convalescent. They perform the last sad offices to the dead; and they seek no other reward than the approval of their own consciences.

These are the true Knights of the present age: these, and the captain who remains at his post on board his shattered ship until the last boat, loaded to the water's edge with passengers and crew, has parted from her side; and then goes calmly down with her into the mysterious depths of the ocean:—the pilot who stands at the wheel while the swift flames eddy round him and scorch away his life:—the fireman who ascends the blazing walls, and plunges amid the flames to save the property or lives of those who have upon him no claim by tie of blood, or friendship, or even of ordinary acquaintance:—these, and others like these:—all men, who, set at the post of duty, stand there manfully; to die, if need be, but not to desert their post: for these, too, are sworn not to recede before the enemy.

To the performance of duties and of acts of heroism like these, you have devoted yourself, my Brother, by becoming a Knight Commander of the Temple. Soldier of the Truth and of Loyalty! Protector of Purity and Innocence! Defier of Plague and Pestilence! Nurser of the Sick and Burier of the Dead! Knight, preferring Death to abandonment of the Post of Duty! Welcome to the bosom of this Order!

XXVIII.

KNIGHT OF THE SUN, OR PRINCE ADEPT.

God is the author of everything that existeth; the Eternal, the Supreme, the Living, and Awful Being; from Whom nothing in the Universe is hidden. Make of Him no idols and visible images; but rather worship Him in the deep solitudes of sequestered forests; for He is invisible, and fills the Universe as its soul, and liveth not in any Temple!

Light and Darkness are the World's Eternal ways. God is the principle of everything that exists, and the Father of all Beings. He is eternal, immovable, and Self-Existent. There are no bounds to His power. At one glance He sees the Past, the Present, and the Future; and the procession of the builders of the Pyramids, with us and our remotest Descendants, is now passing before Him. He reads our thoughts before they are known to ourselves. He rules the movements of the Universe, and all events and revolutions are the creatures of His will. For He is the Infinite Mind and Supreme Intelligence.

In the beginning Man had the WORD, and that WORD was from God: and out of the living power which, in and by that WORD, was communicated to man, came the LIGHT of his existence. Let no man speak the WORD, for by it THE FATHER made light and darkness, the world and living creatures!

The Chaldean upon his plains worshipped me, and the sea-loving Phœnician. They builded me temples and towers, and burned sacrifices to me upon a thousand altars. Light was divine to them, and they thought me a God. But I am nothing—*nothing;* and LIGHT is the creature of the unseen GOD that taught the true religion to the Ancient Patriarchs: AWFUL, MYSTERIOUS, THE ABSOLUTE.

Man was created pure; and God gave him TRUTH, as He gave him LIGHT. He has lost the *truth* and found *error.* He has wandered far into darkness; and round him Sin and Shame hover evermore. The Soul that is impure, and sinful, and defiled with earthly stains, cannot again unite with God, until, by long trials and many purifications, it is finally delivered from the old calamity; and Light overcomes Darkness and dethrones it, in the Soul.

God is the First; indestructible, eternal, UNCREATED, INDIVISIBLE. *Wisdom, Justice, Truth,* and *Mercy,* with *Harmony* and *Love,* are of His essence, and *Eternity* and *Infinitude of Extension.* He is silent, and consents with MIND, and is known to Souls through MIND alone. In Him were all things originally contained, and from Him all things were evolved. For out of His Divine SILENCE and REST, after an infinitude of time, was unfolded the WORD, or the Divine POWER; and then in turn the Mighty, ever-acting, measureless INTELLECT; and from the WORD were evolved the myriads of suns and systems that make the Universe; and *fire,* and *light,* and the electric HARMONY, which is the harmony of spheres and numbers: and from the INTELLECT all Souls and intellects of men.

In the Beginning, the Universe was but ONE SOUL. HE was THE ALL, alone with TIME and SPACE, and Infinite as they.

—— HE HAD THIS THOUGHT: *"I Create Worlds:"* and lo! *the Universe,* and the laws of *harmony* and *motion* that rule it, the expression of a thought of God; and bird and beast, and every living thing but Man: and light and air, and the mysterious currents, and the dominion of mysterious numbers!

—— HE HAD THIS THOUGHT: *"I Create Man, whose Soul shall be my image, and he shall rule."* And lo! *Man,* with senses, instinct, and a reasoning mind!

—— And yet not MAN! but an *animal* that breathed, and saw, and thought: until an immaterial spark from God's own

Infinite Being penetrated the brain, and became the Soul: and lo, MAN THE IMMORTAL! Thus, threefold, fruit of God's thought, is Man; that sees and hears and feels; that thinks and reasons; that loves and is in harmony with the Universe.

Before the world grew old, the primitive Truth faded out from men's Souls. Then man asked himself, *"What am I? and how and whence am I? and whither do I go?"* And the Soul, looking inward upon itself, strove to learn whether that "I" were mere matter; its thought and reason and its passions and affections mere results of material combination; or a material Being enveloping an immaterial Spirit: . . and further it strove, by self-examination, to learn whether that Spirit were an individual essence, with a separate immortal existence, or an infinitesimal portion of a Great First Principle, inter-penetrating the Universe and the infinitude of space, and undulating like light and heat: . . and so they wandered further amid the mazes of error; and imagined vain philosophies; wallowing in the sloughs of materialism and sensualism, of beating their wings vainly in the vacuum of abstractions and idealities.

While yet the first oaks still put forth their leaves, man lost the perfect knowledge of the One True God, the Ancient Absolute Existence, the Infinite Mind and Supreme Intelligence; and floated helplessly out upon the shoreless ocean of conjecture. Then the soul vexed itself with seeking to learn whether the material Universe was a mere chance combination of atoms, or the work of Infinite, Uncreated Wisdom: . . whether the Deity was a concentrated, and the Universe an extended immateriality; or whether He was a personal existence, an Omnipotent, Eternal, Supreme Essence, regulating matter at will; or subjecting it to unchangeable laws throughout eternity; and to Whom, Himself Infinite and Eternal, Space and Time are unknown. With their finite limited vision they sought to learn the source and explain the existence of Evil, and Pain, and Sorrow; and so they wandered ever deeper into the darkness, and were lost; and there was for them no longer any God; but only a great, dumb, soulless Universe, full of mere emblems and symbols.

You have heretofore, in some of the Degrees through which you have passed, heard much of the ancient worship of the Sun, the Moon, and the other bright luminaries of Heaven, and of the Elements and Powers of Universal Nature. You have been made, to some extent, familiar with their personifications as Heroes suffering or triumphant, or as personal Gods or Goddesses, with human characteristics and passions, and with the multitude of legends and fables that do but allegorically represent their risings and settings, their courses, their conjunctions and oppositions, their domiciles and places of exaltation.

Perhaps you have supposed that we, like many who have written on these subjects, have intended to represent this worship to you as the most ancient and original worship of the first men that lived. To undeceive you, if such was your conclusion, we have caused the Personifications of the Great Luminary of Heaven, under the names by which he was known to the most ancient nations, to proclaim the old primitive truths that were known to the Fathers of our race, before men came to worship the visible manifestations of the Supreme Power and Magnificence and the Supposed Attributes of the Universal Deity in the Elements and in the glittering armies that Night regularly marshals and arrays upon the blue field of the firmament.

We ask now your attention to a still further development of these truths, after we shall have added something to what we have already said in regard to the Chief Luminary of Heaven, in explanation of the names and characteristics of the several imaginary Deities that represented him among the ancient races of men.

ATHOM or ATHOM-RE, was the Chief and Oldest Supreme God of Upper Egypt, worshipped at Thebes; the same as the OM or AUM of the Hindūs, whose name was unpronounceable, and who, like the BREHM of the latter People, was "The Being that was, and is, and is to come; the Great God, the Great Omnipotent, Omniscient, and Omnipresent One, the Greatest in the Universe, the Lord;" whose emblem was a perfect sphere, showing that He was first, last, midst, and without end; superior to all Nature-Gods, and all personifications of Powers, Elements, and Luminaries; symbolized by Light, the Principle of Life.

AMUN was the Nature-God, or Spirit of Nature, called by that name or AMUN-RE, and worshipped at Memphis in Lower Egypt, and in Libya, as well as in Upper Egypt. He was the Libyan Jupiter, and represented the intelligent and organizing force that develops itself in Nature, when the intellectual types or forms of bodies are revealed to the senses in the world's order, by their union with matter, whereby the generation of bodies is effected. He was the same with Kneph, from whose mouth issued the Orphic egg out of which came the Universe.

DIONUSOS was the Nature-God of the Greeks, as AMUN was of the Egyptians. In the popular legend, Dionusos, as well as Hercules, was a Theban Hero, born of a mortal mother. Both were sons of Zeus, both persecuted by Heré. But in Hercules the God is subordinate to the Hero; while Dionusos, even in poetry, retains his divine character, and is identical with Iacchus, the presiding genius of the Mysteries. Personification of the Sun in Taurus, as his ox-hoofs showed, he delivered earth from the harsh dominion of Winter, conducted the mighty chorus of the Stars, and the celestial revolution of the year, changed with the seasons, and underwent their periodical decay. He was the Sun as invoked by the Eleans, Πυριγενης, ushered into the world amidst lightning and thunder, the Mighty Hunter of the Zodiac, Zagreus the Golden or ruddy-faced. The Mysteries taught the doctrine of Divine Unity; and that Power whose Oneness is a seeming mystery, but really a truism, was Dionusos, the God of Nature, or of that moisture, which is the life of Nature, who prepares in darkness, in Hades or Iasion, the return of life and vegetation, or is himself the light and change evolving their varieties. In the Egean Islands he was Butes, Dardanus, Himeros or Imbros; in Crete he appears as Iasius or even Zeus, whose orgiastic worship, remaining unveiled by the usual forms of mystery, betrayed to profane curiosity the symbols which, if irreverently contemplated, were sure to be misunderstood.

He was the same with the dismembered Zagreus, the son of Persephone, an Ancient Subterranean Dionusos, the horned progeny of Zeus in the Constellation of the Serpent, entrusted by his father with the thunderbolt, and encircled with the protecting dance of Curetes. Through the envious artifices of Heré, the Titans eluded the vigilance of his guardians and tore him to pieces; but Pallas restored the still palpitating heart to his father, who commanded Apollo to bury the dismembered remains upon Parnassus.

Dionusos, as well as Apollo, was leader of the Muses; the tomb of one accompanied the worship of the other; they were the same, yet different, contrasted, yet only as filling separate parts in the same drama; and the mystic and heroic personifications, the God of Nature and of Art, seem, at some remote period, to have proceeded from a common source. Their separation was one of form rather than of substance: and from the time when Hercules obtained initiation from Triptolemus, or Pythagoras received Orphic tenets, the two conceptions were tending to re-combine. It was said that Dionusos or Poseidon had preceded Apollo in the Oracular office; and Dionusos continued to be esteemed in Greek Theology as Healer and Saviour, Author of Life and Immortality. The dispersed Pythagoreans, "Sons of Apollo," immediately betook themselves to the Orphic Service of Dionusos, and there are indications that there was always something Dionysiac in the worship of Apollo.

Dionusos is the Sun, that liberator of the elements; and his spiritual meditation was suggested by the same imagery which made the Zodiac the supposed path of the Spirits in their descent and their return. His second birth, as offspring of the highest, is a type of the spiritual regeneration of man. He, as well as Apollo, was precentor of the Muses and source of inspiration. His rule prescribed no unnatural mortification: its yoke was easy, and its mirthful choruses, combining the gay with the severe, did but commemorate that golden age when earth enjoyed eternal spring, and when fountains of honey, milk, and wine burst forth out of its bosom at the touch of the thyrsus. He is the "Liberator." Like Osiris, he frees the soul, and guides it in its migrations beyond the grave, preserving it from the risk of again falling under the slavery of matter or of some inferior animal form. All soul is part of the Universal Soul, whose totality is Dionusos; and he leads back the vagrant spirit to its home, and accompanies it through the purifying processes, both real and symbolical, of its earthly transit. He died and descended to the Shades; and his suffering was the great secret of the Mysteries, as death is the grand mystery of existence. He is the immortal suitor of Psyche (the Soul), the Divine influence which physically called the world into being, and which, awakening the soul from its Stygian trance, restores it from earth to Heaven.

Of HERMES, the Mercury of the Greeks, the Thoth of the Egyptians, and the Taaut of the Phœnicians, we have heretofore spoken sufficiently at length. He was the inventor of letters and of Oratory, the winged messenger of the Gods, bearing the Caduceus wreathed with serpents; and in our Council he is represented by the ORATOR.

The *Hindūs* called the Sun SURYA; the *Persians*, MITHRAS;

the *Egyptians,* OSIRIS; the *Assyrians* and *Chaldæans,* BEL; the *Scythians* and *Etruscans* and the ancient *Pelasgi,* ARKALEUS or HERCULES; the *Phœnicians,* ADONAI or ADON; and the *Scandinavians,* ODIN.

From the name SURYA, given by the Hindūs to the Sun, the Sect who paid him particular adoration were called *Souras.* Their painters describe his car as drawn by seven green horses. In the Temple of Visweswara, at Benares, there is an ancient piece of sculpture, well executed in stone, representing him sitting in a car drawn by a horse with twelve heads. His charioteer, by whom he is preceded, is ARUN [from אור, AUR the *Crepusculum?*], or the Dawn; and among his many titles are twelve that denote his distinct powers in each of the twelve months. Those powers are called Adityas, each of whom has a particular name. Surya is supposed frequently to have descended upon earth, in a human shape, and to have left a race on earth, equally renowned in Indian story with the Heliades of Greece. He is often styled King of the Stars and Planets, and thus reminds us of the Adon-Tsbauth (Lord of the Starry Hosts) of the Hebrew writings.

MITHRAS was the Sun-God of the Persians; and was fabled to have been born in a grotto or cave, at the Winter Solstice. His feasts were celebrated at that period, at the moment when the sun commenced to return Northward, and to increase the length of the days. This was the great Feast of the Magian religion. The Roman Calendar, published in the time of Constantine, at which period his worship began to gain ground in the Occident, fixed his feast-day on the 25th of December. His statues and images were inscribed, *Deo-Soli invicto Mithræ*—to the invincible Sun-God Mithras. *Nomen invictum Sol Mithra. . Soli Omnipotenti Mithræ.* To him, gold, incense, and myrrh were consecrated. "Thee," says Martianus Capella, in his hymn to the Sun, "the dwellers on the Nile adore as Serapis, and Memphis worships as Osiris; in the sacred rites of Persia thou art Mithras, in Phrygia, Atys, and Libya bows down to thee as Ammon, and Phœnician Byblos as Adonis; and thus the whole world adores thee under different names."

OSIRIS was the son of Helios (Phra), the "divine offspring congenerate with the dawn," and at the same time an incarnation of Kneph or Agathodæmon, the Good Spirit, including all his possible manifestations, either physical or moral. He represented in a familiar form the beneficent aspect of all higher emanations and in him was developed the conception of a Being purely good, so that it became necessary to set up another power as his adversary, called Seth, Babys or Typhon, to account for the injurious influences of Nature.

With the phenomena of agriculture, supposed to be the invention of Osiris, the Egyptians connected the highest truths of their religion. The soul of man was as the seed hidden in the ground, and the mortal framework, similarly consigned to its dark resting-place, awaited its restoration to life's unfailing source. Osiris was not only benefactor of the living; he was also Hades, Serapis, and Rhadamanthus, the monarch of the dead. Death, therefore, in Egyptian opinion, was only another name for *renovation,* since its God is the same power who incessantly renews vitality in Nature. Every corpse duly embalmed was called "Osiris," and in the grave was supposed to be united, or at least brought into approximation, to the Divinity. For when God became incarnate for man's benefit, it was implied that, in analogy with His assumed character, He should submit to *all* the conditions of visible existence. In death, as in life, Isis and Osiris were patterns and precursors of mankind; their sepulchres stood within the temples of the Superior Gods; yet though their remains might be entombed at Memphis or Abydus, their divinity was unimpeached, and they either shone as luminaries in the heavens, or in the unseen world presided over the futurity of the disembodied spirits whom death had brought nearer to them.

The notion of a dying God, so frequent in Oriental legend, and of which we have already said much in former Degrees, was the natural inference from a literal interpretation of nature-worship; since nature, which in the vicissitudes of the seasons seems to undergo a dissolution, was to the earliest religionists the express image of the Deity, and at a remote period one and the same with the "varied God," whose attributes were seen not only in its vitality, but in its changes. The unseen Mover of the Universe was rashly identified with its obvious fluctuations. The speculative Deity suggested by the drama of nature, was worshipped with imitative and sympathetic rites. A period of mourning about the Autumnal Equinox, and of joy at the return of Spring, was almost universal. Phrygians and Paphlagonians, Bœotians, and even Athenians, were all more or less attached to such observances; the Syrian damsels sat weeping for Thammuz or Adoni, mortally wounded by the tooth of Winter, symbolized by the boar, its very general emblem: and these rites, and those of Atys and Osiris, were evidently suggested by the arrest of vegetation, when the Sun, descending from his altitude, seems deprived of his generating power.

Osiris is a being analogous to the Syrian Adoni; and the fable of his history, which we need not here repeat, is a narrative form of the popular religion of Egypt, of which the Sun is the Hero, and the agricultural calendar the moral. The moist valley of the Nile, owing its fertility to the annual inundation, appeared, in contrast with the surrounding desert, like life in the midst of death. The inundation was in evident dependence on the Sun, and Egypt, environed with arid deserts, like a heart within a burning censer, was the female power, dependent on the influences personified in its God. Typhon his brother, the type of darkness, drought, and sterility, threw his body into the Nile; and thus Osiris, the "good," the "Saviour," perished, in the 28th year of his life or reign, and on the 17th day of the month Athor, or the 13th of November. He is also made to die during the heats of the early Summer, when, from March to July, the earth was parched with intolerable heat, vegetation was scorched, and the languid Nile exhausted. From that death he rises when the Solstitial Sun brings the inundation, and Egypt is filled with mirth and acclamation anticipatory of the second harvest. From his Wintry death he rises with the early flowers of Spring, and then the joyful festival of Osiris found was celebrated.

So the pride of Jemsheed, one of the Persian Sun-heroes, or the solar year personified, was abruptly cut off by Zohak, the tyrant of the West. He was sawn asunder by a fish-bone, and immediately the brightness of Iran changed to gloom. Ganymede and Adonis, like Osiris, were hurried off in all their strength and beauty; the premature death of Linus, the burthen of the ancient lament of Greece, was like that of the Persian Siamek, the Bithynian Hylas, and the Egyptian Maneros, Son of Menes or the Eternal. The elegy called Maneros was sung at Egyptian banquets, and an effigy enclosed within a diminutive Sarcophagus was handed round to remind the guests of their brief tenure of existence. The beautiful Memnon, also, perished in his prime; and Enoch, whose early death was lamented at Iconium, lived 365 years, the number of days of the solar year; a brief space when compared with the longevity of his patriarchal kindred.

The story of Osiris is reflected in those of Orpheus and Dionusos Zagreus, and perhaps in the legends of Absyrtus and Pelias, of Æson, Thyestes, Melicertes, Itys, and Pelops. Io is the disconsolate Isis or Niobe: and Rhea mourns her dismembered Lord, Hyperion, and the death of her son Helios, drowned in the Eridanus; and if Apollo and Dionusos are immortal, they had died under other names, as Orpheus, Linus, or Hyacinthus. The sepulchre of Zeus was shown in Crete. Hippolytus was associated in divine honors with Apollo, and after he had been torn to pieces like Osiris, was restored to life by the Pæonian herbs of Diana, and kept darkling in the secret grove of Egeria. Zeus deserted Olympus to visit the Ethiopians; Apollo underwent servitude to Admetus; Theseus, Peirithous, Hercules, and other heroes, descended for a time to Hades; a dying Nature-God was exhibited in the Mysteries, the Attic women fasted, sitting on the ground, during the Thesmophoria, and the Bœotians lamented the descent of Cora-Proserpine to the Shades.

But the death of the Deity, as understood by the Orientals, was not inconsistent with His immortality. The temporary decline of the Sons of Light is but an episode in their endless continuity; and as the day and year are more convenient subdivisions of the Infinite, so the fiery deaths of Phaëthon or Hercules are but breaks in the same Phœnix process of perpetual regeneration, by which the spirit of Osiris lives forever in the succession of the Memphian Apis. Every year witnesses the revival of Adonis; and the amber tears shed by the Heliades for the premature death of their brother, are the golden shower full of prolific hope, in which Zeus descends from the brazen vault of Heaven into the bosom of the parched ground.

BAL, representative or personification of the sun, was one of the Great Gods of Syria, Assyria, and Chaldea, and his name is found upon the monuments of Nimroud, and frequently occurs in the Hebrew writings. He was the Great Nature-God of Babylonia, the Power of heat, life, and generation. His symbol was the Sun, and he was figured seated on a bull. All the accessories of his great temple at Babylon, described by Herodotus, are repeated with singular fidelity, but on a smaller scale, in the Hebrew tabernacle and temple. The golden statue alone is wanted to complete the resemblance. The word *Bal* or *Baal,* like the word *Adon,* signifies Lord and Master. He was also the Supreme Deity of the Moabites, Amonites, and Carthaginians, and of the Sabeans in general; the Gauls worshipped the Sun under the name of Belin or Belinus: and Bela is found among the Celtic Deities upon the ancient monuments.

The Northern ancestors of the Greeks maintained with hardier habits a more manly style of religious symbolism than the effeminate enthusiasts of the South, and had embodied in their *Perseus,* Hercules and Mithras, the consummation of the qualities they esteemed and exercised.

Almost every nation will be found to have had a mythical being, whose strength or weakness, virtues or defects, more or less nearly describe the Sun's career through the seasons. There was a Celtic, a Teutonic, a Scythian, an Etruscan, a Lydian Hercules, all whose legends became tributary to those of the Greek hero. The name of Hercules was found by Herodotus to have been long familiar in Egypt and the East, and to have originally belonged to a much higher personage than the comparatively modern hero known in Greece as the Son of Alcmena. The temple of the Hercules of Tyre was reported to have been built 2300 years before the time of Herodotus; and Hercules, whose Greek name has been sometimes supposed to be of Phœnician origin, in the sense of Circuitor, *i. e.* "rover" and "perambulator" of earth, as well as "Hyperion" of the sky, was the patron and model of those famous navigators who spread his altars from coast to coast through the Mediterranean, to the extremities of the West, where "Arkaleus" built the City of Gades, and where a perpetual fire burned in his service. He was the lineal descendant of Perseus, the luminous child of darkness, conceived within a subterranean vault of brass; and he a representation of the Persian Mithras, rearing his emblematic lions above the gates of Mycenæ, and bringing the sword of Jemsheed to battle against the Gorgons of the West. Mithras is similarly described in the Zend-Avesta as the "mighty hero, the rapid runner, whose piercing eye embraces all, whose arm bears the club for the destruction of the Darood."

Hercules Ingeniculus, who, bending on one knee, uplifts his club and tramples on the Serpent's head, was, like Prometheus and Tantalus, one of the varying aspects of the struggling and declining Sun. The victories of Hercules are but exhibitions of

Solar power which have ever to be repeated. It was in the far North, among the Hyperboreans, that, divested of his Lion's skin, he lay down to sleep, and for a time lost the horses of his chariot. Henceforth that Northern region of gloom, called the "place of the death and revival of Adonis," that Caucasus whose summit was so lofty, that, like the Indian Meru, it seemed to be both the goal and commencement of the Sun's career, became to Greek imaginations the final bourne of all things, the abode of Winter and desolation, the pinnacle of the arch connecting the upper and lower world, and consequently the appropriate place for the banishment of Prometheus. The daughters of Israel, weeping for Thammuz, mentioned by Ezekiel, sat looking to the North, and waiting for his return from that region. It was while Cybele with the Sun-God was absent among the Hyperboreans, that Phrygia, abandoned by her, suffered the horrors of famine. Delos and Delphi awaited the return of Apollo from the Hyperboreans, and Hercules brought thence to Olympia the olive. To all Masons, the North has immemorially been the place of darkness; and of the great lights of the Lodge, none is in the North.

Mithras, the rock-born hero (Πετρογενης), heralded the Sun's return in Spring, as Prometheus, chained in his cavern, betokened the continuance of Winter. The Persian beacon on the mountain-top represented the Rock-born Divinity enshrined in his worthiest temple; and the funeral conflagration of Hercules was the sun dying in glory behind the Western hills. But though the transitory manifestation suffers or dies, the abiding and eternal power liberates and saves. It was an essential attribute of a Titan, that he should arise again after his fall; for the revival of Nature is as certain as its decline, and its alternations are subject to the appointment of a power which controls them both.

"God," says Maximus Tyrius, "did not spare His own Son [Hercules], or exempt Him from the calamities incidental to humanity. The Theban progeny of Jove had his share of pain and trial. By vanquishing earthly difficulties he proved his affinity with Heaven. His life was a continuous struggle. He fainted before Typhon in the desert; and in the commencement of the Autumnal season (cum longæ redit hora noctis), descended under the guidance of Minerva to Hades. He died; but first applied for initiation to Eumolpus, in order to foreshadow that state of religious preparation which should precede the momentous change. Even in Hades he rescued Theseus and removed the stone of Ascalaphus, reanimated the bloodless spirits, and dragged into the light of day the monster Cerberus, justly reputed invincible because an emblem of Time itself; he burst the chains of the grave (for Busiris is the grave personified), and triumphant at the close as in the dawn of his career, was received after his labors into the repose of the heavenly mansions, living forever with Zeus in the arms of Eternal Youth.

ODIN is said to have borne twelve names among the old Germans, and to have had 114 names besides. He was the Apollo of the Scandinavians, and is represented in the Voluspa as destined to slay the monstrous snake. Then the Sun will be extinguished, the earth be dissolved in the ocean, the stars lose their brightness, and all Nature be destroyed in order that it may be renewed again. From the bosom of the waters a new world will emerge clad in verdure; harvests will be seen to ripen where no seed was sown, and evil will disappear.

The free fancy of the ancients, which wove the web of their myths and legends, was consecrated by faith. It had not, like the modern mind, set apart a petty sanctuary of borrowed beliefs, beyond which all the rest was common and unclean. Imagination, reason, and religion circled round the same symbol; and in all their symbols there was serious meaning, if we could but find it out. They did not devise fictions in the same vapid spirit in which we, cramped by conventionalities, read them. In endeavoring to interpret creations of fancy, fancy as well as reason must guide: and much of modern controversy arises out of heavy misapprehensions of ancient symbolism.

To those ancient peoples, this earth was the centre of the Universe. To them there were no other worlds, peopled with living beings, to divide the care and attention of the Deity. To them the world was a great plain, of unknown, perhaps inconceivable limits, and the Sun, the Moon, and the Stars journeyed above it, to give them light. The worship of the Sun became the basis of all the religions of antiquity. To them light and heat were mysteries; as indeed they still are to us. As the Sun caused the day, and his absence the night; as, when he journeyed Northward, Spring and Summer followed him; and when he again turned to the South, Autumn and inclement Winter, and cold and long dark nights ruled the earth; . . . as his influence produced the leaves and flowers, and ripened the harvests, and brought regular inundation, he necessarily became to them the most interesting object of the material Universe. To them he was the innate fire of bodies, the fire of nature. Author of Life, heat, and ignition, he was to them the efficient cause of all generation, for without him there was no movement, no existence, no form. He was to them immense, indivisible, imperishable, and everywhere present. It was their need of light, and of his creative energy, that was felt by all men; and nothing was more fearful to them than his absence. His beneficent influences caused his identification with the Principle of Good; and the BRAHMA of the Hindūs, the MITHRAS of the Persians, and ATHOM, AMUN, PHTHA, and OSIRIS, of the Egyptians, the BEL of the Chaldeans, the ADONAI of the Phœnicians, the ADONIS and APOLLO of the Greeks became but personifications of the Sun, the regenerating Principle, image of that fecundity which perpetuates and rejuvenates the world's existence.

So too the struggle between the Good and Evil Principles was personified, as was that between life and death, destruction and re-creation; in allegories and fables which poetically represented the apparent course of the Sun; who, descending toward the Southern Hemisphere, was figuratively said to be conquered and put to death by darkness, or the genius of Evil; but, returning again toward the Northern Hemisphere, he seemed to be victorious, and to arise from the tomb. This death and resurrection were also figurative of the succession of day and night, of death, which is a necessity of life, and of life which is born of death; and everywhere the ancients still saw the combat between the two Principles that ruled the world. Everywhere this contest was embodied in allegories and fictitious histories: into which were ingeniously woven all the astronomical phenomena that accompanied, preceded, or followed the different movements of the Sun, and the changes of Seasons, the approach or withdrawal of inundation. And thus grew into stature and strange proportions the histories of the contests between Typhon and Osiris, Hercules and Juno, the Titans and Jupiter, Ormuzd and Ahriman, the rebellious Angels and the Deity, the Evil Genii and the Good; and the other like fables, found not only in Asia, but in the North of Europe, and even among the Mexicans and Peruvians of the New World; carried thither, in all probability, by those Phœnician voyagers who bore thither civilization and the arts. The Scythians lamented the death of Acmon, the Persians that of Zohak conquered by Pheridoun, the Hindūs that of Soura-Parama slain by Soupra-Muni, as the Scandinavians did that of Balder, torn to pieces by the blind Hother.

The primitive idea of infinite space existed in the first men, as it exists in us. It and the idea of infinite time are the first two innate ideas. Man cannot conceive how thing can be added to thing, or event follow event, forever. The idea will ever return, that no matter how long bulk is added to bulk, there must be, still beyond, an empty void *without* limit; in which is *nothing*. In the same way the idea of time without beginning or end forces itself on him. *Time,* without events, is also a *void,* and *nothing.*

In that empty void space the primitive men knew there was no light nor warmth. They *felt,* what we know scientifically, that there must be a thick darkness there, and an intensity of cold of which we have no conception. Into that void they thought the Sun, the Planets, and the Stars went down when they set under the Western Horizon. Darkness was to them an enemy, a harm, a vague dread and terror. It was the very embodiment of the evil principle; and out of it they said that he was formed. As the Sun bent Southward toward that void, they shuddered with dread: and when, at the Winter Solstice, he again commenced his Northward march, they rejoiced and feasted; as they did at the Summer Solstice, when most he appeared to smile upon them in his pride of place. These days have been celebrated by all civilized nations ever since. The Christian has made them feast-days of the church, and appropriated them to the two Saints John; and Masonry has done the same.

We, to whom the vast Universe has become but a great *machine,* not instinct with a great Soul, but a *clockwork* of proportions unimaginable, but still infinitely less than infinite; and part at least of which we with our orreries can imitate; we, who have measured the distances and dimensions, and learned the specific gravity and determined the orbits of the moon and the planets; we, who know the distance to the sun, and his size; have measured the orbits of the flashing comets, and the distances of the fixed stars; and know the latter to be suns like our sun, each with his retinue of worlds, and all governed by the same unerring, mechanical laws and outwardly imposed forces, centripetal and centrifugal; we, who with our telescopes have separated the galaxy and the nebulæ into other stars and groups of stars; discovered new planets, by first discovering their disturbing forces upon those already known; and learned that they all, Jupiter, Venus, and the fiery Mars, and Saturn and the others, as well as the bright, mild, and ever-changing Moon, are mere dark, dull, opaque clods like our earth, and not living orbs of brilliant fire and heavenly light; we, who have counted the mountains and chasms in the moon, with glasses that could distinctly reveal to us the temple of Solomon, if it stood there in its old original glory; we, who no longer imagine that the stars control our destinies, and who can calculate the eclipses of the sun and moon, backward and forward, for ten thousand years; we, with our vastly increased conceptions of the powers of the Grand Architect of the Universe, but our wholly material and mechanical view of that Universe itself; we cannot, even in the remotest degree, *feel,* though we may partially and imperfectly *imagine,* how those great, primitive, simple-hearted children of Nature felt in regard to the Starry Hosts, there upon the slopes of the Himalayas, on the Chaldean plains, in the Persian and Median deserts, and upon the banks of that great, strange River, the Nile. To them the Universe was *alive*—instinct with forces and powers, mysterious and beyond their comprehension. To them it was no machine, no great system of clockwork; but a great live creature, an army of creatures, in sympathy with or inimical to man. To them, all was a mystery and a miracle, and the stars flashing overhead spoke to their hearts almost in an audible language. Jupiter, with his kingly splendors, was the Emperor of the starry legions. Venus looked lovingly on the earth and blessed it; Mars, with his crimson fires, threatened war and misfortune; and Saturn, cold and grave, chilled and repelled them. The ever-changing Moon, faithful companion of the Sun, was a constant miracle and wonder; the Sun himself the visible emblem of the creative and generative power. To them the earth was a great plain, over which the sun, the moon, and the planets revolved, its servants, framed to give it light. Of the stars, some were beneficent existences that brought with them Spring-time and fruits and flowers,—some, faithful sentinels, advising them of coming inundation, of the season of storm and of deadly winds; some heralds of evil, which, steadily foretelling, they seemed to cause. To them the eclipses were portents of evil, and their causes hidden in mystery, and supernatural. The regular returns of the stars, the comings of Arcturus, Orion,

Sirius, the Pleiades, and Aldebaran, and the journeyings of the Sun, were voluntary and not mechanical to them. What wonder that astronomy became to them the most important of sciences; that those who learned it became rulers; and that vast edifices, the Pyramids, the tower or temple of Bel, and other like erections everywhere in the East, were builded for astronomical purposes? —and what wonder that, in their great child-like simplicity, they worshipped Light, the Sun, the Planets, and the Stars, and personified them, and eagerly believed in the histories invented for them; in that age when the capacity for belief was infinite; as indeed, if we but reflect, it still is and ever will be?

If we adhered to the literally historic sense, antiquity would be a mere inexplicable, hideous chaos, and all the Sages deranged: and so it would be with Masonry and those who instituted it. But when these allegories are explained, they cease to be absurd fables, or facts purely local; and become lessons of wisdom for entire humanity. No one can doubt, who studies them, that they all came from a common source.

And he greatly errs who imagines that, because the mythological legends and fables of antiquity are referable to and have their foundation in the phenomena of the Heavens, and all the Heathen Gods are but mere names given to the Sun, the Stars, the Planets, the Zodiacal Signs, the Elements, the Powers of Nature, and Universal Nature herself, therefore the first men worshipped the Stars, and whatever things, animate and inanimate, seemed to them to possess and exercise a power or influence, evident or imagined, over human fortunes and human destiny.

For ever, in all the nations, ascending to the remotest antiquity to which the light of History or the glimmerings of tradition reach, we find, seated above all the gods which represent the luminaries and the elements, and those which personify the innate Powers of universal nature, a still higher Deity, silent, undefined, incomprehensible, the Supreme, one God, from Whom all the rest flow or emanate, or by Him are created. Above the Time-God Horus, the Moon-Goddess or Earth-Goddess Isis, and the Sun-God Osiris, of the Egyptians, was Amun, the Nature-God; and above him, again, the Infinite, Incomprehensible Deity, Athom. Brehm, the silent, self-contemplative, one original God, was the Source, to the Hindūs, of Brahma, Vishnu, and Siva. Above Zeus, or before him, were Kronos and Ouranos. Over the Alohayim was the great

Nature-God AL, and still beyond him, Abstract Existence, IHUH —He that IS, WAS, and SHALL BE. Above all the Persian Deities was the Unlimited Time, ZERUANE-AKHERENE; and over Odin and Thor was the Great Scandinavian Deity ALFADIR.

The worship of Universal Nature as a God was too near akin to the worship of a Universal Soul, to have been the instinctive creed of any savage people or rude race of men. To imagine all nature, with all its apparently independent parts, as forming one consistent whole, and as itself a unit, required an amount of experience and a faculty of generalization not possessed by the rude uncivilized mind, and is but a step below the idea of a universal Soul.

In the beginning man had the WORD; and that WORD was from God; and out of the living POWER communicated to man in and by that WORD, came THE LIGHT of His Existence.

God made man in His own likeness. When, by a long succession of geological changes, He had prepared the earth to be his habitation, He created him, and placed him in that part of Asia which all the old nations agreed in calling the cradle of the human race, and whence afterward the stream of human life flowed forth to India, China, Egypt, Persia, Arabia, and Phœnicia. HE communicated to him a knowledge of the nature of his Creator, and of the pure, primitive, undefiled religion. The peculiar and distinctive excellence and real essence of the primitive man, and his true nature and destiny, consisted in his likeness to God. HE stamped HIS own image upon man's soul. That image has been, in the breast of every individual man and of mankind in general, greatly altered, impaired, and defaced; but its old, half-obliterated characters are still to be found on all the pages of primitive history; and the impress, not entirely effaced, every reflecting mind may discover in its own interior.

Of the original revelation to mankind, of the primitive WORD of Divine TRUTH, we find clear indications and scattered traces in the sacred traditions of all the primitive Nations; traces which, when separately examined, appear like the broken remnants, the mysterious and hieroglyphic characters, of a mighty edifice that has been destroyed; and its fragments, like those of the old Temples and Palaces of Nimroud, wrought incongruously into edifices many centuries younger. And, although amid the ever-growing degeneracy of mankind, this primeval word of revelation was falsified by the admixture of various errors, and overlaid and obscured by numberless and manifold fictions, inextricably confused, and disfigured almost beyond the power of recognition, still a profound inquiry will discover in heathenism many luminous vestiges of primitive Truth.

For the old Heathenism had everywhere a foundation in Truth; and if we could separate that pure intuition into nature and into the simple symbols of nature, that constituted the basis of all Heathenism, from the alloy of error and the additions of fiction, those first hieroglyphic traits of the instinctive science of the first men, would be found to agree with truth and a true knowledge of nature, and to afford an image of a free, pure, comprehensive, and finished philosophy of life.

The struggle, thenceforward to be eternal, between the Divine will and the natural will in the souls of men, commenced immediately after the creation. Cain slew his brother Abel, and went forth to people parts of the earth with an impious race, forgetters and defiers of the true God. The other Descendants of the Common Father of the race intermarried with the daughters of Cain's Descendants: and all nations preserved the remembrance of that division of the human family into the righteous and impious, in their distorted legends of the wars between the Gods, and the Giants and Titans. When, afterward, another similar division occurred, the Descendants of Seth alone preserved the true primitive religion and science, and transmitted them to posterity in the ancient symbolical character, on monuments of stone: and many nations preserved in their legendary traditions the memory of the columns of Enoch and Seth.

Then the world declined from its original happy condition and fortunate estate, into idolatry and barbarism: but all nations retained the memory of that old estate; and the poets, in those early days the only historians, commemorated the succession of the ages of gold, silver, brass, and iron.

In the lapse of those ages, the sacred tradition followed various courses among each of the most ancient nations; and from its original source, as from a common centre, its various streams flowed downward; some diffusing through favored regions of the world fertility and life; but others soon losing themselves, and being dried up in the sterile sands of human error.

After the internal and Divine WORD originally communicated

by God to man, had become obscured; after man's connection with his Creator had been broken, even outward language necessarily fell into disorder and confusion. The simple and Divine Truth was overlaid with various and sensual fictions, buried under illusive symbols, and at last perverted into horrible phantoms.

For in the progress of idolatry it needs came to pass, that what was originally revered as the symbol of a higher principle, became gradually confounded or identified with the object itself, and was worshipped; until this error led to a more degraded form of idolatry. The early nations received much from the primeval source of sacred tradition; but that haughty pride which seems an inherent part of human nature led each to represent these fragmentary relics of original truth as a possession peculiar to themselves; thus exaggerating their value, and their own importance, as peculiar favorites of the Deity, who had chosen them as the favored people to whom to commit these truths. To make these fragments, as far as possible, their private property, they reproduced them under peculiar forms, wrapped them up in symbols, concealed them in allegories, and invented fables to account for their own special possession of them. So that, instead of preserving in their primitive simplicity and purity these blessings of original revelation, they overlaid them with poetical ornament; and the whole wears a fabulous aspect, until by close and severe examination we discover the truth which the apparent fable contains.

These being the conflicting elements in the breast of man; the old inheritance or original dowry of truth, imparted to him by God in the primitive revelation; and error, or the foundation for error, in his degraded sense and spirit now turned from God to nature, false faiths easily sprung up and grew rank and luxuriant, when the Divine Truth was no longer guarded with jealous care, nor preserved in its pristine purity. This soon happened among most Eastern nations, and especially the Indians, the Chaldeans, the Arabians, the Persians, and the Egyptians; with whom imagination, and a very deep but still sensual feeling for nature, were very predominant. The Northern firmament, visible to their eyes, possesses by far the largest and most brilliant constellations; and they were more alive to the impressions made by such objects, than are the men of the present day.

With the Chinese, a patriarchal, simple, and secluded people, idolatry long made but little progress. They invented writing within three or four generations after the flood; and they long preserved the memory of much of the primitive revelation; less overlaid with fiction than those fragments which other nations have remembered. They were among those who stood nearest to the source of sacred tradition; and many passages in their old writings contain remarkable vestiges of eternal truth, and of the WORD of primitive revelation, the heritage of old thought, which attest to us their original eminence.

But among the other early nations, a wild enthusiasm and a sensual idolatry of nature soon superseded the simple worship of the Almighty God, and set aside or disfigured the pure belief in the Eternal Uncreated Spirit. The great powers and elements of nature, and the vital principle of production and procreation through all generations; then the celestial spirits or heavenly Host, the luminous armies of the Stars, and the great Sun, and mysterious, ever-changing Moon (all of which the whole ancient world regarded not as mere globes of light or bodies of fire, but as animated living substances, potent over man's fate and destinies); next the genii and tutelar spirits, and even the souls of the dead, received divine worship. The animals, representing the starry constellations, first reverenced as symbols merely, came to be worshipped as gods; the heavens, earth, and the operations of nature were personified; and fictitious personages invented to account for the introduction of science and arts, and the fragments of the old religious truths; and the good and bad principles personified, became also objects of worship; while, through all, still shone the silver threads of the old primitive revelation.

Increasing familiarity with early oriental records seems more and more to confirm the probability that they all originally emanated from one source. The eastern and southern slopes of the Paropismus, or Hindukusch, appear to have been inhabited by kindred Iranian races, similar in habits, language, and religion. The earliest Indian and Persian Deities are for the most part symbols of celestial light, their agency being regarded as an eternal warfare with the powers of Winter, storm, and darkness. The religion of both was originally a worship of outward nature, especially the manifestations of fire and light; the coincidences being too marked to be merely accidental. Deva, God, is derived from the root *div*, to shine. Indra, like Ormuzd or Ahura-Mazda, is the bright firmament; Sura or Surya, the Heavenly, a name of the Sun, recurs in the Zend word Huare, the Sun, whence Khur and Khorshid or Corasch. Uschas and Mitra are Medic as well as Zend Deities and the Amschaspands or "immortal Holy Ones" of the Zend-Avesta may be compared with the seven Rishis or Vedic Star-God, of the constellation of the Bear. Zoroastrianism, like Buddhism, was an innovation in regard to an older religion; and between the Parsee and Brahmin may be found traces of disruption as well as of coincidence. The original Nature-worship, in which were combined the conceptions both of a Universal Presence and perpetuity of action, took different directions of development, according to the difference between the Indian and Persian mind.

The early shepherds of the Punjaub, then called the country of the Seven Rivers, to whose intuitional or inspired wisdom (Veda) we owe what are perhaps the most ancient religious effusions extant in any language, apostrophized as living beings the physical objects of their worship. First in this order of Deities stands Indra, the God of the "blue" or "glittering" firmament, called Devaspiti, Father of the Devas or Elemental Powers, who measured out the circle of the sky, and made fast the foundations of the Earth; the ideal domain of Varouna, "the All-encompasser," is almost equally extensive, including air, water, night, the expanse between Heaven and Earth; Agni, who lives on the fire of the sacrifice, on the domestic hearth, and in the lightnings of the sky, is the great Mediator between God and Man; Uschas, or the Dawn, leads forth the Gods in the morning to make their daily repast in the intoxicating Soma of Nature's offertory, of which the Priest could only compound from simples a symbolical imitation. Then came the various Sun-Gods, Adityas or Solar Attributes, Surya the Heavenly, Savitri the Progenitor, Pashan the Nourisher, Bagha the Felicitous, and Mitra the Friend.

The coming forth of the Eternal Being to the work of creation was represented as a marriage, his first emanation being a universal mother, supposed to have potentially existed with him from Eternity, or, in metaphorical language, to have been "his sister and his spouse." She became eventually promoted to be the Mother of the Indian Trinity, of the Deity under His three Attributes, of Creation, Preservation, and Change or Regeneration.

The most popular forms or manifestations of Vishnu the Preserver, were his successive avataras or historic impersonations.

which represented the Deity coming forth out of the incomprehensible mystery of His nature, and revealing Himself at those critical epochs which either in the physical or moral world seemed to mark a new commencement of prosperity and order. Combating the power of Evil in the various departments of Nature, and in successive periods of time, the Divinity, though varying in form, is ever in reality the same, whether seen in useful agricultural or social inventions, in traditional victories over rival creeds, or in physical changes faintly discovered through tradition, or suggested by cosmogonical theory. As Rama, the Epic hero armed with sword, club, and arrows, the prototype of Hercules and Mithras, he wrestles like the Hebrew Patriarch with the Powers of Darkness; as Chrishna-Govinda, the Divine Shepherd, he is the Messenger of Peace, overmastering the world by music and love. Under the human form he never ceases to be the Supreme Being. "The foolish" (he says, in Bhagavad Ghita), "unacquainted with my Supreme Nature, despise me in this human form, while men of great minds, enlightened by the Divine principle within them, acknowledge me as incorruptible and before all things, and serve me with undivided hearts." "I am not recognized by all," he says again, "because concealed by the supernatural power which is in me; yet to me are known all things past, present, and to come; I existed before Vaivaswata and Menou. I am the Most High God, the Creator of the World, the Eternal Poorooscha (Man-World or Genius of the World). And although in my own nature I am exempt from liability to birth or death, and am Lord of all created things, yet as often as in the world virtue is enfeebled, and vice and injustice prevail, so often do I become manifest and am revealed from age to age, to save the just, to destroy the guilty, and to reassure the faltering steps of virtue. He who acknowledgeth me as even so, doth not on quitting this mortal frame enter into another, for he entereth into me; and many who have trusted in me have already entered into me, being purified by the power of wisdom. I help those who walk in my path, even as they serve me."

Brahma, the creating agent, sacrificed himself, when, by descending into material forms, he became incorporated with his work; and his mythological history was interwoven with that of the Universe. Thus, although spiritually allied to the Supreme, and Lord of all creatures (Prajapati), he shared the imperfection and corruption of an inferior nature, and, steeped in manifold and perishable forms, might be said, like the Greek Uranus, to be mutilated and fallen. He thus combined two characters, formless form, immortal and mortal, being and non-being, motion and rest. As Incarnate Intelligence, or THE WORD, he communicated to man what had been revealed to himself by the Eternal, since he is creation's Soul as well as Body, within which the Divine Word is written in those living letters which it is the prerogative of the self-conscious spirit to interpret.

The fundamental principles of the religion of the Hindūs consisted in the belief in the existence of One Being only, of the immortality of the soul, and of a future state of rewards and punishments. Their precepts of morality inculcate the practice of virtue as necessary for procuring happiness even in this transient life; and their religious doctrines make their felicity in a future state to depend upon it.

Besides their doctrine of the transmigration of souls, their dogmas may be epitomized under the following heads: 1st. The existence of one God, from Whom all things proceed, and to Whom all must return. To him they constantly apply these expressions—The Universal and Eternal Essence; that which has ever been and will ever continue; that which vivifies and pervades all things; He who is everywhere present, and causes the celestial bodies to revolve in the course He has prescribed to them. 2d. A tripartite division of the Good Principle, for the purposes of Creation, Preservation, and Renovation by change and death. 3d. The necessary existence of an Evil Principle, occupied in counteracting the benevolent purposes of the first, in their execution by the Devata or Subordinate Genii, to whom is entrusted the control over the various operations of nature.

And this was part of their doctrine: "One great and incomprehensible Being has alone existed from all Eternity. Everything we behold and we ourselves are portions of Him. The soul, mind or intellect, of gods and men, and of all sentient creatures, are detached portions of the Universal Soul, to which at stated periods they are destined to return. But the mind of finite beings is impressed by one uninterrupted series of illusions, which they consider as real, until again united to the great fountain of truth. Of these illusions, the first and most essential is individuality. By its influence, when detached from its source, the soul becomes

ignorant of its own nature, origin, and destiny. It considers itself
as a separate existence, and no longer a spark of the Divinity, a
link of one immeasurable chain, an infinitely small but indispensable portion of one great whole."

Their love of imagery caused them to personify what they conceived to be some of the attributes of God, perhaps in order to
present things in a way better adapted to the comprehensions of
the vulgar, than the abstruse idea of an indescribable, invisible
God; and hence the invention of a Brahma, a Vishnu, and a Siva
or Iswara. These were represented under various forms; but no
emblem or visible sign of Brihm or Brehm, the Omnipotent, is to
be found. They considered the great mystery of the existence of
the Supreme Ruler of the Universe, as beyond human comprehension. Every creature endowed with the faculty of thinking,
they held, must be conscious of the existence of a God, a first
cause; but the attempt to explain the nature of that Being, or in
any way to assimilate it with our own, they considered not only a
proof of folly, but of extreme impiety.

The following extracts from their books will serve to show
what were the real tenets of their creed:

"By one Supreme Ruler is this Universe pervaded; even every
world in the whole circle of nature. . . . There is one Supreme
Spirit, which nothing can shake, more swift than the thought of
man. That Supreme Spirit moves at pleasure, but in itself is
immovable; it is distant from us, yet near us; it pervades this
whole system of worlds; yet it is infinitely beyond it. That man
who considers all beings as existing even in the Supreme Spirit,
and the Supreme Spirit as pervading all beings, henceforth views
no creature with contempt. . . . All spiritual beings are the same
in kind with the Supreme Spirit. . . . The pure enlightened soul
assumes a luminous form, with no gross body, with no perfora-
tion, with no veins or tendons, unblemished, untainted by sin;
itself being a ray from the Infinite Spirit, which knows the Past
and the Future, which pervades all, which existed with no cause
but itself, which created all things as they are, in ages most remote.
That all-pervading Spirit which gives light to the visible Sun,
even the same in *kind* am I, though infinitely distant in *degree*.
Let my soul return to the immortal Spirit of God, and then let
my body, which ends in ashes, return to dust! O Spirit, who per-
vadest fire, lead us in a straight path to the riches of beatitude.

Thou, O God, possessest all the treasures of knowledge! Remove each foul taint from our souls!

"From what root springs mortal man, when felled by the hand of death? Who can make him spring again to birth? God, who is perfect wisdom, perfect happiness. He is the final refuge of the man who has liberally bestowed his wealth, who has been firm in virtue, who knows and adores that Great One. . . . Let us adore the supremacy of that Divine Sun, the Godhead who illuminates all, who re-creates all, from whom all proceed, to whom all must return, whom we invoke to direct our understandings aright, in our progress toward his holy seat. . . . What the Sun and Light are to this visible world, such is truth to the intellectual and visible Universe. . . . Our souls acquire certain knowledge, by meditating on the light of Truth, which emanates from the Being of Beings. . . . That Being, without eyes sees, without ears hears all; he knows whatever can be known, but there is none who knows him; him the wise call the Great, Supreme, Pervading Spirit. . . . Perfect Truth, Perfect Happiness, without equal, immortal; absolute unity, whom neither speech can describe, nor mind comprehend: all-pervading, all-transcending, delighted with his own boundless intelligence, nor limited by space or time; without feet, running swiftly; without hands, grasping all worlds; without eyes, all-surveying; without ears, all-hearing; without an intelligent guide, understanding all; without cause, the first of all causes; all-ruling, all-powerful, the Creator, Preserver, Transformer of all things: such is the Great One; this the Vedas declare.

"May that soul of mine, which mounts aloft in my waking hours as an ethereal spark, and which, even in my slumber, has a like ascent, soaring to a great distance, as an emanation from the Light of Lights, be united by devout meditation with the Spirit supremely blest, and supremely intelligent! . . . . May that soul of mine, which was itself the primeval oblation placed within all creatures. . . . which is a ray of perfect wisdom, which is the inextinguishable light fixed within created bodies, without which no good act is performed. . . . in which as an immortal essence may be comprised whatever has passed, is present, or will be hereafter. . . . be united by devout meditation with the Spirit supremely blest and supremely intelligent!

"The Being of Beings is the Only God, eternal and everywhere present, Who comprises everything. There is no God but He. . . .

The Supreme Being is invisible, incomprehensible, immovable, without figure or shape. No one has ever seen Him; time never comprised Him; His essence pervades everything; all was derived from Him.

"The duty of a good man, even in the moment of his destruction, consists not only in forgiving, but even in a desire of benefiting his destroyer; as the sandal-tree, in the instant of its overthrow, sheds perfume on the axe which fells it."

The Vedanta and Nyaya philosophers acknowledge a Supreme Eternal Being, and the immortality of the soul: though, like the Greeks, they differ in their ideas of those subjects. They speak of the Supreme Being as an eternal essence that pervades space, and gives life or existence. Of that universal and eternal pervading spirit, the Vedanti suppose four modifications; but as these do not change its nature, and as it would be erroneous to ascribe to each of them a distinct essence, so it is equally erroneous, they say, to imagine that the various modifications by which the All-pervading Being exists, or displays His power, are individual existences. Creation is not considered as the instant production of things, but only as the manifestation of that which exists eternally in the one Universal Being. The Nyaya philosophers believe that spirit and matter are eternal; but they do not suppose that the world in its present form has existed from eternity, but only the primary matter from which it sprang when operated on by the almighty Word of God, the Intelligent Cause and Supreme Being, Who produced the combinations or aggregations which compose the material Universe. Though they believe that soul is an emanation from the Supreme Being, they distinguish it from that Being, in its individual existence. Truth and Intelligence are the eternal attributes of God, not, they say, of the individual soul, which is susceptible both of knowledge and ignorance, of pleasure and pain; and therefore God and it are distinct. Even when it returns to the Eternal, and attains supreme bliss, it undoubtedly does not cease. Though *united* to the Supreme Being, it is not *absorbed* in it, but still retains the abstract nature of definite or visible existence.

"The dissolution of the world," they say, "consists in the destruction of the visible forms and qualities of things; but their material essence remains, and from it new worlds are formed by the creative energy of God; and thus the Universe is dissolved and renewed in endless succession." ·

The Jainas, a sect at Mysore and elsewhere, say that the ancient religion of India and of the whole world consisted in the belief in one God, a pure Spirit, indivisible, omniscient and all-powerful; that God, having given to all things their appointed order and course of action, and to man a sufficient portion of reason, or understanding, to guide him in his conduct, leaves him to the operation of free will, without the entire exercise of which he could not be held answerable for his conduct.

Menou, the Hindū lawgiver, adored, not the visible, material Sun, but "that divine and incomparably greater light," to use the words of the most venerable text in the Indian Scripture, "which illumines all, delights all, from which all proceed, to which all must return, and which alone can irradiate our intellects." He thus commences his Institutes:

"Be it heard!

"This Universe existed only in the first divine idea yet unexpanded, as if involved in darkness, imperceptible, undefinable, undiscoverable by reason, and undiscovered by revelation, as if it were wholly immersed in sleep:

"Then the Sole Self-existing Power, Himself undiscovered, but making this world discernible, with five elements, and other principles of nature, appeared with undiminished glory, *expanding His idea,* or dispelling the gloom.

"He Whom the mind alone can perceive, whose essence eludes the eternal organs, who has no visible parts, who exists from Eternity, even He, the soul of all beings, Whom no being can comprehend, shone forth.

"He, having willed to produce various beings from His own divine Substance, first with a thought created the waters.... From *that which is* [precisely the Hebrew יהוה], the first cause, not the object of sense, existing everywhere in substance, not existing to our perception, without beginning or end" [the A∴ and Ω∴, or the I∴ A∴ Ω∴], "was produced the divine male famed in all worlds under the appellation of Brahma."

Then recapitulating the different things created by Brahma, he adds: "He," meaning Brahma [the Λογος, the WORD], "whose powers are incomprehensible, having thus created this Universe, was again absorbed in the Supreme Spirit, changing the time of energy for the time of repose."

The *Antareya A'ran'ya,* one of the Vedas, gives this primitive idea of the creation: "In the beginning, the Universe was but a Soul: nothing else, active or inactive, existed. Then HE had this thought, *I will create worlds;* and thus HE created these different worlds; air, the light, mortal beings, and the waters.

"HE had this thought: *Behold the worlds; I will create guardians for the worlds.* So HE took of the water and fashioned a being clothed with the human form. He looked upon him, and of that being so contemplated, the mouth opened like an egg, and speech came forth, and from the speech fire. The nostrils opened, and through them went the breath of respiration, and by it the air was propagated. The eyes opened; from them came a luminous ray, and from it was produced the sun. The ears dilated; from them came hearing, and from hearing space:" . . . and, after the body of man, with the senses, was formed;—"HE, the Universal Soul, thus reflected: *How can this body exist without Me?* He examined through what extremity He could penetrate it. He said to Himself: If, *without Me, the World is articulated, breath exhales, and sight sees; if hearing hears, the skin feels, and the mind reflects, deglutition swallows, and the generative organ fulfils its functions, what then am I?* And separating the suture of the cranium, He penetrated into man."

Behold the great fundamental primitive truths! God, an infinite Eternal Soul or Spirit. Matter, not eternal nor self-existent, but created—created by a thought of God. After matter, and worlds, then man, by a like thought: and finally, after endowing him with the senses and a thinking mind, a portion, a spark, of God Himself penetrates the man, and becomes a living spirit within him.

The Vedas thus detail the creation of the world:

"In the beginning there was a single God, existing of Himself; Who, after having passed an eternity absorbed in the contemplation of His own being, desired to manifest His perfections outwardly of Himself; and created the matter of the world. The four elements being thus produced, but still mingled in confusion, He breathed upon the waters, which swelled up into an immense ball in the shape of an egg, and, developing themselves, became the vault and orb of Heaven which encircles the earth. Having made the earth and the bodies of animal beings, this God, the essence of movement, gave to them, to animate them, a portion of His own being. Thus, the soul of everything that breathes being a fraction of the universal soul, none perishes; but each soul merely changes its mould and form, by passing successively into different bodies. Of all forms, that which most pleases the Divine Being is Man, as nearest approaching His own perfections. When a man, absolutely disengaging himself from his senses, absorbs himself in self-contemplation, he comes to discern the Divinity, and becomes part of Him."

The Ancient Persians in many respects resembled the Hindūs,—in their language, their poetry, and their poetic legends. Their conquests brought them in contact with China; and they subdued Egypt and Judea. Their views of God and religion more resembled those of the Hebrews than those of any other nation; and indeed the latter people borrowed from them some prominent doctrines, that we are in the habit of regarding as an essential part of the original Hebrew creed.

Of the King of Heaven and Father of Eternal Light, of the pure World of LIGHT, of the Eternal WORD by which all things were created, of the Seven Mighty Spirits that stand next to the Throne of Light and Omnipotence, and of the glory of those Heavenly Hosts that encompass that Throne, of the Origin of Evil, and the Prince of Darkness, Monarch of the rebellious spirits, enemies of all good, they entertained tenets very similar to those of the Hebrews. Toward Egyptian idolatry they felt the strongest abhorrence, and under Cambyses pursued a regular plan for its utter extirpation. Xerxes, when he invaded Greece, destroyed the Temples and erected fire-chapels along the whole course of his march. Their religion was eminently spiritual, and the earthly fire and earthly sacrifice were but the signs and emblems of another devotion and a higher power.

Thus the fundamental doctrine of the ancient religion of India and Persia was at first nothing more than a simple veneration of nature, its pure elements and its primary energies, the sacred fire, and above all, Light,—the air, not the lower atmospheric air, but the purer and brighter air of Heaven, the breath that animates and pervades the breath of mortal life. This pure and simple veneration of nature is perhaps the most ancient, and was by far the most generally prevalent in the primitive and patriarchal world. It was not originally a deification of nature, or a denial of the sovereignty of God. Those pure elements and primitive essences of created nature offered to the first men, still in a close communication with the Deity, not a likeness of resemblance, nor a mere fanciful image or a poetical figure, but a natural and true symbol of Divine power. Everywhere in the Hebrew writings the pure light or sacred fire is employed as an image of the all-pervading and all-consuming power and omnipresence of the Divinity. His breath was the first source of life; and the faint whisper of the breeze announced to the prophet His immediate presence.

"All things are the progeny of one fire. The Father perfected all things, and delivered them over to the Second Mind, whom all nations of men call the First. Natural works co-exist with the intellectual light of the Father; for it is the Soul which adorns the great Heaven, and which adorns it after the Father. The Soul, being a bright fire, by the power of the Father, remains immortal, and is mistress of life, and fills up the recesses of the world. For the fire which is first beyond, did not shut up his power in matter by works, but by mind, for the framer of the fiery world is the mind of mind, who first sprang from mind, clothing fire with fire. Father-begotten Light! for He alone, having from the Father's power received the essence of intellect, is enabled to understand the mind of the Father; and to instill into all sources and principles the capacity of understanding, and of ever continuing in ceaseless revolving motion." Such was the language of Zoroaster, embodying the old Persian ideas.

And the same ancient sage thus spoke of the Sun and Stars: "The Father made the whole Universe of fire and water and earth, and all-nourishing ether. He fixed a great multitude of moveless stars, that stand still forever, not by compulsion and unwillingly, but without desire to wander, fire acting upon fire. He congregated the seven firmaments of the world, and so surrounded the earth with the convexity of the Heavens; and therein set seven living existences, arranging their apparent disorder in regular orbits, six of them planets, and the Sun, placed in the centre, the seventh;—in that centre from which all lines, diverging which way soever, are equal; and the swift sun himself, revolving around a principal centre, and ever striving to reach the central and all-pervading light, bearing with him the bright Moon."

And yet Zoroaster added: "Measure not the journeyings of the Sun, nor attempt to reduce them to rule; for he is carried by the eternal will of the Father, not for your sake. Do not endeavor to understand the impetuous course of the Moon; for she runs evermore under the impulse of necessity; and the progression of the Stars was not generated to serve any purpose of yours."

Ormuzd says to Zoroaster, in the Boundehesch: "I am he who holds the Star-Spangled Heaven in ethereal space; who makes this sphere, which once was buried in darkness, a flood of light. Through me the Earth became a world firm and lasting—the earth on which walks the Lord of the world. I am he who makes the light of Sun, Moon, and Stars pierce the clouds. I make the corn seed, which perishing in the ground sprouts anew. . . . I created man, whose eye is light, whose life is the breath of his nostrils. I placed within him life's unextinguishable power."

Ormuzd or Ahura-Mazda himself represented the primal light, distinct from the heavenly bodies, yet necessary to their existence, and the source of their splendor. The Amschaspands (Ameschaspenta, "immortal Holy Ones"), each presided over a special department of nature. Earth and Heaven, fire and water, the Sun and Moon, the rivers, trees, and mountains, even the artificial divisions of the day and year were addressed in prayer as tenanted by Divine beings, each separately ruling within his several sphere. Fire, in particular, that "most energetic of immortal powers," the visible representative of the primal light, was invoked as "Son of Ormuzd." The Sun, the Archimagus, that noblest and most powerful agent of divine power, who "steps forth as a Conqueror from the top of the terrible Alborj to rule over the world which he enlightens from the throne of Ormuzd," was worshipped among other symbols by the name of MITHRAS, a beneficent and friendly genius, who, in the hymn addressed to him in the Zend-Avesta, bears the names given him by the Greeks, as the "Invincible" and the "Mediator"; the former, because in his daily strife with darkness he is the most active confederate of Ormuzd; the latter, as being the medium through which Heaven's choicest blessings are communicated to men. He is called "the eye of Ormuzd, the effulgent Hero, pursuing his course triumphantly, fertilizer of deserts, most exalted of the Izeds or Yezatas, the never-sleeping, the protector of the land." "When the dragon foe devastates my provinces," says Ormuzd, "and afflicts them with famine, then is he struck down by the strong arm of Mithras, together with the Devs of Mazanderan. With his lance and his immortal club, the Sleepless Chief hurls down the Devs into the dust, when as Mediator he interposes to guard the City from evil."

Ahriman was by some Parsee sects considered older than Ormuzd, as darkness is older than light; he is imagined to have been unknown as a Malevolent Being in the early ages of the world, and the fall of man is attributed in the Boundehesch to an apostate worship of him, from which men were converted by a succession of prophets terminating with Zoroaster.

Mithras is not only light, but intelligence; that luminary which, though born in obscurity, will not only dispel darkness but conquer death. The warfare through which this consummation is to be reached, is mainly carried on through the instrumentality of the "Word," that "ever-living emanation of the Deity, by virtue of which the world exists," and of which the revealed formulas incessantly repeated in the liturgies of the Magi are but the expression. "What shall I do," cried Zoroaster, "O Ormuzd, steeped in brightness, in order to battle with Daroodj-Ahriman, father of the Evil Law; how shall I make men pure and holy?" Ormuzd answered and said: "Invoke, O Zoroaster, the pure law of the Servants of Ormuzd; invoke the Amschaspands who shed abundance throughout the seven Keshwars; invoke the Heaven, Zeruana-Akarana, the birds travailing on high, the swift wind, the Earth; invoke my Spirit, me who am Ahura-Mazda, the purest, strongest, wisest, best of beings; me who have the most majestic body, who through purity am Supreme, whose Soul is the Excellent Word; and ye, all people, invoke me as I have commanded Zoroaster."

Ahura-Mazda himself is the living WORD; he is called "Firstborn of all things, express image of the Eternal, very light of very light, the Creator, who by power of the Word which he never ceases to pronounce, made in 365 days the Heaven and the Earth." The Word is said in the Yashna to have existed before all, and to be itself a Yazata, a personified object of prayer. It was revealed in Serosch, in Homa, and again, under Gushtasp, was manifested in Zoroaster.

Between life and death, between sunshine and shade, Mithras is the present exemplification of the Primal Unity from which all things arose, and into which, through his mediation, all contrarieties will ultimately be absorbed. His annual sacrifice is the passover of the Magi, a symbolical atonement or pledge of moral and physical regeneration. He created the world in the beginning; and as at the close of each successive year he sets free the current of life to invigorate a fresh circle of being, so in the

end of all things he will bring the weary sum of ages as a heca-
tomb before God, releasing by a final sacrifice the Soul of Nature
from her perishable frame, to commence a brighter and purer
existence.

Iamblichus (*De Mys.* viii. 4) says: "The Egyptians are far from
ascribing all things to physical causes; life and intellect they
distinguish from physical being, both in man and in the Universe.
They place intellect and reason first as self-existent, and from these
they derive the created world. As Parent of generated things
they constitute a Demiurge, and acknowledge a vital force both in
the Heavens and before the Heavens. They place Pure Intellect
above and beyond the Universe, and another (that is, Mind revealed in the Material World), consisting of one continuous mind
pervading the Universe, and apportioned to all its parts and
spheres." The Egyptian idea, then, was that of all transcendental
philosophy—that of a Deity both immanent and transcendent—
spirit passing into its manifestations, but not exhausted by so
doing.

The wisdom recorded in the canonical rolls of Hermes quickly
attained in this transcendental lore, all that human curiosity can
ever discover. Thebes especially is said to have acknowledged a
being without beginning or end, called Amun or Amun-Kneph,
the all-prevading Spirit or Breath of Nature, or perhaps even some
still more lofty object of reverential reflection, whom it was
forbidden even to name. Such a being would in theory stand at
the head of the three orders of Gods mentioned by Herodotus,
these being regarded as arbitrary classifications of similar or equal
beings, arranged in successive emanations, according to an estimate of their comparative dignity. The Eight Great Gods, or
primary class, were probably manifestations of the emanated God
in the several parts and powers of the Universe, each potentially
comprising the whole Godhead.

In the ancient Hermetic books, as quoted by Iamblichus, occurred the following passage in regard to the Supreme Being:—

"Before all the things that actually exist, and before all beginnings, there is one God, prior even to the first God and King,
remaining unmoved in the singleness of his own Unity: for neither
is anything conceived by intellect inwoven with him, nor anything
else; but he is established as the exemplar of the God who is
good, who is his own father, self-begotten, and has only one

Parent. For he is something greater and prior to, and the fountain of all things, and the foundation of things conceived by the intellect, which are the first species. And from this ONE, the self-originated God caused himself to shine forth; for which reason he is his own father, and self-originated. For he is both a beginning and God of Gods, a Monad from the One, prior to substance and the beginning of substance; for from him is substantiality and substance, whence also he is called the beginning of things conceived by the intellect. These then are the most ancient beginnings of all things, which Hermes places before the ethereal and empyrean and celestial Gods."

"CHANG-TI, or the Supreme Lord or Being," said the old Chinese creed, "is the principle of everything that exists, and Father of all living. He is eternal, immovable, and independent: His power knows no bounds: His sight equally comprehends the Past, the Present, and the Future, and penetrates even to the inmost recesses of the heart. Heaven and earth are under his government: all events, all revolutions, are the consequences of his dispensation and will. He is pure, holy, and impartial; wickedness offends his sight; but he beholds with an eye of complacency the virtuous actions of men. Severe, yet just, he punishes vice in an exemplary manner, even in Princes and Rulers; and often casts down the guilty, to crown with honor the man who walks after his own heart, and whom he raises from obscurity. Good, merciful, and full of pity, he forgives the wicked upon their repentance: and public calamities and the irregularity of the seasons are but salutary warnings, which his fatherly goodness gives to men, to induce them to reform and amend."

Controlled by reason infinitely more than by the imagination, that people, occupying the extreme East of Asia, did not fall into idolatry until after the time of Confucius, and within two centuries of the birth of Christ; when the religion of BUDDHA or Fo was carried thither from India. Their system was long regulated by the pure worship of God, and the foundation of their moral and political existence laid in a sound, upright reason, conformable to true ideas of the Deity. They had no false gods or images, and their third Emperor *Hoam-ti* erected a Temple, the first probably ever erected, to the Great Architect of the Universe. And though they offered sacrifices to divers tutelary angels, yet they honored them infinitely less than XAM-TI or CHANG-TI, the Sovereign Lord of the World.

Confucius forbade making images or representations of the Deity. He attached no idea of personality to Him; but considered Him as a Power or Principle, pervading all Nature. And the Chinese designated the Divinity by the name of THE DIVINE REASON.

The Japanese believe in a Supreme Invisible Being, not to be represented by images or worshipped in Temples. They styled him AMIDA or OMITH; and say that he is without beginning or end; that he came on earth, where he remained a thousand years, and became the Redeemer of our fallen race: that he is to judge all men; and the good are to live forever, while the bad are to be condemned to Hell.

"The Chang-ti is represented," said Confucius, "under the general emblem of the visible firmament, as well as under the particular symbols of the Sun, the Moon, and the Earth, because by their means we enjoy the gifts of the Chang-ti. The Sun is the source of life and light: the Moon illuminates the world by night. By observing the course of these luminaries, mankind are enabled to distinguish times and seasons. The Ancients, with the view of connecting the act with its object, when they established the practice of sacrificing to the Chang-ti, fixed the day of the Winter Solstice, because the Sun, after having passed through the twelve places assigned apparently by the Chang-ti as its annual residence, began its career anew, to distribute blessings throughout the Earth."

He said: "The TEEN is the universal principle and prolific source of all things. . . . The Chang-ti is the universal principle of existence."

The Arabians never possessed a poetical, high-wrought, and scientifically arranged system of Polytheism. Their historical traditions had much analogy with those of the Hebrews, and coincided with them in a variety of points. The tradition of a purer faith and the simple Patriarchal worship of the Deity, appear never to have been totally extinguished among them; nor did idolatry gain much foothold until near the time of Mahomet; who, adopting the old primeval faith, taught again the doctrine of one God, adding to it that he was His Prophet.

To the mass of Hebrews, as well as to other nations, seem to have come fragments only of the primitive revelation: nor do they seem, until after their captivity among the Persians, to have concerned themselves about metaphysical speculations in regard to the Divine Nature and essence; although it is evident, from the Psalms of David, that a select body among them preserved a knowledge, in regard to the Deity, which was wholly unknown to the mass of the people; and those chosen few were made the medium of transition for certain truths, to later ages.

Among the Greeks, the scholars of the Egyptians, all the higher ideas and severer doctrines on the Divinity, his Sovereign Nature and Infinite Might, the Eternal Wisdom and Providence that conducts and directs all things to their proper end, the Infinite Mind and Supreme Intelligence that created all things, and is raised far above external nature,—all these loftier ideas and nobler doctrines were expounded more or less perfectly by Pythagoras, Anaxagoras, and Socrates, and developed in the most beautiful and luminous manner by Plato, and the philosophers that succeeded him. And even in the popular religion of the Greeks are many things capable of a deeper import and more spiritual signification; though they seem only rare vestiges of ancient truth, vague presentiments, fugitive tones, and momentary flashes, revealing a belief in a Supreme Being, Almighty Creator of the Universe, and Common Father of Mankind.

Much of the primitive Truth was taught to Pythagoras by Zoroaster, who himself received it from the Indians. His disciples rejected the use of Temples, of Altars, and of Statues; and smiled at the folly of those nations who imagined that the Deity sprang from or had any affinity with human nature. The tops of the highest mountains were the places chosen for sacrifices. Hymns and prayers were their principal worship. The Supreme God, who fills the wide circle of Heaven, was the object to Whom they were addressed. Such is the testimony of Herodotus. Light they considered not so much as an object of worship, as rather the most pure and lively emblem of, and first emanation from, the Eternal God; and thought that man required something visible or tangible to exalt his mind to that degree of adoration which is due to the Divine Being.

There was a surprising similarity between the Temples, Priests, doctrines, and worship of the Persian Magi and the British Druids. The latter did not worship idols in the human shape, because they held that the Divinity, being invisible, ought to be adored without being seen. They asserted the Unity of the Godhead. Their invocations were made to the One All-preserving Power; and they argued that, as this power was not matter, it must necessarily be the Deity; and the secret symbol used to express his name was O. I. W. They believed that the earth had sustained one general destruction by water; and would again be destroyed by fire. They admitted the doctrines of the immortality of the soul, a future state, and a day of judgment, which would be conducted on the principle of man's responsibility. They even retained some idea of the redemption of mankind through the death of a Mediator. They retained a tradition of the Deluge, perverted and localized. But, around these fragments of primitive truth they wove a web of idolatry, worshipped two Subordinate Deities under the names of Hu and Ceridwen, male and female (doubtless the same as Osiris and Isis), and held the doctrine of transmigration.

The early inhabitants of Scandinavia believed in a God who was "the Author of everything that existeth; the Eternal, the Ancient, the Living and Awful Being, the Searcher into concealed things, the Being that never changeth." Idols and visible representations of the Deity were originally forbidden, and He was directed to be worshipped in the lonely solitude of sequestered forests, where He was said to dwell, invisible, and in perfect silence.

The Druids, like their Eastern ancestors, paid the most sacred regard to the odd numbers, which, traced backward, ended in Unity or Deity, while the even numbers ended in nothing. 3 was particularly reverenced. $19 (7+3+3^2)$: $30 (7\times3+3\times3)$: and $21 (7\times3)$ were numbers observed in the erection of their temples, constantly appearing in their dimensions, and the number and distances of the huge stones.

They were the sole interpreters of religion. They superintended all sacrifices; for no private person could offer one without their permission. They exercised the power of excommunication; and without their concurrence war could not be declared nor peace made: and they even had the power of inflicting the punishment of death. They professed to possess a knowledge of magic, and practised augury for the public service.

They cultivated many of the liberal sciences, and particularly astronomy, the favorite science of the Orient; in which they attained considerable proficiency. They considered day as the off-spring of night, and therefore made their computations by nights instead of days; and we, from them, still use the words fortnight and sen'night. They knew the division of the heavens into con-stellations; and finally, they practised the strictest morality, having particularly the most sacred regard for that peculiarly Masonic virtue, Truth.

In the Icelandic Prose Edda is the following dialogue:

"Who is the first or eldest of the Gods?

"In our language he is called ALFADIR (All-Father, or the Father of All) ; but in the old Asgard he had twelve names.

"Where is this God? What is his power? and what hath he done to display his glory?

"He liveth from all ages, he governeth all realms, and swayeth all things both great and small.

"He hath formed Heaven and earth, and the air, and all things thereunto belonging.

"He hath made man and given him a soul which shall live and never perish, though the body shall have mouldered away or have been burnt to ashes. And all that are righteous shall dwell with him in the place called *Gimli* or *Vingolf;* but the wicked shall go to *Hel* and thence to *Niflhel* which is below, in the ninth world."

Almost every heathen nation, so far as we have any knowledge of their mythology, believed in one Supreme Overruling God, whose name it was not lawful to utter.

"When we ascend," says Müller, to the most distant heights of Greek history, the idea of God as the Supreme Being stands before us as a simple fact. Next to this adoration of One God, the Father of Heaven, the Father of men, we find in Greece a Worship of Nature." The original Ζεὺς was the God or Gods, called by the Greeks the Son of Time, meaning that there was no God before Him, but He was Eternal. "Zeus," says the Orphic line, "is the Beginning, Zeus the Middle; out of Zeus all things have been made." And the Peleides of Dodona said, "Zeus was, Zeus is, Zeus will be; O great Zeus!" Ζεὺς νῆ, Ζεὺς ἐστὶν, Ζεὺς ἐσσε-ται· ὦ μεγάλη Ζεῦ: and he was Ζεὺς, κύδιστος, μέγιστος, Zeus, Best and Greatest.

The Parsees, retaining the old religion taught by Zaradisht, say in their catechism: "We believe in only one God, and do not believe in any beside Him; Who created the Heavens, the Earth, the Angels. . . . Our God has neither face nor form, color nor shape, nor fixed place. There is no other like Him, nor can our mind comprehend Him."

The Tetragrammaton, *or some other word covered by it,* was forbidden to be pronounced. But that its pronunciation might not be lost among the Levites, the High-Priest uttered it in the Temple once a year, on the 10th day of the Month Tisri, the day of the great feast of expiation. During this ceremony, the people were directed to make a great noise, that the Sacred Word might not be heard by any who had not a right to it; for every other, said the Jews, would be incontinently stricken dead.

The Great Egyptian Initiates, before the time of the Jews, did the same thing in regard to the word Isis; which they regarded as sacred and incommunicable.

Origen says: "There are names which have a natural potency. Such as those which the Sages used among the Egyptians, the Magi in Persia, the Brahmins in India. What is called Magic is not a vain and chimerical act, as the Stoics and Epicureans pretend. The names SABAOTH and ADONAI were not made for created beings; but they belong to a mysterious theology, which goes back to the Creator. From Him comes the virtue of these names, when they are arranged and pronounced according to the rules."

The Hindū word AUM represented the three Powers combined in their Deity: Brahma, Vishnu, and Siva; or the Creating, Preserving, and Destroying Powers: A, the first; U or Ŏ-Ŏ, the, second; and M, the third. This word could not be pronounced, except by the letters: for its pronunciation as one word was said to make Earth tremble, and even the Angels of Heaven to quake for fear.

The word AUM, says the Ramayan, represents "The Being of Beings, One Substance in three forms; without mode, without quality, without passion: Immense, Incomprehensible, Infinite, Indivisible, Immutable, Incorporeal, Irresistible."

An old passage in the Purana says: "All the rites ordained in the Vedas, the sacrifices to the fire, and all other solemn purifications, shall pass away; but that which shall never pass away is the word A∴Ŏ-Ŏ∴M∴ for it is the symbol of the Lord of all things."

Herodotus says that the Ancient Pelasgi built no temples and worshipped no idols, and had a sacred name of Deity, which it was not permissible to pronounce.

The Clarian Oracle, which was of unknown antiquity, being asked which of the Deities was named IAΩ, answered in these remarkable words: "The Initiated are bound to conceal the mysterious secrets. Learn, then, that IAΩ is the Great God Supreme, that ruleth over all."

The Jews consider the True Name of God to be irrecoverably lost by disuse, and regard its pronunciation as one of the Mysteries that will be revealed at the coming of their Messiah. And they attribute its loss to the illegality of applying the Masoretic points to so sacred a Name, by which a knowledge of the proper vowels is forgotten. It is even said, in the Gemara of Abodah Zara, that God permitted a celebrated Hebrew Scholar to be burned by a Roman Emperor, because he had been heard to pronounce the Sacred Name with points.

The Jews feared that the Heathen would get possession of the Name: and therefore, in their copies of the Scriptures, they wrote it in the Samaritan character, instead of the Hebrew or Chaldaic, that the adversary might not make an improper use of it: for they believed it capable of working miracles; and held that the wonders in Egypt were performed by Moses, in virtue of this name being engraved on his rod: and that any person who knew the true pronunciation would be able to do as much as he did.

Josephus says it was unknown until God communicated it to Moses in the wilderness: and that it was lost through the wickedness of man.

The followers of Mahomet have a tradition that there is a secret name of the Deity which possesses wonderful properties; and that the only method of becoming acquainted with it, is by being initiated into the Mysteries of the *Ism Abla*.

H∴O∴M∴ was the first framer of the new religion among the Persians, and His Name was Ineffable.

AMUN, among the Egyptians, was a name pronounceable by none save the Priests.

The old Germans adored God with profound reverence, without daring to name Him, or to worship Him in Temples.

The Druids expressed the name of Deity by the letters O.·.I.·.
W.·.

Among all the nations of primitive antiquity, the doctrine of the
immortality of the soul was not a mere probable hypothesis, needing laborious researches and diffuse argumentation to produce
conviction of its truth. Nor can we hardly give it the name of
Faith; for it was a lively *certainty,* like the feeling of one's own
existence and identity, and of what is actually present; exerting
its influence on all sublunary affairs, and the motive of mightier
deeds and enterprises than any mere earthly interest could inspire.

Even the doctrine of transmigration of souls, universal among
the Ancient Hindūs and Egyptians, rested on a basis of the old
primitive religion, and was connected with a sentiment purely
religious. It involved this noble element of truth: That since
man had gone astray, and wandered far from God, he must needs
make many efforts, and undergo a long and painful pilgrimage,
before he could rejoin the Source of all Perfection: and the firm
conviction and positive certainty, that nothing defective, impure,
or defiled with earthy stains, could enter the pure region of perfect spirits, or be eternally united to God; wherefore the soul had
to pass through long trials and many purifications before it could
attain that blissful end. And the end and aim of all these systems
of philosophy was the final deliverance of the soul from the old
calamity, the dreaded fate and frightful lot of being compelled to
wander through the dark regions of nature and the various forms
of the brute creation, ever changing its terrestrial shape, and its
union with God, which they held to be the lofty destiny of the
wise and virtuous soul.

Pythagoras gave to the doctrine of the transmigration of souls
that meaning which the wise Egyptians gave to it in their Mysteries. He never taught the doctrine in that literal sense in which
it was understood by the people. Of that literal doctrine not the
least vestige is to be found in such of his symbols as remain, nor
in his precepts collected by his disciple Lysias. He held that men
always remain, in their essence, such as they were created; and
can degrade themselves only by vice, and ennoble themselves only
by virtue.

Hierocles, one of his most zealous and celebrated disciples,
expressly says that he who believes that the soul of man, after his
death, will enter the body of a beast, for his vices, or become a

plant for his stupidity, is deceived; and is absolutely ignorant of the eternal form of the soul, which can never change; for, always remaining man, it is said to become God or beast, through virtue or vice, though it can become neither one nor the other by nature, but solely by resemblance of its inclinations to theirs.

And Timæus of Locria, another disciple, says that to alarm men and prevent them from committing crimes, they menaced them with strange humiliations and punishments; even declaring that their souls would pass into new bodies,—that of a coward into the body of a deer; that of a ravisher into the body of a wolf; that of a murderer into the body of some still more ferocious animal; and that of an impure sensualist into the body of a hog.

So, too, the doctrine is explained in the Phædo. And Lysias says, that after the soul, purified of its crimes, has left the body and returned to Heaven, it is no longer subject to change or death, but enjoys an eternal felicity. According to the Indians, it returned to, and became a part of, the universal soul which animates everything.

The Hindūs held that Buddha descended on earth to raise all human beings up to the perfect state. He will ultimately succeed, and all, himself included, be merged in Unity.

Vishnu is to judge the world at the last day. It is to be consumed by fire: The Sun and Moon are to lose their light; the Stars to fall; and a New Heaven and Earth to be created.

The legend of the fall of the Spirits, obscured and distorted, is preserved in the Hindū Mythology. And their traditions acknowledged, and they revered, the succession of the first ancestors of mankind, or the Holy Patriarchs of the primitive world, under the name of the Seven Great RISHIS, or Sages of hoary antiquity; though they invested their history with a cloud of fictions.

The Egyptians held that the soul was immortal; and that Osiris was to judge the world.

And thus reads the Persian legend:

"After Ahriman shall have ruled the world until the end of time, SOSIOSCH, the promised Redeemer, will come and annihilate the power of the DEVS (or Evil Spirits), awaken the dead, and sit in final judgment upon spirits and men. After that the comet *Gurzsher* will be thrown down, and a general conflagration take place, which will consume the whole world. The remains of the earth will then sink down into *Duzakh,* and become for three periods a place of punishment for the wicked. Then, by degrees, all will be pardoned, even *Ahriman* and the *Devs,* and admitted to the regions of bliss, and thus there will be a new Heaven and a new earth."

In the doctrines of Lamaism also, we find, obscured, and partly concealed in fiction, fragments of the primitive truth. For, according to that faith, "There is to be a final judgment before ESLIK KHAN: The good are to be admitted to Paradise, the bad to be banished to hell, where there are eight regions burning hot and eight freezing cold."

In the Mysteries, wherever they were practised, was taught that truth of the primitive revelation, the existence of One Great Being, Infinite and pervading the Universe, Who was there worshipped without superstition; and His marvellous nature, essence, and attributes taught to the Initiates; while the vulgar attributed His works to Secondary Gods, personified, and isolated from Him in fabulous independence.

These truths were covered from the common people as with a veil; and the Mysteries were carried into every country, that, without disturbing the popular beliefs, truth, the arts, and the sciences might be known to those who were capable of understanding them, and maintaining the true doctrine incorrupt; which the people, prone to superstition and idolatry, have in no age been able to do; nor, as many strange aberrations and superstitions of the present day prove, any more now than heretofore. For we need but point to the doctrines of so many sects that degrade the Creator to the rank, and assign to Him the passions of humanity, to prove that now, as always, the old truths must be committed to a few, or they will be overlaid with fiction and error, and irretrievably lost.

Though Masonry is identical with the Ancient Mysteries, it is so in this qualified sense; that it presents but an imperfect image of their brilliancy; the ruins only of their grandeur, and a system that has experienced progressive alterations, the fruits of social events and political circumstances. Upon leaving Egypt, the Mysteries were modified by the habits of the different nations among whom they were introduced. Though originally more moral and political than religious, they soon became the heritage, as it were, of the priests, and essentially religious, though in reality limiting the sacerdotal power, by teaching the intelligent laity the folly and absurdity of the creeds of the populace. They were therefore necessarily changed by the religious systems of the countries into which they were transplanted. In Greece, they were the Mysteries of Ceres; in Rome, of *Bona Dea,* the Good Goddess; in Gaul, the School of Mars; in Sicily, the Academy of the Sciences; among the Hebrews, they partook of the rites and ceremonies of a religion which placed all the powers of government, and all the knowledge, in the hands of the Priests and Levites. The pagodas of India, the retreats of the Magi of Persia and Chaldea, and the pyramids of Egypt, were no longer the sources at which men drank in knowledge. Each people, at all informed, had its Mysteries. After a time the Temples of Greece and the School of Pythagoras lost their reputation, and Freemasonry took their place.

Masonry, when properly expounded, is at once the interpretation of the great book of nature, the recital of physical and astronomical phenomena, the purest philosophy, and the place of deposit, where, as in a Treasury, are kept in safety all the great truths of the primitive revelation, that form the basis of all religions. In the modern Degrees three things are to be recognized: The image of primeval times, the tableau of the efficient causes of the Universe, and the book in which are written the morality of all peoples, and the code by which they must govern themselves if they would be prosperous.

The Kabalistic doctrine was long the religion of the Sage and the Savant; because, like Freemasonry, it incessantly tends toward spiritual perfection, and the fusion of the creeds and Nationalities of Mankind. In the eyes of the Kabalist, all men are his brothers; and their relative ignorance is, to him, but a reason for instructing them. There were illustrious Kabalists among the Egyptians and Greeks, whose doctrines the Orthodox Church has accepted; and among the Arabs were many, whose wisdom was not slighted by the Mediæval Church.

The Sages proudly wore the name of Kabalists. The Kabalah embodied a noble philosophy, pure, not mysterious, but symbolic. It taught the doctrine of the Unity of God, the art of knowing and explaining the essence and operations of the Supreme Being, of spiritual powers and natural forces, and of determining their action by symbolic figures; by the arrangement of the alphabet,

the combinations of numbers, the inversion of letters in writing
and the concealed meanings which they claimed to discover therein. The Kabalah is the key of the occult sciences; and the Gnostics
were born of the Kabalists.

The science of numbers represented not only arithmetical qualities, but also all grandeur, all proportion. By it we necessarily
arrive at the discovery of the Principle or First Cause of things,
called at the present day THE ABSOLUTE.

Or UNITY,—that loftiest term to which all philosophy directs
itself; that imperious necessity of the human mind, that pivot
round which it is compelled to group the aggregate of its ideas:
Unity, this source, this centre of all systematic order, this principle of existence, this central point, unknown in its essence, but
manifest in its effects; Unity, that sublime centre to which the
chain of causes necessarily ascends, was the august Idea toward
which all the ideas of Pythagoras converged. He refused the title
of *Sage,* which means *one who knows.* He invented, and applied
to himself that of *Philosopher,* signifying one who *is fond of* or
studies things secret and occult. The astronomy which he mysteriously taught, was *astrology:* his science of numbers was based
on Kabalistical principles.

The Ancients, and Pythagoras himself, whose real principles
have not been always understood, never meant to ascribe to numbers, that is to say, to abstract signs, any special virtue. But the
Sages of Antiquity concurred in recognizing a ONE FIRST CAUSE
(material or spiritual) of the existence of the Universe. Thence,
UNITY became the symbol of the Supreme Deity. It was made to
express, to represent God; but without attributing to *the mere
number* ONE any divine or supernatural virtue.

The Pythagorean ideas as to particular numbers are partially
expressed in the following

LECTURE OF THE KABALISTS.

Qu.·. Why did you seek to be received a Knight of the Kabalah?

Ans.·. To know, by means of numbers, the admirable harmony
which there is between nature and religion.

Qu.·. How were you announced?

Ans.·. By twelve raps.

Qu.·. What do they signify?

Ans∴ The twelve bases of our temporal and spiritual happiness.

Qu∴ What is a Kabalist?

Ans∴ A man who has learned, by tradition, the Sacerdotal Art and the Royal Art.

Qu∴ What means the device, *Omnia in numeris sita sunt?*

Ans∴ That everything lies veiled in numbers.

Qu∴ Explain me that.

Ans∴ I will do so, as far as the number 12. Your sagacity will discern the rest.

Qu∴ What signifies the *unit* in the number 10?

Ans∴ GOD, creating and animating matter, expressed by 0, which, alone, is of no value.

Qu∴ What does the unit *mean?*

Ans∴ In the moral order, a Word incarnate in the bosom of a virgin—or religion. . . . In the physical, a spirit embodied in the virgin earth—or nature.

Qu∴ What do you mean by the number *two?*

Ans∴ In the moral order, *man* and *woman*. . . . In the physical, the *active* and the *passive*.

Qu∴ What do you mean by the number 3?

Ans∴ In the moral order, the three theological virtues. . . . In the physical, the three principles of bodies.

Qu∴ What do you mean by the number 4?

Ans∴ The four cardinal virtues. . . . The four elementary qualities.

Qu∴ What do you mean by the number 5?

Ans∴ The quintessence of religion. . . . The quintessence of matter.

Qu∴ What do you mean by the number 6?

Ans∴ The theological cube . . . The physical cube.

Qu∴ What do you mean by the number 7?

Ans∴ The seven sacraments . . . The seven planets.

Qu∴ What do you mean by the number 8?

Ans∴ The small number of Elus . . . The small number of wise men.

Qu∴ What do you mean by the number 9?

Ans∴ The exaltation of religion . . . The exaltation of matter.

Qu∴ What do you mean by the number 10?

Ans∴ The ten commandments . . . The ten precepts of nature.

Qu∴ What do you mean by the number 11?

Ans.·. The multiplication of religion . . . The multiplication of nature.

Qu.·. What do you mean by the number 12?

Ans.·. The twelve Articles of Faith; the twelve Apostles, foundation of the Holy City, who preached throughout the whole world, for our happiness and spiritual joy . . . The twelve operations of nature: The twelve signs of the Zodiac, foundation of the *Primum Mobile,* extending it throughout the Universe for our temporal felicity.

[The Rabbi (President of the Sanhedrim) adds: From all that you have said, it results that the unit develops itself in 2, is completed in three internally, and so produces 4 externally; whence, through 6, 7, 8, 9, it arrives at 5, half of the spherical number 10, to ascend, passing through 11, to 12, and to raise itself, by the number 4 times 10, to the number 6 times 12, the final term and summit of our eternal happiness.]

Qu.·. What is the generative number?

Ans.·. In the Divinity, it is the unit; in created things, the number 2: Because the Divinity, 1, engenders 2, and in created things 2 engenders 1.

Qu.·. What is the most majestic number?

Ans.·. 3, because it denotes the triple divine essence.

Qu.·. What is the most mysterious number?

Ans.·. 4, because it contains all the mysteries of nature.

Qu.·. What is the most occult number?

Ans.·. 5, because it is inclosed in the centre of the series.

Qu.·. What is the most salutary number?

Ans.·. 6, because it contains the source of our spiritual and corporeal happiness.

Qu.·. What is the most fortunate number?

Ans.·. 7, because it leads us to the decade, the perfect number.

Qu.·. Which is the number most to be desired?

Ans.·. 8, because he who possesses it, is of the number of the Elus and Sages.

Qu.·. Which is the most sublime number?

Ans.·. 9, because by it religion and nature are exalted.

Qu.·. Which is the most perfect number?

Ans.·. 10, because it includes unity, which created everything, and zero, symbol of matter and chaos, whence everything emerged.

In its figures it comprehends the created and uncreated, the commencement and the end, power and force, life and annihilation. By the study of this number, we find the relations of all things; the power of the Creator, the faculties of the creature, the Alpha and Omega of divine knowledge.

Qu.·. Which is the most multiplying number?

Ans.·. 11, because with the possession of two units, we arrive at the multiplication of things.

Qu.·. Which is the most solid number?

Ans.·. 12, because it is the foundation of our spiritual and temporal happiness.

Qu.·. Which is the favorite number of religion and nature?

Ans.·. 4 times 10, because it enables us, rejecting everything impure, eternally to enjoy the number 6 times 12, term and summit of our felicity.

Qu.·. What is the meaning of the square?

Ans.·. It is the symbol of the four elements contained in the triangle, or the emblem of the three chemical principles: these things united form absolute unity in the primal matter.

Qu.·. What is the meaning of the centre of the circumference?

Ans.·. It signifies the universal spirit, vivifying centre of nature.

Qu.·. What do you mean by the quadrature of the circle?

Ans.·. The investigation of the quadrature of the circle indicates the knowledge of the four vulgar elements, which are themselves composed of elementary spirits or chief principles; as the circle, though round, is composed of lines, which escape the sight, and are seen only by the mind.

Qu.·. What is the profoundest meaning of the figure 3?

Ans.·. The Father, the Son, and the Holy Spirit. From the action of these three results the triangle within the square; and from the seven angles, the decade or perfect number.

Qu.·. Which is the most confused figure?

Ans.·. Zero,—the emblem of chaos, formless mixture of the elements.

Qu.·. What do the four devices of the Degree signify?

Ans.·. That we are to hear, see, be silent, and enjoy our happiness.

The *unit* is the symbol of identity, equality, existence, conservation, and general harmony; the Central Fire, the Point within the Circle.

Two, or the *duad,* is the symbol of diversity, inequality, division, separation, and vicissitudes.

The figure 1 signifies the living man [a body standing upright]; man being the only living being possessed of this faculty. Adding to it a head, we have the letter P, the sign of Paternity, Creative Power; and with a further addition, R, signifying man in motion, going, *Iens, Iturus.*

The Duad is the origin of contrasts. It is the imperfect condition into which, according to the Pythagoreans, a being falls, when he detaches himself from the Monad, or God. Spiritual beings, emanating from God, are enveloped in the duad, and therefore receive only illusory impressions.

As formerly the number ONE designated harmony, order, or the Good Principle (the ONE and ONLY GOD, expressed in Latin by *Solus,* whence the words *Sol, Soleil,* symbol of this God), the number Two expressed the contrary idea. There commenced the fatal knowledge of good and evil. Everything double, false, opposed to the single and sole reality, was expressed by the Binary number. It expressed also that state of contrariety in which nature exists, where everything is double; night and day, light and darkness, cold and heat, wet and dry, health and sickness, error and truth, one and the other sex, etc. Hence the Romans dedicated the second month in the year to Pluto, the God of Hell, and the second day of that month to the *manès* of the dead.

The number *One,* with the Chinese, signified unity, harmony, order, the Good Principle, or God; *Two,* disorder, duplicity, falsehood. That people, in the earliest ages, based their whole philosophical system on the two primary figures or lines, one straight and unbroken, and the other broken or divided into two; doubling which, by placing one under the other, and trebling by placing three under each other, they made the four symbols and eight *Koua;* which referred to the natural elements, and the primary principles of all things, and served symbolically or scientifically to express them. Plato terms unity and duality the original elements of nature, and first principles of all existence: and the oldest sacred book of the Chinese says: "The Great First Principle has produced two equations and differences, or primary rules of existence; but the two primary rules or two oppositions, namely YN and YANG, or repose and motion, have produced four signs or symbols, and the four symbols have produced the eight KOUA or further combinations."

The interpretation of the Hermetic fables shows, among every ancient people, in their principal gods, first, 1, the Creating Monad, then 3, then 3 times 3, 3 times 9, and 3 times 27. This triple progression has for its foundation the three ages of Nature, the Past, the Present, and the Future; or the three degrees of universal generation. . . Birth, Life, Death. . . Beginning, middle, end.

The Monad was male, because its action produces no change *in* itself, but only *out* of itself. It represented the creative principle.

The Duad, for a contrary reason, was female, ever changing by addition, subtraction, or multiplication. It represents matter capable of form.

The union of the Monad and Duad produces the Triad, signifying the world formed by the creative principle out of matter. Pythagoras represented the world by the right-angled triangle, in which the squares of the two shortest sides are equal, added together, to the square of the longest one; as the world, as formed, is equal to the creative cause, and matter clothed with form.

The ternary is the first of the unequal numbers. The Triad, mysterious number, which plays so great a part in the traditions of Asia and the philosophy of Plato, image of the Supreme Being, includes in itself the properties of the first two numbers. It was, to the Philosophers, the most excellent and favorite number: a mysterious type, revered by all antiquity, and consecrated in the Mysteries; wherefore there are but three essential Degrees among Masons; who venerate, in the triangle, the most august mystery, that of the Sacred Triad, object of their homage and study.

In geometry, a line cannot represent a body absolutely perfect. As little do two lines constitute a figure demonstratively perfect. But three lines form, by their junction, the TRIANGLE, or the first figure regularly perfect; and this is why it has served and still serves to characterize The Eternal; Who, infinitely perfect in His nature, is, as Universal Creator, the first Being, and consequently the first Perfection.

The Quadrangle or Square, perfect as it appears, being but the second perfection, can in no wise represent God; Who is the first. It is to be noted that the name of God in Latin and French (Deus, Dieu), has for its initial the Delta or Greek Triangle. Such is the reason, among ancients and moderns, for the consecration of the Triangle, whose three sides are emblems of the three Kingdoms, or Nature, or God. In the centre is the Hebrew Jod (initial of יהוה), the Animating Spirit of Fire, the generative principle, represented by the letter G., initial of the name of Deity in the languages of the North, and the meaning whereof is Generation.

The first side of the Triangle, offered to the study of the Apprentice, is the mineral kingdom, symbolized by Tub.∴.

The second side, the subject of the meditations of the Fellow Craft, is the vegetable kingdom, symbolized by Schib.∴ (an ear of corn). In this reign begins the Generation of bodies; and this is why the letter G., in its radiance, is presented to the eyes of the adept.

The third side, the study whereof is devoted to the animal kingdom, and completes the instruction of the Master, is symbolized by Mach.∴ (Son of putrefaction).

The figure 3 symbolizes the Earth. It is a figure of the terrestrial bodies. The 2, upper half of 3, symbolizes the vegetable world, the lower half being hidden from our sight.

Three also referred to harmony, friendship, peace, concord, and temperance; and was so highly esteemed among the Pythagoreans that they called it perfect harmony.

Three, four, ten, and twelve were sacred numbers among the Etrurians, as they were among the Jews, Egyptians, and Hindūs.

The name of Deity, in many Nations, consisted of three letters: among the Greeks, I.∴A.∴Ω.∴; among the Persians, H.∴O.∴M.∴; among the Hindūs, Aum; among the Scandinavians, I.∴O.∴W.∴. On the upright Tablet of the King, discovered at Nimroud, no less than five of the thirteen names of the Great Gods consist of three letters each,—Anu, San, Yav, Bar, and Bel.

The quaternary is the most perfect number, and the root of other numbers, and of all things. The tetrad expresses the first mathematical power. Four represents also the generative power, from which all combinations are derived. The Initiates considered it the emblem of Movement and the Infinite, representing everything that is neither corporeal nor sensible. Pythagoras communicated it to his disciples as a symbol of the Eternal and Creative Principle, under the name of Quaternary, the Ineffable Name of God, which signifies Source of everything that has received existence; and which, in Hebrew, is composed of four letters.

In the Quaternary we find the first solid figure, the universal symbol of immortality, the pyramid. The Gnostics claimed that the whole edifice of their science rested on a square whose angles were . . . Σιγή, *Silence:* Βυθος, *Profundity:* Noos, *Intelligence:* and Αληθεια, *Truth.* For if the Triangle, figured by the number 3, forms the triangular base of the pyramid, it is unity which forms its point or summit.

Lysias and Timæus of Locria said that not a single thing could be named, which did not depend on the quaternary as its root.

There is, according to the Pythagoreans, a connection between the gods and numbers, which constitutes the kind of Divination called Arithmomancy. The soul is a number: it is moved of itself: it contains in itself the quaternary number.

Matter being represented by the number 9, or 3 times 3, and the Immortal Spirit having for its essential hieroglyphic the quaternary or the number 4, the Sages said that Man, having gone astray and become entangled in an inextricable labyrinth, in going from *four* to *nine,* the only way which he could take to emerge from these deceitful paths, these disastrous detours, and the abyss of evil into which he had plunged, was to retrace his steps, and go from *nine* to *four.*

The ingenious and mystical idea which caused the Triangle to be venerated, was applied to the figure 4 (4). It was said that it expressed a living being, I, bearer of the Triangle Δ, the emblem of God; *i. e.,* man bearing with himself a Divine principle.

Four was a divine number; it referred to the Deity, and many Ancient Nations gave God a name of four letters; as the Hebrews יהוה, the Egyptians AMUN, the Persians SURA, the Greeks ΘΕΟΣ, and the Latins DEUS. This was the Tetragrammaton of the Hebrews, and the Pythagoreans called it Tetractys, and swore their most solemn oath by it. So too ODIN among the Scandinavians, ZEYΣ among the Greeks, PHTA among the Egyptians, THOTH among the Phœnicians, and AS-UR and NEBO among the Assyrians. The list might be indefinitely extended.

The number 5 was considered as mysterious, because it was compounded of the Binary, Symbol of the False and Double, and the Ternary, so interesting in its results. It thus energetically expresses the state of imperfection, of order and disorder, of happiness and misfortune, of life and death, which we see upon the earth. To the Mysterious Societies it offered the fearful image of the Bad Principle, bringing trouble into the inferior order,—in a word, the Binary acting in the Ternary.

Under another aspect it was the emblem of marriage; because it is composed of 2, the first equal number, and of 3, the first unequal number. Wherefore Juno, the Goddess of Marriage, had for her hieroglyphic the number 5.

Moreover, it has one of the properties of the number 9, that of reproducing itself, when multiplied by itself: there being always a 5 on the right hand of the product; a result which led to its use as a symbol of material changes.

The ancients represented the world by the number 5. A reason for it, given by Diodorus, is, that it represents earth, water, air, fire, and ether or spirit. Thence the origin of πεντε (5) and Παν the Universe, as the whole.

The number 5 designated the universal quintessence, and symbolized, by its form   s, the vital essence, the animating spirit, which flows [*serpentat*] through all nature. In fact, this ingenious figure is the union of the two Greek accents ' ', placed over those vowels which ought to be or ought not to be aspirated. The first sign ' bears the name of potent spirit; and signifies the Superior Spirit, the Spirit of God aspirated (*spiratus*), respired by man. The second sign ' is styled mild spirit, and represents the secondary spirit, the spirit purely human.

The triple triangle, a figure of five lines uniting in five points, was among the Pythagoreans an emblem of Health.

It is the Pentalpha of Pythagoras, or Pentangle of Solomon; has five lines and five angles; and is, among Masons, the outline or origin of the five-pointed Star, and an emblem of Fellowship.

The number 6 was, in the Ancient Mysteries, a striking emblem of nature; as presenting the six dimensions of all bodies; the six lines which make up their form, viz., the four lines of direction, toward the North, South, East, and West; with the two lines of height and depth, responding to the zenith and nadir. The sages applied the senary to the physical man; while the septenary was, for them, the symbol of his immortal spirit.

The hieroglyphical senary (the double equilateral triangle) is the symbol of Deity.

Six is also an emblem of health, and the symbol of justice; because it is the first perfect number; that is, the first whose aliquot parts (1/2, 1/3, 1/6, or 3, 2, and 1), added together, make itself.

Ormuzd created six good spirits, and Ahriman six evil ones. These typify the six Summer and the six Winter months.

No number has ever been so universally in repute as the septenary. Its celebrity is due, no doubt, to the planets being *seven* in number. It belongs also to sacred things. The Pythagoreans regarded it as formed of the numbers 3 and 4; the first whereof was, in their eyes, the image of the three material elements, and the second the principle of everything that is neither corporeal nor sensible. It presented them, from that point of view, the emblem of everything that is perfect.

Considered as composed of 6 and unity, it serves to designate the invisible centre or soul of everything; because no body exists, of which six lines do not constitute the form, nor without a seventh interior point, as the centre and reality of the body, whereof the external dimensions give only the appearance.

The numerous applications of the septenary confirmed the ancient sages in the use of this symbol. Moreover, they exalted the properties of the number 7, as having, in a subordinate manner, the perfection of the unit: for if the unit is uncreated, if no number produces it, the seven is also not engendered by any number contained in the interval between 1 and 10. The number 4 occupies an arithmetical middle-ground between the unit and 7, inasmuch as it is as much over 1, as it is under 7, the difference each way being 3.

The number 7, among the Egyptians, symbolized life; and this is why the letter Z of the Greeks was the initial of the verb Ζάω, I live; and Ζεὺς (Jupiter), Father of Life.

The number 8, or the octary, is composed of the sacred numbers 3 and 5. Of the heavens, of the seven planets, and of the sphere of the fixed stars, or of the eternal unity and the mysterious number 7, is composed the ogdoade, the number 8, the first cube of equal numbers, regarded as sacred in the arithmetical philosophy.

The Gnostic ogdoade had eight stars, which represented the eight Cabiri of Samothrace, the eight Egyptian and Phœnician principles, the eight gods of Xenocrates, the eight angles of the cubic stone.

The number eight symbolizes perfection: and its figure, 8 or ∞ indicates the perpetual and regular course of the Universe.

It is the first cube $(2 \times 2 \times 2)$, and signifies friendship, prudence, counsel, and justice. It was a symbol of the primeval law which regarded all men as equal.

The novary, or triple ternary. If the number three was celebrated among the ancient sages, that of three times three had no less celebrity; because, according to them, each of the three elements which constitute our bodies is ternary: the water containing earth and fire; the earth containing igneous and aqueous particles; and the fire being tempered by globules of water and terrestrial corpuscles which serve to feed it. No one of the three elements being entirely separated from the others, all material beings composed of these three elements, whereof each is triple, may be designated by the figurative number of three times three, which has become the symbol of all formations of bodies. Hence the name of ninth envelope, given to matter. Every material extension, every circular line, has for representative sign the number nine, among the Pythagoreans; who had observed the property which this number possesses, of reproducing itself incessantly and entire, in every multiplication; thus offering to the mind a very striking emblem of matter which is incessantly composed before our eyes, after having undergone a thousand decompositions.

The number nine was consecrated to the Spheres and the Muses. It is the sign of every circumference; because a circle of 360 degrees is equal to 9, that is to say, $3 + 6 + 0 = 9$. Nevertheless, the ancients regarded this number with a sort of terror: they considered it a bad presage; as the symbol of versatility, of change, and the emblem of the frailty of human affairs. Wherefore they avoided all numbers where nine appears, and chiefly 81, the product of 9 multiplied by itself, and the addition whereof, $8 + 1$, again presents the number 9.

As the figure of the number 6 was the symbol of the terrestrial globe, animated by a divine spirit, the figure of the number 9 symbolized the earth, under the influence of the Evil Principle; and thence the terror it inspired. Nevertheless, according to the Kabalists, the figure 9 symbolizes the generative egg, or the image of a little globular being, from whose lower side seems to flow its spirit of life.

The Ennead, signifying an aggregate of 9 things or persons, is the first square of unequal numbers.

Every one is aware of the singular properties of the number 9, which, multiplied by itself or any other number whatever, gives a result whose final sum is always 9, or always divisible by 9.

Nine, multiplied by each of the ordinary numbers, produces an arithmetical progression, each member whereof, composed of two figures, presents a remarkable fact; for example: .

$$1\ldots2\ldots3\ldots4\ldots5\ldots6\ldots7\ldots8\ldots9\ldots10$$
$$9\ldots18\ldots27\ldots36\ldots45\ldots54\ldots63\ldots72\ldots81\ldots90$$

The first line of figures gives the regular series, from 1 to 10.

The second reproduces this line doubly; first ascending, from the first figure of 18, and then returning from the second figure of 81.

It follows, from the curious fact, that the half of the numbers which compose this progression represents, in inverse order, the figures of the second half:

$$9\ldots18\ldots27\ldots36\ldots45 = 135 = 9\ldots and\ 1+3+5 = 45 = 9$$
$$90\ldots81\ldots72\ldots63\ldots54 = 360 = 9.$$

$$99 \quad 99 \quad 99 \quad 99 \quad 99 \quad\quad 495 = 18 = 9.$$

So $9^2 = 81\ldots81^2 = 6561 = 18 = 9\ldots9\times2 = 18\ldots18^2 = 324 = 9.$

$9\times3 = 27\ldots27^2 = 729 = 18 = 9. \quad 9\times4 = 36\ldots36^2 = 1296 = 18 = 9.$

And so with every multiple of 9—say 45, 54, 63, 72, etc.

Thus $9 \times 8 = 72\ldots72^2 = 5184 = 18 = 9.$

And further:

18	27	36	72
18	27	36	72
144 = 9	189 = 18 = 9	216 = 9	144 = 9
18 = 9	54 = 9 =	108 = 9	504 = 9
324 = 9...18 = 9	729 = 18 = 9	1296 = 18 = 9	5184 = 18 = 9

108
108
___
864 = 18
108 = 9
___
11664 = 18 = 9.

And so the cubes:

$$27^2 = 729 \times 729 = 18 = 9 \quad 18^2 = 324 = 9 \quad 9^2 = 81 \quad 81^2 = ..6561 = 18 = 9$$

$$729 \qquad\qquad\qquad 324 \qquad\qquad\qquad 6561$$

6561 =18=9	1296=18=9	6561=18=9
1458 =18=9	648 =18=9	39366 =27=9
5103 =9	972 =18=9	32805 =18=9
		39366 =27=9

$$531441 = 18 = 9 \qquad 104976 = 27 = 9 \qquad 43{,}046{,}721 = 27 = 9.$$

The number 10, or the Denary, is the measure of everything; and reduces multiplied numbers to unity. Containing all the numerical and harmonic relations, and all the properties of the numbers which precede it, it concludes the Abacus or Table of Pythagoras. To the Mysterious Societies, this number typified the assemblage of all the wonders of the Universe. They wrote it thus θ, that is to say, Unity in the middle of Zero, as the centre of a circle, or symbol of Deity. They saw in this figure everything that should lead to reflection: the centre, the ray, and the circumference, represented to them God, Man, and the Universe.

This number was, among the Sages, a sign of concord, love, and peace. To Masons it is a sign of union and good faith; because it is expressed by joining two hands, or the Master's grip, when the number of fingers gives 10: and it was represented by the Tetractys of Pythagoras.

The number 12, like the number 7, is celebrated in the worship of nature. The two most famous divisions of the heavens, that by 7, which is that of the planets, and that by 12, which is that of the Signs of the Zodiac, are found upon the religious monuments of all the peoples of the Ancient World, even to the remote extremes of the East. Although Pythagoras does not speak of the number 12, it is none the less a sacred number. It is the image of the Zodiac; and consequently that of the Sun, which rules over it.

Such are the ancient ideas in regard to those numbers which so often appear in Masonry; and rightly understood, as the old Sages understood them, they contain many a pregnant lesson.

Before we enter upon the final lesson of Masonic Philosophy, we will delay a few moments to repeat to you the Christian interpretations of the Blue Degrees.

In the First Degree, they said, there are three symbols to be applied.

1st. Man, after the fall, was left naked and defenceless against the just anger of the Deity. Prone to evil, the human race staggered blindly onward into the thick darkness of unbelief, bound fast by the strong cable-tow of the natural and sinful will. Moral corruption was followed by physical misery. Want and destitution invaded the earth. War and Famine and Pestilence filled up the measure of evil, and over the sharp flints of misfortune and wretchedness man toiled with naked and bleeding feet. This condition of blindness, destitution, misery, and bondage, from which to save the world the Redeemer came, is symbolized by the condition of the candidate, when he is brought up for the first time to the door of the Lodge.

2d. Notwithstanding the death of the Redeemer, man can be saved only by faith, repentance, and reformation. To repent, he must feel the sharp sting of conscience and remorse, like a sword piercing his bosom. His confidence in his guide, whom he is told to follow and fear no danger; his trust in God, which he is caused to profess; and the point of the sword that is pressed against his naked left breast over the heart, are symbolical of the faith, repentance and reformation necessary to bring him to the light of a life in Christ the Crucified.

3d. Having repented and reformed, and bound himself to the service of God by a firm promise and obligation, the light of Christian hope shines down into the darkness of the heart of the humble penitent, and blazes upon his pathway to Heaven. And this is symbolized by the candidate's being brought to light, after he is obligated, by the Worshipful Master, who in that is a symbol of the Redeemer, and so brings him to light, with the help of the brethren, as He taught the Word with the aid of the Apostles.

In the Second Degree there are two symbols:

4th. The Christian assumes new duties toward God and his fellows. Toward God, of love, gratitude, and veneration, and an anxious desire to serve and glorify Him; toward his fellows, of kindness, sympathy, and justice. And this assumption of duty, this entering upon good works, is symbolized by the Fellow-Craft's obligation; by which, bound as an apprentice to secrecy merely, and set in the Northeast corner of the Lodge, he descends as a Fellow-Craft into the body of the brethren, and assumes the active duties of a good Mason.

5th. The Christian, reconciled to God, sees the world in a new light. This great Universe is no longer a mere machine, wound up and set going six thousand or sixty millions years ago, and left to run on afterward forever, by virtue of a law of mechanics created at the beginning, without further care or consideration on the part of the Deity; but it has now become to him a great emanation from God, the product of His thought, not a mere dead machine, but a thing of life, over which God watches continually, and every movement of which is immediately produced by His present action, the law of harmony being the essence of the Deity, re-enacted every instant. And this is symbolized by the imperfect instruction given in the Fellow-Craft's Degree, in the sciences, and particularly geometry, connected as the latter is with God Himself in the mind of a Mason, because the same letter, suspended in the East, represents both; and astronomy, or the knowledge of the laws of motion and harmony that govern the spheres, is but a portion of the wider science of geometry. It is so symbolized, because it is here, in the Second Degree, that the candidate first receives an other than moral instruction.

There are also two symbols in the Third Degree, which, with the 3 in the first, and 2 in the second, make the 7.

6th. The candidate, after passing through the first part of the ceremony, imagines himself a Master; and is surprised to be informed that as yet he is not, and that it is uncertain whether he ever will be. He is told of a difficult and dangerous path yet to be travelled, and is advised that upon that journey it depends whether he will become a Master. This is symbolical of that which our Saviour said to Nicodemus, that, notwithstanding his morals might be beyond reproach, he could not enter the Kingdom of Heaven unless he were born again; symbolically dying, and again entering the world regenerate, like a spotless infant.

7th. The murder of Hiram, his burial, and his being raised again by the Master, are symbols, both of the death, burial, and resurrection of the Redeemer; and of the death and burial in sins of the natural man, and his being raised again to a new life, or born again, by the direct action of the Redeemer; after Morality (symbolized by the Entered Apprentice's grip), and Philosophy (symbolized by the grip of the Fellow-Craft), had failed to raise him. That of the Lion of the House of Judah is the strong grip, never to be broken, with which Christ, of the royal line of that House, has clasped to Himself the whole human race, and embraces them in His wide arms as closely and affectionately as brethren embrace each other on the five points of fellowship.

As Entered Apprentices and Fellow-Crafts, Masons are taught to imitate the laudable example of those Masons who labored at the building of King Solomon's Temple; and to plant firmly and deep in their hearts those foundation-stones of principle, truth, justice, temperance, fortitude, prudence, and charity, on which to erect that Christian character which all the storms of misfortune and all the powers and temptations of Hell shall not prevail against; those feelings and noble affections which are the most proper homage that can be paid to the Grand Architect and Great Father of the Universe, and which make the heart a living temple builded to Him: when the unruly passions are made to submit to rule and measurement, and their excesses are struck off with the gavel of self-restraint; and when every action and every principle is accurately corrected and adjusted by the square of wisdom, the level of humility, and the plumb of justice.

The two columns, Jachin and Boaz, are the symbols of that profound faith and implicit trust in God and the Redeemer that are the Christian's *strength;* and of those good works by which alone that faith can be *established* and made operative and effectual to salvation.

The three pillars that support the Lodge are symbols of a Christian's HOPE in a future state of happiness; FAITH in the promises and the divine character and mission of the Redeemer; and CHARITABLE JUDGMENT of other men.

The three murderers of Khir-Om symbolize Pontius Pilate, Caiaphas the High-Priest, and Judas Iscariot: and the three blows given him are the betrayal by the last, the refusal of Roman protection by Pilate, and the condemnation by the High-Priest. They also symbolize the blow on the ear, the scourging, and the crown of thorns. The twelve fellow-crafts sent in search of the body are the twelve disciples, in doubt whether to believe that the Redeemer would rise from the dead.

The Master's word, supposed to be lost, symbolizes the Christian faith and religion, supposed to have been crushed and destroyed when the Saviour was crucified, after Iscariot had betrayed Him, and Peter deserted Him, and when the other disciples doubted whether He would arise from the dead; but which rose from His tomb and flowed rapidly over the civilized world; and so that which was supposed to be *lost* was *found*. It symbolizes also the Saviour Himself; the WORD that was in the beginning—that was *with* God, and that *was* God; the Word of life, that was made flesh and dwelt among us, and was supposed to be lost, while He lay in the tomb, for three days, and His disciples "as yet knew not the scripture that He must rise again from the dead," and doubted when they heard of it, and were amazed and frightened and still doubted when He appeared among them.

The bush of acacia placed at the head of the grave of Khir-Om is an emblem of resurrection and immortality.

Such are the explanations of our Christian brethren; entitled, like those of all other Masons, to a respectful consideration.

CLOSING INSTRUCTION.

There is no pretence to infallibility in Masonry. It is not for us to dictate to any man what he shall believe. We have hitherto, in the instruction of the several Degrees, confined ourselves to laying before you the great thoughts that have found expression in the different ages of the world, leaving you to decide for yourself as to the orthodoxy or heterodoxy of each, and what proportion of truth, if any, each contained. We shall pursue no other course in this closing Philosophical instruction; in which we propose to deal with the highest questions that have ever exercised the human mind,—with the existence and the nature of a God, with the existence and the nature of the human soul, and with the relations of the divine and human spirit with the merely material Universe. There can be no questions more important to an intelligent being, none that have for him a more direct and personal interest; and to this last word of Scottish Masonry we invite your serious and attentive consideration. And, as what we shall now say will be but the completion and rounding-off of what we have already said in several of the preceding Degrees, in regard to the Old Thought and the Ancient Philosophies, we hope that you have noted and not forgotten our previous lessons, without which this would seem imperfect and fragmentary.

In its idea of rewarding a faithful and intelligent workman by conferring upon him a knowledge of the True Word, Masonry has perpetuated a very great truth, because it involves the proposition that the idea which a man forms of God is always the most important element in his speculative theory of the Universe, and in his particular practical plan of action for the Church, the State, the Community, the Family, and his own individual life. It will ever make a vast difference in the conduct of a people in war or peace, whether they believe the Supreme God to be a cruel Deity, delighting in sacrifice and blood, or a God of Love; and an individual's speculative theory as to the mode and extent of God's government, and as to the nature and reality of his own free-will and consequent responsibility, will needs have great influence in shaping the course of his life and conversation.

We see every day the vast influence of the popular idea of God. All the great historical civilizations of the race have grown out of the national ideas which were formed of God; or have been intimately connected with those ideas. The popular Theology, which at first is only an abstract idea in the heads of philosophers, by and by shows itself in the laws, and in the punishments for crime, in the churches, the ceremonies and the sacraments, the festivals and the fasts, the weddings, the baptisms and the funerals, in the hospitals, the colleges, the schools, and all the social charities, in the relations of husband and wife, parent and child, in the daily work and the daily prayer of every man.

As the world grows in its development, it necessarily *out*grows its ancient ideas of God, which were only temporary and provisional. A man who has a higher conception of God than those about him, and who denies that their conception *is* God, is very likely to be called an Atheist by men who are really far less believers in a God than he. Thus the Christians, who said the Heathen idols were no Gods, were accounted Atheists by the People, and accordingly put to death; and Jesus of Nazareth was crucified as an unbelieving blasphemer, by the Jews.

There is a mere formal Atheism, which is a denial of God in *terms*, but not in *reality*. A man says, There is no God; that is, no God that is self-originated, or that never originated, but always WAS and HAD BEEN, who is the cause of existence, who is the Mind and the Providence of the Universe; and so the order, beauty, and harmony of the world of matter and mind do not indicate any plan or purpose of Deity. But, he says, NATURE,— meaning by that the whole sum-total of existence,—*that* is powerful, active, wise, and good; *Nature* is self-originated, or always was and had been, the cause of its own existence, the mind of the Universe and the Providence of itself. There is obviously a plan and purpose whereby order, beauty, and harmony are brought about; but all that is the plan and purpose of nature.

In such cases, the absolute denial of God is only formal and not real. The *qualities* of God are admitted, and affirmed to be real; and it is a mere change of name to call the possessor of those qualities, *Nature,* and not *God.* The real question is, whether such Qualities exist, as we call God; and not, by what particular name we shall designate the Qualities. One man may call the sum total of these Qualities, Nature; another, Heaven; a third, Universe, a fourth, Matter; a fifth, Spirit; a sixth, God, Theos, Zeus, Alfadir, Allah, or what he pleases. All admit the existence of the Being, Power, or Ens, thus diversely named. The name is of the smallest consequence.

Real Atheism is the denial of the existence of *any* God, of the actuality of all possible ideas of God. It denies that there is *any* Mind, Intelligence, or Ens, that is the Cause and Providence of the Universe, and of any Thing or any Existence, Soul, Spirit, or Being, that *intentionally* or *intelligently* produces the Order, Beauty, and Harmony thereof, and the constant and regular modes of operation therein. It must necessarily deny that there is any law, order, or harmony in existence, or any constant mode of operation in the world; for it is utterly impossible for any human creature to conceive, however much he may *pretend* to do so, of either of these, except as a consequence of the action of Intelligence; which is, indeed, that otherwise unknown thing, the existence of which these alone prove; otherwise than as the cause of these, not a thing at all; a mere *name* for the wholly uncognizable cause of these.

The *real* atheist must deny the existence of the Qualities of God, deny that there is any mind of or in the Universe, any self-conscious Providence, any Providence at all. He must deny that there is any Being or Cause of Finite things, that is self-consciously powerful, wise, just, loving, and faithful to itself and its own nature. He must deny that there is any *plan* in the Universe or any part of it. He must hold, either that matter is eternal, or that it originated itself, which is absurd, or that it was originated by an Intelligence, or at least by a Cause; and then he admits a God,

No doubt it is beyond the reach of our faculties to imagine *how* matter originated,—how it began to *be,* in space where before was nothing, or God only. But it is equally beyond the reach of our faculties to imagine it eternal and *un*originated. To hold it to be eternal, without thought or will; that the specific forms of it, the seed, the rock, the tree, the man, the solar system, all came with no forethought planning or producing them, by "chance" or "the fortuitous concourse of atoms" of matter that has no thought or will; and that they indicate no mind, no plan, no purpose, no providence, is absurd. It is not to deny the *existence* of what we understand by mind, plan, purpose, Providence; but to insist that these words shall have some other meaning than that which the human race has ever attached to them: shall mean some unknown thing, for which the human race has no *name,* because it has of such a thing no possible idea. Either there never was any such thing as a "plan," and the word is nonsense, or the Universe exists in conformity to a plan. The *word* never meant, and never can mean, any other *thing* than that which the Universe exhibits. So with the word *"purpose;"* so with the word *"Providence."* They mean nothing, or else only what the Universe proves.

It was soon found that the denial of a Conscious Power, the cause of man and of his life, of a Providence, or a Mind and Intelligence arranging man in reference to the world, and the world in reference to man, would not satisfy the instinctive desires of *human* nature, or account for the facts of *material* nature. It did not long answer to say, if it ever *was* said, that the Universe was drifting in the void inane, and neither it, nor any mind within or without it, knew of its whence, its whither, or its whereabouts; that man was drifting in the Universe, knowing little of his whereabouts, nothing of his whence or whither; that there was no Mind, no Providence, no Power, that knew any better; nothing that guided and directed man in his drifting, or the Universe in the weltering waste of Time. To say to man and woman, "your heroism, your bravery, your self-denial all comes to nothing: your nobleness will do you no good: you will die, and your nobleness will do mankind no service; for there is no plan or order in all these things; everything comes and goes by the fortuitous concourse of atoms;" did not, nor ever will, long satisfy the human mind.

True, the theory of Atheism has been uttered. It has been said, "Death is the end: this is a world without a God: you are a body without a soul: there is a Here, but no Hereafter for you; an Earth, but no Heaven. Die, and return to your dust. Man is bones, blood, bowels, and brain; mind is matter: there is no soul in the brain, nothing but nerves. We can see all the way to a little star in the nebula of Orion's belt; so distant that it will take light a thousand millions of years to come from it to the earth, journeying at the rate of twelve millions of miles a minute. There is no Heaven this side of that: you see all the way through: there is not a speck of Heaven; and do you think there is any beyond it; and if so, when would you reach it? There is no Providence. Nature is a forfuitous concourse of atoms; thought is a fortuitous function of matter, a fortuitous result of a fortuitous result, a chance-shot from the great wind-gun of the Universe, accidentally loaded, pointed at random, and fired off by chance. Things *happen;* they are not *arranged.* There is luck, and there is ill-luck; but there is no Providence. Die you into dust!" Does all this satisfy the human instinct of immortality, that makes us ever long, with unutterable longing, to join ourselves again to our dear ones who have gone away before us, and to mankind, for eternal life? Does it satisfy our mighty hungering and thirst for immortality, our anxious longing to come nearer to, and to know more of, the Eternal Cause of all things?

Men never could be content to believe that there was no mind that thought for man, no conscience to enact eternal laws, no heart to love those whom nothing of earth loves or cares for, no will of the Universe to marshal the nations in the way of wisdom, justice, and love. History is not—thank God! we *know* it is not,—the fortuitous concourse of events, or Nature that of atoms. We cannot believe that there is no plan nor purpose in Nature, to guide our going out and coming in: that there is a mighty going, but it goes nowhere; that all beauty, wisdom, affection, justice, morality in the world, is an accident, and may end to-morrow.

All over the world there is heroism unrequited, or paid with misery; vice on thrones, corruption in high places, nobleness in poverty or even in chains, the gentle devotion of woman rewarded oy brutal neglect or more brutal abuse and violence; everywhere want, misery, over-work, and under-wages. Add to these the Atheist's creed,—a body without a soul, an earth without a

Heaven, a world without a God; and what a Pandemonium would we make of this world!

The intellect of the Atheist would find matter everywhere; but no Causing and Providing Mind: his moral sense would find no Equitable Will, no Beauty of Moral Excellence, no Conscience enacting justice into the unchanging law of right, no spiritual Order or spiritual Providence, but only material Fate and Chance. His affections would find only finite things to love; and to them the dead who *were* loved and who died yesterday, are like the rainbow that yesterday evening lived a moment and then passed away. His soul, flying through the vast Inane, and feeling the darkness with its wings, seeking the Soul of all, which at once is Reason, Conscience, and the Heart of all that is, would find no God, but a Universe all disorder; no Infinite, no Reason, no Conscience, no Heart, no Soul of things; nothing to reverence, to esteem, to love, to worship, to trust in; but only an Ugly Force, alien and foreign to us, that strikes down those we love, and makes us mere worms on the hot sand of the world. No voice would speak from the Earth to comfort him. It is a cruel mother, that great Earth, that devours her young,—a Force and nothing more. Out of the sky would smile no kind Providence, in all its thousand starry eyes; and in storms a malignant violence, with its lightning-sword, would stab into the darkness, seeking for men to murder.

No man ever was or ever can be content with that. The evidence of God has been ploughed into Nature so deeply, and so deeply woven into the texture of the human soul, that Atheism has never become a faith, though it has sometimes assumed the shape of theory. Religion is natural to man. Instinctively he turns to God and reverences and relies on Him. In the Mathematics of the Heavens, written in gorgeous diagrams of fire, he sees law, order, beauty, harmony without end: in the ethics of the little nations that inhabit the ant-hills he sees the same; in all Nature, animate and inanimate, he sees the evidences of a Design, a Will, an Intelligence, and a God,—of a God beneficent and loving as well as wise, and merciful and indulgent as well as powerful.

To man, surrounded by the material Universe, and conscious of the influence that his material environments exercised upon his fortunes and his present destiny;—to man, ever confronted with the splendors of the starry heavens, the regular march of the seasons, the phenomena of sunrise and moonrise, and all the evidences of intelligence and design that everywhere pressed upon and overwhelmed him, all imaginable questions as to the nature and cause of these phenomena constantly recurred, demanding to be solved, and refusing to be sent away unanswered. And still, after the lapse of ages, press upon the human mind and demand solution, the same great questions—perhaps still demanding it in vain.

Advancing to the period when man had ceased to look upon the separate parts and individual forces of the Universe as gods,—when he had come to look upon it as a whole, this question, among the earliest, occurred to him, and insisted on being answered: "Is this material Universe self-existent, or was it created? Is it eternal, or did it originate?"

And then in succession came crowding on the human mind these other questions:

"Is this material Universe a mere aggregate of fortuitous combinations of matter, or is it the result and work of intelligence, acting upon a plan?

"If there *be* such an Intelligence, what and where is it? Is the material Universe *itself* an Intelligent being? Is it like man, a body and a soul? Does Nature act upon itself, or is there a Cause beyond it that acts upon it?

"If there is a *personal* God, *separate from* the material Universe, that created all things, Himself uncreated, is He corporeal or incorporeal, material or spiritual, the soul of the Universe or wholly apart from it? and if He be Spirit, what then is spirit?

"Was that Supreme Deity active or quiescent before the creation; and if quiescent during a previous eternity, what necessity of His nature moved Him at last to create a world; or was it a mere whim that had no motive?

"Was matter co-existent with Him, or absolutely created by him out of nothing? Did He *create* it, or only *mould* and *shape* and *fashion* a chaos already existing, co-existent with Himself?

"Did the Deity *directly* create matter, or was creation the work of inferior deities, emanations from Himself?

"If He be good and just, whence comes it that, foreknowing everything, He has allowed sorrow and evil to exist; and how to reconcile with His benevolence and wisdom the prosperity of vice and the misfortunes of virtue in this world?"

And then, as to man himself, recurred these other questions, as they continue to recur to all of us:

"What is it in us that thinks? Is Thought the mere result of material organization; or is there in us a *soul* that thinks, separate from and resident in the body? If the latter, is it eternal and uncreated; and if not, how created? Is it distinct from God, or an emanation from Him? Is it *inherently* immortal, or only so by destination, because God has willed it? Is it to return to and be merged in Him, or ever to exist, separately from Him, with its present identity?

"If God has fore-seen and fore-arranged all that occurs, how has man any real free-will, or the least control over circumstances? How can anything be done *against* the will of Infinite Omnipotence; and if all is done *according* to that will, how is there any wrong or evil, in what Infinite Wisdom and Infinite Power does not choose to prevent?

"What is the foundation of the moral law? Did God enact it of His own mere pleasure; and if so, can He not, when He pleases, repeal it? Who shall assure us He will not repeal it, and make right wrong, and virtue vice? Or is the moral law a necessity of His nature; and if so, who enacted it; and does not that assert a power, like the old Necessity, superior to Deity?"

And, close-following after these, came the great question of HEREAFTER, of another Life, of the soul's Destiny; and the thousand other collateral and subordinate questions, as to matter, spirit, futurity, and God, that have produced all the systems of philosophy, all metaphysics, and all theology, since the world began.

What the old philosophic mind thought upon these great questions, we have already, to some extent, developed. With the Emanation-doctrine of the Gnostics and the Orient, we have endeavored to make you familiar. We have brought you face to face with the Kabalists, the Essenes, and Philo the Jew. We have shown that, and how, much of the old mythology was derived from the daily and yearly recurring phenomena of the heavens. We have exhibited to you the ancient notions by which they endeavored to explain to themselves the existence and prevalence of evil; and we have in some degree made known to you their metaphysical ideas as to the nature of the Deity. Much more remains to be done than it is within our power to do.

We stand upon the sounding shore of the great ocean of Time. In front of us stretches out the heaving waste of the illimitable Past; and its waves, as they roll up to our feet along the sparkling slope of the yellow sands, bring to us, now and then, from the depths of that boundless ocean, a shell, a few specimens of algæ torn rudely from their stems, a rounded pebble; and that is all; of all the vast treasures of ancient thought that lie buried there, with the mighty anthem of the boundless ocean thundering over them forever and forever.

Let us once more, and for the last time, along the shore of that great ocean, gather a few more relics of the Past, and listen to its mighty voices, as they come, in fragmentary music, in broken and interrupted rhythm, whispering to us from the great bosom of the Past.

Rites, creeds, and legends express, directly or symbolically, some leading idea, according to which the Mysteries of Being are supposed to be explained in Deity. The intricacies of mythical genealogies are a practical acknowledgment of the mysterious nature of the Omnipotent Deity; displaying in their beautiful but ineffectual imagery the first efforts of the mind to communicate with nature: the flowers which fancy strewed before the youthful steps of Psyche, when she first set out in pursuit of the immortal object of her love. Theories and notions, in all their varieties of truth and falsehood, are a machinery more or less efficacious, directed to the same end. Every religion was, in its origin, an embryo philosophy, or an attempt to interpret the unknown by mind; and it was only when philosophy, which is essentially progress, outgrew its first acquisitions, that religion became a thing apart, cherishing as unalterable dogmas the notions which philosophy had abandoned. Separated from philosophy, it became arrogant and fantastical, professing to have already attained what its more authentic representative was ever pursuing in vain; and discovering, through its initiations and Mysteries, all that to its contracted view seemed wanting to restore the well-being of mankind, the means of purification and expiation, remedies for disease, expedients to cure the disorders of the soul, and to propitiate the gods.

Why should we attempt to confine the idea of the Supreme Mind within an arbitrary barrier, or exclude from the limits of veracity any conception of the Deity, which, if imperfect and inadequate, may be only a little more so than our own? "The name of God," says Hobbes, "is used not to make us *conceive* Him, for He is inconceivable, but that we may *honor* Him." "Believe in God, and adore Him," said the Greek Poet, "but investigate Him not; the inquiry is fruitless, seek not to discover who God is; for, by the desire to know, you offend Him who chooses to remain unknown." "When we attempt," says Philo, "to investigate the essence of the Absolute Being, we fall into an abyss of perplexity; and the only benefit to be derived from such researches is the conviction of their absurdity."

Yet man, though ignorant of the constitution of the dust on which he treads, has ventured, and still ventures, to speculate on the nature of God, and to define dogmatically in creeds the subject least within the compass of his faculties; and even to hate and persecute those who will not accept his views as true.

But though a knowledge of the Divine Essence is impossible, the conceptions formed respecting it are interesting, as indications of intellectual development. The history of religion is the history of the human mind; and the conception formed by it of Deity is always in exact relation to its moral and intellectual attainments. The one is the index and the measure of the other.

The *negative* notion of God, which consists in abstracting the inferior and finite, is, according to Philo, the only way in which it is possible for man worthily to apprehend the nature of God. After exhausting the varieties of symbolism, we contrast the Divine Greatness with human littleness, and employ expressions apparently affirmative, such as "Infinite," "Almighty," "All-wise," "Omnipotent," "Eternal," and the like; which in reality amount only to denying, in regard to God, those limits which confine the faculties of man; and thus we remain content with a name which is a mere conventional sign and confession of our ignorance.

The Hebrew יהוה and the Greek *To ON* expressed abstract existence, without outward manifestation or development. Of the same nature are the definitions, "God is a sphere whose centre is everywhere, and whose circumference nowhere;" "God is He who sees all, Himself unseen:" and finally, that of Proclus and Hegel —"the *To* μη ον—that which has no outward and positive existence." Most of the so-called ideas or definitions of the "Absolute" are only a collection of negations; from which, as they affirm nothing, nothing is learned.

God was first recognized in the heavenly bodies and in the elements. When man's consciousness of his own intellectuality was matured, and he became convinced that the internal faculty of thought was something more subtle than even the most subtle elements, he transferred that new conception to the object of his worship, and deified a mental principle instead of a physical one. He in every case makes God after his own image; for do what we will, the highest efforts of human thought can conceive nothing higher than the supremacy of intellect; and so he ever comes back to some familiar type of exalted humanity. He at first deifies nature, and afterward himself.

The eternal aspiration of the religious sentiment in man is to become united with God. In his earliest development, the wish and its fulfillment were simultaneous, through unquestioning belief. In proportion as the conception of Deity was exalted, the notion of His terrestrial presence or proximity was abandoned; and the difficulty of comprehending the Divine Government, together with the glaring superstitious evils arising out of its misinterpretation, endangered the belief in it altogether.

Even the lights of Heaven, which, as "bright potentates of the sky," were formerly the vigilant directors of the economy of earth, now shine dim and distant, and Uriel no more descends upon a sunbeam. But the real change has been in the progressive ascent of man's own faculties, and not in the Divine Nature; as the Stars are no more distant now than when they were supposed to rest on the shoulders of Atlas. And yet a little sense of disappointment and humiliation attended the first awakening of the soul, when reason, looking upward toward the Deity, was impressed with a dizzy sense of having fallen.

But hope revives in despondency; and every nation that ever advanced beyond the most elementary conceptions, felt the necessity of an attempt to fill the chasm, real or imaginary, separating man from God. To do this was the great task of poetry, philosophy, and religion. Hence the personifications of God's attributes, developments, and manifestations, as "Powers," "Intelligences," "Angels," "Emanations;" through which and the oracular faculty in himself, man could place himself in communion with God.

The various ranks and orders of mythical beings imagined by Persians, Indians, Egyptians, or Etrurians, to preside over the various departments of nature, had each his share in a scheme to bring man into closer approximation to the Deity; they eventually gave way only before an analogous though less picturesque symbolism; and the Deities and Dæmons of Greece and Rome were perpetuated with only a change of names, when their offices were transferred to Saints and Martyrs. The attempts by which reason had sometimes endeavored to span the unknown by a bridge of metaphysics, such as the idealistic systems of Zoroaster, Pythagoras, or Plato, were only a more refined form of the poetical illusions which satisfied the vulgar; and man still looked back with longing to the lost golden age, when his ancestors communed face to face with the Gods; and hoped that, by propitiating Heaven, he might accelerate the renewal of it in the islands of the Far West, under the sceptre of Kronos, or in a centralization of political power at Jerusalem. His eager hope overcame even the terrors of the grave; for the Divine power was as infinite as human expectation, and the Egyptian, duly ensepulchred in the Lybian Catacombs, was supposed to be already on his way to the Fortunate Abodes under the guidance of Hermes, there to obtain a perfect association and reunion with his God.

Remembering what we have already said elsewhere in regard to the old ideas concerning the Deity, and repeating it as little as possible, let us once more put ourselves in communion with the Ancient poetic and philosophic mind, and endeavor to learn of it what it thought, and how it solved the great problems that have ever tortured the human intellect.

The division of the First and Supreme Cause into two parts, one Active and the other Passive, the Universe Agent and Patient, or the hermaphroditic God-World, is one of the most ancient and widespread dogmas of philosophy or natural theology. Almost every ancient people gave it a place in their worship, their mysteries, and their ceremonies.

Ocellus Lucanus, who seems to have lived shortly after Pythagoras opened his School in Italy, five or six hundred years before our era, and in the time of Solon, Thales, and the other Sages who had studied in the Schools of Egypt, not only recognizes the eternity of the Universe, and its divine character as an unproduced and indestructible being, but also the distinction of Active and Passive causes in what he terms the Grand Whole, or the single hermaphroditic Being that comprehends all existences, as well causes as effects; and which is a system regularly ordered, perfect and complete, of all Natures. He well apprehended the dividing-line that separates existence eternally the same, from that which eternally changes; the nature of celestial from that of terrestrial bodies, that of causes from that of effects, that which IS from that which only BECOMES,—a distinction that naturally struck every thinking man.

We shall not quote his language at full length. The heavenly bodies, he thought, are first and most noble; they move of themselves, and ever revolve, without change of form or essence. Fire, water, earth, and air change incessantly and continually, not place, but form. Then, as in the Universe there are generation and cause of generation,—as generation is where there are change and displacement of parts, and cause where there is stability of nature, evidently it belongs to what is the cause of generation, to move and to act, and to the recipient, to be made and moved. In his view, everything above the Moon was the habitation of the gods; all below, that of Nature and discord; *this* operates dissolution of things made; *that,* production of those that are being made. As the world is unproduced and indestructible, as it had no beginning, and will have no end, necessarily the principle that operates generation in another than itself, and that which operates it *in* itself, have co-existed.

The former is all above the moon, and especially the sun: the latter is the sublunary world. Of these two parts, one active, the other passive—one divine and always the same, the other mortal and ever changing, all that we call the "world" or "universe" is composed.

These accorded with the principles of the Egyptian philosophy, which held that man and the animals had always existed together with the world; that they were its effects, eternal like itself. The chief divisions of nature into active and passive causes, its system of generation and destruction, and the concurrence of the two great principles, Heaven and earth, uniting to form all things, will, according to Ocellus, always continue to exist. "Enough," he concludes, "as to the Universe, the generations and destructions effected in it, the mode in which it now exists, the mode in which it will ever exist, by the eternal qualities of the two principles, one always moving, the other always moved; one always *governing,* the other always *governed.*"

Such is a brief summary of the doctrine of this philosopher, whose work is one of the most ancient that has survived to us. The subject on which he treated occupied in his time all men's minds: the poets sang of cosmogonies and theogonies, and the philosophers wrote treatises on the birth of the world and the elements of its composition. The cosmogony of the Hebrews, attributed to Moses; that of the Phœnicians, ascribed to Sanchoniathon; that of the Greeks, composed by Hesiod; that of the Egyptians, the Atlantes, and the Cretans, preserved by Diodorus Siculus; the fragments of the theology of Orpheus, divided among different writers; the books of the Persians, or their Boundehesh; those of the Hindūs; the traditions of the Chinese and the people of Macassar; the cosmogonic chants which Virgil puts in the mouth of Iopas at Carthage; and those of the old Silenus, the first book of the Metamorphoses of Ovid; all testify to the antiquity and universality of these fictions as to the origin of the world and its causes.

At the head of the causes of nature, Heaven and earth were placed; and the most apparent parts of each, the sun, the moon, the fixed stars and planets, and, above all, the zodiac, among the *active* causes of generation; and among the *passive,* the several elements. These causes were not only classed in the progressive order of their energy, Heaven and earth heading the respective lists, but distinct sexes were in some sort assigned to them, and characteristics analogous to the mode in which they concur in universal generation.

The doctrine of Ocellus was the general doctrine everywhere, it naturally occurring to all to make the same distinction. The Egyptians did so, in selecting those animals in which they recognized these emblematic qualities, in order to symbolize the double sex of the Universe. Their God KNEPH, out of whose mouth issued the Orphic egg, whence the author of the Clementine Recognitions makes a hermaphroditic figure to emerge, uniting in itself the two principles whereof Heaven and the earth are forms, and which enter into the organization of all beings which the heavens and the earth engender by their concourse, furnishes another emblem of the double power, active and passive, which the ancients saw in the Universe, and which they symbolized by the egg. Orpheus, who studied in Egypt, borrowed from the theologians of that country the mysterious forms under which the science of nature was veiled, and carried into Greece the symbolic egg, with its division into two parts or causes figured by the hermaphroditic being that issued from it, and whereof Heaven and earth are composed.

The Brahmins of India expressed the same cosmogonic idea by a statue, representative of the Universe, uniting in itself both sexes. The male sex offered an image of the sun, centre of the active principle, and the female sex that of the moon, at the sphere whereof, proceeding downward, the passive portion of nature begins. The Lingam, unto the present day revered in the Indian temples, being but the conjunction of the organs of generation of the two sexes, was an emblem of the same. The Hindūs have ever had the greatest veneration for this symbol of ever-reproductive nature. The Greeks consecrated the same symbols of universal fruitfulness in their Mysteries; and they were exhibited in the sanctuaries of Eleusis. They appear among the sculptured ornaments of all the Indian temples. Tertullian accuses the Valentinians of having adopted the custom of venerating them; a custom, he says, introduced by Melampus from Egypt into Greece. The Egyptians consecrated the Phallus in the Mysteries of Osiris and Isis, as we learn from Plutarch and Diodorus Siculus; and the latter assures us that these emblems were not consecrated by the Egyptians alone, but by every people. They certainly were so among the Persians and Assyrians; and they were regarded everywhere as symbolic of the generative and productive powers of all animated beings. In those early ages, the works of Nature and all her agents were sacred like herself.

For the union of Nature with herself is a chaste marriage, of which the union of man and woman was a natural image, and their organs were an expressive emblem of the double energy which manifests itself in Heaven and Earth uniting together to produce all beings. "The Heavens," says Plutarch, "seemed to men to fulfill the functions of father, and the Earth of mother. The former impregnated the earth with its fertilizing rains, and the earth, receiving them, became fruitful and brought forth." Heaven, which covers and embraces the earth everywhere, is her potent spouse, uniting himself to her to make her fruitful, without which she would languish in everlasting sterility, buried in the shades of chaos and of night. Their union is their marriage; their productions or parts are their children. The skies are our Father, and Nature the great Mother of us all.

This idea was not the dogma of a single sect, but the general opinion of all the Sages. "Nature was divided," says Cicero, "into two parts, one active, and the other that submitted itself to this action, which it received, and which modified it. The former was deemed to be a Force, and the latter the material on which that Force exerted itself." Macrobius repeated almost literally the doctrine of Ocellus. Aristotle termed the earth the fruitful mother, environed on all sides by the air. Above it was Heaven, the dwelling-place of the gods and the divine stars, its substance ether, or a fire incessantly moving in circles, divine and incorruptible, and subject to no change. Below it, nature, and the elements, mutable and acted on, corruptible and mortal.

Synesius said that generations were effected in the portions of the Universe which we inhabit; while the cause of generations resided in the portions above us, whence descend to us the germs of the effects produced here below. Proclus and Simplicius deemed Heaven the Active Cause and Father, relatively to the earth. The former says that the World or the Whole is a single Animal; what is done *in* it, is done *by* it; the same World *acts*, and *acts upon itself*. He divides it into "Heaven" and "Generation." In the former, he says, are placed and arranged the conservative causes of generation, superintended by the Genii and Gods. The Earth, or Rhea, associated ever with Saturn in production, is mother of the effects of which Heaven is Father; the womb or bosom that receives the fertilizing energy of the God that engenders ages. The great work of generation is operated, he says, primarily by the action of the Sun, and secondarily by that of the Moon, so that the Sun is the primitive source of this energy, as father and chief of the male gods that form his court. He follows the action of the male and female principles through all the portions and divisions of nature, attributing to the former the origin of stability and identity, to the latter, that of diversity and mobility. Heaven is to the earth, he says, as the male to the female. It is the movement of the heavens that, by their revolutions, furnished the seminal incitements and forces, whose emanations received by the earth, make it fruitful, and cause it to produce animals and plants of every kind.

Philo says that Moses recognized this doctrine of two causes, active and passive; but made the former to reside in the Mind or Intelligence external to matter.

The ancient astrologers divided the twelve signs of the Zodiac into six male and six female, and assigned them to six male and six female Great Gods. Heaven and Earth, or Ouranos and Ghê, were among most ancient nations, the first and most ancient Divinities. We find them in the Phœnician history of Sanchoniathon, and in the Grecian Genealogy of the Gods given by Hesiod. Everywhere they marry, and by their union produce the later Gods. "In the beginning," says Apollodorus, "Ouranos or the Heavens was Lord of all the Universe: he took to wife Ghê or the earth, and had by her many children." They were the first Gods of the Cretans, and under other names, of the Armenians, as we learn from Berosus, and of Panchaia, an island South of Arabia, as we learn from Euhemerus. Orpheus made the Divinity, or the "Great Whole," male and female, because, he said, it could produce nothing, unless it united in itself the productive force of both sexes. He called Heaven PANGENETOR, the Father of all things, most ancient of Beings, beginning and end of all, containing in Himself the incorruptible and unwearying force of Necessity.

The same idea obtained in the rude North of Europe. The Scythians made the earth to be the wife of Jupiter; and the Germans adored her under the name of HERTA. The Celts worshipped the Heavens and the Earth, and said that without the former the latter would be sterile, and that their marriage produced all things. The Scandinavians acknowledged BÖR or the Heavens, and gave FURTUR, his son, the Earth as his wife. Olaus Rudbeck adds, that their ancestors were persuaded that Heaven intermarried with the Earth, and thus uniting his forces with hers, produced animals and plants. This marriage of Heaven and Earth produced the AZES, Genii famous in the theology of the North. In the theology of the Phrygians and Lydians, the ASII were born of the marriage of the Supreme God with the Earth, and Firmicus informs us that the Phrygians attributed to the Earth supremacy over the other elements, and considered her the Great Mother of all things.

Virgil sings the impregnation of the joyous earth, by the Ether, its spouse, that descends upon its bosom, fertilizing it with rains. Columella sings the loves of Nature and her marriage with Heaven annually consummated at the sweet Spring-time. He describes the Spirit of Life, the soul that animates the world, fired with the passion of Love, uniting with Nature and itself, itself a part of

Nature, and filling its own bosom with new productions. This union of the Universe with itself, this mutual action of two sexes, he terms "the great Secrets of Nature," "the Mysteries of the Union of Heaven with Earth, imaged in the Sacred Mysteries of Atys and Bacchus."

Varro tells us that the great Divinities adored at Samothrace were the Heavens and the Earth, considered as First Causes or Primal Gods, and as male and female agents, one bearing to the other the relations that the Soul and Principle of Movement bear to the body or the matter that receives them. These were the gods revered in the Mysteries of that Island, as they were in the orgies of Phœnicia.

Everywhere the sacred body of Nature was covered with the veil of allegory, which concealed it from the profane, and allowed it to be seen only by the sage who thought it worthy to be the object of his study and investigation. She showed herself to those only who loved her in spirit and in truth, and she abandoned the indifferent and careless to error and to ignorance. "The Sages of Greece," says Pausanias, "never wrote otherwise than in an enigmatical manner, never naturally and directly." "Nature," says Sallust the Philosopher, "should be sung only in a language that imitates the secrecy of her processes and operations. She is herself an enigma. We see only bodies in movement; the forces and springs that move them are hidden from us." The poets inspired by the Divinity, the wisest philosophers, all the theologians, the chiefs of the initiations and Mysteries, even the gods uttering their oracles, have borrowed the figurative language of allegory. "The Egyptians," says Proclus, "preferred that mode of teaching, and spoke of the great secrets of Nature, only in mythological enigmas." The Gymnosophists of India and the Druids of Gaul lent to science the same enigmatic language, and in the same style wrote the Hierophants of Phœnicia.

The division of things into the active and the passive cause leads to that of the two Principles of Light and Darkness, connected with and corresponding with it. For Light comes from the ethereal substance that composes the active cause, and darkness from earth or the gross matter which composes the passive cause. In Hesiod, the Earth, by its union with Tartarus, engenders Typhon. Chief of the Powers or Genii of Darkness. But it unites itself with the Ether or Ouranos, when it engenders the Gods of Olympus, or the Stars, children of Starry Ouranos.

Light was the first Divinity worshipped by men. To it they owed the brilliant spectacle of Nature. It seems an emanation from the Creator of all things, making known to our senses the Universe which darkness hides from our eyes, and, as it were, giving it existence. Darkness, as it were, reduces all nature again to nothingness, and almost entirely annihilates man.

Naturally, therefore, two substances of opposite natures were imagined, to each of which the world was in turn subjected, one contributing to its felicity and the other to its misfortune. Light multiplied its enjoyments; Darkness despoiled it of them: the former was its friend, the latter its enemy. To one all good was attributed; to the other all evil; and thus the words "Light" and "Good" became synonymous, and the words "Darkness" and "Evil." It seeming that Good and Evil could not flow from one and the same source, any more than could Light and Darkness, men naturally imagined two Causes or Principles, of different natures and opposite in their effects, one of which shed Light and Good, and the other Darkness and Evil, on the Universe.

This distinction of the two Principles was admitted in all the Theologies, and formed one of the principal bases of all religions. It entered as a primary element into the sacred fables, the cosmogonies and the Mysteries of antiquity. "We are not to suppose," says Plutarch, "that the Principles of the Universe are inanimate bodies, as Democritus and Epicurus thought; nor that a matter devoid of qualities is organized and arranged by a single Reason or Providence, Sovereign over all things, as the Stoics held; for it is not possible that a single Being, good or evil, is the cause of all, inasmuch as God can in nowise be the cause of any evil. The harmony of the Universe is a combination of contraries, like the strings of a lyre, or that of a bow, which alternately is stretched and relaxed." "The good," says Euripides, "is never separated from the Evil. The two must mingle, that all may go well." And this opinion as to the two principles, continues Plutarch, "is that of all antiquity. From the Theologians and Legislators it passed to the Poets and Philosophers. Its author is unknown; but the opinion itself is established by the traditions of the whole human race, and consecrated in the mysteries and sacrifices both of the Greeks and Barbarians, wherein was recognized the dogma of opposing principles in nature, which, by their contrariety, produce the mixture of good and evil. We must admit two contrary causes, two opposing powers, which lead, one to the right and the other to the left, and thus control our life, as they do the sublunary world, which is therefore subject to so many changes and irregularities of every kind. For if there can be no effect without a cause, and if the Good cannot be the cause of the Evil, it is absolutely necessary that there should be a cause for the Evil, as there is one for the Good." This doctrine, he adds, has been generally received among most nations, and especially by those who have had the greatest reputation for wisdom. All have admitted two gods, with different occupations, one making the good and the other the evil found in nature. The former has been styled "God," the latter "Demon." The Persians, or Zoroaster, named the former Ormuzd and the latter Ahriman; of whom they said one was of the nature of Light, the other of that of Darkness. The Egyptians called the former Osiris, and the latter Typhon, his eternal enemy.

The Hebrews, at least after their return from the Persian captivity, had their good Deity, and the Devil, a bad and malicious Spirit, ever opposing God, and Chief of the Angels of Darkness, as God was of those of Light. The word "Satan" means, in Hebrew, simply, "The Adversary."

The Chaldeans, Plutarch says, had their good and evil stars. The Greeks had their Jupiter and Pluto, and their Giants and Titans, to whom were assigned the attributes of the Serpent with which Pluto or Serapis was encircled, and the shape whereof was assumed by Typhon, Ahriman, and the Satan of the Hebrews. Every people had something equivalent to this.

The People of Pegu believe in two Principles, one author of Good and the other of Evil, and strive to propitiate the latter, while they think it needless to worship the former, as he is incapable of doing evil. The people of Java, of the Moluccas, of the Gold Coast, the Hottentots, the people of Teneriffe and Madagascar, and the Savage Tribes of America, all worship and strive to avert the anger and propitiate the good-will of the Evil Spirit.

But among the Greeks, Egyptians, Chaldeans, Persians, and Assyrians, the doctrine of the two Principles formed a complete and regularly arranged theological system. It was the basis of the religion of the Magi and of Egypt. The author of an ancient

work, attributed to Origen, says that Pythagoras learned from
Zarastha, a Magus at Babylon (the same, perhaps, as Zerdusht or
Zoroaster), that there are two principles of all things, whereof one
is the *father* and the other the *mother;* the former, Light, and
the latter, Darkness. Pythagoras thought that the Dependencies
on Light were warmth, dryness, lightness, swiftness; and those on
Darkness, cold, wet, weight, and slowness; and that the world
derived its existence from these two principles, as from the male
and the female. According to Porphyry, he conceived two opposing powers, one good, which he termed Unity, the Light, Right,
the Equal, the Stable, the Straight; the other evil, which he
termed Binary, Darkness, the Left, the Unequal, the Unstable, the
Crooked. These ideas he received from the Orientals, for he
dwelt twelve years at Babylon, studying with the Magi. Varro
says he recognized two Principles of all things,—the Finite and
the Infinite, Good and Evil, Life and Death, Day and Night.
White he thought was of the nature of the Good Principle, and
Black of that of the Evil; that Light and Darkness, Heat and
Cold, the Dry and the Wet, mingled in equal proportions; that
Summer was the triumph of heat, and Winter of cold; that their
equal combination produced Spring and Autumn, the former producing verdure and favorable to health, and the latter, deteriorat-
ing everything, giving birth to maladies. He applied the same
idea to the rising and setting of the sun; and, like the Magi, held
that God or Ormuzd in the body resembled light, and in the soul,
truth.

Aristotle, like Plato, admitted a principle of Evil, resident in
matter and in its eternal imperfection.

The Persians said that Ormuzd, born of the pure Light, and
Ahriman, born of darkness, were ever at war. Ormuzd produced
six Gods, Beneficence, Truth, Good Order, Wisdom, Riches, and
Virtuous Joy. These were so many emanations from the Good
Principle, so many blessings bestowed by it on men. Ahriman, in
his turn, produced six Devs, opponents of the six emanations
from Ormuzd. Then Ormuzd made himself three times as great
as before, ascended as far above the sun as the sun is above the
earth, and adorned the heavens with stars, of which he made
Sirius the sentinel or advance-guard: that he then created twenty-
four other Deities, and placed them in an egg, where Ahriman
also placed twenty-four others, created by him, who broke the egg,

and so intermingled Good and Evil. Theopompus adds that, according to the Magi, for two terms of three thousand years, each of the two Principles is to be by turns victor and the other vanquished; then for three thousand more for each they are to contend with each other, each destroying reciprocally the works of the other; after which Ahriman is to perish, and men, wearing transparent bodies, to enjoy unutterable happiness.

The twelve great Deities of the Persians, the six Amshaspands and six Devs, marshalled, the former under the banner of Light, and the latter under that of Darkness, are the twelve Zodiacal Signs or Months; the six supreme signs, or those of Light, or of Spring and Summer, commencing with Aries, and the six inferior, of Darkness, or of Autumn and Winter, commencing with Libra. Limited Time, as contradistinguished from Time without limits, or Eternity, is Time created and measured by the celestial revolutions. It is comprehended in a period divided into twelve parts, each subdivided into a thousand parts, which the Persians termed years. Thus the circle annually traversed by the Sun was divided into 12,000 parts, or each sign into 3,000: and thus, each year, the Principle of Light and Good triumphed for 3,000 years, that of Evil and Darkness for 3,000, and they mutually destroyed each other's labors for 6,000, or 3,000 for each: so that the Zodiac was equally divided between them. And accordingly Ocellus Lucanus, the Disciple of Pythagoras, held that the principal cause of all sublunary effects resided in the Zodiac, and that from it flowed the good or bad influences of the planets that revolved therein.

The twenty-four good and twenty-four evil Deities, enclosed in the Egg, are the forty-eight constellations of the ancient sphere, equally divided between the realms of Light and Darkness, on the concavity of the celestial sphere which was apportioned among them; and which, enclosing the world and planets, was the mystic and sacred egg of the Magi, the Indians, and the Egyptians,—the egg that issued from the mouth of the God Kneph, that figured as the Orphic Egg in the Mysteries of Greece, that issued from the God Chumong of the Coresians, and from the Egyptian Osiris and the God Phanes of the Modern Orphics, Principle of Light,—the egg crushed by the Sacred Bull of the Japanese, and from which the world emerged; that placed by the Greeks at the feet of Bacchus the bull-horned God, and from which Aristophanes makes Love emerge, who with Night organizes Chaos.

Thus the Balance, the Scorpion, the Serpent of Ophiucus, and the Dragon of the Hesperides became malevolent Signs and Evil Genii; and entire nature was divided between the two principles, and between the agents or partial causes subordinate to them. Hence Michael and his Archangels, and Satan and his fallen compeers. Hence the wars of Jupiter and the Giants, in which the Gods of Olympus fought on the side of the Light-God, against the dark progeny of earth and Chaos; a war which Proclus regarded as symbolizing the resistance opposed by dark and chaotic matter to the active and beneficent force which gives it organization; an idea which in part appears in the old theory of two Principles, one innate in the active and luminous substance of Heaven, and the other in the inert and dark substance of matter that resists the order and the good that Heaven communicates to it.

Osiris conquers Typhon, and Ormuzd, Ahriman, when, at the Vernal Equinox, the creative action of Heaven and its demiourgic energy is most strongly manifested. Then the principle of Light and Good overcomes that of Darkness and Evil, and the world rejoices, redeemed from cold and wintry darkness by the beneficent Sign into which the Sun then enters triumphant and rejoicing, after his resurrection.

From the doctrine of the two Principles, Active and Passive, grew that of the Universe, animated by a Principle of Eternal Life, and by a Universal Soul, from which every isolated and temporary being received at its birth an emanation, which, at the death of such being, returned to its source. The life of matter as much belonged to nature as did matter itself; and as life is manifested by movement, the sources of life must needs seem to be placed in those luminous and eternal bodies, and above all in the Heaven in which they revolve, and which whirls them along with itself in that rapid course that is swifter than all other movement. And fire and heat have so great an analogy with life, that cold, like absence of movement, seemed the distinctive characteristic of death. Accordingly, the vital fire that blazes in the Sun and produces the heat that vivifies everything, was regarded as the principle of organization and life of all sublunary beings.

According to this doctrine, the Universe is not to be regarded, in its creative and eternal action, merely as an immense machine, moved by powerful springs and forced into a continual movement, which, emanating from the circumference, extends to the centre, acts and re-acts in every possible direction, and re-produces in succession all the varied forms which matter receives. So to regard it would be to recognize a cold and purely mechanical action, the energy of which could never produce life.

On the contrary, it was thought, the Universe should be deemed an immense Being, always living, always moved and always moving in an eternal activity inherent in itself, and which, subordinate to no foreign cause, is communicated to all its parts, connects them together, and makes of the world of things a complete and perfect whole. The order and harmony which reign therein seem to belong to and be a part of it, and the design of the various plans of construction of organized beings would seem to be graven in its Supreme Intelligence, source of all the other Intelligences which it communicates together with life to man. Nothing existing out of it, it must be regarded as the principle and term of all things.

Chæremon had no reason for saying that the Ancient Egyptians, inventors of the sacred fables, and adorers of the Sun and the other luminaries, saw in the Universe only a machine, without life and without intelligence, either in its whole or in its parts; and that their cosmogony was a pure Epicureanism, which required only matter and movement to organize its world and govern it. Such an opinion would necessarily exclude all religious worship. Wherever we suppose a worship, there we must suppose intelligent Deities who receive it, and are sensible to the homage of their adorers; and no other people were so religious as the Egyptians.

On the contrary, with them the immense, immutable, and Eternal Being, termed "God" or "the Universe," had eminently, and in all their plenitude, that life and intelligence which sublunary beings, each an infinitely small and temporary portion of itself, possess in a far inferior degree and infinitely less quantity. It was to them, in some sort, like the Ocean, whence the springs, brooks, and rivers have risen by evaporation, and to the bosom whereof they return by a longer or shorter course, and after a longer or shorter separation from the immense mass of its waters. The machine of the Universe was, in their view, like that of man, moved by a Principle of Life which kept it in eternal activity, and circulated in all its parts. The Universe was a living and animated being, like man and the other animals; or rather they were so only because the Universe was essentially so, and for a few moments communicated to each an infinitely minute portion of its eternal life, breathed by it into the inert and gross matter of sublunary bodies. That withdrawn, man or the animal died; and the Universe alone, living and circulating around the wrecks of their bodies, by its eternal movement, organized and animated new bodies, returning to them the eternal fire and subtle substance which vivifies itself, and which, incorporated in its immense mass, was its universal soul.

These were the ancient ideas as to this Great God, Father of all the gods, or of the World; of this BEING, Principle of all things, and of which nothing other than itself is Principle,—the Universal cause that was termed God. Soul of the Universe, eternal like it, immense like it, supremely active and potent in its varied operations, penetrating all parts of this vast body, impressing a regular and symmetrical movement on the spheres, making the elements instinct with activity and order, mingling with everything, organizing everything, vivifying and preserving everything,—this was the UNIVERSE-GOD which the ancients adored as Supreme Cause and God of Gods.

Anchises, in the Æneid, taught Æneas this doctrine of Pythagoras, learned by him from his Masters, the Egyptians, in regard to the Soul and Intelligence of the Universe, from which *our* souls and intelligences, as well as our life and that of the animals, emanate, Heaven, Earth, the Sea, the Moon and the Stars, he said, are moved by a principle of internal life which perpetuates their existence; a great intelligent soul, that penetrates every part of the vast body of the Universe, and, mingling with everything, agitates it by an eternal movement. It is the source of life in all living things. The force which animates all, emanates from the eternal fire that burns in Heaven. In the Georgics, Virgil repeats the same doctrine; and that, at the death of every animal, the life that animated it, part of the universal life, returns to its Principle and to the source of life that circulates in the sphere of the Stars.

Servius makes God the active Cause that organizes the elements into bodies, the vivifying breath or spirit, that, spreading through matter or the elements, produces and engenders all things. The elements compose the substance of our bodies: God composes the souls that vivify these bodies. From it come the instincts of animals, from it their life, he says: and when they die, that life returns to and re-eners into the Universal Soul, and their bodies into Universal Matter.

Timæus of Locria and Plato his Commentator wrote of the Soul of the World, developing the doctrine of Pythagoras, who thought, says Cicero, that God is the Universal Soul, resident everywhere in nature, and of which our Souls are but emanations. "*God is one,*" says Pythagoras, as cited by Justin Martyr: "He is not, as some think, *without* the world, but within it, and entire in its entirety. He sees all that *becomes,* forms all immortal beings, is the author of their powers and performances, the origin of all things, the Light of Heaven, the *Father,* the *Intelligence,* the *Soul* of all beings, the Mover of all spheres."

God, in the view of Pythagoras, was ONE, a single substance, whose continuous parts extended through all the Universe, without separation, difference, or inequality, like the soul in the human body. He denied the doctrine of the spiritualists, who had severed the Divinity from the Universe, making Him exist apart from the Universe, which thus became no more than a material work, on which acted the Abstract Cause, a God, isolated from it. The Ancient Theology did not so separate God from the Universe. This Eusebius attests, in saying that but a small number of wise men, like Moses, had sought for God or the Cause of all, outside of that ALL; while the Philosophers of Egypt and Phœnicia, real authors of all the old Cosmogonies, had placed the Supreme Cause *in* the Universe itself, and in its parts, so that, in their view, the world and all its parts are *in* God.

The World or Universe was thus compared to man: the Principle of Life that moves it, to that which moves man; the Soul of the World to that of man. Therefore Pythagoras called man a *microcosm,* or little world, as possessing in miniature all the qualities found on a great scale in the Universe; by his reason and intelligence partaking of the Divine Nature: and by his faculty of changing aliments into other substances, of growing, and reproducing himself, partaking of elementary Nature. Thus he made the Universe a great intelligent Being, like man—an immense Deity, having in itself, what man has in himself, movement, life, and intelligence, and besides, a perpetuity of existence, which man has not; and, as having in itself perpetuity of movement and life, therefore the Supreme Cause of all.

Everywhere extended, this Universal Soul does not, in the view of Pythagoras, act everywhere equally nor in the same manner. The highest portion of the Universe, being as it were its head, seemed to him its principal seat, and there was the guiding power of the rest of the world. In the seven concentric spheres is resident an eternal order, fruit of the intelligence, the Universal Soul that moves, by a constant and regular progression, the immortal bodies that form the harmonious system of the heavens.

Manilius says: "I sing the invisible and potent Soul of Nature; that Divine Substance which, everywhere inherent in Heaven, Earth, and the Waters of the Ocean, forms the bond that holds together and makes one all the parts of the vast body of the Universe. It, balancing all Forces, and harmoniously arranging the varied relations of the many members of the world, maintains in it the life and regular movement that agitate it, as a result of the action of the living breath or single spirit that dwells in all its parts, circulates in all the channels of universal nature, flashes with rapidity to all its points, and gives to animated bodies the configurations appropriate to the organization of each . . . . This eternal Law, this Divine Force, that maintains the harmony of the world, makes use of the Celestial Signs to organize and guide the animated creatures that breathe upon the earth; and gives to each of them the character and habits most appropriate. By the action of this Force Heaven rules the condition of the Earth and of its fields cultivated by the husbandman: it gives us or takes from us vegetation and harvests: it makes the great ocean overpass its limits at the flow, and retire within them again at the ebbing, of the tide."

Thus it is no longer by means of a poetic fiction only that the heavens and the earth become animated and personified, and are deemed living existences, from which other existences proceed. For now they live, with their own life, a life eternal like their bodies, each gifted with a life and perhaps a soul, like those of man, a portion of the universal life and universal soul; and the other bodies that they form, and which they contain in their bosoms, live only through them and with their life, as the embryo lives in the bosom of its mother, in consequence and by means of the life communicated to it, and which the mother ever maintains by the active power of her own life. Such is the universal life of the world, reproduced in all the beings which its superior portion creates in its inferior portion, that is as it were the *matrix* of the world, or of the beings that the heavens engender in its bosom.

"The soul of the world," says Macrobius, "is nature itself" [as the soul of man is man himself], "always acting through the celestial spheres which it moves, and which but follow the irresistible impulse it impresses on them. The heavens, the sun, great seat of generative power, the signs, the stars, and the planets act only with the activity of the soul of the Universe. From that soul, through them, come all the variations and changes of sublunary nature, of which the heavens and celestial bodies are but the secondary causes. The zodiac, with its signs, is an existence, immortal and divine, organized by the universal soul, and producing, or gathering in itself, all the varied emanations of the different powers that make up the nature of the Divinity."

This doctrine, that gave to the heavens and the spheres living souls, each a portion of the universal soul, was of extreme antiquity. It was held by the old Sabæans. It was taught by Timæus, Plato, Speusippus, Iamblichus, Macrobius, Marcus Aurelius, and Pythagoras. When once men had assigned a soul to the Universe, containing in itself the plenitude of the animal life of particular beings, and even of the stars, they soon supposed that soul to be essentially intelligent, and the source of intelligence of all intelligent beings. Then the Universe became to them not only animated but intelligent, and of that intelligence the different parts of nature partook. Each soul was the vehicle, and, as it were, the envelope of the intelligence that attached itself to it, and could repose nowhere else. Without a soul there could be no intelligence; and as there was a universal soul, source of all souls, the universal soul was gifted with a universal intelligence, source of all particular intelligences. So the soul of the world contained in itself the intelligence of the world. All the agents of nature into which the universal soul entered, received also a portion of its intelligence, and the Universe, in its totality and in its parts, was filled with intelligences, that might be regarded as so many emanations from the sovereign and universal intelligence. Wherever the divine soul acted as a cause, there also was intelligence; and thus Heaven, the stars, the elements, and all parts of the Universe, became the seats of so many divine intelligences. Every minutest portion of the great soul became a partial intelligence, and the more it was disengaged from gross matter, the more active and intelligent it was. And all the old adorers of nature, the theologians, astrologers, and poets, and the most distinguished philosophers, supposed that the stars were so many animated and intelligent beings, or eternal bodies, active causes of effects here below, whom a principle of life animated, and whom an intelligence directed, which was but an emanation from, and a portion of, the universal life and intelligence of the world.

The Universe itself was regarded as a supremely intelligent being. Such was the doctrine of Timæus of Locria. The soul of man was part of the intelligent soul of the Universe, and therefore itself intelligent. His opinion was that of many other philosophers. Cleanthes, a disciple of ZENO, regarded the Universe as God, or as the unproduced and universal cause of all effects produced. He ascribed a soul and intelligence to universal nature, and to this intelligent soul, in his view, divinity belonged. From it the intelligence of man was an emanation, and shared its divinity. Chrysippus, the most subtle of the Stoics, placed in the universal reason that forms the soul and intelligence of nature, that divine force or essence of the Divinity which he assigned to the world moved by the universal soul that pervades its every part.

An interlocutor in Cicero's work, *De Natura Deorum,* formally argues that the Universe is necessarily intelligent and wise, because man, an infinitely small portion of it, is so. Cicero makes the same argument in his oration for Milo. The physicists came to the same conclusion as the philosophers. They supposed that movement essentially belonged to the soul, and the direction of regular and ordered movements to the intelligence. And, as both movement and order exist in the Universe, therefore, they held, there must be in it a soul and an intelligence that rule it, and are not to be distinguished from itself; because the idea of the Universe is but the aggregate of all the particular ideas of all things that exist.

The argument was, that the Heavens, and the Stars which make part of them, are *animated,* because they possess a portion of the Universal Soul: they are *intelligent* beings, because that Universal Soul, part whereof they possess, is supremely intelligent; and they share *Divinity* with Universal Nature, because Divinity resides in the Universal Soul and Intelligence which move and rule the world, and of each of which they hold a share. By this process of logic, the interlocutor in Cicero assigned Divinity to the Stars, as animated beings gifted with sensibility and intelligence, and composed of the noblest and purest portions of the ethereal substance, unmixed with matter of an alien nature, and essentially containing light and heat. Hence he concluded them to be so many gods, of an intelligence superior to that of other existences, corresponding to the lofty height in which they moved with such perfect regularity and admirable harmony, with a movement spontaneous and free. Hence he made them "Gods," active, eternal, and intelligent "Causes"; and peopled the realm of Heaven with a host of Eternal Intelligences, celestial Genii or Angels, sharing the universal Divinity, and associated with it in the administration of the Universe, and the dominion exercised over sublunary nature and man.

We make the motive-force of the planets to be a mechanical law, which we explain by the combination of two forces, the centripetal and centrifugal, whose *origin* we cannot demonstrate, but whose *force* we can calculate. The ancients regarded them as moved by an intelligent force that had its origin in the first and universal Intelligence. Is it so certain, after all, that we are any nearer the truth than they were; or that we know what our "centripetal and centrifugal forces" *mean;* for what *is* a *force?* With us, the entire Deity acts upon and moves each planet, as He does the sap that circulates in the little blade of grass, and in the particles of blood in the tiny veins of the invisible rotifer. With the Ancients, the Deity of each Star was but a portion of the Universal God, the Soul of Nature. Each Star and Planet, with them, was moved of *itself,* and directed by *its own* special intelligence. And this opinion of Achilles Tatius, Diodorus, Chrysippus, Aristotle, Plato, Heraclides of Pontus, Theophrastus, Simplicius, Macrobius, and Proclus, that in each Star there is an immortal Soul and Intelligence,—part of the Universal Soul and Intelligence of the Whole,—this opinion of Orpheus, Plotinus, and the Stoics, was in reality, that of many Christian philosophers. For Origen held the same opinion; and Augustin held that every visible thing in the world was superintended by an Aneglic Power: and Cosma. the Monk, believed that every Star was under the guidance of an Angel; and the author of the Octateuch, written in the time of the Emperor Justin, says that they are moved by the impulse communicated to them by Angels stationed above the firmament. Whether the stars were animated beings, was a question that Christian antiquity did not decide. Many of the Christian doctors believed they were. Saint Augustin hesitates, Saint Jerome doubts, if Solomon did not assign souls to the Stars. Saint

Ambrose does not doubt they *have* souls; and Pamphilus says that many of the Church believe they are reasonable beings, while many think otherwise, but that neither one nor the other opinion is heretical.

Thus the Ancient Thought, earnest and sincere, wrought out the idea of a Soul *inherent* in the Universe and in its several parts. The next step was to *separate* that Soul from the Universe, and give to it an external and independent existence and personality; still omnipresent, in every inch of space and in every particle of matter, and yet not a part of Nature, but its Cause and its Creator. This is the middle ground between the two doctrines, of Pantheism (or that all is God, and God is *in* all and is all), on the one side, and Atheism (or that all is nature, and there is no other God), on the other; which doctrines, after all, when reduced to their simplest terms, seem to be the same.

We complacently congratulate ourselves on our recognition of a *personal* God, as being the conception most suited to human sympathies, and exempt from the mystifications of Pantheism. But the Divinity remains still a mystery, notwithstanding all the devices which symbolism, either from the organic or inorganic creation, can supply; and personification is itself a symbol, liable to misapprehension as much as, if not more so than, any other, since it is apt to degenerate into a mere reflection of our own infirmities; and hence *any* affirmative idea or conception that we can, in our own minds, picture of the Deity, must needs be infinitely inadequate.

The spirit of the Vedas (or sacred Indian Books, of great antiquity), as understood by their earliest as well as most recent expositors, is decidedly a pantheistic monotheism—one God, and He all in all; the many divinities, numerous as the prayers addressed to them, being resolvable into the titles and attributes of a few, and ultimately into THE ONE. The machinery of personification was understood to have been unconsciously assumed as a mere expedient to supply the deficiencies of language; and the Mimansa justly considered itself as only interpreting the true meaning of the Mantras, when it proclaimed that, in the beginning, "Nothing was but Mind, the Creative Thought of Him which existed alone from the beginning, and breathed without afflation." The idea suggested in the Mantras is dogmatically asserted and developed in the Upanischadas. The Vedanta philosophy, assuming the mystery of the "ONE IN MANY" as the fundamental article of faith, maintained not only the Divine Unity, but the identity of matter and spirit. The unity which it advocates is that of mind. Mind is the Universal Element, the One God, the Great Soul, Mahaatma. He is the material as well as efficient cause, and the world is a texture of which he is both the web and the weaver. He is the Macrocosmos, the universal organism called Pooroosha, of which Fire, Air, and Sun are only the chief members. His head is light, his eyes the sun and moon, his breath the wind, his voice the opened Vedas. All proceeds from Brahm, like the web from the spider and the grass from the earth.

Yet it is only the impossibility of expressing in language the origination of matter from spirit, which gives to Hindū philosophy the appearance of materialism. Formless Himself, the Deity is present in all forms. His glory is displayed in the Universe as the image of the sun in water, which is, yet is not, the luminary itself. All maternal agency and appearance, the subjective world, are to a great extent phantasms, the notional representations of ignorance. They occupy, however, a middle ground between reality and non-reality; they are unreal, because nothing exists but Brahm; yet in some degree real, inasmuch as they constitute an outward manifestation of him. They are a self-induced hypostasis of the Deity, under which He *presents to Himself* the whole of animate and inanimate Nature, the actuality of the moment, the diversified *appearances* which successively invest the one Pantheistic Spirit.

The great aim of reason is to generalize; to discover unity in multiplicity, order in apparent confusion; to separate from the accidental and the transitory, the stable and universal. In the contemplation of Nature, and the vague, but almost intuitive perception of a general uniformity of plan among endless varieties of operation and form, arise those solemn and reverential feelings, which, if accompanied by intellectual activity, may eventually ripen into philosophy.

Consciousness of self and of personal identity is co-existent with our existence. We cannot conceive of mental existence without it. It is not the work of reflection nor of logic, nor the result of observation, experiment, and experience. It is a gift from God, like instinct; and that consciousness of a thinking soul which is really the person that we are, and other than our body, is the best and most solid proof of the soul's existence. We have the same consciousness of a Power on which we are dependent; which we can *define* and form an idea or picture of, as little as we can of the soul, and yet which we *feel,* and therefore *know,* exists. True and correct ideas of that Power, of the Absolute Existence from which all proceeds, we cannot trace; if by true and correct we mean *adequate* ideas; for of such we are not, with our limited faculties, capable. And ideas of His nature, so far correct as we are capable of entertaining, can only be attained either by direct inspiration or by the investigations of philosophy.

The idea of the universal preceded the recognition of any system for its explanation. It was *felt* rather than understood; and it was long before the grand conception on which all philosophy rests received through deliberate investigation that analytical development which might properly entitle it to the name. The sentiment, when first observed by the self-conscious mind, was, says Plato, "a Divine gift, communicated to mankind by some Prometheus, or by those ancients who lived nearer to the gods than our degenerate selves." The mind deduced from its first experiences the notion of a general Cause or Antecedent, to which it shortly gave a name and personified it. This was the statement of a theorem, obscure in proportion to its generality. *It explained all things but itself*. It was *a true* cause, but an *incomprehensible* one. Ages had to pass before the nature of the theorem could be rightly appreciated, and before men, acknowledging the First Cause to be an object of faith rather than science, were contented to confine their researches to those nearer relations of existence and succession, which are really within the reach of their faculties. At first, and for a long time, the intellect deserted the real for a hastily-formed ideal world, and the imagination usurped the place of reason, in attempting to put a construction on the most general and inadequate of conceptions, by transmuting its symbols into realities, and by substantializing it under a thousand arbitrary forms.

In poetry, the idea of Divine unity became, as in Nature, obscured by a multifarious symbolism; and the notionalities of transcendental philosophy reposed on views of nature scarcely more profound than those of the earliest symbolists. Yet the idea of unity was rather obscured than extinguished; and Xenophanes appeared as an enemy of Homer, only because he more emphatic-ally insisted on the monotheistic element, which, in poetry, has been comparatively overlooked. The first philosophy reasserted the unity which poetry had lost; but being unequal to investigate its nature, it again resigned it to the world of approximate sensa-tions, and became bewildered in materialism, considering the con-ceptional whole or First Element as some refinement of matter, unchangeable in its essence, though subject to mutations of qual-ity and form in an eternal succession of seeming decay and regen-eration; comparing it to water, air, or fire, as each endeavored to refine on the doctrine of his predecessor, or was influenced by a different class of theological traditions.

In the philosophical systems, the Divine Activity, divided by the poets and by popular belief among a race of personifications, in whom the idea of descent replaced that of cause, or of pantheistic evolution, was restored, without subdivision or reservation, to nature as a whole; at first as a mechanical *force* or *life;* afterward as an all-pervading *soul* or inherent *thought;* and lastly as an external directing *Intelligence.*

The Ionian revival of pantheism was materialistic. The Moving Force was inseparable from a material element, a subtle yet visible ingredient. Under the form of *air* or *fire,* the principle of life was associated with the most obvious material machinery of nature. Everything, it was said, is alive and full of gods. The wonders of the volcano, the magnet, the ebb and flow of the tide, were vital indications, the breathing or moving of the Great World-Animal. The imperceptible ether of Anaximenes had no *positive* quality beyond the atmospheric air with which it was easily confused: and even the "Infinite" of Anaximander, though free of the conditions of quality or quantity, was only an ideal chaos, relieved of its coarseness by negations. It was the illimit-able storehouse or Pleroma, out of which is evolved the endless circle of phenomenal change. A moving Force was recognized *in,* but not clearly distinguished *from,* the material. Space, Time, Figure, and Number, and other common forms or properties, which exist only as *attributes,* were treated as *substances,* or at least as making a substantial connection between the objects to which they belong: and all the conditions of material existence were supposed to have been evolved out of the Pythagorean Monad.

The Eleatic philosophers treated conceptions not only as

entities, but as the only entities, alone possessing the stability and certainty and reality vainly sought among phenomena. The only reality was Thought. "All *real* existence," they said, "is *mental* existence; non-existence, being inconceivable, is therefore impossible; existence fills up the whole range of thought, and is inseparable from its exercise; thought and its object are one."

Xenophanes used ambiguous language, applicable to the material as well as to the mental, and exclusively appropriate to neither. In other words, he availed himself of material imagery to illustrate an indefinite meaning. In announcing the universal being, he appealed to the heavens as the visible manifestation, calling it *spherical,* a term borrowed from the material world. He said that God was neither moved nor unmoved, limited nor unlimited. He did not even attempt to express clearly what cannot be conceived clearly; admitting, says Simplicius, that such speculations were above physics. Parmenides employed similar expedients, comparing his metaphysical Deity to a sphere, or to heat, an aggregate or a continuity, and so involuntarily withdrawing its nominal attributes.

The Atomic school, dividing the All into Matter and Force, deemed matter unchangeable in its ultimate constitution, though infinitely variable in its resultant forms. They made all variety proceed from the varied combinations of atoms; but they required no mover nor director of the atoms external to themselves; no universal Reason; but a Mechanical Eternal *Necessity,* like that of the Poets. Still it is doubtful whether there ever was a time when reason could be said to be entirely asleep, a stranger to its own existence, notwithstanding this apparent materialism. The earliest contemplation of the external world, which brings it into an imagined association with ourselves, assigns, either to its whole or its parts, the sensation and volition which belong to our own souls.

Anaxagoras admitted the existence of ultimate elementary particles, as Empedocles did, from the combinations whereof all material phenomena resulted. But he asserted the Moving Force to be Mind; and yet, though he clearly saw the impossibility of advancing by illustration or definition beyond a reasonable faith, or a simple negation of materiality, yet he could not wholly desist from the endeavor to illustrate the nature of this non-matter or mind, by symbols drawn from those physical considerations which decided him in placing it in a separate category. Whether as human reason, or as the regulating Principle in nature, he held it different from all other things in character and effect, and that therefore it must necessarily differ in its essential constitution. It was neither Matter, nor a Force conjoined with matter, or homogeneous with it, but independent and generically distinct, especially in this, that, being the source of all motion, separation, and cognition, it is something entirely unique, pure, and unmixed; and so, being unhindered by any interfering influence limiting its independence of individual action, it has Supreme Empire over all things, over the vortex of worlds. as well as over all that live in them. It is most penetrating and powerful, mixing with other things, though no other thing mixes with it; exercises universal control and cognition, and includes the *Necessity* of the Poets, as well as the independent power of thought which we exercise within ourselves. In short, it is the self-conscious power of thought extended to the Universe, and exalted into the Supreme External Mind which sees, knows, and directs all things.

Thus Pantheism and Materialism were both avoided; and matter, though as infinitely varied as the senses represent it, was held in a bond of unity transferred to a ruling power apart from it. That Power could not be Prime Mover, if it were itself moved; nor All-Governing, if not apart from the things it governs. If the arranging Principle were *inherent* in matter, it would have been impossible to account for the existence of a chaos: if something *external,* then the old Ionian doctrine of a "beginning" became more easily conceivable, as being the epoch at which the Arranging Intelligence commenced its operations.

But this grand idea of an all-governing independent mind involved difficulties which proved insuperable; because it gave to matter, in the form of chaos, an independent and eternal self-existence, and so introduced a dualism of mind and matter. In the Mind or Intelligence, Anaxagoras included not only life and motion, but the moral principles of the noble and good; and probably used the term on account of the popular misapplication of the word "God," and as being less liable to misconstruction, and more specifically marking his idea. His "Intelligence" principle remained practically liable to many of the same defects as the "Necessity" of the poets. It was the presentiment of a great idea, which it was for the time impossible to explain or follow out.

It was not yet intelligible, nor was even the road opened through which it might be approached.

Mind cannot advance in metaphysics beyond self-deification. In attempting to go further, it only enacts the apotheosis of its own subtle conceptions, and so sinks below the simpler ground already taken. The realities which Plato could not recognize in phenomena, he discovered within his own mind, and as unhesitatingly as the old Theosophists installed its creations among the gods. He, like most philosophers after Anaxagoras, made the Supreme Being to be Intelligence; but in other respects left His nature undefined, or rather indefinite through the variety of definitions, a conception vaguely floating between Theism and Pantheism. Though deprecating the demoralizing tendencies of poetry, he was too wise to attempt to replace them by other representations of a positive kind. He justly says, that spiritual things can be made intelligible only through figures; and the forms of allegorical expression which, in a rude age, had been adopted unconsciously, were designedly chosen by the philosopher as the most appropriate vehicles for theological ideas.

As the devices of symbolism were gradually stripped away, in order, if possible, to reach the fundamental conception, the religious feeling habitually connected with it seemed to evaporate under the process. And yet the advocates of Monotheism, Xenophanes and Heraclitus, declaimed only against the making of gods in human form. They did not attempt to strip nature of its divinity, but rather to recall religious contemplation from an exploded symbolism to a purer one. They continued the veneration which, in the background of poetry, has been maintained for Sun and Stars, the Fire or Ether. Socrates prostrated himself before the rising luminary; and the eternal spheres, which seem to have shared the religious homage of Xenophanes, retained a secondary and qualified Divinity in the Schools of the Peripatetics and Stoics.

The unseen being or beings revealed only to the Intellect became the theme of philosophy; and their more ancient symbols, if not openly discredited, were passed over with evasive generality, as beings respecting whose problematical existence we must be "content with what has been reported by those ancients, who, assuming to be their descendants, must therefore be supposed to have been well acquainted with their own ancestors and family connections." And the Theism of Anaxagoras was still more decidedly subversive, not only of Mythology, but of the whole religion of outward nature; it being an appeal from the world without, to the consciousness of spiritual dignity within man.

In the doctrines of Aristotle, the world moves on uninterruptedly, always changing, yet ever the same, like Time, the Eternal Now, knowing neither repose nor death. There is a principle which makes good the failure of *identity*, by multiplying *resemblances;* the destruction of the *individual* by an eternal renewal of the *form* in which matter is manifested. This regular eternal *movement* implies an Eternal Mover; not an inert Eternity, such as the Platonic *Eidos*, but one always *acting*, His *essence* being *to act*, for otherwise he might *never* have acted, and the existence of the world would be an accident; for what should have, in that case, decided Him to act, after long inactivity? Nor can He be partly *in act* and partly *potential*, that is, quiescent and undetermined to act or not to act, for even in that case motion would not be eternal, but contingent and precarious. He is therefore *wholly in act*, a pure, untiring activity, and for the same reasons wholly immaterial. Thus Aristotle avoided the idea that God was inactive and self-contemplative for an eternity, and then for some unknown reason, or by some unknown motive, commenced to act outwardly and produce; but he incurred the opposite hazard, of making the result of His action, matter and the Universe, be coexistent with Himself; or, in other words, of denying that there was any time when His outward action *commenced*.

The First Cause, he said, unmoved, moves all. *Act* was *first*, and the Universe has existed forever; one persistent cause directing its continuity. The *unity* of the First Mover follows from His immateriality. If He were not Himself unmoved, the series of motions and causes of motion would be infinite. Unmoved, therefore, and unchangeable Himself, all movement, even that in space, is caused by Him: He is necessary: He cannot be otherwise than as He is; and it is only through the necessity of His being that we can account for those necessary eternal relations which make a science of Being possible. Thus Aristotle leaned to a seemingly personal God; not a Being of parts and passions, like the God of the Hebrews, or that of the mass even of educated men in our own day, but a Substantial Head of all the categories of being, an Individuality of Intelligence, the dogma of Anaxagoras revived out of a more elaborate and profound analysis of Nature; something like that living unambiguous Principle which the old poets, in advance of the materialistic cosmogonists from Night and Chaos, had discovered in Ouranos or Zeus. Soon, however, the vision of personality is withdrawn, and we reach that culminating point of thought where the real blends with the ideal; where moral action and objective thought (that is, thought exercised as to anything outside of itself), as well as the material body, are excluded; and where the divine action in the world retains its veil of impenetrable mystery, and to the utmost ingenuity of research presents but a contradiction. At this extreme, the series of efficient causes resolves itself into the Final Cause. That which moves, itself *unmoved*, can only be the immobility of Thought or Form. God is both formal, efficient, and final cause; the One Form comprising all forms, the one good including all good, the goal of the longing of the University, moving the world as the object of love or rational desire moves the individual. He is the internal or self-realized Final Cause, having no end beyond Himself. He is no moral agent; for if He were, He would be but an instrument for producing something still higher and greater. One sort of act only, activity of mind or thought, can be assigned to Him who is at once all act yet all repose. What we call our highest pleasure, which distinguishes wakefulness and sensation, and which gives a reflected charm to hope and memory, is with Him perpetual. His existence is unbroken enjoyment of that which is most excellent but only temporary with us. The divine quality of active and yet tranquil self-contemplation characterizing intelligence, is pre-eminently possessed by the divine mind; His thought, which is His existence, being, unlike ours, unconditional and wholly *act*. If He can receive any gratification or enjoyment from that which exists beyond Himself, He can also be displeased and pained with it, and then He would be an imperfect being. To suppose pleasure experienced by Him from anything outward, supposes an insufficient *prior* enjoyment and happiness, and a sort of dependency. Man's Good is beyond himself; not so God's. The eternal act which produces the world's life is the eternal desire of good. The object of the Absolute Thought is the Absolute Good. Nature is all movement, and Thought all repose. In contemplating that absolute good, the Finality can contemplate only itself; and thus, all material interference being excluded, the distinction of subject and object vanishes in complete identification, and the Divine Thought is "the thinking of thought." The energy of mind is life, and God is that energy in its purity and perfection. He is therefore life itself, eternal and perfect; and this sums up all that is meant by the term "God." And yet, after all this transcendentalism, the very essence of thought consists in its mobility and power of transference from object to object; and we can conceive of no thought, without an object beyond itself, about which to think, or of any activity in mere self-contemplation, without outward act, movement, or manifestation.

Plato endeavors to show how the Divine Principle of Good becomes realized in Nature: Aristotle's system is a vast analogical induction to prove how all Nature tends toward a final good. Plato considered Soul as a principle of movement, and made his Deity realize, that is, turn into realities, his ideas as a free, intelligent Force. Aristotle, for whom Soul is the motionless centre from which motion radiates, and to which it converges, conceives a correspondingly unmoved God. The Deity of Plato creates, superintends, and rejoices in the universal joy of, His creatures. That of Aristotle is the perfection of man's intellectual activity extended to the Universe. When he makes the Deity to be an eternal act of self-contemplation, the world is not excluded from His cognizance, for He contemplates it within Himself. Apart from and beyond the world, He yet mysteriously intermingles with it. He is universal as well as individual; His agency is necessary and general, yet also makes the real and the good of the particular.

When Plato had given to the unformed world the animal life of the Ionians, and added to that the Anaxagorean Intelligence, overruling the wild principle of Necessity; and when to Intelligence was added Beneficence; and the dread Wardours, Force and Strength, were made subordinate to Mildness and Goodness, it seemed as if a further advance were impossible, and that the Deity could not be more than The Wise and The Good.

But the contemplation of the Good implies that of its opposite, Evil. When God is held to be "The Good," it is not because Evil is unknown, but because it is designedly excluded from His attributes. But if Evil be a separate and independent existence, how would it fare with His prerogative of Unity and Supremacy? To meet this dilemma, it remained only to fall back on something more or less akin to the vagueness of antiquity; to make a virtual confession of ignorance, to deny the ultimate reality of evil, like Plato and Aristotle, or, with Speusippus, the eternity of its antithetical existence, to surmise that it is only one of those notions which are indeed provisionally indispensable in a condition of finite knowledge, but of which so many have been already discredited by the advance of philosophy; to revert, in short, to the original conception of "The Absolute," or of a single Being, in whom all mysteries are explained, and before whom the disturbing principle is reduced to a mere turbid spot on the ocean of Eternity, which to the eye of faith may be said no longer to exist.

But the absolute is nearly allied to the non-existent. Matter and evil obtruded themselves too constantly and convincingly to be confuted or cancelled by subtleties of Logic. It is in vain to attempt to merge the world in God, while the world of experience exhibits contrariety, imperfection, and mutability, instead of the immutability of its source. Philosophy was but another name for uncertainty; and after the mind had successively deified Nature and its own conceptions, without any practical result but toilsome occupation; when the reality it sought, without or within, seemed ever to elude its grasp, the intellect, baffled in its higher flights, sought advantage and repose in aiming at truth of a lower but more applicable kind.

The Deity of Plato is a Being proportioned to human sympathies; the Father of the World, as well as its Creator; the author of good only, not of evil. "Envy," he says, "is far removed from celestial beings, and man, if willing, and braced for the effort, is permitted to aspire to a communion with the solemn troops and sweet societies of Heaven. God is the Idea or Essence of Goodness, the Good itself [τὸ ἀγαθόν]: in goodness, He created the World, and gave to it the greatest perfection of which it was susceptible; making it, as far as possible, an image of Himself. The sublime type of all excellence is an object not only of veneration but love." The Sages of old had already intimated in enigmas that God is the Author of Good; that like the Sun in Heaven, or Æsculapius on earth, He is "Healer," "Saviour," and "Redeemer," the destroyer and averter of Evil, ever healing the mischiefs inflicted by Herè, the wanton or irrational power of nature.

Plato only asserts with more distinctness the dogma of antiquity when he recognizes LOVE as the highest and most beneficent of gods, who gives to nature the invigorating energy restored by the art of medicine to the body; since Love is emphatically the physician of the Universe, the Æsculapius to whom Socrates wished to sacrifice in the hour of his death.

A figurative idea, adopted from familiar imagery, gave that endearing aspect to the divine connection with the Universe which had commanded the earliest assent of the sentiments, until, rising in refinement with the progress of mental cultivation, it ultimately established itself as firmly in the deliberate approbation of the understanding, as it had ever responded to the sympathies. Even the rude Scythians, Bithynians, and Scandinavians, called God their "Father"; all nations traced their ancestry more or less directly to Heaven. The Hyperborean Olen, one of the oldest symbols of the religious antiquity of Greece, made Love the First-born of Nature. Who will venture to pronounce at what time God was first worthily and truly honored, or when man first began to feel aright the mute eloquence of nature? In the obscure physics of the mystical Theologers who preceded Greek philosophy, Love was the Great First Cause and Parent of the Universe. "Zeus," says Proclus, "when entering upon the work of creation, changed Himself into the form of Love: and He brought forward Aphroditè, the principle of Unity and Universal Harmony, to display her light to all. In the depths of His mysterious being, He contains the principle of love within Himself; in Him creative wisdom and blessed love are united."

> "From the first
> Of Days on these his love divine be fixed,
> His admiration; till in time complete
> What he admired and loved, his vital smile
> Unfolded into being."

The speculators of the venerable East, who had conceived the idea of an Eternal Being superior to all affection and change, in his own sufficiency enjoying a plenitude of serene and independent bliss, were led to inquire into the apparently inconsistent fact of the creation of the world. Why, they asked, did He, who required nothing external to Himself to complete His already-existing Perfection, come forth out of His unrevealed and perfect existence, and become incorporated in the vicissitudes of nature? The solution of the difficulty was Love. The Great Being beheld the beauty of His own conception, which dwelt with Him alone from the beginning, Maia, or Nature's loveliness, at once the germ of passion and the source of worlds. Love became the universal parent, when the Deity, before remote and inscrutable, became ideally separated into the loving and the beloved.

And here again recurs the ancient difficulty; that, at whatever early period this creation occurred, an eternity had previously elapsed, during which God, dwelling alone in His unimpeached unity, had no object for His love; and that the very word implies to us an existing object toward which the love is directed; so that we cannot conceive of love in the absence of any object to be loved; and therefore we again return to this point, that if love is of God's essence, and He is unchangeable, the same necessity of His nature, supposed to have caused creation, must ever have made His existence without an object to love impossible: and so that the Universe must have been co-existent with Himself.

The questions how and why evil exists in the Universe: how its existence is to be reconciled with the admitted wisdom and goodness and omnipotence of God; and how far man is a free agent, or controlled by an inexorable necessity or destiny, have two sides. On one, they are questions as to the qualities and attributes of God; for we must infer His moral nature from His mode of governing the Universe, and they ever enter into any consideration of His intellectual nature: and on the other, they directly concern the moral responsibility, and therefore the destiny, of man. All-important, therefore, in both points of view, they have been much discussed in all ages of the world, and have no doubt urged men, more than all other questions have, to endeavor to fathom the profound mysteries of the Nature and the mode of Existence and action of an incomprehensible God.

And, with these, still another question also presents itself: whether the Deity governs the Universe by fixed and unalterable laws, or by special Providences and interferences, so that He may be induced to change His course and the results of human or material action, by prayer and supplication.

God alone is all-powerful; but the human soul has in all ages asserted its claim to be considered as part of the Divine. "The purity of the spirit," says Van Helmont, "is shown through energy and efficaciousness of will. God, by the agency of an infinite will, created the Universe, and the same sort of power in an inferior degree, limited more or less by external hindrances, exists in all spiritual beings." The higher we ascend in antiquity, the more does prayer take the form of incantation; and that form it still in a great degree retains, since the rites of public worship are generally considered not merely as an expression of trust or reverence, as real spiritual acts, the effect of which is looked for only within the mind of the worshipper, but as acts from which some direct outward result is anticipated, the attainment of some desired object, of health or wealth, of supernatural gifts for body or soul, of exemption from danger, or vengeance upon enemies. Prayer was able to change the purposes of Heaven, and to make the Devs tremble under the abyss. It exercised a compulsory influence over the gods. It promoted the magnetic sympathy of spirit with spirit; and the Hindū and Persian liturgies, addressed not only to the Deity Himself, but to His diversified manifestations, were considered wholesome and necessary iterations of the living or creative Word which at first effectuated the divine will, and which from instant to instant supports the universal frame by its eternal repetition.

In the narrative of the Fall, we have the Hebrew mode of explaining the great moral mystery, the origin of evil and the apparent estrangement from Heaven; and a similar idea, variously modified, obtained in all the ancient creeds. Everywhere, man had at the beginning been innocent and happy, and had lapsed, by temptation and his own weakness, from his first estate. Thus was accounted for the presumed connection of increase of knowledge with increase of misery, and, in particular, the great penalty of death was reconciled with Divine Justice. Subordinate to these greater points were the questions, Why is the earth covered with thorns and weeds? whence the origin of clothing, of sexual shame and passion? whence the infliction of labor, and how to justify the degraded condition of woman in the East, or account for the loathing so generally felt toward the Serpent Tribe?

The hypothesis of a fall, required under some of its modifications in all systems, to account for the apparent imperfection in the work of a Perfect Being, was, in Eastern philosophy, the unavoidable accompaniment and condition of limited or individual existence; since the Soul, considered as a fragment of the Universal Mind, might be said to have lapsed from its pre-eminence when parted from its source, and ceasing to form part of integral perfection. The theory of its reunion was correspondent to the assumed cause of its degradation. To reach its prior condition, its individuality must cease; it must be emancipated by re-absorption into the Infinite, the consummation of all things in God, to be promoted by human effort in spiritual meditation or self-mortification, and completed in the magical transformation of death.

And as man had fallen, so it was held that the Angels of Evil had, from their first estate, to which, like men, they were, in God's good time, to be restored, and the reign of evil was then to cease forever. To this great result all the Ancient Theologies point; and thus they all endeavored to reconcile the existence of Sin and Evil with the perfect and undeniable wisdom and beneficence of God.

With man's exercise of thought are inseparably connected freedom and responsibility. Man assumes his proper rank as a moral agent, when with a sense of the limitations of his nature arise the consciousness of freedom, and of the obligations accompanying its exercise, the sense of duty and of the capacity to perform it. To suppose that man ever imagined himself not to be a free agent until he had argued himself into that belief, would be to suppose that he was in that below the brutes; for he, like them, is *conscious* of his freedom to act. Experience alone teaches him that this freedom of action is limited and controlled; and when what is outward to him restrains and limits this freedom of action, he instinctively rebels against it as a wrong. The rule of duty and the materials of experience are derived from an acquaintance with the conditions of the external world, in which the faculties are exerted; and thus the problem of man involves those of Nature and God. Our freedom, we learn by experience, is determined by an agency external to us; our happiness is intimately dependent on the relations of the outward World, and on the moral character of its Ruler.

Then at once arises this problem: The God of Nature must be One, and His character cannot be suspected to be other than good. Whence, then, came the evil, the consciousness of which must invariably have preceded or accompanied man's moral development? On this subject human opinion has ebbed and flowed between two contradictory extremes, one of which seems inconsistent with God's Omnipotence, and the other with His beneficence. If God, it was said, is perfectly wise and good, evil must arise from some *independent* and *hostile* principle: if, on the other hand, all agencies are subordinate to One, it is difficult, if evil does indeed exist, if there is any such thing as Evil, to avoid the impiety of making God the Author of it.

The recognition of a moral and physical dualism in nature was adverse to the doctrine of Divine Unity. Many of the Ancients thought it absurd to imagine one Supreme Being, like Homer's Jove, distributing good and evil out of two urns. They therefore substituted, as we have seen, the doctrine of two distinct and eternal principles; some making the cause of evil to be the inherent imperfection of matter and the flesh, without explaining how God was not the cause of that; while others personified the required agency, and fancifully invented an Evil Principle, the question of whose origin indeed involved all the difficulty of the original problem, but whose existence, if once taken for granted, was sufficient as a popular solution of the mystery; the difficulty being supposed no longer to exist when pushed a step further off, as the difficulty of conceiving the world upheld by an elephant was supposed to be got rid of when it was said that the elephant was supported by a tortoise.

The simpler, and probably the older, notion, treated the one only God as the Author of all things. "I form the light," says Jehovah, "and create darkness; I cause prosperity and create evil; I, the Lord, do all these things." "All mankind," says Maximus Tyrius, "are agreed that there exists one only Universal King and Father, and that the many gods are His Children." There is nothing improbable in the supposition that the primitive idea was that there was but one God. A vague sense of Nature's Unity, blended with a dim perception of an all-pervading Spiritual Essence, has been remarked among the earliest manifestations of the Human Mind. Everywhere it was the dim remembrance, uncertain and indefinite, of the original truth taught by God to the first men.

The Deity of the Old Testament is everywhere represented as the direct author of Evil, commissioning evil and lying spirits to men, hardening the heart of Pharaoh, and visiting the iniquity of the individual sinner on the whole people. The rude conception of sternness predominating over mercy in the Deity, can alone account for the human sacrifices, purposed, if not executed, by Abraham and Jephthah. It has not been uncommon, in any age or country of the world, for men to recognize the existence of one God, without forming any becoming estimate of His dignity. The causes of both good and ill are referred to a mysterious centre, to which each assigns such attributes as correspond with his own intellect and advance in civilization. Hence the assignment to the Deity of the feelings of envy and jealousy. Hence the provocation given by the healing skill of Æsculapius and the humane theft of fire by Prometheus. The very spirit of Nature, personified in Orpheus, Tantalus, or Phineus was supposed to have been killed, confined, or blinded, for having too freely divulged the Divine Mysteries to mankind. This Divine Envy still exists in a modified form, and varies according to circumstances. In Hesiod it appears in the lowest type of human malignity. In the God of Moses, it is jealousy of the infringement of the autocratic power, the check to political treason; and even the penalties denounced for worshipping other gods often seem dictated rather by a jealous regard for His own greatness in Deity, than by the immorality and degraded nature of the worship itself. In Herodotus and other writers it assumes a more philosophical shape, as a strict adherence to a moral equilibrium in the government of the world, in the punishment of pride, arrogance, and insolent pretension.

God acts providentially in Nature by regular and universal laws, by constant modes of operation; and so takes care of material things without violating their constitution, acting always according to the nature of the things which He has made. It is a fact of observation that, in the material and unconscious world, He works *by* its materiality and unconsciousness, not against them; in the animal world, *by* its animality and partial consciousness, not against them. So in the providential government of the world, He acts by regular and universal laws, and constant modes of operation; and so takes care of human things without violating their constitution, acting always according to the human nature of man, not against it, working in the human world by means of man's consciousness and partial freedom, not against them.

God acts by general laws for general purposes. The attraction of gravitation is a good thing, for it keeps the world together; and if the tower of Siloam, thereby falling to the ground, slays eighteen men of Jerusalem, that number is too small to think of, considering the myriad millions who are upheld by the same law. It could not well be repealed for *their* sake, and to hold up that tower; nor could it remain in force, and the tower stand.

It is difficult to conceive of a Perfect *Will* without confounding it with something like mechanism; since language has no name for that combination of the Inexorable with the Moral, which the old poets personified separately in Ananke or Eimarmene and Zeus. How combine understandingly the Perfect Freedom of the Supreme and All-Sovereign Will of God with the inflexible necessity, as part of His Essence, that He should and must continue to be, in all His great attributes, of justice and mercy for example, what He is now and always has been, and with the impossibility of His changing His nature and becoming unjust, merciless, cruel, fickle, or of His repealing the great moral laws which make crime wrong and the practice of virtue right?

For all that we familiarly know of Free-Will is that capricious exercise of it which we experience in ourselves and other men; and therefore the notion of Supreme Will, still guided by Infallible Law, even if that law be self-imposed, is always in danger of being either stripped of the essential quality of Freedom, or degraded under the ill-name of Necessity to something of even less moral and intellectual dignity than the fluctuating course of human operations.

It is not until we elevate the idea of law above that of partiality or tyranny, that we discover that the self-imposed limitations of the Supreme Cause, constituting an array of certain alternatives, regulating moral choice, are the very sources and safeguards of human freedom; and the doubt recurs, whether we do not set a law above God Himself; or whether laws self-imposed may not be self-repealed: and if not, what power prevents it.

The Zeus of Homer, like that of Hesiod, is an array of antitheses, combining strength with weakness, wisdom with folly, universal parentage with narrow family limitation, omnipotent control over events with submission to a superior destiny;—DESTINY, a name by means of which the theological problem was cast back into the original obscurity out of which the powers of the human mind have proved themselves as incapable of rescuing it, as the efforts of a fly caught in a spider's web to do more than increase its entanglement.

The oldest notion of Deity was rather indefinite than repulsive. The positive degradation was of later growth. The God of nature reflects the changeful character of the seasons, varying from dark to bright. Alternately angry and serene, and lavishing abundance which she again withdraws, nature seems inexplicably capricious, and though capable of responding to the highest requirements of the moral sentiment through a general comprehension of her mysteries, more liable by a partial or hasty view to become darkened into a Siva, a Saturn, or a Mexitli, a patron of fierce orgies or blood-stained altars. All the older poetical personifications exhibit traces of this ambiguity. They are neither wholly immoral nor purely beneficent.

No people have ever deliberately made their Deity a malevolent or guilty Being. The simple piety which ascribed the origin of all things to God, took all in good part, trusting and hoping all things. The Supreme Ruler was at first looked up to with unquestioning reverence. No startling discords or contradictions had yet raised a doubt as to His beneficence, or made men dissatisfied with His government. Fear might cause anxiety, but could not banish hope, still less inspire aversion. It was only later, when abstract notions began to assume the semblance of realities, and when new or more distinct ideas suggested new words for their expression, that it became necessary to fix a definite barrier between Evil and Good.

To account for moral evil, it became necessary to devise some new expedient suited both to the piety and self-complacency of the inventor, such as the perversity of woman, or an agent distinct from God, a Typhon or Ahriman, obtained either by dividing the Gods into two classes, or by dethroning the Ancient Divinity, and changing him into a Dev or Dæmon. Through a similar want, the Orientals devised the inherent corruption of the fleshy and material; the Hebrew transferred to Satan everything illegal and immoral; and the Greek reflection, occasionally adopting the older and truer view, retorted upon man the obloquy cast on these creatures of his imagination, and showed how he has to thank himself alone for his calamities, while his good things are the voluntary *gifts,* not the *plunder* of Heaven. Homer had already made Zeus exclaim, in the Assembly of Olympus, "Grievous it is to hear these mortals accuse the Gods; they pretend that evils come from us; but they themselves occasion them gratuitously by their own wanton folly." "It is the fault of man," said Solon, in reference to the social evils of his day, "not of God, that destruction comes;" and Euripides, after a formal discussion of the origin of evil, comes to the conclusion that men act wrongly, not from want of natural good sense and feeling, but because know-

ing what is good, they yet for various reasons neglect to practise it.

And at last reaching the highest truth, Pindar, Hesiod, Æschylus, Æsop, and Horace said, "All virtue is a struggle; life is not a
scene of repose, but of energetic action. Suffering is but another
name for the teaching of experience, appointed by Zeus himself,
the giver of all understanding, to be the parent of instruction, the
schoolmaster of life. He indeed put an end to the golden age;
he gave venom to serpents and predacity to wolves; he shook the
honey from the leaf, and stopped the flow of wine in the rivulets;
he concealed the element of fire, and made the means of life scanty
and precarious. But in all this his object was beneficent; it was
not to destroy life, but to improve it. It was a blessing to man,
not a curse, to be sentenced to earn his bread by the sweat of his
brow; for nothing great or excellent is attainable without exertion; safe and easy virtues are prized neither by gods nor men;
and the parsimoniousness of nature is justified by its powerful
effect in rousing the dormant faculties, and forcing on mankind
the invention of useful arts by means of meditation and thought."

Ancient religious reformers pronounced the worship of "idols"
to be the root of all evil; and there have been many iconoclasts in
different ages of the world. The maxim still holds good; for the
worship of idols, that is, of fanciful conceits, if not the source of
all evil, is still the cause of much; and it prevails as extensively
now as it ever did. Men are ever engaged in worshipping the
picturesque fancies of their own imaginations.

Human wisdom must always be limited and incorrect; and
even right opinion is only a something intermediate between
ignorance and knowledge. The normal condition of man is that
of progress. Philosophy is a kind of journey, ever learning, yet
never arriving at the ideal perfection of truth. A Mason should,
like the wise Socrates, assume the modest title of a "lover of
wisdom"; for he must ever long after something more excellent
than he possesses, something still beyond his reach, which he
desires to make eternally his own.

Thus the philosophic sentiment came to be associated with the
poetical and the religious, under the comprehensive name of Love.
Before the birth of Philosophy, Love had received but scanty and
inadequate homage. This mightiest and most ancient of gods,
coeval with the existence of religion and of the world, had been

indeed unconsciously felt, but had neither been worthily honored nor directly celebrated in hymn or pæan. In the old days of ignorance it could scarcely have been recognized. In order that it might exercise its proper influence over religion and philosophy, it was necessary that the God of Nature should cease to be a God of terrors, a personification of mere Power or arbitrary Will, a pure and stern Intelligence, an inflictor of evil, and an unrelenting Judge. The philosophy of Plato, in which this charge became forever established, was emphatically a mediation of Love. With him, the inspiration of Love first kindled the light of arts and imparted them to mankind; and not only the arts of mere existence, but the heavenly art of wisdom, which supports the Universe. It inspires high and generous deeds and noble self-devotion. Without it, neither State nor individual could do anything beautiful or great. Love is our best pilot, confederate, supporter, and saviour; the ornament and governor of all things human and divine; and he with divine harmony forever soothes the minds of men and gods.

Man is capable of a higher Love, which, marrying mind with mind and with the Universe, brings forth all that is noblest in his faculties, and lifts him beyond himself. This higher love is neither mortal nor immortal, but a power intermediate between the human and the Divine, filling up the mighty interval, and binding the Universe together. He is chief of those celestial emissaries who carry to the gods the prayers of men, and bring down to men the gifts of the gods. "He is forever poor, and far from being beautiful as mankind imagine, for he is squalid and withered; he flies low along the ground, is homeless and unsandalled; sleeping without covering before the doors and in the unsheltered streets, and possessing so far his mother's nature as being ever the companion of want. Yet, sharing also that of his father, he is forever scheming to obtain things good and beautiful; he is fearless, vehement, and strong; always devising some new contrivance; strictly cautious and full of inventive resource; a philosopher through his whole existence, a powerful enchanter, and a subtle sophist."

The ideal consummation of Platonic science is the arrival at the contemplation of that of which earth exhibits no express image or adequate similitude, the Supreme Prototype of all beauty, pure and uncontaminated with human intermixture of flesh or color, the Divine Original itself. To one so qualified is given the prerogative of bringing forth not mere images and shadows of virtue, but virtue itself, as having been conversant not with shadows, but with the truth; and having so brought forth and nurtured a progeny of virtue, he becomes the friend of God, and, so far as such a privilege can belong to any human being, immortal.

Socrates believed, like Heraclitus, in a Universal Reason pervading all things and all minds, and consequently revealing itself in ideas. He therefore sought truth in general opinion, and perceived in the communication of mind with mind one of the greatest prerogatives of wisdom and the most powerful means of advancement. He believed true wisdom to be an attainable idea, and that the moral convictions of the mind, those eternal instincts of temperance, conscientiousness, and justice, implanted in it by the gods, could not deceive, if rightly interpreted.

This metaphysical direction given to philosophy ended in visionary extravagance. Having assumed truth to be discoverable in thought, it proceeded to treat thoughts as truths. It thus became an idolatry of notions, which it considered either as phantoms exhaled from objects, or as portions of the divine pre-existent thought; thus creating a mythology of its own, and escaping from one thraldom only to enslave itself afresh. Theories and notions indiscriminately formed and defended are the false gods or "idols" of philosophy. For the word *idolon* means *image,* and a false *mind*-picture of God is as much an idol as a false *wooden* image of Him. Fearlessly launching into the problem of universal being, the first philosophy attempted to supply a compendious and decisive solution of every doubt. To do this, it was obliged to make the most sweeping assumptions; and as poetry had already filled the vast void between the human and the divine, by personifying its Deity as man, so philosophy bowed down before the supposed reflection of the divine image in the mind of the inquirer, who, in worshipping his own notions, had unconsciously deified himself. Nature thus was enslaved to common notions, and notions very often to words.

By the clashing of incompatible opinions, philosophy was gradually reduced to the ignominious confession of utter incapacity, and found its check or intellectual fall in skepticism. Xenophanes and Heraclitus mournfully acknowledged the unsatisfactory result of all the struggles of philosophy, in the admission of a universality of doubt; and the memorable effort of Socrates to rally the discomfited champions of truth, ended in a similar confession.

The worship of abstractions continued the error which personified Evil or deified Fortune; ·and when mystical philosophy resigned its place to mystical religion, it changed not its nature, but only its name. The great task remained unperformed, of reducing the outward world and its principles to the dominion of the intellect, and of reconciling the conception of the supreme unalterable power asserted by reason, with the requisitions of human sympathies.

A general idea of purpose and regularity in nature had been suggested by common appearances to the earliest reflection. The ancients perceived a natural order, a divine legislation, from which human institutions were supposed to be derived, laws emblazoned in Heaven, and thence revealed to earth. But the divine law was little more than an analogical inference from human law, taken in the vulgar sense of arbitrary will or partial covenant. It was surmised rather than discovered, and remained unmoral because unintelligible. It mattered little, under the circumstances, whether the Universe were said to be governed by chance or by reason, since the latter, if misunderstood, was virtually one with the former. "Better far," said Epicurus, "acquiesce in the fables of tradition, than acknowledge the oppressive necessity of the physicists"; and Menander speaks of God, Chance, and Intelligence as undistinguishable. Law unacknowledged goes under the name of *Chance:* perceived, but not understood, it becomes *Necessity.* The wisdom of the Stoic was a dogged submission to the arbitrary behests of one; that of the Epicurean an advantage snatched by more or less dexterous management from the equal tyranny of the other.

Ignorance sees nothing necessary, and is self abandoned to a power tyrannical because defined by no rule, and paradoxical because permitting evil, while itself assumed to be unlimited, all-powerful, and perfectly good. A little knowledge, presuming the identification of the Supreme Cause with the inevitable certainty of perfect reason, but omitting the analysis or interpretation of it, leaves the mind chain-bound in the ascetic fatalism of the Stoic. Free-will, coupled with the universal rule of Chance; or Fatalism and Necessity, coupled with Omniscience and fixed and unalterable Law,—these are the alternatives, between which the human mind has eternally vacillated. The Supernaturalists, contemplating a Being acting through impulse, though with superhuman wisdom, and considering the best courtier to be the most favored subject, combines contradictory expedients, inconsistently mixing the assertion of free action with the enervating service of petition; while he admits, in the words of a learned archbishop, that "if the production of the things we ask for depend on antecedent, natural, and necessary causes, our desires will be answered no less by the omission than the offering of prayers, which, therefore, are a vain thing."

The last stage is that in which the religion of action is made legitimate through comprehension of its proper objects and conditions. Man becomes morally free only when both notions, that of Chance and that of incomprehensible Necessity, are displaced by that of Law. Law, as applied to the Universe, means that universal, providential pre-arrangement, whose conditions can be discerned and discretionally acted on by human intelligence. The sense of freedom arises when the individual independence develops itself according to its own laws, without external collisions or hindrance; that of constraint, where it is thwarted or confined by other Natures, or where, by combination of external forces, the individual force is compelled into a new direction. Moral choice would not exist safely, or even at all, unless it were bounded by conditions determining its preferences. Duty supposes a rule both intelligible and certain, since an uncertain rule would be unintelligible, and if unintelligible, there could be no responsibility. No law that is unknown can be obligatory; and that Roman Emperor was justly execrated, who pretended to promulgate his penal laws, by putting them up at such a height that none could read them.

Man commands results, only by selecting among the contingent the pre-ordained results most suited to his purposes. In regard to absolute or divine morality, meaning the final cause or purpose of those comprehensive laws which often seem harsh to the individual, because inflexibly just and impartial to the universal, speculation must take refuge in faith; the immediate and obvious purpose often bearing so small a proportion to a wider and unknown one, as to be relatively absorbed or lost. The rain that, unseasonable to me, ruins my hopes of an abundant crop, does so because it could not otherwise have blessed and prospered the crops of another kind of a whole neighboring district of country. The obvious purpose of a sudden storm of snow, or an unexpected change of wind, exposed to which I lose my life, bears small proportion to the great results which are to flow from that storm or wind over a whole continent. So always, of the good and ill which at first seemed irreconcilable and capriciously distributed, the one holds its ground, the other diminishes by being explained. In a world of a multitude of individuals, a world of action and exertion, a world affording, by the conflict of interests and the clashing of passions, any scope for the exercise of the manly and generous virtues, even Omnipotence cannot make it, that the comfort and convenience of one man alone shall always be consulted.

Thus the educated mind soon begins to appreciate the moral superiority of a system of law over one of capricious interference; and as the jumble of means and ends is brought into more intelligible perspective, partial or seeming good is cheerfully resigned for the disinterested and universal. Self-restraint is found not to imply self-sacrifice. The true meaning of what appeared to be Necessity is found to be, not arbitrary Power, but Strength and Force enlisted in the service of Intelligence. God having made us men, and placed us in a world of change and eternal renovation, with ample capacity and abundant means for rational enjoyment, we learn that it is folly to repine because we are not angels, inhabiting a world in which change and the clashing of interests and the conflicts of passion are unknown.

The mystery of the world remains, but is sufficiently cleared up to inspire confidence. We are constrained to admit that if every man would but do the best in his power to do, and that which he knows he ought to do, we should need no better world than this. Man, surrounded by necessity, is free, not in a dogged determination of isolated will, because, though inevitably complying with nature's laws, he is able, proportionately to his knowledge, to modify, in regard to himself, the conditions of their action, and so to preserve an average uniformity between their forces and his own.

Such are some of the conflicting opinions of antiquity; and we have to some extent presented to you a picture of the Ancient Thought. Faithful, as far as it goes, it exhibits to us Man's Intellect ever struggling to pass beyond the narrow bounds of the circle in which its limited powers and its short vision confine it; and ever we find it travelling round the circle, like one lost in a wood, to meet the same unavoidable and insoluble difficulties. Science with her many instruments, Astronomy, particularly, with her telescope, Physics with the microscope, and Chemistry with its analyses and combinations, have greatly enlarged our ideas of the Deity, by discovering to us the vast extent of the Universe in both directions, its star-systems and its invisible swarms of minutest animal life; by acquainting us with the new and wonderful Force or Substance we call Electricity, apparently a link between Matter and Spirit: and still the Deity only becomes more incomprehensible to us than ever, and we find that in our speculations we but reproduce over and over again the Ancient Thought.

Where, then, amid all these conflicting opinions, is the True Word of a Mason?

My Brother, most of the questions which have thus tortured men's minds, it is not within the reach and grasp of the Human Intellect to understand; but without understanding, as we have explained to you heretofore, we may and must *believe*.

The True Word of a Mason is to be found in the concealed and profound meaning of the Ineffable Name of Deity, communicated by God to Moses; and which meaning was long lost by the very precautions taken to conceal it. The true pronunciation of that name was in truth a secret, in which, however, was involved the far more profound secret of its meaning. In that meaning is included all the truth than can be known by us, in regard to the nature of God.

Long known as AL, AL SCHADAI, ALOHAYIM, and ADONAI; as the Chief or Commander of the Heavenly Armies; as the aggregate of the Forces [ALOHAYIM] of Nature; as the Mighty, the Victorious, the Rival of Bal and Osiris; as the Soul of Nature, Nature itself, a God that was but Man personified, a God with human passions, the God of the Heathen with but a mere change of name, He assumes, in His communications to Moses, the name יהוה [IHUH], and says to Him, אהיה אשר אהיה [AHIH ASHR AHIH], I AM WHAT I AM. Let us examine the esoteric or inner meaning of this Ineffable Name.

היה [HIH] is the imperfect tense of the verb TO BE, of which יהיה [IHIH] is the present; אהי [AHI— א being the personal pronoun "I" affixed] the first person, by apocope; and יהי [IHI] the third. The verb has the following forms: . . . Preterite, 3d person, masculine singular, היה [HIH], did exist, was; 3d person com.

plural, הִיוּ [HIU] . . . Present, 3d pers. masc. sing. יִהְיֶה [IHIH], once יִהְוֶא [IHUA], by apocope יְהִי, אֱהִי [AHI, IHI] . . Infinitive, הֱיֹה, הָיֹן [HIH, HIU] . . . Imperative, 2d pers. masc. sing. הֱיֵה [HIH], fem. הֱוִי [HUI] . . . Participle, masc. sing. הֹוֶה [HUH], ENS— EXISTING . . EXISTENCE.

The verb is never used, as the mere logical copula or connecting word, *is, was,* etc., is used with the Greeks, Latins, and ourselves. It always implies *existence, actuality.* The *present* form also includes the *future* sense, . . *shall* or *may* be or exist. And הֹוֶה and הוּא [HUH and HUA] Chaldaic forms of the imperfect tense of the verb, are the same as the Hebrew הָיָה and הֹוֶה [HUH and HIH], and mean *was, existed, became.*

Now הוּא and הִיא [HUA and HIA] are the Personal Pronoun [Masculine and Feminine], HE, SHE. Thus in Gen. iv. 20 we have the phrase, הוּא הָיָה [HUA HIH], HE WAS: and in Lev. xxi. 9, אֶת אָבִיהָ הִיא [ATH ABIH HIA], HER Father. This feminine pronoun, however, is often written הוּא [HUA], and הִיא [HIA] occurs only eleven times in the Pentateuch. Sometimes the feminine form means IT; but *that* pronoun is generally in the masculine form.

When either י, ו, ה, or א [Yod, Vav, He, or Aleph] terminates a word, and has no vowel either immediately preceding or following it, it is often rejected; as in גִי [GI], for גִיא [GIA], a valley.

So הוּא-הִיא [HUA-HIA], He-She, could properly be written הו-הי [Hu-Hi]; or by transposition of the letters, common with the Talmudists, יה-וה [IH-UH], which is the Tetragrammaton or Ineffable Name.

In Gen. i. 27, it is said, "So the ALHIM created man in His image: *in the image* of ALHIM created He him: MALE and FEMALE created He them."

Sometimes the word was thus expressed; triangularly:

<pre>
                    ה
                 ה   ו
              ה   י   ה
           ה   ו   ה   י
</pre>

And we learn that this designation of the Ineffable Name was, among the Hebrews, a symbol of Creation. The mysterious union *of God with His creatures* was in the letter ה, which they considered to be the Agent of Almighty Power; and to enable the possessor of the Name to work miracles.

The Personal Pronoun הוּא [HUA], HE, is often used *by itself,* to express the Deity. Lee says that in such cases, IHUH, IH, or ALHIM, or some other name of God, is *understood;* but there is no necessity for that. It means in such cases the Male, Generative, or Creative Principle or Power.

It was a common practice with the Talmudists to conceal secret meanings and sounds of words by transposing the letters.

The reversal of the letters of words was, indeed, anciently common everywhere. Thus from *Neitha,* the name of an Egyptian Goddess, the Greeks, writing backward, formed *Athenè,* the name of Minerva. In Arabic we have *Nahid,* a name of the planet Venus, which, reversed, gives *Dihan,* Greek, in Persian, *Nihad,* Nature; which Sir William Jones writes also *Nahid.* Strabo informs us that the Armenian name of Venus was *Anaitis.*

Tien, Heaven, in Chinese, reversed, is *Neit,* or *Neith,* worshipped at *Sais* in Egypt. Reverse *Neitha,* drop the *i,* and add an *e,* and we, as before said, *Athenè. Mitra* was the name of Venus among the ancient Persians. Herodotus, who tells us this, also informs us that her name, among the Scythians, was *Artim pasa. Artim* is *Mitra,* reversed. So, by reversing it, the Greeks formed Artemis, Diana.

One of the meanings of *Rama,* in Sanscrit, is *Kama,* the Deity of *Love.* Reverse this, and we have *Amar,* and by changing *a* into *o, Amor,* the Latin word for *Love.* Probably, as the verb is *Amare,* the oldest reading was *Amar* and not *Amor.* So *Dipaka,* in Sanscrit, one of the meanings whereof is *love,* is often written *Dipuc.* Reverse this, and we have, adding *o,* the Latin word *Cupido.*

In Arabic, the radical letters *rhm,* pronounced *rahm,* signify the *trunk, compassion, mercy;* this reversed, we have *mhr,* in Persic, *love* and the *Sun.* In Hebrew we have *Lab,* the *heart;* and in Chaldee, *Bal,* the *heart;* the radical letters of both being *b* and *l.*

The Persic word for *head* is *Sar.* Reversed, this becomes *Ras* in Arabic and Hebrew, Raish in Chaldee, Rash in Samaritan, and Ryas in Ethiopic; all meaning *head, chief,* etc. In Arabic we have *Kid,* in the sense of *rule,* regulation, article of agreement, obligation; which, reversed, becomes, adding *e,* the Greek *dikè* justice. In Coptic we have *Chlom,* a crown. Reversed, we have in Hebrew, *Moloch* or *Malec,* a King, or he who wears a crown.

In the Kou-onen, or oldest Chinese writing, by Hieroglyphics, ⊙ *Ge* [*Hi* or *Khi,* with the initial letter modified], was the Sun: in Persic, *Gaw;* and in Turkish *Giun. Yue* [☽], was the Moon;

in Sanscrit *Uh,* and in Turkish *Ai.* It will be remembered that, in Egypt and elsewhere, the Sun was originally feminine, and the Moon masculine. In Egypt, *Ioh* was the moon: and in the feasts of Bacchus they cried incessantly, *Euoï Sabvi! Euoï Bakhè! Io Bakhe! Io Bakhe!*

Bunsen gives the following personal pronouns for *he* and *she:*

	He	She
Christian Aramtic	Hû	Hî
Jewish Aramaic	Hû	Hî
Hebrew	Hû'	Hî'
Arabic	Huwa	Hiya

Thus the Ineffable Name not only embodies the Great Philosophical Idea, that the Deity is the ENS, the To ON, the Absolute Existence, that of which the Essence is To Exist, the only Substance of Spinoza, the BEING, that never could *not* have existed, as contradistinguished from that which only *becomes,* not Nature or the Soul of Nature, but that which created Nature; but also the idea of the Male and Female Principles, in its highest and most profound sense; to wit, that God originally comprehended in Himself all that is: that matter was not co-existent with Him, or independent of Him; that He did not merely fashion and shape a pre-existing chaos into a Universe; but that His Thought manifested itself outwardly in that Universe, which so *became,* and before *was not,* except as comprehended in Him: that the Generative Power or Spirit, and Productive Matter, ever among the ancients deemed the Female, originally were in God; and that He Was and Is all that Was, that Is, and that Shall be: *in* Whom all else lives, moves, and has its being.

This was the great Mystery of the Ineffable Name; and this true arrangement of its letters, and of course its true pronunciation and its meaning, soon became lost to all except the select few to whom it was confided; it being concealed from the common people, because the Deity thus metaphysically named was not that personal and capricious, and as it were tangible God in whom they believed, and who alone was within the reach of their rude capacities.

Diodorus says that the name given by Moses to God was IAΩ. Theodorus says that the Samaritans termed God *IABE,* but the Jews IAΩ. Philo Byblius gives the form IEYΩ; and Clemens of Alexandria IAOY.   Macrobius says that it was an admitted axiom among the Heathen, that the triliteral IAΩ was the sacred name of the Supreme God.   And the Clarian oracle said: "Learn thou that IAΩ is the great God Supreme, that ruleth over all." The letter I signified Unity.   A and Ω are the first and last letters of the Greek Alphabet.

Hence the frequent expression: "I am the First, and I am the Last; and besides Me there is no other God. I am A and Ω, the First and the Last.   I am A and Ω, the Beginning and the Ending, which Is, and Was, and Is to come: the Omnipotent."   For in this we are shadowed forth the same great truth; that God is all in all—the Cause and the Effect—the beginning, or Impulse, or Generative Power: and the Ending, or Result, or that which is produced; that He is in reality all that is, all that ever was, and all that ever will be; in this sense, that nothing besides Himself has existed eternally, and co-eternally with Him, independent of Him, and self-existent, or self-originated.

And thus the meaning of the expression, ALOHAYIM, a *plural* noun, used, in the account of the Creation with which Genesis commences, with a singular verb, and of the name or title IHUH-ALHIM, used for the first time in the 4th verse of the 2d chapter of the same book, becomes clear.   The ALHIM is the aggregate unity of the manifested Creative Forces or Powers of Deity, His Emanations; and IHUH-ALHIM is the ABSOLUTE Existence, or Essence of these Powers and Forces, of which they are Active Manifestations and Emanations.

This was the profound truth hidden in the ancient allegory and covered from the general view with a double veil.   This was the esoteric meaning of the generation and production of the Indian, Chaldean, and Phœnician cosmognies; and the Active and Passive Powers, of the Male and Female Principles; of Heaven and its Luminaries generating, and the Earth producing; all hiding from vulgar view, as above its comprehension, the doctrine that matter is not eternal, but that God was the only original Existence, the ABSOLUTE, from Whom everything has proceeded, and to Whom all returns: and that all moral law springs not from the relation of things, but from His Wisdom and Essential Justice, as the Omnipotent Legislator.   And this TRUE WORD is with entire accuracy said to have been *lost;* because its *meaning* was lost, even among the Hebrews, although we still find the name (its real meaning unsuspected), in the Hu of the Druids and the Fo-Hi of the Chinese.

When we conceive of the Absolute Truth, Beauty, or Good, we cannot stop short at the abstraction of either. We are forced to refer each to some living and substantial Being, in which they have their foundations, some being that is the first and last principle of each.

Moral Truth, like every other universal and necessary truth, cannot remain a mere abstraction. Abstractions are unrealities. In ourselves, moral truth is merely conceived of. There must be *somewhere* a Being that not only *conceives* of, but *constitutes* it. It has this characteristic; that it is not only, to the eyes of our intelligence, an universal and necessary truth, but one obligatory on our will. It is A LAW. *We* do not establish that law ourselves. It is imposed on us *despite* ourselves: its principle must be *without* us. It supposes a *legislator*. He cannot be the being to whom the law applies; but must be one that possesses in the highest degree all the characteristics of moral truth. The moral law, universal and necessary, necessarily has as its author a necessary being;—composed of justice and charity, its author must be a being possessing the plenitude of both.

As all *beautiful* and all *true* things refer themselves, *these* to a Unity which is absolute TRUTH, and those to a Unity which is absolute BEAUTY, so all the *moral* principles centre in a single principle, which is THE GOOD. Thus we arrive at the conception of THE GOOD *in itself,* the ABSOLUTE Good, superior to all *particular* duties, and determinate in those duties. This Absolute *Good* must necessarily be an attribute of the Absolute BEING. There cannot be *several* Absolute Beings; the one in whom are realized Absolute Truth and Absolute Beauty being different from the one in whom is realized Absolute Good. The Absolute necessarily implies absolute Unity. The True, the Beautiful, and the Good are not three distinct essences: but they are one and the same essence, considered in its fundamental attributes: the different phases which, in our eyes, the Absolute and Infinite Perfection assumes. Manifested in the World of the Finite and Relative, these three attributes separate from each other, and are distinguished by our minds, which can comprehend nothing except by division. But in the Being from Whom they emanate, they are indivisibly united; and this Being, at once triple and one, Who sums up in Himself perfect *Beauty*, perfect *Truth*, and the perfect *Good*, is GOD.

God is necessarily the principle of Moral Truth, and of personal morality. Man is a moral person, that is to say, one endowed with reason and liberty. He is capable of Virtue: and Virtue has with him two principal forms, respect for others and love of others,—*justice* and *charity*.

The *creature* can possess no real and essential attribute which the *Creator* does not possess. The *effect* can draw its reality and existence only from its *cause*. The *cause* contains in itself, at least, what is essential in the *effect*. The characteristic of the effect is inferiority, short-coming, imperfection. Dependent and derivate, it bears in itself the marks and conditions of dependence; and its imperfection proves the perfection of the cause; or else there would be in the effect something immanent, without a cause.

God is not a logical Being, whose Nature may be explained by deduction, and by means of algebraic equations. When, setting out with a primary attribute, the attributes of God are deduced one from the other, after the manner of the Geometricians and Scholastics, we have nothing but abstractions. We must emerge from this empty dialetic, to arrive at a true and living God. The first notion which we have of God, that of an *Infinite* Being, is not given us *à priori*, independently of all experience. It is our consciousness of ourself, as at once a Being and a limited Being, that immediately raises us to the conception of a Being, the principle of *our* being, and Himself without limits. If the existence that we possess forces us to recur to a cause possessing the same existence in an infinite degree, all the substantial attributes of existence that we possess equally require each an infinite cause. God, then, is no longer the Infinite, Abstract, Indeterminate Being, of which reason and the heart cannot lay hold, but a real Being, determinate like ourselves, a moral person like ourself; and the study of our own souls will conduct us, without resort to hypothesis, to a conception of God, both sublime and having a connection with ourselves.

If man be free, God must be so. It would be strange if, while the creature has that marvellous power of disposing of himself, of choosing and willing freely, the Being that has made him should be subject to a necessary development, the cause of which, though in Himself, is a sort of abstract, mechanical, or metaphysical power, inferior to the personal, voluntary cause which we are, and of which we have the clearest consciousness. God is free *because* we are: but he is not free *as* we are. He is at once *everything* that we are, and *nothing* that we are. He possesses the same attributes as we, but extended to infinity. He possesses, then, an infinite liberty, united to an infinite intelligence; and as His intelligence is infallible, exempt from the uncertainty of deliberation, and perceiving at a glance where the Good is, so His liberty accomplishes it spontaneously and without effort.

As we assign to God that liberty which is the basis of our existence, so also we transfer to His character, from our own, justice and charity. In man they are virtues: in God, His attributes. What is in us the laborious conquest of liberty, is in Him His very nature. The idea of the right, and the respect paid to the right, are signs of the dignity of our existence. If respect of rights is the very essence of justice, the Perfect Being must know and respect the rights of the lowest of His creatures; for He assigned them those rights. In God resides a sovereign justice, that renders to every one what is due him, not according to deceitful appearances, but according to the truth of things. And if man, a limited being, has the power to go out of himself, to forget his own person, to love another like himself, and devote himself to his happiness, dignity, and perfection, the Perfect Being must have, in an infinite degree, that disinterested tenderness, that Charity, the Supreme Virtue of the human person. There is in God an infinite tenderness for His creatures, manifested in His giving us existence, which He might have withheld; and every day it appears in innumerable marks of His Divine Providence.

Plato well understood that love of God, and expresses it in these great words: "Let us speak of the cause which led the Supreme Arranger of the Universe to produce and regulate that Universe. He was good; and he who is good has no kind of ill-will. Exempt from that, He willed that created things should be, as far as possible, like Himself." And Christianity in its turn said, *"God has so loved men that He has given them His only Son."*

It is not correct to affirm, as is often done, that Christianity has in some sort *discovered* this noble sentiment. We must not lower human nature, to raise Christianity. Antiquity knew, described, and practised charity; the first feature of which, so touching, and thank God! so common, is goodness, as its loftiest one is heroism. Charity is devotion to another; and it is ridiculously senseless to pretend that there ever was an age of the world, when the human soul was deprived of that part of its heritage, the power of devotion. But it is certain that Christianity has diffused and popularized this virtue, and that, before Christ, these words were never spoken: "LOVE ONE ANOTHER; FOR THAT IS THE WHOLE LAW." *Charity* presupposes *Justice*. He who truly loves his brother respects the rights of his brother; but he does more, he forgets his own. Egoism *sells* or *takes*. Love delights in *giving*. In God, love is what it is in us; but in an infinite degree. God is inexhaustible in His charity, as He is inexhaustible in His essence. That Infinite Omnipotence and Infinite Charity, which, by an admirable good-will, draws from the bosom of its immense love the favors which it incessantly bestows on the world and on humanity, teaches us that the more we give, the more we possess.

God being all just and all good, He can will nothing but what is good and just. Being Omnipotent, whatever He wills He can do, and consequently does. The world is the work of God: it is therefore perfectly made.

Yet there is disorder in the world, that seems to impugn the justice and goodness of God.

A principle indissolubly connected with the very idea of good, tells us that every moral agent deserves reward when he does well, and punishment when he does ill. This principle is universal and necessary. It is absolute. If it does not apply in this world, it is false, or the world is badly ordered.

But good actions are not always followed by happiness, nor evil ones by misery. Though often this fact is more apparent than real; though virtue, a war against the passions, full of dignity but full of sorrow and pain, has the latter as its condition, yet the pains that follow vice are greater; and virtue conduces most to health, strength, and long life;—though the peaceful conscience that accompanies virtue creates internal happiness; though public opinion generally decides correctly on men's characters, and rewards virtue with esteem and consideration, and vice with contempt and infamy; and though, after all, justice reigns in the world, and the surest road to happiness is still that of virtue, yet there are exceptions. Virtue is not always rewarded, nor vice punished, in this life.

The data of this problem are these: 1st. The principle of merit and demerit within us is absolute: every good action *ought* to be rewarded, every bad one punished: 2d. God is just as He is all-powerful: 3d. There are in this world particular cases, contradicting the necessary and universal law of merit and demerit. What is the result?

To reject the two principles, that God is just, and the law of merit and demerit absolute, is to raze to the foundations the whole edifice of human faith.

To maintain them, is to admit that the present life is to be terminated or continued elsewhere. The moral person who acts well or ill, and awaits reward or punishment, is connected with a body, lives with it, makes use of it, depends upon it in a measure, but is not *it*. The *body* is composed of parts. It diminishes or increases, it is divisible even to infinity. But this *something* which has a consciousness of itself, and says "I, ME"; that feels itself free and responsible, feels too that it is incapable of division, that it is a being *one* and *simple;* that the ME cannot be halved, that if a limb is cut off and thrown away, no part of the ME goes with it: that it remains identical with itself under the variety of phenomena which successively manifest it. This identity, indivisibility, and absolute unity of the person, are its *spirituality,* the very essence of the person. It is not in the least an hypothesis to affirm that the soul differs essentially from the body. By the soul we mean *the person,* not separated from the consciousness of the attributes which constitute it,—*thought* and *will.* The Existence without consciousness is an abstract being, and not a person. It is *the person,* that is *identical, one, simple.* Its attributes, developing it, do not divide it. Indivisible, it is indissoluble, and may be immortal. If absolute justice requires this immortality, it does not require what is impossible. The spirituality of the soul is the condition and necessary foundation of immortality: the law of merit and demerit the direct demonstration of it. The first is the metaphysical, the second the moral proof. Add to these the tendency of all the powers of the soul toward the Infinite, and the principle of final causes, and the proof of the immortality of the soul is complete.

God, therefore, in the Masonic creed, is INFINITE TRUTH, INFINITE BEAUTY, INFINITE GOODNESS. He is the Holy of Holies, as Author of the Moral Law, as the PRINCIPLE of Liberty, of

Justice, and of Charity, Dispenser of Reward and Punishment. Such a God is not an abstract God; but an intelligent and free *person,* Who has made us in His image, from Whom we receive the law that presides over our destiny, and Whose judgment we await. It is His love that inspires us in *our* acts of charity: it is His justice that governs *our* justice, and that of society and the laws. We continually remind ourselves that He is infinite; because otherwise we should degrade His nature: but He would be for us as if He were not, if His infinite nature had not forms inherent in ourselves, the forms of our own reason and soul.

When we love Truth, Justice, and Nobility of Soul, we should know that it is God we love underneath these special forms, and should unite them all into one great act of total piety. We should feel that we go in and out continually in the midst of the vast forces of the Universe, which are only the Forces of God; that in our studies, when we attain a truth, we confront the thought of God; when we learn the right, we learn the will of God laid down as a rule of conduct for the Universe; and when we feel disinterested love, we should know that we partake the feeling of the Infinite God. Then, when we reverence the mighty cosmic force, it will not be a blind Fate in an Atheistic or Pantheistic world, but the Infinite God, that we shall confront and feel and know. Then we shall be mindful of the mind of God, conscious of God's conscience, sensible of His sentiments, and our own existence will be in the infinite being of God.

The world is a whole, which has its harmony; for a God who is One, could make none but a complete and harmonious work. The harmony of the Universe responds to the unity of God, as the indefinite quantity is the defective sign of the infinitude of God. To say that the Universe is God, is to admit the world only, and deny God. Give it what name you please, it is atheism at bottom. On the other hand, to suppose that the Universe is void of God, and that He is wholly apart from it, is an insupportable and almost impossible abstraction. To distinguish is not to separate. I distinguish, but do not separate myself from my qualities and effects. So God is not the Universe, although He is everywhere present in spirit and in truth.

To us, as to Plato, absolute truth is in God. It is God Himself under one of His phases. In God, as their original, are the immutable principles of reality and cognizance. In Him things receive

at once their existence and their intelligibility. It is by partici-
pating in the Divine reason that our own reason possesses something of the Absolute. Every judgment of reason envelopes a
necessary truth, and every necessary truth supposes the necessary
Existence.

Thus, from every direction,—from metaphysics, æsthetics, and
morality above all, we rise to the same Principle, the common
centre, and ultimate foundation of all truth, all beauty, all good.
The True, the Beautiful, the Good, are but diverse revelations of
one and the same Being. Thus we reach the threshold of religion,
and are in communion with the great philosophies which all proclaim a God; and at the same time with the religions which cover
the earth, and all repose on the sacred foundation of natural religion; of that religion which reveals to us the natural light given
to all men, without the aid of a particular revelation. So long as
philosophy does not arrive at religion, it is below all worships,
even the most imperfect; for they at least give man a Father, a
Witness, a Consoler, a Judge. By religion, philosophy connects
itself with humanity, which, from one end of the world to the
other, aspires to God, believes in God, hopes in God. Philosophy
contains in itself the common basis of all religious beliefs; it, as
it were, borrows from them their principle, and returns it to them
surrounded with light, elevated above uncertainty, secure against
all attack.

From the necessity of His Nature, the Infinite Being must
create and preserve the Finite, and to the Finite must, in its
forms, give and communicate of His own kind. We cannot conceive of any finite thing existing without God, the Infinite basis
and ground thereof; nor of God existing without something. God
is the necessary logical condition of a world, its necessitating
cause; a world, the necessary logical condition of God, His neces-
sitated consequence. It is according to His Infinite Perfection to
create, and then to preserve and bless whatever He creates. That
is the conclusion of modern metaphysical science. The stream
of philosophy runs down from Aristotle to Hegel, and breaks off
with this conclusion: and then again recurs the ancient difficulty.
If it be of His nature to create,—if we cannot conceive of His
existing *alone,* without creating, without *having* created, then
what He created was co-existent with Himself. If He could
exist an instant without creating, He could as well do so for a

myriad of eternities. And so again comes round to us the old doctrine of a God, the Soul of the Universe, and co-existent with it. For what He created had a *beginning;* and however long since that creation occurred, an eternity had before elapsed. The difference between *a* beginning and *no* beginning is infinite.

But of some things we can be certain. We are conscious of ourselves—of ourselves if not as substances, at least as Powers to be, to do, to suffer. We are conscious of ourselves not as self-originated at all or as self-sustained alone; but only as dependent, first for existence, ever since for support.

Among the primary ideas of consciousness, that are inseparable from it, the atoms of self-consciousness, we find the idea of God. Carefully examined by the scrutizing intellect, it is the idea of God as infinite, perfectly powerful, wise, just, loving, holy; absolute being with no limitation. This made us, made all, sustains us, sustains all; made our body, not by a single act, but by a series of acts extending over a vast succession of years,—for man's body is the resultant of all created things,—made our spirit, our mind, conscience, affections, soul, will, appointed for each its natural mode of action, set each at its several aim. Thus self-consciousness leads us to consciousness of God, and at last to consciousness of an infinite God. That is the highest evidence of our own existence, and it is the highest evidence of His.

If there is a God at all, He must be omnipresent in space. Beyond the last Stars He must be, as He is here. There can be no mote that peoples the sunbeams, no little cell of life that the microscope discovers in the seed-sporule of a moss, but He is there.

He must also be omnipresent in time. There was no second of time before the Stars began to burn, but God was in that second. In the most distant nebulous spot in Orion's belt, and in every one of the millions that people a square inch of limestone, God is alike present. He is in the smallest imaginable or even unimaginable portion of time, and in every second of its most vast and unimaginable volume; His Here conterminous with the All of Space, His Now coeval with the All of Time.

Through all this Space, in all this Time, His Being extends, spreads undivided, operates unspent; God in all His infinity, perfectly powerful, wise, just, loving, and holy. His being is an infinite activity, a creating, and so a giving of Himself to the

World. The World's being is a *becoming*, a being created and
continued. It is so now, and was so, incalculable and unimaginable millions of ages ago.

All this is philosophy, the unavoidable conclusion of the human
mind. It is not the *opinion* of Coleridge and Kant, but their
science; not what they *guess,* but what they *know.*

In virtue of this in-dwelling of God in matter, we say that the
world is a revelation of Him, its existence a show of His. He is
in His work. The manifold action of the Universe is only His
mode of operation, and all material things are in communion with
Him. All grow and move and live in Him, and by means of Him,
and only so. Let Him withdraw from the space occupied by anything, and it ceases to be. Let Him withdraw any quality of His
nature from anything, and it ceases to be. All must partake of
Him, He dwelling in each, and yet transcending all.

The failure of fanciful religion to become philosophy, does not
preclude philosophy from coinciding with true religion. Philosophy, or rather its object, the divine order of the Universe, is the
intellectual guide which the religious sentiment needs; while
exploring the real relations of the finite, it obtains a constantly
improving and self-correcting measure of the perfect law of the
Gospel of Love and Liberty, and a means of carrying into effect
the spiritualism of revealed religion. It establishes law, by ascer-
taining its terms; it guides the spirit to see its way to the amelioration of life and the increase of happiness. While religion was
stationary, science could not walk alone; when both are admitted
to be progressive, their interests and aims become identified.
Aristotle began to show how religion may be founded on an intellectual basis; but the basis he laid was too narrow. Bacon, by
giving to philosophy a definite aim and method, gave it at the
same time a safer and self-enlarging basis. Our position is that
of intellectual beings surrounded by limitations; and the latter
being constant, have to intelligence the practical value of laws, in
whose investigation and application consists that seemingly endless
career of intellectual and moral progress which the sentiment of
religion inspires and ennobles. The title of Saint has commonly
been claimed for those whose boast it has been to despise philosophy; yet faith will stumble and sentiment mislead, unless knowledge be present, in amount and quality sufficient to purify the one
and to give beneficial direction to the other.

Science consists of those matured inferences from experience which all other experience confirms. It is no fixed system superior to revision, but that progressive mediation between ignorance and wisdom in part conceived by Plato, whose immediate object is happiness, and its impulse the highest kind of love. Science realizes and unites all that was truly valuable in both the old schemes of mediation; the heroic, or system of action and effort; and the mystical theory of spiritual, contemplative communion. "Listen to me," says Galen, "as to the voice of the Eleusinian Hierophant, and believe that the study of nature is a mystery no less important than theirs, nor less adapted to display the wisdom and power of the Great Creator. Their lessons and demonstrations were obscure, but ours are clear and unmistakable."

To science we owe it that no man is any longer entitled to consider himself the central point around which the whole Universe of life and motion revolves—the immensely important individual for whose convenience and even luxurious ease and indulgence the whole Universe was made. On one side it has shown us an infinite Universe of stars and suns and worlds at incalculable distances from each other, in whose majestic and awful presence we sink and even our world sinks into insignificance; while, on the other side, the microscope has placed us in communication with new worlds of organized livings beings, gifted with senses, nerves, appetites, and instincts, in every tear and in every drop of putrid water.

Thus science teaches us that we are but an infinitesimal portion of a great whole, that stretches out on every side of us, and above and below us, infinite in its complications, and which infinite wisdom alone can comprehend. Infinite wisdom has arranged the infinite succession of beings, involving the necessity of birth, decay, and death, and made the loftiest virtues possible by providing those conflicts, reverses, trials, and hardships, without which even their names could never have been invented.

Knowledge is convertible into power, and axioms into rules of utility and duty. Modern science is social and communicative. It is moral as well as intellectual; powerful, yet pacific and disinterested; binding man to man as well as to the Universe; filling up the details of obligation, and cherishing impulses of virtue, and, by affording clear proof of the consistency and identity of all interests, substituting co-operation for rivalry, liberality for jealousy, and tending far more powerfully than any other means to realize the spirit of religion, by healing those inveterate disorders which, traced to their real origin, will be found rooted in an ignorant assumption as to the penurious severity of Providence, and the consequent greed of selfish men to confine what seemed as if extorted from it to themselves, or to steal from each other rather than quietly to enjoy their own.

We shall probably never reach those higher forms containing the true differences of things, involving the full discovery and correct expression of their very self or essence. We shall ever fall short of the most general and most simple nature, the ultimate or most comprehensive law. Our widest axioms explain many phenomena, but so too in a degree did the principles or elements of the old philosophers, and the cycles and epicycles of ancient astronomy. We cannot in any case of causation assign the whole of the conditions, nor though we may reproduce them in practice, can we mentally distinguish them all, without knowing the essences of the things including them; and we therefore must not unconsciously ascribe that absolute certainty to axioms, which the ancient religionists did to creeds, nor allow the mind, which ever strives to insulate itself and its acquisitions, to forget the nature of the process by which it substituted scientific for common notions, and so with one as with the other lay the basis of self-deception by a pedantic and superstitious employment of them.

Doubt, the essential preliminary of all improvement and discovery, must accompany all the stages of man's onward progress. His intellectual life is a perpetual beginning, a preparation for a birth. The faculty of doubting and questioning, without which those of comparison and judgment would be useless, is itself a divine prerogative of the reason. Knowledge is always imperfect, or complete only in a prospectively boundless career, in which discovery multiplies doubt, and doubt leads on to new discovery. The boast of science is not so much its manifested results, as its admitted imperfection and capacity of unlimited progress. The true religious philosophy of an imperfect being is not a system of creed, but, as Socrates thought, an infinite search or approximation. Finality is but another name for bewilderment or defeat. Science gratifies the religious feeling without arresting it, and opens out the unfathomable mystery of the One Supreme into more explicit and manageable Forms, which express not indeed His Essence, which is wholly beyond our reach and higher than our faculties can climb, but His Will, and so feeds an endless enthusiasm by accumulating forever new objects of pursuit. We have long experienced that knowledge is profitable, we are beginning to find out that it is moral, and we shall at last discover it to be religious.

God and truth are inseparable; a knowledge of God is possession of the saving oracles of truth. In proportion as the thought and purpose of the individual are trained to conformity with the rule of right prescribed by Supreme Intelligence, so far is his happiness promoted, and the purpose of his existence fulfilled. In this way a new life arises in him; he is no longer isolated, but is a part of the eternal harmonies around him. His erring will is directed by the influence of a higher will, informing and moulding it in the path of his true happiness.

Man's power of apprehending outward truth is a qualified privilege; the mental like the physical inspiration passing through a diluted medium; and yet, even when truth, imparted, as it were, by intuition, has been specious, or at least imperfect, the intoxication of sudden discovery has ever claimed it as full, infallible, and divine. And while human weakness needed ever to recur to the pure and perfect source, the revelations once popularly accepted and valued assumed an independent substantiality, perpetuating not themselves only, but the whole mass of derivitive forms accidentally connected with them, and legalized in their names. The mists of error thickened under the shadows of prescription, until the free light again broke in upon the night of ages, redeeming the genuine treasure from the superstition which obstinately doted on its accessories.

Even to the Barbarian, Nature reveals a mighty power and a wondrous wisdom, and continually points to God. It is no wonder that men worshipped the several things of the world. The world of matter is a revelation of fear to the savage in Northern climes; he trembles at his deity throned in ice and snow. The lightning, the storm, the earthquake startle the rude man, and he sees the divine in the extraordinary.

The grand objects of Nature perpetually constrain men to think of their Author. The Alps are the great altar of Europe; the noc-

turnal sky has been to mankind the dome of a temple, starred all
over with admonitions to reverence, trust, and love. The Scriptures for the human race are writ in earth and Heaven. No organ
or miserere touches the heart like the sonorous swell of the sea
or the ocean-wave's immeasurable laugh. Every year the old world
puts on new bridal beauty, and celebrates its Whit-Sunday, when
in the sweet Spring each bush and tree dons reverently its new
glories. Autumn is a long All-Saints' day; and the harvest is
Hallowmass to Mankind. Before the human race marched down
from the slopes of the Himalayas to take possession of Asia,
Chaldea, and Egypt, men marked each annual crisis, the solstices
and the equinoxes, and celebrated religious festivals therein; and
even then, and ever since, the material was and has been the element of communion between man and God.

Nature is full of religious lessons to a thoughtful man. He dissolves the matter of the Universe, leaving only its forces; he dissolves away the phenomena of human history, leaving only
immortal spirit; he studies the law, the mode of action of these
forces and this spirit, which make up the material and the human
world, and cannot fail to be filled with reverence, with trust, with
boundless love of the Infinite God, who devised these laws of matter and of mind, and thereby bears up this marvellous Universe
of things and men. Science has its New Testament; and the
beatitudes of Philosophy are profoundly touching. An undevout
astronomer is mad. Familiarity with the grass and the trees
teaches us deeper lessons of love and trust than we can glean from
the writings of Fénélon and Augustine. The great Bible of God
is ever open before mankind. The eternal flowers of Heaven seem
to shed sweet influence on the perishable blossoms of the earth.
The great sermon of Jesus was preached on a mountain, which
preached to Him as He did to the people, and His figures of
speech were first natural figures of fact.

If to-morrow I am to perish utterly, then I shall only take
counsel for to-day, and ask for qualities which last no longer.
My fathers will be to me only as the ground out of which my
bread-corn is grown; dead, they are but the rotten mould of
earth, their memory of small concern to me. Posterity!—I shall
care nothing for the future generations of mankind! I am one
atom in the trunk of a tree, and care nothing for the roots below,
or the branch above. I shall sow such seed only as will bear har-

vest to-day. Passion may enact my statutes to-day, and ambition repeal them to-morrow. I will know no other legislators. Morality will vanish, and expediency take its place. Heroism will be gone; and instead of it there will be the savage ferocity of the he-wolf, the brute cunning of the she-fox, the rapacity of the vulture, and the headlong daring of the wild bull; but no longer the cool, calm courage that, for truth's sake, and for love's sake, looks death firmly in the face, and then wheels into line ready to be slain. Affection, friendship, philanthropy, will be but the wild fancies of the monomaniac, fit subjects for smiles or laughter or for pity.

But knowing that we shall live forever, and that the Infinite God loves all of us, we can look on all the evils of the world, and see that it is only the hour before sunrise, and that the light is coming; and so we also, even we, may light a little taper, to illuminate the darkness while it lasts, and help until the day-spring come. Eternal morning follows the night: a rainbow scarfs the shoulders of every cloud that weeps its rain away to be flowers on land and pearls at sea: Life rises out of the grave, the soul cannot be held by fettering flesh. No dawn is hopeless; and disaster is only the threshold of delight.

Beautifully, above the great wide chaos of human errors, shines the calm, clear light of natural human religion, revealing to us God as the Infinite Parent of all, perfectly powerful, wise, just, loving, and perfectly holy too. Beautiful around stretches off every way the Universe, the Great Bible of God. Material nature is its Old Testament, millions of years old, thick with eternal truths under our feet, glittering with everlasting glories over our heads; and Human Nature is the New Testament from the Infinite God, every day revealing a new page as Time turns over the leaves. Immortality stands waiting to give a recompense for every virtue not rewarded, for every tear not wiped away, for every sorrow undeserved, for every prayer, for every pure intention and emotion of the heart. And over the whole, over Nature, Material and Human, over this Mortal Life and over the eternal Past and Future, the infinite Loving-kindness of God the Father comes enfolding all and blessing everything that ever was, that is, that ever shall be.

Everything is a thought of the Infinite God. Nature is His prose, and man His Poetry. There is no Chance, no Fate; but God's Great Providence, enfolding the whole Universe in its bosom, and feeding it with everlasting life. In times past there has been evil which we cannot understand; now there are evils which we cannot solve, nor make square with God's perfect goodness by any theory our feeble intellect enables us to frame. There are sufferings, follies, and sins for all mankind, for every nation, for every man and every woman. They were all foreseen by the infinite wisdom of God, all provided for by His infinite power and justice, and all are consistent with His infinite love. To believe otherwise would be to believe that He made the world, to amuse His idle hours with the follies and agonies of mankind, as Domitian was wont to do with the wrigglings and contortions of insect agonies. Then indeed we might despairingly unite in that horrible utterance of Heine: "Alas, God's Satire weighs heavily on me! The Great Author of the Universe, the Aristophanes of Heaven, is bent on demonstrating, with crushing force, to me, the little, earthly, German Aristophanes, how my wittiest sarcasms are only pitiful attempts at jesting, in comparison with His, and how miserably I am beneath Him, in humor, in colossal mockery."

No, no! God is not thus amused with and prodigal of human suffering. The world is neither a Here without a Hereafter, a body without a soul, a chaos with no God; nor a body blasted by a soul, a Here with a worse Hereafter, a world with a God that hates more than half the creatures He has made. There is no Savage, Revengeful, and Evil God: but there is an Infinite God, seen everywhere as Perfect Cause, everywhere as Perfect Providence, transcending all, yet in-dwelling everywhere, with perfect power, wisdom, justice, holiness, and love, providing for the future welfare of each and all, foreseeing and forecaring for every bubble that breaks on the great stream of human life and human history.

The end of man and the object of existence in this world, being not only happiness, but happiness in virtue and through virtue, virtue in this world is the condition of happiness in another life, and the condition of virtue in this world is suffering, more or less frequent, briefer or longer continued, more or less intense. Take away suffering, and there is no longer any resignation or humanity, no more self-sacrifice, no more devotedness, no more heroic virtues, no more sublime morality. We are subjected to suffering, both because we are sensible, and because we ought to be virtuous. If there were no physical evil, there would be no possible virtue, and the world would be badly adapted to the destiny of man.

The apparent disorders of the physical world, and the evils that result from them, are not disorders and evils that occur despite the power and goodness of God. God not only allows, but wills them. It is His will that there shall be in the physical world causes enough of pain for man, to afford him occasions for resignation and courage.

Whatever is favorable to virtue, whatever gives the moral liberty more energy, whatever can serve the greater moral development of the human race, is good. Suffering is not the worst condition of man on earth. The worst condition is the moral brutalization which the absence of physical evil would engender.

External or internal physical evil connects itself with the object of existence, which is to accomplish the moral law here below, whatever the consequences, with the firm hope that virtue unfortunate will not fail to be rewarded in another life. The moral law has its sanction and its reason in itself. It owes nothing to that law of merit and demerit that accompanies it, but is not its basis. But, though the principle of merit and demerit ought not to be the determining principle of virtuous action, it powerfully concurs with the moral law, because it offers virtue a legitimate ground of consolation and hope.

Morality is the recognition of duty, as duty, and its accomplishment, whatever the consequences.

Religion is the recognition of duty in its necessary harmony with goodness; a harmony that must have its realization in another life, through the justice and omnipotence of God.

Religion is as true as morality; for once morality is admitted, its consequences must be admitted.

The whole moral existence is included in these two words, harmonious with each other: DUTY and HOPE.

Masonry teaches that God is infinitely good. What motive, what reason, and, morally speaking, what possibility can there be to Infinite Power and Infinite Wisdom, to be anything but good? Our very sorrows, proclaiming the loss of objects inexpressibly dear to us, demonstrate His Goodness. The Being that made us intelligent cannot Himself be without intelligence; and He Who has made us so to love and to sorrow for what we love, must number love for the creatures He has made, among His infinite attributes. Amid all our sorrows, we take refuge in the assurance that He loves us; that He does not capriciously, or through indifference, and still less in mere anger, grieve and afflict us; that He chastens us, in order that by His chastisements, which are by His universal law only the consequences of our acts, we may be profited; and that He could not show so much love for His creatures, by leaving them unchastened, untried, undisciplined. We have faith in the Infinite; faith in God's Infinite Love; and it is that faith that must save us.

No dispensations of God's Providence, no suffering or bereavement is a messenger of wrath: none of its circumstances are indications of God's Anger. He is incapable of Anger; higher above any such feelings than the distant stars are above the earth. Bad men do not die because God hates them. They die because it is best for them that they should do so; and, bad as they are, it is better for them to be in the hands of the infinitely good God, than anywhere else.

Darkness and gloom lie upon the paths of men. They stumble at difficulties, are ensnared by temptations, and perplexed by trouble. They are anxious, and troubled, and fearful. Pain and affliction and sorrow often gather around the steps of their earthly pilgrimage. All this is written indelibly upon the tablets of the human heart. It is not to be erased; but Masonry sees and reads it in a new light. It does not expect these ills and trials and sufferings to be removed from life; but that the great truth will at some time be believed by all men, that they are the means, selected by infinite wisdom, to purify the heart, and to invigorate the soul whose inheritance is immortality, and the world its school.

Masonry propagates no creed except its own most simple and Sublime One; that universal religion, taught by Nature and by Reason. Its Lodges are neither Jewish, Moslem, nor Christian Temples. It reiterates the precepts of morality of all religions. It venerates the character and commends the teachings of the great and good of all ages and of all countries. It extracts the good and not the evil, the truth, and not the error, from all creeds; and acknowledges that there is much which is good and true in all.

Above all the other great teachers of morality and virtue, it reveres the character of the Great Master Who, submissive to the will of His and our Father, died upon the Cross. All must admit, that if the world were filled with beings like Him, the great ills of society would be at once relieved. For all coercion, injury, selfishness, and revenge, and all the wrongs and the greatest sufferings of life, would disappear at once. These human years would be happy; and the eternal ages would roll on in brightness and beauty; and the still, sad music of Humanity, that sounds through the world, now in the accents of grief, and now in pensive melancholy, would change to anthems, sounding to the March of Time, and bursting out from the heart of the world.

If every man were a perfect imitator of that Great, Wise, Good Teacher, clothed with all His faith and all His virtues, how the circle of Life's ills and trials would be narrowed! The sensual passions would assail the heart in vain. Want would no longer successfully tempt men to act wrongly, nor curiosity to do rashly. Ambition, spreading before men its Kingdoms and its Thrones, and offices and honors, would cause none to swerve from their great allegiance. Injury and insult would be shamed by forgiveness. "Father," men would say, "forgive them; for they know not what they do." None would seek to be enriched at another's loss or expense. Every man would feel that the whole human race were his brothers. All sorrow and pain and anguish would be soothed by a perfect faith and an entire trust in the Infinite Goodness of God. The world around us would be new, and the Heavens above us; for here, and there, and everywhere, through all the ample glories and splendors of the Universe, all men would recognize and feel the presence and the beneficent care of a loving Father.

However the Mason may believe as to creeds, and churches, and miracles, and missions from Heaven, he must admit that the Life and character of Him who taught in Galilee, and fragments of Whose teachings have come down to us, are worthy of all imitation. That Life is an undenied and undeniable Gospel. Its teachings cannot be passed by and discarded. All must admit that it would be happiness to follow and perfection to imitate Him. None ever felt for Him a sincere emotion of contempt, nor in anger accused Him of sophistry, nor saw immorality lurking in His doctrines; however they may judge of those who succeeded Him, and claimed to be His apostles. Divine or human, inspired or only a reforming Essene, it must be agreed that His teachings are far nobler, far purer, far less alloyed with error and imperfection, far less of the earth earthly, than those of Socrates, Plato, Seneca, or Mahomet, or any other of the great moralists and Reformers of the world.

If our aims went as completely as His beyond personal care and selfish gratification; if our thoughts and words and actions were as entirely employed upon the great work of benefiting our kind— the true work which we have been placed here to do—as His were; if our nature were as gentle and as tender as His; and if society, country, kindred, friendship, and home were as dear to us as they were to Him, we should be at once relieved of more than half the difficulties and the diseased and painful affections of our lives. Simple obedience to rectitude, instead of self-interest; simple self-culture and self-improvement, instead of constant cultivation of the good opinion of others; single-hearted aims and purposes, instead of improper objects, sought and approached by devious and crooked ways, would free our meditations of many disturbing and irritating questions.

Not to renounce the nobler and better affections of our natures, nor happiness, nor our just dues of love and honor from men; not to vilify ourselves, nor to renounce our self-respect, nor a just and reasonable sense of our merits and deserts, nor our own righteousness of virtue, does Masonry require, nor would our imitation of Him require; but to renounce our vices, our faults, our passions, our self-flattering delusions; to forego all outward advantages, which are to be gained only through a sacrifice of our inward integrity, or by anxious and petty contrivances and appliances; to choose and keep the better part; to secure that, and let the worst take care of itself; to keep a good conscience, and let opinion come and go as it will; to retain a lofty self-respect, and let low self-indulgence go; to keep inward happiness, and let outward advantages hold a subordinate place; to renounce our selfishness, and that eternal anxiety as to what we are to have, and what men think of us; and be content with the plenitude of God's great mercies, and so to be happy. For it is the inordinate devotion to self, and consideration of self, that is ever a stumbling-block in the way; that spreads questions, snares, and difficulties around us, darkens the way of Providence, and makes the world a far less happy one to us than it might be.

As He taught, so Masonry teaches, affection to our kindred, tenderness to our friends, gentleness and forbearance toward our inferiors, pity for the suffering, forgiveness of our enemies; and to wear an affectionate nature and gentle disposition as the garment of our life, investing pain, and toil, and agony, and even death, with a serene and holy beauty. It does not teach us to wrap our-selves in the garments of reserve and pride, to care nothing for the world because it cares nothing for us, to withdraw our thoughts from society because it does us not justice, and see how patiently we can live within the confines of our own bosoms, or in quiet communion, through books, with the mighty dead. No man ever found peace or light in that way. Every relation, of hate, scorn, or neglect, to mankind, is full of vexation and torment. There is nothing to do with men but to love them, to admire their virtues, pity and bear with their faults, and forgive their injuries. To hate your adversary will not help you; to kill him will help you still less: nothing within the compass of the Universe will help you, but to pity, forgive, and love him.

If we possessed His gentle and affectionate disposition, His love and compassion for all that err and all that offend, how many difficulties, both within and without us, would they relieve! How many depressed minds should we console! How many troubles in society should we compose! How many enmities soften! How many a knot of mystery and misunderstanding would be untied by a single word, spoken in simple and confiding truth! How many a rough path would be made smooth, and how many a crooked path be made straight! Very many places, now solitary, would be made glad; very many dark places be filled with light.

Morality has its axioms, like the other sciences; and these axioms are, in all languages, justly termed moral truths. Moral truths, considered in themselves, are equally as certain as mathematical truths. Given the idea of a deposit, the idea of keeping it faithfully is attached to it as necessarily, as to the idea of a triangle is attached the idea that its three angles are equal to two right angles. You may violate a deposit; but in doing so, do not imagine that you change the nature of things, or make what is in itself a deposit become your own property. The two ideas exclude each other. You have but a false semblance of property: and all the efforts of the passions, all the sophisms of interest, will not overturn essential differences. Therefore it is that a moral truth is so imperious; because, like all truth, it is what it is, and shapes itself to please no caprice. Always the same, and always present, little as we may like it, it inexorably condemns, with a voice always heard, but not always regarded, the insensate and guilty will which thinks to prevent its existing, by denying, or rather by pretending to deny, its existence.

The moral truths are distinguished from other truths by this singular characteristic: so soon as we perceive them, they appear to us as the rule of our conduct. If it is true that a deposit is made in order to be returned to its legitimate possessor, it *must* be returned. To the necessity of *believing* the truth, the necessity of *practising* it is added.

The necessity of practising the moral truths is obligation. The moral truths, necessary to the eye of reason, are obligatory on the will. The moral obligation, like the moral truth which is its basis, is absolute. As necessary truths are not *more* or *less* necessary, so obligation is not more or less *obligatory*. There are degrees of importance among different obligations; but there are no degrees in *the obligation itself*. One is not *nearly* obliged, *almost* obliged; but *wholly* so, or *not at all*. If there be any place of refuge against the obligation, it ceases to exist.

If the obligation is *absolute*, it is *immutable* and *universal*. For if what is obligation *to-day* may not be so *to-morrow*, if what is obligatory for *me* may not be so for *you*, the obligation differing from itself, it would be relative and contingent. This fact of absolute, immutable, universal obligation is certain and manifest. *The good* is the foundation of obligation. If it be not, obligation has *no* foundation; and that is impossible. If one act ought to be done, and another ought not, it must be because evidently there is an essential difference between the two acts. If one be not good and the other bad, the obligation imposed on us is arbitrary.

To make the Good a *consequence,* of anything whatever, is to annihilate it. It is the first, or it is nothing. When we ask an honest man why, despite his urgent necessities, he has respected the sanctity of a deposit, he answers, because it was *his duty*. Asked why it was his duty, he answers, because it was *right*, was *just,* was *good*. Beyond that there is no answer to be made, but there is also no question to be asked. No one permits a duty to be imposed on him without giving himself a reason for it: but when it is admitted that the duty is commanded by justice, the mind is satisfied; for it has arrived at a principle beyond which there is nothing to seek, justice being its own principle. The primary truths include their own reason: and justice, the essential distinction between good and evil, is the first truth of morality.

Justice is not a *consequence;* because we cannot ascend to any principle above it. Moral truth *forces itself* on man, and does not *emanate from him.* It no more becomes subjective, by appearing to us obligatory, than truth does by appearing to us necessary. It is in the very nature of the true and the good that we must seek for the reason of necessity and obligation. Obligation is founded on the necessary distinction between the good and the evil; and it is itself the foundation of liberty. If man has his duties to perform, he must have the faculty of accomplishing them, of resisting desire, passion, and interest, in order to obey the law. He must be free; therefore he is so, or human nature is in contradiction with itself. The certainty of the *obligation* involves the corresponding certainty of *free will.*

It is the *will* that is free: though sometimes that will may be ineffectual. The power *to do* must not be confounded with the power *to will.* The former may be *limited:* the latter is *sovereign.* The *external effects* may be prevented: *the resolution* itself cannot. Of this sovereign power of the will we are conscious. We feel in ourselves, before it becomes determinate, the force which can determine itself in one way or another. At the same time when I will this or that, I am equally conscious that I *can* will the contrary. I am conscious that I am the master of my resolution: that I may check it, continue it, retake it. When *the act* has ceased, the consciousness of *the power* which produced it has *not.* That consciousness and the power remain, superior to all the manifestations of the power. Wherefore free-will is the essential and ever-subsisting attribute of the will itself.

At the same time that we judge that a free agent has done a good or a bad act, we form another judgment, as necessary as the first; that if he has done well, he deserves compensation; if ill, punishment. That judgment may be expressed in a manner more or less vivid, according as it is mingled with sentiments more or less ardent. Sometimes it will be a merely kind feeling toward a virtuous agent, and moderately hostile to a guilty one; sometimes enthusiasm or indignation. The judgment of merit and demerit is intimately connected with the judgment of good and evil. Merit is the natural right which we have to be rewarded; demerit the natural right which others have to punish us. But whether the reward is received, or the punishment undergone, or not, the merit or demerit equally subsists. Punishment and reward are the satisfaction of merit and demerit, but do not constitute them. Take away the former, and the latter continue. Take away the latter, and there are no longer real rewards or punishments. When a base man encompasses our merited honors, he has obtained but the mere appearance of a reward; a mere material advantage. The reward is essentially moral; and its value is independent of its form. One of those simple crowns of oak with which the early Romans rewarded heroism, was of more real value than all the wealth of the world, when it was the sign of the gratitude and admiration of a people. Reward accorded to merit is a debt; without merit it is an alms or a theft.

The Good is good in itself, and to be accomplished, whatever the consequences. The results of the Good cannot but be fortunate. Happiness, separated from the Good, is but a fact to which no moral idea is attached. As an effect of the Good, it enters into the moral order, completes and crowns it.

Virtue without happiness, and crime without misery, is a contradiction and disorder. If virtue suppose sacrifice (that is, suffering), eternal justice requires that sacrifice generously accepted and courageously borne, shall have for its reward the same happiness that was sacrificed: and it also requires that crime shall be punished with unhappiness, for the guilty happiness which it attempted to procure.

This law that attaches pleasure and sorrow to the good and the evil, is, in general, accomplished even here below. For order rules in the world; because the world lasts. Is that order sometimes disturbed? Are happiness and sorrow not always distributed in legitimate proportion to crime and virtue? The absolute judgment of the Good, the absolute judgment of obligation, the absolute judgment of merit and demerit, continue to subsist, inviolable and imprescriptible; and we cannot help but believe that He Who has implanted in us the sentiment and idea of order, cannot therein Himself be wanting; and that He will, sooner or later, reestablish the holy harmony of virtue and happiness, by means belonging to Himself.

The Judgment of the Good, the decision that such a thing is good, and that such another is not,—this is the primitive fact, and reposes on itself. By its intimate resemblances to the judgment of the true and the beautiful, it shows us the secret affinities of morality, metaphysics, and æsthetics. The good, so especially united to the true, is distinguished from it, only because it is truth put in practice. The good is obligatory. These are two indivisible but not identical ideas. The idea of obligation reposes on the idea of the Good. In this intimate alliance, the former borrows from the latter its universal and absolute character.

The obligatory good is the moral law. That is the foundation of all morality. By it we separate ourselves from the morality of interest and the morality of sentiment. We admit the existence of those facts, and their influence; but we do not assign them the same rank.

To the moral law, in the reason of man, corresponds liberty in action. Liberty is deduced from obligation, and is a fact irresistibly evident. Man, as free, and subject to obligation, is a moral person; and that involves the idea of rights. To these ideas is added that of merit and demerit; which supposes the distinction between good and evil, obligation and liberty; and creates the idea of reward and punishment.

The sentiments play no unimportant part in morality. All the moral judgments are accompanied by sentiments that respond to them. From the secret sources of enthusiasm the human will draws the mysterious virtue that makes heroes. Truth enlightens and illumines. Sentiment warms and inclines to action. Interest also bears its part; and the hope of happiness is the work of God, and one of the motive powers of human action.

Such is the admirable economy of the moral constitution of man. His Supreme Object, the Good: his law, Virtue, which often imposes upon him suffering, thus making him to excel all other created beings known to us. But this law is harsh, and in contradiction with the instinctive desire for happiness. Wherefore the Beneficent Author of his being has placed in his soul, by the side of the severe law of duty, the sweet, delightful force of sentiment. Generally he attaches happiness to virtue; and for the exceptions, for such there are, he has placed Hope at the end of the journey to be travelled.

Thus there is a side on which morality touches religion. It is a sublime necessity of Humanity to see in God the Legislator supremely wise, the Witness always present, the infallible Judge of virtue. The human mind, ever climbing up to God, would deem the foundations of morality too unstable, if it did not place in God the first principle of the moral law. Wishing to give to the moral law a *religious* character, we run the risk of taking from it its *moral* character. We may refer it so entirely to God as to make His will an arbitrary degree. But the will of God, whence we deduce morality, in order to give it authority, itself has no moral authority, except as it is just. The Good comes from the will of God alone; but from His will, in so far as it is the expression of His wisdom and justice. The Eternal Justice of God is the sole foundation of Justice, such as Humanity perceives and practises it. The Good, duty, merit and demerit, are referred to God, as everything is referred to Him; but they have none the less a proper evidence and authority. Religion is the crown of Morality, not its base. The base of Morality is in itself.

The Moral Code of Masonry is still more extensive than that developed by philosophy. To the requisitions of the law of Nature and the law of God, it adds the imperative obligation of a contract. Upon entering the Order, the Initiate binds to himself every Mason in the world. Once enrolled among the children of Light, every Mason on earth becomes his brother, and owes him the duties, the kindnesses, and the sympathies of a brother. On every one he may call for assistance in need, protection against danger, sympathy in sorrow, attention in sickness, and decent burial after death. There is not a Mason in the world who is not bound to go to his relief, when he is in danger, if there be a greater probability of saving his life than of losing his own. No Mason can wrong him to the value of anything, knowingly, himself, nor suffer it to be done by others, if it be in his power to prevent it. No Mason can speak evil of him, to his face or behind his back. Every Mason must keep his lawful secrets, and aid him in his business, defend his character when unjustly assailed, and protect, counsel, and assist his widow and his orphans. What so many thousands owe to him, he owes to each of them. He has solemnly bound himself to be ever ready to discharge this sacred debt. If he fails to do it he is dishonest and forsworn; and it is an unparalleled meanness in him to obtain good offices by false pretences, to receive kindness and service, rendered him under the confident expectation that he will in his turn render the same, and then to disappoint, without ample reason, that just expectation.

Masonry holds him also, by his solemn promise, to a purer life, a nobler generosity, a more perfect charity of opinion and action; to be tolerant, catholic in his love for his race, ardent in his zeal for the interest of mankind, the advancement and progress of humanity.

Such are, we think, the Philosophy and the Morality, such the TRUE WORD of a Master Mason.

The world, the ancients believed, was governed by Seven Secondary Causes; and these were the universal forces, known to the Hebrews by the plural name ELOHIM. These forces, analogous and contrary one to the other, produce equilibrium by their contrasts, and regulate the movements of the spheres. The Hebrews called them the Seven great Archangels, and gave them names, each of which, being a combination of another word with AL, the first Phœnician Nature-God, considered as the Principle of Light, represented them as His manifestations. Other peoples assigned to these Spirits the government of the Seven Planets then known, and gave them the names of their great divinities.

So, in the Kabala, the last Seven Sephiroth constituted ATIK YOMIN, the Ancient of Days; and these, as well as the Seven planets, correspond with the Seven colors separated by the prism, and the Seven notes of the musical octave.

Seven is the sacred number in all theogonies and all symbols, because it is composed of 3 and 4. It represents the magical power in its full force. It is the Spirit assisted by all the Elementary Powers, the Soul served by Nature, the Holy Empire spoken of in the clavicules of Solomon, symbolized by a warrior, crowned, bearing a triangle on his cuirass, and standing on a cube, to which are harnessed two Sphinxes, one white and the other black, pulling contrary ways, and turning the head to look backward.

The vices are Seven, like the virtues; and the latter were anciently symbolized by the Seven Celestial bodies then known as planets. FAITH, as the converse of arrogant Confidence, was represented by the *Sun;* HOPE, enemy of Avarice, by the *Moon;* CHARITY, opposed to Luxury, by *Venus;* FORCE, stronger than Rage, by *Mars;* PRUDENCE, the opposite of Indolence, by *Mercury;* TEMPERANCE, the antipodes of Gluttony, by *Saturn;* and JUSTICE, the opposite of Envy, by *Jupiter.*

The Kabalistic book of the Apocalypse is represented as closed with Seven Seals. In it we find the Seven genii of the Ancient Mythologies; and the doctrine concealed under its emblems is the pure Kabala, already lost by the Pharisees at the advent of the Saviour. The pictures that follow in this wondrous epic are so many pantacles, of which the numbers 3, 4, 7, and 12 are the keys.

The Cherub, or symbolic bull, which Moses places at the gate of the Edenic world, holding a blazing sword, is a Sphinx, with the body of a bull and a human head; the old Assyrian Sphinx whereof the combat and victory of Mithras were the hieroglyphic analysis. This armed Sphinx represents the law of the Mystery, which keeps watch at the door of initiation, to repulse the Profane. It also represents the grand Magical Mystery, all the elements whereof the number 7 expresses, still without giving its last word. This "unspeakable word" of the Sages of the school of Alexandria, this word, which the Hebrew Kabalists wrote יהוה [Ihuh], and translated by אראריתא, [Ararita,] so expressing the threefoldness of the Secondary Principle, the dualism of the middle ones, and the Unity as well of the first Principle as of the end; and also the junction of the number 3 with the number 4 in a word composed of four letters, but formed of seven by one triplicate and two repeated,—this word is pronounced *Ararita.*

The vowels in the Greek language are also *Seven* in number, and were used to designate the Seven planets.

Tsadok or Sydyc was the Supreme God in Phœnicia. His Seven Sons were probably the Seven Cabiri; and he was the Heptaktis, the God of Seven Rays.

Kronos, the Greek Saturn, Philo makes Sanchoniathon say, had six sons, and by Astarte Seven daughters, the Titanides. The Persians adored Ahura Masda or Ormuzd and the Six Amshaspands, the first three of whom were Lords of the Empires of Light, Fire, and Splendor; the Babylonians, Bal and the Gods; the Chinese, Shangti, and the Six Chief Spirits; and the Greeks, Kronos, and the Six great Male Gods, his progeny, Zeus, Poseidon, Apollo, Arēs, Hēphaistos, and Hermes; while the female deities were also Seven: Rhea, wife of Kronos, Hērē, Athēnē, Artemis, Aphroditē, Hestia, and Dēmētēi. In the Orphic Theogony, Gaia produced the fourteen Titans, Seven male and Seven female, Kronos being the most potent of the males; and as the number *Seven* appears in these, nine by threes, or the triple triangle, is found in the three Mœraê or Fates, the three Centimanēs, and the three Cyclopēs, offspring of Ouranos and Gaia, or Heaven and Earth.

The metals, like the colors, were deemed to be Seven in number, and a metal and color were assigned to each planet. Of the metals, gold was assigned to the Sun and silver to the Moon.

The palace of Deioces in Ecbatana had Seven circular walls of different colors, the two innermost having their battlements covered respectively with silvering and gilding.

And the Seven Spheres of Borsippa were represented by the Seven Stories, each of a different color, of the tower or truncated pyramid of Bel at Babylon.

Pharaoh saw in his dream, which Joseph interpreted, *Seven* ears of wheat on one stalk, full and good, and after them *Seven* ears, withered, thin, and blasted with the East wind; and the Seven thin ears devoured the Seven good ears; and Joseph interpreted these to mean Seven years of plenty succeeded by Seven years of famine.

Connected with this Ebn Hesham relates that a flood of rain laid bare to view a sepulchre in Yemen, in which lay a woman having on her neck *Seven* collars of *pearls,* and on her hands and feet bracelets and ankle-rings and armlets, Seven on each, with an inscription on a tablet showing that, after attempting in vain to purchase grain of Joseph, she, Tajah, daughter of Dzu Shefar, and her people, died of famine.

Hear again the words of an adept, who had profoundly studied the mysteries of science, and wrote, as the Ancient Oracles spoke, in enigmas; but who knew that the theory of mechanical forces and of the materiality of the most potent agents of Divinity, explains nothing, and ought to satisfy no one!

Through the veil of all the hieratic and mystic allegories of the ancient dogmas, under the seal of all the sacred writings, in the ruins of Nineveh or Thebes, on the worn stones of the ancient temples, and on the blackened face of the sphinx of Assyria or Egypt, in the monstrous or marvellous pictures which the sacred pages of the Vedas translate for the believers of India, in the strange emblems of our old books of alchemy, in the ceremonies of reception practised by all the mysterious Societies, we find the traces of a doctrine, everywhere the same, and everywhere carefully concealed. The occult philosophy seems to have been the nurse or the godmother of all religions, the secret lever of all the intellectual forces, the key of all divine obscurities, and the absolute Queen of Society, in the ages when it was exclusively reserved for the education of the Priests and Kings.

It had reigned in Persia with the Magi, who perished one day, as the masters of the world had perished, for having abused their power. It had endowed India with the most marvellous traditions, and an incredible luxury of poetry, grace, and terror in its emblems: it had civilized Greece by the sounds of the lyre of Orpheus: it hid the principles of all the sciences, and of the whole progression of the human spirit, in the audacious calculations of Pythagoras: fable teemed with its miracles; and history, when it undertook to judge of this unknown power, confounded itself with fable: it shook or enfeebled empires by its oracles; made tyrants turn pale on their thrones, and ruled over all minds by means of curiosity or fear. To this science, said the crowd, nothing is impossible; it commands the elements, knows the language of the planets, and controls the movements of the stars; the moon, at its voice, falls, reeking with blood, from Heaven; the dead rise upright on their graves, and shape into fatal words the wind that breathes through their skulls. Controller of Love or Hate, this science can at pleasure confer on human hearts Paradise or Hell: it disposes at will of all forms, and distributes beauty or deformity as it pleases: it changes in turn, with the rod of Circe, men into brutes and animals into men: it even disposes of Life or of Death, and can bestow on its adepts riches by the transmutation of metals, and immortality by its quintessence and elixir, compounded of gold and light.

This is what magic had been, from Zoroaster to Manes, from Orpheus to Apollonius Thyaneus; when positive Christianity, triumphing over the splendid dreams and gigantic aspirations of the school of Alexandria, publicly crushed this philosophy with its anathemas, and compelled it to become more occult and more mysterious than ever.

At the bottom of magic, nevertheless, was science, as at the bottom of Christianity there was love; and in the Evangelic Symbols we see the incarnate WORD adored in its infancy by three magi whom a star guides (the ternary and the sign of the microcosm), and receiving from them gold, frankincense, and myrrh; another mysterious ternary, under the emblem whereof are allegorically contained the highest secrets of the Kabala.

Christianity should not have hated magic; but human ignorance always fears the unknown. Science was obliged to conceal itself, to avoid the impassioned aggressions of a blind love. It enveloped itself in new hieroglyphs, concealed its efforts, disguised its hopes. Then was created the jargon of alchemy, a continual deception for the vulgar herd, greedy of gold, and a living language for the true disciples of Hermes alone.

Resorting to Masonry, the alchemists there invented Degrees, and partly unveiled their doctrine to their Initiates; not by the language of their receptions, but by oral instruction afterward; for their rituals, to one who has not the key, are but incomprehensible and absurd jargon.

Among the sacred books of the Christians are two works which the infallible church does not pretend to understand, and never attempts to explain,—the prophecy of Ezekiel and the Apocalypse; two cabalistic clavicules, reserved, no doubt, in Heaven, for the exposition of the Magian kings; closed with Seven seals for all faithful believers; and perfectly clear to the unbeliever initiated in the occult sciences.

For Christians, and in their opinion, the scientific and magical clavicules of Solomon are lost. Nevertheless, it is certain that, in the domain of intelligence governed by the WORD, nothing that is written is lost. Only those things which men cease to understand no longer exist for them, at least as WORD; then they enter into the domain of enigmas and mystery.

The mysterious founder of the Christian Church was saluted in His cradle by the three Magi, that is to say by the hieratic ambassadors from the three parts of the known world, and from the three analogical worlds of the occult philosophy.

In the school of Alexandria, Magic and Christianity almost take each other by the hand under the auspices of Ammonius Saccos and Plato. The dogma of Hermes is found almost entire in the writings attributed to Dionysius the Areopagite. Synesius traces the plan of a treatise on dreams, which was subsequently to be commented on by Cardan, and composes hymns which might serve for the liturgy of the Church of Swedenborg, if a church of illuminati could have a liturgy.

To this epoch of ardent abstractions and impassioned logomachies belongs the philosophical reign of Julian, an illuminatus and Initiate of the first order, who believed in the unity of God and the universal Dogma of the Trinity, and regretted the loss of nothing of the old world but its magnificent symbols and too graceful images. He was no Pagan, but a Gnostic, infected with the allegories of Grecian polytheism, and whose misfortune it was to find the name of Jesus Christ less sonorous than that of Orpheus.

We may be sure that so soon as Religion and Philosophy become distinct departments, the mental activity of the age is in advance of its Faith; and that, though habit may sustain the latter for a time, its vitality is gone.

The dunces who led primitive Christianity astray, by substituting faith for science, reverie for experience, the fantastic for the reality; and the inquisitors who for so many ages waged against Magism a war of extermination, have succeeded in shrouding in darkness the ancient discoveries of the human mind; so that we now grope in the dark to find again the key of the phenomena of nature. But all natural phenomena depend on a single and immutable law, represented by the philosophal stone and its symbolic form, which is that of a cube. This law, expressed in the Kabala by the number 4, furnished the Hebrews with all the mysteries of their divine Tetragram.

Everything is contained in that word of four letters. It is the *Azot* of the Alchemists, the *Thot* of the Bohemians, the *Taro* of the Kabalists. It supplies to the Adept the last word of the human Sciences, and the Key of the Divine Power: but he alone understands how to avail himself of it who comprehends the necessity of never revealing it. If Œdipus, in place of *slaying* the Sphynx, had *conquered* it, and driven it into Thebes harnessed to his chariot, he would have been King, without incest, calamities, or exile. If Psyche, by submission and caresses, had persuaded Love to reveal himself, she would never have lost him. Love is one of the mythological images of the grand secret and the grand agent, because it expresses at once an action and a passion, a void and a plenitude, an arrow and a wound. The Initiates ought to understand this, and, lest the profane should overhear, Masonry never says too much.

When Science had been overcome in Alexandria by the fanaticism of the murderers of Hypatia, it became Christian, or, rather, it concealed itself under Christian disguises, with Ammonius, Synosius, and the author of the books of Dionysius the Areopagite. Then it was necessary to win the pardon of miracles by the appearances of superstition, and of science by a language unintelligible. Hieroglyphic writing was revived, and pantacles and characters were invented, that summed up a whole doctrine in a sign, a whole series of tendencies and revelations in a word. What was the object of the aspirants to knowledge? They sought for the secret of the great work, or the Philosophal Stone, or the perpetual motion, or the squaring of the circle, or the universal medicine; formulas which often saved them from persecution and general ill-will, by exposing them to the charge of folly; and each of which expressed one of the forces of the grand magical secret. This lasted until the time of the Roman de la Rose, which also expresses the mysterious and magical meaning of the poem of Dante, borrowed from the High Kabalah, that immense and concealed source of the universal philosophy.

It is not strange that man knows but little of the powers of the human will, and imperfectly appreciates them; since he knows nothing as to the nature of the will and its mode of operation. That his own will can move his arm, or compel another to obey him; that his thoughts, symbolically expressed by the signs of writing, can influence and lead other men, are mysteries as incomprehensible to him, as that the will of Deity could effect the creation of a Universe.

The powers of the will are as yet chiefly indefinite and unknown. Whether a multitude of well-established phenomena are to be ascribed to the power of the will alone, or to magnetism or some other natural agent, is a point as yet unsettled; but it is agreed by all that a concentrated effort of the will is in every case necessary to success.

That the phenomena are real is not to be doubted, unless credit is no longer to be given to human testimony; and if they are real, there is no reason for doubting the exercise heretofore, by many adepts, of the powers that were then termed magical. Nothing is better vouched for than the extraordinary performances of the Brahmins. No religion is supported by stronger testimony; nor has any one ever even attempted to explain what may well be termed their miracles.

How far, in this life, the mind and soul can act without and independently of the body, no one as yet knows. That the will can act at all without bodily contact, and the phenomena of dreams, are mysteries that confound the wisest and most learned, whose explanations are but a Babel of words.

Man as yet knows little of the forces of nature. Surrounded, controlled, and governed by them, while he vainly thinks himself independent, not only of his race, but the universal nature and her infinite manifold forces, he is the slave of these forces, unless he becomes their master. He can neither ignore their existence nor be simply their neighbor.

There is in nature one most potent force, by means whereof a single man, who could possess himself of it, and should know how to direct it, could revolutionize and change the face of the world.

This force was known to the ancients. It is a universal agent, whose Supreme law is equilibrium; and whereby, if science can but learn how to control it, it will be possible to change the order of the Seasons, to produce in night the phenomena of day, to send a thought in an instant round the world, to heal or slay at a distance, to give our words universal success, and make them reverberate everywhere.

This agent, partially revealed by the blind guesses of the disciples of Mesmer, is precisely what the Adepts of the middle ages called the elementary matter of the great work. The Gnostics held that it composed the igneous body of the Holy Spirit; and it was adored in the secret rites of the Sabbat or the Temple, under the hieroglyphic figure of Baphomet or the hermaphroditic goat of Mendes.

There is a Life-Principle of the world, a universal agent, wherein are two natures and a double current, of love and wrath. This ambient fluid penetrates everything. It is a ray detached from the glory of the Sun, and fixed by the weight of the atmosphere and the central attraction. It is the body of the Holy Spirit, the universal Agent, the Serpent devouring his own tail. With this electro-magnetic ether, this vital and luminous caloric, the ancients and the alchemists were familiar. Of this agent, that phase of modern ignorance termed physical science talks incoherently, knowing naught of it save its effects; and theology might apply to it all its pretended definitions of spirit. Quiescent, it is appreciable by no human sense; disturbed or in movement, none can explain its mode of action; and to term it a "fluid," and speak of its "currents," is but to veil a profound ignorance under a cloud of words.

Force attracts force, life attracts life, health attracts health. It is a law of nature.

is *necessary*. He *can* exist only in virtue of a Supreme and inevitable REASON. That REASON, then, is THE ABSOLUTE; for it is in IT we must believe, if we would that our faith should have a reasonable and solid basis. It has been said in our times, that God is a Hypothesis; but Absolute Reason is not one: it is essential to Existence.

Saint Thomas said, "*A thing is not just because God wills it,* BUT GOD WILLS IT BECAUSE IT IS JUST." If he had deduced all the consequences of this fine thought, he would have discovered the true Philosopher's Stone; the magical elixir, to convert all the trials of the world into golden mercies. Precisely as it is a necessity for God to BE, so it is a necessity for Him to be just, loving, and merciful. He cannot be unjust, cruel, merciless. He cannot repeal the law of right and wrong, of merit and demerit; for the moral laws are as absolute as the physical laws. There are impossible things. As it is impossible to make two and two be five and not four; as it is impossible to make a thing be and not be at the same time; so it is impossible for the Deity to make crime a merit, and love and gratitude crimes. So, too, it was impossible to make Man perfect, with his bodily senses and appetites, as it was to make his nerves susceptible of pleasure and not also of pain.

Therefore, according to the idea of Saint Thomas, the moral laws are the *enactments* of the Divine WILL, only because they are the *decisions* of the Absolute WISDOM and REASON, and the *Revelations* of the Divine NATURE. In this alone consists the *right* of Deity to enact them; and thus only do we attain the certainty in Faith that the Universe is one Harmony.

To believe in the Reason of God, and in the God of Reason, is to make Atheism impossible. It is the Idolaters who have made the Atheists.

Analogy gives the Sage all the forces of Nature. It is the key of the Grand Arcanum, the root of the Tree of Life, the science of Good and Evil.

The Absolute, is REASON. Reason IS, by means of Itself. It IS BECAUSE IT IS, and not because we suppose it. IT IS, where nothing *exists;* but nothing could possibly exist without IT. Reason is Necessity, Law, the Rule of all Liberty, and the direction of every Initiative. If God IS, HE IS by Reason. The conception of an Absolute Deity, outside of, or independent of, Reason, is the IDOL of Black Magic, the PHANTOM of the Dæmon.

The Supreme Intelligence is necessarily *rational*. God, in philosophy, can be no more than a Hypothesis; but a Hypothesis imposed by good sense on Human Reason. To personify the Absolute Reason, is to determine the Divine Ideal.

NECESSITY, LIBERTY, and REASON! Behold the great and Supreme Triangle of the Kabalists!

FATALITY, WILL, and POWER! Such is the magical ternary which, in human things, corresponds with the Divine Triangle.

FATALITY is the inevitable linking together, in succession, of effects and causes, in a given order.

WILL is the faculty that directs the forces of the Intellect, so as to reconcile the liberty of persons with the necessity of things.

The argument from these premises must be made by yourself. Each one of us does that. "Seek," say the Holy Writings, "and ye shall find." Yet discussion is not forbidden; and without doubt the subject will be fully treated of in your hearing hereafter. Affirmation, negation, discussion,—it is by these the truth is attained.

To explore the great Mysteries of the Universe and seek to solve its manifold enigmas, is the chief use of Thought, and constitutes the principal distinction between Man and the animals. Accordingly, in all ages the Intellect has labored to understand and explain to itself the Nature of the Supreme Deity.

That one Reason and one Will created and governed the Universe was too evident not to be at once admitted by the *philosophers* of all ages. It was the ancient *religions* that sought to multiply gods. The *Nature* of the One Deity, and the mode in which the Universe had its beginning, are questions that have always been the racks in which the human intellect has been tortured: and it is chiefly with these that the Kabalists have dealt.

It is true that, in one sense, we can have no actual knowledge of the Absolute Itself, the *very* Deity. Our means of obtaining what is commonly termed *actual* knowledge, are our senses only. If to *see* and *feel* be *knowledge*, we have none of our own Soul, of electricity, of magnetism. We see and feel and taste an acid or an alkali, and know something of the *qualities* of each; but it is only when we use them in combination with other substances, and learn their *effects*, that we really begin to know their *nature*. It is the combination and experiments of Chemistry that give us a knowledge of the nature and powers of most animal and vegetable substances. As these are cognizable by inspection by our senses, we may partially know them by that alone: but the Soul, either of ourself or of another, being beyond that cognizance, can only be known by the acts and words which are its effects. Magnetism and electricity, when at rest, are equally beyond the jurisdiction of the senses; and when they are in action, we see, feel, hear, taste, and smell only their effects. We do not know what they *are,* but only what they *do.* We can know the attributes of Deity only through His manifestations. To ask anything more, is to ask, not *knowledge,* but something else, for which we have no name. God is a Power; and we know nothing of any Power *itself,* but only its effects, results, and action, and what Reason teaches us by analogy.

In these later days, in laboring to escape from all *material* ideas in regard to Deity, we have so refined away our notions of GOD, as to have no idea of Him at all. In struggling to regard Him as a pure immaterial Spirit, we have made the word *Spirit* synonymous with *nothing,* and can only say that He is a *Somewhat,* with certain attributes, such as Power, Wisdom, and Intelligence. To compare Him to LIGHT, would now be deemed not only unphilosophical, but the equivalent of Atheism; and we find it necessary to excuse and pity the ancients for their inadequate and gross ideas of Deity, expressed in considering Him as the Light-Principle, the invisible essence or substance from which visible Light flows.

Yet our own holy writings continually speak of Him as Light; and therefore the Tsabeans and the Kabala may well be pardoned for doing the same; especially since they did not regard Him as the *visible* Light known to us, but as the Primordial Ether-Ocean from which light flows.

Before the creation, did the Deity dwell alone in the Darkness, or in the Light? Did the Light co-exist with Him, or was it created, after an eternity of darkness? and if it co-existed, was it an effluence from Him, filling all space as He also filled it, He and the Light at the same time filling the same place and every place?

MILTON says, expressing the Hebraic doctrine:

> "Hail, Holy Light, offspring of Heaven first-born,
> Or of th' Eternal, co-eternal beam!
> May I express thee unblamed, *since God is Light.*

And never but in unapproached Light
Dwelt from Eternity; dwelt then in Thee,
Bright effluence of bright Essence uncreate."

"The LIGHT," says the Book *Omschim,* or Introduction to the
Kabala, "Supremest of all things, and most Lofty, and Limitless,
and styled INFINITE, can be attained unto by no cogitation or
speculation; and its VERY SELF is evidently withdrawn and
removed beyond all intellection. It WAS, before all things whatever, produced, created, formed, and made by Emanation; and in
it was neither Time, Head, or Beginning; since it always existed,
and remains forever, without commencement or end."

"Before the Emanations flowed forth, and created things were
created, the Supreme Light was infinitely extended, and filled the
whole WHERE; so that with reference to Light no vacuum
could be affirmed, nor any unoccupied space; but the ALL was
filled with that Light of the Infinite, thus extended, whereto in
every regard was no end, inasmuch as nothing was, except that
extended Light, which, with a certain single and simple equality,
was everywhere like unto itself."

AINSOPH is called *Light,* says the Introduction to the Sohar,
because it is impossible to express it by any other word.

To conceive of God as an actuality, and not as a mere non-
substance or name, which involved non-*existence,* the Kabala, like
the Egyptians, imagined Him to be "a most occult Light," AUR;
not our material and visible Light, but the Substance out of which
Light flows, the *fire,* as relative to its heat and flame. Of this
Light or Ether, the Sun was to the Tsabeans the only manifestation or out-shining, and as such it was worshipped, and not as the
type of dominion and power. God was the *Phōs Noëton,* the Light
cognizable only by the Intellect, the Light-Principle, the Light-
Ether, from which souls emanate, and to which they return.

Light, Fire, and Flame, with the Phœnicians, were the sons of
Kronos. They are the Trinity in the Chaldæan Oracles, the AOR
of the Deity, manifested in *flame,* that issues out of the invisible
Fire.

In the first three Persian Amshaspands, Lords of LIGHT, FIRE,
and SPLENDOR, we recognize the AOR, ZOHAR, and ZAYO, *Light,
Splendor,* and *Brightness,* of the Kabalah. The first of these is
termed AOR MUPALA, *Wonderful* or *Hidden* Light, unrevealed,
undisplayed—which is KETHER, the first Emanation or *Sephirah,*

the *Will* of Deity: the second is NESTAR, *Concealed*—which is HAKEMAH, the second *Sephirah,* or the Intellectual Potence of the Deity: and the third is METANOTSATS, *coruscating*—which is BINAH, the third *Sephirah,* or the intellectual *producing* capacity. In other words, they are THE VERY SUBSTANCE of light, *in* the Deity: *Fire,* which is that light, limited and furnished with attributes, so that it *can* be revealed, but yet remains unrevealed, and its *splendor* or out-shining, or the *light* that goes out from the fire.

Masonry is a search after Light. That search leads us directly back, as you see, to the Kabalah. In that ancient and little understood medley of absurdity and philosophy, the Initiate will find the source of many doctrines; and may in time come to understand the Hermetic philosophers, the Alchemists, all the Antipapal Thinkers of the Middle Ages, and Emanuel Swedenborg.

The Hansavati Rich, a celebrated Sanscrit Stanza, says: "He is Hansa (the Sun), dwelling in light; Vasu, the atmosphere dwelling in the firmament; the invoker of the gods (Agni), dwelling on the altar (*i. e.,* the altar fire) ; the guest (of the worshipper), dwelling in the house (the domestic fire) ; the dweller amongst men (as consciousness) ; the dweller in the most excellent orb, (the Sun) ; the dweller in truth; the dweller in the sky (the air) ; born in the waters, in the rays of light, in the verity (of manifestation), in the Eastern mountains; the Truth (itself)."

"In the beginning," says a Sanscrit hymn, "arose the Source of golden light. *He was the only born Lord of all that is.* He established the earth and the sky. Who is the God to Whom we shall offer our sacrifice?"

"He who gives life, He who gives strength; Whose blessing all the bright gods desire; *Whose shadow is immortality; Whose shadow is death;* Who is the God, etc?"

"He through Whom the sky is bright and the earth for us; He through Whom the Heaven was established, nay, the highest Heaven; He who measured out the light in the air; Who is the God, etc?"

"He to Whom the Heaven and earth, standing firm by His will, look up trembling inwardly; He over Whom the rising sun shines forth; Who is the God, etc?"

"Wherever the mighty water-clouds went, where they placed

the seed and lit the fire, thence arose He Who is the only life of
the bright gods; Who is the God, etc?"

The WORD of God, said the Indian philosophy, is the universal
and invisible Light, cognizable by the senses, that emits its blaze
in the Sun, Moon, Planets, and other Stars. Philo calls it the
"Universal Light," which loses a portion of its purity and splendor
in descending from the intellectual to the sensible world, manifesting itself outwardly from the Deity; and the Kabalah represents that only so much of the Infinite Light flowed into the circular void prepared for creation within the Infinite Light and
Wisdom, as could pass by a canal like a line or thread. The Sephiroth, emanating from the Deity, were the rays of His splendor.

The Chaldæan Oracles said: "The intellect of the Generator,
stirred to action, out-spoke, forming within itself, by intellection,
universals of every possible form and fashion, which issued out,
flowing forth from the One Source . . . For Deity, impersonated
as Dominion, before fabricating the manifold Universe, posited an
intellected and unchangeable universal, the impression of the form
whereof goes forth through the Universe; and that Universe,
formed and fashioned accordingly, becomes visibly beautified in
infinitely varying types and forms, the Source and fountain
whereof is one. . . . Intellectual conceptions and forms from the
Generative source, succeeding each other, considered in relation
to ever-progressing Time, and intimately partaking of THE PRIMAL
ETHER or FIRE; but yet all these Universals and Primal Types
and Ideas flowed forth from, and are part of, the first Source of
the Generative Power, perfect in itself."

The Chaldeans termed the Supreme Deity ARAOR, Father of
Light. From Him was supposed to flow the light above the world,
which illuminates the heavenly regions. This Light or Fire was
considered as the Symbol of the Divine Essence, extending itself
to inferior spiritual natures. Hence the Chaldean oracles say:
"The Father took from Himself, and did not confine His proper
fire within His intellectual potency:" . . "All things are begotten
from one Fire."

The Tsabeans held that all inferior spiritual beings were emanations from the Supreme Deity; and therefore Proclus says:
"The progression of the gods is one and continuous, proceeding
downward from the intelligible and latent unities, and terminating
in the last partition of the Divine cause."

It is impossible to speak clearly of the Divinity. Whoever attempts to express His attributes by the help of abstractions, confines himself to negatives, and at once loses sight of his ideas, in wandering through a wilderness of words. To heap Superlatives on Superlatives, and call Him *best, wisest, greatest,* is but to exaggerate qualities which are found in man. That there exists one only God, and that He is a Perfect and Beneficent Being, Reason legitimately teaches us; but of the Divine *Nature,* of the *Substance* of the Deity, of the manner of His Existence, or of the mode of creation of His Universe, the human mind is inadequate to form any just conception. We can affix no clear ideas to Omnipotence, Omniscience, Infinity or Eternity; and we have no more right to attribute intelligence to Him, than any other mental quality of ourselves, extended indefinitely; or than we have to attribute our senses to Him, and our bodily organs, as the Hebrew writings do.

We satisfy ourselves with negativing in the Deity everything that constitutes existence, so far as we are capable of conceiving of existence. Thus He becomes to us logically nothing, *Non-Ens.* The Ancients saw no difference between that and Atheism, and sought to conceive of Him as something real. It is a necessity of Human Nature. The theological idea, or rather non-idea, of the Deity, is not shared or appreciated by the unlearned. To them, God will always be The Father Who is in Heaven, a Monarch on His Throne, a Being with human feelings and human sympathies, angry at their misdeeds, lenient if they repent, accessible to their supplications. It is the Humanity, far more than the Divinity, of Christ, that makes the mass of Christians worship Him, far more than they do the Father.

"The Light of the Substance of The Infinite," is the Kabalistic expression. Christ was, according to Saint John, "the Light that lighteth every man that cometh into the world"; and "that Light was the life of men." "The Light shone in the darkness, and the darkness comprehended it not."

The ancient ideas in respect to Light were perhaps quite as correct as our own. It does not appear that they ascribed to Light any of the qualities of matter. But modern Science defines it to be a flood of particles of *matter,* flowing or shot out from the Sun and Stars, and moving through space to come to us. On the theories of mechanism and force, what force of attraction here or repulsion at the Sun or at the most distant Star could draw or drive these impalpable, weightless, infinitely minute particles, appreciably by the Sense of Sight alone, so far through space? What has become of the immense aggregate of particles that have reached the earth since the creation? Have they increased its bulk? Why cannot chemistry detect and analyze them? If matter, why can they travel only in right lines?

No characteristic of matter belongs to Light, or Heat, or flame, or to Galvanism, Electricity, and Magnetism. The electric spark is light, and so is that produced by the flint, when it cuts off particles of steel. Iron, melted or heated, radiates light; and insects, infusoria, and decayed wood emit it. Heat is produced by friction and by pressure; to explain which, Science tells us of *latent* Caloric, thus representing it to us as existing without its only known distinctive quality. What quality of matter enables lightning, blazing from the Heavens, to rend the oak? What quality of matter enables it to make the circuit of the earth in a score of seconds?

Profoundly ignorant of the nature of these mighty agents of Divine Power, we conceal our ignorance by words that have no meaning; and we might well be asked *why* Light may not be an effluence from the Deity, as has been agreed by all the religions of all the Ages of the World.

All truly dogmatic religions have issued from the Kabalah and return to it: everything scientific and grand in the religious dreams of all the illuminati, Jacob Bœhme, Swedenborg, Saint-Martin, and others, is borrowed from the Kabalah; all the Masonic associations owe to it their Secrets and their Symbols.

The Kabalah alone consecrates the alliance of the Universal Reason and the Divine Word; it establishes, by the counterpoises of two forces apparently opposite, the eternal balance of being; it alone reconciles Reason with Faith, Power with Liberty, Science with Mystery; it has the keys of the Present, the Past, and the Future.

The Bible, with all the allegories it contains, expresses, in an incomplete and veiled manner only, the religious science of the Hebrews. The doctrine of Moses and the Prophets, identical at bottom with that of the ancient Egyptians, also had its outward meaning and its veils. The Hebrew books were written only to recall to memory the traditions; and they were written in Sym-

bols unintelligible to the Profane. The Pentateuch and the prophetic poems were merely elementary books of doctrine, morals,
or liturgy; and the true secret and traditional philosophy was
only written afterward, under veils still less transparent. Thus
was a second Bible born, unknown to, or rather uncomprehended
by, the Christians; a collection, *they* say, of monstrous absurdities; a monument, the adept says, wherein is everything that the
genius of philosophy and that of religion have ever formed or
imagined of the sublime; a treasure surrounded by thorns; a
diamond concealed in a rough dark stone.

One is filled with admiration, on penetrating into the Sanctuary
of the Kabalah, at seeing a doctrine so logical, so simple, and at
the same time so absolute. The necessary union of ideas and
signs, the consecration of the most fundamental realities by the
primitive characters; the Trinity of Words, Letters, and Numbers; a philosophy simple as the alphabet, profound and infinite
as the Word; theorems more complete and luminous than those
of Pythagoras; a theology summed up by counting on one's fingers; an Infinite which can be held in the hollow of an infant's
hand; ten ciphers, and twenty-two letters, a triangle, a square,
and a circle,—these are all the elements of the Kabalah. These
are the elementary principles of the written Word, reflection of
that spoken Word that created the world!

This is the doctrine of the Kabalah, with which you will no
doubt seek to make yourself acquainted, as to the Creation.

The Absolute Deity, with the Kabalists, has no name. The
terms applied to Him are אור פשוט, Aor Pasot, the Most Simple
[or Pure] Light, "called אין סוף, Ayen Soph, or Infinite, before
any Emanation. For then there was no space or vacant place,
but all was infinite Light."

Before the Deity created any Ideal, any limited and intelligible
Nature, or any form whatever, He was alone, and without form
or similitude, and there could be no cognition or comprehension of
Him in any wise. He was without Idea or Figure, and it is forbidden to form any Idea or Figure of Him, neither by the letter
He (ה), nor by the letter Yōd (י), though these are contained
in the Holy Name; nor by any other letter or point in the
world.

But after He created this Idea [this limited and existing-in-
intellection Nature, which the ten Numerations, Sephiroth or

Rays are], of the Medium, the First Man Adam Kadmon, He descended therein, that, by means of this Idea, He might be called by the name Tetragrammaton; that created things might have cognition of Him, in His own likeness.

When the Infinite God willed to emit what were to flow forth, He contracted Himself in the centre of His light, in such manner that that most intense light should recede to a certain circumference, and on all sides upon itself. And this is the first contraction, and termed צמצם, *Tsemsum.*

אדם קדמון, Adam Kadmon, the Primal or First Man, is the first Aziluthic emanant from the Infinite Light, immitted into the evacuated Space, and from which, afterward, all the other degrees and systems had their beginnings. It is called the Adam prior to all the first. In it are imparted ten spherical numerations; and thereafter issued forth the rectilinear figure of a man in his sephirothic decade, as it were the diameter of the said circles; as it were the axis of these spheres, reaching from their highest point to their lowest; and from it depend all the systems.

But now, as the Infinite Light would be too excellent and great to be borne and endured, except through the medium of this Adam Kadmon, its most Secret Nature preventing this, its illuminating light had again to emanate in streams out of itself, by certain apertures, as it were, like windows, and which are termed the ears, eyes, nostrils, and mouth.

The light proceeding from this Adam Kadmon is indeed but one; but in proportion to its remoteness from the place of outflowing, and to the grades of its descent, it is more dense.

From the word אצל, Atsil, to emanate or flow forth, comes the word אצילות, Atsiloth or Aziluth, Emanation, or the System of Emanants. When the primal space was evacuated, the surrounding Light of the Infinite, and the Light immitted into the void, did not touch each other; but the Light of the Infinite flowed into that void through a line or certain slender canal; and that Light is the Emanative and emitting Principle, or the out-flow and origin of Emanation: but the Light within the void is the emanant subordinate; and the two cohere only by means of the aforesaid line.

Aziluth means specifically and principally the first system of the four Olamoth [עלמות], worlds or systems; which is thence called the Aziluthic World.

The ten Sephiroth of the general Aziluthic system are ten Nekudoth or Points.

אין‌סוף, Ainsoph, Aensoph, or Ayensoph, is the title of the Cause of Causes, its meaning being *"endless,"* because there is no limit to Its loftiness, and nothing can comprehend it. Sometimes, also, the name is applied to Kether, or the Crown, the first emanation, because that is the Throne of the Infinite, that is, its first and highest Seat, than which none is higher, and because Ainsoph resides and is concealed therein: hence it rejoices in the same name.

Before that anything was, says the *Emech Hammelech,* He, of His mere will, proposed to Himself to make worlds . . . but at that time there was no vacant space for worlds; but all space was filled with the light of His Substance, which He had with fixed limits placed in the centre of Himself, and of the parts whereof, and wherein, He was thereafter to effect a folding together.

What then did the Lord of the Will, that most perfectly free Agent, do? By His own estimation, He measured off within His own Substance the width and length of a circular space to be made vacant, and wherein might be posited the worlds aforesaid; and of that Light which was included within the circle so measured, He compressed and folded over a certain portion . . . and that Light He lifted higher up, and so a place was left unoccupied by the Primal Light.

But yet was not this space left altogether empty of that Light; for the vestiges of the Primal Light still remained in the place where Itself had been; and they did not recede therefrom.

Before the Emanations out-flowed, and created things were created, the Supreme Light was infinitely extended, and filled the whole *Where:* nothing *was,* except that extended light, called Aor h' Ainsoph, the Light of the non-finite.

When it came into the mind of the Extended to will to make worlds, and by forth-flowing to utter Emanations, and to emit as Light the perfection of His active powers, and of His aspects and attributes, which was the impelling cause of the creation of worlds; then that Light, in some measure compressed, receded in every direction from a particular central point, and on all sides of it drew back, and so a certain vacuum was left, called void space, its circumference everywhere equidistant from that point which was exactly in the centre of the space . . . a certain void place and space left in Mid-Infinite: a certain *Where* was thereby constituted wherein Emanations might BE, and the Created, the Fashioned and the Fabricated.

This world of the *garmenting,*—this circular vacant space, with the vestiges of the withdrawn light of the Infinite yet remaining, is the inmost garment, nearest to His substance; and to it belongs the name AOR PENAI-AL, *Light of the Countenance of God.*

An interspace surrounds this great circle, established *between* the light of the *very* substance, surrounding the circle on its outside, and the substance contained *within* the circle. This is called SPLENDOR EXCELSUS, in contradistinction to Simple Splendor.

This light "of the vestige of the garment," is said to be, relatively to that of the vestige of the substance, like a point in the centre of a circle. This light, a point in the centre of the Great Light, is called Auir, Ether, or Space.

This Ether is somewhat more gross than the Light—not so Subtle—*though not perceptible by the Senses*—is termed the Primal Ether—extends everywhere; Philosophers call it *the Soul of the World.*

The Light so *forth-shown* from the Deity, cannot be said to be *severed* or *diverse* from Him. "It is flashed forth from Him, and yet all continues to be perfect unity . . . The Sephiroth, sometimes called the *Persons* of the Deity, *are His rays,* by which He is enabled most perfectly to manifest Himself.

The Introduction to the Book SOHAR says:

The first compression was effected, in order that the Primal Light might be upraised, and a space become vacant. The second compression occurred when the vestiges of the removed Light, remaining were compressed into points; and that compression was effected by means of the emotion of joy; the Deity rejoicing, it had already been said, on account of His Holy People, thereafter to come into being; and that joy being vehement, and a commotion and exhilaration in the Deity being caused by it, so that He flowed forth in His delight; and of this commotion an abstract power of judgment being generated, which is a collection of the letters generated by the points of the vestiges of Light left within the circle. *For He writes the finite expressions, or limited manifestations of Himself upon the Book, in single letters.*

Like as when water or fire, it had been said, is blown upon by the wind, it is wont to be greatly moved, and with flashes like lightning to smite the eyes, and gleam and coruscate hither and thither, even so The Infinite was moved within Himself, and shone and coruscated in that circle, from the centre outward and again to the centre: and that commotion we term exhilaration; and from that exhilaration, variously divided within Himself, was generated the potency of determining the fashioning of the letters.

Of that exhilaration, it had also been said, was generated the determination of *forms,* by which determination the Infinite determined them within Himself, as if by saying: "Let this Sphere be the appointed place. wherein let all worlds be created!"

He, by radiating and coruscating, effected the points, so that their sparkling should smite the eyes like lightning. Then He combined diversely the single points, until *letters* were fashioned thereof, in the similitude and image of those wherewith THE BLESSED had set forth the decrees of His Wisdom.

It is not possible to attain to an understanding of the creation of man, except by the mystery of letters; and in these worlds of The Infinite is nothing, except the letters of the Alphabet and their combinations. All the worlds are Letters and Names; but He Who is the Author of all, has no name.

This world of the covering [or *garment—vestimenti*], [that is, the circular vacant space, with the vestiges of the removed Light of The Infinite still remaining after the first contraction and compression], is the *inmost* covering, *nearest* to His substance; and to this covering belongs the general name AUR PENIAL, *Light of the Countenance of God:* by which we are to understand the Light of The Substance.

And after this covering was effected, He contracted it, so as to lift up the lower moiety; . . . and this is the *third* contraction; and in this manner He made vacant a space for the worlds, which had not the capacity to use the great Light of the covering, the end whereof was lucid and excellent as its beginning. And so [by drawing up the lower half and half the letters], are made the *Male* and *Female,* that is, the anterior and posterior adhering mutually to one another.

The vacant space effected by this retraction is called AUIR KADMON, the PRIMAL SPACE: for it was the first of all Spaces; nor was it allowable to call it *covering,* which is AUR PENI-BAL, the Light of the Countenance of God.

The vestiges of the Light of the Garment still remained there.
And this world of the garment has a name *that includes all things,*
which is the name IHUH. Before the world of the vacant space
was created, HE was, and His Name, and they alone; that is,
AINSOPH and His garmenting.

The EMECH HAMMELECH says again:

The lower half of the garment [by the third retraction], was
left empty of the light of the garment. But the vestiges of that
light remained in the place so vacated . . . and *this* garment is
called SHEKINAH, God in-dwelling; that is, the place where יה
Yōd He, of the anterior [or male], and וה Vav He, of the posterior [or female], combinations of letters dwelt.

This vacant space was square, and is called the *Primal Space;*
and in Kabalah it is called *Auira Kadmah,* or *Rasimu Ailah,* The
Primal Space, or The Sublime Vestige. It is the vestige of the
Light of the Garment, with which is intermingled somewhat of
the vestige of the Very Substance. It is called *Primal Ether,* but
not void Space. . . The Light of the Vestige still remains in the
place it occupied, and adheres there, like somewhat spiritual, of
extreme tenuity.

In this Ether are two Lights; that is, the Light of the SUB-
STANCE, which was taken away, and that of the Garment. There
is a vast difference between the two; for that of the Vestige of the
Garment is, relatively to that of the Vestige of the Substance, *like
a point in the centre of a circle.* And as the only appropriate
name for the Light of the Vestige of Ainsoph is AUR, *Light,*
therefore the Light of the Vestige of the Garment could not be
called by *that* name; and so we term it a *point,* that is, Yōd [' or
י], which is that point in the centre of Light . . . and *this* Light,
a point in the centre of the Great Light, is called *Auir,* Ether, or
Space.

This Ether is somewhat more gross than The Light . . . . not so
subtle, though not perceptible by the senses . . . is termed the Primal Ether . . . extends everywhere; whence the Philosophers call
it The Soul of the World . . . Light is visible, though not perceptible. *This Ether is neither perceptible nor visible.*

The Introduction to the Book Sohar continues, in the Section
of the Letter Yōd, etc:

Worlds could not be framed in this Primal Ether, on account
of its extreme tenuity and the excess of Light; and also because

in it remained the vital Spirit of the Vestige of the Light Ain-soph, and that of the Vestige of the Light of the Garment; whereby such manifestation was prevented.

Wherefore HE directed the letter Yōd, since it was not so brilliant as the Primal Ether, to descend, and take to itself the light remaining in the Primal Ether, and return above, with that Vestige which so impeded the manifestation; which Yōd did.

It descended below five times, to remove the vital Spirit of the Vestige of the Light Ainsoph; and the Vestige of the Light and vital Spirit of the Garment from the Sphere of Splendor, so as to make of it ADAM, called KADMON. And by its return, manifestation is effected in the space below, and a Vestige of the Sublime Brilliance yet remains there, existing as a Spherical Shape, and termed in the Sohar simply *Tehiru*, that is, Splendor; and it is styled The First Matter. . . . it being, as it were, vapor, and, as it were, smoke. And as smoke is formless, not comprehended under any fixed definite form, so this Sphere is a formless somewhat, since it seems to be somewhat that is spherical, and yet is not limited.

The letter Yōd, while adhering to the Shekinah, had adhering to himself the Light of the Shekinah, though his light was not so great as that of the Shekinah. But when he descended, he left that light of his own below, and the Splendor consisted of it. After which there was left in Yōd only a vestige of that light, inasmuch as he could not re-ascend to the Shekinah and adhere to it. Wherefore The Holy and Blessed directed the letter He [ח, the female letter], to communicate to Yōd of her Light; and sent him forth, to descend and share with *that* light in the Splendor aforesaid . . . and when he re-descended into the Sphere of Splendor, he diffused abroad in it the Light communicated to him by the letter He.

And when he again ascended he left behind him the productive light of the letter He, and thereof was constituted another Sphere, *within* the Sphere of Splendor; which *lesser* Sphere is termed in the Sohar KETHER AILAH, CORONA SUMMA, *The Supreme Crown*, and also ATIKA DE ATIKIM, *Antiquus Antiquum, The Ancient of Ancients*, and even AILIT H' AILIT, *Causa Causarum, the Cause of Causes*. But the Crown is very far smaller than the Sphere of Splendor, so that within the latter an immense unoccupied place and space is still left.

The Beth Alohim says:

Before the Infinite God, the Supreme and First Good, formed objectively within Himself a particular conception, definite, limited, and the object of intellection, and gave form and shape to an intellectual conception and image. He was alone, companionless, without form or similitude, utterly without Ideal or Figure ... It is forbidden to make of Him any figure whatever, by any image in the world, neither by the letter He nor by the letter Yōd, nor by any other letter or point in the world.

But after He had formed this Idea, the particular conception, limited and intelligible, which the Ten Numerations are, of the medium of transmission, Adam Kadmon, the Primal or Supreme Man, He by that medium descended, and may, through that Idea, be called by the name Ihuh, and so created things have cognizance of Him, by means of His proper likeness.

Woe unto him who makes God to be like unto any mode or attribute whatever, even were it to one of His own; and still more if he make Him like unto the Sons of Men, whose elements are earthly, and so are consumed and perish!

There can be no conception had of Him, except in so far as He manifests Himself, in exercising dominion by and through some attribute ... Abstracted from this, there can be no attribute, conception, or ideal of Him. He is comparable only to the Sea, filling some great reservoir, its bed in the earth, for example; wherein it fashions for itself a certain concavity, so that thereby we may begin to compute the dimensions of the Sea itself.

For example, the Spring and Source of the Ocean is a somewhat, which is *one*. If from this Source or Spring there issues forth a certain fountain, proportioned to the space occupied by the Sea in that hemispherical reservoir, such as is the letter Yōd, there the Source of Spring is the first somewhat, and the fountain that flows forth from it is the second. Then let there be made a great reservoir, as by excavation, and let this be called the Ocean, and we have the third thing, a vessel [*Vas*]. Now let this great reservoir be divided into seven beds of rivers, that is, into seven oblong reservoirs, so that from this ocean the waters may flow forth in seven rivers; and the Source, Fountain, and Ocean thus make *ten* in all.

The Cause of Causes made ten Numerations, and called the Source of Spring Kether, *Corona,* the Crown, in which the idea of circularity is involved, for there is no *end* to the out-flow of Light; and therefore He called this, like Himself, *endless;* for this also, like Him, has no similitude or configuration, nor hath it any vessel or receptacle wherein it may be contained, or by means whereof any possible cognizance can be had of it.

After thus forming the Crown, He constituted a certain smaller receptacle, the letter Yōd, and filled it from that source; and this is called "The Fountain gushing with Wisdom," and, manifested in this, He called Himself WISE, and the vessel He called HAKE-MAH, *Wisdom, Sapientia.*

Then He also constituted a great reservoir, which He called the Ocean; and to it He gave the name of BINAH, Understanding, *Intelligentia.* In this He characterized Himself as Intelligent or *Conceiver.* HE is indeed the Absolutely Wise and Intelligent, but Hakemah is not Absolute Wisdom of itself, *but is wise by means of Binah,* who fills Himself from it, and if this supply were taken from it, would be dry and unintelligent.

And thereupon seven precious vessels become, to which are given the following names: GEDULAH, *Magnificence* or *Benignity* [or KHASED, *Mercy*]; GEBURAH, *Austerity, Rigor* or *Severity;* TEPHARETH, *Beauty;* NETSAKH, *Victory;* HŌD, *Glory;* YESOD, *Foundation* or *Basis;* and MALAKOTH, *Rule, Reign, Royalty, Dominion* or *Power.* And in GEDULAH He took the character of *Great* and *Benignant;* in GEBURAH, of *Severe;* in TEPHARETH, of *Beautiful;* in NETSAKH, of *Overcoming;* in HŌD, of OUR GLORI-OUS AUTHOR; in YESOD, of *Just,* by Yesod all vessels and worlds being upheld; and in MALAKOTH He applied to Himself the title of *King.*

These numerations or Sephiroths are held in the Kabala to have been originally contained in each other; that is, Kether contained the nine others, Hakemah contained Binah, and Binah contained the last seven.

For all things, says the commentary of Rabbi *Jizchak Lorja,* in a certain most abstruse manner, consist or reside and are con-tained in Binah, and it projects them, and sends them downward, species by species, into the several worlds of Emanation, Creation, Formation, and Fabrication; all whereof are derived from what are above them, and are termed their out-flowings; for, from the potency which was their state there, they descend into actual-ity.

The INTRODUCTION says:

It is said in many places in the Sohar, that all things that emanate or are created have their root above. Hence also the Ten Sephiroth have their root above, in the world of the garment, with the very Substance of HIM. And AINSOPH had full conscious-ness and appreciation, prior to their actual existence, of all the Grades and Impersonations contained unmanifested within Him-self, with regard to the essence of each, and its domination then in potency . . . When He came to the Sephirah of the Impersonation Malakoth, which He then contained hidden within Himself, He concluded within Himself that therein worlds should be framed; since the scale of the first nine Sephiroths was so constituted, that it was neither fit nor necessary for worlds to be framed from *them;* for all the attributes of these nine Superior Sephiroth could be assigned to Himself, even if He should never operate out-wardly; but Malakoth, which is Empire or Dominion, could not be attributed to Him, unless He ruled over other Existences; whence from the point Malakoth He produced all the worlds into actuality.

These circles are ten in number. Originated by points, they expanded in circular shape. Ten Circles, under the mystery of the ten Sephiroth, and between them ten Spaces; whence it ap·pears that the sphere of Splendor is in the centre of the space Malakoth of the First Occult Adam.

The First Adam, *in the ten circles above the Splendor,* is called the First *occult* Adam; and in each of these spaces are formed many thousand worlds. The first Adam is *involved* in the Primal Ether, and is the analogue of the world Binah.

Again the Introduction repeats the first and second descent of Yōd into the vacated space, to make the light there less great and subtile; the constitution of the *Tehiru,* Splendor, from the light left behind there by him; the communication of Light to him by the female letter He; the emission by him of that Light, within the sphere of Splendor, and the formation thereof, within the sphere, "of a certain sphere called the Supreme Crown," *Corona Summa,* KETHER, "wherein were contained, in potence, all the remaining Numerations, so that they were not distinguishable from it. Pre-cisely as in man exist the four elements, in potence specifically undistinguishable, so in this Corona were in potence all the ten Numerations, specifically undistinguishable." This Crown, it is added, was called, after the restoration, The Cause of Causes, and the Ancient of the Ancients.

The point, Kether, adds the Introduction, was the aggregate of all the Ten... when it first emanated, it consisted of all the Ten; and the Light which extended from the Emanative Principle simultaneously flowed into *it;* and beheld the two *Universals* [that is, the Unities out of which manifoldness flows; as, for example, the *idea,* within the Deity, of Humanity as a Unit, out of which the individuals were to flow], the Vessel or Receptacle containing this immitted Light, and the Light Itself within it. And *this Light is the Substance of the point Kether; for the* WILL *of God is the Soul of all things that are.*

The Ainsophic Light, it had said, was infinite in every direction, and without end or limit. To prevent it from flowing into and re-filling the quasi-vacant space, occupied by an infinitely less Splendor, a partition between the greater and lesser Splendor was necessary; and this partition, the boundary of the sphere of Splendor, and a like one bounding the sphere Kether, were called *Vessels* or *Receptacles, containing,* including, and enclosing within themselves the light of the sphere. Imagine a sea of pellucid water, and in the centre of it a spherical mass of denser and darker water. The outer surface of this sphere, or its limits every way, is the vessel containing it. The Kabalah regards the vessels "as by their nature somewhat opaque, and not so splendid as the light they enclose."

The contained Light is the *Soul* of the vessels, and is active in them, like the Human Soul in the human body. The Light of the Emanative Principle [Ainsoph] *inheres* in the vessels, as their *Life,* internal *Light,* and *Soul. . .* Kether emanated, with its Very Substance, at the same time as Substance and Vessel, in like manner as the flame is annexed to the live coal, and as the Soul pervades, and is within, the body. All the Numerations were potentially contained in it.

And this potentiality is thus explained: When a woman conceives, a Soul is immediately sent into the embryo which is to become the infant, in which Soul are then, potentially, all the members and veins of the body, which afterward, from that potency of the Soul, *become* in the human body of the child to be born.

Then the wisdom of God commanded that these Numerations

potentially in Kether, should be produced from potentiality into actuality, in order that worlds might consist; and HE directed Yōd again to descend, and to enter into and shine within Kether, and then to re-ascend: which was so done. From which illumination and re-ascension, all the other numerations, potentially in Kether, were manifested and disclosed; but they continued still compacted together, remaining within Kether in a circle.

When God willed to produce the other emanations or numerations from Kether, it is added, HE sent Yōd down again, to the upper part of Kether, one-half of him to remain without and one-half to penetrate within the sphere of Kether. Then HE sent the letter Vav into the Splendor, to pour out its light on Yōd: and thus,—

Yōd received light from Vav, and thereby so directed his countenance that it should illuminate and confer exceeding great energy on Hakemah, which yet remained in Kether; so giving it the faculty to proceed forth therefrom; and that it might collect and contain within itself, and there reveal, all the other eight numerations, until that time in Kether.

The sphere of Kether opened, and thereout issued Hakemah, to remain below Kether, containing in itself all the other numerations.

By a similar process, Binah, illuminated within Hakemah by a second Yōd, "issued forth out of Hakemah, having within itself the Seven lower Numerations."

And since the vessel of Binah was excellent, and coruscated with rays of the color of sapphire, and was so nearly of the same color as the vessel of Hakemah that there was scarcely any difference between them, hence it would not quietly remain below Hakemah, but rose, and placed itself on his left side.

And because the light from above profusely flowed into and accumulated in the vessel of Hakemah, to so great an extent that it overflowed, and escaped, coruscating, outside of that vessel, and, flowing off to the left, communicated potency and increase to the vessel of Binah . . . . For Binah is *female* . . . .

Binah, therefore, by means of this energy that flowed into it from the left side of Hakemah, by virtue of the second Yōd, came to possess such virtue and potency, as to project beyond itself the Seven remaining vessels contained within itself, and so emitted them all, continuously, one after the other . . . all connected and linked one with the other, like the links of a chain.

Three points first emanated, one under the other; Kether, Hakemah, and Binah; and, so far, there was no copulation. But afterward the positions of Hakemah and Binah changed, so that they were side by side, Kether remaining above them; and then conjunction of the Male and Female, ABA and IMMA, *Father* and *Mother*, as points.

He, from Whom all emanated, created Adam Kadmon, consisting of all the worlds, so that in him should be somewhat from those above, and somewhat from those below. Hence in Him was NEPHESCH [PSYCHE, *anima infima,* the lowest spiritual part of man, *Soul*], from the world ASIAH, which is one letter *He* of the Tetragrammaton; RUACH [SPIRITUS, *anima media,* the next higher spiritual part, or *Spirit*], from the world YEZIRAH, which is the *Vav* of the Tetragrammaton; NESCHAMAH [the highest spiritual part, *mens* or *anima superior*], from the world BRIAH, which is the other letter *He;* and NESCHAMAH LENESCHAMAH, from the world ATSILUTH, which is the YŌD of the Tetragrammaton.

And these letters [the Sephiroth] were changed from the spherical form into the form of a person, the symbol of which person is the BALANCE, it being *Male* and *Female* . . . Hakemah on one side, Binah on the other, and Kether over them: and so Gedulah on one side, Geburah on the other, and Tephareth under them.

The Book *Omschim* says: Some hold that the ten Sephiroth succeeded one another in ten degrees, one above the other, in regular gradation, one connected with the other in a direct line, from the highest to the lowest. Others hold that they issued forth in three lines, parallel with each other, one on the right hand, one on the left, and one in the middle; so that, beginning with the highest and going down to the lowest, Hakemah, Khased [or Gedulah], and Netsach are one over the other, in a perpendicular line, on the right hand; Binah, Geburah, and Hōd on the left; and Kether, Tephareth, Yesod, and Malakoth in the middle: and many hold that all the ten subsist in circles, one within the other, and all homocentric.

It is also to be noted, that the Sephirothic tables contain still another numeration, sometimes called also a Sephirah, which is called Daath, cognition. It is in the middle, below Hakemah and Binah, and is the result of the conjunction of these two.

To Adam Kadmon, the Idea of the Universe, the Kabalah assigns a human form. In this, Kether is the cranium, Hakemah and

Binah the two lobes of the brain, Gedulah and Geburah the two arms, Tephareth the trunk, Netsach and Hōd the thighs, Yesod the male organ, and Malkuth the female organ, of generation.

Yōd is Hakemah, and He Binah; Vav is Tephareth, and the last He, Malkuth.

The whole, say the Books *Mysterii* or of *Occultation,* is thus summed up: The intention of God The Blessed was to form Impersonations, in order to diminish the Light. Wherefore HE constituted, in Macroprosopos, Adam Kadmon, or Arik Anpin, three Heads. The first is called, "The Head whereof is no cognition"; the second, "The Head of that which is non-existent"; and the third, "The Very Head of Macroprosopos"; and these three are *Corona, Sapientia,* and *Informatio,* Kether, Hakemah, and Binah, existent in the Corona of the World of Emanation, or in Macroprosopos; and these three are called in the Sohar ATIKA KADISCHA, *Senex Sanctissimus,* The Most Holy Ancient. But the Seven inferior Royalties of the first Adam are called "The Ancient of Days"; and this Ancient of Days is the internal part, or Soul, of Macroprosopos.

The human mind has never struggled harder to understand and explain to itself the process of creation, and of Divine manifestation, *and at the same time to conceal its thoughts from all but the initiated,* than in the Kabalah. Hence, much of it seems at first like jargon. Macroprosopos or Adam Kadmon is, we have said, the idea or intellectual aggregate of the whole Universe, included and contained unevolved in the manifested Deity, Himself yet contained unmanifested in the Absolute. The Head, Kether, "whereof is no cognition," is the *Will* of the Deity, or the Deity *as* Will. Hakemah, the head "of that which is non-existent," is the Generative Power of begetting or producing Thought; yet *in* the Deity, not in action, and therefore non-existent. Binah, "the very or actual head" of Macroprosopos, is the productive intellectual capacity, which, impregnated by Hakemah, is to *produce* the Thought. This Thought is Daath; or rather, the result is Intellection, Thinking; the Unity, of which Thoughts are the manifold outflowings.

This may be illustrated by a comparison. Pain, in the human being, is a feeling or sensation. It must be *produced.* To produce it, there must be, not only the *capacity* to *produce* it, in the nerves, but also the *power* of *generating* it by means of that capacity.

This generative Power, the Passive Capacity which produces, and the pain produced, are like Hakemah, Binah, and Daath.

The four Worlds or Universals, Aziluth, Briah, Yetzirah, and Asiah, of Emanation, Creation, Formation, and Fabrication, are another enigma of the Kabalah. The first three are wholly *within* the Deity. The first is the Universe, as it exists potentially in the Deity, determined and imagined, but as yet wholly formless and undeveloped, except so far as it is contained in His Emanations. The second is the Universe in idea, distinct within the Deity, but not invested with forms; a simple unity. The third is the same Universe in potence in the Deity, unmanifested, but invested with forms,—the idea developed into manifoldness and individuality, and succession of species and individuals; and the fourth is the potentiality become the Actuality, the Universe fabricated, and existing as it exists for us.

The Sephiroth, says the *Porta Cœlorum,* by the virtue of their Infinite Emanator, who uses them as a workman uses his tools, and who operates with and through them, are the cause of existence of everything created, formed, and fashioned, employing in their production certain *media.* But these same *Sephiroth, Persons* and *Lights,* are not creatures *per se,* but *ideas,* and *Rays* of THE INFINITE, which, by different gradations, so descended from the Supreme Source as still not to be severed from It; but It, through them, is extended to the production and government of all Entities, and is the Single and Perfect Universal Cause of All, though becoming determinate for this or the other operation, through this or that Sephiroth or MODE.

God produced all things by His Intellect and Will and free Determination. He willed to produce them by the mediation of His Sephiroth, and Persons . . . . . by which He is enabled most perfectly to manifest Himself; and that the *more* perfectly, by producing the causes themselves, and the Causes of Causes, and not merely the viler effects.

God produced, in the first Originate, all the remaining causates. For, as He Himself is most simply One, and from One Simple Being One only can *im*mediately proceed, hence it results that from the First Supreme Infinite Unity flowed forth at the same time All and One. One, that is, in so far as flowing from the Most Simple Unity, and being like unto It; but also All, in so far as, departing from that perfect Singleness which can be measured by no other Singleness, it became, to a certain extent, manifold, though still Absolute and Perfect.

Emanation, says the same, is the Resulting displayed from the Unresulting, the Finite from the Infinite, the Manifold and Composite from the Perfect Single and Simple, Potentiality from that which is Infinite Power *and* Act, the mobile from that which is perennially permanent; and therefore in a more imperfect and diminished mode than His Infinite Perfection is. As the First Cause is all things, in an unresulting and Infinite mode, so the Entities that flow from Him are the First Causes, in a resulting and finite mode.

The Necessary Entity, subsisting of Itself, as It cannot be dissevered into the manifold, yet becomes, as it were, multiplied in the Causates, in respect of their Nature, or of the Subsistences, Vessels, and openings assigned to them; whereby the Single and Infinite Essence, being inclosed or comprehended in these limits, bounds, or externalnesses, takes on Itself Definiteness of dimension, and becomes Itself manifold, by the manifoldness of these envelopes.

As man [the unit of Humanity] is a microcosm, so Adam Kadmon is a macrocosm, containing all the Causates of the First Cause . . . . . as the Material Man is the end and completion of all creation, so in the Divine Man is the beginning thereof. As the inferior Adam *receives* all things *from* all, so the superior Adam *supplies* all things *to* all. As the former is the principle of *reflected* light, so the latter is of *Direct* Light. The former is the terminus of the Light, descending; the latter its terminus, ascending. As the Inferior man ascends from the lowest matter even to the First Cause, so the Superior Adam descends from the Simple and Infinite Act, even to the lowest and most attenuated Potence.

The Ternary is the bringing back of duality to unity.

The Ternary is the Principle of Number, because, bringing back the binary to unity, it restores to it the same quantity whereby it had departed from unity. It is the first odd number, containing in itself the first even number and the unit, which are the Father and Mother of all Numbers; and it has in itself the beginning, middle, and end.

Now, Adam Kadmon emanated from the Absolute Unity, and so is himself a unit; but he also descends and flows downward into his own Nature, and so is duality. Again, he returns to the Unity, which he hath in himself, and to The Highest, and so is the Ternary and Quaternary.

And this is why the Essential Name has four letters,—three different ones, and one of them once repeated; since the first He is the wife of the Yōd, and the second He is the wife of the Vav.

Those *media* which manifest the First Cause, in Himself profoundly hidden, are the Sephiroth, which emanate immediately from that First Cause, and by Its Nature have produced and do control all the rest.

These Sephiroth were put forth from the One First and Simple, manifesting His Infinite Goodness. They are the mirrors of His Truth, and the analogues of His Supremest Essence, the Ideas of His Wisdom, and the representations of His will; the receptacles of His Potency, and the instruments with which He operates; the Treasury of His Felicity, the dispensers of His Benignity, the Judges of His Kingdom, and reveal His Law; and finally, the Denominations, Attributes, and Names of Him Who is above all and the Cause of all . . . . . the ten categories, wherein all things are contained; the universal genera, which in themselves include all things, and utter them outwardly . . . . the Second Causes, whereby the First Cause effects, preserves, and governs all things; the rays of the Divinity, whereby all things are illumined and manifested; the Forms and Ideas and Species, out whereof all things issue forth; the Souls and Potencies, whereby essence, life, and movement are given to all things; the Standard of times, whereby all things are measured; the incorporeal Spaces which, in themselves, hold and inclose the Universe; the Supernal Monads to which all manifolds are referred, and through them to The One and Simple; and finally the Formal Perfections, flowing forth from and still connected with the One Eminent Limitless Perfection, are the Causes of all dependent Perfections, and so illuminate the elementary Intelligences, not adjoined to matter, and the intellectual Souls, and the Celestial, Elemental and Element-produced bodies.

The IDRA SUTA says:

HE, the Most Holy Hidden Eldest, separates Himself, and is ever more and more separated from all that are; nor yet does HE in very deed separate Himself; because all things cohere with

Him and HE with All.   HE is All that is, the Most Holy Eldest
of All, the Occult by all possible occultations.

When HE takes shape, HE produces nine Lights, which shine
forth from Him, from His outforming.   And those Lights out-
shine from Him and emit flames, and go forth and spread out on
every side; as from one elevated Lamp the Rays are poured forth
in every direction, and these Rays thus diverging, are found to be,
when one approaching has cognizance of them, but a single Lamp.

The Space in which to create is fixed by THE MOST HOLY
ANCIENT, and illuminated by His inflowing, which is the Light
of Wisdom, and the Beginning from which manifestation flows.

And HE is conformed in three Heads, which are but one Head;
and these three are extended into Microprosopos, and from them
shines out all that is.

Then this Wisdom instituted investiture with form, whereby
the unmanifested and informous became manifested, putting on
form; and produced a certain outflow.

When this Wisdom is thus expanded by flowing forth, then it
is called "Father of Fathers," the whole Universe of Things being
contained and comprehended in it.   This Wisdom is the principle
of all things, and in it beginning and end are found.

The Book of the Abstruse, says the *Siphra de Zeniutha,* is that
which describes the equilibrium of the Balance.   Before the
Balance was, face did not look toward face.

And the *Commentary* on it says: The Scales of the Balance are
designated as Male and Female.   In the Spiritual world Evil and
Good are *in equilibrio,* and it will be restored, when of the Evil
Good becomes, until all is Good.   Also this other world is called
the World of the Balance.   For, as in the Balance are two scales,
one on either side and the beam and needle between them, so too
in this world of restoration, the Numerations are arranged as distinct persons.   For Hakemah is on the right hand, on the side
of Gedulah, and Binah on the left, on the side of Geburah; and
Kether is the beam of the Balance above them in the middle.   So
Gedulah or Khased is on one hand, and Geburah on the other,
and under these Tephareth; and Netsach is on one side, and Hōd
on the other, and under these Yesōd.

The Supreme Crown, which is the Ancient Most Holy, the most
Hidden of the Hidden, is fashioned, *within* the occult Wisdom,
of both sexes, Male and Female.

Hakemah, and Binah, the Mother, whom it impregnates, are quantitatively equal. Wisdom and the Mother of Intellection go forth at once and dwell together; for when the Intellectual Power emanates, the productive *Source* of intellection is included in Him.

Before Adam Kadmon was fashioned into Male and Female, and the state of equilibrium introduced, the Father and Mother did not look each other in the face; for the Father denotes most perfect Love, and the Mother most perfect Rigor; and she averted her face.

There is no *left* [female], says the *Idra Rabba*, in the Ancient and Hidden One; but His totality is Right [male]. The totality of things is HUA, HE, and HE is hidden on every side.

Macroprosopos [Adam Kadmon] is not so near unto us as to speak to us in the first person; but is designated in the third person, HUA, HE.

Of the letters it says:

Yōd is male, He is female, Vav is both.

In Yōd [◟] are three Yōds, the upper and the lower apex, and Vav in the middle. By the upper apex is denoted the Supreme Kether; by Vav in the middle, Hakemah; and by the lower apex, Binah.

The IDRA SUTA says:

The Universe was out-formed in the form of Male and Female. Wisdom, pregnant with all that is, when it flowed and shone forth, shone altogether under the form of male and female. Hakemah is the Father, and Binah is the Mother; and so the two are in equilibrium as male and female, and for this reason, all things whatsoever are constituted in the form of male and female; *and if it were not so they would not exist.*

This Principle, Hakemah, is the Generator of all things; and He and Binah conjoin, and she shines within Him. When they thus conjoin, she conceives, and the out-flow is Truth.

Yōd impregnates the letter He and begets a son; and she, thus pregnant, brings forth. The Principle called Father [the Male or Generative Principle] is comprehended in Yōd, which itself flows downward from the energy of the Absolute Holy One.

Yōd is the beginning and the end of all things that are. The stream that flows forth is the Universe of things, which always *becomes*. having no cessation. And this *becoming* world is created by Yōd: for Yōd includes two letters. All things are included in Yōd; wherefore it is called the Father of all.

All Categories whatever go forth from Hakemah; and in it are contained all things, unmanifested; and the aggregate of all things, or the Unity *in* which the many *are,* and *out* of which all flow, is the Sacred Name IHUH.

In the view of the Kabalists, all individuals are *contained* in species, and all species in genera, and all particulars in a Universal, which is an idea, abstracted from all consideration of individuals; not an *aggregate* of individuals; but, as it were, an *Ens,* Entity or Being, ideal or intellectual, but none the less real; prior to *any* individual, *containing* them all, and out of which they are all in succession evolved.

If this discontents you, reflect that, supposing the theory correct, that *all* was originally in the Deity, and that the Universe has proceeded forth from Him, and not been *created* by Him out of nothing, the *idea* of the Universe, existing in the Deity before its out-flow, must have been as real as the Deity Himself. The whole Human race, or Humanity, for example, then existed in the Deity, not distinguished into individuals, but as a Unit, out of which the Manifold was to flow.

Everything *actual* must also first have been *possible,* before having actual existence; and this possibility or potentiality was to the Kabalists a real Ens. Before the evolvement of the Universe, it had to exist *potentially,* the whole of it, with all its individuals, included in a single Unity. This was the Idea or Plan of the Universe; and this had to be *formed.* It had to emanate from the Infinite Deity, and be *of* Himself, though not His Very Self.

Geburah, Severity, the Sephirah opposite to and conjoined sexually with Gedulah, to produce Tephareth, Harmony and Beauty, is also called in the Kabalah *"Judgment,"* in which term are included the ideas of *limitation* and *conditioning,* which often seems, indeed, to be its principal sense; while Benignity is as often styled *Infinite.* Thus it is obscurely taught that in everything that is, not only the *Finite* but also the *Infinite* is present; and that the rigor of the stern law of limitation, by which everything below or beside the Infinite Absolute is limited, bounded, and conditioned, is tempered and modified by the *grace,* which so relaxes it that the Infinite, Unlimited, Unconditioned, is also everywhere present; and that it is thus the Spiritual and Material Natures are *in equilibrio,* Good everywhere counterbalancing Evil, Light everywhere in equilibrium with Darkness: from which again results the Universal Harmony of things. In the vacant space effected for creation, there at last remained a faint vestige or trace of Ainsophic Light, of the Light of the Substance of the Infinite. Man is thus both human and divine: and the *apparent* antagonisms in his Nature are a real equilibrium, *if he wills it shall be so;* from which results the Harmony, not only of Life and Action, but of Virtue and Perfection.

To understand the Kabalistic idea of the Sephiroth, it must be borne in mind that they were assigned, not only to the world of Emanation, Aziluth, but also to each of the other worlds, Briah, Jezirah, and Asiah. They were not only attributes of the Unmanifested Deity, not only Himself in limitation, but His actual manifestations, or His qualities made apparent as modes; and they were also qualities of the Universal Nature—Spiritual, Mental, and Material, produced and made existent by the outflow of Himself.

In the view of the Kabalah, God and the Universe were One, and in the One General, as the type or source, were included and involved, and from it have been evolved and issued forth, the manifold and all particulars. Where, indeed, does individuality begin? Is it the Hidden Source and Spring alone that is the individual, the Unit, or is it the flowing fountain that fills the ocean, or the ocean itself, or its waves, or the drops, or the vaporous particles, that are the individuals? The Sea and the River—these are each One; but the drops of each are many. The tree is one; but its leaves are a multitude: they drop with the frosts, and fall upon his roots; but the tree still continues to grow, and new leaves come again in the Spring. Is the Human Race not the Tree, and are not individual men the leaves? How else explain the force of will and sympathy, and the dependence of one man at every instant of his·life on others, except by the oneness of the race? The links that bind all created things together are the links of a single Unity, and the whole Universe is One, developing itself into the manifold.

Obtuse commentators have said that the Kabalah assigns sexual characteristics to the very Deity. There is no warrant for such an assertion, anywhere in the Sohar or in any commentary upon it. On the contrary, the whole doctrine of the Kabalah is based on the fundamental proposition, that the Very Deity is Infinite, everywhere extended, without limitation or determination, and therefore without any conformation whatever. In order to commence the process of creation, it was necessary for Him, first of all, to effect a vacant space within Himself. To this end the Deity, whose Nature is approximately expressed by describing Him as Light filling all space, formless, limitless, contracts Himself on all sides from a point within Himself, and thus effects a quasi-vacant space, in which only a vestige of His Light remains; and into this circular or spherical space He immits His Emanations, portions of His Light or Nature; and to some of these, sexual characteristics are symbolically assigned.

The Infinite first limits Himself by flowing forth in the shape of *Will,* of determination to act. This *Will* of the Deity, or the Deity *as* will, is *Kether,* or the *Crown,* the first Sephirah. In it are *included* all other Emanations. This is a philosophical necessity. The Infinite does not *first* will, and *then,* as a sequence to, or consequence of, that determination, *subsequently* perform. To will and to act must be, with Him, not only simultaneous, but in reality *the same* . . Nor does He, by His Omniscience, *learn* that a particular action will be wise, and then, in consequence of being so convinced, first *determine* to do the act, and *then* do it. His Wisdom and His Will, also, act simultaneously; and, with Him, to decide that it was wise to create, *was* to create. Thus His will contains in itself all the Sephiroth. This will, determining Him to the exercise of intellection, to thought, to frame the Idea of the Universe, caused the Power in Him to excite the intellectual. Faculty to exercise, and *was* that Power. Its SELF, which had flowed forth from Ainsoph as Will, now flows forth as the Generative Power to beget intellectual action in the Intellectual Faculty, or Intelligence, Binah. The *Act* itself, the Thought, the Intellection, producing the Idea, is *Daath;* and as the text of the *Siphra de Zeniutha* says, The Power and Faculty, the Generative and Productive, the Active and Passive, the Will .and Capacity, which unite to produce that Act of reflection or Thought or Intellection, are *always* in conjunction. As is elsewhere said in the Kabalah, both of them are *contained* and essentially *involved* in the result. And the Will, *as* Wisdom or Intellectual Power, and the Capacity or Faculty, are really the Father and Mother of all that is; for to the creation of *anything,* it was absolutely necessary that The Infinite should form for Himself and *in* Himself, an idea of what HE willed to produce or create: and, as there is no Time with Him, to *will was* to *create,* to *plan* was to *will* and to *create;* and in the Idea, the Universe in potence, the universal succession of things was included. Thenceforward all was merely evolution and development.

Netsach and Hōd, the Seventh and Eighth Sephiroth, are usually called in the Kabalah, Victory and Glory. Netsach is the perfect *Success,* which, with the Deity, to Whom the Future is present, *attends,* and to His creatures is to *result,* from the plan of Equilibrium everywhere adopted by Him. It is the reconciliation of Light and Darkness, Good and Evil, Free-will and Necessity, God's omnipotence and Man's liberty; and the harmonious issue and result of all, without which the Universe would be a failure. It is the inherent Perfection of the Deity, manifested in His Idea of the Universe, and in all the departments or worlds, spiritual, mental, or material, of that Universe; but it is that Perfection regarded as the successful *result,* which it both causes or produces and *is;* the *perfection* of the plan *being* its *success.* It is the prevailing of Wisdom over Accident; and it, in turn, both produces and *is* the Glory and Laudation of the Great Infinite Contriver, whose plan is thus Successful and Victorious.

From these two, which are one,—from the excellence and perfection of the Divine Nature and Wisdom, considered as Success and Glory, as the opposites of Failure and Mortification, results what the Kabalah, styling it Yesod, Foundation or Basis, characterizes as the Generative member of the Symbolical human figure by which the ten Sephiroth are represented, and from this flows Malakoth, Empire, Dominion, or Rule. Yesod is the Stability and Permanence, which would, in ordinary language, be said to *result* from the perfection of the Idea or Intellectual Universal, out of which all particulars are evolved; from the *success* of that scheme, and the consequent *Glory* or Self-Satisfaction of the Deity; but which Stability and Permanence that Perfection, Success, and Glory really Is; since the Deity, infinitely Wise, and to Whom the Past, Present, and Future were and always will be one Now, and all space one HERE, had not to await the operation and evolution of His plan, as men do the result of an experiment, in order to see if it would succeed, and so to determine whether it should stand, and be stable and permanent, or fall and be temporary. Its *Perfection* was its *Success;* His *Glory,* its *permanence* and *stability:* and the Attributes of Permanence and Stability belong, like the others, to the Universe, material, mental, spiritual, and real, *because* and *as* they belong to the Infinite Himself.

This Stability and Permanence causes continuance and generates succession. It *is* Perpetuity, and continuity without solution; and by this continuous succession, whereby out of Death comes new Life, out of dissolution and resolution comes reconstruction, Necessity and Fatality result as a consequence: that is to say, the absolute control and dominion (Malakoth) of The Infinite Deity over all that He produces, and over chance and accident; and the absolute non-existence in the Universe, in Time and in Space, of any other powers or influences than those which, proceeding from Him, are and cannot *not* be perfectly submissive to His will. This *results,* humanly speaking; but in reality, the Perfection of the plan, which *is* its *success,* His *glory,* and its *stability,* is also His Absolute Autocracy, and the utter absence of Chance, Accident, or Antagonism. And, as the Infinite Wisdom or Absolute Reason rules in the Divine Nature itself, so also it does in its Emanations, and in the worlds or systems of Spirit, Soul, and Matter; in each of which there is as little Chance or Accident or Unreasoning Fate, as in the Divine Nature unmanifested.

This is the Kabalistic theory as to each of the four worlds;— 1st, of the Divine Nature, or Divinity itself, quantitatively limited and determined, but not manifested into Entities, which is the world of *Emanation;* 2d, of the first Entities, that is, of Spirits and Angels, which is the world of *Creation;* 3d, of the first *forms,* souls, or psychical natures, which is the world of *Formation* or *Fashioning;* and, 4th, of Matter and Bodies, which is the world of *Fabrication,* or, as it were, of manufacture. In each of these the Deity is *present, as, in,* and *through* the Ten Sephiroth. First of these, in each, is Kether, the Crown, ring, or circlet, the HEAD. Next, *in* that Head, as the two Hemispheres of the Brain, are Hakemah and Binah, and their result and progeny, Daath. These three are found also in the Spiritual world, and are universals in the psychical and material world, producing the lower Sephiroth. Then follow, in perfect Equilibrium, Law and Equity, Justice and Mercy, the Divine Infinite Nature and the Human Finite Nature, Good and Evil, Light and Darkness, Benignity and Severity, the Male and the Female again, as Hakemah and Binah are, mutually tempering each other, and by their intimate union producing the other Sephiroth.

The whole Universe, and all the succession of entities and events were present to The Infinite, before any act of creation; and His Benignity and Leniency, tempering and qualifying the law of rigorous Justice and inflexible Retribution, enabled Him to create: because, but for it, and if He could not but have administered the strict and stern law of justice, that would have compelled Him to destroy, immediately after its inception, the Universe He purposed to create, and so would have *prevented* its creation. This Leniency, therefore, was, as it were, the very essence and quintessence of the Permanence and Stability of the plan of Creation, and part of the Very Nature of the Deity. The Kabalah, therefore, designates it as *Light* and *Whiteness,* by which the Very Substance of Deity is symbolized. With this agree Paul's ideas as to Law and Grace; for Paul had studied the Kabalah at the feet of Gamaliel the Rabbi.

With this Benignity, the Autocracy of the dominion and control of the Deity is imbued and interpenetrated. The former, *poured,* as it were, into the latter, is an integral and essential *part* of it, and causes it to give birth to the succession and continuance of the Universe. For Malakoth, in the Kabalah, is *female,* and the matrix or womb out of which all creation is born.

☞ *The Sephiroth may be arranged as on page* 770.

The Kabalah is the primitive tradition, and its entirety rests on the single dogma of Magism, "the visible is for us the proportional measure of the invisible." The Ancients, observing that equilibrium is in physics the universal law, and that it results from the apparent opposition of two forces, concluded from the physical to the metaphysical equilibrium, and thought that in God, that is to say, in the first living and active cause, two properties necessary to each other, should be recognized; stability and movement, necessity and liberty, order dictated by reason and the self-rule of Supreme Will, Justice, and Love, and consequently Severity and Grace, Mercy or Benignity.

The idea of equilibrium among all the impersonations; of the male on one side, and the female on the other, with the Supreme Will, which *is* also the Absolute Reason, above each two, holding the balance, is, according to the Kabalah, the foundation of all religions and all sciences, the primary and immutable idea of things. The Sephiroth are a triple triangle and a circle, the idea of the Ternary explained by the balance and multiplied by itself in the

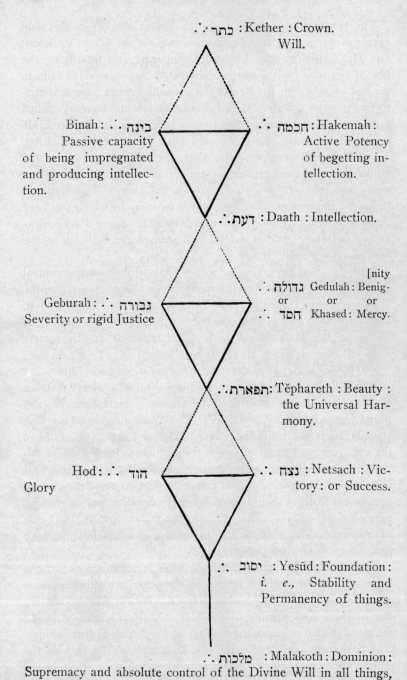

‏כתר‏ ∴ : Kether : Crown.
Will.

Binah : ∴ ‏בינה‏

Passive capacity
of being impregnated
and producing intellec-
tion.

∴ ‏חכמה‏ : Hakemah :

Active Potency
of begetting in-
tellection.

∴ ‏דעת‏ : Daath : Intellection.

[nity

∴ ‏גדולה‏ Gedulah : Benig-

or   or   or

∴ ‏חסד‏ Khased : Mercy.

Geburah : ∴ ‏גבורה‏

Severity or rigid Justice

∴ ‏תפארת‏ : Tĕphareth : Beauty :

the Universal Har-
mony.

Hod : ∴ ‏הוד‏

Glory

∴ ‏נצח‏ : Netsach : Vic-

tory : or Success.

∴ ‏יסוב‏ ∴ : Yesūd : Foundation :

i. e., Stability and
Permanency of things.

∴ ‏מלכות‏ : Malakoth : Dominion :

Supremacy and absolute control of the Divine Will in all things, domain of the Ideal; then the realization of this Idea in forms.

Unity can only be manifested by the Binary. Unity itself and the idea of Unity are already two.

The human unity is made complete by the right and left. The primitive man was of both sexes.

The Divinity, one in its essence, has two essential conditions as fundamental bases of its existence—Necessity and Liberty.

The laws of the Supreme Reason necessitate and regulate liberty in God, Who is necessarily reasonable and wise.

Knowledge supposes the binary. An object known is indispensable to the being that knows.

The binary is the generator of Society and the law. It is also the number of the *gnosis*, a word adopted in lieu of *Science*, and expressing only the idea of cognizance by intuition. It is Unity, multiplying itself by itself to create; and therefore it is that the Sacred Symbols make Eve issue from the very chest of Adam.

Adam is the human Tetragram, which is summed up in the mysterious Yōd of the Kabalah, image of the Kabalistic Phallus. Add to this Yōd [י], the ternary name of Eve, and you form the name of Jehova, the *Divine* Tetragram, the transcendent Kabalistic and magical word:

יהוה

Thus it is that Unity, complete in the fecundity of the Ternary, forms, with it, the Quaternary, which is the key of all numbers, movements, and forms.

The Square, turning upon itself, produces the circle equal to itself, and the circular movement of four equal angles turning around one point, is the quadrature of the circle.

The Binary serves as a measure for Unity; and the relation of equality between the Above and the Below, forms with them the Ternary.

To us, Creation is Mechanism: to the Ancients it was Generation. The world-producing egg figures in all cosmogonies; and modern science has discovered that all animal production is oviparous. From this idea of generation came the reverence everywhere paid the image of generative power, which formed the Stauros of the Gnostics, and the philosophical Cross of the Masons.

Aleph is the man; *Beth* is the woman. *One* is the Principle;

two is the Word. A∴ is the Active; B∴ is the Passive. **Unity is** Boaz, and the Binary is Jachin.

The two columns, Boaz and Jachin, explain in the Kabalah all the mysteries of natural, political, and religious antagonism.

Woman is man's creation; and universal creation is the female of the First Principle. When the Principle of Existence made Himself Creator, He produced by emanation an ideal Yōd; and to make room for it in the plenitude of the uncreated Light, He had to hollow out a pit of shadow, equal to the dimension determined by His creative desire; and attributed by Him to the ideal Yōd of radiating Light.

The nature of the Active Principle is to diffuse: of the Passive Principle, to collect and make fruitful.

Creation is the habitation of the Creator-Word. To create, the Generative Power and Productive Capacity must unite, the Binary become Unity again by the conjunction. The WORD is the First-BEGOTTEN, not the first *created* Son of God.

SANCTA SANCTIS, we repeat again; the Holy things to the Holy, and to him who is so, the mysteries of the Kabalah will be holy. Seek and ye shall find, say the Scriptures: knock and it shall be opened unto you. If you desire to find and to gain admission to the Sanctuary, we have said enough to show you the way. If you do not, it is useless for us to say more, as it has been useless to say so much.

The Hermetic philosophers also drew their doctrines from the Kabalah; and more particularly from the Treatise *Beth Alohim* or *Domus Dei*, known as the *Pneumatica Kabalistica,* of Rabbi Abraham Cohen Irira, and the Treatise *De Revolutionibus Animarum* of Rabbi Jitz-chak Lorja.

This philosophy was concealed by the Alchemists under their Symbols, and in the jargon of a rude Chemistry,—a jargon incomprehensible and absurd except to the Initiates; but the key to which is within your reach; and the philosophy, it may be, worth studying. The labors of the human intellect are always interesting and instructive.

To be always rich, always young, and never to die: such has been in all times the dream of the Alchemists.

To change into gold, lead, mercury, and all the other metals; to possess the universal medicine and elixir of life; such is the problem to be resolved, in order to accomplish this desire and realize this dream.

Like all the Mysteries of Magism, the Secrets of "the Great Work" have a threefold signification: they are religious, philosophical, and natural.

The philosophal gold, in religion, is the Absolute and Supreme Reason: in philosophy, it is the Truth; in visible nature, the Sun; in the subterranean and mineral world, the most perfect and pure gold.

It is for this that the pursuit of the Great Work is called the Search for the Absolute; and the work itself, the work of the Sun.

All the masters of the Science admit that it is impossible to attain the material results, unless there are found in the two higher Degrees all the analogies of the universal medicine and of the philosophal stone.

Then, they say, the work is simple, easy, and inexpensive; otherwise, it consumes fruitlessly the fortune and lives of the seekers.

The universal medicine for the Soul is the Supreme Reason and Absolute Justice; for the mind, mathematical and practical Truth; for the body, the Quintessence, a combination of light and gold.

The prima materia of the Great Work, in the Superior World, is enthusiasm and activity; in the intermediate world, intelligence and industry; in the lower world, labor: and, in Science, it is the Sulphur, Mercury, and Salt, which by turns volatilized and fixed, compose the AZOTH of the Sages.

The Sulphur corresponds with the elementary form of the Fire; Mercury with the Air and Water; and Salt with the Earth.

The Great Work is, above all things, the creation of man by himself; that is to say, the full and entire conquest which he effects of his faculties and his future. It is, above all, the perfect emancipation of his will, which assures him the universal empire of Azoth, and the domain of magnetism, that is, complete power over the universal Magical agent.

This Magical agent, which the Ancient Hermetic philosophers disguised under the name of *"Prima Materia,"* determines the forms of the modifiable Substance; and the Alchemists said that by means of it they could attain the transmutation of metals and the universal medicine.

There are two Hermetic operations, one spiritual, the other material, dependent the one on the other.

The whole Hermetic Science is contained in the dogma of Hermes, engraven originally, it is said, on a tablet of emerald. Its sentences that relate to operating the Great Work are as follows:

"Thou shalt separate the earth from the fire, the subtile from the gross, gently, with much industry.

"It ascends from earth to Heaven, and again descends to earth, and receives the force of things above and below.

"Thou shalt by this means possess the glory of the whole world, and therefore all obscurity shall flee away from thee.

"This is the potent force of all force, for it will overcome everything subtile, and penetrate everything solid.

"So the world was created."

All the Masters in Alchemy who have written of the Great Work, have employed symbolic and figurative expressions; being constrained to do so, as well to repel the profane from a work that would be dangerous for them, as to be well understood by Adepts, in revealing to them the whole world of analogies governed by the single and sovereign dogma of Hermes.

So, in their language, gold and silver are the King and Queen, or the Sun and Moon; Sulphur, the flying Eagle; Mercury, the Man-woman, winged, bearded, mounted on a cube, and crowned with flames; Matter or Salt, the winged Dragon; the Metals in ebullition, Lions of different colors; and, finally, the entire work has for its symbols the Pelican and the Phœnix.

The Hermetic Art is, therefore, at the same time a religion, a philosophy, and a natural science. As a religion, it is that of the Ancient Magi and the Initiates of all ages; as a philosophy, we may find its principles in the school of Alexandria and the theories of Pythagoras; as a science, we must inquire for its processes of Paracelsus, Nicholas Flamel, and Raymond Lulle.

The Science is a real one only for those who admit and understand the philosophy and the religion; and its process will succeed only for the Adept who has attained the sovereignty of will, and so become the King of the elementary world: for the grand agent of the operation of the Sun, is that force described in the Symbol of Hermes, of the table of emerald; it is the universal magical power; the spiritual, fiery, motive power; it is the Od, according to the Hebrews, and the Astral light, according to others.

Therein is the secret fire, living and philosophical, of which all the Hermetic philosophers speak with the most mysterious reserve: the Universal Seed, the secret whereof they kept, and which they represented only under the figure of the Caduceus of Hermes.

This is the grand Hermetic arcanum. What the Adepts call dead matter are bodies as found in nature; living matters are substances assimilated and magnetized by the science and will of the operator.

So that the Great Work is more than a chemical operation; it is a real creation of the human word initiated into the power of the Word of God.

The creation of gold in the Great Work is effected by transmutation and multiplication.

Raymond Lulle says, that to make gold, one must have gold and mercury; and to make silver, silver and mercury. And he adds: "I mean by mercury, that mineral spirit so fine and pure that it gilds even the seed of gold, and silvers that of silver." He meant by this, either electricity, or Od, the astral light.

The Salt and Sulphur serve in the work only to prepare the mercury, and it is to the mercury especially that we must assimilate, and, as it were, incorporate with it, the magnetic agent. Paracelsus, Lulle, and Flamel alone seem to have perfectly known this mystery.

The Great Work of Hermes is, therefore, an operation essentially magical, and the highest of all, for it supposes the Absolute in Science and in Will. There is light in gold, gold in light, and light in all things.

The disciples of Hermes, before promising their adepts the elixir of long life or the powder of projection, advised them to seek for the Philosophal *Stone.*

The Ancients adored the *Sun,* under the form of a black Stone, called Elagabalus, or Heliogabalus. The faithful are promised, in the Apocalypse, a white Stone.

This *Stone,* says the Masters in Alchemy, is the true *Salt* of the philosophers, which enters as one-third into the composition of Azoth. But Azoth is, as we know, the name of the grand Hermetic Agent, and the true philosophical Agent: wherefore they represent their Salt under the form of a cubical Stone.

The Philosophal Stone is the foundation of the Absolute philosophy, the Supreme and unalterable Reason. Before thinking of the Metallic work, we must be firmly fixed on the Absolute principles of Wisdom; we must be in possession of this Reason, which is the touchstone of Truth. A man who is the slave of prejudices will never become the King of Nature and the Master of transmutations. The Philosophal Stone, therefore, is necessary above all things. How shall it be found? Hermes tells us, in his "Table of Emerald," we must separate the subtile from the fixed, with great care and extreme attention. So we ought to separate our certainties from our beliefs, and make perfectly distinct the respective domains of science and faith; and to comprehend that we do not know the things we believe, nor believe anything that we come to know; and that thus the essence of the things of Faith are the unknown and indefinite, while it is precisely the contrary with the things of Science. Whence we shall conclude, that Science rests on reason and experience, and Faith has for its bases sentiment and reason.

The Sun and Moon of the Alchemists concur in perfecting and giving stability to the Philosophal Stone. They correspond to the two columns of the Temple, Jachin and Boaz. The Sun is the hieroglyphical sign of Truth, because it is the source of Light; and the rough Stone is the symbol of Stability. Hence the Mediæval Alchemists indicated the Philosophal Stone as the first means of making the philosophical gold, that is to say, of transforming all the vital powers figured by the six metals into Sun, that is, into Truth and Light; which is the first and indispensable operation of the Great Work, which leads to the secondary adaptation, and enables the creators of the spiritual and living gold, the possessors of the true philosophical Salt, Mercury, and Sulphur, to discover, by the analogies of Nature, the natural and palpable gold.

To find the Philosophal Stone, is to have discovered the Absolute, as all the Masters say. But the Absolute is that which admits of no errors, is the Fixed from the Volatile, is the Law of the Imagination, is the very necessity of Being, is the immutable Law of Reason and Truth. The Absolute is that which IS.

To find the Absolute in the Infinite, in the Indefinite, and in the Finite, this is the Magnum Opus, the Great Work of the Sages, which Hermes called the Work of the Sun.

To find the immovable bases of true religious Faith, of Philosophical Truth, and of Metallic transmutation, this is the secret of Hermes in its entirety, the Philosophal Stone.

This stone is one and manifold; it is decomposed by Analysis, and re-compounded by Synthesis. In Analysis, it is a powder, the powder of projection of the Alchemists; before Analysis, and in Synthesis, it is a stone.

The Philosophal Stone, say the Masters, must not be exposed to the atmosphere, nor to the gaze of the Profane; but it must be kept concealed and carefully preserved in the most secret place of the laboratory, and the possessor must always carry on his person the key of the place where it is kept.

He who possesses the Grand Arcanum is a genuine King, and more than a king, for he is inaccessible to all fear and all empty hopes. In all maladies of soul and body, a single particle from the precious stone, a single grain of the divine powder, is more than sufficient to cure him. "Let him hear, who hath ears to hear!" the Master said.

The Salt, Sulphur, and Mercury are but the accessorial elements and passive instruments of the Great Work. All depends, as we have said, on the internal Magnet of Paracelsus. The entire work consists in *projection:* and the projection is perfectly accomplished by the effective and realizable understanding of a single word.

There is but a single important operation in the work; this consists in *Sublimation,* which is nothing else, according to Geber than the elevation of dry matter, by means of fire, with adhesion to its proper vessel.

He who desires to attain to the understanding of the Grand Word and the possession of the Great Secret, ought carefully to read the Hermetic philosophers, and will undoubtedly attain initiation, as others have done; but he must take, for the key of their allegories, the single dogma of Hermes, contained in his table of Emerald, and follow, to class his acquisitions of knowledge and direct the operation, the order indicated in the Kabalistic alphabet of the Tarot.

Raymond Lulle has said that, to make gold, we must first have gold. Nothing is made out of nothing; we do not absolutely *create* wealth; we increase and multiply it. Let aspirants to science well understand, then, that neither the juggler's tricks nor miracles are to be asked of the adept. The Hermetic science, like all the *real* sciences, is mathematically demonstrable. Its results, even material, are as rigorous as that of a correct equation.

The Hermetic Gold is not only a true dogma, a light without Shadow, a Truth without alloy of falsehood; it is also a material gold, real, pure, the most precious that can be found in the mines of the earth.

But the living gold, the living sulphur, or the true fire of the philosophers, is to be sought for in the house of Mercury. This fire is fed by the air : to express its attractive and expansive power, no better comparison can be used than that of the lightning, which is at first only a dry and earthly exhalation, united to the moist vapor, but which, by self-exhalation, takes a fiery nature, acts on the humidity inherent in it, which it attracts to itself and transmutes in its nature; after which it precipitates itself rapidly toward the earth, whither it is attracted by a fixed nature like unto its own.

These words, in form enigmatic, but clear at bottom, distinctly express what the philosophers mean by their Mercury, fecundated by Sulphur, and which becomes the Master and regenerator of the Salt. It is the AzoTH, the universal magnetic force, the grand magical agent, the Astral light, the light of life, fecundated by the mental force, the intellectual energy, which they compare to sulphur, on account of its affinities with the Divine fire.

As to the Salt, it is Absolute Matter. Whatever is matter contains salt; and all salt [nitre] may be converted into pure gold by the combined action of Sulphur and Mercury, which sometimes act so rapidly, that the transmutation may be effected in an instant, in an hour, without fatigue to the operator, and almost without expense. At other times, and according to the more refractory temper of the atmospheric *media*, the operation requires several days, several months, and sometimes even several years.

Two primary laws exist in nature, two essential laws, which produce, by counterbalancing each other, the universal equilibrium of things. These are fixedness and movement, analogous, in philosophy, to Truth and Fiction, and, in Absolute Conception, to Necessity and Liberty, which are the very essence of Deity. The Hermetic philosophers gave the name *fixed* to everything ponderable, to everything that tends by its natural to central repose and immobility; they term *volatile* everything that more naturally and more readily obeys the law of movement; and they form their stone by analysis, that is to say, by the volatilization of the Fixed, and then by synthesis, that is, by fixing the volatile, which they effect by applying to the fixed, which they call their salt, the sulphurated Mercury, or the light of life, directed and made omnipotent by a Sovereign Will. Thus they master entire Nature, and their stone is found wherever there is salt, which is the reason for saying that no substance is foreign to the Great Work, and that even the most despicable and apparently vile matters may be changed into gold, which is true in this sense, that they all contain the original salt-principle, represented in our emblems by the cubical stone.

To know how to extract from all matter the pure salt concealed in it, is to have the Secret of the Stone. Wherefore this is a Saline stone, which the Od or universal astral light decomposes or re-compounds: it is single and manifold; for it may be dissolved like ordinary salt, and incorporated with other substances. Obtained by analysis, we might term it' *the Universal Sublimate:* found by way of synthesis, it is the true *panacea* of the ancients, for it cures all maladies of soul and body, and has been styled, *par-excellence,* the medicine of all nature. When one, by absolute initiation, comes to control the forces of the universal agent, he always has this stone at his disposal, for its extraction is then a simple and easy operation, very distinct from the metallic projection or realization. This stone, when in a state of sublimation, must not be exposed to contact with the atmospheric air, which might partially dissolve it and deprive it of its virtue; nor could its emanations be inhaled without danger. The Sage prefers to preserve it in its natural envelopes, assured as he is of extracting it by a single effort of his will, and a single application of the Universal Agent to the envelopes, which the Kabalists call *cortices,* the shells, bark, or integuments.

Hieroglyphically to express this law of prudence, they gave their Mercury, personified in Egypt as Hermanubis, a dog's head; and to their Sulphur, represented by the Baphomet of the Temple, that goat's head which brought into such disrepute the occult Mediæval associations.

Let us listen for a few moments to the Alchemists themselves, and endeavor to learn the hidden meaning of their mysterious words.

The RITUAL of the Degree of Scottish Elder MASTER, and Knight of Saint Andrew, being the fourth Degree of Ramsay, it is said upon the title-page, or of the Reformed or Rectified Rite of Dresden, has these passages:

"O how great and glorious is the *presence* of the Almighty God which gloriously *shines* from between the Cherubim!

"How adorable and astonishing are the *rays* of that glorious *Light,* that sends forth its bright and brilliant beams from the Holy Ark of Alliance and Covenant!

"Let us with the deepest veneration and devotion adore the great Source of Life, that Glorious Spirit Who is the Most Merciful and Beneficent Ruler of the Universe and of all the creatures it contains!

"The secret knowledge of the Grand Scottish Master relates to the combination and transmutation of different substances; whereof that you may obtain a clear idea and proper understanding, you are to know that all matter and all material substances are composed of combinations of three several substances, extracted from the four elements, which three substances in combination are, ⊖, *Salt,* △, *Sulphur,* and △, *Spirit.* The first ⊖ of these ⊖ produces *Solidi-*⌐⌐△ *ty,* the second *Softness,* and the third the *Spiritual,* vaporous particles. These three compound substances work potently together; and therein consists the true process for the transmutation of metals.

"To these three substances allude the three golden basins, in the first of which was engraved the letter M.·., in the second, the letter G.·., and in the third nothing. The first, M.·., is the initial letter of the Hebrew word *Malakh,* which signifies *Salt;* and the second, G.·., of the Hebrew word *Geparaith,* which signifies *Sulphur;* and as there is no word in Hebrew to express the vaporous and intangible *Spirit,* there is no letter in the third basin.

"With these three principal substances you may effect the transmutation of metals, which must be done by means of the five points or rules of the Scottish Mastership.

"The first Master's point shows us the Brazen Sea, wherein must always be rain-water; and out of this rain-water the Scottish Masters extract the first substance, which is Salt; which salt must afterward undergo a *seven-fold* manipulation and purification, before it will be properly prepared. This sevenfold purification is symbolized by the Seven Steps of Solomon's Temple, which symbol is furnished us by the first point or rule of the Scottish Masters.

"After preparing the first substance, you are to extract the second, Sulphur, out of the purest gold, to which must then be added the purified or celestial Salt. They are to be mixed as the Art directs, and then placed in a vessel in the form of a SHIP, in which it is to remain, as the Ark of Noah was afloat, one hundred and fifty days, being brought to the first damp, warm degree of fire, that it may putrefy and produce the mineral fermentation. This is the second point or rule of the Scottish Masters."

If you reflect, my Brother, that it was impossible for any one to imagine that either common salt or nitre could be extracted from rain-water, or sulphur from pure gold, you will no doubt suspect that some secret meaning was concealed in these words.

The Kabalah considers the immaterial part of man as threefold, consisting of NEPHESCH, RUACH, and NESCHAMAH, *Psyche, Spiritus,* and *Mens,* or *Soul, Spirit,* and *Intellect.* There are Seven Holy Palaces, Seven Heavens and Seven Thrones; and Souls are purified by ascending through Seven Spheres. A *Ship,* in Hebrew, is *Ani;* and the same word means *I, Me,* or *Myself.*

The RITUAL continues:

"Multiplying the substance thus obtained, is the third operation, which is done by adding to them the animate, volatile *Spirit;* which is done by means of the water of the Celestial Salt, as well as by the Salt, which must daily be added to it very carefully, and strictly observing to put neither too much nor too little; inasmuch as, if you add too much, you will destroy that growing and multiplying substance; and if too little, it will be self-consumed and destroyed, and shrink away, not having sufficient substantiality for its preservation. This third point or rule of the Scottish Masters gives us the emblem of the building of the Tower of Babel, used by our Scottish Masters, because by irregularity and want of due proportion and harmony that work was stopped; and the workmen could proceed no further.

"Next comes the fourth operation, represented by the Cubical Stone, whose faces and angles are all equal. As soon as the work is brought to the necessary point of multiplication, it is to be submitted to the third Degree of Fire, wherein it will receive the due proportion of the strength and substance of the metallic particles of the Cubical Stone; and this is the fourth point or rule of the Scottish Masters.

"Finally, we come to the fifth and last operation, indicated to us by the Flaming Star. After the work has become a duly-proportioned substance, it is to be subjected to the fourth and strongest Degree of fire, wherein it must remain three times twenty-seven hours; until it is thoroughly glowing, by which means it becomes a bright and shining tincture, wherewith the lighter metals may be changed, by the use of one part to a thousand of the metal. Wherefore this Flaming Star shows us the fifth and last point of the Scottish Masters.

"You should pass practically through the five points or rules of the Master, and by the use of one part to a thousand, transmute and ennoble metals. You may then in reality say that your age is a thousand years."

In the oration of the Degree, the following hints are given as to its true meaning:

"The three divisions of the Temple, the Outer Court, Sanctuary, and Holy of Holies, signify the three Principles of our Holy Order, which direct to the knowledge of morality, and teach those most practical virtues that ought to be practised by mankind. Therefore the Seven Steps which lead up to the Outer Court of the Temple, are the emblem of the Seven-fold Light which we need to possess, before we can arrive at the height of knowledge, in which consist the ultimate limits of our order.

"In the Brazen Sea we are symbolically to purify ourselves from all pollutions, all faults and wrongful actions, as well those committed through error of judgment and mistaken opinion, as those intentionally done; inasmuch as they equally prevent us from arriving at the knowledge of True Wisdom. We must thoroughly cleanse and purify our hearts to their inmost recesses, before we can of right contemplate that *Flaming Star,* which is the emblem of the Divine and Glorious Shekinah, or presence of God; before we may dare approach the Throne of Supreme Wisdom."

In the Degree of The True Mason [*Le Vrai Maçon*], styled in the title-page of its Ritual the 23d Degree of Masonry, or the 12th of the 5th class, the Tracing-board displays a luminous Triangle, with a great Yōd in the centre.

"The Triangle," says the Ritual, "represents one God in three Persons; and the great Yōd is the initial letter of the last word.

"The Dark Circle represents the Chaos, which in the beginning God created.

"The Cross within the Circle, the Light by means whereof He developed the Chaos.

"The Square, the four Elements into which it was resolved.

"The Triangle, again, the three *Principles* [Salt, Sulphur, and Mercury], which the intermingling of the elements produced.

"God *creates;* Nature *produces;* Art *multiplies.* God created Chaos; Nature produced it; God, Nature, and Art, have perfected it.

"The Altar of Perfumes indicates the *Fire* that is to be applied to Nature. The two *towers* are the two furnaces, moist and dry, in which it is to be worked. The bowl is the mould of oak that is to inclose the philosophal egg.

"The two figures surmounted by a Cross are the two vases, Nature and Art, in which is to be consummated the double marriage of the white woman with the red Servitor, from which marriage will spring a most Potent King.

"Chaos means universal matter, formless, but susceptible of all forms. Form is the Light inclosed in the seeds of all species; and its home is in the Universal Spirit.

"To work on universal matter, use the internal and external fire: the four elements result, the *Principia Principiorum* and *Inmediata;* Fire, Air, Water, Earth. There are four qualities of these elements—the warm and dry, the cold and moist. Two appertain to each element: The dry and cold, to the Earth; the cold and moist, to Water; the moist and warm, to the Air; and the warm and dry, to Fire: whereby the Fire connects with the Earth; all the elements, as Hermes said, moving in circles.

"From the mixture of the four Elements and of their four qualities, result the three Principles,—Mercury, Sulphur, and Salt. These are the philosophical, not the vulgar.

"The philosophical *Mercury* is a *Water* and SPIRIT, which dissolves and sublimates the Sun; the philosophical *Sulphur,* a *fire* and a SOUL, which mollifies and colors it; the philosophical *Salt,* an *Earth* and a BODY, which coagulates and fixes it; and the whole is done in the bosom of the *Air.*

"From these three Principles result the four Elements duplicated, or the Grand Elements, *Mercury, Sulphur, Salt,* and *Glass;* two of which are volatile,—the Water [Mercury] and the Air [Sulphur], which is oil; for all substances liquid in their nature avoid fire, which takes from the one [water] and burns the other [oil]; but the other two are dry and solid, to wit, the Salt, wherein Fire is contained, and the pure *Earth,* which is the *Glass;* on both of which the Fire has no other action than to melt and refine them, unless one makes use of the liquid alkali; for, just as each element consists of two qualities, so these great duplicated Elements partáke, each of two of the simple elements, or, more properly speaking, of all the four, according to the greater or less degree of each,—the Mercury partaking more of the Water, to which it is assigned; the Oil or Sulphur, more of the Air; the Salt, of the Fire; and the Glass, of the Earth; which is found, pure and clear, in the centre of all the elementary composites, and is the last to disengage itself from the others.

"The four Elements and three Principles reside in all the Compounds, Animal, Vegetable, and Mineral; but more potently in some than in others.

"The Fire gives them Movement; the Air, Sensation; the Water, Nutriment; and the Earth, Subsistence.

"The four duplicated Elements engender THE STONE, if one is careful enough to supply them with the proper quantity of fire, and to combine them according to their natural weight. Ten parts of Air make one of Water; ten of Water, one of Earth; and ten of Earth, one of Fire; the whole by the Active Symbol of the one, and the Passive Symbol of the other, whereby the conversion of the Elements is effected."

The Allusion of the Ritual, here, is obviously to the four Worlds of the Kabalah. The ten Sephiroth of the world Briah proceed from Malakoth, the last of the ten Emanations of the world Aziluth; the ten Sephiroth of the world Yezirah, from Malakoth of Briah; and the ten of the world Asiah, from Malakoth of Yezirah. The Pass-word of the Degree is given as *Metralon,* which is a corruption of METATRON, the Cherub, who and Sandalphon are in the Kabalah the Chief of the Angels. The Active and Passive Symbols are the Male and Female.

The Ritual continues:

"It is thereby evident that, in the Great Work, we must employ ten parts of philosophical Mercury to one of Sun or Moon.

"This is attained by *Solution* and *Coagulation.* These words mean that we must dissolve the body and coagulate the spirit; which operations are effected by the moist and dry bath.

"Of colors, *black* is the Earth; *white,* the Water; *blue,* the Air; and *red,* the Fire; wherein also are involved very great secrets and mysteries.

"The apparatus employed in 'The Great Work' consists of the Moist bath, the Dry bath, the Vases of Nature and Art, the bowl of oak, *lutum sapientiæ*, the Seal of Hermes, the tube, the physical lamp, and the iron rod.

"The work is perfected in seventeen philosophical months, according to the mixture of ingredients. The benefits reaped from it are of two kinds—one affecting the soul, and the other the body. *The former consist in knowing God, Nature, and ourself;* and those to the body are wealth and health.

"The Initiate traverses Heaven and Earth. Heaven is the World manifest to the Intelligence, subdivided into Paradise and Hell; Earth is the World manifest to the Senses, also subdivided into the Celestial and that of the Elements.

"There are Sciences specially connected with each of these. *The one is ordinary and common; the other, mystic and secret.* The World cognizable by the Intellect has the Hermetic Theology and the Kabalah; the Celestial Astrology; and that of the Elements, Chemistry, which by its decompositions and separations, effected by fire, reveals all the most hidden secrets of Nature, in the three kinds of Compound Substances. This last science is styled 'Hermetic,' or 'The operating of the Great Work.'"

The Ritual of the Degree of Kabalistic and Hermetic Rose ✠, has these passages:

"The true Philosophy, known and practised by Solomon, is the basis on which Masonry is founded.

"Our Ancient Masons have concealed from us the most important point of this Divine Art, under hieroglyphical characters, which are but enigmas and parables, to all the Senseless, the Wicked, and the Ambitious.

"He will be supremely fortunate, who shall, by arduous labor, discover this sacred place of deposite, wherein all naked the sublime Truth is hidden; for he may be assured that he has found the True Light, the True Felicity, the True Heavenly Good. Then may it truly be said that he is one of the True Elect; for it *is the only real and most Sublime Science of all those to which a mortal can aspire:* his days will be prolonged, and his soul freed of all vices and corruption; into which" (it is added, to mislead, as if from fear too much would be disclosed), *"the human race is often led by indigence."*

As the symbolism of the Hall and the language of the ritual mutually explain each other, it should be noted here, that in this Degree the columns of the hall, 12 in number, are white variegated with black and red. The hangings are black, and over that crimson.

Over the throne is a great Eagle, in gold, on a black ground. In the centre of the Canopy the Blazing Star in gold, with the letter Yōd in its centre. On the right and left of the throne are the Sun in gold and the Moon in silver. The throne is ascended to by *three* Steps. The hall and ante-room are each lighted by *ten* lights, and a single one at the entrance. The colors, black, white, and crimson appear in the clothing; and the Key and Balance are among the symbols.

The duty of the Second Grand Prior, says the Ritual, is "to see if the Chapter is hermetically sealed; whether the materials are ready, and the elements; whether the Black gives place to the White, and the White to the Red."

"Be laborious," it says, "like the Star, and procure the light of the Sages, and hide yourself from the Stupid Profane and the Ambitious, and be like the Owl, which sees only by night, and hides itself from treacherous curiosity."

"The Sun, on entering each of his houses, should be received there by the four elements, which you must be careful to invite to accompany you, that they may aid you in your undertaking; for without them the House would be melancholy: wherefore you will give him to feast upon the four elements.

"When he shall have visited his twelve houses, and seen you attentive there to receive him, you will become one of his chiefest favorites, and he will allow you to share all his gifts. Matter will then no longer have power over you; you will, so to say, be no longer a dweller on the earth; but after certain periods you will give back to it a body which is its own, to take in its stead one altogether Spiritual. Matter is then deemed to be dead to the world.

"Therefore it must be re-vivified, and made to be born again from its ashes, which you will effect by virtue of the vegetation of the Tree of Life, represented to us by the branch of acacia. Whoever shall learn to comprehend and execute this great work, will know great things, say the Sages of the work; but whenever you depart from the centre of the Square and the Compass you will no longer be able to work with success.

"Another Jewel is necessary for you, and in certain undertakings cannot be dispensed with. It is what is termed the Kabalistic pantacle . . . This carries with it the power of commanding the spirits of the elements. It is necessary for you to know how to use it, and that you will learn by perseverance if you are a lover of the science of our predecessors the Sages.

"A great Black Eagle, the King of Birds. He alone it is that can fire the Sun, material in its nature, that has no form, and yet by its form develops color. The black is a complete harbinger of the work: it changes color and assumes a natural form, out whereof will emerge a brilliant Sun.

"The birth of the Sun is always announced by its Star, represented by the Blazing Star, which you will know by its fiery color; and it is followed in its course by the silvery lustre of the Moon.

"A rough Ashlar is the shapeless stone which is to be prepared in order to commence the philosophical work; and to be developed, in order to change its form from triangular to cubic, after the separation from it of its Salt, Sulphur, and Mercury, by the aid of the Square, Level, Plumb, and Balance, and all the other Masonic implements *which we use symbolically*.

"Here me put them to philosophical use, to constitute a well-proportioned edifice, through which you are to make pass the crude material, analogous to a candidate commencing his initiation into our Mysteries. When we build we must observe all the rules and proportions; for otherwise the Spirit of Life cannot lodge therein. So you will build the great tower, in which is to burn the fire of the Sages, or, in other words, the fire of Heaven; as also the Sea of the Sages, in which the Sun and Moon are to bathe. That is the basin of Purification, in which will be the water of Celestial Grace, water that doth not soil the hands, but purifies all leprous bodies.

"Let us labor to instruct our Brother, to the end that by his toils he may succeed in discovering the principle of life contained in the profundity of matter, and known by the name of *Alkahest*.

"The most potent of the names of Deity is ADONAI. Its power is to put the Universe in movement; and the Knights who shall be fortunate enough to possess it, with weight and measure, shall have at their disposition all the potences that inhabit it, the Ele-

ments, and the cognizance of all the virtues and sciences that man
is capable of knowing. By its power they would succeed in discovering the primary metal of the Sun, which holds within itself
the Principle of the germ, and wherewith we can put in alliance
and six other metals, each of which contains the principles and
primitive seed of the grand philosophical work.

"The six other metals are Saturn, Jupiter, Mars, Venus, Mercury, and Luna; vulgarly known as Lead, Tin, Iron, Copper,
Quicksilver, and Silver. Gold is not included; because it is not in
its nature a metal. It is all Spirit and incorruptible; wherefore it
is the emblem of the Sun, which presides over the Light.

"The vivifying Spirit, called Alkahest, has in itself the generative virtue of producing the triangular Cubical Stone, and contains in itself all the virtues to render men happy in this world
and in that to come. To arrive at the composition of that Alkahest, we begin by laboring at the science of the union of the four
Elements which are to be educed from the three Kingdoms of
Nature, Mineral, Vegetable, and Animal; the rule, measure,
weight, and equipoise whereof have each their key. We then
employ in one work the animals, vegetables, and minerals, each
in his season, which make the space of the Houses of the Sun,
where they have all the virtues required.

"Something from each of the three Kingdoms of Nature is
assigned to each Celestial House, to the end that everything may
be done in accordance with sound philosophical rules; and that
everything may be thoroughly purified in its proper time and place
in order to be presented at the wedding-table of the Spouse and
the six virgins who hold the mystic shovel, without a common fire,
but with an elementary fire, that comes primarily by *attraction,*
and by digestion in the philosophical bed lighted by the four
elements.

"At the banquet of the Spouses, the viands, being thoroughly,
purified, are served in Salt, Sulphur, Spirit, and Oil; a sufficient
quantity thereof is taken every month, and therewith is compounded, by means of the Balance of Solomon, the Alkahest, to
serve the Spouses, when they are laid on the nuptial bed, there to
engender their embryo, producing for the human race immense
treasures, that will last as long as the world endures.

"Few are capable of engaging in this great work. Only the
true Free-Masons may of right aspire to it; and even of them,

very few are worthy to attain it, because most of them are ignorant of the Clavicules and their contents, and of the Pantacle of Solomon, which teaches how to labor at the great work.

"The weight raised by Solomon with his balance was 1, 2, 3, 4, 5; which contains 25 times unity, 2 multiplied by 2; 3 multiplied by 3; 4 multiplied by 4; 5 multiplied by 5, and once 9; these numbers thus involving the squares of 5 and 2, the cube of 2, the square of the square of 2, and the square of 3."

Thus far the Ritual, in the numbers mentioned by it, is an allusion to the 47th problem of Euclid, a symbol of Blue Masonry, entirely out of place there, and its meaning unknown. The base of the right-angled triangle being 3, and the perpendicular 4, the hypothenuse is 5, by the rule that the sum of the squares of the two former equals the square of the latter,—3×3 being 9; and 4×4, 16; and 9+16 being 25, the square of 5. The triangle contains in its sides the numbers 1, 2, and 3. The Perpendicular is the Male; the Base, the Female; the Hypothenuse, the product of the two.

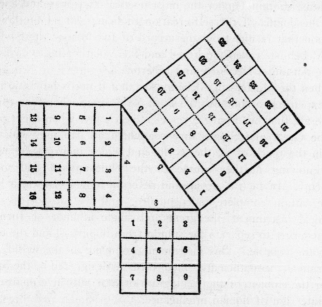

To fix the volatile, in the Hermetic language, means to materialize the spirit; to volatilize the fixed is to spiritualize matter.

To separate the subtile from the gross, in the first operation, which is wholly internal, is to free our soul from all prejudice and all vice. This is effected by the use of the philosophical SALT, that is to say, of WISDOM; of MERCURY, that is to say, of personal aptitude and labor; and of SULPHUR, which represents the vital energy, and the ardor of the will. Thus we succeed in changing into spiritual gold such things even as are of least value, and even the foul things of the earth.

It is in this sense we are to understand the parables of the Hermetic philosophers and the prophets of Alchemy; but in their works, as in the Great Work, we must skillfully separate the subtile from the gross, the mystic from the positive, allegory from theory. If you would read them with pleasure and understandingly, you must first understand them allegorically in their entirety and then descend from allegories to realities by way of the correspondences or analogies indicated in the single dogma:

"What is above is like what is below; and what is below is like what is above."

The treatise "*Minerva Mundi,*" attributed to Hermes Trismegistus, contains, under the most poetical and profound allegories, the dogma of the self-creation of beings, or of the law of creation that results from the accord of two forces, these which the Alchemists called the Fixed and the Volatile, and which are, in the Absolute, Necessity and Liberty.

When the Masters in Alchemy say that it needs but little time and expense to accomplish the works of Science. when they affirm, above all, that but a single vessel is necessary, when they speak of the Great and Single furnace, which all can use, which is within the reach of all the world, and which men possess without knowing it, they allude to the philosophical and moral Alchemy. In fact, a strong and determined will can, in a little while, attain complete independence; and we all possess that chemical instrument, the great and single athanor or furnace, which serves to separate the subtile from the gross, and the fixed from the volatile. This instrument, complete as the world, and accurate as the mathematics themselves, is designated by the Sages under the emblem of the Pentagram or Star with five points, the absolute sign of human intelligence.

The end and perfection of the Great Work is expressed, in alchemy, by a triangle surmounted by a cross: and the letter Tau, ת, the last of the Sacred alphabet, has the same meaning.

The "elementary fire," that comes primarily by attraction, is evidently Electricity or the Electric Force, primarily developed as magnetism, and in which is perhaps the secret of life or the vital force.

Paracelsus, the great Reformer in medicine, discovered magnetism long before Mesmer, and pushed to its last consequences this luminous discovery, or rather this initiation into the magic of the ancients, who understood the grand magical agent better than we do, and did not regard the Astral Light, Azoth, the universal magnetism of the Sages, as an animal and particular fluid, emanating only from certain special beings.

The four Elements, the four symbolic animals, and the re-duplicated Principles correspond with each other, and are thus arranged by the Hermetic Masons:

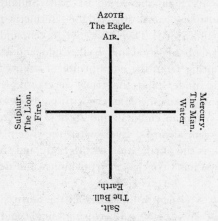

The Air and Earth represent the *Male* Principle; and the Fire and Water belong to the *Female* Principle.

To these four forms correspond the four following philosophical ideas.

Spirit: Matter: Movement: Repose.

Alchemy reduces these four things to three:

The Absolute: the Fixed: the Volatile.

Reason: Necessity; Liberty: are the synonyms of these three words.

As all the great Mysteries of God and the Universe are thus hidden in the Ternary, it everywhere appears in Masonry and in the Hermetic Philosophy under its mask of Alchemy. It even appears where Masons do not suspect it; to teach the doctrine of the equilibrium of Contraries, and the resultant Harmony.

The double triangle of Solomon is explained by Saint John in a remarkable manner: There are, he says, three witnesses in Heaven,—the Father, the Word, and the Holy Spirit; and three witnesses on earth,—the breath, water, and blood. He thus agrees with the Masters of the Hermetic Philosophy, who give to their Sulphur the name of Ether, to their Mercury the name of philosophical water, to their Salt that of blood of the dragon, or menstruum of the earth. The blood, or Salt, corresponds by opposition with the Father; the Azothic, or Mercurial water, with the Word, or Logos; and the breath, with the Holy Spirit. But the things of High Symbolism can be well understood only by the true children of Science.

Alchemy has its Symbolic Triad of Salt, Sulphur, and Mercury,—man consisting, according to the Hermetic philosophers, of Body, Soul, and Spirit. The Dove, the Raven, and the Phœnix are striking Symbols of Good and Evil, Light and Darkness, and the Beauty resulting from the equilibrium of the two.

If you would understand the true secrets of Alchemy, you must study the works of the Masters with patience and assiduity. Every word is often an enigma; and to him who reads in haste, the whole will seem absurd. Even when they seem to teach that the Great Work is the purification of the Soul, and so to deal only with morals, they most conceal their meaning, and deceive all but the Initiates.

Yōd [s or י] is termed in the Kabalah the *opifex, workman* of the Deity. It is, says the *Porta Cælorum,* single and primal, like *one,* which is the first among numbers; and like a *point,* the first before all bodies. Moved lengthwise, it produces a *line,* which is Vau, and this moved sidewise produces a *superficies,* which is Daleth. Thus Vau [י] becomes Daleth [ד]; for movement tends from right to left; and all communication is from above to below. The *plenitude* of Yōd, that is, the *name* of this letter, spelled, is יוד, Y-O-D. Vau [which represents 6] and Daleth [4] are 10; like Yōd, their principle.

Yōd, says the *Siphra de Zeniutha,* is the Symbol of Wisdom and of the Father.

The Principle called Father, says the *Idra Suta,* is comprehended in Yōd, which flows downward from the Holy influence, wherefore Yōd is the most occult of all the letters; for he is the beginning and end of all things. The Supernal Wisdom is Yōd; and all things are included in Yōd, who is therefore called Father of Fathers, or the Generator of the Universal. The Principle of all things is called the House of all things: wherefore Yōd is the beginning and end of all things; as it is written: *"Thou hast made all things in Wisdom."* For The All is termed Wisdom; and in it The All is contained; and the summary of all things is the Holy Name.

Yōd, says the *Siphra de Zeniutha,* signifying the Father, approaches the letter He, which is the Mother; and by the combination of these two is denoted that luminous influence wherewith Binah is imbued by the Supernal Wisdom.

In the name יהו, says the same, are included the Father, Mother, and Microprosopos, their issue. He, impregnated by Vau, produced Microprosopos, or Seir Anpin.

Wisdom, Hakemah, is the Principle of all things: it is the Father of Fathers, and in it are the beginning and end of all things. Microprosopos, the second Universal, is the issue of Wisdom, the Father, and Binah, the Mother, and is composed of the six Numerations, Geburah, Gedulah, and Tephareth, Netsach, Hod, and Yesod; is represented under the form of a man, and said to have at first occupied the place afterward filled by the world Briah [of Creation], but afterward to have been raised to the Aziluthic sphere, and received Wisdom, Intelligence, and Cognition [Daath] from the Supernal Wisdom and Intellectuality.

Vau, in the tri-literal word, denotes these six members of Microprosopos. For this latter is formed after the fashion of Macroprosopos, but without Kether, the will, which remains in the first prototype or Universal; though invested with a portion of the Divine Intellectual Power and Capacity. The first Universal does not use the first person, and is called in the third person, הוא, HUA, He: but the second Universal speaks in the first person, using the word אני, ANI, I.

The IDRA RABBA, or Synodus Magna, one of the books of the Sohar, says:

The Eldest of the Eldest [the Absolute Deity] is in Microprosopos. All things are one: all was, all is, all will be: there neither will be, nor is, nor has been, mutation.

But He conformed Himself, by the formings, into a form that contains all forms, in a form which comprehends all genera.

This form is in the likeness of His form; and is not that form but its analogue: wherefore the human form is the form of all above and below, which are included in it: and because it embraces all above and below. The Most Holy so took form, and so Microprosopos was configured. All things are equally one, in each of the two Universals; but in the second His ways are divided, and judgment is on our side, and on the side that looks toward us, also, they differ.

These Secrets are made known only to the reapers in the Holy Field.

The Most Holy Ancient is not called ATHAH, Thou, but HUA, He: but in Microprosopos, where is the beginning of things, He has the name ATHAH, and also AB, Father. From Him is the beginning, and He is called Thou, and is the Father of Fathers. He issues from the Non-Ens; and therefore is beyond cognition.

Wisdom is the Principle of the Universe, and from it thirty-two ways diverge: and in them the law is contained, in twenty-two letters and ten words. Wisdom is the Father of Fathers, and in this Wisdom is found the Beginning and the End: wherefore there is a wisdom in each Universal, one above, the other below.

The *Commentary* of *Rabbi Chajun Vital,* on the *Siphra de Zeniutha,* says: At the beginning of emanation, Microprosopos issued from the Father, and was intermingled with the Mother, under the mysteries of the letter ה [He], resolved in רו, that is, Daleth and Vau; by which Vau is denoted Microprosopos: because Vau is six, and he is constituted of the six parts that follow Hakemah and Binah. And, according to this conception, the Father is called Father of Fathers, because from Him these Fathers proceed, Benignity, Severity, and Beauty. Microprosopos was then like the letter Vau in the letter He, because He had no head; but when He was now born, three brains were constituted for Him, by the flow of Divine Light from above.

And as the world of restitution [after the vessels of the Sephiroth below Binah had been broken, that from the fragments evil might be created] is instituted after the fashion of the Balance, so also is it formed throughout in the human form. But Malakoth, Regnum, is a complete and separate person, behind Microprosopos, and in conjunction with him, and the two are called man.

The first world [of Inanity] could not continue and did not subsist, because it had no human conformation nor the system of the Balance, the Sephiroth being points, one below the other. The first Adam [Microprosopos, as distinguished from Macroprosopos, the first *Occult* Adam] was the beginning, wherein the ten Numerations proceeded forth from potence into act.

Microprosopos is the second garment or interposed medium, with respect to the Elder Most Holy, who is the name Tetragrammaton; and he is called Alohim; because the former is Absolute Commiseration; while in Macroprosopos his lights have the nature of Severities, with respect to the elder Universal; though they are Commiseration, with respect to the lights of Malakoth and the three lower worlds.

All the conformations of Macroprosopos come from the first Adam; who, to interpose a second covering, caused a single spark to issue from the sphere of Severity, of whose five letters is generated the name Alohim. With this issued from the brain a most subtle air, which takes its place on the right hand, while the spark of fire is on the left. Thus the white and red do not intermix, that is, the Air and Fire, which are Mercy and Judgment.

Microprosopos is the Tree of the Knowledge of Good and Evil, his Severities being the Evil.

REGNUM, to which is given the name of Word of The Lord, superinvests Heaven, as the six members of the Degree Tephareth are called, and these become and are constituted by that superior vestiture. For every conformation and constitution is effected by means of veiling, because occultation here is the same as manifestation, the excess of light being veiled, so that, diminished in intensity and degree, it may be received by those below. Those six members conceived of as contained in Binah, are said to be in the World of Creation; as in Tephareth, in that of Formation; and as in Malakoth, in that of Fabrication.

Before the institution of equilibrium, face was not toward face: Microprosopos and his wife issuing forth back to back, and yet cohering. So above; before the prior Adam was conformed into male and female, and the state of equilibrium established, the Father and Mother were not face to face. For the Father denotes the most perfect Love; and the Mother the most perfect Rigor. And the seven supernal sons who proceeded from her, from Binah, who brought forth seven, were all most perfect rigors, having no connection with a root in the Most Holy Ancient; that is, they were all *dead,* destroyed, shattered; but they were placed in equilibrium, in the equipoise of the Occult Wisdom, when it was conformed into male and female, Rigor and Love, and they were then restored, and there was given them a root above.

The Father is Love and Mercy, and with a pure and subtle Aur or Benignity impregnates the Mother, who is Rigor and Severity of Judgments; and the product is the brain of Microprosopos.

It was determined, says the *Introduction* to the Book *Sohar,* by the Deity, to create Good and Evil in the world, according to what is said in Isaiah, *"who makes the Light and creates the Evil."* But the Evil was at first occult, and could not be generated and brought forth, except by the sinning of the First Adam. Wherefore He determined that the numerations first emanated, from Benignity downward, should be destroyed and shattered by the excessive influx of His Light; His intention being to create of them the worlds of Evils. But the first three were to remain and subsist, that among the fragments should be neither Will, Intellectual Power, nor the Capacity of Intellection of the Divinity. The last seven numerations were *points,* like the first three, each subsisting independently, unsustained by companionship; which was the cause of their dying and being shattered.

There was then no Love between them, but only a two-fold Fear; Wisdom, for example, fearing lest it should ascend again to its Source in Kether; and also lest it should descend into Binah. Hence there was no union between any two, except Hakemah and Binah, and this imperfect, with averted faces. This is the meaning of the saying, that the world was created by Judgment, which is fear. And so that world could not subsist, and the Seven Kings were dethroned, until the attribute of Compassion was adjoined to it, and then restoration took place. Thence came Love and Union, and six of the parts were united into one person; for Love is the attribute of Compassion or Mercy.

Binah produced the Seven Kings, not successively, but all together. The Seventh is Regnum, called a stone, the corner-stone, because on it are builded the palaces of the three lower worlds.

The first six were shattered into fragments; but Regnum was crushed into a formless mass, lest the malignant demons created from the fragments of the others should receive bodies from it, since from it came bodies and vitality [Nephesch].

From the fragments of the vessels came all Evils; judgments, turbid waters, impurities, the Serpent, and Adam Belial [Baal]. But their internal light re-ascended to Binah, and then flowed down again into the worlds Briah and Yezirah, there to form vestiges of the Seven Numerations. The Sparks of the great Influence of the shattered vases descending into the four spiritual elements, Fire, Air, Water, and Earth, and thence into the inanimate, vegetable, living, and speaking kingdoms, became Souls.

Selecting the suitable from the unsuitable lights, and separating the good from the evil, the Deity first restored the universality of the Seven Kings of the World Aziluth, and afterward the three other Worlds.

And though in them were both good and evil, still this evil did not develop itself in act, since the Severities remained, though mitigated; some portion of them being necessary to prevent the fragments of the integuments from ascending. These were also left, because connection of two is necessary to generation. And this necessity for the existence of Severity is the mystery of the pleasure and warmth of the generative appetite; and thence Love between husband and wife.

If the Deity, says the *Introduction,* had not created worlds and then destroyed them, there could have been no evil in the world, but all things must have been good. There would have been neither reward nor punishment in the world. There would have been no merit in righteousness, for the Good is known by the evil, nor would there have been fruitfulness or multiplication in the world. If all carnal concupiscence were enchained for three days in the mouth of the great abyss, the egg of one of the days would be wanting to the sick man. In time to come it will be called Laban [לבן—*white*], because it will be whitened of its impurity, and will return to the realm Israel, and they will pray the Lord to give them the appetite of carnal concupiscence, for the begetting of children.

The intention of God was, when He created the world, that His creatures should recognize His existence. Therefore He created evils, to afflict them withal when they should sin, and Light and Blessing to reward the just. And therefore man necessarily has free-will and election, since Good and Evil are in the World.

And these kings died, says the *Commentary,* because the condition of equilibrium did not yet exist, nor was Adam Kadmon formed male and female. They were not in contact with what was alive: nor had any root in Adam Kadmon; nor was Wisdom which outflowed from Him, their root, nor did they connect with it. For all these were pure mercies and most simple Love; but those were rigorous judgments. Whence face looked not toward face; nor the Father toward the Mother, because from her proceeded judgments. Nor Macroprosopos toward Microprosopos. And Regnum, the last numeration, was empty and inane. It has nothing of itself; and, as it were, was nothing, receiving nothing from them. Its need was, to receive Love from the Male; for it is mere rigor and judgment; and the Love and Rigor must temper each other, to produce creation, and its multitudes above and below. For it was made to be inhabited; and when rigorous judgments rule in it, it is inane because its processes cannot be carried on.

Wherefore the Balance must needs be instituted, that there might be a root above, so that judgments might be restored and tempered, and live and not again die. And Seven Conformations descend; and all things become in equilibrium, and the needle of the Balance is the root above.

In the world Yezirah, says the *Pneumatica Kabalistica*, ‎י denotes Kether; יה, Hakemah and Binah; and יהו, Gedulah, Geburah, and Tephareth; and thus Vau is Beauty and Harmony. The *Man* is Hakemah; the *Eagle,* Binah; the *Lion,* Gedulah; and the *Ox,* Geburah. And the mysterious circle is thus formed by the Sohar and all the Kabalists: Michael and the face of the Lion are on the South, and the right hand, with the letter ‎י, Yod, and Water; Gabriel and the face of the Ox, on the North, and left hand, with the first ה of the Tetragrammaton and Fire; Uriel and the face of the Eagle, on the East and forward, with   and Air; and Raphael and the face of the Man, on the West, and backward with the last ה, and Earth. In the same order, the four letters represent the four worlds.

Rabbi Schimeon Ben Jochai says that the four animals of the Mysterious Chariot, whose wheels are Netsach and Hōd, are Gedulah, whose face is the Lion's; Geburah, with that of the Ox; Tephareth, with that of the Eagle; and Malakoth, with that of the Man.

The Seven lower Sephiroth, says the *Æsch Mezareph,* will represent Seven Metals; Gedulah and Geburah, Silver and Gold;

Tephareth, Iron; Netsach and Hod, Tin and Copper; Yesod, Lead; and Malakoth will be the metallic Woman and Morn of the Sages, the field wherein are to be sowed the Seeds of the Secret Minerals, to wit, the Water of Gold; but in these such mysteries are concealed as no tongue can utter.

The word אמש, Amas, is composed of the initials of the three Hebrew words that signify Air, Water, and Fire; by which, say the Kabalists, are denoted Benignity, Judicial Rigor, and Mercy or Compassion mediating between them.

Malakoth, says the *Apparatus,* is called *Haikal,* Temple or Palace, because it is the Palace of the Degree Tephareth, which is concealed and contained in it, and Haikal denotes the place in which all things are contained.

For the better understanding of the Kabalah, remember that Kether, or the Crown, is treated of as a person, composed of the ten Numerations, and as such termed Arik Anpin, or Macroprosopos:

That Hakemah is a person, and termed *Abba,* or *Father:*

That Binah is a person, and termed *Mother, Imma:*

That Tephareth, including all the Numerations from Khased or Gedulah to Yesod, is a person, called Seir Anpin, or Microprosopos. These Numerations are six in number, and are represented by the interlaced triangle, or the Seal of Solomon.

And Malakoth is a person, and called the wife of Microprosopos. Vau represents the Beauty or Harmony, consisting of the six parts which constitute Seir Anpin.

The wife, Malakoth, is said to be *behind* the husband, Seir, and to have no other cognition of him. And this is thus explained: That every cognizable object is to be known in two ways: *à priori,* which is when it is known by means of its cause, or of itself; or, *à posteriori* when it is known by its effects. The most nearly perfect mode of cognition is, when the intellect knows the thing itself, in itself, and through itself. But if it knows the thing by its similitude or idea, or species separate from it, or by its effects and operations, the cognition is much feebler and more imperfect. And it is thus only that Regnum, the wife of Seir, knows her husband, until face is turned to face, when they unite, and she has the more nearly perfect knowledge. For then the Deity, as limited and manifested in Seir and the Universe are one.

Vau is Tephareth, considered as the Unity in which are

the six members, of which itself is one. Tephareth, Beauty, is the column which supports the world, symbolized by the column of the junior Warden in the Blue Lodges. The world was first created by Judgment: and as it could not so subsist, Mercy was conjoined with Judgment, and the Divine Mercies sustain the Universe.

God, says the *Idra Suta,* formed all things in the form of male and female, since otherwise the continuance of things was impossible. The All-embracing Wisdom, issuing and shining from the Most Holy Ancient, shines not otherwise than as male and female. Wisdom as the Father, Intelligence the Mother, are in equilibrium as male and female, and they are conjoined, and one shines in the other. Then they generate, and are expanded in the Truth. Then the two are the Perfection of all things, when they are coupled; and when the Son is in them, the summary of all things is in one.

These things are intrusted only to the Holy Superiors, who have entered and gone out and known the ways of the Most Holy God, so as not to err in them, to the right hand or to the left? For these things are hidden; and the lofty Holinesses shine in them, as light flows from the splendor of a lamp.

These things are committed only to those who have entered and not withdrawn; for he who has not done so had better never have been born.

All things are comprehended in the letters Vau and He; and all are one system; and these are the letters, תבונה. Tabunah, Intelligence.

XXIX.

GRAND SCOTTISH KNIGHT OF ST. ANDREW.

A MIRACULOUS tradition, something like that connected with the *labarum* of Constantine, hallows the Ancient Cross of St. Andrew. Hungus, who in the ninth century reigned over the Picts in Scotland, is said to have seen in a vision, on the night before a battle, the Apostle Saint Andrew, who promised him the victory; and for an assured token thereof, he told him that there should appear over the Pictish host, in the air, such a fashioned cross as he had suffered upon. Hungus, awakened, looking up at the sky, saw the promised cross, as did all of both armies; and Hungus and the Picts, after rendering thanks to the Apostle for their victory, and making their offerings with humble devotion, vowed that from thenceforth, as well they as their posterity, in time of war, would wear a cross of St. Andrew for their badge and cognizance.

John Leslie, Bishop of Ross, says that this cross appeared to Achaius, King of the Scots, and Hungus, King of the Picts, the night before the battle was fought betwixt them and Athelstane, King of England, as they were on their knees at prayer.

Every cross of Knighthood is a symbol of the nine qualities of a Knight of St. Andrew of Scotland; for every order of chivalry required of its votaries the same virtues and the same excellencies.

Humility, Patience, and Self-denial are the three essential qualities of a Knight of St. Andrew of Scotland. The Cross, sanctified by the blood of the holy ones who have died upon it; the

801

Cross, which Jesus of Nazareth bore, fainting, along the streets of Jerusalem and up to Calvary, upon which He cried, "Not My will, O Father! but Thine be done," is an unmistakable and eloquent symbol of these three virtues. He suffered upon it, because He consorted with and taught the poor and lowly, and found His disciples among the fishermen of Galilee and the despised publicans. His life was one of Humility, Patience, and Self-denial.

The Hospitallers and Templars took upon themselves vows of obedience, poverty, and chastity. The Lamb, which became the device of the Seal of the Order of the Poor Fellow Soldiery of the Temple of Solomon, conveyed the same lessons of humility and self-denial as the original device of two Knights riding a single horse. The Grand Commander warned every candidate not to be induced to enter the Order by a vain hope of enjoying earthly pomp and splendor. He told him that he would have to endure many things, sorely against his inclinations; and that he would be compelled to give up his own will, and submit entirely to that of his superiors.

The religious Houses of the Hospitallers, despoiled by Henry the Eighth's worthy daughter, Elizabeth, because they would not take the oath to maintain her supremacy, had been Alms-houses, and Dispensaries, and Foundling-asyla, relieving the State of many orphan and outcast children, and ministering to their necessities, God's ravens in the wilderness, bread and flesh in the morning, bread and flesh in the evening. They had been Inns to the wayfaring man, who heard from afar the sound of the Vesper-bell, inviting him to repose and devotion at once, and who might sing his matins with the Morning Star, and go on his way rejoicing. And the Knights were no less distinguished by bravery in battle, than by tenderness and zeal in their ministrations to the sick and dying.

The Knights of St. Andrew vowed to defend all orphans, maidens, and widows of good family, and wherever they heard of murderers, robbers, or masterful thieves who oppressed the people, to bring them to the laws, to the best of their power.

"If fortune fail you," so ran the vows of Rouge-Croix, "in divers lands or countries wherever you go or ride that you find any gentleman of name and arms, which hath lost goods, in worship and Knighthood, in the King's service, or in any other place of worship, and is fallen into poverty, you shall aid, and support, and succor him, in that you may; and he ask of you your goods to his sustenance, you shall give him part of such goods as God hath sent you to your power, and as you may bear."

Thus CHARITY and GENEROSITY are even *more* essential qualities of a true and gentle Knight, and have been so in all ages; and so also hath CLEMENCY. It is a mark of a noble nature to spare the conquered. Valor is then best tempered, when it can turn out a stern fortitude into the mild strains of pity, which never shines more brightly than when she is clad in steel. A martial man, compassionate, shall conquer both in peace and war; and by a twofold way, get victory with honor. The most famed men in the world have had in them both courage and compassion. An enemy reconciled hath a greater value than the long train of captives of a Roman triumph.

VIRTUE, TRUTH, and HONOR are the three MOST essential qualities of a Knight of St. Andrew. "Ye shall love God above all things, and be steadfast in the Faith," it was said to the Knights, in their charge, "and ye shall be true unto your Sovereign Lord, and true to your word and promise. Also, ye shall sit in no place where that any judgment should be given wrongfully against any body, to your knowledge."

The law hath not power to strike the virtuous, nor can fortune subvert the wise. Virtue and Wisdom, only, perfect and defend man. Virtue's garment is a sanctuary so sacred, that even Princes dare not strike the man that is thus robed. It is the livery of the King of Heaven. It protects us when we are unarmed; and is an armor that we cannot lose, unless we be false to ourselves. It is the tenure by which we hold of Heaven, without which we are but outlaws, that cannot claim protection. Nor is there wisdom without virtue, but only a cunning way of procuring our own undoing.

> Peace is nigh
> Where Wisdom's voice has found a listening heart.
> Amid the howl of more than winter storms,
> The halcyon hears the voice of vernal hours,
> Already on the wing.

Sir Launcelot thought no chivalry equal to that of Virtue. This word means not continence only, but chiefly manliness, and so includes what in the old English was called *souffrance,* that patient endurance which is like the emerald, ever green and flowering; and also that other virtue, *droicture,* uprightness, a virtue so strong and so puissant, that by means of it all earthly things almost attain to be unchangeable. Even our swords are formed to remind us of the Cross, and you and any other of us may live to show how much men bear and do not die; for this world is a place of sorrow and tears, of great evils and a constant calamity, and if we would win true honor in it, we must permit no virtue of a Knight to become unfamiliar to us, as men's friends, coldly entreated and not greatly valued, become mere ordinary acquaintances.

We must not view with impatience or anger those who injure us; for it is very inconsistent with philosophy, and particularly with the Divine Wisdom that should govern every Prince Adept, to betray any great concern about the evils which the world, which the vulgar, whether in robes or tatters, can inflict upon the brave. The favor of God and the love of our Brethren rest upon a basis which the strength of malice cannot overthrow; and with these and a generous temper and noble equanimity, we have everything. To be consistent with our professions as Masons, to retain the dignity of our nature, the consciousness of our own honor, the spirit of the high chivalry that is our boast, we must disdain the evils that are only material and bodily, and therefore can be no bigger than a blow or a cozenage, than a wound or a dream.

Look to the ancient days, Sir E....., for excellent examples of VIRTUE, TRUTH, and HONOR, and imitate with a noble emulation the Ancient Knights, the first Hospitallers and Templars, and Bayard, and Sydney, and Saint Louis; in the words of Pliny to his friend Maximus, Revere the ancient glory, and that old age which in man is venerable, in cities sacred. Honor antiquity and great deeds, and detract nothing from the dignity and liberty of any one. If those who now pretend to be the great and mighty, the learned and wise of the world, shall agree in condemning the memory of the heroic Knights of former ages, and in charging with folly us who think that they should be held in eternal remembrance, and that we should defend them from an evil hearing, do you remember that if these who now claim to rule and teach the world should condemn or scorn your poor tribute of fidelity, still it is for you to bear therewith modestly, and yet not to be ashamed, since a day will come when these who now scorn those who were of infinitely higher and finer natures than they are, will be pronounced to have lived poor and pitiful lives, and the world will make haste to forget them.

But neither must you believe that, even in this very different age, of commerce and trade, of the vast riches of many, and the poverty of thousands, of thriving towns and tenement houses swarming with paupers, of churches with rented pews, and theatres, opera-houses, custom-houses, and banks, of steam and telegraph, of shops and commercial palaces, of manufactories and trades-unions, the Gold-room and the Stock Exchange, of newspapers, elections, Congresses, and Legislatures, of the frightful struggle for wealth and the constant wrangle for place and power, of the worship paid to the children of mammon, and covetousness of official station, there are no men of the antique stamp for you to revere, no heroic and knightly souls, that preserve their nobleness and equanimity in the chaos of conflicting passions, of ambition and baseness that welters around them.

It is quite true that Government tends always to become a conspiracy against liberty; or, where votes give place, to fall habitually into such hands that little which is noble or chivalric is found among those who rule and lead the people. It is true that men, in this present age, become distinguished for other things, and may have name and fame, and flatterers and lacqueys, and the oblation of flattery, who would, in a knightly age, have been despised for the want in them of all true gentility and courage; and that such men are as likely as any to be voted for by the multitude, who rarely love or discern or receive truth; who run after fortune, hating what is oppressed, and ready to worship the prosperous; who love accusation and hate apologies; and who are always glad to hear and ready to believe evil of those who care not for their favor and seek not their applause.

But no country can ever be wholly without men of the old heroic strain and stamp, whose word no man will dare to doubt, whose virtue shines resplendent in all calamities and reverses and amid all temptations, and whose honor scintillates and glitters as purely and perfectly as the diamond—men who are not wholly the slaves of the material occupations and pleasures of life, wholly engrossed in trade, in the breeding of cattle, in the framing and enforcing of revenue regulations, in the chicanery of the law, the objects of political envy, in the base trade of the lower literature, or in the heartless, hollow vanities of an eternal dissipation. Every generation, in every country, will bequeath to those who succeed it splendid examples and great images of the dead, to be admired and imitated; there were such among the Romans, under the basest Emperors; such in England when the Long Parliament ruled; such in France during its Saturnalia of irreligion and murder, and some such have made the annals of America illustrious.

When things tend to that state and condition in which, in any country under the sun, the management of its affairs and the customs of its people shall require men to entertain a disbelief in the virtue and honor of those who make and those who are charged to execute the laws; when there shall be everywhere a spirit of suspicion and scorn of all who hold or seek office, or have amassed wealth; when falsehood shall no longer dishonor a man, and oaths give no assurance of true testimony, and one man hardly expect another to keep faith with him, or to utter his real sentiments, or to be true to any party or to any cause when another approaches him with a bribe; when no one shall expect what he says to be printed without additions, perversions, and misrepresentations; when public misfortunes shall be turned to private profit, the press pander to licentiousness, the pulpit ring with political harangues, long prayers to God, eloquently delivered to admiring auditors, be written out for publication, like poems and political speeches; when the uprightness of judges shall be doubted, and the honesty of legislators be a standing jest; then men may come to doubt whether the old days were not better than the new, the Monastery than the Opera Bouffe, the little chapel than the drinking-saloon, the Convents than the buildings as large as they, without their antiquity, without their beauty, without their holiness, true Acherusian Temples, where the passer-by hears from within the never-ceasing din and clang and clashing of machinery, and where, when the bell rings, it is to call wretches to their work and not to their prayers; where, says an animated writer, they keep up a perennial laudation of the Devil, before furnaces which are never suffered to cool.

It has been well said, that whatever withdraws us from the power of our senses, whatever makes the Past, the Distant, or the Future, predominate over the Present, advances us in the dignity of thinking beings. The modern rivals of the German Spa, with their flaunting pretences and cheap finery, their follies and frivolities, their chronicles of dances and inelegant feasts, and their bulletins of women's names and dresses, are poor substitutes for the Monastery and Church which our ancestors would have built in the deep sequestered valleys, shut up between rugged mountains and forests of sombre pine; and a man of meditative temper, learned, and of poetic feeling, would be glad if he could exchange the showy hotel, amid the roar and tumult of the city, or the pretentious tavern of the country-town, for one old humble Monastery by the wayside, where he could refresh himself and his horse without having to fear either pride, impertinence, or knavery, or to pay for pomp, glitter, and gaudy ornamentation; then where he could make his orisons in a church which resounded with divine harmony, and there were no pews for wealth to isolate itself within; where he could behold the poor happy and edified and strengthened with the thoughts of Heaven; where he could then converse with learned and holy and gentle men, and before he took his departure could exalt and calm his spirits by hearing the evening song.

Even Free-Masonry has so multiplied its members that its obligations are less regarded than the simple promises which men make to one another upon the streets and in the markets. It clamors for public notice and courts notoriety by scores of injudicious journals; it wrangles in these, or, incorporated by law, carries its controversies into the Courts. Its elections are, in some Orients, conducted with all the heat and eagerness, the office-seeking and management of political struggles for place. And an empty pomp, with semi-military dress and drill, of peaceful citizens, glittering with painted banners, plumes, and jewels, gaudy and ostentatious, commends to the public favor and female admiration an Order that challenges comparison with the noble Knights, the heroic soldiery encased in steel and mail, stern despisers of danger and death, who made themselves immortal memories, and won Jerusalem from the infidels and fought at Acre and Ascalon, and were the bulwark of Christendom against the Saracenic legions that swarmed after the green banner of the Prophet Mohammed.

If you, Sir E....., would be respectable as a Knight, and not a mere tinselled pretender and Knight of straw, you must practise, and be diligent and ardent in the practice of, the virtues you have professed in this Degree. How can a Mason vow to be tolerant, and straightway denounce another for his political opinions? How vow to be zealous and constant in the service of the Order, and be as useless to it as if he were dead and buried? What does the symbolism of the Compass and Square profit him, if his sensual appetites and baser passions are not governed by, but domineer over his moral sense and reason, the animal over the divine, the earthly over the spiritual, both points of the compass *remaining* below the Square? What a hideous mockery to call one "Brother," whom he maligns to the Profane, lends money unto at usury, defrauds in trade, or plunders at law by chicanery?

VIRTUE, TRUTH, HONOR!—possessing these and never proving false to your vows, you will be worthy to call yourself a Knight, to whom Sir John Chandos might, if living, give his hand, and whom St. Louis and Falkland, Tancred and Baldassar Castiglione would recognize as worthy of their friendship.

Chivalry, a noble Spaniard said, is a religious Order, and there are Knights in the fraternity of Saints in Heaven. Therefore do you here, and for all time to come, lay aside all uncharitable and repining feeling; be proof henceforward against the suggestions of undisciplined passion and inhuman zeal; learn to hate the vices and not the vicious; be content with the discharge of the duties which your Masonic and Knightly professions require; be governed by the old principles of honor and chivalry, and reverence with constancy that Truth which is as sacred and immutable as God Himself. And above all, remember always, that jealousy is not our life, nor disputation our end, nor disunion our health, nor revenge our happiness; but loving-kindness is all these, greater than Hope, greater than Faith, which can remove mountains, properly the only thing which God requires of us, and in the possession of which lies the fulfillment of all our duties.

[*By Ill∴ Bro∴ Rev∴ W. W. Lord, 32°.*]

We are constrained to confess it to be true, that men, in this Age of Iron, worship gods of wood and iron and brass, the work of their own hands. The Steam-Engine is the pre-eminent god of the nineteenth century, whose idolaters are everywhere, and those, who wield its tremendous power securely account themselves gods, everywhere in the civilized world.

Others confess it everywhere, and we must confess here, how reluctantly soever, that the age which we represent is narrowed and not enlarged by its discoveries, and has lost a larger world than it has gained. If we cannot go as far as the satirist who says that our self-adored century

——its broad clown's back turns broadly on the glory of the stars,

we can go with him when he adds,

We are gods by our own reckoning, and may as well shut up our temples
And wield on amidst the incense-steam, the thunder of our cars:
For we throw out acclamations of self-thanking, self-admiring,
With, at every step, "Run faster, O the wondrous, wondrous age!"
Little heeding if our souls are wrought as nobly as our iron,
Or if angels will commend us at the goal of pilgrimage.

Deceived by their increased but still very imperfect knowledge and limited mastery of the brute forces of nature, men imagine that they have discovered the secrets of Divine Wisdom, and do not hesitate, in their own thoughts, to put human prudence in the place of the Divine. Destruction was denounced by the Prophets against Tyre and Sidon, Babylon, and Damascus, and Jerusalem, as a consequence of the sins of their people; but if fire now consumes or earthquake shatters or the tornado crushes a great city, those are scoffed at as fanatics and sneered at for indulging in cant, or rebuked for Pharisaic uncharitableness, who venture to believe and say that there are divine retributions and God's judgment in the ruin wrought by His mighty agencies.

Science, wandering in error, struggles to remove God's Providence to a distance from us and the material Universe, and to substitute for its supervision and care and constant overseeing, what it calls Forces—Forces of Nature—Forces of Matter. It will not see that the Forces of Nature are the varied actions of God. Hence it becomes antagonistic to all Religion, and to all the old Faith that has from the beginning illuminated human souls and constituted their consciousness of their own dignity, their divine origin, and their immortality; that Faith which is the *Light* by which the human soul is enabled, as it were, to see itself.

It is not one religion only, but the basis of all religions, the *Truth* that is in all religions, even the religious creed of Masonry, that is in danger. For all religions have owed all of life that they have had, and their very being, to the foundation on which they were reared; the proposition, deemed undeniable and an axiom, that the Providence of God rules directly in all the affairs and changes of material things. The Science of the age has its hands upon the pillars of the Temple, and rocks it to its foundation. As yet its destructive efforts have but torn from the ancient structure the worm-eaten fret-work of superstition, and shaken down some incoherent additions—owl-inhabited turrets of ignorance, and massive props that supported nothing. The structure itself will be overthrown, when, in the vivid language of a living writer, "Human reason leaps into the throne of God and waves her torch over the ruins of the Universe."

Science deals only with phenomena, and is but charlatanism when it babbles about the powers or causes that produce these, or what the things are, in essence, of which it gives us merely the names. It no more knows what Light or Sound or Perfume *is*, than the Aryan cattle-herders did, when they counted the Dawn and Fire, Flame and Light and Heat as gods. And that Atheistic Science is not even half-science, which ascribes the Universe and its powers and forces to a system of natural laws or to an inherent energy of Nature, or to causes unknown, existing and operating independently of a Divine and Supra-natural power.

That theory would be greatly fortified, if science were always capable of protecting life and property, and, with anything like the *certainty* of which it boasts, securing human interests even against the destructive agencies that man himself develops in his endeavors to subserve them. Fire, the fourth element, as the old philosophers deemed it, is his most useful and abject servant. Why cannot man prevent his ever breaking that ancient indenture, old as Prometheus, old as Adam? Why can he not be certain that at any moment his terrible subject may not break forth and tower up into his master, tyrant, destroyer? It is because it also is a power of nature; which, in ultimate trial of forces, is always superior to man. It is also because, in a different sense from that in which it is the servant of man, it is the servant of Him Who makes His ministers a flame of fire, and Who is over nature, as nature is over man.

There are powers of nature which man does not even attempt to check or control. Naples does nothing against Vesuvius. Valparaiso only trembles with the trembling earth before the coming earthquake. The sixty thousand people who went down alive into the grave when Lisbon buried her population under both earth and sea had no knowledge of the causes, and no possible control over the power, that effected their destruction.

But here the servant, and, in a sense, the creature of man, the drudge of kitchen and factory, the humble slave of the lamp, engaged in his most servile employment, appearing as a little point of flame, or perhaps a feeble spark, suddenly snaps his brittle chain, breaks from his prison, and leaps with destructive fury, as if from the very bosom of Hell, upon the doomed dwellings of fifty thousand human beings, each of whom, but a moment before, conceived himself his master. And those daring fire-brigades, with their water-artillery, his conquerors, it seemed, upon so many midnight fields, stand paralyzed in the presence of their conqueror.

In other matters relative to human safety and interests we have observed how confident science becomes upon the strength of some slight success in the war of man with nature, and how much inclined to put itself in the place of Providence, which, by the very force of the term, is the only absolute science. Near the beginning of this century, for instance, medical and sanitary science had made, in the course of a few years, great and wonderful progress. The great plague which wasted Europe in the fourteenth and fifteenth centuries, and reappeared in the seventeenth, had been identified with a disease which yields to enlightened treatment, and its ancient virulence was attributed to ignorance of hygiene, and the filthy habits of a former age. Another fatal and disfiguring scourge had to a great extent been checked by the discovery of vaccination. From Sangrado to Sydenham, from Paracelsus to Jenner, the healing art had indeed taken a long stride. The Faculty might be excused had it then said, "Man is mortal, disease will be often fatal; but there shall be no more unresisted and unnecessary slaughter by infectious disease, no more general carnage, no more carnivals of terror and high festivals of death."

The conceited boast would hardly have died upon the lip, when, from the mysterious depths of remotest India a spectre stalked forth, or rather a monster crept, more fearful than human eye had ever yet beheld. And not with surer instinct does the tiger of the jungles, where this terrible pestilence was born, catch the scent of blood upon the air, than did this invisible Destroyer, this fearful agent of Almighty Power, this tremendous Consequence of some Sufficient Cause, scent the tainted atmosphere of Europe and turn Westward his devastating march. The millions of dead left in his path through Asia proved nothing. They were unarmed, ignorant, defenceless, unaided by science, undefended by art. The cholera was to them inscrutable and irresistible as Azrael, the Angel of Death.

But it came to Europe and swept the halls of science as it had swept the Indian village and the Persian khan. It leaped as noise-lessly and descended as destructively upon the population of many a high-towered, wide-paved, purified, and disinfected city of the West as upon the Pariahs of Tanjore and the filthy streets of Stamboul. In Vienna, Paris, London, the scenes of the great plague were re-enacted.

> The sick man started in his bed,
> The watcher leaped upon the floor,
> At the cry, Bring out your dead,
> The cart is at the door!

Was *this* the judgment of Almighty God? He would be bold who should say that it was; he would be bolder who should say it was not. To Paris, at least, that European Babylon, how often have the further words of the prophet to the daughter of the Chal-dæans, the lady of kingdoms, been fulfilled? "Thy wisdom and thy knowledge have perverted thee, and thou hast said in thy heart I am and none else beside me. Therefore shall evil come upon thee; thou shalt not know whence it riseth; and mischief shall fall upon thee; thou shalt not be able to put it off; desolation shall come upon thee suddenly."

And as to London—it looked like judgment, if it be true that the Asiatic cholera had its origin in English avarice and cruelty, as they suppose who trace it to the tax which Warren Hastings, when Governor-General of India, imposed on salt, thus cutting off its use from millions of the vegetable-eating races of the East: just as that disease whose spectral shadow lies always upon America's threshold, originated in the avarice and cruelty of the slave-trade, translating the African coast fever to the congenial climate of the West Indies and Southern America—the yellow fever of the former, and the *vomito negro* of the latter.

But we should be slow to make inferences from our petty human logic to the ethics of the Almighty. Whatever the cruelty of the slave-trade, or the severity of slavery on the continents or islands of America, we should still, in regard to its supposed con-sequences, be wiser, perhaps, to say with that great and simple Casuist Who gave the world the Christian religion: "Suppose ye that these Galileans were sinners above all the Galileans because they suffered such things? or those eighteen upon whom the tower of Siloam fell and slew them, think ye that they were sinners above all the men that dwelt in Jerusalem?"

Retribution bars retaliation, even in words. A city shattered, burned, destroyed, desolate, a land wasted, humiliated, made a desert and a wilderness, or wearing the thorny crown of humiliation and subjugation, is invested with the sacred prerogatives and immunities of the dead. The base human revenge of exultation at its fall and ruin should shrink back abashed in the presence of the infinite Divine chastisement. "Forgiveness is wiser than revenge," our Freemasonry teaches us, "and it is better to love than to hate." Let him who sees in great calamities the hand of God, be silent, and fear His judgments.

Men are great or small in stature as it pleases God. But their nature is great or small as it pleases themselves. Men are not born, some with great souls and some with little souls. One by taking thought cannot add to his stature, but he can enlarge his soul. By an act of the will he can make himself a moral giant, or dwarf himself to a pigmy.

There are two natures in man, the higher and the lower, the great and the mean, the noble and the ignoble; and he can and must, by his own voluntary act, identify himself with the one or with the other. Freemasonry is continual effort to exalt the nobler nature over the ignoble, the spiritual over the material, the divine in man over the human. In this great effort and purpose the chivalric Degrees concur and co-operate with those that teach the magnificent lessons of morality and philosophy. Magnanimity, mercy, clemency, a forgiving temper, are virtues indispensable to the character of a perfect Knight. When the low and evil principle in our nature says, "Do not give; reserve your beneficence for impoverished friends, or at least unobjectionable strangers, Do not bestow it on successful enemies,—friends only in virtue, of our misfortunes," the diviner principle whose voice spake by the despised Galilean says, "Do good to them that hate you, for if ye love them (only) who love you, what reward have you? Do not publicans and sinners the same"—that is, the tax-gathers and wicked oppressors, armed Romans and renegade Jews, whom ye count your enemies?

XXX.

KNIGHT KADOSH.

WE often profit more by our enemies than by our friends. *"We support ourselves only on that which resists,"* and owe our success to opposition. The best friends of Masonry in America were the Anti-Masons of 1826, and at the same time they were its worst enemies. Men are but the automata of Providence, and it uses the demagogue, the fanatic, and the knave, a common trinity in Republics, as its tools and instruments to effect that of which they do not dream, and which they imagine themselves commissioned to prevent.

The Anti-Masons, traitors and perjurors some, and some mere political knaves, purified Masonry by persecution, and so proved to be its benefactors; for that which is persecuted, grows. To them its present popularity is due, the cheapening of its Degrees, the invasion of its Lodges, that are no longer Sanctuaries, by the multitude; its pomp and pageantry and overdone display.

An hundred years ago it had become known that the קדש were the Templars under a veil, and therefore the Degree was proscribed, and, ceasing to be worked, became a mere brief and formal ceremony, under another name. Now, from the tomb in which after his murders he rotted, Clement the Fifth howls against the successors of his victims, in the Allocution of Pio Nono against the Free-Masons. The ghosts of the dead Templars

814

haunt the Vatican and disturb the slumbers of the paralyzed Papacy, which, dreading the dead, shrieks out its excommunications and impotent anathemas against the living. It is a declaration of war, and was needed to arouse apathy and inertness to action.

An enemy of the Templars shall tell us the secret of this Papal hostility against an Order that has existed for centuries in despite of its anathemas, and has its Sanctuaries and Asyla even in Rome.

It will be easy, as we read, to separate the false from the true, the audacious conjectures from the simple facts.

"A power that ruled without antagonism and without concurrence, and consequently without control, proved fatal to the Sacerdotal Royalties; while the Republics, on the other hand, had perished by the conflict of liberties and franchises, which, in the absence of all duty hierarchically sanctioned and enforced, had soon become mere tyrannies, rivals one of the other. To find a stable medium between these two abysses, the idea of the Christian Hierophants was to create a society devoted to abnegation by solemn vows, protected by severe regulations; which should be recruited by initiation, and which, sole depositary of the great religious and social secrets, should make Kings and Pontiffs, without exposing it to the corruptions of Power. In that was the secret of that kingdom of Jesus Christ, which, without being of this world, would govern all its grandeurs.

"This idea presided at the foundation of the great religious orders, so often at war with the secular authorities, ecclesiastical or civil. Its realization was also the dream of the dissident sects of Gnostics or Illuminati who pretended to connect their faith with the primitive tradition of the Christianity of Saint John. It at length became a menace for the Church and Society, when a rich and dissolute Order, initiated in the mysterious doctrines of the Kabalah, seemed disposed to turn against legitimate authority the conservative principle of Hierarchy, and threatened the entire world with an immense revolution.

"The Templars, whose history is so imperfectly known, were those terrible conspirators. In 1118, nine Knights Crusaders in the East, among whom were Geoffroi de Saint-Omer and Hugues de Payens, consecrated themselves to religion, and took an oath between the hands of the Patriarch of Constantinople, a See always secretly or openly hostile to that of Rome from the time of Photius. The avowed object of the Templars was to protect the Christians who came to visit the Holy Places: their secret object was the re-building of the Temple of Solomon on the model prophesied by Ezekiel.

"This re-building, formally predicted by the Judaïzing Mystics of the earlier ages, had become the secret dream of the Patriarchs of the Orient. The Temple of Solomon, re-built and consecrated to the Catholic worship would become, in effect, the Metropolis of the Universe; the East would prevail over the West, and the Patriarchs of Constantinople would possess themselves of the Papal power.

"The Templars, or *Poor Fellow-Soldiery of the Holy House of the Temple* intended to be re-built, took as their models, in the Bible, the Warrior-Masons of Zorobabel, who worked, holding the sword in one hand and the trowel in the other. Therefore it was that the Sword and the Trowel were the insignia of the Templars, who subsequently, as will be seen, concealed themselves under the name of *Brethren Masons*. [This name, *Frères Maçons* in the French, adopted by way of secret reference to the Builders of the Second Temple, was corrupted in English into *Free*-Masons, as *Pythagore de Crotone* was into *Peter Gower* of *Groton* in England. *Khairūm* or *Khūr-ūm,* (a name mis-rendered into *Hiram*) from an artificer in brass and other metals, became the Chief Builder of the *Haikal Kadosh,* the Holy House, of the Temple, the Ἱερος Δομος; and the words *Bonai* and *Banaim* yet appear in the Masonic Degrees, meaning Builder and Builders.]

"The trowel of the Templars is quadruple, and the triangular plates of it are arranged in the form of a cross, making the Kabalistic pantacle known by the name of the Cross of the East. The Knight of the East, and the Knight of the East and West, have in their titles secret allusions to the Templars of whom they were at first the successors.

"The secret thought of Hugues de Payens, in founding his Order, was not exactly to serve the ambition of the Patriarchs of Constantinople. There existed at that period in the East a Sect of Johannite Christians, who claimed to be the only true Initiates into the real mysteries of the religion of the Saviour. They pretended to know the real history of YESUS the ANOINTED, and, adopting in part the Jewish traditions and the tales of the Talmud, they held that the facts recounted in the Evangels are but allegories, the key of which Saint John gives, in saying that the world might be filled with the books that could be written upon the words and deeds of Jesus Christ; words which, they thought, would be only a ridiculous exaggeration, if he were not speaking of an allegory and a legend, that might be varied and prolonged to infinity.

"The Johannites ascribed to Saint John the foundation of their Secret Church, and the Grand Pontiffs of the Sect assumed the title of *Christos, Anointed,* or *Consecrated,* and claimed to have succeeded one another from Saint John by an uninterrupted succession of pontifical powers. He who, at the period of the foundation of the Order of the Temple, claimed these imaginary prerogatives, was named THEOCLET; he knew HUGUES DE PAYENS, he initiated him into the Mysteries and hopes of his pretended church, he seduced him by the notions of Sovereign Priesthood and Supreme royalty, and finally designated him as his successor.

"Thus the Order of Knights of the Temple was at its very origin devoted to the cause of opposition to the tiara of Rome and the crowns of Kings, and the Apostolate of Kabalistic Gnosticism was vested in its chiefs. For Saint John himself was the Father of the Gnostics, and the current translation of his polemic against the heretical of his Sect and the pagans who denied that Christ was the Word, is throughout a misrepresentation, or misunderstanding at least, of the whole Spirit of that Evangel.

"The tendencies and tenets of the Order were enveloped in profound mystery, and it externally professed the most perfect orthodoxy. The Chiefs alone knew the aim of the Order: the Subalterns followed them without distrust.

"To acquire influence and wealth, then to intrigue, and at need to fight, to establish the Johannite or Gnostic and Kabalistic dogma, were the object and means proposed to the initiated Brethren. The Papacy and the rival monarchies, they said to them, are sold and bought in these days, become corrupt, and to-morrow, perhaps, will destroy each other. All that will become the heritage of the Temple: the World will soon come to us for its Sovereigns and Pontiffs. We shall constitute the equilibrium of the Universe, and be rulers over the Masters of the World.

"The Templars, like all other Secret Orders and Associations, had two doctrines, one concealed and reserved for the Masters, which was Johannism; the other public, which was the *Roman Catholic.* Thus they deceived the adversaries whom they sought

to supplant. Hence Free-Masonry, vulgarly imagined to have begun with the Dionysian Architects or the German Stone-workers,
adopted Saint John the Evangelist as one of its patrons, associ-
ating with him, in order not to arouse the suspicions of Rome,
Saint John the Baptist, and thus covertly proclaiming itself the
child of the Kabalah and Essenism together."

[For the Johannism of the Adepts was the Kabalah of the
earlier Gnostics, degenerating afterward into those heretical forms
which Gnosticism developed, so that even Manes had his followers
among them. Many adopted his doctrines of the two Principles,
the recollection of which is perpetuated by the handle of the dagger and the tesselated pavement or floor of the Lodge, stupidly
called *"the Indented Tessel,"* and represented by great hanging
tassels, when it really means a *tesserated* floor (from the Latin
tessera) of white and black lozenges, with a necessarily *denticulated* or *indented* border or edging. And wherever, in the higher
Degrees, the two colors white and black, are in juxtaposition, the
two Principles of Zoroaster and Manes are alluded to. With
others the doctrine became a mystic Pantheism, descended from
that of the Brahmins, and even pushed to an idolatry of Nature
and hatred of every revealed dogma.

[To all this the absurd reading of the established Church, taking literally the figurative, allegorical, and mythical language of a
collection of Oriental books of different ages, directly and inevitably led. The same result long after followed the folly of regarding the Hebrew books as if they had been written by the un-
imaginative, hard, practical intellect of the England of James the
First and the bigoted stolidity of Scottish Presbyterianism.]

"The better to succeed and win partisans, the Templars sympa-
thized with regrets for dethroned creeds and encouraged the hopes
of new worships, promising to all liberty of conscience and a new
orthodoxy that should be the synthesis of all the persecuted
creeds."

[It is absurd to suppose that men of intellect adored a monstrous
idol called Baphomet, or recognized Mahomet as an inspired
prophet. Their symbolism, invented ages before, to conceal what
it was dangerous to avow, was of course misunderstood by those
who were not adepts, and to their enemies seemed to be pantheistic. The calf of gold, made by Aaron for the Israelites, was but one
of the oxen under the laver of bronze, and the Karobim on the Pro-
pitiatory, misunderstood. The symbols of the wise always become

the idols of the ignorant multitude. What the Chiefs of the Order really believed and taught, is indicated to the Adepts by the hints contained in the high Degrees of Free-Masonry, and by the symbols which only the Adepts understand.

[The Blue Degrees are but the outer court or portico of the Temple. Part of the symbols are displayed there to the Initiate, but he is intentionally misled by false interpretations. It is not intended that he shall understand them; but it is intended that he shall imagine he understands them. Their true explication is reserved for the Adepts, the Princes of Masonry. The whole body of the Royal and Sacerdotal Art was hidden so carefully, centuries since, in the High Degrees, as that it is even yet impossible to solve many of the enigmas which they contain. It is well enough for the mass of those called Masons, to imagine that all is contained in the Blue Degrees; and whoso attempts to undeceive them will labor in vain, and without any true reward violate his obligations as an Adept. Masonry is the veritable Sphinx, buried to the head in the sands heaped round it by the ages.]

"The seeds of decay were sown in the Order of the Temple at its origin. Hypocrisy is a mortal disease. It had conceived a great work which it was incapable of executing, because it knew neither humility nor personal abnegation, because Rome was then invincible, and because the later Chiefs of the Order did not comprehend its mission. Moreover, the Templars were in general uneducated, and capable only of wielding the sword, with no qualifications for governing, and at need enchaining, that queen of the world called Opinion." [The doctrines of the Chiefs would, if expounded to the masses, have seemed to them the babblings of folly. The symbols of the wise are the idols of the vulgar, or else as meaningless as the hieroglyphics of Egypt to the nomadic Arabs. There must always be a common-place interpretation for the mass of Initiates, of the symbols that are eloquent to the Adepts.]

"Hugues de Payens himself had not that keen and far-sighted intellect nor that grandeur of purpose which afterward distinguished the military founder of another soldiery that became formidable to kings. The Templars were unintelligent and therefore unsuccessful Jesuits.

"Their watchword was, to become wealthy, in order to buy the world. They became so, and in 1312 they possessed in Europe alone more than nine thousand seignories. Riches were the shoal on which they were wrecked. They became insolent, and unwisely showed their contempt for the religious and social institutions which they aimed to overthrow. Their ambition was fatal to them. Their projects were divined and prevented. [Rome, more intolerant of heresy than of vice and crime, came to fear the Order, and fear is always cruel. It has always deemed philosophical truth the most dangerous of heresies, and has never been at a loss for a false accusation, by means of which to crush free thought.] Pope Clement V. and King Philip le Bel gave the signal to Europe, and the Templars, taken as it were in an immense net, were arrested, disarmed, and cast into prison. Never was a *Coup d' Etat* accomplished with a more formidable concert of action. The whole world was struck with stupor, and eagerly waited for the strange revelations of a process that was to echo through so many ages.

"It was impossible to unfold to the people the conspiracy of the Templars against the Thrones and the Tiara. It was impossible to expose to them the doctrines of the Chiefs of the Order. [This would have been to initiate the multitude into the secrets of the Masters, and to have uplifted the veil of Isis. Recourse was therefore had to the charge of magic, and denouncers and false witnesses were easily found. When the temporal and spiritual tyrannies unite to crush a victim they never want for serviceable instruments.] The Templars were gravely accused of spitting upon Christ and denying God at their receptions, of gross obscenities, conversations with female devils, and the worship of a monstrous idol.

"The end of the drama is well known, and how Jacques de Molai and his fellows perished in the flames. But before his execution, the Chief of the doomed Order organized and instituted what afterward came to be called the Occult, Hermetic, or Scottish Masonry. In the gloom of his prison, the Grand Master created four Metropolitan Lodges, at Naples for the East, at Edinburg for the West, at Stockholm for the North, and at Paris for the South." [The initials of his name, J∴ B∴ M∴ found in the same order in the first three Degrees, are but one of the many internal and cogent proofs that such was the origin of modern Free-Masonry. The legend of Osiris was revived and adopted, to symbolize the destruction of the Order, and the resurrection of

Khūrūm, slain in the body of the Temple, of Khūrūm Abai, the Master, as the martyr of fidelity to obligation, of Truth and Conscience, prophesied the restoration to life of the buried association.]

"The Pope and the King soon after perished in a strange and sudden manner. Squin de Florian, the chief denouncer of the Order, died assassinated. In breaking the sword of the Templars, they made of it a poniard; and their proscribed trowels thenceforward built only tombs."

[The Order disappeared at once. Its estates and wealth were confiscated, and it seemed to have ceased to exist. Nevertheless it lived, under other names and governed by unknown Chiefs, revealing itself only to those who, in passing through a series of Degrees, had proven themselves worthy to be entrusted with the dangerous Secret. The modern Orders that style themselves Templars have assumed a name to which they have not the shadow of a title.]

"The Successors of the Ancient Adepts Rose-Croix, abandoning by degrees the austere and hierarchial Science of their Ancestors in initiation, became a Mystic Sect, united with many of the Templars, the dogmas of the two intermingling, and believed themselves to be the sole depositaries of the secrets of the Gospel of St. John, seeing in its recitals an allegorical series of rites proper to complete the initiation.

"The Initiates, in fact, thought in the eighteenth century that their time had arrived, some to found a new Hierarchy, others to overturn all authority, and to press down all the summits of the Social Order under the level of Equality."

The mystical meanings of the Rose as a Symbol are to be looked for in the Kabalistic Commentaries on the Canticles.

The Rose was for the Initiates the living and blooming symbol of the revelation of the harmonies of being. It was the emblem of beauty, life, love, and pleasure. Flamel, or the Book of the Jew Abraham, made it the hieroglyphical sign of the accomplishment of the great Work. Such is the key of the Roman de la Rose. The Conquest of the Rose was the problem propounded to Science by Initiation, while Religion was laboring to prepare and establish the universal triumph, exclusive and definitive, of the Cross.

To unite the Rose to the Cross, was the problem proposed by the High Initiation; and in fact the Occult philosophy being the

Universal Synthesis, ought to explain all the phenomena of Being. Religion, considered solely as a physiological fact, is the revelation and satisfaction of a necessity of souls. Its existence is a scientific fact; to deny it, would be to deny humanity itself.

The Rose-Croix Adepts respected the dominant, hierarchical, and revealed religion. Consequently they could no more be the enemies of the Papacy than of legitimate Monarchy; and if they conspired against the Popes and Kings, it was because they considered them personally as apostates from duty and supreme favorers of anarchy.

What, in fact, is a despot, spiritual or temporal, but a crowned anarchist?

One of the magnificent pantacles that express the esoteric and unutterable part of Science, is a Rose of Light, in the centre of which a human form extends its arms in the form of a cross.

Commentaries and studies have been multiplied upon the *Divine Comedy,* the work of DANTE, and yet no one, so far as we know, has pointed out its especial character. The work of the great Ghibellin is a declaration of war against the Papacy, by bold revelations of the Mysteries. The Epic of Dante is Johannite and Gnostic, an audacious application, like that of the Apocalypse, of the figures and numbers of the Kabalah to the Christian dogmas, and a secret negation of every thing absolute in these dogmas. His journey through the supernatural worlds is accomplished like the initiation into the Mysteries of Eleusis and Thebes. He escapes from that gulf of Hell over the gate of which the sentence of despair was written, *by reversing the positions of his head and feet,* that is to say, *by accepting the direct opposite of the Catholic dogma;* and then he reascends to the light, by using the Devil himself as a monstrous ladder. Faust ascends to Heaven, by stepping on the head of the vanquished Mephistopheles. Hell is impassable for those only who know not how to turn back from it. We free ourselves from its bondage by audacity.

His Hell is but a negative Purgatory. His Heaven is composed of a series of Kabalistic circles, divided by a cross, like the Pantacle of Ezekiel. In the centre of this cross blooms a rose, and we see the symbol of the Adepts of the Rose-Croix for the first time publicly expounded and almost categorically explained.

For the first time, because Guillaume de Lorris, who died in 1260, five years before the birth of Alighieri, had not completed his *Roman de la Rose,* which was continued by Chopinel, a half century afterward. One is astonished to discover that the Roman de la Rose and the Divina Commedia are two opposite forms of one and the same work, initiation into independence of spirit, a satire on all contemporary institutions, and the allegorical formula of the great Secrets of the Society of the Roses-Croix.

The important manifestations of Occultism coincide with the period of the fall of the Templars; since Jean de Meung or Chopinel, contemporary of the old age of Dante, flourished during the best years of his life at the Court of Philippe le Bel. The Roman de la Rose is the Epic of old France. It is a profound book, under the form of levity, a revelation as learned as that of Apuleius, of the Mysteries of Occultism. The Rose of Flamel, that of Jean de Meung, and that of Dante, grew on the same stem.

Swedenborg's system was nothing else than the Kabalah, minus the principle of the Hierarchy. It is the Temple, without the keystone and the foundation.

Cagliostro was the Agent of the Templars, and therefore wrote to the Free-Masons of London that the time had come to begin the work of re-building the Temple of the Eternal. He had introduced into Masonry a new Rite called the *Egyptian,* and endeavored to resuscitate the mysterious worship of Isis. The three letters L∴ P∴ D∴ on his seal, were the initials of the words *"Lilia pedibus destrue;" tread under foot the Lilies* [of France], and a Masonic medal of the sixteenth or seventeenth century has upon it a sword cutting off the stalk of a lily, and the words *"talem dabit ultio messem,"* such harvest revenge will give.

A Lodge inaugurated under the auspices of Rousseau, the fanatic of Geneva, became the centre of the revolutionary movement in France, and a Prince of the blood-royal went thither to swear the destruction of the successors of Philippe le Bel on the tomb of Jacques de Molai. The registers of the Order of Templars attest that the Regent, the Duc d' Orleans, was Grand Master of that formidable Secret Society, and that his successors were the Duc de Maine, the Prince of Bourbon-Condé, and the Duc de Cossé-Brissac.

The Templars compromitted the King; they saved him from the rage of the People, to exasperate that rage and bring on the catastrophe prepared for centuries; it was a scaffold that the vengeance of the Templars demanded. The secret movers of the

French Revolution had sworn to overturn the Throne and the
Altar upon the Tomb of Jacques de Molai. When Louis XVI.
was executed, half the work was done; and thenceforward the
Army of the Temple was to direct all its efforts against the Pope.

Jacques de Molai and his companions were perhaps martyrs,
but their avengers dishonored their memory. Royalty was regenerated on the scaffold of Louis XVI., the Church triumphed in
the captivity of Pius VI., carried a prisoner to Valence, and dying
of fatigue and sorrow, but the successors of the Ancient Knights
of the Temple perished, overwhelmed in their fatal victory.

Morals and Dogma.

Consistory.

XXXI.

GRAND INSPECTOR INQUISITOR COMMANDER.

[Inspector Inquisitor.]

To hear patiently, to weigh deliberately and dispassionately, and to decide impartially;—these are the chief duties of a Judge. After the lessons you have received, I need not further enlarge upon them. You will be ever eloquently reminded of them by the furniture upon our Altar, and the decorations of the Tribunal.

The Holy Bible will remind you of your obligation; and that as you judge here below, so you will be yourself judged hereafter, by One who has not to submit, like an earthly judge, to the sad necessity of inferring the motives, intentions, and purposes of men [of which all crime essentially consists] from the uncertain and often unsafe testimony of their acts and words; as men in thick darkness grope their way, with hands outstretched before them: but before Whom every thought, feeling, impulse, and intention of every soul that now is, or ever was, or ever will be on earth, is, and ever will be through the whole infinite duration of eternity, present and visible.

The Square and Compass, the Plumb and Level, are well known to you as a Mason. Upon you as a Judge, they peculiarly inculcate uprightness, impartiality, careful consideration of facts and circumstances, accuracy in judgment, and uniformity in decision. As a Judge, too, you are to bring up square work and square work only. Like a temple erected by the plumb, you are to lean neither to one side nor the other. Like a building well squared and levelled, you are to be firm and steadfast in your convictions of right and justice. Like the circle swept with the compasses, you are to be true. In the scales of justice you are to weigh the facts and the law alone, nor place in either scale personal friendship or personal dislike, neither fear nor favor: and when reformation is no longer to be hoped for, you are to smite relentlessly with the sword of justice.

The peculiar and principal symbol of this Degree is the Tetractys of Pythagoras, suspended in the East, where ordinarily the sacred word or letter glitters, like it, representing the Deity. Its nine external points form the triangle, the chief symbol in Masonry, with many of the meanings of which you are familiar.

To us, its three sides represent the three principal attributes of the Deity, which created, and now, as ever, support, uphold, and guide the Universe in its eternal movement; the three supports of the Masonic Temple, itself an emblem of the Universe:—Wisdom, or the Infinite Divine Intelligence; Strength, or Power, the Infinite Divine Will; and Beauty, or the Infinite Divine Harmony, the Eternal Law, by virtue of which the infinite myriads of suns and worlds flash ever onward in their ceaseless revolutions, without clash or conflict, in the Infinite of space, and change and movement are the law of all created existences.

To us, as Masonic Judges, the triangle figures forth the Pyramids, which, planted firmly as the everlasting hills, and accurately adjusted to the four cardinal points, defiant of all assaults of men and time, teach us to stand firm and unshaken as they, when our feet are planted upon the solid truth.

It includes a multitude of geometrical figures, all having a deep significance to Masons. The triple triangle is peculiarly sacred, having ever been among all nations a symbol of the Deity. Prolonging all the external lines of the Hexagon, which also it includes, we have six smaller triangles, whose bases cut each other in the central point of the Tetractys, itself always the symbol of the generative power of the Universe, the Sun, Brahma, Osiris, Apollo, Bel, and the Deity Himself. Thus, too, we form twelve still smaller triangles, three times three of which compose the Tetractys itself.

I refrain from enumerating all the figures that you may trace within it: but one may not be passed unnoticed. The Hexagon itself faintly images to us a cube, not visible at the first glance, and therefore the fit emblem of that faith in things invisible, most essential to salvation. The first perfect solid, and reminding you of the cubical stone that sweated blood, and of that deposited by Enoch, it teaches justice, accuracy, and consistency.

The infinite divisibility of the triangle teaches the infinity of the Universe, of time, of space, and of the Deity, as do the lines that, diverging from the common centre, ever increase their distance from each other as they are infinitely prolonged. As they may be infinite in number, so are the attributes of Deity infinite; and as they emanate from one centre and are projected into space, so the whole Universe has emanated from God.

Remember also, my Brother, that you have other duties to perform than those of a judge. You are to inquire into and scrutinize carefully the work of the subordinate Bodies in Masonry. You are to see that recipients of the higher Degrees are not unnecessarily multiplied; that improper persons are carefully excluded from membership, and that in their life and conversation Masons bear testimony to the excellence of our doctrines and the incalculable value of the institution itself. You are to inquire also into your own heart and conduct, and keep careful watch over yourself, that you go not astray. If you harbor ill-will and jealousy, if you are hospitable to intolerance and bigotry, and churlish to gentleness and kind affections, opening wide your heart to one and closing its portals to the other, it is time for you to set in order your own temple, or else you wear in vain the name and insignia of a Mason, while yet uninvested with the Masonic nature.

Everywhere in the world there is a natural law, that is, a constant mode of action, which seems to belong to the nature of things, to the constitution of the Universe. This fact is universal. In different departments we call this mode of action by different names, as the law of Matter, the law of Mind, the law of Morals, and the like. We mean by this, a certain mode of action which belongs to the material, mental, or moral forces, the mode in

which commonly they are found to act, and in which it is their
ideal to act always. The ideal laws of matter we know only from
the fact that they are always obeyed. To us the actual *obedience*
is the only evidence of the ideal rule; for in respect to the conduct of the material world, the *ideal* and the *actual* are the same.

The laws of matter we learn only by observation and experience. Before experience of the fact, no man could foretell that a
body, falling toward the earth, would descend sixteen feet the first
second, twice that the next, four times the third, and sixteen times
the fourth. No mode of action in our consciousness anticipates
this rule of action in the outer world. The same is true of all the
laws of matter. The ideal law is known because it is a fact. The
law is imperative. It must be obeyed without hesitation. Laws
of crystallization, laws of proportion in chemical combination,—
neither in these nor in any other law of Nature is there any mar-
gin left for oscillation of disobedience. Only the primal will of
God works in the material world, and no secondary finite will.

There are no exceptions to the great general law of Attraction,
which binds atom to atom in the body of a rotifer visible only by
aid of a microscope, orb to orb, system to system; gives unity to
the world of things, and rounds these worlds of systems to a Universe. At first there seem to be exceptions to this law, as in
growth and decomposition, in the repulsions of electricity; but at
length all these are found to be special cases of the one great law
of attraction acting in various modes.

The variety of effect of this law at first surprises the senses;
but in the end the unity of cause astonishes the cultivated mind.
Looked at in reference to this globe, an earthquake is no more
than a chink that opens in a garden-walk of a dry day in Summer. A sponge is porous, having small spaces between the solid
parts: the solar system is only *more* porous, having larger room
between the several orbs: the Universe yet more so, with spaces
between the systems, as small, compared with *infinite* space, as
those between the atoms that compose the bulk of the smallest invisible animalcule, of which millions swim in a drop of salt-water.
The same attraction holds together the animalcule, the sponge, the
system, and the Universe. Every particle of matter in that Universe is related to each and all the other particles; and attraction
is their common bond.

In the spiritual world, the world of human consciousness, there is also a law, an ideal mode of action for the spiritual forces of man. The law of Justice is as universal an one as the law of Attraction; though we are very far from being able to reconcile all the phenomena of Nature with it. The lark has the same right, in our view, to live, to sing, to dart at pleasure through the ambient atmosphere, as the hawk has to ply his strong wings in the Summer sunshine: and yet the hawk pounces on and devours the harmless lark, as *it* devours the worm, and as the worm devours the animalcule; and, so far as we know, there is nowhere, in any future state of animal existence, any compensation for this apparent injustice. Among the bees, one rules, while the others obey—some work, while others are idle. With the small ants, the soldiers feed on the proceeds of the workmen's labor. The lion lies in wait for and devours the antelope that has apparently as good a right to life as he. Among men, some govern and others serve, capital commands and labor obeys, and one race, superior in intellect, avails itself of the strong muscles of another that is inferior; and yet, for all this, no one impeaches the justice of God.

No doubt all these varied phenomena are consistent with one great law of justice; and the only difficulty is that we do not, and no doubt we cannot, understand that law. It is very easy for some dreaming and visionary theorist to say that it is most evidently unjust for the lion to devour the deer, and for the eagle to tear and eat the wren; but the trouble is, that we know of no other way, according to the frame, the constitution, and the organs which God has given them, in which the lion and the eagle could manage to live at all. Our little measure of justice is not God's measure. His justice does not require us to relieve the hard-working millions of all labor, to emancipate the serf or slave, unfitted to be free, from all control.

No doubt, underneath all the little bubbles, which are the lives, the wishes, the wills, and the plans of the two thousand millions or more of human beings on this earth (for bubbles they are, judging by the space and time they occupy in this great and age-outlasting sea of human-kind),—no doubt, underneath them all resides one and the same eternal force, which they shape into this or the other special form; and over all the same paternal Providence presides, keeping eternal watch over the little and the great, and producing variety of effect from Unity of Force.

It is entirely true to say that justice is the constitution or funda-

mental law of the moral Universe, the law of right, a rule of conduct for man (as it is for every other living creature), in all his
moral relations. No doubt all human affairs (like all other affairs), must be subject to that as the law paramount; and what
is *right* agrees therewith and stands, while what is *wrong* conflicts
with it and falls. The difficulty is that we ever erect *our* notions
of what is right and just into the *law* of justice, and insist that
God shall adopt that as His law; instead of striving to learn by
observation and reflection what His law *is,* and then believing that
law to be consistent with *His* infinite justice, whether it corresponds with *our* limited notion of justice, or does not so correspond. We are too wise in our own conceit, and ever strive to
enact our own little notions into the Universal Laws of God.

It might be difficult for man to prove, even to his own satisfaction, how it is right or just for him to subjugate the horse and ox
to his service, giving them in return only their daily food, which
God has spread out for them on all the green meadows and savan-
nas of the world: or how it is just that we should slay and eat
the harmless deer that only crops the green herbage, the buds, and
the young leaves, and drinks the free-running water that God
made common to all; or the gentle dove, the innocent kid, the
many other living things that so confidently trust to our protection;—quite as difficult, perhaps, as to prove it just for one man's
intellect or even his wealth to make another's strong arms his
servants, for daily wages or for a bare subsistence.

To find out this universal law of justice is one thing—to undertake to measure off something with our own little tape-line, and
call *that* God's law of justice, is another. The great general plan
and system, and the great general laws enacted by God, continually produce what to our limited notions is wrong and injustice,
which hitherto men have been able to explain to their own satisfaction only by the hypothesis of another existence in which all
inequalities and injustices in this life will be remedied and com-
pensated for. To our ideas of justice, it is very unjust that the
child is made miserable for life by deformity or organic disease, in
consequence of the vices of its father; and yet that is part of the
universal law. The ancients said that the child was *punished* for
the sins of its father. *We* say that this its deformity or disease is
the *consequence* of its father's vices; but so far as concerns the
question of justice or injustice, that is merely the change of a word.

It is very easy to lay down a broad, general principle, embodying our own idea of what is absolute justice, and to insist that everything shall conform to that: to say, "all human affairs must be subject to that as the law paramount; what is right agrees therewith and stands, what is wrong conflicts and falls. Private cohesions of self-love, of friendship, or of patriotism, must all be subordinate to this universal gravitation toward the eternal right." The difficulty is that this Universe of necessities God-created, of sequences of cause and effect, and of life evolved from death, this interminable succession and aggregate of cruelties, will not conform to any such absolute principle or arbitrary theory, no matter in what sounding words and glittering phrases it may be embodied.

Impracticable rules in morals are always injurious; for as all men fall short of compliance with them, they turn real virtues into imaginary offences against a forged law. Justice as between man and man and as between man and the animals below him, is that which, under and according to the God-created relations existing between them, and the whole aggregate of circumstances surrounding them, is fit and right and proper to be done, with a view to the general as well as to the individual interest. It is not a theoretical principle by which the very relations that God has created and imposed on us are to be tried, and approved or condemned.

God has made this great system of the Universe, and enacted general laws for its government. Those laws environ everything that lives with a mighty network of necessity. He chose to create the tiger with such organs that he cannot crop the grass, but must eat other flesh or starve. He has made man carnivorous also; and some of the smallest birds are as much so as the tiger. In every step we take, in every breath we draw, is involved the destruction of a multitude of animate existences, each, no matter how minute, as much a living creature as ourself. He has made necessary among mankind a division of labor, intellectual and moral. He has made necessary the varied relations of society and dependence, of obedience and control.

What is thus made necessary cannot be unjust; for if it be, then God the great Lawgiver is Himself unjust. The evil to be avoided is, the legalization of injustice and wrong under the *false* plea of necessity. Out of all the relations of life grow duties,—

as naturally grow and as undeniably, as the leaves grow upon the trees. If we have the right, created by God's law of necessity, to slay the lamb that we may eat and live, we have no right to torture it in doing so, because that is in no wise necessary. We have the right to live, if we fairly can, by the legitimate exercise of our intellect, and hire or buy the labor of the strong arms of others, to till our grounds, to dig in our mines, to toil in our manufactories; but we have no right to overwork or underpay them.

It is not only true that we may learn the moral law of justice, the law of right, by experience and observation; but that God has given us a moral faculty, our conscience, which is able to perceive this law directly and immediately, by intuitive perception of it; and it is true that man has in his nature a rule of conduct higher than what he has ever yet come up to,—an ideal of nature that shames his actual of history: because man has ever been prone to make necessity, his own necessity, the necessities of society, a plea for injustice. But this notion must not be pushed too far—for if we substitute this ideality for actuality, then it is equally true that we have within us an ideal rule of right and wrong, to which God Himself in His government of the world has never come, and against which He (we say it reverentially) every day offends. We detest the tiger and the wolf for the rapacity and love of blood which are their nature; we revolt against the law by which the crooked limbs and diseased organism of the child are the fruits of the father's vices; we even think that a God Omnipotent and Omniscient ought to have permitted no pain, no poverty, no servitude; our ideal of justice is more lofty than the actualities of God. It is well, as all else is well. He has given us that moral sense for wise and beneficent purposes. We accept it as a significant proof of the inherent loftiness of human nature, that it can entertain an ideal so exalted; and should strive to attain it, as far as we can do so consistently with the relations which He has created, and the circumstances which surround us and hold us captive.

If we faithfully use this faculty of conscience; if, applying it to the existing relations and circumstances, we develop it and all its kindred powers, and so deduce the duties that out of these relations and those circumstances, and limited and qualified by them, arise and become obligatory upon us, then we learn justice, the law of right, the divine rule of conduct for human life. But if we undertake to define and settle "the mode of action that belongs to the infinitely perfect nature of God," and so set up any ideal rule, beyond all human reach, we soon come to judge and condemn His work and the relations which it has pleased Him in His infinite wisdom to create.

A sense of justice belongs to human nature, and is a part of it. Men find a deep, permanent, and instinctive delight in justice, not only in the outward effects, but in the inward cause, and by their nature love this law of right, this reasonable rule of conduct, this justice, with a deep and abiding love. Justice is the object of the conscience, and fits it as light fits the eye and truth the mind.

Justice keeps just relations between men. It holds the balance between nation and nation, between a man and his family, tribe, nation, and race, so that his *absolute* rights and theirs do not interfere, nor their *ultimate* interests ever clash, nor the eternal interests of the one prove antagonistic to those of all or of any other one. This we must believe, if we believe that God is just. We must do justice to all, and demand it of all; it is a universal human debt, a universal human claim. But we may err greatly in defining what that justice is. The *temporary* interests, and what to human view are the rights, of men, do often interfere and clash. The life-interests of the individual often conflict with the permanent interests and welfare of society; and what may seem to be the natural rights of one class or race, with those of another.

It is not true to say that "one man, however little, must not be sacrificed to another, however great, to a majority, or to all men." That is not only a fallacy, but a most dangerous one. Often one man and many men must be sacrificed, in the ordinary sense of the term, to the interest of the many. It is a comfortable fallacy to the selfish; for if they cannot, by the law of justice, be sacrificed for the common good, then their country has no right to demand of them *self*-sacrifice; and he is a fool who lays down his life, or sacrifices his estate, or even his luxuries, to insure the safety or prosperity of his country. According to that doctrine, Curtius was a fool, and Leonidas an idiot; and to die for one's country is no longer beautiful and glorious, but a mere absurdity. Then it is no longer to be asked that the common soldier shall receive in his bosom the sword or bayonet-thrust which otherwise would let out the life of the great commander on whose fate hang the liberties of his country, and the welfare of millions yet unborn.

On the contrary, it is certain that necessity rules in all the affairs of men, and that the interest and even the life of one man must often be sacrificed to the interest and welfare of his country. Some must ever lead the forlorn hope: the missionary must go among savages, bearing his life in his hand; the physician must expose himself to pestilence for the sake of others; the sailor, in the frail boat upon the wide ocean, escaped from the foundering or burning ship, must step calmly into the hungry waters, if the lives of the passengers can be saved only by the sacrifice of his own; the pilot must stand firm at the wheel, and let the flames scorch away his own life to insure the common safety of those whom the doomed vessel bears.

The mass of men are always looking for what is just. All the vast machinery which makes up a State, a world of States, is, on the part of the people, an attempt to organize, not that ideal justice which finds fault with God's ordinances, but that practical justice which may be attained in the actual organization of the world. The minute and wide-extending civil machinery which makes up the law and the courts, with all their officers and implements, on the part of mankind, is chiefly an effort to reduce to practice the theory of right. Constitutions are made to establish justice; the decisions of courts are reported to help us judge more wisely in time to come. The nation aims to get together the most nearly just men in the State, that they may incorporate into statutes their aggregate sense of what is right. The people wish law to be embodied justice, administered without passion. Even in the wildest ages there has been a wild popular justice, but always mixed with passion and administered in hate; for justice takes a rude form with rude men, and becomes less mixed with hate and passion in more civilized communities. Every progressive State revises its statutes and revolutionizes its constitution from time to time, seeking to come closer to the utmost possible practical justice and right; and sometimes, following theorists and dreamers in their adoration for the ideal, by erecting into law positive principles of theoretical right, works practical injustice, and then has to retrace its steps.

In literature men always look for practical justice, and desire that virtue should have its own reward, and vice its appropriate punishment. They are ever on the side of justice and humanity; and the majority of them have an ideal justice, better than the things about them, juster than the law: for the law is ever imperfect, not attaining even to the utmost *practicable* degree of perfection; and no man is as just as his own idea of possible and practicable justice. His passions and his necessities ever cause him to sink below his own ideal. The ideal justice which men ever look up to and strive to rise toward, is true; but it will not be realized in this world. Yet we must approach as near to it as practicable, as we should do toward that ideal democracy that "now floats before the eyes of earnest and religious men,—fairer than the Republic of Plato, or More's Utopia, or the Golden Age of fabled memory," only taking care that we do not, in striving to reach and ascend to the impossible ideal, neglect to seize upon and hold fast to the possible actual. To aim at the best, but be content with the best possible, is the only true wisdom. To insist on the absolute right, and throw out of the calculation the important and all-controlling element of necessity, is the folly of a mere dreamer.

In a world inhabited by men with bodies, and necessarily with bodily wants and animal passions, the time will never come when there will be no want, no oppression, nor servitude, no fear of man, no fear of God, but only Love. That can never be while there are inferior intellect, indulgence in low vice, improvidence, indolence, awful visitations of pestilence and war and famine, earthquake and volcano, that must of necessity cause men to want, and serve, and suffer, and fear.

But still the ploughshare of justice is ever drawn through and through the field of the world, uprooting the savage plants. Ever we see a continual and progressive triumph of the right. The injustice of England lost her America, the fairest jewel of her crown. The injustice of Napoleon bore him to the ground more than the snows of Russia did, and exiled him to a barren rock, there to pine away and die, his life a warning to bid mankind be just.

We intuitively understand what justice is, better than we can depict it. What it is in a given case depends so much on circumstances, that definitions of it are wholly deceitful. Often it would be unjust to society to do what would, in the absence of that consideration, be pronounced just to the individual. General propositions of man's right to this or that are ever fallacious: and not infrequently it would be most unjust to the individual himself to do for him what the theorist, as a general proposition, would say was right and his due.

We should ever do unto others what, under the same circumstances, we *ought* to wish, and should have *the right* to wish they should do unto us. There are many cases, cases constantly occurring, where one man must take care of himself, in preference to another, as where two struggle for the possession of a plank that will save one, but cannot uphold both; or where, assailed, he can save his own life only by slaying his adversary. So one must prefer the safety of his country to the lives of her enemies; and sometimes, to insure it, to those of her own innocent citizens. The retreating general may cut away a bridge behind him, to delay pursuit and save the main body of his army, though he thereby surrenders a detachment, a battalion, or even a corps of his own force to certain destruction.

These are not departures from justice; though, like other instances where the injury or death of the individual is the safety of the many, where the interest of one individual, class, or race is postponed to that of the public, or of the superior race, they may infringe some dreamer's ideal rule of justice. But every departure from real, practical justice is no doubt attended with loss to the unjust man, though the loss is not reported to the public. Injustice, public or private, like every other sin and wrong, is inevitably followed by its consequences. The selfish, the grasping, the inhuman, the traudulently unjust, the ungenerous employer, and the cruel master, are detested by the great popular heart; while the kind master, the liberal employer, the generous, the humane, and the just have the good opinion of all men, and even envy is a tribute to their virtues. Men honor all who stand up for truth and right, and never shrink. The world builds monuments to its patriots. Four great statesmen, organizers of the right, embalmed in stone, look down upon the lawgivers of France as they pass to their hall of legislation, silent orators to tell how nations love the just. How we revere the marble lineaments of those just judges, Jay and Marshall, that look so calmly toward the living Bench of the Supreme Court of the United States! What a monument Washington has built in the heart of America and all the world, not because he dreamed of an impracticable ideal justice, but by his constant effort to be practically just!

But necessity alone, and the greatest good of the greatest number, can legitimately interfere with the dominion of absolute and ideal justice. Government should not foster the strong at the expense of the weak, nor protect the capitalist and tax the laborer. The powerful should not seek a monopoly of development and enjoyment; not prudence only and the expedient for to-day should be appealed to by statesmen, but conscience and the right: justice should not be forgotten in looking at interest, nor political morality neglected for political economy: we should not have national housekeeping instead of national organization on the basis of right.

We may well differ as to the abstract right of many things; for every such question has many sides, and few men look at all of them, many only at one. But we all readily recognize cruelty, unfairness, inhumanity, partiality, over-reaching, hard-dealing, by their ugly and familiar lineaments, and in order to know and to hate and despise *them,* we do not need to sit as a Court of Errors and Appeals to revise and reverse God's Providences.

There are certainly great evils of civilization at this day, and many questions of humanity long adjourned and put off. The hideous aspect of pauperism, the debasement and vice in our cities, tell us by their eloquent silence or in inarticulate mutterings, that the rich and the powerful and the intellectual do not do their duty by the poor, the feeble, and the ignorant; and every wretched woman who lives, Heaven scarce knows how, by making shirts at sixpence each, attests the injustice and inhumanity of man. There are cruelties to slaves, and worse cruelties to animals, each disgraceful to their perpetrators, and equally unwarranted by the lawful relation of control and dependence which it has pleased God to create.

A sentence is written against all that is unjust, written by God in the nature of man and in the nature of the Universe, because it is in the nature of the Infinite God. Fidelity to your faculties, trust in their convictions, that is justice to yourself; a life in obedience thereto, that is justice toward men. No wrong is really successful. The gain of injustice is a loss, its pleasure suffering. Iniquity often seems to prosper, but its success is its defeat and shame. After a long while, the day of reckoning ever comes, to nation as to individual. The knave deceives himself. The miser, starving his brother's body, starves also his own soul, and at death shall creep out of his great estate of injustice, poor and naked and miserable. Whoso escapes a duty avoids a gain. Outward judgment often fails, inward justice never. Let a man try to love the wrong and to do the wrong, it is eating stones and not bread, the swift feet of justice are upon him, following with woolen tread, and her iron hands are round his neck. No man can escape from this, any more than from himself. Justice is the angel of God that flies from East to West; and where she stoops her broad wings, it is to bring the counsel of God, and feed mankind with angel's bread.

We cannot understand the moral Universe. The arc is a long one, and our eyes reach but a little way; we cannot calculate the curve and complete the figure by the experience of sight; but we can divine it by conscience, and we surely know that it bends toward justice. Justice will not fail, though wickedness appears strong, and has on its side the armies and thrones of power, the riches and the glory of the world, and though poor men crouch down in despair. Justice will not fail and perish out from the world of men, nor will what is really wrong and contrary to God's real law of justice continually endure. The Power, the Wisdom, and the Justice of God are on the side of every just thought, and it cannot fail, any more than God Himself can perish.

In human affairs, the justice of God must work by human means. Men are the instruments of God's principles; our morality is the instrument of His justice, which, incomprehensible to us, seems to our short vision often to work injustice, but will at some time still the oppressor's brutal laugh. Justice is the rule of conduct written in the nature of mankind. We may, in our daily life, in house or field or shop, in the office or in the court, help to prepare the way for the commonwealth of justice which is slowly, but, we would fain hope, surely approaching. All the justice we mature will bless us here and hereafter, and at our death we shall leave it added to the common store of human-kind. And every Mason who, content to do that which is possible and practicable, does and enforces justice, may help deepen the channel of human morality in which God's justice runs; and so the wrecks of evil that now check and obstruct the stream may the sooner be swept out and borne away by the resistless tide of Omnipotent Right. Let us, my Brother, in this, as in all else, endeavor always to perform the duties of a good Mason and a good man.

XXXII.

SUBLIME PRINCE OF THE ROYAL SECRET.

[Master of Royal Secret.]

THE Occult Science of the Ancient Magi was concealed under the shadows of the Ancient Mysteries: it was imperfectly revealed or rather disfigured by the Gnostics: it is guessed at under the obscurities that cover the pretended crimes of the Templars; and it is found enveloped in enigmas that seem impenetrable, in the Rites of the Highest Masonry.

Magism was the Science of Abraham and Orpheus, of Confucius and Zoroaster. It was the dogmas of this Science that were engraven on the tables of stone by Hanoch and Trismegistus. Moses purified and re-*veiled* them, for that is the meaning of the word *reveal*. He covered them with a new veil, when he made of the Holy Kabalah the exclusive heritage of the people of Israel, and the inviolable Secret of its priests. The Mysteries of Thebes and Eleusis preserved among the nations some symbols of it, already altered, and the mysterious key whereof was lost among the instruments of an ever-growing superstition. Jerusalem, the murderess of her prophets, and so often prostituted to the false gods of the Syrians and Babylonians, had at length in its turn lost the Holy Word, when a Prophet announced to the Magi by the consecrated Star of Initiation, came to rend asunder the worn veil of the old Temple, in order to give the Church a new tissue of legends and symbols, that still and ever conceals from the Profane, and ever preserves to the Elect the same truths.

It was the remembrance of this scientific and religious Absolute, of this doctrine that is summed up in a word, of this Word, in fine, alternately lost and found again, that was transmitted to the Elect of all the Ancient Initiations: it was this same remembrance, preserved, or perhaps profaned in the celebrated Order of the Templars, that became for all the secret associations, of the Rose-Croix, of the Illuminati, and of the Hermetic Freemasons, the reason of their strange rites, of their signs more or less conventional, and, above all, of their mutual devotedness and of their power.

The Gnostics caused the Gnosis to be proscribed by the Christians, and the official Sanctuary was closed against the high initiation. Thus the Hierarchy of Knowledge was compromitted by the violences of usurping ignorance, and the disorders of the Sanctuary are reproduced in the State; for always, willingly or unwillingly, the King is sustained by the Priest, and it is from the eternal Sanctuary of the Divine instruction that the Powers of the Earth, to insure themselves durability, must receive their consecration and their force.

The Hermetic Science of the early Christian ages, cultivated also by Geber, Alfarabius, and others of the Arabs, studied by the Chiefs of the Templars, and embodied in certain symbols of the higher Degrees of Freemasonry, may be accurately defined as the Kabalah in active realization, or the Magic of Works. It has three analogous Degrees, religious, philosophical, and physical realization.

Its religious realization is the durable foundation of the true Empire and the true Priesthood that rule in the realm of human intellect: its philosophical realization is the establishment of an absolute Doctrine, known in all times as the "HOLY Doctrine," and of which PLUTARCH, in the Treatise *"de Iside et Osiride,"* speaks at large but mysteriously; and of a Hierarchical instruction to secure the uninterrupted succession of Adepts among the Initiates: its physical realization is the discovery and application, in the Microcosm, or Little World, of the creative law that incessantly peoples the great Universe.

Measure a corner of the Creation, and multiply that space in proportional progression, and the entire Infinite will multiply its circles filled with universes, which will pass in proportional segments between the ideal and elongating branches of your Compass. Now suppose that from any point whatever of the Infinite above you a hand holds another Compass or a Square, the lines of the Celestial triangle will necessarily meet those of the Compass of Science, to form the Mysterious Star of Solomon.

All hypotheses scientifically probable are the last gleams of the twilight of knowledge, or its last shadows. Faith begins where Reason sinks exhausted. Beyond the human Reason is the Divine Reason, to our feebleness the great Absurdity, the Infinite Absurd, which confounds us and which we believe. For the Master, the Compass of Faith is *above* the Square of Reason; but *both* rest upon the Holy Scriptures and combine to form the Blazing Star of Truth.

All eyes do not see alike. Even the visible creation is not, for all who look upon it, of one form and one color. Our brain is a book printed within and without, and the two writings are, with all men, more or less confused.

The primary tradition of the single revelation has been preserved under the name of the "Kabalah," by the Priesthood of Israel. The Kabalistic doctrine, which was also the dogma of the Magi and of Hermes, is contained in the Sepher Yetsairah, the Sohar, and the Talmud. According to that doctrine, the Absolute is the Being, in which The Word Is, the Word that is the utterance and expression of being and life.

Magic is that which it is; it is by itself, like the mathematics; for it is the exact and absolute science of Nature and its laws.

Magic is the science of the Ancient Magi: and the Christian religion, which has imposed silence on the lying oracles, and put an end to the prestiges of the false Gods, itself reveres those Magi who came from the East, guided by a Star, to adore the Saviour of the world in His cradle.

Tradition also gives these Magi the title of *"Kings,"* because initiation into Magism constitutes a genuine royalty; and because the grand art of the Magi is styled by all the Adepts, *"The Royal Art,"* or the *Holy Realm* or *Empire, Sanctum Regnum.*

The Star which guided them is that same Blazing Star, the image whereof we find in all initiations. To the Alchemists it is the sign of the Quintessence; to the Magists, the Grand Arcanum; to the Kabalists, the Sacred Pentagram. The study of this Pentagram could not but lead the Magi to the knowledge of the New Name which was about to raise itself above all names, and cause all creatures capable of adoration to bend the knee.

Magic unites in one and the same science, whatsoever Philosophy can possess that is most certain, and Religion of the Infallible and the Eternal. It perfectly and incontestably reconciles these two terms that at first blush seem so opposed to each other; faith and reason, science and creed, authority and liberty.

It supplies the human mind with an instrument of philosophical and religious certainty, exact as the mathematics, and accounting for the infallibility of the mathematics themselves.

Thus there is an Absolute, in the matters of the Intelligence and of Faith. The Supreme Reason has not left the gleams of the human understanding to vacillate at hazard. There is an incontestable verity, there is an infallible method of knowing this verity, and by the knowledge of it, those who accept it as a rule may give their will a sovereign power that will make them the masters of all inferior things and of all errant spirits; that is to say, will make them the Arbiters and Kings of the World.

Science has its nights and its dawns, because it gives the intellectual world a life which has its regulated movements and its progressive phases. It is with Truths, as with the luminous rays: nothing of what is concealed is lost; but also, nothing of what is discovered is absolutely new. God has been pleased to give to Science, which is the reflection of His Glory, the Seal of His Eternity.

It is not in the books of the Philosophers, but in the religious symbolism of the Ancients, that we must look for the footprints of Science, and re-discover the Mysteries of Knowledge. The Priests of Egypt knew, better than we do, the laws of movement and of life. They knew how to temper or intensify action by reaction; and readily foresaw the realization of these effects, the causes of which they had determined. The Columns of Seth, Enoch, Solomon, and Hercules have symbolized in the Magian traditions this universal law of the Equilibrium; and the Science of the Equilibrium or balancing of Forces had led the Initiates to that of the universal gravitation around the centres of Life, Heat, and Light.

Thales and Pythagoras learned in the Sanctuaries of Egypt that the Earth revolved around the Sun; but they did not attempt to make this generally known, because to do so it would have been necessary to reveal one of the great Secrets of the Temple, that double law of attraction and radiation or of sympathy and antipathy, of fixedness and movement, which is the principle of Creation, and the perpetual cause of life. This Truth was ridiculed by the Christian Lactantius, as it was long after sought to be proven a falsehood by persecution, by Papal Rome.

So the philosophers reasoned, while the Priests, without replying to them or even smiling at their errors, wrote, in those Hieroglyphics that created all dogmas and all poetry, the Secrets of the Truth.

When Truth comes into the world, the Star of Knowledge advises the Magi of it, and they hasten to adore the Infant who creates the Future. It is by means of the Intelligence of the Hierarchy and the practice of obedience, that one obtains Initiation. If the Rulers have the Divine Right to govern, the true Initiate will cheerfully obey.

The orthodox traditions were carried from Chaldea by Abraham. They reigned in Egypt in the time of Joseph, together with the knowledge of the True God. Moses carried Orthodoxy out of Egypt, and in the Secret Traditions of the Kabalah we find a Theology entire, perfect, unique, like that which in Christianity is most grand and best explained by the Fathers and the Doctors, the whole with a consistency and a harmoniousness which it is not as yet given to the world to comprehend. The Sohar, which is the Key of the Holy Books, opens also all the depths and lights, all the obscurities of the Ancient Mythologies and of the Sciences originally concealed in the Sanctuaries. It is true that the Secret of this Key must be known, to enable one to make use of it, and that for even the most penetrating intellects, not initiated in this Secret, the Sohar is absolutely incomprehensible and almost illegible.

The Secret of the Occult Sciences is that of Nature itself, the
Secret of the generation of the Angels and Worlds, that of the
Omnipotence of God.

"Ye shall be like the Elohim, knowing good and evil," had the
Serpent of Genesis said, and the Tree of Knowledge became the
Tree of Death.

For six thousand years the Martyrs of Knowledge toil and die
at the foot of this tree, that it may again become the Tree of Life.

The Absolute sought for unsuccessfully by the insensate and
found by the Sages, is the TRUTH, the REALITY, and the REASON
of the universal equilibrium!

Equilibrium is the Harmony that results from the analogy of
Contraries.

Until now, Humanity has been endeavoring to stand on one
foot; sometimes on one, sometimes on the other.

Civilizations have risen and perished, either by the anarchical
insanity of Despotism, or by the despotic anarchy of Revolt.

To organize Anarchy, is the problem which the revolutionists
have and will eternally have to resolve. It is the rock of Sisyphus
that will always fall back upon them. To exist a single instant,
they are and always will be by fatality reduced to improvise a despotism without other reason of existence than necessity, and
which, consequently, is violent and blind as Necessity. We escape
from the harmonious monarchy of Reason, only to fall under the
irregular dictatorship of Folly.

Sometimes superstitious enthusiasms, sometimes the miserable
calculations of the materialist instinct have led astray the nations,
and God at last urges the world on toward believing Reason and
reasonable Beliefs.

We have had prophets enough without philosophy, and philosophers without religion; the blind believers and the skeptics resemble each other, and are as far the one as the other from the eternal
salvation.

In the chaos of universal doubt and of the conflicts of Reason
and Faith, the great men and Seers have been but infirm and
morbid artists, seeking the beau-ideal at the risk and peril of their
reason and life.

Living only in the hope to be crowned, they are the first to do
what Pythagoras in so touching a manner prohibits in his admirable Symbols; they rend crowns, and tread them under foot.

Light is the equilibrium of Shadow and Lucidity.

Movement is the equilibrium of Inertia and Activity.

Authority is the equilibrium of Liberty and Power.

Wisdom is equilibrium in the Thoughts, which are the scintillations and rays of the Intellect.

Virtue is equilibrium in the Affections: Beauty is harmonious proportion in Forms.

The beautiful lives are the accurate ones, and the magnificences of Nature are an algebra of graces and splendors.

Everything just is beautiful; everything beautiful ought to be just.

There is, in fact, no Nothing, no void Emptiness, in the Universe. From the upper or outer surface of our atmosphere to that of the Sun, and to those of the Planets and remote Stars, in different directions, Science has for hundreds of centuries imagined that there was simple, void, empty Space. Comparing finite knowledge with the Infinite, the Philosophers know little more than the apes! In all that "void" space are the Infinite Forces of God, acting in an infinite variety of directions, back and forth, and never for an instant inactive. In all of it, active through the whole of its Infinity, is the Light that is the Visible Manifestation of God. The earth and every other planet and sphere that is not a Centre of Light, carries its cone of shadow with it as it flies and flashes round in its orbit; but the darkness has no *home* in the Universe. To illuminate the sphere on one side, is to project a cone of darkness on the other; and Error also is the Shadow of the Truth with which God illuminates the Soul.

In all that "Void," also, is the Mysterious and ever Active Electricity, and Heat, and the Omnipresent Ether. At the will of God the Invisible becomes Visible. Two invisible gases, combined by the action of a Force of God, and compressed, become and remain the water that fills the great basins of the seas, flows in the rivers and rivulets, leaps forth from the rocks or springs, drops upon the earth in rains, or whitens it with snows, and bridges the Danubes with ice, or gathers in vast reservoirs in the earth's bosom. God manifested fills all the extension that we foolishly call Empty Space and the Void.

And everywhere in the Universe, what we call Life and Movement results from a continual conflict of Forces or Impulses.
Whenever that active antagonism ceases, the immobility and
inertia, which are Death, result.

If, says the Kabalah, the Justice of God, which is Severity or
the Female, alone reigned, creation of imperfect beings such as
man would from the beginning have been impossible, because Sin
being congenital with Humanity, the Infinite Justice, measuring
the Sin by the Infinity of the God offended against, must have
annihilated Humanity at the instant of its creation; and not
only Humanity but the Angels, since these also, like all created
by God and less than perfect, are sinful. Nothing imperfect
would have been possible. If, on the other hand, the Mercy or
Benignity of God, the Male, were in no wise counteracted, Sin
would go unpunished, and the Universe fall into a chaos of corruption.

Let God but repeal a single principle or law of chemical attraction or sympathy, and the antagonistic forces equilibrated in matter, released from constraint, would instantaneously expand all
that we term matter into impalpable and invisible gases, such as
water or steam is, when, confined in a cylinder and subjected to
an immense degree of that mysterious force of the Deity which
we call "heat," it is by its expansion released.

Incessantly the great currents and rivers of air flow and rush
and roll from the equator to the frozen polar regions, and
back from these to the torrid equatorial realms. Necessarily
incident to these great, immense, equilibrated and beneficent
movements, caused by the antagonism of equatorial heat and
polar cold, are the typhoons, tornadoes, and cyclones that result
from conflicts between the rushing currents. These and the
benign trade-winds result from the same great law. God is
omnipotent; but effects without causes are impossible, and these
effects cannot but sometimes be evil. The fire would not warm,
if it could not also burn, the human flesh. The most virulent
poisons are the most sovereign remedies, when given in due proportion. The Evil is the shadow of the Good, and inseparable
from it.

The Divine Wisdom limits by equipoise the Omnipotence of
the Divine Will or Power, and the result is Beauty or Harmony.
The arch rests not on a single column, but springs from one on

either side. So is it also with the Divine Justice and Mercy, and with the Human Reason and Human Faith.

That purely scholastic Theology, issue of the Categories of Aristotle and of the Sentences of Peter Lombard, that logic of the syllogism which argues instead of reasoning, and finds a response to every thing by subtilizing on terms, wholly ignored the Kabalistic dogma and wandered off into the drear vacuity of darkness. It was less a philosophy or a wisdom than a philosophical automaton, replying by means of springs, and uncoiling its theses like a wheeled movement. It was not the human verb but the monotonous cry of a machine, the inanimate speech of an Androïd. It was the fatal precision of mechanism, instead of a free application of rational necessities. St. Thomas Aquinas crushed with a single blow all this scaffolding of words built one upon the other, by proclaiming the eternal Empire of Reason, in that magnificent sentence, *"A thing is not just because* God *wills it; but* God *wills it because it is just."* The proximate consequence of this proposition, arguing from the greater to the less, was this: *"A thing is not true because* Aristotle *has said it; but* Aristotle *could not reasonably say it unless it was true. Seek then, first of all, the* Truth *and* Justice, *and the Science of* Aristotle *will be given you in addition."*

It is the fine dream of the greatest of the Poets, that Hell, become useless, is to be closed at length, by the aggrandizement of Heaven; that the problem of Evil is to receive its final solution, and Good alone, necessary and triumphant, is to reign in Eternity. So the Persian dogma taught that Ahriman and his subordinate ministers of Evil were at last, by means of a Redeemer and Mediator, to be reconciled with Deity, and all Evil to end. But unfortunately, the philosopher forgets all the laws of equilibrium, and seeks to absorb the Light in a splendor without shadow, and movement in an absolute repose that would be the cessation of life. So long as there shall be a visible light, there will be a shadow proportional to this Light, and whatever is illuminated will cast its cone of shadow. Repose will never be happiness, if it is not balanced by an analogous and contrary movement. This is the immutable law of Nature, the Eternal Will of the Justice which is GOD.

The same reason necessitates Evil and Sorrow in Humanity, which renders indispensable the bitterness of the waters of the seas. Here also, Harmony can result only from the analogy of contraries, and what is above exists by reason of what is below. It is the depth that determines the height; and if the valleys are filled up, the mountains disappear: so, if the shadows are effaced, the Light is annulled, which is only visible by the graduated contrast of gloom and splendor, and universal obscurity will be produced by an immense dazzling. Even the colors in the Light only exist by the presence of the shadow: it is the threefold alliance of the day and night, the luminous image of the dogma, the Light made Shadow, as the Saviour is the Logos made man: and all this reposes on the same law, the primary law of creation, the single and absolute law of Nature, that of the distinction and harmonious ponderation of the contrary forces in the universal equipoise.

The two great columns of the Temple that symbolizes the Universe are Necessity, or the omnipotent Will of God, which nothing can disobey, and Liberty, or the free-will of His creatures. Apparently and to our human reason antagonistic, the same Reason is not incapable of comprehending how they can be in equipoise. The Infinite Power and Wisdom could so plan the Universe and the Infinite Succession of things as to leave man free to act, and, foreseeing what each would at every instant think and do, to make of the free-will and free-action of each an instrument to aid in effecting its general purpose. For even a man, foreseeing that another will do a certain act, and in nowise controlling or even influencing him may use that action as an instrument to effect his own purposes.

The Infinite Wisdom of God foresees what each will do, and uses it as an instrument, by the exertion of His Infinite Power, which yet does not control the Human action so as to annihilate its freedom. The result is Harmony, the third column that upholds the Lodge. The same Harmony results from the equipoise of Necessity and Liberty. The will of God is not for an instant defeated nor thwarted, and this is the Divine Victory; and yet He does not tempt nor constrain men to do Evil, and thus His Infinite Glory is unimpaired. The result is Stability, Cohesion, and Permanence in the Universe, and undivided Dominion and Autocracy in the Deity. And these, Victory, Glory, Stability, and Dominion, are the last four Sephiroth of the Kabalah.

I Am, God said to Moses, that which Is, Was and Shall forever

Be. But the Very God, in His unmanifested Essence, conceived of as not yet having created and as Alone, has no Name. Such was the doctrine of all the ancient Sages, and it is so expressly declared in the Kabalah. יהוה is the Name of the Deity manifested in a single act, that of Creation, and containing within Himself, in idea and actuality, the whole Universe, to be invested with form and be materially developed during the eternal succession of ages. As God never WAS NOT, so He never THOUGHT not, and the Universe has no more had a beginning than the Divine Thought of which it is the utterance,—no more than the Deity Himself. The duration of the Universe is but a point halfway upon the infinite line of eternity; and God was not inert and uncreative during the eternity that stretches behind that point. The Archetype of the Universe did never not exist in the Divine Mind. The Word was in the BEGINNING with God, and WAS God. And the Ineffable NAME is that, not of the Very Essence but of the Absolute, manifested as Being or Existence. For Existence or Being, said the Philosophers, is limitation; and the Very Deity is not limited nor defined, but is all that *may possibly be,* besides all that is, was, and shall be.

Reversing the letters of the Ineffable Name, and dividing it, it becomes bi-sexual, as the word יה, *Yud-He* or JAH is, and discloses the meaning of much of the obscure language of the Kabalah, and is The Highest of which the Columns Jachin and Boaz are the symbol. "In the image of Deity," we are told, "God created the Man; Male and Female created He *them:*" and the writer, symbolizing the Divine by the Human, then tells us that the woman, at first contained in the man, was taken from his side. So Minerva, Goddess of Wisdom, was born, a woman and in armor, of the brain of Jove; Isis was the sister before she was the wife of Osiris, and within BRAHM, the Source of all, the Very God, without sex or name, was developed MAYA, the Mother of all that is. The WORD is the First and Only-begotten of the Father; and the awe with which the Highest Mysteries were regarded has imposed silence in respect to the Nature of the Holy Spirit. The Word is Light, and the Life of Humanity.

It is for the Adepts to understand the meaning of the Symbols.

Return now, with us, to the Degrees of the Blue Masonry, and for your last lesson, receive the explanation of one of their Symbols.

You see upon the altar of those Degrees the SQUARE and the COMPASS, and you remember how they lay upon the altar in each Degree.

The SQUARE is an instrument adapted for plane surfaces only, and therefore appropriate to Geometry, or measurement of the Earth, which appears to be, and was by the Ancients supposed to be, a plane. The COMPASS is an instrument that has relation to spheres and spherical surfaces, and is adapted to spherical trigonometry, or that branch of mathematics which deals with the Heavens and the orbits of the planetary bodies.

The SQUARE, therefore, is a natural and appropriate Symbol of this Earth and the things that belong to it, are of it, or concern it. The Compass is an equally natural and appropriate Symbol of the Heavens, and of all celestial things and celestial natures.

You see at the beginning of this reading, an old Hermetic Symbol, copied from the "MATERIA PRIMA" of Valentinus, printed at Franckfurt, in 1613, with a treatise entitled "AZOTH." Upon it you see a Triangle upon a Square, both of these contained in a circle; and above this, standing upon a dragon, a human body, with two arms only, but two heads, one male and the other female. By the side of the male head is the Sun, and by that of the female head, the Moon, the crescent within the circle of the full moon. And the hand on the *male* side holds a *Compass,* and that on the *female* side, a *Square.*

The Heavens and the Earth were personified as Deities, even among the Aryan Ancestors of the European nations of the Hindus, Zends, Bactrians, and Persians; and the Rig Veda Sanhita contains hymns addressed to them as gods. They were deified also among the Phœnicians; and among the Greeks OURANOS and GÆA, Heaven and Earth, were sung as the most ancient of the Deities, by Hesiod.

It is the great, fertile, beautiful MOTHER, Earth, that produces, with limitless profusion of beneficence, everything that ministers to the needs, to the comfort, and to the luxury of man. From her teeming and inexhaustible bosom come the fruits, the grain, the flowers, in their season. From it comes all that feeds the animals which serve man as laborers and for food. She, in the fair

Springtime, is green with abundant grass, and the trees spring from her soil, and from her teeming vitality take their wealth of green leaves. In her womb are found the useful and valuable minerals; hers are the seas the swarm with life; hers the rivers that furnish food and irrigation, and the mountains that send down the streams which swell into these rivers; hers the forests that feed the sacred fires for the sacrifices, and blaze upon the domestic hearths. The EARTH, therefore, the great PRODUCER, was always represented as a *female,* as the MOTHER,—Great, Bounteous, Beneficent Mother Earth.

On the other hand, it is the light and heat of the Sun in the Heavens, and the rains that seem to come from them, that in the Springtime make fruitful this bountifully-producing Earth, that restore life and warmth to her veins, chilled by Winter, set running free her streams, and *beget,* as it were, that greenness and that abundance of which she is so prolific. As the procreative and generative agents, the Heavens and the Sun have always been regarded as *male;* as the generators that fructify the Earth and cause it to produce.

The Hermaphroditic figure is the Symbol of the double nature anciently assigned to the Deity, as Generator and Producer, as BRAHM and MAYA among the Aryans, Osiris and Isis among the Egyptians. As the Sun was male, so the Moon was female; and Isis was both the sister and the wife of Osiris. The Compass, therefore, is the Hermetic Symbol of the Creative Deity, and the Square of the productive Earth or Universe.

From the Heavens come the spiritual and immortal portion of man; from the Earth his material and mortal portion. The Hebrew Genesis says that YEHOUAH formed man of the dust of the Earth, and breathed into his nostrils the breath of life. Through the seven planetary spheres, represented by the Mystic Ladder of the Mithriac Initiations, and it by that which Jacob saw in his dream (not with *three,* but with *seven* steps), the Souls, emanating from the Deity, descended, to be united to their human bodies; and through those seven spheres they must re-ascend, to return to their origin and home in the bosom of the Deity.

The COMPASS, therefore, as the Symbol of the *Heavens,* represents the spiritual, intellectual, and moral portion of this double nature of Humanity; and the SQUARE, as the Symbol of the *Earth,* its material, sensual, and baser portion.

"Truth and Intelligence," said one of the Ancient Indian Sects of Philosophers, "are the Eternal attributes of God, not of the individual Soul, which is susceptible both of knowledge and ignorance, of pleasure and pain; therefore God and the individual Soul are distinct:" and this expression of the ancient Nyaya Philosophers, in regard to Truth, has been handed down to us through the long succession of ages, in the lessons of Freemasonry, wherein we read, that "Truth is a Divine Attribute, and the foundation of every virtue."

"While embodied in matter," they said, "the Soul is in a state of imprisonment, and is under the influence of evil passions; but having, by intense study, arrived at the knowledge of the elements and principles of Nature, it attains unto the place of THE ETERNAL; in which state of happiness, its individuality does not cease."

The vitality which animates the mortal frame, the Breath of Life of the Hebrew Genesis, the Hindu Philosophers in general held, perishes with it; but the Soul is divine, an emanation of the Spirit of God, but not a *portion* of that Spirit. For they compared it to the heat and light sent forth from the Sun, or to a *ray* of that light, which neither lessens nor divides its own essence.

However created, or invested with separate existence, the Soul, which is but the creature of the Deity, cannot know the mode of its creation, nor comprehend its own individuality. It cannot even comprehend how the being which it and the body constitute, can feel pain, or see, or hear. It has pleased the Universal Creator to set bounds to the scope of our human and finite reason, beyond which it cannot reach; and if we are capable of comprehending the mode and manner of the creation or generation of the Universe of things, He has been pleased to conceal it from us by an impenetrable veil, while the words used to express the act have no other definite meaning than that He caused that Universe to commence to exist.

It is enough for us to know, what Masonry teaches, that we are not all mortal; that the Soul or Spirit, the intellectual and reasoning portion of ourself, is our Very Self, is not subject to decay and dissolution, but is simple and immaterial, survives the death of the body, and is *capable* of immortality; that it is also capable of improvement and advancement, of increase of knowledge of the things that are divine, of becoming wiser and better, and more and more worthy of immortality; and that to become so, and to help to improve and benefit others and all our race, is the noblest ambition and highest glory that we can entertain and attain unto, in this momentary and imperfect life.

In every human being the Divine and the Human are intermingled. In every one there are the Reason and the Moral sense, the passions that prompt to evil, and the sensual appetites. "If ye live after the flesh, ye shall die," said Paul, writing to the Christians at Rome, "but if ye through the spirit do mortify the deeds of the body, ye shall live. For as many as are led by the Spirit of God, they are the sons of God." "The flesh lusteth against the spirit, and the spirit against the flesh," he said, writing to the Christians of Galatia, "and these are contrary the one to the other, so that ye cannot do the things that ye would." "That which I do, I do not willingly do," he wrote to the Romans, "for what I wish to do, that I do not do, but that which I hate I do. It is no more I that do it, but sin that dwelleth in me. To will, is present with me; but how to perform that which is good, I find not. For, I do not do the good that I desire to do; and the evil that I do not wish to do, that I do do. I find then *a law,* that when I desire to do good, evil is present with me; for I delight in the law of God after the inward man, but I see another law in my members, warring against the law of my mind, and bringing me into captivity to the law of sin which is in my members. . . So then, with the mind I myself serve the law of God, but with the flesh the law of sin."

Life is a battle, and to fight that battle heroically and well is the great purpose of every man's existence, who is worthy and fit to live at all. To stem the strong currents of adversity, to advance in despite of all obstacles, to snatch victory from the jealous grasp of fortune, to become a chief and a leader among men, to rise to rank and power by eloquence, courage, perseverance, study, energy, activity, discouraged by no reverses, impatient of no delays, deterred by no hazards; to win wealth, to subjugate men by our intellect, the very elements by our audacity, to succeed, to prosper, to thrive;—thus it is, according to the general understanding, that one fights well the battle of life. Even to succeed in business by that boldness which halts for no risks, that audacity which stakes all upon hazardous chances; by the shrewdness of the close dealer, the boldness of the unscrupulous operator, even by the knaveries of the stock-board and the gold-room; to crawl up into place by disreputable means or the votes of brutal ignorance,—these also are deemed to be among the great successes of life.

But that which is the greatest battle, and in which the truest honor and most real success are to be won, is that which our intellect and reason and moral sense, our spiritual natures, fight against our sensual appetites and evil passions, our earthly and material or animal nature. Therein only are the true glories of heroism to be won, there only the successes that entitle us to triumphs.

In every human life that battle is fought; and those who win elsewhere, often suffer ignominious defeat and disastrous rout, and discomfiture and shameful downfall in this encounter.

You have heard more than one definition of Freemasonry. The truest and the most significant you have yet to hear. It is taught to the entered Apprentice, the Fellow-Craft, and the Master, and it is taught in every Degree through which you have advanced to this. It is a definition of what Freemasonry is, of what its purposes and its very essence and spirit are; and it has for every one of us the force and sanctity of a divine law, and imposes on every one of us a solemn obligation.

It is symbolized and taught, to the Apprentice as well as to you, by the COMPASS *and the* SQUARE; upon which, as well as upon the Book of your Religion and the Book of the law of the Scottish Freemasonry, you have taken so many obligations. As a Knight, you have been taught it by the Swords, the symbols of HONOR and DUTY, on which you have taken your vows: it was taught you by the BALANCE, the symbol of all Equilibrium, and by the CROSS, the symbol of devotedness and self-sacrifice; but all that these teach and contain is taught and contained, for Entered Apprentice, Knight, and Prince alike, by the Compass and the Square.

For the Apprentice, the points of the Compass are beneath the Square. For the Fellow-Craft, one is above and one beneath. For the Master, both are dominant, and have rule, control, and empire over the symbol of the earthly and the material.

FREEMASONRY *is the subjugation of the Human that is in man by the Divine; the Conquest of the Appetites and Passions by the Moral Sense and the Reason; a continual effort, struggle, and warfare of the Spiritual against the Material and Sensual.* That victory, when it has been achieved and secured, and the conqueror may rest upon his shield and wear the well-earned laurels, is the true HOLY EMPIRE.

To achieve it, the Mason must first attain a solid conviction, founded upon reason, that he hath within him a spiritual nature, a soul that is not to die when the body is dissolved, but is to continue to exist and to advance toward perfection through all the ages of eternity, and to see more and more clearly, as it draws nearer unto God, the Light of the Divine Presence. This the Philosophy of the Ancient and Accepted Rite teaches him; and it encourages him to persevere by helping him to believe that his free will is entirely consistent with God's Omnipotence and Omniscience; that He is not only infinite in power, and of infinite wisdom, but of infinite mercy, and an infinitely tender pity and love for the frail and imperfect creatures that He has made.

Every Degree of the Ancient and Accepted Scottish Rite, from the first to the thirty-second, teaches by its ceremonial as well as by its instruction, that the noblest purpose of life and the highest duty of a man are to strive incessantly and vigorously to win the mastery of everything, of that which in him is spiritual and divine, over that which is material and sensual; so that in him also, as in the Universe which God governs, Harmony and Beauty may be the result of a just equilibrium.

You have been taught this in those Degrees, conferred in the Lodge of Perfection, which inculcate particularly the practical morality of Freemasonry. To be true, under whatever temptation to be false; to be honest in all your dealings, even if great losses should be the consequence; to be charitable, when selfishness would prompt you to close your hand, and deprivation of luxury or comfort must follow the charitable act; to judge justly and impartially, even in your own case, when baser impulses prompt you to do an injustice in order that you may be benefited or justified; to be tolerant, when passion prompts to intolerance and persecution; to do that which is right, when the wrong seems to promise larger profit; and to wrong no man of anything that is his, however easy it may seem so to enrich yourself;—in all these things and others which you promised in those Degrees, your spiritual nature is taught and encouraged to assert its rightful dominion over your appetites and passions.

The philosophical Degrees have taught you the value of knowledge, the excellence of truth, the superiority of intellectual labor, the dignity and value of your soul, the worth of great and noble thoughts; and thus endeavored to assist you to rise above the level of the animal appetites and passions, the pursuits of greed and the miserable struggles of ambition, and to find purer pleasure and nobler prizes and rewards in the acquisition of knowledge, the enlargement of the intellect, the interpretation of the sacred writing of God upon the great pages of the Book of Nature.

And the Chivalric Degrees have led you on the same path, by showing you the excellence of generosity, clemency, forgiveness of injuries, magnanimity, contempt of danger, and the paramount obligations of Duty and Honor. They have taught you to overcome the fear of death, to devote yourself to the great cause of civil and religious Liberty, to be the Soldier of all that is just, right, and true; in the midst of pestilence to deserve your title of Knight Commander of the Temple, and neither there nor elsewhere to desert your post and flee dastard-like from the foe. In all this, you assert the superiority and right to dominion of that in you which is spiritual and divine. No base fear of danger or death, no sordid ambitions or pitiful greeds or base considerations can tempt a true Scottish Knight to dishonor, and so make his intellect, his reason, his soul, the bond-slave of his appetites, of his passions, of that which is material and animal, selfish and brutish in his nature.

It is not possible to create a true and genuine Brotherhood upon any theory of the baseness of human nature: nor by a community of belief in abstract propositions as to the nature of the Deity, the number of His persons, or other theorems of religious faith: nor by the establishment of a system of association simply for mutual relief, and by which, in consideration of certain payments regularly made, each becomes entitled to a certain stipend in case of sickness, to attention then, and to the ceremonies of burial after death.

There can be no genuine Brotherhood without mutual regard, good opinion and esteem, mutual charity, and mutual allowance for faults and failings. It is those only who learn habitually to think better of each other, to look habitually for the good that is in each other, and expect, allow for, and overlook, the evil, who can be Brethren one of the other, in any truse sense of the word. Those who gloat over the failings of one another, who think each other to be naturally base and low, of a nature in which the Evil predominates and excellence is not to be looked for, cannot be even friends, and much less Brethren.

No one can have a right to think meanly of his race, unless he also thinks meanly of himself. If, from a single fault or error, he judges of the character of another, and takes the single act as evidence of the whole nature of the man and of the whole course of his life, he ought to consent to be judged by the same rule, and to admit it to be right that others should thus uncharitably condemn himself. But such judgments will become impossible when he incessantly reminds himself that in every man who lives there is an immortal Soul endeavoring to do that which is right and just; a Ray, however small, and almost inappreciable, from the Great Source of Light and Intelligence, which ever struggles upward amid all the impediments of sense and the obstructions of the passions; and that in every man this ray continually wages war against his evil passions and his unruly appetites, or, if it has succumbed, is never wholly extinguished and annihilated. For he will then see that it is not victory, but the struggle that deserves honor; since in this as in all else no man can always command success. Amid a cloud of errors, of failure, and shortcomings, he will look for the struggling Soul, for that which is good in every one amid the evil, and, believing that each is better than from his acts and omissions he seems to be, and that God cares for him still, and pities him and loves him, he will feel that even the erring sinner is still his brother, still entitled to his sympathy, and bound to him by the indissoluble ties of fellowship.

If there be nothing of the divine in man, what is he, after all, but a more intelligent animal? He hath no fault nor vice which some beast hath not; and therefore in his vices he is but a beast of a higher order; and he hath hardly any moral excellence, perhaps none, which some animal hath not in as great a degree,— even the more excellent of these, such as generosity, fidelity, and magnanimity.

Bardesan, the Syrian Christian, in his Book of the Laws of Countries, says, of men, that "in the things belonging to their bodies, they maintain their nature like animals, and in the things which belong to their minds, they do that which they wish, as being free and with power, and as the likeness of God"; and Meliton, Bishop of Sardis, in his Oration to Antoninus Cæsar,

says, "Let Him, the ever-living God, be always present in thy
mind; for thy mind itself is His likeness, for it, too, is invisible
and impalpable, and without form. . . As He exists forever, so
thou also, when thou shalt have put off this which is visible and
corruptible, shalt stand before Him forever, living and endowed
with knowledge."

As a matter far above our comprehension, and in the Hebrew Genesis the words that are used to express the origin of
things are of uncertain meaning, and with equal propriety may
be translated by the word "generated," "produced," "made," or
"created," we need not dispute nor debate whether the Soul or
Spirit of man be a ray that has emanated or flowed forth from the
Supreme Intelligence, or whether the Infinite Power hath called
each into existence from nothing, by a mere exertion of Its will,
and endowed it with immortality, and with intelligence like unto
the Divine Intelligence: for, in either case it may be said that in
man the Divine is united to the Human. Of this union the equilateral Triangle inscribed within the Square is a Symbol.

We see the Soul, Plato said, as men see the statue of Glaucus,
recovered from the sea wherein it had lain many years—which
viewing, it was not easy, if possible, to discern what was its original nature, its limbs having been partly broken and partly worn
and by defacement changed, by the action of the waves, and shells,
weeds, and pebbles adhering to it, so that it more resembled some
strange monster than that which it was when it left its Divine
Source. Even so, he said, we see the Soul, deformed by innumerable things that have done it harm, have mutilated and defaced it.
But the Mason who hath the ROYAL SECRET can also with him
argue, from beholding its love of wisdom, its tendency toward association with what is divine and immortal, its larger aspirations,
its struggles, though they may have ended in defeat, with the impediments and enthralments of the senses and the passions, that
when it shall have been rescued from the material environments
that now prove too strong for it, and be freed from the deforming
and disfiguring accretions that here adhere to it, it will again be
seen in its true nature, and by degrees ascend by the mystic ladder
of the Spheres, to its first home and place of origin.

The ROYAL SECRET, of which you are Prince, if you are a true
Adept, if knowledge seems to you advisable, and Philosophy is,
for you, radiant with a divine beauty, is that which the Sohar

terms *The Mystery of the* BALANCE. It is the Secret of the UNI-
VERSAL EQUILIBRIUM :—

—Of that Equilibrium in the Deity, between the Infinite Divine WISDOM and the Infinite Divine POWER, from which result
the Stability of the Universe, the unchangeableness of the Divine
Law, and the Principles of Truth, Justice, and Right which are
a part of it; and the Supreme Obligation of the Divine Law upon
all men, as superior to all other law, and forming a part of all
the laws of men and nations.

—Of that Equilibrium also, between the Infinite Divine JUS-
TICE and the Infinite Divine MERCY, the result of which is the
Infinite Divine EQUITY, and the Moral Harmony or Beauty of
the Universe. By it the endurance of created and imperfect natures in the presence of a Perfect Deity is made possible; and for
Him, also, as for us, to love is better than to hate, and Forgiveness is wiser than Revenge or Punishment.

—Of that Equilibrium between NECESSITY and LIBERTY, between the action of the DIVINE Omnipotence and the Free-will
of man, by which vices and base actions, and ungenerous thoughts
and words are crimes and wrongs, justly punished by the law of
cause and consequence, though nothing in the Universe can happen or be done contrary to the will of God; and without which
co-existence of Liberty and Necessity, of Free-will in the creature
and Omnipotence in the Creator, there could be no religion, nor
any law of right and wrong, or merit and demerit, nor any justice
in human punishments or penal laws.

—Of that Equilibrium between Good and Evil, and Light and
Darkness in the world, which assures us that all is the work of the
Infinite Wisdom and of an Infinite Love; and that there is no
rebellious demon of Evil, or Principle of Darkness co-existent and
in eternal controversy with God, or the Principle of Light and
of Good: by attaining to the knowledge of which equilibrium we
can, through Faith, see that the existence of Evil, Sin, Suffering,
and Sorrow in the world, is consistent with the Infinite Goodness
as well as with the Infinite Wisdom of the Almighty.

Sympathy and Antipathy, Attraction and Repulsion, each a
Force of nature, are contraries, in the souls of men and in the
Universe of spheres and worlds; and from the action and opposition of each against the other, result Harmony, and that movement which is the Life of the Universe and the Soul alike.

They are not antagonists of each other. The force that repels a Planet from the Sun is no more an *evil* force, than that which attracts the Planet toward the central Luminary; for each is created and exerted by the Deity, and the result is the harmonious movement of the obedient Planets in their elliptic orbits, and the mathematical accuracy and unvarying regularity of their movements.

—Of that Equilibrium between Authority and Individual Action which constitutes Free Government, by settling on immutable foundations Liberty with Obedience to Law, Equality with Subjection to Authority, and Fraternity with Subordination to the Wisest and the Best: and of that Equilibrium between the *Active* Energy of the Will of the Present, expressed by the Vote of the People, and the Passive Stability and Permanence of the Will of the Past, expressed in constitutions of government, written or unwritten, and in the laws and customs, gray with age and sanctified by time, as precedents and authority; which is represented by the arch resting on the two columns, Jachin and Boaz, that stand at the portals of the Temple builded by Wisdom, on one of which Masonry sets the celestial Globe, symbol of the spiritual part of our composite nature, and on the other the terrestrial Globe, symbol of the material part.

—And, finally, of that Equilibrium, possible in ourselves, and which Masonry incessantly labors to accomplish in its Initiates, and demands of its Adepts and Princes (else unworthy of their titles), between the Spiritual and Divine and the Material and Human in man; between the Intellect, Reason, and Moral Sense on one side, and the Appetites and Passions on the other, from which result the Harmony and Beauty of a well-regulated life.

Which possible Equilibrium proves to us that our Appetites and Senses also are Forces given unto us by God, for purposes of good, and not the fruits of the malignancy of a Devil, to be detested, mortified, and, if possible, rendered inert and dead: that they are given us to be the means by which we shall be strengthened and incited to great and good deeds, and are to be wisely used, and not abused; to be controlled and kept within due bounds by the Reason and the Moral Sense; to be made useful instruments and servants, and not permitted to become the managers and masters, using our intellect and reason as base instruments for their gratification.

And this Equilibrium teaches us, above all, to reverence ourselves as immortal souls, and to have respect and charity for others, who are even such as we are, partakers with us of the Divine Nature, lighted by a ray of the Divine Intelligence, struggling, like us, toward the light; capable, like us, of progress upward toward perfection, and deserving to be loved and pitied, but never to be hated nor despised; to be aided and encouraged in this life-struggle, and not to be abandoned nor left to wander in the darkness alone, still less to be trampled upon in our own efforts to ascend.

From the mutual action and re-action of each of these pairs of opposites and contraries results that which with them forms the Triangle, to all the Ancient Sages the expressive symbol of the Deity; as from Osiris and Isis, Har-oeri, the Master of Light and Life, and the Creative Word. At the angles of one stand, symbolically, the three columns that support the Lodge, itself a symbol of the Universe, Wisdom, Power, and Harmony or Beauty. One of these symbols, found on the Tracing-Board of the Apprentice's Degree, teaches this last lesson of Freemasonry. It is the right-angled Triangle, representing man, as a union of the spiritual and material, of the divine and human. The base, measured by the number 3, the number of the Triangle, represents the Deity and the Divine; the perpendicular, measured by the number 4, the number of the Square, represents the Earth, the Material, and the Human; and the hypothenuse, measured by 5, represents that nature which is produced by the union of the Divine and Human, the Soul and the Body; the squares, 9 and 16, of the base and perpendicular, added together, producing 25, the square root whereof is 5, the measure of the hypothenuse.

And as in each Triangle of Perfection, one is three and three are one, so man is one, though of a double nature; and he attains the purposes of his being only when the two natures that are in him are in just equilibrium; and his life is a success only when it too is a harmony, and beautiful, like the great Harmonies of God and the Universe.

Such, my Brother, is the TRUE WORD of a Master Mason; such the true ROYAL SECRET, which makes possible, and shall at length make real, the HOLY EMPIRE of true Masonic Brotherhood.

GLORIA DEI EST CELARE VERBUM. AMEN.

DIGEST—INDEX

OF

"MORALS AND DOGMA,"

OF

ALBERT PIKE 33°

BY

T. W. HUGO, G∴C∴C∴H∴

Published by
The Supreme Council, 33°
A∴ & A∴S∴R∴ for the
Southern Jurisdiction, U. S. A.

WASHINGTON, D. C.

L. H. JENKINS, INC.
RICHMOND, VIRGINIA

PREFACE.

The following Digest of the contents of Brother Albert Pike's monumental work, "Morals and Dogma," the text book of the Ancient and Accepted Scottish Rite for the southern jurisdiction, issued by the Supreme Council, grew out of the desire of the writer to have an index of the contents for his own personal use as the presiding officer, for twenty years, of each of the Scottish Rite Bodies in Duluth, Minnesota, and it can be imagined that in that time, dating from the first organization, many questions have been propounded which could only be properly answered by reference to that epitome of Scottish Rite Free Masonry; the book referred to.

From the very nature of "Morals and Dogma," different subjects are hard to find; the book is very naturally divided under the headings of Degrees; there are no sub-headings; and as most of the important subjects are touched on, to a greater or lesser extent, in all the Degrees it meant a perusal of the entire book if all the information on any of those subjects was desired.

The writer started to compile an Index (in the ordinary acceptation of the term), giving the pages where such and such words would be found, but he had not progressed very far before it became evident that that was only half a solution of the problem; so many references were found that it would have been necessary to spend a great length of time looking up the several pages to see if that particular reference was to what the searcher was after; the procedure was entirely changed and it was decided, although it would consume very much more time, and entail more arduous labor, to digest the contents and then Index that, so that when a person wanted to find out what, for instance, the Egyptians understood by "The Universe," it was not necessary to look in "Morals and Dogma," at all the pages on which "Universe" was mentioned but by following down the column, under the heading "Universe," come to "Universe of the Egyptians a living, animated being like man, page 665-1;" if that is not enough in detail turn to page 665, and in the lower third of the page will be found the paragraph of which the line just quoted is the boiled down meaning; most of the time it will not be necessary to consult the "Morals and Dogma" at all.

When the Digest (so called for want of a better name) was completed, a meeting of the Duluth Brethren was called to secure the assistance of some of them in making a few copies on the typewriter, but they decided that each of them wanted a copy and the only thing to do was to print; hence the book.

In the opinion of the writer no one who has not carefully studied "Morals and Dogma," or the several subjects of which it is the epitome, is or can be a Master of the Royal Secret in the true meaning of the term, no matter how many patents he may have, nor how completely they are countersigned by distinguished Masons of the Thirty-third Degree, and it is for those who do not wish to sail along under false colors and assume titles of which they know not the meaning that this volume is prepared, believing it will assist them to acquire an interest in the subject which they otherwise would be much slower in gaining, if not deterred altogether by the apparent difficulty in following up the several subjects.

Honored with the personal friendship and confidence of the author of "Morals and Dogma," receiving the highest honors at his hands and cherishing a lively recollection of his many splendid qualities of mind and heart, the writer can conceive of no higher ambition than that of shewing by deeds that he has appreciated the privileges of that friendship and has absorbed some of the inspiration which personal intercourse with Brother Pike made possible therefore.

This volume is dedicated in grateful memory of the Prince Adept, Albert Pike, 33°, Mystic, Poet, Scholar, who through his researches and his study of the Symbolism of Free Masonry has raised that Institution far above the commonplace and enthroned it on the lofty plane of a sublime system of Philosophy, embracing the accumulated Wisdom of the ages fitted to make men wiser, happier, better.

No attempts have been made to standardize the spelling of some words, nor make any changes in phraseology; for instance, "Cabala," "Kabalah," "Kabala," are different spellings of the one word; "Deity" and "God" are used indiscriminately, etc., etc.; this volume is a Digest of "Morals and Dogma" as it is, and nothing else.

T. W. HUGO.

Duluth, Minn., October 1st, 1909.

EXPLANATION.

In explanation of the characters used in the Index; the letters "u," "m," "l" after a number signifies that the subject mentioned will be found on the page represented by the number and in the upper, middle, or lower thirds of that page, respectively; thus "Unity of God taught in the Kabalah, 625-l," means that on the lower third of page 625 will be found the paragraph of which the notation in question is a shortened statement.

Where no final letter is given it means that the notation refers to the entire page, as "Universe, questions concerning the creation or self existence of, 648," means that all of page 648 refers to that notation just quoted.

Where a dash (—) appears at the end of the words, it means that for the completion of the sentence reference must be made to the page whose number follows; for instance, "Universe must have been co-existent with Deity because—, 684-u," means that the reader must consult page 684-u, and complete the sentence, as it is of such a nature that it could not be boiled down very well and preserve the true sense.

Where a dash (—) appears between two numbers of pages it means that both of those pages and the intervening ones refer to the subject matter of the notation opposite those numbers.

DIGEST OF "MORALS AND DOGMA"

A

1

B

C

D

E

F

G

H

I

J

K

L

M

N

O

P

Q

R

S

178   DIGEST OF "MORALS AND DOGMA"

T

W

X

Y

Z